DICTIONARY OF THE NORTH-WEST SEMITIC INSCRIPTIONS

PART TWO

HANDBUCH DER ORIENTALISTIK
HANDBOOK OF ORIENTAL STUDIES

ERSTE ABTEILUNG

DER NAHE UND MITTLERE OSTEN
THE NEAR AND MIDDLE EAST

HERAUSGEGEBEN VON

H. ALTENMÜLLER · B. HROUDA · B.A. LEVINE
K.R. VEENHOF

EINUNDZWANZIGSTER BAND

DICTIONARY OF THE NORTH-WEST SEMITIC INSCRIPTIONS

PART TWO

DICTIONARY OF THE NORTH-WEST SEMITIC INSCRIPTIONS

BY

J. HOFTIJZER AND K. JONGELING

WITH APPENDICES BY
R.C. STEINER, A. MOSAK MOSHAVI AND B. PORTEN

PART TWO

M – T

E.J. BRILL
LEIDEN · NEW YORK · KÖLN
1995

The paper in this book meets the guidelines for permanence and durability of the Committee on Production Guidelines for Book Longevity of the Council on Library Resources.

Library of Congress Cataloging-in-Publication Data

Hoftijzer, J. (Jacob)
Dictionary of the North-West Semitic inscriptions /J. Hoftijzer & K. Jongeling : with appendices by R.C. Steiner, A. Mosak Moshavi and B. Porten.
p. cm.— (Handbuch der Orientalistik. Erste Abteilung, Der Nahe und Mittlere Osten ; 21. Bd., T. 1-2
Based on: Dicxtionnaire des inscriptions sémitiques de l'ouest / C.F. Jean and J. Hoftijzer.
Includes bibliographical references.
ISBN 9004098178 (v. 1). — ISBN 9004098208 (v. 2)
1. Inscriptions, Semitic—Dictionaries—English. 2. Semitic languages, Northwest—Dictionaries—English. I. Jongeling, K. II. Steiner, Richard C. III. Moshavi, A. Mosak. IV. Porten, Bezalel. V. Jean, Charles-F.
(Charles-François), b. 1874. Dictionnaire des inscriptions sémitiques de l'ouest. V. Title. VI. Series.
PJ3085.H63 1995
492—dc20 94-39945
CIP

ISSN 0169-9423
ISBN 90 04 09817 8 (*Vol. 1*)
ISBN 90 04 09820 8 (*Vol. 2*)
ISBN 90 04 09821 6 (*Set*)

PRINTED IN THE NETHERLANDS

Contents

PART ONE

PART TWO

M - T

M

m_1 v. *m›h_2*.
m_2 v. *mkl_1*.
m_3 v. *mlk_3*.
m_4 v. *mmlkh*.
m_5 v. *mnh_2*.
m_6 v. *m‹h_1*.
m_7 v. *mqdš*.
m_8 v. *mr›*.
m_9 v. *mry*.
m_{10} v. *mzḥ*.
m_{11} v. *mh*, v. also *n$š_1$*.
m_{12} v. *mn_5*.
m_{13} v. *‹m_1*.
m_{14} abbrev. in CIS ii 3971[7] (mile stone) of Greek μίλιον = Roman mile, cf. also Rosenthal Sprache 92.
m_{15} abbrev. with unknown meaning in CIS ii 53[1].
m›$_1$ v. *mkl_1*.
m›$_2$ v. *m›h_2*.
m›$_3$ v. *mh_2*.
m›$_4$ on coins from Arad, poss. = abbrev. of *mlk ›rwd* (= the king of A.), cf. J.& A.G.Elayi JANES xviii 16, also for older litt.
m›d **Hebr** TA-H 111[3] (dam. context), AMB 1[1] - ¶ adv. (originally subst., v. also *m›h_2*) very, much.
v. *hwy_1*.
m›h_1 (< Iran., cf. Humbach IPAA 10) - **OffAr** Sing. abs. *m›h* IPAA 11[1] - ¶ subst. month.
m›h_2 **Ph** Sing. abs. *m›t* RES 1502, Hill xxii, Mus li 286[8] (*m[›]t*) - **Pun** Sing. abs. *m›t* KAI 66[1], 69[6], 101[2,3], 130[2], CIS i 171[4,6]; Dual *m›tm* KAI 76B 9, 141[5] - **Mo** Sing. abs. *m›t* KAI 181[29] (cf. e.g. Cooke NSI p. 3, Röllig KAI a.l. × e.g. Gibson SSI i p. 77, Lipiński Or xl 340, Dahood FS Horn 438f., Smelik HDAI 35: = Plur. abs.; cf. also Segert ArchOr xxix 265); Dual *m›tn* KAI 181[20] - **Hebr** Sing. abs. *m›h* Mosc var. 10 (cf. e.g. Maisler JNES x 266, Gibson SSI i p. 17, Lemaire IH i p. 252 :: Catastini Hen vi 137: l. *m›d* (= Sing. abs. of *m›d* (= strength))); cstr. *m[›]t* KAI 189[5f.]; Dual *m›tym* KAI 189[5], AMB 4[16]; Plur. abs. *m›wt* SM 13 (= Frey 977), AMB 4[18] - **Samal** Sing. abs. *m›h* KAI 214[28] (for the reading, cf. Gibson SSI ii p. 68, 75, Lipiński BiOr xxxiii 232, OLP viii 101 (cf. also Dahood Or xlv 382) :: e.g. D.H.Müller WZKM vii 53, 67, 134, Halévy RS ii 57, Garb 261, Friedr 33*a, Dion p. 139, Oelsner OLZ '80, 555 n.: l. *mṣ‹h* (= Sing. abs. of *mṣ‹h*) :: Lidzbarski Handb 315, Cooke NSI p. 170: l. *mṣ‹h* = Sing. + suff. 3 p.s.m. of

mṣʿ (= midst; cf. also Poeb 49 n. 1, Donner KAI a.l. (cf. also Degen ZDMG cxxi 124, 132: l. *mṣʿh* or *mṣʿ<t>h* = Sing. + suff. 3 p.s.m. of *mṣʿh*)) :: Sader EAS 162: l. *mṣʿt* = Sing. cstr. of *mṣʿh*) - **OldAr** Sing. abs. *mʾh* Tell F 20, 21, 22 (Akkad. par. *mē*) - **OffAr** Sing. abs. *mʾh* Cowl $26^{14,15,17}$, *mh* IEJ xxv 118^2 (for script and language, cf. Naveh ibid. 120ff.); cstr. *mʾt* Cowl 2^8, $22^{19,20}$; emph. *mʾtʾ* Cowl 3^{11}; + suff. 3 p.s.m. *mʾth* Cowl $2^{6,10}$; Dual *mʾtyn* Cowl $26^{13\text{-}16}$ (for the form, cf. Leand 60q :: BL 67q); Plur. + suff. 3 p.pl.m. *mʾwthm* Cowl 80^3 (for the reading, cf. also Porten & Yardeni sub TADAE A 5.5 :: RES sub 247^3: l. *mʾrthm* (= Sing. + suff. 3 p.pl.m. of *mʾrh* (= decrease))) - **Nab** Sing. abs. *mʾh* CIS ii 200^9, 205^9, 209^8, 963^1, J 17^5, MPAT 64 iii 2; Dual *mʾtyn* CIS ii 333^7, J 386^5, BAGN ii 88^6 - **Palm** Sing. abs. *mʾh* CIS ii 3948^4, 4053^4, 4173^1, 4174^8, 4199^{15}, InscrP 32^4, Inv x 13^7 (*mʾ[h]*, dam. context), 54^5, RB xxxix 548^4, MUSJ xxxviii 106^1, Sem xxxvi $89^{3,4,5,6}$; Dual *mʾtn* Sem xxxvi 89^2 (*mtʾn* misprint) - **JAr** Sing. abs. *mʾh* MPAT 48^3, MPAT-A 52^6, Syn D A 2 (= SM 88), $C_1{}^2$ (= SM 89), DBKP 17^{41}, 18^{77} (diff. reading), Mas 570, 571^2, *mʾ*MPAT-A 50^6, 51^6; cstr. *mʾt* MPAT-A 11^3 (= SM 49); Dual abs. *mʾtyn* MPAT 48^2, Mas 582^2 (*[m]ʾtyn*), *mtyn* AMB 9^3 - ¶ cardinal number, hundred passim; Dual two hundred - with special meaning "company of hundred men", "century": RES 1502, KAI $101^{2,3}$, Cowl $2^{6,8,10}$, 3^{11}, $22^{19,20}$, 80^3 (v. also *rb*$_2$); for *mʾh* as military term in Elephantine, cf. also Temerev FS Freedman 523f. - Aharoni TA a.l.: l. *ʾmtym* in TA-H 10^3, lapsus for *mʾtym* (= Dual abs.; highly uncert. reading and interpret., cf. Pardee UF x 308, HAHL 43f.) - Périkhanian REA-NS a.l.: the *m*in REA-NS viii 9 = abbrev. of *mʾh* (poss. interpret.).
v. *tmʾ*$_2$.

mʾwzn v. *mʾzn*$_1$.

mʾwm v. *mʾwmh*.

mʾwmh **Hebr** *mʾwm[h]* KAI 193^{13} (for the reading, cf. e.g. Torczyner Lach i p. 51, Albright BASOR lxxiii 18 (cf. also Gibson SSI i p. 38, Cross FS Iwry 45): l. *mʾwmh* :: de Vaux RB xlviii 192 (div. otherwise): l. *mʾwm* (= Sing. abs. (= small stain, point)) + horizontal stroke) - ¶ indef. pronoun, something: KAI 193^{13} (for the interpret. and reading of the context, cf. also Cross FS Iwry 42f., 46).

mʾz v. *mʾzn*$_2$.

mʾzl **OffAr** Segal ATNS a.l.: l. *mʾzlh* (= Sing. + suff. 3 p.s.m. of *mʾzl* (departure)) in ATNS 2^3 (?, or = Qal Inf. + suff. 3 p.s.m. of *ʾzl*?); uncert. reading, cf. Shaked Or lvi 408 (div. otherwise): l. perhaps *tmʾw* (= Qal Impf. 2 p.pl.m. of *ymʾ*)+ *lh* (= *l*$_5$ + suff. 3 p.s.m.), cf. also Porten & Yardeni sub TADAE B 8.9.

mʾzn$_1$ **Hebr** Dual abs. *mʾznym* Frey 1162^7 (= SM 45), *mʾwznyym* SM 70^4, *mwznym* SM 27^7, *mwznyym* Frey 1206^7 (= SM 67) - **OffAr** Sing.

emph. *mwznʾ* Cowl 15[24], Krael 7[26]; cf. Frah xix 4 (*mzynʾ*) - ¶ subst. scales, pair of scales; in Frey 1162[7], 1206[7], SM 27[7], 70[4] indicating sign of the Zodiac - for the root, cf. also Segert AAG p. 122.

m ʾzn$_2$ Pun a subst. *mʾzn$_2$* (Sing. or Plur. + suff. 3 p.pl.m. *mʾznm* (cf. also Clermont-Ganneau RAO iii 9 n. 1: meaning of *mʾzn* unknown)) in KAI 81[3]?? or rather = subst. *mʾz* (Sing. + suff. 3 p.pl.m., cf. e.g. Cooke NSI p. 128, Clermont-Ganneau RAO iii 9, Prätorius ZDMG lx 166 n. 1, Chabot RES sub 17, 132, 1589) or verbal form (PIʿEL or YIPH Part. pl.m. abs.) of root *ʾzn$_1$*? (cf. Halévy RS ix 81: = PIʿEL Part. Plur. (= those charged with the management of the objects necessary inside the buildings)) :: cf. v.d.Branden PO i 208, BiOr xxxvi 202: Plur. cstr. of *mʾznm* (< root *znm*; = annex (to a building)).

m ʾznm v. *mʾzn$_2$*.

m ʾkl OffAr Sing. abs. *mkl* Cowl 24[35], 49[4] (:: Ungnad ArPap sub no. 45: or = *mn$_5$* + Sing. abs. of *kl$_1$*; cf. Degen NESE iii 25, Porten BASOR cclviii 50), *mʾkl* ATNS 26[8,10,11], 29[5], 38[19] (dam. context); emph. *mʾklʾ* KAI 279[3], ATNS 26[13,16] - ¶ subst. food - Milik DFD 205ff.: this word in Greek transcr., μαχολ in FDE inscr no. 50[1] (p. 404), highly uncert. interpret.
v. *mkl$_1$*.

m ʾkn v. *mkn$_1$*.

m ʾlh v. *mlʾ$_3$*.

m ʾmr Hebr Sing. + suff. 3 p.s.m. *mʾmrh* DJD ii 24C 20 - **JAr** Sing. abs. *mʾmr* AMB 3[23] - ¶ subst. order: DJD ii 24C 20 (dam. context); *mlʾkyh dm[mnyn ʿ]l ʾšth ... ʾswn ʾl[ʿzr b]mʾmr qdyš* AMB 3[21ff.]: oh angels appointed over fever, ... cure E. by a holy command.
v. *šhd$_2$*.

m ʾn OldAr Plur. emph. *mʾnyʾ* Tell F 16 (Akkad. par. *ú-nu-te*) - **OffAr** Sing. abs. *mʾn* Cowl 65 i 3 (or cstr.?, dam. context), Aḥiq 109, Sem xiv 72 conc. 2 (dam. context), 3; cstr. *mʾn* KAI 226[6], Krael 11[11], ATNS 39[6]; Plur. abs. *mʾnn* Cowl 72[4], Krael 7[15] (*[m]ʾn[n]*; for the reading, cf. Porten & Yardeni sub TADAE B 3.8), ATNS 9[5] (prob. reading, cf. Porten & Yardeni sub TADAE B 8.6 :: Segal ATNS a.l.: l. *mkns* (= Sing. abs. of *mkns* (= trousers))), 41[6]; cstr. *mʾny* Cowl 20[5], Krael 7[13]; + suff. 3 p.s.m. *mʾnwhy* ATNS 67b 6, *mʾnhy* RES 1792A 7; cf. Frah v 7 (*mʾnh*; cf. Toll ZDMG-Suppl viii 29) - **JAr** Sing. cstr. *mn* Mas 556[3] - ¶ subst. m. vessel, vase, recipient, passim; made of silver: KAI 226[6f.]; made of bronze: KAI 226[6f.], Cowl 20[5], Krael 7[13], 11[11]; made of iron: Cowl 20[5], Krael 11[11]; made of clay: Mas 556[3]; made of wood: Cowl 20[5]; made of palm-leaves (?): Cowl 20[5f.] (v. *ḥṣ$_4$*); used for wine: Cowl 72[4] (cf. also Grelot Sem xxiii 103); in Tell F 16 Plur. prob. indicating movable objects - for Aḥiq 109, v. *mlh* - on this word, cf. Kottsieper SAS 113.

v. *'mn$_4$*, *mnm*, *mšr*.

m'nn Pun Plur. abs. *m'nnm* RCL '66, 201[6] - ¶ subst. indicating profession, Fantar RCL '66, 208: poss. = maker of vases (cf. also Dupont-Sommer CRAI '68, 129) :: Ferron Mus xcviii 59, 61: = the equipment of vessels.

m'nš' Pun diff. word in KAI 119[6]; prob. subst. (Sing. abs. or + suff. 3 p.s.m.), poss. meaning, offering, contribution (related to root *'nš$_1$* or less prob. *nš'$_1$*?), cf. however Février RA l 187f.: = OPH Part. s.m. abs. or + suff. 3 p.s.m. of *nš'$_1$*, *m'nš'* = (his) offering (cf. v.d.Branden GP p. 85) :: Röllig KAI a.l.: = PI'EL Part. s.m. abs. of *nš'$_1$*, *m'nš'* = giving help/assistence :: Levi Della Vida RCL '55, 560: = PU'AL Part. s.m. abs. subst. (= what is paid).

m's' v. *m'šh*.

m'sp Pun Sing. abs. *m'sp* KAI 122[1] - ¶ subst. poss. meaning: whole, in the comb. *m'sp šhnskt š'lm 'wgsṭs* KAI 122[1] (for the reading *šhnskt*, cf. Amadasi IPT 54f. :: Levi Della Vida AfrIt vi 18, Röllig KAI a.l.: l. *hnskt*): poss. = the whole of the statue of the divine A.

m'sph Pun Sing. cstr. *m'spt* CIS i 6000bis 4 (= TPC 84) - ¶ subst. place or object, where something is gathered; *m'spt 'ṣmy* CIS i 6000bis 4: the place/object, where his bones are gathered.

v. *mḥsp*, *n'sph*.

m''ms v. *my'ms*.

m'rh v. *m'h$_2$*.

m'rḥ v. *'rḥ$_1$*.

m'rk v. *'rk$_1$*.

m'š$_1$ Ph Sing. abs. *mš* KAI 6[1] (prob. reading), 43[1] (cf. Honeyman JEA xxvi 58f., v.d.Branden OA iii 248f., Lipiński RTAT 250, Gibson SSI iii p. 135f. :: e.g. Cooke NSI p. 84, Harr 123, Röllig KAI a.l., FR 47 (div. otherwise): l. *mšl* (= Sing. cstr. of *mšl$_4$*, variant of *mzl* (= fortune)) :: Dahood Or li 283: l. *mšl* = Sing. abs. of *mšl$_5$* (= rule)),[2] (cf. e.g. Honeyman JEA xxvi 58f., v.d.Branden OA iii 248f., Lipiński RTAT 250 × Lane BASOR cxciv 44: = Sing. + suff. 1 p.s., cf. also Röllig KAI a.l., Gibson SSI iii p. 135f.), Mus li 286[2] (:: Lane BASOR cxciv 44: = Sing. + suff. 1 p.s.); cstr. *mš* KAI 43[7]; + suff. 3 p.s.m. *m'šy* DD 13[2] (cf. Caquot Sem xv 30f., Milik DFD 426, Gibson SSI iii p. 121f. (v. however infra), Pardee Mem Craigie 56 (n. 5) :: Dunand & Duru DD p. 192f. (div. otherwise): l. *km'š* (= *km$_2$* + *'š$_4$* (= *š$_{10}$*)) *ylh* (= QAL Impf. 3 p.pl. of *lhy/lhh* (= to ask)) :: Krahmalkov RSO xlvi 35f. (div. otherwise): l. *km* (= *km$_2$*) *'my* (= Sing. + suff. 3 p.s.m. of *'m$_1$*) *l* (= *l$_5$* + suff. 3 p.s.m.)) - **Pun** Sing. abs. *m'š* KAI 119[1] (or cstr.?, dam. context), 127, 16[3], 172[4]; *mš* Antas 7; cstr. *m'š* KAI 118[1] (v. infra), 119[4], 277[9] (for this text, cf. e.g. Friedrich BAGN i 209 :: Février CRAI '65, 14f.: *lm'š* = *l$_5$* + *m$_{12}$* (= *mn$_5$*) + *'š$_4$* (= *š$_{10}$*) = since (the time)

that; cf. also Dupont-Sommer CRAI '65, 17), *mš* CIS i 3777[1], Antas 1[1], 5[1], 9[1], 13 (or = abs.?. *mš[* ; heavily dam. context) - ¶ subst. prob. meaning, votive donation, statue as votive donation (cf. e.g. Garbini AION xviii 230ff., xix 321ff., FSR 209ff., cf. also Honeyman Mus li 289f. (cf. already Bruston EtPhen 40), Bordreuil Syr lii 113ff. :: CIS i sub 3777: = stele). For parallels, cf. KAI 127 (*mʾš//sac(rum)*), KAI 172 (*mʾš//statuam*); *mš ʾbn* CIS i 3777[1]: stone statue (v. supra :: Dussaud BAr '22, 244f., CRAI '46, 383 (div. otherwise): l. *mšʾ* (= Sing. cstr.) *bn* = offering of a son, cf. however Dussaud Syr xvi 408 n. 1: l. *mš ʾbn* - stele of stone); *mš ʾbn ḥrṣ* Antas 5[1]: statue of carved stone (v. *ḥrṣ*$_5$); *mš ʾlm* KAI 277[9]: statue of the deity (:: Garbini AION xviii 230ff.: = sacred place corresponding with *ʾšr qdš* in l. 1), cf. also KAI 118[1] (for the context, v. *pʿr*$_2$); *mʾš hnḥšt* KAI 119[4]: statue of bronze (cf. Antas 1[1]); *mš pn ʾby* KAI 43[7]: a statue representing my father (for the context, v. *pnh*$_1$); *mš lnʿm* KAI 43[1]: effigy for good fortune (v. supra); for *sml z mš* in KAI 43[2] and *sml mš z* Mus li 286[2], v. *sml*$_1$; *mš šdrpʾ* Antas 9[1]: statue of Sh. (or votive offering for Sh.??) - the diff. *thmʾʾʾst* in CIS i 151[2] to be divided in *t*$_1$ + *hmʾʾ* (= lapsus for *hmʾš* (= *h*$_1$ + Sing. abs. of *mʾš*$_1$)) + *ʾst* (v. *z*$_1$)?? (cf. Clermont-Ganneau RAO vii 91 n. 2, Février JA ccxlvi 443, Amadasi sub ICO-Sard Np 2 :: v.d.Branden BO xix 275f.: *hmʾʾ* = Sing. abs. of *ḥmh*$_5$ (= hot spring) :: Pili BO xxii 214ff. l. poss. *trmʾʾ* = Latin *thermae*) - for the etymology and derivation of the word, cf. Rocco AION xx 396ff.: < root *ʾwš/ʾyš* (cf. also Teixidor Syr xlix 415f., liii 318, Bordreuil Syr lii 115f.), cf. however also Gibson SSI iii p. 136ff. (cf. also p. 21): etymology unclear, prob. two words *m(ʾ)š*?, one of which might be < Egypt. (cf. Lidzbarski OLZ '27, 456, cf. however Montet Syr ix 172) - on this word, cf. also Hvidberg-Hansen TNT ii 34 n. 312 - for the *mʾš* in Herr SANSS-Ph 5, v. *š*$_{10}$.
v. *mzl*.

mʾš$_2$ v. *mh*$_2$.

mbʾ **Ph** Sing. cstr. *mbʾ* KAI 26A i 18; + suff. 3 p.s.m. *mbʾy* KAI 26A i 5, ii 3 - **Pun** Sing. cstr. *mbʾ* KAI 78[5], *mbw* KAI 161[3] (for this reading and interpret., cf. Roschinski Num 112, 114 :: Février RA xlv 142, Röllig KAI a.l. (div. otherwise): l. *md* (= Sing. abs. of *md*$_1$ (= garment)) :: v.d.Branden RSF ii 143: l. *md* = Sing. abs. of *md*$_2$ (= measure), *bmd* = in natural size, life-size); + suff. 1 p.s., cf. Poen 941: *mbae* (or l. rather *mbai*?, cf. Sznycer PPP 121) - **Amm** Plur. abs. *mbʾt* BASOR cxciii 8[1] (for this interpret., cf. Horn BASOR cxciii 8f., Albright BASOR cxcviii 38f., R.Kutscher Qadm v 28, Puech & Rofé RB lxxx 534f., v.Selms BiOr xxxii 8, Dion RB lxxxii 32, Shea PEQ '79, 18, Sasson PEQ '79, 118ff., Jackson ALIA 10, 14f., 25, Smelik HDAI 84, Aufrecht sub CAI 59 × Cross BASOR cxciii 18, Fulco BASOR ccxxx

41f., Shea PEQ '81, 105f.: = Plur. cstr.; cf. however Garbini AION xx 253f.: or = Sing. abs. of *mb'h*?; for the context, v. *sbb*$_2$) - ¶ subst. - **1)** coming: Poen 941 - **2)** setting (sc. of the sun), west: KAI 26A i 5, 18, ii 3, 78^5 - **3)** entrance; *bmbw 'ḥdr* KAI 161^3: at the entrance of the room.
v. *rzm*$_1$.

mb'h v. *mb'*.

mbw v. *mb'*.

mbṭ **Nab** Sing. + suff. 3 p.s.m. *mbṭh* CIS ii 618^3, 656^3 - ¶ subst. expectation, hope; in the expression *bṭb mbṭh* CIS ii 618^3, 656$^{2f.}$: for his good expectation.

mbky v. *mšky*.

mbn v. *pslh*.

mbnh **Ph** Sing. (or Plur.?) cstr. *mbnt* KAI 60^2 - **OffAr** Plur. (?) emph. *mbnt'* Krael 11^{11} (v. infra) - ¶ subst. - **1)** used coll. (?) constructions, buildings (in stone); *mbnt ḥṣr bt 'lm* KAI 60^2: the buildings in the temple court - **2)** building: Krael 11^{11}, interpret. of context highly uncert. (cf. Ginsberg JNES xviii 149 n. 20: = lapsus for *mdnt'* (= Sing. emph. of *mdnh* (= province)) :: Yaron JNES xx 127 (cf. Grelot DAE p. 253, Porten Arch 78, Porten & Greenfield JEAS p. 66, Porten & Yardeni sub TADAE B 3.13): l. *mdnt'* = Sing. emph. of *mdnh*).
v. *nbnh*.

mbny **OffAr** Sing. abs. *mbny* Krael 12^{12}; cstr. *mnby* Krael 9^{12}, 10^{2,3}, 12^{13} (for all instances :: Porten & Greenfield JEAS p. 58, 63, 68: Part. pass. s.m. abs. of *bny*$_1$ (in derived stem), cf. however Grelot RB lxxxii 290 :: Krael p. 241: = QAL Inf. of *bny*$_1$)- ¶ subst. building, construction; *mbny drgh* Krael 10^3: construction of a stairway (v. also *drg*); *mbny* combined with *by tḥty*, v. *tḥty*.

mb'l **Pun** Sing. cstr. *mb'l* on coins, cf. Müll iii 145f., 155 (or abs.?), 156, CHC 618 no. 1, cf. also Mazard no. 597-599, 611, 630, 631-634 (or abs.?), 638 (or abs.?), 639, 641 (or abs.?) - ¶ subst. poss. meaning community (of the citizens, cf. Müll iii 149ff., Müll Suppl 79f. (:: Lidzbarski Handb 239, Harr 88, Ginsberg FS Gaster 145: = *mn*$_5$ + Plur. cstr. of *b'l*$_2$)).

mb'lh **Pun** Sing. abs. *mb'lt* on coins, cf. Mazard no. 619, 635, 636 - ¶ subst. poss. meaning community (of the citizens), cf. also Mazard p. 180 - reading *mb'ltt* on coin, cf. Mazard no. 62, prob. = *mb'lt* (Sing. cstr.) + *t* (= abbrev. of n.l.).

mb'r₁ **Mo** Sing. abs. *mb'r* SSI i 83^2 (v. infra) - ¶ subst. of unknown meaning; poss. denoting an object (in relig. context), cf. Reed & Winnett BASOR clxxii 8f.: = altar? (cf. also Weippert ZDPV lxxx 171f., cf. also Swiggers AION xlii 523ff.: = burning-place), cf. however Gibson SSI i a.l.: = act of purgation :: Schiffmann ZAW lxxvii 324f.: =

pillager (= HIPH Part. s.m. abs. of *b‘r$_1$*;cf. also Weippert ZDPV lxxxii 330: or = Part. pass., pillaged one).

mb‘r$_2$ Palm Sing. (or Plur.) emph. *mb‘r’* Syr xiv 188[3] (for the reading, cf. Milik DFD 33; v. also infra) - ¶ subst. (?) of unknown meaning; Milik DFD 33: = merchandise; or poss. to be related to *b‘d$_1$*,and l. *mb‘d’*?; Cantineau Syr xiv a.l.: l. *md‘r’* without interpret.

mbṣ‘ Pun Sing. abs. *mbṣ‘* KAI 119[6] (cf. however Février RA l 185, 187f.: poss. = PU‘AL Part. s.m. abs. of *bṣ‘$_2$*, *mbṣ‘* = contribution (cf. v.d.Branden GP p. 79) :: Röllig KAI a.l., BiOr xxvii 379: prob. = PI‘EL Part. s.m. abs. of *bṣ‘$_2$*, *mbṣ‘* = contributing :: Levi Della Vida RCL ’55, 552, 560: l. *nbṣ‘* = NIPH Part. s.m. abs. of *bṣ‘$_2$*, *nbṣ‘* = what is acquired) - ¶ subst. (v. however supra), poss. meaning, gain, contribution.

mbq v. *mrq‘*.

mbš v. *npš*.

mg$_1$ OffAr Kottsieper UF xx 131ff.: l. *mg* (= Sing. abs. (= garrison)) in Aḥiq 159; highly uncert. reading, cf. Cowl a.l., Lindenberger APA 159ff.: l. *mt[*.

mg$_2$ v. *rbmg*.

mgd$_1$ Palm PA‘EL Pf. 3 p.s.m. *mgd* CIS ii 3927[3], 3934[4], Inv xii 24, RIP 162[3] - ¶ verb PA‘EL to give generously - **1)** + obj.: Inv xii 24 (dam. context) - **2)** + *l$_5$* + obj.: CIS ii 3927[3], 3934[4] (cf. also RIP 162[3f.]) - denominative verb < *mgd$_2$*?, cf. Rosenthal Sprache 95.

mgd$_2$ (< Arab.?, cf. Cantineau Gramm 101, cf. however Rosenthal Sprache 95) - **Palm** Sing. (or Plur.) emph. *mgd’* CIS ii 3924[5], Inv xii 23[3]; + suff. 3 p.pl.m. *mgdyhwn* CIS ii 3914[3] - ¶ subst. liberality, generous ġift, offering.
v. *mgd$_1$*.

mgdl Mo Plur. + suff. 3 p.s.f. *mgdlth* KAI 181[22] (on this form, cf. Garr DGSP 98, Jackson & Dearman SMIM 118) - ¶ subst. tower; cf. Marrassini FLEM 114ff. (cf. also Garbini AION xxiii 276); cf. also Harr p. 93.

mgdr v. *gdr*.

mghṭ = metal utensil, scraper (for cleaning of brick) > Akkad. *magattu*, cf. v.Soden Or xxxv 16, xlvi 190, AHW s.v. *magattu* (Plur. *magaṭātu*), cf. also CAD s.v. *magattu*.

mgwš (< Iran., v. *mgšy*) - **OffAr** Sing. emph. *mgwš’* Beh 60 (for the reading, cf. Greenfield & Porten BIDG p. 50f. l. 75; Akkad. par. *ma-gu-šú*), PF 1798 - ¶ subst. magian, cf. *mgš$_1$*, *mgšy*.

mglb Pun Sing. cstr. *mglb* CIS i 6065 (for the reading, cf. Lidzbarski Eph i 171, Garbini StudMagr xi 19ff. :: Février CIS i a.l.: l. *myglb* (= *mglb*) :: Chabot sub RES 1598 (div. otherwise): l. *glb* = Sing. abs. of *glb$_2$* (= barber; for the reading problems, cf. also RES sub 125) ::

Ferron Mus lxxix 445, 448f.: l. *št* (= QAL Pf. 3 p.s.m. of *šty*$_1$ (= to drink)) *lb* (= Sing. cstr. of *lb* (= soul))) - ¶ subst. razor.

mglh **Ph** Sing. abs. *mglt* Syr xlviii 403[7] (cf. e.g. Caquot Syr xlviii 406, Röllig NESE ii 35, v.d.Branden BiOr xxxiii 13, Lipiński RSF ii 53f., Garbini OA xx 292, Sem xxxviii 134, de Moor JEOL xxvii 111 :: Gaster BASOR ccix 19, 26: = Plur. abs. :: Baldacci BiOr xl 130: poss. = PU<AL Part. s.f. abs. of *gly* (= what is uncovered) :: Avishur PIB 267, 272, UF x 32, 36, Gibson SSI iii p. 90: *kmglt* = *km*$_2$+ *glt* (= Sing. or Plur. of *glh* (= ball (of the eye))) :: Cross CBQ xxxvi 488f.: pro *kmglt* l. *mmglt* = *m*$_{12}$ (= *mn*$_5$) + Sing. abs. of *mglh*) - **OffAr**, cf. Frah xv 4 (*mglt*›; v. also *mnrtwyn*) - ¶ subst. scroll, book - > Akkad. *magallatu*, cf. v.Soden Or xxxv 15, xlvi 189, AHW s.v., CAD s.v.

mgmr$_1$ **Ph** diff. word *mgmr* in Syr xlviii 403[3], uncert. interpret.; Caquot Syr xlviii 404, 406: = PI‹EL Part. s.m. abs. of *gmr*$_1$ (= to destroy (cf. also Gaster BASOR ccix 19, 25, Garbini OA xx 290, 292, Baldacci BiOr xl 129, Cross CBQ xxxvi 488f.; Lipiński RSF ii 53: = PI‹EL Part. s.m. abs. of *gmr*$_1$ (= to achieve); cf. also de Moor JEOL xxvii 111); Röllig NESE ii 29, 32f.: = Sing. abs. of *mgmr*$_3$ (= destruction) :: v.d.Branden BiOr xxxiii 13: = HOPH Part. s.m. abs. of *gmr*$_1$ (= to be intoxicated by burnt incense) :: Avishur PIB 267, 271, UF x 32, 35f.: = Sing. abs. of *mgmr*$_4$ (= door, bolt); on the subject, cf. also Gibson SSI iii p. 91.

mgmr$_2$ **Nab** Sing. abs. *mgmr* CIS ii 199[8] - ¶ subst. totality; *ldmy mgmr* CIS ii 199[8]: at the full price; cf. *gmr*$_4$.

mgmr$_3$ v. *mgmr*$_1$.

mgmr$_4$ v. *mgmr*$_1$.

mgn$_1$ (poss. denominative verb, cf. v.Soden JEOL xviii 340f.; v. *mgn*$_3$) - **Ph** PI‹EL Pf. 3 p.s.f. *mgn* KAI 29[1] (:: v.Soden JEOL xviii 341: or = form of *mgn*$_3$?) - ¶ verb PI‹EL to offer; *›rn zn* (v. however *znh*) *mgn ›mtb‹l ... mtt l‹štrt* KAI 29[1f.]: A. offered this box ... (as) a gift to A. - on this root, cf. v.Soden BAO 51ff.

mgn$_2$ **Ph** Sing. abs. *mgn* KAI 26A i 7 - ¶ subst. shield - Safar Sumer xviii 61f.: l. *mgn›* (= Plur. emph. (= shields/discs)) in Hatra 201[2] (cf. Caquot Syr xli 270; cf. also - a) Milik DFD 407: = n.l. - b) Altheim & Stiehl AAW iv 248, 259: < Lat. *magna*), improb. reading, cf. Aggoula MUSJ xlvii 42, Vattioni IH a.l.: l. *m‹n›* = n.p. - v.Soden Or xxxv 16, xlvi 190, AHW s.v. *maginnu*: > Akkad. *maginnu* (less prob. interpret., cf. CAD s.v. *maginnu*: = type of headgear).

mgn$_3$ (< Hurr. (?), cf. v.Soden JEOL xviii 339ff., cf. also Kaufman AIA 67 (n. 184), cf. however Margain Sem xxxv 80 n. 31, O'Connor JAOS cix 25ff.) - **Pun** Sing. abs. *mgn* BAr-NS i/ii 228[3] (cf. Garbini AION xxv 260f. :: Février BAr a.l.: = n.p.) - **Palm** Sing. abs. (v. infra) *mgn* CIS ii 3936[4] - ¶ subst. gift: BAr-NS i/ii 228[3] (v. supra), KAI 78[3f.] (v.

supra) - used adverbially: CIS ii 3936[4] (gratuitously, for nothing), cf. also Rundgren OrSu xv 81ff. - v.Soden Or xxxv 15, xlvi 189, AHW s.v. *magānu*: > Akkad. in the expression *ana maganu* (= in vain, for nothing), cf. also CAD s.v. *magannu* A, v.Soden BAO 52 - Röllig sub KAI 78: the *mgnm* in KAI 78[3f.] = Plur. abs. (uncert. interpret., cf. also Chabot CIS i sub 3778: *bʿl mgnm* = B. the protector; for the problem, cf. also Garbini RSF xviii 211).
v. *mgn*$_1$, *mlh*.

mgnh **Pun** Garbini AION xix 327: the *mgnt* in Antas 4[5] poss. = Sing. abs. of *mgnh* (= gift, offering); cf. however Fantar Antas a.l.: prob. = n.p.

mgr$_1$ **OffAr** PA ʿEL Pf. 3 p.pl.m. *mgrw* Cowl 30[14] - ¶ verb PA ʿEL to overthrow + obj. (temples).

mgr$_2$ **Pun**, cf. Corpus Glossariorum Latinorum (ed. G. Goetz, Lipsiae 1894) 82: *quia mager punica villa dicitur* (*mager* = country-house, farm); cf. also Lewis & Short Latin Dict. s.v. *magalia* (= little dwellings, huts), *Magalia* (= suburbs of Carthage); cf. also *mply*.

mgrd **Pun** Plur. abs. *mgrdm* CIS i 338[4] - ¶ subst. scraper, scratcher.

mgš$_1$ (< Iran. v. *mgšy*) - **OffAr** PA ʿEL Pf. 3 p.s.m. *mgyš* KAI 265[2] (Greek par. ἐμάγευσε; cf. Lidzbarski Eph iii 67 :: Lipiński Stud 176, 179ff.: = QAL pass. Pf. 3 p.s.m. (cf. however Degen WO ix 170f.)) - ¶ verb PA ʿEL to act as a magian, to be a magian - cf. *mgwš*, *mgšy*.

mgš$_2$ v. *mgšh*.

mgšh **Ph** Sing. + suff. 2 p.s.m. *mgštk* KAI 3[4] (:: McCarter & Coote BASOR ccxii 22: = Plur. + suff. 2 p.s.m. :: Albright BASOR xc 36 (n. 9): = Plur. + suff. 2 p.s.m. of *mgš*$_2$ (= offering) :: v.d.Branden RSF ii 138ff.: l. *mgšt* (Sing. abs.) + word divider; v. infra); + suff. 1 p.s. *mgšt* KAI 3[5] (:: McCarter & Coote BASOR ccxii 22: = Plur. + suff. 1 p.s. :: Albright BASOR xc 36 (n. 9): = Plur. + suff. 1 p.s. of *mgš*$_2$ (= offering; cf. idem JAOS lxvii 158f. (n. 48) and also Dunand BG 157 n. 1) :: v.d.Branden RSF ii 140: = Sing. abs.; v. infra) - ¶ subst. of unknown meaning; Iwry JAOS lxxxi 32ff.: = divining implement (i.e. the spatula on which the text is written; cf. also Cross EI viii 9* n. 9); Lane BASOR cxciv 41: = oracle?; CF 13 (n. 7): = offering; Dunand BMB ii 104f.: credit, right to a debt; McCarter & Coote BASOR ccxii 19, 22 (n. 33; v. also supra): = obligation :: v.d.Branden RSF ii 138 (v. also supra): l. prob. *mgšt* = battle (cf. also idem BiOr xxxvi 202) :: Obermann JBL lviii 236, 238, 242: = dominion; for the reading *mgšt-*, v. also Talmon JAOS lxxxiii 182 n. 43; :: Dupont-Sommer ArchOr xvii[1] 160, 164: l. *mpšt-* (= Sing. of *mpšh* (= possession)), cf. also FR 237, Röllig KAI a.l. :: Torczyner Lesh xiv 162ff.: l. *mpšt-* = *m*$_{10}$ (= *mn*$_5$) + Sing. of *pšt*; on this word, cf. also Gibson SSI iii p. 10f., Garr DGSP 40, 97.

mgšy (< Iran., cf. Telegdi JA ccxxvi 229, de Menasce BiOr xi 161f., Eilers AfO xvii 333, Chaumont JA cclvi 24) - **OffAr** Sing. emph. *mgšy*› Krael 4[24] - ¶ subst. m. magian, Magus; cf. *mgwš*, *mgš*$_1$.
md$_1$ v. *mb*›, *mr*›.
md$_2$ v. *mb*›, *mr*$_5$.
md$_3$ v. *mdy*$_1$.
md$_4$ v. *dy*$_1$, *mdy*$_2$.
md›n›mwp› **OffAr** diff. group of signs in AM ii 174[2]; Henning AM a.l.: comb. of two n.p.'s unlikely, cf. also Altheim & Stiehl Suppl 94, ASA 273: pro *md*› l. *myd*› = something (highly uncert. reading and interpret.).
mdbḥ v. *mzbḥ*, *mrḥb*.
mdbr **Hebr** Sing. abs. *mydbr* SM 49[18] - **OffAr** Sing. emph. *mdbr*› KAI 233[5] - **JAr** Sing. emph. *mdbrh* AMB 9[7] - ¶ subst. desert, steppe - v.Soden Or xxxv 15, xlvi 189, AHW s.v. *madbaru*: > Akkad. *madbaru*, *mud(a)baru*.
mdgl v. *rgl*$_1$.
mdd$_1$ **Pun** QAL Part. act. s.m. abs. *mdd* CIS i 349[5] - **Hebr** QAL Part. act. s.m. abs. *mwdd* DJD ii 24A 16, C 17, E 11, F 15 - ¶ verb QAL to measure, Part. act.: measurer: CIS i 349[5]; > to pay, *t ḥkyr ... mwdd lk b[hr]wdys* DJD ii 24E 10f.: the rent .. (I will be) paying to you in H.; *t* *›lh ... mwdd ‹l gg ›wṣrh* DJD ii 24C 16f.: paying these (sc. the tithes) on the roof of the treasury (v. also *gg*$_1$),cf. also DJD ii 24F 15.
v. *mdr*$_2$, *mwddw*.
mdd$_2$ = to escape; v.Soden Or xxxv 14f., xlvi 189: > Akkad. *madādu* (cf. id. AHW s.v. *madādu* III; cf. however CAD s.v. *madādu* B: meaning uncert.).
mdd$_3$ v. *mddh*.
mdd$_4$ v. *mdr*$_2$.
mddh **OffAr** Sing. abs. *mddh* Aḥiq 159 (for interpret. as Sing. abs., cf. Cowl p. 244, Lindenberger APA 159, 265 n. 477 (:: Cowl ibid.: *mddh* stands for *mdh*$_1$) × Grelot RB lxviii 190: = Sing. + suff. 3 p.s.m. of *mdd*$_3$ (= conduct; cf. also Lindenberger APA 265 n. 477) :: Epstein ZAW xxxii 137: l. *mrdh* (= Sing. abs. of *mrdh* (= conduct)) :: Sach p. 174, Halévy RB xx 69: l. *mdrh* (= Sing. + suff. 3 p.s.m. of *mdr*$_3$ (= dwelling)) :: Kottsieper SAS 17, 230: l. *mrdh* = QAL Inf. of *rdy* (= to rule, to walk, Inf. = behaviour)) - ¶ subst. conduct; *›yš [šp]yr mddh* Aḥiq 159: a man whose conduct is excellent.
mdh$_1$ **Ph** Sing. cstr. *mdt* KAI 14[19] (cf. e.g. Cooke NSI p. 38f., Röllig KAI a.l., Gibson SSI iii p. 109, 114 :: Lipiński RSF ii 56, 58 (cf. also Peckham DLPS 80 n. 54, Puech RB lxxxviii 100, Polselli OA xxiii 178 n. 10): = Sing. cstr. of *mdh*$_2$ (= tribute)) - **Pun** Sing. abs. (?, v. infra) *mdt* KAI 145[15] (cf. e.g. Cooke NSI p. 155, Clermont-Ganneau RAO iii

341, Février Sem vi 27, Röllig KAI a.l., v.d.Branden RSF i 166, 172 :: Lipiński RSF ii 59 (div. otherwise): l. *lmd* (= QAL Imper. s.m. of *lmd*$_1$ (= to learn)) + *t* (= *t*$_1$; cf. however Elayi RCP 23f., SCA 53: l. *mrt* prob. = lapsus for *mdt*); cstr. *mdt* KAI 69^{17} - **Hebr** Sing. abs. *mydh* SM 49^4 - ¶ subst. measure - **1)** prec. by prep. *b*, *hnymkryn bmydh* SM 49^4: (goods) which are sold by measure (i.e. by retail) - **2)** prec. by prep. *k*$_1$, *kmdt št bktb* KAI 69^{17}: according as is set down in the document - **3)** prec. by prep. *l*$_5$, *ytn ln ... ʾyt dʾr wypy ... lmdt ʿṣmt ʾš pʿlt* KAI $14^{18f.}$: he gave us D. and Y. ... according to the measure of (i.e. as reward for) the striking deeds which I performed; Clermont-Ganneau RAO iii 341, Février Sem vi 27: l. in KAI 145^{15} *lmdt s* = according to this rule (uncert. reading and interpret., cf. Cooke NSI p. 151, Röllig KAI a.l.: l. *lmdt t*, without interpret., cf. also v.d.Branden RSF i 166, 172: l. *lmdt tm ...* = according to the generosity of ... (for the context, v. *mʿzrh*)).
v. *mddh*.

mdh_2 v. *mdh*$_1$.

mdwbr Sznycer Sem v 78: *mdwbr* in Nisa 17^4, 18^5, 19^4, 20^4, 22^4, etc., etc. derivative of *dbr*$_2$??,improb. interpret., cf. Diakonov & Livshitz Nisa-b p. 42, Chaumont JA cclvi 14: < Iran. = conveyor of wine (:: I.M.Diakonov, M.M.Diakonov & Livshitz VDI xlvi ('53,4) 122, Vinnikov VDI xlviii ('54,2) 125, Altheim & Stiehl WZKMU '55/56, 283, ASA 142, 145, 273, GMA 483: < Iran. = cup-bearer).

mdy_1 (< Greek μόδιος, cf. Cantineau Gramm 156, Rosenthal Sprache 92) - **Palm** Sing. emph. *mdyʾ* CIS ii 3913 ii 69, 73, 133, *mdʾ* CIS ii 3913 ii 71 (for this form, cf. Rosenthal Sprache 15) - ¶ subst. dry measure (for e.g. salt), *modius*, bushel (8 à 9 litres) - for CIS ii 3913 ii 69, v. *qsṭwn*.

mdy_2 **Ph** the diff. *mdy* in MUSJ xlv 262^3 poss. = n.g. *Media* (cf. Starcky MUSJ xlv 266, v.d.Branden BiOr xxxiii 12, Schiffmann RSF iv 172, 175 :: Röllig NESE ii 6f.: or = *md*$_4$ (= *mn*$_5$ + *dy*$_1$))?

mdy_3 v. *mrʾ*.

mdynh v. *mdnh*.

mdytʾ **Pun** Sing. abs. *mdytʾ* KAI 153^2, *mdyty* CRAI '16, 128a 4, 130^3, *mdty* CRAI '16, 128b 5 - ¶ subst. (?) or nisbe-adj. (?) related to tribal name (?, cf. Chabot CRAI '16, 130, Jongeling NINPI 180, cf. also Rössler KAI ii p. 147) or title/function indication? (cf. Février JA ccxxxvii 86, Garbini StudMagr ii 120).

mdk v. *bdmrk*.

mdl **OffAr** Sing. emph. *mdlʾ* Cowl $81^{20,21}$ (v. infra) - ¶ subst. (?) of unknown meaning, cf. Cowl p. 198: meaning 'property' unsuitable; Harmatta ActAntHung vii 349: = APH Part. pass. s.m. abs. of *dly*$_1$/*dlʾ*?(= lifted up, extended; highly uncert. interpret.); to be connected to the obscure *mydlh* in Cowl 81^{42}?? (cf. Cowl a.l., cf. however Harmatta ActAntHung vii 356f.: l. poss. *mgdlh* = n.l.?? (cf. also Grelot DAE p. 111 n. j)).

mdm$_1$ (< Iran., cf. Bowman Pers p. 46, 63, Hinz AISN 155) - **OffAr** Sing. m. abs. *mdm* Pers 2^4, 17^5, 21^4, 23^5, 41^3, 55^3 (*[m]dm*), 56^3, 57^4, 80^3, 97^3, 124^3, 149^3 (*md[m]*) - ¶ adj. medium-sized; *ʾbšwn mdm* Pers $21^{3f.}$: a medium-sized pestle (cf. Pers $2^{3f.}$, 17^5, etc.).

mdm$_2$ **OffAr**, cf. Frah xxv 1, Paik 898, Syr xxxv 321^{53}, 323^{55}, 325^{59}, explained by Iran. *apar* = on, upon; *mdm* = misreading of *qdm$_3$* (cf. Nyberg FP p. 101 (cf. also Schaed 42), :: Ebeling Frah a.l.: misreading uncertain).

mdmr v. *mhdmr.*

mdnh **Hebr** Sing. abs. *mdynh*SM 49^4 - **OffAr** Sing. abs. *mdynh*Driv 6^5, Or lvii 50 iv (prob. reading, heavily dam. context), *mdynʾ*Cowl 37^6; cstr. *mdynt*Cowl 17^6 (for the reading, cf. Porten RB xc 406, 413, Porten & Yardeni sub TADAE A 6.1), 24^{36}, 27^9, 37^6, 68 xi rev. 2, TA-Ar 12^1 (dam. context); emph. *mdyntʾ*Cowl $17^{1,2}$, 73^{14}, ATNS 103^2, Samar 4^1, 5^1, *mdntʾ* Cowl 16^7; Plur. + suff. 2 p.pl.m. *mdyntkm*Driv 6^2; cf. Frah ii 7 (*mdynʾ*)- **Nab** Sing. emph. *mdtʾ* RES 675^2 (reading uncert., cf. Lidzbarski Eph iii 89 :: Chabot sub RES 675: l. *mdwtʾ*?) - **Palm** Sing. cstr. *mdynt* Syr xii 122^3; emph. *mdyntʾ*CIS ii 3994abc 1, *mdytʾ* CIS ii 3913 ii 57, 58, 147, DFD 37^3 (for this form, cf. Kaufman JAOS civ 92); + suff. 3 p.s.m. *mdynth*Syr xiv 175^3, DFD 13^3, Inv x 62^2 (*mdynt[h]*; diff. reading), *mdyth* InscrP 6^3, 32^3, Inv x $115^{2,3}$, xii 23^3, DFD 37^4 (reading uncert.), *mdth* CIS ii 3932^7 (cf. Rosenthal Sprache 16 :: Cantineau sub Inv iii 22: = lapsus for *mdyth* :: CIS ii sub 3932: l. *mdyth*); + suff. 3 p.pl.m. *mdythwn* CIS ii 3914^3, 3930^3, 3931^4; Plur. emph. *mdyntʾ*CIS ii 3913 ii 116 (on the Palm. forms, cf. Kaufman AAALT 52f.) - ¶ subst. f. - **1)** jurisdiction, department, province: Driv $6^{2,5}$, Cowl 16^7, 17^2, 73^{14}; *mdynt nʾ* Cowl 37^6: the province of Thebes, cf. Cowl 17^6 (v. supra), 24^{36}, 27^9, 68 xi rev. 2; *ḥth rbʾ mdyntʾ* ATNS 103^2: the province of Great Ch., cf. Samar 4^1, 5^1; *spry mdyntʾ* Cowl $17^{1,6}$: the scribes of the province; *bṣlyn bny mdynh* SM 49^4: the onions raised within the district - **2)** town: CIS ii 3913 ii 57, 58, cf. *mdynt bbl* Syr xii $122^{3f.}$: the town of B. - **3)** city, state: CIS ii 3913 ii 116; *bthwmy mdytʾ* DFD 37^3: within the borders of the state; cf. *rḥym mdynth* Syr xiv $175^{2f.}$ (Lat. par. *[phi]lopatrin*, Greek par. [φιλ]όπατριν; cf. also CIS ii 3914^3, 3930^3, InscrP 32^3, etc.): patriotic - **4)** > the citizens: CIS ii 3994abc 1, InscrP 6^3, Inv x $115^{2,3}$ - for this word and its derivation, cf. e.g. Marrassini FLEM 87 (cf. also Magnanini AION xviii 371f., Lipiński Trans iii 96) :: M.Fraenkel ZAW lxxvii 215: < root *mdn*.

mdnḥ **OffAr** Sing. cstr. *mdnḥ* Krael 6^7 - **Nab** Sing. cstr. *mdḥ* CIS ii 213^6 (lapsus for *mdnḥ* :: Milik RB lxvi 557: l. *mrḥ* = *mn$_5$* + Sing. cstr.

of *rḥ*$_1$ (= at the side of ...)); emph. *mdnḥ›* CIS ii 213^5 - **Palm** Sing. emph. *mdnḥ›* CIS ii 3946^2, 3971^3, RB xxxix 548^6 - **JAr** Sing. emph. *mdnḥ›* MPAT 44 i 4, 51^8, 52^3, *mdnḥh* IEJ xxxvi 206^{2,3} (*mdnḥ[h]*, diff. reading)^{,4} - ¶ subst. Orient, East: passim; cf. *mdnḥ›* CIS ii 213^5, MPAT 44 i 4, 51^8, 52^3: at the east side (cf. IEJ xxxvi 206^4); *mdnḥ šmš* Krael 6^7: at the east side; *mdḥ* (v. supra) *ymyn›* CIS ii 213^6: at the south-east side; *lmdnḥh* IEJ xxxvi 206^2: at the east side.

mdnḥy **Palm** Sing. m. emph. *mdnḥy›* CIS ii 4173^1, 4174^4, Ber ii 86^9, Syr xix 156^1 (Greek par. ἀνατολικὸν); Plur. m. abs. *mdnḥyyn* Ber v 124^6; m. emph. *mdnḥy›* Ber ii 99 i 2, 100 i 2 - **Hatra** Sing. f. emph. *mdnḥyt›* 408^7 (:: As-Salihi Sumer xlv 102 (n. 34; div. otherwise): l. *mr* (= Sing. abs. of *mr*$_4$ (=mr')) *nḥyt›* (= Qal Part. s.m. emph. of *nḥt*$_1$ (= to descend > to live)) - ¶ adj. oriental, eastern.

md‹m **OffAr** *md‹m* Cowl 49^{3,4}, Herm 1^{10}, 4^{10}, 5^2, *mnd‹m* Cowl 21^7, 27^2, 30^{14}, Aḥiq 101, Beh 11 (Akkad. par. *šá-ni-ti girri*), Herm 5^4, etc. (on this form, cf. Kottsieper SAS 51ff., 206); Plur. f. emph. *mnd‹mt›* Cowl 27^{23}, 30^{12}, ATNS 83^2 (*[m]nd‹mt›*, dam. context); + suff. 3 p.s.m. *mnd‹mth* KAI 260^8; cf. Frah xvi 9 (*mnd‹m*), Paik 640 (*mnd‹m*), DEP 154 verso 2, 3, GIPP 29, SaSt 20 - **Nab** *mnd‹m* CIS ii 350^5 - **Palm** *md‹m* CIS ii 3913 i 8, 11, ii 78, 90, RIP 154^2, SBS 45^9, *md‹n* CIS ii 3913 i 5, 3959^5 (= SBS 44), MUSJ xxxviii 106^{7,9,10}; emph. *md‹m›* CIS ii 3913 i 8, 9 (cf. however Rosenthal Sprache 52: prob. = Sing. f. abs.) - **Hatra** *md‹n* 74^8 (for this reading, cf. Vattioni IH a.l.) - **JAr** *mnd‹m* DBKP 17^{42} - ¶ indefinite pronoun, something; *mnd‹m qšh* Aḥiq 101: something hard (cf. Cowl 49^4, for the context, v. *m›kl*); *›th lkn md‹m* Herm 4^{10}: I shall send you something; *mnd‹m ksntw* Driv 7^8: any sort of loss; *nmws› md‹m* CIS ii 3913 ii 78: any law whatever; *mnh md‹m* RIP 154^2: any portion whatever; *s[y‹] šyr[t›] ... bmd‹m* SBS 45$^{8f.}$: he has helped the caravan ... in every way; *brbw‹t› ... md‹n* MUSJ xxxviii 106$^{6f.}$: in the recess ... whatever it is (for the context, v. also *kl*$_1$); *y‹bd bsṭr› dydh ḥwlwh md‹n* MUSJ xxxviii 106^{10}: he will make anything in his wall, i.e. his niches (cf. MUSJ xxxviii 106^9; :: Ingholt MUSJ xxxviii 115f.: *md‹n* in both instances = adverb: in some way, to some extent); *md‹n dbš* Hatra 74^8: something evil - **1)** in clauses with negation, *w›yš mnd‹m b›gwr› zk l› ḥbl* Cowl 30^{14}: no one did any harm to that temple; *k‹t md‹m ›l tzbny bkst* Herm 1^{10}: do not buy anything as clothing; *lh hwšr ly spr wmnd‹m* Herm 5^4: he has not sent me a letter or anything else (cf. Cowl 27^2, Driv 5^8, 7^2, 10^2, 11^2, KAI 269^2, Herm 5^2, CIS ii 3913 i 11) - **2)** for *kl md‹m* and variants, v. *kl*$_1$ - **3)** *lmd‹m› md‹m›* CIS ii 3913 i 8f.: each article (Greek par. ἑκάστῳ εἴδει) - **4)** + *zy* and variants, *md‹n dy hw› mtktb* CIS ii 3913 i 5: what was written; *md‹m dy l› msq bnmws›* CIS ii 3913 i 8: what was not specified in the law (cf. Greek par. τὰ μὴ ἀνειλημμένα τῷ νόμῳ); cf. also *mnd‹[m] ›ḥrn zy lqḥt*

Driv 12[6f.]: anything else that you have taken - **5)** Plur. f. everything; *wmzrqy› zy zhb› wksp wmnd‘mt› zy hwh b›gwr› zk kl› lqḥw* Cowl 30[12]: the bowls of gold and silver and everything which was in the temple, all of it, they took (cf. Cowl 27[23]); *trbṣh byth qnynh ṭyn wmyn mnd‘mth ybdrwnh* KAI 260[7f.]: his courtyard, his house, his acquest ground and water, and everything that is his, may they scatter it (for the context, v. also bdr_1) - for this word, cf. also Kaufman AIA 72.

md‘n v. *mnd‘m*.

md‘r v. $mb‘r_2$.

mdr_1 **DA** the *mdr* in ii 5 poss. = Sing. abs. of mdr_1 (= soil), cf. Hoftijzer DA a.l., cf. also Caquot & Lemaire Syr liv 203, Garbini Hen i 185, cf. however Levine JAOS ci 201: = Sing. abs. of mdr_3 (= slope); on this word, cf. also Hackett BTDA 57f., 83, 131: poss. = mdr_4 (= fire-pit)?? (cf. however Levine JAOS cvi 365).

mdr_2 **Nab** Sing. emph. *mdr›* IEJ xi 133[1], 135[1], xiii 113[1] (for the reading, cf. Naveh IEJ xvii 187 × Eissfeldt MiOr xv 225: l. poss. *mdd›* = Sing. emph. of mdd_4 (< root mdd_1;= receptacle used to measure (liquids)), cf. however Teixidor Syr xlviii 481 :: Eissfeldt MiOr xv 227: or perhaps = charitable foundation < root *ydd* :: Negev IEJ xi & xiii a.l.: l. *skr›* = Sing. emph. of skr_6 (= dam; the same word as skr_6 = bolt?; cf. also Levinson NAI 193)) - ¶ subst. of unknown meaning; Naveh IEJ xvii 187: poss. related to J.Ar. *mdr* = watercourse (for this word, cf. also Kaufman AIA 72: < Akkad.).

mdr_3 v. *mddh*, mdr_1.

mdr_4 v. mdr_1.

mdrš **Hebr** Sing. + suff. 3 p.s.m. *mdršw* SM 6[2] - ¶ subst. learning; *zh byt mdršw š...* SM 6[1ff.]: this is the Beth Midrash of ...

mdš v. *mrš*.

mdšh v. *ndš*.

mh_1 v. $m›h_2$.

mh_2 **Ph** *m* KAI 14[21], 24[4] - **Pun** *m›*BAr '21, p. cclx[1] (for the reading, cf. Levi Della Vida OA ii 79f., Jongeling NINPI 10f.), Trip 39[1], cf. Plautus Caecus Fragm. x: *mu*, Poen 1010: *mu* (cf. Schroed 295, FR 120c, Sznycer PPP 142, Garbini AION xxii 268, cf. however Clermont-Ganneau RAO iv 216: *mu* = contraction of mh_2 + *hw›* (= $h›_1$) :: Gray AJSL xxxix 81 (div. otherwise): l. *muphursa* = Sing. abs. of *mpršh* (= explanation) :: J.J.Glück & Maurach Sem ii 120f. (div. otherwise): l.: *muphursa* = *mprš* (= Hoph Part. s.m. emph. of $prš_1$ (= excretion > dung))), cf. IRT 877[2] (cf. Levi Della Vida OA ii 87, iv 60), 901[1,4] (cf. Levi Della Vida OA ii 79, Krahmalkov JSS xxiv 27, Polselli StudMagr xi 39): *mu* (:: Vattioni AION xvi 50 (on IRT 901[1f.,4]) (dividing otherwise): l. *muphela* = Hoph (?) Part. s.m. + suff. 3 p.s.m. of $p‘l_1$)), cf. prob. also IRT 828[1]: *[m]u* (cf. Levi Della Vida OA ii 78 :: Vattioni AION xvi

48 (div. otherwise): l. *[mu]fel* = pass. form of *pʿl*$_1$) - **Hebr** *mh* KAI 195[9], DJD ii 43[6], 46[9] (in *mhw* = *mh*$_2$ + *hw*$_1$ (dam. context)), SM 75[4] - **DA** *mh* i 7 - **Samal** *mh* KAI 214[12], *m* (in *mz* = *m*$_{11}$ (= *mh*$_2$) + *z*$_2$ (= *zy*)), KAI 214[3,4,22] - **OldAr** *mh* KAI 216[15], 222B 26, C 1, 224[3,16,28,29] - **OffAr** *mh* Cowl 38[6,8,9], Aḥiq 36, 119, 165, Driv 12[7], Herm 4[5], 5[7] (in *mhy* = *mh*$_2$ + *hy*$_1$), Sem ii 31 conc. 3, etc., *m*ʾKAI 276[7]; cf. Frah xxv 5 (*mh*), Paik 614, 615 (*mh*), Syr xxxv 327[61] (*mh*), GIPP 28, 56, 57, SaSt 19 - **Nab** *mh* CIS ii 199[6], 209[2], MPAT 64 i 10, BASOR cclxiii 77[1], 78[3] - **Palm** *mh* Syr xvii 351[10], 353[8], *m*ʾCIS ii 3913 i 13, ii 15, 70, 4218[7], RIP 199[13], *m* (in *mdy* (= *m*$_{11}$ + *dy*)) CIS ii 3913 i 4, 9, ii 60, 106, 111, 114, 128 - **Hatra** *m*ʾ74[6] (for the reading, v. *kl*$_1$) - **JAr** *mh* AMB 15[13], cf. *lmt* in AMB 7[19,20,21] = contraction of *lmh* + ʾ*t*$_4$ (= ʾ*nty*), cf. Scholem JGM 86, 91f., Naveh & Shaked AMB a.l., Sokoloff DJPA s.v. *lmh* (cf. also Beyer ATTM 372f.) :: Dupont-Sommer JKF i 203, 210: = m. Sing. abs. of *mt*$_5$ - ¶ pronoun - **1)** interrogative pronoun, what?: passim; *mh tbʿy* JRAS '29, 108[15]: what do you want?; *mh ṭb šg[yʾ] kby[k]* Aḥiq 165: what is the good of your many thorns? (cf. e.g. Cowl a.l., Ginsberg ANET 429, Grelot DAE p. 445 :: Lipiński BiOr xxxi 120: how good is ...); *mhy dh zy spr lh hwšrtn* Herm 5[7]: what is the reason that you did not send a letter?; cf. poss. also KAI 195[9] (for the context, v. *yṭb*) - prec. by prep. *l*$_5$ - a) why?; *lmh hw yḥbl mtʾ ʿlyn* Aḥiq 36: why should he ruin the land against us? (cf. prob. Aḥiq 201); *lmt kpnh* AMB 7[19f.]: why are you hungry? (v. supra; cf. AMB 7[20,21]) - b) in the expression *lmh ly*, *wʾmrt lnmrʾ lmy ly* Aḥiq 119: she said to the leopard, what use is it to me? (cf. Job xxx 2; cf. also Lindenberger APA 109; for the reading *ly*, cf. idem ibid. 249 n. 313) - c) > conj., lest (cf. Tomback JNSL xii 122f.); *wʾl yšʾ ʾyt ḥlt mškby lm ysgrnm ʾlnm hqdšm ʾl* KAI 14[21f.]: and let no one lift up the sarcophagus in which I lie, lest these holy gods deliver them ... (cf. Aḥiq 126, Driv 12[7]); cf. also *lmh hn yʾbd* Sem ii 31 conc. 3: lest they should be spoiled - d) > indef. negation, *wlḥm wmn lmʾ yšbʿ* CIS ii 4218[7]: that he will not be satisfied with bread and water - **2)** indefinite pronoun, that which; *mh ʾšʾl mn ʾlhy* KAI 214[12]: whatever I will ask from the gods ...; *mh ṭb bʿyny* KAI 224[3]: whatever is good in my eyes (cf. KAI 222C 1, Cowl 38[6,8,9], Aḥiq 163, 177, DA i 7, Herm 4[5] (for the context, v. *ytr*$_1$), CRAI '70, 163[2,2bis] (diff. context), IPAA 11[4] (diff. context)) - a) for *mz*, *mh z/dy*, *mʾ dy*, *mdy*, v. *zy*; for KAI 276[7f.], v. *prnwš* - b) *mh š*, *m ʾš*, that which; *m ʾš pʿlt bl pʿl hlpnyhm* KAI 24[4f.]: whatever I accomplished their predecessors did not accomplish (cf. SM 75[4]) - c) *mh š* prec. by prep. *k*$_1$, *kmh šʿsyt[y]* DJD ii 43[6]: like I did - **3)** relative pronoun, *mnṣbt mʾ bʿnʾ* ... BAr '21, cclx 1f.: stele which has built ... (v. supra, v. also *bny*$_1$; cf. Trip 39[1]); *mmemoria mu fela thualath* IRT 901[1f.]: memorial stele which T. has made ... (cf. also IRT 877[2], 901[4]; v.

also supra); cf. also Levi Della Vida FS Cohen 274ff., Amadasi Guzzo VO iv/2, 3f., IPT 113, Polselli StudMagr xi 39 - a) for *kl mh/m›*, v. *kl$_1$* - Vattioni Aug xvi 542: the *ymu* in IRT 873[2] to be divided in *-y* and *mu* (= rel. pronoun; prob. interpret.) :: Levi Della Vida OA ii 79, Polselli OAC xiii 237: *ymu* = variant of *mu* :: Vattioni AION xvi 45 (div. otherwise): l. *ymufel* = Impf. pass. form of *p‹l$_1$* - Hoftijzer DA p. 239f., 285: *bm* in DA ii 13 = prep. *b$_2$* + *m$_{11}$* (= *mh*) = why? (uncert. interpret.; for the reading, cf. also Rofé SB 63, 68, Levine JAOS ci 200, 202) :: Caquot & Lemaire Syr liv 206 (div. otherwise): l. *bmy* = *b$_2$* + Dual cstr. of *mym* (for the context, v. also *lqḥ*) - Hoftijzer DA p. 247, 285: *m* in DA ii 17 (in *mlqb*) = *m$_{11}$* (= *mh*; uncert. interpret.) :: Caquot & Lemaire Syr liv 207f.: l. *nlqy* (v. *qbb*) - the *mdy* in TMP 569[3] = *m$_{11}$* + *dy$_2$*, du Mesnil du Buisson TMP a.l.: *mdy* = when, Gawlikowksi Sem xxiii 122f.: *mdy* = because of (uncert. interpretations, diff. context).
v. *dm$_1$*, *ḥzy$_1$*, *klmh$_1$*, *lm$_2$*, *mhdmr*, *mḥr$_3$*, *nš$_1$*, *‹dm$_2$*.

mhb **JAr** Sing. emph. *mhbh* Syr xlv 101[19] (dam. context) - ¶ subst. gift.

mhdmr **Palm** Plur. abs. *mhdmryn* InscrP 31[3] (for this reading, cf. Gawlikowski Syr xlviii 413ff., Sem xxiii 122, TP 76 :: du Mesnil du Buisson RES '45, 77: l. *mhr* (= Sing. cstr. of *mhr$_2$*) *mryn* (= Plur. abs. of *mr›*) :: Milik DFD 270ff.: l. *mh* (= *mh$_2$*) *d* (= *d$_3$* (= *zy*)) *qryn* (= QAL Part. pass. pl.m. abs. of *qr›$_1$*) :: Cantineau sub InscrP 31, sub Inv ix 28: l. *mhrqryn* = Plur. abs. of *mhrqr* (= one who makes incantations (cf. also Benveniste with Cantineau sub InscrP 31: < Iran.?); for the reading, cf. Cantineau Syr xii 119; cf. also Littmann with Cantineau Syr xii 118) :: Aggoula Sem xxxii 111ff.: l. *mhrqdyn* poss. = *mhr* (= Sing. abs. of *mhr$_1$* (= tax)) *qdyn* (= QAL Part. act. pl.m. abs. of *qdy* (= to collect)) or l. *mhrqryn* = Plur. abs. of *mhrqr* (< Iran.; = those who possess the seal, the functionaries)); Plur. emph. *[m]dmry›*TMP 569[2] (for the reading and interpret., cf. Gawlikowski Sem xxiii 121ff., Syr li 91f. :: du Mesnil du Buisson TMP a.l.: l. *[t]dmry›* (= Plur. emph. of *tdmry* (= Tadmorean, Palmyrenean)) - ¶ subst. (prob. < HAPH/APH Part. of *dmr$_1$*;cf. also Starcky with Gawlikowski Syr xlviii 415) guard, protector (cf. also Gawlikowski Sem xxiii 123f.).

mhyr v. *mhr$_2$*.

mhlm **Pun** Müll ii 31: l. subst. *mhlm* (= coin) on Pun. coin from Spain (highly uncert. interpret.).

mhny **OffAr** this subst. (Sing. abs. or cstr.?) = profit in Cowl 81[14]? (cf. also Harmatta ActAntHung vii 357f., also for the context).

mhr$_1$ **OffAr** Sing. cstr. *mhr* Cowl 15[4], Krael 7[4]; emph. *mhr›* Krael 7[15]; + suff. 3 p.s.f. *mhrh* Cowl 15[27], Krael 7[25] (cf. Cowl a.l., Yaron JSS iii 14 n. 2; cf. however Krael a.l., Ginsberg JAOS lxxiv 159, Muffs 59: = + suff. 3 p.s.m.) - ¶ subst. m. dowry (properly, the price paid

for a wife to the head of her family); *mhr brtk mptḥyh* Cowl 15[4f.]: the dowry (paid) for your daughter M.; for *mhr* in Elephantine, cf. Wag 196, Yaron Law 47ff., 57ff., Verger RGP 121ff., Muffs 59f., 181; cf. also Porten Arch 221f. n. 65, 252f., Fitzmyer FS Albright ii 143ff., WA 253f.
v. *mhdmr*.

mhr$_2$ **Pun** Sing. f. abs. *mhrt* NP 130[1] (cf. Dérenbourg CRAI 1875, 260f., Krahmalkov JSS xxiv 27 (cf. also Cooke NSI p. 147) :: Février RHR cxli 19f., FR 156: l. *mhbt* (poss. reading; = PU ʿAL Part. s.f. abs. of *ʾhb$_1$* (= loved)) - **OffAr** Sing. m. abs. *mhyr* Aḥiq 1 - ¶ adj. capable, efficient, skilled; *skr drʾ lʾšt nʿmt mhrt* NP 130[3]: memorial stone from her family for an agreeable (and) capable woman; *spr ḥkym wmhyr* Aḥiq 1: a scribe wise (i.e. skilful) and and expert (cf. also Castellino FS Ziegler ii 29ff.).
v. *mhdmr*.

mhrh **Hebr** TA-H 12[3], 17[5] - ¶ adv. quickly; *wšlḥ lzp mhrh* TA-H 17[4f.]: and send (it) quickly to Z.

mhryt **Palm** CIS ii 4047[2] - ¶ adv. quickly.

mhrqr v. *mhdmr*.

mw **OffAr** Segal ATNS a.l.: l. *mw* (= Greek letter μῦ used as slave mark) in ATNS 164a 1 (uncert. reading, dam. context).

mwʾtr **OffAr** word (?) of unknown meaning in RES 1785i; for interpretations proposed, cf. Chabot sub RES 1785.

mwbl **OffAr** Sing. abs. *mwbl* RES 957[3,6]; Sach 80 vii B; Plur. abs. *mwbln* RES 957[2,5,7,9] - ¶ subst. of uncert. meaning, certain type of weight/coin? (worth less than a *zz*; cf. Montgomery JAOS xxix 207ff., Chabot sub RES 957) :: Lidzbarski Eph iii 63f.: rather = burden, load :: Montgomery JAOS xxix 207ff.: > Greek ὀβολός).
v. *ybl$_1$*, *mʿh$_1$*.

mwdd **Samal** Plur. + Suff 3 p.s.m. *mwddyh* KAI 214[27]; + suff. 1 p.s. *mwddy* KAI 214[24] - **OldAr** Plur. + suff. 3 p.s.m. *mwddwh* KAI 224[14] - ¶ subst. m. friend (cf. however Gibson SSI ii p. 49, 69: = relative).

mwddw **OldAr** Sing. cstr. *mwddt* Tell F 13 (for the reading, cf. also v.Soden ZA lxxii 295; v. infra) - ¶ subst. love, occurring in the comb. *lʾr mwddt krsʾh* Tell F 13 (Akkad. par. *ana ti-ri-iṣ* [iš]*kussî-šu*): to a light of loving-kindness for his throne (uncert. and diff. interpret.) × Kaufman Maarav iii 159, 162, 167 (cf. also id. JAOS liv 572): l. *ltrṣ* (= *l$_5$* + PA ʿEL Inf. of *trṣ* (= to set aright); for this reading, cf. also Puech RB xc 596) *wd/rdt* (= Sing. cstr. of noun of uncert. meaning (= foundation?); cf. also Greenfield & Shaffer Irâq xlv 113, 115, Greenfield OrSu xxxiii-xxxv 151f.; cf. also Gropp & Lewis BASOR cclix 46, 51f.: l. *lʾrm* (unexplained) *wrdt* = *w* + Sing. cstr. of *rdh$_2$* (= dominion)??) :: Abou-Assaf MDOG cxiii 13f., 18: l. *lʾrm* (= *l$_5$* + APH Inf. of *rwm$_1$*??, cf. also Sader EAS 20 n. 40: < root *rwm$_1$*) *wddt* (= Sing. cstr. of *wddh*) *krs'h* (= to further the love for his throne) :: Berger with v.Soden ZA lxxii 295f.: l. *'rmwddt* poss. = cstr. state of ITP Inf. of mdd_1 (= to extend, to stretch) :: Abou-Assaf, Bordreuil & Millard Tell F a.l.: l. *l'rm* (= l_5 + Sing. abs. of *'rm* (= exaltation)) *wrdt* (= *w* + Sing. cstr. of rdh_1 (= succession, perpetuation)) *krs'h* (= for the exaltation and the perpetuation of his throne) :: Fales Syr lx 249: l. *l'rm* (= l_5 + Sing. abs. of *'rm* (= exaltation)) *wrdt* (= Sing. cstr. of *wrdt* (< Akkad.; = vassalage)) :: Wesselius SV 56, 58: l. *'rmwddt krs'h* = that his throne may be solid? (transl. based on context) :: Vattioni AION xlvi 361f.: l. *l'rṣ* (= l_5 + Sing. abs. of *'rṣ*$_2$ (= help, assistance)) *wrdt* (= *w* + Sing. cstr. of rdh_2 < root *rdy* (= to rule)) - on this text, cf. also Geller BSOAS xlvi 546, Sasson ZAW xcvii 98 (n. 10).

mwhbh **Nab** Sing. abs. *mwhbh* CIS ii 209[6], 219[5], J 5[6], 38[7] (for the reading in J 5, 38, cf. Cantineau Nab ii 103; J a.l: l. *mwhb'*); emph. *mwhbt'* CIS ii 204[4] - ¶ subst. f. - **1)** gift; *šṭr mwhbt'* CIS ii 204[3f]: deed of a gift - **2)** deed of gift: CIS ii 209[6], 219[5], J 5[6], 38[7].

mwzn v. $m'zn_1$.

mwḥth v. *msḥth*.

mwṭ **Palm** Sing. abs. *mwṭ* CIS ii 3913 ii 57 - ¶ subst. poss. meaning: hesitation, unsteadiness; in the diff. comb. *yhn mwṭ mks'* CIS ii 3913 ii 57: they shall be unsteadiness in taxation (i.e. their tax shall be undetermined)?

mwk v. *mk*.

mwkrw **Samal** Sing. abs. *mwkrw* KAI 215[10] - ¶ subst. price - on this word, cf. Cooke NSI p. 177, Dion p. 76, Rosenthal JBL xcv 155, Gibson SSI ii p. 84.

mwl$_1$ v. ll_2.

mwl$_2$ v. ll_2.

mwl$_3$ **OffAr** Altheim & Stiehl FuF xxxv 173, 175, ASA 273: the *mwl* in FuF xxv 173[3,4] = Sing. abs. and the *mwly* in FuF xxxv 173[3] = Sing. + suff. 1 p.s. of mwl_3 (= possession(s)) - **Waw** Dupont-Sommer Waw p. 30: l. *mwl* = Sing. abs. of mwl_3 (= power, might) in AMB 6[15] (cf. also idem AIPHOS xi 127 n.; highly uncert. interpret., cf. also Gordon Or xviii 339 (div. otherwise): l. *dm.llk* (without interpret., reading more prob.); for the text, cf. also Naveh & Shaked AMB a.l.

mwly$_1$ v. *yly*.

mwly$_2$ v. *yly*.

mwm **OffAr** poss. a Plur. emph. *mwmy'* (= defects) in ATNS 76[2] (context however heavily dam., uncert. interpret.) :: Segal ATNS a.l.: or = Plur. emph. of *mwm'* (v. *mwm'h*).

v. *ym'*.

mwm' v. *mwm'h*.

mwm'h **OffAr** Sing. abs. *mwm'h* Cowl 6[6] (:: Segert AAG p. 191: =

Sing. emph. of *mwm›* = oath;cf. however Naveh IEJ xxviii 206), 14[4,6,9], Cowl 44[1] (*mwm[›h]*; for the reading, cf. Porten & Yardeni sub TADAE B 7.3), *mwmh* Cowl 59, *mwm›*Cowl 8[24], ATNS 2[5] - ¶ subst. f. oath (cf. Verger RCL '64, 90ff., RGP 186ff., Porten Arch 152ff.); *spr mwmh* Cowl 59: deed of an affidavit.
v. *mwm*.

mwmh v. *mwm›h*.

mwmt **Samal** the diff. *mwmt* in KAI 214[24] (for the reading, cf. e.g. Gibson SSI ii p. 68, Dion p. 32, 74 :: Donner KAI a.l.: poss. (div. otherwise): l. *[mn mn b]ty*, whoever from my dynasty) and in KAI 214[26] (for the reading, cf. e.g. Donner KAI a.l., Dion p. 33, 74 :: Gibson SSI ii p. 68 (div. otherwise): l. *ywmw/ywmy* (= lapsus for *ywmt* (= Hoph Impf. 3 p.s.m. of mwt_1)) . *mt* (= derivation of root mwt_1)) poss. = Hoph Part. s.m. abs. of mwt_1, cf. e.g. Lidzbarski Handb 306, Cooke NSI p. 169, Garb 262f., Friedrich Or xxvi 38, Koopmans 38, Donner sub KAI 214[26], Gibson SSI ii p. 74 (for l. 24), diff. and dam. context; cf. however Montgomery JAOS liv 422: = Sing. abs. of *mwmt* (= *coniuratio*, conspiracy (cf. also Dion p. 402f. (for the context, cf. p. 383): < Akkad. *manūtu*, less prob. interpret.)).

mwsr **DA** Sing. abs. *mwsr* i 12 (cf. Hoftijzer DA a.l., Puech FS Grelot 23, 28 :: Caquot & Lemaire Syr liv 200, Garbini Hen i 180, 185, McCarter BASOR ccxxxix 51: = Sing. cstr.) - ¶ subst. exhortation (:: Garbini Hen i 180, 185: = punishment); on the context, v. *gry*.

mw‹ v. *mwṣ›*.

mw‹› v. *mwṣ›*.

mw‹d **DA** Sing. abs. *mw‹d* i 8 - ¶ subst. assembly: **DA** i 8 (cf. also Hoftijzer DA a.l., McCarter BASOR ccxxxix 57 :: Lemaire BAT 318: = term?).
v. *yḥ›*.

mw‹h v. *mwṣ›*.

mw‹ṭ **Hebr** Sing. cstr. *mw‹ṭ* AMB 4[20] - ¶ subst. waning; *mw‹ṭ lbnh* AMB 4[20]: the waning of the moon (cf. also Naveh & Shaked AMB a.l.).

mwṣ› **Ph** Sing. cstr. *mṣ›* KAI 19[1], 26A i 4, 21, ii 2 - **Pun** Sing. cstr. *mṣ›* KAI 78[6] - **Hebr** Sing. abs. *mwṣ›* KAI 189[5] - **Samal** Sing. cstr. *mwq›* KAI 215[13,14] - **OffAr** Sing. abs. *mw‹›*Cowl 8[4], 13[14], ATNS 24[9] (or = Sing. cstr.?, dam. context), 68[7], *mw‹h*Krael 4[7], 9[6], 12[7]; cstr. *mw‹›* Cowl 8[6], *mw‹h*Cowl 25[6], Krael 3[9], 4[10], 9[3,8], 10[3], 12[9,15,17], *mw‹* Cowl 6[8]; + suff. 1 p.pl. *mw‹n›* ATNS 110[1] - ¶ subst. - **1)** place of outflow (sc. of water), spring; *wylkw hmym mn hmwṣ› ›l* ... KAI 189[4f.]: the water flowed from the spring to ... - **2)** rising (sc. of the sun); *mṣ› šmš* KAI 19[1], 26A i 4f., 21, ii 2, *mṣ› hšmš* KAI 78[6], *mwq› šmš* KAI 215[13,14], *mw‹h šmš* Krael 12[15]: (the rising of the sun >) East, Orient (cf. *mw‹h* Krael 4[7], 9[6], 12[7]: (rising >) East, Orient); cf. also *mw‹› šmš*

l Cowl 8[6]: at the east side of (cf. *mw‘h šmš l* Cowl 25[6], Krael 3[9], 4[10], 9[8], 10[3], 12[9,17]); cf. with the same meaning: *mw‘› l* Cowl 13[14], ATNS 68[7] (dam. context), *mw‘h šmš mn* Krael 9[3], *lmw‘ šmš mn* Cowl 6[8]; *mw‘n›* ATNS 110[1]: east of us (sc. of our house); for *bnt mwq› šmš* in KAI 215[14], v. *br*$_1$.
v. *zt*$_3$, *ms‘*.

mwq› v. *mwṣ›*.

mwr$_1$ CAD s.v. *mâru*: Ar. root *mwr* (= to buy) > Akkad. (cf. also v.Soden Or xxxv 18, xlvi 190 and for an instance of this Akkad. verb Lambert JSS xiv 249).

mwr$_2$ v. *mr*$_1$.

mwš v.Soden Or xxxv 20, xlvi 191, AHW s.v. *muāšu*: > Akkad. *muāšu/mâšu* = to check, to look over (cf. also CAD s.v. *măšu*).

mwt$_1$ **OldCan** HIPH Impf. 2 p.s.m. + suff. 1 p.pl. *ti-mi-tu-na-nu* EA 238[33] (for this form, cf. Steiner JAOS c 515, Sivan GAG 175, 250) - **Pun** QAL Pf. 3 p.s.f. *mt‘* KAI 136[2] (cf. Hoftijzer VT xi 344f., Röllig KAI a.l. :: Février Sem v 63f. (div. otherwise): l. *mn‘bt* = PI‘EL Part. s.f. abs. of *nwb* (= to grow), *mn‘bt* = having lived); Part. act. s.m. abs. *mt* KAI 128[3], cf. IRT 827[1]: *myth* (cf. Levi Della Vida OA ii 84f., Krahmalkov JSS xvii 72 :: Vattioni Aug xvi 539: or = part of n.p.); pl.m. abs., cf. IRT 828[2]: *mythem* (cf. Levi Della Vida OA ii 78, 91, Krahmalkov JSS xvii 72 :: Vattioni AION xvi 48f. (div. otherwise): l. *ihim* (= Dual abs. of *›ḥ*$_1$) *ythem* (= causative form of *tmm*$_1$) :: Vattioni Aug xvi 538: *ythem* = *›t*$_6$+ suff. 3 p.s.m.) - **Amm** QAL Impf. 3 p.pl.m. *ymtn* BASOR cxciii 8[2] (for this prob. interpret., cf. Cross BASOR cxciii 18, Fulco BASOR ccxxx 41, Shea PEQ ’79, 18, ’81, 105f., Sasson PEQ ’79, 120, Dion RB lxxxii 32 (n. 50), Sivan UF xix 230, Jackson ALIA 10, 16, 25, Garr DGSP 127, Smelik HDAI 84, Aufrecht sub CAI 59 (cf. Puech & Rofé RB lxxx 535f.: or = HOPH Impf. 3 p.pl.m.; cf. also Zayadine & Thompson Ber xxii 136 n. 53: = QAL Impf. 3 p.s.m.? (with emphatic ending) and Baldacci AION xlv 519: *ymtn* = QAL Impf. 3 p.s.m. + energic ending) :: Horn BASOR cxciii 8 (div. otherwise): l. *mtymtn* = *m*$_{12}$ (= *mn*$_5$) + n.p. or n.l. (cf. also Albright BASOR cxcviii 38f.: *tymtn* = n.l.) :: Garbini AION xx 255f. (dividing otherwise): l. *mtymtn* = < root *tym* (to be a servant or to be double), prob. nominal form f. Plur. :: v.Selms BiOr xxxii 6f. (div. otherwise): l. *mtymtn* = *m*$_{12}$ (= *mn*$_5$) + *t*$_2$ (= *›t*$_6$)+ *ymtn* (= Sing. abs. (= highest part))); Inf. abs. *mt* BASOR cxciii 8[2] (v. supra) - **Hebr** QAL Pf. 3 p.s.f. *mth* IEJ vii 239[2,6]; Impf. 2 p.pl.m. *tmwtw* Mas 643 (on the problems of the text, cf. also Yadin & Naveh Mas a.l.) - **Samal** QAL Pf. 3 p.s.m. *mt* KAI 215[16] - **OldAr** QAL Impf. 3 p.s.m. *ymwt* KAI 224[16] (cf. e.g. Segert ArchOr xxxii 125f., Fitzmyer AIS 115, 145, Garbini AION xix 13, xx 276, Röllig WO vi 130, Beyer ZDMG cxx 200, Lipiński Stud 38, Gibson SSI ii p.

54 :: Degen AAG p. 28: or = presens (cp. Akkadian *iparras*-type; cf. also Donner BiOr xxvii 248, Meyer OLZ '74, 473); Inf. (or *mwt*$_2$ used as Inf.?) *mwt* KAI 222B 30f. (cf. Segert ArchOr xxxii 125, Fitzmyer AIS 69, Lipiński Stud 38, Degen GGA '79, 35, Sader EAS 131, Garr DGSP 132); HAPH Inf. *hmtt* KAI 224^{11,15,16}; + suff. 1 p.s. *hmtty* KAI 224^{11,15} - **OffAr** QAL Pf. 3 p.s.m. *myt* Cowl 5^8, 62^3 (reading uncert.), Aḥiq 210 (diff. context), ATNS 3^2, 36^1 (dam. and diff. context); 2 p.s.f. *mytty* Krael 4^{17}; 1 p.s. *mtt* KAI 226^4, *mytt* Cowl 10^{14}, *m'tt* Krael 11^8 (for the reading, cf. Milik RB lxi 251: prob. lapsus for *mytt* (for the reading, cf. also Porten & Yardeni sub TADAE B 3.13) :: Krael a.l., Porten & Greenfield JEAS p. 66: l. *mytt*); Impf. 3 p.s.m. *ymwt* Cowl 15^{17}, Krael 2^{11}, 7^{28}; 3 p.s.f. *tmwt* Cowl 15^{20}, Krael 2^{12}, 6^{18}, 7^{34}; 2 p.s.m. *tmwt* Aḥiq 82; 1 p.s. *'mwt* Krael 4^{18}, CRAI '47, 181 conc. 1; 3 p.pl.m. *ymwtwn* Aḥiq 174; Part. act. s.m. abs. *myt* Herm 5^8 (cf. Porten & Greenfield ZAW lxxx 225 n. 32, Milik Bibl xlviii 618, Gibson SSI ii p. 140 :: Bresciani & Kamil Herm a.l.: *myt* = rather Sing. m. abs. of adj. *myt*$_4$ (= *mt*$_5$; = dead)); s.f. emph. *mytt'* ATNS 186^1 (?, heavily dam. and diff. context); pl.m. abs. *m'ytyn* KAI 276^{11} (Greek par. ἀπέθανε; prob. ideogrammatic use (cf. Segert ArchOr xxxviii 225, cf. also Nyberg Eranos xliv 241); or rather = lapsus for *m'ytt*? (cf. Stiehl NouvClio iii 76 n. 3, Altheim & Stiehl WZKMU '55/56, 284, Suppl 82f., GH i 431, EW x 252f., ASA 46 :: Kutscher & Naveh Lesh xxxiv 310, 313: l. *m'ytt*), *m'ytt* prob. = QAL Pf. 3 p.s.f. (cf. Kutscher & Naveh o.c. 313 :: Altheim & Stiehl opera citata: = QAL Part. act. s.f. + ending - *t*); :: Altheim & Stiehl EW x 253f., ASA 46f. (cf. AAW i 656): or l. *m'ytyn* = QAL Part. act. + enclit. pron. 1 p.s. (cf. also Altheim GH ii 178f.); cf. also Grelot Sem viii 18f., Donner KAI a.l., Degen ZDMG cxxi 138); cf. Frah xxii 5 (*ymytwn*), Syn 305^4 (cf. Altheim & Stiehl Suppl 122), 309^4, 311^4 (cf. also Toll ZDMG-Suppl viii 36), GIPP 38, 57 - **Nab** QAL Pf. 3 p.s.m. *myt* J 386^4, IEJ xxi 50^4, ADAJ x 44 ii 3 (= RB lxxii 95), MPAT 64 i 7; 3 p.s.f. *mytt* BAGN ii 88^5; Part. act. s.m. abs. *m't* MPAT 64 i 9 - **Palm** QAL Pf. 3 p.s.m. *myt* CIS ii 3920^3, 3927^5 (for the reading, v. *btr*), 4261^5, 4261bis 6, 4562^8, 4616^9, Inv x 4, RIP 24^4, 25^9 (Greek par. [τ]ελευ[τήσαν]το); 3 p.s.f. *mytt* CIS ii 3954^3 (*m[y]tt*), 4258^6, AAS iii 20^1 - **Hatra** QAL Pf. 3 p.s.f. *mytt* 30^4; Impf. 3 p.s.m. *lmwt* 344^{12} - **JAr** QAL Pf. 3 p.s.m. *myt* MPAT-A 50^3; 3 p.s.f. *mytt* MPAT-A 51^3, 52^2; Impf. 3 p.s.m. *ymwt* MPAT-A 45^4; Part. act. s.m. abs. *m'yt* MPAT-A 46^5 - ¶ verb QAL to die (passim); for Krael 4^{18}, cf. Ginsberg JAOS lxxiv 158, Porten Arch 185 (n. 141); for Hatra 344^{12}, v. *mwt*$_2$; Part. act. dying, dead; cf. also *'nh nktny ḥwyh whwt myt* Herm 5^8: a snake has bitten me and I was almost dead (cf. Bresciani & Kamil Herm a.l., cf. also Hoftijzer SV 117: ... I was critically ill (cf. also Milik Bibl xlviii 554, 584)) - HIPH/HAPH to let (someone) die, to kill; + obj., *wyš' 'l šptwh*

lhmtt ʿqry KAI 224[16]: he takes it upon his lips to kill my descendant (cf. KAI 224[11,15], EA 238[33]) - a QAL form of this root (Part.?, *mt*) poss. in KAI 142[4] (cf. Cooke NSI p. 141f., Röllig KAI a.l.) - a form of this root (*myt*) in Aḥiq 210 (= QAL Part. act. s.m. abs.?, cf. however Kottsieper SAS 23, 213 = Sing. m. abs. of myt_4 (= mt_5)) - du Mesnil du Buisson TMP 544: the *mytʾ* in RTP 720: = QAL Part. act. s.m. emph. (less prob. interpret., cf. Caquot RTP p. 174f.: = n.p. (cf. also Gawlikowski TP 38)) - the *mt* in DJD ii 49 ii poss. = QAL Pf. 3 p.s.m. (heavily dam. context) - Segal ATNS a.l.: l. poss. *myt* in ATNS 28b 1 (= QAL Part. pass. s.m. abs.), highly uncert. reading, cf. Porten & Yardeni sub TADAE B 8.4.
v. $hʾ_1$, *mwmt*, *mṣbh*, mt_5, *mtrḥ*.

mwt₂ **OldCan** Sing. abs. *mu-tu-mi* EA 362[47] - **DA** Sing. abs. *mwt* ii 13 (diff. context; v. *lqḥ*) - **OffAr** Sing. abs. *mwt* KAI 225[10]; emph. *mwtʾ* Aḥiq 106; + suff. 2 p.s.m. *mwtk* Krael 5[12,14]; + suff. 2 p.s.f. *mwtky* Krael 4[18]; + suff. 1 p.s. *mwty* Cowl 8[3,8], 44 (*scriptio anterior* l. 2; for the reading, cf. Porten & Yardeni sub TADAE B 7.3), Krael 4[21], 5[4], 9[17,18], 10[11,13] - **Nab** Sing. abs. *mwt* CIS ii 212[6] - **Palm** Sing. emph. *mwtʾ* Inv x 53[3]; + suff. 3 p.s.m. *mwth* RIP 103c 4; + suff. 3 p.pl.m. *mwthm* Inv x 119b 1 - **Hatra** Sing. emph. 343[7], 344[12] ¶ subst. m. - **1)** death: passim; *mwtʾ dy ʾlhʾ* Hatra 343[7f.]: the death of the gods (for the interpret. of this expression, cf. Aggoula Syr lxiv 93, 94); v. also $ḥy_1$, $ḥlp_3$ - **2)** plague, pestilence: EA 362[47], Aḥiq 106 (prob. interpret.; cf. Ginsberg ANET 429, cf. also Lindenberger APA 91, 243 n. 256; cf. however Muraoka JSS xxxii 188).
v. ll_2, mwt_1, mt_1.

mwtb₁ v. $mšb_1$.

mwtbw **Nab** word of unknown meaning in RES 2067. For interpret. proposals, cf. RES a.l., Cantineau Nab ii 113.

mwtn **OldAr** Sing. abs. *mwtn* Tell F 23 (cf. in Akkad. par. *di<-li>-ip-te*; cf. Zadok TeAv ix 118f., Fales Syr lx 247) - ¶ subst. m. pest - on this word, cf. Kaufman AIA 74, Gropp & Lewis BASOR cclix 54.

mz **JAr** Yadin & Naveh Mas a.l.: l. poss. *mz* (= Sing. cstr. of *mz* (= squash, juice)) in Mas 544 (uncert. reading).

mzbḥ **Ph** Sing. abs. *mzbḥ* KAI 10[4] (cf. Gibson SSI iii p. 96 :: Baldacci BiOr xl 130: = Sing. cstr.),[11f.], 32[2] (= Kition A 2), 42[4] (Greek par. βω[μὸ]ν), 58; Plur. abs. *mzbḥt* KAI 43[10] - **Pun** Sing. abs. *mzbḥ* KAI 126[10] (Lat. par. *aram*), 138[3], CIS i 170[1,2], Mont-Sirai ii 80[1] (*[mz]bḥ*), StudMagr iv 3[1]; cstr. *mzbḥ* KAI 66[1], 77[1], CIS i 140[1] (for all instances :: FR 309: = Sing. abs.); Plur. abs. *mzbḥm* KAI 173[1], CIS i 3918[1] (cf. FR 304,3b) - **OffAr** Sing. emph. *mdbḥʾ* Cowl 30[26], 31[25], 32[3,10], LA ix 331[3] - ¶ subst. m. altar, passim; cf. *mzbḥ ʾbn* KAI 77[1]: a stone altar; *mzbḥ nḥ[št]* CIS i 140[1]: an altar of bronze (cf. KAI 66[1]); *hmzbḥ*

nḥšt zn KAI 10[4]; this altar of bronze; *mzbḥ šhmqnt* KAI 138[3]: an altar for sacrifying cattle; *mdbḥ› zy YHW ›lh›* Cowl 30[26], 31[25]: the altar of the God Y.; cf. also the n.d. Μαδβάχῳ in IGLS ii no. 465, 467, 469, 471 (Μα[δβ]άχῳ), 472, 473 (Μάδραχο), cf. Clermont-Ganneau RAO iv 164f., vii 81ff., Jalabert & Mouterde IGLS ii p. 259, Milik Bibl xlviii 578); for *byt mdbḥ›*, v. *byt₂*.
v. *mzrḥ₁*, *mrḥb*.

mzg₁ **OffAr** QAL Part. act. s.f. abs., cf. Warka 6, 9: *ma-zi-ga-›* (for this form, cf. Kaufman JAOS civ 89) - ¶ verb QAL to mix; + obj. (poison): Warka 6, 9 - for this root, cf. also Brown VT xix 153, Lipiński UF ii 84.

mzg₂ **JAr** Sing. + suff. 3 p.pl.m. *mzghw[n]* MPAT 42[12] (× Milik sub DJD ii 21: l. *mzghy[n]* = QAL Inf. + suff. 3 p.pl.f. of *zwg* (= to match, to marry)) - ¶ subst. (v. however supra) matching (diff. and heavily dam. context).

mzd› v. *ydy₁*.

mzdyzn (< Iran., cf. Schaed 267, Hinz AISN 164) - **OffAr** Sing. abs. *mzdyzn* Cowl 37[6] - ¶ subst. m. mazdaean (cf. Cowl a.l., Porten & Greenfield JEAS p. 81, but rather = n.p., cf. Benveniste BSOAS xxxiii 5ff., Grelot DAE p. 389 (n. i), 478); for a related n.p. *mzdymn›* in RTP 23, cf. Milik DFD 279 (:: RTP a.l.: l. *mnd/rymn›*, cf. also RTP p. 188, s.v. *mnrmn›*).

mzh₁ v. *z₁*.

mzh₂ **Ph** Lipiński RSF ii 51: the *mzh* in Syr xlviii 396[1] = YIPH Part. s.m. abs. of *nzy* (= the sprinkler, i.e. the priest appointed to do the sprinkling), cf. idem RTAT 266, cf. also v.d.Branden BiOr xxxiii 13, xxxvi 202: the sprinkler = epithet of Ba‹al; *mzh* = rather name or epithet of a demon cf. (Dupont-Sommer with) Caquot Syr xlviii 397ff., Gaster BASOR ccix 19ff., Röllig NESE ii 29f., Avishur PIB 267f., Gibson SSI iii p. 89f., de Moor JEOL xxvii 111 (n. 16), Cross CBQ xxxvi 488 (n. 17), 489 (relating the name to different roots like *nzy*, *zhy*, *mzy* or *mzh* = *my* or *mh* + *zh*).

mzwn **JAr** Sing. abs. *m[z]wn* MPAT 62[12] (diff. reading, cf. Yadin & Greenfield sub DBKP 27; cf. Greek par. [τρ]οφίων) - ¶ subst. food, maintenance; *lkswt [wl]m[z]wn* MPAT 62[12]: for clothing and food (cf. Greek par. text ἰς λόγο[ν τρ]οφίων καὶ ἀμφιαζμοῦ).

mzwr **OffAr** Sing. abs. *mzwr* FuF xxxv 173[9]; Plur. abs. *mzwryn* FuF xxxv 173[6] - ¶ subst. (?) of uncert. meaning; Altheim & Stiehl FuF xxxv 173, 176, ASA 273: = adj. strong > subst. warrior.

mzzh **Ph** Plur. abs. *mzzt* KAI 27[26] (diff. context; for reading and interpret., cf. Cross & Saley BASOR cxcvii 46f. (n. 33), Caquot FS Gaster 51, Röllig NESE ii 19, 26, Lipiński RTAT 266, Avishur PIB 248, Garbini OA xx 286, Gibson SSI iii p. 83, 88, de Moor JEOL xxvii

108, 110 :: Albright BASOR lxxvi 9f. (n. 35): l. *szyt*? = n.p. (cf. also Röllig KAI a.l.) :: du Mesnil du Buisson FS Dussaud 424f., 433: l. *sz.zt* = n.d. (cf. Gaster Or xi 67: l. *sz zt*= onomatopaeic representation of hissing and spitting; cf. also Rosenthal ANET 658) :: v.d.Branden BiOr xxxiii 13 (div. otherwise): l. *mʿy* = Sing. abs. or Sing. + suff. 3 p.s.f. of *mʿh$_2$* (= belly) :: Torczyner JNES vi 27, 29: l. *ʿd$_7$*) - ¶ subst. doorpost - for KAI 27[22], v. *zt$_3$*.

mzḥ **Palm** Milik DFD 156: l. this subst. (*mzḥ*, Sing. abs.) in RTP 160, 161 (= liturgical procession), cf. however Seyrig sub RTP 160, 161: l. in both instances *m* (= abbrev. of *mšḥ$_3$*) *1 ḥ* (= abbrev. of *ḥmr$_5$*), cf. also Teixidor PP 51.

mzy$_1$ cf. Frah x 8: hair.

mzy$_2$ v. *ḥl$_2$*.

mzyn v. *mʾzn$_1$*.

mzyšt (< Iran., cf. Benveniste JA ccxlvi 43, Altheim & Stiehl GH i 404f., EW ix 196f., x 245, ASA 28, 273, GMA 351, Altheim GH ii 174, Humbach MSSW xxvi 41f. n. 5, Schwarzschild JAOS lxxx 156, Garbini Kand 16, Kutscher, Naveh & Shaked Lesh xxxiv 135, Donner KAI a.l., Hinz AISN 164) - **OffAr** Plur. emph. *mzyštyʾ* KAI 279[6] (cf. e.g. Dupont-Sommer JA ccxlvi 30, Garbini Kand 15, 18, Donner KAI a.l. :: Altheim & Stiehl EW ix 196f., x 245, ASA 28, 273: or = Iran. acc. plur.; cf. Greek par. τῶν πρεσβυτέρων for *mzyštyʾ ʾnšn*) - ¶ subst. elder (for this meaning, cf. Benveniste JA ccxlvi 43, Altheim & Stiehl ASA 28 (cf. also Hinz AISN 164) :: Nober VD xxxvii 373: rather = presbyter, priest).

mzkr **Mo** (cf. Abu Taleb ZDPV ci 23ff., cf. however Zayadine Syr lxii 158) Sing. abs. *mzkr* ZDPV ci 22[2f.] (= Syr lxii 156) - ¶ subst. indicating high official, mazkīr; on this function in ancient Israel, cf. e.g. de Vaux IAT i 202f., Mettinger SSO 21ff., 52ff., Ahlström RANR 28 (cf. also Abu Taleb ZDPV ci 28f.).

mzl **Ph** Sing. abs. *mzl* KAI 42[5] (diff. reading, cf. Bruston sub RES 1515: l. *mš* (= Sing. abs. of *mʾš$_1$*)+ *l$_5$*) - **Hebr** Plur. + suff. 3 p.s.f. *mzlwtyh* AMB 4[20] - ¶ subst. - **1)** sign/constellation of the Zodiac: AMB 4[20] - **2)** fortune; *[l]mzl nʿm* KAI 42[5]: for good fortune (Greek par. ἀγα[θ]ῆ τύχῃ) - for this word, cf. e.g. Kaufman AIA 69f., Emerton JSS xiv 27, Delcor FS Cazelles 96f.

v. *mʾš$_1$*.

mzlh v. *mslh$_2$*

mzrʾ v. *mzrḥ*.

mzrḥ$_1$ **Pun** Sing. abs. *mzrḥ* KAI 69[16], 145[1,12,16], 147[1] (or cstr.?, dam. context), 159[4] (for this reading, cf. e.g. Clermont-Ganneau RAO iii 31f., Röllig KAI a.l. (cf. also Cooke NSI p. 145) :: e.g. Lidzbarski Handb 265, 437 sub a: l. *mzbḥ*), *mzrʾ* Karth xii 53[2] - ¶ subst. of uncert. meaning, indicating a certain community, assembly; Clermont-Ganneau RAO iii 22ff.: = the Roman *curia* (?, cf. Picard Karthago viii 62f.: rather = a professional or religious board (cf. also Krahmalkov RSF iii 189f.)) :: Lidzbarski Handb 268: = native?, cf. however idem Eph i 47f. :: v.d.Branden BMB xiii 94: *mzrḥ* in KAI 69[16] = YIPH Part. of *zrḥ* (= to singe (a lighter)); for other interpretations, cf. CIS i sub 165, Sznycer Sem xxii 36ff. (cf. also Garbini RSO xliii 16f., AION xix 326f., Huss 464, 503 (n. 79), 551) - cf. also *mrzḥ*.

mzrḥ$_2$ Hebr Sing. abs. *mzrḥ* DJD ii 22[11], 30[3,16] - ¶ subst. East; *mzrḥ hmkyr m‹rb hdrk* DJD ii 30[3,16]: at the east side the vendor, at the west side the road - cf. *myzrḥ*.

mzr‹ Pun Sing. abs. *mzr‹* Karth xii 54[1] (cf. Krahmalkov RSF iii 178f., 186, 202, v.d.Branden RSF v 56f., 62 :: Février & Fantar Karth xii a.l. (div. otherwise): l. *zr‹* (= Sing. abs. of *zr‹$_2$*))- ¶ subst. cultivated land.

mzrq OffAr Plur. emph. *mzrqy›* Cowl 30[12], 31[11] - ¶ subst. bowl, basin (used to sprinkle).

mḥ$_1$ Ph Masson & Sznycer RPC 95f., Puech Sem xxix 27: the *mḥ* in RPC 95B prob. = Sing. abs. of subst. *mḥ$_1$* (= fat) :: Honeyman with Karageorghis BCH '63, 333f.: = either measure of capacity or abbrev. of n.p.?
v. *›r›l*.

mḥ$_2$ Pun Sing. m. abs. *mḥ* KAI 76A 5 - ¶ adj. fat, rich (dam. context).

mḥ› OldAr Pf. 3 p.pl.m. *mḥ›w* KAI 202A 15, 16; Impf. 3 p.s.m. *ymḥ›* KAI 222A 42 (for this interpret., cf. e.g. Donner KAI a.l., Fitzmyer AIS 57, Gibson SSI ii p. 43 :: Dupont-Sommer Sf p. 60, Koopmans 55: Impf. pass.) - **OffAr** QAL Pf. 3 p.s.m. *mḥ›* ATNS 20[5]; 3 p.pl.m. *mḥ›w* ATNS 189; Impf. 3 p.s.m. + suff. 2 p.s.m. *y[m]ḥnk* MAI xiv/2, 66[9] (for this reading, cf. Dupont-Sommer MAI xiv/2, 78 (cf. also Grelot DAE p. 73, Porten & Yardeni sub TADAE B 1.1) :: Bauer & Meissner SbPAW '36, 415, 420: l. *y[n]ḥnk* or *y[hn]ḥnk* = APH Impf. 3 p.s.m. + suff. 2 p.s.m. of *nwḥ$_1$* (= to satisfy)); 1 p.s. + suff. 2 p.s.m. *›mḥn›nk* Aḥiq 82; cf. Frah xxi 4 (*mḥytwn*), GIPP 28, SaSt 19 - ¶ verb QAL - **1)** to beat + obj.: Aḥiq 82, ATNS 20[5] (v. *ṯḥnh*), 189; cf. also MAI xiv/2, 66[9], exact meaning unknown; Dupont-Sommer MAI xiv/2, 67, 78: to beat > to harm, cf. however Yaron BiOr xv 19: > to bring suit against, to interfere with (cf. also Porten & Yardeni sub TADAE B 1.1; on this text, cf. also Koopmans 97f.; v. also *qns$_1$*); cf. Frah xxi 4 - **2)** + *‹l$_7$*, *ymḥ› ‹l ›pyh* KAI 222A 42: one strikes (her) on her face - **3)** + *‹l$_7$* + obj., *mḥ›w ‹lyk mṣr* KAI 202A 15: they have forced a siege upon you (cf. Greenfield FS Fitzmyer 50, Ṣader EAS 209 (n. 30)) - on the root, cf. Degen AAG 42 n. 21, Greenfield Proc v CJS i 177, Lipiński Stud 19ff. :: e.g. Held JAOS lxxix 171 (n. 38), Greenfield JAOS lxxxii 290 n. 7, (Kutscher with) Silverman JAOS lxxxix 694 n. 15, xciv 270, Beyer

ZDMG cxx 200, Halpern FS Lambdin 123: *mḥ'* < *mḥ'* < *mḥḏ*; cf. also Gibson SSI ii p. 16, Lindenberger APA 225 n. 44 - Beyer ATTM 329, 621: l. *mḥ'* = QAL Part. pass. s.m. abs. in MPAT 89[4] (highly uncert. interpret.) - cf. also *mḥy$_1$*.

mḥ'h **OffAr** Sing. abs. *mḥ'h* Aḥiq 83 - ¶ subst. blow.

mḥ'r v. *mḥr$_3$*.

mḥbl v. *ḥbl$_1$*.

mḥgh **OldAr** Sing. cstr. (?, dam. context) *mḥgt* KAI 202B 5 - ¶ subst. of uncert. meaning, poss. = territory, environment, district < root *ḥwg*, cf. e.g. Lidzbarski Eph iii 9, 11, Donner KAI a.l., Degen AAG p. 48, OLZ '71, 271, Dupont-Sommer AH i/2, 3, Gibson SSI ii p. 11, 16, de Moor UF xx 162, Delsman TUAT i 627 (Greenfield Proc v CJS i 175: = encirclement, wall) :: Nöldeke ZA xxi 382: = place for (rel.) festival > holy place < root *ḥgg* (cf. also Koopmans 28).

mḥwz v. *mḥz$_1$*, *mḥzy$_2$*.

mḥz$_1$ (< Akkad.?; cf. Zimmern Fremdw 9, Littmann with Cantineau Syr xix 171, Rosenthal Sprache 90, Marrassini FLEM 79f., cf. also Kaufman AIA 68, 149, 161 n. 90, Kutscher Lesh xxxiv 5ff., R.Kutscher Lesh xxxiv 267ff., Borger UF i 1ff., Cooper Or xliii 83ff.; cf. however also the discussion of Amadasi MLE i 31ff.; cf. also Del Olmo Lete AO i 307) - **Pun** Sing. abs. *mḥz* KAI 124[2] (Lat. par. *forum*) - **OffAr**, cf. GIPP 57 (*mḥwz'*)- **Palm** Sing. + suff. 3 p.s.m. *mḥwzh* InscrP 6[2]; + suff. 3 p.pl.m. *mḥwzhwn* Syr xii 124[4] - ¶ subst. - **1)** *forum*: KAI 124[2] - **2)** city; *rḥym mḥwzh* InscrP 6[2]: lover of his town; *[mn d]y špr lhwn wlmḥwzhwn wlbt 'lhyhwn* Syr xii 124[4]: because he has favoured them and their city and the temple(s) of their gods; cf. however Teixidor UF xv 309f.: = portus, i.e. the place in which the rights to enter or to pass. through with merchandise were paid, par. of *lmn* (uncert. interpret.) - **3)** region, cf. GIPP 57.
v. *mḥzy$_2$*.

mḥz$_2$ (or *mḥzy$_2$*) - **Pun** Plur. abs. *mḥzm* KAI 130[3,5] (cf. Lat. par. *aediles*) - ¶ subst. m. *aedilis*, superintendent of the market (rel. to *mḥz$_1$*), for this interpret., cf. Levi Della Vida RCL '49, 402 n. 1 (cf. also idem RSO xxxix 307), Röllig KAI a.l. (cf. also Friedrich Or xxiv 156f., Angeli Bertinelli CISFP i 256, Amadasi IPT 44) :: Levi Della Vida Lib iii/ii 13, Février RA xlii 84: related to root *'ḥz* or *ḥzy$_1$*.

mḥz$_3$ v. *mḥr$_3$*.

mḥzh$_1$ v. *mḥzt*.

mḥzh$_2$ v. *mḥzt*.

mḥzh$_3$ v. *mḥzt*.

mḥzh$_4$ **DA** (Hamilton with) Hackett BTDA 25, 33 (combining DA v e 2 and xv c): l. *mḥzh* (= Sing. abs.) = vision (poss. reading), cf. also Puech BAT 360.

mḥzwry **JAr** Sing. emph. *mḥzwryt[ʾ]* (?, heavily dam. context) MPAT 33 v 1 - ¶ subst. return.

mḥzy$_1$ **OffAr** Sing. abs. *mḥzy* Cowl 15[11], Krael 2[5], 7[13]; emph., cf. Warka 6: *ma-aḫ-zi-ia-ʾ* (cf. e.g. Driver AfO iii 50 :: e.g. Dupont-Sommer RA xxxix 44: = QAL Inf. cstr. of *ḥzy$_1$*)- ¶ subst. f. (cf. Krael 2[5]), m. (cf. Cowl 15[11]; cf. Fitzmyer FS Albright ii 155) - **1)** mirror: Cowl 15[11], Krael 2[5], 7[13] - **2)** vision; *ma-aḫ-zi-ia-ʾ di-ʾ ḫa-za-ú-ni* Warka 6f.: as soon as they saw me (cf. (Epstein with) Gordon AfO xii 106 n. 4, Dupont-Sommer RA xxxix 44).
v. *mḥzy$_2$*.

mḥzy$_2$ **Hatra** Sing. emph. *mḥzyʾ* app. 3[2] (= KAI 257; for this reading, cf. Naveh BASOR ccxvi 9, Teixidor Syr liii 337, Vattioni IH a.l. :: du Mesnil du Buisson Syr xix 147: l. *mḥwzʾ* = Sing. emph. of *mḥwz* (= *mḥz$_1$*;= town) :: Dussaud Syr xix 152: l. *mḥznʾ* = Sing. emph. of *mḥzn* (= epithet of person mentioned) :: Torrey with Ingholt YClSt xiv 133f., Caquot Syr xxx 245: l. *mḥybʾ* (= PA ʿEL Part. pass. s.m. abs. of *ḥwb$_1$*, resp. "someone under an obligation" and "guilty one") :: Ingholt YClSt xiv 134: l. *mḥybʾ* = noun < root *ḥbb$_1$*)- ¶ subst. of uncert. meaning; Naveh BASOR ccxvi 9f.: = townsman or harbor-master (= nisbe of *mḥz$_1$*)?,or = form of *mḥzy$_3$* (= mirror-maker? (= nisbe of *mḥzy$_1$*)), cf. also Vattioni IH a.l.: = caus. Part. s.m. emph. of *ḥzy$_1$* (= seer).

mḥzy$_3$ v. *mḥzy$_2$*.

mḥzy$_4$ v. *pḥz$_2$*.

mḥzn v. *mḥzy$_2$*.

mḥzt **Pun** the diff. *mḥzt* in KAI 145[2] prob. = Plur. abs. of *mḥzh$_1$* (= light, window), cf. Cooke NSI p. 152f. :: v.d.Branden RSF i 166f.: = Sing./Plur. abs. of *mḥzh$_2$* (= *forum*; cf. already Lidzbarski Eph i 303: = Sing. abs. of *mḥzh$_2$*) :: Février Sem vi 17: = PU ʿAL Part. s.f. abs. of *ʾḥz* (= closed) :: Röllig KAI iii p. 14 = Sing. abs. of *mḥzh$_3$* (= place where divination takes place) :: Berger MAIBL xxxvi/2, 150f.: = *m$_{12}$* (= *mn$_5$*) + Sing. cstr. of *ḥzw*:: Krahmalkov RSF iii 190, 202: = *mn$_5$* + *zt$_2$* (= on this side); for a discussion, cf. Halévy RS ix 270f.; cf. also Sznycer Sem xxii 40f.: *mḥzt* = independent architectural construction - Kornfeld sub Abydos 15: l. poss. *mḥzt* (= Sing. abs.) in RES 1349[2] (highly uncert. reading and interpret.).

mḥy$_1$ **Ph** QAL Pf. 3 p.pl. *mḥ* KAI 26A iii 18 (cf. e.g. Bron RIPK 118, Gibson SSI iii p. 63 × FR 174: = Pf. 3 p.s.m. (cf. Swiggers BiOr xxxvii 341)); Impf. 3 p.s.m. *ymḥ* KAI 26A iii 13; Inf. cstr. *mḥt* KAI 26C iv 15 (cf. e.g. Röllig KAI a.l., Bron RIPK 126, Gibson SSI iii p. 64 :: Dupont-Sommer RA xlii 179: = QAL Pf. 1 p.s.); NIPH Impf. 3 p.s.m. *ymḥ* KAI 1[2] (:: Butterweck TUAT ii 583: = QAL Impf. 3 p.s.m.) - **Hebr** QAL Pf. 3 p.pl. *mḥw* NESE ii 45[3] (dam. context); Impf. 3 p.s.m. *ymḥh* IEJ xxv 229[1] (dam. context) - ¶ verb QAL to efface; *ʾdm šm ʾš ymḥ šm* *ˀztwd bšˁr z wšt šm* KAI 26A iii 13f.: a man of reknown who effaces the name of A. from this gate and puts up his own name (cf. also KAI 26C iv 15); cf. also *wmḥ bˁlšmm ... ˀyt hmmlkt hˀ* KAI 26A iii 18f.: may B.-Sh. efface (i.e. destroy) ... that kingdom (cf. also Pardee JNES xlii 67) - NIPH to be effaced (said of an inscription): KAI 1[2] - Bar-Adon IEJ xxv 231: for the diff. *mḥr* in IEJ xiii 79[2] l. <*y*>*mḥh* (= QAL Impf. 3 p.s.m.), cf. also Lemaire RB lxxiii 561f.: *ˀˀrr yšr mḥh* mistake for *ˀrr ˀšr* (v. *ˀšr₇*) *ymḥh* (highly uncert. interpretations; cf. also Naveh IEJ xiii 79f., Miller SVT xxxii 332) - Porten Or lvii 18: the *mḥyn* in Or lvii 16[2] poss. = QAL Part. act. pl.m. abs. or QAL Pf. 1 p.pl. (heavily dam. context) - cf.also *mḥˀ*.

v. *mḥt₁*.

mḥy₂ v. *mḥy₃*, *mḥt₁*.

mḥy₃ **OffAr** Grelot RB lxviii 183, DAE p. 437 n. e: l. *m[ḥ]y* in Aḥiq 99 (= QAL Imper. s.m. of *mḥy₂* (= to weave > to consider, to plot)), uncert. restoration, cf. Lindenberger APA 77, 237 n. 180: l. *m[š]y* (= PAˁEL Imper. s.m. of *mšy₂* (= to choose, to select), Kottsieper SAS 12, 20, 176, 217: l. *m[š]y* = QAL Imper. s.m. of *mšy₃* (= to remove), Cowl a.l., Ginsberg ANET 428: l. *m[n]y* = QAL Imper. s.m. of *mny*).

mḥy₄ v. *mḥˀ*.

mḥy₅ **Pun** Sing. + suff. 3 p.s.m. *mḥyˀ* Trip 8[3] (cf. Levi Della Vida Lib iii/ii 7, FR 253) - ¶ subst. life; *lmbmḥyˀ* Trip 8[3]: during his lifetime; Berger RA ii 36, 42, Levi Della Vida Lib iii/ii 7 (cf. also Cooke NSI p. 148, 150): l. *mḥ[yˀ]* = Sing. + suff. 3 p.s.m. in KAI 161[6] (highly uncert. interpret.; cf. also Février RA xlv 145, Röllig KAI a.l.) - cf. also *ḥy₁*.

mḥyh v. *mḥyr*.

mḥyr **JAr** Sing. + suff. 3 p.pl.m. *mḥyrhwn* MPAT-A 27[4] (for the reading, cf. Naveh sub SM 33, Beyer ATTM 385 :: Sukenik JPOS xv 138, 143, Frey sub 857, Fitzmyer & Harrington MPAT a.l.: l. *mḥythwn* = Plur. + suff. 3 p.pl.m. of *mḥyh* (= woven good, cloth); cf. also Hüttenmeister ASI 156) - ¶ subst. gift (cf. however Beyer ATTM 385, 622: = equivalent, counter-value, in the context: counter-value of the gift in goods).

mḥkl **OffAr**, cf. Frah xxvii 8: the day after tomorrow (cf. Syriac *mèkkēl*? :: Ebeling Frah a.l.: related to *mḥr₃*).

mḥlph **Ph** Sing. (?) abs. *mḥlpt* RES 921[4] - ¶ subst. lock of hair (cf. Honeyman Irâq vi 105f. :: Lidzbarski Eph iii 54 (div. otherwise): l. *ḥlpt* (= Sing. cstr. of *ḥlpḥ₁*)).

mḥnh **Ph** Sing. abs. *mḥnt* KAI 1[2], 26A i 7, 8 - **Pun** Sing. abs. *mḥnt* KAI 118[2], 120[1], CIS i 5866[3], on coins, cf. Müller ii 74f., CHC 585 no. 7-12 (on these coins, cf. Cutroni Tusa CISFP i 142) - **Hebr** Sing. abs. *mḥnh* DJD ii 24E 3, *mḥnyh* DJD ii 42[2] (cf. Milik DJD a.l. :: Ginsberg BASOR cxxxi 26, Sonne PAAJR xxiii 87: l. *mḥnh* (cf. Birnbaum PEQ

'55, 22) :: Yeivin At i 96: l. *mḥnyh* = APH Part. s.m. emph. of *ḥn'₁*) - **Samal** Sing. abs./cstr. *mḥnt* KAI 215[13] (× e.g. Cooke NSI p. 178, Donner KAI a.l., Gibson SSI ii p. 81, 84, Dion p. 140 (cf. also p. 434 n. 2): = Plur. abs./cstr.); abs. *mḥnt* KAI 215[16] (cf. e.g. Cooke NSI p. 178, Donner KAI a.l. :: Gibson SSI ii p. 81, 84, Dion p. 140 (cf. also p. 434 n. 2): = Plur. abs.),[17] - **OldAr** Sing. + suff. 3 p.s.m. *mḥnth* KAI 202A 5, 6 (:: Altheim & Stiehl AAW i 232 n. 9: or = Plur.); Plur. + suff. 3 p.pl.m. *mḥnwt.hm* KAI 202A 9 - **JAr** Sing. emph. *mḥnyh* MPAT 57[2], 60[3,4] - ¶ subst. f. camp, encampment (*castra*), army, host (the shades of meaning difficult to differentiate), passim; for *'m hmḥnt*, v. *'m₁*;, for *rb mḥnt*, v. *rb₂*; for *rwš hmḥnyh*, v. *r'š₁*; for *tm' mḥnt*, v. *tm'₂*; cf. *mt 'by ... bmḥnt* KAI 215[16]: my father died in the encampment (cf. e.g. Cooke NSI p. 174 :: Gibson SSI ii p. 81: in the campaigns :: Donner KAI a.l.: during the battle); cf. also *šm'wn bn k[ws]b' nsy' [yš]r'l bmḥnh šywšb bhrwdys* DJD ii 24E 2f.: Sh. the son of K. the prince of Y. in the encampment (i.e. in the field), who lives at H. (on this text, cf. also Schäfer BKA 123f.) - Yadin & Naveh Mas a.l.: l. *mḥnw* or *mḥny* (both variants of *mḥnh*) in Mas 566[2] (uncert. interpret.).
v. *ytn₁*.

mḥnw v. *mḥnh*.

mḥny v. *mḥnh*.

mḥsm **Ph** Sing. cstr. *mḥsm* KAI 11 - ¶ subst. implement to close lips, bridle, clip, leaf of metal (cf. e.g. Ehelolf with Friedrich OLZ '35, 348f., Röllig KAI a.l., Gibson SSI iii p. 100, Butterweck TUAT ii 589 :: Dunand FB i 31: = mask (cf. also Dussaud Syr xvii 99)).

mḥsp **Pun** Sing. abs. *mḥsp* CIS i 6002; cstr. *mḥsp* RES 596 (dam. context, for the reading, cf. Clermont-Ganneau sub RES 596 :: Lidzbarski Eph iii 61 (div. otherwise): l. *mḥspt* (= orthogr. variant of *m'spt* (Sing. cstr.))) - ¶ subst. of uncert. meaning, poss. = vase, urn (cf. e.g. Lidzbarski Eph i 170, Février sub CIS i 6002, Ferron OA v 199), cf. however Clermont-Ganneau with RES 10: place where vases are made, factory of urns (or fabrication of vases)? - this word poss. also in BAr '14, 345a 1 (Sing. cstr. *[m]ḥsp*, dam. context), 345b 1 (Sing. abs. *[m]ḥsp*, dam. context), cf. also Dussaud BAr a.l. - on this word, cf. also Bénichou-Safar TPC p. 187f.

mḥsr **OldCan** Sing. + suff. 3 p.pl.m. *ma-aḫ-sí-ra-mu* EA 287[16] - **Pun** Sing. abs. *mḥsr* KAI 69[5] - **JAr** Sing. abs. *mḥ[s]r* MPAT 52[2] (uncert. reading, cf. Beyer ATTM 322: l. *hn ḥ[s]yr*) - ¶ subst. - **1)** need; *ma-aḫ-sí-ra-mu* EA 287[16]: their needs - **2)** lack, defect; *mḥ[s]r [wly]tyr* MPAT 52[2f.]: more or less (prob. interpret.); *'š qrny lmbmḥsr* KAI 69[5]: whose horns are wanting.

mḥṣ₁ **OldCan** QAL Pf. 3 p.pl. + suff. 3 p.s.m. (cf. FR 188) *ma-aḫ-ṣú-ú* EA 245[14] (cf. Sivan GAG 138, 247) - ¶ verb QAL to strike, to kill (?);

+ obj.: EA 245[14].
v. *pḥṣ*.

mḥṣ₂ **Ph** Sing. cstr. *mḥṣ* on coins from Tyre, cf. Hill cxxvii - ¶ subst. half; *mḥṣ k(sp)* half a silver obol (cf. also *ksp₂*) :: Betlyon CMP 40f.: l. *mḥṣt* = Sing. abs. of *mḥṣt* (= half; cf. also Puech RB xcii 287).

mḥṣb **Pun** Sing. abs. *mḥṣb* KAI 62[7] - ¶ subst. quarry.

mḥṣh Zadok JAOS cii 116: this word (= wall, partition-wall) poss. > Akkad. *maḫaṣṣat* in *Bīt-Maḫaṣṣat* (uncert. interpret.; cf. also CAD s.v. *maḫazzatu*).

mḥṣrt v. *ḥṣr₁*.

mḥṣt v. *mḥṣ₂*.

mḥq v. *ḥqq₁*.

mḥqh v. *ḥṣr₁*.

mḥr₁ v. *tl*.

mḥr₂ v. *mḥr₃*.

mḥr₃ **Hebr** *mḥr* KAI 197[8f.] (for the reading, cf. e.g. Albright BASOR lxxxii 23 n. 28, Röllig KAI a.l., Gibson SSI i p. 47, Lemaire IH i 127 :: Torczyner Lach i p. 137: l. *mhw* = *mh₂*+ *hw₁*),TA-H 2[6] (cf. e.g. Aharoni TA a.l., Lemaire IH i 161f., Pardee UF x 297 :: Lipiński BiOr xxxv 287, xli 157: *mḥr* poss. = Sing. abs. of *mḥr₂* (= exchange value, equivalent, payment)) - **DA** *mḥr* i 5 (for the reading, cf. Hoftijzer DA a.l. :: Dahood Bibl lxii 125: l. *mḥz* = Sing. abs. of *mḥz₃* (= vision); cf. however H.& M.Weippert ZDPV xcviii 86 (n. 35)) - **OffAr** *mḥr* Cowl 5[6,8], 8[18], Krael 2[7,9,10], Sem ii 31 conc. 2, etc., etc.; cf. Frah xxvii 7 (*mḥ*ʾ*l*) - ¶ adv. tomorrow: passim; *lmḥr* Krael 11[10]: tomorrow; *mn mḥr* DA i 5: the next morning; for the expression *(l)mḥr (*ʾ*w) ywm* ʾ*ḥrn*, v. ʾ*ḥrn*; the reading *lmhr* in Cowl 1[4] incorrect, cf. Porten & Greenfield JEAS p. 106, Porten & Yardeni sub TADAE B 5.1: l. *mḥr*.
v. ʾ*ḥr₃*, *hkl₂*, *mḥkl*, *mkr₂*, *mlh*.

mḥrm **OffAr** Aggoula Syr lxii 64, 69, 71f.: the *mḥrm* in KAI 228A 16 = Sing. abs. of *mḥrm* (= sanctuary, in the context indicating the main sanctuary of Têma; cf. also Knauf Trans ii 213f.), less prob. interpret., cf. e.g. Cooke NSI p. 196, 198, Donner KAI a.l., Gibson SSI ii p. 150: = n.l.

mḥrmh **Nab** Sing. cstr. *mḥrmt* RES 2093[1]; emph. *mḥrmt*ʾ CIS ii 158[1,5] (:: Cooke NSI p. 256f.: = Plur. emph.),[6], RB lxiv 215[1] - ¶ subst. f. - **1)** cultic place, sanctuary: CIS ii 158[1,5,6], RB lxiv 215[1] - **2)** reserved place: RES 2093[1] (the same word also in RES 2094?) - on this word, cf. also Starcky RB lxiv 199f., Brekelmans Ḥerem 23f., Gawlikowski Ber xxiv 38 - l. this word prob. also in CIS ii 3927[4] (*mḥrmn* (Plur. abs.); Greek par. ἀναθέματα), for the reading, cf. Chabot CIS ii a.l., Cantineau Gramm 111, Milik DFD 3f., Gawlikowski TP 51 (meaning: objects dedicated).

mḥšb$_1$ **Pun** Plur. abs. *mḥšbm* CIS i 5547^{5} - ¶ subst. engine, cf. Février CIS i a.l. :: Heltzer UF xix 434: = Pi ʿel Part. pl.m. abs. of *ḥšb*$_1$ (or = Plur. abs. of *mḥšb*$_2$).

mḥšb$_2$ v. *ḥšb*$_1$, *mḥšb*$_1$.

mḥt$_1$ **Ph/Pun** the diff. *lmḥt* in KAI $60^{3,6}$, $119^{6,7}$ prob. = *l*$_5$ + *mḥt* (poss. = Qal/Pi ʿel Inf. cstr. of a root *mḥy/mḥt*); cf. Cooke NSI p. 97 (following Hoffmann; on KAI 60): < root *mḥy*$_1$= to wipe off into the measure (i.e. to fill up to the full weight), cf. also Février RA l 187, Röllig KAI a.l. (on KAI 60), Garbini RSO xliii 13: < root *mḥy*$_1$= to strike (i.e. to coin); cf. also v.d.Branden BiOr xxxvi 160 (n. 38); Lipiński UF iii 89f.: < root *mḥy*$_2$= to overflow (to make overflow > to pay/weigh to the full weight; cf. also the remarks of Gibson SSI iii p. 150); Levi Della Vida RCL '55, 559f.: < root *mḥy*$_1$ = to cancel (sc. a debt) > to pay (cf. also Röllig sub KAI 119, Garbini RSO xliii 13, Amadasi IPT 80f.) :: Février RA l 187: < root *mḥy*$_1$= to strike > to engrave - *drknm 20 lmḥt* KAI $60^{3,6}$: twenty drachms to the full weight (?, v. supra); exact meaning in KAI 119 unclear; cf. also Bonnet SEL vii 120f.
v. *mḥth*.

mḥt$_2$ v.Soden Or xxxv 16, xlvi 190: *mḥt*$_2$ = whip > Akkad. (cf. also idem AHW s.v. *māḫītu* (improb. interpret., cf. CAD s.v. *maḫītu*)).

mḥth **Pun** Plur. (?) abs. *mḥtt* RCL '66, 201^{5} - ¶ subst. of unknown meaning in the comb. *šql mḥtt*, poss. related to money/weight matters, cf. Garbini RSO xliii 13: *mḥtt* = the weight (sc. of money; related to *mḥt*$_1$),cf. also Dupont-Sommer CRAI '68, 128: *mḥtt* = something broken, something small > small coin (< root *ḥtt*$_1$;cf. also Ferron Mus xcviii 61); cf. however also Mahjoubi & Fantar RCL '66, 208: *mḥth* = brazier.

mṭ **Ph** Sing. abs. *mṭ* KAI 14^{11} - **Pun** Sing. abs. *mtʾ* KAI 145^{14} (?, cf. Lidzbarski Eph i 50, Cooke NSI p. 155, Février Sem vi 27, FR 39, 248a, Röllig KAI a.l., v.d.Branden RSF i 171 :: Halévy RS ix 284f.: = Hoph Part. s.m. abs. of *ʾty*$_1$) - ¶ subst. what is below; *lmṭ* KAI 14^{11}: below; *lmmʿlʾ mtʾ* KAI 145^{15}: from the top to the bottom (v. also *mʿl*$_2$).
v. *mṭh*.

mṭʾ **OffAr** Qal Pf. 3 p.s.m. *mṭʾ* Cowl 7^{7}, 10^{7}, 35^{8} (*[m]ṭʾ*, for the reading, cf. Porten & Yardeni sub TADAE B 4.6; for the context cf. also Porten JNES xlviii 166), 38^{3}, 83^{2}; + suff. 2 p.s.m. *mṭʾk* Cowl $28^{3,7,9,10,12}$, Herm 3^{6}; + suff. 1 p.s. *mṭʾny* Cowl 28^{5}; 3 p.s.f. *mṭʾt* Cowl 41^{2}, Krael 13^{7} (*[m]ṭʾt*), Sach 76 i A 3 (for the reading, cf. Lidzbarski Eph iii 256), *mṭt* Cowl 10^{6}; + suff. 2 p.s.f. *mṭtky* Cowl 1^{4}; + suff. 1 p.s. *mṭtny* Herm 4^{4}; 3 p.pl.m. *mṭʾ[w]* KAI 266^{4} (for the reading, cf. Porten BiAr xliv 36, 50, Porten & Yardeni sub TADAE A 1.1 :: Milik Bibl xlviii 562: l. *mʿb[r]t* = Sing. cstr. of *mʿbrh* (poss. = defile); cf. also

Lipiński OLP viii 104), *mṭw* Cowl 37[15]; Impf. 3 p.s.m. *ymṭ'* Driv 6[5], NESE i 11[8]; 3 p.s.f. *[t]mṭ'* Cowl 42[7], *tmṭh* Herm 6[5f.]; + suff. 2 p.s.m. *tmṭ'nk* JRAS '29, 108[11] (prob. reading), *tmṭnk* Krael 13[2]; 3 p.pl.m. *ymṭ'n* AE '23, 42 no. 12[2] (dam. context); Imper. s.m./f. *mṭy* ATNS 133[1] (?, heavily dam. context); Inf. *mmṭh* Beh 8 (Akkad. par. *ka-šá-du*), 12 (Akkad. par. *ka-šá-di*); Part. act. s.f. abs. *mṭ'h* Cowl 14[5], Herm 3[4]; cf. Frah xxiii 4 (*yḥmtwn*), Paik 483 (*ymṭ'*), 484, 485 (*ymṭ'h*), 486-490 (*yḥmtwn*), GIPP 37, 68, SaSt 25 (cf. also Lemosín AO ii 108, Toll ZDMG-Suppl 37) - **Palm** QAL Pf. 3 p.s.m. *mṭ'* CIS ii 4027[1] - **JAr** APH Impf. 3 p.pl.m. *ymṭwn* MPAT 60[4] - ¶ verb QAL to reach, to arrive; cf. *mṭ' tnyn šnh* Cowl 10[7]: a second year arrives - **1)** with *yd* as subject, *kdy mṭ'h ydy* Herm 3[4]: as far as I am able (cf. Herm 6[5f.]; cf. Greenfield FS Fitzmyer 49) - **2)** + obj. (or orig. acc. loci?), *mṭtny ktnt zy ...* Herm 4[4]: the tunic which ... has reached me (cf. Herm 3[6], JRAS '29, 108[11] (diff. context), Krael 13[2] (dam. context)); *ymṭ' mṣryn* Driv 6[5]: he will reach Egypt (cf. Cowl 83[2], KAI 266[4]); cf. *plg mnt' zy mṭtky* Cowl 1[3f.]: half the share which came to you (cf. Cowl 28[3,5,7,9,10,12]; on Cowl 1 and 28, cf. Porten & Szubin JAOS cii 653) - **3)** + l_5, *mṭ' l'bwṭ* Cowl 38[3]: he came to Abydos; cf. *mṭ' l'ty ... gwmḥ'* CIS ii 4227[1f.]: the niche came to A. (i.e. belongs to A.); cf. also *mṭt mrbyt' lrš'* Cowl 10[6]: the interest is added to the capital - **4)** + l_5 + Inf., *mṭ't lmgz* Sach 76 i A 3: she (sc. the ewe) has reached shearing (for the transl., cf. Greenfield Or xxix 99f.) - **5)** + *'l*$_7$, *'grt' z' [t]mṭ' 'lyk* Cowl 42[7]: this letter will reach you (cf. Dion RB lxxxix 561f.); *[m]ṭ't spynt' tnh 'lyn* Krael 13[7]: the ship has reached us here (cf. Cowl 41[2] (:: Dion RB lxxxix 557: *mṭ't 'ly* belonging to foll. clause); cf. prob. also NESE i 11[8], cf. Degen ibid. 20); cf. also *mwm'h mṭ'h 'lyky* Cowl 14[4f.]: an oath is imposed upon you (cf. Cowl 7[6f.]) - APH to bring; *wymṭwn lk hdsyn* (v. *hds*) MPAT 60[4]: let them bring to you myrtle branches - a form of this root poss. in Assur 27g (*mṭy/w*), Aggoula sub Assur 27: = have been delivered (highly uncert. interpret.).

mṭ'r v. *mṭr*$_3$.

mṭbḥ **Pun** Sing. abs. *mṭbḥ* KAI 80[1] - ¶ subst. construction on which animals were slaughtered before being sacrificed (for the context, v. *dl*$_6$, *p'm*$_2$).

mṭh **DA** Sing. abs. *mṭh* i 11 (cf. also Puech FS Grelot 23 (n. 44) :: Lemaire BAT 318: = *mṭ*+ adv. ending (= below)) - ¶ subst. rod: DA i 11 (dam. context); poss. > punishment, cf. Hoftijzer DA a.l., cf. however Caquot & Lemaire Syr liv 199 (v. also *ḥṭr*$_1$), cf. also *mṭy*.

mṭw v. *mṭy*.

mṭwl v. *mṭl*.

mṭwtw **Palm** the diff. *mṭwtwt'* in Syr xvii 271[6] poss. = Sing. emph. of *mṭwtw* (cf. Cantineau Syr xvii 273, Gawlikowski Syr li 98f.: fast, order of the fast (cf. also Lipiński BiOr xxxiii 233f.: *mṭwtw* = favour, pardon), cf. however Cantineau Syr xvii 273 (div. *mṭ* (= word of unknown meaning) + *w* + *ṭwt’* (= Sing. emph. of *ṭwt* (= mulberry)), less prob. interpret.) :: Milik DFD 297 (div. otherwise): l. *mṭw* (= QAL Pf. 3 p.pl.m. of *mṭy* (= *mṣ’*$_1$)) + *t*$_1$ (= *’yt*$_3$) + suff. 3 p.s.m. + *t’* (= *’t*$_6$ + suff. 3 p.s.m./f.)).

mṭḥ Pun Sing. abs. *mṭḥ* KAI 137[3] - ¶ subst. prob. meaning, plastering: KAI 137[3] (for litt., cf. RES sub 942).

mṭy Palm the diff. *mṭy’* in InvD 47 (diff. reading) = Sing. emph. of *mṭy* (= camel rider)?? (cf. Ingholt YClSt xiv 138f.), cf. however du Mesnil du Buisson TMP 235: l. *mṭw’* = Sing. emph. of *mṭw* (= lance; cf. also *mṭḥ*;:: du Mesnil du Buisson sub InvD 47: l. *mṭw’* = *mṭwh* (= Sing. + suff. 3 p.s.m. of *mṭw*)).

mṭl Palm *mṭl* CIS ii 3913 i 6, 3932[6], MUSJ xxxviii 106[7] - **JAr** *mṭwl*Syr xlv 101[17] (dam. context) - ¶ orig. subst. used as prep., because of; for *mṭl kwt*, v. *kwt*; for *kl lmṭl dy*, v. *kl*$_1$ - on this word, cf. also Rundgren OrSu xv 79 ff.

mṭlh Palm Sing. emph. *mṭlt’* SBS 1A 1, 2ABCD 1, 3[1], 4ABCDEF 1, Syr xii 130[1], xvii 268[5] (for the reading, cf. Milik DFD 220, cf. also Gawlikowski TP 61 :: Cantineau Syr xvii a.l.: *[‘]lt’* = Sing. emph. of *‘lh*$_1$), 274[1] (*[m]ṭlt’*), InscrP 30[1] (= Inv i 5[1] = SBS1 B1; *m[ṭ]lt’*; for this reading, cf. Rosenthal Sprache 73 n. 5, Dunant sub SBS 1B, cf. also Cantineau Syr xvii 276 :: Cantineau InscrP a.l., Inv i 5 a.l.: l. *m[‘]lt’* = Sing. emph. of *m‘lh* (= entry)), Inv xii 30[1] (*mṭ[lt’]*), etc. - ¶ subst. f. portico, (part of) roofed collonade (cf. Dunant SBS p. 13f., Garbini OA xiv 176, cf. already Rosenthal Sprache 73 n. 5, 111f. (: = στοά), cf. also Bounni & Teixidor sub Inv xii 30 :: Cantineau Syr xvii 275ff.: prob. = small building with religious character, providing a shelter for the image of a divinity or for a sacred object (cf. also Gaster Syr xviii 230ff., Driver CanMyths 160 n. 21)).

mṭll OffAr Sing. cstr. *mṭll* Cowl 30[11], 31[10] - ¶ subst. roof.

mṭmr OffAr Sing. cstr. *mṭmr* Atlal vii 112 i 1 (for this uncert. reading, cf. Beyer & Livingstone ZDMG cxxxvii 292 :: Livingstone Atlal vii a.l: l. *m‘mr* = Sing. cstr. of *m‘mr* (= monument?)) - ¶ subst. of uncert. meaning (v. supra), poss. indicating a certain type of tomb/grave.

mṭn’ Ph Sing. abs. *mṭn’* KAI 48[1], RES 1513B - **Pun** Sing. abs. *mṭn’* ICO-Spa 16[1] (for this diff. reading, cf. also Delcor CISFP i 777f., Fuentes Estañol sub CIFE 14.01 :: Puech RSF v 85ff. (dividing otherwise): l. poss. *ks’* = Sing. cstr. of *ks’*$_3$:: Cross HThR lxiv 189f.: l. *nš’* = Sing. cstr. of *nš’*$_3$ :: Heltzer OA vi 266: = orthogr. var. of *mtn’* (= offering; on the reading, cf. also Teixidor Syr lvi 386f.)) - ¶ subst. (votive) offering; in KAI 48[1] on a stele, in RES 1513B on an urn, in ICO-Spa 16[1] on a statuette (:: Krahmalkov OA xi 210: = statuette).

mṭ‘ Pun Février RA xlv 147: this subst. (Plur. cstr. *mṭ‘’*) = plantation

in KAI 161[9]?? (cf. also Roschinski Num 112, 115); highly uncert. interpret., diff. context; cf. however Mosca & Russell EpAn ix 9 (n. 30): l. poss. *nṭʿm* (= Plur. abs. of *nṭʿ₂*).
mṭr₁ **OffAr**, cf. Frah i 17: to rain (*yntlwn* lapsus for *ymṭlwn*).
mṭr₂ **OffAr**, cf. Frah i 16 (*mtlʾ*) - **Hatra** Sing. emph. *mṭrʾ*, cf. Assur 27e 1 - ¶ subst. rain.
mṭr₃ **OffAr**, Ebeling Frah a.l.: l. *mṭʾrin* Frah xxx 31 = form of *mṭr₃* (= part, section), less prob. interpret., cf. Nyberg FP p. 58, 110: l. here Iran. word.
mṭrʾ v. *qry₁*.
mṭrh **JAr** Patrick & Rubin RB xci 382: l. *mṭrn* (= Plur. abs. of *mṭrh* (= guard)) RB xci 382 (uncert. interpret., diff. context; for the reading problems, cf. Patrick RB xcii 273 (cf. also idem EI xviii 159)).
my₁ **Ph** *my* KAI 13[3], 24[10,11,12,13,15] - **Pun** KAI 126[7] (for this reading, cf. Amadasi Guzzo StudMagr xi 31, VO iv/2, 5f. :: Levi Della Vida RCL '49, 405f., Röllig KAI a.l.: l. *ʾš* (= *š₁₀*)), cf. Poen 1010: *mi* - **Hebr** KAI 192[3], 195[3], 196[2], DJD ii 44[8] -
1) interrogative pronoun, who?: Poen 1010; *my ʿbdk klb ky zkr ʾdny ʾt [ʿ]bdh* KAI 192[3ff.]: who is your servant but a dog, that my lord remembers his servant? (cf. KAI 195[3f.], 196[2f.]) - **2)** indefinite pronoun, whoever; *my bl ḥz ...* KAI 24[11]: he who had never seen ..., cf. KAI 24[12,15]; cf. also *my bbny ʾš ...* KAI 24[13f.]: anyone of my sons who ...; *my ʾt kl ʾdm ʾš ...* KAI 13[3]: whoever you are, any man at all who ...; *pqdty t my š ytn ...* DJD ii 44[8f.]: I have ordered anyone who will give ...; in the comb. *my ... my*, *lmy kt ʾb wlmy kt ʾm wlmy kt ʾḥ* KAI 24[10f.]: to some I was a father, to some I was a mother and to some I was a brother (cf. Sperling UF xx 335) - **3)** relative pronoun: KAI 126[7] (cf. Amadasi Guzzo VO iv/2, 5f.).
v. *qnmy*.
my₂ v. *myṭb*.
my₃ **OffAr** word of highly uncert. interpret. in FuF xxxv 173[4]; Altheim & Stiehl FuF xxxv 173, 176, ASA 273: = Sing. abs. of *mym* (= water), incorrectly derived from Plur. emph. *myʾ* (improb. interpret.).
myglb v. *mglb*.
mydʾ v. *mdʾnʾmwpʾ*.
mydbr v. *mdbr*.
mydh v. *mdh₁*.
mydlh v. *mdl*.
myh v. *z₁*.
myzrḥ **Hebr** Sing. abs. *myzrḥ* SM 49[8] - ¶ subst. east (side); *mn hmyzrḥ* SM 49[8]: at the east side; cf. *mzrḥ*.
myṭb **Pun** Plur. cstr. *myṭbʾ* 172[2] (cf. Friedrich AfO x 82, FR 105, 225b, Röllig KAI a.l.; v. also infra) - ¶ subst. Plur. approbation; *ʿl*

myṭb› rš› hslky KAI 172²: with the approbation of the senate of Sulcis (Lat. par. *ex s(enatus) c(onsulto)*) :: Levi Della Vida RSO xxxix 310, idem with Garbini OA iv 42, Amadasi ICO p. 131 (div. otherwise): l. *‹l myṭb* (= Sing. cstr.) *›rš›* (= QAL Part. pass. pl.m. cstr. of *›rš*$_1$ (= the chosen ones, the senate) *hslky*) :: Garbini AION xix 132: l. *›rš›* = quaestores < root *›rš*$_2$ (= to possess), cf. also Polselli StudMagr xii 84f. :: CIS i sub 149 (cf. also Cooke NSI p. 158 (div. otherwise): l. *my.ṭb›rš›*without interpret.; cf. also CIS i sub 149 for older litt.).

myṭryn **JAr** Dupont-Sommer JKF i 203, 206: l. *myṭryn* (= Sing. abs. of *myṭryn* < Greek μήτρα) = womb in AMB 7a 8, 7b 4 (improb. interpret., cf. Naveh & Shaked AMB a.l. (div. otherwise): l. *dmyṭryn* = n.p. (cf. also Beyer ATTM 372f.)).

myl **Pun** Milik with Vattioni AION xvi 48: the diff. *vmylthe* in IRT 827³ poss. = *v* (= article) + *myl* + *the* (= *t*$_1$+ suff. 3 p.s.m.), *myl* being a derivative of the root *myl* (= to be loved; improb. interpret.); cf. Krahmalkov JSS xvii 72f., Vattioni Aug xvi 539: *vmylthe* = n.p. (cf. also Levi Della Vida OA ii 85, *umylthe* unexplained).

mylḥ v. *mlḥ*$_2$.

myll **Pun** the diff. *myll* in KAI 161² poss. = PU‹AL Part. s.m. abs. of *yll*$_1$ (= the regretted), cf. Cooke NSI p. 149, Février RA xlv 142, FR 158 (cf. also Lidzbarski Handb 288) :: v.d.Branden GP § 239: = PU‹AL Part. s.m. abs. of *hll* (= the praiseworthy one; cf. however v.d.Branden BiOr xxxvi 202) :: Roschinski Num 114: = PI‹EL Part. s.m. abs. of *‹ll*$_2$ (= to bring about, to effectuate) :: Berger RA ii 37, 40: = PU‹AL Part. s.m. abs. of *yll*$_1$ (= the glorious one; cf. Cooke NSI p. 149) or = HIPH Part. s.m. abs. of *yll*$_1$ (= the victor).

mym **OldCan** Plur. (or Dual?, cf. Sivan GAG 14 n. 3) abs. *mu-mi* TeAv iii 137¹, *mé-ma* EA 148¹², 155¹⁰, *mé-e-ma* EA 148³¹ - **Ph** Plur. abs. *mym* KAI 37B 4 (v. infra) - **Hebr** Plur. abs. *mym* KAI 189⁵, TA-H 111⁸ (dam. context), IEJ xxxii 195² (heavily dam. context), *myn* Mas 449² (dam. context); cstr. *my* SM 49¹⁴ - **OldAr** Plur. cstr. *my* KAI 222B 33, 34; + suff. 3 p.s.m. *mwh* Tell F 17, 18 (Akkad. par. twice *mî-šú* ; on the form, cf. Greenfield & Shaffer Shn v/vi 123) - **OffAr** Plur. abs. *myn* Cowl 27⁷, Aḥiq 113, 192, KAI 260 8, 266⁴ (for this reading, cf. Porten & Yardeni sub TADAE A 1.1 (cf. already Naveh AramScript 16) :: Porten BiAr xliv 36, Dion RB lxxxix 532 n. 30: l. *rmyn* = Plur. m. abs. of *rm*$_2$ (cf. also Delsman TUAT i 633) :: e.g. Dupont-Sommer Sem i 44, 48, Ginsberg BASOR cxi 25f., Fitzmyer Bibl xlvi 44, 49f., WA 237, Donner KAI a.l., Gibson SSI ii p. 113ff., Briend TPOA 136: l. *›myn* = Sing. m. abs. of *›myn* (= firm, stable, enduring) :: Rosenthal JBL xci 552: l. *›myn* = lapsus for *myn*), 269³, FS Driver 54 conc. 3; emph. *my›* Cowl 6¹¹, 8⁸, 27⁸, Krael 12²⁰, ATNS 65b 5, 69b 3; cf. Frah iii 1, 2 (*my›*), GIPP 29, SaSt 20 - **Nab** Plur. emph. *my›* CIS ii 350²

- **Palm** Plur. abs. *mn* (contraction? :: Rosenthal Sprache 16f.: *mn* = *mîn*) CI ii 4218[7]; emph. *my*ʾ CIS ii 3913 ii 1, 63, RIP 162[2] - **Waw** Plur. emph. *my*ʾ AMB 6[5] - ¶ subst. m. Plur. water: passim; for *lḥm wmyn* v. *lḥm*$_4$; for *mḥm my*ʾ, v. *ḥmm*$_1$; *bʿl mym* KAI 37B 4: prob. meaning, the master of the water (cf. Masson & Sznycer RPC 27, 58f. (cf. also Yon Mem Saidah 260ff.), cf. Garbini AION xxiii 134: *bʿl* = Plur. cstr. of *bʿl*$_2$, *bʿl mym* = the personnel charged with the water basin (cf. also Teixidor AJA lxxviii 189f.; cf. Amadasi sub Kition C 1; for the reading, cf. already Peckham Or xxxvii 318, 319 (n. 1): = the owner(s) of the water, less prob. interpret.)) :: Healy BASOR ccxvi 53, 56: l. *bʿlm* (= Plur. cstr. of *bʿl*$_2$ + enclitic *m*) *ym* (= Sing. abs. of *ym*$_1$ (= Sea, ritual object)) :: e.g. CIS i sub 86, Cooke NSI p. 68f., Röllig KAI a.l.: l. *bʿl* (= Plur. cstr. of *bʿl*$_2$) *ymm* (= Plur. abs. of *ywm*)= the lords of the days (i.e. the gods who preside over the different days of the month; cf. also Gibson SSI iii p. 127, 130) - with special meaning: brook; *r*ʾ*š my gy*ʾ*tw wgy*ʾ*tw* ʿ*ṣmh* SM 49[14]: the head of the brook of G. and G. itself (cf. also Jastrow s.v. *gʿtwn*) - Rosenthal Sprache 16: l. *m[n]* in CIS ii 3913 ii 58 (= Plur. abs.) pro *m[y]*, cf. also Reckendorf ZDMG xlii 409, Cooke NSI p. 326, 337: = Sing. cstr. (cf. also CIS ii a.l.) - CIS ii a.l.: the *my* in CIS ii 129[3] = Plur. cstr. of *myn*$_1$ (improb. interpret., cf. e.g. RES sub 1367, Grelot DAE p. 339, 494: = part of n.p.).
v. *ym*ʾ, *kry*$_4$, *lqḥ*, *mh*$_2$, *my*$_3$, *mʿyn*, *qny*.

myn$_1$ v. *mym*.

myn$_2$ **Palm** Plur. abs. *mynyn* Sem xxvii 117[8] - ¶ subst. poss. meaning: tribe, clan (cf. Aggoula Sem xxvii 119), uncert. interpret., cf. also Teixidor Syr lvi 399 :: Starcky with Teixidor Syr lvi 399: *mynyn* < Lat. *mina*, Greek μνᾶ.

myn$_3$ v. *mn*$_5$.

mynwq **JAr** Naveh SM sub 33 and 35: l. *mynwqh* (= Sing. + suff. 3 p.s.m. of *mynwq* (= child, boy)) in MPAT-A 27[1] (= SM 33) and 29[3] (= SM 35), uncert. interpret., cf. also Sukenik JPOS xv 140, 146, Fitzmyer & Harrington MPAT a.l.: l. *mwnyqh* = n.p. (< Greek Μόνιχος) and Fitzmyer & Harrington MPAT a.l.: = n.p. (< Greek Μόνικα).

mynkd (< Lib., cf. Levi Della Vida AfrIt vi 4ff., RSO xxxix 307, Friedrich Or xxiv 156, (Rössler with) Röllig KAI a.l., FR 211, Garbini StudMagr ii 118ff. :: Schiffmann Klio lxiii 425: = Punic < root *ngd*$_2$; on this word, cf. also Février MC 86) - **Pun** Sing. abs. *mynkd* KAI 120[1,2] (Lat. par. *imp(erator)*) - ¶ subst. used to indicate the Roman emperor (cf. also litt. mentioned supra).

mynṭh (< Greek μίνθα, μίνθη) - **Hebr** Sing. abs. *mynṭh* (or l. *mynth*?) - ¶ subst. f. mint.

myst **Pun** Sing./Plur. abs. (or cstr., cf. v.d.Branden RSF v 57, 60), *myst* Karth xii 51[3] (for the reading problems, cf. Février & Fantar

Karth xii a.l. :: Krahmalkov RSF iii 177f., 181, 202: l. *kyst=* Plur. cstr. of *ks*’$_3$ (= position)) - ¶ subst. of unknown meaning; v.d.Branden RSF v 57, 60: = authorisation, authority; Février & Fantar Karth xii 51: = foundation??

my‘ms Pun diff. word (Sing. or Plur. cstr. or abs.?) occurring in votive texts in the following expressions: *lmy‘ms ‘m qrtḥdšt* CIS i 270[3], 271[3f.] (*[lmy‘m]s ‘m qrtḥd[št]*), 290[6f.] (*[lmy]‘ms ‘m q[rtḥdšt]*), 291[5f.] (*lmy‘ms ‘m qrt[ḥdšt]*), 4909[4f.] (*lmy‘m[s ‘]m qrtḥdšt*), *lm*’‘*ms*’ *‘m qrtḥdšt* CIS i 4908[4f.], *[lmy]‘ms ‘m* CIS i 272[4f.], *lmy‘ms* CIS i 273[4], 274[2f.] (*[lm]y‘ms*), 275[5f.], 2822[3] (*[lmy‘]ms*); except in CIS i 4909 (and perhaps CIS i 2822??) occurring in texts in which also the diff. expression *’š ṣdn* (v. *ṣdn*) is attested; meaning of *lmy‘ms* uncert. (*‘m qrtḥdšt* = the people of C. (or their representatives) :: v.d.Branden BiOr xxxvi 158: = the group of Carthage, i.e. the group of *’š ṣdn* living in the town of C.) - for *lmy‘ms*, cf. CIS i sub 270: = *ex decreto*? (cf. also Slouschz TPI p. 251, Huss 498f.), cf. however Sznycer Sem xxv 57ff.: rather = selon ... l'ordonnance (ou le relevé) du ... :: v.d.Branden BiOr xxxvi 157f.: by vote of :: Heltzer OA xxiv 81ff.: by the power of :: Good SEL iii 99ff.: *m‘yms* = indication of Maioumas festival (= *m* (form of *mym*) + *y‘ms* (= Yoph Inf. of *‘ms*)/ *’‘ms* (= Oph Inf. of *‘ms*), cf. also idem SHP 24) :: Février Sem iv 17f.: *my‘ms* = good weight, *lmy‘ms* = with complete payment of the sum due for the manumission, or rather (div. otherwise *lm y‘ms* = that they may not take (it, i.e. the stele) away (cf. already Hoffmann AGWG xxxvi/1 (1889), 5; against this solution, cf. also CIS i sub 4908) - cf. prob. also CIS 269[5] with only *‘m qrtḥdšt.*

myp’ v. *yp’*.

myph(h) Ph Plur. abs. *myphṭ* EI xviii 117[6] (= IEJ xxxv 83; reading of *y* and *p* not absolutely certain) - ¶ subst. of uncert. meaning indicating a certain kind of object; Dothan EI xviii 118, IEJ xxxv 83, 88: = object made by blowing or hammering and not by casting.

myp‘l Pun Sing. cstr. *myp‘l* CIS i 5522[2] (cf. Levi Della Vida with Février SOLDV i 276, Sem xi 5 n. 2, v.d.Branden BiOr xxiii 143f., Février sub CIS i a.l. :: Chabot BAr '43/45, 160 (div. otherwise): l. *bmy p‘l* (without interpret.) :: Février Sem iv 15 (div. otherwise): l. *bmyp‘ l* (= b_2 + nomen mensis) + l_5) - ¶ subst. prob. meaning, act (v.d.Branden BiOr xxiii 143f., GP p. 118: = authority); for the context, v. *trš*$_2$ - cf. also *p‘l*$_2$.

myqdš v. *mqdš*.

myqm v. *qwm*$_1$.

myqn’ v. *qny*.

myryt OffAr Sing. emph. *myryt’* Cowl 83[29] (cf. Leand 43g'''') - ¶ subst. heritage (?).

myšṭr v. *mšṭr*.

myškb v. *mškb*$_1$.
myšql v. *šql*$_1$.
myšr v. *yšr*$_1$, *mkr*$_2$.
myšrt v. *mšrt*$_2$.
myt$_1$ v. *mwt*$_1$.
myt$_2$ v. *mšb*$_1$.
myt$_3$ v. *ʿtd*$_1$.
myt$_4$ **Hebr** Plur. abs. *mytyn* DJD ii 46[5] - ¶ adj. dead (for the context of DJD ii 46[5], v. *qbr*$_1$).
v. *mwt*$_1$.
mytb v. *mrḥb*, *mšb*$_1$.
myth v. *ʿtd*$_1$.
mytwyh **Palm** Sing. emph. *mytwytʾ* CIS ii 3932[2] (cf. Rosenthal Sprache 73 n. 6 × Cantineau sub Inv iii 22: = Sing. emph. of *mytwyt*, type *maqtôlît*?) - ¶ subst. advent, arrival.
mytwyt v. *mytwyh*.
mk **OldAr** the diff. *mk* in KAI 224[22] poss. = lapsus for *mnk* (= *mn*$_5$ + suff. 2 p.s.m.), cf. e.g. Fitzmyer CBQ xx 462 (cf. also idem AIS 118), Rosenthal BASOR clviii 30, Gibson SSI ii p. 55 :: Koopmans 68, Donner KAI a.l., Dahood Bibl lvi 94f.: *mk* < *mnk* by assimilation :: Lipiński BiOr xxxiii 234, Stud 48 (div. otherwise): l. *lṭbh* (= *l*$_5$ + Sing. + suff. 3 p.s.m. of *ṭb*$_2$) + *ʾmk* (= QAL Impf. 1 p.s. of *mwk*= (to go down, to resign)) :: Nober VD xxxvii 172: = interjection < root *mwk*,down! - *ky lṭb hʾ mk* KAI 224[22]: for he is not better than you (cf. Vogt Bibl xxxix 273, Rosenthal BASOR clviii 30, Fitzmyer JAOS lxxxi 213, AIS 101, Dahood Bibl lvi 94f., Gibson SSI ii p. 51 :: Dupont-Sommer BMB xiii 29, Sf p. 131, 146, Donner KAI a.l.: for it would not be right from your part).
mkʾwb **JAr** Sing. emph. *mkʾwbʾ* AMB 1[11] - ¶ subst. pain.
mkbrh **Pun** Février RA xlv 145: l. this word *mʿkbrt* (Sing. abs.?) = perfuming pan in KAI 161[7] (cf. also v.d.Branden RSF ii 144f.; for the reading, cf. also Röllig KAI a.l., cf. however also Berger RA ii 36f., Cooke NSI p. 148, 150, Roschinski Num 112, 115: different word division, without interpret.).
mky **OffAr** Milik Bibl xlviii 551, 582, 618: the *mky* in Herm 2[9] = Sing. abs. of *mky* (= bad condition), *ʿl mky* = in bad condition, of inferior quality (improb. interpret., cf. e.g. Bresciani & Kamil Herm. a.l., Gibson SSI ii p. 133f., Porten & Greenfield JEAS p. 154, Porten & Yardeni sub TADAE A 2.2: *mky* = n.p. (cf. also Grelot DAE 154 (n. d)).
mkyl **Palm** Sing. cstr. (with prosth. alef) *ʾmkyl* Sem xxxvi 89[1] (:: Gawlikowski Sem xxxvi 89, 92 (div. otherwise): l. *mkyl* (= Sing. abs.)) - ¶ subst. of uncert. meaning: investment (??) :: Gawlikowski Sem

xxxvi 89, 92: = account - poss. same word as *mkl*$_1$.

mkyr **Hebr** Sing. abs. *mkyr* DJD ii 30[3,16] - ¶ subst. prob. meaning vendor.

mkyt$_1$ **OldCan** the *mi-ki-tu* in EA 64[22] poss. = Plur. abs. of *mkyt* (= attractive girl)??, cf. Loretz & Mayer UF vi 493f. :: Krahmalkov JNES xxx 141ff.: = Sing. abs. of *mkyt*$_2$ (= attack, plague) :: Knudtzon EA p. 355, 1461: poss. = the forgotten ones < root *makû*.

mkyt$_2$ v. *mkyt*$_1$.

mkl$_1$ **Palm** Sing. abs. *mkl* RTP 39, 127, 284, 563, 564, 690, 694-704 - ¶ subst. prob. meaning some kind of liquid measure, cf. Caquot RTP p. 145, du Mesnil du Buisson TMP 475ff., Sznycer Sem xiii 34 :: Milik DFD 184f.: = variant of *m*ʾ*kl* (cf. also Lipiński EI xx 131*) - the *m*in RTP 350, 689, 691-693 poss. abbrev. of *mkl*$_1$ (cf. Caquot RTP a.l., du Mesnil du Buisson TMP 33, 475ff., Sznycer Sem xiii 34), cf. however Milik DFD 185ff.: = abbrev. indicating certain kind of coin - RTP a.l.: the diff. *m*ʾin RTP 572 = *m 1* (cf. also Milik DFD 187), uncert. interpret., cf. du Mesnil du Buisson TMP 33 - the poss. *m*in RTP 758 abbrev. of *mkl*?, cf. Starcky RTP a.l. (cf. however Milik DFD 186: = a certain type of coin, a submultiple of the Roman *denarius*), cf. however Starcky RTP a.l.: or l. *2*? (for the context, v. also *rb*ʿ$_3$).
v. *mkyl*, *mkl*$_2$.

mkl$_2$ **Hatra** Sing. (or Plur.?) emph. *mkl*ʾ 281[6] - ¶ subst. denoting certain object; Safar Sumer xxvii 5, Aggoula Syr lii 182, lxv 209, Vattioni IH a.l.: = bar, lever, cf. however Degen NESE iii 68, 70: = certain measure (= *mkl*$_1$).

mkl$_3$ v. *m*ʾ*kl*.

mkn$_1$ **Ph** Sing. abs. *mkn* KAI 37B 7 (v. infra) - **Pun** Sing. + suff. 3 p.s.m. *m*ʾ*kn*ʾ KAI 119[4] - ¶ subst. pedestal (of a statue): KAI 119[4] - the interpret. in KAI 37B 7 (: = place, office, cf. Peckham Or xxxvii 322f.; cf. Healy BASOR ccxvi 53, 57: Post = terminus technicus precise meaning unknown) uncert., cf. Masson & Sznycer RPC 63: = socle, pedestal? (cf. Puech Sem xxix 33; for the problems, cf. also Amadasi Kition p. 118, 123f.), cf. however Gibson SSI iii p. 131 (div. otherwise): l. *mknbm* (= Sing. + suff. 3 p.pl.m. of *mknb*, meaning unknown) :: e.g. CIS i sub 86, Cooke NSI p. 69, Röllig KAI a.l., FR 56c (div. otherwise): l. *knbm*= lapsus or variant of *klbm* (= Plur. abs. of *klb*$_1$)= hierodules :: v.d.Branden BMB xiii 92, BO viii 248f., 261: l. *knrm* (= Plur. abs. of *knr* (= cither)) - the same word as *mkn*$_2$?
v. *kwn*$_1$, *mlh*.

mkn$_2$ **Hatra** Sing. emph. *mkn*ʾ 202[5,18,21:1,2], 232a 1, d - ¶ subst. (fire) altar (cf. Teixidor Sumer xxi 86*ff., Safar Sumer xxiv 9 n. 5, Aggoula MUSJ xlvii 6 :: Aggoula Ber xviii 100, Milik DFD 368, 405, Vattioni IH a.l..: = stele :: Degen JEOL xxiii 404: = platform, dais) - same

word as *mkn$_1$*?
mknb v. *mkn$_1$*.
mkns v. *m›n*.
mks$_1$ (< Akkad., cf. Zimmern Fremdw 10, Ellenbogen 102, Kaufman AIA 72; on this word, cf. also Masing WGAV 521ff.) - **OffAr** Sing. abs. *mks* Cowl 81^{112}; cstr. ATNS 19^{4,6} - **Palm** Sing. abs. *mks* CIS ii 3913 ii 108, 113, 122; emph. *mks›* CIS ii 3913 i 4, 5, 14, ii 1, 57, 95, etc., etc.; + suff. 3 p.s.m. *mksh* CIS ii 3913 i 9; Plur. emph. *mksy›* CIS ii 3913 ii 105 (cf. also CIS ii 3913 ii 76?) - ¶ subst. m. tax; *mks pṭ›sy* ATNS 19^4: the tax to be paid by P. (cf. ATNS 19^6); in the Palm. texts mostly duties on import and export; *nmws› dy mks›* CIS ii 3913 i 4: the law of taxation (cf. Greek par. τῷ τελωνικῷ νόμῳ); *mks› gby* CIS ii 3913 i 14: the tax shall be levied (cf. Greek par. τέλος ἐπράχθη); *mks› dy qṣb›* CIS ii 3913 ii 102: the tax which the butchers (v. however *qṣb$_2$*) have to pay (Greek par. τὸ τοῦ σφάκτρου τέλος; cf. CIS ii 3913 ii 125); cf. also *mks› mlḥ›* CIS ii 3913 ii 134, prob. lapsus for *mks› dy mlḥ›*: the tax levied on salt (cf. CIS ii 3913 i 9) :: Schlumberger Syr xviii 283: *mks› mlḥ›* = salt used to pay tax with (cf. also Teixidor AO i 245f., Sem xxxiv 80).
mks$_2$ (< Akkad., v. *mks$_1$*; cf. also Kaufman AIA 72 - **Palm** Sing. emph. *mks›* CIS ii 3913 i 6, ii 38, 47, 59, 80, 106, 126, 149, 4235^2; Plur. emph. *mksy›* CIS ii 3913 i 7 - ¶ subst. m. tax-collector (Greek par. e.g. τὸν τελωνοῦντα, ὁ τελώνης), cf. also Kinnier Wilson NWL 17f., Gawlikowski TP 44f.
mks$_3$ = a kind of date < Akkad., on Babyl. docket, cf. Kaufman AIA 69.
mks› **Pun** Sing. abs./cstr. *mks›* KAI 76A 6 - ¶ subst. prob. meaning covering (diff. and dam. context).
mksh **Hebr** Sing. abs. *mksh* DJD ii 24E 10 (*[m]ksh*), F 12 (dam. context) - ¶ subst. tax, taxation; *šny [m]ksh* DJD ii 24E 10: fiscal years - the meaning of the diff. *mkst* in MUSJ xlv 262^4 (Sing./Plur. abs./cstr.) unknown; Starcky MUSJ xlv 262, 270: poss. = tax (Plur. abs.; cf. also Mazar with Cross IEJ xxix 44); Röllig NESE ii 2, 9: = sum, amount (Sing. cstr.), cf. also Schiffmann RSF vi 176, Cross IEJ xxix 44; v.d.Branden BiOr xxxiii 12: = covering, roof (Sing. cstr.).
mkpṣ v. *kpṣ*.
mkr$_1$ **Pun** Qal Impf. 3 p.s.m. *ymkr* KAI 75^5 (dam. context); 3 p.pl.m. *ymkr›* Trip 51^5 (cf. Amadasi IPT 134, cf. also Levi Della Vida Or xxxiii 12: or = Impf. 3 p.s.m. + suff. 3 p.s.m.?; dam. and diff. context); Part. act. s.m. abs. *mkr* CIS i 333^2, 334^3, 335^3, 407^4, 3889^3, 4874^2; cstr. CIS i 3885^1 - **Hebr** Qal Pf. 3 p.s.m. *mkr* DJD ii 29 recto 10, 13^{10} (dam. context); 1 p.s. *mkrty* DJD ii 30^{4,20}; 3 p.pl.m. *mkrw* Frey 562^1 (Hebr.?); Niph Part. pl.m. abs. *nymkryn* SM 49^4 - **OffAr** Qal Part. pass. s.m. abs. *mkyr* Samar 3^{3,8} (dam. context) - ¶ verb Qal to sell; + obj.:

DJD ii 29 recto 10; + obj. + *l*$_5$ + *b*$_2$, *kl ... mkrty lk b 88* DJD ii 30[4f.]: everything I sold to you for 88 (sc. *zuz*), cf. also DJD ii 30[26]; Part. act. merchant - NIPH to be sold: SM 49[4] - Delavault & Lemaire RSF vii 20: l. *hmk[r]* (= *h*$_1$ + QAL Part. act. s.m. abs. (?) of *mkr*$_1$) in Orient ix 23 (prob. interpret.) :: e.g. Naveh FS Glueck 278, Goto Orient ix 5ff. (div. otherwise): l. *ʾlsmk* (= n.p.).
v. *mqr*, *mtr*$_1$.

mkr$_2$ Hebr Sing. abs. *mkr* DJD ii 22[12], 30[4,7,16,17,22,24,28] - ¶ Subst. sale of land > the land sold; *tḥwm[y] hmkr hzh* DJD ii 30[16]: the boundaries of this sold plot (cf. DJD ii 30 passim) - Sznycer PPP 141f.: l. poss. in Poen 1002 *mechar* pro *mephar* (variant *mehar*) = Sing. abs. of *mkr*$_2$ (= merchandise; poss. interpret., diff. context, v. also *ḥk*) :: L.H.Gray AJSL xxxix 80: *mehar* = *mḥr*$_3$:: Schroed 294, 316: l. *meshar* = *my*$_1$ + QAL Pf. 3 p.s.m. of *škr*$_1$ (= to thank) :: J.J.Glück & Maurach Semitics ii 119: l. *meshar* = *myšr* (= honesty, trust).

mkr$_3$ OffAr Epstein ZAW xxxiii 233: the *]mkrʾ* in Aḥiq 203 = Sing. emph. of *mkr*$_3$ (= acquaintance, friend), cf. however Ungnad ArPap p. 80, cf. also Lindenberger APA 202, Kottsieper SAS 215.

mkrt v. *mkrth*.

mkrth Mo Plur. (or Sing.?) abs. *mkrtt* KAI 181[25] - ¶ subst. of uncert. meaning and derivation; for interpret. proposals, cf. - **1)** < *krt*$_1$, Albright ANET 320, Michaud PA 40 (n. 1): *krty mkrtt* KAI 181[25]: I cut beams (cf. also Lidzbarski Handb 299) :: Andersen Or xxxv 106ff.: = I cut the covenant tokens? (cf. de Geus SV 26; cf. also Lipiński Or xl 336ff.: = *mkrtt* = PUʿAL Part. pl.f. abs. of *krt*$_1$ (= dissected, sc. animals in covenant ceremony)) - **2)** < *kry*$_1$, Plur. abs. of *mkrt*,cf. e.g. Segert ArchOr xxix 242, Röllig KAI a.l., Gibson SSI i p. 77, 82, Jackson & Dearman SMIM 98, 119f.: I had the ditches dug; cf. also Yadin IEJ xix 18: I quarried the quarried (system; cf. idem BiAr xxxii 70 n. 18); on this word, cf. also Nöldeke Inschrift 15, Cooke NSI p. 13, Reviv CSI p. 28.

mktb Pun Sing. abs. *mktb* CIS i 6000bis 6 (= TPC 84) - **Hebr** Sing. abs. *mktb* TA-H 40[12] (:: Dion with Pardee HAHL 65: = PIʿEL Part. s.m. abs. of *ktb*$_1$ (= to write)) - ¶ subst. - **1)** text: CIS i 6000bis 6 (cf. also Ferron StudMagr i 75, 78 (for the context, v. also *šm*$_1$)) - 2) document: TA-H 40[12].
v. *ktb*$_1$.

ml$_1$ v. *mlk*$_3$.

ml$_2$ OffAr this word (= might, power) Sing. + suff. 2 p.s.m. *mlk* poss. in MAI xiv/2, 66[11] (cf. Dupont-Sommer ibid. p. 80 (n. 1), cf. also Grelot DAE p. 73 :: Bauer & Meissner SbPAW '36, 420, 423: *mlk* = Sing. abs. of *mlk*$_8$ (= goods, possessions)? :: Yaron BiOr xv 19, Koopmans 98, Porten & Yardeni sub TADAE B 1.1: = Sing. abs. of *mlk*$_3$).

ml$_3$ v. *mlš$_1$*.

mlʾ$_1$ **Ph** PI ʿEL (or QAL?) Pf. 3 p.s.m. *mlʾ* KAI 26A i 6 (cf. FR 174, 267b also for litt.; interpret. as Inf. abs. (cf. also Amadasi Guzzo VO iii 89f., Gai Or li 254ff.) less prob.) - **Samal** PA ʿEL (or QAL?) Pf. 3 p.s.m. *mlʾ* KAI 215^4 (cf. e.g. Cooke NSI p. 173, Donner KAI a.l., Gibson SSI ii p. 79, 82, Dion p. 211 :: Lipiński BiOr xxxiii 232, OLP viii 102: = Sing. cstr. of *mlʾ$_2$* (= quantity)) - **OldAr** PA ʿEL Impf. 3 p.pl.f. + suff. 3 p.s.m. *ymlʾnh* Tell F 22 (Akkad. par. *ú<-mal>-la-a*) - **OffAr** QAL Pf. 2 p.s.f. *mlty* Herm 1^6 (cf. Porten & Greenfield ZAW lxxx 222, 228, Porten Arch 269f. (n. 12), Kutscher IOS i 112f., Grelot DAE p. 151 (n. f), Gibson SSI ii p. 130f., Kaufman AIA 66 n. 177, Fitzmyer WA 225f., Degen GGA '79, 34f. (n. 64), 36, Hoftijzer SV 108, Porten & Yardeni sub TADAE A 2.3 :: Hayes & Hoftijzer VT xx 99: = QAL Pf. 2 p.s.f. of *mll$_1$* :: Bresciani & Kamil Herm a.l.: = PA ʿEL Pf. 2 p.s.f. of *mll$_1$* (cf. also Milik Bibl xlviii 581); on this instance, cf. also Swiggers AION xli 145); Impf. 3 p.s.m. *ymlʾ* Cowl 71^7; 2 p.s.m. *tmly* SSI ii 28 rev. 3; 1 p.s. *ʾmlʾ* NESE iii 34 conc. 6 (dam. context); Inf. *mmlʾ* (cf. Leand 40h, Kottsieper SAS 215; ?, or rather = subst.?, v. also infra) Aḥiq 131 (:: Lindenberger APA 124: or = PA ʿEL/APH Part. act. s.m. abs. (cf. also idem ibid. 254 n. 370, against this interpret., cf. Muraoka JSS xxxii 188)); ITP (cf. Joüon MUSJ xviii 59) Impf. 2 p.s.m. *ttmlʾ* Cowl 2^{17}, 10^{11,17}; 2 p.s.f. *ttml[ʾy]* TADAE B 4.6^{17} (prob. reading; heavily dam. context) - ¶ verb QAL to be full; *ʾl tmly lbt* SSI ii 28 rev. 3: do not be angry (cf. also Greenfield FS Fitzmyer 50; for the context, v. *lbh*);*mlty lbty* Herm 1^6: you are angry with me (v. supra, v. also *lbh*);for the expression, cf. Baneth OLZ '14, 251, Kutscher IOS i 112f., Degen Or xliv 123, Kaufman AIA 66 - QAL/PI ʿEL (PA ʿEL) to fill - **1)** + obj., KAI 26A i 6, Tell F 22 - 2) + double object, *wlʾ ymlʾ b[ṭn]hm lḥ[m]* (?, uncert. reading) Cowl 71^1: he shall not fill their belly with bread; *wytrh .. mlʾ msgrt* KAI 215^4: and with the rest of them ... he filled the prisons (v. supra) - **3)** *wmšlmwth mmlʾ [b]y* Aḥiq 131: the payment of it is the filling of a house (cf. Cowl a.l., Kottsieper SAS 15 × Grelot RB lxviii 187, DAE p. 441, Lindenberger APA 124f.: the repayment of it is the contents of a house (*mmlʾ* = subst.?) :: Ginsberg ANET 429: *wmšlmwth mmlʾ* = its repayment is grief (cf. also idem ibid. 1st edition: its repayment is trouble for the house, cf. also Epstein OLZ '16, 207) :: Baneth OLZ '14, 350: *mmlʾ* is lapsus for *mlʾ* = Pf. 3 p.s.m.) - ITP to be indemnified in full, to have full payment; *ʿd ttmlʾ bʿbwrʾ* Cowl 2^{17}: until you are indemnified in full for the corn; *ʿd ttmlʾ bkspk* Cowl 10^{11}: until you have full payment of your silver (cf. Cowl 10$^{17f.}$) - a form of this root (*mlʾt*) prob. in KAI 50^4, cf. Aimé-Giron ASAE xl 440, 443: = PI ʿEL Pf. 1 p.s./2 p.s., v.d.Branden BO xii 218: = PI ʿEL Pf. 1 p.s., cf. also Silverman JAOS xciv 269: = Pf. 2 p.s. - the diff. *mly[*

in Hatra 30[10] poss. = form of this root, cf. also Safar Sumer viii 187 n. 17: l. poss. *mly[']* = Plur. emph. of *mly* (= filling), cf. however Aggoula MUSJ xlvii 29, Vattioni IH a.l.: = verbal form of *ml'*$_1$ :: Milik DFD 381: l. *mly[ṭn?]* = form of *mlyṭn* (< root *lwṭ*;= slanderer) :: Silverman JAOS xciv 271: = QAL Part. m. pl. emph. of *mll*$_1$ - a form of this root poss. in KAI 200[12] (*'ml'*) = NIPH Impf. 1 p.s. (= to be confirmed, to be corroborated?), cf. also Gibson SSI i p. 29f. (= to be given satisfaction) and Sasson BASOR ccxxxii 57ff. (= to be vindicated; cf. also idem JNSL xii 115ff., Lipiński BiOr xxxv 287), cf. however (Albright with) Cross BASOR clxv 45 n. 49, 50, Albright ANET 568 (n. 12), Röllig KAI a.l., Delekat Bibl li 468f., Briend TPOA 135 (div. otherwise): l. *'m* (= *'m*$_3$) *l'* (= *l'*$_1$)= if not, (then) ... (:: Vinnikov ArchOr xxxiii 547, 551, Lemaire Sem xxi 74f., IH i p. 261, Pardee Maarav i 37, 52f., HAHL 21f.: *'m l'* connected with foll. *l*... = if it is not incumbent upon ..., cf. also Pardee BASOR ccxxxix 47f.) :: Naveh IEJ x 134f.: *'ml'* = PI'EL Impf. 1 p.s. of *ml'*$_1$ (= to pay, to compensate, cf. Suzuki AJBI viii 5, 20ff.: to count out; Yeivin BiOr xix 5f.: = to fulfill, cf. also Vogt Bibl xli 183, Michaud VT x 455; cf. Talmon BASOR clxxvi 34: = to be able to prove one's faultlessness; cf. Amusin & Heltzer IEJ xiv 150, 153f.: = to cry in a full voice > to appeal) - Lemaire & Vernus Or xlix a.l.: l. poss. *ml'* (= PI'EL Imper. s.m.) in Or xlix 342 i 1 (highly uncert. reading, diff. context).
v. *hrg*$_1$, *ml'*$_{2,4}$, *škm*$_1$, *šml'*.

ml'$_2$ **Hebr** Sing. cstr. *ml'* TA-H 2[5] (cf. Aharoni a.l., Pardee UF x 298f., HAHL 33 :: Lemaire IH i 161f., Dahood Bibl xlvi 330, v.Dyke Parunak BASOR ccxxx 25: = PI'EL Imper. s.m. of *ml'*$_1$)- ¶ subst. fullness; *ml' hḥmr* TA-H 2[5]: a full *ḥomer* (v. *ḥmr*$_6$).
v. *ml'*$_1$.

ml'$_3$ **Hatra** Sing. abs. 343[5] - ¶ subst. poss. = artificial terrace, cf. Steiner BASOR cclxxvi 15ff. :: e.g. Aggoula Syr lxiv 93: = ditch :: Segal JSS xxxi 73: store.

ml'$_4$ **OffAr** Sing. m. abs. *ml'* KAI 233[19,20], Cowl 41[4], 82[8], cf. Warka 4, 7: *ma-li-e*; Sing. f. abs. *ml'h* Sach 80 vi A 3 (??, highly uncert. context); Plur. m. abs. *mlyn* Cowl 37[11]; cf. Frah xxv 30 (*m'lh*), GIPP 27, SaSt 19, cf. Toll ZDMG-Suppl viii 29 - ¶ adj. (or QAL Part. act. of *ml'*$_1$?)full; *ba-a-a ma-li-e mi-il-in-ni* Warka 4: the house full of words (cf. Warka 7); *ml' lbtk* Cowl 41[4]: full of wrath against you (cf. KAI 233[19,20], Cowl 37[11]).
v. *mlh*.

ml'$_5$ **Nab** the diff. *ml'* in J 134 of uncert. reading and interpret. = n.p.??; Chabot sub RES 1123D: l. poss. *psl'* = Sing. emph. of *psl*$_2$.

ml'h$_1$ (or *ml't*?) - **OffAr** Sing. emph. *ml't'* MAI xiv/2, 66[9] - ¶ subst. of uncert. meaning; Bauer & Meissner SbPAW '36, 423, Dupont-

Sommer MAI xiv/2, 67, 77, Koopmans 97: = totality, *bml't'* = completely (cf. also Porten & Yardeni sub TADAE B 1.1) - v.Soden Or xxxv 16, xlvi 190: > Akkad. *malâtu* (= Sing.; total offering), cf. idem AHW s.v. (uncert. interpret.; cf. also CAD s.v. *malītu* A: *malâtu* = Plur.).

ml'h$_2$ Palm Milik DFD 148: l. this noun (= symposium) Sing. emph. in Syr xix 80[2] (*[ml]'t'*), Inv iv 16[1] (*ml['t']*) and SOLDV ii 512[2] (*ml['t']*). Highly uncert. interpret., cf. also Starcky SOLDV ii 512: l. in SOLDV ii 512[2] poss. *ml[qṭ']* = Sing. emph. of *mlqṭ* (= tweezers, snuffers); Gawlikowski TP 93 n. 29: uncert. interpret., in Syr xix 80[2]: l. *[gb]'t'* = Sing. emph. of *gb't*.

ml'k$_1$ Ph Sing. abs. *ml'k* EpAn ix 5[9] - **OldAr** Sing. + suff. 3 p.s.m. *ml'kh* KAI 224[8] - **OffAr**, cf. GIPP 56 (*ml'kh*); + suff. 1 p.s. *ml'ky* KAI 224[8] - **JAr** Sing. emph. *ml'kh* AMB 11[6,7] (*ml'[kh]*); Plur. emph. *ml'kyh* AMB 3[21], 7[4] (cf. Naveh & Shaked AMB a.l. :: Dupont-Sommer JKF i 203, 205 (div. otherwise): l. *ml'ky* = Plur. cstr.), 10[3] - ¶ subst. - **1)** delegate, envoy; *w'šlḥ ml'ky '[l]wh* KAI 224[8]: I (i.e. a king) send my envoy to him (i.e. another king), cf. KAI 224[8], EpAn ix 5[9] - **2)** angel: AMB 3[21], 10[3], 11[6]; *ml'kyh qdšyh* AMB 7[4]: the holy angels - the *ml'k* in the comb. *ml'k mlk'štrt* KAI 19[2], DD 13[3] prob. = part of n.d., cf. Caquot Sem xv 31f., Milik DFD 424ff. (cf. also Gibson SSI iii p. 119f.) :: e.g. Cooke NSI p. 48, Chabot sub RES 1205, Meyer ZAW xlix 8, Dunand & Duru DD p. 186f. (: = the inspired ones, cf. also v.d.Branden BO vii 70,72), Röllig KAI a.l., FS Friedrich 407, H.P.Müller UF ii 182, Baldacci BiOr xl 131: in KAI 19[2] = Plur. cstr. of *ml'k$_1$* :: Seyrig Syr xl 27: in KAI 19[2] = Sing. cstr. of *ml'k$_1$* :: Dunand & Duru DD p. 192f.: in DD 13[3] *ml'k* = Sing. cstr. of *ml'k$_1$* (v. also *'l$_1$*) - Milik DFD 199: the *mlk'* in PNO 57 = Sing. (or Dual?) emph. of *ml'k* (angel), poss. interpret., cf. however Ingholt & Starcky PNO a.l.: *mlk'* = n.d. - Milik DFD 195: l. *mlk[w]hy* in CIS ii 4060[1f.]: = Plur. (or Dual) + suff. 3 p.s.m. of *ml'k* (angel; cf. already Cantineau Syr xii 137; cf. also du Mesnil du Buisson TMP 274, 329: l. *mlk[y]hy*), cf. however Chabot sub CIS ii 4060: = Plur. + suff. 3 p.s.m. of *mlk$_6$* (= counsellor) :: Cantineau Syr xii 137: or = Sing. (abs.) of *mlk$_3$*.

v. *mlk$_5$*, *mr'*.

ml'k$_2$ v. *hn$_3$*.

ml'k$_3$ v. *mlk$_5$*.

ml'kh$_1$ Ph Sing. abs. *ml'kt* KAI 10[11,13,14] (*m[l']kt*), 37A 13 - **Pun** Sing. abs. *ml'kt* Antas 70[2], *mlkt* KAI 96[5], 101[5], Trip 1 (heavily dam. context; × Vattioni RB lxxviii 242ff.: = Sing. cstr. (cf. also Hoftijzer DA p. 224 n. 113), cf. however also Lipiński RAI xvii 37, 57: = name of female deity), 18[1], RCL '66, 201[3]; cstr. *mlkt* KAI 81[2], 119[6,7], 137[2,3], CIS i 3919[2]; + suff. 1 p.s., cf. Poen 931: *mlachthi* (for this reading

and for the context, v. *hn$_3$*); + suff. 3 p.pl. *mlktm* KAI 124[2], 126[11] (:: v.d.Branden RSF v 62f.: the forms *mlkt(-)* < root *hlk$_1$*) - **Hebr** Sing. abs. *ml'kh* Lach 13[1] - ¶ subst. - **1)** labour; *ṭn'm ʿl hmlkt z* KAI 101[5]: those appointed over this work (cf. KAI 96[5], RCL '66, 201[3]); *mlkt hmqm* KAI 119[6,7]: the labour on this (holy) place; *mlkt hbn'* KAI 137[2]: the building activities; *mlkt hmṭḥ* KAI 137[3]: the plastering activities (v. *mṭḥ*); cf. also the diff. expression *lmbmlktm* KAI 124[2], 126[11]: (poss. transl.) according to the work necessary for them (cf. Levi Della Vida RCL '49, 402 × FR 253: their manufacturing included) - **2)** the result of the labour, piece of work; *šm 'nk ... [tšt] ... ʿl ml'kt h'* KAI 10[12f.]: you shall put my name on that work (cf. KAI 10[11,14]); *pʿl mlkt* Trip 18[1]: he has made the piece of work; *mlkt hḥrṣ* KAI 81[2]: goldsmith's work - **3)** cult: KAI 37A 13 (for the context, v. Masson & Sznycer RPC 50f. :: v.d.Branden RSF v 62: secular labour indicated here) - the *hmlkt* in KAI 138[4] (:: Lidzbarski Eph iii 288: l. *ḥmlkt*) prob. = *h$_1$* + Sing. abs. of *ml'kh$_1$* (cf. Röllig KAI a.l., Sznycer Sem xxx 39ff. :: Février Sem ii 25f.: = Sing. cstr. of *ml'kh$_1$*), or = n.p. (= variant of n.p. *ḥmlkt*?), cf. also Lidzbarski Eph iii 288; diff. context.
v. *drh$_1$*, *ml'kh$_2$*, *mlk$_3$*, *ʿybydh*, *ṣb'$_3$*.

ml'kh$_2$ (or *ml'kt*?) - **OffAr** Sing. + suff. 1 p.s. *ml'kty* KAI 233[19] (v. infra) - Février & Fantar xii a.l.: restore poss. *mlʿ[kt]* (= Sing. abs. of *ml'kh$_2$*) in Karth xii 54[3] (cf. also v.d.Branden RSF v 56f., 62f. (prob. restoration)) - ¶ subst. prob. meaning message (cf. Dupont-Sommer Syr xxiv 48, Donner KAI a.l., Gibson SSI ii p. 105, 110) :: Lidzbarski ZA xxxi 202: = Sing. + suff. 1 p.s. of *ml'kh$_1$* (cf. also Dupont-Sommer Syr xxiv 48, Koopmans 86) :: R.A.Bowman UMS xx 278: = messenger - cf. also Cunchillos SVT xxxii 44f.: *ml'kh$_1$* identical with *ml'kh$_2$*.

ml'kn v. *hn$_3$*.

mlbwn **OffAr**, cf. Frah iv 23: melon (cf. also Löw AP 351f.).

mlbn **Palm** Sing. + suff. 3 p.s.m. *mlbnh* Inv xii 49[6] - ¶ subst. doorframe, door (cf. Dupont-Sommer CRAI '66, 189, Wiet CRAI '66, 190, Teixidor Syr xlv 380, Inv xii a.l., Gawlikowski TP 83, Aggoula Sem xxix 118); in Inv xii 49[6] used // with *trʿwhy* in Inv xii 48[2].

mlbš **OldCan** Sing. (or Plur.?) abs. *ma-al-ba-ši* EA 369[9] - ¶ subst. garment.

mlgprt **Pun** word (?) of unknown meaning in RES 1925.

mld v. *lwd*.

mlh **OldAr** Sing. abs. *[m]lh* KAI 222B 41 (dam. and diff. context; cf. Fitzmyer AIS 18, 72, Lipiński Stud 43f.); Plur. abs. *m[l]n* KAI 223C 4f. (diff. context; cf. Dupont-Sommer Sf p. 118, 120, 145, Veenhof BiOr xx 144 n. 19, Donner KAI a.l. × Lipiński Stud 47: l. *m[k]n* = Sing. abs. of *mkn$_1$* (= foundation) :: Gibson SSI ii p. 44f.: l. *m[ḥr]* (= *mḥr$_3$*;cf. also Rosenthal ANET 660) :: (Glanzman with) Fitzmyer AIS 83, 91:

l. *m[g]n* (= *mgn*$_3$), *lm[g]n* = with impunity), 224^{2}; cstr. *mly* KAI 222B 8, C 17; emph. *mly*ʾ KAI 224^{2}; + suff. 3 p.s.m. *mlwh* KAI 222C 18f. - **OffAr** Sing. abs. *mlh* Cowl 37^{16}, 38^{6}, 40^{4}, Aḥiq 93, 98, 109, Krael 13^{6}; cstr. *mlt* MAI xiv/2, 66^{12}, Aḥiq 100, 104, RES 1792B 6, ATNS 18^{3} (?, *mlt[*); emph. *mlt*ʾ RES 1792B 8, ATNS 171^{3} (heavily dam. context); + suff. 1 p.pl. *mltn* ATNS 171^{4} (heavily dam. context); Plur. abs. *mlyn* Cowl 37^{9}, *mln* KAI 226^{4}, Aḥiq 29, 92, cf. Warka 4, 7: *mi-il-in-ni* (on this form, cf. also Garbini HDS 32); cstr. *mly* ATNS 4^{2}, 58b 8 (?, *mly[*); emph. *mly*ʾ KAI 233^{12}, Cowl 30^{29}, 31^{28}, 71^{12}, Krael 13^{5}, Driv 8^{3}, RES 1785B 4, ATNS 4^{3}, 13^{1}, Samar 1^{7} (= EI xviii 8*), 3^{7}; + suff. 3 p.s.m. *mlwhy* Aḥiq 43, 60, 114, Krael 9^{16}, ATNS 52b 8; + suff. 1 p.s. *mly* Aḥiq 4; + suff. 3 p.pl.m. *mlyhm* Cowl 42^{13}, ATNS 6^{1}; cf. Frah x 23 (*mry*ʾ), Paik 637 (*mlt[*; ?), GIPP 57 - **Hatra** Sing. cstr. *mlt* 344^{1} - **JAr** Plur. abs. *mlyn* MPAT 51^{12}; emph. *mlyh* AMB 7^{14} (cf. Scholem JGM 86, Levine with Neusner HJB v 361, Naveh & Shaked AMB p. 71 :: Dupont-Sommer JKF i 208: = Sing. m. emph. of *ml*ʾ$_4$; cf. also Beyer ATTM 372f.) - ¶ subst. f. - **1)** word: KAI 222B 8, Cowl 37^{9}, 71^{12}, Aḥiq 93, 98, 100, ATNS 4^{2,3}, AMB 7^{14}; *kmly*ʾ ʾ*lh* Driv 8^{3}: as described in this account; *ba-a-a ma-li-e mi-il-in-ni* Warka 4, 7: the house full of words (i.e the house of the sorcerer and the sorceress, resounding with the words of their maledictions, cf. Dupont-Sommer RA xxxix 44); *[b]mlt [š]mšḥrt* Hatra 344^{1}: by the word (i.e. order) of Š; for KAI 224^{2}, v. *lḥy*$_2$, *lqḥ*; for Aḥiq 114, v. *rby*$_1$; for MAI xiv/2, 66^{12}, v. *mlk*$_3$ - **2)** thing, matter: Cowl 37^{16}, 38^{6}, 40^{4}, Aḥiq 92, Krael 13^{5}, RES 1792B 8; *mlh mlh* Krael 13^{6}: each thing (heavily dam. context); *kl*ʾ *mly*ʾ Cowl 30^{29}: the whole matter (cf. Cowl 31^{28}); *byt*ʾ *zy tḥwmwhy ... ktybn wmlwhy ktybn bspr*ʾ *znh* Krael 9^{16}: the house the boundaries of which are described and the details of which are described in this document; *mlyn l*ʾ*yty ly* MPAT 51$^{12f.}$: there is no claim for me (cf. J.J.Rabinowitz BASOR cxxxvi 16, Geller BSOAS li 316); for Cowl 38^{6}, v. *b*ʾ*š*$_2$; cf. also *m*ʾ*n ṭb ks[h] mlh blbbh* Aḥiq 109: a good vessel (allusion to a good man) hides a thing (/word) within itself (/ his heart); for ATNS 52b 8, v. *šml*ʾ - the *mlwhy* (= Plur. + suff. 3 p.s.m.) in KAI 270A 6 (cf. CIS ii sub 137, Cooke NSI p. 202f., Donner KAI a.l., Grelot DAE p. 138, Levine JAOS lxxxiv 19, Fuhs HZH 46f. :: Sach p. 239f.: l. *mlph* (= PA ʿEL Part. s.f. abs. of ʾ*lp*$_1$)= instructing), prob. to be read *mlyh* (= part of n.p.), cf. Dupont-Sommer ASAE xlviii 120, 125 - Yadin & Naveh sub Mas 438: the *mlt*ʾ in Mas 438 = Sing. emph. of *mlh* used as a nickname (highly uncert. interpret.) - Segal ATNS a.l.: l. *mlh* (= Sing. abs.) in ATNS 2^{6} (improb. reading, cf. Porten & Yardeni sub TADAE B 8.9: l. *[*ʾ*y]ty ly*).

v. *lylh*, *mlk*$_3$, *spr*$_3$, *škm*$_1$.

mlw v. *hlw*.

mlwkh **OffAr** Sing. emph. *mlwkt>* Cowl 6[1] - ¶ subst. reign (:: Leand 43y[00]? *mlwkt>* prob. = lapsus for *mlkwt>* = Sing. emph. of *mlkw* :: Lidzbarski Eph iii 78: < Hebr.); for Cowl 6[1], cf. also (Ginsberg with) Muffs 192f.

mlḥ₁ (< Akkad. < Sum., cf. Zimmern Fremdw 45, v.Soden AHW s.v. *mallāḫu* I, Kaufman AIA 69, cf. also Lipiński ZAH i 69) - **Ph** Sing. abs. *mlḥ* KAI 49[2] (:: Lidzbarski Eph iii 96, Chabot sub RES 1319, Röllig KAI a.l.: l. *mlḥm* (= Plur. abs.), combining with *m* in foll. line); Plur. abs. *mlḥm* MUSJ xlv 262[5] (prob. interpret., dam. context; cf. Starcky MUSJ xlv 262, 271 (cf. also Cross IEJ xxix 44) :: Schiffmann RSF iv 172, 176f.: prob. l. *mlḥm[t]* = Plur. abs. of *mlḥmh* (= war, battle) :: Röllig NESE ii 2, 11: *mlḥm* prob. = Plur. abs. of *mlḥ₃* (= torn cloth)) - **OffAr** Sing. abs. *mlḥ* Cowl 6[11], 8[8]; emph. *mlḥ>* Cowl 5[13], AG 87b 11, 18; Plur. abs. *mlḥn* Krael 12[20], AG 88[4] - ¶ subst. m. boatman, sailor, passim; cf. Krael 12[20]: *mlḥn zy my>*, boatmen of the waters (:: Rundgren SL xi 57f.: = abbrev. for *mlḥn zy my> qšy>*); *mlḥ zy my> qšy>* Cowl 6[11], 8[8]: boatman of the cataract (for this expression, cf. Rundgren SL xi 58).

mlḥ₂ **OldAr** Sing. abs. *mlḥ* KAI 222A 36 (× Degen ZDMG cxxi 134: or = *mlḥ₄* (= salt-herb/salt-plant)?) - **OffAr** Sing. abs. *mlḥ* Aḥiq 111, RSO xxxii 403[5], ASAE xlviii 112A 2, RES '41/42, 67 conc. 2, 3, conv. 1, ATNS 77[2]; emph. *mlḥ>* OLZ '27, 1043[3]; cf. Frah xvi 12 (*myl>*, *mlḥ>*) - **Palm** Sing. abs. *mlḥ* CIS ii 3913 ii 72; emph. *mlḥ>* CIS ii 3913 ii 130, 134 (*[m]lḥ>*) - ¶ subst. m. (ASAE xlviii 112A 2f., CIS ii 3913 ii 72) and f. (CIS ii 3913 ii 130, 134) salt, passim; for *ksp mlḥ>* OLZ '27, 1043[3], v. *ksp₂* - on this word, cf. also Cardascia FS Seidl 27ff.

mlḥ₃ v. *mlḥ₁*.

mlḥ₄ v. *mlḥ₂*.

mlḥ₅ **Hatra** the *mlḥ>* in app. 4[9] poss. = n.g. (place or district called the Salt-mine, the Salt-district, cf. Safar Sumer xvii 39f. n. 99, Teixidor Syr xli 275, Altheim & Stiehl AAW v/1, 83f., Aggoula Sem xxvii 140, Tubach ISS 402, 403 n. 702), cf. however also Caquot Syr xl 13, Vattioni IH a.l.: = Sing. emph. of *mlḥ₅* (= salt-mine); cf. also Milik DFD 396, 398.

mlḥ₆ v. *mlk₃*.

mlḥm **OffAr** Sing. abs. *mlḥm* Aḥiq 99 - ¶ subst. war; :: Joüon MUSJ xviii 13f.: < Hebr. (cp. Kottsieper SAS 214: < Canaanite; cf. however Lindenberger APA 237 n. 189).

mlḥmh **Hebr** Sing. abs. *mlḥ[mh]* DJD ii 48[4] (??, heavily dam. context) - ¶ subst. war.

v. *mlḥ₁*.

mlṭ (< Greek μηλωτή, cf. Cantineau Gramm 156, Rosenthal Sprache 92) - **Palm** Sing. emph. *mlṭ>* CIS ii 3913 ii 11, 67 - ¶ subst. fleece.

mly v. *ml'*$_1$.
mlyḥ **Palm** Plur. m. emph. *mlyḥy'* CIS ii 3913 ii 34 - ¶ adj. salted (said of fish, v. *nwn*).
mlyṭn v. *ml'*$_1$.
mlyk v. *mlk*$_1$.
mlk$_1$ **Ph** QAL Pf. 3 p.s.m. *mlk* KAI 24[2]; Inf. cstr. + suff. 3 p.s.m. *mlky* KAI 14[1], 38[2], RES 453[1] (:: Chabot RES a.l.: = Inf. cstr. + suff. 1 p.s.), CIS i 4[1f.] (*m[l]ky*; for this reading, cf. also Elayi SCA 57f.), 92[2], 114 (*mlk[y]*; for the interpret. of *-y* as suff. 3 p.s.m., cf. e.g. Ringgren Oriens ii 127f., Honeyman JRAS '53, 57, FR 137 :: Lidzbarski Handb 310 (cf. also Lipiński Or xl 337f.): *-y* = *yod compaginis*), *mlkh* KAI 1[2] - **Pun** QAL Inf. cstr. + suff. 3 p.s.m. *mlky* KAI 110[4], 111[4], 277[7], RES 336[5], 337[3], 338[4], Hofra 57[4f.], 61[4], 62, 64[3], *mlkm* KAI 141[4], Hofra 59[4f.] (*[ml]km*), 60[5] (?, dam. context); + suff. 3 p.pl.m. *mlknm* KAI 112[5] - **Mo** QAL Pf. 3 p.s.m. *mlk* KAI 181[2]; 1 p.s. *mlkty* KAI 181[2f.,28f.] (*mlkt[y]*; diff. context, cf. also Auffret UF xii 121f. n. 26; cf. e.g. Röllig KAI a.l., Gibson SSI i p. 77 :: Lipiński Or xl 339f., Stud 21f., OLP viii 102 = PI'EL Pf. 1 p.s. (cf. also de Geus SV 28 n. s)) - **Hebr** QAL Pf. 1 p.s. *mlkty* TA-H 88[1] - **Samal** QAL Impf. 3 p.s.m. *yml[k]* KAI 214[25]; PA'EL Pf. 3 p.s.m. + suff. 3 p.s.m. *mlkh* KAI 215[7] - **OldAr** QAL Impf. 3 p.s.m. *ymlk* KAI 222A 25 (:: Gibson SSI ii p. 30f., 39 (div. otherwise): = QAL Impf. 3 p.s.m. of *mll*$_2$ (= to fade away), cf. already Rosenthal ANET 659 (cf. also Lemaire & Durand IAS 133, (Daniels with) Pardee JNES xxxvii 197)); 3 p.pl.m. *ymlkn* KAI 222B 22; HAPH Pf. 3 p.s.m. + suff. 1 p.s. *hmlkny* KAI 202A 3; 1 p.s. + suff. 2 p.s.m. *hml[ktk]* KAI 202A 13 - **OffAr** QAL Pf. 3 p.s.m. *mlk* AE '23, 41 no. 5[6] (?; or = QAL Part. act. s.m. abs.?); Part. act. s.m. abs. *mlyk*FuF xxxv 173[1] (:: Altheim & Stiehl FuF xxxv 174, ASA 273: or = Sing. abs. of *mlyk* (= *mlk*$_3$) = king) - ¶ verb QAL to become a king, to be a king, to reign, passim - **1)** + *b*$_2$ (in): KAI 222B 22 (cf. poss. also TA-H 88[1] (dam. context)) - **2)** + *'l*$_7$, *mlk gbr 'l y'dy* KAI 24[2]: G. was king over Y. (cf. KAI 38[2], 181[2], CIS i 92[2]); Inf. cstr. = reign, *ks' mlkh* KAI 1[2]: his royal throne; ... *mkwsn hmmlkt bšt* ... *lmlkm* KAI 141[3f.]: ... king Micipsa in the ...th year of his reign (cf. KAI 14[1], 38[2], 112[5], etc.), cf. also the remarkable *lmlky* (= of his reign; the name of the king not being mentioned): RES 336[5], 337[3], KAI 110[4], Hofra 57[4f.], etc. (Berthier & Charlier Hofra p. 52: poss. indication of the reign of king Massinissa :: Lidzbarski Eph i 43: = abbrev. for *mlk ywb'y* (?; = the reign of king Iuba)) - PA'EL to make king; + obj. + *'l*$_7$ (over), KAI 215[7] - HAPH to make king; + obj.: KAI 202A 3 - Lemaire IAS 115, 139: l. *ymlk* (= QAL Impf. 3 p.s.m.) in KAI 222B 36 (highly uncert. reading), cf. Lipiński Stud 41: l. *ym'n* = QAL Pf. 1 p.pl. of *ym'* (highly uncert. reading), cf. also Dupont-Sommer Sf p. 62, 64, 83, Donner KAI a.l., Fitzmyer AIS 18f. (div. otherwise): l.

ʾymʾm = n.l. (highly uncert. reading) - for constructions of forms of this root with b_2 or $ʿl_7$, cf. Buccellati FS Oppenheim 56, Yadin IEJ xxvi 9ff.
v. *ṭby*$_3$, *mlk*$_{3,5}$, *tmk*.

mlk_2 **DA** Itp Impf. 3 p.s.m. *ytmlk* ii 9 - **OffAr** Qal Pf. 3 p.pl.m. *mlkw* Driv 12[4] - **Palm** Aph (pass.??, cf. Cantineau Gramm 90) Pf. 3 p.s.m. *ʾmlk* CIS ii 4064[5] - ¶ verb Qal + l_5 + obj., to promise something to someone: Driv 12[4] - Aph meaning uncert.; Cantineau Gramm 90: Aph pass. = to be established?? - Itp to seek someone's advice: DA ii 9 (for the context, cf. Hoftijzer DA a.l.; v. also *mlkh*$_2$).
v. *mlk*$_5$.

mlk_3 **Ph** m. Sing. abs. *mlk* KAI 1[1,2], 4[6], 10[9], 14[1], 26A i 12, Kition A 29[1], IEJ xviii 227A 1, EpAn ix 5[8], etc., etc.; cstr. *mlk* KAI 1[1], 4[1], 10[1], 13[1], 14[1], 24[7,8], 26A i 2, 32[2] (= Kition A 2), 33[1] (= Kition A 1), Kition A 29[2], Mem Saidah 180[2], on coins from Byblos, cf. Betlyon CMP 116ff., 120, etc., etc. (cf. *mlkty* in KAI 33[2], haplography for *mlk kty* attested in KAI 33[1], RSF i 130[1], etc.); Plur. abs. *mlkm* KAI 1[2], 14[18], 18[5], 19[6] (:: Milik DFD 424: = Plur. abs. of *mlk*$_4$ (= reign)), 24[5,6,9f.], 26A i 19, iii 12, C iv 13, MUSJ xlv 262[3], etc. (for *ʾdmlkm* in KAI 42[2], v. *ʾdn*$_1$; Greek par. βασιλέως); f. Sing. abs. *mlkt* KAI 14[15] (on this text, cf. Elayi RCP 23, SCA 108f.), 37A 7, 10 (dam. context; for both KAI 37 instances, v. infra) - **Pun** m. Sing. abs. *mlk* KAI 145[5], 277[3] (cf. e.g. Röllig KAI a.l., WO v 112, Amadasi sub ICO-App 2, Fitzmyer JAOS lxxxvi 286, 290 :: Ferron OA iv 184, Lipiński RTAT 261, BiOr xxxiii 232: = Qal Part. act. s.m. abs. of *mlk*$_1$ (cf. also Gibson SSI iii p. 154, 156)); cstr. *mlk* KAI 161[1]; f. Sing. abs. *mlkt* KAI 89[1] (= CIS i 6068; v. however infra) - **Mo** m. Sing. abs. KAI 181[23]; cstr. *mlk* KAI 181[1,5] (cf. e.g. Lidzbarski KI p. 6, Röllig KAI a.l., Gibson SSI p. 76 :: Segert ArchOr xxix 210 (n. 63), 260: = Qal Pf. 3 p.s.m. of *mlk*$_1$ (cf. also Halévy RS viii 238, 297, Cooke NSI p. 8, Lidzbarski Eph i 145)),[10,18], SSI i p. 83[1], ADAJ xxx 302 (?, heavily dam. context) - **Amm** m. Sing. abs. *mlk* AUSS xiii 2[1] (= CAI 80), BASOR ccxxv 63 (= Vatt sig. eb. 401 (= Jackson ALIA 72 no. 17 = CAI 102); cf. Teixidor Syr liv 263 :: Avigad BASOR a.l.: poss. = Sing. cstr. with omission of *ʿmn*); cstr. *mlk* Ber xxii 120[1,2,3] (= CAI 78) - **Edom** Sing. abs. *mlk* SANSS-Edom 3 (cf. also Lemaire Levant vii 18f.), 4; cstr. *mlk* SANSS-Edom 1 (= RB lxxiii 399,2[2]; cf. also PEQ '66, 125, Lipiński RTAT 263) - **Hebr** m. Sing. abs. *mlk* KAI 193[19], 195[10], 196[4,11] (diff. reading, dam. context), Dir boll 10, 30-34, sig. 69-72 (= Vatt sig. eb. 69-72; 69 = SANSS-Hebr. 46 (= IS 5), 72 = SANSS-Hebr. 148), Mosc sig. 2 (= Vatt sig. eb. 125), var. 2, 10 (cf. e.g. Maisler JNES x 266, Gibson SSI i p. 17, Lemaire IH i p. 252; cf. however Catastini Hen vi 137 (div. otherwise): = part of n.p.), Vatt sig. eb. 209 (= SANSS-Hebr 114; or = Mo.?, cf. Naveh BASOR clxxxiii

29 n. 24, Avigad FS Glueck 289, 294 n. 52), HBTJ 4, 5, 6, 7, 8, EI xv 304, NESE ii 45^{2}, on coins of the Hasmonean period: JC no. 5, 5a, 6, 8, 9, etc., etc., cf. also Meshorer Mas coin 19 (Greek par. βασιλέως), *nmlk* Mosc p. 92β (lapsus for *mlk* in *lnmlk*); cstr. *mlk* TA-H 40^{13}, 88^{3}, AMB 1^{24}, 15^{24}; m. Plur. abs. *mlky[m]* AMB 1^{24} - **DA** m. Sing. abs. *mlk* ii 15 (:: Hackett BTDA 72: or = form of *mlk$_5$*?), 18 (*mlk[*; ??, dam. and diff. context); m. Plur. abs. *mlkn* ii 13 (diff. context :: H.P.Müller ZAW xciv 219, 236 = Plur. abs. of *mlk$_6$* (= councellor)?) - **Samal** m. Sing. abs. *mlk* KAI 214^{20} (cf. e.g. Cooke NSI p. 162, Donner KAI a.l., Gibson SSI ii p. 67, Dion p. 31, 131, 241 × Lipiński BiOr xxxiii 232, OLP viii 102: = QAL Part. act. s.m. abs. of *mlk$_1$*),215^{3}; cstr. *mlk* KAI 214^{1,14}, 215^{1,7,11,12,13,15,16,17,21} (??, heavily dam. context); m. Plur. abs. (nom.) *mlkw* KAI 215^{17}; cstr. (cas. obl.) *mlky* KAI 215^{10} (diff. and uncert. reading, cf. also Gibson SSI ii p. 84)^{,12} (v. *kbr$_2$*) - **OldAr** m. Sing. abs. *mlk* KAI 222A 6, B 2, 6 (cf. Lipiński Stud 33, Rössler TUAT i 182, cf. also Fitzmyer AIS 60: or = Sing. cstr. of *mlk$_4$* (= reign, kingship); v. also *ṭby$_2$*), 7, 26, 224^{28}; cstr. *mlk* KAI 201^{3}, 202A 1, 2, 4, 6, 7, B 17, 216^{2,9}, 217^{1}, 222A 1, 3, 14, Tell F 6, 7, 13 (Akkad. par. *šakin māti*, cf. Stefanovic COAI 53f., 228; on the Akkad. par., cf. also Millard Irâq xlv 105, Garr JAOS cv 798); emph. *mlkh* KAI 203 (cf. Garb 252 n. 2, Donner KAI a.l., Kutscher IOS i 104 n. 4, Gibson SSI ii p. 17 × Segert ArchOr xxvi 581: = f. Sing. abs.? (= queen) :: Degen AAG p. 8 n. 40, Kottsieper SAS 48: or = Sing. + suff. 3 p.s.m. :: Ingholt Hama 117, Koopmans 23: l. *mlk*ʾ (= Sing. emph.; on the reading problems, cf. also Andersen & Freedman FS Fitzmyer 8; on the form, cf. also Garr DGSP 87f.)); + suff. 3 p.s.f. (?; cf. Degen AAG p. 56 (n. 30)) *mlkh* KAI 202B 3, 223C 5f.; m. Plur. abs. *mlkn* KAI 202A 5, 216^{10,13}, 219^{3} (*mlk[n]*), 222B 26, 28, 224^{19} (*[m]lkn*); cstr. *mlky* KAI 216$^{16f.}$, 222B 41 (cf. e.g. Dupont-Sommer Sf p. 85, Fitzmyer AIS 72, Donner KAI a.l. :: Noth ZDPV lxxvii 135 n. 48 (dividing otherwise): l. *mlky*ʾ (= Plur. emph.)??), C 15, 224^{1,3} (*[m]lky*); emph. *mlky*ʾ KAI 202A 9, 16, 216$^{14f.}$, 222B 22, 224^{7} - **OffAr** Sing. abs. *mlk* Aḥiq 5, 15, 100, 103, 104, 107, 108, Beh 17 (v. infra), 50 (Akkad. par. *šarru*), KAI 276^{3,5} (Greek par. βασιλέως)^{,7}, MAI xiv/2, 66^{12} (cf. e.g. Dupont-Sommer a.l. :: Grelot DAE p. 74 (n. k), Lipiński BiOr xxxi 119, Stud 139: = Sing. abs. of *mlk$_7$* (= ownership) :: Bauer & Meissner SbPAW '36, 420: = *mlk$_8$* (= goods)), RES 1299A 2, CIS ii 1c, 2c, WO vi 44A 2, C 1, D 4, REA-NS viii 170A 1, B 1 (cf. Périkhanian REA-NS iii 18, 19ff., viii 170 × Naveh WO vi 45: or (div. otherwise) l. *mlk*ʾ (= Sing. emph., v. also *rwndkn*)), FuF xxxv 173^{1,6}, etc.; cstr. *mlk* Aḥiq 3, 4, 10, 11, 14, 32, KAI 227 vs. 5 (dam. context), 233^{4}, 266^{4}, JNES xv 2C (= SSI ii 25), AE '23, 41 no. 5^{6} (diff. context); emph. *mlk*ʾ Cowl 1^{1,3}, 2^{12}, Aḥiq 15, 27, Beh 37 (Akkad. par. *šarru*), Cowl p. 269 iii 5 (cf. Greenfield &

Porten BIDG 24 l. 8; Akkad. par. *šarru*), Krael 1[1], 2[1], Driv 2[1], KAI 228A 19, 233[8,17], 260B 1, Syr xli 285[2], FX 136[2], ATNS 10a i 12 (cf. Segal ATNS a.l.; Porten & Yardeni sub TADAE B 8.2: or l. *mlky* (= Sing. + suff. 1 p.s.)), 17[3], Samar 1[1] (= EI xviii 8*), etc., etc.; m. Plur. abs. *mlkn* KAI 266[1,6] (for both instances, cf. e.g. Dupont-Sommer Sem i 45f., Donner KAI a.l., Horn AUSS vi 31 (n. 8), Gibson SSI ii p. 114, Porten BiAr xliv 36 :: Ginsberg BASOR cxi 25 n. 5: = Plur. abs. of *mlk*$_4$ (= kingdom)); cstr. *mlky* Cowl 31[12] (the *mlk* in Cowl 30[13] lapsus for *mlky*? (cf. Cowl p. 116) or rather = Sing. cstr.?, cf. Leand 53c), KAI 233[16]; cf. Frah xii 2 (*mlkʾ*), Paik 545, 632-634 (*mlkʾ*), 635 (*mlk*), Sogd ii 223B 258, Ta 478, Ve 114, Nisa-b 1760[1], 1949[5], Nisa-c 100 + 91[2] (*mlkʾ*), ZDMG xcii 441[3,4,5], 442A 7, 8, 12, 14, B 3, 4, 5, 7, 8, 11, Syr xxxv 305[1,2], 317[41,42], 319[46-48], 321[49-53], 323[55,56], 325[59], 327[60], Chw Ir 57, BSOAS xxxiii 147[2,4], 152[8], GIPP 28, 29, 57, SaSt 20 (on the ideogrammatic use of *mlk-*, *mlkt-*, cf. Benveniste Titres 11, 18f., 22f., 27; cf. also Lemosín AO ii 265, Toll ZDMG-Suppl viii 29); f. Sing. emph. *mlktʾ* LA ix 331[1], cf. Frah xii 11 (*mlktʾ*), Paik 636 (*mlktʾ*), Syr xxxv 317[40], 319[47,48], 321[50], 323[56], 327[60], 329[64], GIPP 28, 57 - **Nab** m. Sing. abs. *mlk* MPAT 64 ii 8 (cf. e.g. Fitzmyer & Harrington MPAT a.l. :: Starcky RB lxi 166, 177: = Sing. + suff. 2 p.s.m. of *ml*$_1$ (= word, counsel)); cstr. *mlk* CIS ii 158[3,6], 195[5], 196[7], HDS 151[4], ADAJ xx 121[5], on coins NC no. 47-49, etc., etc.; emph. *mlkʾ* CIS ii 161[9], 174[3], 184[4], 199[8], on coins NC no. 37, 46 (*mlk[ʾ]*), etc., etc. (cf. Meshorer Mas coin 3603; cf. also Spijkerman CDPA p. 32f.); m. Plur. cstr. *mlky* RB lxxiii 244[3] (reading of *y* highly uncert.; Starcky & Strugnell RB lxxiii 246f.: or = lapsus for *mlkt* (= f. Sing. cstr.?)); f. Sing. cstr. *mlkt* CIS ii 351[2], 354[3], RES 1434[9], ADAJ xx 112, BASOR cclxix 48[4] (uncert. instance, at the end of l. 5), on coins, cf. NC no. 48-51, etc., etc. (cf. Meshorer Mas coin 3604; cf. also Spijkerman CDPA p. 32f.); f. Plur. cstr. *[m]lkt* RES 1434[7,11], *mlkwt* RB xlii 408[3] (for the reading, cf. Savignac ibid. 409) - **Palm** m. Sing. abs. (or cstr.?, dam. context) *mlk* FS Dussaud i 278[3]; cstr. *mlk* CIS ii 3946[1], 3971[2,6]; emph. *mlkʾ* InvD 40[2], PNO 21a; m. Plur. emph. *mlkʾ* CIS ii 3946[1], 3971[2,4,6]; f. Sing. emph. *mlktʾ* CIS ii 3947[2], 3971[6], RTP 198, 200 - **Hatra** m. Sing. abs. *mlk* 195[1], 198[2] (for the reading of both instances, cf. Vattioni IH a.l., cf. also Caquot Syr xli 269, Ingholt AH i/1, 47: l. *mlk*<ʾ> = Sing. emph. :: Safar Sumer xviii 57, 59: l. *mlkʾ* = Sing. emph. (cf. also Milik DFD 363)); emph. *mlkʾ* 16[1,2] (for the reading of both instances, cf. e.g. Caquot Syr xxix 98, Donner sub KAI 241, Degen WO v 234, Vattioni IH a.l., cf. however Safar Sumer vii 179, Altheim & Stiehl AAW ii 196: reading of *l* uncert. × Milik RN vi/iv 53: l. *mrkʾ* = variant of *mlkʾ*), 17, 21[1] (:: Aggoula Sem xxvii 136f. (div. otherwise): l. *mlk* (Sing. cstr.) *ʾntwn ʾšryʾ* = the king of A. (n.l.) the Assyrian (town)), 28[3,5] (*mlk[ʾ]*), 36[3,4],

37[3], 79[3,11,13], Mašr xv 512[2,4], etc. (cf. also Assur 15a 3 (*mlk[›]*; :: Milik DFD 347: = f. Sing. abs.), 15b 1 (for both texts, v. infra), 29j 3) - **JAr** m. Sing. cstr. *mlk* MPAT 70[3] (against the authenticity of this text, cf. however Garbini OA xxiv 67ff.), MPAT-A 10[2] (= SM 4), 26[9] (= SM 32), 27[2,4] (= SM 33), 28[2,3] (= SM 34), SM 83 (dam. context), etc., on Hasmonean coins, cf. Meshorer Mas coin 21 (Greek par. βασιλέως); emph. *mlkh* MPAT-A 11 (for the reading, cf. Naveh sub SM 43), SM 107[20] (for the reading, cf. Naveh a.l.); + suff. 3 p.s.m. *mlkyh* MPAT-A 34[3] (= SM 69); f. Sing. emph. *mlkth* MPAT 132b - ¶ subst. m. king, f. queen, passim (on the par. of *mlk* and Lib. *gld*, cf. Février MC 85f.) - **1)** used for human beings, *yhwntn hmlk* on coins, cf. JC 5, 6, 8: king Y. (cf. *yhwntn mlk* IEJ xxv 245 (on this text, cf. Sarfatti IEJ xxvii 204f.); *mlk› ›lksndrws* IEJ xviii 22; *drywhš mlk›* Syr xli 285[2] (on word order, cf. e.g. Naveh IEJ xviii 23 (nn. 14, 15)); cf. also *mlkt qlptrw* BASOR cclxix 48[4f.] (v. also supra), *sr› mlkt›* LA ix 331[1], *myhrdt mlk* FuF xxxv 173[6]); cf. e.g. *mlk ›šr* KAI 24[8]: the king of A.; *mlk bbl* KAI 233[4], 260[4]: the king of B.; *mlk ›mr* Mem Saidah 180[2]: the king of Amurru (cf. however Mazza OA xxvi 191ff.: fake??); *mlk gbl* KAI 6[1], 7[1f.]: the king of Byblos (cf. *mlk kty* KAI 32[2], 33[1] (for *mlkty* KAI 33[2], v. supra), *mlk gwzn* Tell F 6, 7, 13 (cf. however Akkad. par., v. supra; cf. also Lemaire & Durand IAS 43ff., Puech RB xc 594f., Greenfield & Shaffer Irâq xlv 110, Stefanovic COAI 52f.), *mlk yhwd[h]* TA-H 40[13], *mlk m›b* SSI i p. 83[1], *mlk mṣrym* TA-H 88[3], *mlk qdr* JNES xv 2C (= SSI ii 25)); *mlk bn ‹mn* Ber xxii 120[1,2,3]: the king of the Ammonites; *mlk ṣdnm* KAI 13, 14[1]: the king of the Sidonians (cf. *mlk dnnym* KAI 26A i 2, *mlk [m]šlyym* KAI 161[1]); *mlk› dy ‹rb* Hatra 193[2]: the king of the Arabs (or: Arabia; cf. Hatra 345[2], 347[2], 353[2], cf. also *mlk d‹rb* Hatra 195[1f.] (v. supra), and *mlk› d‹rby›* Hatra 287[3f.]; on the exact meaning of *‹rb/‹rby›*, cf. Aggoula Syr lii 197ff., cf. also Tubach ISS 246f. (n. 46)); *mlky nb[ṭw]* RB lxxiii 244[3]: the sovereigns of Nabatea (said of the king and queen; v. however supra); for formulae containing *mlk₃* as *nomen regens*, cf. also Shea Maarav i 159ff.; *mlk ‹l y‹dy* KAI 214[20]: king over Y. (v. however supra); *mlk ‹l kyšry›* KAI 277[3f]: king over K. (v. supra; for the construction with *‹l₇*, cf. also Garbini OA iv 39f., Röllig WO v 112; v. also *mlk₁*)- cf. *[b]yt mlkh* KAI 203: the royal household (v. however supra); cf. also the foll. titles: *›dn mlkm* (v. *›dn₁*), *mr› mlkn* (v. *mr›*), *mlk mlk›* CIS ii 3946[1], 3971[2,6]: king of kings (title of the Palmyrenean king); on these titles, cf. also Huss ZDPV xciii 131ff., Teixidor Syr lvi 359; for *mlk gdl* (prob. indicating the king of Assyria), v. *gdl₂*; for *mlk rb*, v. *rb₂*; for KAI 1[2], 26A iii 12, v. *skn₂*, *rzn* - the title *bn hmlk* in Dir sig. 72 (= Vatt sig. eb. 72 = SANSS-Hebr 148), bol 10 (= Vatt sig. eb. 110 = SANSS-Hebr 39 = IS 7), Vatt sig. eb. 209 (= SANSS-Hebr 114; v. supra), 252 (= SANSS-Hebr 97 = IS

6), HBTJ 6, 7, 8 (= IEJ xxviii 53 ii), Sem xxix 71, EI xv 304, BiAr xlix 51, poss. indication of function (bearer not being (necessarily) of royal blood), cf. Clermont-Ganneau RAO i 36, EM ii 160, de Vaux IAT i 183f., Brin Lesh xxxi 5ff., 85ff., 240, AION xix 433ff., Avigad EI ix 9, FS Glueck 289 (cf. also idem IEJ xxviii 147: official of royal descendance (cf. also idem FS Cross 202f.)), Gibson SSI i p. 64, cf. however e.g. Torrey AASOR ii/iii 108, Avigad IEJ xiii 133ff., xxviii 54f., EI xv 304, Rainey Lesh xxxiii 304ff., UF vii 427ff., Lemaire Sem xxix 59ff.: = son of the king = prince, member of the royal family (on the subject, cf. also Dir p. 232, Heltzer AION xxi 183ff., Imparati Or xliv 88ff.); the title *bt hmlk* IEJ xxviii 146 poss. indicating female member of the royal family (cf. Avigad IEJ xxviii 146f.; or = high female official?); the *br mlkʾ* in CIS ii 38^{2}, 39$^{1f.}$ (cf. 40^{2} (*br m[lkʾ]*); = Del 21-23) prob. title indicating a function (cf. also Koschaker ZA xlviii 184); for the function indications *ʾrdkl zy mlkʾ*, *dyny mlkʾ*, *ʿbd hmlk*, v. resp. *ʾrdkl*, *dyn*$_3$, *ʿbd*$_2$; cf. also the foll. instances - a) *qblt mlk wdyn* MPAT 64 ii 8: a complaint before king and judge (dam. context, v. supra, *dyn*$_3$ and *qblh*) - b) *mlk ʿlyhm ʿbdw [prdʾ]* Beh 17f.: they made P. a king over them (cf. the Akkad. par. *ištēn amelu pa-ra-da-ʾ šu-um-šú amelu mar-gu-ma-a-a šu-u a-na ra-bu-ú ina UGU-šú-nu it-tur*) - c) for the comb. *ʾbny mlkʾ*, *ʾrḥ mlkʾ*, *byt mlkʾ* (*/bt mlk*), *mnh mlk*, *mtqlt mlkʾ*, v. resp. *ʾbn*$_2$, *ʾrḥ*$_2$, *byt*$_2$, *mnh*$_2$, *mtqlh* - d) for *lmlk* (used - α) independently: Dir boll. 30-34, Mosc p. 92ff., etc., etc. (cf. on Ph. jar, RPC 87, on Ar. weight CISFP i 767 i) - β) in the comb. *bt lmlk* Mosc var. 2 - γ) in the comb. *ḥṣy lmlk* TeAv ii 160 - δ) in the comb. *2 lmlk* Dir pes. 19 (cf. Shany PEQ '67, 55 (n. 11)); cf. also *25 lmlk* IEJ xviii 227A 1, B 1 (cf. Cross IEJ xviii a.l., EI ix 22*, cf. however Delavault & Lemaire RSF vii 15f.: l. *b25 lmlk* = in the 25th year of the king, poss. interpret.)) = of (/ for) the king, royal (cf. also IEJ xl 262); on *lmlk*, cf. Dir p. 147f., Mosc p. 85ff., Sukenik Kedem i 32ff., Scott BASOR cliii 32, clxxiii 56, Lapp. BASOR clviii 11ff., clxxii 28, 34, AASOR xlv 111f., Yadin SH viii 13ff., BASOR clxiii 6ff., Kutscher SY 173f., Aharoni IEJ ix 273, Pritchard HISG 18ff., Gibeon 117f., Rainey BASOR clxxix 34ff., ccxlv 57ff., IEJ xvi 187ff., PEQ '67, 32, '70, 48f., EI xvi 179f., de Vaux RB lxxiii 271, Yeivin Lesh xxxi 243ff., Cross EI ix 20*ff., Welten passim, Tushingham BASOR cc 78 (n. 19), cci 25f., Lance HThR lxiv 315ff., Mettinger SSO 93ff., Lang RB lxxix 441ff., Millard BASOR ccviii 5ff., Cotella RB lxxx 552f., Lemaire RB lxxxii 15ff., VT xxv 678ff., EI xv 54*ff, Stern BiAr xxxviii 49ff., Goldwasser & Naveh IEJ xxvi 15ff., Ussishkin BASOR ccxxiii 1ff., Barkay IEJ xxviii 212f., Lemaire & Vernus Sem xxviii 54f., Hestrin ASB 52ff., Eshel IEJ xxxi 60ff., Mommsen, Perlman & Yellin IEJ xxxiv 89ff., Kelm & Mazar BASOR ccxlviii 29ff., Na'aman VT xxix 70ff., BASOR cclxi 11ff., Biran & Cohen EI xv 265, Garfinkel BASOR cclxxi 69ff., EI xviii 108ff., Israel RivBib xxxii 103ff., Avigad SVT xl 13, Borowski AIAI 28f., 112 - Ben-David IEJ xxiii 176f.: the *l* on weight (IEJ xxiii 176,1) = abbrev. of *lmlk*, uncert. interpret. - cf. also *lmlk* in seal impression (Syr lxiii 313); for *gmr lmlk*, v. *gmr*$_2$ - e) the diff. expression *mn bl‘dy mlt mlk* MAI xiv/2, 66[11f.]: without a word of the king (cf. Dupont-Sommer MAI xiv/2, 80, Koopmans p. 98, Yaron BiOr xv 19, Rabinowitz Law 121 (cf. also Porten & Yardeni sub TADAE B 1.1: except for a word of the king) :: Bauer & Meissner SbPAW '36, 421, 423 n. 5: = without the expression 'possession' (without it being said *expressis verbis* that it is your possession)) - **2)** used for divine beings - a) used as epithet of Assur: Assur 29j 3 - b) used as epithet of Bel: KAI 264[3] - c) used as epithet of Ba‘alshemin: Hatra 16[1,2], 17; Vattioni sub IH 164: the *mlk’* in Hatra 164[2] also indication of Ba‘alshemin (uncert. interpret., cf. e.g. Safar Sumer xviii 48, Caquot Syr xli 263: = the king (sc. of Hatra)) - d) used as epithet of *ḥṭr myskr*: KAI 145[5] - e) used as epithet of Nanai (*nny mlk’*): Assur 15a 3, 15b 1 (m. form used for female deity; v. also *ṣlm*$_1$; cf. Aggoula Assur p. 18ff.) - f) *mlk ‘lm* MPAT-A 27[4], *mlk ‘lmh* MPAT-A 26[9], 28[2,3], *mlk h‘wlm* AMB 15[24]: king of the universe, epithet of God (cf. also MPAT-A 34[3]), cf. also AMB 3[1] (*mlk ‘lm[yh]*) - g) *mlkt qdšt* KAI 37A 7: holy queen, prob. epithet of Ashtarte, cf. Peckham Or xxxvii 306, 312f., Healy BASOR ccxvi 53, Amadasi sub Kition C 1, Delcor UF xi 153f., FS v.d.Ploeg 110f., Gibson SSI iii p. 128 (cf. already Harr 118; cf. also Winter FG 570) :: e.g. CIS i sub 86, Cooke NSI p. 67, Röllig KAI a.l., FR 202c, v.d.Branden BO viii 248, 252: *mlkt* (= Sing. abs. of *ml’kh*$_1$) *qdšt* = holy service, cult; the same words prob. in l. 10 (dam. context) - h) *mlk ml[ky h]mlky[m]* AMB 1[24]: king of the kings of kings, epithet of God - i) as epithet of the goddess *b‘ltk* (v. *b‘l*$_2$): RTP 200 - j) *mlkt šmyn* Herm 4[1]: queen of heavens, epithet of Ashtarte or ‘Anat, cf. Bresciani & Kamil Herm a.l., Milik Bibl xlviii 560f., Porten JNES xxviii 120f., Delcor FS v.d.Ploeg 120ff., Winter FG 502ff., Hoftijzer SV 115 n. b, Hvidberg-Hansen TNT i 96f. - k) as epithet of the goddess *ḥwt*: KAI 89[1] (= CIS 6068), cf. e.g. Clermont-Ganneau RAO iii 305, Lidzbarski Eph i 30, 34 (cf. ibid. 175), sub KI 85, Halévy RS ix 264, Chabot sub RES 18, Février sub CIS i 6068, Milik Bibl xlviii 561 :: Levi Della Vida RSO xiv 312: *mlkt* = Sing. abs. of *ml’kh*$_1$:: Clermont-Ganneau RAO iv 90, Cooke NSI p. 135: *mlkt* = n.d. - l) as epithet of goddess Ishtarbad: RTP 198 - Naveh IEJ xvii 189: l. *mlk* in IEJ xi 130 no. 4 (reading of *m* uncert., heavily dam. context; = Sing. abs./cstr.) :: Negev IEJ xi a.l.: l. *nyw* (without interpret.) - Lemaire Sem xxvi 34: the *m*in Sem xxvi 33,2 poss. = abbrev. of *mlk*$_3$ (i.e. *lmlk*) or = abbrev. of *m‘h*$_1$??, both interpret. uncert. - the *mlkyh* in KAI 271B 7 prob. = n.p. (cf. Degen NESE i 30) :: CIS ii sub 138, Cooke NSI p. 204f.,

Donner KAI a.l.: = Plur. emph. of *mlk$_3$* - this word (Sing. abs.) in Syr lxv 418 (in inscription on mortar)?, cf. Zayadine & Worschech Syr lxv 419f. (uncert. interpret.; = part of n.p.?) - Lipiński RTAT 260, Gibson SSI iii p. 55, 64: instead of *mlḥ* l. poss. *mlk* (= Sing. abs.) in KAI 26C iv 20 (highly uncert. reading; cf. however Lipiński SV 50 (n. j; div. otherwise): l. *ʾm* (= *ʾm$_3$*) *lṭb* (= *l$_5$* + Sing. abs. of *ṭb$_2$*)??,cf. also Bron RIPK 21, 127f.: l. *mlṭ* = part of a word of unknown meaning.) - Bordreuil sub CSOI-Ph 7: l. *lmlk* (= *l$_5$*+ Sing. cstr.) *ṣrm* (= Tyrians) in SANSS-Ph 15 (uncert. reading, cf. Naveh IEJ xxxiii 115) instead of *lmlkḥrm* (= *l$_5$*+ n.p.; less prob. reading).
v. *hlk$_1$*, *mʾ$_4$*, *ml$_2$*, *mlʾk$_1$*, *mlk$_{1,5}$*, *mlky*, *mrʾ*, *šlk$_1$*, *ṣbʾ$_3$*.

mlk$_4$ v. *mlk$_3$*.

mlk$_5$ **Ph** m. Sing. abs. *mlk* RES 367 i 1 (cf. Delavault & Lemaire RB lxxxiii 569ff., cf. however Lidzbarski Eph i 285ff.: = fraud; cf. also Delcor Hen iv 215) - **Pun** m. Sing. abs. *mlk* Hofra 42^3, 43^4 (diff. and uncert. reading, cf. Berthier & Charlier Hofra a.l. × Février BAr '55/56, 157: l. *šlm* (= PIʿEL Pf. 3 p.s.m. of *šlm$_1$*)); cstr. *mlk* KAI 61A 1, B 1, 98^2, 99^2, 103^1, etc., etc., *mlʾk* Hofra 54^2 (:: Charlier Karth iv 12f.: = Sing. abs. of *mlʾk$_1$* (= (divine) messenger)); f. Sing. abs. *mlkt* CIS i 198^4, SMI 7^1 (dam. context), Moz vi 105^1 (for the reading, cf. Amadasi Guzzo sub SMI 24 :: id. sub Moz vi 105: l. *mtnt* (= Sing. abs. of *mtnt*)); cstr. *mlkt* CIS i 5684^1, Moz vi 110^2 (= SMI 31), RSF v 135^2 (for f. forms, v. also infra) - ¶ subst. m. prob. indicating certain type of sacrifice (for the derivation of this word from the root *ylk*, cf. v.Soden ThLZ lxi 46, Alt WO i 282f., Février RHR cxliii 8f., JA ccxliii 52f., ccxlviii 168, Hoftijzer VT viii 289 n. 4, Röllig sub KAI 61, BiOr xxvii 377f., FR 202b, De Vaux SAT 70, Lipiński RTAT 252, Delavault & Lemaire RB lxxxiii 575, Segert GPP p. 85, (cf. also Garbini SAB i 130: *mlk* = YOPH Part. of *ylk*/*hlk$_1$*) :: Chabot CRAI '31, 27: < root *mlk$_2$*:vow, fulfillment of a vow (cf. Eissfeldt Molk 12: = vow, sacrifice, cf. also de Vaux RB xlv 278, 280, cf. v.d.Branden GP §80) :: Dussaud CRAI '46, 375: < root *mlk$_1$*= possession, i.e. (sacrifice which is) the possession of ... :: Albright Religion 180f.: *mlk$_2$*and *mlk$_5$* (= vow) both < name of deity *Malik*, *Muluk*, poss. = patron of oath and vow :: v.d.Branden BO xv 199: *mlk$_5$* = name of deity used with meaning 'sacrifice' (*mlk* short for *zbḥ mlk*, a sacrfice to Molk) :: Dussaud Syr xxxiv 394: for *mlk$_5$*, cf. Arab. *mulk* = power > sacrifice which has compelling influence on the deity :: CIS i sub 294: = *mlk$_3$* (cf. also Harr 118: = *mlk$_3$*or *mlk$_9$* (= *mlʾk$_1$*) as part of title?) :: Cazelles SDB v 1342: = sacrifice connected with first-born children either to obtain their birth or to preserve their lives; for this word, cf. also the surveys of Berthier & Charlier Hofra p. 29ff., Cazelles SDB v 1337ff., Amadasi ICO p. 20f., and cf. Dussaud Orig 352ff., Dhorme AnSt vi 60, Donkert MOT 123ff., de Vaux IAT ii

331f., Février JA ccl 1ff., Mulder KGOT 57ff., Schaeffer Ugaritica iv 77ff., Green RHS 179ff., M.Smith JAOS xcv 477ff., Garbini StudMagr vii 47ff., Picard Karth xvii 67ff., xviii 5ff., RB lxxxiii 584ff., Sem xxxix 77ff., Rebuffat RevEtAnc lxxiv 17ff., Hvidberg-Hansen TNT i 37f., ii 35f. n. 331, Garbini FSR 155ff., 193f., H.P.Müller ThWAT iv 957ff., Martelli CISFP i 425ff., Heider CM 35ff., 185ff., 196ff., Day MGHS 4ff., Del Olmo Lete Sem xxxix 67ff., cf. also Botterweck TUAT ii 597, v. also infra) - for the attestations, cf. the foll. types - **1)** *mlk* (used absolutely); *l›dn ... ndr NP ... mlk šm‹ ql›* Hofra 42: to the lord ... NP has vowed a *mlk*-sacrfice, he has heard his voice; *nṣb mlk* RES 367 i 1: a stele commemorating a *mlk*-sacrifice (v. however supra; cf. also Gianto Bibl lxviii 398f.: another word to be restored foll. *mlk*?; on this text, cf. also Heider CM 182ff.) - **2)** *mlk ›dm* KAI $103^{1f.}$, 105^3, $106^{1f.}$, 107^4, RES 335^3, 336^2, Hofra 29^1, $30^{1f.}$, 31^1 (reading of *m* in *›dm* diff., cf. Berthier & Charlier a.l.: reading *r* poss., *m* prob.), 32^2, $34^{3f.}$, $36^{2f.}$, 37^2, $38^{1f.}$, 39^1, 40^3, 41^3, Eph i 42 iii 1 (= RSF ix 11 = Sem xxxii 60): sacrifice of a human being (cf. Hoftijzer VT viii 289, Röllig sub KAI 103, cf. also de Vaux SAT 71, v.d.Branden RSF ix 13f., Huss 538f. (n. 280), Day MGHS 5f. (n. 6) :: Mosca with Heider CM 83, 187: = *mlk* of a lower-class child :: Eissfeldt Molk 19: = sacrifice made by a layman (cf. Dussaud CRAI '46, 380, Lipiński RTAT 252f., Gibson SSI iii p. 75, cf. also v.d.Branden BO xv 200) :: Février JA ccxlviii 186 n. 17: = offering of blood (*›dm* = dm_1, *aleph* being the first radical of the root; cf. Février RHR cxliii 11: *›dm* = dm_1+ *aleph* prosth.), cf. also idem JA ccxliii 54 :: CIS i sub 294: = king of mankind (cf. also Charlier Karth iv 21ff., Weinfeld UF iv 137ff.) :: Slouschz TPI p. 223: = human king :: Ryckmans with Berthier & Charlier Hofra p. 30: = king of the earth (*›dm* = $›dm_3$ (= variant of *›dmh*)) :: Lidzbarski NGWG '16, 90: *mlk ›dm* = indication of deity, cf. also Lidzbarski Eph i 42 :: Buber KG 215, Kornfeld WZKM li 290ff.: *mlk ›dm* = cultic exclamation, Malk is Lord (*›dm* = $›dm_4$ (= variant of $›dn_1$))); v.d.Branden RSF ix 15: the *›dm* in Eph i 42 iii 3 = abbrev. of *mlk ›dm* (improb. interpret., cf. Sznycer Sem xxxii 60, 64f.: = part of n.p.) - **3)** *mlk ›mr* CIS i $307^{4f.}$ (*[›]mr* :: Slouschz TPI p. 247: pro *[›]mr* l. *[b]šr*), KAI 61B 1f. (for the reading which remains diff., cf. e.g. Dussaud CRAI '46, 376f., Röllig KAI a.l., de Vaux SAT 69ff., Amadasi sub ICO-MaltaPu 5, Gibson SSI iii p. 76f. :: CIS i a.l.: l. *›sr* = n.d. (part of composite n.d., cf. Slouschz TPI p. 126); cf. Garbini RSO xliii 5ff., 10f., FSR 195ff.: *mlk ›sr* = king Osiris; cf. also Eissfeldt Molk 27f.: = king Osiris or n.p. and Lidzbarski NGWG '16, 90f.: *mlk ›sr* = indication of deity), $109^{1f.}$, 110^1 (reading of *m* in *›mr* uncert., reading *t* poss., cf. also Berthier & Charlier Hofra 56 sub :: Cazelles SDB v 1342: l. *›tr* = $›tr_2$ (= holy place), cf. also Charlier Karth iv 19ff.), Punica xviii/i 58^3, *ml›k ›mr* Hofra 54^2 (cf. also the Lat. expressions *molchomor*, *morchomor*, *mochomor*, *morcomor*, cf. CRAI '31, 22ff., Eissfeldt Molk 1ff.): sacrifice of a lamb (cf. e.g. Chabot CRAI '31, 26f., Carcopino RHR cvi 592ff., Eissfeldt Molk a.l., Dussaud Orig 353, Février JA ccxliii 54, Cazelles SDB v 1341, Röllig KAI a.l., de Vaux SAT 70, Amadasi sub ICO-MaltaPu 5, Weinfeld UF iv 135f., Delcor Hen iv 214, cf. also Heider CM 186, Roschinski TUAT ii 609 (for the exact interpret. of *mlk* in these instances, v. however supra) :: v.d.Branden BO xv 200: = sacrifice of the one who commands (i.e. the head of the family), *ʾmr* being QAL Part. act. s.m. abs. of *ʾmr*$_1$ :: Lipiński RTAT 252f., Gibson SSI iii p. 76: = sacrifice of one promising (it), *ʾmr* being QAL Part. act. (or pass.?) s.m. abs. of *ʾmr*$_1$:: Buber KG 214, Kornfeld WZKM li 288ff.: *mlk ʾmr* = cultic exclamation, 'Malk has spoken' (*ʾmr* = QAL Pf. 3 p.s.m. of *ʾmr*$_1$, cf. also Charlier Karth iv 9 ff.)) - **4)** *mlk ʾzrm* and related forms occurring in the foll. comb.: - a) *mlk ʾzrm hʾš* Punica xi 20$^{2f.}$, *[m]l[k ʾz]rm ʿš* Punica xi 23^{3}, *[mlk ʾzr]m ʾ[š]* Punica xi 33$^{2f.}$, *mlk ʾzm* (lapsus for *ʾzrm*, cf. also Chabot Punica a.l.) *ʿš* Punica xi 34^{2}, *mlk hzrm ʾhš* Punica xi 26$^{3f.}$, *mlk ʾšrm ʾyš* Punica xi 24$^{2f.}$, *mlk [ʾ]šrm hʾyš* Punica xi 27$^{3f.}$, *mlk ʾšrm hyš* Punica xi 19$^{2f.}$, 31$^{2f.}$ - b) *mlk ʾzrm ʾzt* Punica xi 25$^{1f.}$, *mlk hzrm hš[t]* Punica xi 18^{2}, *mlk ʾšrm ʾšt* Punica xi 22$^{2f.}$ (= KAI 167), 32$^{6f.}$ (*ʾš[t]*), *mlk ʾ[š]r[m] ʿst* (or l. rather *ʿšt*?) Punica xi 28$^{2f.}$, *mlk hšr[m] št* Punica xi 21$^{2f.}$ (in the texts from Guelma (Punica xi) it is extremely diff. to distinguish between *z* and *š*, cf. also Chabot sub Punica xi 35) - c) *mlk ʾdm ʾzrm ʾš* Hofra 37^{2} - d) *mlk bʿl ʾzrm ʾš* KAI 98^{2} - e) cf. also *ʾzrm ʾš* Hofra 162$^{1f.}$, CIS i 3781^{2}, *ʾšrm hʾš* Punica xi 35ter 2, *ʾzrš* CIS i 3783^{2} (lapsus for *ʾzrm*?, or l. *ʾzrm*?, cf. Février BAr '46/49, 169; or rather lapsus for *ʾzrm ʾš*??), cf. also *ʿzrm* in BAr-NS i-ii 224^{2} (Février a.l.: = *ʾzrm*) - highly diff. expressions, *ʾš*/*ʾšt* and related forms poss. = resp. man/woman, male/female (cf. Février JA ccxliii 60f., ccxlviii 171f., Röllig sub KAI 98, cf. also Cazelles SDB v 1341f., v.d.Branden BO xv 201, RSF ix 13f., Roschinski TUAT ii 609 :: Chabot sub Punica xi 35 (cf. also FR 113, Segert GPP p. 105f.): *ʾš* (etc.) = variant of *ʾz*$_1$ (= *z*$_1$), *ʾšt* (etc.) = variant of *zt* (variant form of *z*$_1$) :: Février BAr '46/49, 170: *ʾš* = *ʾš*$_2$:: Berger WO xiii 56 n. 31: *ʾš* prob. = *ʾš*$_2$, *ʾšt* = *ʾšh*$_3$ (= fire offering), cf. also id. ibid. 57 n. 12 :: Eissfeldt Molk 25: *ʾš* related to *ʾšh*$_3$ (= fire offering), or to *š*$_1$?; the *ʾš* in KAI 98^{2} prob. however = *ʾš*$_4$ (variant form of *š*$_{10}$),cf. Röllig KAI a.l.); the meaning of *ʾzrm*, etc. highly uncert., cf. Chabot sub Punica xi 35, Eissfeldt Molk 24ff., CIS i sub 3781, Berthier & Charlier sub Hofra 37 :: Février JA ccxliii 61, ccxlviii 170f., BAr-NS i-ii 224: poss. = lamb (cf. also Roschinski TUAT ii 609) :: Février BAr '46/49, 170: = offspring :: v.d.Branden BO xv 201f., 206f.: = adolescent, young boy:: Gibson SSI iii p. 110: = one afflicted < root *zrm* :: v.d.Branden RSF ix 13f.: = holocaust, burnt-offering? :: Slouschz TPI p. 213: = epithet of deity :: Dussaud CRAI '46, 375 n. 3: = notorious (referring to the sacrifice as such; cf. also Albright JAOS lxxi 262f.: *mlk ʾzrm* = a glorious *mulk*-vow, *ʾzrm* < root *ʾzr* (= to be honoured, to be excellent; cf. however Tsevat UF xviii 347)); cf. Garbini JSS xii 112: poss. the same word as *ʾzr*$_1$; cf. also the poss. relationship with Ug. *ʾuzr*, cf. e.g. de Vaux RB xlvi 442, Dijkstra & de Moor UF vii 172 (for litt., cf. also Dressler UF vii 221ff.), Sanmartín UF ix 369f., Cazelles CISFP i 674ff. - **5)** *mlk bʿl* CIS i 147$^{1f.}$ (*b[ʿ]l*), 194^1, 380^1, 5685^1 (*bʿ[l]*), KAI 61A 1, 98^2 (v. supra), 99^2 (in all instances, except KAI 99^2, preceded by *nṣb*$_3$; in KAI 99^2 preceded by *mtnt mtntʾ*), meaning uncert.; Gibson SSI iii p. 74f.: prob. = sacrifice of one making it (*bʿl* = sacrificer, offerer, cf. *bʿl hzbḥ*; cf. Lipiński RTAT 252f. (n. 38), Baldacci BiOr xl 127; cf. also v.d.Branden BO xv 200f., RSF ix 13: = sacrifice of the husband/head of the family); Dussaud CRAI '46, 375f.: = sacrifice dedicated to (properly: possession of) Baʿal (cf. also Roschinski TUAT ii 609 (cf. Coxon PEQ '83, 76: = sacrifice to Baʿal, v however infra)) :: Mosca with Heider CM 83, 187: = *mlk* of a noble child :: CIS i sub 123: *mlk bʿl* = compound n.d. (cf. also Lidzbarski sub KI 54, Eissfeldt Molk 27f. (: or = n.p.?), Weinfeld UF iv 139) :: Slouschz TPI p. 126: = king Baʿal :: Février RHR cxliii 16: *bʿl* = *b*$_2$ + Sing. abs. of *ʿl*$_5$ (= child), *mlk bʿl* = offering instead of a child (cf. also idem JA ccxliii 54, ccxlviii 177, Röllig sub KAI 61, Delcor Hen iv 214f., cf. also Coxon PEQ '83, 76: or = sacrifice in place of an infant) :: Cazelles SDB v 1342: = offering of a citizen :: Garbini RSO xliii 8ff.: *mlk* = *mlk*$_3$ (= the human sacrifice represented as king); cf. also Rosenthal ANET 658, cf. however Levi Della Vida RSO xxxix 303, Teixidor Syr li 312, Huss 533 n. 213, 539f., Day MGHS 6f. (n. 13), Gras, Rouillard & Teixidor UP 181ff. - **6)** *mlk bšr* CIS i 306^4: sacrifice of a child (for this and other interpret. of *bšr* and variants, v. *bšr*$_2$) - **7)** for the f. form *mlkt* indicating a certain type of sacrifice or gift, cf. also Amadasi Guzzo SMI p. 48 - **8)** *mlkt* in *mlkt bmṣrm* CIS i 198$^{4f.}$ (preceded by *nṣb*, v. also *nṣb*$_3$) :: Février SOLDV i 276: *mlkt* lapsus (cf. however idem JA ccxlviii 176) :: Lidzbarski NGWG '16, 91: *mlkt* = f. form of *mlk*$_3$;diff. expression, *mlkt* poss. = f. form parallel to *mlk*$_5$ (cf. also Day MGHS 7, cf. however Lipiński RTAT 253 (n. 39): *mlkt* = Plur. of *mlk*$_5$; on this subject, cf. also Gras, Rouillard & Teixidor UP 181), cf. Eissfeldt Molk 28ff., Dussaud CRAI '46, 382f., Garbini SAB i 132; meaning of *bmṣrm* uncert., Eissfeldt Molk 29f.: poss. = *b*$_2$ + Plur. abs. of *mṣr*$_1$ (= distress), cf. also Dussaud CRAI '46, 383: *mlkt bmṣrm* = sacrifice made in distress (cf. Roschinksi TUAT ii 616, cf. also Février JA ccxlviii 176, Africa i 16) :: CIS i sub 198: = *b*$_2$ + n.g. (Egypt; cf. also Slouschz TPI p. 296) - **9)** *mlkt* in *mlkt bʿl* CIS i 5684^1 (preceded by *nṣb*, v. *nṣb*$_3$), Mozia vi 110^2 (= SMI 31;

not preceded by *nṣb* nor *mtnt*), meaning uncert.; Dussaud CRAI '46, 382f.: = sacrifice dedicated to (properly: possession of) Ba‘al (on this sacrifice, cf. also Guzzo Amadasi Kokalos xviii/xix 281); Huss 533 n. 213, 539f.: = offering instead of a child (less prob. interpret., v. supra); for *Moloch*, cf. also Israel RSF xviii 151ff.
v. *ywm*, *mlk$_3$*.
mlk$_6$ v. *ml’k$_1$*.
mlk$_7$ v. *mlk$_3$*.
mlk$_8$ v. *ml$_2$*, *mlk$_3$*.
mlk$_9$ v. *ml’k$_1$*, *mlk$_5$*.
mlk$_{10}$ **Hatra** Sing. emph. *mlk’* 336[3] - ¶ subst. counsel.
mlkh$_1$ v. *mlk$_3$*.
mlkh$_2$ **DA** Sing. abs. *mlkh* ii 9 (:: Caquot & Lemaire Syr liv 204: = QAL Inf. abs. of *mlk$_2$*) - ¶ subst. advice (for the context, v. *mlk$_2$*).
mlkh$_3$ v. *mlk$_5$*.
mlkh$_4$ v. *ml’kh$_1$*, *mlk$_3$*.
mlkw **Hebr** Sing. cstr. *mlkwt* AMB 4[25] - **OldAr** Sing. cstr. *mlkt* KAI 222A 25; + suff. 3 p.s.m. *mlkth* KAI 222A 25 - **OffAr** Sing. cstr. *mlkwt* Samar 1[1] (= EI xviii 8*); emph. *mlkwt’* Cowl 6[1], Aḥiq 95; cf. Frah xii 2 (*mlkwt’*) - **Hatra** Sing. + suff. 3 p.s.m. *mlkwth* 79[9] - **JAr** Sing. + suff. 3 p.s.m. *mlkwth* MPAT-A 11[2] (for the reading, cf. also Naveh sub SM 43) - ¶ subst. - **1)** kingdom: KAI 222A 25 (for the context, v. *ḥl$_2$*) - **2)** kingship: Aḥiq 95 (said of wisdom), Hatra 79[9] (said of a god), cf. prob. also AMB 4[25] - **3)** reign: Cowl 6[1], MPAT-A 11[2]; *r’š mlkwt [d]ryhwš* Samar 1[1]: the accession year of D.
v. *mlwkh*, *mlky*.
mlky **Ph** Plur. f. abs. *mlkyt* KAI 11 (cf. e.g. Röllig KAI a.l., Gibson SSI iii p. 100 :: FR 204a, 230a: = Sing. f. abs. :: (Bauer with) Dussaud Syr xvii 99 n. 1: = Plur. abs. of *mlkw* (= royal persons) :: Silverman JAOS xciv 268: = Plur. f. abs. of *mlk$_3$*) - **OffAr**, cf. Frah ii 13 (:: Ebeling Frah a.l.: l. *[ḥ]ml’* = royal treasure (< *ḥml*))- ¶ adj. - **1)** royal: Frah ii 13 - **2)** substantivated adj., someone belonging to the royal family: KAI 11 (cf. Elayi RCP 25: *mlkyt* poss. = title of the mother of the king) - Beyer & Livingstone ZDMG cxxxvii 286f.: l. *[m]lky* in Atlal vii 109[3] (= Sing. m. cstr. (= royal official)), uncert. interpret., cf. Aggoula Syr lxii 66f.: = m. Plur. cstr. of *mlk$_3$*and Livingstone Atlal vii a.l.: l. *[m]lky* = n.p. :: Cross CBQ xlviii 392: l. *mlk* (= m. Sing. cstr. of *mlk$_3$*)+ *z* (damaged as result of erasure).
mlkt v. *ṣb’$_3$*.
mll$_1$ **OldAr** PA‘EL Impf. 3 p.s.m. *ymll* KAI 224[2] - **OffAr** PA‘EL Pf. 3 p.s.m. *mll* Cowl 69[2,8] (for the reading, cf. Porten & Yardeni sub TADAE B 8.5),[11] (for the reading, cf. Porten & Yardeni sub TADAE B 8.5 :: Cowl a.l.: l. *ymll* (= PA‘EL Impf. 3 p.s.m.)), ATNS 1[4,7],

9[3,7], 196[3] (heavily dam. context), *mlyl* RES 1785B 4; Impf. 3 p.s.m. *ymll* ATNS 1[8]; 2 p.s.m. *tmll* ATNS 2[2] (dam. context; highly uncert. reading, cf. Porten & Yardeni sub TADAE B 8.9: l. poss. *ʾytyly*); Part. act. s.m. abs. *mmll* Aḥiq 178; cf. Frah xviii 3 (*ymllwn*, *ymrrwn*), Paik 492, 493 (*ymll*), 494, 495 (*ymllwn*), BSOAS xxxiii 148[3], GIPP 38, 67, 68, SaSt 26, cf. also Lemosín AO ii 266, Toll ZDMG-Suppl viii 39 - **JAr** PA‘EL Part. s.m. abs. *mml* (lapsus for *mmll*) AMB 3[3] - ¶ verb PA‘EL to speak; *gbrʾ zk šʾln wlʾ mll* ATNS 1[7]: we interrogated this man, but he did not speak - **1)** + obj.: RES 1785B 4 - **2)** + obj. + *l‘l* (= l_5 + ‘l_7), *wymll mln lḥyt l‘ly* KAI 224[2]: he will speak evil words against me (cf. Rosenthal BASOR clviii 28, Fitzmyer AIS 97, 104f.; for *l‘l*, cf. Fitzmyer AIS 105 (cf. also Lipiński Stud 55: about me) :: Gibson SSI ii p. 46f., 52: *l‘l* = l_5 + ‘l_7 (= over, beyond [justification] > unjustified) :: Dupont-Sommer Sf p. 129, 148: l. *l‘ly[lw]ty* = l_5 + Sing. + suff. 1 p.s. of *‘lylw* (= conduct) :: Röllig KAI a.l.: *l‘ly[lw]ty* = l_5 + Plur. + suff. 1 p.s. of *‘lylw*) > he will stir up strife against me (cf. Greenfield ActOr xxix 8f., cf. also Tawil JNES xxxii 478 nn. 19, 20) - **3)** + b_2 + ʾl_5, *mml* (v. supra) *brwz prwš ʾl kl rwḥ byšh* AMB 3[3]: who speaks with distinct mystery to every evil spirit (epithet of God) - **4)** + ‘l_7 (= to): ATNS 9[3,7] (in both instances however dam. context), cf. prob. also: Cowl 69[2,8] (v. supra),[11] (v. supra; dam. context; to speak to/against?) and KAI 224[1] (dam. context; for a discussion, cf. Tawil JNES xxxii 478 (n. 19)) - **5)** + ‘m_4 + ‘l_7, *lʾ tmll ‘mhm ‘l znh* ... ATNS 2[2]: you shall not speak with them about this ... .
v. *hlw*, *ll₂*, *mlʾ₁*.

mll₂ v. *ll₂*, *mlk₁*.

mll₃ v. *ll₂*.

mllwt v. *mnrtwyn*.

mls v. *lyṣ*.

ml‘t v. *tl‘*.

mlṣ₁ v. *lyṣ*.

mlṣ₂ v. *lyṣ*.

mlṣ₃ v. *lyṣ*.

mlṣh **Pun** Février BAr '46/49, a.l.: the *mlṣʾt* in BAr '46/49, 253[4] poss. = Plur. abs. of *mlṣh* (< root ʾ*lṣ₂*= to press, to oppress (highly uncert. interpret.)).

mlqh v. *qbb*.

mlqḥ **Pun** Sing. abs. *mlqḥ* CIS i 344[4]; Plur. abs. *[m]lqḥm* CIS i 345[3] - ¶ subst. of uncert. meaning; Lidzbarski Handb 304: = object to catch something with (plaited or woven) :: CIS i sub 344: poss. = pincers or candle-snuffer (cf. however the *ʾrgʾmlqḥ* in CIS i 344[3f.]: the weaver of *m...*) :: Harr 115: = trap (or tongs?), cf. however also CIS i 344[3f.]; cf. also Slouschz TPI p. 243 and p. 265 for CIS i 345[3] (*mlqḥ* = sack?).

mlqṭ v. *ml'h₂*.
mlqy₁ v. *qbb*.
mlqy₂ v. *nṣb₃*.
mlš₁ **Ph** The *mlš* in Kition D 21[1] poss. = Sing. cstr. of *mlš₁* (= kneading > fLat. cake), cf. Liverani RSF iii 39, cf. also Amadasi sub Kition D 21 :: Liverani RSF iii 38f. (div. otherwise): or l. *ml* (= Sing. cstr. of *ml₃* (= lock)) *š'r* (= Sing. abs. of *š'r₄* (= hair)) :: Dupont-Sommer MAIBL xliv 281, 292ff., Puech RSF iii 13: l. *ml* (= n.p.) *š'r* (= Sing. abs. of *š'r₄*) :: Coote BASOR ccxx 47, 49: *mlš* = *mlš₂* (= variant of *mlḥš* (= incantation)) :: Teixidor Syr xlix 434: text poss. in non-Semitic language; the same word prob. ibid. in l. 2 (cf. Liverani RSF iii 40, Amadasi sub Kition D 21 :: Dupont-Sommer MAI xliv 281 (div. otherwise): l. *ml* (= n.p.) *š* (= Sing. abs. of *š₁*), cf. also Puech RSF iv 12f. :: Coote BASOR ccxx 47, 49: *mlš* = *mlš₂* (= variant of *mlḥš* (= incantation)); the same word prob. in l. 3 (cf. Amadasi sub Kition D 21 :: Dupont-Sommer MAIBL xliv 281 (div. otherwise): l. *ml* (= n.p.) *š'* (= Sing. abs. of *š₁*), cf. also Puech RSF iv 12f.) :: Coote BASOR ccxx 47, 49: *mlš* = *mlš₂* (= variant of *mlḥš* (= incantation)); the same word prob. in l. 4 (cf. Amadasi sub Kition D 21) :: Dupont-Sommer MAIBL xliv 292ff. (div. otherwise): l. *ml* (= n.p.) *š'r* (= Sing. abs. of *š'r₄*), cf. also Puech RSF iii 13f. :: Coote BASOR ccxx 47, 49: *mlš* = *mlš₂* (= variant of *mlḥš* (= incantation))).
mlš₂ v. *mlš₁*.
mmzgn **Palm** Sing. emph. *mmzgn'* Syr vii 129[9] - ¶ subst. m. mixer, cup-bearer (cf. also Milik DFD 152).
mml' **Ph** Plur. abs. *mml'm* EI xviii 117[3] (= IEJ xxxv 83) - ¶ subst. of uncert. meaning indicating a certain object; Dothan EI xviii 118, IEJ xxxv 87: = round ringstand or vessel with inlay?
v. *ml'₁*.
mmlhh **Pun** Sing. abs. *mmlht* (variant of *mmlḥt*, cf. FR 35a) KAI 66[1] - ¶ subst. salt-mine (cf. Greek par. for *'š bmmlht*: ὁ ἐπὶ τῶν ἁλῶν, Lat. par. *salari(us)*; cf. also Slouschz TPI p. 135).
mmlḥ **Pun** Sing. abs. *mmlḥ* CIS i 351[4] - ¶ subst. m. indication of function/occupation: salt-maker, salt-merchant.
mmlḥh v. *mmlhh*.
mmlkh **Ph** Sing. abs. *mmlkt* KAI 10[2,11], 14[4,6,10,20,22], 26A iii 19, *mmlk* KAI 14[9] (lapsus), *mmlt* KAI 14[11] (lapsus) - **Pun** Sing. abs. *mmlkt* KAI 101[1,2,3] (*[mml]kt*)[,4], 111[5], 141[3], Hofra 59[5f.] (*mm[l]kt*), 61[4f.], on coins, cf. Müll iii 42f., 88, 90, 98, 100, CHC 611 no. 5-7, Mazard no. 1-16, 18, 84-87, 90-93, 99-101, 113-118, CB iii 93, 95, 97, vi 371f., Libyca '55, 371; Plur. abs. *mmlkt* KAI 112[6], *mmlk't* KAI 161[2] (cf. Février RA xlv 142, Röllig KAI a.l., Roschinski Num 112 :: Cooke NSI p. 149: = Sing. abs. (cf. also Berger RA ii 37, 40); v. also *rb₂*) - ¶ subst. m. (cf. FR

306,2) (kingship >) prince, king; *bššt ʾrbʿm št lmlky msnsn hmmlkt* KAI $111^{3ff.}$: in the 46th year of the reign of king M. (cf. e.g. KAI $112^{4ff.}$); cf. for *mmlkt* as distinct from *ʾdm* KAI 10^{11}, $14^{6f.,10,22}$ and as distinct from both *mlk* and *ʾdm* KAI 26A iii 19f. (cf. also KAI 26A iii 12f. for *mlk* as distinct from *rzn* and *ʾdm*, cf. also Dupont-Sommer RA xlii 175), cf. Dupont-Sommer RA xlii 168, 175 :: Röllig KAI a.l.: *mmlkt* in KAI 26A iii 19 = kingdom (cf. also Gibson SSI iii p. 53, 63) - cf. also *mmlk<t> ʾdr* KAI 14^9: a mighty king (cf. e.g. Cooke NSI p. 31, 35, Röllig KAI a.l.; cf. however Dahood Bibl l 341f., lii 351: = the Awesome King = Death, cf. also Kuhnigk NSH 54, 55f., Gibson SSI iii p. 111) - for Lib. par. cf. Chaker AION xlvi 543f. - the *mmlkʾt* in KAI 161^2 (Plur.) indication of one king? (v. however *rb*$_2$) - abbrev. *m*on coins (in *hm* = *hmmlkt*), cf. Mazard 19, 20, 22, 79 - abbrev. *mt* on coins (in *hmt* = *hmmlkt*), cf. Mazard 112, 120, 120bis, 121 - Betlyon CMP 82, 84, 86, 89ff., 100 n. 46-48: the *m* (in *mʾ*) on coins from Aradus = abbrev. of *mmlkt* (*mʾ* = *m(mlkt)* (= Sing. cstr.) *ʾ(rd)* = king of Aradus), poss. interpret. :: *m* = *mn*$_5$.
v. *ṣbʾ*$_3$.

mmll **OffAr** Sing. cstr. *mmll* Aḥiq 100 - ¶ subst. m. word.

mmlppwn (< Greek μηλοπέπων) - **Hebr** Plur. abs. *mmlppwnwt* (lapsus for *mylppwnwt*?) SM 49^2 - ¶ subst. some sort of melon.

mmn **Pun**, cf. August. de Serm Dom ii/xiv 47, Sermones 113, cap. 2: *mammon* - ¶ subst. advantage, profit, fortune (cf. also Penna CISFP i 888f., Martin Bibl lxv 89f.) - Caquot HDS 9, 13, 15: l. *mmnhy* in HDS 9^4 = Plur. + suff. 3 p.s.m. of *mmn* = profit (highly uncert. reading and interpret.) :: Lipiński Stud 79, 81, WGAV 375f.: *mmnhy* = PAʿEL Part. pass. s.m. + suff. 3 p.s.m. of *mny* (= assigned (part), due (cf. also idem ActAntHung xxii 376)) :: Fales AION xxviii 275ff.: l. *yṭmnhy* (= QAL Impf. 3 p.s.m. of *ṭmn* (= to hide)).

mmry (< Lat. *memoria*) - **Pun** Sing. abs., cf. IRT 901^1 (cf. e.g. Vattioni Aug xvi 552): *mmemoria* - ¶ subst. memorial.

mmrqn , cf. Akkad. *mumarriqānu*, *mumarraqqānu* (= guarantor) sub *mrq*$_1$.

mmth **OffAr** Sing. + suff. 3 p.s.m. *mmtth* KAI 226^{10} (on this form, cf. Kottsieper SAS 82) - ¶ subst. dying (cf. Donner KAI a.l, Gibson SSI ii p.98).

mn$_1$ v. *mym*.

mn$_2$ **OldAr** Sing. abs. *mn* KAI 222A 30 (cf. Tawil BASOR ccxxv 60f. :: Dupont-Sommer Sf p. 20, 46, Gibson SSI ii p. 31, 40: = *mn*$_5$ :: Fitzmyer AIS 15, 48, Donner KAI a.l.: = *mn*$_5$ or *mn*$_4$ (cf. also Lemaire & Durand IAS 114, 122)) - ¶ subst. caterpillar (for the context, cf. Tawil BASOR ccxxv 60f.).

mn$_3$ v. *mnm*.

mn_4 **DA** ii 12 (:: Hackett BTDA 26, 68: no *mn* to be read) - **Samal** KAI 214[15] (reading however uncert., cf. Gibson SSI ii p. 66, 72) - **OldAr** KAI 202B 16 (for the reading, cf. also e.g. Gibson SSI ii p. 10), 21, 222C 16, 223B 9, 224[9,10,26], Tell F 10, 16 (Akkad. par. in both instances *ma-nu*) - **OffAr** KAI 225[5], 226[8], 258[3], 259[2], 260[4,6], 262, Cowl 8[9,19], Aḥiq 107, 139, Krael 3[12,14], Sem xxiii 95 verso 4 (cf. Fales AION xxvi 545, 547, Kaufman Conn xix 124f.: l. *mn ‘l mn* :: Bordreuil Sem xxiii 101f.: l. *mn* (= *mn_5*) *‘lmn* (= Plur. abs. of *‘lm_4*); v. *šwb*), etc., etc., cf. Warka 19, 20: *man-nu* (cf. Dupont-Sommer RA xxxix 49: = *mn_4* × e.g. Driver AfO iii 52, Garbini HDS 31: < *mn_4* + *hw_1*),*mnw* (< *mn_4* + *hw_1*)FuF xxxv 173[4]; cf. Frah xxv 6 (*mnw*), Paik 641 (*mnw*), ZDMG xcii 441[5], 442A 7, 13, B 7, Syr xxxv 305[1], 321[53], 323[55], 325[59], BSOAS xxxiii 152[11,16] (*mnw*), GIPP 29, 58, SaSt 20, cf. also Lemosín AO ii 267 - **Nab** CIS ii 197[2,3,6,8], 198[4], etc., etc. - **Palm** CIS ii 3913 ii 48, 49, 51, 72 (Greek par. ὃς), SBS 34[4], etc., etc., *mnw* Ber v 133[1] (< *mn_4* + *hw_1*)- **Hatra** 20[4], 23[3], 24[2], 25[2], etc., etc. (cf. also Assur 11 ii 2, 14[4]) - **JAr** MPAT 49 i 4, MPAT-A 5[1], 22[2,4], etc., etc., cf. PEQ ’38, 238[1]: μαν (cf. Peters OLZ ’40, 218f., Beyer ATTM 353; cf. also Milik LA x 154f.) - ¶ pronoun - **1)** interrog. pronoun, who?: DA ii 12 (for the context, cf. Hoftijzer a.l., Caquot & Lemaire Syr liv 205), Warka 19, 20; cf. *mn hw zy yqwm qdmwhy lhn* Aḥiq 107: who is he that can stand before him, except ... (i.e. no one can stand before him, except ...); *mn ’pw ṣdqny* Aḥiq 140: who then has justified me?, cf. also Aḥiq 139, 140, 161 - **2)** indefinite pronoun, who, whoever: KAI 202B 16, 214[15], 222C 16, Tell F 10, 16, CIS ii 198[4,5], 3913 ii 132, MPAT 49 i 4, etc.; cf. the remarkable expression *mn ḥd* in *mn ḥd ’ḥy ’w mn ḥd byt ’by ’w mn ḥd ...* KAI 224[9f.]: anyone of my brothers or any member of my father’s house or anyone ... (for the interpret. of *mn* as *mn_4*, cf. e.g. Dupont-Sommer BMB xiii 32, Koopmans 65, Fitzmyer AIS 112, 152, Donner KAI a.l., Degen AAG p. 62 n. 39, 119 (n. 1), ZDMG cxix 175, Gibson SSI ii p. 54, Segert AAG p. 325 × Ben-Chayyim Lesh xxxv 251, Kaufman BiOr xxxiv 96: = *mn_5*; cf. also KAI 222B 30 *mn ḥd mlk*, this *mn* = *mn_5*, cf. Degen AAG p. 62 (n. 39) :: Fitzmyer AIS 69, 152: = *mn_4* (cf. also Donner KAI a.l.) :: Lipiński Stud 36, 38 (div. otherwise): l. *[y’]mn* = NIPH Impf. 3 p.s.m. of *’mn_1* (= to be true)); *mn ’t thns ṣlm’ znh* KAI 225[5ff.]: whoever you are who takes away this picture (cf. KAI 226[8]), cf. also *mn zy ’t* KAI 259[2]: whoever you are, who ... and *mnw dy* Ber v 133[1f.]: whosoever who ...; for *mn zy* and variants, v. *zy*; for *kl mn dy* and variants, v. *kl_1* - cf. also the expression *mn ‘l mn yšb* Sem xxiii 95 verso 4: whoever will turn himself against the other ... (for this interpret., cf. Lipiński ActOrHung xii 377 (= WGAV 377), Fales AION xxvi 545ff., sub AECT 58, Kaufman Conn xix 124f., Teixidor Syr lvi 392) - l. poss. *wmn* in Hatra 24[3] (cf. Degen ZDMG cxxi 125 ::

Safar Sumer vii 183: l. *šmn* (without interpret.), cf. also Caquot Syr xxix 103, Donner sub KAI 245 :: Safar Sumer ix 14*: = part of n.d. :: Vattioni IH a.l.: l. *smn* (without interpret.) :: Pennacchietti FO xvi 60f.: l. *šmn* = part of n.p. :: Milik RN vi/iv 55 (div. otherwise): l. *l>š* (= form of *>šš* (= to be long, to be numerous)) + *mn* (= mn_4).
v. *>mr*$_1$, *dlmn*, *zrnyk*, *mn*$_{2,5}$, *nṣb*$_3$, *qrb*$_2$.

mn_5 in **Ph/Pun** (only relatively few examples) and **Hebr** (frequently) assimilation of *n* to the foll. consonant, normally not to foll. *h*, cf. however *mhbn>* Trip 41[1], *mhm<rb* DJD ii 30[15]; for **Mo**, cf. poss. also *h<m [m]hqr* KAI 181[11f.]?, cf. also J.Ar. MPAT 42[13], 62[12] (= DBKP 27), MPAT-A 50[4]; in Hatra 292[7] occurs the variant orthography *myn*, cf. Aggoula Syr lii 194, Degen NESE iii 91, Vattioni IH a.l. :: Safar Sumer xxvii 14: = Plur.? abs. of *mnh*$_2$ (cf. also Aggoula Syr lii 194, Vattioni IH a.l.: l. also *myn*in Hatra 292[4] :: Degen NESE iii 89f.: l. *mn*); for a poss. *myn*in J.Ar., cf. Milik sub Syr xlv 101[20]; in **Ph** poss. variant *bn*KAI 43[13] (cf. e.g. Lidzbarski Handb 312, Cooke NSI p. 87, Harr 120, FR 54 b, 251 I, v.d.Branden GP § 203a, 304b, cf. also Röllig KAI a.l., Segert GPP p. 162), another poss. interpret., however, is: QAL Pf. 3 p.pl. of *bny*$_1$,cf. Honeyman JEA xxvi 64 (n. 12), Röllig KAI a.l. :: Honeyman JEA xxvi 64: = *bn*$_5$ (= *byn*$_2$),cf. Röllig KAI a.l., Segert GPP p. 162 :: Clermont-Ganneau Et ii 176, Gibson SSI iii p. 141: = *bn*$_6$ (= allomorph of *b*$_2$)+ suff. 3 p.s.f. (cf. also Honeyman JEA xxvi 64); for the variant form *hm* (= *hm*$_2$; in *hmk* = *hm*$_2$+ suff. 2 p.s.m.) in DJD ii 24B 7, 13, C 6, 11, E 5, 8, EI xx 256[8] (on the reading, cf. (Naveh with) Broshi & Qimron EI xx 258), cf. Milik DJD ii p. 127, Broshi & Qimron EI xx 260 - for transcriptions, cf. Poen 949: *mim* (var. *nim*, *mum*; lapsus for *min*, cf. Sznycer PPP 129), Poen 939: *mon* (lapsus for *min*, cf. Sznycer PPP 107 :: Gottheil 916, J.J.Glück & Maurach Semitics ii 113f. (n. 46): = *mn*$_4$ (imposs. interpret.)), Warka 1, 2, 14, etc., etc.: *mi-in*, Warka 34: *mi-in-ni* (cf. also Garbini HDS 30); cf. also Frah xxv 34 (*mn*), Paik 638 (*mn*), 639, 690 (in the comb. *mn npšh*), Nisa 1[2], 2[2], 3[2], 4[2], 5[2], etc., etc., *dn/rn/<n* Nisa 121[2] (diff. reading, prob. lapsus), Sogd B 258, Bb 141, Ka 15, 19-22, R 50, Ta 476, 478, 483, ZDMG xcii 441[5], 442A 7, 9, 10, 13, B 5, 7, 9, Syr xxxv 315[34], 331[66], DEP 153[1], ChwIr 57, IrAnt vii 148, BSOAS xxxiii 148[8], 152[18], FS Nyberg 271 ii, 273 vii, 275 xii, xiii, GIPP 26, 28, 29, 33, 52, 57, 60, SaSt 19, cf. Lemosín AO ii 266 - ¶ prep. (on this prep., cf. also Pennacchietti AION xxiv 181ff.) - **1)** local, indicating separation: from; *mon* (v. supra) *cho th lusim* (lapsus for *iusim*, v. *yṣ>*) Poen 939: those who are going out from here, cf. also Poen 949 (cf. Sznycer PPP 107f., 129 :: Zevit JANES vii 107 (div. otherwise): l. *lymmon* (Poen 939), *limin* (Poen 949) = *l*$_5$ + *mn*$_5$ (= from)); *wylkw hmym mn hmwṣ> >l hbrkh* KAI 189[4f.]: the water flowed from the spring to the pool; *kṣ>ty mbytk* TA-H 16[3f.]: when I left your house; *wh‘br ʾby mn dmšq lʾšr* KAI 215[18]: he brought across my father from D. to A.; *mn mwqʾ šmš w‘d m‘rb* KAI 215[13]: from the East to the West; *thns ṣlmʾ znh ... mn ʾšrh* KAI 225[6ff.]: you will drag this picture away from its place; *yqrq mny qr[q] ḥd pqdy* KAI 224[4]: one of my officers will flee from me as a fugitive; *wmn qlqltʾ llqṭw ʾnšwh š‘rn* Tell F 22: may his men gather barley from the dunghill (Akkad. par. *eli tup-qí-na-te ...*); *ltrkwth mn byth* Cowl 15[30]: to drive her away from his house; *nksn ... hnpqt mn byty* Cowl 7[5]: you have removed goods from my house; *mn tmh* ATNS 26[12]: from there; *npqtm mn mṣryn* SSI ii 28 obv. 3: you have left Egypt; *mn tḥtyʾ l‘lyʾ* Krael 9[6]: from the South to the North (v. *tḥtyh*, *‘lyh*); *mn ʾr‘ʾ w‘d ‘lʾ* Cowl 5[5]: from the ground upwards; *lh mns ʾnh lh mn mpy* Herm 2[3]: I will not let him leave Memphis; *ʾdwnʾ zy mn mdynh ‘d mdynh* Driv 6[5]: the journey from province to province; *ʾl yrḥq mnkm ‘d ymṭʾ* NESE i 11[8]: let he not remove himself from you until he arrives ...; *ʾgwrʾ... yh‘dw mn tmh* Cowl 30[6]: let them remove the temple ... from there (i.e. let they destroy it); *na-šá-a-a-tú qi-ta-ri mi-in ig-ga-ri* Warka 1: I have taken a knot from the wall; *md‘m lh mpqn ln mn swn* Herm 5[2f.]: they do not send anything out to us from S.; *ynpq mnh gt* CIS ii 198[5f.]: he will take out the corpse from it; *dy slqw ‘mh mn krkʾ* CIS ii 3948[2f.]: those who came up with him from K.; *lnsb mšknʾ ... mn ‘bdʾ dy brmryn* Hatra 281[3/7f.]: he will take a tent ... from the building site of B.; *lnsb ... mn dy brmryn* Hatra 281[9f.]: he will take away from what belongs to B. (:: Degen NESE iii 68, 71: pro *mn dy* l. *mn* <*‘bdʾ*> *dy*); *slqt mn tmn* MPAT 49 i 10: I went from there; etc., etc.; cf. *m‘lyk mn bbʾ* Ber ii 60[1]: when you enter from the gate (cf. also RIP 163[3]; cf. the par. expression *m‘lyk bbʾ* Ber ii 101[6]: when you enter the gate); *wšm‘w ḥršn mn rḥq* DA i 15: the deaf ones heard from afar - a) with the meaning "coming from, from"; *bšt h‘šrt lšmryw mbʾrym nbl yn yšn* KAI 183[1ff.]: in the tenth year, for Sh. from B. a jar of old wine; *wrmh mn gdš* DA ii 8: and vermin from the grave; *mn ḥqlʾ dqln 16 wmn šymtʾ zy mlkʾ dqln 5* KAI 228[18f.]: 16 date palms from the field and 5 date palms from the royal treasury (for the context, v. *šymh*); *ytntn ly ptpʾ mn byt mlkʾ* Krael 11[5f.]: a ration will be given to me from the treasury; *brkth mn šmyh* Syn D A 12 (= SM 88): a blessing from heaven, etc., etc.; used of persons originating from a certain place, *zbdy mn kpr nbšmn* AECT F 1: Z. from the village of N.; *hṣlyhw mmqdh* EI xviii 94[4]: H. from M. (cf. EI xviii 94[2,3]; for the reading of l. 3, cf. also Misgav IEJ xl 206f.); *šptw ... mn ʾyrsy* BSOAS xxvii 272 iv 3f.: Sh. ... from A. (cf. also Sznycer JA ccliii 7f.), cf. also AM '52, 174[3], Syr lxv 444; *ʾšlm mn ‘qw* J 284: A. from U.; *wʾlw ... dy mn ‘ylʾ* J 189: W. from A.; *ʾbšlwm br ḥnyn mn ṣwyh* MPAT 39[2]: A., the son of Ch., from Ṣ. (cf. IEJ xxxvi 206[1]); *ḥ... br yhwdh mn kprbbyw ʾmr lʾl‘zr ... šṭrʾ mn tmn* MPAT 51[2f.]: Ch.

the son of Y. from K. said to E. ... the scribe from there ...; cf. *kwl ʾnš mtqwʿ* MPAT 59[2]: every man from T.; cf. also *qrbn ʾlh mn dbgwh* MPAT 69[2]: an offering to God from the one within it - b) in the introductory formula of a message/letter, *mšmʿwn bn kwsbh lyšʿ bn glglh wlʾnšy ... šlwm* DJD ii 43[1ff.]: from Sh. the son of K. to Y. the son of G. and the men of ... greetings; *mn hprnsyn ... mn yšwʿ wmn ʾlʿzr lyšwʿ ... šlwm* DJD ii 42[1f.]: from the administrators ... from Y. and E. to Y. ... greetings (cf. I.Rabinowitz BASOR cxxxi 21f., Lehmann & Stern VT iii 392, Bardtke ThLZ lxxix 301, Yeivin At i 95f., Milik DJD ii a.l.; cf. however - a) Sonne PAAJR xxiii 87: pro the second and third *mn* l. *kn* (= *kn*$_4$)- b) de Vaux RB lx 270, Ginsberg BASOR cxxxi 26, Birnbaum PEQ '55, 21, 32f.: pro *mn* l. *kn* (= *kn*$_4$) :: Albright BASOR cxxxi 24: pro *mn* l. *kn* = *kn*$_5$ (= *kʾn* (= here))); *šlm byt nbw ʾl ʾḥty rʿyh mn ʾḥky mkbnt* Herm 1[1]: greetings to the temple of N., to my sister R. from your brother M. (cf. also the address on the same letter, l. 14: *ʾl ʾby psmy ... mn mkbnt swn ybl*, to my father P. ... from M., to be delivered to S.); *mn ʾršm ʿl mrdk* Driv 6[1]: from A. to M. (cf. Driv 3[1], 4[1], 5[1]); *mn mykyh ʿl ʾ[ḥwṭb] šlmky* Sem xxi 85 conc. 1f.: from M. to A. greetings to you; etc. (cf. also Alexander JSS xxiii 161f., Fitzmyer JBL xciii 211, 219, WA 189, 195f., Porten EI xiv 167, Pardee JBL xcvii 333, Fales JAOS cvii 454f., Greenfield IrJu 4ff.); cf. also the greeting formula at the end of a letter, *šlm ʾby psmy mn ʿbdk nbwšh* Herm 4[13]: greetings to my father P. from your servant N., etc., etc. - c) with meaning "born from"; *bnyk mn mbtḥyh brty* Cowl 9[7]: your children by my daughter M.; *br dkr wnqbh lʾ ʾyty lh mn ʾsḥwr bʿlh* Cowl 15[20f.]: she has no male or female child by her husband A.; etc. - d) used in connection with verbal forms indicating acquisition and related concepts, *wlqḥt mšm* TA-H 17[3f.]: take from there; *šlqḥ yhwsp ... mn yʿqb* DJD ii 42[3]: which Y. ... has acquired from Y.; *ḥkrty hmk* DJD ii 24B 13: I have rented from you; *ḥkrt mšmʿwn* DJD ii 24C 8: I have rented from Sh.; *yqḥw mn ydy* KAI 214[12]: they accepted from my hand; *lḥmh wmwh ʾl ylqḥ mn ydh* Tell F 17f.: may he not accept the bread and water he offers from his hand (cf. Tell F 18); *bytn zy zbn ... mn bgzšt* Krael 12[3f.]: our house which we bought ... from B.; *hwy lqḥ šʿrn mn tšy* Herm 3[9]: acquire barley from T.; *ʾsḥwr ʾbwkm lqḥ mn šlwmm* Cowl 20[6]: A. your father received from Sh.; *yzpt mnk* Krael 11[3]: I borrowed from you; *ʾp ygbʾ mksʾ mn znytʾ* CIS ii 3913 ii 47: the tax collector will also levy from the prostitute; *ʾtqblyh* (v. *qbl*$_1$) *mn šmʿwn* MPAT 62[11]: I have received from Sh. (cf. Greek par. ἀπέσχον παρὰ Σίμωνι, cf. EI viii 50); etc.; cf. also *ʾyš mtwm yhnṣl mn kndwṣ ʾlhʾ* FX 136[21f.]: someone will take away something from the god K. (cf. Greek par. μετακινήσειν μηδαμὰ), etc.; cf. also *lhwy lky mny spr trkyn* MPAT 40[7]: you have from me a bill of repudiation - e) used in connection with verbal forms indicating removal and absence, used figuratively, *wlmld mrq mnh* Tell F 9: to remove illness from him (for the context, v. also *lwd*; cf. also Tell F 23); *ʾnh rḥyq mn kl dyn wdbb* Cowl 14^{11}: I renounce all suit and process; *rḥqt mnh* Cowl 13^{7}: I resigned all claim to it (i.e. the house); *rḥqt mnky* Cowl 14^{6}: I renounced all claim on you; *rḥqt mn ʾksdrʾ* RIP 163B 2: she has ceded the exedra; etc. etc.; cf. *[y]klʾw mnh lḥm wmym* FS Driver 54 conc. 3: they will withhold from him bread and water; *wʾprq mnk šṭr ...* MPAT 64 i 9: I shall redeem from you the document of ...; cf. also *lʾ ytkswn mn ʿnny* Cowl 38^{11}: they will not be hidden from A.; *prš lylyʾ mn ymmʾ* J 2^{4}: he who separates the night from the day; *mn kl ḥrr [w]tgr* MPAT 45^{5}: without any litigation and claim - f) used in connection with verbal forms indicating a demand (etc.) from someone, *wmh ʾšʾl mn ʾlhy* KAI 214^{12}: and whatever I asked from the gods; *ʾzd ytʿbd mn dynyʾ* Cowl $27^{8f.}$: an inquiry (v. *ʾzd*) will be made from the judges; *wbʿyt mnk* MPAT 64 i 9: I requested of you; etc.; cf. also *ʾlhyʾ ybʿwn mnh* FX $137^{26f.}$: may the gods require (it) from him (i.e. punish him); *mnkn prʿnwtʾ ttʿbd* MPAT 53^{2}: punishment is to be exacted from you; etc. - g) used in connection with verbal forms indicating rescue/deliverance, *hšʿny mkl h[š]lkn* KAI 181^{4}: he delivered me from all assaults (v. *šlk*$_1$); *šwzbh mn qdns rb* SBS 45^{9}: he has delivered it from great danger (Greek par. διασώσαντα ... ἐκ τοῦ ... μεγάλου κινδύνου) - **2)** local, indicating the place where, on, at; *mhmʿrb whdrwm* DJD ii 30^{15}: at the west and the south side (cf. SM $49^{6,7,8}$); *mʾḥryk* AMB 1^{2}: behind you; *mn tnn* Sem xxvii 117^{7}: here (for the context, v. *šwy*$_1$); *mn ymynk* CIS ii 4195^{7}: at your right; *mn ʿlʾ* MPAT 52^{9}: above (cf. *mmʿlʾ* MPAT 42^{13}); etc. - **3)** temporal, since; *mʿlm* KAI 181^{10}: from of old; *mbqʿ hšḥr ʿd ṣhrm* KAI 181^{15}: from break of dawn till noon; *mn hšlšh ʿšr lḥdš ʿd hšmnh ʿšr lḥdš* TA-H $8^{2ff.}$: from the 13th of the month till the 18th; *mn hywm ʿd swp ʿrb hšmṭh* DJD ii 24B 13f.: from this day until the end of the year preceding the sabbatical year (cf. DJD ii 24C 11f., E 8f.); *mn hʿṣrt ʿd hḥnwkh* SM 49^{3}: from the Concluding Feast until the Channukkah-festival; *mn yrḥ tmwz šnt 14 dryhwš mlkʾ wʿd znh* Cowl $30^{19f.}$: from the month T. in the 14th year of king D. until now; *mn ywm mlky mṣryn ʾbhyn bnw ʾgwrʾ zk* Cowl 31^{12}: since the time of the kings of Egypt our fathers have built that temple (i.e. already in the time of ...); *mn ywm [z]y npqtm* SSI ii 28 obv. 3: from the day you left; *mn ywmʾ dnh ʿd ʿlm* J 38^{4}: from this day until forever; *wyhb kprʾ dnh lʾmh ʾntth ... mn zmn šṭr mwhbtʾ ... mn 26 bʾb* CIS ii $204^{2ff.}$: he has given this tomb to A. his wife ... from the date of the deed of gift ... from the 26th of Ab (i.e. the tomb is the possession of the woman since that date); *mn ywm 26 bšbṭ ʿdmʾ lywm 12 bnysn* Assur 27e 1f.: from the 26th day of Sh. until the 12th day of N.; *mn ymh* *dnh wl‘lm* MPAT 51[11f.]: from this day and forever; *mšbt lšbt* AMB 4[30]: from week to week (cf. AMB 4[29,30f.,31]); *mḥd* (for the reading, v. *›ḥd₄*) *1 btmwz* (reading *tmwz* improb.) *w‘dy tlt{l}yn b›lwl›* MPAT 62[12f.] (= DBKP 27): from the first of Tammuz until the 30th in Elul (cf. Greek par. ἀπὸ μηνὸς ... μέχρι ..., cf. EI viii 50); etc. - **4)** temporal, indicating the time on/during which something happens, *mn mḥr* DA i 5: next morning; *mn ›ḥry znh* Samar 6[5]: hereafter; cf. also *mn* used in connection with derivative of root *qdm*, *mn qdmn qdm knbwzy* Cowl 32[5]: formerly, before Cambyzes; *mn qdmt dn›* MPAT 40[17]: before this time (cf. MPAT 52[4]); cf. also *bnwhy mn ›ḥrwhy* Samar 1[4]: his sons after him (cf. Samar 1[6]) - **5)** partitive, belonging to, among, from; *mrym yw‘zr šm‘wn ... mn bny yšb›b* MPAT 91a 2: M., Y., Sh. ... belonging to the sons of Y.; *m›lw ›bdw bḥrb* DJD ii 45[7]: a part of them perished by the sword; *mn hgll›ym šhṣlkm kl ›dm* DJD ii 43[4f.]: every person whosoever of the Galileans who are with you; *myyn h›gnt ttn* TA-H1[9f.]: give from the wine in the craters; *m‘wd hqmḥ hr›šn* TA-H 1[5f.]: from the rest of the first flour; *mn mn bny* KAI 214[15]: someone among my sons; *wyšlḥn ›lhn mn kl mh ›kl* KAI 222A 30: and the gods will send all manner of devourer; *ḥdh mn mly spr› zn[h]* KAI 222B 8: one of the words of this inscription; *[ḥ]d mn rby ›by* Aḥiq 33: one of the nobles of my father; *qṣt mn byty* Krael 9[3]: a part of my house; *wtlqḥ lk mn by zy lbnn ‘bd w›mh* ... Krael 11[10f.]: and you may take for yourself from among the house of bricks, the slave and the slave-girl ... (cf. Hoftijzer VT ix 315, Porten & Greenfield JEAS p. 66 :: Krael a.l.: *mn* has separative meaning; cf. also Yaron JSS xvi 241 (n. 7)); *zy ykl› mnhm* Cowl 5[10]: the one who will restrain one of them; *l› ›št›r ln ‘lyk mn dmy›* Krael 12[6]: none of the price was outstanding to us from you; *w›šlm[nh]y lk ... mn prsy* Cowl 11[5f.]: I will pay it to you ... out of my salary; *mn dgl* ... TA-Ar 18[1]: belonging to the detachment of ... (contrast with normal *ldgl*, v. *l₅*); *mn ‘bdy* Samar 5[7]: one of my slaves; *›ḥd mn ›rb‘› ›ḥy›* CIS ii 4158[1f.]: one of the four brothers; *gys ... qṭrywn› dy mn lgywn› dy* ... Inv xii 33[1]: G. ... the *centurion* belonging to the legion of ...; *mn mn tdmry›* CIS ii 3913 ii 132: whoever from the Palmyreneans; *‘gylw ... dy mn bny knn›* CIS ii 3922[1f.]: O. ... belonging to the Bene K.; *mn pḥd bny khnbw* Inv xi 100[4]: belonging to the tribe of the Bene K.; *‘bdt mdynt› ... mn ksp ‘nwšt›* CIS ii 3994[1ff.]: the city ... made it from the money of (i.e. at the expense of) the Treasury; *zbn zbd‘th ... mn mnth* Inv xii 14[1f.] (= RIP 51): Z. has sold ... from his portion; *wqrb mn kysh* Inv xii 19[1]: and he has offered from his purse (i.e. at his own expense; cf. Greek par. ἐξ ἰδί[ων]); *mn dylh* CIS ii 158[3]: from what is his (i.e. at his own expense); *wl› ršy ›nwš klh mn š‘ydw w›ḥwhy ... dy yzbn* CIS ii 209[4f.]: and no man, either Sh. or his brothers, ... shall be allowed to sell; *kl mn dy y‘yr mn kl dy* ... CIS ii 206[8f.]: anyone who shall change anything whatever which ...; *ḥlqh mn kpr› hw* CIS ii 200[4]: his part of that tomb; *klbw br ‹mrw mn ›l ḥttw* CIS ii 2604: K. the son of A. belonging to the tribe of Ch.; *mnw ... dy mn ›l ‹mlt* ADAJ xxiv 42: M. ... who belongs to the tribe A.; *hn›w ... dy mnhm* ADAJ xxiv 43: H. who belongs to them (cf. Syr xxxv 244[3f.]); *mh dy y›t› lh mn ksp wdhb* BASOR cclxiii 77[1]: whatever comes to him of silver and gold (cf. also Jones BASOR cclxxv 42); *ḥd mn grb›* Hatra 281[9]: one of the jars (??, v. *grb$_3$*); *›nš mn bn› ddhwn* Hatra 79[12]: one of their sons; *›qym ›rz› ... mn kyshwn* Hatra 214[1f.]: they erected the mystery temple (v. *›rz$_3$*) ... at their own expense; *mn bny ›lyšyb* MPAT 41[2]: belonging to the sons of E.; *tšlwm[t›] lk mnksy* MPAT 39[7f.]: the indemnity for you from my possessions; *dyhb ṭymy psypsh mn dydh* MPAT-A 2[1ff.] (= SM 58): who gave the cost of the mosaic from his own resources (v. also *zy*); *wyhbyn lk mn dlnh* MPAT 46[4]: and giving to you from what is ours; *dyhb ḥd ṭr[ym]ysyn mn p‹l[h]* MPAT-A 56[2f.] (for the reading, cf. Naveh sub SM 74): who has given one *trimesion* from his possessions (v. *p‹l$_2$*; cf. also MPAT-A 16[3] (= SM 17)); *yrḥ mrḥšwn mšth qdmyth d* ... MPAT-A 50[3ff.]: the month M. from the first year of the ...; *šnt tlt m› [wtlt] mn šnyn lḥrbn byt mqdšh* MPAT-A 51[6ff.]: the year 303 from the years after the destruction of the Temple; etc., etc.; cf. also *›p ygb› [mks]› mn gnsy› klhwn* CIS ii 3913 ii 68: also the tax-collector shall levy from goods of all kinds; Aggoula Syr lii 191: *mn byth dnpš[h]* in Hatra 290[3] = at the expense of his own house (:: Degen NESE iii 85f.: from his own family; diff. and dam. context); cf. poss. also *›syqw mn ‹bwr* BSh 5[2]: they brought from the corn (reading uncert., dam. context) - **6)** indicating cause or reason, both personal and impersonal, because of, through; *šl› thy ›mwr mn bšrwn* DJD ii 42[6]: that you will not say out of disdain ...; *mrṣwny* DJD ii 24E 5: from my own free will (cf. DJD ii 24B 6, C 6); *mšmnyty 30 šnh wšnh* DJD ii 30[26f.]: on the condition that I am paid 30 (dinars?) yearly; *›grt mn mr›y tštlḥ* Driv 10[2]: let a letter be sent from my lord; *l‹lym ›ḥrn zyly mny l› yhyb* Driv 8[5]: it is not given by me to any other of my servants; *yštb‹ k‹s mn lḥm* Aḥiq 189: let him that is vexed be satisfied by bread; *mn mt› yhybn ksp [m]nh ḥd wplg* FX 136[13f.]: by the government there is given 11/2 *mina* silver (cf, Greek par. καὶ δίδοται .. τρία ἡμιμναῖα παρὰ τῆς πόλεως); *bwl› knyš› mn nmws›* CIS ii 3913 i 3: the Council was assembled by law (cf. Greek par. βουλῆς νομίμου ἀγομένης); *mn ‹yd›* CIS ii 3913 i 5: by custom (cf. Greek par. ἐκ συνηθείας); *mn twḥyt bwl› wdmws* CIS ii 3959[1]: by an edict of Senate and People; *mn rḥm›* CIS ii 3935[4]: out of love; *kl ›nwš dy ynpq bydh ktb mn khln* CIS ii 206[5]: every man who shall produce in his hand a writ from K.; *kl mn ynpq bydh mn šby ... ktb* CIS ii 215[2]: whosoever shall produce in his hand from Sh. ... a writ; *mn dy ynpq bydh ktb mn yd kmkm* CIS ii 198[9f.]: whosoever shall produce in his hand a writ from the hand of K.; *mn r'ty* MPAT 40[2]: out of my own free will; *mn šṭr* ... MPAT 64 i 3: in accordance with the document of ...; *dškn* (v. *škn*$_1$) ... *mn drḥmnh wmn 'mly* MPAT-A 39[1ff.] (= SM 42[2ff.]; for the reading, cf. Naveh sub SM 42): (we) who have established ... out of our own generosity and out of my toil; etc.; cf. also with the meaning "with regard to, as to", *br 'ynš l' dm' yhwh mn ṭbwt* KAI 276[9ff.]: no one was (her) equal in goodness (for Greek par., v. *dm'*); *yṣrw 'lhn mn ywmh wmn byth* KAI 222C 15f.: may the gods preserve (him) as to his days and as to his house (cf. Rosenthal ANET 660 :: Ben-Chayyim Lesh xxxv 246: *mn ywmh wmn byth* = during his days and in his house (cf. also Beyer ZDMG cxx 202) :: Rosenthal ANET 660 n. 9: or = during his lifetime and that of his posterity :: Fitzmyer AIS 21, 75: may the gods keep [all evils] away from his day and from his house (cf. Donner KAI a.l., Lipiński Stud 53, Lemaire & Durand IAS 125 (cf. also ibid. 143 for KAI 223C 16f.)) :: Gibson SSI ii p. 33, 40: may the gods keep (him) all his days and his house as long as it lasts :: Dupont-Sommer Sf p. 88, 91f.: *mn* = *mn*$_4$with accusative function or perhaps *mn* = *mn*$_6$ (= adv., certainly, surely)) - **7)** used in comparison, *whyṭbh mn qdmth* KAI 215[9]: he made it better than it was before; *wbyt 'by 'ml mn kl* KAI 216[7]: my father's house laboured more than all (others); *whrmw šr mn šr ḥzrk* KAI 202A 10: they put up a wall higher than the wall of Ch. (cf. e.g. Donner KAI a.l., Gibson SSI ii p. 9 :: Garbini OA iv 144: *mn šr* = near the wall of ...); *ky 'zyz 'rb pm mn 'rb mlḥm* Aḥiq 99: the ambush of the mouth is stronger than the ambush of the war (v. also *'rb*); *wṣdqh yhwh lk ... mn gbr zy yqrb* ... Cowl 30[27f.]: your merit will be greater ... than that of the man who offers ...; *ṣdyq mnk* Aḥiq 128: one more righteous than you (?; cf. e.g. Cowl p. 128, Lindenberger APA 118f. (cf. also Kottsieper SAS 15: 'gerecht vor dir'), for less prob. word division, cf. Grimme OLZ '11, 537, Joüon MUSJ xviii 86f., Ginsberg ANET 429, Grelot RB lxviii 187, DAE p. 441: combine *mnk ḥṭ'*; v. also *h'*$_1$, *ḥṣ*$_1$); *špyr' 'nt mn 'lhn* KAI 264[6]: you are more beautiful than the goddesses; etc. - cf. also *mn* with the meaning "different from", *wkl 'nwš dy yktb bqbr' dnh ktb mn kl dy 'l'* CIS ii 206[6]: every man who shall write on this tomb any writing other than what is (written) above - **8)** indicating identity (*mn* explicativum), *wh' mšḥt byt' zk zy 'nh ... yhbt lky ... mn plg try rbt' wtwnh* Krael 4[5f.]: and behold the measurements of that house which I ... gave to you ... to wit the half of the great *try* (v. *try*$_1$) and the chamber ... (cf. Hoftijzer VT ix 314f. :: Grelot DAE p. 222 n. c: = *mn* here used with partitive meaning; cf. also Krael a.l., Porten & Greenfield JEAS p. 45, Porten & Yardeni sub TADAE B 3.5 (v. *plg*$_3$)); *lšydw brh w'ḥwhy mh dy ytyld lḥlpw dnh mn dkryn* CIS ii 209[1f.]: for Sh. his son and his brothers as many as there will be born from Ch. mentioned above ... i.e. the male children; this use of *mn* poss. also in Herm 2[7] (cf. Hayes & Hoftijzer VT xx 102, Hoftijzer SV 111; v. also *qṣt*$_1$) - **9)** indicating a position with respect to another one, *lmw‘ šmš mn[h]* Cowl 6[8]: to the east of it; *tḥty› mnh* Krael 9[10]: to the south of it (v. *tḥty*); *gw› mnhm* MPAT 64 iii 5: within them (or: behind them??; v. also *gw*$_2$); *w›sṭw› dy l‘l mnh* Inv xii 49[5]: and the portico which is above it; *‘mwdyh d‘l mn kpth* MPAT-A 17[1f.] (= SM 7): the columns which are above the arches (v. also *‘l*$_1$); etc. - **10)** indicating the material of which a certain object is made, *[s]mlt ›[z] ›š ytn wyṭn› mnḥšt y›š* KAI 33[2]: this is the statue which Y. gave and erected in bronze (v. however *nḥšt*) - **11)** with the meaning "without (the necessity of)"; *kl šyš ly wš›qnh ›ḥr›ym ... mkl ḥrr wtgr* DJD ii 30[23ff.]: everything I possess and which I will acquire are the guarantees .. without any litigation or claim being necessary (cf. MPAT 45[5]) - **12)** cf. the following prep. compounds - a) for *m›t* (= *mn*$_5$ + *›t*$_6$), v. *›t*$_6$ and for KAI 124[3], v. *‘ly*$_1$ - b) for *mn ›ḥr(y)*, v. *›ḥr*$_5$ - c) for *mn bl‘dy*, v. *bl‘d*, v. also *mlk*$_3$ - d) for *mn btr*, v. *btr*, v. also *›šr*$_4$ for *mn b›tr d* - e) for *mlwt* (= *mn*$_5$ + *l*$_5$ + *wt*), v. *›yt*$_3$ - f) for *mn l*, v. *l*$_5$ - g) for *mn ‘l*, v. *‘l*$_7$, v. also *ṭ‘m*$_2$ - h) for *mn qdm*, v. *qdm*$_3$ - i) for *mn tḥt*, v. *tḥt* - j) for *br mn*, v. *br*$_3$ - k) for *lmn*, v. *l*$_5$ - l) for *lmb* (= *l*$_5$ + *mn*$_5$ + *b*$_2$), v. *l*$_5$ - Beyer ATTM 330: l. *mnn›* = *mn*$_5$ + suff. 1 p.pl. in MPAT 37[1] (poss. reading and interpret.; heavily dam. context) - in KAI 270A 2 l. *wmn* (cf. e.g. CIS ii sub 137, Dupont-Sommer ASAE xlviii 122, Donner KAI a.l., Gibson SSI ii p. 124 :: Sach p. 239f.: l. *tmn* (cf. also Leand 61a, Segert AAG p. 237)).

v. *›dyn*, *›mn*$_1$, *›np*$_2$, *›rk*$_4$, *b*$_2$, *byt*$_4$, *bl*$_3$, *bn*$_1$, *zbnwt*, *z*$_1$, *zy*, *ṭl*$_2$, *kn*$_4$, *mḥzt*, *mmlkh*, *mk*, *mn*$_{2,4}$, *mnh*$_{1,2}$, *ntn*, *‘l*$_1$, *pnh*$_1$, *prh*$_2$, *qdmh*$_1$, *qny*$_1$, *šwb*, *šṭr*$_3$.

mn$_6$ v. *mn*$_5$.

mn› v. *mny*.

mnbṣbh v. *mṣbh*.

mngl **OffAr**, cf. Frah-S$_1$ 1 (*mngl›*): sickle.

mndh$_1$ (< Akkad., cf. Zimmern Fremdw 9, Kaufman AIA 67, cf. also Ellenbogen 98, Lipiński ZAH i 68) - **OffAr** Sing. abs. *mndh* Driv F viii 1[2], ATNS 75a 1; cstr. *mnd[t]* Cowl 69C 2 (for this poss. reading, cf. Porten & Yardeni sub TADAE B 8.5), p. 318[6], Krael 5[7], Driv 10[3,4], 11[3], ATNS 24[11]; emph. *mndt›* Driv 10[3], 11[5], ATNS 21[2,3] - ¶ subst. - **1)** tax; *mndt ḥyl›* Cowl p. 318[6]: tax paid by the military colony (cf. ATNS 24[11]; cf. also Kaufman AIA 44) - **2)** revenue, rent: Driv 10[3,4], 11[3,5]; *mndt bgy›* Driv 10[3,4]: the rent on the domains - **3)** payment; *mndt ksp* Krael 5[7]: payment of silver (for the context, v. also *zwl*) - the exact meaning in ATNS 21[2,3] uncert., dam. context.

mndh$_2$ v. *bny*$_1$.

mnd‘$_1$ **OffAr** Sing. abs. *mnd‘* Aḥiq 53 - **JAr** Sing. cstr. *mnd‘* DBKP

17^{40} - ¶ subst. (or QAL Inf. of *yd*'$_1$)knowledge - **1)** prec. by prep. *b*$_2$, *qblt mn bbt' ... bmnd' ... 'dwnh ... ksp* DBKP $17^{40f.}$: I have received from B. ... with the knowledge of her guardian ... the sum of ... - **2)** in the expression *kmnd'* Aḥiq 53: as is known (cf. Torczyner OLZ '12, 398; cf. also Driver JRAS '32, 87: > assuredly :: Cowl p. 232: *mnd'* = *mnd'*$_2$ (= someone?; cf. also Leand 18d, Ginsberg ANET 428, Segert AAG p. 179, Grelot DAE p. 450 (n. d): = something)).

mnd'$_2$ v. *bny*$_1$, *mnd'*$_1$.

mnd'h = information > Akkad., cf. v.Soden Or xxxv 17, xlvi 190, AHW s.v. *mandētu*, CAD s.v. *mandētu*.

mnd'm v. *md'm*.

mnh$_1$ **OffAr** Sing. abs. *mnh* Cowl 37^{12} (dam. context; uncert. interpret.; cf. e.g. Cowl a.l., Grelot DAE p. 390, Porten & Greenfield JEAS p. 80, cf. however Porten & Yardeni sub TADAE A 4.2: = *mn*$_5$ + suff. 3 p.s.m.); emph. *mnt'* Cowl $1^{3,4,6}$, 17^2 (for the reading of the context, cf. Porten RB xc 406, 410f., Porten & Yardeni sub TADAE A 6.1); + suff. 2 p.s.m. *mntk* Aḥiq 144 (dam. context); + suff. 2 p.s.f. *mntky* Cowl 1^7 (for the reading, cf. Porten & Greenfield JEAS p. 106, Porten & Yardeni sub TADAE B 5.1 :: Cowl a.l.: l. *mnt'* (= Sing. emph.)); + suff. 1 p.s. (?) *mnty* Cowl 66 xii 1 (heavily dam. context) - **Palm** Sing. abs. *mnh* RIP 154^2, *mnt* RB xxxix 548^7; emph. *mnt'* RB xxxix 547^2, 548^4 (*mnt['] *), RTP 270; + suff. 3 p.s.m. *mnth* CIS ii 4206^2, RB xxxix 547^2, Inv viii 72^1 (for the reading, cf. Rosenthal Syr xix 165; or = + suff. 3 p.s.f.?, dam. context), xii 14^2 (= RIP 51), MUSJ xxxviii 106^8, FS Collart 161^9; Plur. abs. *mnwn* RB xxxix 548^5 - ¶ subst. f. share, portion, instalment; *plg mnt' zy mṭtky* Cowl $1^{3f.}$: half the share which accrued to you (for the nature of the share in this text, cf. Porten & Szubin JAOS cii 651ff.); *yhb mnt' mnth dy m'rt'* RB xxxix 547^2: he gave as instalment his part of the hypogee (cf. Greek par. ἔδωκεν κατάδοσιν τὸ προσῆκον αὐτῷ μέρος τοῦ σπηλαίο[υ]); *p[l]gwt mnt['] 'ḥd' dydh mn mnwn tlt dy m'rt'* RB xxxix $548^{4f.}$: half of the one part that is hers from the three parts of the hypogee (cf. Cowl $1^{4,6,7}$, Inv xvii 72^1, xii 14^2 (= RIP 51), RIP 154^2 (v. *md'm*), CIS ii 4206^2, RTP 270, RB xxxix 548^7, MUSJ xxxviii 106^8); *[ylqḥ] mn mntk* Aḥiq 143f.: he will take from your part (i.e. from your possessions); *štp tym' ... bmnth šm'wn* FS Collart 161^9: T. associated himself with Sh. for his share (sc. of the tomb), i.e. he ceded a part to him; for the diff. text Cowl 17^2, cf. e.g. Cowl p. 54, Porten Arch 52 n. 90, Grelot DAE p. 281 (n. f), Porten RB xc 411; Lipiński Stud 118, 121: l. *mnt[']* (= Sing. emph.) in TH i rs 1 (uncert. reading; cf. Friedrich AfO Beih. vi 71ff.: l. *rnn*? = part of n.l.; cf. also Degen NESE i 51f.) - Sach a.l.: l. *mnty* (= Sing. + suff. 1 p.s.) in Sach 77 i 1 (highly uncert. reading, cf. also SC p. 76: l. *'nty* without interpret.).

v. *ʾyt$_3$*, *mnt$_2$*.

mnh$_2$ (< Akkad., cf. Zimmern Fremdw 20f., Kaufman AIA 69) - **OffAr** Sing. abs. *mnh* CIS ii 6^2, FX 136^{14} (*[m]nh*), Samar 2^{10}, 5^{10}, 8^{10}; cstr. *mnh* CIS ii 6^1, 8, 9, 19^2 (= Del 12; for the reading, cf. Fales sub AECT 17; poss. reading, Delaporte sub Del 12: l. *mny* = Plur. cstr.); Plur. abs. *mnn* CIS ii 1a, 2a 1, 3a 1, 5^1, Cowl 26^{17}, Samar 1^{10} (= EI xviii 8*), 2^9, 3^9, 7^{15}, *mnyn* CIS ii 1c, 4a 1; cstr. *mny* CIS ii 2c (*m[n]y*), 3c (*mn[y]*); emph. *mnyʾ* Samar 7^5 (*mny[ʾ]*, diff. reading)^{,12} - **Palm** Plur. abs. *mnyn* Sem xxxvi 89^6 - **Hatra** Plur. abs. *mnyn* 241^1, 243^2, 244^2; emph. *mnyʾ* 240^2 (?, cf. Aggoula MUSJ xlvii 14; cf. however Degen JEOL xxiii 408, Vattioni IH a.l.: = Dual emph. :: Safar Sumer xxiv 14: = Sing. emph.) - **JAr** Plur. abs. *mnyn* EI xx 305 ii (heavily dam. context) - ¶ subst. m. certain weight, coin, *mine*; *ksp [m]nh ḥd wplg* FX 136$^{13f.}$: one *mine* and a half in silver (cf. Greek par. τρία ἡμιμναῖα); *mnh mlk* CIS ii 6^1, 8, 9: official *mine* (cf. CIS ii 1b, 2b, 3b, 4b); *mnn 15 b* CIS ii 1c: fifteen double *mines* (??, cf. CIS ii sub 1), cf. CIS ii 2a 1, 3a 1, 4a 1; cf. also *mn(y)n ... b zy ʾrqʾ* CIS ii 2a, 3a, 4a // with *mny mlkʾ*, *mnyn zy mlkʾ* and with *ma-na ša šarri* in the Akkad. par. (a comb. *mn(y)n/mnh ... b zy mlk* deest: *mnyn [b z]y mlk* in CIS ii 1c highly uncert. reconstruction) - for the problems of the Palm. text Sem xxxvi 89, cf. Gawlikowski Sem xxxvi 95ff. - for the poss. reading *mn[y]n* in Hatra 191^2, v. *ʾs$_1$* - the *mn[* in FuB xiv 13^1, 23^1 prob. first part of forms of this word - abbrev. *m*in Ph. text PEQ '75, 122: *1 m*, cf. also Ben-David PEQ '75, 121ff. - Segal Maarav iv 71: l. *mnyn* (= Plur. abs.) in AG 4bis 3 (uncert. reading, diff. context), Aimé-Giron AG a.l.: l. *mnʾnh* (without interpret.) - the *mnn* in ATNS 54^{10} poss. = Plur. abs. of *mnh$_2$* (Segal ATNS a.l.: *mnn* preferably = *mn$_5$*+ suff. 1 p.pl.) - Segal ATNS a.l.: l. *mnn* in ATNS 44 ii 8 (*scriptio anterior*), highly uncert. reading, cf. also Porten & Yardeni sub TADAE B 8.2 - on this weight, cf. also Barrois ii 253ff., Wambacq VD xxix 342f., Trinquet SDB v 1241ff., EM iv 863ff. - > Greek μνᾶ, cf. Masson RPAE 32ff.

v. *mn$_5$*, *mnyn*, *mʿh$_1$*, *ʿlm$_5$*, *prs$_2$*, *šlšn$_2$*.

mnw v. *mn$_4$*.

mnwḥ **Hebr** this word (Sing. abs. *mnwḥ*) in Mas 644; = rest, resting-place?, cf. also Yadin & Naveh Mas a.l.

mnwḥh v. *mnḥh$_2$*.

mnwrh **OffAr** this subst. (Sing. cstr. *mnwrt*) = candelabrum in the *scriptio anterior* of Sach Pap 49?, cf. Ungnad ArPap sub no. 50.

mnḥ **Hatra** Sing. abs. *mnḥ* 200^1 (for the reading, cf. Teixidor Sumer xxi 88f., Milik DFD 405, Vattioni IH a.l. :: Safar Sumer xviii 60 (n. 25), Caquot Syr xli 269f.: l. *nḥ* (= part of n.p.)) - ¶ subst. offering, gift (cf. also Teixidor Sumer xxi 89 :: Milik DFD 406: = dedication, the object which is dedicated (i.e. the altar) < root *nwḥ*$_1$).

mnḥh$_1$ **Ph** Sing. abs. *mnḥt* RES 930[1]; cstr. *mnḥt* KAI 43[13]; Plur. abs. *mnḥt* CIS i 14[5] - **Pun** Sing. abs. *mnḥt* KAI 69[14] (*mnḥ[t]*), 74[10], 145[13] (cf. e.g. Cooke NSI p. 152, Février Sem vi 28, Röllig KAI a.l. × v.d.Branden RSF i 166, 177: = Plur. abs.), 159[8] (*m[n]ḥt*; for this reading, cf. e.g. Lidzbarski Handb 313, Cooke NSI p. 144, Février RHR cxliii 17) - **OffAr** Sing. abs. *mnḥh* Cowl 27[14] (*mnḥ[h]*; for the reading, cf. also Porten & Yardeni sub TADAE A 4.5), 30[21], 31[21], 33[11]; emph. *mnḥt*ʾ Cowl 32[9], *mḥt*ʾ Cowl 30[25] (lapsus?) - ¶ subst. f. offering made to the gods - a) said of a stele: RES 930[1] (:: Milik DFD 406: < root *nwḥ*$_1$) - b) said of a meal-offering: KAI 69[14], 74[10], 159[8], Cowl 30[21,25], 31[21], 32[9], 33[11] (for the Pun. texts, cf. also Dussaud Orig 147 n. 3, 153) - for *mnḥt ḥny* in KAI 43[13], v. *ḥn*$_1$ - exact meaning in KAI 145[13] uncert.: either = a) the gift of the temple itself together with appertenances or b) meal offerings? - the *mnḥt* in KAI 141[2] (cf. Février BAr '51/52, 116, Röllig KAI a.l.) false reading, cf. Garbini RSO xliii 15f.: l. *bn* = Plur. cstr. of *bn*$_1$ followed by (part of) n.p. - for this word, cf. also Dahood Bibl xlix 357f.

mnḥh$_2$ **Hebr** Sing. abs. *mnwḥh* AMB 1[2];+ suff. 2 p.s.m. *mnwḥtk* Frey 558; + suff. 3 p.s.m. *mnwḥtw* Frey 622[5]; + suff. 3 p.pl.m. *mnwḥtm* Frey 630b 5; Plur. cstr. *mnḥwt* IEJ vii 239[1] - ¶ subst. - **1)** repose: AMB 1[2] - **2)** resting-place, tomb: Frey 558, 622[5], 630b 5, IEJ vii 239[1].

mnḥh$_3$ (< Egypt., cf. e.g. CIS ii sub 141, Cooke NSI p. 205, Lévy JA ccxi 294ff., Janssen with Koopmans 168, Donner KAI a.l., REHR 38, Grelot Sem xvii 73, Couroyer Sem xx 18, Lipiński OLP viii 112 (n. 148)) - **OffAr** Sing. m. abs. *mnḥh* KAI 272; f. abs. *tmnḥh* KAI 269[1] (*t* functioning as f. article in Egypt.) - ¶ adj. perfect, pious (epithet of a deceased person); *mnḥh zy* ʾ*wsry* ʾ*lh*ʾ KAI 272: the one devoted to the god O. (:: Lévy JA ccxi 295: *zy* in this construction of diff. explanation).

mnḥlh **Pun** Février Sem xi 8: l. this subst. (Sing. + suff. 3 p.s.m. *mnltm*) = heritage in KAI 166[4] (improb. interpret.; cf. Chabot sub Punica xi 7, Jongeling NINPI 198 :: Lidzbarski Handb 438, Röllig KAI a.l.: = part of n.p.).

mnḥm v. *nḥm*$_1$.

mnṭr = covering, bast > Akkad., cf. v.Soden Or xxxv 17, xlvi 90 (cf. also Landsberger with v.Soden Or xxxvii 270), cf. also v.Soden AHW s.v. *manṭaru*, CAD s.v. *manṭaru*.

mnṭrh **OffAr** Sing. abs. *mnṭrh* Aḥiq 98; Plur. + suff. 1 p.pl. (or Sing. + suff. 1 p.pl.?) *mnṭrtn* Cowl 27[1] - ¶ subst. - **1)** guarding post: Cowl 27[1] - **2)** watch, watchfulness; *mn kl mnṭrh ṭr pmk* Aḥiq 98: more than all watchfulness watch your mouth (i.e. watch your mouth more than anything; cf. also Kottsieper SAS 20, 218, Lindenberger APA 75, 235f.

n. 162).

mny **Pun** QAL Pf. 3 p.s.m. *mn*ʾ Trip 51^5 (cf. Levi Della Vida Or xxxiii 12, 14, Amadasi IPT 134; diff. and uncert. context) - **OffAr** QAL Imper. pl.m. *mnw* Cowl 21^4; Part. act. pl.m. abs. *mnyn* JRAS '29, 108^{12} (for the reading, cf. Cowley JRAS '29, 111 :: Grelot DAE p. 142 n. i: l. *mnyw* = PA ʿEL Pf. 3 p.pl.m.); PA ʿEL Pf. 3 p.s.m. *mny* Aḥiq 37; Imper. s.m. *mny* ATNS 26^7; Part. pass. pl.m. abs. *mmnyn* Cowl 27^9, Driv 5^5, ATNS 15^2; cf. Frah xxiii 6 (*mnytwn*), GIPP 29, SaSt 20 - **Nab** QAL Pf. 2 p.s.m. *mnyt* MPAT 64 i 11 - **JAr** QAL Part. pass.m. emph. *mnyh* MPAT 39^3 (for the reading, cf. Milik DJD ii p. 102; :: Milik DJD ii p. 103: = QAL Part. pass. s.m. + suff. 3 p.s.m.); PA ʿEL Part. pass. s.m. abs. *mmny* AMB 12^2; ITP Part. s.f. abs. *mmnyh* MPAT 38^5 (cf. Milik DJD ii sub 8 :: Fitzmyer & Harrington MPAT p. 328: = QAL Inf.) - ¶ verb QAL to count - **1)** + obj.: Cowl 21^4 (for this text, cf. Grelot VT iv 357, Porten Arch 312f.), JRAS '29, $108^{12f.}$ (v. supra) - **2)** + l_5: MPAT 64 i 11 (diff. context) - **3)** + $ʿm_4$, *mnyh ʿmy ... ksp zwzyn ʿs[ry]n* MPAT $39^{3f.}$: there is counted out with me (i.e. there is paid out to me) ... silver twenty *zwz* - PA ʿEL to appoint - **1)** + obj., *mny ʿmh gbrn 2 ʾḥrnn* Aḥiq 37: he appointed with him two other men; *gbrn kšyrn mny byn bbyʾ* ATNS 26^7: appoint capable men in the gates (v. byn_2; i.e. post them there) - 2) Part. pass. appointed: ATNS 15^2, AMB 12^2 (both instances dam. context) - a) + b_2, *gwškyʾ zy mmnyn bmdynt tšṭrs* Cowl 27^9: the hearers (v. *gwšk*) which are appointed in the province of T. - b) + byn_2, *mmnyn hww byn bgyʾ zyly* Driv 5^5: they were appointed in my domains - ITP Part. counted out > delivered: MPAT 38^5 (diff. context, cf. Milik DJD ii p. 89) - Honeyman JEA xxvi 58, 63: l. *ymn* = NIPH Impf. 3 p.s.m. (= to be allocated) in KAI 43^{10} (improb. interpret.; diff. and dam. context, cf. e.g. Cooke NSI p. 83, 85, Röllig KAI a.l.; cf. also Lipiński RTAT 251 (n. 30): l. *[š]mn* (= Sing. abs. of ($šmn_2$ = fat); highly uncert. interpret.) and Gibson SSI iii p. 136: l. *]ym*, without interpret. and v.d.Branden OA iii 248, 256f.: l. *[lʾln]m* (highly uncert. interpret.) - a prob. instance of this root in KAI 188^3 (*ymnh*), cf. Galling ZDPV lxxvii 178f., Milik DJD ii p. 97 n. 2, Lipiński OLP viii 86, Zevit MLAHE 14: = QAL Impf. 3 p.s.m. × Gibson SSI i p. 15: or = NIPH Impf. 3 p.s.m.? (cf. also Lemaire RB lxxix 569, IH p. 246) × Michaud PA 63 n. 1: = PI ʿEL Impf. 3 p.s.m. :: Albright PEQ '36, 212, ANET 321: = n.p. (cf. also Birnbaum sub Sam 1, Röllig KAI a.l.: or = n.p.), for a discussion, cf. also Sukenik PEQ '33, 154, Dir p. 72 - the *mny* in RTP 211 prob. = n.p., v. sub br_1 (l. *bny* pro *gny*) :: Caquot RTP p. 146: = QAL Part. pass. s.m. abs. (= counted, portion?)) - Milik sub DJD ii 30: the *mnyty* in DJD ii 30^{26} = QAL Pf. 1 p.s. (= to receive; highly uncert. interpret., diff. context).
v. *ʾmnh*, zmn_2, $mḥy_3$, *mmn*, mnt_2, $pʿl_1$, *škḥ*.

mnyn **OffAr** Sing. abs. *mnyn* Cowl 2^{14}, 3^{13}, ATNS 30a 5 (for this uncert. reading, cf. Porten & Yardeni sub TADAE B 8.4; for the reading problems, cf. also Segal ATNS a.l.), JAOS liv 31^4 (reading highly uncert., cf. Torrey JAOS liv 31f.); cstr. *mnyn* Cowl 29^3 (cf. Sach p. 62, Grelot DAE p. 86 (n. b), Porten JNES xlviii 163, Porten & Yardeni sub TADAE B 4.5 :: Cowl p. 107f.: = Plur. abs. of *mnh*$_2$ (cf. also Sach p. 62)), Krael 12^{14} - **Nab** Sing. cstr. *mnyn* CIS ii 161^7 - **JAr** Sing. abs. *mnyn* MPAT 36^2 (?, dam. context), 38^1; cstr. *mnyn* Mas 554^2 (?, dam. context; :: Beyer ATTM 349: = Plur. abs. of *mnh*$_2$) - ¶ subst. - **1)** number - a) *bmnyn sttry 6* Krael 12^{14}: in the amount of 6 staters - b) *bmnyn* Cowl 2^{14}, 3^{13}: completely, in full (both instances in dam. context; Porten & Yardeni sub TADAE B 4.3/4: = by amount, Grelot DAE p. 269: = according to the number) - **2)** way of reckoning; *bmnyn ʾrhwmyʾ* CIS ii 161^7: according to the reckoning of the Romans - **3)** account; *lmnyn* MPAT 38^1: on account; with the meaning 'prescription' (*ʿl mnyn* = according to the prescription) in JAOS liv $31^{3f.}$ (??, uncert. interpret., v. also supra); cf. poss. also Mas 554^2.

mnm **Ph** KAI 13^5, 14^5 - **Pun** KAI 74^6, $81^{2,3}$ - ¶ indefinite pronoun, something (cf. e.g. FR 124a, v.d.Branden GP p. 62, Segert GPP p. 109, Avishur PIB 171, 174 :: e.g. Lidzbarski Handb 305, Cooke NSI p. 29, Harr 120, Slouschz TPI p. 17: = Plur. abs. of *mn*$_3$ (= *mʾn*) :: Tomback CSL s.v., Faber FUCUS 223: = anything, nothing); + neg., nothing: KAI 14^5, 74^6; *kl mnm* KAI 13^5, $81^{2,3}$: everything whatsoever.
v. *ʿlm*$_5$.

mnsb **OffAr** Sing. cstr. *mnsb* Del 99^1 - **Nab** Sing. abs./cstr. *mnsb* MPAT 64 ii 3 (heavily dam. context; cf. also Starcky RB lxi 176) - ¶ subst. (:: Del p. 80: = QAL Inf. of *nsb*): removal; *mnsb ʿpry zy sngl* Del 99 (cf. also Vattioni Aug x 513): the removal of the debris of the Esagila.

mnʿ **Samal** QAL Impf. 3 p.s.m. *lmnʿ* (v. *l*$_1$) KAI 214^{24} (cf. Friedr 17*, Donner KAI a.l., Gibson SSI ii p. 69, 74, Dion p. 166, 192 :: Dahood Or xlv 383: = *l*$_1$ + QAL Pf. 3 p.s.m. :: Garb 262: = *l*$_5$ + QAL Inf. :: Driver AnOr xii 47: = *l*$_1$ + QAL pass. Pf. 3 p.s.m.) - **OffAr** QAL pass. Impf. 3 p.s.m. *ymnʿ* Aḥiq 136 (cf. e.g. Leand 21j, Lindenberger APA 133, 285, Kottsieper SAS 16, 144, 216 × Joüon MUSJ xviii 87f.: = ITP Impf. 3 p.s.m. × e.g. Grimme OLZ '11, 538: = OPH Impf. 3 p.s.m. :: Garbini ISNO 197: = QAL act. Impf. 3 p.s.m.) - ¶ verb QAL to deny, to withhold; + obj. + *mn*$_5$, *wšnh lmnʿ mnh* KAI 214^{24}: and may he withhold sleep from him - QAL pass. to be denied to (+ *mn*$_5$): Aḥiq 136.

mnʿbd v. *ʿbd*$_3$.

mnʿl_1 **Ph** Sing. abs. *mnʿl* Syr xlviii 403^1 (cf. e.g. Caquot ibid. 403f., Röllig NESE ii 29, 32, Cross CBQ xxxvi 488f. (n. 27), Gaster BASOR ccix 19, Avishur PIB 267, 270, UF x 32, 35, Garbini OA xx 292, Gibson SSI iii p. 89, 91 :: v.d.Branden BiOr xxxiii 13, Lipiński RSF ii 52f. (div. otherwise): l. *mn‘lm* = Plur. abs.; for the reading problems, cf. Teixidor AO i 108) - ¶ subst. bolt.

mn‘l$_2$ v. *m‘l$_1$*.

mn‘m **Ph** Sing. abs. *mn‘m* KAI 26A i 6, ii 7, 13, 16 - ¶ subst. fine food, dainty (cf. Barré Maarav iii 193: = fullness, abundance).

mnpq **Nab** Sing. + suff. 3 p.pl.m. *mnpqhm* MPAT 64 iii 5, iv 2 - **JAr** Sing. abs. *mpq*MPAT 51[10]; emph. *mpq’* MPAT 44 i 3, 52[6], *mp[q]h* IEJ xxxvi 206[5] (diff. reading, cf. also Broshi & Qimron IEJ xxxvi 209f.) - ¶ subst. - **1)** exit; *mn‘lhm wmnpqhm* MPAT 64 iii 5: their entrances and their exits (cf. MPAT 44 i 3, 64 iv 2) - **2)** egress; *wl’ m‘l wl[’] mpq ‘ly* MPAT 51[10]: there is no entrance nor egress (i.e. no right of way) against my will (cf. MPAT 52[6]), cf. also J.J.Rabinowitz Bibl xxxix 486.

mnṣbh v. *mṣbh*.

mnṣy‘h **OffAr** Sing. cstr. *mnṣy‘t* Cowl 27[5,6] (:: RES sub 361: l. *mpṣy‘t* = Sing. cstr. of *mpṣy‘h* (= breach)) - ¶ subst. middle, midst; *bmnṣy‘t byrt’* Cowl 27[6]: in the midst of the fortress (cf. Cowl 27[5]).

mnṣp **Nab** Sing. cstr. *mnṣp* J 58 - ¶ subst. of unknown meaning, cf. Jaussen & Savignac in J i p. 216 n. 1, Lidzbarski Eph iii 270.

mnr **Nab** Sing. cstr. *mnr* CIS ii 183[1] (reading uncert.) - ¶ subst. of uncert. meaning: candelabrum??

mnrt **Ph** on coin (QDAP ii 5 no. 4): *mnrt*, word (?) of unknown meaning; poss. = n.p. :: Lambert ibid. 3, 5 n. 2: poss. = transliteration with metathesis of n.p. *Mentor*.

mnrtwyn **OffAr** Ebeling Frah a.l.: l. *mnrtwyn* in Frah xv 4, as variant reading of *mllwt* (= lapsus for *mglt’*?; v. also *mglh*), *mnrtyn* = *m* (?) + *nr$_2$* (< Akkad. *narû* = inscription on stone) + *twyn* (< Akkad. *tew/mennu* = foundation (improb. interpret., prob. l. Iran. word here).

mnt$_1$ v. *mnh$_1$*.

mnt$_2$ **Ph** Sing. + suff. 1 p.s. *mnty* Syr xlviii 403[7] (cf. however Caquot Syr xlviii 406: or + suff. 3 p.s.m.? (cf. also Cross CBQ xxxvi 488f. (n. 31)) :: Lipiński RSF ii 53: or = Plur. + suff. 1 p.s. :: v.d.Branden BiOr xxxiii 13, xxxvi 202: = Plur. + suff. 1 p.s. of *mnh$_1$* (= my extracts) :: Baldacci BiOr xl 130: = QAL Pf. 1 p.s. of *mny* (= to register) :: Avishur PIB 267, 271f., UF x 32, 36: *mnty* = nomen demonis (cf. also Watson UF xiii 187 n. 45)) - ¶ subst. prob. meaning spell.

ms$_1$ **Hebr** Sing. abs. *ms* IEJ xxx 171[3] - **OffAr** Sing. + suff. 2 p.s.m. *msk* Irâq xxxi 174[3] (cf. Segal Irâq a.l. (highly uncert. interpret.); or = Sing. cstr. of *msk$_5$* (= noun of unknown meaning)) - ¶ subst. forced labour; *’šr ‘l hms* IEJ xxx 171[2f.]: who is over the corvée (cf. also Mettinger SSO 128ff., Avigad IEJ xxx 172f., FS Cross 203f., Ahlström RANR 31) - Segal ibid.: *ms* in Irâq xxxi 174[3]: = tax? (uncert. interpret.) -

Aggoula Syr lxvii 10: the *ms*ʾ in Hatra 408[8] = Sing. emph. of ms_3 (= forum), *mr ms*ʾ = master of the agora, or of ms_1, *mr ms*ʾ = publican, or rather *ms*ʾ = Sing. abs. of mst_2 (= balance, plummet), *mr ms*ʾ = architect :: As-Salihi Sumer xlv 102 (n.35): l. *mr mt*ʾ (Sing. emph. of mt_1) the lord of the town).
v. ms_2.

ms$_2$ **DA** this word (Sing. abs. or cstr. *ms*) poss. in ix a 2 (or (div. otherwise): l. *]dms* (derivative of root $dms_3$of unknown meaning?)); meaning unknown, cf. Hoftijzer DA a.l.: = Sing. abs./cstr. of ms_1 (= forced labour)? or = derivative of root *mss*?

ms$_3$ v. ms_1.

msb v. sbb_1.

msbb$_1$ v. sbb_1.

msbb$_2$ v. *mskn*.

msgd **OffAr** Sing. emph. *msgd*ʾ Cowl 44[3] - **Nab** Sing. abs. *msgd* RES 2052[1] (cf. however Milik Syr xxxv 230: l. *msgd[*ʾ*]* = Sing. emph.); emph. *msgd*ʾ CIS ii 161[1] (*[m]sgd*ʾ), 176[1], 185[1f.] (*ms[g]d*ʾ), 188[1], 218[1], RES 83[1], 676[1], 2051[1], J 82 (cf. Jaussen & Savignac J a.l.: or l. *msgdy*ʾ (= Plur. emph.)??; cf. however also Milik sub ARNA-Nab 111[1]: l. *[m]sgd*ʾ), Syr xxxv 231[1], *mšgd*ʾ CIS ii 190[1] (for the reading, cf. Chabot sub RES 1096; for the orthography, cf. Diem Or xlix 76f., l 354f.) - ¶ subst. m. - **1)** place of prostration/worship, temple: Cowl 44[3] (cf. e.g. Cowl a.l., Joüon MUSJ xviii 80, Porten Arch 154ff., Grelot DAE p. 95, Porten & Greenfield JEAS p. 123, Aggoula MUSJ xlix 514 n. 2, Porten & Yardeni sub TADAE B 7.3 × Milik Bibl xlviii 578f., Teixidor JAOS xc 544: > n.d.; cf. also Greenfield FS Cross 70) - **2)** object serving as a permanent sign of adoration of the god to whom it is dedicated - a) said of a stele: CIS ii 161[1], 185[1f.], 190[1] - b) said of an altar: RES 2051[1], 2052[1], Syr xxxv 231[1] - **3)** mentioned at the side of a niche: J 82 - in several instances indicating a monument dedicated to a god to acknowledge a favour or to obtain one - for this word, cf. also Cooke NSI p. 238, Joüon MUSJ xviii 80-83, Aggoula MUSJ xlix 514 n. 2 (on CIS ii 188 = RES 2024).

msgr **Hebr** Sing. abs. *msgr* SVT xl 10 - **OffAr** Sing. emph. *[m]sgr*ʾ FS Driver 54[2] - ¶ subst. prison.

msgrh **Samal** Plur. abs. *msgrt* KAI 215[4,8] - ¶ subst. prison.

msh Zadok WO xii 199: this subst. (= decay, failure, whithering) poss. > Akkad. *massātu*.

mswyh **Pun** Plur. abs. *mswy*ʾ*t* KAI 122[2] - ¶ subst. clothing, dress (in the context indicating the attire of a statue; cf. Levi Della Vida AfrIt vi 22, Amadasi IPT 55) - v. also $mšwt_1$.

msḥth **OffAr** Porten & Yardeni sub TADAE B 6.2: l. *msḥth* (= Sing. abs.); or l. *mwḥth/mrḥth* (cf. also Porten AN xxvii 90, 93 (n. 12)) in

Cowl 36[3] = subst. of uncert. meaning, prob. indicating some kind of garment; reading uncert., cf. Porten & Greenfield JEAS p. 118: poss. l. *mr[ṭ]th* = garment of plucked wool (cf. also Porten GCAV 259).

msy‘n **Palm** Plur. emph. *msy‘n’* Syr vii 129[9] (cf. Ingholt Syr vii 140, Rosenthal Sprache 76 :: Cantineau Gramm 113: = Sing. emph.) - ¶ subst. m. Plur. auxiliary personnel (cf. also Milik DFD 152, 188).

msyq **Hatra** Sing. abs. *msyq* 218[2] (cf. Safar Sumer xxi 36 :: Degen WO v 225f.: l. *msyq’* (= Sing. emph.; cf. also Vattionio IH a.l.) :: Aggoula MUSJ xlvii 41, 43: l. *msyqr’* (= Sing. emph. of *msyqr* (= musician)) - ¶ subst. tax collector (cf. Safar Sumer xxi 36 n. 12, Degen WO v 226 :: Vattioni IH a.l.: = musician).

msyqr v. *msyq*.

$\mathbf{msk_1}$ v. nsk_1.

$\mathbf{msk_2}$ v. nsk_1.

$\mathbf{msk_3}$ **Ph** Sing. cstr. *msk* KAI 14[3,12f.] - ¶ subst. word of uncert. meaning in the expression *bn msk ymm ’zrm* KAI 14[3,12f.]: a son of a short number of days (v. also $’zr_2$)??; *msk* derived from root - 1) *skk*, cf. e.g. Lidzbarski Handb 328, Cooke NSI p. 33, Harr 120, Röllig KAI a.l.: *msk* = (limited) number - **2)** *sky*, cf. e.g. Röllig KAI a.l., Gibson SSI iii p. 109: *msk* = (limited) number - **3)** *swk/śwk*, cf. Slouschz TPI p. 19, Gibson SSI iii p. 109: *msk* = limited number; cf. also Avishur PIB 191 :: Cazelles CISFP i 674ff.: = YIPH Part. s.m. abs. of nsk_1 (cf. also Puech RB lxxxviii 99, xcii 292) :: Lipiński RSF ii 56f. (div. otherwise): l. *bnm* (= b_2 + QAL Inf. cstr. of *nwm*) *sk* (= Sing. m. abs. of sk_2 (= deaf) :: v.d.Branden BiOr xxxvi 202: = Sing. cstr. of msk_6 (= misfortune; < Akkad.).

$\mathbf{msk_4}$ **Pun** Sing. abs. *msk* CIS i 153 (= ICO-Sard-Pu 5) - ¶ subst. of unknown meaning in an inscription on a stone hemisphere: *msk lmgn bn ḥnb‘l* = *msk* of M. the son of Ch.; Amadasi ICO a.l.: = whetstone?, Slouschz TPI p. 138: indication of a molten statue :: Harr p. 120: = mixer, mixing-vessel; cf. however Praetorius ZDMG lxvii 132 (div. otherwise): l. *mskl* (= Sing. cstr. of *mskl* (= whetstone)); cf. also CIS i sub 153.

$\mathbf{msk_5}$ v. ms_1.

$\mathbf{msk_6}$ v. msk_3.

$\mathbf{mskh_1}$ **Ph** Plur. abs. *mskt* KAI 26A iii 1, C iv 3 (cf. e.g. Dupont-Sommer RA xlii 178, Gibson SSI iii p. 53 :: Röllig KAI a.l.: = Sing. abs. (cf. also Lipiński SV 49, 50 n. h); v. also infra) - ¶ subst. molten image (cf. e.g. Dupont-Sommer RA xlii 173, 178f., Röllig KAI a.l., v.d.Branden Meltô i 77, Avishur PIB 224, Bron RIPK 24, 96f. :: Levi Della Vida RCL ’49, 285f.: = libation :: Garbini AION xli 160: = covenantal ceremony :: Gordon JNES viii 11: = Sing. abs. (= ritual?; cf. also Alt WO i 283, cf. also id. ThLZ lxxv 574: = dedication, foundation)) :: Dunand BMB viii 32 (div. otherwise): l. *klhm skt* = *kl*$_1$ + suff. 3 p.pl.m. + Plur. abs. of *skh*$_1$ (= chapel) :: Morpurgo Davies & Hawkins Heth viii 270ff., 289f. n. 15: = Plur. abs. of *mskh*$_2$ (poss. = variant of *mšqh*; = riverland) :: Del Olmo Lete AO i 289: poss. = Plur. abs. of *mskh*$_3$ (= type); on this word, cf. also Pardee JNES xlvi 141.

mskh$_2$ v. *mskh*$_1$.

mskh$_3$ v. *mskh*$_1$.

mskl v. *msk*$_4$.

mskn (< Akkad., cf. Zimmern Fremdw 47, Kaufman AIA 74, cf. also Lipiński ZAH i 69) - **OffAr** Sing. abs. *mskn* Beh 54 (cf. Ungnad ArPap p. 90 (with reserve), Greenfield & Porten BIDG p. 48f. :: Cowl a.l.: l. prob. *msbb* (= Sing. abs. of *msbb*$_2$of unknown meaning)) - ¶ subst. poor man.

mslh$_1$ **Mo** Sing. abs. *mslt* KAI 181[26] (cf. e.g. Gibson SSI i p. 82 :: Blau Maarav ii 157 (n. 60): or = Plur. abs.?) - ¶ subst. highway.

mslh$_2$ **Ph** Sing. abs. *mslt* BIFAO xxxviii 20, 21 (= RES 1847), 22 - ¶ subst. of unknown meaning (cf. Lidzbarski Handb 314); Aimé-Giron BIFAO xxxviii 22f.: = liquid measure, *mslt 1 lp 340* BIFAO xxxviii 21 (text on an alabaster vase): (containing) 1340 *m* (highly uncert. interpret., cf. BIFAO xxxviii 22: *mslt 1 p 24* (text on an alabaster vase 17 times smaller than the one just mentioned; the interpret. of Aimé-Giron ibid. 24ff., highly improb.); Renan CIS i sub 87: = *gradus* (uncert. interpret.); RES sub 1847: = equivalent of *mzlt*??, subst. belonging to the sphere of the horoscope?? (less. prob. interpret.).

msmr **OffAr** Plur. abs. *msmryn* Cowl 26[16]; cstr. *msmry* Cowl 26[12,15]; + suff. 3 p.pl.m. *msmryhm* Cowl 26[16] - ¶ subst. nail; made of bronze (Cowl 26[12,15]) or iron (Cowl 26[12]).

msn **OffAr**, cf. Frah vii 23, xiv 9 (*msn*›): shoe - cf. *mšn*$_1$.

mss$_1$ **OffAr** Qal (?) Impf. 1 p.s. ›*ms* MAI xiv/2, 66[9] (v. also infra; interpret. however uncert., cf. also Porten & Yardeni sub TADAE B 1.1) - ¶ verb Qal (?) uncert. meaning (v. also supra); Dupont-Sommer MAI xiv/2, 77: = to pay tax? (cf. Grelot DAE p. 73 (n. h)) :: Bauer & Meissner SbPAW '36, 419f.: = Qal Impf. 1 p.s. of *mss*$_2$ (= to beat, to thresh), or = Qal Impf. 1 p.s. of ›*ms*$_1$ (= ‹*ms*; = to bear, to take over); cf. also Koopmans 97.

mss$_2$ v. *mss*$_1$.

ms‘ **Pun** Sing. + suff. 1 p.s., cf. Poen 931: *mysehi* (cf. Sznycer PPP 59f., or = Sing. + suff. 1 p.s. of *mṣ*›$_2$ (= *mwṣ*›),cf. e.g. L.H.Gray AJSL xxxix 77f., FR 86b (cf. also Zadok FS Loewenstamm i 172) :: Schroed 286, 289f., 306 (div. otherwise): l. *im ischi* = ›*m*$_3$ (with demonstrative meaning) + Sing. + suff. 1 p.s. of *ḥšq* (= wish) :: J.J.Glück & Maurach Semitics ii 104: *mysehi* = Sing. + suff. 1 p.s. of *mš*› (= gift or endeavour)) - ¶ subst. voyage.

ms‘r v. *s‘r.*
ms‘rh v.Soden Or xxxv 19, xlvi 190: the Akkad. *masartu/masārtu* < Ar. *ms‘rh* = investigation (cf. also idem AHW s.v. *masārtu*), cf. however CAD s.v. *māšartu* (in *ekal māšarti*) = arsenal.
mspn **Pun** Sing. cstr. *mspn* KAI 122² - ¶ subst. prob. meaning roof, cf. Levi Della Vida AfrIt vi 23, Röllig KAI a.l.
mspnh **Ph** Sing. + suff. 3 p.s.f. *mspnth* KAI 10⁶ - ¶ subst. roof.
mspr **Ph** Sing. + suff. 3 p.pl.m. *msprm* Mus li 286^{4,7} - **Pun** Sing. cstr. *mspr* Punica xv 2^4 (v. infra); + suff. 3 p.pl.m. *msprm* RES 1543^4 (v. infra) - **Hebr** Sing. cstr. *mspr* SM 13^1 (= Frey 977) - ¶ subst. number: Mus li $286^{4,7}$, cf. *wktbt msprm ’rb‘m wšlš* RES $1543^{4f.}$: and I have written (v. ktb_1) their number 43 (i.e. the number of signs in the inscription) :: Février BAr '51/52, 262: *msprm* = Plur. abs. (= letters (of the alphabet)); cf. also Chabot sub Punica xv 2 (n.); *w‘w’ š‘nt mspr š‘t* Punica xv $2^{3f.}$: and he lived years, the number of the year(s) (prob. interpret., cf. Chabot a.l. (n.)); *lmspr ’rb‘ m’wt wtyš‘ym w’rb‘ šnh lḥrbn hbyt* SM $13^{1f.}$: in the year 494 of the destruction of the Temple (cf. also Avigad BIES xxiv 140, BLRF iii 52).
msqh v.Soden Or xxxv 19, xlvi 190: for the Akkad. *maššaktu* l. *massaqtu* = burnt offering < Ar. *msqh* (cf. also id. AHW s.v. *massaqtu*), less prob. interpret., cf. CAD s.v. *maššaktu.*
msrw‘ **Pun** Sing. abs. *msrw‘* CIS i 353^3 - ¶ subst. of unknown meaning, prob. function indication (cf. also Slouschz TPI p. 247).
msrsr v. $srsr_1$.
mst₁ **Pun** Sing. abs. *mst* Trip 51^4 (diff. context, cf. Levi Della Vida ibid. 11, 14, Amadasi IPT 134) - **OffAr** Sing. cstr. *mst* Herm 2^4, 3^8, Beh 23, ATNS 41^1 - ¶ subst. amount, complete/sufficient amount; *mst ksph zy hwh bydy* Herm $2^{4f.}$: the amount of silver which was in my hand (cf. Bresciani & Kamil Herm a.l., Grelot DAE p. 154, Porten & Greenfield JEAS p. 155, Hoftijzer SV 111 × an amount of the silver ... :: Porten & Yardeni sub TADAE A 2.2: an amount of money (cf. also Grelot RB xcv 296) :: Milik Bibl xlviii 582: a part of the silver (cf. also Gibson SSI ii p. 133f.: a due amount of the money)); *mškn mst lbš mšk 1* Herm $3^{7f.}$: skins sufficient to make one leather garment; *mst ywm’ qmḥ ’ 2* ... ATNS 41^1: the daily amount (is) two *ardab* of flour ... - preceded by the prep. k_1, *kmst zy bbty’* Beh 23: (troops) as many as were in the palaces; Levi Della Vida Or xxxiii 11f., 14, Amadasi IPT 134: *kmst* in Trip 51^4 = in the measure of of/in conformity with (context however diff.) - this subst. (Sing. emph. *mst’*) prob. also in Or lvii $35^{4,5}$, 39 ii 1, FS Volterra vi 530A 3, in the expression *tḥt mst’* (on the problems, cf. Porten Or lvii 36).
mst₂ v. ms_1.
mstr **Ph** Sing. + suff. 3 p.s.m. *mstrw* KAI 10^{15} (for the reading, cf.

e.g. Dupont-Sommer Sem iii 43f., Röllig KAI a.l., Gibson SSI iii p. 95, 99) - ¶ subst. hiding-place.

m‘bd **Amm** Plur. cstr. *m‘bd* Ber xxii 120[1] (cf. Thompson & Zayadine Ber xxii 129, BASOR ccxii 9, Dion RB lxxxii 25f., Jackson ALIA 36, 37f., 40, cf. also Briend TPOA 141, Smelik HDAI 85 :: Loretz UF ix 170: = Sing. cstr. (= object; cf. also Coote BASOR ccxl 93: = Sing. cstr. (= product, referring to contents of the bottle on which the inscription is found; cf. also Block AUSS xxii 208f., Thompson BASOR ccxlix 88f., Aufrecht BASOR cclxvi 89, sub CAI 78; cf. also Becking BiOr xxxviii 273f.: fruits/produce of agriculture, also referring to the contents of the bottle)) :: Shea PEQ '78, 108, 110: = m_{12} (= mn_5) + Sing. cstr. of *‘bd*$_3$ :: Krahmalkov BASOR ccxxiii 56, Emerton FS v.d.Ploeg 369ff., 376: = Sing. cstr. of *m‘bd* (= poem), v. also infra) - ¶ subst. work: Ber xxii 120[1] (said of vineyard, garden, etc., laid out by a king), on this text, cf. also Ahlström PEQ '84, 12.
v. *‘bd*$_3$.

m‘br **Pun** Sing. abs. *m‘br* KAI 145[7] (cf. Février Sem vi 21, Röllig KAI a.l., v.d.Branden RSF i 166, 169, Krahmalkov RSF iii 189, 193, cf. already Clermont-Ganneau RAO iii 337 n. 2 :: Clermont-Ganneau RAO iii 337: or l. *m‘rb* (= Sing. abs. of *m‘rb*$_1$ (= west)) :: Cooke NSI p. 151, 154f. (dividing otherwise): l. *‘bd* = part of n.p., cf. also Halévy RS ix 280, 285) - ¶ subst. passage: KAI 145[7], poss. to be connected *m‘br yrd b‘mq* KAI 145[7f.]: a passage leading downwards into the valley (v. however *yrd*) :: Krahmalkov RSF iii 189, 193 = mountain-pass.

m‘brh **Waw** Sing. emph. *m‘brt’* AMB 6[3f.] (for this prob. reading, cf. Naveh & Shaked AMB a.l. :: Dupont-Sommer Waw p. 15 (div. otherwise): l. *gbrt’* = Sing. emph. of *gbrh*$_2$ (= power),cf. also id. AIPHOS xi 120f. :: Gordon Or xviii 339f.: l. *gbrt’* = f. Sing. emph. of *gbr*$_2$),[6]- ¶ subst. f. ford; *m‘brt’ rbt’ d’wqynws* AMB 6[3ff.]: the great ford of the ocean.
v. *mṭ’*.

m‘gb v. *mšgb*.

m‘gh v. *‘ly*$_1$.

m‘dd v. *‘dr*$_2$.

m‘dw v. *t‘dwz*.

m‘dt v. *m‘rh*.

m‘h$_1$ - **Nab** Sing. cstr. *m‘h*, on coins, cf. Meshorer NC no. 79, 79a, 83 - **Palm** Plur. abs. *m‘yn* Sem xxxvi 89[3,5,7] (uncert. reading, cf. Gawlikowski Sem xxxvi 92) - ¶ subst. certain coin, *obolos*; *m‘h ksp* on Nab coins (v. supra): a silver *obolos* (cf. also Meshorer NC p. 51); for the problems of the Palm. text Sem xxxvi 89, cf. Gawlikowski Sem xxxvi 93ff.; the *min* Cowl 81[70,71,79,87,94,96-98,106,126,137] poss. = abbrev. of *m‘h*$_1$, cf. Driver JRAS '32, 85f. or perhaps = abbrev. of *mwbl*?;the *m*

in RES 1794[3,4,7,9], etc., etc. = abbrev. of *m‘ḥ₁*? (cf. Lidzbarski Eph ii 245) or perhaps = abbrev. of *mwbl*?; the *m* in RES 1298B 3 poss. = abbrev. of *m‘ḥ₁*? (cf. Lidzbarski Eph iii 22: or = abbrev. of *mnḥ₂*?)or perhaps = abbrev. of *mwbl*?;the *m* in REJ lxv 18[1-5] poss. = abbrev. of *m‘ḥ₁* (cf. Weil REJ lxv 21f.) or = abbrev. of *mwbl*?; the *m* in BIFAO xxxviii 58[2,3,5,6,8,9,11] poss. = abbrev. of *m‘ḥ₁* or *mwbl*;for the interpret. as abbrev. of *mwbl*,cf. also Chabot sub RES 1298, 1794; the *m* in BSh 37[3,4], 38 obv. 2, 5, rev. 5 poss. = abbrev. of *m‘ḥ₁*, cf. Naveh TeAv vi a.l.: or = abbrev. of *mnḥ₂*?,cf. also the *m* in AG 88[1,3,8]; the *m*in DJD ii 9[1], 10 i 2, 4 prob. = abbrev. of *m‘ḥ₁* (cf. Milik DJD ii a.l.), cf. also the *m* in Mas 597-599; cf. also Milik DJD ii p. 90: l. also *m*in Syr iv 245[2-8,10-14,16,17], 246[18,23,26,27] as abbrev. of *m‘ḥ₁*? (cf. also Naveh TeAv vi 188 :: Dussaud Syr iv a.l.: = symbol of *20*); the second *m* in BIFAO xxxviii 58[9] of uncert. and diff. interpret., Segal Maarav iv 73: for the first *m* l. *k* = abbrev. of *krš₁* (poss. reading) - Segal ATNS a.l.: the *m*in ATNS 37[2], 127[3], xvi 2 = abbrev. of *m‘ḥ₁* (uncert. interpret., diff. and dam. context) - Segal ATNS a.l.: the *m*in ATNS 41[4] = abbrev. of *m‘ḥ₁* (improb. interpret.) - the *m*in IEJ xxxviii 164B ii 4, 7 = abbrev. of *m‘ḥ₁*? (cf. Eshel and Mishgav IEJ xxxviii 165f. (in IEJ xxxviii 164B ii 7: l. *š 8 m*?)) - for the *m* in Frah xvi 7 as abbrev. of *m‘ḥ₁*, cf. Nyberg FP 86 - on the abbrev., cf. also Mayer Or liv 203 n. 1 - for the *m‘ḥ*, cf. also Ben-David PEQ '68, 145ff., '71, 109ff., Meshorer Proc v CJS i 83 (Hebr.) - > Akkad. *māḫăt*, *māḫt*, cf. (Sachs with) Oppenheim Or xlii 327, v.Soden xlvi 190.
v. *mlk₃*.

m‘h₂ v. *mzzh*.

m‘wn **Pun** a subst. (Sing. abs./cstr.) *m‘wn* = temple poss. in BAr '50, 111. Context however heavily dam., cf. Février BAr '50, 112.

m‘z **Ph** Sing. cstr. *m‘z* KAI 42[1] (for this reading, cf. Hall JAOS x p. cxxxvi, Chabot sub RES 1515, Röllig KAI a.l. :: CIS i sub 95: l. *‘z* = Sing. cstr. of *‘z₁*) - ¶ subst. bulwark; *‘nt m‘z ḥym* KAI 42[1]: Anat the stronghold of life.

m‘zyn **Palm** for the tribe/clan of the *bny m‘zyn* in Palmyre, as originally the tribe of the goat-herds, cf. Gawlikowski TP 38ff.

m‘zrh] **Pun** a subst. *m‘zrt* in KAI 145[15]; uncert. interpret., cf. Clermont-Ganneau RAO iii 341: = Plur. abs. of *m‘zrh* (= subsidy, aid); cf. also Halévy RS ix 284f., Röllig KAI a.l.: aids; Lidzbarski Eph i 50 (cf. however ibid. 304), Cooke NSI p. 152, 155: = Sing. abs. of *m‘zrh* (= help); cf. however Février Sem vi 27: *m‘zrt* = *m₁₂* (= *mn₅*) + *‘zrt* (pro *’zrt* = Sing. abs. of *’zrh₁* (= family)); v.d.Branden RSF i 166, 172 (div. otherwise): l. *tm* (= Sing. cstr. of *tm₁* (= perfection > generosity)) *‘zrt* (= Sing. abs. of *‘zrh* (= group of benefactors)) :: Clermont-Ganneau RAO iii 341: or l. *m‘šrt* (= Plur. abs. of *m‘šr* (= tithe)).

m‘ṭ **OffAr** Lipiński Stud 140f.: l. *[m]‘ṭ* in TH 5 obv. 2 (= AECT 57) = Sing. m. abs./cstr. of adj. *m‘ṭ* (= small); highly uncert. reading (cf. Friedrich sub TH 5, Degen NESE i 56), less prob. interpret.

m‘ṭh v. *mtnt*.

m‘ṭpt v. *mtnt*.

m‘yn **Mo** Sing. abs. *[m‘]yn* KAI 181[23] (for this reading, cf. e.g. CF 41f., Röllig KAI ii p. 178, Lipiński Or xl 335, Gibson SSI i p. 75, 81, ii p. 37 :: e.g. Lidzbarski Handb 308, 416, Cooke NSI p. 2, 13: l. *[m]yn* = Dual abs. of myn_1 (= *mym*);cf. also Segert ArchOr xxix 267, Andersen Or xxxv 83, 96: or l. *[m]yn*) - **OldAr** Plur. abs. *m‘ynn* KAI 222A 12 - ¶ subst. spring, source: KAI 181[23]; in KAI 222A 12: indicating the primeval springs, called as witnesses.

m‘kbrh v. *mkbrh*.

m‘l₁ **Nab** Sing. + suff. 3 p.pl.m. *mn‘lhm* MPAT 64 iii 5 (for the reading, cf. however also Starcky RB lxi 179) - **Palm** Sing. abs. *m‘l* CIS ii 4172[2], 4174[4], RIP 163B 3 (??; diff. reading, Gawlikowski MFP 216: l. *m‘lyk* = Plur. + suff. 2 p.s.m., Michałowski FP '59, 214 (div. otherwise): l. *‘lt* :: Gawlikowski sub RIP 163: l. *m‘l<k>* (= Sing. + suff. 2 p.s.m.)); emph. *m‘l’* RB xxxix 538[1,2]; + suff. 2 p.s.m. *m‘lk* RB xxxix 541[3], Ber ii 76[1] (for the reading, cf. Ingholt Ber iii 126), 77[1], 78[2], 85[10], Inv xii 14[2] (= RIP 51), FS Collart 161[3], etc.; + suff. 1 p.pl. *m‘ln* Ber ii 86[10]; Plur. + suff. 2 p.s.m. *m‘lyk* CIS ii 4173[2], 4204[1,2], Syr xix 156[1], Ber ii 60[1], 86[7], 91[3], 101[6], FS Miles 38[1], etc., etc. - **JAr** Sing. abs. *m‘l* MPAT 51[10]; emph. *m‘l’* MPAT 44 i 3, 52[6]; + suff. 3 p.s.m. At xiv 55[1] (diff. context; Naveh At xiv 56, 58: or = Qal Inf. + suff. 3 p.s.m. of *‘ll₁*? :: Cross IEJ xxxiii 246: = Qal Inf. of *‘ly₁* (= to go up, sc. from the grave)) - ¶ subst. - **1)** entrance; *trty ḥnwt’ ... wmn‘lhm wmnpqhm* MPAT 64 iii 5: two shops ... with their entrances and exits (cf. MPAT 44 i 3) - **2)** entrance, right of way; *wl’ m‘l wl[’] mpq ‘ly* MPAT 51[10]: there is no entrance nor egress (i.e. no right of way) against my will (cf. MPAT 52[6]); cf. J.J.Rabinowitz Bibl xxxix 486 - **3)** action of entering; *’ksdr’ dy m‘l m‘rt’ dh ‘l smlk* CIS ii 4174[4f.]: the exedra at your left side when entering this hypogee; *plg’ m‘l’ ‘l šml’* RB xxxix 538[1]: the part at the left when you enter; *šṭr’ grbyy’ dy hw m‘lk bb’ ‘l ymyn’* Ber ii 98[1]: the northern wall which is to the right when you enter the door; *’ksdr’ dnh ... m‘lyk mn bb’ ‘l ymyn’* Ber ii 60[1]: this exedra ... to the right when you enter from the door; *b’ksdr’ m‘lyk bb’ ‘l ymynk* Ber ii 101[5f.]: in the exedra to the right when you enter the door; *gwmḥy’ ’ln tlt’ ... dy bplṭy’ m‘lyk bplṭy’ ‘l smlk* Ber ii 84: these three niches ... which are in the exedra (v. *plṭy₁*), when you enter the exedra at your left side; etc. - on the use of *m‘l₁* in Palm. texts, cf. O'Connor FUCUS 358ff.

v. *‘ll₁*.

m‘l$_2$ **Ph** Sing. abs. *m‘l* KAI 14[12] - **Pun** Sing. abs. + loc. ending *m‘l’* KAI 145[14] (for the form, cf. v.d.Branden RSF i 171, Segert GPP p. 158, Pardee UF x 313 n. 98 :: FR 252a = *m*$_{12}$ (= *mn*$_5$) + *‘l*$_7$ + suff. 3 p.s.m.) - **Hebr** Sing. abs. *m‘l* AMB 14[8]; + loc. ending *m‘lh* AMB 1[3] - **JAr** Sing. emph. *m‘l’* MPAT 42[13], 44 xiii 2 (*m‘l[’]*; cf. however Beyer ATTM 312: l. *mn* (= *mn*$_5$) + *‘l[’]* (= Sing. emph. of *‘l*$_1$)) - ¶ subst. what is above; *šrš lmṭ wpr lm‘l* KAI 14[11f.]: roots below and branches above (v. *pry*$_2$); *šk[yn]t ’l lm‘l mr‘šy* AMB 14[8]: God's divine Presence above my head (on the context, cf. Naveh & Shaked AMB a.l.); *lmm‘l’ mt’* KAI 145[14]: from above to below (cf. Février Sem vi 26f.; cf. also FR 248, 253, Röllig KAI a.l., v.d.Branden GP p. 117: = *l*$_5$ + *m*$_{12}$ (= *mn*$_5$) + *m‘l’* :: e.g. Halévy RS ix 284f., Lidzbarski Eph i 46, 50, Cooke NSI p. 151, 155, RES sub 2221, Friedr 276 (div. otherwise): l. *lm* (= *l*$_5$ (indicating object) + suff. 3 p.pl.m.) *m‘l’*); *mm‘l’* MPAT 42[13]: above (dam. context); *m‘l[’]*, cf. MPAT 44 xiii 2: above (heavily dam. context); *mlm‘lh m’lh škynt ’l* AMB 1[3]: above these is God's divine Presence (on the context, cf. Naveh & Shaked AMB a.l.).

m‘lh v. *mṭlh*, *‘ly*$_1$.

m‘ln **Palm** Sing. abs. *m‘ln* CIS ii 3913 ii 66; abs. or cstr. *m‘ln* CIS ii 3913 ii 92 (dam. context); cstr. *m‘ln* CIS ii 3913 ii 24, 27 (*m‘l[n]*), 142; emph. *m‘ln’* CIS ii 3913 ii 8, 10 (cf. however Teixidor AO i 248: l. *mpqn’* = Sing. emph. of *mpqn*), 30, 32, 33, 67 - ¶ subst. entry, import; *lm‘ln ṭ‘wn g[m]l’ d 13 wlmpqn’ d 1[3]* CIS ii 3913 ii 24f.: for import the camel-load 13 *denarii* and for export 13 *denarii*, etc.; cf. *mn ṭ‘wn dhn’ ... dy ṭ‘wn gml m‘ln’ d 13 wl[mpq]n’ d 13* CIS ii 3913 ii 29f.: from a load of fat ... for a camel-load, import 13 *denarii*, for export 13 *denarii* (CIS ii sub 3913: *gml m‘ln’* = haplography for *gml lm‘ln’*, poss. interpret., cf. however *lk[l] ṭ‘wn dy gml m‘ln d 4 wmpqn d 4* CIS ii 3913 ii 66: of every camel-load import 4 *denarii*, export 4 *denarii*); cf. e.g. in the Greek par. ἑκάστου γόμο[υ καμηλικοῦ] εἰσκομισ[θέ]ντος ἐκκομισθ[έντ]ος [γόμου καμηλικοῦ] ἑκάστου (etc.).

m‘md **Palm** Teixidor sub Inv xi 28: poss. l. pro *]md/r’* in Inv xi 28[1] *[m‘]md’* = Sing. emph. of *m‘md* (= raised, erected object > altar), highly uncert. reading (cf. also Aggoula Sem xxix 112: l. *‘mwd’* (= Sing. emph. of *‘md*$_2$)).

m‘mq **DA** this noun (derivative of the root *‘mq*$_1$ (= to be deep)) poss. in xi b (cf. Hoftijzer DA a.l.).

m‘mr v. *mṭmr*.

m‘n **OldAr** Sing. abs. *m‘n* Tell F 14 - **OffAr** Sing. abs. *m‘n* KAI 226[7] - ¶ subst. intention; occurring in comb. with *l*$_5$: *lm‘n* = in order that; *wlm‘n ’mrt pmh ... tyṭb dmwt’ z’t ‘bd* Tell F 14f.: in order that the word of his mouth may please ..., he has made this statue; *wlšmw ‘my m’n ksp wnḥš ... lm‘n ... lthns ’rṣty* KAI 226[6ff.]: they did not lay with me any vessel of silver or bronze in order that you may not remove (v. *hns*) my sarcophagus (v. *ʼrṣh*).

m‘nh v. *‘ly*$_1$.

m‘s v. *‘ly*$_1$.

m‘ṣrh **Pun** word of unknown meaning *m‘ṣrt* in Karth xii 52[2]; Février & Fantar ibid.: = subst. Sing. abs. (= wall, enclosure (< root *ṣwr*; cf. also v.d.Branden RSF v 57, 60f.) :: Krahmalkov RSF iii 178, 183, 202: = variant form of *mšrt* (= Sing. abs. of *mšrt*$_1$ (= public service)); or derivative of root *‘ṣr*?; for the context, v. also *mplh*).

m‘q v. *mqm*$_1$, *mrq‘*.

m‘qʼm v. *mqm*$_1$.

m‘rb$_1$ **Hebr** Sing. abs. *m‘rb* SM 49[6], DJD ii 22[3,11], 30[3,15,16], AMB 4[13] - **Samal** Sing. abs. *m‘rb* KAI 215[13,14] - **OffAr** Sing. abs. *m‘rb* Cowl 8[5,7], 9[3], 66 xv (or cstr.?; dam. context), Krael 4[7], 9[6], 12[15], ATNS 49[3] (*[m‘]rb*); cstr. *m‘rb* Cowl 6[9], 13[15], 21[8], 25[7], Krael 3[9], 4[11], 6[7] (or abs.?; dam. context), 9[11], 10[4], 12[7,18] - **JAr** Sing. emph. *m‘rbʼ* MPAT 51[9], 52[3], *m‘rbh* IEJ xxxvi 206[4] - ¶ subst. - **1)** setting (of the sun); *m‘rb šmšʼ* Cowl 21[8]: at sunset - **2)** the west, passim; *m‘rb l* Cowl 8[7], 9[3]: to the west of (cf. *m‘rb šmš l* Cowl 13[15], Krael 4[11], 9[11], 10[4], 12[18], *lm‘rb šmš l* Cowl 6[9], Krael 3[9]); *m‘rb* DJD ii 22[3,11], 30[3,15,16]: at the west side; *m‘rbʼ* MPAT 51[9], 52[3]: at the west side (cf. IEJ xxxvi 206[4]); *mn hm‘rb* SM 49[6]: at the west side.
v. *m‘br*, *m‘rb*$_2$, *‘rb*$_{2,3}$.

m‘rb$_2$ **OffAr** Sing. abs. *m‘rb* Cowl 2[5] (v. however infra) - **Palm** Sing. emph. *m‘rbʼ* Syr vii 129[6] (cf. Milik DFD 153 :: Ingholt Syr vii 136f., 141: = Sing. emph. of *m‘rb*$_1$)- ¶ subst. (:: Leand 33f: = PA‘EL Part. act. s.m. abs. of *‘rb*$_3$ (= to mix)) - **1)** something mixed, mixture; *wʼsq ḥmr lʼ ‘tyqʼ ... ʼyty mn m‘rbʼ* Syr vii 129[4,6]: he brought old wine ... there was nothing mixed - **2)** used adverbially, *š‘rn wṭlpḥn m‘rb ʼrdbn 55* Cowl 2[5]: barley and beans together 55 *ardab* (cf. Cowl a.l. (cf. also Porten & Yardeni sub TADAE B 4.4) × Grelot DAE p. 268: = Sing. cstr. of *m‘rb*$_3$ (= load)).

m‘rb$_3$ v. *m‘rb*$_2$.

m‘rb$_4$ **Pun** Sing. abs., cf. Poen 933: *marob* (var. *rnarob*) - ¶ subst. guarantee, protection (cf. Sznycer PPP 70f., Krahmalkov Or lvii 60 (n. 14), cf. also J.J.Glück & Maurach Semitics ii 105: = promise :: Lipiński UF vi 171: = Sing. abs. of *mrḥb* (= extent, extensiveness)); cf. also Lipiński ibid. (n. 11): pro *nesubi* in Poen 943 l. *merubi* = Sing. abs. of *mrḥb* (= width, extent), highly uncert. interpret.

m‘rb$_5$ v. *‘rb*$_2$.

m‘rbh **Waw** Sing. emph. *m‘rbtʼ* AMB 6[6] - ¶ subst. ford.

m‘rby **Hatra** Sing. f. emph. *m‘rbytʼ* 408[8] - **Palm** Sing. m. abs. *m‘rby* Ber ii 112[5]; cstr. *m‘rby* Ber v 110[5] (cf. Brockelmann OLZ ’42, 369 ::

Ingholt Ber v 110, 112: = Sing. abs. used adverbially); emph. *mʿrbyʾ* CIS ii 4171[2], 4198B 3 (dam. context), 4204[1], Ber ii 102 ii 2, v 95[5]; Plur. abs. *mʿrbyyn* Ber ii 88[5], v 124[7]; emph. *mʿrbyʾ* Ber ii 99 i 2; Sing. f. emph. *mʿrbytʾ* CIS ii 4175[7], Syr xvii 271[1] - ¶ adj. western: passim; *ʾtrʾ ... mʿrby ʾksdrʾ* Ber v 110[4f.]: the place ... at the westside of the exedra (v. supra); cf. also *mʿrby wsmly* = North-western in *mnhwn smlyn tltʾ wʾḥrnʾ mʿrby wsmly* Ber ii 112[3ff.]: three of them at the north side and the other one at the North-western side (cf. Bauer with Ingholt Ber iii 127).

m ʿrh **OffAr** Sing. cstr. *mʿrt* TA-Ar 38[1] (cf. (Naveh with) Aharoni & Amiran IEJ xiv 141 (n. 13), Naveh AION xvi 31, TA a.l. :: Weippert ZDPV lxxx 182: l. *mʿdt* (meaning unknown) :: Aharoni BIES xxvii 228f.: l. *mʿdt*, poss. = mn_{12} (= mn_5) + *ʿdh* (= part of n.l.) or preferably = Sing. abs. of *ʿ*dh_1); emph. *mʿrtʾ* KAI 260[2,5] - **Palm** Sing. emph. *mʿrtʾ* CIS ii 4122[1], 4124[1], 4159[1], 4166[1] (= Inv xii 16; reading *mʿrt* in Inv xii mistaken), Ber ii 59[1], 60[1], Inv xii 1[1], RIP 24[6], 28[3], Syr lxii 273[1] (Greek par. σπηλαίῳ), etc., etc. - **JAr** Sing. emph. *mʿrth* MPAT 68[6f.]. - ¶ subst. f. (in KAI 260[5] with dem. pron. m., however, cf. also Donner KAI a.l., Lipiński Stud 159) - **1)** cave: TA-Ar 38[1] (cf. Aharoni & Amiran IEJ xiv 141f.: cave used as storehouse; cf. however Naveh AION xvi 31: cave used to live in) - **2)** > burial cave, tomb, hypogee: passim - the *mʿrt* in CIS i 248[3] (cf. also *m[ʿr]t* in CIS i 247[5f.]) prob. = n.l. (cf. CIS i sub 247, Harr 135, Slouschz TPI p. 261) - cf. poss. also μέγαρον/μέγαρα/μάγαρα, pits sacred to Demeter and Persephone, cf. PW ix s.v. *Isis* (col. 2125), xv.1 s.v. *Megaron*, PW Suppl vii s.v. Μέγαρον: < Ph. *mʿrt* (cf. however Masson RPAE 87f.) - cf. also Lipiński Stud 163: l. in KAI 262 *mʿ[rtʾ]* = Sing. emph. (poss. restoration) - Israel BiOr xxxvii 6f.: l. *mʿrt* (= Sing. cstr.) in NESE ii 66[5] (poss. reading, less prob. interpret., cf. Degen NESE ii a.l.: l. *mʿdt* = n.p.).

m ʿrkh **Hebr** Plur. abs. *mʿrkwt* AMB 4[24] - ¶ subst. battle-line; *ʾlhy mʿrkwt* AMB 4[24]: God of battles.

v. *ʿ*rb_2.

m ʿšh **Pun** Plur. cstr. *mʾsʾ*KAI 126[8]; + suff. 3 p.s.m. *mʾsm* KAI 126[8] (cf. Amadasi Guzzo StudMagr xi 32f. :: Levi Della Vida RCL '49, 405f., Röllig KAI a.l.: l. *mʾsʾ*= Plur. cstr.) - **Hebr** Plur. + suff. 3 p.s.m. *mʿyw* SM 1 (= Frey 974; lapsus for *mʿšyw*) - ¶ subst. act, deed, cf. SM 1; > merit; cf. *lpy mʾsʾ ʾbty* KAI 126[8]: because of the merits of his ancestors (cf. Lat. par. *ob merita maiorum eius*); cf. on this text also Amadasi Guzzo StudMagr xi 32f.

m ʿšn **Pun** Sing. abs. *mʿšn* RES 950D 1; cstr. *mʿšn* RES 906[1] - ¶ subst. urne, vase; cf. *mʿšn ʿṣmm* RES 906[1], *mʿšn šʿṣmm* RES 950D 1: urne for the bones of ...; Harr 135: < root *ʿ*$šn_1$ = to burn (cf. also FR 200c), uncert. interpret. - on this word, cf. also Bénichou-Safar TPC p.

187f.

m‘šr **Hebr** Sing. cstr. *m‘šr* Mas 441 - **OffAr** Sing. cstr. *m‘šr* ATNS 92[1] - ¶ subst. tithe; *m‘šr khn* Mas 441: priest's tithe; *m‘šr tqm* ATNS 92[1]: a tithe of castor oil; Aharoni sub TA-H 5: l. *m‘[šr]* (= Sing. abs.? (= tithe)) in TA-H 5[11f.], diff. and dam. context, cf. also Pardee JBL xcvii 328, UF x 304, HAHL 38.
v. *m‘zrh*.

m‘šrh v. *yšr₁*.

mp’lh v. *mplh*.

mph the Lat. *mappa* (= tablecloth) < Ph./Pun., cf. Quintilianus i 5,57 (cf. Harr 125: < root *npy₁* (= to weave), cf. also v.Selms UF iii 236, FS Gonin 191ff.)
v. *mpt*.

mpḥr v. *mpḥrh*.

mpḥrh **Ph** Sing. cstr. *mpḥrt* KAI 4[4] (:: Levi Della Vida RSO xxxix 301 (div. otherwise): l. poss. *mpḥr* = Sing. cstr. of *mpḥr* (= assembly)) - ¶ subst. assembly, totality; *mpḥrt ’l gbl* KAI 4[4]: the assembly of the gods of G.; cf. also *npḥr*.

mpṭr v. *mptḥ*.

mpl v. *mply*.

mplh **Ph** Sing. (?) cstr. *mplt* KAI 4[2] - ¶ subst. ruins; *mplt hbtm ’l* KAI 4[2f.]: the ruins of these temples - this word (Sing./Plur. abs.?) poss. also in Karth xii 52[3] (*mp’lt*) :: Février & Fantar Karth xii a.l. (div. otherwise): l. *km₂*+ *p’lt* (= variant of *p‘lt*, Sing. cstr. of *p‘lh*), cf. also Krahmalkov RSF iii 178, 183, 203.
v. *plt’*.

mplṭ **Samal** Gibson SSI ii p. 78f., 82: l. poss. *mplṭ[h]* = Sing. + suff. 3 p.s.m. of *mplṭ* (= deliverance) in KAI 215[1] (uncert. reading, dam. context; for a comparable reading, cf. already Sachau AS i 68, 70: l. poss. *nplṭ* (root *plṭ*)).

mply (or *mpl*?)the Lat. *mapalia* (gen. *mapalium*; = huts, cottages (of African aborigines)) poss. < root Pun., cf. Lewis & Short LatDict. s.v. *mapalia*; cf. also Gsell HAAN i 313 n. 6, v 219 (cf. also id. HAAN ii 17f., v 219f.: *mapalia* identical with the also attested *magalia*); cf. also *mgr₂*.

mp‘m **Pun** Sing. cstr. *mp‘m* Müll iii 155 - ¶ subst. coin? (cf. Müll ibid. 158f.).

mpṣy‘h v. *mnṣy‘h*.

mpq v. *mnpq*.

mpqd₁ **Ph** Sing. abs. *mpqd* CIS i 88[4,5] (= Kition F 1) - ¶ subst. of uncert. meaning; poss. part of a temple (cf. e.g. Cooke NSI p. 74f., cf. also Slouschz TPI p. 98, Garfinkel Lesh lii 72 (cf. also v.d.Branden FS Rinaldi 65f.: = temple court where the animals destined for the sacrifice were examined) :: Lidzbarski Handb 353: = care (cf. Amadasi Kition a.l.: this interpret. preferable; cf. CIS i sub 88: either = part of temple (portico, peristyle) or = care) :: Harr 139: = appointed work, appointed place).

$mpqd_2$ **Pun** Sing. abs. *mpqd* on coins, cf. Müll ii 3, CHC 579 no. 1-5 (v. infra) - **Hebr** Sing. abs. *mpqd* PEQ '83, 105[1] (:: Garfinkel PEQ '86, 22, Lesh lii 68ff.: = Sing. cstr.; v. also infra) - ¶ subst. prob. meaning in Pun.: administration (cf. e.g. Müll ii 10, Harr 139 :: Müll ii 10, iii 192: or *mpqd* = m_{12} (= mn_5) + *pqd* (= Sing. abs. of pqd_2 (= magistrate, officer)), cf. also Müll-Suppl 34); *mpqd lpqy* on Pun. coins = the administration of Lepcis; in the Hebr. text *mpqd* is followed by four n.p., Beit Arieh PEQ '83, 105f., 108: = roll-call, census for military purposes :: Garfinkel PEQ '86, 19ff., Lesh lii 68ff.: = guard.

mpqn **Palm** Sing. abs. *mpqn* CIS ii 3913 ii 66; emph. *mpqn*ʾ CIS ii 3913 ii 12 (*mpqn[*ʾ*]*), 18 (*mpq[n*ʾ*]*), 20, 22 (*[m]pqn*ʾ), 25, 27, 67, 95, *pqn*ʾ (lapsus) CIS ii 3913 ii 28, *mpq*ʾ (lapsus) CIS ii 3913 ii 97, *mmpqn*ʾ (lapsus, dittography, cf. Rosenthal Sprache 13, 40 n. 1) CIS ii 3913 ii 143 - ¶ subst. export - for the context and for Greek par., v. *m*ʿ*ln*.

mprnsny **Palm** f. Sing. emph. *mprsnyt*ʾ Ber v 124[5] (lapsus for *mprnsnyt*ʾ, cf. Cantineau Gramm 116, Brockelmann OLZ '42, 370; Ingholt's reading Ber v 124, 130 (*mprnsyt*ʾ) mistaken; cf. also the *mprnsnyt*ʾ in unpubl. text, cf. Ingholt Ber v 130, on the form, cf. also Nöldeke Gramm 71[1], Cantineau Gramm 116) - ¶ subst. f. (female) provider, cf. Ingholt Ber v 130ff.

mprš v. $pr\check{s}_1$.

mpršh v. mh_2.

mpšh v. *mgšh*.

mpt **Ph** word of unknown meaning *mpt* in KAI 30[1]; (Albright with) Honeyman Irâq vi 107: < root pty_2 = magistrate (cf. also H.P.Müller UF ii 236 (n. 78)); Albright BASOR lxxxiii 16 (n. 7): = miracle, sign > dignitary, cf. Hebrew *mōp̱ēt* (cf. also Gibson SSI iii p. 29: = note, ʾ*y mpt* = there is nothing of note; :: Dupont-Sommer RA xli 203: = miracle, ʾ*y mpt* = the peninsula of the miracle :: Puech Sem xxix 21: ʾ*y mpt* = there are no miracles); H.P.Müller ZA lxv 107f., 113: = PIʿEL or YIPH Part. s.m. abs. of *pwt/pyt* or pty_2 = leader (cf. also Dahood Bibl lx 433); v.Selms FS Gonin 194: = Plur. abs. of *mph* (= fabrics) :: v.d.Branden OA iii 253: = wicked man; on this word, cf. also Röllig KAI a.l., Masson & Sznycer RPC 15ff.; :: Teixidor Syr l 423: poss. l. *bpt* (without interpret.).
v. *mpt$\underset{.}{h}$*.

mpt$\underset{.}{h}$ **OffAr** Sing. cstr. *mpt$\underset{.}{h}$* A$\underset{.}{h}$iq 114, 178 - **JAr** Sing. emph. *mpt$\underset{.}{h}$h* IEJ xxxvi 206[4] - ¶ subst. - **1)** opening: A$\underset{.}{h}$iq 114, 178 (or = QAL Inf. of $pt\underset{.}{h}_1$?, cf. Kottsieper SAS 227); *mpt$\underset{.}{h}$ pmh* A$\underset{.}{h}$iq 114: the opening of his mouth (cf. also Aḥiq 178; cf. Lindenberger APA 102) - **2)** key: IEJ xxxvi 206[4] - Vattioni Aug xvi 545: l. in IRT 886a 6f.: *bymyft* = b_2 + Sing. abs. of *mptḥ* (uncert. interpret.), cf. however Levi Della Vida OA ii 81: l. *bymy/t* = deformated from *manṣabt* = *mṣbh* (highly uncert. interpret.) :: Polselli StudMagr xi 42: l. *bymyft* = b_2 + Sing. abs. of *mpt* (= dignitary) :: Vattioni AION xvi 47 (div. otherwise): l. *bymyftyr* = b_2 + Sing. abs. of *mpṭr* (= removal > demise).

mṣ v. *ršw*₁.

mṣʾ₁ **Ph** QAL Pf. 3 p.s.m. *mṣʾ* EpAn ix 5[9] (for this prob. interpret., cf. Mosca & Russell EpAn ix 21) - **Hebr** QAL Impf. 3 p.s.f. *tmṣʾ* Frey 634[5] - ¶ verb to find; *wtmṣʾ pny ʾl ḥnyh* Frey 634[5f.]: and may she find grace with God; *mṣʾ lpny phlš hmlʾk* EpAn ix 5[9]: one found before him P. the envoy (i.e. P. the envoy was in his presence) - Dupont-Sommer Sem ii 31, 38: l. *mṣʾth* (= QAL Pf. 3 p.s.f. + suff. 3 p.s.m.) in Sem ii 31 conv. 3 (cf. also Segert AAG p. 432: l. *mṣʾt* = QAL Pf. 3 p.s.f.); highly uncert. reading, cf. Rosenthal AH i/1, 13: l. *[.....]*, cf. also Grelot DAE p. 371 (n. o) - Levi Della Vida OA iv 63, 65ff.: l. *mʿṣʾ* in KAI 165[4] (= QAL Pf. 3 p.s.m.; for this division of words, cf. also Chabot sub Punica xvi 1), poss. interpret. (for other division of words, v. *ʾṣl*₂and *ktm*) - l. *mṣy[t]* (= QAL Pf. 1 p.s.) in AG 90??, reading highly uncert. - Schroed 298: *musti* in Poen 1141 = QAL Pf. 1 p.s. (highly uncert. interpret.); :: L.H.Gray AJSL xxxix 83 (div. otherwise): l. *mustine* poss. = HITP Part. s.m. + suff. 1 p.s. of *šwn* (= to enjoy) :: J.J.Glück & Maurach Semitics ii 124 (div. otherwise): l. *mustine* = HITP Part. s.m. abs. of *šny*₁ (= to be changed) - Shunnar GMA 115, 117: l. *ytmṣ* in NESE i 11[5] (= ITP Inf. (= to be delivered, to be shipped)), highly improb. reading and interpret., cf. Degen NESE i 11, 18, Grelot DAE p. 504: l. *ytmʾ* = n.p. (cf. also Shunnar CRM ii 282f., 287).
v. *zt*₃, *mṭwtw*, *nšṭ*.

mṣʾ₂ v. *zt*₃, *mwṣʾ*, *msʿ*.

mṣb **Nab** Sing. emph. *mṣbʾ* Syr xxxv 246[1] - **Palm** Sing. cstr. *mṣb* CIS ii 4064[6], 4065[4]; emph. *mṣbʾ* CIS ii 3972[1], Syr xiv 182[2], Inv xi 87[2], InvD 23[2], 33[2], RIP 143[3], AAS xv 90[1], Sem xxii 59[1], xxvii 117[2], FS Collart 327[1] (*[m]ṣbʾ*; for the restoration, cf. Starcky ibid. 328); Plur. emph. *mṣbyʾ* PNO 35c - ¶ subst. m. (bas-)relief, image in bas-relief (:: e.g. CIS ii sub 3972, Cantineau Gramm 111: = stele, cf. also Gawlikowski Ber xxi 15: = votive stele): CIS ii 3972[1], Syr xiv 182[2], Inv xi 87[2] (cf. Aggoula Sem xxix 114), InvD 23[2] (Greek par. ἀνδριάντα), PNO 35c, Sem xxii 59[1], AAS xv 90[1]; in Syr xxxv 246[1] indication of sacred stone with "cross with two bars", cf. Milik ibid. 248f.; *mṣbʾ dy ʿynʾ* InvD 33[2f.]: epithet of the god Yarḥibol, idol of the spring, cf. Ingholt & Starcky PNO p. 155, cf. also *ʾpkl[ʾ dy] mṣb ʿynʾ* CIS ii 4064[5f.], *ʾ[pk]lʾ dy mṣb ʿynʾ* CIS ii 4065[4], prob. indicating priest of Yarḥibol (cf. also

Gawlikowski TP 112f. (n. 9), 118), and cf. *mrt byt' mṣb' dy nṣb mtny* RIP 143[3]: the Lady of the temple, the idol which M. has erected; cf. also *mṣb' dy bṣr'* Syr xxxv 246[1f.]: the sacred stone (v. supra) of Bosra (cf. Milik Syr xxxv 247f.).
v. *mṣbh*, *ṣb'*$_3$.

mṣbh Ph Sing. abs. *mṣbt* CIS i 44[1] (= Kition B 40), 57[1] (= Kition B 2), 58[1] (= Kition B 3), 59[1] (= Kition B 4), 61[1] (*[m]ṣbt*; = Kition B 6), KAI 34[1] (= Kition B 45), 35[1] (= Kition B 1), 60[6] (= Kition B 5), RES 1208[2] (= Kition B 40), RDAC '84, 104[1]; cstr. *mṣbt* KAI 53[1], 60[5] (= Kition B 5), KI 15[1] (= RES 250 = DD 5), DD 9[1], 10[1], 11[1], NESE i 3[1] - **Pun** Sing. abs. *mṣbt* CIS i 6000bis 3 (= TPC 84), KAI 100[1] (*[m]ṣbt* × Alvarez Delgado ILC 179: l. *[mn]ṣbt*), *mnṣbt* KAI 163[2] (diff. context), 165[2], NP 130[1], Punica xx 1[1], BAr '21, cclx 1, Karth x 131[1], Trip 39[1], 40[1] (for this form, cf. FR 58c), *mnbṣbt* KAI 149[1] (lapsus), cf. IRT 873[1] (cf. Levi Della Vida OA ii 79, Polselli OAC xiii 237), 906[1f.] (cf. Levi Della Vida OA ii 71; dam. context): *mynṣysth* (cf. also IRTS 20[1], for this text, cf. Levi Della Vida OA ii 77, Vattioni Aug xvi 553; and cf. IRT 828[1]: *[m]y/inṣyst[h]* (cf. Levi Della Vida OA ii 78, Vattioni AION xvi 48 :: Vattioni Aug xvi 538: l. *[m]inṣisth*); on the form, cf. also Jongeling JEOL xxix 127); cstr. *mnṣbt* CIS i 159[1], KAI 78[4], cf. poss. IRT 879[1]: *mysyst* (:: Levi Della Vida OA ii 85: l. *mysysy* :: Vattioni AION xvi 41, Aug xvi 544 (div. otherwise): l. *m* (= part of n.p.) *ysy* (= Sing. + suff. 3 p.s.m. of *'š*$_1$) *sy* (= *š*$_{10}$) :: Krahmalkov RSF iii 184f.: l. *m ys* (= Sing. abs. of *'š*$_1$)+ *ysy* (= dem. pronoun)) - **Palm** Plur. abs. *mṣbt* SBS 45B 5 (Greek par. ἀνδριᾶσι; peculiar form, Gawlikowski Ber xxii 146: = < Ph.?; or lapsus for *mṣb'* = Plur. emph. of *mṣb*?;Dunant SBS p. 92 s.v. *mṣb*: = form of *mṣb*) - ¶ subst. - **1)** stele, passim (cf. Amadasi sub Kition B 1); in most instances funerary stele: CIS i 44[1], 57[1], 58[1], 61[1], KAI 34[1], 35[1], NP 130[1], Trip 39[1], 40[1], DD 9[1], etc.; in CIS i 6000bis 3, KAI 100[1] prob. indicating mausoleum on which the inscription was engraved (cf. Ferron StudMagr i 71f.); cf. also *mṣbt skr* KI 15[1], DD 10[1], 11[1]: memorial stele and *mṣbt skr bḥym* KAI 53[1]: memorial stele among the living and cf. *mṣbt qbry* NESE i 3[1]: the stele on my grave (v. *qbr*$_3$); in some instances stele of another (non-funerary) character: KAI 60[5] (v. *ḥrṣ*$_5$), 78[4] (v. *pslh*) - **2)** image, statue: SBS 45B 5 (v. however supra) - Février AIPHOS xiii 166f.: l. *mṣbt* (= Sing. abs.) in KAI 163[2] (prob. reading, interpret. of context highly uncert.) - Dérenbourg RevArch ii/xxxi 178 n. 2: l. *mnṣbt* (= Sing. cstr.) pro *mt* (= QAL Part. pass. of *mwt*$_1$?) *qbr* (= Sing. cstr. of *qbr*$_3$) in KAI 142[4] (poss. reading; for the reading of *n*, cf. also Lidzbarski Handb 435 n. 4) - Levi Della Vida OA ii 82: l. *bimst* in IRT 886h, Dréd 17 (= transcription of *mnṣbh*?),less prob. reading, cf. Vattioni Aug xvi 548f.: l. *t imst* in both instances (without interpret.) - on this word, cf. also

Bénichou-Safar TPC p. 201ff.
v. *byt*$_2$, *mptḥ*, *mṣr*$_3$.

mṣdyt v. *mṣryt*.

mṣwh **Hebr** Plur. cstr. *mṣwwt* Frey 634^{4} (dam. context) - **JAr** Sing. emph. *mṣwth* MPAT-A 30^{1,2} (or in both instances = Sing. + suff. 3 p.s.m.?, cf. also Naveh sub SM 26); Plur. + suff. 3 p.pl.m. *myṣwtwn* MPAT-A 26^{7} (= SM 32) - ¶ subst. - **1)** law, prescription: Frey 634^{4} - **2)** act of charity: MPAT- A 26^{7} - **3)** donation: MPAT-A 30^{1,2}.

mṣy v. *šnṣy*.

mṣy‘ **JAr** Sing. abs./cstr. *mṣy[‘]* Syr xlv 101^{5} (?, heavily dam. context) - ¶ subst. midst, middle.

mṣlh **OldAr** this word (Sing. abs. *[mṣ]lh*) = abyss prob. to be restored in KAI 222A 11f., for this solution, cf. already Dupont-Sommer Sf p. 35, cf. also Fitzmyer AIS 38, Degen AAG p. 10 (n. 45), ZDMG cxix 173, 175, Gibson SSI ii p. 28, 37 :: Dupont-Sommer Sf p. 17, 35, AH i/1, 3, i/2, 6, Donner KAI a.l.: l. *[ṣw]lh* = abyss.

mṣn **OffAr** word of unknown meaning in Cowl 26^{17}, for the problems of the context, v. *ršw*$_1$.

mṣ‘ v. *m’h*$_2$, *mṣ‘h*.

mṣ‘h **Samal** Sing. cstr. *mṣ‘t* KAI 215^{10} (reading of *t* uncert., for this reading, cf. e.g. Cooke NSI p. 177, Dion p. 39, 295 :: Gibson SSI ii p. 78, 84: l. prob. *mṣ‘h* = Sing. + suff. 3 p.s.f. of *mṣ‘* (= midst, middle)) - **OldAr** Sing. cstr. *mṣ‘t* KAI 216$^{9f.}$ - ¶ subst. midst, middle; *bmṣ‘t mlkn* KAI 216$^{9f.}$: in the midst of kings, cf. KAI 215^{10} (cf. also Hoffmann ZA xi 319: > of equal rank with the (other) kings; v. also supra).
v. *m’h*$_2$.

mṣ‘y **Palm** Sing. f. emph. *mṣ‘yt’* SBS 40^{6} - ¶ adj. situated in the middle: SBS 40^{6} (same text as the one quoted by Cantineau Gramm 114?).

mṣṣkwy **Pun** Sing. abs. *mṣṣkwy* KAI 101^{3} - ¶ subst. prob. function indication < Lib., cf. Lib. par. of this text: *mṣṣkw* (cf. also FR 211, Rössler with Röllig KAI a.l. (uncert. interpret.)), cf. also Chaker AION xlvi 545ff.: = the one who orders (others) to build, an architect?

mṣr$_1$ **OldAr** Sing. abs. *mṣr* KAI 202A 9, 15 - ¶ subst. siege: KAI 202A 9, 15 (for the context, v. *mḥ’*, *šym*$_1$; Donner KAI a.l.: = siege-rampart with wall) - this word (Plur. abs. *mṣrm*) poss. in KAI 5^{2}, *bmṣrm* = in distress, cf. Février Africa i 13ff., cf. however e.g. Dussaud Syr v 146, Albright JAOS lxvii 157f. (nn. 40, 42), Röllig KAI a.l., Dahood JNSL ii 21: *mṣrm* = n.g. (Egypt), cf. also Gibson SSI iii p. 21, Swiggers AO v 153.
v. *’rr*$_1$, *mlk*$_5$.

mṣr$_2$ (< Akkad., cf. Zimmern Fremdw 9, Kaufman AIA 72f., cf. also Marrassini FLEM 103) - **JAr** Sing. + suff. 3 p.s.m. *mṣrh* MPAT 52^{6} - ¶

subst. border, limit; *btḥwmh wbmṣrh* MPAT $52^{5f.}$: within its boundary and within its border.

mṣr$_3$ **Pun** Vattioni Aug xvi 545: l. *bmṣir* in IRT 886b 4f. (= b_2 + word derived from the root *ṣwr*$_1$ (= to form)), highly uncert. interpret. :: Levi Della Vida OA ii 82f. n. 40, 92: l. *bmṣt* = variant form of *mṣbt* (= *mṣbh*).

mṣr$_4$ v.Soden Or xxxv 19, xlvi 190 (cf. also id. AHW s.v. *maṣīru*): = bridge > Akkad. (less prob. interpret., cf. also CAD s.v. *maṣīru*: = a kind of toll).

mṣry v. *ʾrr*$_1$.

mṣryt **OffAr** Krael 6^5, 9^4 (for the reading, cf. Milik RB lxi 250, Ginsberg JAOS lxxiv 160, Kutscher JAOS lxxiv 237, Grelot DAE p. 243 (n. d), 250 (n. h), Porten & Greenfield JEAS p. 48, 58, Porten & Yardeni sub TADAE B 3.7/10 :: Krael a.l.: l. *mṣdyt* (= Sing. abs.) = open space?) - **Nab** BASOR cclxix 48^4 - ¶ adj. f. used adverbially: in Egyptian (sc. language); *bdpnʾ mṣryt* BASOR cclxix 48^4: in D. (as it is known, in the Egyptian language), cf. Jones, Hammond, Johnson & Fiema BASOR cclxix 48, 51, 52, cf. however id. ibid. p. 52: or = D. of Egypt or D. of the Egyptians.
v. *mqwyt*.

mqbr **Nab** Sing. emph. *mqbrʾ* RES 805^7, ADAJ xxi 143^1 (*mqb[rʾ]*, cf. Greek par. [μ]νημεῖο[ν]); Plur. abs. *mqbryn* CIS ii 350^1 - ¶ subst. m. tomb, sepulchre (cf. also Negev IEJ xxi 115); for CIS ii 350^1, cf. also Milik RB lxvi 558.

mqbrh **Nab** Sing. cstr. *mqbrt* CIS ii 181 (= RES 481); emph. *mqbrtʾ* CIS ii 196^1, RES 1090^6 (= 2033), Syr xxxv 244^1 - **Palm** Sing. emph. *mqbrtʾ* RB xxxix 539^4, CIS ii 4170, Syr xvii 355^1; Plur. abs. *mqbrn* CIS ii 4175^8, 4186^1 (cf. however Lidzbarski Eph i 205: l. prob. *mqbrt[ʾ]* = Sing. emph.), Ber v 95^9 - ¶ subst. f. - **1)** tomb, sepulchre: CIS ii 181, 196^1, RES 1090^6, cf. also *mqbrtʾ wnpšʾ dy ʿlʾ mnh* Syr xxxv $244^{1f.}$: the tomb and the monument which is upon it - **2)** burial place; *ʾyt bgwmḥʾ mqbrn št* CIS ii $4175^{7f.}$: in (each) *loculus* there are six burial places, cf. RB xxxix 539^4, Ber v 95^9; cf. also *bt mqbrtʾ* CIS ii 4170: house of burial = tomb - on this word, cf. also Negev IEJ xxi 115f., Gawlikowski Ber xxi 11f.

mqdr v. *ʿdr*$_2$.

mqdš **Ph** Sing. cstr. *mqdš* KAI $43^{3,7}$ - **Pun** Sing. abs. *mqdš* KAI 72A 1 (*mqd[š]*), 101^1, 122^2, 145^1 (:: Berger MAIBL xxxvi/2, 144, 149: = Sing. cstr.), 159^8, 172^3, CIS i 6051^2, Sem xxxviii 114^1; cstr. *mqdš* KAI $62^{2,3}$, 118^1, *myqdš*KAI 161^1; + suff. 3 p.s.m. *mqdʿšʾ* Karth xii 52^2 (for this poss. interpret., cf. Février & Fantar Karth xii a.l. :: Krahmalkov RSF iii 178, 183, v.d.Branden RSF v 56f. (div. otherwise): l. *mqdʿš* (= Sing. abs.)); Plur. abs. *mqdšm* KAI 80^1, $81^{1,2,3,4}$, $137^{1,2,5,6}$, 159^5 - **JAr**

Sing. emph. *mqdšh* MPAT-A 50^8, 51^8, 52^8 - ¶ subst. sanctuary; for *mqdš bt n.d.* and *byt mqdšh*, v. *byt$_2$* - Chabot sub Punica xiii, Amadasi sub ICO-Sard 36, Schiffmann RSF iv 50f.: l. *[mq]dš* (= Sing. abs.) in KAI 65^1 (prob. interpret.) :: Guidi with Taramelli NdS '13, 87ff., Lidzbarski Eph iii 283f., Röllig KAI a.l.: l. *[ʾ]rš* = n.p. - Avigad IEJ xxv 11f.: the *min* IEJ xxv 8^4: poss. = *mqdš* or = 40 (both interpret. uncert.).
v. *brk$_1$*.

mqwyt **OffAr** Segal ATNS a.l.: l. *mqwyt* (= Sing. abs. of *mqwyt* (= reservoir)) in ATNS 55a i 1 (highly uncert. reading and interpret.; l. *mṣryt*??).

mqwm v. *mqm$_1$*.

mqymw v. *mqmw*.

mqlw (< Akkad., cf. Cowl p. 126, Leand 43t'''', Kaufman AIA 70) - **OffAr** Sing. abs. *mqlw* Cowl 33^{10} - **Palm** Sing. emph. *[m]qlwtʾ* CIS ii 3927^3 (for the reading, cf. Milik DFD 3f. :: Chabot sub CIS ii 3927: l. *[ʾ]qlwtʾ*= Plur. emph. < Greek ἀκόλουθα (= things which are fitting, consistent (*consentanea*)) :: Cantineau Gramm 155: < Greek ἀκόλουθα = which follows) - ¶ subst. holocaust (in CIS ii 3927, Greek par. θυσίαν) - Milik DFD 147: l. *[m]qlwtʾ* in Inv x 13^6 (= Plur. emph.; uncert. reading) - Gawlikowski sub RIP 130, TP 94: l. *[mql]wtʾ* (= Sing. emph.) in CIS ii 3998B 3 (= Inv vi 5 = RIP 130), uncert. restoration, cf. e.g. Chabot CIS ii a.l.: l. *[ʾs]wtʾ* = Sing. emph. of *ʾsw* (= cure, recovery), Cantineau sub Inv vi 5: l. *[ʾsy]wtʾ* = Sing. emph. of *ʾsyw* (= cure, recovery), Lidzbarski Eph ii 297: l. *[šyzb]wtʾ* = Sing. emph. of *šyzbw* (= deliverance), Aggoula Syr liv 283: or l. *[ḥlym]wtʾ* = Sing. emph. of *ḥlymw* (= health, well-being) - Milik DFD 317: l. *mq[lwt]* (= Plur. cstr.) in Syr xii 138^4 (highly uncert. restoration, cf. also Gawlikowski TP 78: l. *mq[lwtʾ]* = Sing. emph.).

mqm$_1$ **Ph** Sing. abs. *mqm* KAI 9A 3 (dam. context), 10^{14}, 14^4; Plur. abs. *mqmm* KAI 26A i 14, 17, ii 3 - **Pun** Sing. abs. *mqm* KAI 119^{5,6} (*mq[m]*),^{7}, 122^2 (cf. Levi Della Vida AfrIt vi 18, 24f., 27, Röllig KAI a.l. (diff. context) :: Février JA ccxxxix 8 (div. otherwise): l. *-m* (= pron. suff.) *bmt* (lapsus for *btm* = *b$_2$* + Sing. abs. of *tm$_1$*)), 146^4, 173^5 (prec. by article in *ʿmmqm*, cf. FR 33, 97b, 117b, cf. also Röllig KAI a.l., Tomback JNSL v 67, Ullendorff BHL 170), Trip 51^7 (dam. context), *[m]ʿqm* Karth xii 52^3 (diff. and dam. context), *mʿqʾm*KAI 124^2 (:: v.d. Branden BiOr xxxvi 203: = Plur. abs. of *mʿq* (subst.)), cf. Poen 930: *macom*, 940: *macom* (var. *macum*); cstr. *mqm* RCL '66, 201^1 - **Hebr** Sing. abs. *mqwm*Frey 973^2 (= SM 3), 974 (= SM 1), 1002^1, SM 49^{13,26}, DJD ii 22^{2,11} (*[m]qwm*), 44^7, 49 i 1 (heavily dam. context); cstr. *mqwm*DJD ii 44^5; Plur. abs. *mqwmwt* SM 49^5; cstr. *mqwmwt*Frey 973^1 (= SM 3), 974 (= SM 1) - **Samal** Sing. cstr. *mqm* KAI 214^{14} - **Nab** Sing. cstr. *mqm* MPAT 61^{25} (= DBKP 15); + suff. 1 p.s. *mqmy*

MPAT 61[25] (= DBKP 15) - **Hatra** Sing. emph. *mqm›* 62[1], 219[1] - ¶ subst. m. - **1)** place; KAI 26A i 14, 17, ii 3, Poen 930, 940, SM 49[13,26]; for *mqwm pnyw* DJD ii 44[5], v. *pnh*$_1$; *ḥzq t mqwm* DJD ii 44[7]: encourage the place (i.e. prob. its inhabitants) - with the foll. spec. meanings: - a) sanctuary: KAI 119[7], 173[5], cf. prob. also Karth xii 52[3]; used for a synagogue, *yhy šlwm bmqwm hzh wbkl mqwmwt yšr›l* Frey 974 (= SM 1): may there be peace upon this synagogue and upon all synagogues of Israel, cf. Frey 973[1] (= SM 3) - b) tomb, grave: KAI 9A 3, 14[4] (:: Swiggers BiOr xxxvii 339: = necropolis), 214[14] (cf. Poeb 48, Gibson SSI ii p. 72, Lipiński AAALT 20, cf. also Sader EAS 163: = funerary stele), Frey 1002 - c) square, open space; *mqm š‹r hḥdš* RCL '66, 201[1]: the open space before the new gate (:: Sznycer GLECS xii/xiii 6: the place of (i.e. the place to be used for) a new gate) - d) plot: DJD ii 22[2,11] - e) poss. meaning, stand, standing-place: Hatra 219[1] (cf. Safar Sumer xxi 36 (n. 13), Degen WO v 226; cf. however Vattioni IH a.l.: = stele) - f) village; *hmqwmwt ... sbybwt byt š›n* SM 49[5]: the villages surrounding B.-Sh. - **2)** in *t ‹mdm wt hm‹q›m* (Lat. par. *columnas cum superficie*) KAI 124[2], *m‹q›m*poss. = some sort of superstructure, cf. on this text Levi Della Vida RCL '49, 401f., Röllig KAI a.l., v.d.Branden PO i 435f. - **3)** in Hatra 62[1] with uncert. meaning; Caquot Syr xxxii 265: = plate or table-top (cf. Donner sub KAI 253), Safar Sumer xi 6 n. 14, 7: = something which is erected (cf. also Vattioni IH a.l.: = stele), Safar Sumer xxi 36 n. 13, Degen WO v 226: = stand, standing-place (less prob. interpret.) - **4)** prec. by prep. *b*$_2$, *bmqm* MPAT 61[25]: in the presence of (for this prob. interpret., cf. Yadin & Greenfield sub DBKP 15) - cf. *qdm*$_3$ - Schroed 314 (cf. ibid. 291f.): restore *mucom* (= Sing. abs. of *mqm*$_1$) in Poen 948 (cf. also Krahmalkov Or lvii 60 (n. 15)) :: LHGray AJSL xxxix 77f., 80: l. *mucop* (= Sing. abs. *mqp* (< *nqp*, = border)).

v. *qwm*$_1$, *tklh*.

mqm₂ v. *qwm*$_1$.

mqm₃ v. *nqm*$_2$.

mqmh **JAr** Sing. abs. *mqmh* MPAT-A 5[5] (= SM 64) - ¶ subst. object.

mqmw **Palm** Sing. cstr. *mqmwt* RB xxxix 548[2] (cf. Milik DFD 301); emph. *mqymt›*Syr xvii 353[3] - ¶ subst. - **1)** place; *bmqmwt ‹gylw* RB xxxix 548[2]: instead of O. (cf. Gawlikowski MFP 206, cf. also Milik DFD 301: > by legal assignment of O.) - **2)** immutability, validity: Syr xvii 353[3].

mqn› **Pun** Sing. abs. *mqn›* KAI 69[15], 74[6] - **OldAr** Plur. + suff. 1 p.s. *mqny* KAI 222B 27 (cf. e.g. Fitzmyer AIS 67, 155, Degen AAG p. 58 × Donner KAI a.l., BiOr xxvii 248: = Sing. + suff. 1 p.s.) - ¶ subst. - **1)** possession: KAI 222B 27 - **2)** cattle: KAI 69[15], 74[6] - Vattioni Aug xvi 547: the *mycnei* in IRT 886f l. 8f. = form of *mqn›/h* (highly

uncert. interpret.).
v. *qny*$_1$.

mqnʾh **Pun** Sing. abs. *mqnʾt* Trip 38[1], *mqnt* KAI 138[3] - ¶ subst. - **1)** cattle: KAI 138[3] - **2)** possession; *mqnʾt ʾtmʾ* Trip 38[1]: complete possession, absolute possession (said of a tomb) - on this word, cf. also Amadasi IPT 118.

mqny v. *qny*$_1$.

mqst **OffAr** word (?) of unknown meaning and uncert. reading in FuB xiv 22 ii 2.

mqp v. *mqm*$_1$.

mqṣ **Palm** this subst. (Sing. cstr. *mqṣ*) = portion, in InvD 40[2]??, reading and interpret. highly uncert.

mqṣr **OffAr** word of unknown meaning in BSh 13; Naveh a.l.: = PUʿAL Part. s.m. abs. of *qṣr*$_2$ (= to clean, to husk), also comparing Syr *qṣrʾ* = chaff; cf. also Naveh Shn i 194.

mqṣt v. *qṣt*$_1$.

mqr **Pun** Plur. abs. *mqrm* Hofra 89[2] - ¶ subst. of uncert. meaning: well, spring?? :: Berthier & Charlier Hofra a.l.: or *mqrm* = variant of *mkrm* (= QAL Part. act. pl.m. abs. of *mkr*$_1$); for the interpret., cf. Berthier & Charlier Hofra p. 77.

mqrʾ$_1$ **OffAr** Sing. abs. *mqrʾ* Cowl 28[4,6]; emph. *mqryʾ* Cowl 7[6] (cf. Leand 54c) - ¶ subst. - **1)** solemn declaration; *mqryʾ ʿl ʾlhn mṭʾ ʿly bdynʾ* Cowl 7[6f.]: a solemn declaration is imposed upon me in the court (cf. e.g. Milik Bibl xlviii 566 (cf. also Porten & Yardeni sub TADAE B 7.2) :: Porten Arch 316, Porten & Greenfield JEAS p. 124: *mqryʾ ʿl* = a call to ... (cf. also Cowl p. 20, Grelot DAE p. 93: = an appeal to) :: Joüon MUSJ xviii 62: = legal summons near ...) - **2)** something to be read, legend; *mqrʾ ʾrmyt kznh lmbṭḥyh* Cowl 28[4f.]: a legend in Aramaic as follows: belonging to M. (cf. Cowl 28[6]), for the context, cf. Ginsberg with Porten Arch 204 n. 15.

mqrʾ$_2$ **Pun** Février JA ccxlvi 445: in CIS i 151[3] (= ICO-Sard Npu 2) pro *bn mqrʾ* (= son of M. (cf. CIS i a.l., Amadasi ICO p. 127f.)) l. *bt* (= Sing. cstr. of *byt*$_2$) *mqrʾ* (= Sing. abs. of *mqrʾ*$_2$ (= timberwork)) = a house of timberwork, small building made of wood (improb. interpret.).

mqrh v.Soden Or xxxv 18, xlvi 190: = vessel (< root *qrr*$_1$ = to be cool) > Akkad., cf. idem AHW s.v. *maqartu*, cf. also CAD s.v. *maqartu*.

mqšh v.d.Branden BO xxii 220, 222: l. *mqšh* = Sing. abs. (= (hammered) work) in RSF vii 18 no. 38.

mqtb **Nab** Plur. emph. *mqtbyʾ* BSOAS xv 13,34[3] (*[m]qtby[ʾ]*), 14,37[3], 16,46a 3 (*mqtby[ʾ]*) - ¶ subst. of uncert. meaning, cameleer? (cf. Littmann BSOAS xv 14: < Arab. *muqtib* = the man who puts the pack-saddle on the camel) - this subst. (Sing. cstr. *mqtb*) also in RB xlvii 98 i?? :: Savignac RB xlvii a.l.: l. *mqtr* (< root *qtr*) = someone attached to.

mqtr v. *mqtb*.

mr$_1$ **OldCan** Sing. abs. *mu-ur-ra* EA 269[16] - **Ph** Sing. abs. *mr* MUSJ xlv 262[1] - **DA** Sing. abs. *mr* i 13 - **JAr** Sing. emph. *m[r]›* Mas 556[2]; + suff. 3 p.s.m. *mrh* Mas 556[2]; + suff. 2 p.s.m. *mwrk*Mas 556[3] - ¶ subst. myrrh; *›nk škb b›rn zn ›sp bmr wbbdl[ḥ]* MUSJ xlv 262[1]: I am lying in this coffin, gathered in myrrh and bdellium (cf. also Nielsen SVT xxxviii 30, Zwickel ZAW ci 267ff.); for the context of DA i 13, v. *rqḥ$_1$*, cf. also Hoftijzer DA p. 212f. - Février RA xlv 146: l. *mr* (= Sing. abs.) in KAI 161[8] (cf. also Röllig KAI a.l.; for the context, v. *dr$_3$*) - v.d.Branden RSF ii 144f. : l. *mr* (= Sing. abs.) in KAI 161[7] (highly uncert. reading and interpret., cf. also Cooke NSI p. 148f., Février RA xlv 145, Röllig KAI a.l.) - the reading *mwr›* (= Sing. emph.) in CIS ii 147AB 4 (= Cowl 73) highly uncert. (cf. also Cowley a.l.: l. *s[...* (?)) - on this word, cf. also Masson RPAE 54ff., Nielsen SVT xxxviii 61.

mr$_2$ (< Akkad., cf. Zimmern Fremdw 41, Kaufman AIA 70) - **Hatra** Sing. (or Plur.) *mr›* 281[4] - ¶ subst. indicating certain tool; Safar Sumer xxvii 4 n. 3, Degen NESE iii 68, 69f.: = spade, shovel; Aggoula Syr lii 182: = something like a chisel (cf. also Vattioni IH a.l.).

mr$_3$ v. *mrḥ$_2$*.

mr$_4$ v. *mdnḥy, ms, mr›*.

mr$_5$ **OffAr** Segal ATNS a.l.: l. poss. *mr* (= Sing. cstr. of *mr$_5$* (= vessel) < Egypt.) in ATNS 52a 8, b 9 (*mr ḥlb* = a vessel of milk?), or l. *md* (= Sing. cstr. of *md$_2$* (= measure))?

mr$_6$ **Hatra** Sing. emph. *mr›* 281[4] - ¶ subst. spade, cf. Aggoula Syr lxv 208.

mr› **Samal** m. Sing. + suff. 3 p.s.m. *mr›h* KAI 215[11] (*m[r]›h*),[12,13,15,16,17]; + suff. 1 p.s. *mr›[y]* KAI 215[19] - **OldAr** m. Sing. abs. *mr›* Tell F 6 (twice; Akkad. par. *bēli, bēli-šú*; or the second *mr›* = Sing. cstr.?, cf. Kaufman Maarav iii 161, JAOS civ 572, or = lapsus for *mr›h* (haplography), cf. Greenfield & Shaffer Irâq xlv 111, Puech RB xc 596, Gropp & Lewis BASOR cclix 49); cstr. *mr›* KAI 216[3], 217[2], Tell F 16 (Akkad. par. *bēl*); + suff. 3 p.s.m. *mr›h* KAI 201[3]; + suff. 1 p.s. *mr›y* KAI 216[5,6,9], 217[3f.] (*[m]r›y*), 218[1], Tell F 17 (Akkad. par. *bēli-ia*); + suff. 2 p.pl.m. *mr›km* KAI 224[21f.]; + suff. 1 p.pl. *mr›n* KAI 232, MDAIA ciii 62; f. Sing. + suff. 1 p.s. *mr›ty* Tell F 18 (Akkad. par. *be-si*) - **OffAr** m. Sing. abs. *mr›* Cowl 47[2], Krael 1[6] (*mr[›]*), 9[19], 10[13], 12[28]; cstr. *mr›* Cowl 30[15], KAI 266[1,6], HDS 9[5]; + suff. 3 p.s.m. *mr›h* Cowl 71[7], Aḥiq 198 (*[m]r›h*), 199 (?, heavily dam. context; cf. Kottsieper SAS 13, 22, 217: l. poss. *mr›[hm]* = Sing. + suff. 3 p.pl.m.); + suff. 3 p.s.f. *mryh* NESE i 11[2]; + suff. 2 p.s.m. *mr›k* Aḥiq 192, RES 1298A 2; + suff. 2 p.s.f. *mr›ky* ANTS 58[3]; + suff. 1 p.s. *mr›y* Cowl 16[8], 39[2], 77[1] (cf. Cowl a.l. :: CIS ii sub 152: l. *rb›* = Sing. m. emph. of *rb$_2$*), Krael 13[1],

Driv 3[2,5], Herm 3[1], KAI 233[7,8,17], AE ’23, 41 no 5[4], etc., *mry* KAI 233[6] (cf. e.g. Dupont-Sommer Syr xxiv 37, Segert AAG p. 121 :: Gibson SSI ii p. 107: poss. = lapsus for *mr᾽y* :: Lidzbarski ZA xxxi 197: l. *mdy* (= n.g.) :: R.A.Bowman UMS xx 279 (div. otherwise): l. *lmdy* = Sing. + suff. 1 p.s. of *lmd*$_2$ (= information)), RHR cxxx 20[1], RES 492A 2, CIS ii 111[2f.] (?); + suff. 1 p.pl. *mr᾽n* Cowl 17[1,5], 27[2,10], KAI 273[9,12] (cf. e.g. Donner KAI a.l., Humbach AIT 8, 11f. :: In Der Smitten BiOr xxviii 310: = Sing. abs. of *mr᾽n* (= subject)), 279[1,3], etc., etc., *mrn* RES 496[2] (diff. context); Plur. + suff. 1 p.s. *mr᾽y* Cowl 37[1,17], 38[1,12], 54[10]; + suff. 3 p.pl.m. *mr᾽yhm* Driv 7[4,5] (cf. Grelot DAE p. 314 :: Driv p. 65: = Sing. + suff. 3 p.pl.m., cf. also Milik RB lxi 594), *mryhm* Cowl 34[6]; + suff. 1 p.pl. *mryn* Aeg xxxix 4 recto 3 (cf. Hoftijzer VT xii 342 × Swiggers Aeg lx 94: = Sing. + suff. 1 p.pl. :: Bresciani Aeg xxxix 4, 6: l. *mdyn* = Plur. abs. of *md*$_1$ (= garment) :: Milik Aeg xl 79, 80: l. *mdyn* = dual (?) abs. of *mdy*$_3$ (= Median)); cf. Frah i 1 (*mrwḥy*, cf. Nyberg FP 60, cf. also Toll ZDMG-Suppl viii 29), xiii 5 (*mr*),Paik 651 (*mrwḥy*), 652 (*mrwḥyn*), Nisa-b 31a 1, Nisa-c 287[9] (*mr᾽y*), Nisa-c 362[1] (*mr᾽n*), Syr xxxv 319[46], 323[57], 327[62] (*mr῾ḥy*; cf. also Benveniste Titres 18ff.), GIPP 29, 58; f. Sing. + suff. 1 p.s. *mr᾽ty* Cowl 39[1,2]; cf. Frah xii 10 (*mr῾t᾽/mr᾽t᾽*), Paik 649 (*mr᾽ty*), 650 (*mr῾t᾽*), Nisa-b 31a 2 (*mr᾽ty*), Syr xxxv 321[49] (*mr᾽ty/ml῾t᾽*; cf. also Benveniste Titres 28, 46), DEP 153[1], ChwIr 57, GIPP 28, 29, 58, SaSt 20 - **Nab** m. Sing. cstr. *mr᾽* CIS ii 235A 2, B, J 58, 59, RES 1088[1], *mr*J 392[5], RB xlii 413[1], *mry* J 17[7], 257 (??); + suff. 1 p.pl. *mr᾽n᾽* CIS ii 185[7], 199[8], 201[4], J 5[9], 30[7] (= CIS ii 200; for this reading, cf. Milik sub ARNA-Nab 79), RES 2054[3], RB xlii 415[3], IEJ xi 135[3], etc., etc., *mrn᾽* RES 2117[1], *mr᾽n* BSOAS xvi 227[3] (= RAO viii 232; for this reading, cf. Strugnell BASOR clvi 32 :: Milik with Starcky Syr xxxii 156: l. *mr᾽y* = Sing. + suff. 1 p.s. :: Littmann BSOAS xvi 228: l. *mr᾽* (= Sing. abs.) *p...* (reading uncert., = part of n.p.)) - **Palm** m. Sing. cstr. *mr᾽* CIS ii 3912[1], 3986[1], 3989[1] (= RIP 131), 3990[1], 3998B 1 (= RIP 130), SBS 25[1], RIP 126[1], 145[2], 154[2], *mr*CIS ii 4218[2] (?, v. infra), Inv xi 78[3f.] (v. infra); + suff. 3 p.s.m. *mrwhy* CIS ii 4011[6] (cf. Cantineau Gramm 102, Odeberg 279 :: CIS ii sub 4011, Díez Merino LA xxi 95: = Plur. + suff. 3 p.s.m.), Inv xi 13[7] (:: Aggoula Sem xxix 111: = Plur. + suff. 3 p.s.m.); + suff. 3 p.pl. *mrhwn* CIS ii 3946[4]; + suff. 1 p.pl. *mrn* CIS ii 3938[3], 3945[2], SBS 45[7] (Greek par. κυρίου); f. Sing. cstr. *mrt* CIS ii 3977[3] (= RIP 132A), SBS 35[1], RIP 143[3]; + suff. 3 p.pl. *mrthwn* CIS ii 3947[4] - **Hatra** m. Sing. abs. *mr᾽* 140[3], 202[6], 232d (cf. e.g. Safar Sumer xxiv 9 (n. 8), Vattioni IH a.l. :: Degen JEOL xxiii 404: l. *mr/d᾽* = n.p. (cf. also Aggoula MUSJ xlvii 10)); cstr. *mr᾽* 78 (?, cf. Vattioni IH a.l. :: Safar Sumer xi 14, Caquot Syr xxxii 271: l. *]qr/d᾽*), 140[2] (uncert. interpret., v. *kph*); emph. *mry᾽* 67[2] (cf. Safar Sumer xi 9f. (n. 32), Milik DFD 361, Vattioni IH a.l. (cf.

also Ingholt AH i/1, 47, i/2, 47) :: Caquot Syr xxxii 267: l. *mdy᾽* = Sing. emph. of mdy_3 (= Median)), 82[4], 123 (cf. Safar Sumer xviii 32 (n. 25), Milik DFD 361, Vattioni IH a.l. :: Caquot Syr xli 256: or l. *mdy᾽* = Sing. emph. of mdy_3 (= Median)), 189[3], 194[2] (cf. e.g. Safar Sumer xviii 56f., xxix 94*, Vattioni IH a.l. :: Caquot Syr xli 268: or l. *mdy᾽* = Sing. emph. of mdy_3 (= Median)), 197, 231[3], 232a 2, 233[1], 250, 272[1,2,3] (*m[r]y᾽*), 273[2,3,4,5], 274[2,4], 288c 5 (cf. also Assur 1[2], 3 ii 6 (*mry[᾽]*), 11 i 3, 16[1]); + suff. 3 p.s.m. *mrh* 223[7] (for this text, cf. e.g. Degen WO v 228; missing in Vattioni IH sub 223), 243[2], app. 5[6] (reading of *m* uncert.); + suff. 1 p.pl. *mrn* 3[1] (v. infra), 24[1], 25[2], 26[2], 29[1], 30[5], 52[4], etc., etc.; Plur. + suff. 1 p.pl. *mryn* 23[2] (cf. Caquot Syr xl 15, Aggoula Ber xviii 90, Vattioni IH a.l. :: Safar Sumer vii 182, Caquot Syr xxix 102 (div. otherwise): l. *mrynw* (= n.p.)), 25[2], 26[2], 30[6], 35[3,7], 50[3], 52[4], 53[6], app. 1 (Greek par. μαρεινος), etc., etc.; f. Sing. + suff. 3 p.s.m. *mr᾽th* 74[5] (diff. reading, cf. Milik DFD 401, 403: or l. *mry᾽th*?; cf. also Vattioni IH a.l. :: Caquot Syr xxxii 270: l. poss. *mr[.]wth* = Sing. emph. or Sing. + suff. 3 p.s.m. of *mr᾽w* (= majesty)), *mrth*, cf. Assur 25g 4, 34a 3; + suff. 1 p.pl. *mrtn* 25[2], 26[2], 29[2], 30[6], 52[4], 53[6], 74[1], 75[1], 81[3], etc. (cf. also Assur 15b 1, 27k 2, 32j 4, 34g 3), *mrt* app. 1 (lapsus) - **JAr** m. Sing. cstr. *mry* MPAT-A 42[4] (= SM 20), SM 75[1] (in Hebr. context), AMB 1[18]; Plur. abs. *mrym* (or l. *mrwm*) MPAT-A 53 (cf. Rahmani IEJ xxii 115f., Kutscher IEJ xxii 117 × Beyer ATTM 369, 736: l. *mrwm* = n.g. :: Yadin IEJ xxii 235f., Rahmani IEJ xxii 236: *mrym* = variant form of *ʿmrym* (= Plur. abs. of $ʿmr_5$ (= citizen)) :: Fitzmyer & Harrington MPAT a.l.: l. <ʿ>*mrym*); f. Sing. cstr. *mrt* MPAT 37 ii 2 (heavily dam. context), Frey 1145[1] (diff. context); + suff. 1 p.s. *mrty* AMB 8[6] - ¶ subst. m. lord, master, f. lady, mistress, passim - **1)** title of a god, *mr᾽y hdd* Tell F 17: my lord H.; *hdd skn ... mr᾽ rb mr᾽* Tell F 1, 6: H. of S. ... the great lord, the lord (Akkad. par. *bēli rabî bēli-šú*, cf. also Abou-Assaf, Bordreuil & Millard Tell F p. 30f.); *lmr᾽h lmlqrt* KAI 201[3f.]: to his lord M.; *mr᾽y rkb᾽l* KAI 216[5]: my lord R. (cf. KAI 218); *swl mr᾽ty* Tell F 18: my lady S.; *sry/w mrth* Assur 25g 4: S. his lady (cf. Assur 34a 3); cf. also *mrty* (my lady) used as epithet of an angel: AMB 8[6] - **2)** indication of a deity whose name is not mentioned - a) *mrn* = our lord in Hatrean texts: 53[1], 77[2] (*[m]rn*), 90, 101[1,2], 152, 153[1], 159, 161[1], 167, 171[2], 174[1], 175, 178[2], 195[2], 202[19], 232c 5, 247[1], 268, 298[2], 299, 311[2], 322[2], 327[2], 328; cf. also *mn dy lmrn* Hatr 311[4]: whoever belongs to our lord; *dkyr ʿwydw bmrn lṭb* Hatra 179[1f.]: may A. be remembered for good by/with our lord (poss. interpret., cf. Caquot Syr xli 205, cf. however Vattioni IH a.l.: *bmrn* poss. = b_1 (= br_1)+ *mrn* (= n.p.)); used in exclamation, *mrn dkyr ʿg᾽ br ... lṭb* Hatra 117: our lord!, may O. the son of ... be remembered for good (cf. Hatra 118, 119, 121, 147 (*[m]rn*), 149, 154, 179[1], 181, 184[1], 230[1],

253^1, 306^1, 324 (*[m]rn*), 326, 331; cf. also *mrn dkyr šmš‘qb br šmšyhb qdm mrn* Hatra 152: our lord!, may Sh. the son of Sh. be remembered before our lord); cf. also *mrn* in combination with other gods - α) in the Hatrean triad, *mrn (w)mrtn wbrmryn* (our lord, our lady and the son of our lords), cf. Hatra 26^2, 50^3, 89^2, $281^{1f.}$, $301^{1f.}$, app. 1; cf. the variant description of the triad in *mrn wmrtn wnrgwl* Hatra 81^3: our lord, our lady and Nergol (cf. Hoftijzer RelAr 52 (n. 2), cf. also (with reserves) Milik DFD 166, cf. however Safar Sumer xxi 38 n. 17, xxiv 5, Aggoula MUSJ xlvii 44, Drijvers ANR ii/8, 831, SV 408f., Tubach ISS 270ff. :: As-Salihi Sumer xxxi 75*ff. *brmryn* = Sin); cf. also the Hatrean triad combined with other gods: *mrn wmrtn wbrmryn wb‘šmyn* Hatra 25^2, *mrn wmrtn wbrmryn ›lt wsmyt› klhwn* Hatra $52^{4f.}$ (cf. also *sm›*; cf. also Hatra $75^{1f.}$, $82^{4f.}$, $151^{1f.}$), *mrn wmrtn wbrmryn w›lt wšḥrw* Hatra $74^{1f.}$, *mrn wmrtn wbrm[ryn] wšḥrw wb‘šm[yn]* Hatra $29^{1ff.}$, *mrn wmrtn wbrmryn wb‘lšmn w›tr‘t* Hatra $30^{5ff.}$, *mrn wmrtn wbrmryn wmrn[...* Hatra $53^{6f.}$, *mrn wmrtn wbrmryn wkwl ›lh kwlyh* Hatra 173^2 (our lord, our lady and the son of our lords, and every god whosoever), *mrn wmrtn wbrmryn wsmy› wgnd› d‘mh* Hatra 235^1 (our lord, our lady and the son of our lords and the standard (v. *sm›*) and the fortune of his people (v. however gd_1); on the triad, cf. also As-Salihi Sumer xxxi 75*ff. (cf. also Downey Syr xlv 105ff.) - β) in the combination *mrn wb‘šmn* Hatra 24^1 - γ) in the combination *mrn wgd› dy ›bwl›* Hatra 297^2 (our lord and the fortune of the gateway) - *mrn* identical with *šmš*?, cf. *dy bn› brmryn lšmš ›bwhy* Hatra $107^{6f.}$: which the son of our lords has built for his father Shamash (cf. also *brmryn br šmš ›lh›* Hatra 280: the son of our lords, the son of the god Shamash), cf. however *mrn wgdh wšmš wmr›th* (v. supra) *wbrh wsmyt› kwlhwn* Hatra $74^{4f.}$: our lord and his fortune and Shamash and his lady and his son and all the *insignia* (cf. Safar Sumer xi 13, Caquot Syr xxxii 270 for l. 4 and Milik DFD 401f., Vattioni IH a.l. for l. 5, Drijvers EM 160ff., CBE 41f.; v. also gd_1), cf. perhaps also Hatra 82, which mentions *šmš ›lh›* in l. 3 and the triad in l. 4f.; for the problem, cf. Aggoula Ber xviii 102, Hoftijzer RelAr 52, Drijvers ANR ii/8, 830f., EM 159ff., Tubach ISS 258ff. - *mrn* poss. not to be identified with *mrn nšr›* (Hatra 79^9, 88^2, 155^2, 232e 1)?, for this problem, cf. e.g. Hoftijzer RelAr 54, Drijvers ANR ii/8, 831, EM 161ff., EM 162ff., Tubach ISS 266ff., cf. also Aggoula MUSJ xlix 511f.; :: Caquot Syr xxix 114ff.: *mrn* = Hadad; cf. in this connection Hatra 3^1, in which *mrn* poss. indicates the Eagle, cf. Milik DFD 407 (for the reading *mrn wdy* (= *w* + dy_2), cf. Krückmann AfO xvi 141 n. 13, Ingholt AH i/1, 44, Pirenne GLECS vii 113, Milik DFD 406, Vattioni IH a.l. :: Caquot Syr xxix 90f.: l. *mrn zry* (= n.p.) :: Safar Sumer vii 173 (n. 13): l. *mr* (= Sing. cstr.) *nzry* (= Plur. emph. of nzr_2 (= ndr_2)) = lord of the vows) - b) *mrtn* = our lady: Hatra 138, cf. also

Assur 15b 1, 27k 2, 32j 4, 34g 3; for *mrtn* as member of the Hatrean triad, v. supra sub a; for the identification of *mrtn*, cf. e.g. Hoftijzer RelAr 52f., Milik DFD 387, Tubach ISS 449ff. (cf. also Caquot Syr xxix 114ff.: prob. = identical with Atargatis (less prob. interpret., cf. Hatra 29[1ff.], 30[5ff.] in which *›tr‹t(›)* is mentioned besides the triad)); in Assur *mrtn* identical with Nanai: Assur 15b 1 (cf. also Aggoula Assur p. 21) - c) *brmryn* = son of our lords: Hatra 23[2], 35[3,7], 107[7], 109, 116[2], 127, 209[1], 215[2], 222[2], 223[4], 224[5], 228[3], 232b 3, 248[2], 281[8,10], 282, 290[2,6] (v. *dyr*), cf. also Assur 15d 1; for *brmryn* as member of the Hatrean triad, v. supra sub a; for *brmryn* in Assur, cf. Aggoula Assur p. 18; used in exclamations, *bl brmryn dkyr zmq br ... lṭb* Hatra 128: Oh! Son of our lords! may Z. the son of ... be remembered for good (cf. also Hatra 271) - cf. the foll. combination, *brmryn wgndh* Hatra 125[2]: the son of our lords and his fortune; for the identification of *brmryn*, v. supra sub a; cf. prob. also the bilingual text InvD 53bis (= Hatra app. 1) *mrn wmrt<n> wbrmryn*, μαρεινος, μαρεινος, μαρι[θ]εν σ[....] μαρινος υἱ[ος ... (for the reading, cf. Milik DFD 334 (cf. Caquot Syr xxx 244f.; cf. also Milik DFD 332f., Syr xliv 302)) - **3)** *mr›* further defined by another subst. or a name, used to indicate a deity - a) *mr› šmy›* Cowl 30[15]: the Lord of Heaven (title of YHW), cf. *mry šwmy›* MPAT-A 42[4f.]: the Lord of Heaven, cf. also *mry šmyh* AMB 1[18] - b) *mr› ‹lm›* CIS ii 3912[1], 3986[1]: the lord of the world, used as title of Ba‹alshemin; cf. also *mr› ‹lm›* used independently (CIS ii 3989[1], 3990[1], SBS 25[1], RIP 126[1]), prob. also indication of Ba‹alshemin, cf. Février Rel 110ff., Díez Merino LA xxi 138f. (n. 180), Greek par. of RIP 125 (*m[r› ‹lm›]*): Διὶ ὑψίστῳ μεγίστῳ καὶ ἐπηκόῳ, cf. also Gawlikowski TP 118f., cf. however Oden CBQ xxxix 468f., 472f.: = lord of eternity; the *mry ‹lm›* in J 17[7] = Dushara? - c) *mr› kl* CIS ii 3998B 1: the lord of everything/the universe, prob. also title of Ba‹alshemin, cf. Février RES '34/1, xvf., cf. also Díez Merino LA xxi 139, cf. however Gawlikowski TP 94, sub RIP 130: l. *mr› kl [‹lm›]* = the lord of the whole world (less prob. interpret.) - d) *mr(›) byt(›)* CIS ii 235A 2, B, J 58, 59, 392[5], RES 1088[1], RB xlii 413[1]: the lord of the temple, cf. *mrt byt›* CIS ii 3977[3], RIP 143[3]: the lady of the temple (cf. also *mr byt› ›lht* J 59: the lord of the temple Ilahat, m. formula used for female deity?, or *mr* = lapsus for *mrt*?); Lidzbarski Eph iii 88: *mr(›) byt(›)* prob. not title of one single deity; cf. also on *mr›/mrt byt›*, Milik DFD 175f., 287f., Gawlikowski Syr xlvii 315, Sem xxiii 118, TP 97 (: *mrt byt›* prob. = Allât); l. prob. also *mr byt›* in Inv xi 78[3f.] (for the reading, cf. Gawlikowski Syr xlviii 423 n. 11, TP 75f., rather than *mr by{y}t›*, cf. Milik DFD 176 :: Teixidor Inv xi a.l.: l. poss. *mrbyyn›* = Sing. emph. of *mrbyn*) - e) for *mr› mytb›*, v. $mšb_1$ - f) for *mr› ›lh›*, *mrlh›*, v. *mrlh›* - g) *mr› ḥbwr* Tell F 16: the lord of Kh. (epithet of Hadad of Sikan) - **2)** designation of a human being - a) title of a king, *mrʾkm* KAI 224$^{21f.}$: your lord (i.e. your king), cf. CIS ii 185^{7}, 199^{8}, 201^{4}, 3938^{3}, 3945^{2}, KAI 232, etc., etc. (cf. in this connection the indication of the king of Aram as *ma-ri-ʾ*, prob. = Sing. abs., cf. Lipiński Stud 19 :: Oppenheim RHA v 112: Sing. + suff. 1 p.s. (cf. also Vattioni Aug ix 366f.) :: Millard & Tadmor Irâq xxxv 63 n. 22: *mariʾ* most prob. = abbrev. form of n.p.); *mrʾy mlkʾ* KAI 233^{7}: my lord the king (cf. KAI 233^{8,17}, cf. also KAI 279^{1,3}, Hatra 223^{7} (v. also supra)); cf. also *mrthwn* CIS ii 3947^{4}: their mistress (i.e. their queen); title given by a vassal to the Assyrian king: KAI 215^{11,12}, KAI 216^{6}, etc.; cf. the following combinations: - α) *mrʾ mlkn* KAI 266^{1,6} (title given to the Pharao): the lord of kings (cf. e.g. Fitzmyer Bibl xlvi 45ff., WA 233ff., Gibson SSI ii p. 114, Porten BiAr xliv 39), v. also *mlk*$_3$ - β) *mrʾ rbʿy ʾrqʾ* KAI 216$^{3f.}$: the lord of the four quarters of the earth (for this title, cf. e.g. Donner KAI ii p. 228, Gibson SSI ii p. 90); cf. also KAI 217^{2} - b) *mryʾ* as title used for the ruler of Hatra before he was called king: Hatra 67^{2}, 82^{4}, 123, 189^{3}, 194^{2}, 197, 231^{3}, 232a 2, 233^{1}, 250, 272^{1,2,3}, 273 (passim), 274^{2,4}, 288c 5 (cf. also *mrʾ* Hatra 140^{3}, 202^{6} (?), 232d (v. supra)), on this title, cf. also Segal Syr lx 108f., Aggoula Syr lxiii 272f.; in Hatra 285 l. prob. *mr[yʾ]* or *mr[ʾ]*, cf. Safar Sumer xxvii 7 (n. 16), Aggoula Syr lii 185, Degen NESE iii 75 :: Vattioni IH a.l.: l. *ml[kʾ]* = Sing. emph. of *mlk*$_3$;for the title *mryʾ/mrʾ* in Hatra, cf. Altheim & Stiehl AAW iv 265ff., Aggoula MUSJ xlvii 55f., Syr lii 196f., 203f., Milik D Sikan) - **2)** designation of a human being - a)

title of a king, *mrʾkm* KAI 224$^{21f.}$: your lord (i.e. your king), cf. CIS ii 185^{7}, 199^{8}, 201^{4}, 3938^{3}, 3945^{2}, KAI 232, etc., etc. (cf. in this connection the indication of the king of Aram as *ma-ri-ʾ*, prob. = Sing. abs., cf. Lipiński Stud 19 :: Oppenheim RHA v 112: Sing. + suff. 1 p.s. (cf. also Vattioni Aug ix 366f.) :: Millard & Tadmor Irâq xxxv 63 n. 22: *mariʾ* most prob. = abbrev. form of n.p.); *mrʾy mlkʾ* KAI 233^{7}: my lord the king (cf. KAI 233^{8,17}, cf. also KAI 279^{1,3}, Hatra 223^{7} (v. also supra)); cf. also *mrthwn* CIS ii 3947^{4}: their mistress (i.e. their queen); title given by a vassal to the Assyrian king: KAI 215^{11,12}, KAI 216^{6}, etc.; cf. the following combinations: - α) *mrʾ mlkn* KAI 266^{1,6} (title given to the Pharao): the lord of kings (cf. e.g. Fitzmyer Bibl xlvi 45ff., WA 233ff., Gibson SSI ii p. 114, Porten BiAr xliv 39), v. also *mlk*$_3$ - β) *mrʾ rbʿy ʾrqʾ* KAI 216$^{3f.}$: the lord of the four quarters of the earth (for this title, cf. e.g. Donner KAI ii p. 228, Gibson SSI ii p. 90); cf. also KAI 217^{2} - b) *mryʾ* as title used for the ruler of Hatra before he was called king: Hatra 67^{2}, 82^{4}, 123, 189^{3}, 194^{2}, 197, 231^{3}, 232a 2, 233^{1}, 250, 272^{1,2,3}, 273 (passim), 274^{2,4}, 288c 5 (cf. also *mrʾ* Hatra 140^{3}, 202^{6} (?), 232d (v. supra)), on this title, cf. also Segal Syr lx 108f., Aggoula Syr lxiii 272f.; in Hatra 285 l. prob. *mr[yʾ]* or *mr[ʾ]*, cf. Safar Sumer xxvii 7 (n. 16), Aggoula Syr lii 185, Degen NESE iii 75 :: Vattioni IH a.l.: l. *ml[k']* = Sing. emph. of *mlk*$_3$;for the title *mry'/mr'* in Hatra, cf. Altheim & Stiehl AAW iv 265ff., Aggoula MUSJ xlvii 55f., Syr lii 196f., 203f., Milik DFD 360f.; cf. also the title *mr' ʿrby'* Hatra 78: the lord of Arabia (reading however uncert., v. supra) - c) *mry'* as title used for the ruler of Assur: Assur 1^2, 3 ii 6, 11 i 3, 16^1; on this title, cf. Aggoula Assur p. 8f., 11 - d) title given to a superior: Cowl 16^8, 17^{1,5}, 27^2, Krael 13^1, Driv 3^3, 7^4, Herm 3^1, Hatra 243^2, app. 5^6; cf. *mry rby 'ysy* SM 75$^{1f.}$: my lord rabbi I.; *hgmwn' mrn* SBS 45^7: the governor our lord; *bn' mrwhy* Inv xi 13$^{6f.}$: the sons of his master; for *mr'* in epistolary style, cf. Porten Arch 284, EI xiv 167, 172 - e) with the meaning 'proprietor', 'owner', *wnksy' zy lqḥw 'tbw ... ʿl mryhm* Cowl 34^6: they gave back to their owners the goods which they took; *'yty ly 'lp ḥdh ... byny wbyn mryh* NESE i 11^2: I have a boat ... (which is) the joint possession of me and its owner (cf. Degen NESE i 14, cf. however Naveh & Shaked JAOS xci 379f.: its lord i.e. its captain) - f) with the meaning 'chief', *mr' byt'* HDS 9^5: the supervisor of the domain (:: Lipiński Stud 79f., WGAV 375, ActAntHung xxii 375f.: = landlord); cf. also the diff. *mr 'gr'* in CIS ii 4218^4: - α) = treasurer?, cf. Clermont-Ganneau Et i 122f. (*'gr'* = Sing. emph. of *'gr*$_2$ (= wages, salary), cf. CIS ii a.l.: *dispensator*) - β) = notary?, cf. Février Rel 188 n. 2 - γ) = *conductor operarum*?, cf. Milik DFD 279 - g) designation of high official connected with the law court, *sgn wmr'* Cowl 47^2, Krael 9^{19}, 10^{13}: prefect and lord; *sgn wmr' wdyn* Krael 12^{28}: prefect, lord and judge; *dyn wmr'* Krael 1^6: judge and lord (for these formulae, cf. Porten Arch 48f., cf. also Verger RGP 185, Greenfield Trans iii 89) - h) citizen; *rš mrym* (v. supra) MPAT-A 53: chief of the citizens (cf. Greek par. πρωτοπολείτης) - Sprengling AJSL xlix 54: l. *mr* (= Sing. cstr.) on seal, less prob. interpret., cf. Kaufman AAALT 53f.: *mr* = part of n.p. - a form of this word poss. also in NESE iii 29 i 3 (*]mr'[*), heavily dam. context - a form of this word prob. also in NESE ii 87^2 (*mr'[*), heavily dam. context - a form of this word (Sing. + suff. 1 p.pl., *mrn*) poss. in Hatra 229b 3, heavily dam. context - Safar Sumer xviii 60f., Caquot Syr xli 269f.: the *mrn* in Hatra 200^2 = Sing. + suff. 1 p.pl. (improb. interpret., *mrn* prob. = part of n.p., cf. Degen WO v 227, Abbadi PIH 22 (n. 2), for the context, cf. also litt. mentioned sub *mnḥ*) - Degen JEOL xxiii 415: the *mrn* in Hatra 258^2 = Sing. + suff. 1 p.pl. (for this division of words, cf. also Safar Sumer xxiv 21), less prob. interpret., *mrn* prob. = part of n.p., cf. Aggoula MUSJ xlvii 20, Vattioni IH a.l. (diff. context, v. also *ḥnn*$_2$) - Mazar, Dothan & Dunayevsky At v 34f., Mazar AOTS 225: l. poss. *mr'* (Sing. abs.) on seal, reading *n* pro *m* however also poss., reading *t* pro ' also poss. (for the interpret. as *mr'*, cf. also Mazar & Dunayevski IEJ xvii 137, Teixidor Syr xlvii 364), cf. Cross EI ix 20 n. 3;Herr sub SANSS-Hebr 29:l. *nr'* = n.p.; the reading *mrt*, however, seems most prob. - Degen NESE iii 108, Abbadi PIH 199: the diff. *mmrn* in Hatra 329 = lapsus for *mrn* (= Sing. + suff. 1 p.pl.), cf. however As-Saliḥi Sumer xxxi 185, Aggoula Sem xxvii 133: *mmrn* = n.p. (cf. also Vattioni IH a.l.: *mmrn* = n.p. or lapsus for *mrn* or lapsus for *qdm mrn*) - Dupont-Sommer sub Lach iii p. 358f.: l. *mr'* (= Sing. cstr.) in NESE i 48[3], cf. also idem AIPHOS xiii 142f.: l. *mr'[h]* (= Sing. + suff. 3 p.s.m.), Aharoni IEJ xviii 163: l. *mr'[nn]* (= Sing. + suff. 1 p.pl.), cf. however Aharoni Lesh xxxv 3ff.: l. *mlk[š]* = m_{12} (= mn_5) + n.l., cf. also Ullendorff JSS xviii 268, Degen NESE i 39ff. (for this reading, cf. also Lemaire RB lxxxi 64ff., Trans i 101f. (div. otherwise): l. *hmlk* = *h* + Sing. abs. of mlk_3);reading with *k* instead of ' more prob. :: Cross BASOR cxciii 23 (dividing otherwise): l. *hml'[k]* = *h* + Sing. abs. of *ml'*k_1 (= courier; cf. also Vattioni Aug xi 180, Albright FS Myers 26ff.) :: Lipiński Stud 144f. (div. otherwise): l. *mn* (= mn_5 (= because of)) *'[š]* (= Sing. abs. of '$š_2$) :: Albright BASOR cxxxii 46f. (div. otherwise): l. *lyh[w?] zk'* (reading uncert.) = l_1+ QAL Impf. 3 p.s.m. of hwy_1+ Sing. m. abs. of *zk'* (= zky_2);on this text, cf. also Milik LA ix 334 n. 4, Dahood CBQ xxii 407, Teixidor Syr l 430 - Vanel BMB xx 48, 54, 65: l. *mrn* (= Sing. + suff. 1 p.pl.) in BMB xx 48[14] (improb. interpret., cf. Betlyon BMB xxvi 32: l. *mgn* = n.p.) - Vattioni Aug xvi 550: l. *mra* (prob. = form of *mr'*) in Aug xvi 550 no. 55[10], less prob. interpret. - Degen JEOL xxiii 406, 416: the *m*in Hatra 233[2], 266, 267 = abbrev. of *mry'* (= Sing. emph.), prob. interpret.; cf. also Aggoula MUSJ xlvii 6ff. :: Safar Sumer xxiv 10, 23: = abbrev. of *mry'* = n.p. :: Vattioni IH a.l.: l. *m[ry']*; v. also *mrlh'* - a form of this word (*mr'[*) in Or lvii 50 i 3 (heavily dam. context) - a form of this word poss. in Atlal vii 109[9] (*mr'[*), cf. Beyer & Livingstone ZDMG cxxxvii 286: l. *mr'[y']* = Plur. emph., cf. also Aggoula Syr lxii 66, 68: l. *mr'[ny]* = Sing. m. abs. of *mr'ny* (= seignorial; less prob. reading); cf. also Cross CBQ xlviii 392: = part of n.p. - Heltzer AAALT 9ff.: the *mr'* on seal impression (AAALT 9) = Sing. abs. of *mr'* (= indication of king of Damascus), cf. also Lipiński WO xx/xxi 302 (uncert. interpret., = n.p.?). v. *'mr*$_2$, *kph*, *mhdmr*, *mrbyn*, *mrd*$_2$, *mrnr*, *p'r*, *šmym*.

mr'h$_1$ **Hebr** Plur. cstr. *mr'wt* AMB 4[27] (reading of *m* uncert.) - ¶ subst. vision.

mr'h$_2$ v. *mr'*.

mr'w v. *mr'*.

mr'lh' v. *mrlh'*.

mr'n v. *mr'*.

mr'ny v. *mr'*.

mr'š$_1$ **Ph** Sing. abs. *mr'š* KAI 11 - ¶ subst. exact meaning unknown, prob. some kind of headdress (cf. e.g. Dunand FB i 31, Friedrich OLZ '35, 348, Röllig KAI a.l. :: Dussaud Syr xvii 99: = diadem (cf. also

Gibson SSI iii p. 100: or = tiara?)).

mr'š$_2$ v. *rwšh*.

mrb v. *'mr$_1$*.

mrbh **OffAr** Lipiński Stud 34f., 51: the *mrbh* in KAI 222B 12 = Sing. abs. of *mrbh* (= quarrel; less prob. interpret., cf. e.g. Dupont-Sommer Sf p. 63, 74, 146 (with reserve), Fitzmyer AIS 17, 65, Donner KAI a.l., Lemaire & Durand IAS 73: = n.l.).

mrby **OffAr** Sing. abs. *mrby* Cowl 11^7, *mrbyt* Cowl 11^5 (acc. form?, cf. also Wesselius AION xxx 265ff. :: Cowl p. 34, Leand 57d: = lapsus for Sing. emph. *mrbyt'* or for Sing. + suff. 3 p.s.m. *mrbyth* :: Joüon MUSJ xviii 8: = defective writing of Sing. emph. *mrbyt'* :: Muffs 202f.: = calque from Akkadian); cstr. *mrbyt* Cowl 11^3; emph. *mrbyt'* Cowl 10^6; + suff. 3 p.s.m. *mrbyth* Cowl 10^{4,8,11,12,14,15,16,18}, 11^{8,9}, 65 i 1 - ¶ subst. f. interest; *mrbyt kspk* Cowl 11$^{3f.}$: the interest of your silver, cf. Cowl 10^{4,8}, etc. etc.

mrbyn **Palm** m. Sing. + suff. 3 p.s.m. *mrbynh* CIS ii 4478B 3 (cf. CIS ii a.l. × Ingholt Ber v 131: = Sing. + suff. 3 p.s.f.); f. Sing. + suff. 3 p.s.m. *mrbyth* CIS ii 4479A 4 (cf. Starcky MUSJ xxxviii 133 n. 4, Milik DFD 176 :: CIS ii a.l. (div. otherwise): l. *mr* (= Sing. cstr. of *mr'*)+ *byth* (= Sing. + suff. 3 p.s.m. of *byt$_2$*));+ suff. 3 p.pl. *mrbythn* Syr xlviii 422c 2,

mrbythwn RB xxxix 542 ii 9 - **Hatra** m. Sing. emph. *mrbyn'* 203^2 - ¶ subst. one who feeds, upbringer, educator (f. poss. wet-nurse, cf. however Ingholt Ber v 131f.) - Gawlikowski RIP a.l.: the *mrbt[']* in RIP 172^3 poss. = f. Sing. emph. of *mrbyn* (uncert. reading and interpret.). v. *byt$_2$*, *mr'*.

mrb' v. *rb'$_1$*.

mrg v. *šmrg*.

mrd$_1$ **OffAr** QAL Pf. 3 p.s.f. *mrdt* Driv 5^6; 3 p.pl.m. *mrdw* Cowl 27^1, Driv 7^1 - ¶ verb to revolt.
v. *mrd$_2$*.

mrd$_2$ **OffAr** Plur. emph. *mrdy'* Cowl 80^9 (for this prob. reading, cf. Porten & Yardeni sub TADAE A 5.5 :: Cowl a.l.: l. *mry'* = lapsus for *mr'y* (= Sing. + suff. 1 p.s. of *mr'*;cf. also Leand 54k) :: Driver JRAS '32, 83: l. *mry'* = Plur. emph. of *mr'*?), Beh 1, 3, 5 (*mr[d]y'*), 7, 8 (*m[rd]y'*), 44 (cf. Akkad. parallels *ni-ik-ru-tu*, *ni-ik-ru-ú-tu*, *ni-ik-ru-tú*, *[ni-]ik-ru-tu$_4$*; cf. also CAD s.v. *nakru*) - ¶ subst. (cf. Leand 44 n''': *qattāl*-form; or rather = QAL Part. act. of *mrd$_1$*?)rebel.

mrdh v. *mddh*.

mrh$_1$ **OffAr** Sing. abs., cf. Warka 6, 9: *mi-ir-ra-'* - ¶ subst. poison (cf. e.g. Gordon AfO xii 108f., 117, Or ix 36, Landsberger AfO xii 254, Dupont-Sommer RA xxxix 39, 44, cf. however Pardee ZAW xci 409ff.: = gall).

mrh$_2$ v. *mlh.*
mrwm v. *mr*ʾ, *rwm*$_1$.
mrwr **Hebr/JAr** this word (Sing. abs. *mrwr*) = bitter herb, to be read in Mas 549? or l. *srwr* (= frame??), cf. Yadin & Naveh Mas a.l.
mrwšh v. *rwšh.*
mrwšt v. *rwšh.*
mrwt **OffAr** Sing. abs. *mrwt* FuF xxxv 173^{3,4} - ¶ subst. rule, kingship - Naveh sub SM 65: l. *mrwt* (= Sing. abs. (= master, lord)) in SM 65^{2}? (uncert. interpret.; cf. also *mrw[* SM 66^{1}; cf. however Vincent & Carrière RB xxx 595f., 600, Fitzmyer & Harrington sub MPAT-A 7 and 8: l. resp. *mrwt[h]*, *mrw[th]* = n.p.; on these texts, cf. also Sukenik ASPG 76).
mrzḥ **Ph** Sing. abs. *mrzḥ* KAI 60^{1}; cstr. *mrzḥ* IEJ xxxii 120 - **Pun** Sing. cstr. *mrzḥ* KAI 69^{16} (cf. e.g. Cooke NSI p. 121, Röllig KAI a.l. :: v.d.Branden BMB xiii 94f.: = Yiph Part. s.m. cstr. of *rzḥ* (= to shout) = the one who presents the food at the sacred banquet, i.e. the servant at this banquet; cf. also CIS i sub 165) - **OffAr** Sing. emph. *mrzḥ*ʾ RES 1295^{3} - **Nab** Sing. cstr. *mrzḥ* RES 1423^{2}, IEJ xiii 113^{2}; emph. *mrzḥ*ʾ IEJ xi 134 i (for the reading, cf. Naveh IEJ xvii 188 :: Negev IEJ xi a.l. (dividing otherwise): l. *dnh drt*ʾ (= *dnh*$_3$ (= *znh*) + Sing. emph. of *drh*$_1$ (= house)), cf. also Levinson NAI 150), IEJ xi 137^{2} (for the reading, cf. Naveh IEJ xvii 188 (cf. also Starcky SDB vii 919) :: Negev IEJ xi 137: l. *srwt*ʾ, *bny srwt*ʾ = religious fraternity, military unit or tribe), IEJ xiii 113^{2} (for the reading, cf. Porten Arch 182 n. 126 :: Negev IEJ xiii a.l.: l. *srwt*ʾ, v. supra), ADAJ xxi 139^{2} (= CIS ii 476; :: CIS ii a.l.: l. *mn* (= *mn*$_5$) + *qdm* (= *qdm*$_3$)) - **Palm** Sing. abs. *mrzḥ* RTP 301 (cf. however Milik DFD 159: l. *mrzḥ*ʾ = Sing. emph.); emph. *mrzḥ*ʾ CIS ii 3980^{2} (*[m]rzḥ*ʾ), RTP 27, 30-34, 35 (*mrzḥ[*ʾ*]*), Syr xxxvi 105 no. 12 (v. infra) - ¶ subst. - **1)** religious feast: KAI 60^{1} (cf. e.g. Clermont-Ganneau BAIBL '98, 354ff., RAO ii 390 n. 2, iii 28f., iv 344f., v 210, Lidzbarski sub KI 52, Röllig KAI a.l., Dombrowski HThR lix 294, Gibson SSI iii p. 149, Elayi RCP 32, cf. however e.g. Lidzbarski Handb 317, Cooke NSI p. 94f., Harr 146, Eissfeldt OA v 168: or = name of a month? (on KAI 60^{1}, cf. also Elayi SCA 112)) - **2)** religious guild, confraternity: CIS ii 3980^{2}; *mrzḥ* ʾ*lm* KAI 69^{16}: confraternity in honour of the gods; *mrzḥ* ʿ*bdt* ʾ*lh*ʾ RES 1423$^{2f.}$: the confraternity of the divine Obodat; *mrzḥ dwšr*ʾ ʾ*lh g*ʾ*y*ʾ IEJ xiii 113$^{2f.}$: the confraternity of Dushara the god of G. (:: Negev IEJ xiii 113: the offering of sacrifices to D. ...); *mrzḥ b*ʿ*ltk* Syr xxxvi 105 no. 12: the confraternity of B. (cf. du Mesnil du Buisson BiOr xvii 238, TMP 365; v. also *b*ʿ*l*$_2$ for *b*ʿ*ltk*), cf. RTP 301 (v. supra); *mrzḥ šmš* IEJ xxxii 120: the confraternity of Sh. (cf. also Avigad & Greenfield ibid. 126ff.); *rb mrzḥ*ʾ ADAJ xxi 139$^{1f.}$ (= CIS ii 476), IEJ xi 134 i (for the reading, cf. Naveh IEJ xvii 188, v. also

supra), RTP 27, 30-33, 35: the chief of the confraternity (cf. also Milik DFD 110, 221f., 227ff.); *rbnwt mrzḥ›* RTP 34: the presidency of the confraternity; *bny mrzḥ(›)* IEJ xi 137[2] (for the reading, v. supra), xiii 113[2] (for the reading, v. supra), RTP 301 (v. supra): the members of the confraternity; *ksp mrzḥ›* RES 1295[2f.]: the funds of the confraternity (cf. Hoftijzer RelAr 28 n. 12 × Porten Arch 179, 184: the contribution (in silver) to the confraternity × Lidzbarski Eph iii 120f., Grelot DAE p. 371ff.: the contribution (in silver) for the feast); for the *mrzḥ* in Pun. texts, cf. Clermont-Ganneau RAO iii 28ff., iv 343, Amadasi Guzzo SSMA 118; for the *mrzḥ* in general, cf. e.g. Clermont-Ganneau RAO iv 380f., v 210, Starcky Syr xxvi 59ff., 62ff., Virolleaud GLECS ix 41, du Mesnil du Buisson TMP 466f., Eissfeldt OA v 166ff., MiOr xv 217ff., Hoftijzer RelAr 28f., Porten Arch 179ff., Teixidor Syr xlviii 458, Miller AnOr xlviii 44ff., Milik DFD 118ff., 141ff. (cf. also Seyrig AAS i 32ff., Schlumberger PNO p. 101ff., Collart AAS vii 73f., Teixidor Sumer xx 77ff., Pope FS Stinespring 190ff., AAS xxix/xxx 141ff., Greenfield ActAntHung xxii 451ff., WGAV 451ff., FS Cross 71, Aggoula Sem xxii 55, L'Heureux HThR lxvii 266ff., 270ff., RACG 206ff., Catastini FS Bresciani 113ff., Zayadine FS Horn 469ff., Spronk BAAI 196ff., Meyer UF xi 603f., O'Connor JANES xviii 70ff., Milano SSMA 78, King EI xx 98*ff, Lipiński EI xx 130*ff - cf. also *mrzḥ* (Sing. abs.) in Sem xxxviii 52[1], in unknown West-Sem dialect; or = fraud?, cf. however Bordreuil & Pardee Sem xxxviii 65ff. - cf. also *mzrḥ*.

mrzḥw **Palm** Sing. cstr. *mrzḥwt* CIS ii 3970[1], Syr vii 129[2], InscrP 31[1] (cf. also Gawlikowski Syr xlviii 414), Syr xlviii 413[1] (= DFD 271); + suff. 3 p.s.m. *mrzḥwth* CIS ii 3919[4], Syr xii 120[4] (= Inv ix 26; Greek par. [σ]υμποσιάρχ[ης]) - ¶ subst. membership of a confraternity; in the comb. *rbnwt mrzḥwt-* CIS ii 3919[4], 3970[1], Syr vii 129[2], xlviii 413[1], InscrP 31[1]: the presidency of a confraternity - in Syr xii 120[3f.] l. prob. *[rbnwt] mrzḥwth*, cf. Gawlikowski TP 75 :: Cantineau sub Inv ix 26 (cf. also idem Syr xii 120): l. *bmrzḥwth*.

mrḥ$_1$ v. *mrr*$_1$.

mrḥ$_2$ **OldAr** Plur. emph. *mrḥy›* KAI 222B 31 (v. however infra) - ¶ subst. (?) of unknown meaning, cf. e.g. Dupont-Sommer Sf p. 80f., 146, Fitzmyer AIS 69, Donner KAI a.l., cf. however Lipiński Stud 38 (div. otherwise): l. *mr* (= Sing. cstr. of *mr*$_3$) *ḥy›* (= Sing. emph. of *ḥy*$_1$)= the bitterness of life (= euphemistic expression to avoid mentioning the king's death; improb. interpret., cf. also Lemaire & Durand IAS 138).

mrḥb Beyer & Livingstone ZDMG cxxxvii 286f., 293: l. *mrḥbh* (= Sing. + suff. 3 p.s.m. of *mrḥb* (= width, extent poss. > temple territory)), or *mdḥbh* (= Sing. + suff. 3 p.s.m. of *mdbḥ* (= altar, cf. also Aggoula Syr lxii 66f.)) in Atlal vii 109[4]; both interpretations uncert., reading of *m* uncert., cf. Cross CBQ xlviii 392 (n. 9): l. *›rḥbh* = n.l. (prob. reading

and interpret.) :: Livingstone Atlal vii a.l.: l. *mytbh* (= Sing. + suff. 3 p.s.m. of *mytb* (=*mšb*$_1$)).
v. *m‘rb*$_4$.

mrḥṣ **Hebr** (?) Sing. abs. *mrḥṣ* Frey 562^2 - ¶ subst. bath, bathhouse.

mrḥq **OffAr** Sing. abs. *mrḥq* Cowl 6^{22}, 8^{23,25}, 14^{14}, 25^{20}, Krael 5^8 - ¶ subst. withdrawal, renunciation: Krael 5^8; *spr mrḥq* Cowl 6^{22}, 8^{23,25}, 14^{14}, 25^{20}: act of renunciation, document of withdrawal, cf. Driver PEQ '55, 93, J.J.Rabinowitz Law 21ff., VT xi 74f., Verger RGP 84f., 88, 134, Porten Arch 203 n. 10, Muffs 17, 25ff., 159, 163.

mrḥth v. *msḥth*.

mrṭ **OffAr** Itp Part. s.m. abs. *mtmrṭ* Sach 76 i 5 - ¶ verb Itp to be pulled out; *mtmrṭ bkb›* Sach 76 i 5 (v. *kb*): pulled out by thorns (said of wool), cf. Lidzbarski Eph iii 256, Greenfield Or xxix 100.

mrṭth v. *msḥth*.

mry **OffAr** Sing. abs. *mry* ATNS 42a 3, 4, 91^{1,2,3} - ¶ subst. indicating a liquid measure prob. related to the *mry* (abbrev. *m*)found in Nisa texts (< Iran., cf. Diakonov & Livshitz Nisa-b p. 39, 60 n. 29), on this measure (cf. also Diakonov & Livshitz Nisa-c p. 138, Chaumont JA cclvi 14), related to Greek μάρις (cf. also Segal sub ATNS 42).

mryr v. *mrr*$_2$.

mryš v. *rwšh*.

mryšt v. *rwšh*.

mrk$_1$ v. *mlk*$_3$.

mrk$_2$ v. *mrkbh*.

mrkbh **Ph** Sing. + suff. 3 p.s.m. *mrkbty* Syr xlviii 396^2 (cf. Caquot Syr xlviii 398, 403, Gaster BASOR ccix 19, Röllig NESE ii 30, Liverani RSF ii 37, Lipiński RSF ii 51, Avishur UF x 30, 33, PIB 267f., de Moor JEOL xxvii 111 :: v.d.Branden BiOr xxxiii 13: = Plur. + suff. 3 p.s.m. :: Gibson SSI iii p. 89f.: = Sing. + suff. 1 p.s. :: Garbini OA xx 288, 292 (div. otherwise): l. *mrk* (= Plur. cstr. of *mrk*$_2$ (= hiding-place)) *bty* (= Sing. + suff. 3 p.s.m. of *byt*$_2$),for this word division, cf. also Teixidor Syr li 321, AO i 108) - ¶ subst. chariot.

mrlh› (< *mr›* (= Sing. cstr. of *mr›*) *›lh›* (= Plur. emph. of *›lh*$_1$)) - **Hatra** *mr›lh›*325^3 (for reading problems, cf. Tubach ISS 404 (n. 709)), *mrlh›* app. 4^3, 8 (prob. non Hatrean text, cf. Aggoula MUSJ xlvii 47ff., Teixidor Syr li 335, cf. also Milik DFD 399), cf. also Assur 15b 2 - ¶ compound subst. the lord of the gods (cf. also in Palm. *mr› ›lh›* RIP 154^2), on the form, cf. also Brock BSOAS xxxvi 133; *qdm mr›lh› klhwn* Hatra 325$^{2f.}$: before the lord of all the gods; *mrlh› dqrqbš* Hatra app. 4$^{3f.}$: M. of Q.; *syn mrlh›* Hatra app. 8 (v. supra): Sin the lord of the gods; for this divine epithet, cf. Walker NumChr vi/xviii 170f. (type B), Caquot Syr xl 12, Teixidor Syr xli 275f., Altheim & Stiehl AAW v/1, 80, Gawlikowski Syr xlvii 316f., Vattioni Aug xi 442ff., Milik DFD

347ff., Aggoula Sem xxvii 140ff., Tubach ISS 386ff., for the *mrlh>* in Sumatar, cf. also Segal AnSt iii 115f., BSOAS xvi 15; in Assur 15b 2 = epithet of Bel (cf. also Aggoula Assur p. 16, 22) - Milik DFD 400: l. *[m]rlh>* in Hatra 17 (poss. interpret., cf. however e.g. Vattioni IH a.l.: l. *w>lh>* (cf. also Tubach ISS 405), v. also *>lh*$_1$ and cf. Aggoula Sem xxvii 141) - Milik DFD 399, Vattioni IH a.l.: l. *mrlh>* in Hatra 48 (less prob. reading, cf. also Aggoula Sem xxvii 141, Tubach ISS 405f. (n. 718)) - v. also *kmr*$_2$.

mrm **Pun** Sing. abs. *mrm* KAI 161[6] (for the reading, cf. e.g. Février RA xlv 144, Roschinski Num 112, 115) - ¶ subst. height, or 'elevated part': KAI 161[6], for the diff. context, cf. Roschinski Num 112, 115, cf. also Février RA xlv 144 (v. however *khn*$_1$) :: v.d.Branden RSF ii 144: > story, floor; uncert. and diff. context.

mrmh **OldAr** Plur. abs. *mrmt* KAI 224[22] (cf. e.g. Dupont-Sommer BMB xiii 29, 31, 35, Sf p. 146, Donner KAI a.l., Fitzmyer AIS 119, 155, Gibson SSI ii p. 51, 55 × Degen AAG p. 49 (n. 12), ZDMG cxix 175, Wesselius AION xxx 265 (n. 2): = Sing. abs. (the interpret. of Rössler with Degen AAG p. 49 n. 12: *marmay-at* > *marmāt* highly uncert. (cf. Degen ZDMG cxix 175), cf. e.g. Hebr. *mirmā*, pl. *mirmōt*)) - ¶ subst. treachery.

mrnr **Pun** Vattioni AION xvi 45f., Aug xvi 551: the *marnar* in IRT 889[3] (= KAI 179) = Sing. abs. of *mrnr* (< Greek μα&/ρμαρ-) = marmor (uncert. interpret.; in the comb. *balars σumarnar* :: Krahmalkov JAOS xciii 62ff. (div. otherwise): l. *śumar* (= n.p.) *nar* (= Sing. abs. of *n<r*$_3$) :: Levi Della Vida RSO xxxix 311 (div. otherwise): l. *šumar* (= QAL Part. act. s.m. abs. of *šmr*$_1$) *nar* (part of n.p.; cf. also id. OA ii 87, cf. also Sznycer GLECS x 100f., Röllig KAI ii p. 341, Polselli OAC xiii 237f., 239) :: Février JA ccxli 467f. (div. otherwise): l. *marn* (= Sing. + suff. 1 p.pl. of *mr>*)+ *a r* (= abbrev. of n.p. *Alexander*); cf. also Röllig sub KAI 179).

mrs v.Soden Or xxxv 18, xlvi 190: *mrs* (= to squash) > Akkad. (cf. CAD s.v. *marāsu* B, cf. also v.Soden AHW s.v. *marāsu* sub C 2); poss. interpret.

mr<$_1$ **JAr** QAL Part. act. + encl. pron. pers. 1 p.s. *mr<n>* Syr xlv 101[3] (heavily dam. context) - ¶ verb QAL to be ill; *mr<n>* Syr xlv 101[3]: I am ill (v. however supra; cf. Milik Syr xlv 103).
v. *mrq*$_3$, *šmrg*.

mr<$_2$ v. *mrq*$_3$.

mr<$_3$ v. *mrq*$_3$.

mrp> v. *rp>*$_1$.

mrṣ$_1$ **Pun** Plur. abs. *mrṣm* KAI 141[5] - ¶ subst. of uncert. meaning; prob. measure of length (of unknown extent), cf. Février BAr '51/52, 118ff., Röllig KAI a.l.

mrṣ₂ v. *šmrg*.

mrq₁ **Hebr** QAL Inf. cstr. *mrq* DJD ii 30[5,24] - **OffAr** QAL (?) Impf. 3 p.s.m. *ymrq* Samar 3[6] - **JAr** PA‹EL Inf. *mrq›* MPAT 45[4], 52[12] - ¶ verb QAL to clear: Samar 3[6] (a contract); *›ḥr›ym w‹rbym lmrq lpnk ›t hmkr hzh* DJD ii 30[24]: a guarantee and surety to clear in your favour this sale of land (> sold plot; v. infra, v. *mkr₂*; cf. also DJD ii 30[5f]) - PA‹EL to clear; *kl dy ›yty ly wdy ›qnh ›ḥr›yn w[‹rbyn] lmrq› wlqym› zbnh dk qdm[kn]* MPAT 52[11f.]: everything which belongs to me and which I shall acquire are a guarantee and surety to clear and confirm that purchase for you (cf. Milik Bibl xxxviii 260, 263, cf. also J.J.Rabinowitz Bibl xxxv 202f., Yaron BASOR cl 27, Koffmahn DWJ 175, Geller BSOAS li 316 > Akkad., cf. v.Soden Or xxxv 18, xlvi 190, cf. id. AHW s.v. *marāqu(m)* D 2, cf. also the related Akkad. words *murruqu* (fine, cleared (of claims)), *mumarriqānu* (with variants: *mumarraqānu, murqannu, murraqu, murruqūnu, murruqu*) = guarantor (cf. also CAD s.v. *mumarriqānu*), on this point, cf. however Greenfield RAI xxv 473. v. *mrq₃*.

mrq₂ v. *mrq₃*, *šmrg*.

mrq₃ **OldAr** Sing. abs. *mrq* Tell F 9 (Akkad. par. *murṣi*), KAI 222A 29 (cf. e.g. Brekelmans VT xiii 226ff., Fitzmyer AIS 48, Rosenthal ANET 660 (n. 5), Gibson SSI ii p. 31, 40 (cf. also Degen AAG p. 37, 46, Gropp & Lewis BASOR cclix 50) :: Brekelmans VT xiii 227: or = oppression (< root *rqq₁*) :: Rosenthal ANET 660 n. 5: or rather = some kind of ominous noise, crushing? :: Dupont-Sommer Sf p. 45, 146: = QAL Part. act. s.m. abs. of *mrq₁* (= to destroy; cf. id. AH i/2, 5, Fitzmyer JAOS lxxxi 197, Donner KAI a.l.; cf. also Segert AAG p. 440: = conqueror) :: Lipiński Stud 49: = QAL Part. act. s.m. abs. of *mrq₂* (= *mr‹₁* (= to be sick))) - **OffAr** Sing. abs. *mr‹*Cowl 75[1,3] (= CIS ii 150; reading of *r* in both instances uncert.; heavily dam. context); emph. *mr‹›*KAI 279[2] (v. infra) - ¶ subst. illness: Tell F 9; for the context of KAI 222A 29, v. *hn₃*; in KAI 279[2] prob. also to be interpreted as illness, cf. Altheim & Stiehl EW ix 193, 198, ASA 274, Coxon ZDMG cxxix 17 :: Dupont-Sommer JA ccxlvi 24, 33, Koopmans 176, Kutscher, Naveh & Shaked Lesh xxxiv 132: > evil (cf. also Levi Della Vida Editto 21f., 33, Donner KAI a.l., Garbini Kand 8f., 18: = evil) :: Rosenthal EI xiv 97*f.: = Sing. emph. of *mr‹₃* (= trouble; < root *r‹‹* = to break); cf. also Koopmans 176: interpret. of *mr‹* in KAI 279[2] as derivative of the root *r‹‹* (= to be evil) less prob.

mrq₄ cf. Akkad. *murraqu, murruqu* = guarantor sub *mrq₁*.

mrq₅ cf. Akkad. *murruqu* = fine, cleared (of claims) sub *mrq₁*.

mrqdn **Hatra** Sing. emph. *mrqdn›* 202[19] (or = Plur.?, cf. Vattioni IH a.l.) - ¶ subst. of uncert. meaning, poss. function indication; Aggoula Ber xviii 100f., MUSJ xlvii 41: = mourner, one who utters elegies ::

Teixidor Sumer xxi 87*, Vattioni IH a.l.: = dancer; cf. also Milik DFD 272: prob. = some sort of sacred functionary (poss. < Iran.; highly uncert. derivation).

mrqḥ v. *rqḥ*$_1$.

mrqn cf. Akkad. *murqannu*, *murruqūnu* = guarantor sub *mrq*$_1$.

mrq῾ **Ph** Sing. cstr. *mrq῾* KAI 38[1] - ¶ subst. indicating certain object in the comb. *mrq῾ ḥrṣ* = a *mrq῾* made of gold; Kellermann ZDPV lxxxvi 30ff., Gibson SSI iii p. 132: = mace, cf. however Harr 147: = beaten plate (cf. CIS i sub 90) :: Cooke NSI p. 75f.: = plating (sc. of a statue) :: Lidzbarski sub KI 31, Röllig KAI a.l., Butterweck TUAT ii 602: prob. = bowl (cf. also Caquot & Masson Syr xlv 306) - the same word has been restored in RES 453 (Sing. abs. *mrq[῾]*), cf. RES sub 453, cf. however Honeyman Irâq vi 104: reading *mrq῾* impossible, l. *m῾q*= parapet, low wall, breastwork (a low wall of masonry serving to demarcate the *temenos*; cf. H.P. Müll VT xxi 562), cf. also (Weippert with) Kellermann ZDPV lxxxvi 24ff.: reading *mrq῾* impossible, l. *m῾[*, followed by one unrecognizable sign and Teixidor Syr xlix 433: l. *mrq[ ]* or *mbq[ ]* (cf. however id. ibid. 413).

mrr$_1$ **OffAr** QAL Impf. 2 p.s.m. *tmr* Aḥiq 148 (:: Epstein ZAW xxxiii 231: l. *tmr[ḥ]* = QAL Impf. 2 p.s.m. of *mrḥ*$_1$ (= to be rash)) - ¶ verb QAL to be bitter.

mrr$_2$ **OffAr** m. Sing. abs. *[m]ryr* Aḥiq 105; f. Sing. emph. *mrrt᾽* Aḥiq 105 (:: Wensinck OLZ '12, 53: = Sing. emph. of *mrrh* (= bitterness; cf. also Kottsieper SAS 20, 75f., 217)) - ¶ adj. bitter; *ṭ῾mt ᾽p z῾rrt᾽ mrrt᾽ w[ṭ῾m]᾽ ḥsyn wl᾽ ᾽yty zy [m]ryr mn ῾nwh* Aḥiq 105: I have tasted the bitter medlar (?, v. *z῾rrh*) and the taste is strong (?, v. *ḥsyn*$_1$), but there is nothing more bitter than poverty (on this text, cf. also Pardee UF x 266 n. 109).

mrrh v. *mrr*$_2$.

mrrw **OffAr** Sing. emph. *mrrwt᾽* Aḥiq 188 (on this form, cf. Kottsieper SAS 75f.) - ¶ subst. bitterness; *kpn yhḥlh mrrwt᾽* Aḥiq 188: hunger makes bitterness (i.e. that which is bitter) sweet.

mrš$_1$ **OffAr** Sing. emph. *mrš᾽* RCL '62, 259 i 2 (v. infra) - ¶ subst. of uncert. meaning; Bresciani RCL '62, 262: poss. = loan (cf. id. ibid. 259, 262: reading *mdš᾽* also poss.; cf. also Naveh AION xvi 35f.).

mrš$_2$ v. *ndš*.

mršh v. *ndš*.

mš v. *m᾽š*$_1$, *mzl*.

mš᾽ **Ph** this subst. (Sing. abs. *[m]š᾽*) poss. in RSF vii 10 no. 14 (heavily dam. context), cf. Delavault & Lemaire RSF vii a.l.: = due - **Pun** this subst. (Sing. abs. *mš᾽*) poss. in CIS i 408[2]? (= offering), or rather lapsus for *nš᾽* (= QAL Pf. 3 p.s.m./f. of *nš᾽*$_1$)? - **Hebr** Sing. cstr. *mš᾽* TA-H 3[4] - ¶ subst. load; *mš᾽ ṣmd ḥmrm* TA-H 3[4f.]: a load of a pair

of donkeys (i.e. two pack donkeys; cf. Aharoni TA a.l., Dahood Or xlvi 330f. :: Pardee UF x 299ff.: a pair of pack donkeys, cf. however id. HAHL 35).
v. *mʾš$_1$*, *msʿ*, *mšt$_1$*, *škm$_1$*.
mšʾh Pun Sing. abs. *mšʾt* KAI $69^{3,6,10,17,18,20,21}$, 75^2; Plur. abs. *mšʾtt* (cf. FR 240,19) KAI 69^1 (*[mš]ʾtt*), 74^1, CIS i 170^1, 3917^1 (*mšʾ[tt]*) - **Hebr** Plur. cstr. *mšʾt* KAI 194^{10} (cf. e.g. Torczyner Lach i p. 79, 83, Cross BASOR cxliv 25, Röllig KAI a.l., Gibson SSI i p. 42f., Sasson VT xxxiii 92 × Lemaire IH i 110, 113, Conrad TUAT i 623: = Sing. cstr.; cf. also Reviv CSI 83) - ¶ subst. - **1)** due, payment: KAI $69^{1,3,6,10,17,18,20,21}$, 74^1, 75^2, CIS i 170^1; *šlšm hʾš ʾš ʿl hmšʾ[tt]* CIS i 3917^1: the thirty men that are over the payments - **2)** signal, beacon: KAI 194^{10} (cf. e.g. Torczyner Lach i p. 83).
v. *mšwt$_1$*.
mšʾlh OffAr Sing. cstr. *mšʾlt* AG 37^1 (?, dam. context, or l. *mšʾlt[ʾ]*? = Sing. emph.); emph. *mšʾltʾ* Cowl 76^4 (for the reading, cf. Porten & Yardeni sub TADAE A 5.4 :: Cowl a.l.: l. *mšʾlt* (= Sing. cstr.)), ATNS 1^6 - ¶ subst. interrogation: Cowl 76^4 (:: Cowl a.l.: = petition), ATNS 1^6; exact meaning in AG 37^1 uncert. (cf. also Segal sub ATNS 1).
mšʾn OffAr Sing. abs. *mšʾn* Cowl 15^{16}, 55^8, Krael 2^5 - ¶ subst. of uncert. meaning, prob. indicating some type of shoe, cf. Grelot RB lxxviii 534: = mule (cf. also Epstein ZAW xxxiii 225, Kutscher JAOS lxxiv 234, Porten Arch 91 (n. 145), Grelot DAE p. 195 (n. q), Porten & Greenfield JEAS p. 20, 39, Porten & Yardeni sub TADAE B 2.6 a.e. (cf. also Rosenthal AH i/2, 12, Fitzmyer FS Albright ii 158, WA 260)); for the comb. *šnn mšʾn* in Cowl 15^{16}, Krael 2^5, v. *šnn*.
mšʾt v. *mšʾh*.
mšb$_1$ Pun Sing. + suff. 3 p.s.m. (?) *mšbʾ* BAr '46/49, 253^3 (diff. and dam. context) - **Samal** Sing. cstr. *mšb* KAI 214^8; + suff. 3 p.s.m. *mšbh* KAI 215^2; + suff. 1 p.s. *mšby* KAI $214^{15,20}$ (diff. reading, cf. also Lipiński BiOr xxxiii 232, OLP viii 102)^{,25} - **OffAr** Sing. cstr. *mytb*Atlal vii 109^6; emph. *mytbʾ* KAI 229^1 (for the reading, cf. Driver PEQ '38, 189) - **Nab** Sing. + suff. 3 p.s.m. *mwtbh*CIS ii 198^4, $350^{3,4}$ (v. infra) - **Palm** Sing. emph. *mytbʾ*RIP 145^2 (*myt[bʾ]*, for the reading, cf. Gawlikowski RIP a.l., TP 96, Ber xxii 145, cf. however Aggoula Syr liv 284: l. *myt[rʾ]* = PAʿEL Part. s.m. emph. of *ytr$_1$*, *mrʾ myt[rʾ]* = supreme lord), SBS 35^1 (for the diff. reading *my[tb]ʾ*, cf. Gawlikowski Ber xxii 145, TP 96 :: Dunant sub SBS 35: l. *mytʾ* = Sing. emph. of *myt$_2$* (= death); cf. also Garbini OA xiv 179: l. *mytʾ* = indication of a tribal or corporate association, the *bny mytʾ*, cf. id. AION xviii 77); + suff. 3 p.s.m. *mwtbh*Inv x 63^3, *mtbh* Inv x 106^2 - ¶ subst. - **1)** seat, throne: KAI $214^{8,15,20,25}$, 215^2, 229^1, Atlal vii 109^6 (in Atlal vii 109 and KAI 229 poss. indicating the pedestal of a statue, cf. e.g. Donner KAI

a.l., Livingstone Atlal vii 109f., Beyer & Livingstone ZDMG cxxxvii 286, cf. however Aggoula Syr lxii 66, 67f.: = seat) - in other instances in religious context: - a) *dwšr› ›lh mr›n› wmwtbh ḥryš› w›lhy› klhm* CIS ii 350[3]: D. the god of our lord, and his sacred (??, v. *ḥrš$_3$*) throne and all the gods (for this prob. interpret. of *mwtb*, cf. e.g. Nöldeke sub CIS ii 198, CIS ii sub 350, Lidzbarski Handb 291, Cooke NSI p. 241, 243, Milik RB lxvi 560 (cf. CIS ii 198[4], 350[4]), cf. also Will Syr lxiii 343ff. :: Lidzbarski Eph i 194: < Arab. (= throne =) pantheon? (cf. Glaser die Abessinier 48: Saf. *mwṯb* = pantheon (cf. also Gawlikowski sub RIP 145)) :: Nöldeke ZA xii 5 (id. sub CIS ii 350): = council? :: Clermont-Ganneau RAO ii 131: compare πάρεδρος or σύνεδρος? = assessor, coadjutor, one who sits with others in council :: Winckler AltorForsch ii 62, 321, Hommel FS de Vogüé 298ff.: = spouse (for a survey, cf. also Cantineau Nab ii 112f.)) - b) *mr› myt[b›]* RIP 145[2]: lord of the throne (epithet of a god), cf. Gawlikowski RIP a.l. (:: id. ibid., TP 96: or = lord of the (divine) assembly); cf. also *mrt my[tb]›* SBS 35[1]: the lady of the throne (epithet of a goddess, v. supra) - CIS ii a.l.: l. *mytb* (Sing. abs.) in CIS ii 117, cf. however Jaussen & Savignac sub J 146 (div. otherwise): l. *myt* (= n.p.) *br* (= Sing. cstr. of *br$_1$*), cf. however also Degen NESE ii 94f. - **2)** (seat >) office (of σύνεδρος (= assessor, coadjutor) or προέδρος (= one who sits in the first place, president, cf. Starcky Inv x p. 43); *dy ‹bdt lh bwl› bmwtbh* Inv x 63[3]: which the Senate made for him during his office (cf. Inv x 106[2]) - 3) indication of tomb: BAr '46/49, 253[3] (diff. and dam. context).
v. *mrḥb*.

mšb$_2$ **Pun** diff. word in RES 237[2] (for the reading of the context, cf. RES 1857). Chabot sub RES 237: = inhabitant (less prob. interpret., cf. also Lidzbarski Eph ii 64: = settler??, context diff.).

mšbq **Nab** Starcky RB lxi 178f.: l. this word (Plur. cstr. *mšbqy*) = legacy? poss. in MPAT 64 iii 4 (reading and interpret. uncert.).

mšgb **DA** Caquot & Lemaire Syr liv 204: l. *mšgb* (Sing. abs.) = fortress in ii 10?? (highly uncert. reading; cf. also v.d. Kooij DA p. 123 :: Garbini Hen i 172, 183, 186: l. *m‹gb* = Sing. abs. of *m‹gb* (= sensual pleasure) :: Levine JAOS ci 200f.: l. *mškb* = Sing. abs. of *mškb$_1$*); cf. Puech RB lxxxv 116: poss. l. *mḥṭbn* < root *ḥṭb*.

mšgd v. *msgd*.

mšd v. *mšr$_2$*.

mšh v. *ršy$_1$*.

mšwt$_1$ **Pun** Sing. + suff. 3 p.s./pl.m. *mšwtm* KAI 119[5] - ¶ subst. of unknown meaning; Levi Della Vida RCL '55, 559, Röllig KAI a.l., Amadasi IPT 79: = *mš›h* (= payment, gift), cf. however Février RA l 186: = *mswyh* (= clothing). Diff. and uncert. context.

mšwt$_2$ **Samal** diff. word in KAI 215[21] (prob. Plur. abs.), poss. meaning offering, contribution, cf. Halévy RS i 238, Cooke NSI p. 180, Lagrange ERS 498, Dion p. 42, 133, 434 n. 3 (cf. also Donner KAI a.l.) :: Dupont-Sommer AH i/2, 5: = smoke :: D.H. Müll WZKM vii 134: derivative of root *mšy*$_1$ (= to wash); cf. however Gibson SSI ii p. 85: = variant of *mšt*$_1$ - on this word, cf. also Garr DGSP 96.

mšḥ$_1$ **Pun** QAL Imper. s.m., cf. August in Ioan Ev xv 27: *messe* (cf. FR 136, Penna CISFP i 890f. :: Harr 122: = Sing. abs. of *mšḥ*$_6$ (= messiah)) - **OldAr** QAL Impf. 3 p.pl.f. *ymšḥ[n]* KAI 222A 21 - **OffAr** QAL Part. pass. pl.m. abs. *mšḥn* Cowl 31[20], *mšḥyn* Cowl 30[20] (:: Cowl p. 298 (cf. also p. 114, 117, 121f.): in both instances = QAL Pf. 1 p.pl., cf. Leand 34a: *mšḥyn* = lapsus, cf. also Grelot DAE p. 411, Porten & Greenfield JEAS p. 93, 96, Porten & Yardeni sub TADAE A 4.7) - **JAr** QAL Pf. 3 p.s.m. *mšḥ* SM 93[2] (= Frey 841a) - ¶ verb QAL to anoint; *mšḥ lʾ mšḥyn* Cowl 30[20]: not anointed with oil (cf. Cowl 31[20]; v. supra); *šmw[ʾl] kd mšḥ [d]wyd* SM 93[1f.]: Sh. when he anointed D.; for the context of KAI 222A 21, cf. Dupont-Sommer Sf p. 39, Hillers TC 61f., Galling ZDPV lxxxiii 134f., cf. however Greenfield ActOr xxix 12 n. 37 - Puech FS Grelot 24: l. *mšḥ* (= QAL Inf. of *mšḥ*$_1$) in DA x d 1.
v. *mšḥ*$_2$.

mšḥ$_2$ **OffAr** QAL Pf. 3 p.s.m. *mšḥ* Cowl 71[17] (uncert. reading, dam. context) - ¶ verb QAL to measure (??): Cowl 71[47]; highly uncert. interpret., cf. also CIS ii sub 145: = *mšḥ*$_1$??- Garbini RSO xliii 14f. (cf. also id. StudMagr vi 27): l. *mšḥ* (= QAL Part. act. s.m. abs. of *mšḥ*$_2$ or nominal derivative of this root (*mšḥ*$_5$) in KAI 141[1] (highly uncert. reading and interpret.); Février BAr '51/52, 116f., 120, Röllig KAI a.l.: l. *wtḥ*? = n.p.?) - on this word, cf. also Kaufman AIA 70 (n. 199).

mšḥ$_3$ **OffAr** Sing. abs. *mšḥ* Cowl 30[20], 31[20], Krael 2[5] (v. infra), 7[19,20] (*mš[ḥ]*), Herm 2[12] (v. infra), 3[10] (v. infra), 4[7], ATNS 19[7], 20[4], 45b 5 (*mšḥ[*), RES 1299A 4, Del 76[3], RCL '62, 259 ii 2, 4, 5, 6, iii 1, 4, iv 1, *mš* (lapsus) RCL '62, 259 ii 3, NESE iii 31[2] (?, heavily dam. context; = Or lvii 43 ii); cstr. *mšḥ* CIS ii 44, Herm 2[11]; emph. *mšḥʾ* RES 496[3]; cf. Frah vii 19 (*mšḥʾ*), Nisa-c 355[3,4] (*mšḥʾ*), GIPP 58 - **Palm** Sing. abs. *mšḥ* CIS ii 3913 ii 28 (Greek par. ἐλεηροῦ), RTP 709 (cf. Milik DFD 190 :: Seyrig sub RTP 709, Caquot RTP p. 146: l. *mšḥ[ʾ]* = Sing. emph.); emph. *mšḥʾ* CIS ii 3913 ii 13, 17 (*[m]šḥʾ*), 19, 21, 46, 98, 3959[3] (= SBS 44), RIP 199[5] (?, dam. context, v. also infra), RTP 131, 132 (:: Caquot RTP p. 146, Starcky MUSJ xxxviii 127f., du Mesnil du Buisson TMP 196: = *mšḥ*$_4$ (= olive tree), cf. also Cantineau sub InscrP 104 (reading here *mšḥyʾ*, *y* being uncert.); on this problem, cf. also Gawlikowski Sem xxiii 117: = *mšḥ*$_3$ (prob. = unction)) - ¶ subst. m. oil (cf. also Grelot Sem xiv 66, RB lxxviii 533); *mšḥ bšm* Herm 2[12]: perfumed oil (cf. Krael 2[5], Herm 3[10f.], cf. also *mšḥʾ bšymʾ* CIS ii 3913 ii 13 (Greek par.

μύρου), 17, 46f. and *mšḥ› b[šym›]* CIS ii 3913 ii 98 (Greek par. μύρου); for Krael 7[20], v. *bšm$_3$*; for Krael 2[5], Herm 2[12], 3[10f.], cf. however Krael p. 146: or *bšm* = *bšm$_1$* (= fragrance), in which case *mšḥ* = Sing. cstr. (poss. interpret.)); *mšḥ zyt* Krael 7[20]: olive-oil (cf. also Herm 2[11]); *byt mšḥ›* RIP 199[5]: the house of the oil (diff. expression, exact meaning unknown; Gawlikowski Sem xxiii 117: poss. interpretations: - a) oil-press (cf. also Teixidor Syr li 333) - b) storehouse for oil - c) locality used for the ceremony of anointing).
v. *mzḥ*, *mšt$_1$*, *qysm*.

mšḥ$_4$ v. *mšḥ$_3$*.

mšḥ$_5$ v. *mšḥ$_2$*.

mšḥ$_6$ v. *mšḥ$_1$*.

mšḥh v. *mšḥt*.

mšḥt (:: Leand 43 k[00]: = subst. *mšḥh*)- **OffAr** Sing. (:: Krael p. 174: Plur.) abs. *mšḥt* Krael 4[12] (v. infra), 12[28]; cstr. *mšḥt* Cowl 9[4], Krael 4[5], 9[5], 12[6,15]; + suff. 3 p.s.m. *mšḥth* Cowl 8[4], Krael 3[21], 9[11] (for the reading, cf. Porten & Greenfield JEAS p. 58, Porten & Yardeni sub TADAE B 3.10 :: Krael a.l.: l. *mšḥt* = Plur. abs.),[16], 12[22] - ¶ subst. measurement; *wh› mšḥt byt› zk* Krael 4[5]: and behold, the measurement (i.e. the measures) of this house; *zn› byt› zy tḥwmwhy wmšḥth ktybn* Krael 9[16] ...: this is the house the boundaries and measures of which are written ...; etc.; *byt› zy mšḥt ktybn wtḥwmwhy* in Krael 4[12] prob. lapsus for *byt› zy mšḥt wtḥwmwhy ktybn* (cf. e.g. Krael 9[11]; :: Krael p. 174: *ktybn* predicate the subject of which is *mšḥt*, cf. also Grelot DAE p. 222).

mšṭr **Pun** Sing. abs. *mšṭr* Hofra 41[2], 79[3], *myšṭr*RES 332[2] (= Punica xi 35b), Hofra 78[2], 81[3] - ¶ subst. indicating a military function, military officer? whose function is administrative (cf. Milik Bibl xxxviii 266f., cf. also Février SOLDV i 285, Roschinski Num 109, Heltzer AO ii 228ff.).
v. *mšn$_2$*.

mšṭrh **Pun** Sing. abs. *mšṭrt* Hofra 74[2], 75[3], 76[2] - ¶ subst. prob. meaning, military administration; *rb (h)mšṭrt* Hofra 74[2], 75[3], 76[2]: head of the military adminstration (cf. Février SOLDV i 285, Heltzer AO ii 228ff.).

mšy$_1$ v. *mšwt$_2$*, *nš$_1$*.

mšy$_2$ v. *mḥy$_3$*.

mšy$_3$ v. *mḥy$_3$*.

mšk$_1$ **OffAr** Sing. abs. *mšk* Herm 3[8]; + suff. 1 p.s. *mšky* Aḥiq 118; Plur. abs. *mškn* Herm 3[7], ATNS 43b ii 2; cstr. *mšky* Cowl 37[10], ATNS 99[2] - **Palm** Sing. abs. *mšk* CIS ii 3913 ii 56 (Greek par. δέρματα), 67 (Greek par. δέρματος); emph. *mšk›* CIS 3913 ii 56 - ¶ subst. skin, hide (cf. also Lozachmeur Sem xxi 92 nn. 3, 4); *mšky ‹prn* ATNS 99[2]: hides of young stags/gazelles; for *mšky ṣl*, v. *ṣl$_1$*.

mšk$_2$ v. *mšn$_1$*.

mškb$_1$ **Ph** Sing. abs. *mškb* KAI 9A 1, 3, B 2 (*mšk[b]*), 3, 13[8], 14[4,6,7,8,10,21]; cstr. *mškb* KAI 34[5], 35[2]; + suff. 1 p.s. *mškby* KAI 14[5,7,21] - **Hebr** Sing. abs. *mškb* Frey 1413[1]; + suff. 3 p.s.m. *mškbw* Frey 569[1], IEJ iv 98[1,2], 99, *mškhbw* Frey 593[5], 613[5], *myškhbw* Frey 595[1f.], 608 (for this reading, cf. Leon JQR xliv 268 n. 4); + suff. 3 p.s.f. *mškbh* Frey 570[1], 611[10] (*mšk[b]h*), 1536[2]; + suff. 2 p.s.m. *myškbk* Frey 1414[6] - **DA** Plur. cstr. *mškby* ii 11 - **Nab** Sing. emph. *mškb*ʾ CIS ii 234[1] - ¶ subst. m. - **1)** lying, resting; *tškb mškby* ‘*lmyk* DA ii 11: you will sleep your eternal sleep, you will sleep the sleep of death (cf. Hoftijzer DA a.l., cf. also Rofé SB 68 :: Levine JAOS ci 200, 202, Hackett BTDA 30, 67, Hoftijzer TUAT ii 146: you shall lie on your eternal bed (cf. also H.P.Müller ZAW xciv 219, 234f.) :: Caquot & Lemaire Syr liv 205: you will cohabitate as in your youth :: Garbini Hen i 186: the embraces of your young men (*tškb* belonging to the prec. clause), v. also ‘*lm$_4$*) - **2)** (couch, resting-place >) ultimate resting-place, tomb (cf. also Marcus JANES vii 89 n. 53): KAI 9A 1, 3, B 2, 3, 14[4,6,7,7f.,10,21], Frey 569[1], 570[1], 611[10], 1413[1], 1414[6], IEJ iv 98[1,2], 99 (cf. also *šlwm* ‘*l mškhbw* Frey 593[5f.]: peace on his resting-place, cf. Frey 595[1f.], 613[5], 1536[20]; cf. also Zunz 356ff.); *ḥlt mškby* KAI 14[5,7,21]: the sarcophagus serving as my ultimate resting-place; *mškb nḥty* KAI 35[2]: the tomb in which I rest (cf. KAI 34[5]), cf. also Teixidor Syr lvi 385; *mškb* ʾ*t rp*ʾ*m* KAI 13[8], 14[8]: a resting-place with the shades - **3)** meaning of the word in CIS ii 234[1] uncert.: seat? (at a cultic banquet?), cf. Milik DJD iii p. 249 (cf. also Teixidor Syr xlviii 482) :: J i p. 206: = tomb? - the same word poss. also in Frey 584, cf. Frey a.l.
v. *mšgb*, *mškb$_2$*.

mškb$_2$ **Ph** Plur. abs. *mškbm* KAI 24[10,13,14,15] - ¶ subst. m. (= Yoph Part. m. of *škb$_1$*, cf. Röllig KAI a.l., Gibson SSI iii p. 38) probably designation of the conquered indigenous population of Samʾal, cf. Lidzbarski Eph iii 233f., Röllig KAI a.l., Gibson SSI iii p. 38 (cf. also Alt ZÄS lxxv 16ff., Sader EAS 158f. n. 19, 177f., Baldacci BiOr xl 126) :: Joüon RES v 91f.: = Pi‘el Part. pl.m. abs. of *škb* (= to lay out for irrigation) > agricultural labourers :: Poeb 36ff.: = *mškb$_1$* (= couch) - cf. also Landsberger Samʾal 55f., Avishur PIB 206, v. *b*‘*rr*.

mškhb v. *mškb$_1$*.

mškwn v. *mškn$_2$*.

mšky **Samal** Sing. abs. *mšky* KAI 215[18] (for this reading, cf. e.g. Halévy RS i 237, Donner KAI a.l., Gibson SSI ii p. 80, 85 (cf. also Landsberger Samʾal 70 n. 184, Dion p. 133, 434 n. 1) :: e.g. Cooke NSI p. 173, 179: prob. l. *mšty* (= Sing. abs. of *mšty* (= *mšth* (= feast))) :: Lidzbarski Handb 236, 443: l. *mbky* (= Sing. abs. of *mbky* (= mourning))) - ¶ subst. stone decorated with an image.

mškn$_1$ **Nab** QAL Impf. 3 p.s.m. *ymškn* CIS ii 199[5], 200[3] (= J 30; for the reading, cf. Milik sub ARNA-Nab 79), 206[4], 223[3], J 38[6]; 3 p.pl.m. *ymšknwn* CIS ii 205[7] (for this text, cf. J 12), 212[3] - ¶ verb (< *mškn$_2$*) QAL to give as a pledge.

mškn$_2$ (< Akkad., cf. Zimmern Fremdw 18, Greenfield Mem Yalon 74, Kaufman AIA 70) - **Nab** Plur. cstr. *mškwny*MPAT 64 iii 4 (diff. reading) - **Palm** Sing. abs. *mškn* Syr xvii 353[9] (cf. Milik DFD 302f. (:: Gawlikowski TP 57: l. *mškn*ʾ (misprint?)) :: Cantineau Syr xvii 354: = *mškn$_3$*); emph. *mškn*ʾ RIP 199[8]; + suff. 3 p.s.m. *mšknh* Syr xvii 353[10] (cf. Milik DFD 302f., Gawlikowski TP 57f. :: Cantineau Syr xvii 354 = *mškn$_3$*) - ¶ subst. pledge - Gawlikowksi RIP a.l.: l. in RIP 199[7] *[mšk]n*ʾ (= Sing. emph.) :: Milik DFD 286: l. *]kwl* (= Sing. abs. of *kl$_1$*).
v. *mškn$_1$*.

mškn$_3$ **Hatra** Sing. emph. *mškn*ʾ 50[3] (cf. Caquot Syr xxxii 54 × Milik DFD 358f., Vattioni IH a.l. = n.l. :: Safar Sumer ix 245 (div. otherwise): l. *dm* (without explanation) + *škn*ʾ (= Sing. emph. of *škn$_2$* (= dwelling, locality)); for the context, v. also *znh*), 79[10] (cf. Caquot Syr xl 4f. (cf. also Hillers BASOR ccvii 54ff. for Hatra 50 & 79) × Teixidor Syr xli 281 (n. 4), Milik DFD 358f., Aggoula Syr lii 201f., Vattioni IH a.l.: = n.l. (cf. also Safar Sumer xvii 14f. n. 21: = *mškn$_3$*, or n.l.) :: Altheim & Stiehl AAW iv 246, 249: = Plur. emph.), 281[3] (or = Plur.?) - ¶ subst. - **1)** tent: Hatra 281[3] (cf. also Aggoula Syr lxv 208 :: v.d.Branden BiOr xxxvi 341: = entrepôt (prob. < Akkad.)) - **2)** dwelling > shrine: Hatra 50[3], 79[10] (v. however supra) :: Haran TTS 196 n. 12: merely = abode, dwelling-place - the same word also in Sumer xx 16 ii 3? (cf. Milik DFD 359: *mškn*ʾ = Sing. emph. (= camp (sc. of bedouins)), cf. however Teixidor Sumer xx 17: *bny mškn*ʾ = indication of a tribe).
v. *mškn$_2$*, *mšn$_1$*.

mšl$_1$ **Ph** QAL Part. act. s.m. abs. *mšl* KAI 14[9], 15 (cf. e.g. RES sub 287, Lidzbarski Eph ii 52, id. sub KI 8, Torrey JAOS xxiii 165, xxiv 212, xxv 331, lvii 405, Milik Bibl xlviii 575f. n. 6, Röllig KAI a.l.; Elayi SCA 61: the *bmšl* pro *mšl* in variant text = lapsus) - **Pun** QAL Part. act. pl.m. abs. *mšlm* KAI 120[1] - **OldAr** QAL Impf. 2 p.s.m. *tmšl* KAI 224[9] - ¶ verb QAL to rule; ʾ*š mšl bnm* KAI 14[9]: who shall have dominion over them; *ltmšl by bz*ʾ KAI 224[9]: you shall not dominate over me in this respect - *mšlt* ʿ*sr hmšlm p*ʿ*m*ʾ*t* ʿ*sr wḥmš* KAI 120[1]: the rule of the ten-rulers (i.e. tribunes of the people) for the 15th time (Lat. par. *trib(unicia) pot(estate) xv*, cf. Angeli Bertinelli CISFP i 256) - *ṣdn mšl* KAI 15 prob. is the name of a ward of Sidon (= Sidon the Ruler; v. also ʾ*rṣ$_1$*), cf. Milik Bibl xlviii 575f. n. 6 (: Sidon which is royal residence or possession), Teixidor Syr xlvi 332, Elayi RCP 15f., cf. also Clermont-Ganneau RAO v 225ff.: *Sidon Michal* = locality near Sidon, cf. also Cooke NSI p. 401, 403 :: Röllig KAI a.l.: poss. name of a temple, *ṣdn*

= n.d. (cf. also Lidzbarski sub KI 8) :: Torrey JAOS xxiii 165, xxiv 212, xxv 331, lvii 405: *bṣdn ... mšl* = reigning over Sidon - Amadasi sub Kition B 2: l. poss. *mšl* (= QAL Part. act. s.m. abs. of *mšl$_1$*) in CIS i 57[2,3] (or = n.p.?), highly uncert. reading and interpret.

mšl$_2$ v. *bḥr.*

mšl$_3$ **Palm** Sing. emph. *mšl›* Syr xvii 268[5] - ¶ subst. of unknown meaning, prob. indicating a (part of a) building, cf. also Milik DFD 220f.: = canalization system (improb. interpret.) :: Cantineau Syr xvii 269: = fork.

mšl$_4$ v. *m›š$_1$*.

mšl$_5$ v. *m›š$_1$*.

mšlh **Pun** Sing. cstr. *mšlt* KAI 120[1] - ¶ subst. rule (for the context, v. *mšl$_1$*).

v. *nšl$_1$*.

mšlḥ **Palm** du Mesnil du Buisson TMP 604f.: l. *bmšlḥ* (= *b$_1$* + Sing. cstr. of *mšlḥ* (= delegation)) in RTP 184 (poss. reading :: Seyrig sub RTP 184: l. *bny* (= Plur. cstr. of *br$_1$*) *šlm* (= tribal name; cf. also Caquot RTP p. 178)).

mšlm **Hebr** the diff. *mšlm* in SM 49[19] poss. = Sing. abs. of *mšlm* (= completion), or = PU‘AL Part. s.m. abs. of *šlm$_1$*??; for the context, cf. Sussmann Tarbiz xliii 130, Lieberman Tarbiz xlv 60.

mšlmw **OffAr** Sing. + suff. 3 p.s.f. *mšlmwth* Aḥiq 131 - ¶ subst. f. payment (or PA‘EL Inf. of *šlm$_1$*?, cf. Leand 31g, Lindenberger APA 124, Kottsieper SAS 235, or APH Inf. of *šlm$_1$*?, cf. e.g. Greenfield Lesh xxxii 367); *mšlmwth* Aḥiq 131: the payment (i.e. prob. the repayment) of it (i.e. of a loan?).

mšlmn **Palm** Plur. m. abs. *mšlmnyn* Ber ii 82[1], 84[1] - ¶ adj. perfect; *gwmḥy› ... mšlmnyn* Ber ii 82[1], 84[1]: prob. = perfect (i.e. undefiled) niches (cf. Ingholt Ber ii 83 :: Gawlikowski MFP 212f.: = complete).

mšmn **Pun** Garbini StudMagr xi 24f.: l. *mšmn* (Sing. abs.; = fatness, richness) in CIS i 6066[1] preceded by ›$_{11}$ (= *›y$_2$* (= negation)), less prob. interpret., cf. Février CIS i a.l. (dividing otherwise): l. *›mšmn* = n.p. (cf. also RES 126, Lidzbarski Eph i 298, Chabot sub RES 1599) :: Ferron Mus lxxix 446f. (div. otherwise): l. *›mšm* (= Plur. abs. of *›mš* (= darkness)).

mšm‘ v. *šm‘$_1$*.

mšm‘h **Mo** Sing. abs. *mšm‘t* KAI 181[28] - ¶ subst. subjects; *ky kl dybn mšm‘t* KAI 181[28]: for all Dibân was subject (to me), cf. Segert ArchOr xxix 220, 226, 230, 245 (cf. also Cooke NSI p. 3, 14, Röllig KAI a.l., Galling TGI 53 (n. 19), Reviv CSI p. 29, Smelik HDAI 35), cf. also Segert ArchOr xxix 226, 230: or = PU‘AL/HOPH Part. s.f. abs. of *šm‘$_1$* :: de Moor UF xx 155: because all Dibon had been a subjected area :: Gibson SSI p. 82: or = HIPH Part. s.f. abs. of *šm‘$_1$* (= to declare, sc.

allegiance) :: Lipiński Or xl 339: = bodyguard (cf. de Geus SV 28).

mšmr **Ph** Sing. abs. *mšmr* KAI 26A ii 14 - **Hebr** Sing. abs. *mšmr* TA-H 111^2 (?; or cstr.?, dam. context), SM $52^{1,2,3}$ (= Frey 962), $106^{1,2,3,4,5,7}$ (*[m]šmr*)^{,8,9,10,11} - ¶ subst. m. - **1)** guard; *lkny mšmr lʿmq ʾdn* KAI 26A ii 14: so that it (i.e. the town) might be a protection for the plain of A.; cf. poss. also TA-H 111^2 (heavily dam. context) - **2)** division of duty for priests and Levites: SM 52^{1-3}, $106^{1-5,7-11}$ (cf. also Steindler AION xxiv 277ff.).

mšmrt **Hebr** Sing. abs. *mšmrt* SM 51^2 (*[mš]mrt*)^{,3} (*[mš]mrt*)^{,4} (*m[šmrt]*)^{,5} (*mš[mrt]*)^{,6} (*mš[mrt]*) - ¶ subst. f. division of duty for priests and Levites.

mšmš cf. Frah iv 22: apricot (cf. Löw AP 150).

mšn$_1$ **Hatra** Sing. abs. *mšn* 29^6 (cf. Milik DFD 214, 359, cf. also Vattioni StudMagr ii 20, IH a.l :: Milik DFD 214: or = QAL Inf. of denominative verb < Akkad. *šênu* (= shoes) :: Caquot Syr xxx 235f., GLECS ix 88, Donner sub KAI 247: l. *mšn* = n.g. :: Safar Sumer viii 186 n. 11: l. poss. *mšn* = Sing. abs. of *mšn*$_3$ (= advanced age > strength, endurance) :: Aggoula MUSJ xlvii 27f.: l. *mšk* = Sing. abs. of *mšk*$_2$, *bmšk* = unduly, in a profane way :: Hillers BASOR ccvi 55f., Degen NESE ii 100, ZDMG cxxi 125, Teixidor Syr l 436: l. *mšk[nʾ]* = Sing. emph. of *mškn*$_3$ (= shrine (cf. however Degen NESE ii 104, Pennacchietti FO xvi 64)) :: Teixidor Syr xli 281 (n. 4), Ingholt AH i/1, 45, i/2, 47: l. *mšk[nʾ]* = n.l. :: Safar Sumer viii 186 (n. 11): l. *lšn* = Sing. abs. of *lšn*)- ¶ subst. footwear (v. supra); *dlʿwl mhkʾ bmšn* Hatra $29^{5f.}$: whoever proceeds from here (i.e. past this point) wearing shoes (for the reading *mhkʾ* (= *m*$_{12}$ (= *mn*$_5$) + *hkʾ*), cf. Caquot Syr xxx 235f., GLECS ix 88, Teixidor Syr xli 281, Donner sub KAI 247, Hillers BASOR ccvi 55, Ingholt AH i/1, 45, i/2, 47, Degen NESE ii 100 :: Safar Sumer viii 185f.: l. *lhkʾ* = *l*$_5$ + *hkʾ*, cf. also Pennacchietti FO xvi 63f., Aggoula MUSJ xlvii 28, Milik DFD 214, 359, Vattioni IH a.l. (reading *lhkh* prob. misprint); for *lʿwl* in this text, v. *ʿll*) - cf. *msn*.

mšn$_2$ **Samal** Lipiński BiOr xxxiii 232, OLP viii 103: l. *mšn* (= Sing. abs. of *mšn*$_2$) in KAI 215^{12} (= vice-regent); highly uncert. reading and interpret.; for the reading *m*, cf. also Halévy RS i 219 (:: id. RS i 219, 232: l. *mšṭr* = Sing. abs./cstr. of *mšṭr* (= government)) :: Halévy RS vii 342f. (div. otherwise): l. *rš* (= Sing. cstr. of *rš*$_1$ (= *rʾš*$_1$)), cf. also Gibson SSI ii p. 81, 84, Dion p. 40, 120, Stefanovic COAI 171 (for the reading *rš*, cf. also Lidzbarski Handb 443, Cooke NSI p. 172, Donner KAI a.l., for the reading *r[* , cf. D.H.Müller WZKM vii 38a).

mšn$_3$ v. *mšn*$_1$.

mšnh v.Soden Or xlvi 191, AHW s.v. *mušannû*: > Akkad. *mušannû* = irresolute?, prob. < Ar. *mšnh* (= PAʿEL Part. of *šny*$_1$) = the one who changes (improb. interpret.; cf. also CAD s.v.: meaning unknown).

mš'$_1$ v. *bny$_1$*, *yš'$_2$*.
mš'$_2$ v. *š''$_2$*.
mš'rt **Pun** diff. word in KAI 136[6], prob. = n.p. (cf. Jongeling NINPI 10, 188), cf. however Février Sem v 64: *mš'rt* = PI'EL Part. pl.f. abs. of *šyr$_1$* (= female singers), cf. also Röllig KAI a.l., Garbini FSR 182 :: v.d.Branden BiOr xxxvi 157 (dividing otherwise): l. *'m* (= Sing. cstr. of *'m$_1$*) *š'rt* (= Sing. cstr. of *šrt$_3$* (= cultic service)).
mšpṭ **Ph** Sing. + suff. 3 p.s.m. *mšpṭh* KAI 1[2] - ¶ subst. rule, dominion; for the context of KAI 1[2], v. *ḥṭr$_1$*.
v. *špṭ$_1$*.
mšplt **OffAr** word of unknown meaning in ATNS 52b ii 11; Segal ATNS a.l.: perhaps to be related to *š'plt* in l. 3 as Part. form (uncert. interpret.; heavily dam. context).
mšpn **Ph** word (?) of unknown meaning in KAI 49[26] (= RES 1303), indication of function??, (part of) n.p.?? or = *m$_{12}$* (= *mn$_5$*) + *špn* (= n.g.??) :: Kornfeld sub Abydos 9: *špn* (Sing. abs. of *špn$_2$*) = dialectal form of *ṣpn$_2$*.
v. *pnh$_1$*.
mšq' **Nab** this word (Sing. abs. or emph.) in CIS ii 2628[2] (prob. also in CIS ii 1491[2]), meaning unknown, prob. appellative or function indication.
mšqh v. *mskh$_1$*.
mšqy$_1$ **OldAr** Sing. abs. *mšqy* Tell F 3 (Akkad. par. *maš-qí-tím*; cf. also Fales Syr lx 246, Greenfield FS Rundgren 151) - ¶ subst. watering place; *wntn r'y wmšqy* Tell F 2f.: and giving pasture and watering-place (on this word, cf. also Abou-Assaf, Bordreuil & Millard Tell F p. 28, Kaufman Maarav iii 164, Gropp & Lewis BASOR cclix 47) :: Andersen & Freedman FS Fensham 16f.: food and drink.
mšqy$_2$ **OldAr** Cross BASOR ccv 37ff.: l. *mšqy'* (= Sing. emph. of *mšqy* (= Damascene)) in KAI 201[2] (reading highly uncert., improb. interpret.); for the problems involved, cf. also Gibson SSI ii p. 3f.
mšql **Ph** Sing. abs. *mšql* KAI 43[14], 50[4] (*mš[q]l*), Mus li 286[7]; + suff. 3 p.s.m./f.? *mšqly* Mus li 286[5]; + suff. 3 p.pl.m. *mšqlm* Mus li 286[4], RES 933 (?, diff. context) - **Pun** Sing. abs. *mšql* KAI 66[1], 69[6] - **OffAr** Sing. cstr. *mtql* REA viii 9 - ¶ subst. weight; *mzbḥ nḥšt mšql lṭrm m't 100* KAI 66[1]: an altar of bronze in weight a hundred 100 pounds; *š'r mšql m't ḥmšm 150* KAI 69[6]: flesh in weight 150 (units); etc. - cf. also *mtqlh*.
mšqn **Ph** word of diff. reading and interpret. in BIFAO xxxviii 3[6]; Aimé-Giron ibid. 6: poss. = the gathering of the olives (improb. interpret.).
mšr$_1$ v. *mšr$_2$*.
mšr$_2$ **Ph** Sing. abs. *mšr* KAI 13[5] - ¶ subst. poss. meaning riches, cf.

Lipiński RSF ii 55f., RTAT 262, Gibson SSI iii p. 103f., Butterweck TUAT ii 590 (cf. also Rosenthal ANET 662: = jewelry?), cf. however Polselli RSF x 8f., OA xxiii 177f.: = *viaticum* and Xella UF xiv 295ff.: = precious gift :: Harr 149: l. *mšd* = m_{12} (= mn_5) + Sing. abs. of $šd_2$ (= booty; cf. Slouschz TPI p. 17, Avishur PIB 171, 174f.; cf. also Röllig KAI a.l.: *šd* = word of unknown meaning, prob. indicating something precious) :: Lagrange ERS 481: l. *mšd* = HOPH Part. s.m. abs. of *šdd* (= to plunder) :: Torrey ZA xxvi 80 (div. otherwise): pro *mnm mšr* l. *mn* (= Sing. abs. of *m›n*) *mmšr* (= PU‹AL Part. s.m. abs. of $mšr_1$ (= to be deposed)).

mšry **OffAr** Sing. abs. *mšry* ATNS 43a 4 - **Nab** Sing. emph. *mšryt›* CIS ii 196[4], RB lxiv 215[1f.] - **Palm** Sing. emph. *mšryt›* CIS ii 3973[3], Inv xi 70[2] (heavily dam. context); + suff. 3 p.s.m. *[mš]ryth* CIS ii 3959[5] (= SBS 44 :: Milik DFD 11, Gawlikowski Ber xxii 145: l. *[m]dyth* = Sing. + suff. 3 p.s.m. of *mdnh*) - ¶ subst. camp; *byt mšry* ATNS 43a 4: poss. = camp, barracks (dam. context); for *rb mšryt›*, v. rb_2.

$mšrt_1$ **Ph** Sing. abs. *mšrt* KAI 60[4,8] - ¶ subst. service; *kl ›š ‹lty mšrt* KAI 60[3f.]: all that was required of him by way of service; *›dmm ›š p‹l mšrt* KAI 60[7f.]: the men who have rendered service.
v. *m‹ṣrh*.

$mšrt_2$ **Pun** Sing. + suff. 3 p.pl.m., cf. Poen 933: *mysyrthoho[m]* (cf. e.g. Sznycer PPP 74) - ¶ subst. justice; Vattioni Aug xvi 547: the *mysyrthim* in IRT 886f l. 6f. (= Dréd 6) = Sing. + suff. 3 p.s.m. of $mšrt_2$ (highly uncert. interpret., diff. context).

$mšrt_3$ v. $šrt_1$.

$mšt_1$ **Samal** word of unknown meaning in KAI 215[6]; for this reading, without interpret., cf. e.g. Cooke NSI p. 172, 176, Lagrange ERS 495, Gibson SSI ii p. 79, 83, Dion p. 37, cf. also D.H.Müller WZKM vii 38, 45: = Sing. abs. of *mšt* (= drink), Halévy RS i 219, 226: *mšt* = Sing. f. of *mš›* (= load, charge; improb. interpret.) :: e.g. Lidzbarski Handb 442, Donner KAI a.l., Sader EAS 165, 167: l. *mšḥ* = Sing. abs. of $mšḥ_3$.
v. *mšwt*.

$mšt_2$ **Nab** word of unknown meaning in CIS ii 340.

mšth **Hebr** Sing. cstr. *mšth* SM 75[4] - ¶ subst. meal; *mh šntndb bmšth rby ywḥnn hkhn* SM 75[4f.]: that which he vowed to donate during a meal of rabbi Y. the priest.
v. *mšky*.

mšty v. *mšky*, $šty_2$.

mt_1 (< Akkad., cf. Zimmern Fremdw 9, Kaufman AIA 71 (n. 201)) - **OldAr** Sing. abs. *mt* Tell F 3, 5; + suff. 3 p.s.m. *mth* Tell F 23 (Akkad. par. *māti-šú*) - **OffAr** Sing. cstr. *mt* CIS ii 31[2] (= Del 30 = AECT 16), HDS 9[2] (v. also infra), ATNS 29[8], FuF xxxv 173[10] (?; or abs.?, cf. Altheim & Stiehl ASA 274; interpret. of context uncert.);

emph. *mt'* ATNS 29[7], Aḥiq 36, Beh 48 (*mt['];* cf. Greenfield & Porten BIDG 46; Akkad. par. *māt*), Cowl p. 268, 56[18] l. 1 (for the reading, cf. Greenfield & Porten BIDG 32; Akkad. par. *māt*), KAI 266[9] (cf. e.g. Ginsberg BASOR cxi 26 n. 10, Fitzmyer Bibl xlvi 55, Horn AUSS vi 31 (n. 13), Gibson SSI ii p. 114f., Porten BiAr xliv 36, Porten & Yardeni sub TADAE A 1.1 :: Dupont-Sommer Sem i 53: = Sing. emph. of mt_2 (= mwt_2)),FX 136[13]; + suff. 2 p.s.m. *mtk* ATNS 2[3] (diff. reading, cf. Porten & Yardeni sub TADAE B 8.9); cf. Frah ii 9 (*mt'*), GIPP 29 - ¶ subst. land, town (as political entity): Aḥiq 36, Tell F 23; *mt 'kdh* HDS 9[2]: the land of Akkad (cf. also *mtkdy* KAI 233[3], cf. Lidzbarski ZA xxxi 196 (cf. also Zadok WO xv 211 n. 3) :: Dupont-Sommer Syr xxiv 35, Donner KAI a.l.: *mt* not to be pronounced, because it is the representation of an Akkad. determinative; cf. also Weidner AfO xvi 14f., Lipiński Stud 79, Fales AION xxviii 280ff.); *mt nbyh* ATNS 29[8]: the land of N.; *nbyh mt'* ATNS 29[7]: the land of N.; *mt kln* Tell F 3 (Akkad. par. *kal ālāni*), 5 (Akkad. par. *kib-ra-ti*): all towns/regions; *mn mt'* FX 136[13]: on behalf of the town (cf. Greek par. παρὰ τῆς πόλεως); *pḥh bmt'* KAI 266[9]: a governor in the land (dam. context; cf. Meyer FS Zucker 258: = town) - Segal ATNS a.l.: l. *mtwh[* (= Plur. + suff. 3 p.s.m.) in ATNS 55 ii 1 (highly uncert. reading) - for CIS ii 31[2] (= Del30), v. *rbšqh*.
v. $'mh_2$, ms_1, mt_6.

mt_2 v. mt_1.

mt_3 v. mt_6.

mt_4 v. mt_6.

mt_5 **OffAr** Sing. m. abs. *mt* KAI 225[2], Herm 5[9], 8[4] (heavily dam. context) - ¶ adj. (or poss. = QAL Part. pass. of mwt_1?, cf. e.g. Donner KAI sub 225, Gibson SSI ii p. 96, 140 :: Degen ZDMG cxxi 135 (for KAI 225): this interpret. imposs. :: Donner KAI sub 225: or = QAL Pf. 3 p.s.m. of mwt_1) dead.
v. ll_2, mh_2, mwt_1.

mt_6 **Samal** KAI 214[12,13,14], 215[4,10] - ¶ diff. word in KAI 214, 215, poss. = adverb: always (cf. Gibson SSI ii p. 72 (cf. however id. ibid. p. 82: this transl. diff. in KAI 215[4]), Faber FUCUS 230, ZDMG cxxxvii 278ff.; for KAI 214[12f.], cf. already Poeb 46) rather than: surely, indeed (for this interpret., cf. Lidzbarski Handb 319, Cooke NSI p. 167, Ginsberg AJSL l 2, Friedr 41*, Donner KAI a.l., de Moor UF i 187, Dion p. 28, Caquot Syr liv 136, Dupont-Sommer AH i/2, 5, Segert AAG p. 233, Garr DGSP 42 (cf. however Garb 264)) :: Halévy RS i 150: = adv. immediately in KAI 214[12,14], 215[4], in 215[10] = Sing. abs. of mt_3 (= man, person), cf. id. RS i 230, cf. already D.H.Müller WZKM vii 52, 58, 60f. for KAI 214[13,14], 215[4] (id. ibid. 58 n. 3: in KAI 214[12] = abbrev. of *mtn* (gift)) :: Landsberger Sam'al 50 n. 127: = pronoun, everyone??

(cf. also Koopmans 35) :: Winckler AltorForsch i 106f., Lipiński BiOr xxxiii 232, OLP viii 100ff. = Sing. abs. of mt_1 (= land), except in KAI 215[10] = (the people of) the land (cf. already D.H.Müller WZKM vii 58 for KAI 215[10]) :: Elliger FS Eissfeldt 85 n. 51: = Sing. abs. of mt_4 (= gift) - the reading of this word in KAI 214[28] (cf. e.g. Lidzbarski Handb 442, Cooke NSI p. 161, Friedr 41*, Donner KAI a.l., Dion p. 33, 179, Gibson SSI ii p. 68, Segert AAG p. 233, P.J.v.Zijl UF vii 508f.) improb., cf. Lipiński BiOr xxxiii 232, OLP viii 101 (dividing otherwise): l. *ntršh* = *ntr* (= Sing. cstr. (or abs.) of ntr_3) + *šh* (= Sing. abs. of $šh_1$ (= $š_1$)) = the dissector of the lamb (prob. reading, highly uncert. interpret.) :: D.H.Müller WZKM vii 53, 67 n. 1, 135 (div. otherwise): l. *mtnšh* = ITP Part. s.m. abs. of $nšy_1$ (= to bring into oblivity) :: Halévy RS i 142, 162: l. *mtwšh* word of unknown meaning; *pbnyt mt* KAI 214[14]: and I built constantly.

mt_7 v. *mmlkh*.

mtʾ v. *mṭ*.

mtb v. $mšb_1$.

mtbn **OffAr** Sing. + suff. 3 p.s.m. (or f.?) *mtbnh* TA-Ar 38[2] (reading uncert.; cf. Naveh TA a.l., cf. also (Naveh with) Aharoni & Amiran IEJ xi 141 (n. 13), Naveh AION xvi 31f.; cf. however Aharoni BIES xxvii 228: l. *mḥbrh* = m_{12} (= mn_5) + *ḥbrh* = n.l. (cf. also Weippert ZDPV lxxx 182), reading uncert., improb. interpret.) - ¶ subst. shed for straw (v. however supra).

mtw **JAr** Sing. + suff. 2 p.s.f. *mtwt[k]* MPAT 42[16] (cf. however Beyer ATTM 310, 642: l. *mntn* = QAL Inf. of *ntn*) - ¶ subst. demise, decease.

mtwm v. *ymʾ*.

mtḥ **Pun** Sing. abs. *mtḥ* RES 952 - ¶ subst. of unknown meaning, prob. function indication.

mtyn v. zwn_1.

mtkh **Ph** Sing. cstr. *mtkt* KAI 24[5] (:: Dahood Bibl lx 433 (div. otherwise): l. *tkt* = Sing. cstr. of *tkh* (= midst)) - ¶ subst. oppression (cf. v.d.Branden RSF ii 140f., cf. also Gibson SSI iii p. 36, H.P.Müller TUAT i 638) × e.g. Lidzbarski Eph iii 227f., 237, Röllig KAI a.l., Rosenthal ANET 654, Avishur PIB 208, 210f. (cf. also Collins WO vi 184, Gibson SSI iii p. 34): = midst.

mtm_1 v. $šʿl_1$.

mtm_2 **Ph** KAI 26A ii 16 - ¶ indefinite pronoun, something, anything (for the context of KAI 26A ii 16 and parallels, v. ll_2), cf. however Gibson SSI iii p. 60: *mtm* = adv. always, cf. also Faber ZDMG cxxxvii 280, 281 (n. 18).

v. *ymʾ*.

mtm_3 **Ph** diff. word in DD 13[1]; Caquot Sem xv 30: = m_{12} (= mn_5) + Sing. abs. of tm_1 (= in totality (uncert. interpret.)); Milik DFD 425f.:

= Sing. abs. of *mtm* (= totality (uncert. interpret.)) :: Dunand & Duru sub DD 13: = HIPH Part. s.m. abs. of *tmm$_1$* :: Gibson SSI iii p. 122: = YOPH Part. s.m. abs. of *tmm$_1$*.

mtn$_1$ v. *zwn$_1$*.

mtn$_2$ **Pun** Sing. abs. *mtn* KAI 277[5] (:: e.g. Nober VD xliii 204 (div. otherwise): l. *mtn*ʾ = Sing. + suff. 3 p.s.m., cf. also Garbini ArchClass xvi 70 :: Levi Della Vida with Garbini ArchClass xvi 70, 75: l. *mtn*ʾ = n.l.), Punica xviii/ii 131 1 (for this reading, cf. Bertrandy & Sznycer sub SPC 109, cf. however id. ibid.: l. *mtn<t>*); cstr. *mtn* CIS i 4730 (or = lapsus for *mt(n)t* (= Sing. cstr. of *mtnh*)) - **OffAr** Sing. emph. *mtn*ʾ Sach 75 ii 7, 11 (*mt[n]*ʾ), 12 - ¶ subst. gift; *bmtn* ʾ*bbt* KAI 277[5]: as a gift in the temple (:: Gibson SSI iii p. 154, 156: as a gift (and) as a temple); *lmtn*ʾ Sach 75 ii 7, 11, 12: as a gift.
v. *ḥnh$_1$*, *mt$_6$*.

mtnʾ v. *mṭn*ʾ.

mtnh **Ph** Sing. abs. *mtt* KAI 29[2] (on the problems of form & context, cf. Amadasi Guzzo Or lix 60f.) - **Pun** Sing. abs. *mtnt* KAI 99[1], 102[2], 104[1], 112[1], 113A 1, CIS i 192[1], 381B 2, 409[2f.] (*mt[n]t*), 410[3], 3712[2f.], 3783[6], 4872[2], 5510[7], Hofra 2[2], 15[1], SMI 12[2], 13[1f], 14[4] , Mozia vi 99[2] (= SMI 19), 100[2] (= SMI 20), 101 (= SMI 21), 104[1f.] (= SMI 23; cf. however Amadasi Guzzo SMI a.l.: l. *mtn<t>t* (lapsus)), ix 156[1] (= SMI 37), etc., etc. (the *ḥmtnt* in Mozia vi 102[1] = lapsus for *ḥmn mtnt*); cstr. *mtnt* RES 335[1]; + suff. 3 p.s.m. *mtnt*ʾ KAI 99[2]; + suff. 1 p.pl. *mtntn* Hofra 103[1f.] (?, cf. Berthier & Charlier Hofra p. 85, or rather lapsus for Sing. cstr. *mtnt*?) - ¶ subst. f. gift; *l*ʾ*dn lb*ʿ*l mtnt mtnt*ʾ *mlk b*ʿ*l* ʾ*š ndr* ... KAI 99[1f.]: for the lord Baʿal a gift, his gift is a *mlk b*ʿ*l* which he has vowed ... (v. *mlk$_5$*); *mtnt* ʾ*š ṭn*ʾ *b*ʿ*lytn* KAI 112[1f.]: the gift which B. has erected; etc. - Milik MUSJ xxxi 8ff. (cf. also Röllig KAI a.l.): the μαθηδ in KAI 174[6f.] = Sing. abs. of *mtnt*/*mtt* (highly uncert. interpret., cf. also Sznycer Sem viii 8f.) :: Ferron MC 76f. (div. otherwise): l. αμαθ (= Sing. abs. of ʾ*mh$_2$*) :: Sznycer Sem viii 8f. (div. otherwise): l. μαθ (= Sing. abs. of *m*ʿ*ṭ(h)* (= garment), or = corrupted form of *m*ʿ*ṭpt* (= garment)), ηδεσαθ (= Sing. f. abs. of *ḥdš$_3$*),v. also *z$_1$*.
v. *mlk$_5$*, *mtn$_2$*.

mtʿ v. *nt*ʿ.

mtql v. *mšql*.

mtqlh **OffAr** Sing. cstr. *mtqlt* Cowl 26[21], 28[11] - ¶ subst. weight; *bmtqlt mlk*ʾ Cowl 28[11]: according to the official weight; *bmtqlt prs* Cowl 26[21]: according to the Persian (i.e. official) weight - cf. also *mšql*.

mtqnn **Palm** Sing. emph. *mtqnn*ʾ CIS ii 3946[2] - ¶ subst. m. restorer; *mtqnn*ʾ *dy mdnḥ*ʾ *klh* CIS ii 3946[2]: the restorer of the whole Orient (title of the Palm. king), cf. Cantineau JA ccxxii 217ff., Altheim & Stiehl AAW ii 253f.; for par. title, v. ʾ*pnrṭt*.

mtr$_1$ **Pun** Plur. abs. *mtrm* Hofra 84[3] (uncert. reading) - ¶ subst. (?) of unknown meaning, in the comb. *rb hmtrm*, poss. function indication (??) or rather *mtrm* = (members of) a tribe (cf. Berthier & Charlier Hofra a.l.)? :: Février BAr '55/56, 157: l. *mkrm* (= QAL Part. act. pl.m. abs. of *mkr$_1$*) :: Garbini RSO xliii 17: l. *mgnm* (= members of the Magonide clan).

mtr$_2$ **OffAr** Israel BiOr xxxvii 6: l. *mtr* in NESE ii 66[1] (= Sing. cstr. of *mtr$_2$* (= oven poker); on this word, cf. Kaufman AIA 74: < Akkad.), uncert. interpret. (cf. Degen NESE ii 67: l. prob. *ntr* = n.p., reading *mtr* poss.).

mtrḥ **Ph** Sing. cstr. (v. infra) *mtrḥ* KAI 44[2] - **Pun** Sing. cstr. (v. infra) *mtrḥ* KAI 93[4] (= TPC 12), CIS i 260[4], 261[5], 3351[5f.], 3352[7], 4864[6], 4865[6], 4866[4], 4867[6], 4868[6], 4869[7], 4870[5f.], 4871[4], 5903[5], 5979[1,2] (= TPC 41) - ¶ subst. of uncert. meaning in the comb. *mtrḥ ʿštrny* (in all instances preceded by *mqm ʾlm* (v. *qwm$_1$*)), poss. indication of cultic function; Honeyman RHR cxxi 8ff.: *mtrḥ* prob. = YIPH Part. s.m. cstr. of *trḥ$_1$* (= consort, bridegroom, spouse; for this transl., cf. de Vaux BMB v 18 (n. 3) and cf. already Février JA ccxxx 298f., cf. also Uffenheimer Lesh xxx 170, Röllig sub KAI 44, Ferron StudMagr i 70 (n. 13; combining *mtrḥ* with preceding *ʾlm* and not taking it as parallel to *mqm*...), Février JA cclvi 5, Lipiński RAI xvii 33f. (n. 10), 48, 53, Hermann MiOr xv 35, cf. however Gibson SSI iii p. 146) :: Röllig FS Friedrich 412f.: *mtrḥ* = Sing. abs. (followed by nisbe-adj.) :: Février JA ccxxx 297ff.: = HITP Part. s.m. cstr. of *ʾrḥ$_1$* (= to determine, to fix), *mtrḥ* = priest assigned to the service of ... :: Berger RHR lxv 1ff.: *mtrḥ* = part of compound n.d. (Mithra) :: Slouschz TPI p. 197 (div. otherwise): l. *mt* (= QAL Part. act. s.m. abs. of *mwt$_1$*)+ *rḥ* (= form of *rḥ$_1$*) - for the diff. interpret. of *ʿštrny*, cf. the litt. quoted above and Seyrig Syr xl 22f. n. 24, Teixidor Syr xlvi 320f., li 308.

mtt v. *mtnh*, *ntn*.

N

n$_1$ v. *bn$_1$*.

n$_2$ v. *nṣp*.

n$_3$ v. *nʾ*.

nʾ **Ph** *n* KAI 50[3] - **Pun**, cf. Poen 942: *na* (?, v. *kʾ$_2$*) - **Hebr** *nʾ* KAI 196[5] - ¶ particle with deprecative function; *ʾpqn* KAI 50[3]: would that I might obtain (v. also *pwq$_1$*); *qrʾ nʾ* KAI 196[5]: you should read!
v. *bdr$_1$*.

nʾb **OldAr** HITP Pf. 3 p.pl.m. *htnʾbw* KAI 216[14] (cf. Poeb 51 n. 5, CF 30, Koopmans 77f., Degen AAG p. 67, Ben-Chayyim Lesh xxxv

250, Gibson SSI ii p. 91, Kaufman AIA 153, Younger JANES xviii 101 n. 38 × Cooke NSI p. 183f., Röllig KAI a.l.: HITNAPH/HITTANAPH of *᾽by* or *y᾽b* (cf. also Garb 274); cf. also Schaed 249, Segert AAG 257) - ¶ verb HITP to long for, to covet; *whtn᾽bw ᾽ḥy mlky᾽ lkl mh ...* KAI 216[14f.]: and my brothers the kings were envious because of everything ... (coveted everything) :: Ben-Chayyim Lesh xxxv 250: root *n᾽b* related to Hebr. root *n᾽p*.

n᾽y v. *᾽yny*.

n᾽lk **Ph** Lidzbarski Eph i 155, sub KI 37 (cf. also Röllig sub KAI 48): l. *n᾽lky* in KAI 48[2] = Sing. + suff. 1 p.s. of *n᾽lk* (= way, journey)?? (highly uncert. reading and interpret., cf. also RES sub 1 (div. otherwise): l. *-n* (end of n.p.) *᾽nky* (= *᾽nk*)) :: Lidzbarski Eph i 155: *lky* poss. = l_5 + suff. 2 p.s.f. (cf. also Milik Bibl xlviii 564).

n᾽n **Pun** Berthier & Charlier sub Hofra 83: the *n᾽nm* in the comb. *rb ḥn᾽nm* in Hofra 83[3] poss. = Plur. abs. of *n᾽n* (= function indication) or *n᾽nm* = tribal name (*ḥ* being $ḥ_1$, variant of h_1), less prob. interpret.: *ḥn᾽nm* poss. = name of clan? (related to n.p. Hannon??).

n᾽sph **Ph** Sing. abs. *n᾽spt* KAI 60[1] (for this form, cf. FR 54a (< *m᾽spt* with dissimilation of *m* to *n*; cf. also Lidzbarski Handb 223, Röllig KAI a.l.) × Gordon Or xxi 121, H.P.Müller ZA lxv 111 (div. otherwise): l. bn_6 (= var. of b_2) + *᾽spt* (= Sing. abs. of *᾽sph* (= community), cf. also Teixidor Syr lvi 382) × Dahood Bibl xxxiii 217f., v.d.Branden BiOr xxxvi 158 (div. otherwise): l. *bn* (= Plur. cstr. of bn_1) + *᾽spt* (= Sing. abs. of *᾽sph* (= community, assembly)); cf. also Gibson SSI iii p. 149; :: Cooke NSI p. 95f.: = NIPH Part. s.f. abs. of $᾽sp_1$ substantivated (= gathering, assembly)) - ¶ subst. gathering, assembly (v. also supra).

nb᾽₁ v. *ndy*.

nb᾽₂ **Hebr** Sing. abs. *nb᾽* KAI 193[20], Lach xvi 5 (?, dam. context) - ¶ subst. m. prophet; *wspr ṭbyhw ... hb᾽ ᾽l šlm ... m᾽t hnb᾽ l᾽mr ...* KAI 193[19ff.]: and the letter (v. spr_3) of T. ... which came (v. *bw᾽*) to Sh. ... from (the side of) the prophet, with the accompanying message ... (v. $᾽mr_1$; cf. e.g. Hempel ZAW lvi 131, de Vaux RB xlviii 190, 193, Lemaire IH i 101, 105, Hoftijzer FS Hospers 87f., 91 nn. 23, 25, 92f. n. 29 (sent by the prophet), Smelik PEQ '90, 136 :: Albright BASOR lxxiii 19 (n. 24), ANET 322, Diringer Lach iii p. 333, Röllig sub KAI 193, H.P.Müller UF ii 240, Gibson SSI i p. 39, 41: *m᾽t* = through (the instrumentality of) :: Torczyner Lach i p. 51, 59f.: l. *wspr ndbyhw ...* = a letter which N. ... had brought to Sh. from the prophet, saying); for the prophet in Lachish, cf. Thomas The Prophet, id. BZAW lxxvii 244ff., cf. also H.P.Müller UF ii 241f., Hoftijzer FS Hospers 89, Smelik PEQ '90, 136.

nbz **OffAr** Sing. abs. *nbz* Cowl 11[6] - ¶ subst. document, receipt; word of uncert. origin and etymology, cf. Kaufman AIA 77 (cf. v.Soden Or xxxvii 261, xlvi 191, AHW s.v. *nibzu*: Aramaic *nbz* > Akkad. (cf. also (Landsberger with) Altheim & Stiehl ASA 102, CAD s.v. *nibzu*, Muffs 186) :: Zimmern Fremdw 19: Akkad. *nibzu* > Ar. *nbz* :: Cowl p. 34: < Iran.).

nbṭ OffAr, cf. Frah app. 18: to grow (*nbṭwn*; cf. Nyberg FP 54, 100 :: Ebeling Frah a.l.: l. *‘b(y)twn* < root *‘by*$_1$ (= to become thick)).

nbṭgtp’š Nab group of signs in CIS ii 459, preceding *dkrwn*; reading uncert. (cf. Euting with Brünnow ProvArab i 210); meaning unknown.

nbl$_1$ v. *ybl*$_1$.

nbl$_2$ v. *ybl*$_1$.

nbl$_3$ **Pun** Sing. abs. *nbl* ICO-Malta-Npu 17[1] (uncert. context; cf. also Amadasi ICO a.l., Sem xxxviii 23); Plur. cstr. *nbl* KAI 137[5] (cf. e.g. Lidzbarski Eph iii 280, RES sub 942, Röllig KAI a.l. :: e.g. Berger RHR lviii 155, Lidzbarski Eph iii 58: l. *nblm* = Plur. abs.) - **Hebr** Sing. cstr. *nbl* KAI 183[2], 185[3], 186[2], 187[2], etc., etc. - ¶ subst. indicating certain type of vessel; *nbl nskt* KAI 137[5f.]: vessels of cast metal; *nbl yn* KAI 185[3]: a vessel containing wine; *nbl šmn* KAI 186[2f.]: a vessel containing oil; etc. - on the type of vessel, cf. e.g. Welten Stempel 54f., M.Aharoni TeAv vi 95ff. (and litt. mentioned there), Amadasi Guzzo Sem xxxviii 23f.

nbl$_4$ = musical instrument with 10 or 12 strings > Greek νάβλα, νάβλας, cf. also Latin *nablium*, *nablum*; cf. Boisacq 655, cf. also Liddell & Scott s.v. - on this word, cf. also Masson RPAE 67ff.

nbl$_5$ v. *nwl*$_1$.

nbnh Février RA xliv 124, 125f.: in KAI 46[6] l. *nbn[t]* (= Sing. abs. of *nbnh* (variant form of *mbnh* = construction)); cf. also Bunnens EPM 36f.: l. *nbn* = derivative of *bny*$_1$ (= monument?), cf. also Lipiński BiOr xlv 63, less prob. reading and interpret., cf. e.g. CIS i sub 144, Cooke NSI p. 111, Peckham Or xli 459, Cross BASOR ccviii 15ff. (div. otherwise): l. *mlktn* (= n.p., v. also *ṣb’*$_3$) + *bn* (= Sing. cstr. of *bn*$_1$), for this reading, cf. also - a) Delcor Syr xlv 331, 348f.: *bn* = Qal Pf. 3 p.s.m. of *bny*$_1$ - b) Albright BASOR lxxxiii 19: l. *wbn* = *w* + *bn*$_5$ (= *byn*$_2$), - c) Ferron RSO xli 285, 287f.: *bn* = Qal Inf. abs. of *bny*$_1$ (= architecture; improb. interpret.) :: Dupont-Sommer CRAI ’48, 15, 17f., JA cclii 301: l. *nrn[k]* = n.l. (cf. also Röllig KAI a.l.) :: v.d.Branden Mašr liv 286, 290f.: l. *bdrt* = *b*$_2$ + Sing. abs. of *drh*$_2$ (= sanctuary).

nb‘ OldAr Qal Impf. 3 p.s.m. *yb‘* KAI 223B 8 (v. however infra) - ¶ verb Qal to boil over, to speak, to stammer (cf. Dupont-Sommer Sf p. 111, Koopmans 60, Donner KAI a.l., Fitzmyer AIS 88) × Thomas JSS v 284: *yb‘* partly dittography of foll. *yb‘h* (cf. also Degen AAG p. 18 n. 73, GGA ’79, 16, Lemaire & Durand IAS 117, 142) :: Lipiński Stud 46f.: = Qal or Pa‘el Impf. 3 p.s.m. of *b‘‘* (= to be impatient, to be anxious) :: Ben-Chayyim Lesh xxxv 246 (div. otherwise): l. *yb‘h*

= QAL Impf. 3 p.s.m. of *b'y$_1$* - a form of this verb *nby't* (= QAL Pf. 1 p.s.) also in CIS ii 4093[2]? (uncert. interpret., cf. Cantineau Gramm 80, Rosenthal Sprache 14 n. 1).

nbr **Hatra** Sing. emph. *nbr'*, cf. Assur 27e 1 - ¶ subst. ardour, passion (?); *nbr' dmṭr'* Assur 27e 1: a torrential rain.

nbršt v. *rwšh*.

nbš v. *npš*.

ngbrg v. *ḥwb$_1$*.

ngg **OffAr** Grelot DAE p. 401f. n. c: l. *[m]tngn* in Cowl 27[1] = ITP Part. pl.m. abs. of *ngg* (= to cry (out)) or l. *[']tngn* = ITP Pf. 1 p.pl. of *ngg* :: Cowl a.l.: l. *[n]tngn* = ITP Impf. 1 p.pl. of *ngn* (QAL = to strike > to inflict an injury; ITP = to be injured).

ngd$_1$ **OffAr** QAL Part. pass. s.f. abs. *ngydh* Cowl 26[8] (v. infra :: Cowl p. 94, Leand 35c: = QAL Part. pass. s.f. abs. of *ngd$_2$* (= to report, to describe) :: Sach p. 46 = n.l. :: Bowman AJSL lviii 309: = Sing. + suff. 3 p.s.f. of *ngyd* (= keel, prow) :: Perles OLZ '11, 498: l. *ngyrh* (without interpret.)); ITP Impf. 3 p.s.m. *ytngd* Cowl 26[4] (cf. e.g. Grelot Sem xx 26 (v. also infra) :: Cowl a.l.: = ITP Impf. 3 p.s.m. of *ngd$_2$* (= to be drawn up (said of a statement), cf. Leand 35e) :: Sach p. 44, 46: l. *ytngr* = ITP Impf. 3 p.s.m. of *ngr$_1$* (= to timber, to do a carpenter's work); cf. also Perles OLZ '11, 498) - ¶ verb QAL to pull, to tow: Cowl 26[8] (cf. e.g. Epstein ZAW xxxiii 141, Grelot Sem xx 26, DAE p. 288, Porten & Yardeni sub TADAE A 6.2; v. also supra) - ITP to be pulled, to be towed: Cowl 26[4] (cf. e.g. Epstein ZAW xxxiii 141, Bowman AJSL lviii 309, Grelot Sem xx 26, DAE p. 286, Porten & Yardeni sub TADAE A 6.2) - a derivative of this root poss. in AJSL lviii 303B 7 (*ngyd[n]* = QAL Part. pass. pl.m./f. abs.?? :: Bowman AJSL lviii 305, 310: = Plur. abs. of *ngyd* (= keel, prow)) - Margolis JQR ii 441, Halévy RS xx 63, Lindenberger APA 118, 252 n. 348: prob. l. *[n]gt* (= QAL Pf. 2 p.s.m. of *ngd$_1$*) in Aḥiq 128 (poss. restoration, cf. however Cowl a.l., Kottsieper SAS 10, 15, 41, 197 : l. *[dr]gt* = QAL Pf. 2 p.s.m. of *drg$_1$*).

ngd$_2$ **Hebr** HIPH Inf. cstr. *hg[d]* KAI 193[2] (reading however uncert., cf. Pardee HAHL 85); HOPH Pf. 3 p.s.m. *hgd* KAI 193[13] - ¶ verb HIPH to report; *šlḥ lhg[d]* KAI 193[1f.]: he sends to report - HOPH to be reported; + *l$_5$*, *wl'bdk hgd l'mr* KAI 193[13f.]: it has been reported to your servant that ...

v. *'mr$_1$*, *mynkd*, *ngd$_1$*.

ngd$_3$ **OldAr** Plur. + suff. 1 p.s. *ngdy* KAI 224[10] (for the reading, cf. Fitzmyer CBQ xx 459, AIS 112f. :: Dupont-Sommer BMB xiii 27, 32f.: l. *ngry* = Plur. + suff. 1 p.s. of *ngr$_3$* (= prefect; cf. Koopmans 65, Degen AAG p. 21, 46, 52, Sader EAS 126, 140; cf. also Donner KAI a.l., Noth ZDPV lxxvii 150 (n. 88), Gibson SSI ii p. 48, 54, Puech lxxxix 584, Lemaire & Durand IAS 119, 129, 145)) - **OffAr** Sing. emph. *ngd'* KAI

266^8 (cf. Fitzmyer Bibl xlvi 44f., 54f., WA 232f., 240f., Porten BiAr xliv 36 (cf. also Dupont-Sommer Sem i 52, Kaufman AIA 75 n. 224, Donner KAI a.l., Delsman TUAT i 634) :: Dupont-Sommer Sem i 52: or l. *ngr*ʾ = Sing. emph. of ngr_3 (= chief, prefect; cf. also Donner KAI a.l., Lipiński Or lvii 434f.) :: Krael p. 144: or l. *ngr*ʾ = Sing. emph. of ngr_3 (= herald) :: Ginsberg BASOR cxi 25 n. 4c, 26, Milik RB lxi 248, Horn AUSS vi 31 (n. 12), Gibson SSI ii p. 113, 115, Shea BASOR ccxxiii 61: l. *ngw*ʾ = Sing. emph. of *ngw* (= region, territory), cf. also Galling TGI 72 (n. 5)); Plur. cstr. *ngdy* ATNS 13^3, 19^8 - ¶ subst. m. officer, overseer, commander - Delcor Syr xlv 331, 349, 351, Peckham Or xli 459, 465, Cross BASOR ccviii 15ff.: l. *ngd* = Sing. abs. of ngd_3 in KAI 46^7 (uncert. reading and interpret.; cf. also CIS i sub 144, Cooke NSI p. 111: l. *ngd* = n.p.) × Dupont-Sommer CRAI '48, 15, 18f., JA cclii 301, Février RA xliv 124, 126, Röllig KAI a.l.: l. *ngr* = n.p. (cf. also Albright BASOR lxxxiii 19: l. *ngr[š]* = NIPH Pf. 3 p.s.m. of $grš_1$) :: Ferron RSO xli 285, 287f.: l. *nr*ʿ = n.l.; on the subject, cf. also Gibson SSI iii p. 27.
v. bny_1, *ngy*, ngr_2.

ngdw v. *ngdwt*ʾ.

ngdwtʾ (< Iran., cf. Humbach AIT p. 9f., Degen Lesh xxxiv 317, Hinz AISN 171) - **OffAr** Sing. abs. *ngdwt*ʾ KAI $273^{3,4}$ (for the reading, cf. Humbach AIT p. 7, 9f., Degen Lesh xxxiv 316f., ZDMG cxxi 125 :: Kutscher, Naveh & Shaked Lesh xxxiv 126: = Sing. emph. of *ngdw* (= leadership) :: Altheim & Stiehl ASA 274, GMA 340: l. *ngrwt*ʾ = Sing. emph. of $ngrw_1$ (= carpenter's workshop; cf. Altheim & Stiehl Suppl 12, Donner KAI a.l.: = group of carpenters, cf. also Andreas NGWG '32, 9, 11, In der Smitten BiOr xxviii 310)) :: In der Smitten BiOr xxviii 310: or = Sing. emph. of $ngrw_2$ (= variant form of NIPH Part. of *ngr*) = what is poured out :: Barnett JRAS '15, 341, Cowley JRAS '15, 343: in l. 3. l. *ngrwt*ʾ = Sing. emph. of $ngrw_3$ (= carving) :: Barnett JRAS '15, 341 (div. otherwise): in l. 4 l. *wšn* (= *w* + *šn* = Sing. cstr. of $šn_1$ (= ivory)) *gbwt*ʾ (< root *gb*ʾ) :: Cowley JRAS '15, 343 (div. otherwise): in l. 4: l. *šnhbwt*ʾ (= Sing. emph. of *šnhbw* (= ivory)) - ¶ subst. not-killing (cf. Humbach AIT p. 9f.).

ngh **DA** Sing. abs. *ngh* i 8 (:: McCarter BASOR ccxxxix 51, 54, Hackett BTDA 29, 44, 102: = Sing. cstr.) - ¶ subst. brightness, light (for the context of DA i 8, v. $ʾl_3$) - Caquot Syr xxxii 54, Milik RN vi/iv 56 n. 2, Syr xliv 297, Altheim & Stiehl AAW iv 265, Vattioni IH a.l.: l. *ngh*ʾ (= Sing. emph.) = dawn in Hatra 49^1 (highly uncert. reading, less prob. interpret.).

nghy v. $nsḥ_2$.

ngw v. ngd_3.

ngy **OffAr** Porten & Yardeni sub TADAE B 4.4: l. prob. *ngy*ʾ (=

Sing. emph. of *ngy* (= district, region)) in Cowl 2^3 (:: Porten Arch 52 n. 93, Grelot DAE p. 267: l. *ngd*ʾ = Sing. emph. of ngd_3 :: Cowl a.l.: l. *ngr*ʾ (= Sing. emph. of ngr_2)) - on this word, cf. also Kaufman AIA 75.

ngyd v. ngd_1.

ngl **Hatra** Safar Sumer xvii 31: the diff. *ngl* in Hatra 95 = QAL Pf. 3 p.s.m. of *ngl* (= to take refuge; uncert. reading, highly uncert. interpret.) :: Caquot Syr xl 10 : = QAL Impf. 1 p.pl. of *gl*ʾ (= to pronounce, to name)? (cf. also Vattioni IH a.l.).

ngn v. gny_2, *ngg*.

ngʿ$_1$ **OldAr** HAPH Impf. 3 p.s.m. *yhg*ʿ KAI 202B 16, 19 (*[y]hg*ʿ; cf. Kutscher with Naveh AION xvi 33 n. 47, Dupont-Sommer AH i/2, 5, Ben-Chayyim Lesh xxxv 252, Tawil JNES xxxii 481 n. 50 (cf. also Torrey JAOS xxxv 363) :: Donner KAI a.l., Degen AAG p. 76: = HAPH Impf. 3 p.s.m. of *gw*ʿ (= to remove; cf. also Lidzbarski Eph iii 10f., Sader EAS 210 (n. 33)) :: Gibson SSI ii p. 11, 16: = QAL Impf. 3 p.s.m. of *hg*ʿ (= to efface); on the subject, cf. also Pognon ISMM 171, Halévy RS xvi 367f., Nöldeke ZA xxi 383) - **OffAr** QAL Part. act. s.m. abs. *ng*ʿ Aḥiq 165 (*[n]g*ʿ), 166 (for the reading, cf. also Lindenberger APA 169, 269 n. 514; cf. also Puech RB xcv 591) - ¶ verb QAL to touch; + b_2, *zy ng*ʿ *bk* Aḥiq 166: whoever touches you - HAPH to take away, to remove, to destroy; + obj.: KAI 202B 16, 19.

ngʿ$_2$ **Hebr** Sing. abs. *ng*ʿ AMB 1^4 - ¶ subst. plague.

ngr$_1$ v. ngd_1.

ngr$_2$ (< Akkad. < Sum., cf. Zimmern Fremdw 25, Widengren HDS 224ff., Kaufman AIA 75) - **Pun** Sing. abs. *ngr* CIS i 354, $5547^{5f.}$ (*ng[r]*), Hofra $95^{1f.}$, 96^1, 97^2 (uncert. reading) - **OffAr** Sing. emph. *ngr*ʾ Cowl 63^9 (cf. Cowl a.l.; heavily dam. context, diff. interpret.; in l. 12 l. *ng[r*ʾ*]*??), IEJ xxxviii 164A 8, B i 6 (*[n]gr*ʾ, uncert. reading, heavily dam. context); Plur. emph. *ngry*ʾ Del 77^1, Cowl $26^{9,22}$ - **Nab** Sing. emph. *ngr*ʾ ADAJ x 47 i 2, *ngrh* CIS ii 2474^2, 3001 (in both instances uncert. reading) - **Palm** Sing. emph. *ngr*ʾ Inv xii 40^1 (cf. Aggoula Sem xxix 115, cf. however Bounni & Teixidor Inv xii a.l.: l. rather *ngd*ʾ = n.p.) - **Hatra** Sing. emph. *ngr*ʾ 202^4, 295^1 (cf. As-Saliḥi Irâq xxxv 67 (n. 12), Sumer xxxi 172, Aggoula Sem xxvii 123f., Degen NESE iii 96, Vattioni IH a.l. × Teixidor Syr li 335: l. *ngd*ʾ = Sing. emph. of ngd_3) - ¶ subst. m. carpenter, passim; *ng[r] šmḥšbm* CIS i $5547^{5f.}$: the carpenter who makes engines.

v. *ngy*.

ngr$_3$ v. bny_1, ngd_3.

ngrbt (< Iran., cf. Segal sub ATNS 26, Shaked Or lvi 412) - **OffAr** Plur. abs. *ngrbt* ATNS 26^6 - ¶ subst. f., meaning uncert., prob. referring to (part of) a ship, or to something related to naval practice; Shaked

Or lvi 412: = vessel for catching ships?? :: Segal ATNS a.l.: = chain.

ngrh v.Soden Or xxxvii 261, xlvi 191, AHW s.v. *nungurtu*: *ngrh* (< root *ngr* = to continue, to be prolonged) > Akkad. *nungurtu* (= kind of property); improb. interpret., cf. CAD s.v.

ngrw$_1$ v. *ngdwt*ʾ.

ngrw$_2$ v. *ngdwt*ʾ.

ngrw$_3$ v. *ngdwt*ʾ.

ngš OffAr diff. word (Sing. abs.) in IrAnt iv 109[2]. Teixidor Syr xliv 184: = task-master, cf. however Dupont-Sommer IrAnt iv 110f.: = n.p. and cf. Garbini AION xvii 93f. remarking on several poss. lines of interpret.

nd Amm diff. word (??) of unknown meaning in BASOR cxciii 8[4] (for this prob. reading, cf. Horn BASOR cxciii 8, 11) or to be connected with preceding *yl*?? (meaning??); Horn BASOR cxciii a.l.: = Sing. abs./cstr. of *nd* (= wall); :: Puech & Rofé RB lxxx 532f., 537f., Fulco BASOR ccxxx 41, Jackson ALIA 10, 19, 25, Aufrecht sub CAI 59: l. *ylnn* = Qal Impf. 3 p.pl.m. of *lyn*$_1$ (cf. Smelik HDAI 84) :: Puech & Rofé RB lxxx 532f., 537f.: or l. *ylnn* = Qal Impf. 3 p.s.m. + *n* of *lyn*$_1$ (cf. Shea PEQ '79, 17, 19) :: Shea PEQ '79, 17, 19: or *ylnn* = Pol Impf. 3 p.s.m. of *lyn*$_1$ (= to spend the night, to be posted nightly) :: Cross BASOR cxciii 17ff. (nn. 12, 13): l. *ylḥn* = n.d. or (dividing otherwise): l. *-y lḥn* (= Sing. abs. of *lḥn*$_2$ (= hierophant)) :: Sasson PEQ '79, 121: = Qal Impf. 3 p.s.m. of *lḥn*$_1$ (= to be skilful > to be masterful, to prevail) :: Albright BASOR cxcviii 38, Dion RB lxxxii 32, Shea PEQ '81, 105, 107: l. *ylḥm* = Niph Impf. 3 p.s.m. of *lḥm*$_1$ (= to fight; cf. however Garr DGSP 121) :: v.Selms BiOr xxxii 7f.: l. *yl ṣd* = lapsus for *kl ṣd* (= Sing. cstr. of *kl*$_1$ + Sing. abs. of *ṣd*$_2$).

ndb$_1$ Hebr Nitp Pf. 3 p.s.m. *ntndb* SM 75[4] - **JAr** Itp Pf. 3 p.pl.m. ʾ*tndbwn* MPAT-A 11[4] (= SM 43); 3 p.s./pl. ʾ*tndb[* SM 25[4] (heavily dam. context) - ¶ verb Nitp/Itp to vow to donate, to volunteer: MPAT-A 11[4], SM 75[4] (for the context, v. *mšth*) - a form of this verb prob. also in *ndb*ʾ RES 907[1] (= Qal Pf. 3 p.s.m. + suff. 3 p.s.m./f. or Pf. 3 p.pl.m., cf. also Février RHR cxliii 18).
v. *dnb*, *kdb*$_1$, *ndb*$_2$, *ndr*$_1$.

ndb$_2$ Samal Sing. + suff. 3 p.s.m. *ndbh* KAI 214[33] (v. litt. mentioned below × Gibson SSI ii p. 76: = Qal Inf. + suff. 3 p.s.m. of *ndb*$_1$) - ¶ subst. (v. however supra) prob. meaning instigation (cf. e.g. D.H.Müller WZKM vii 54, 69, Cooke NSI p. 163, 171, Koopmans p. 41, Donner KAI a.l., Gibson SSI ii p. 69, 76 :: e.g. Halévy RS i 164, ii 57, Lidzbarski Handb 321, Dion p. 131: = generosity (cf. however Dion p. 35: = 'promptitude') :: Sader EAS 165 (n. 35): = complaint).

ndd verb Qal to flee - v.Soden Or xxxvii 261, xlvi 191: > Akkad. *nadādu* (= to make way, to yield; cf. also idem AHW s.v.), less prob.

interpret., also CAD s.v. - Dupont-Sommer JKF i 203, 210: l. *nd'n* = QAL Imper. pl.f. in AMB 7[22] (improb. interpret., cf. also Naveh & Shaked AMB a.l. (div. otherwise): l. *d'n* (= magic word) or = *d*$_3$ + *'n*$_4$ (= yes), cf. also Beyer ATTM 372f.: l. *d'n* = QAL Pf. 3 p.s.m. of *dyn*$_1$ (= to decide)).

ndḥ v. *dḥy*.

ndy Mo Lipiński Or xl 340: l. *[n]dh* = PI'EL Pf. 3 p.s.m. in KAI 181[33] (= to exclude), highly uncert. interpret. - cf. Frah xviii 19: to separate (*ndyḥwn*, *ndywn*), cf. Nyberg FP 49, 90 (cf. also Toll ZDMG-Suppl viii 37) :: Ebeling Frah a.l.: l. *nby'wn* from *np'*$_1$ = to seave.

ndm v. *dm*$_1$.

ndr$_1$ Ph QAL Pf. 3 p.s.m. *ndr* KAI 18[1], 40[5] (cf. Harr 65, 123, FR 262,3 n., Röllig KAI a.l., Dahood Bibl xliii 361, Segert GPP p. 192: preceded by QAL Pf. 3 p.s.m. of *kwn*$_1$ used as indication of Plusquampf.; or = QAL Part. s.m. abs.? or rather = Sing. cstr. of *ndr*$_2$?, cf. M.Cohen SVS 163f., Bron RIPK 69), 45[1] (heavily dam. context), CIS i 8[2] (= DD 2), 9[2] (= DD 3; *nd[r]*), 15[2] (= Kition A 4), RES 504A 2 (= DD 7), B 2 (= DD 8), 1204[3] (dam. context), DD 14[1], Kition A 30[2]; 3 p.pl.m. *ndr* RES 367 i 2 (cf. Delavault & Lemaire RB lxxxiii 569ff., cf. however also Lidzbarski Eph i 285ff. :: Teixidor Syr lvi 383: with s.f. subject) - **Pun** QAL Pf. 3 p.s.m. *ndr* KAI 63[1], 64[1], 66[1], 72A 2, B 1, 82 (or = Sing. cstr. of *ndr*$_2$?), 84 (*[n]dr*; or = Sing. cstr. of *ndr*$_2$?), 114[1] (or = Sing. cstr. of *ndr*$_2$?; Röllig KAI a.l.: = Sing. cstr. of *ndr*$_2$, cf. however idem sub KAI 84), CIS i 180[2f.], 5707[3] (or = Sing. cstr. of *ndr*$_2$?), 5727[3] (or = Sing. cstr. of *ndr*$_2$?), Hofra 1[2], 5[1] (or = Sing. cstr. of *ndr*$_2$?), 10[1] (or = Sing. cstr. of *ndr*$_2$?), 14[1] (or = Sing. cstr. of *ndr*$_2$?), Punica iv A 2[1], xvii 10[1] (or = Sing. cstr. of *ndr*$_2$?), Antas 51[1], Mozia ii 111[2] (= SMI 1), iii 71[2] (= SMI 5; or = Sing. cstr. of *ndr*$_2$?; cf. Garbini Mozia iii p. 72f., Amadasi Guzzo SMI a.l.), iv 97[2] (= SMI 11), vi 96 ii 2b (= SMI 16), ix 158[1] (= SMI 39), MontSir ii 80[1], ICO-Malta 9[1], etc., etc., *n'dr* CIS i 3763[3], *n'dr* KAI 156[1], CIS i 186[2], 358[3], Hofra 107[2], Punica xi 35c 1, Sem xxxvi 26[1], etc., etc., *nd'r* CIS i 3992[3f.], 4475[3] (*[nd]'r*), 4564[4], *nd'r* KAI 147[2] (or = 3 p.s.f.?, or rather = Sing. abs. of *ndr*$_2$??), CIS i 1697[2f.] (*[n]d'r?*, dam. context), 4961[1] (*[n]d'r*; or = Sing. cstr. of *ndr*$_2$?), Hofra 153[3] (or = Sing. cstr. of *ndr*$_2$?), Sem xxxvi 30[1], BAr-NS ii 229, *n'd'r* Punica xvii 1 (cf. FR 132b, Röllig sub KAI 175), *ndwr* CIS i 2522[3], *nndr* (lapsus) CIS i 1292[2f.], *bdr* (lapsus) CIS i 1456[2], 3233[4], *ldr* (lapsus) CIS i 2586[3], *mdr* (lapsus) CIS i 840[2], *nnr* (lapsus) CIS i 3265[8], 3867[3], *nbr* (lapsus) CIS i 735[3f.], *n'r* (lapsus?) CIS i 805[2], 1110[3], 3753[2], 4825[2], RES 179[1], *nr* (lapsus?) CIS i 336[2], 941[2f.], 1358[3], etc., *mr* (lapsus) CIS i 403[2], *nd'* (lapsus) CIS i 3392[2], *nd* (lapsus) CIS i 1358[3], 2207[2], *dr* (lapsus) CIS i 360[2], 804[3], 1339[3f.] (*d[r]*), *ndrr* (?, lapsus) Hofra 168[2f.], *r* (lapsus) CIS i 3240[3], cf. KAI 175[3]: ναδωρ (cf. FR 131, 132b,

Röllig KAI a.l.); + suff. 3 p.s.m. (or f.) *ndrʾ* RES 891^{2} (or rather = Pf. 3 p.pl.?), KAI 159^{9} (or = Sing. + suff. 3 p.s.m. of *ndr*$_2$? :: Février RHR cxliii 17f.: l. *ndbʾ* = QAL Pf. 3 p.pl. of *ndb*$_1$); 3 p.s.f. *ndr* KAI 109^{2}, CIS i 191^{2}, 228^{2}, 279^{3}, 302^{3}, 304^{4}, 5521^{1} (dam. context), 5779$^{4f.}$ (or = Sing. cstr. of *ndr*$_2$?), 5863^{3}, 5870^{3} (or = Sing. cstr. of *ndr*$_2$?), Punica xvii 9^{1} (or = Sing. cstr. of *ndr*$_2$?), etc., etc., *ndrʾ* KAI 88$^{2f.}$, 164^{2}, CIS i 216$^{3f.}$, 280$^{2f.}$, 371^{3}, 5547^{3}, 5692$^{2f.}$, 5733$^{2f.}$, 5761^{2}, 5771^{4}, 5773^{2}, 5823^{3}, 5834 (*[n]drʾ*?; diff. and dam. context), 5844^{4}, 5878^{2}, 5911$^{3f.}$, RSF iii 51 ii 2, Hofra 24^{2}, Punica xii 3^{2}, 5^{1}, xviii/ii 129^{2}, *ndrʿ* CIS i 232^{3}, 281^{3}, 320^{3}, 349^{3}, 515^{2}, 3244^{2}, *nʿdr* KAI 87^{4}, *nʾdrʿ* CIS i 3546^{2}, *nʿdrʾ* Punica xvii 2$^{1f.}$, *ndrt* (lapsus?) CIS i 417$^{3f.}$ (cf. CIS i 1200^{2}??), *bdr* (lapsus) CIS i 605^{4}, *bdrʿ* (lapsus) CIS i 1717^{2}, *ldr* (lapsus) CIS i 2670^{3}, *nddr* (lapsus) CIS i 375$^{3f.}$, *nrdʿ* (lapsus; originally *nrʿ*, the *d* added later at the wrong place) CIS i 3616^{5}, *nrʾ* (lapsus?) CIS i 4607^{3}, *drʾ* (lapsus), CIS i 3010^{3}, *drʿ* (lapsus) CIS i 1428^{3}; 3 p.pl. *ndr* KAI 47^{1} (or = 3 p.s.m.? :: Röllig KAI a.l.: = Sing./Plur. cstr. of *ndr*$_2$), CIS i 348^{3}, 4596$^{3f.}$, 5702^{3}, *ndrʾ* KAI 159^{1}, *nʿdrʾ* KAI 155$^{1f.}$ (cf. Chabot sub Punica v 5, Jongeling NINPI 181; or = s.f.? (cf. RES sub 179, Röllig KAI a.l.) or div. otherwise l. *ndr* = QAL Pf. 3 p.s.m.), Sem xxxvi 28^{1} - **Amm** QAL Pf. 3 p.s.m. *ndr* SANSS-Amm 36 (= Jackson ALIA 77 no. 49 = CAI 56 = CSOI-Amm 80; for this text, cf. also Bordreuil & Lemaire Sem xxix 80f.) - **OldAr** QAL Pf. 3 p.s.m. *nzr* KAI 201^{4} (same root as *ndr*??; for the problems involved, cf. e.g. Albright BASOR lxxxvii 26, Levi Della Vida BASOR xc 30 n. 1, Ginsberg Ginzberg Vol. (Engl.) 161 n. 8, Garbini ISNO 195, Degen AAG p. 35 n. 16, Macintosh VT xxi 55f., Gibson SSI ii p. 4, de Moor & Dijkstra UF vii 173 (nn. 15-17), Priebatsch UF xii 322, Boyd UF xvii 61ff., Stefanovic COAI 118f.) - **OffAr** QAL Pf. 3 p.s.m. *ndr* Sam 15 (same root as in Ph./Pun.?, v. sub OldAr.), THP 146^{4} (or = Sing. cstr. of *ndr*$_2$?, dam. context; Greek par. εὐχην) - **Palm** QAL Pf. 3 p.s.m. *ndr* PNO 14^{5} - ¶ verb QAL to vow, passim - **1)** + obj., *mtnt ndr* CIS i 4935^{3} (or = lapsus for *mtnt ʾš ndr*?; cf. also *ʾš ndr ndr* CIS i 3732$^{3f.}$: which he vowed as a vow, cf. however Chabot sub CIS i a.l.: = lapsus for *ndr ʾš ndr* or *ʾš ndr*) - **2)** + *l*$_5$, *zy nzr lh* KAI 201^{4}: to whom he made a vow, cf. Punica ix 9 i 1, xvii 5^{1}, SANSS-Amm 36, PNO 14^{5}; cf. also in Punic texts, *lrbt ... ndr bdʿštrt* CIS i 5727$^{1,3f.}$: to the lady ... B. has made a vow (v. however supra), cf. CIS i 3794^{1,3}, 3795^{1,3}, 3800$^{1ff.}$, 5707^{1,3}, 5779$^{1,4f.}$, Hofra 20$^{1f.}$, Mozia iii 71$^{1f.}$ (= SMI 3), THP 146^{4}, etc. - **3)** + *ʿl*$_7$, *[n]dr bʿlšlk ... ʿl bnm* KAI 84: B. has made a vow ... for the sake of his son (v. however supra), cf. CIS i 15^{2} (= Kition A 4) - **4)** cf. also the foll. combinations - a) *ʾš ndr wṭynʾ ʾdrbʿl* KAI 119^{2}: which A. has vowed and erected, cf. KAI 170^{1} - b) *ʾš ndr wytn ... lʾdnnm* RES 367 i 2 (v. supra): which they vowed and gave ... to their lord - c) *pʿl wndr wḥdš ʾyt hgzt* (v. however *gzt) st ʿbdʾšmn ... ltnt* KAI 72B 1ff.: A. has made, vowed and restored this *gzt* (?, v. *gzt*) to T. - d) *ʾš ndr wyṭnʾ ... ʿl bny ... lʾdny* Kition A 30[2]: which he vowed and erected for the sake of his son... to his lord - Ginsberg Ginzberg Vol. (Engl.) 161 n. 8: l. *ndrʾ* (= QAL Pf. 3 p.s.m. + suff. 3 p.s.m.) in RES 907[1] :: Chabot sub RES 907: l. *ndbʾ* = QAL Pf. 3 p.s.m. + suff. 3 p.s.m. of ndb_1 (= to present, to offer) (cf. also Berger RevArch '89 ii 38) - the *ndrʾ* in CIS i 5352[3], 5353[3], 5354[3] of diff. interpret. because of foll. lacuna - the uncert. *[nd]hr* in Hofra 170[2] poss. = QAL Impf. 3 p.s.m. or = Sing. cstr. of ndr_2 - RES sub 53: l. *ndr* = QAL Pf. 3 p.s.m. in RES 53[1] (improb. reading, cf. Lidzbarski Eph i 74, Chabot sub RES 806, Cantineau Nab ii 70: l. *bdr* = n.p.) - a form of this root in Kition D 21[2], cf. Liverani RSF iii 37, 40: l. *ytdr* = HITP Impf. 3 p.s.m. (uncert. interpret.; cf. Amadasi sub Kition D 21: or l. *ytdr[k]* = HITP Impf. 3 p.s.m. of drk_1 (= to press (uncert. interpret.)) :: Dupont-Sommer MAIBL xliv 281: l. *ytqr[b]* (= HITP Impf. 3 p.s.m. of qrb_1), cf. also Puech RSF iii 12f. :: Coote BASOR ccxx 47, 49 (div. otherwise): l. *yt* (= QAL Impf. 3 p.s.m. of $ʾty_1$) :: Teixidor Syr xlix 434: text non-Semitic ?

v. ndr_2, *ndrn*.

ndr₂ Ph Sing. abs. *ndr* KAI 40[5] - **Pun** Sing. abs. *ndr* KAI 103[2], 105[2], 107[2], 108[2], CIS i 3732[3] (?; v. ndr_1), Hofra 3[1], 8[1], Punica xii 9[1], 11[1], etc., etc., *nʿdr* Hofra 228[1], Punica iv A 2[2] (for the context, cf. also Hoftijzer OMRO xliv 94), BAr-NS i-ii 229, *ndʿr* KAI 147[4] (?, dam. context), 155[1], 156, Trip 43, Hofra 44[1], 88[2], Punica ix 9 i 1, xi 35c 1, xii 8[1], Sem xxxvi 26[1], etc., etc. (for this orthography, cf. FR 96c), *ndʾr* Hofra 142[2], *ldr* (lapsus) Hofra 227[1]; + suff. 3 p.s.m./f. *ndrʾ* KAI 147[2] (or rather = QAL Pf. 3 p.s.f. or 3 p.pl. of ndr_1??); + suff. 3 p.s.m. *ndrm* KAI 115[2] (= Hofra 27; reading *ndrʾ* in KAI mistake), Hofra 43[5] (for the reading, cf. Février BAr '55/56, 157 :: Berthier & Charlier Hofra a.l.: l. *ndr š* (= z_1)), 121[3]; *ndʿrm* Punica xi 38[3] (= RES 303; :: Chabot Punica a.l., Garbini BO xx 111, GP p. 29: = Plur. abs.); + suff. 1 p.s. *ndry* Punica xviii/i 31[3f.]; Plur. abs. *ndrm* Hofra 118[1] - **OffAr** Sing. abs. *ndr* Cowl 72[18] - ¶ subst. vow, more specifically: votive offering, passim; *ywm lndr* Cowl 72[18]: day of a vow (prob. a day on which a vow was made/fulfilled).

v. dr_1, *mrʾ*, ndr_1.

ndr₃ v. $ʿbr_4$.

ndrn Ph inscription on fragment of a dish (poss. a fish plate) Ber xi 136 (prob. reading); Ingholt Ber xi a.l.: = Sing. abs. of *ndrn* (= vow) or = QAL Pf. 3 p.s.m. + suff. 1 p.s. of ndr_1 (highly uncert. interpret.).

ndš OffAr QAL Pf. 3 p.s.m. *ndš* Cowl 32[6]; 3 p.pl.m. *ndšw* Cowl 27[5,24], 30[10]; + suff. 3 p.s.m. *ndšwhy* Cowl 30[9], 31[8]; Impf. 3 p.pl.m. *yndšw* Cowl 30[8], 31[7] - ¶ verb QAL to destroy, passim; + obj., *qṣt mn ywdnʾ*

(v. *ywdn*) *zy mlk›* ... *ndšw* Cowl 27[4f.]: a part of the royal barley-house they destroyed, cf. Cowl 30[7f.,9,10], 31[7,8] - the diff. *mdšh* in Krael 9[14] poss. = PA ‹EL (or APH?) Part. pass. s.m. emph. (or rather + suff. 3 p.s.m. or f.?) = what is destroyed (cf. also Driver PEQ '55, 93; and cf. Grelot DAE p. 245 (n. 1): = PA ‹EL/APH Part. pass. of root *dšy*, *ršy*$_2$ (= what is deteriorated?) :: Milik RB lxi 251: *mdšh* = noun indicating what is destructed :: Kutscher JAOS lxxiv 237: l. *mršh* = Sing. + suff. 3 p.s.m. of *mrš*$_2$ (= beam; cf. also Porten & Greenfield JEAS p. 58, Porten & Yardeni sub TADAE B 3.10 :: Wesselius AION xlv 503ff.: l. *mršh* = Sing. abs. of *mršh* (= mortar)).

nh v. *bdr*$_1$.

nhg Pun Elayi Sem xxxviii 104f.: l. poss. *nhg* (< root *nhg* (= to lead)) in Sem xxxviii 104 (uncert. reading and interpret.).

nhwyg OffAr word of unknown meaning in FX 136[22]; Dupont-Sommer FX p. 154: = lapsus for *nhwy›* = NIPH Part. s.m. emph. of *hwy*$_1$ (= being present; highly uncert. interpret.) :: for a reading *nhwy›*, cf. Teixidor JNES xxxvii 184 (n. 19), Syr lvi 394: *nhwy›* = Impf. 3 p.s.m. with *n*- prefix of *hwy*$_1$ (improb. interpret.); on the subject, cf. also Contini OA xx 233, Frei BiOr xxxviii 367f.

nhwryt Palm Inv x 44[7] (Greek par. λαμπρῶς), DFD 13[4] (?; *nhw[ryt]*, heavily dam. context) - ¶ adv. brilliantly.

nhy v. *hn*$_3$.

nhyr v. *nhr*$_4$.

nhr$_1$ **Waw** APH Imper. s.m. *›nhr* AMB 6[10] (cf. Naveh & Shaked AMB a.l. :: Dupont-Sommer Waw p. 11, 23f. = Pf. 3 p.s.m.) - ¶ verb APH to illuminate; + obj.: AMB 6[10].

nhr$_2$ **OldAr** Sing. abs. *nhr* Tell F 4 (Akkad. par. *nārāti*), MDAIA ciii 62 (for this interpret., cf. Bron & Lemaire RA lxxxiii 40, Eph‹al & Naveh IEJ xxxix 193, 195f. :: Kyrielleis & Röllig MDAIA ciii 67: = Sing. m. abs. of *nhr*$_4$) - ¶ subst. river, water-course; *gwgl nhr klm* Tell F 4: inspector of all the water-courses (epithet of a god) - in MDAIA ciii 62 indication of Euphrates.

v. *‹br*$_5$.

nhr$_3$ v. *bl›*$_1$.

nhr$_4$ **Palm** Sing. m. emph. *nhyr›* CIS ii 3944[2], 3945[2] (Greek par. λαμ[πρότατον]), Syr xlviii 413[2] (= DFD 271), Syr lxii 257 (Greek par. λα[μ]πρότατον), AAS xxxvi/xxxvii 169 no. 10[3] (Greek par. λα[μ]πρότατον); Plur. m. abs. *nhryn* CIS ii 3914[3]; Sing. f. emph. *nhyrt›* CIS ii 3947[1] (Greek par. λαμπροτάτην), 3971[5] (Greek par. λαμπροτάτης) - ¶ adj. illustrious; epithet of - a) the Palm. ruler/king: CIS ii 3945[2], Syr lxii 257, AAS xxxvi/xxxvii 169 no. 10[3] (× Cooke NSI p. 287: *nhyr› hpṭyq›* // with Latin *vir clarissimus consularis*) - b) the Palm. queen, *nhyrt› wzdqt[›]* CIS ii 3947[1]: the illustrious and just one, cf. CIS ii

3971[5] - c) of a senator, *snqlṭyq*ʾ *nhyr*ʾ CIS ii 3944[2]: the illustrious senator (cf. Greek par. τὸν λαμπρότατον συνκλητικὸν; cf. also Syr xlviii 413[1f.]); cf. *nhryn bmgdyhwn* CIS ii 3914[3]: those illustrious because of their generous gifts (cf. Greek par. φιλοτείμους ἐν πολλοῖς [πράγ]μασιν).
v. nhr_2.

nhtm v. *nḥtm*.

nwb v. mwt_1.

nwdyt **OffAr** word of unknown meaning in FuF xxxv 173[9], Altheim & Stiehl FuF xxxv 173, ASA 274: = n.l.

nwh **OffAr** the diff. *nwh* in KAI 258[2] (for the reading, v. infra) poss. = Sing. cstr. of *nwh* (= dwelling; cf. Teixidor Syr xlvii 374; cf. also Lipiński Stud 149: > tomb (cf. Millard JSS xxi 177; cf. however Degen WO ix 169)) :: Hanson BASOR cxcii 4f.: *nwh* = PAʿEL Pf. 3 p.s.m. of *nwy* (= to adorn; cf. also Segert AAG p. 516, 542) :: Gibson SSI ii p. 153f.: *nwh* = lapsus for or variant of *nwḥ* (= PAʿEL Pf. 3 p.s.m. of $nwḥ_1$ (= to give rest)) :: Teixidor Syr lvi 393: = Pf. 3 p.s.m. of root *nwy* (related to root $ʾwy_3$ (= to mark)?) :: Albright with Hanson BASOR cxcii 5, Degen ZDMG cxxi 136: l. *znh* :: Torrey JAOS xxxv 372, 374, Donner KAI a.l. (cf. also Cross BASOR clxxxiv 10): pro *wnwh* l. *gnnh* (= QAL Inf. cstr. + suff. 3 p.s.m. of gnn_1 (= to protect), cf. also Koopmans 168: l. *gnnh* = QAL or PAʿEL Inf. cstr. + suff. 3 p.s.m. of gnn_1).
v. nqy_1.

nwz **OffAr** Plur. abs. *nwzyn* AJSL lviii 304C 4 - ¶ subst. of uncert. meaning; AG p. 27, Bowman AJSL lviii 305: = cordage or sails?; Shaked Or lvi 412: prob. < Iran., meaning prob. = sail.

nwḥ₁ **OldCan** QAL Pf. 1 p.s. *nu-uḫ-ti* EA 147[56] (cf. Sivan GAG 144, 256) - **Ph** YIPH Pf. 3 p.s.m. *ynḥ* KAI 58 - **Hebr** QAL Impf. 3 p.s.m. *ynwḥ* Frey 621[1] (f. subject), 622[1], 624[1], 630b 1 - **JAr** QAL Part. act. s.m. cstr. *nyḥ* MPAT-A 12[3] (= SM 71; :: Frey sub 1195, Fitzmyer & Harrington MPAT a.l.: = Sing. cstr. of *nyḥ*; or l. *nwḥ*?? (= Sing. m. cstr. of $nwḥ_3$)); ITP Impf. 3 p.s.f. *ttnyḥ* MPAT-A 50[1] (:: Frey sub 1208: l. *tḥnyt* = Sing. cstr. (= resting place)), 52[1] - ¶ verb QAL to be calm, to be at rest - **1)** said of someone who is in safe condition: EA 147[56] - 2) said of someone who is at rest in his grave: Frey 621[1], 622[1], 624[1], 630b 1; cf. also *NP nyḥ npš* MPAT-A 12[3] (= SM 71): NP the deceased - YIPH to erect (sc. an altar) + l_5: KAI 58 - ITP to be at rest; *ttnyḥ npšh dšʾwl* MPAT-A 50[1f.]: may the soul of Sh. be at rest (cf. MPAT-A 52[1]).
v. $ʾnḥn_1$, $brḥ_1$, *mḥ*ʾ, *mnḥ*, $mnḥh_1$, *nwh*, $nḥt_2$.

nwḥ₂ v. $nwḥ_3$.

nwḥ₃ **Hebr** Sing. m. cstr. *nwḥ* Frey 569[4], 611[11], 892[2], 900[4], 988 (= MPAT 109) - **JAr** Sing. f. abs. *nwḥh* Frey 1416 (:: Frey a.l.: l. *nwḥ*

+ *h* (= n.d.)) - ¶ adj. calm, at rest; only in the expression *nwḥ npš* following a n.p.; *sw‘m br mnḥm nwḥ npš* Frey 988: S. the son of M., the deceased one (cf. Frey 569[4], 611[11], 892[2], 900[4], 1416), cf. Pedersen InscrSem sub 1 (cf. also Lieberman Greek 70) :: Frey a.l., Gawlikowski Ber xxi 7: *nwḥ* = Sing. cstr. of *nwḥ*$_2$ (= rest), *nwḥ npš* = the rest of the soul (= rest for the soul; cf. Fitzmyer & Harrington MPAT a.l.).
v. *nwḥ*$_1$.

nwḥr **JAr** Sing. + suff. 3 p.s.m. *nwḥrh* AMB 5[5] (reading uncert.) - ¶ subst. nostril.

nwṭ v.Soden Or xxxvii 262, xlvi 191: Akkad. *nūtu* (= leather container, bag) most prob. < Ar.; highly uncert. interpret.; cf. also AHW and CAD s.v.

nwy v. *nwh*.

nwyšh **OffAr** Sing. abs. *nwyš’* JAOS liv 31[2]; + suff. 3 p.pl.m. *nwyšthwn* JAOS liv 31[3] (in both instances uncert. reading) - ¶ subst. of uncert. meaning; Torrey JAOS liv 31f.: = cemetery (< Arab. < Greek ναός), uncert. interpret., v. also *wd‘y*.

nwyt **Palm** MUSJ xxxviii 106[8], DFD 37[4] - ¶ word of uncert. meaning, prob. prep. (:: Ingholt MUSJ a.l., Milik DFD a.l.: = adverb), poss. meaning - **1)** next to; *plgh ... nwyt gmḥwhy* MUSJ xxxviii 106[8]: his half ... next to his niches - **2)** together with, besides; *’qymw lh bny kmr’ nwyt š’wr pḥz’ bt ’lhwhwn* DFD 37[4f.]: the Benē K. have erected (it; i.e. a statue) as did the rest of the tribes, in their own temples (cf. Greek par. Syr xiii 279: ἔφιππον ἀνδριάντα καὶ αἱ τέσσαρες φυλαὶ ἐν ἰδίοις ἱεροῖς ἐξ ἰδίων ἀνδριάντας τέσσαρες, ὧν τοῦτον Χωνειτῶν φυλή).

nwl$_1$ v.Soden Or xlvi 191: Akkad. *nablu* (= something woven) < Ar. **nbl* (= *nbl*$_5$), *nwl* (cf. also idem AHW s.v. *nablu* II); highly uncert. interpret., cf. also CAD s.v. *nablu* C.

nwl$_2$ **Nab** Sing. emph. *nwl’* ARNA-Nab 125 - ¶ subst. weaver.

nwlh v. *‘l*$_7$.

nwm **JAr** QAL Part. act. s.f. abs. *nymh* AMB 7[18,21]; emph. *n’mt* AMB 7[21] (lapsus for *n’mth*, cf. already Dupont-Sommer JKF i 210) - ¶ verb QAL to be sleepy, to slumber; *ḥdh nymh wl’ dmkh* AMB 7[18f.]: a woman who is sleepy but does not sleep (cf. AMB 7[21f.]).
v. *ḥly*$_2$, *ywm*, *msk*$_3$.

nwn **OffAr** Plur. abs. *nwnn* Cowl 45[4], RSO xxxii 404[2], *nwnyn* Cowl 45[3,6] (for this reading, cf. Porten & Yardeni sub TADAE B 7.1 :: Cowl a.l., Grelot DAE p. 97: l. *nwnyk* = Plur. + suff. 2 p.s.m.); emph. *nwny’* KAI 279[4]; + suff. 2 p.s.m. *nwnyk* Cowl 45[5] - ¶ subst. fish - this word (*n[wny]’* = Plur. emph.) prob. to be restored in CIS ii 3913 ii 34, in the comb. *n[wny]’ mlyḥy’* = salted fish (cf. also Milik DFD 210) - *zy nwny’ ’ḥdn* KAI 279[4]: the fishermen (cf. Greek par. ἁλιεῖς; v. *’ḥz*) - on this word, cf. also Rundgren FS Widengren 72ff.

v. *rwndkn*.

nws$_1$ **OffAr** APH Part. s.m. abs. *mns* Herm 2[3] - ¶ verb APH meaning derived from context: to make to leave, to give the opportunity to leave (the transl. a) to send/to take away (cf. Bresciani & Kamil Herm a.l., Porten Arch 269, Grelot DAE p. 154, Porten & Greenfield JEAS p. 155, Porten & Yardeni sub TADAE A 2.2) b) to give the opportunity to flee (cf. Milik Bibl xlviii 582) less prob.) - Krahmalkov RSF iv 156: the *nws* in CIS i 5510[11] = derivative of this root (they put to flight), improb. interpret., meaning of *nws* unknown (Février sub CIS i 5510: = part of n.p.) :: v.d.Branden RSF v 139, 142f.: l. *nks* (= Sing. abs. of *nks$_3$*; *b'l nks* = the notables), for the improb. reading *nks*, cf. also Février sub CIS i 5510.

v. *hns*.

nws$_2$ (< Greek ναός, cf. Altheim & Stiehl AAW v/2, 24f., Teixidor Syr xlvii 378, Milik BIA x 56) - **Nab** Sing. emph. *nws'* BIA x 55[4] - **Palm** Sing. emph. *nws'* JSS xxxiii 171[2] - ¶ subst. m. temple.

nwp **Hebr** for a poss. reading *mn[yp]m* (= HIPH Part. pl.m. abs. (= to handle)) in KAI 189[1], cf. Puech RB lxxxi 200.

nwph v.Soden Or xxxvii 262, xlvi 191: Akkad. *nūptu* (= additional payment, present) < Ar. *nwph*? (cf. also idem AHW s.v.); highly uncert. interpret.

nwpy' v. *np'$_2$*.

nwpt (< Iran., cf. e.g. Schaed 265, Grelot Sem xx 27 n. 2, Hinz AISN 174) - **OffAr** Sing. emph. *nwpt'* Cowl 26[2,7]; Plur. emph. *nwpty'* Cowl 26[8], ATNS 64b 11 - ¶ subst. boatman; Hinz AISN 174: = captain.

v. *np'$_2$*.

nwq v. *ynq$_1$*.

nwr$_1$ **Palm** Sing. abs. (?) *nwr* CIS ii 3948[3] (for the reading, cf. Chabot sub CIS ii 3948, Cantineau sub Inv iii 28 :: Cooke NSI p. 273f.: l. *zwd* (= Sing. abs.) = expenses, cf. also Teixidor Sem xxxiv 17f.) - ¶ subst. of uncert. meaning, poss. interpret.: expenses (cf. Greek par. ἀναλ[ωμ]άτω[ν]; cf. Cantineau sub Inv iii 28), cf. also Chabot CIS ii a.l.: = lapsus for *zwd*.

v. *nwr$_3$*.

nwr$_2$ cf. Frah i 19 (*nwl'*) = fire, cf. GIPP 30, SaSt 20.

v. *nr$_1$*, *nkr$_3$*.

nwr$_3$ Milik DFD 299: the diff. *nwr/d* in Syr xvii 271[10] (diff. text in Palm. script) poss. = *nwr$_1$* (= expenses) :: Milik ibid.: l. *nwr* < *n'r$_3$*? :: Cantineau Syr xvii 274 (dividing otherwise): l. *nwd/rz* = (part of) Persian n.p. :: Gawlikowski Syr li 99 (div. otherwise): l. *-nw* (apocopated form of pron. suff. 3 p.pl.m. *-nwn*) *rz* (= secret).

nzy **DA** the diff. *]nzyt* in v d 2 poss. form of this root (= to splash, to be sprinkled; on the context, cf. Dijkstra GTT xc 163 (n. 21)); cf.

however Puech FS Grelot 17, 24, 28 (dividing otherwise): l. *zyt* = Sing. abs. of *zyt*; cf. also Garr DGSP 24.
v. *mzh*$_2$.
nzyr v. *nzr*$_3$.
nzl v. *dbr*$_2$.
nzq$_1$ **Ph** YIPH Impf. 3 p.s.m. *yzq* KAI 24[14] (cf. e.g. FR 151, Gibson SSI iii p. 39 :: Torrey JAOS xxxv 368: rather = QAL Impf. 3 p.s.m. (cf. also Röllig KAI a.l.: or = QAL Impf. 3 p.s.m.) of *nzq* (= to damage) :: Landsberger Samʾal 52f.: = QAL Impf. 3 p.s.m. of *nzq* (= to take offence) :: Bauer ZDMG lxvii 689: = QAL Impf. 3 p.s.m. of *yzq* (= to pour out, to make an oblation)) - **OffAr** QAL (or PAʿEL) Pf. 3 p.s.m. *nzq* Cowl 37[14] (for this interpret., cf. Cowl a.l. × Porten & Greenfield JEAS p. 80, Porten & Yardeni sub TADAE A 4.2: = Sing. cstr. of *nzq*$_2$ (= damage; dam. context)) - **JAr** APH Part. s.m. emph. *mzqh* AMB 7a 13, 7b 2; pl.m. abs. *mzqyn* AMB 11[8], 13[5] (*[m]zqyn*)[,9] - ¶ verb QAL (or PAʿEL): Cowl 37[14], v. however supra; uncert. meaning, to suffer damage? (cf. Grelot DAE p. 390), cf. however Cowl a.l.: = to give damages against + obj.; cf. also Sach p. 53, Wag 28: = to determine an indemnity - YIPH/APH to damage; + *b*$_2$: KAI 24[14] (cf. also Dahood Bibl lx 433 :: Gevirtz VT xi 141 n. 4: l. *wyzq* <*šm*> *bspr z*?; cf. however Torrey JAOS xxxv 368, Sperling UF xx 337); Part.: the Evildoer, name of an evil spirit: AMB 7a 13, 7b 2, 11[8], 13[5,9] (cf. also Dupont-Sommer JKF i 208).
v. *zqn*$_1$.
nzq$_2$ v. *nzq*$_1$.
nzqh **JAr** Plur. abs. *nzqn* MPAT 40[9] (cf. Milik DJD ii p. 108f.) - ¶ subst. damage, damaged goods.
nzr$_1$ v. *ndr*$_1$.
nzr$_2$ v. *mrʾ*.
nzr$_3$ **Hebr** Sing. abs. *nzr* MPAT 121, *nzyr* MPAT 122 (in Ar. context) - ¶ subst. nazirite.
nḥdṭ **OffAr** word of unknown meaning in FuF xxxv 173[8]; Altheim & Stiehl FuF xxxv 173, 175, ASA 274: = title (< Iran.).
nḥw **Pun** Rocco StudMagr vii a.l.: l. *ḥ* in StudMagr vii 12[2] = QAL Imper. pl.m. of *nḥw* (= to attack), highly improb. reading and interpret.
nḥl **Ph** QAL Impf. 2 p.s.m. *tnḥl* KAI 3[4] (cf. e.g. FR 58b, Gibson SSI iii p. 11); Inf. abs. *nḥl* KAI 3[3] - ¶ verb QAL to take possession of, to inherit (diff. context, v. also *mgšh*), cf. Albright BASOR lxxiii 73, xc 36, JAOS lxvii 159, Obermann JBL lviii 235, 242, Dupont-Sommer ArchOr xvii[1] 161, 163f., Torczyner Lesh xiv 162f., 165, Röllig KAI a.l. (:: v.d.Branden RSF ii 139, 147: = to take possession of > to choose, to prefer) :: Dunand BMB ii 103, 105: = to recover :: McCarter & Coote BASOR ccxii 19ff.: = to receive a grant :: Iwry JAOS lxxxi 33:

= to share by (casting) lots - for the context, cf. also Gibson SSI iii p. 11.
v. *nṣl*.

nḥm$_1$ **OffAr** PA ʿEL Part. pl.m. abs. *mnḥmn* KAI 271A 2 (v. infra) - **JAr** PA ʿEL Part. s.m. emph. *mnḥmh* MPAT-A 55 (= SM 77; v. infra) - ¶ verb PA ʿEL Part. consoler > counsellor, legal assistant, supporting witness in legal action; for KAI 271A 2, cf. CIS ii sub 138, Cooke NSI p. 204, Donner KAI a.l. (highly uncert. interpret., heavily dam. context) :: Donner KAI a.l.: or = derivative of root *nḥm$_2$* (< Egypt.) = to protect, to save - for MPAT-A 55, cf. Fitzmyer & Harrington MPAT a.l., Naveh sub SM 77, FS Loewenstamm ii 307, cf. however Gutman, Z.Yeivin, Netzer Qadm v 51: *mnḥmh* = n.p. (cf. also Fitzmyer & Harrington MPAT p. 303: poss. = fem. n.p.).
v. *rḥm$_1$*.

nḥm$_2$ v. *nḥm$_1$*.

nḥn$_1$ v. *ḥnn$_1$*.

nḥn$_2$ v. *ḥnn$_1$*.

nḥnw v. *ʾnḥn$_1$*.

nḥq v. *ḥqq$_1$*.

nḥṣ$_1$ **DA** Sing. abs. *nḥṣ* i 10 (v. infra) - ¶ subst. prob. meaning: distress (dam. context, cf. Hoftijzer DA a.l., TUAT ii 142, Garbini Hen i 178, 185, Kaufman BASOR ccxxxix 73, Levine JAOS ci 197, 199, H.P.Müller ZAW xciv 218, 226, H. & M.Weippert ZDPV xcviii 95, 103, Smelik HDAI 79 :: Caquot & Lemaire Syr liv 198, McCarter BASOR ccxxxix 51, 55, Ringgren Mem Scligmann 94, Hackett BTDA 29, 48, 132, Sasson UF xvii 299: = *nḥṣ$_2$* (= certain kind of bird) :: Lemaire BAT 317f., CRAI '85, 280, Puech BAT 359, 362, FS Grelot 17, 22, 28: l. *nṣṣ* = Sing. abs. of *nṣṣ* (= falcon, hawk)).

nḥṣ$_2$ v. *nḥṣ$_1$*.

nḥq v. *ḥqq$_1$*.

nḥr$_1$ **Palm** Plur. emph. *nḥryʾ* Syr xvii 268[5] - ¶ subst. of uncert. meaning ((cultic) slaughtering?), in the comb. *bt nḥryʾ* Syr xvii 268[5]: the locality where (cultic) slaughtering takes place (?; cf. Cantineau Syr xvii 269, Gawlikowski TP 62, cf. also Teixidor PP 112).

nḥr$_2$ **Pun** word (?) of unknown meaning in KAI 165[3], cf. Chabot sub Punica xvi 1, Röllig KAI a.l.; Levi Della Vida OA iv 65, 67: *nḥr* = Sing. abs. of *nʿr$_3$* (uncert. interpret.); v.d.Branden RSF ii 145ff., BiOr xxxvi 203: *nḥr* = Sing. abs. of *nḥr$_2$* (= dolphin; uncert. interpret.); on the problems, cf. also Février BAr '51/52, 41; for the context, v. also *kwn$_1$*.

nḥrg **Nab** Sing. emph. *nḥrgʾ* ARNA-Nab 67 (highly uncert. reading) - ¶ subst. of uncert. meaning. Milik sub ARNA-Nab 67: = sacred slave, temple-slave?

nḥš₁ **Hebr** Impf. 2 p.s.m. of this root (*]tnḥš*; reading uncert.) in TA-H 28^3??, heavily dam. context, meaning uncert.

nḥš₂ **OffAr** Sing. abs. *nḥš* Cowl 10^{10}, 14^4, $15^{11,12,13}$, $26^{12,15,16}$, 30^{11}, 31^{10}, 36^4, 81^{37}, Krael $7^{13,14,15}$ (for the reading, cf. Porten & Yardeni sub TADAE B 3.8), ATNS 9^5, KAI 226^7; emph. *nḥšʾ* Aḥiq 186 (diff. and dam. context, cf. Lindenberger APA 183f.: or = Sing. emph. of *nḥš₇* (= serpent)?? or of *nḥš₄* (= diviner)??), Krael 13^5; Plur. abs. *nḥšn* ATNS 30a 5 - **Nab** Sing. emph. *nḥ[šʾ]* BASOR cclxiii 77^1 - **Palm** Sing. abs. *nḥš* SBS $48^{7,8}$; emph. *nḥšʾ* CIS ii 3913 ii 128, 3952^4, Inv xii 48^2, 49^6 (*nḥš[ʾ]*), Syr xvii 274^3, JSS xxxiii 171^1 (*[n]ḥšʾ*) - **JAr** Sing. abs. *[n]ḥš* AMB 11^6 - ¶ subst. bronze; Plur. prob. = bronze chains: ATNS 30a 5 - cf. also *nḥšt*.
v. *nḥš₆*.

nḥš₃ **Nab** Sing. emph. *nḥšʾ* CIS ii 158^1 - ¶ subst. m. of uncert. meaning, poss.: bronze smith, someone working in bronze (or = *nḥš₄* (= diviner, soothsayer)?) - cf. also the *nḥšʾ* in RES 1785B 1, 4??

nḥš₄ v. *nḥš₂, ₃*.

nḥš₅ **Hatra** Sing. emph. *nḥšʾ* 67^1 - ¶ subst. augury, omen; *bnḥšʾ ṭ[bʾ ʿ]l ḥyʾ nšrw* Hatra $67^{1f.}$: as a good augury for the life of N.

nḥš₆ **OffAr** Plur. emph. *nḥšyʾ* Cowl 81^{111} - ¶ subst. of unknown meaning; Cowl a.l.: = form of *nḥš₂* (= bronze-bands); Grelot DAE p. 116: = form of *nḥš₂* (= pieces of bronze); *nḥšyʾ zy yhbw ʿl tmryʾ zy pḥy* Cowl 81^{111}: objects (v. supra) which they put (or: were put) on the date-palms of P. (diff. interpret.; cf. Grelot DAE p. 116: which they gave for the date-palms of P.); Harmatta ActAntHung vii 371: poss. = 'Unterbett, Unterdecke'.

nḥš₇ v. *nḥš₂*.

nḥšrpṭ (< Iran., cf. Safar Sumer xviii 32 n. 20, Caquot Syr xli 254, Altheim & Stiehl AAW iv 257, GMA 544f.) - **Hatra** Sing. abs. *nḥšrpṭ* 112^3 (cf. e.g. Altheim & Stiehl AAW iv 257, Vattioni IH a.l., cf. however Safar Sumer xviii 32, Caquot Syr xli 254: l. *nḥšrpṭ[ʾ]* = Sing. emph.) - ¶ subst. master of the hunt.

nḥšt **OldCan** Sing. abs. *nu-uḫ-uš-tum* EA 69^{28} - **Ph** Sing. abs. *nḥšt* KAI 10^4, 31^1, $43^{7,12}$, Mus li 286^2 - **Pun** Sing. abs. *nḥšt* KAI 66^1, 119^4, 122^2, CIS i 330^4, 331^3, 332^4, Antas p. 51^1 - ¶ subst. bronze: passim; for the context of KAI 31^1, v. *rʾšt* - CIS i sub 11, Cooke NSI p. 58, Röllig KAI a.l., Amadasi sub Kition A 1: l. *mnḥšt* (= *m₁₀* (= *mn₅*) + Sing. abs.) in KAI 33^2 (v. *mn₅*; reading of *š* highly uncert.; interpret. uncert., cf. Ginsberg JANES v 145 n. 60 :: Ginsberg ibid.: *mnḥšt* = n.p. (or = lapsus for *mnḥmt* (= n.p.)) :: Teixidor Syr li 322: l. poss. *mnḥmt* = n.p. (cf. also idem Syr lvi 384)) - cf. also *nḥš₂*.

nḥt₁ **OldAr** HAPH Part. s.m. abs./cstr. *mhnḥt* Tell F 2 (Akkad. par. *mu-šá-az-nin*) - **OffAr** QAL Pf. 2 p.s.m. *nḥt* Cowl 42^{11} (cf. Leand 35c

:: Cowl p. 144: = QAL Part. act. s.m. abs.); 3 p.pl.m. *nḥtw* ATNS 62[1] (dam. context), 124[3] (*[n]ḥtw*; heavily dam. context); Impf. 1 p.s. *ʾnḥt* ATNS 6[3] (dam. context; or APH??; highly uncert. reading, cf. Porten & Yardeni sub TADAE B 8.12: poss. l. *hnḥt* = HAPH Pf. 3 p.s.m.); 3 p.pl.m. *yḥtwn* Cowl 71[5]; Imper. s.m. *ḥt* Cowl 42[7,8,13]; Inf. *mnḥt* Krael 6[10] (*[m]nḥt*),[13], 9[15]; HAPH/APH Pf. 1 p.s. + suff. 3 p.s.m., cf. Warka 3: *aḫ-ḫi-te-e*; Imper. s.m. *hnḥt* Cowl 42[13]; Inf. *mḥth* Herm 5[6]; + suff. 3 p.s.f. *mnḥtwth* Aḥiq 123 (:: Kottsieper SAS 148, 217: = PAʿEL Inf.); + suff. 3 p.pl. *mnḥtwthm* Aḥiq 122 (:: Kottsieper SAS 148: = PAʿEL Inf. + suff. :: Baneth OLZ '14, 349 n. 1, Kottsieper SAS 179: = lapsus for *mnḥtwth* = + suff. 3 p.s.f.; :: Lindenberger APA 111, 250 n. 327: or in both Aḥiq instances poss. = PAʿEL?); cf. Frah xxi 15 (*ḥnḥtwn*), Paik 408 (*ḥnḥtwn*), GIPP 23, SaSt 17, cf. Lemosín AO ii 266f. - **Nab** QAL Pf. 3 p.s.m. *nḥt* J 109[2] (= CIS ii 298; reading uncert., cf. Chabot sub RES 1187) - **Palm** QAL Pf. 3 p.s.f. *nḥtt* Syr xix 75 i 3; 3 p.pl.m. *nḥtw* Inv x 124[3], *nḥt* CIS ii 3933[4] (Greek par. κατελθόντες) - ¶ verb QAL to descend, to go: passim - **1)** + n.l., *ḥt mnpy* Cowl 42[7]: go to Memphis; *lʾ yḥtwn šʾwl* Cowl 71[15]: they shall not go down to the netherworld - **2)** + *l₅*, *nḥtt lkrkʾ* Syr xix 75 i 3: (the caravan) descended to K. (cf. Cowl 42[11], J 109[2] (v. however supra)) - **3)** + *ʿm₄* + *l₅*, *nḥt ʿmh lʾlgšyʾ* CIS ii 3933[4]: they descended with him to V. - **4)** + *ʿm₄* + *mn₅* (from) + *l₅*: Inv x 124[3f.] - HAPH/APH to put (down), to lower, to bring - **1)** + obj., *mhnḥt ʿsr* Tell F 2: he who brings riches (epithet of a god; cf. Sasson ZAW xcvii 93; on the context, cf. Dion FS Delcor 142f.); *lʾ bydyk m[nš]ʾ rglk [w]lmnḥtwth* Aḥiq 123: it is not in your power to lift up your foot and to put it down (cf. Aḥiq 122) - **2)** + obj. + *tḥt*, *aḫ-ḫi-te-e ti-ḫu-ú-tú li-iš-šá-ni-ʾ* Warka 3: I put it under my tongue - **3)** + *l₅* + obj., *lmḥth lbmršry ʾtryh* Herm 5[6]: to bring to B. the *ʾtryh* (v. *ʾtr₄*) - **4)** + *l₅* + obj. + *byd* + *ʿl₇* (?, dam. context), *hnḥt ly ktwn 1 bydk ʿl [mnpy]* Cowl 42[13]: bring down to me one tunic with you to M. - a form of this root also in RES 492A 4? (Grelot DAE p. 139: = QAL Pf. 3 p.s.m.) - a form of this root in Herm 8[5] (*nḥt*), heavily dam. context - a form of this root (QAL Impf. 3 p.s.m. *ynḥt*) also in the Ph. or Ar. text Krug 35?? (dam. context).
v. *mdnḥy*.

nḥt₂ **Ph** Sing. abs. *nḥt* KAI 1[2] (cf. e.g. Röllig KAI a.l., Gibson SSI iii p. 14, 16 (cf. also Zevit UF ix 318 n. 19) :: Lane BASOR cxciv 42: = Sing. + suff. 3 p.s.m. :: Dussaud Syr xi 184 (n. 4; cf. already Syr v 136): = QAL Pf. 3 p.s.f. of *nwḥ₁*); cstr. *nḥt* KAI 26A i 18, ii 8, 13; + suff. 1 p.s. *nḥty* KAI 35[2] (= Kition B 1); + suff. 3 p.pl.m. *nḥtnm* KAI 34[5] (= Kition B 45) - **Pun** Sing. abs. (?, v. infra) *nḥt* RES 1975 - **OldAr** Sing. abs. (or cstr.?, dam. context) *nḥt* KAI 223B 4 - ¶ subst. f. peace, rest, well-being (for the context of KAI 1[2], v. *brḥ₁*; for the context of KAI 26A i 18f., cf. Greenfield EI xiv 74f.; for the context of KAI 35[2] (= Kition B 1), cf. Teixidor Syr lvi 385); *bnḥt* RES 1975: in peace? (on a jar from a tomb).

nḥt₃ **OffAr** Plur. abs. *nḥtn* Cowl 81[30] (uncert. reading; v. infra) - ¶ subst. tray (cf. Cowl a.l., Grelot DAE p. 109 n. x, cf. however Harmatta ActAntHung vii 351: l. poss. *pḥtn* = Plur. abs. of *pḥt* (= hollow cask, 'Hohlgefäss')).

nḥt₄ **Palm** Plur. emph. *nḥty*ʾ CIS ii 3913 ii 57 (for this reading, cf. CIS ii sub 3913: l. *[mzbn]y nḥty*ʾ :: Cooke NSI p. 337: or l. ... *h]ymnty*ʾ (= Plur. emph. of *hymnt*) = clothiers?, cf. Greek par. ἱματιοπῶλαι (cf. Reckendorff ZDMG xlii 409) :: Lidzbarski Handb 288: l. ... *ymnty*ʾ (= Plur. emph. of *ymnt*) = Greek ἱμάτια (= clothes)) - ¶ subst. garment, piece of clothing.

nḥtwm v. *nḥtm*.

nḥtm **Hebr** Sing. abs. *nhtm* Mas 429 (var. form of *nḥtm*) - **Palm** Sing. emph. *nḥtwm*ʾ Inv xi 32[5] (v. infra) - ¶ subst. baker; for Inv xi 32[5], cf. Aggoula Sem xxix 113 (prob. interpret.) :: Stark PNPI 39, 99: = n.p.; in Mas 429 *hnhtm* poss. = nickname.

nṭbwn v. *ṭb₂*.

nṭḥ₁ **OffAr** QAL Part. act. pl.m. + suff. 3 p.s.m. *nṭḥwhy* Aḥiq 167 (v. infra; :: Epstein ZAW xxxii 138: = Plur. + suff. 3 p.s.m. of *nṭḥ₂* (= glorious deed)) - ¶ verb QAL prob. meaning to beat, to hit; *ṣdyq* ʾ*nš*ʾ *b*ʿ*drh kl nṭḥwhy hwyn* Aḥiq 167: as to the righteous one, people are helping him (:: Lindenberger APA 170: it is best to support a righteous man), everyone beating him (cf. also Lindenberger APA 170, 288: who clashes with him) falls/perishes (cf. Grimme OLZ '11, 538f., Grelot RB lxviii 191, DAE p. 445 n. e, Lindenberger APA 170, 270 n. 521 (*hwyn* being QAL Part. act. pl.m. abs. of *hwy₂* (= to fall)), cf. also Kottsieper SAS 17, 170, 198, 217) :: Cowl a.l.: the righteous among men, all who meet him are for his help (*nṭḥwhy* being QAL Part. act. pl.m. + suff. 3 p.s.m. of *nṭḥ* (= to meet), *hwyn* being QAL Part. act. pl.m. abs. of *hwy₁*); cf. also Ginsberg ANET 430 and v. ʿ*dr₃*.

nṭḥ₂ v. *nṭḥ₁*.

nṭy **Hebr** HIPH Pf. 3 p.s.m. *hṭh* TA-H 40[4] - ¶ verb HIPH to incline; *hṭh [*ʿ*]bdk [l]bh* ʾ*l* ʾ*šr* ʾ*m[rt]* TA-H 40[4f.]: your servant has inclined his heart (i.e. has paid attention) to what you have said - Rocco StudMagr vii a.l.: l. *ṭ* (= QAL Imper. pl.m.) in StudMagr vii 12[4] (highly uncert. reading and interpret.).

nṭl **Hebr** QAL Pf. 1 p.s. *nṭlty* TA-H 60[1f.] (for the reading, cf. Aharoni TA a.l., v.Dyke Parunak BASOR ccxxx 26, cf. however Lemaire IH i p. 216f. (div. otherwise): l. *hb*ʿ*l ty* (= n.p., cf. ibid. p. 293; less prob. interpret.); Impf. 3 p.pl. + suff. 3 p.pl.f. *yṭlwn* DJD ii 44[10] - **OffAr** QAL Pf. 1 p.s. *nṭlt* Aḥiq 169 - **Hatra** QAL Impf. 3 p.s.m. *yṭwl* 173[3] (for the reading, cf. Caquot Syr xli 264f. :: Milik DFD 105 (div. otherwise): l. *yṭy* = QAL/APH Impf. 3 p.s.m. of *ʾty₁* (with sec. change *t* > *ṭ*, cf. also Vattioni IH a.l.: *yty*) + *l₅*, v. also *ʾrnwh*; diff. and uncert. context) - ¶ verb QAL - **1)** to lift; *ʿyny zy nṭlt ʿlyk* Aḥiq 169: my eyes which I lifted up unto you (cf. Greenfield FS Fitzmyer 50); Aharoni TA sub 60: in TA-H 60[1f.] = to load, or to weigh (diff. context, v. also *h₆*) - **2)** to bring; + obj.: DJD ii 44[10].

nṭs **Nab** a form of this root (QAL (or PAʿEL?) Impf. 3 p.s.m. *ynṭs*) in CIS ii 373?? (for the reading, cf. Chabot sub RES 1472; meaning unknown; or rather = n.p.?).

nṭʿ₁ **Ph** QAL Pf. 3 p.s.m. *nṭʿ* EpAn ix 5[1] - ¶ verb QAL to plant; + obj. + *b₂*, *nṭʿ hʾ nṭʿm bšd* ... EpAn ix 5[1f.]: he planted plantations in the field of ...
v. *lyṭʾ*.

nṭʿ₂ Plur. abs. *nṭʿm* EpAn ix 5[2] - ¶ subst. plantation: EpAn ix 5[2]; Mosca & Russell EpAn ix 9 (n. 30): the same word poss. also in KAI 161[9].
v. *mtʿ*.

nṭp **DA** QAL Impf. 3 p.s.f. *tṭpn* ii 35, 36 (for the reading, cf. v.d.Kooij DA p. 144, Hoftijzer DA p. 251f.; for the interpret., cf. Hoftijzer DA p. 297 × Rofé SB 68, Garr DGSP 128: = QAL Impf. 3 p.pl.f.) - ¶ verb QAL to drip; *tṭpn ṭl* DA ii 36: she (v. however supra) will drip of dew (cf. ii 35; cf. Hoftijzer DA p. 252).

nṭr₁ v. *nṣr₁*, *sṭr₁*.

nṭr₂ v. *nṣr₁*.

nṭrh **OffAr** Sing. emph. *nṭrtʾ* ATNS 33b - ¶ subst. guard: ATNS 33b (context however dam.).

nṭš v.Soden Or xxxvii 261 (cf. idem AHW s.v. *naṭāšu*): Akkad. *naṭāšu* < Ar. *nṭš* = to give up, to abandon (ghost-word with false interpret., cf. CAD s.v. and v.Soden Or xlvi 191).

ny₁ **JAr** Sing. emph. *nyʾ* AMB 11[5] (diff. reading), *nyh* AMB 11[10] (or = + suff. 3 p.s.f.?) - ¶ subst. of uncert. meaning, prob. indicating part of body; Naveh & Shaked AMB a.l.: compare prob. Syriac *nʿ*, J.Ar *nyʿ* = chest (uncert. interpret.).

ny₂ v. *ʾyny*.

nydbh **JAr** Sing./Plur. cstr. *nydbt* SM 85[2] (uncert., partly lost context, cf. Yeivin IEJ xxiv 207, Naveh SM a.l.) - ¶ subst. donation.

nyḥ **OffAr** Sing. emph. *nyḥ[ʾ]* Aḥiq 108 (for the reading, cf. Montgomery OLZ '12, 536, Cowl p. 216, 238, Grelot RB lxviii 184, DAE p. 438, Lipiński BiOr xxxi 120, Lindenberger APA 94, 245 nn. 268, 269 × Kottsieper SAS 12, 21, 217: l. *nyḥ[h]* = Sing. + suff. 3 p.s.m. :: Epstein ZAW xxxiii 229f. (div. otherwise): l. *bny* (= Plur. cstr. of *br₁*) *ḥ[lwp]* = Sing. abs. of *ḥlwp* (= passing away) :: Grimme OLZ '14, 532: l. *bny* (=

Plur. cstr. of *br*₁) *ḥ[l*ʾ*]* = Sing. emph. of *ḥl*₂) - **Nab** Sing. emph. *nyḥ*ʾ Syr xxxv 242 (cf. Greek par. ἀνά[πα]υμα) - **Palm** Sing. emph. *nyḥ*ʾ Inv xi 67[1] (dam. context) - ¶ subst. - **1)** rest, tranquillity: Aḥiq 108 - **2)** resting place: Syr xxxv 242; cf. also Teixidor sub Inv xi 67: l. poss. *[b]t nyḥ*ʾ in Inv xi 67[1] (= house of rest).
v. *nwḥ*₁.

nyḥh **Palm** Sing. cstr. *nyḥt* CIS ii 3907[1] - **JAr** Sing. abs. *nyḥh* AMB 8[12] (dam. context) - ¶ subst. rest; *npš*ʾ *dnyḥt ṭm*ʾ *brll* CIS ii 3907[1f.]: tomb, where the bones of B. rest.

nyr v. *nkr*₃.

nyš v. *nš*₁.

nk v. *nky*₂.

nkʾt **Amm** Sing. abs. *nkʾt* AUSS xiii 2[4,5] (= CAI 80; for the reading problems, cf. Cross AUSS xiii 5; or = Plur.? cf. Sivan UF xiv 227) - ¶ subst. aromatic resin, laudanum gum (on this word, cf. Nielsen SVT xxxviii 63, Knauf IUGP 15) - Février Sem iv 22, Röllig KAI a.l.: the *nkʾt* in KAI 160[3] = Sing. abs. (highly uncert. interpret., heavily dam. context).

nkd v. *yrd*, *nky*₂, *ʿbd*₂.

nkh v. *nky*₁.

nkḥ v. *ntn*.

nky₁ **Hebr** Hiph Pf. 3 p.pl. *hkw* KAI 189[4]; Part. s.m. abs. *mkh* AMB 1[20] - **OldAr** Qal Inf. abs. *nkh* KAI 224[12,13] (cf. Fitzmyer CBQ xx 459, AIS 114, 156, Degen AAG p. 77 × Dupont-Sommer BMB xiii 33: *nkh* = Sing. abs. of *nkh* (= blow, hit); for the reading, cf. also Puech RB lxxxix 585) - ¶ verb Qal to beat, to hit: KAI 224[12,13] (v. however supra; for the context, v. *tpp*) - Hiph to strike, to hit: KAI 189[4]; *[brwk] hmkh whmrp*ʾ *lrwḥ grmyh* AMB 1[20]: Blessed be He who afflicts and heals the spirit of the bones (i.e. the actual illness) - a form of this verb poss. in EA 250[45]: *ia[-a]n-[na-]ki-en-n[i]*? (cf. also Albright ANET 486) - Rocco AION xxiv 476, 478: l. *k* (= Qal Imper. s.m. of *nky*₁ (= to beat)) in GR ii 36 no. 20[3] (highly uncert. reading and interpret.).
v. *nkt*₁, *tk*₁, *tpp*.

nky₂ **Hatra** the diff. *nkyhwn* in 79[8] poss. = Sing./Plur. + suff. 3 p.pl.m. of *nky*₂? (or Plur. + suff. 3 p.pl.m. of *nk*?), word of unknown meaning; Safar Sumer xvii 13 (n. 14): = far > further descendant; Aggoula Ber xviii 96: = variant of *nqy*₂ (= sheep; less prob. interpret.); cf. however also Caquot Syr xl 4: *nkyhwn* = lapsus for *nksyhwn* (= Plur. + suff. 3 p.pl.m. of *nks*₃) and Teixidor Syr xli 280 n. 3: *nkyhwn* = lapsus for *nkdyhwn* (= Plur. + suff. 3 p.pl.m. of *nkd* (= little child, descendant)).

nkyr Ebeling Frah a.l.: the *nkyr* in Frah x 14 = look, gaze (Semitic word), less prob. interpret., cf. Nyberg FP 75: = Iran. word (cf. also Schaeder with Ebeling Frah a.l.).

nkl$_1$ v.Soden Or xxxvii 261, xlvi 191: Akkad. *nikla nakālu* (= to deceive, to play a trick) < Ar. *nkl*$_2$ (= deception, trick) + *nkl*$_1$ (= to deceive), cf. also idem AHW s.v. *nakālu(m)* sub G 3 and *niklu* sub 2; less prob. interpret., cf. also CAD s.v. *nakālu*, *niklu*.
v. *qr*ʾ$_1$.

nkl$_2$ v. *nkl*$_1$.

nkl$_3$ **OffAr** Sing. abs. *nkl* NESE iii 34 conc. 6 (Degen NESE iii 34, 37: reading uncert.) - ¶ subst. of unknown meaning; Degen NESE iii 37: < Egypt.??

nkl$_4$ **Hebr** Sing. m. abs. *nkl* AMB 4^{18} - ¶ adj. evil; for the context of AMB 4^{18}, v. also *šyt*$_1$.

nklh **OffAr**, cf. Frah xiii 11: cleverness > clever (for the reading *nklt*ʾ, cf. Ebeling Frah a.l.; reading *rklt*ʾ less prob.), cf. however Nyberg FP 47, 83: l. *lkw*ʾ*n*ʾ = form of *rqwn* (= intelligent)?

nks$_1$ **Pun** QAL Part. act. s.f. abs. *nkst* CIS i 3783^{6} (cf. CIS i a.l., Chabot Mus xxxvii 161, Gevirtz VT xi 151 n. 6 :: Février CB viii 27: = QAL Pf. 3 p.s.f. :: Dahood Bibl xlix 364, lx 432: = QAL pass. Pf. 2 p.s.m.) - **OffAr** cf. Frah xxii 3 (*nkswn*) - ¶ verb QAL to slaughter, to kill :: Slouschz TPI p. 347: poss. = *nks*$_2$ (= to call to account, to punish).

nks$_2$ v. *nks*$_1$.

nks$_3$ (< Akkad., cf. Zimmern Fremdw 20, Kaufman AIA 77, cf. also Lipiński ZAH i 69f.) - **Hebr** Plur. + suff. 1 p.s. *nksy* EI xx 256^{11} - **OffAr** Plur. abs. *nksn* Cowl $7^{5,9}$, 13^{5}, 14^{4}, 20^{6} (for this prob. reading, cf. e.g. Porten & Yardeni sub TADAE B 2.9 :: e.g. Cowl a.l.: l. poss. *wršyn* = *w* + QAL Pf. 1 p.pl. of *ršy*$_1$)^{,12}, 27^{4}, 38^{9}, 44 (*scriptio anterior*, l. 2; for this reading, cf. Ungnad sub ArPap 33a 2, Porten & Yardeni sub TADAE B 7.3), Aḥiq 66, 74, Krael $2^{11,12}$, Driv 12^{9}, *nksyn* Cowl 30^{16}, 31^{5}; cstr. *nksy* Driv 7^{4}; emph. *nksy*ʾ Cowl $14^{6,8}$, 15^{14}, 18^{2}, $20^{5,8,15}$, 34^{6}, 35^{4}, Krael 2^{6}, $7^{23,41}$ (*nks[y]*ʾ; for the reading, cf. Porten & Yardeni sub TADAE B 3.8), Driv $7^{1,6,8}$, ATNS 50^{10}; + suff. 3 p.s.m. *nkswhy* Cowl 15^{30}, Krael 7^{29}; + suff. 3 p.s.f. *nksyh* Cowl 13^{4} (for the reading, cf. e.g. Porten & Greenfield JEAS p. 14, Porten & Yardeni sub TADAE B 2.7, cf. also Grelot DAE p. 185 :: e.g. Cowl a.l.: l. *nksy*ʾ = Plur. emph.), 15^{21}, Krael $7^{27,35}$; + suff. 2 p.s.f. *nksyky* Cowl 13^{6} (cf. however Porten & Yardeni sub TADAE B 2.7: l. *nksyk*); + suff. 1 p.s. *nksy* Cowl 15^{35}, Driv 3^{5}; + suff. 3 p.pl.m. *nksyhwm* Cowl p. 265^{2} (cf. Greenfield & Porten BIDG p. 54); cf. Frah xvi 1 (*nksy*ʾ), GIPP 30 - **Palm** Plur. + suff. 3 p.pl.m. *nksyhwn* RIP 132B 1 (cf. Milik DFD 287, Aggoula Syr liv 283 × Cantineau sub Inv vi 11b (cf. also Gawlikowski RIP a.l.): = Plur. + suff. 3 p.pl.m. of *nks*$_4$ (= victim)) - **JAr** Plur. cstr. *nksy* MPAT 46^{3} (v. ʾ*ḥry*$_1$); + suff. 1 p.s. *nksy* MPAT 39^{8}, 41^{4} (v. infra); + suff. 1 p.pl. *nksy[nh]* MPAT 45^{6} (heavily dam. context; uncert. restoration)

- ¶ subst. Plur. possessions, passim; cf. the following comb. - **1)** *ksp wnksn* Cowl 13^5: silver and goods (cf. Cowl 18^2, 27^4, 31^5, 35^4, Krael 2^6, $7^{27,35}$); cf. also *nksn wksp ʿbwr wʾḥrn* Cowl 20^{12}: the possessions and the silver, corn and other (things) - **2)** *nksyh wqnynh* Cowl $15^{21f.}$: her goods and possessions (cf. Cowl $15^{19,30,35}$); cf. also *ksp 10 wʿbwr wlbwš wnḥš wprzl kl nksn wqnyn wspr ʾntw* Cowl $14^{3f.}$: the silver and the corn and garments and bronze and iron, all the goods and possessions, and the marriage contract (cf. also *byth wnkswhy wqnynh* Krael $7^{29f.}$: his house, his goods and his possessions) - **3)** *nksyhwm wbtyhm* Cowl p. 265^2 (for the reading, v. byt_2; dam. context): their goods and their houses (for parallels, cf. Greenfield and Porten BIDG p. 54) - **4)** *grdʾ wnksyʾ zylnʾ* Driv $7^{1f.}$: our domestic staff and property (cf. Driv $7^{4,5f.,8}$, 12^9) - **5)** *kl dmy lbšʾ wnksyʾ* ATNS 50^{10}: the value of the clothing and the goods - the *nks nksy* in MPAT 41^4 prob. lapsus for *nksy* (cf. already Milik DJD ii p. 111) - Puech & Rofé RB lxxx 532, 541: l. *nksm* in BASOR cxciii 8^7 (= Plur. abs.), less prob. reading, cf. also Puech RB lxxx 546 (div. otherwise): l. *nṭh* (without interpret., improb. reading), for the reading problems, cf. also Fulco BASOR ccxxx 42.
v. $ḥsn_4$, nws_1, nky_2.

nks_4 v. nks_3.

nkr_1 v. bkr_1.

nkr_2 v. $ḥrš_7$.

nkr_3 **OffAr**, cf. Frah i 19 (*nklyʾ*) = transcendent, holy (cf. Nyberg FP 62 :: Schaeder with Ebeling Frah a.l.: l. *nyr[y]ʾ* = lapsus for *nwrʾ* (= form of nwr_2 (= light, fire)).

nkry **OffAr** Plur. m. emph. *nkryʾ* Aḥiq 139 - **Palm** Sing. m. abs. *nkry* Syr xiv 184^2 - ¶ substantivated adj., stranger, foreigner: Aḥiq 139; *swm nkry dy lwʾ mn bnwhy* Syr xiv 184^2: the corpse of a stranger, who is not one of his sons (v. also *swm*).

nkš v. *npš*.

nkt_1 **OffAr** QAL Pf. 3 p.s.m. + suff. 1 p.s. *nktny* Herm 5^8 (:: Bresciani & Kamil Herm a.l.: = QAL Pf. 3 p.s.f. + suff. 1 p.s. of nky_1) - ¶ verb QAL to bite; + obj., *nktny ḥwyh* Herm 5^8: a snake has bitten me - a form of this root poss. in Cowl 64 xxiii 2 (*]nkt*), cf. Lindenberger APA 220.

nkt_2 v. *hnkt*.

nktḥt v. pth_2.

nlnwn **OffAr** word of unknown meaning in RES 1301^8; prob. designating a certain measure; prob. Plur. form; cf. Lidzbarski Eph iii 26.

nmws v. *nms*.

nmwš v. *nms*.

nmḥl word of unknown meaning (on seal of unknown provenance) in SANSS-Hebr 163; Avigad IEJ xvi 245f.: *nmḥl* written boustrophedonwise, l. *lḥmn* = l_5 + n.d. (improb. interpret., cf. Herr SANSS a.l.; most prob. forgery).

nmlh v. *nmr*$_1$.

nmlk v. *mlk*$_3$.

nms (< Greek νόμος, cf. Cantineau Gramm 156, Rosenthal Sprache 92, cf. also Brown Bibl lxx 208) - **Palm** Sing. emph. *nmwsʾ* CIS ii 3913 i 3, 4, 6, 8, 9, etc., etc. - **JAr** Sing. cstr. *nmwš* DBKP 17[42] (cf. Yadin & Greenfield DBKP p. 137); emph. *nmsʾ* MPAT 42[11] - ¶ subst. law, passim; *knmsʾ* MPAT 42[11]: legitimately; *mn nmwsʾ* CIS ii 3913 i 3: legitimately, by law (cf. Greek par. νομίμου); *knmwš pqdnh* DBKP 17[42]: according to the law of deposit.

nmʿty (< Egypt., v. infra) - **OffAr** diff. word in KAI 269[4]; (Quaegebeur with) Lipiński OLP viii 113, 115: < Egypt. *nʾ mʾʿ.ty(w)* = the righteous ones (poss. interpret.); Lévy JA ccxxi 289: < Egypt. *nʾ mʾʿty* = the two 'Maʿat' (to be identified with Isis and Nephtys (cf. also Grelot Sem xx 21f.)) :: Couroyer Sem xx 18ff., RB lxxxvii 594ff., Gibson SSI ii p. 121f.: < Egypt. *nb mʾʿty* = the lord of the two Justices (cf. also Grelot Sem xx 21, DAE p. 342f. (n. s)) :: Grelot Sem xvii 74f.: < Egypt. *n mʾʿ.t*, *n* = Egypt. prep. + *mʾʿ.t* = the barque of the sun-god (cf. also Greenfield IEJ xix 202 (n. 16)) :: e.g. Cooke NSI p. 206, Torrey JAOS xl 244, 247: or = lapsus for *nʿmty* (= f. Sing. + suff. 1 p.s. of *nʿm*$_3$; cf. also CIS i sub 141, Koopmans 169, Donner KAI a.l.).

nmr$_1$ **DA** m. Sing. abs. *nmr* i 17 - **OldAr** f. Sing. abs. *nmrh* KAI 222A 31 (for this reading, cf. e.g. Dupont-Sommer Sf p. 46, 146, Donner KAI a.l., Fitzmyer AIS 49, Degen AAG p. 11, 48, Gibson SSI ii p. 30, Wittstruck JBL xcvii 100 × Rimbach JBL xcvii 565f., Lemaire & Durand IAS 114, 134 (cf. already Rosenthal ANET 660 n. 6): l. *nmlh* (= Sing. abs.) = ant), 223A 9 (*nmr[h]*, diff. reading, dam. context :: Lemaire & Durand IAS 117 (div. otherwise): l. *nmr* (= m. Sing. abs.)) - **OffAr** m. Sing. emph. *nmrʾ* Aḥiq 118, 119; cf. Frah S_2 99 (*nmrʾ*) - ¶ subst. m. and f. panther; for KAI 222A 31, 223A 9, cf. Thomas JSS v 283, Hillers TC 54f. (v. however supra).

nmr$_2$ **Hatra** word of diff. reading and unknown meaning *nmr[* in 30[11] (cf. Safar Sumer viii 187, Caquot Syr xxx 236f., cf. however Aggoula MUSJ xlvii 29: l. *nsk* = Qal Pf. 3 p.pl. of *nsk*$_1$ (highly uncert. interpret.) :: Milik DFD 381: l. *tmr[ʾ]* = Sing. emph. of *tmr*$_4$ (= ex-voto) :: Vattioni IH a.l. with incorrect interpret. of Aggoula's remarks in MUSJ xlvii 28f.).

nmrh v. *nmr*$_1$.

nmrsy (< Lib., cf. *nmrsh* in Lib. par.) - **Pun** Sing. abs. *nmrsy* RIL 451 - ¶ subst. of unknown meaning, prob. indication of function.

nmš v. *npš*.

nn **Pun** Février AIPHOS xiii 164, 170: the *nn* in KAI 162[4] = Sing. abs. of *nn* (= descendant), cf. also Röllig KAI a.l., v.d.Branden BO xiv 199, RSF ix 16; highly uncert. interpret., diff. context.
v. *šnym*.
ns v. *bny*$_1$.
nsʾ$_1$ v. *nst*, *nšʾ*$_1$.
nsʾ$_2$ **Ph** Zauzich & Röllig Or lix 327: the *msʾ* in Or lix 325[2] poss. = QAL Inf. cstr. of *nsʾ*$_2$ (= to pull out); highly uncert. interpret.
nsb **OffAr** QAL Pf. 1 p.s. *nsbt* Aḥiq 112; Part. act. s.m. abs. (or cstr.?) *nʾsyb* AM-NS ii 169, 171 i 4, ii 4, 173 v (*nʾ[s]yb*), vi (*nʾ[sy]b*), 174[4]; cf. Frah xxi 11 (*ynsbwn*), GIPP 38, SaSt 26 - **Palm** QAL Pf. 3 p.s.m. *nsb* MUSJ xxxviii 106[7] (× Ingholt MUSJ xxxviii 113 = QAL Part. act. s.m. abs.); Impf. 3 p.s.m. *ysb* CIS ii 4050[3], Syr xvii 353[10] (diff. and dam. context; cf. Milik DFD 303, Gawlikowski TP 58 :: Cantineau Syr xvii 354: < root *sb*$_1$ = to burn); QAL pass. Pf. 3 p.s.m. *nsyb* CIS ii 3977[4] (= RIP 132; or = QAL Part. pass. s.m. abs.?) - **Hatra** QAL Impf. 3 p.s.m. *lnsb* 281[3,9] - ¶ verb QAL to take, to take away, passim - **1)** + obj., *nšʾyt tbn wnsbt prn* Aḥiq 112: I have lifted bruised straw and taken up bran; *lnsb mšknʾ* Hatra 281[3]: he will take away the tent (cf. CIS ii 4050[9] (?; dam. context), Hatra 281[9]); *wrwd nʾsyb kwrsyʾ* AM-NS ii 169: O. who takes the stool (cf. Shaked BSOAS xxvii 287ff., cf. however Henning AM-NS ii a.l.: assuming the throne; cf. AM-NS 171 i 4, ii 4f., 173 v, vi 2, 174[4]; cf. also Altheim & Stiehl Suppl 91, ASA 274) - **2)** + double obj., *plg nsb mnth* MUSJ xxxviii 106[7f.]: the half he takes as his share - QAL pass. to be taken (away), to be transported; *lb[t b]l nsyb knwnʾ dnh* CIS ii 3977[4]: this altar (v. *knwn*) was transported to the temple of B. (cf. Milik DFD 175; heavily dam. context).
v. *bʿy*$_1$, *mnsb*, *šbt*$_1$.
nsbh v. *bny*$_1$.
nsh v. *nst*.
nsḥ$_1$ **OffAr** QAL Impf. 3 p.s.m. *ynsḥ* Aḥiq 156, 211 (reading uncert.); 3 p.pl.m. *ysḥw* KAI 225[9]; + suff. 3 p.s.m. *ynsḥwhy* KAI 228A 14; cf. SbPAW '33, 140? - ¶ verb QAL to tear (out) - **1)** + obj., *wynsḥ lšn[h]* Aḥiq 156: and he shall tear out his tongue (cf. also Greenfield HDS 54ff., Lindenberger APA 157, 265 n. 473) - **2)** + obj. + *mn*$_5$; *ynsḥwhy wzrʿh wšmh mn ʾnpy tymʾ* KAI 228A 14f.: let they remove (> eliminate, cf. Aggoula Syr lxii 64) him and his seed and his name from T.; *ysḥw šmk wʾšrk mn ḥyn* KAI 225[9f.]: may they pluck out your name and the traces of your existence from among the living (v. also *ʾšr*$_4$ and *ḥy*$_2$); for Aḥiq 211, v. *dm*$_1$ - a form of this root also in DA iv a 2: *[n]sḥn?*, cf. Hoftijzer DA a.l. - a form of this root (*nsḥ/nsḥh*) poss. in IEJ xxxii 195[4] (heavily dam. context).
nsḥ$_2$ **OffAr** (Arnaud with) Bordreuil Sem xxiii 98f.: the diff. *nsḥnghy*

in Sem xxiii 95 recto 3, verso 2 = *nsḥ₂* (= Sing. cstr. (= governor) < Akkad.) + *nghy* (= Sing. abs. (= district) < Akkad.), less prob. interpret., cf. also Fales AION xxvi 542 n. 6, 544, 547 (cf. idem sub AECT 58), Kaufman Conn xix 121, JAOS cix 100, Lipiński WGAV 377f., ActAntHung xxii 377: *nsḥnghy* = n.p.

nsḥ₃ OffAr word of unknown meaning (subst., Sing. abs.??) in PF 1955, 2075.

nsḥh (< Akkad. cf. Zimmern Fremdw 29, Kaufman AIA 78, cf. also O'Connor JNES xlv 218) - **Nab** Sing. cstr. *nsḥt* CIS ii 209[9] - ¶ subst. extract, copy.

nsy₁ Hebr PI'EL Pf. 3 p.s.m. *nsh* KAI 193[9] - ¶ verb PI'EL to try, to dare; + *l₅* + Inf., *'m nsh 'yš lqr' ly spr lnṣḥ* KAI 193[9f.]: no man has ever dared to read a letter for me (for this text, cf. Pardee HAHL 86) - Milik Bibl xlviii 549: the *]wnsy* in Herm 8[6] = *w* + form of the root *nsy₁*, cf. however Bresciani & Kamil Herm a.l.: *nsy* poss. = n.p. - Milik Bibl xlviii 549: in Herm 8[12] l. *'tns[h]* = ITP - form of *nsy* (poss. reading and interpret.) :: Bresciani & Kamil Herm a.l.: l. *'tnn[h]* = QAL Impf. 1 p.s. + suff. 3 p.s.m./f. of *ntn*.

nsy₂ v. *nš'₄*.

nsy' v. *nš'₄*.

nsyk OffAr Sing. + suff. 1 p.s. *nsyky* Aḥiq 119 (for the reading, cf. Lindenberger APA 249 n. 314 :: Kottsieper SAS 13, 21, 131 n. 254, 210: l. poss. *ksyky* = Sing. + suff. 2 p.s.f. of *ksy₂* (= covering), suff. 2 p.s.f. lapsus for suff. 2 p.s.m.) - ¶ subst. prince - > Akkad. *nasīku* (= chieftain), cf. e.g. v.Soden Or xxxvii 261, xlvi 191 (cf. also idem AHW s.v.); cf. also CAD s.v.: *nasīku* = foreign word.

v. *nsk₃*.

nsk₁ Ph QAL Part. act. s.m. abs. *nsk* SE xlv 60 (v. infra), RSF vii 4 ii 2, RDAC '85, 253[2] (for the context, cf. also Puech Sem xxxix 108f.); cstr. *nsk* CIS i 67[4] (= Kition B 12) - **Pun** QAL Part. act. s.m. abs. *nsk* CIS i 4880[2], 5984[2] (= TPC 46); cstr. (or abs.?) *nsk* CIS i 327[4], 328[4], 329[3f.] (*n[s]k*), 331[2f.] (*[n]sk*; ??, cf. Slouschz TPI p. 287, cf. however CIS i a.l.: l. poss. *[m]sk*, v. infra), 1293[4] (or abs.?), 3014[3], 3275[3], 5943[1] (= TPC 5); pl.m. abs. *nskm* KAI 100[7]; cstr. *nsk* RCL '66, 201[6] (cf. Dupont-Sommer CRAI '68, 117, 129 :: Mahjoubi & Fantar RCL '66, 208f.: = Sing. cstr. of *nsk₂* (= founding (in metal))); YIPH Part. s.m. cstr. *msk* CIS i 330[3f.] (??; or = lapsus for *nsk*? (QAL Part. act.; cf. Harr 124) or = Sing. cstr. of noun *msk₂* (= founder (in metal))?? :: Dérenbourg JA vii/v 36 n. 1: = QAL Part. s.m. cstr. of *msk₁* (= to mix; cf. also Harr 124)) - **OldAr** QAL Impf. 2 p.s.m. *tsk* KAI 222B 38, 224[5] (*ts[k]*),[7]; 3 p.s.m. *ysk* KAI 222A 26 - ¶ verb QAL to pour out, to found (in metal), to provide :: Dohmen UF xv 42: in Ph./Pun. *nsk₁* = to hammer, to forge - **1)** + *l₅* + obj., *wtsk lhm lḥm* KAI 224[7]: and you will provide them with food (cf. Greenfield ActOr xxix 7f., FS Fitzmyer 50, FS Moran 201, Ben-Chayyim Lesh xxxv 247, Hoftijzer FS Beek 92f. (cf. KAI 224[5], cf. also KAI 222B 38)) - **2)** + *ʿl_7* + obj., to pour out over, to shower upon: KAI 222A 26f. - Part. act. substantivated, founder (in metal), passim; cf. the foll. combinations with metals - a) ***nsk brzl*** CIS i 67[4f.], ***nsk hbrzl*** CIS i 3014[3], 5943[1f]: the founder in iron; ***hnskm šbrzl*** KAI 100[7]: the founders in iron - b) ***nsk hḥrṣ*** CIS i 327[4f.], ***nsk ʾḥrṣ*** CIS i 328[4], ***ʾn[s]k ʾḥrṣ*** CIS i 329[3f.]: the founder in gold; cf. RCL '66, 201[6] (v. supra) - c) ***nsk hnskt***, v. ***nskh*** - cf. also ***bn nsk*** SE xlv 60: (litt.:) son of the founder, caster, i.e. belonging to the corporation of the casters (cf. Garbini SE xlv 60f., FSR 111, Heltzer CISFP i 118ff. (cf. also Dothan IEJ xxxv 84f. n. 9)) - YIPH Part. substantivated (?; v. supra) founder; *msk hnḥšt* CIS i 330[3f.]: the founder in bronze; for founding in bronze, cf. also CIS i 331[2f.], v. also supra - on this root, cf. also Collini SEL iv 10ff., 26ff.

v. *ysk*, *$msk_{1,3}$* , *nmr_2*, *$nsk_{2,3}$*, *nskh*.

nsk_2 Ebeling Frah a.l.: l. *nskh* (= form of *nsk_2* (= libation)) in Frah xix 13 (less prob. reading), Nyberg FP 50, 91: l. *ʾsgdh* (v. *ʾsgd*) - Yadin & Naveh Mas a.l.: l. *nsk* (= Sing. abs. of *nsk_2*) in Mas 672, 673 (*[n]sk*), in both instances diff. reading - this word poss. in RPC 92[2] (*nsk*), cf. Avigad BCH '67, 302 (cf. also Puech Sem xxix 26: l. *nsky* (= Sing. + suff. 3 p.s.m.)) :: Masson & Sznycer RPC 93: = QAL Part. act. s.m. of *nsk_1* or = Sing. abs. of *nsk_5* (= melting).

v. *$nsk_{1, 3}$*.

nsk_3 **OffAr** word of unknown meaning (prob. noun Sing. emph. *nskʾ*) in RES 492B 1 (= RES 1800); Driver AnOr xii 57: = weaving; Grelot DAE p. 140: = *nsk_2* (= libation) :: e.g. Lidzbarski Eph ii 238f.: = either QAL Part. act. s.m. emph. of *nsk_1* or = Sing. emph. of *nsk_4* (= *nsyk*).

nsk_4 v. *nsk_3*.

nsk_5 v. *nsk_2*.

nskh **Pun** Sing. abs. *nskt* CIS i 3275[3], KAI 122[1,2], 137[6] (cf. Lidzbarski Eph iii 59f., Harr 124 :: FR 139, 151, Segert GPP p. 137: = QAL Part. pass. pl.f. abs. of *nsk_1*) - ¶ subst. - **1)** molten/cast metal; ***nsk hnskt*** CIS i 3275[3]: the founder in metal; ***nbl nskt*** KAI 137[5f.]: vessels of cast metal (:: Berger RHR lviii 156: ... for libations; v. also *nbl_2*) - **2)** statue of cast metal; ***hnskt šʾlm ʿwgsṭs*** KAI 122[1]: the statue in cast metal of the divine August (cf. KAI 122[2]).

nss_1 **Ph** the diff. *nss* in KAI 27[26a] (for the reading, v. infra) as read by Caquot FS Gaster 51 (= QAL Pf. 3 p.pl. of *nss* (= to be/become weak; cf. also Lipiński RTAT 266 (n. 96): = to groan)), Garbini OA xx 286 (= QAL Pf. 3 p.s.m.) and Avishur PIB 248, 255f. (= QAL Inf. abs. or Imper. s.f. of *nss* (= to flee, to fly)), poss. to be read *ssm* (cf. Gibson

SSI iii p. 82, 88; cf. also Cross & Saley BASOR cxcvii 47, Röllig NESE ii 19, 26: l. *l*$_3$ (= oh) + *ssm* (= name of a demon) :: v.d.Branden BiOr xxxiii 13: l. *pr* (= Sing. abs. of *pry*$_2$) :: e.g. du Mesnil du Buisson FS Dussaud 424, Albright BASOR lxxvi 10, Gaster Or xi 44, Torczyner JNES vi 29, Röllig KAI a.l.: no text between ll. 26 and 27.

nss$_2$ **Amm** the diff. *nss* in SANSS-Amm 14 (= Vatt sig. eb. 261, IS 10 = Jackson ALIA 83 no. 59 = CAI 68) poss. indication of function/title (cf. Herr SANSS p. 209), cf. also Avigad FS Glueck 287: *nss* = noun (Sing. abs.) = standard-bearer (cf. also Jackson ALIA 83f.).

nssh v. *n ʿsst*.

ns ʿ **Ph** Qal Impf. 3 p.s.m. *ys ʿ* KAI 26A iii 15, 17 - ¶ verb to pull down; + obj., *wys ʿ hšʿr z* KAI 26A iii 15: and he will pull down this gate (cf. KAI 26A iii 17f.).
v. *šyʿ*$_1$.

nst **Pun** diff. word in RCL '66, 201[5]; Mahjoubi & Fantar RCL '66, 207, 209: = Part. pl. f. abs. < root *ns*ʾ$_1$ < *nś*ʾ (= distinguished; improb. interpret.); Ferron Mus xcviii 55f., 61: = adj. Plur. f. abs. < root *nss* (= most prominent, most outstanding; highly uncert. interpret.); Garbini RSO xliii 12: = Sing. abs. of noun *nsh* (= ordinance, regulation; uncert. interpret.); Dupont-Sommer CRAI '68, 117, 126f.: = Qal Part. act. s.f. abs. of *ns*ʾ (= *nś*ʾ) > collective noun (= porters; improb. interpret.).

n ʿbṣ **OffAr** Plur. abs. *n ʿbṣn* Cowl 15[15], Krael 7[18] - ¶ subst. of uncert. meaning indicating something made of stone/alabaster (v. *šš*$_1$); Epstein Tarbiz i 53, Gottlieb JAOS c 512f.: = vessel, cf. however Krael p. 213, Grelot RB lxxviii 517, 520ff., DAE p. 194 (n.l.), 235, Porten & Greenfield JEAS p. 20, 55, Porten & Yardeni sub TADAE B 2.6 a.e.: = inlaid work, inlay? (cf. also Porten Arch 94, Delsman TUAT i 261) :: Cowl p. 48: = support (of a bed)? (cf. Wag 61 n. 3), cf. also Perles OLZ '11, 28, Fitzmyer FS Albright ii 156f., WA 259.

n ʿwr **Hatra** Aggoula MUSJ xlvii 41: the *n ʿwr*ʾ in 220 = Sing. emph. of *n ʿwr* (= herald), improb. interpret.; *n ʿwr*ʾ prob. = n.p., cf. Safar Sumer xxi 37, Degen WO v 226, Vattioni IH a.l., Abbadi PIH 28, 129 (Vattioni a.l.: or l. *ngwr*ʾ*?*).

n ʿl$_1$ **OffAr** Pa ʿel Impf. 3 p.s.m. *yn ʿl* Aḥiq 206 (cf. Driver JRAS '32, 89 (uncert. interpret.) × Grelot RB lxviii 193 (cf. idem DAE p. 447): = Qal Impf. 3 p.s.m. of *ʿll*$_1$ (= to enter, to penetrate) × Cowl p. 226, 304: = Aph Impf. 3 p.s.m. of *ʿll*$_1$ (= to make to enter, to make to penetrate); cf. also Gressmann ATAT 462: = to put, to lay down; :: Kottsieper SAS 23, 51, 219: = Qal pass. Impf. 3 p.s.m. of *n ʿl*$_2$; cf. also Lindenberger APA 205, 283; for the reading problems, cf. Teixidor AO i 108) - ¶ verb Pa ʿel to cause a sore: Aḥiq 206 (v. however supra; for the context, cf. also Watson AO ii 259).

n ʿl$_2$ **Ph** Qal Pf. 1 p.s. *n ʿlt* Syr xlviii 403[1] (on this form, cf. also Garr

DGSP 123) - ¶ verb QAL to fasten (sc. a bolt); for the context, v. also *mnʿl*.
v. *nʿl*$_1$.
nʿl$_3$ v. *ʿll*$_1$.
nʿm$_1$ **Pun** Levi Della Vida OA ii 85, 92, Polselli OAC xiii 239: the diff. *ynim* in IRT 879[1] poss. = QAL Impf. 3 p.s.m. of *nʿm*$_1$ (= to be pleasant; improb. interpret., cf. Vattioni AION xvi 41: = part of n.p.) :: Krahmalkov RSF iii 184: = Plur. abs. of *ʾwn*$_2$, *adom ynim* = man of substance :: Krahmalkov RSF vi 29: or = Plur. abs. of *ʾwn*$_4$ (= deceit, injustice), *adom ynim* = scoundrel - a form of this root (*tnʿm*) poss. in BAr '55/56, 31 no. 3[1] (for the reading problems, cf. Février sub IAM 3).
nʿm$_2$ **Ph** Sing. abs. *nʿm* KAI 10[8], 19[6], 26A i 5, 10, 43[1] (cf. Honeyman JEA xxvi 58f., v.d.Branden OA iii 248f., Lipiński RTAT 250, Gibson SSI iii p. 135f. (cf. also Harr 124) :: e.g. Cooke NSI p. 84, Röllig KAI a.l., Dahood Or li 283: = Sing. m. abs. of *nʿm*$_3$; for the context, v. *mʾš*$_1$)^{,15}; cstr. *nʿm* KAI 26A i 13 - **Pun** Sing. abs. *nʿm* KAI 161[2], Punica xviii/ii 92[4], *nm* CIS i 6000bis 7 (= TPC 84; cf. e.g. Février BAr '51/52, 78, CIS i a.l., Ferron StudMagr i 76, 78, v.d.Branden BO xxiii 156), Punica xviii/iii 4[7] (cf. Février JA cclv 63) - ¶ subst. good, fortune; *kn bymty kl nʿm ldnnym* KAI 26A i 5f.: and in my days the D. had everything (that was) good (cf. KAI 43[15]); *yṭnʾ ʾnk bt ʾdny bnʿm* KAI 26A i 9f.: and I put the house of my lord into good order (for the context, v. also *byt*$_2$); *pʿl ly nʿm* KAI 10[8]: she did kindness to me (cf. KAI 26A i 10; cf. *pʿl nʿm* KAI 19[6]: the beneficient, epithet of the Ptolemean king, prob. representation of Greek εὐεργέτης); *ytn lʾ nʿm* Punica xviii/ii 92[4]: he gave him goodness (i.e. was good to him); *ḥšb nʿm* KAI 161[2]: who devises good, the well-dispersed (epithet of Numidian king); for the context of Punica xviii/iii 4[7], v. *rḥm*$_1$ - Février AIPHOS xiii 169f.: the *nm* in KAI 162[5] poss. = Sing. abs. of *nʿm*$_2$ (highly uncert. interpret., diff. context) - Vattioni AION xvi 50: the *nema* in IRT 901[5] = Sing. + suff. 3 p.s.f. of *nʿm*$_2$ :: Milik (with Vattioni) AION xvi 50: = Sing. + suff. 3 p.s.m. of *nʿm*$_2$ (cf. also Polselli StudMagr xi 40) :: Krahmalkov JSS xxiv 26: = Sing. f. abs. of *nʿm*$_3$ - Honeyman JEA xxvi 58 (n. 4): l. *nʿm* (= Sing. abs. of *nʿm*$_2$) in KAI 43[16] (cf. also Lipiński RTAT 251) - cf. also Augustine Epist xvii 2: n.p. *Namphamio* = *bonipedis hominem*.
v. *hwn*$_3$, *nʿm*$_3$.
nʿm$_3$ **Ph** Sing. m. abs. *nʿm* KAI 18[6] (cf. however Harr 124: = Sing. abs. of *nʿm*$_2$), 42[5] (cf. however Harr 124: = Sing. abs. of *nʿm*$_2$); Sing. f. abs. *nʿmt* KAI 26A ii 8, 13, iii 6, C iii 20 (v. *ršʾt*; :: Lipiński OLZ '82, 458: = Sing. abs. of *nʿmh* (= pleasure)) - **Pun** Sing. m. abs. *nʿm* KAI 113B 1f., 163[5] (poss. interpret.), RES 303[1], 304[1], 305, 331[4], Hofra 98[4], Punica xii 29[3], xviii/iii 1[2], xix 1, MAIBL xvi 397[1], 407[1], 408[1], 409[1],

etc., *n’m* CRAI ’16, 128a 1, b 1, MAIBL xvi 410[1], *nm* MAIBL xvi 401[1], 403[1], BAr-NS i-ii 226[1]; Plur. m. abs. *n‘mm* KAI 119[6], 162[3]; Sing. f. abs. *n‘mt* NP 130[1] (cf. Février RHR cxli 19) - ¶ adj. agreeable, good, favourable, passim; *’lm n‘mm* KAI 162[3]: the favourable gods; *’št n‘mt mhrt* NP 130[1]: an agreeable (and) capable woman (v. also *mhr*$_2$); *šm n‘m* KAI 18[6], Punica xii 29[3]: a good name, a good reputation; *[l]mzl n‘m* KAI 42[5]: for good fortune (Greek par. ἀγα[θ]ῆ τύχῃ); *šbt n‘mt* KAI 26A ii 7f.: gracious living (v. *yšb*$_1$), cf. also KAI 26A ii 13; *ym n‘m hym z lmgn* KAI 113b: a favourable day is this day for M. (for parallels, v. also *ywm*); for *rš’t n‘mt* KAI 26C iii 20, v. *rš’t*, for *bṣ‘m n‘mm* KAI 119[6], v. *bṣ‘*$_3$.
v. *hwn*$_3$, *nm‘ty*, *n‘m*$_2$.

n‘mh v. *n‘m*$_3$.

n‘sst **Pun** diff. word in ICO-Malta-NPu 13. Garbini Malta ’65, p. 65: *n‘sst* = Sing. abs. of *nssh* (= illness; highly uncert. interpret.).

n‘s‘y’ **Pun** word of unknown meaning in KAI 168[4]; FR 237, Röllig KAI a.l.: *-y’* = suff. 3 p.s.m.; Röllig KAI a.l.: *n‘s‘* = noun indicating the relationship between the woman described by this word and the man for whom she erected the tombstone (cf. also Chabot sub Punica xi 9).

n‘‘ym v. *n‘r*$_3$.

n‘r$_1$ **OffAr** QAL Part. act. s.m. abs. *n‘r* Aḥiq 79 - ¶ verb QAL uncert. meaning; Perles OLZ ’11, 500f., Cowl p. 222, 233, Gressmann ATAT 457, Grelot DAE p. 435, Kottsieper SAS 18, 219: = to foam (said of wine), to ferment × e.g. Sach p. 160, Nöldeke AGWG xiv/4, 10, Baneth OLZ ’14, 296, Ginsberg ANET 428, Lindenberger APA 43f., 221 n. 7: = to bray (said of an ass) :: Torczyner OLZ ’12, 402: = Sing. abs. of *n‘r*$_5$ (= fool), v. also *ḥmr*$_5$, cf. also Grelot RB lxviii 180, Stähli KJK 26ff.

n‘r$_2$ **Hebr** NIPH Impf. 3 p.s.f. *tn‘r* AMB 4[15] - ¶ verb NIPH to be shaken, to be removed; *tn‘r hṭlnyt ... mn ’qmw* AMB 4[15f.]: the shadow-spirit will be removed from A.

n‘r$_3$ **Ph** Sing. cstr. *n‘r* IEJ xxxvii 26; Plur. abs. *n‘rm* KAI 37A 8, 12, B 11 (= Kition C 1) - **Amm** Sing. cstr. *n‘r* SANSS-Amm 31 (= Vat sig. eb. 221 = Jackson ALIA 81 no. 53 = CAI 54), 44 (= Vatt sig. eb. 217 = Jackson ALIA 80 no. 50 = CAI 53) - **Hebr** Sing. abs. *n‘r* Frey 668[1]; cstr. *n‘r* TA-H 110[1,2], Dir boll 9 (= SANSS-Hebr 31 = IS 8), SANSS-Hebr 82 (= Vatt sig. eb. 407), 113 (= Vatt sig. eb. 406), Vatt sig. eb. 108, 277, EI xv 303; a form of this noun (*n‘r[*) prob. in TA-H 15[4] (heavily dam. context) - ¶ subst. - **1)** young boy: Frey 668[1] - **2)** servant - a) in KAI 37A 8, 12, B 11 prob. certain kind of temple servant, cf. e.g. Peckham Or xxxvii 313, Masson & Sznycer RPC 46f., Delcor UF xi 154, Stähli KJK 66ff. - b) in Amm. and older

Hebr. texts (: SANSS-Amm 31, 44, SANSS-Hebr 31, 82, 113, Vatt sig. eb. 108, 277 and prob. also TA-H 110[1,2]) and prob. also in IEJ xxxvii 26 prob. indication of high (sometimes military) function, cf. e.g. Dir p. 126, Rainey JNES xxiv 21, TA p. 122f., Mettinger SSO 88, Ussishkin BASOR ccxxiii 11, Cutler & MacDonald UF viii 27ff., MacDonald UF x 170, JNES xxxv 147ff., FS Isserlin 60ff., Stähli KJK 167ff., 179ff. (cf. also 136ff.), Avigad EI xv 303f., Mem Wright 294ff., FS Cross 205, Garfinkel BiAr liii 77f., and the litt. quoted by Mosc p. 82 - Kornfeld sub Abydos 14: l. poss. *nʿr* (= Sing. cstr. of *nʿr*$_3$) in RES 1335[2] (= KAI 49,45; uncert. reading and interpret.); Lidzbarski Eph iii 113 (div. otherwise): l. *nʿrym* (without interpret.); RES sub 1335: l. *nʿʿym* (without interpret.).
v. *mrnr*, *nwr*$_3$, *nḥr*$_2$.

nʿr$_4$ **Ph** Plur. + suff. 3 p.s.m. *nʿry* KAI 24[12] - ¶ subst. Plur. youth; *lmnʿry* KAI 24[12]: from his youth :: Sader EAS 159 n. 22: or = since his deprivation (noun < root *ʿry*$_1$).

nʿr$_5$ v. *nʿr*$_1$.

nʿr$_6$ v. *ṯnʾ*$_2$.

nʿtr **Pun** word (?) of unknown meaning in KAI 122[2] (cf. Amadasi IPT 57). Levi Della Vida AfrIt vi 25, 27: = NIPH Part. s.m. abs. of *ytr*$_1$ (= remaining), cf. also FR 161 (improb. interpret.), cf. also Février JA ccxxxix 8, v.d.Branden BiOr xxxvi 202 (div. otherwise): l. *ʿt r* (for this expression, v. *r*$_1$); diff. and uncert. interpret. (for the context, v. also *mqm*$_1$).

npʾ$_1$ v. *ndy*.

npʾ$_2$ **OffAr** word of unknown meaning in Cowl 7[4] (*bnpʾ*) and 20[4] (*bdyn npʾ*), indicating type of tribunal or process?? (cf. also J.J.Rabinowitz Bibl xxxix 81f., xli 72 :: idem ibid.: perhaps *npʾ* corruption of Greek ἐμπόριον??) × Cowl p. 21, 59, Grelot DAE p. 93, 198: = n.l. (cf. also Verger RCL '64, 83 (n. 28), RGP 181f. (n. 6), Porten Arch 315) :: Andreas with Schulthess AGG '07, 185 n. 3: < Iran. = family, cf. also Wag 68 n. 2, 206f. (improb. interpret., cf. Cowl p. 59, Schaed 258) :: Lidzbarski Eph iii 127: = n.p. - the diff. *nwpyʾ* in ATNS 15[4] related to this word? (context heavily dam. and uncert.); Segal ATNS a.l.: or = lapsus for *nwptyʾ* (= Plur. emph. of *nwpt*) or = n.p.?

npg v. *npq*$_1$.

npḥ Beyer ATTM 388, 638: l. *ʾpḥ* = APH Pf. 3 p.s.m. in MPAT-A 35[1] (= SM 16; (= to forge)), highly uncert. reading and interpret.

npḥr (< Akkad., cf. Cowl p. 264, Kaufman AIA 76, Greenfield & Porten BIDG p. 45) - **OffAr** Sing. cstr. *npḥr* Beh 35 (*np[ḥr]*, for the reading, cf. Greenfield & Porten BIDG p. 40f.; Akkad. par. l. 78: *napḫar*), 47* (Akkad. par. l. 83: *napḫar*) - ¶ subst. totality, cf. *mpḥrh* - on this word, cf. also Greenfield FS Rundgren 152f.

npy$_1$ v. *mph.*

npy$_2$ **OffAr** QAL Impf. 3 p.s.m. *ynpy* Sem xxi 85 conc. 4 - ¶ verb QAL to sieve, to sift (diff. and dam. context).

npl$_1$ **OffAr** QAL Pf. 3 p.s.f. *nplt* Aḥiq 184 (*[n]plt*), 186; cf. Frah xx 6 (*nplwn*), Paik 688 (*nplt*), GIPP 59 - **Nab** QAL Pf. 3 p.s.m. *npl* J 14[2] (= CIS ii 203) - **Palm** QAL Part. act. s.m. emph. *npl›* InscrP 34[7] (cf. Rosenthal Sprache 65 × Cantineau sub InscrP 34, Gramm 98: = Sing. emph. of *npl*$_2$ (= chance, hazard)) - ¶ verb QAL to fall: Aḥiq 186 (dam. context) - **1)** + *b*$_2$: Aḥiq 184 (dam. context) - **2)** *wnpl ḥlq hgrw ymyn›* J 14[2f.]: the portion of H. has fallen at the right side (i.e. the right side has fallen to H.'s share; on this text, cf. Greenfield Mem Yalon 71f.) - **3)** *kl ṣbw dnpl›* InscrP 34[7] (dam. context), Rosenthal Sprache 51 n. 3: *npl* in this text = to be necessary, *kl ṣbw dnpl›* = everything necessary (highly uncert. interpret.), Cantineau (v. supra): *kl ṣbw dnpl›* = every chance event? - Février & Fantar Karth xii 52: the *np›l* in Karth xii 52 ii 2 = QAL Part. act. s.m. abs. of *npl*$_1$ (cf. also Krahmalkov RSF iii 178, 183, 202, v.d.Branden RSF v 57; poss. interpret., diff. context) - Aggoula Syr lxii 62, 65: l. *yhn[p]l* = HAPH Impf. 3 p.s.m. (= to eliminate) in KAI 228A 21 (poss. reading), cf. however Cooke NSI p. 195, 199, Donner KAI a.l., Gibson SSI ii p. 149, 151: l. *yhn[pq]* = HAPH Impf. 3 p.s.m. of *npq*$_1$.
v. *ybl*$_1$, *npl*$_1$.

npl$_2$ v. *npl*$_1$.

nps v. *npš.*

npṣ **OffAr**, cf. Frah app. 13 (*npṣwn*): to press, to crush, cf. Nyberg FP 54, 99 :: Ebeling Frah a.l.: l. *‹pṣwn* (< root *›pṣ* (= to squeeze, to press)) - on this root, cf. also Blau PC 62 - v.Soden Or xxxvii 261, xlvi 191: > Akkad. *napāṣu* = to shake out (cf. also idem AHW s.v. *napāṣu* II), highly uncert. interpret., cf. also CAD s.v. *napāṣu* B: meaning uncert.
v. *kpṣ.*

npq$_1$ **OldAr** QAL Impf. 3 p.s.m. *ypq* KAI 222A 28 - **OffAr** QAL Pf. 3 p.s.m. *npq* Cowl 30[5], 31[4], RES 1785B 3, F 5; 3 p.s.f. *npqt* Aḥiq 135, 139, 140; 2 p.s.m. *npqt* SSI ii 28 obv. 6; 1 p.s. *npqt* Herm 5[3]; 2 p.pl.m. *npqtm* SSI ii 28 obv. 3; Impf. 3 p.s.m. *ynpq* FS Driver 54 conv. 2; 3 p.s.f. *tnpq* Cowl 9[9], Aḥiq 124, Krael 7[26], 12[22]; 2 p.s.m. *tnpq* Cowl 5[12], Sach 76 i B 1, 4; Inf. *mnpq* Cowl 5[14], Krael 6[14], 9[14], 10[3,4], ATNS 26[3]; Part. act. s.f. abs. *npqh* Aḥiq 123; HAPH/APH Pf. 3 p.s.m. + suff. 3 p.s.f. *hnpqh* Aḥiq 109; + suff. 1 p.s. *›pqny* Herm 6[4]; 3 p.s.f. *hnpqt* AG 8 recto 2 (?, dam. context); 2 p.s.m. *hnpqt* Cowl 7[5]; 1 p.s. *hnpgt* ATNS 46[3] (?, dam. context; for the orthogr., cf. Segal ATNS a.l., Shaked Or lvi 410); 3 p.pl.m. *hnpqw* Cowl 30[16], 31[15]; Impf. 3 p.s.m. *yhnpq* Cowl 13[11,12], Krael 10[16], Driv 10[3,5], *ynpq* Krael 12[29], *yhpq* Sach 76 ii B 3; 3 p.s.f. *thnpq* Cowl 15[25,28], Krael 2[8,10], *tpq* ASAE xlviii 112B 3; 3 p.pl.m.

yhnpqwn Cowl $8^{15,17}$, *ynpqwn* Krael 9^{21}, 10^{15}; Imper. s.m. *hnpq* Aḥiq 99, *ʾpq* ASAE xlviii 112B 1; s.f. *hnpqy* Cowl 8^{27}; Part. pl.m. abs. *mpqn* Herm 5^{3}; ITP Pf. 3 p.s.m. *ʾtnpq* Cowl 71^{29}; cf. Frah xxi 9 (*ynpkwn*; cf. Nyberg FP 95), GIPP 38 - **Nab** APH Pf. 2 p.s.m. *ʾnpqt* MPAT 64 i 11; Impf. 3 p.s.m. *ynpq* CIS ii 197^{2}, $198^{5,9}$, 206^{5}, 207^{3}, $211^{3,7}$, 212^{7}, 215^{2}, 221^{4}, 222^{3}, 224^{2}, J 2^{5}, 5^{2}; 2 p.s.m. *tnpq* MPAT 64 i 9; HOPH Pf. 3 p.s.m. *hnpq* MPAT 64 i 3 (uncert. reading; cf. Fitzmyer & Harrington MPAT a.l.; or l. *ynpq*? (= APH Impf. 3 p.s.m.?) :: Starcky RB lxi 163, 169: l. *p* (= p_1) + *npq* (= QAL Pf. 3 p.s.m.)) - **Palm** APH Pf. 3 p.s.m. *ʾpq* Inv x 44^{5}; Impf. 3 p.s.m. *ypq* CIS ii 3913 ii 6; Part. s.m. abs. *mpq* CIS ii 3913 ii 35, 81, 82 (*[m]pq*), 85, 86, 112; Part. pass. s.m. abs. *mʾpq* CIS ii 3913 ii 111 (for the reading, cf. Rosenthal Sprache 29) - **Hatra** QAL Part. s.m. abs. *npyq* 336^{6} - APH Impf. 3 p.s.m. *lnpq* 342^{8} - **JAr** QAL Pf. 3 p.s.m. *npq* Frey 834 (= SM 91); Impf. 3 p.s.m. *lypwq* Syr xlv 101^{18} (dam. and diff. context) - ¶ verb QAL to leave, to go forth; *kdy ʾršm npq* Cowl $30^{4f.}$: when A. departed (cf. Cowl 31^{4}); cf. *bbʾ zylk lmnpq* Krael 10^{4}: your gate (through which) to go forth (for the context, cf. also Porten & Szubin JAOS cvii 233f.; cf. Krael 10^{3}); *kl dy ʿl wnpyq* Hatra 336^{6} everyone who enters or leaves; said of vegetation, *wʾl ypq ḥṣr* KAI 222A 28: let the grass not come forth; cf. also the foll. comb. - **1)** + b_2, *šlyṭʾ ʾnt lmnpq btrʿ* Krael $9^{14f.}$: you have the right to go forth through the gate; *wlʾ tnpq bšwqʾ zy bynyn wbyn byt ppṭʿwnyt* Cowl $5^{12f.}$: you shall not go forth into the street which is between us and the house of P. (cf. Cowl 5^{14}) - **2)** + l_5, *lmnpq lṣd* ... ATNS 26^{3}: to go forth in the direction of ... - **3)** + mn_5, *ywm [z]y npqtm mn mṣryn* SSI ii 28 obv. 3: the day you left Egypt (cf. Herm 5^{3}); *mšh kd npq mn mn mṣryn* Frey 834 (= SM 91): Moshe when he left Egypt; *mn tmh tnpq* Krael 12^{22}: from there you may go forth (sc. from that gate; v. tmh_3); *hn npqh ṭbh mn pm* ... Aḥiq 123: if a good thing comes forth from the mouth of ... (cf. Aḥiq 124, 140); *brty tšnʾnk wtnpq mnk* Cowl $9^{8f.}$: my daughter divorces you and goes away from you; cf. *wtnpq mnh ʿm šʿrt* ... Krael 7^{26}: and she will go away from him with the rest of ...; *wmn ʾlhn lʾ npqt* Aḥiq 135: it does not come forth from the gods (for the context, cf. Lindenberger APA 132, 258 n. 410) - 4) + $ʿl_7$, *ynpq ʿly* FS Driver 54 conv. 2: he must make his way to me - HAPH/APH to remove, to produce, to export, passim - **1)** + obj., *wtpq ʾḥṭb ʿmr 1* ASAE xlviii 112B 3ff.: and that A. may bring one *ʿomer* ...; *wlʾ ynpq yth ʾnwš* CIS ii 212^{7}: and nobody shall remove him (cf. J 2^{5}); *whn zbwnʾ ypq ʿly[m]yn* CIS ii 3913 ii 6: and if the buyer shall export slaves (sc. from the town; cf. CIS ii 3913 ii 86); *dy lnpq zmrt[ʾ]* Hatra $342^{8f.}$ whoever makes a female singer leave; *wkl zy hnʿlt bydh thnpq* Cowl $15^{24f.}$: and everything she brought with her, she may take away (v. $ʿll_1$), cf. Cowl $15^{27f.}$, Krael $2^{8,10}$; cf. also the foll.

instances, *w[hw zy] tbyr hnpqh br›* Aḥiq 109: the one (sc. the vessel) that is broken lets it (sc. its contents) go forth; *spr› zk hnpqy* Cowl 8[27]: produce this deed (cf. MPAT 64 i 11; cf. also Muffs 182f., Yaron RB lxxvii 414f.; for the producing of a document, cf. also Greenfield Mem Yalon 74f.); *mndt bgy› ›lk yhnpq* Driv 10[3]: he will collect the rent for these domains (cf. Driv 10[4f.]); *w›pqny ›nh wbry* Herm 6[4]: and he released me and my son (cf. Gibson SSI ii p. 141 × Hillers UF xi 380f.: he redeemed me, me and my son, cf. also Hoftijzer SV 118 (nn. e, h) (cf. also Wesselius FS Lebram 10: he liberated us (from prison or some other kind of custody)), cf. however Grelot RB lxxiv 436: he let me pay me and my son (cf. also Bresciani & Kamil Herm a.l.) :: Milik Bibl xlviii 548: he has delivered (them) to me and my son :: Porten & Greenfield IOS iv 19f.: he brought me forth, me and my son (cf. also Porten & Greenfield JEAS p. 163, Porten & Yardeni sub TADAE A 2.6)) - **2)** + obj. + l_5, *›pq ly ... ktwn 1* ASAE xlviii 112B 1f.: send me (// with form of HAPH of $yšr_1$) ... one garment; *tnpq ly šṭr ... hw* MPAT 64 i 9: you will produce for me this document of ... - **3)** + obj. + l_5 + mn_5, *md‹m lh mpqn ln mn swn* Herm 5[2f.]: they have sent us nothing from S. - **4)** + obj. + mn_5, *nksn kḥsn hnpqt mn byty* Cowl 7[5]: you have removed goods from my house forcibly (v. $ḥsn_4$); *ynpq mnh gt* CIS ii 198[5f.]: he will remove a body from it (i.e. from the tomb); cf. also the foll. instances, *›pq mn kysh npqn rbrbn* Inv x 44[5f.]: he has extracted great sums from his purse; *hnpqw kblwhy mn rglwhy* Cowl 31[15]: they have removed his anklets (?, v. kbl_3) from his feet - **5)** + *byd* + obj., *ynpq bydh ktb* CIS ii 197[2f.]: he will bring forward with his own hand a document (cf. CIS ii 198[9], 206[5], 207[3], 215[2f.], 221[4f.], 222[3f.], 224[2f.], J 5[2f.]) - **6)** + l_5, *mn dy mpq l ...* CIS ii 3913 ii 112: whoever exports to ... - **7)** + mn_5, *hnpqt mn tmh* AG 8 recto 2: she has removed from there (?, dam. context) - **8)** + $‹l_7$, *spr› zy hnpqwn ‹lyky* Cowl 8[16f.]: a deed which they produce against you - **9)** + $‹l_7$ + obj., *wl› ykhlwn yhnpqwn ‹lyky spr ḥdt* Cowl 8[15f.]: they shall not have the right to produce any new deed against you (cf. Cowl 13[11,12], Krael 9[21f.], 10[15], 12[29]) - **10)** Part. pass. *m›pq* CIS ii 3913 ii 111: exported - ITP to be taken away, to be taken out: Cowl 71[29] (?, heavily dam. context) - Porten & Yardeni sub TADAE A 3.9: l. a form of this root (*[hn]pq*) in Krael 13[5] (poss. reading, dam. context).
v. $ḥpṣ_1$, npl_1, pwq_1, *pqh*.

npq₂ v.Soden Or xlvi 191: the Akkad. *nipqū* < Ar. *npq* = excrements (cf. also idem AHW s.v.), highly uncert. interpret. (cf. also CAD s.v.).

npqh **OffAr** Sing. abs. *npqh* Cowl 83[28], ATNS 37[1]; cstr. *npqt* Cowl 73[7] (*[n]pqt*),[14]; emph. *npqt›* Cowl 24[31,33] (*npq[t›]*), ATNS 36[4] (heavily dam. context), 38[14], 51[5] (heavily dam. context), *npqth* Cowl 72[1] (?, uncert. context); + suff. 3 p.s.m./f. *npqth* ATNS 56[3] (reading uncert.; heavily dam. context) - **Nab** Sing. cstr. *npqt* RES 805^9 - **Palm** Plur. abs. *npqn* Inv x 44^6 - ¶ subst. f. - **1)** expenditure, costs; cf. *npqth byrḥ p›py* Cowl 72^1: expenses in the month P.; *[n]pqt npšh* Cowl 73^7: personal expenses; *bnpqt npšh* RES 805^9: on his own costs; *npqt mdynt›* Cowl 73^{14}: expenses of the department (i.e. official expenses) - **2)** what was paid; *kl npq[t› zy y]hyb lḥyl›* Cowl 24^{33}: everything that was paid (/distributed) that was given to the garrison ... (cf. Cowl 24^{31} (heavily dam. context), ATNS 38^{14} (dam. context)) - for this word, cf. Kaufman AIA 96 (n. 330).

npr$_1$ **OffAr** QAL Pf. 3 p.s.m. *npr* JAOS liv 31^4 - ¶ verb meaning unknown; Torrey JAOS liv 32f.: < Arab., *pnpr ‹ly ḥyl gšm* ... = and he went forth in command of the army of G.

npr$_2$ **OffAr** QAL (??) Pf. 1 p.s. *nprt* Cowl 14^3 (:: Nöldeke ZA xx 147, Cowl p. 43 = QAL Impf. 1 p.pl. of *prt* (= to separate, to divide) :: Segal sub ATNS 2: = Sing. abs. of *nprt$_2$* (= curse (v. infra)) :: Blau Lesh xlviii/xlix 216: = oath :: Porten & Yardeni sub TADAE B 2.8: = Sing. abs. of *nprt$_1$* (= litigation?; v. infra) :: Joüon MUSJ xviii 62, Porten & Greenfield JEAS p. 19: = *nprt$_3$*, adj. Sing. f. abs. (< Egypt.) = beautiful (*swn nprt* = beautiful Syene?) :: Joüon MUSJ xviii 62: or = name of quarter of Syene?; v. infra), ATNS 2^5 (:: Shaked Or lvi 412: = Sing. abs. of *nprt$_1$* (< Iran. = litigation, legal proceedings (cf. also Porten & Yardeni sub TADAE B 8.9)) :: Segal ATNS a.l.: = Sing. abs. of *nprt$_2$* (< Iran. = curse)) - ¶ verb QAL (??) meaning uncert., to take legal action?, in ATNS 2^5 + obj. (oath; against), in Cowl 14^3 + *‹l$_7$* (= concerning), cf. Wag 66, Grelot DAE p. 190 (n. d), cf. also Teixidor JAOS cv 732 :: Halévy RS xv 110f.: = to withdraw, to abstain + *‹l$_7$* (with regard to), cf. also Porten Arch 247 n. 21 (cf. also Krael p. 53 n. 13: = to surrender to the court) - on the problems of *npr$_2$*, cf. also Williamson JEA lxxiii 268f.

nprt$_1$ v. *npr$_2$*.

nprt$_2$ v. *npr$_2$*.

nprt$_3$ v. *npr$_2$*.

npš (for the variant *nbš* in the diff. languages, cf. Harris DCD 71, Garbini Ant xxxi 310f., xxxii 427f., RSO xxxiv 43, ISNO 25 (cf. also Garb 258), Weippert LIS 78ff., Degen AAG p. 31f., Dahood Bibl l 74f., Aharoni BASOR cxcvii 20 n. 13, TA p. 48, FR 40 n. 1, 96b n. 1, Heltzer AION xxi 195, Lemaire Sem xxiii 16, Dion 88f., 413, Gibson SSI ii p. 88, iii p. 38, Segert AAG p. 109, Rosenthal JBL xcv 154, Pardee UF x 321f. (n. 136), JNES xliv 70, Grabbe UF xi 311f., Sarfatti Maarav iii 69ff., Fales VO v 75ff., Muraoka AN xxii 88f., Baldacci BiOr xl 126, Macuch Maarav v/vi 230, Zevit Maarav v/vi 337ff.) - **Ph** Sing. abs. *nbš* KAI 24^{13}; cstr. *npš* KAI 37B 5, *nbš* KAI 24^{13} (:: Sperling UF xx 324, 336f.: = Sing. abs.) - **Pun** Sing. cstr. *npš* KAI 128^3 - **Hebr** Sing.

abs. *npš* Frey 569^{4}, 611^{11}, 892^{2}, 904, 988, 1096 (uncert. reading), 1114; cstr. *npš* Frey 1009; + suff. 3 p.s.m. *npšh* DJD ii 24C 19, D 20, 42^{10} (or = Ar.?); + suff. 3 p.s.f. *npšh* DJD ii 29 verso 3, Frey 661^{5}; + suff. 2 p.pl.m. *nbškm* TA-H 24^{18} - **Samal** Sing. cstr. *nbš* KAI $214^{17,21,22}$; + suff. 3 p.s.m. *nbšh* KAI 215^{18} - **OldAr** Sing. cstr. *nbš* KAI 222B 40; + suff. 3 p.s.m. *nbšh* Tell F 7 (Akkad. par. *napšāti-šu*), KAI 222A 37 (diff. reading, cf. e.g. Dupont-Sommer Sf p. 54, Fitzmyer AIS 14, 54, Donner KAI a.l., Gibson SSI ii p. 32, cf. however Lemaire & Durand IAS 114, 122, 135: or l. *rbwh*? (= Plur. + suff. 3 p.s.m. of rb_2) or eventually *bnwh* (= Plur. + suff. 3 p.s.m. of br_1) and Lipiński Stud 31: l. *mbšh* = Sing. + suff. 3 p.s.m. of *mbš* (= shame)); + suff. 2 p.s.m. *nbšk* KAI 222B 39, 42; + suff. 1 p.s. *nbšy* KAI 222B 40; + suff. 3 p.pl.m. *nbšhm* KAI $224^{5f., 6f.}$; Plur. + suff. 3 p.pl.m. *nbšthm* KAI 217^{7} (between noun and suff. a word divider; dam. context) - **OffAr** Sing. abs. *npš* Cowl $24^{27,30}$ (*[n]pš*), ATNS 44 ii 5 (*scriptio anterior*), Samar 2^{10}, 5^{12}, 8^{9}, 9^{12}; cstr. *npš* CIS ii 115, 116 (for the reading, cf. also Degen NESE ii 83), Or lvii 34^{4}, 39 i 3 (*[n]pš*), 41 i 5, NESE ii 89^{1}, 90^{1}, Atlal vii 106^{1}, 107 i 1, ii 1, iii 1, 108 i 1, 3, 109^{8}, *np* (lapsus for *npš*) NESE ii 87 ii 1 (for the reading, cf. Degen NESE ii a.l. :: Stiehl AAW v/1, 75 (div. otherwise): l. *l* (= l_5) + *p* (= part of n.p.)); + suff. 3 p.s.m. *npšh* Cowl 13^{18}, 73^{7}, Driv 12^{6}, KAI 229^{4}, SSI ii 37^{2}, NESE ii 87^{5} (*npš[h]*, for the reading, cf. Segal Irâq xxxi 170ff., Degen NESE ii a.l. :: Stiehl AAW v/1, 75 (div. otherwise): l. *ynkš[* = APH Impf. form of *nkš* (= to beat); heavily dam. context), ZDMG cxl 2^{2}, Atlal vii 109^{10}; + suff. 2 p.s.m. *npšk* Cowl 7^{6} (*npš[k]*), Aḥiq 130, 153, MAI xiv/2, $66^{7,14}$; + suff. 2 p.s.f. *npšky* Sem ii 31 conc. 3 (*npšk[y]*; for the reading, cf. Rosenthal AH i/1, 12, Porten Arch 126, JNES xxviii 116, Teixidor Syr xlviii 480 :: Dupont-Sommer Sem ii 31, 35: l. *knšn* = Plur. abs. of $kn\check{s}_2$ (= wheat) :: Dupont-Sommer Sem ii 35 n. 2: or l. *kn* (= kn_4) + *šn* = Sing. abs. of $\check{s}n_1$ (= ivory)), 8; + suff. 1 p.s. *npšy* Aḥiq 187, Krael 6^{15} (for the reading *npšy ṣbyt* (v. $\d{s}by_1$), cf. Milik RB lxi 250, Grelot DAE p. 231 (n. t), Yaron JSS xviii 276, Porten & Greenfield JEAS p. 50, Porten & Yardeni sub TADAE B 3.7 :: Krael a.l., Muffs 38 (n. 3; cf. also Porten Arch 226): l. *npš* (= Sing. abs.) + *ʾḥryt*): the form *npšy* in KAI 258^{3} poss. = Sing. + suff. 1 p.s., the suffix having lost its original meaning, but not used ideographically (cf. also the comparable use of *bry*, v. br_1 :: Torrey JAOS xxxv 372, 374, Donner KAI a.l.; Gibson SSI ii p. 153, Lipiński Stud 147, 149f., 171, Delsman TUAT ii 578: = Sing. + suff. 1 p.s. functioning as such :: Cross BASOR clxxxiv 10 n. 25: = lapsus or orthogr. variant of *npšh* = Sing. + suff. 3 p.s.m. (cf. also Hanson BASOR cxcii 5, Teixidor Syr xlvii 374)); + suff. 3 p.pl.m. *npšhwm* Cowl 27^{18} (*npš[hwm]*), 30^{13}, ZDMG cxl 2^{3}; cf. Frah xi 21 (in comb. *bnpšh*), 22 (*npšh*), Paik 639, 690 (in comb. *mn npšh*), 689 (*npšh*), 691 (in comb. *bnpšh*), Nisa-b 148^{1}, 525^{1},

587[2], 672[2], 675[2], 916[2], 925[1], 1725[4], Nisa-c 240[2], 280 bis 1 (in comb. *mn npšh*), ZDMG xcii 442A 10, DEP 153[2], FS Nyberg 270 i, 271 iii, 272 iv, v, 273 vi, vii, 274 ix, 275 xi, xiii, 276 xiv, GIPP 20, 30, 49, 57, 59, SaSt 15, 20 - **Nab** Sing. cstr. *npš* CIS ii 159[1], 191[1], 195[1], 352, 353[1], 465, RES 624 (= CIS ii 466), 833[1], ADAJ x 44 ii 1 (= RB lxxii 95[1]), 47 ii 1, iii, 48 ii, iii, iv, ADAJ xx 129[1], Atlal vii 105[2f.], *npšw* RES 1097[1] (= CIS ii 192, *-w* < Arab., cf. also Diem ZDMG cxxiii 229f. (n. 23), also for litt.); emph. *npš*ʾ CIS ii 169[3], 194[1], 323[1], 332[1], 333[1], RES 1093[2], 2063[1], 2126[1,2], J 386[1] (prob. reading), Syr xxxv 244[1], BAGN ii 88[1] (*[n]pš[*ʾ*]*), *[n]ps*ʾ RES 2059[1] (cf. Cantineau Nab i 43, Diem Or xlix 76f., 82); + suff. 3 p.s.m. *npšh* CIS ii 197[2], 199[2], 201[3], 202[2], 204[2], 206[1], 207[1], 208[2], 209[1], 210[1] (*npš[h]*), 212[1], 214[2], 219[2], 220[1], 337[1], ARNA-Nab 16[1], RES 805[10], J 38[2], RHR lxxx 4[4] (= BSOAS xvi 227), Atlal vii 105[2]; + suff. 3 p.s.f. *npšh* CIS ii 162, 211[2], 224[1], 225[2]; + suff. 3 p.pl.m. *npšhm* CIS ii 200[2] (idem, used instead of f. in CIS ii 198[2], 203[2], cf. Cantineau Nab i 56, Ben-Chayyim EI i 137); Plur. emph. *npšt*ʾ RES 674[1] - **Palm** Sing. abs. *npš* MUSJ xxviii 46[1]; cstr. *npš* CIS ii 3905[1], 4597[1]; emph. *npš*ʾ CIS ii 3907[1], 3908[1], 3908bis 1, 3909[1], 4164, 4328[1], Inv viii 6[3], 8[3], 37b 1, 64[1], RIP 104[1], RB xxxix 530[1], Ber i 38[12], CRAI '32, 266A 1, B 1, Syr lxii 273[1], 274 ii 1 (Greek par. [μν]ημεῖον), *nmš*ʾ CIS ii 4157[3] (lapsus?, cf. Rosenthal Sprache 79 n. 1, cf. however Cantineau Gramm 39: poss. *p* > *m*), *npšh* CIS ii 4210[1] (or rather = Sing. + suff. 3 p.s.m.?); + suff. 3 p.s.m. *npšh* Ber v 133[9], DFD 37[3] - **Hatra** Sing. emph. *npš*ʾ 293[2] (cf. As-Salihi Sumer xxviii 20*, Degen NESE iii 92, cf. however Aggoula MUSJ xlix 471f., Vattioni IH a.l.: = Plur. emph.); + suff. 3 p.s.m. *npšh* 20[2], 290[3] (*npš[h]*); + suff. 3 p.s.f. *npšh* 35[5] - **JAr** Sing. abs. *npš* MPAT 109[3] (= Frey 988), MPAT-A 12[3] (= SM 71); cstr. *npš* Frey 1009 (or = Hebr.?), 1081 (or = Hebr.?); emph. *npš*ʾ Frey 1024[1] (v. infra), 1077[1], *npšh* SM 49[8] (or = Sing. + suff. 3 p.s.m./f.?); + suff. 3 p.s.m. *npšh* MPAT 39[9], 40[26] (*npš[h]*), 42[21], 46[6], 47 verso 1 (*npš[h]*), 2, MPAT-A 50[1] (or = Sing. emph.?), Frey 1389, 1416, EI xx 256[14] (Ar. in Hebr. context; diff. reading), *npšyh* MPAT-A 44[2] (dam. context), *pšh* (lapsus) MPAT 51[15]; + suff. 3 p.s.f. *npšh* MPAT 42[23] (?, heavily dam. context), 51[16], MPAT-A 51[1] (or = Sing. emph.?), 52[1] (or = Sing. emph.?); + suff. 2 p.s.f. *npšky* MPAT 40[6,18]; + suff. 1 p.pl. *npšn*ʾ MPAT 37 ii 3 (dam. context) - ¶ subst. f. (for *npš* construed with m. dem. pronoun, cf. Cantineau Nab i 50f., Gramm 145, Rosenthal Sprache 50) - (orig. throat, breath) > - **1)** life; *npšk[y]* ʾ*lqḥ* Sem ii 31 conc. 3f. (v. supra): I will take your life; *dbr hmlk* ʾ*tkm bnbškm* TA-H 24[17f.]: the word of the king is incumbent upon you for your very life (cf. also Levine Shn iii 292, Pardee HAHL 60f.) - **2)** person; *wtb*ʿ*h nbšk* KAI 222B 39: your person (i.e. you) will seek (cf. e.g. Donner KAI a.l., Fitzmyer AIS 18, 72, Lemaire & Durand IAS 125, 140,cf. also Dupont-Sommer Sf p.

84, Rosenthal BASOR clviii 28 n. 1 :: Lipiński Stud 43: your throat seeks (i.e. you are hungry); cf. also KAI 224[5f]); *npšy l› td‹ ›rḥh* Aḥiq 187: my person does not know its path (i.e. I do not know my path); *ḥmr npšk* MAI xiv/2, 66[13f.]: the donkey of your person (i.e. your own donkey); *ktb ... bkpy npšh* Cowl 13[17f.]: he wrote with his own hands (for the reading, v. *kp*$_1$); *ḥyy npšh* KAI 229[4]: the life of his person (i.e his own life; cf. also Tell F 7); *dnh qbr› dy ‹bd ‹ydw ... lnpšh* CIS ii 197[1f.]: this is the tomb which A. made for his person (i.e. for himself), cf. ARNA-Nab 16[1], CIS ii 219[2]; *lḥyy npšh wnpš ›ḥrth* Atlal vii 105[2f.]: for his own life and that of his posterity (cf. also Atlal vii 109[8f.]); *‹l npšh ḥṭ›* Ber v 133[8ff.]: he has sinned against his person (i.e. against himself); *wl› ›ḥ[y]s npšh* DFD 37[3]: he did not spare himself (interpret. uncert. however, v. also *ḥws*); *mn byth dnpš[h]* Hatra 290[3]: from the house of his person (i.e. from his own house; cf. Aggoula Syr lii 191, Degen NESE iii 86; dam. context); cf. also - a) preceded by prep. *b*$_2$, *bnpšh* Frah xi 21: self; *›t ršy› bnpšky lmhk* MPAT 40[5f.]: you are free on your part to go (cf. also MPAT 40[17f.]); for *‹bd lnpšh*, v. *‹bd*$_1$ - b) preceded by prep. *l*$_5$, *lnpš lnpš* Samar 2[10]: per person, cf. Samar 5[12], 9[11f] (*[lnpš] lnpš*), cf. also Samar 8[9] - c) preceded by prep. *mn*$_5$, *mn npšh* Nisa-b 148[1]: on his own accord (cf. also Nisa-b 525[1], 587[2], 687[2], Nisa-c 240[2], etc. (v. *mn*$_5$)); *mn npšh ktb* MPAT 42[23]: she wrote (v. *ktb*$_1$) for herself (for the meaning v. sub d)) - d) preceded by prep. *‹l*$_7$, *‹l npšh* MPAT 51[16]: for herself (written after the name of a signatory of a document or contract who is an interested party, not a witness; cf. Ginsberg BASOR cxxxi 27, Birnbaum PEQ '55, 31, J.J.Rabinowitz BASOR cxlv 33f., cf. also Yaron Law 17, Volterra FS Tisserant i 443ff., Koffmahn DWJ 64, 180, Beyer ATTM 640, Pardee JBL xcvii 342 (cf. also Pardee HAHL 124, 125f.: = principal party) :: I.Rabinowitz BASOR cxxxi 22: *‹l npšh* in DJD ii 42[10] = concerning its essence, cf. also MPAT 39[9], 40[26], 42[21], 46[6], 47 verso 1, 2, 51[15], DJD ii 24C 19, D 20, 29 verso 3, 42[10], EI xx 256[14] (diff. reading)); the context of MPAT-A 44[2] heavily dam. - e) with coll. meaning: persons, people; *[k]l npš 54* Cowl 24[27]: in total 54 persons (cf. Or lvii 34[4], 41 i 5, ATNS 44 ii 5 (*scriptio anterior*); for the reading, cf. Porten & Yardeni sub TADAE B 8.2); *npš bt* KAI 37B 5: people of the temple (i.e. temple personnel, cf. e.g. Masson & Sznycer RPC 60, Amadasi sub Kition C 1, Gibson SSI iii p. 131 :: e.g. CIS i sub 86, Cooke NSI p. 69, Lidzbarski sub KI 29, Röllig KAI a.l.: = temple-slaves); cf. also *lnbšy [wlk]l nbš byty* KAI 222B 40: for myself and all those belonging to my house - **3)** soul (of a deceased person; cf. also Lifshitz ZDPV lxxvi 159f.); *wtšty nbš pnmw ‹m h[d]d* KAI 214[22]: may the soul of P. drink with Hadad (cf. KAI 214[17,21]), for the contexts, cf. e.g. Greenfield RB lxxx 49, De Moor ZAW lxxxviii 338f., Astour RAI xxvi 228, Spronk BAAI 207f.; *ttnyḥ npšh dš›wl* MPAT-A 50[1f.]:

may the soul of S. be at rest (cf. MPAT-A 52[1]); *NP nwḥ npš nšmtw lḥy[y] ʿwlm* Frey 569[3ff.]: NP the deceased, may his soul have part in everlasting life (cf. Frey 611[11], 892[2], 904, 988 (= MPAT 109), 1416); *NP nyḥ npš* MPAT-A 12 (= SM 71): NP the deceased - **4)** disposition; *št nbš km nbš ytm bʾm* KAI 24[13]: they put (their) disposition like the disposition of ... (i.e. they behaved (towards me) like a fatherless orphan towards his mother; cf. also Zevit Maarav v/vi 339ff.); cf. *np/bš* used as indication of the centre of reflexions, *tʾmr bnbšk wtʿšt blbb[k]* KAI 223B 5: you will say in yourself and will think in your heart (cf. e.g. Dupont-Sommer Sf p. 106, Donner KAI a.l., Fitzmyer AIS 81, Zevit Maarav v/vi 340 :: Lipiński Stud 54: *nbš* = throat) - **5)** funerary monument (cf. e.g. Cooke NSI p. 214, Starcky SDB vi 1088, 1091, Caskell MUSJ xlv 375, Negev IEJ xxi 115ff., Gawlikowski MFP 22ff., Ber xxi 5ff., xxiv 35ff., Aggoula MUSJ xlix 484ff., Pardee Maarav i 28f., Hachlili PEQ '81, 33ff.): CIS ii 116[1], 159[1], 169[3], 3905[1], 3908[1], 3908bis 1, KAI 230, NESE ii 89[1], ADAJ x 44 ii 1, 47 ii 1, xx 129[1], Atlal vii 106[1], 107 i 1, ii 1, RIP 104[1], MPAT-A 51[1], Frey 1009, 1081, etc., etc. (cf. poss. also Hatra 293[2], diff. context, cf. Degen NESE iii 92f., Aggoula Syr lxv 207), cf. RES 1093[1] (Greek par. μνημεῖον), Inv viii 64[1] (Greek par. μνημῖον), *npšʾ dh wmʿrtʾ* RB xxxix 530[1]: this funerary monument and hypogee (Greek par. τὸ σπήλαιον καὶ τὸ ἐπὶ τουτῷ μνημεῖον), *npšʾ dh wmʿrtʾ* Syr lxii 273[1] (Greek par. τὸ μνημεῖον συν τῷ σπηλαίῳ) - a) sometimes indicating the stele on the tomb, cf. CIS ii 162 (Greek par. στήλην), RES 1097[1] (Greek par. στήλη), cf. also *dʾ mqbrtʾ wtrty npštʾ dy ʿlʾ mnh* CIS ii 196[1f.]: this is the sepulchre and the two monuments above it (cf. Syr xxxv 244[1f.]; cf. also *dnh n[p]š[ʾ wq]brtʾ* in BAGN ii 88[1]); cf. also CIS ii 4328[1], 4597[1] in which *npš* indicates a portrait of the deceased, parallel with normally used *ṣlm* (cf. also Starcky RB lxxiii 241), the same meaning prob. also in Ber i 38[12] (:: Cantineau Gramm 81, Ingholt Ber iii 126: = stele (and Ingholt Ber i 38, 39f.: = funerary stele representing a person and buried in a tomb)), for the context, v. *qbr*$_1$ - b) indicating the complete tomb, *npšʾ dnyḥt ṭmʾ brll* CIS ii 3907[1]: tomb where the bones of B. rest - c) in the comb. *bt npšʾ* Frey 1077[1]: tomb; cf. *bnpšʾ* Frey 1024[1] (< *byt npšʾ*); cf. also the diff. *nwh npšy zy lh* KAI 258[2f.]: = his tomb (< dwelling of his soul (cf. Teixidor Syr xlvii 374)) or dwelling being his tomb? (v. also supra and v. *nwh*) - d) cf. also *ʾlh ṣlmh zy ʾlnp ... hw ʿbd lnpšh* SSI ii 37[1f.]: these are the picture(s) of E., he made (them) as/for his funeral monument (cf. Cross BASOR clxxxiv 8f., Teixidor Syr xlv 376, li 303f., Gibson SSI ii p. 157f., Lipiński VT xxiii 369, Stud 151 :: Dupont-Sommer CRAI '66, 47, Delcor Mus lxxx 307, 312: *lnpšh* = for himself) - **6)** in the comb. *npš mt* KAI 128[3], uncert. interpret., Levi Della Vida RCL '49, 410: = soul of a deceased person or monument of a deceased person (cf. also

Levi Della Vida FS Friedrich 313f.); cf. also Röllig KAI a.l., Amadasi IPT 71f.: = monument for a deceased person - Naveh AION xvi 21f. n. 9: l. *nbšh* (= Sing. + suff. 3 p.s.m.) in IrAnt iv 115 (improb. reading, cf. Dupont-Sommer IrAnt iv 115ff.: l. *nbšg* = n.p.; cf. also Dion p. 413 n. 7, Lipiński BiOr xxxiii 234) - Hoftijzer VT xi 345: l. *n*ʾ*pš* (= Sing. abs.) in KAI 136[1] (cf. also Röllig KAI a.l., Février MC 94f.; reading of *n* highly uncert.; :: Février Sem v 63: l. *ṭpš* (= Sing. abs. of *ṭpš* < Greek τάφος (= grave, tomb)) :: Chabot BAr '36/37, 170: poss. l. *b*ʿ*l*...) - on this word, cf. also Aggoula MUSJ xlix 480ff.
v. *ḥpṣ*$_3$.

npt **Pun** Sing. abs. (?) *npt* KAI 76B 8 - ¶ subst. honey (uncert. and heavily dam. context) :: v. Selms FS Gonin 195: = some kind of textile covering?

npthṭ v. *ptḥ*$_2$.

nṣb$_1$ **Pun** QAL Pf. 3 p.s.m. *nṣb* KAI 136[6] (cf. Jongeling NINPI 10 :: Février Sem v 64, Röllig KAI a.l.: = Sing. abs. of *nṣb*$_3$ :: Chabot BAr '36/37, 170 (div. otherwise): poss. l. *tnṣb* (without interpret.)); YIPH Pf. 3 p.s.m., cf. IRT 873[4]: *in*ʃ*er* (lapsus for *in*ʃ*eb*; for this prob. interpret., cf. Levi Della Vida OA ii 80, 92, Polselli OAC xiii 236f., 239, cf. however Vattioni AION xvi 45, Aug xvi 542 (div. otherwise): l. *vin*ʃ*er* = n.p.), cf. IRT 886a 8f.: *useb* (cf. Levi Della Vida OA ii 80, 92, Vattioni AION xvi 47, Aug xvi 545, Polselli OAC xiii 239 (n. 54), StudMagr xi 42 :: Beguinot RSO xxiv 17: l. *uzeb* = *w* + QAL Pf. 3 p.s.m. of *zbḥ*$_1$), cf. IRT 886e: *u*ʃ*eb* (Vattioni Aug xvi 546: l. *y*ʃ*eb*), IRT 892[5]: *u*ʃ*eb* (Vattioni Aug xvi 551: pro *vv*ʃ*eb* l. *yu*ʃ*eb*, without interpret., for the reading, cf. also Goodchild AJ xxx 140 :: Beguinot RSO xxiv 17: pro *u*ʃ*eb* l. *zeb* = QAL Pf. 3 p.s.m. of *zbḥ*$_1$), cf. IRT 893[6]: *uxeb* (cf. Levi Della Vida OA ii 92, Vattioni Aug xvi 552) - **DA** NIPH Pf. 3 p.pl.m. *nṣbw* i 8 (cf. Hoftijzer DA a.l., McCarter BASOR ccxxxix 54, H. & M.Weippert ZDPV xcviii 88, 103, Hackett BTDA 40, 95, Knauf ZAH iii 17 :: H.P.Müller ZAW xciv 218, 223: = QAL/PAʿEL Pf. 3 p.pl.m. (= to convocate (sc. a meeting)) :: Lemaire DAT 318, CRAI '85, 280: = PAʿEL Pf. 3 p.pl.m. (= to fix) :: Lemaire GLECS xxiv-xxviii 326: or = QAL? (on the form, cf. also Halpern FS Lambdin 129 (n. 46))) - **OffAr** QAL Pf. 3 p.s.m. *nṣb* Sumer xx 13[2] - **Nab** QAL Pf. 3 p.s.m. *nṣb* CIS ii 182[2] - **Palm** QAL Pf. 3 p.s.m. *nṣb* CIS ii 3972[2], Inv xi 87[2], SBS 33[2], RIP 143[3], PNO 79[1]; 3 p.pl.m. *nṣb* Inv D 23[2] - ¶ verb QAL to erect, to raise: KAI 136[6], PNO 79[1], RIP 143[3], Sumer xx 13[2] (cf. Milik DFD 258 :: Safar Sumer xx 13: = to plant > to camp); context of CIS ii 182[1f.] diff. (*dnh byt*ʾ *dy bnh rwḥw br mlkw ... l*ʾ*lt ... dy bṣlḥd wdy nṣb rwḥw br qṣyw ...*), cf. Milik Syr xxxv 228: this is the temple which R. the son of M. rebuilt ... for Allat ... who is in S. and which R. the son of Q. had founded × e.g. Lidzbarski Handb 150f. n.

7, Cooke NSI p. 252f.: this is the temple which R. the son of M. built ... to Allat ... who is in S. and whom R. the son of Q. had established (cf. also CIS ii a.l.: who erected (sc. the statue of the goddess)) - **1)** + obj.: CIS ii 3972[1f.], RIP 143[2], Inv xi 87[2] (in all instances *nṣb*$_3$ object) - **2)** + obj. + *l*$_5$: Inv D 23[24] (*nṣb* object), SBS 33[2f] (*[mṣb]ʾ* object) - YIPH to erect: in Latino-Punic texts (v. supra, diff. context) - NIPH to gather, to come together; *wnṣbw šdyn mwʿd* DA i 8: the Sh. gods came together in an assembly (:: Sasson AUSS xxiv 152f.: sc. for the sake of rebellion), cf. also Weinfeld Shn v/vi 142.

v. *nṣb*$_5$, *ṣbʾ*$_3$.

nṣb$_2$ v. *bʿy*$_1$.

nṣb$_3$ **Ph** Sing. cstr. *[n]ṣb* RES 367 i 1 (cf. Delavault & Lemaire RB lxxxiii 569ff., cf. however also Lidzbarski Eph i 285ff.: = fraud; cf. also Delcor Hen iv 215) - **Pun** Sing. abs. *nṣb* CIS i 5632[5], Mozia iii 74[1] (= SMI 3); cstr. *nṣb* CIS i 147[1], 194[1], 198[4], 380[1], 2613[1], 5684[1], 5685[1], KAI 61A 1, B 1, 98[1] (*[nṣ]b*); Plur. abs. *nṣbm* KAI 64[1] - **Samal** Sing. abs. (on the absence of emphatic state in Samalian, cf. Dion p. 135ff.) *nṣb* KAI 214[1,15] (cf. however Gibson SSI ii p. 66, 72: pro *ʿm nṣb* l. *wmn* (= *mn*$_4$) *ʾn*$_4$ (var. of *hn*$_3$), less prob. reading), 215[1,20]; cstr. *nṣb* KAI 214[14] - **OldAr** Sing. emph. *nṣbʾ* KAI 201[1], 202A 1 (*[n]ṣbʾ*), B 14, 18, 19, 222C 17 - **Nab** Plur. cstr. *nṣyby* RES 1088[1] (:: Torrey JAOS xxviii 350 (div. otherwise): l. *mlqy* = Sing. abs. of *mlqy*$_2$ (= meeting-place), cf. also Levinson NAI 182) - ¶ subst. m. raised stone - **1)** indicating stele: KAI 201[1], 202A 1, B 14, 18, 19, 222C 17, RES 1088[1]; in Ph. and Pun. texts used to indicate votive stele, cf. KAI 64[1], cf. also the foll. comb. - a) *nṣb mlk* RES 367 i 1 (v. however supra): stele commemorating a *mlk* (cf. KAI 98[1f.]; v. *mlk*$_5$) - b) *nṣb mlk ʾmr* KAI 61B 1f.: stele commemorating a *mlk ʾmr* (v. *mlk*$_5$) - c) *nṣb mlk bʿl* CIS i 147[1f.], 194[1], 380[1], 2613[1], 5685[1], KAI 61A 1: stele commemorating a *mlk bʿl* (v. *mlk*$_5$) - d) *nṣb mlkt bʿl* CIS i 5684[1]: stele commemorating a *mlkt bʿl* (v. *mlk*$_5$), cf. also *nṣb mlkt bmṣrm* CIS i 198[4f.]: stele commemorating a certain type of offering (v. *mlk*$_5$) :: CIS i sub 198, Harr 125: *nṣb* = Sing. cstr. of *nṣb*$_6$ (= prefect, deputy?) - **2)** indicating a statue: KAI 214[1,14], 215[1,20] (cf. also Dion p. 380) - l. prob. also *[nṣ]b* (= Sing. abs.) in KAI 170[1].

v. *nṣb*$_{1, 4, 5}$, *rtb*$_2$.

nṣb$_4$ **OffAr** the diff. *nṣbʾ* (Sing. emph.) in Sam 15[1] rather = *nṣb*$_3$ (cf. Birnbaum sub Sam 15) than *nṣb*$_4$ (= vineyard, plantation; cf. Sukenik PEQ '33, 155f.); interpret. diff., text written on sherd (ostracon?).

nṣb$_5$ **Samal** the diff. *nṣb* in KAI 214[10] (in the comb. *lnṣb qyrt* (v. infra) *wlnṣb zrry*) is either a) Sing. cstr. of *nṣb*$_6$ (= prefect (cf. e.g. D.H.Müller WZKM vii 52, 57)) or b) QAL Inf. of *nṣb*$_1$ (cf. e.g. Cooke NSI p. 161, 166, Lagrange ERS 493f., Landsberger Samʾal 64 n. 165,

Friedr 20*, Garb 262, Donner KAI a.l., Dion p. 28, 215, Gibson SSI ii p. 67, cf. also Garr DGSP 42f.: or = PA ʿEL Inf.?), cf. also Koopmans 34 :: Halévy RS i 82, 141, ii 57f., vii 336: = Sing. cstr. of *nṣb₃* for both instances. Interpret. of *nṣb* depends also upon the interpret. of *qyrt* and *zrry*. For *qyrt* (= Plur. abs. of *qyrh₂* (= town)), cf. Cooke NSI p. 161, Lagrange ERS 493f., Friedr 34*, Garb 261 (cf. also Garbini AION xxvi 125), Koopmans 34 (cf. Gibson SSI ii p. 67, 71: = Plur. abs. of *qr₁*?; cf. also Donner KAI a.l.: = Plur. abs. of *qyrh₂* > n.l.) :: Halévy RS i 141, ii 58 (cf. however idem RS vii 338): *qyrt* = Sing. abs. of *qyrh₂*, cf. however also Ronzevalle FS de Vogüé 525: l. *qyst* (Dion p. 28, 140: l. *qyst* = Plur. abs. of *qysh* (= tree) :: D.H.Müller WZKM vii 50a: l. *ymt* (= n.g.??, cf. idem ibid. p. 52)); for *zrry* of uncert. interpret. (cf. Cooke NSI p. 166, Lagrange ERS 493, Dion p. 28, 130), cf. the foll. proposals: a) = n.l. (cf. Donner KAI a.l.; cf. also D.H.Müller WZKM vii 52: = tribal name; cf. Koopmans 34: name?) - b) = Plur. abs. (cas. obl.) of *zrr* (= town??; cf. Gibson SSI ii p. 67, 71) :: Dreyer FS v.Selms p. 18 n. 3, 20 n. 4: = Plur. abs. (cas. obl.) of *zrr* (= open village) :: Sader EAS 163 (n. 32): = Plur. abs. (cas. obl.) of *zrr* (= (wine/oil) press) :: Koopmans 34: = Plur. abs. (cas. obl.) = those who live scattered (< root *zwr/zry*) :: Halévy RS i 82, 141, 148, 166, ii 55, 57: *zrry* lapsus for *zkry* = Sing. + suff. 1 p.s. of *zkr₂*.

nṣb₆ v. *nṣb₃,₅*, *ṣbʾ₃*.

nṣbh₁ **OffAr** Sing. emph. *nṣbtʾ* Cowl 81[2] - ¶ subst. plantation (> field, farm).

nṣbh₂ **Nab** Sing. cstr. *nṣbt* RB xliii 574,16[1] (for the reading, cf. Starcky with Milik Syr xxxv 247 (n. 1), Milik ADAJ xxi 144 n. 3) - **Palm** Sing. emph. *nṣbtʾ* Inv xii 31[3] - ¶ subst. f. raised stone; in RB xliii 574,16[1] indication of betyle (cf. Milik Syr xxxv 247); in Inv xii 31[3] inscribed on votive altar (cf. Aggoula Sem xxix 114) - v.d.Branden BO xiv 196, 198: l. *nṣbt* (= Sing. abs.) in KAI 162[2] (reading highly uncert.).

nṣwlʿt v. *knṣwlʿt*.

nṣwḥn v. *pṣy*.

nṣḥ₁ **Ph** QAL (cf. FR 151, v.d.Branden GP p. 83; or rather PIʿEL?, cf. Harr 125) Pf. 1 p.s. *nṣḥt* CIS i 91[2] - **OffAr** ITP Pf. 3 p.pl.m. *ʾtnṣḥw* Beh 60; Imper. s.m. *ʾtnṣḥ* Driv 13[1]; pl.m. *ʾtnṣḥw* Driv 7[5] (*[ʾ]tnṣḥw*), 11[3] (*ʾtnṣḥ[w]*); Part. pl.m. abs. *mtnṣḥn* Driv 7[4] - ¶ verb QAL (v. supra) + obj., to conquer, to gain a victory over: CIS i 91[2] - ITP - **1)** to excel, to be active; *šgyʾ ʿm[y] ʾtnṣḥw* Beh 60: they were very active together with me (Akkad. par. *šá kit-ru-ia il-li-[ku-ʾ]* = who came to my aid) - **2)** to do one's best, to exert oneself to the utmost: Driv 7[5], 11[3]; + *b₂*: Driv 7[4], 13[1f.] (cf. Kutscher Kedem ii 73, cf. also Grelot DAE p. 314 n. g :: Driver p. 65: to show oneself active, vigorous :: Cazelles Syr xxxii 94 n. 1: to take the initiative :: Benveniste JA ccxlii 305: Persian

influence (cf. however also Whitehead JNES xxxvii 134 (n. 105))) - on *nṣḥ*, cf. also Greenfield FS Rundgren 152 - Segal ATNS a.l.: l. *ynṣḥ* (= QAL Impf. 3 p.s.m., he will triumph) in ATNS 82b 2 (dam. context, uncert. reading).
v. *nṣyḥ*, *šny$_1$*.

nṣḥ$_2$ **Hebr** Sing. abs. *nṣḥ* KAI 193[10] - ¶ subst. eternity; *ʾm nsh ʾyš lqrʾ ly spr lnṣḥ* KAI 193[9f.]: no man has dared to read a letter for me ever before (cf. H.P.Müller UF ii 238 n. 87, WO viii 66 n. 4) - Vattioni AION xvi 40f.: l. *nvṣyn* in OA ii 83[4] = Sing. + suff. 3 p.s.m. (= his eternity or something similar), highly improb. interpret., cf. also Sznycer GLECS x 102 (: reading completely uncert.), Levi Della Vida OA ii 83f. ((div. otherwise): l. *vnv?yn*, without interpret.), Vattioni Aug xvi 539 (: l. *ynvθ sin* without interpret.), cf. also Polselli StudMagr xi 41 (div. otherwise): l. *lyn*, poss. = form of *lyn$_1$* (highly uncert. reading).

nṣḥ$_3$ v. *ṯlḥ$_2$*.

nṣḥ$_4$ **Hebr** (or **JAr**?) the *nṣḥ* on jar fragment (Mas 545) = juice? (cf. Yadin & Naveh Mas a.l.).

nṣy **OffAr** a nominal form of this root (= to quarrel) prob. to be restored in Aḥiq 142 (*n[ṣy-*), cf. e.g. Cowl a.l., Grelot RB lxviii 189, Lindenberger APA 142 (l. *nṣ[y-*), Kottsieper SAS 9, 16, 219 (*n[ṣyn]*).

nṣyb v. *nṣb$_3$*.

nṣyḥ **OffAr** Sing. m. abs. *nṣyḥ* KAI 276[3] (v. infra) - ¶ adj. (cf. e.g. Nyberg Eranos xliv 238, Grelot Sem viii 15, Donner KAI a.l.) × Kutscher & Naveh Lesh xxxiv 312: = poss. functioning as present perfect or as present of *nṣḥ$_1$*; cf. also Altheim GH i 249, 266, Altheim & Stiehl EW x 251, Suppl 80, 85, ASA 43, 45, 246, 274: adj. or QAL Part. act., victorious (:: Altheim & Stiehl EW x 250f., Suppl 85, ASA 43, 45: = he won) in the diff. comb. *nṣyḥ wkbyr ʾrwst ʿbydʾ* KAI 276[3f.] (:: Altheim GH i 249, Altheim & Stiehl EW x 250f., ASA 42f., 274, AAW i 651f.: pro *ʿbydʾ* l. *ʿbydwʾ* = QAL Part. act. s.m. abs. of *ʿbd$_1$* + encl. *wʾ* < Pf. 3 p.s.m. of *hwy$_1$*; cf. also Altheim GH ii 296 :: Altheim & Stiehl Suppl 84f.: l. *ʿbydwʾ*: = QAL Part. pass. s.m. abs. of *ʿbd$_1$* + enclitic *wʾ*), prob. meaning: victorious and mighty, acting (in) perfection (*ʿbydʾ* = QAL Part. pass. s.m. emph. with active meaning, cf. e.g. Kutscher PICS 141, Kutscher & Naveh Lesh xxxiv 312 :: Grelot Sem viii 14ff.: *ʿbydʾ* = QAL Part. pass. (having been made (i.e. showing oneself)) and combining *kbyr ʾrwst* (= great in accomplishment) :: Bailey JRAS '43, 2: combining *kbyr ʾrwst* = mighty deeds, cf. Metzger JNES xv 20, Altheim & Stiehl EW x 250f., Suppl 85, ASA 42, Kutscher & Naveh Lesh xxxiv 310 :: Donner KAI a.l.: combining *kbyr ʾrwst ʿbydʾ* = mighty in victorious deed; cf. also Henning Ir 38, Diakonov & Livshitz Nisa-b p. 64 n. 76: = Iranian text using Ar. ideograms).

nṣyḥn v. *pṣy*.

nṣl **Hebr** HIPH Imper. s.m. + coh. ending *hṣylh* AMB 1^3 - **OffAr** HAPH/APH Pf. 3 p.s.m. *hnṣl* FX 136^{20} (for the reading, v. *ym*ʾ); 3 p.s.m. + suff. 1 p.s. *hnṣlny* ATNS 9^4 (for the reading, cf. Naveh IEJ xxxv 211, Shaked Or lvi 409, Porten & Yardeni sub TADAE B 8.6 :: Segal ATNS a.l.: l. *hnḥlny* = HAPH Pf. 3 p.s.m. + suff. 1 p.s. of *nḥl* (= to give as inheritance)); 1 p.s. + suff. 3 p.s.m. *hnṣlth* Krael 2^{13b}; 3 p.pl.m. + suff. 1 p.s. *hnṣlwny* ATNS 44 i 6 (for the reading, cf. Naveh IEJ xxxv 211, Porten & Yardeni sub TADAE B 8.2 :: Segal ATNS a.l.: l. *hnḥlwny* = HAPH Pf. 3 p.pl.m. + suff. 1 p.s. of *nḥl* (= to give as inheritance)); Impf. 3 p.s.m. *yhnṣl* Krael 4^{20}; 3 p.s.f. *thnṣl* Cowl 9^{10} (cf. Nöldeke ZA xx 146, Epstein JJLG vi 360, Ginsberg ANET 222 (n. 2), Porten Arch 242 n. 15, Porten & Greenfield JEAS p. 12, Yaron JSS xvi 243, Grelot DAE p. 183, Porten & Yardeni sub TADAE B 2.4 :: Cowl p. 28f., Leand 35h, Yaron Bibl xli 272: = Impf. 2 p.s.m.); 2 p.s.m. + suff. 3 p.s.m. *thnṣln[hy]* Aḥiq 81; 1 p.s. *ʾhnṣl* Cowl 8^{18}, 18^3, Krael 6^{15}, 10^{10}, *ʾnṣl* Krael 2^{13}, *ʾṣl* MAI xiv/2, 66^{14} (cf. Dupont-Sommer MAI xiv/2, 83 :: Bauer & Meissner SbPAW '36, 421: = QAL); Part. s.m. abs. *mhnṣl* FX 136^{23}, 137^{26} (:: Dupont-Sommer FX 154f.: = HOPH Part. (cf. also Teixidor Syr lvi 394), v. infra); cf. Frah xxi 13 (*yḥnṣlwn*) - ¶ verb HIPH/HAPH/APH - **1)** to take, to retake, to remove (or in Elephantine contracts rather to recover, to reclaim, to revoke, cf. Szubin & Porten BASOR cclii 36) - a) + obj., *ṣbyt ʾhnṣl hm* Cowl $18^{2f.}$: I desire to take them away (cf. Krael 7^{42}); with double object, *hnṣlny ksp kršn 20* ATNS 9^4: he took away from me 20 *karaš* silver; *bytʾ hnṣlwny* ATNS 44 i 6: they took the house away from me (or: reclaimed it) - b) + obj. + mn_5, *gbrʾ zy yhnṣl byty ... mn plṭy* Krael $4^{20f.}$: the person who shall take away my house from P. (cf. Krael 2^{13b}, MAI xiv/2, $66^{14f.}$ (cf. also Porten & Yardeni sub TADAE B 1.1), cf. also FX $136^{20f.}$ (for the context and Greek par., v. *ym*ʾ)) - c) + l_5 + mn_5, *lʾ ʾkl ʾnṣl lplṭy mn tḥt lbbk* Krael $2^{13f.}$: I will not be able to take P. away from under your heart - d) + mn_5 (= from): Cowl 8^{18} (for this text, cf. Greenfield Conn xix 91), Krael 6^{15}, 10^{10} (for this text, cf. Porten & Szubin JAOS cvii 235f.); *mn kndws ʾlhʾ ... mhnṣl wmn ʾlhʾ lʾtw ... mhnṣl* FX $136^{22ff.}$: taking away from the god K. and taking away from the god L. ... (cf. also Teixidor JNES xxxvii 184 :: Dupont-Sommer FX 137, 155: may he be taken away by ...; for this text, cf. also Frei BiOr xxxviii 368); *hn thnṣl mnk plg bytʾ [yhwh] lh ...* Cowl $9^{10f.}$: if she takes away from you half the house, it shall be hers to ... (i.e. if she wants to sell the house or give it to a third party :: Ginsberg ANET 222 n. 2: i.e. in the event of your divorcing her in which case she does not forfeit all rights as when she divorces you; v. also supra) - **2)** to save, to preserve: Aḥiq 81 (dam. context); + obj. + mn_5, *hṣylh [N]P mpgʿ* AMB $1^{3f.}$: save NP from affliction - a form of the HAPH of this root (*hnṣl[*) prob. in ATNS

28a 2 + 30b 2 (for the reading, cf. Porten & Yardeni sub TADAE B 8.4 :: Segal sub ATNS 28: l. *hnḥ[l]* (= HAPH Pf. 3 p.s.m. of *nḥl*)) - on this root, cf. also Greenfield SVT xxxii 129f., FS Molin 115ff., Conn xix 91. v. *ʾṣl₂*, *ḥṣl₁*, *ymʾ*, *pṣl*, *špl*.

nṣn **Nab** Naveh IEJ xxix 113, 117: l. this noun (Sing. emph. *nṣnʾ*) = sprouting, blossom in IEJ xxix 112[4] (highly uncert. interpret.).

nṣp **Hebr** Sing. abs. *nṣp* Dir pes. 1-10 (or Dir pes. 10 = Ph.?, cf. Delavault & Lemaire RSF vii 31, Bron & Lemaire CISFP i 769f.), Mosc pes. 2-4, PEQ '65, 129 (two examples), HUCA xl/xli 180f. (two examples), Sem xxvi 42 xxv, 43 xxvi, ANET 373 (= ANET Suppl 33; for a list of the prec. examples and 4 other ones, cf. Scott BASOR cc 65f.), Sem xxvi 34 iii, 35 iv, BS i pl. 39,1 (cf. description of plate), IEJ xxxii 251, cf. also de Vaux mentioning *nṣp*-weights RB lxxi 253 - ¶ subst. certain weight (the *nṣp*-weights ranging from 8.68 gr. to 10.85 gr.; on the precise weight, cf. Scott PEQ '65, 135ff.) poss. identical with light shekel; for a discussion, cf. Barrois RB xli 65ff., Barrois ii 257, Dir p. 272f., Mosc p. 99, Wambacq VD xxix 347f., Trinquet SDB v 1247, EM iv 869ff., Scott BASOR clxxiii 55ff., cc 62ff., Dever HUCA xl/xli 180, Lemaire Sem xxvi 37, Lemaire & Vernus Sem xxviii 56, Puech Lev ix 16, Ben-David UF xi 41ff. (cf. also Sarfatti Maarav iii 73); *rbʿ nṣp* Dir pes. 10: a quarter of a *nṣp* (v. also *šql₃*) - for a poss. abbrev. *n*, cf. Lev ix 15 no. 5 - cf. also Ben-David IEJ xxiii 176f.: l. *1 n l* (abbrev. of *1 nṣp lmlk*) in IEJ xxiii 176 on stone weight weighing 9.516 gr. (uncert. interpret.).

nṣṣ v. *nḥṣ₁*.

nṣr₁ **Pun** QAL Part. pass. s.m. abs. *nṣr* CIS i 6067a 1, b 1 (= RES 1591[1]; cf. Lidzbarski Eph i 172, FR 151 × RES sub 19, 20, 1591, Février sub CIS i 6067: = QAL Imper. s.m.; on this text cf. also Greenfield Sem xxxviii 156) - **OldAr** QAL Impf. 3 p.s.m. *yṣr* KAI 222C 17; 3 p.pl.m. *yṣrw* KAI 222C 15, *yṣrn* KAI 222B 8 - **OffAr** QAL Pf. 3 p.s.m. *nṭr* Driv 7[2]; Impf. 3 p.s.m. *ynṭr* ATNS 37[5] (dam. context); + suff. 3 p.s.m. *y[n]ṭrnhy* Aḥiq 209; 2 p.s.m. *tnṣr* KAI 225[12] (cf. however Garr DGSP 42: or = PA ʿEL?); 3 p.pl.m. *ynṭrw* ATNS 26[7], 77b 2 (dam. context); Imper. s.m. *ṭr* Aḥiq 98, Irâq xxxi 174[4] (dam. context), ATNS 26[5]; pl.m. *ṭrw* Driv 7[6]; Inf. *mnṭr* Aḥiq 192; Part. act. s.m. abs. *nṣr* KAI 266[8] (cf. Meyer FS Zucker 257 × Dupont-Sommer Sem i 45, Koopmans 88, Fitzmyer Bibl xlvi 45, 52, Donner KAI a.l., Altheim & Stiehl AAW i 221, Gibson SSI ii p. 114f.: = QAL Pf. 3 p.s.m.); pl.m. abs. *nṭrn* Driv 7[4]; QAL pass. Impf. 3 p.s.m. *ynṣr* KAI 225[13] (cf. Dupont-Sommer AH i/2, 5, Gibson SSI ii p. 96f., Segert AAG p. 395, cf. also Koopmans 93, Donner KAI a.l. (cf. however Garr DGSP 42: or = PU ʿAL?) :: Lidzbarski Handb 325, Cooke NSI p. 186: = QAL Impf. 3 p.s.m. (cf. also Koopmans 93, Stefanovic COAI 194, 289 n. 1 (cf. however idem ibid. 289)) :: Donner

KAI a.l.: or = NIPH Impf. 3 p.s.m.); ITP Impf. 3 p.s.m. *ytnṭr* Aḥiq 160; cf. Frah xx 10, Paik 700 (*ntlwn*), 701 (*ntrwn*), 702 (*[n]tlwn*), GIPP 30, 59 - **Nab** QAL Part. act. pl.m. abs. *nṭryn* J 246 - **Palm** QAL Part. act. pl.m. emph. *nṭrʾ* InscrP 31[9] (cf. Rosenthal Sprache 76, Milik Bibl xlviii 564, 618, DFD 277, Gawlikowski TP 76, 80 (cf. also idem Syr xlviii 414f.) × Cantineau sub InscrP 31, Gramm 103, du Mesnil du Buisson RES '42-45, 78, 81: = Sing. emph. of *nṭr$_2$* (= guard, observation; cf. also Gawlikowski Syr xlviii 414) - **Hatra** QAL Impf. 3 p.s.m. *lṭr* Syr lx 256[6]; + suff. 3 p.s.m. *lṭrh* 232e 4 (cf. Degen JEOL xxiii 405 :: Tubach ISS 269 (n. 87): = QAL Impf. 3 p.s.m. + suff. 3 p.s.m. of *ṭrʾ$_1$* (= to repair, to restore) :: Aggoula MUSJ xlvii 10f., Vattioni sub IH 232: = QAL Impf. 3 p.s.m. + suff. 3 p.s.m. of *ṭrʾ$_2$* (= to attack)) - **JAr** QAL Imper. s.m. *ṭwr* AMB 12[4]; Part. act. s.m. abs./cstr. *nṭr* AMB 12[3] - ¶ verb QAL to guard, to protect, passim (for the context of KAI 222C 15, v. *mn$_5$* sub 6) - **1)** + obj., *grdʾ wnksyʾ zylnʾ ... nṭr* Driv 7[1f.]: he protected our domestic staff and property, cf. KAI 225[12], Driv 7[4,6], Aḥiq 209, Hatra 232e 4; cf. also *mn kl mnṭrh ṭr pmk* Aḥiq 98: more than all watchfulness watch your mouth (i.e. watch your mouth more than anything else; on this text, cf. e.g. Lindenberger APA 75); *lyṣr mly sprʾ* KAI 222C 17: he will not keep the words of the inscription; cf. also AMB 12[2] (dam. context); for the context of KAI 222B 8, cf. e.g. Greenfield ActOr xxix 9 (n. 27); for KAI 266[8], v. *ṭbh$_1$* - **2)** + obj. + *ʿm$_4$*, *wywnyʾ wkrkyʾ zy tʾḥd ṭr ʿmk* ATNS 26[5]: and guard (i.e. keep) the Ionians and the Carians that you will seize with you - **3)** + *byn$_2$*, *byn bbyʾ ... ynṭrw* ATNS 26[7]: let them guard between the gates - **4)** Part. act. substantivated, guard, guardian; *pršyʾ nṭryn* J 246: the horsemen-guardians (i.e. the horsemen charged with the guard (cf. also Starcky HDS 158f.)); *bt nṭrʾ* InscrP 31[9]: the house of the guards (cf. also Aggoula Sem xxxii 111, 115f.: = prison; and v. supra); *nṭr ṭlyʾ* AMB 12[3]: guardian of the boys (epithet of an angel) - **5)** Part. pass., protected: RES 1591[1] (cf. also *nṣr wšmr* CIS i 6067a 1, *šmr wnṣr* CIS i 6067b 1), v. however supra - QAL pass. to be protected; *ynṣr zy lk* KAI 225[13f.]: may what is yours be guarded (v. supra) - ITP + *ʿl$_7$*, *mh ytnṭr ʿl ʾwn gwh* Aḥiq 160: how can he be protected (or: protect himself) by his own force (v. however *gw$_2$*) - Segal ATNS a.l.: l. *ṣr* (= QAL Imper. s.m.) in ATNS 4[8] (highly uncert. reading and interpret., cf. also Porten & Yardeni sub TADAE B 8.7: l. poss. *byn* (= *byn$_2$*)) - du Mesnil du Buisson sub InvD 39/40: l. *nṭryn* (= QAL Part. act. pl.m. abs.) in InvD 39[3] and *n[ṭ]ry* (= QAL Part. act. pl.m. cstr.) in InvD 40[2] (both readings highly uncert., cf. Milik Bibl xlviii 564 n. 3) - Caquot Syr xlvii 413: l. *nṭrw* (= QAL Pf. 3 p.pl.m.) in Syr xlvii 413[4] (highly uncert. reading, cf. Teixidor Syr xlix 443) - a derivative of this root (*nṣr*) prob. in Syr lxvii 321[2] (dam. context), cf. Sader Syr lxvii a.l.

v. *'rr$_1$*, *ṭr'$_1$*, *kṣr$_5$*, *nṣr$_2$*, *sṭr$_1$*.

nṣr$_2$ **Hatra** Safar Sumer ix 18*, Caquot Syr xxx 238f.: l. *nṣr* (= Sing. cstr. of *nṣr$_2$* (= victory)) in 33 (cf. also Safar Sumer viii 189 (n. 22): l. *nṣr* (< *nṣr$_1$* = to guard, to watch); on this text, cf. also Degen Or xxxvi 79 (n. 6)); false reading and interpret., cf. Milik DFD 363, Vattioni IH a.l.: l. *nṣrw* = n.p.

nṣr$_3$ v. *kṣr$_5$*.

nṣt v. *qṣt$_1$*.

nq$_1$ **Pun** Praetorius ZDMG lx 167: the *nqy* in CIS i 124[2] = Sing. + suff. 3 p.s.m. of *nq$_1$* (= cave, rock cleft; cf. also Harr 125, Lidzbarski sub KI 55, FR 234, Amadasi sub ICO-Malta Pu 2) :: CIS i sub 124: *nqy* = Sing. + suff. 3 p.s.m. of *nq$_2$* (= purification); uncert. interpret. (*nqy* = n.p.??).

nq$_2$ v. *nq$_1$*.

nq'$_1$ v. *dyb$_1$*.

nq'$_2$ **Waw** this adj. (Plur. f. cstr. *nqwt*) = pure, clear, brilliant (Plur. f. = splendours) in AMB 6[15]??, cf. Dupont-Sommer **Waw** p. 31 (highly uncert. interpret.), cf. also Gordon Or xviii 339, 341 (div. otherwise): l. *nqwt'* (= Plur. emph. of *nqy$_3$* (= libation); less prob. interpret.); cf. also Naveh & Shaked AMB a.l.

nqb$_1$ **Hebr** NIPH Inf. cstr. *hnqb* KAI 189[2] (for the reading, cf. e.g. Puech RB lxxxi 200 :: Shea FUCUS 431, 433: l. *hnqb[h]* = article + Sing. abs. of *nqbh* (cf. also Sasson PEQ '82, 112: or l. *hn[qbh]*?)) - **Nab** QAL Part. pass. pl.m. abs. *nqybyn* MPAT 64 iii 6 - ¶ verb QAL (to pierce >) to designate, to mark; *kdy 'nw nqybyn bšmhn* MPAT 64 iii 6: as these are marked by their names (cf. also J.J.Rabinowitz BASOR cxxxix 14, Dijkstra & de Moor UF vii 182 :: Starcky RB lxi 179: this meaning < Arab.) - NIPH to be pierced, to be cut through (said of rock): KAI 189[2] - on this root, cf. also Collini SEL vi 32.
v. *ktb$_1$*, *nqbh*, *qbb*.

nqb$_2$ cf. Frah xxx 26: hole.

nqb$_3$ **Hebr** Sing. f. abs. *nqbh* AMB 4[15] - **OffAr** Sing. f. abs. *nqbh* Cowl 15[17,20], Krael 3[21], 7[29,34]; cf. Frah xi 7 (*nkb*), xxx 25 (*nkb*) - **Nab** Sing. f. emph. *nqbt'* J 12[6] (= CIS ii 205) - **JAr** Sing. f. abs. *nqbh* AMB 7[7] - ¶ adj. female, belonging to the female sex.

nqbh **Hebr** Sing. abs. *nqbh* KAI 189[1,4] (cf. e.g. Lidzbarski Handb 325, Cooke NSI p. 17, Kutscher SY 170, Röllig KAI a.l., Gibson SSI i p. 23 :: CF 49: *hnqbh* = NIPH Inf. cstr. + suff. 3 p.s.m. of *nqb$_1$* :: Fischer ZDMG lvi 800ff., Sasson PEQ '82, 114: *hnqbh* = NIPH Inf. cstr. + suff. 3 p.s.f. of *nqb$_1$* (cf. also Albright JBL lxii 370); on this word, cf. also Zevit MLAHE 19) - ¶ subst. piercing, tunnel (cf. also Puech RB lxxxi 199f., Conrad TUAT ii 555) - on KAI 189, cf. also Levi Della Vida BZAW ciii 162ff., Jepsen MiOr xv 2ff.

v. *nqb$_1$*.

nqd **OffAr** PA ʿEL Pf. 3 p.s.m. *nqd* JAOS liv 31[3] - ¶ verb PA ʿEL to clear the ground (of stones); + obj., cf. Torrey JAOS liv 31f. (highly uncert. interpret.).

nqdn **OffAr**, cf. Frah-S$_2$ 95 (*nkdʾn*): dainty, delicate.

nqdš **Hatra** Sing. emph. *nqdšʾ* Syr lx 251[2] - ¶ subst. sanctuary (on this word, cf. Aggoula Syr lx 252f.).

nqh v. *nqy$_4$*.

nqwh **OffAr** Sing. abs. *nqwh* FX 136[15] (Greek par. ἱερεῖον) - ¶ subst. sheep (cf. also Dion with Teixidor Syr liii 335: < Akkad.; less prob. interpret.) - cf. *nqyh$_2$*.

nqwr v. *nqr$_1$*.

nqḥ v. *ṣʿqh*.

nqy$_1$ **Hebr** NIPH Pf. 1 p.s. *nqty* KAI 200[11] (for this division of words, v. *ʾmn$_5$* :: Delekat Bibl li 468f. (cf. also Weippert FS Rendtorff 461 (n. 32); div. otherwise): l. *nnqty* (= NIPH Pf. 1 p.s. of *nqy$_1$*) :: Weippert FS Rendtorrf 461 (n. 32; div. otherwise): or l. *nnqty* = lapsus for *nqty*) :: Yeivin BiOr xix 5 (div. otherwise): l. *nksty* (= NIPH Pf. 1 p.s. of *kss* (= to be found short of the task allotted)); Impf. 3 p.s.m. *[yn]qh* DJD ii 46[9] - **OffAr** PA ʿEL Pf. 1 p.s. *nqt* MAI xiv/2, 66[11]; Impf. 1 p.s. *ʾnqh* MAI xiv/2, 66[10] - ¶ verb PA ʿEL to clean, to clear: MAI xiv/2, 66[10,11] (used in legal sense, cf. Dupont-Sommer MAI xiv/2, 79f., Yaron BiOr xv 17f., cf. also Kutscher JAOS lxxiv 247 n. 131, J.J.Rabinowitz Bibl xxxv 202f., VT xi 72 :: Bauer & Meissner SbPAW '36, 420: = to clean (sc. the corn), i.e. to thresh) - NIPH - **1)** to be innocent; *ʾmn nqty* KAI 200[11]: truly, I am innocent (cf. Suzuki AJBI viii 18f.) - **2)** to be cleared, cf. DJD ii 46[9] (on this term, cf. also Kutscher JAOS lxxiv 240, 248) - Cross FS Glueck 302, 305f. nn. 12a, 16: l. *nqh* (= PI ʿEL Imper. s.m. of *nqy$_1$*) twice in SSI i p. 58B (= to absolve; poss. reading and interpret.; cf. also Lipiński OLP viii 94, Smelik HDAI 149; for the second *nqh*, cf. also Lemaire RB lxxxiii 560, 566, Miller SVT xxxii 328ff.) :: Lemaire RB lxxxiii 560f., 566: for the first *nqh* l. *pqd* (= QAL Imper. s.m. of *pqd$_1$* (= to intervene, to visit, indicating a positive intervention from God), cf. also Miller SVT xxxii 328 (n. 36), 330, Conrad TUAT ii 560 :: Naveh IEJ xiii 85f.: for the first *nqh* l. (div. otherwise) *hmwryh* (= article + n.g.), for the second *nqh* l. *nwh* (= Sing. cstr. of *nwh* (= dwelling)), cf. also Gibson SSI i a.l.).

v. *ynq$_1$*, *nqt*.

nqy$_2$ v. *nky$_2$*, *nqyh$_2$*.

nqy$_3$ v. *nqʾ$_2$*, *nqyh$_1$*.

nqy$_4$ **Hebr** Sing. m. abs. *nqy* Mas 581; Plur. f. abs. *nqywt* DJD ii 24B 17, C 15 (*nq[ywt]*), D 16 - **JAr** Sing. m. abs. *nqy* Mas 567[2], 572[2], 577[3] (diff. reading), *nqh* Mas 569[2] (dam. context) - ¶ adj. pure; *ḥnṭyn ypwt* *wnqywt* DJD ii 24D 15f.: wheat of good quality and pure (cf. DJD ii 24B 16f., C 15); *lḥm nqy* Mas 567[2]: white bread (cf. Mas 572[2]); *hnqy* Mas 581: the white (sc. bread).

$nqyh_1$ OffAr Sing. abs. *nqyh* Cowl 72[15,16] (or = Sing. emph. of *nqy_3* (= libation)?; cf. CIS ii sub 146, v. also infra :: Dupont-Sommer FX 149: = Sing. abs. of *$nqyh_2$*) - ¶ subst. prob. meaning libation (cf. CIS ii sub 146, Grelot Sem xxiii 103, Kaufman AIA 77 :: Cowl p. 83: = *$nqyh_3$* (= purification), cf. also Grelot DAE p. 100).

$nqyh_2$ OffAr Sing. abs. *nqyh* Herm 2[8] (cf. also Gibson SSI ii p. 134 × Kaufman AIA 77, BiOr xxxiv 93, Sokoloff JBL xcv 278: = Sing. emph. of *nqy_2* (= lamb, sheep)) - ¶ subst. lamb, sheep - cf. *nqwh*.
v. *$nqyh_1$*.

$nqyh_3$ v. *$nqyh_1$*.

nql OffAr, cf. Frah app. 20 (*yḥnklwn*) = to cause to pass, to transport, cf. Nyberg FP 54, 100 (: = HAPH-form) :: Ebeling Frah a.l.: l. *sʿklwn* < root *skl_2* (= to pass over, to let (someone) pass a border, < Akkad. *šagālu* (which in itself might be Akkad. Š-stem of West-semitic root *galû*, cf. v.Soden AHW s.v. *galû* II)).

nqm_1 OldAr QAL Impf. 3 p.s.m. *yqm* KAI 224[12,22]; 2 p.s.m. *tqm* KAI 224[11] - ¶ verb QAL to avenge: KAI 224[22] - **1)** + obj., *yqm dm ʿqry* KAI 224[12]: he shall avenge my descendant's blood - **2)** + obj. + *mn_5*, *yqm dm bry mn šnʾwh* KAI 224[12]: he shall avenge my son's blood upon his enemies - **3)** + obj. + *mn yd*, *tqm dmy mn yd šnʾy* KAI 224[11]: you shall avenge my blood upon my ennemies (cf. Greenfield FS Fitzmyer 50).

nqm_2 OffAr Plur. abs. *[nq]mn* Cowl 7[8]; emph. *[n]qmyʾ* Cowl 7[10] (cf. however Porten Or lvi 90f., Porten & Yardeni sub TADAE B 7.2, Lipiński Or lix 553: l. prob. *[m]qmn* in Cowl 7[8] and *mqmyʾ* in Cowl 7[10] = resp. Plur. abs. and Plur. emph. of *mqm_3* (= court bailiff?/supporter/(oath) administrator?)) - ¶ subst. avenger; exact meaning in context diff., poss. meaning: divine avenger (cf. Kaufmann with Porten Arch 157 (n. 20), 316, cf. also Grelot DAE p. 93 n. d), cf. however J.J.Rabinowitz Bibl xxxviii 272f. = oath helper :: Milik Bibl xlviii 566 n. 1: = prosecuting attorney :: Cowl p. 21: = judges (cf. also Verger RCL '64, 84 (n. 31)); cf. also Wag 208, Yaron JSS xvi 242f. - *qryt lk byn [n]qmyʾ* Cowl 7[10]: I declared (solemnly) for you among the avengers (poss. = in the presence of the divine avengers, v. also supra), cf. Cowl 7[7f.]; v however supra.
v. *nqm_3*.

nqm_3 Hebr Prignaud RB lxxvii 51f., 56ff.: the diff. *nqm* in comb. *nqm gdl[* in RB lxxvii 51 prob. = Sing. abs. of *nqm_2* (but poss. = Sing. abs. of *nqm_3* (= revenge, vengeance)), less prob. interpret., cf. also Teixidor Syr xlviii 468: = n.p.? (less prob. interpret.).

nqmh v.Soden Or xxxvii 261, xlvi 191, AHW s.v. *miqittu* II: = revenge > Akkad. (highly uncert. interpret.); cf. also CAD s.v. *miqittu*: = West-Sem. loanword of unknown meaning.

nqp **Pun** Rocco AION xxiv 475, 478: the *qp* in GR ii 36 no. 20^{3} = QAL Imper. s.m. of *nqp* (= to cut (down)), highly uncert. reading and interpret., cf. Polselli sub GR ii 20: illegible.
v. yqp_1.

nqpr **OffAr** Sing. abs. *nqpr* WO vi 44D 7 (v. infra), REA-NS viii 170A 3, B 3 - ¶ subst. of uncert. meaning, prob. honorific title, epithet of a king (cf. also Périkhanian REA-NS viii 170, 172f. (div. otherwise): l. *wnqpr* < Iran. = victor), cf. also Teixidor Syr l 434 :: Périkhanian REA-NS iii 22f., Naveh WO vi 44: = n.p. < Greek.

$\mathbf{nqr_1}$ **DA** Hoftijzer DA p. 237: the *nqr* in ii 12, 14 poss. = QAL Part. pass. s.m. abs. of nqr_1 (= to pierce; Part. pass. = the blinded one), cf. also Rofé SB 68 (poss. interpret.), cf. however Caquot & Lemaire Syr liv 205f. (cf. also Garbini Hen i 185f., Delcor SVT xxxii 60, H.P.Müller ZAW xciv 219, 235f., Ringgren Mem Seeligmann 97, Hackett BTDA 29, 57, 79ff., 91, 132, FS Cross 126, Wesselius BiOr xliv 592, 599, Dijkstra GTT xc 179f. (n. 77)): = Sing. abs. of nqr_2 (= sprout, offshoot used metaphorically > offspring) :: Levine JAOS ci 200ff., BAT 329, 336: = Sing. abs. of nqr_3 (= corpse); on the subject cf. also Levine JAOS cvi 365 :: H.Weippert LJPM 95 n. 52: = QAL Part. pass. of nqr_1 (= to pierce > to curse); the same word also in DA ii 5? (cf. also Caquot & Lemaire Syr liv 202f., 205f.) :: Dijkstra GTT xc 164 (n. 22): = verbal form of root qry_1; for the context of DA ii 12, v. also *lbb* - **OffAr** QAL Part. act. pl.m. cstr. *nqry* PF 1587^{2} - ¶ verb QAL to dig, to pierce; *nqry gll* PF 1587^{2}: the diggers of stone (indication of the makers of stone sculptures; for the problems of this interpret., cf. Williamson BASOR cclxxx 84ff.); for DA ii 5, 12, 14, v. supra - RABowman Pers p. 67 and sub Pers 160: l. poss. *nqwr* (= derivative of this root (= chiseled)) in Pers 160^{2} (highly uncert. reading and interpret.).

$\mathbf{nqr_2}$ v. nqr_1.

$\mathbf{nqr_3}$ v. nqr_1.

nqt **Ph** Sing. abs. *nqt* KAI 50^{6} (:: Aimé-Giron ASAE xl 442 (div. otherwise): l. *hnqt* = NIPH Inf. cstr. of nqy_1) - ¶ subst. of uncert. meaning, in the comb. *spr hnqt* KAI 50^{6}: (poss. meaning) document of acquittal (cf. for this interpret. also Aimé-Giron ASAE xl 442f. (v. supra), Röllig KAI a.l., v.d.Branden BO xii 219; cf. also Pardee HAHL 167: *nqt* = freedom of obligation?).

$\mathbf{nr_1}$ Ebeling Frah a.l.: l. in Frah xi 13 *br nr* = Sing. cstr. of br_1 + Sing. abs. of nr_1 (= nwr_2 (= fire)); less prob. reading, cf. Nyberg FP 46, 79: l. Iran. word.

$\mathbf{nr_2}$ v. *mnrtwyn*.

nrg **Hatra** Sing. (or Plur.) emph. *nrg'* 281[5] - ¶ subst. axe (cf. Safar Sumer xxvii 4 n. 4, Degen NESE iii 70, Aggoula Syr lxv 208).
nrh v. *krt*$_1$.
nrq v. *'rṣ*.
nrqys **Palm** The *nrqys* in InscrP 31[7] poss. to be explained as n.p. (< Greek), cf. Cantineau Gramm 157, Gawlikowski Syr xlviii 414 n. 3, 415, Milik DFD 274 (cf. also Aggoula Sem xxxii 111, 114f. (div. otherwise): l. *nrqysw* (= n.p.)) × du Mesnil du Buisson RES '45, 80: = Sing. abs. of *nrqys* (= narthex (architect. term; < Greek νάρθηξ)) :: Cantineau sub InscrP 31: or = Sing. abs. of *nrqys* (= numbness, torpor (< Greek νάρκη)).
nrtwyn v. *mnrtwyn*.
nš$_1$ **Samal** Sing. + suff. 3 p.s.m. *nšh* KAI 214[29] (poss. interpret., cf. Montgomery JAOS xxxvii 329f., Donner KAI a.l., Gibson SSI ii p. 72f., Dion p. 383 n. 20 (cf. also P.J.v.Zijl UF vii 508f.) × Lipiński BiOr xxxiii 232, OLP viii 101: l. *ršh* = Qal Part. act. s.m. abs. of *ršy*$_1$ (= to accuse) :: Donner KAI a.l.: or *nšh* = Qal Pf. 3 p.s.m. of *nš'*$_1$ :: Halévy RS i 142, 162f., 323, ii 57: l. *mšh* = *m*$_{11}$ (= *mh*$_2$) + *šh* (= *š*$_{10}$) :: D.H.Müller WZKM vii 53, 67: l. *mšh* = *m*$_{11}$ (= *my*$_1$) + *š*$_{10}$ + *h*$_3$ (= *hw*$_1$) = whoever; cf. also P.J.v.Zijl JNSL iv 76ff.) - **Hatra** Sing. emph. *nš'* 209[2] (cf. Aggoula Ber xviii 99, Milik DFD 391, Vattioni IH a.l. :: Teixidor Sumer xx 79: = Qal Pf. 3 p.s.m. of *nš'*$_1$), *nyš'* 3[1], 65[2], Ibr 14[2] - ¶ subst. - **1)** oath: KAI 214[29] (v. supra) - **2)** image: Hatra 3[1], 65[2], 209[2] (cf. Milik DFD 391, 406, Vattioni IH a.l., cf. also Safar Sumer xi 8f. (n. 22)), Ibr 14[2]; transl. 'emblem' (cf. Caquot Syr xxxii 266), 'standard' (cf. Aggoula Ber xviii 99) less apt - Gibson SSI ii p. 67, 72: the diff. *]nšy* in KAI 214[16]: = *nš*$_1$ + suff. 1 p.s. (highly uncert. interpret. :: D.H.Müller WZKM vii 134: l. *[y]mšy* = Qal Impf. 3 p.s.m. of *mšy*$_1$ (= to clean) :: Halévy RS i 141, 152: l. *[']nšy* = Plur. abs. of *'š*$_1$) - Montgomery JAOS xxxvii 329f., Donner KAI a.l., Gibson SSI ii p. 72f.: the *nšh* in KAI 214[28] = Sing. + suff. 3 p.s.m. of *nš*$_1$ (:: Donner KAI a.l.: or = Qal Pf. 3 p.s.m. of *nš'*$_1$), improb. interpret., v. also *mt*$_6$ - Montgomery JAOS xxxvii 329f., Dion p. 126, Gibson SSI ii p. 72f. (cf. also Koopmans 40): < Akkad. *nīšu* (less prob. interpret. (cf. also Kaufman AIA 153)).
nš$_2$ v. *'nš*$_3$.
nš'$_1$ **OldCan** Qal Pf. 3 p.s.m. *na-aš-ša-a* EA 366[13] (v. however infra sub 6)) - **Ph** Qal Pf. 3 p.s.m., cf. KAI 174[5]: νεσεο (poss. interpret., cf. Milik MUSJ xxxi 7f., FR 170, Röllig KAI a.l., cf. also Sznycer Sem viii 7, Ferron MC 76f. :: Sznycer Sem viii 7f.: or (div. otherwise): l. νεσεοθ = Qal Pf. 1 p.s.); Impf. 3 p.s.m. *yš'* KAI 14[5,7,10,21]; 3 p.pl. *yš'n* KAI 60[6] - **Pun** Qal Pf. 3 p.s.m. *nš'* CIS i 411[3], 412[3], 413[2f.] (*n[š]'*), 416[3] (or = f.?, dam. context), 1108[4], 1943[4] (or = Sing. cstr.

of *nš'₃*), 3696[4], 3740[3], 3781[1], 3783[3], 4682[3] (?, dam. context), 4915[3], 4916[2], 4917[4], 4920[4], 4921[4], 4922[4], 4923[3], 4926[3], 4927[1f.], 4928[3], 4929[1], 4930[3f.], 4931[3], 5632[7] (*n[š']*; for the reading, cf. Krahmalkov RSF iv 154), *n'š'* KAI 167[1,3] (diff. context, v. infra), *n'š'* Punica xi 24[1], *tnš'* (prob. lapsus) CIS i 4924[3]; 3 p.s.f. *nš'* CIS i 401[3] (or = Sing. cstr. of *nš'₃*), 414[3], 415[2] (?, dam. context), 580[2] (?, uncert. reading, cf. CIS i a.l.; FR 151: l. *n'š*), 1165[3], 3830[4], 4925[4]; 1 p.s., cf. Poen 947: *nasot* (var. either *nasoc* or *nasoct* :: Krahmalkov Or lvii 63, 65 (div. otherwise): l. *nasote*), Poen 937: *naso[t]* (reading *naso[ti]* less prob., cf. Sznycer PPP 98 :: Sznycer PPP 98: l. *naso* = QAL Part. pass. s.m. abs. or Inf. abs. :: J.J.Glück & Maurach Semitics ii 111: l. *naso* = QAL Part. act. s.m. abs.; on the form *nasot*, cf. also Garr DGSP 32, 49)); Inf. cstr. + suff. 3 p.s.m. *š't'* CIS i 6001[2] (cf. Lidzbarski Eph i 295, Tomback JNSL 105f. (uncert. interpret.) :: Février sub CIS i 6001: = $š_{10}$ + *'t'* (= $'t_6$ + suff. 3 p.s.m.) :: Berger sub RES 16: = $š_9$ + *'t'* (= $'nth_2$ or = QAL Pf. 3 p.s.m. of $'ty_1$) :: Slouschz TPI p. 206: $š_{10}$ + *'t'* (n.p.)); Part. act. s.m. abs. *nš'* KAI 119[6] (poss. interpret.; cf. Février RA l 187, Röllig KAI a.l., cf. also Sznycer APCI 214 n. 16: interpret. as Sing. form not absolutely cert.; cf. however Levi Della Vida RCL '55, 560: the comb. *nš'y'gn* = *nš'* (= Sing. cstr. of *nš'₃*) + *y'gn* (unexplained) or *nš'y* (= Plur. cstr. of *nš'₃*) + *'gn* (unexplained) or *nš'y'* (= Plur. + suff. 3 p.s.f. of *nš'₃*) + *gn* (unexplained)); Part. pass. pl.m. abs. *ns'm* Karth xii 51 ii 1 (cf. Février & Fantar Karth a.l. :: Krahmalkov RSF iii 177f., 183, 202: = QAL Pf. 3 p.s.m. + suff. 3 p.s.m.; v. $kwlb_1$) - **Mo** QAL Impf. 1 p.s. *'š'* KAI 181[30]; + suff. 3 p.s.m. *'š'h* KAI 181[20] (cf. e.g. Cooke NSI p. 13, Gibson SSI i p. 81 :: Dahood FS Horn 436: = QAL Impf. 1 p.s. + suff. 3 p.s.m. of $š'y_1$ (= to storm, to assault)) - **Hebr** QAL Impf. 1 p.s. *'šh* EI xx 256[9]; 3 p.pl. + suff. 3 p.s.m. *yš'whw* SM 36 - **OldAr** QAL Pf. 3 p.s.m. *nš'* KAI 222B 37 (poss. interpret.; cf. Lipiński Stud 42); Impf. 3 p.s.m. *yš'* KAI 224[15,16,26]; 2 p.s.m. *tš'* KAI 222B 38 (*[t]š'*), 39, 224[14]; 1 p.s. *'š'* KAI 202A 11; 3 p.pl.m. *yš'n* KAI 223C 13 - **OffAr** QAL Pf. 3 p.s.m. *nš'* TA-Ar 41 obv. 1, rev. 1 (heavily dam. context; uncert. interpret., cf. also Lemaire Or lii 447, Dion JAOS ciii 472); + suff. 3 p.s.f. *nš'[h]* Aḥiq 95; 1 p.s. *nš't* ATNS 2[1] (or = 2 p.s.m.?, cf. Naveh Or lvi 408, Porten & Yardeni sub TADAE B 8.9; highly uncert. context), *nš'yt* Aḥiq 111, 112 (on this form, cf. Lindenberger APA 283, Kottsieper SAS 79, 81f.); cf. Warka 1, 27, 32: *na-šá-a-a-tú*; Impf. 3 p.s.m. *ynš'* Aḥiq 90; 2 p.s.m. *tš'* MAI xiv/2, 66[13], *t[n]š'* Aḥiq 121; Inf. *mnš'* Krael 7[19], Driv 2[4], Aḥiq 122 (*m[nš]'*), 123 (*m[nš]'*), ATNS 29 ii 5; Imper. s.m. *š'* Aḥiq 121; Part. act. pl.m. abs. *nš'n* ATNS 26[4] - ¶ verb QAL - **1)** to lift up, to carry, passim - a) + obj., *nasot ers ahelicot* Poen 947: I brought the sherd of hospitality (cf. Poen 937); *'šh 't hšṭr hz'* EI xx 256[9]: I will bring this document (cf.

Broshi & Qimron EI xx 258); *nš'yt ḥl'* Aḥiq 111: I have lifted sand (cf. Aḥiq 112); *'zl lmnš' m'kl* ATNS 29 ii 5: he came to carry food; *kpn lmnš' mšḥ* Krael 7^{19}: tools (v. *kp*$_1$) to ladle oil; cf. *nš'[h]* Aḥiq 95: he has exalted it - b) + obj. + *'l*$_6$, *w'š' ydy 'l b'lš[my]n* KAI 202A 11: and I lifted up my hands to B. (cf. also Greenfield Proc v CJS i 177, 183f., FS Fitzmyer 49, Ross HThR lxiii 3 n. 9) - c) + *'l*$_7$ + *l*$_5$ + Inf., *wtš' 'l šptyk lhmtty* KAI 224$^{14f.}$: you will raise to your lips (i.e. you shall express yourself with the intention) to kill me (cf. also Greenfield ActOr xxi 3, 5, FS Fitzmyer 50, Fitzmyer AIS 115, Gibson SSI ii p. 54, Lemaire & Durand IAS 145f.) - α) cf. poss. also the Part. pass. in Karth xii 51 ii 1 (erected?; v. also *kwlb*$_1$) - **2)** to take (away) - a) + obj., *w'l yš' 'yt ḥlt mškby* KAI 14^5: and let no one take away the sarcophagus which serves as my resting-place (cf. KAI 14$^{7,10f.,21}$, cf. also KAI 222B 39) - b) + obj. + *b*$_2$, *wtš' [š']ry 'dr bḥmr npšk* MAI xiv/2, 66$^{13f.}$: you will take the barley of the threshing floor (v. *š'rh*) on your own donkey - c) + obj. + *mn*$_5$, *na-šá-a-a-tú ki-ṭa-ri mi–in ig-ga-ri* Warka 1: I have taken a knot from the wall (cf. Warka 27, 32 and poss. also Aḥiq 90 (for the diff. context, v. also *bwt*$_2$)) - d) + *l*$_5$ + obj., *š'lk zy t[n]š'* Aḥiq 121: take for you whichever you want (cf. also KAI 222B 38) - e) + *mn*$_5$, *zy t[n]š' mnn* Aḥiq 121: whichever you want to take from us - f) + *'lt* + *b*$_2$ + obj., *'lt mṣbt z yš'n bksp 'lm b'l ṣdn drkmnm 20* KAI 60^6: for this stele the citizens of S. shall draw 20 d. from the temple treasury (for the context, v. *'lt*) - **3)** to accept, to take up; *brh šlyṭ yhwh lmnš' dšn' zky* Driv 2^4: his son shall have the right to accept that donation (sc. the one given by the king to his father; on this text, cf. also Greenfield IrJu 8) - **4)** to offer: CIS i 411^3, 412^3, 413^2, 414^3, etc., etc. - a) + obj.: CIS i 3783$^{2f.}$, 3830^4 (?), SM 36 - b) + obj. + *l*$_5$: CIS i 3781$^{1f.}$ - c) + *l*$_5$: CIS i 3696^4 - d) + *l*$_5$ + *b*$_2$, *l'dn b'lmn n'š' pnṭn' bn mgnm bmlk ... n'š'* KAI 167$^{1ff.}$: to the lord B. F. the son of M. has offered as a *mlk*-offering ... he has offered (it) .. (or take the second *n'š'* = Sing. abs. of *nš'*$_3$??); *n'š' šdbr l'dn b'lmn bmlk* Punica xi 24$^{1f.}$: Sh. has offered to the lord B. as a *mlk*-offering - **5)** to lead; + obj., *w'š'h byhṣ* KAI 181^{20}: and I led it (i.e. the army) against Y. (cf. also Demsky Shn vii/viii 256f.); *w'š' šm 't* ... KAI 181^{30}: and I led up there the ... - **6)** in the meaning 'to bear arms'?? EA 366^{13} (cf. however Rainey EA p. 33, 85: or = NIPH?? (= to rise up (against))) - Tomback JNSL viii 105f.: the *š't'* in RES 16^2 (= QAL Inf. + suff. 3 p.s.m.) = payment, uncert. interpret., cf. Lidzbarski Eph i 296: = taking away, v. also supra - L.H.Gray AJSL xxxix 77f.: the *neso* in Poen 943 = QAL Part. pass. s.m. abs. (highly uncert. interpret., cf. Sznycer PPP 126: text too corrupted to be interpreted, cf. also Schroed 291) - Torczyner JNES vi 21, 28: the *š'* in KAI 27^3 = QAL Imper. s.m. of *nš'*$_1$ (= to take up (sc. the curse), i.e. to recite; cf. also Caquot FS Gaster 47,

Lipiński RTAT 265, Garbini OA xx 281, 283, Sperling HUCA liii 3, 5), improb. interpret., cf. du Mesnil du Buisson FS Dussaud 424, 426, Albright BASOR lxxvi 7f. (n. 10), Dupont-Sommer RHR cxx 135f. (n. 3), Gaster Or xi 44, 52ff., Röllig KAI a.l., Cross & Saley BASOR cxcvii 45, Avishur PIB 248, 250, Gibson SSI iii p. 83f., de Moor JEOL xxvii 108: = part of n.d. *pdršš'* (on this god, cf. also Fauth ZDMG cxx 238ff.; on the problems of the reading of this divine name, cf. also Teixidor AO i 106) - a form of this root in DA x d 3 (*nš'*), cf. also Puech FS Grelot 24 - Kottsieper SAS 13, 22, 220: l. *ynš['] =* QAL Impf. 3 p.s.m. of *nš'$_1$* in Aḥiq 194 (uncert. reading, cf. Cowl a.l.: l. *ypšr* (without interpret.), Lindenberger APA 192: l. *ynš[r]* (without interpret.), Ungnad ArPap 79: l. *ynšk* (*k* uncert.; without interpret.)) - the diff. *ns'm* in Karth xii 51 ii 1 poss. = Pf. 3 p.s.m. + suff. 3 p.s.m. (cf. v.d.Branden RSF v 60 (cf. also Krahmalkov RSF iii 178, 183, 202) :: Février & Fantar Karth xii a.l.: = QAL Part. pass. pl.m. abs.).
v. *hns, m'nš', mš', nsb, nst, nš$_1$, nš'$_4$, nš'h, šyt$_1$*.

nš'$_2$ v. *'š$_1$*.

nš'$_3$ **Pun** Sing. abs. *nš'* Hofra 87[2] - ¶ subst. offering; *nš' l'lm* Hofra 87[2]: offering to the gods; cf. also in Lat. inscriptions *nasililim* CIL viii 14950[3f.], 14987[3f.], 15072[3f.], 15075[4], 15098[3f.], 15115[3].
v. *mṯn', nš'$_1$*.

nš'$_4$ **Ph** Sing. cstr. *nš'* KAI 60[2]; Plur. abs. *nš'm* KAI 60[4] - **Hebr** Sing. abs. *nsy* MPAT 53[1] (Hebr. in Ar. context); cstr. *nšy'* EI xx 256[3], DJD ii 24D 3 (*[n]š[y]'*), F 3, G 3 (*nš[y']*), and on coins of the second revolt (cf. Meshorer JC no. 169, 170, 172, 193), *nsy'* DJD ii 24B 3, C 3, D 18, E 2, 7, I 3, *nšy* on weights from the second revolt: IEJ xl 61, 62, 67 (cf. EI xx 347f.) - **JAr** Sing. cstr. *nšy* IEJ xxxvi 206[1] - ¶ subst. ruler, chief; *nš' hgw* KAI 60[2]: the superintendent of the community; *h'dmm 'š nš'm ln ʿl bt 'lm* KAI 60[4f.]: the men who are our superintendents in charge of the temple; *šmʿwn nsy' yšr'l* DJD ii 24E 7: Sh. the ruler of Israel (cf. DJD ii 24 passim, IEJ xxxvi 206[1], EI xx 256[3], JC no. 169, 170, 172, 193, IEJ xl 61, 62; on this title, cf. Schäfer BKA 67); *šmʿwn br kwsbh hnsy ʿl yšr'l* MPAT 53[1]: Sh. the son of K., the ruler over Israel (for this title, cf. also Philonenko CRAI '74, 183ff.) - Hoftijzer DA a.l.: the *nš'* in DA i 14 = Sing. abs. of *nš'$_4$* (diff. context; cf. also Sasson UF xvii 288, 303, Lemaire CRAI '85, 281), cf. however Caquot & Lemaire Syr liv 201, Rofé SB 67, McCarter BASOR ccxxxix 51, 56, Levine JAOS ci 197, H.P.Müller ZAW xciv 218, 228, Puech BAT 359, 362: = QAL Part. act. s.m. abs./cstr. of *nš'$_1$* :: Puech FS Grelot 24, 28: = QAL Inf. of *nš'$_1$* :: Caquot & Lemaire Syr liv 201: or = f. Plur. emph. of *'š$_1$*? (improb. interpret.); for the interpret. as form of *nš'$_1$*, cf. also Garbini Hen i 185; on the form, cf. also Hackett BTDA 52.

nš'h **OffAr** Segal ATNS a.l.: the *nš'n* in ATNS 4[7] = Plur. abs. of *nš'h*

(= load); heavily dam. context, highly uncert. interpret. (poss. = QAL Part. act. pl.m. abs. of *nš'$_1$*?), reading uncert. (cf. Porten & Yardeni sub TADAE B 8.7).
v. *kšt*, *šnt$_2$*.
nšb$_1$ v. *šbt$_1$*.
nšb$_2$ v. *šbt$_1$*.
nšb$_3$ **OffAr** Sing. emph. *nšb'* ATNS 38[5] - ¶ subst. (?) of unknown meaning, in the comb. *ksp nšb'* ATNS 38[5]: the silver of ...; the same word in ATNS 38[2]: *nšb[*.
v. *šbt$_1$*.
nšg **OffAr** HAPH Impf. 3 p.s.m. *yhnšg* Aḥiq 200; 3 p.pl.m. (used for f.?, cf. also Ben-Chayyim EI i 136; v. infra) *[yh]nšgwn* Aḥiq 133; ITP Impf. 3 p.s.m. *ytnšg* HDS 9[2] - ¶ verb HAPH to reach, to find, to overtake: Aḥiq 200 (heavily dam. context); *[yh]nšgwn kdbth* Aḥiq 133: they will overtake (i.e. find out) his lie(s) (v. *kdbh*), for this interpret., cf. e.g. Cowl p. 242, Ginsberg ANET 429, Grelot RB lxviii 188, DAE p. 441 × Cowl p. 224, Ben-Chayyim EI i 136, Lindenberger APA 127, 129: his lies will find (him) out - ITP to be found, to be encountered: HDS 9[2] (cf. Lipiński Stud 79f., WGAV 375) × Fales AION xxviii 277f., 282: = to find for oneself, to encounter :: Caquot HDS 12f., 15: = to obtain for oneself.
nšh v. *nš$_1$*.
nšḥṭ v. *šḥṭ$_1$*.
nšṭ **Pun** L.H.Gray AJSL xxxix 83: the *neste* in Poen 1142 = Sing. + suff. 1 p.s. of *nšṭ* (= gaiety; highly uncert. interpret.); cf. Schroed 298f., 321: l. *mest a* (*mest* = QAL Pf. 1 p.s. of *mṣ'$_1$*; highly uncert. interpret.) :: J.J.Glück & Maurach Semitics ii 124 (div. otherwise): l. *este* = *'th$_2$* (= *'nth$_2$*); cf. also Sznycer PPP 145: unexplainable.
nšy$_1$ **OldAr** ITP Impf. 3 p.s.m. *[y]tnšy* KAI 223A 4 (heavily dam. context; cf. also Greenfield Lesh xxxii 363 (n. 26)) - ¶ verb ITP to be forgotten.
v. *mt$_6$*, *šy$_1$*.
nšy$_2$ v. *nš'$_4$*.
nšy' v. *nš'$_4$*.
nšyb (< Arab., cf. Cantineau Nab ii 172, O'Connor JNES xlv 217ff.) - **Nab** Sing. abs. *nšyb* CIS ii 209[7] - ¶ subst. father-in-law (?, cf. CIS ii a.l., cf. also Cantineau Nab ii 122, Levinson NAI 191: stepfather; cf. however Mitchell VT xix 110f.: or = blood relation?).
nšyn v. *'š$_1$*.
nšk$_1$ **OffAr**, cf. Nisa-b 211[2] (*[n]škn*), 605[2], 798[5], 1852[4] (*nškn*; ?, cf. Altheim & Stiehl AAW ii 223: or = Plur. abs. of *nškh$_1$*? (v. also infra); cf. also Diakonov & Livshitz Nisa-b p. 40, 61 n. 38), GIPP 59: interest (cf. Diakonov & Livshitz Nisa-b p. 40 and texts a.l. (in comb. *'l nškn*);

uncert. interpret., cf. also Altheim & Stiehl AAW ii 223, GMA 476: = *nšk*$_2$ or *nškh*$_1$ (= outpour(ing), gift (uncert. interpret.)) - Israel BiOr xxxvii 6: l. a form of this word (Sing. abs. *ntk*) in NESE ii 66[3] (highly uncert. reading, cf. also Degen NESE ii a.l. (div. otherwise): l. *ntbʿl* = n.p.).

nšk$_2$ v. *nšk*$_1$.

nškh$_1$ v. *nšk*$_1$.

nškh$_2$ **OffAr** Sing. emph. *nšktʾ* LA ix 331[3] (ʾ poss. corrected from original. *h*, cf. also Milik LA ix 332) - ¶ subst. room (in the context of LA ix 331[3]: room in a sanctuary).

nšl$_1$ **Pun** the *mšlt* in Karth xii 51[3] poss. = Yoph Part. s.f. (?) abs. (?) of *nšl*$_1$ (= to fall; Part. = ruin, ruined), cf. Février & Fantar Karth xii 51, 57; cf. however Krahmalkov RSF iii 178, 181f., 202, v.d.Branden RSF v 57, 60: = Sing. abs. of *mšlh* (= government).

nšl$_2$ **Pun** Krahmalkov RSF iii 178, 184, 202: l. *nʾšl* (= Qal Pf. 3 p.s.m. of *nšl*$_2$ (= to clear away)) in Karth xii 53[1] (improb. interpret., cf. also Février & Fantar Karth xii 53, 57 (dividing otherwise): l. -*n* (v. *ʿn*$_3$) + *ʾš* (= *ʾš*$_4$) + *l*$_5$ ...

nšmh **Hebr** Sing. + suff. 3 p.s.m. *nšmtw* Frey 569[5]; + suff. 3 p.s.f. *nšmth* Frey 661[4], 1536[3] - ¶ subst. soul: Frey 569[5], 661[4], 1536[3].
v. *bqʾ*, *šmym*.

nšn v. *ʾš*$_1$.

nšp v. *šbt*$_1$.

nšq$_1$ **OffAr** Qal Pf. 3 p.s.m. *nšq* Aḥiq 222 (or = Qal Part. act. s.m. abs.?, cf. Kottsieper SAS 220, v. also infra) - ¶ verb Qal to catch fire; *byt rʿh nšq bʾšh* Aḥiq 222: the house of his neighbour caught fire (heavily dam. context; cf. however Lindenberger APA 219, 275 n. 576: poss. l. *[th]nšq* = Haph Impf. form).
v. *hwn*$_1$.

nšq$_2$ v. *zʿq*.

nšr$_1$ v. *nšrt*.

nšr$_2$ **DA** Sing. abs. *nšr* i 10 - **Nab** Sing. emph. *nšrʾ* Souéïda 196, Syr xxxv 236a - **Hatra** Sing. emph. *nšrʾ* 49[3] (cf. e.g. Milik RN vi/iv 56 n. 2, Syr xliv 297, Vattioni IH a.l. :: Caquot Syr xxxii 54: pro *dnšrʾ* l. *tšr* (without interpret.) :: Safar Sumer ix 245: pro *dnšr* l. *tšry* (= *nomen mensis*)) - ¶ subst. eagle (for DA i 10, cf. also Hoftijzer DA a.l.); in Hatra 49[3] prob. indication of statue of an eagle (v. also *dmn*$_1$) representing the god *nšrʾ*; elsewhere in Hatra (88[2], 155[2], 232e 1 and prob. 341[2]) *nšrʾ* = n.d., poss. also in Hatra 229b 2 (cf. Milik DFD 407, v. however *gdy*$_4$).
v. *gd*$_1$, *šr*$_2$.

nšrt **DA** Sing. abs. *nšrt* i 10 (cf. e.g. Caquot & Lemaire Syr liv 198f., Garbini Hen i 178 :: Hoftijzer DA a.l.: = Sing. cstr. :: McCarter

BASOR ccxxxix 51, 55: = PA ʿEL Pf. 3 p.s.f. of *nšr*$_1$ (= to belittle), cf. also Hackett BTDA 29, 49, 132 = to tear, to lacerate (cf. also Puech FS Grelot 28)) - ¶ subst. birds of prey (or indication of special kind of bird?, cf. H. & M.Weippert ZDPV xcviii 95f.).

nštwn (< Iran., cf. e.g. Schaed 265, Ellenbogen 116, Nyberg HP 161f., Herzfeld API 317f., Cowl p. 54, Hinz NWAP 43f., AISN 176, Porten RB xc 412, cf. also Rundgren OrSu xxx 175f.) - **OffAr** Sing. emph. *nštwnʾ* Cowl 17^{2} - ¶ subst. m. instruction, rescript (cf. Grelot DAE p. 282 (n. i) :: Cowl a.l.: = document; cf. also *hwnštwn*).

nt word of unknown meaning on seal of unknown provenance in SANSS-Hebr 163; Avigad IEJ xvi 244f.: l. *nt<n>* = QAL Pf. 3 p.s.m. of *ntn* (improb. interpret., cf. Herr SANSS a.l.; most prob. forgery).

ntʾ **DA** the diff. *nntʾ* in DA x b 2 (reading highly uncert., cf. v.d.Kooij DA p. 159) poss. derivative of this root (uncert. interpret., heavily dam. context).

ntw v. *tw*$_1$.

ntyn **Hatra** Safar Sumer vii 181 (n. 34): l. in 21^{1} *ntynʾ* (= adj. (or QAL Part. pass. of *ntn*) s.m. emph. (= generous, liberal, munificent)) + *šryʾ* (= Sing. emph. of *šry*$_4$ (= sultan, king); cf. Caquot Syr xxix 101 (*šryʾ* = Faʿīl-form s.m. emph. of *šry*$_1$ (= the one who loosens > the liberal one)), cf. also Altheim & Stiehl AAW ii 200f., Levine FS Gordon i 103), cf. however Donner sub KAI 243: = QAL Part. pass. of *ntn* (= someone dedicated (to a sanctuary (cf. also Krückmann AfO xvi 147)), *šryʾ* = QAL Part. pass. s.m. emph. of *šry*$_1$ (= purified from sin)?); cf. however also Krückmann AfO xvi 147 n. 54: pro *-y-* l. rather *-w-*, cf. also Milik RN vi/iv 51ff. (div. otherwise): l. *ntwnʾšryʾ* (= nisbe adj. (Sing. m. emph.) of n.l.), cf. Ingholt AH i/1, 45, i/2, 48, Teixidor Ber xvii 1, Syr xliv 189, Aggoula Ber xviii 89f., Vattioni IH a.l. (cf. also Degen ZDMG cxxi 125; cf. also Altheim & Stiehl AAW iv 264: reading *ntwnʾ* possible) :: Aggoula Sem xxvii 136f. (div. otherwise): l. *ʾntwn* (= n.l.) *ʾšryʾ* (= Sing. m. emph. of *ʾšry* (= Assyrian)).

ntyrh **OffAr** the diff. *ntyrh* in NESE iii 48^{11} word of unknown meaning in the phrase *gbryʾ zy ʿbwrʾ ntyrh ʿmhwn* NESE iii 48$^{10ff.}$: the men with whom the grain is ... (*ntyrh* = QAL Part. pass. s.m. emph. of *ntr*$_2$ of unknown meaning??) :: Degen NESE iii 50, 54f.: l. *ktyrh* = PA ʿEL Imper. s.m. + suff. 3 p.s.f. of *ktr*$_1$ (improb. reading and interpret.).

ntk$_1$ v. *btk*, *prr*$_1$.

ntk$_2$ v. *tkk*.

ntk$_3$ v. *nšk*$_1$.

ntn **Hebr** QAL Pf. 3 p.s.m. *ntn* TA-H 17^{8}, KA 9B 2 (cf. e.g. Scagliarini RSO lxiii208f.(with literature)); 2 p.s.m. *ntt* TA-H 2$^{7f.}$ (cf. Scagliarini Hen xii 137); 1 p.s. + suff. 3 p.pl.m. *nttm* TA-H 40^{10} (for the reading, cf. Aharoni TA a.l., EI xii 75f., cf. also Pardee UF x 323, 325; reading of *n* uncert., however, *m* preferable?, cf. also Aharoni BASOR cxcvii 30, 32 (n. 48): l. *mttk* = Sing. + suff. 2 p.s.m. of *mtt* (= gift)); Impf. 3 p.s.m. *ytn* DJD ii 44[9]; 2 p.s.m. *ttn* TA-H 1[10], 18[6], DJD ii 46[3]; 1 p.s. + suff. 3 p.s.m. *ʾtnnhw* KAI 193[12] (cf. e.g. Ginsberg BASOR lxxi 26, for the reading, cf. also de Vaux RB xlviii 189, 192, Lemaire IH i p. 102f. (v. infra), Gibson JSS xxiv 114, Cross FS Iwry 45, Pardee HAHL 84, 86 :: Torczyner Lach i p. 51, 57 (n. 1 (div. otherwise)): l. *rʾt* (= QAL Pf. 1 p.s. of *rʾy*) *mnhw* (= mn_5 + suff. 3 p.s.m.) :: Birnbaum PEQ '39, 98: l. *ʾtn* (= QAL Impf. 1 p.s.) *bh* (= b_2 + suff. 3 p.s.m.), cf. e.g. Albright BASOR lxxxii 20, Röllig KAI a.l., Gibson SSI i p. 38f. :: Albright BASOR lxxiii 18 (div. otherwise): l. *qrʾt* (= QAL Pf. 1 p.s. of $qrʾ_1$) *nkḥ* (= subst. used as prep.: in the presence of)); Inf. abs. *ntn* TA- H 1[2], 2[1], 7[2], 8[1], 11[2] (cf. e.g. Aharoni TA a.l., Gibson SSI i p. 52, Pardee UF x 293, HAHL 31, 237 :: Sarfatti Maarav iii 71: or = Imper. s.m.?); Imper. s.m. *tn* TA-H 3[2], 4[1,3], 12[2], 18[4], 60[4], 71[1]; Part. act. s.m. abs. *ntn* KAI 194[11] (cf. Torczyner Lach i p. 84, de Vaux RB xlviii 195 × e.g. Albright BASOR lxi 14, Gordon BASOR lxvii 32, Cassuto RSO xvi 176, Hempel ZAW lvi 133, Röllig KAI a.l., Gibson SSI i p. 42, Lemaire IH i p. 110: = QAL Pf. 3 p.s.m.), DJD ii 43[5] - **Amm** QAL Pf. 3 p.s.m. *ntn* AUSS xiii 2[6] (= CAI 80; cf. Cross AUSS xiii 6; uncert. interpret., dam. context); Impf. 1 p.s. *ʾtn* BASOR cclxvi 47[2] (= CAI 144); Imper. s.m. *tn* BASOR cclxvi 47[4] (= CAI 144) - **Edom** QAL Imper. s.m. *tn* TeAv xii 97[3] - **Samal** QAL Pf. 3 p.s.m. *ntn* KAI 214[2] (cf. e.g. Lidzbarski Handb 327, Friedr 20*, Dion p. 215, Gibson SSI ii p. 70 :: Koopmans 32: = QAL Pf. 3 p.pl.m.), 8, 13, 14, 24 (cf. e.g. Lagrange ERS 493f., Dahood Or xlv 383, cf. also v.Dijk VT xviii 27, cf. however Driver AnOr xii 47: = QAL pass. Pf. 3 p.s.m. and Dion p. 128, 215 = QAL Part. pass. s.m. abs. (cf. also Gibson SSI ii p. 74) and Donner KAI a.l.: poss. = QAL Part. act. s.m. abs. :: Koopmans 38: = QAL Inf. :: D.H.Müller WZKM vii 50bis, 135: l. *mtn*); + suff. 3 p.s.f. *ntnh* KAI 214[11] (cf. e.g. Lagrange ERS 493, Donner KAI a.l., Dion p. 28, 215, 225 × Gibson SSI ii p. 71: = QAL Part. pass. s.f. abs. :: Driver AnOr xii 46 = QAL Pass Pf. 3 p.s.f. :: Koopmans 35: = QAL Pf. 3 p.pl.m. + suff. 3 p.s.f., cf. also Lidzbarski Handb 327, Cooke NSI p. 167 :: D.H.Müller WZKM vii 58: l. prob. *ntnw* (= QAL Pf. 3 p.pl.m.)); 3 p.pl.m. *ntnw* KAI 214[20]; Impf. 3 p.s.m. *ytn* KAI 25[5], 214[23]; 3 p.pl.m. KAI 214[4] - **OldAr** QAL Pf. 3 p.s.m. MDAIA ciii 62 (cf. alsoEphʿal & Naveh IEJ xxxix 193f.); Part. act. s.m. abs./cstr. *ntn* Tell F 2, 3 (Akkad. par. *na-din*) - **OffAr** QAL Pf. 3 p.s.m. *ntn* RES 1795A 2 (highly uncert. interpret., dam. context; rather = n.p.?, cf. Milik Bibl xlviii 555), TH i vs. 4 (= AECT 53), BASOR ccxx 55[3] (for the reading, cf. Skaist IEJ xxviii 107 (cf. also Geraty AUSS xix 138, 140) :: Geraty BASOR ccxx 55, 58: pro *hw ntn* l. poss. *hzpt* = HAPH Pf. 1 p.s. of *yzp* (= to loan), cf. however

Geraty ibid. 58 (n. 17): or l. *kzpt* = k_1 + *zpt* (= form of *zph*) or l. *ky ntn* or *hw ntn*); 2 p.s.m. *ntnt* Cowl 3^{12} (*ntnt[*, dam. context), 11^{1}, MAI xiv/2, 66^{12}; 1 p.s. *ntnt* Cowl 69^{12} (?, dam. context), MAI xiv/2, 66^{2,11}, *nttn* Herm 2^{5} (lapsus, cf. Gibson SSI ii p. 134, cf. also Porten & Greenfield ZAW lxxx 219 n. 10, Hoftijzer SV 112, Porten & Yardeni sub TADAE A 2.2 :: Hayes & Hoftijzer VT xx 102, Donner FS Albright ii 83f., Lipiński Or lvii 435, Swiggers AION xli 146: = Pf. 2 p.pl. (cf. also Bresciani & Kamil Herm a.l.: = Pf. 2 p.pl.m./f.) :: Milik RB xlviii 551, 582: = Pf. 1 p.s. + emph. suff. 3 p.s.m.); 3 p.pl.m. *ntnw* RES 496^{1} (cf. SC p. 76, Cowley PSBA xxv 314 :: Sach p. 236, Driver AnOr xii 58: pro *zy ntnw* l. *wyntnw* (= Impf. 3 p.pl.m.)); Impf. 3 p.s.m. *yntn* Cowl 1^{6}, 5^{10}, 6^{14}, 42^{4} (*[y]ntn*; for the reading, cf. Porten & Yardeni sub TADAE A 3.8), 81^{24} (cf. Harmatta ActAntHung vii 349f., Grelot DAE p. 108 n. q :: Cowl a.l.: l. *ttn* = Impf. 3 p.s.f.), Aḥiq 172, Krael 2^{8}, 4^{16}, TH i recto 2 (= AECT 53; for the reading, cf. Friedrich TH a.l.; for the interpret., cf. also Degen NESE i 52, Lipiński Stud 118), Samar 2^{6}, 3^{6}, etc., etc., *ytn* Cowl 81^{64} (cf. Cowl a.l., cf. however Grelot DAE p. 113 (n. c): = n.p. (preferable interpret.) :: Harmatta ActAntHung vii 366: l. poss. *ywnn* or *ywny* (= Greek)); + suff. 3 p.s.m. *yntnhy* RES 1295^{9}; 3 p.s.f. *tntn* Krael 2^{10}, 7^{26}, Sach 78 i B 2; 2 p.s.m. *tntn* Cowl 28^{7,12}, Aḥiq 127, 129, Krael 12^{23,26,28,31}; 2 p.s.f. *tntnn* Cowl 8$^{9f.}$, Krael 9^{21}; + suff. 3 p.s.m. *tntnnh* Cowl 13^{8}; 1 p.s. *ʾntn* Cowl 5^{7,13}, Aḥiq 61, Krael 1^{8,9}, MAI xiv/2, 66^{10}, Samar 1^{9} (*[ʾ]ntn*; = EI xviii 8*), AE '23, 40 no. 2^{5}, etc., etc.; + suff. 3 p.s.m. *ʾntnnh* Cowl 35^{5}, RES 1295^{5}, *ʾtnnhy* MAI xiv/2, 66^{11}, *ʾtnn[h]* Herm 8^{12} (?, heavily dam. context); + suff. 3 p.s.f. *ʾtnnh* Herm 4^{5}; 3 p.pl.m. *yntnwn* Cowl 11^{6} (on the reading, cf. Porten BASOR cclviii 43, cf. also Porten & Yardeni sub TADAE B 4.2), Krael 3^{18}, NESE iii 48 conc. 12, KAI 271B 2 (*[yn]tnwn*; for the reading, cf. Ungnad ArPap p. 115, Degen NESE i 25, 27), *yntnw* Cowl 26^{6}, Driv 8^{3}, JRAS '29, 108^{10}, Sach 76 iii B 2, *ytnwn* Cowl 82^{8,9}; 2 p.pl.m. *tntnwn* Cowl 66 xvi 1, *tntnw* Cowl 25^{14}, Driv 6^{6}, *tntwn* (lapsus) Cowl 25^{11}; + suff. 3 p.s.m. *tntnwnh* Cowl 25^{9}; 1 p.pl. *nntn* Cowl 2^{11}, 28^{10}, 33^{13}, Krael 3^{15,20,21,22a}, Samar 4^{8,10,11}, 7^{13} (*[n]ntn*)^{,14}, *ntn* Cowl 33^{13} (for this reading, cf. Ungnad ArPap p. 11, Porten & Greenfield JEAS p. 100, Porten & Yardeni sub TADAE A 4.10 :: Cowl a.l.: l. *nntn*?); + suff. 3 p.s.m. *ntnhy* Herm 4^{7} (on this form, cf. Kutscher IOS i 118, Gibson SSI ii p. 139 × Degen GGA '79, 40: = Pf. 1 p.pl. + suff. 3 p.s.m. :: Swiggers AION xlii 139: = QAL Impf. 3 p.pl.m. + suff. 3 p.s.m. (with syncope of *y* between preceding *w* and the first root radical)); Inf. *mntn* Cowl 8^{16,19}, 9^{6}, 15^{3}, 50^{14}, 64 xviii 2, Krael 2^{3}, 3^{12,14,15,16}, Driv 12^{2}, ATNS 77a 3, NESE i 11^{4}; + suff. 3 p.s.f. *mntnh* Cowl 9^{9}; ITP Impf. 3 p.s.m. *ytntn* Krael 11^{5}; cf. Paik 498, 499 (*yntn*), 500 (*yntnw*), 501 (*yntnwn*), 502 (*yntn[]*), Nisa-b 211^{2}, 798^{4} (*yntn-t*, on this form, cf.

Naveh & Shaked Or xlii 454 (n. 61) :: Altheim & Stiehl AAW ii 216: l. poss. *yntntwn*), Nisa-b 605[1], 1852[3] (*yntnw*), Syn 315 i 2, GIPP 68 - **Nab** QAL Impf. 3 p.s.m. *yntn* CIS ii 197[3,6], 198[5] - **Palm** QAL Impf. 3 p.s.m. *yntn* RIP 199[7], Syr xvii 353[8] (for the reading, cf. Milik DFD 301), *ytn* CIS ii 3913 ii 6, 70 - **JAr** QAL Impf. 3 p.s.m. *ytn* MPAT-A 22[6], 26[9], 27[4], 28[2,3]; + suff. 2 p.s.m. *ytnk* MPAT 44 i 7 (dam. context); + suff. 2 p.pl. *[y]tnkn* MPAT 45[5] (dam. context); 2 p.s.m. *tntn* Mas 555[3] (?, dam. context); 2 p.pl.m. *ttnwn* MPAT 53[1] - ¶ verb QAL - **1)** to give (sometimes requiring special translation: to pay, to lend), passim - a) + obj., *mn yzbn kpr› dnh ›w mn yzbn ›w yrhn ›w yntn yth* CIS ii 198[4f.]: whoever shall sell this tomb or who shall buy it or mortgage it or who shall give it away; *lmntn ḥlkyn [.... 5] ... wl› yhb ly* Driv 12[2f.]: to assign Cilicians, 5 ..., but did not deliver (them) to me; cf. also Tell F 2, 3, RIP 199[7] - b) + obj. + b_2, *wntnhy bmšḥ* Herm 4[7]: we will (v. supra) exchange it (i.e. castor oil) for (other) oil (v. also infra; :: Bresciani & Kamil Herm a.l.: we put it (i.e. the castor oil) in the oil; cf. Herm 4[5]); *ttnwn ythn b›sply›* MPAT 53[1f.]: you must give them for a bond (:: Fitzmyer & Harrington MPAT a.l.: ... with assurance; v. also *›sply*); cf. also the diff. text Cowl 81[24] (v. supra and v. byt_2) - c) + obj. + *byd*, *ntn nḥm šmn byd hkty* TA-H 17[8f.]: N. gave oil to the Kitti - d) + obj. + l_5, *yyn ... tn lhm* TA-H 4[3]: wine ... you must give them; *wḥyn ›rykn yntn lk* Cowl 30[3]: may he grant you long life (cf. also Dion RB lxxxix 532 (n. 30)); *š[›]rt nksy› ... yntn lh* Krael 7[23f.]: and the rest of the goods ... he shall give her; *ytyr ptp ›l tntnw lhm* Driv 6[6]: you must not assign to them more than (their) ration; cf. Cowl 9[9], BASOR cclxiv 47[2f.], TeAv xii 97[3], etc.; cf. also the construction *lmntn rḥmt l›ḥrnn* Cowl 9[6f.]: to give (it) as a present to others (cf. Weinfeld JAOS xc 190 (n. 45)) - e) + b_2, *›yty ksp š 8 yhbt ... lmntn b‹bwr* NESE i 11[3f.]: there is silver, 8 sh., (which) I gave ... in order to buy corn (for this construction with b_2 (v. also supra), cf. Naveh Lesh xxix 186, Kutscher IOS i 119, Porten & Greenfield ZAW lxxx 223 (n. 21), Milik Bibl xlviii 553, Naveh & Shaked JAOS xci 381); for a construction with *b(ksp)*, v. infra - f) + *byd* + obj., *ntn bydy hdd ... ḥṭr* KAI 214[2f.]: Hadad gave the sceptre into my hands, cf. KAI 214[8f.] (for the context, cf. Tawil Or xliii 46) - g) + l_5, *wntt lhm* TA-H 2[7f.]: and you must give (it) to them; *lmn zy rḥmty tntnn* Cowl 8[9f.]: to whom you wish you may give (it; cf. J.J.Rabinowitz VT xi 63, Greenfield Mem Yalon 69f.); *wtntn lbnyk* Aḥiq 127: you shall give (it) to your children; *yntnw ly* Driv 8[3]: they will assign to me; cf. MDAIA ciii 62, Cowl 8[16,19], 25[11], Krael 1[9], 3[12,14,20], AE '23, 40 no. 2[5], Samar 1[9], 2[6], 3[6], 4[8,11], 7[13], BASOR cclxiv 47[4], Mas 555[3] - h) + l_5 + obj., *ntn lktym yyn* TA-H 1[2f.]: give the K. wine; *ytn lk tḥṭyn* DJD ii 44[9]: he will give you wheat; *yntn lky ksp kršn 5* Cowl 1[6f.]: he shall pay to you 5 k. silver; *ntnt ly ksp* Cowl 11[1]: you have lent me silver; *ntnt lk ḥqly* MAI xiv/2, 66[2f.]: I have let you my field; *'šlm w'ntn lk kntny'* Krael 11[4]: I shall pay and give to you the emmer ...; *l' 'ntn lk bh mrbyt* Cowl 11[4f.]: I will not pay you interest in it (i.e. in the month); cf. TA-H 2[1f.], 4[1f.], 7[2ff.], DJD ii 46[3], KAI 25[5f.], 214[20], Cowl 5[7,10], 13[8], Krael 8[7], 9[20], 12[31], Samar 7[14], etc., etc.; cf. also *wyntnwn ly šlṭn' bh lzbnwth* NESE iii 48[12f.]: and they will give me full power in this to sell it; *ytn lkl rgly [d] 12* CIS ii 3913 ii 6: he shall pay for each person 12 d. - i) + l_5 + b_2, *tntn lh bksp 'w rḥmt* Krael 12[26]: you will sell it to him for silver or (give it) as a gift - j) + l_5 + k_1: *wntn lh YḤW klbbh* KA 9B 2: and the Lord will give to him according to his wish - k) + l_5 + l_5 obj. + *l'ntw*, *lmntn ly ltmt ... l'ntw* Krael 2[3]: to give to me T. ... in marriage; cf. Cowl 15[3] (on both texts, cf. Fitzmyer FS Albright ii 149) - l) + l_5 + ‘l_7 + obj., *wyntn lky w‘l bnyky ... ksp kršn 30* Krael 10[13f.]: he shall pay to you and to your children ... 30 k. silver - m) + l_5 + *mn*$_5$, *prsy zy yn[t]nwn ly mn 'wṣr'* Cowl 11[6]: my salary which they will give me from the treasury - n) + *mn*$_5$, *myyn h'gnt ttn* TA-H 1[9f.]: you must give from the wine in the craters - o) + *mn*$_5$ + obj., *tn mhyyn 3b* TA-H 3[2]: give from the wine 3 b. - p) + ‘l_7 + obj., *nntn ‘l byt mr'n k[sp]* Cowl 33[13]: we will pay to the house of our lord silver; cf. also ATNS 77a 3 (dam. context) - **2)** to place, to put; + obj. + b_2, *'ny ntn tkblym brglkm* DJD ii 43[5f.]: I will put fetters on your feet; *hw' ytn 'pwh bgbrh hhw* MPAT-A 22[6]: He may set His face against this man; *mlk ‘lmh ytn brkth b‘mlhwn* MPAT-A 26[9f.]: may the King of the Universe set His blessing (v. *brkh*$_1$) on their undertaking (cf. MPAT-A 27[4f.], 28[2,3]) - **3)** to give permission; *dy yntn wyqbr bh ‘ydw* CIS ii 197[3f.]: whomsoever A. shall give leave to bury in it; *'l ytn lh l'kl* KAI 214[23]: may he not allow him to eat - ITP to be given; *[k]zy ytntn ly ptp' mn byt mlk'* Krael 11[5f.]: when the ration is given to me from the house of the king - Pardee HAHL 105: l. *tn* = QAL Imper. s.m. in KAI 197[3] (cf. also Lemaire IH i p. 127) - a form of this root in TA-H 28[2] (*ntn*; heavily dam. context), cf. Aharoni TA p. 54, 197 - Gibson SSI ii p. 66: l. *yt[n]w* (= QAL Impf. 3 p.pl.m.) in KAI 214[12] (cf. also Lipiński BiOr xxxiii 232, OLP viii 101), cf. however e.g. Cooke NSI p. 159, 162: l. *ytr* (cf. also Donner KAI a.l.: l. *ytr* = QAL Impf. 3 p.pl.m.; Dion p. 216: *ytr* = QAL Pf. 3 p.s.m. of *ytr*$_1$ (= to grant abundantly, to have abundance)) - Segal Maarav iv 71: l. *'ntnh* = QAL Impf. 1 p.s. + suff. 3 p.s.m./f. (pro *'ntnnh* in AG 4bis 3 (uncert. reading) :: Aimé-Giron AG a.l.: l. *'nḥnh* - a form of this root in ATNS 43a 8 (*ntnh*), heavily dam. context - cf. also *ytn*$_1$.

v. *'mn*$_5$, *'nth*$_2$, *dn*$_1$, *hwn*$_1$, *ktn*$_1$, *mtw*, *nsy*$_1$, *nt*, *ntyn*, *škḥ*, *tny*$_3$.

nt‘ **OldAr** Fitzmyer JAOS lxxxi 205, AIS 18, 68, 158: l. *tnt‘* (= QAL Impf. 2 p.s.m. of *nt‘* (= to draw)) *ly* (= l_5 + suff. 1 p.s.) in KAI 223B 29? (cf. also Donner KAI a.l., Sader EAS 131 (n. 52); highly uncert.

interpret., cf. also Degen AAG p. 14 n. 63, Garr DGSP 42) :: Dupont-Sommer Sf p. 62 (div. otherwise): l. *tnt* *ʿlyh* (without interpret.), cf. however also Lipiński Stud 36f. (div. otherwise): l. *tkt* (= QAL Impf. 2 p.s.m. of *ktt* (= to shatter, to strike)) *ʿlyh* (= *ʿ*l_7 + suff. 3 p.s.m.) and Lemaire & Durand IAS 115, 124, 138: l. *tmtʿ* (= QAL Impf. 2 p.s.m. of *mtʿ* (= to save)).

ntq **DA** the form *ʾtntq* in v c 3 = ITP Pf. 3 p.s.m. or Impf. 1 p.s. of *ntq* (= to pull, to draw; heavily dam. context) - **OffAr** APH Part. s.m. abs. *mtq* FuF xxxv 173^{10}; abs./cstr. *mtq* FuF xxxv $173^{6,7}$ - ¶ verb APH to loosen, to take away, to conquer: FuF xxxv $173^{6,7,10}$ (cf. also Altheim & Stiehl FuF xxxv 176, ASA 274), interpret. of context uncert.

ntr$_1$ **Hebr** HIPH Pf. 3 p.s.m. *hytyr* SM 49^{10}; HOPH Part. s.m. abs. *mwtr* SM 49^9; pl.m. abs. *mwtryn* SM $49^{6,23}$; pl.f. abs. *mwrwt* (lapsus for *mwtrwt*) SM 49^{27} - **OffAr** HAPH Pf. 1 p.s. *hnt[r]t* ATNS 4^4 (for this reading, cf. Segal ATNS a.l.); Impf. 3 p.s.m. *yntr* (*yntr[*; ?, heavily dam. context) ATNS 142^3; 1 p.s. *ʾntr* ATNS 5^6 - ¶ verb HIPH/HAPH - **1)** to allow; + obj.: SM 49^{10} - **2)** to release; + obj. (slaves): ATNS 4^4, 5^6 - HOPH to be allowed, to be permitted; *ʾylw hmqwmwt hmwtryn sbybwt byt šʾn* SM $49^{5f.}$: these are the permitted places around B.Sh. - a form of this root prob. to be restored in Cowl 15^{35} (*[ʾhn]tr* = HAPH Impf. 1 p.s.), cf. e.g. Cowl a.l., Yaron JSS iii 25, Porten & Greenfield JEAS p. 22, Porten & Yardeni sub TADAE B 2.6 (on the problem, cf. also Fitzmyer FS Albright ii 166) - a form of this root (*ntr*) also in ATNS 109^2 (?, or = Sing. abs. of *ntr*$_5$ (= natron)??), reading however uncert., cf. also Ullendorff JRAS '85, 69 - Segal ATNS a.l.: l. poss. a form of this root in ATNS 4^5 (*hnt[*), reading however highly uncert., cf. Shaked Or lvi 409: l. *hmw* (poss. reading), cf. also Porten & Yardeni sub TADAE B 8.7.
v. *hʾ*$_1$.

ntr$_2$ v. *ntyrh*.

ntr$_3$ v. *mt*$_6$.

ntr$_4$ **Nab** a word *ntrʾ* (reading uncert.) in J 34^8 (= CIS ii 224), poss. = Sing. emph. of *ntr*$_4$, meaning unknown, cf. Jaussen & Savignac in J i p. 198.

ntr$_5$ **OffAr** Sing. emph. *ntrʾ* ATNS 24^9 - ¶ subst. natron; *ntrʾ zy mwʿʾ* ATNS 24^9: natron of the East.
v. *ntr*$_1$.

S

s$_1$ v. *z*$_1$.

s$_2$ v. *sʾh*$_1$.

s_3 v. *smyd.*

s_4 abbrev. of uncert. interpret. in ATNS 66a 9.

s'h_1 **Hebr** Sing. abs. *s'h* DJD ii 24K 2 (heavily dam. context); Plur. abs. *s'ym* DJD ii 30[14], *s'yn* DJD ii 24B 17a - **OffAr** Sing. abs. *s'h* Del 77[3]; cstr. *s't* Del 69[2], 83[1], 84[1], 86; Plur. abs. *s'n* Cowl 63[3], Krael 11[3,4] - **Nab** Plur. abs. *s'yn* DBKP 22[33] (Greek par. σάτα) - **JAr** Plur. abs. *s'yn* MPAT 52[2], *š'yn* DBKP 21 back (Greek par. σάτα) - ¶ subst. f. - **1)** measure of capacity (used in connection with grain), *seah* (for this measure, cf. e.g. Barrois ii 248ff., Trinquet SDB v 1224, 1229ff., Yeivin PEQ '69, 64, and also EM iv 853ff.): DJD ii 24B 17a, 30[14], Cowl 63[3], Krael 11[3,4], MPAT 52[2], DBKP 21 back, 22[33]; for abbrev. *s*,cf. in Off.Ar TA-Ar 1[2], 2[1], 3[2], 4[1], 5[1], 6[2], 7[3], 8[3], 9[1,2], BSh 1[2], 2[2], 3[2], 5[3], 6[4], 8[3], 27[2], 28[2], 29[2] (*s[*), 30[3], 32[3], in JA DJD ii 8 i 1, 2, 3 (= MPAT 38), 8 ii, Bibl xl 986 (cf. DJD iii 37), IEJ xl 135[9], 142[2], Mas 590, etc., etc. - the same abbrev. prob. also in Cowl 81[3,4,134,136] (cf. also Grelot DAE p. 106, 118), Krael 17[3,4] (cf. Allrik BASOR cxxxvi 24 n. 2, Porten & Greenfield JAOS lxxxix 156 n. 22) - **2)** rent: Del 77[3], 86; *s't 'rq'* Del 69[2], 83[1], 84[1]: rent for a plot - Gordon BASOR lxxviii 10f.: l. this subst. (Plur. abs. *sn*) poss. in BASOR lxxviii 11B (highly uncert. interpret.) - Zimmern Fremdw 21, v.Soden AHW s.v. *sūtu(m)*, Salonen Hausgeräte ii 297, Lipiński ZAH i 70: < Akkad. (cf. also Ellenbogen 118; highly uncert. interpret.), cf. also HAL s.v. *s'h*; > Greek σάτον.

v. *ḥpn.*

s'h_2 v. *š'h_2*.

sb_1 v. *nsb.*

sb_2 v. *šb.*

sbb_1 **Ph** YIPH Pf. 3 p.s.m. *ysb* EpAn ix 5[8]; + suff. 3 p.s.f. *ysb* EpAn ix 5C 2 (for the form, cf. Mosca & Russell EpAn ix 23f.) - **Hebr** HIPH Pf. 2 p.s.m. *hsbt* TA-H 2[5f.] (cf. Scagliarini Hen xii 137) - **OldAr** QAL Impf. 3 p.s.m. *ysb* KAI 222B 34 (reading uncert.); + suff. 1 p.s. *ysbny* KAI 222B 28 (on this poss. case of haplography, cf. Fitzmyer JAOS lxxxi 204, AIS 67, Donner KAI a.l., Degen AAG p. 14 n. 62, p. 72, 79, GGA '79, 39f., Watson Bibl lii 47 n. 9, Lindenberger APA 226 n. 48, cf. however Lipiński Stud 36 (cf. also Lemaire & Durand IAS 115, 124, 138: l. *ysbbny* (poss. reading; = PAL Impf. 3 p.s.m. + suff. 1 p.s.; without haplography), v. also *'ty_1* :: Grelot RB lxxv 283f.: = QAL Impf. 3 p.s.m. + *n paragogicum* :: Ben-Chayyim Lesh xxxv 246, Segert AAG p. 308: l. *ysbn* = QAL Impf. 3 p.s.m. + suff. 1 p.s., cf. also Dupont-Sommer Sf p. 147) - ¶ verb QAL to encircle, to surround: KAI 222B 34 (dam. context); + obj.: KAI 222B 28 (to surround someone inimically) - HIPH prob. meaning, to send out (sc. on a tour to distribute supplies; cf. Pardee UF x 298f. :: Aharoni TA a.l.: to bring supplies during a daily inspection tour :: Sasson ZAW xciv 106ff.: to hand over): TA-H

2[5f.] (cf. also Levine Shn iii 288: to bring :: Lipiński BiOr xli 157: = to bring back; v. also *mḥr$_3$*) - YIPH to turn over; -a) + *l$_5$* (to): EpAn ix 5C 2 -b) + *l$_5$* + obj., *ysb mlk ... lmsn›zmš kl hšdyt ›l* EpAn ix 5[8]: the king turned over to M. all these fields (for this meaning of *sbb$_1$*, cf. also Greenfield Sem xxxviii 157) - Puech & Rofé RB lxxx 533ff.: the *msbb* in BASOR cxciii 8[2] = PI‹EL Part. m. s. abs. of *sbb$_1$* (*msbb ‹lk* = those who accompany you), poss. interpret., diff. and uncert. context (cf. also R.Kutscher Qadm v 27f.: l. *msbb lk* = your enemies, and Jackson ALIA 10, 15f., 251 (anyone) who surrounds you (*msbb ‹lk*), cf. also Smelik HDAI 84) :: Dion RB lxxxii 32f. n. 50: *msbb* = *mn$_5$* + *sbb$_2$* (l. *msbb lk* = those who surround you, or l. rather *msbb ‹lk* = those who surround you inimically (cf. Aufrecht sub CAI 59: l. prob. *msbb ‹lk* = from round about > who surrounds you, cf. also Cross BASOR cxciii 18: l. *msbb lk* = around you; Shea PEQ '79, 17, '81, 105f.: l. *msbb ‹lk* = from round about (come) against you; Albright BASOR cxcviii 38f.: l. *msbb lk* = your foreign relations; cf. also Horn BASOR cxciii 9f.)) :: v.Selms BiOr xxxii 5, 8: l. *msbb* (= PU‹AL Part. s.m. abs.) = what is enclosed :: Fulco BASOR ccxxx 41f.: l. *msbb* = QAL Part. s.m. abs. (*msbb ‹lk* = those who threaten you) :: Sasson PEQ '79, 118, 120: l. *msbb lk* = your surrounding fronts :: Garbini AION xx 253f.: *msbb*= subst. Sing. abs. :: Horn BASOR cxciii 9f. (div. otherwise): or l. *msb* (= Sing. cstr. of *msb* (= surroundings)) + *b‹lk* (= Sing. + suff. 2 p.s.m. of *b‹l$_2$*)= round about your master.
v. *sbb$_2$*.

sbb$_2$ **Ph** Sing. m. cstr. *sbb* KAI 37B 4 (for the reading, cf. Peckham Or xxxvii 305, 318f. :: e.g. CIS i sub 86, Cooke NSI p. 68, Röllig KAI a.l.: l. *rb* = Sing. m. cstr. of *rb$_2$*; v. also infra) - **Amm** Plur. f. cstr. *sbbt* BASOR cxciii 8[1] (cf. e.g. Horn BASOR cxciii 8f., R.Kutscher Qadm v 28, Dion RB lxxxii 32, Shea PEQ '79, 18; or = Plur. f. abs.?, cf. also Puech & Rofé RB lxxx 534f., Jackson ALIA 15 × Albright BASOR cxcviii 39: = QAL Part. act. pl.f. abs./cstr. of *sbb$_1$*:: Shea PEQ '81, 105f.: = Plur. abs. of *sbbh* (= round tower)) - **Hebr** Sing. m. abs. *sbyb* SM 49[25]; Plur. f. cstr. *sbybwt* SM 49[6] - ¶ adj. surrounding (cf. Horn BASOR cxciii 8, Dion RB lxxxii 32, Shea PEQ '79, 18, cf. also R.Kutscher Qadm v 27f., Sasson PEQ '79, 118, Aufrecht sub CAI 59), peripheral (cf. Puech & Rofé RB lxxx 534f.): BASOR cxciii 8[1] × Cross BASOR cxciii 18, v.Selms BiOr xxxii 5, 8, Fulco BASOR ccxxx 41f.: *sbbt* = courts, precincts, enclosures × Jackson ALIA 10, 15, 26: *sbbt* used as prep.; *hmqwmwt hmwtryn sbybwt byt š›n* SM 49[5f.]: the permitted places around B-Sh. - a) preceded by prep. *b$_2$*: KAI 37B 4 (for the reading, v. supra), Peckham Or xxxvii 306: round about (cf. Amadasi Kition sub C 1, Masson & Sznycer RPC 27, 59: in the entourage of ...), cf. however Healey BASOR ccxvi 53, 56, 60 n. 16:

in the precinct of ... and Gibson SSI iii p. 127, 130: at the procession around (less prob. interpret.) - b) followed by prep. l_5, *sbyb lqysryn* SM 49[25]: around C. - for the *sb/d/rb/d/rt* in BASOR cxciii 8[4] of diff. interpret., cf. Cross BASOR cxciii 17: l. *s[b]bt* = Plur. f. cstr. of sbb_2 (= precincts; :: Cross ibid. (n. 13): or (div. otherwise) l. *s[b]bty* = Plur. f. cstr.; cf. also v.Selms BiOr xxxii 5, 7f., R.Kutscher Qadm v 27f., Dion RB lxxxii 32, Shea PEQ '79, 17, 18f., Sasson PEQ '79, 118, 121: l. *s[bb]t* = Plur. f. abs.), cf. however Albright BASOR cxcviii 39: l. *s[dr]t* = Plur. (or Sing.) abs. of $sdrh_1$ (= rank; for this reading, cf. also Fulco BASOR ccxxx 41f.: l. *s[d]rt* (= Sing. abs. of $sdrh_1$ (= architectonial term)), Puech & Rofé RB lxxx 533f., 537: l. *sdrt* (= Plur. abs. of $sdrh_1$ (= colonnades), Jackson ALIA 10, 18f. 25: l. prob. *sdrt* prob. = Sing. abs. of $sdrh_1$ (= hall?), Baldacci AION xlv 519: = porch?) :: Shea PEQ '81, 107: l. *sbbt* (= Plur. abs. of *sbbh* (= round tower)); cf. also Aufrecht sub CAI 59) :: Horn BASOR cxciii 11 (div. otherwise): l. *s[p]* (= Sing. abs./cstr. of sp_3 (= threshold)) - Lipiński Stud 30: l. *[sb]bt* (= Plur. f. abs.) in KAI 222A 35f. (poss. restoration; :: e.g. Dupont-Sommer Sf p. 51, Donner KAI a.l., Lemaire & Durand IAS 135: l. *[r]bt* (= Plur. f. abs. of rb_2 (for problems with this restoration, cf. e.g. Fitzmyer AIS 53, Degen ZDMG cxix 173)) :: Gibson SSI ii p. 31, 42: l. *rbt* = adverb (= utterly), cf. also Rosenthal ANET 660).
v. sbb_1.

sbbh v. sbb_2.

sbwl v. sbl_2.

sbyb v. sbb_2.

sbk **OffAr** word of uncert. meaning in RES 1795B 1; Clermont-Ganneau RAO viii 135: = net?, cf. also Porten Arch 276: = (fishing) net :: Sach p. 239: = n.l.?

$\mathbf{sbl_1}$ **OffAr** QAL (cf. Joüon MUSJ xviii 52 :: Leand 28d, 31h: = PA ʿEL) Impf. 3 p.s.m. + suff. 3 p.s.m. *ysblnhy* Aḥiq 90; PA ʿEL Pf. 3 p.s.f. + suff. 1 p.s. *sbltny* Krael 9[17]; Impf. 3 p.s.m. *ysbl* Krael 5[11,12,13]; 1 p.s. + suff. 2 p.s.m. *ʾsblnk* Aḥiq 204; 1 p.pl. *nsbl* Krael 5[12]; + suff. 2 p.s.m. *nsblnk* Krael 5[13]; Imper. s.m. *sbl* Beh 63 (cf. Driver JRAS '32, 89f., Greenfield & Porten BIDG p. 52f.; Akkad. par. *su-ud-di-id*; dam. context); Part. act. s.m. abs. *msbl* Aḥiq 48, 72; pl.f. abs. *msbln* Herm 1[5]; ITP Impf. 3 p.pl.m. *ystblwn* Aḥiq 73 - ¶ verb QAL to carry + obj.: Aḥiq 90 (cf. also Held JAOS lxxxviii 92 (n. 52); :: Seidel ZAW xxxii 295: *sbl* here = to provide for, to support) - PA ʿEL to support, to sustain, to provide for (cf. also Muffs 39 n. 4, 198) - **1)** + obj., *nsblnk* Krael 5[13]: we will provide for you (cf. Krael 9[17]); cf. also Aḥiq 204 (*ʾsblnk*), cf. e.g. Cowl a.l., Ginsberg ANET 430, Grelot DAE p. 447 × Grelot RB lxviii 193 n. 106: or = I will burden (/load) you; cf. also Lindenberger APA 203 - **2)** + l_5 (obj.), *nsbl lzkwr* Krael 5[12]: we will provide for Z. (cf. Krael

5[11,12], Aḥiq 48, 72, Herm 1[5]; for *sbl* in Krael 5, cf. also J.J.Rabinowitz Law 26ff., Verger RCL '64, 308, RGP 172f., Greenfield EI xvi 57ff.) - ITP to be supported; + *qdm*$_3$, *lḥm wmyn ystblwn qdm mr*ʾ*y* Aḥiq 72f.: bread and water shall be carried to my lord.
v. *sbl*$_2$.

sbl$_2$ **OffAr** Sing. abs. *sbl* Aḥiq 74 (:: Cowl a.l.: or = QAL Pf. 3 p.s.m. of *sbl*$_1$?),*sbwl*Cowl 43[4]; Plur. + suff. 2 p.s.m. *sbwlyk*Aḥiq 205 - ¶ subst. support, sustenance: Cowl 43[4], Aḥiq 74, cf. also Aḥiq 205 (Plur.; cf. Cowl a.l., Ginsberg ANET 430, Grelot DAE p. 447, Lindenberger APA 203f. :: Grelot RB lxviii 193 n. 106: or *sbwlyk* = your loads).

sbl$_3$ **JAr** Plur. emph. *sbly*ʾ Mas 560[1] - ¶ subst. porter.

sbs$_1$ > Akkad. *subbusu* = to assemble (persons), cf. v.Soden Or xxxvii 266, xlvi 194, AHW s.v. *subbusu* II, CAD s.v. *subbusu* v.; cf. also *sbs*$_2$ > *subbusu* adj. = gathered, congregated.

sbs$_2$ v. *sbs*$_1$.

sbsb **OffAr** cf. Frah x 8 (*sbsb*ʾ), word of uncert. meaning (cf. Ebeling Frah a.l., Nyberg FP 75).

sbʿm v. *šbʿm*.

sbq **Pun** QAL (?) Imper. s.m. *sbq* KAI 165[1] (for the reading, cf. Levi Della Vida OA iv 65, cf. already Chabot sub Punica xvi 1 :: Février BAr '51/52, 40f., 43, Röllig KAI a.l., v.d.Branden RSF ii 145f. (div. otherwise): l. *tbqy* (= QAL Impf. 2 p.s.m. of *bqy*= to stop; v. also *y*$_1$) - ¶ verb QAL (?) meaning unknown; Levi Della Vida OA iv 65, 67: = to stop; or rather: = to do or say (something) spontaneously (cf. Arab. *sabaqa*)?

sbr$_1$ **OffAr** QAL Pf. 1 p.s. *sbrt* Cowl 37[7] (reading uncert., cf. Cowl a.l.; cf. also Porten & Greenfield JEAS p. 80f., Grelot DAE p. 389; cf. however Porten & Yardeni sub TADAE A 4.2: l. *sbrw* (= QAL Pf. 3 p.pl.m. (they favoured)), and Sach p. 52: l. *kbrḡ*; dam. context) - ¶ verb QAL to think (v. however supra)
v. *šbr*$_2$.

sbr$_2$ **Palm** Sing. emph. *sbr*ʾ Inv ix 4[2] (Greek par. καθηγητής) - ¶ subst. m. guide, teacher (cf. also Milik DFD 158; cf. however Cantineau sub Inv ix 4: = master workman, master mason (cf. also Díez Merino LA xxi 112 (n. 71))) - Milik DFD 157: l. *sbry*ʾ in RTP 301 (= Plur. emph. (= experts)); uncert. reading and interpret.; on the reading, cf. also Ingholt, Seyrig & Starcky RTP a.l.).

sbr$_3$ cf. Ebeling Frah a.l.: l. *sbr* in Frah vii 14 = sheep (< Akkad.), less prob. interpret., cf. Nyberg FP 71: l. *tasū-brīt* (= Iran. word).

sg$_1$ v. *šḥsgm*.

sg$_2$ v. *ksp*$_2$.

sgd$_1$ **OffAr** QAL Pf. 1 p.s. *sgd[t]* Aḥiq 13 - ¶ verb QAL to bow down, to prosternate; + *qdm*$_3$ (= before): Aḥiq 13 - Naveh sub SM 88: l. in

SM 88[23] *sgyd* (= QAL Part. act. s.m.), cf. however Torrey sub Syn D B 8 (div. otherwise): l. *prsyn* (= QAL Part. act. pl.m. abs. of *prs*$_1$ (= to spread out)) and Obermann Ber vii 113, 116: l. *dsgy* (= *d*$_3$ + Sing. abs. of *sgy*$_3$ (= *šg'*$_3$)), diff. reading, heavily dam. context - QAL Part. act. f. > Akkad. *sāgittu* (certain kind of priestess), cf. v.Soden Or xxxvii 271, xlvi 193, AHW s.v., cf. also CAD sv.
v. *sgd*$_2$.

sgd$_2$ **OffAr** Plur. + suff. 3 p.s.m. *sgdwhy* Aḥiq 10 - ¶ subst. (cf. Leand 43j'''; or rather = QAL Part. act. of *sgd*$_1$?),courtier.

sgd$_3$ **Palm** this subst. (Sing. emph. *šgd'*) poss. in Inv xi 26[1] (cf. Aggoula Sem xxix 112).
v. *'sgd*, *sgdh*.

sgdh **OffAr**, cf. GIPP 33: worship (or form of *sgd*$_3$?).

sgwb v. *sprb*.

sgwl v. *sgyl*.

sgy$_1$ **OffAr** PA'EL Impf. 3 p.s.m. *ysgh* Aḥiq 126 (:: Lindenberger APA 118, 280, UF xiv 108: poss. = lapsus for *ysgwn* (= QAL Impf. 3 p.pl.m.)); cf. Frah xx 4 (*sgytwn*), 19 (*ḥsgwn*; for this prob. interpret. as HAPH form, cf. Nyberg FP 94 (cf. also Toll ZDMG-Suppl viii 39) :: Ebeling Frah a.l.: l. *hytywn* = form of *'ty*$_1$;var. in FP p. 54 sub 2: *sṣytwn*), Paik 707-709 (*sgytn*), SaSt 23, cf. also MP 2 s.v. *sgytn*, GIPP 33 - ¶ verb PA'EL to come; *ysgh b'drh* Aḥiq 126: he will come to his aid - > Akkad. *segû* = to move about, cf. v.Soden Or xxxvii 266, xlvi 194, AHW s.v., cf. also CAD sv.

sgy$_2$ v. *sgyl*.

sgy$_3$ v. *sgd*$_1$, *sgyl*, *šg'*$_3$.

sgyl (< Akkad. < Sum.?, cf. e.g. Vattioni IH p. 57, Leemhuis JSS xxvii 54f.) - **Hatra** Sing. abs. (or rather name?) *sgyl* 107[6] (cf. Degen JEOL xxiii 409, Vattioni IH a.l. :: Aggoula Ber xviii 98, MUSJ xlvii 40: = Sing. cstr. :: Milik DFD 377f., 386: l. *sgwl* (= Sing. cstr.) = possession :: Caquot Syr xli 253 (div. otherwise): l. *sgy* (= PA'EL Pf. 3 p.s.m. of *sgy*$_2$ (= *šg'*$_2$; = to augment, to add)) + *l*$_5$ :: Safar Sumer xviii 29f. (n. 14), As-Saliḥi Sumer xxxi 77*: l. *sgy* (= Sing. m. abs. of *sgy*$_3$ (= *šg'*$_3$;= the greater part)) + *l*$_5$ (= of)), 191[1] (*[s]gyl*, cf. Aggoula MUSJ xlvii 41, Vattioni IH a.l. :: Safar Sumer xviii 55, Caquot Syr xli 267 (div. otherwise): l. *'lm*$_3$without interpret.; for the context, v. also *'s*$_1$), 225[1] (cf. Aggoula MUSJ xlvii 45, Degen JEOL xxiii 422 add, Vattioni IH a.l. :: Safar Sumer xxi 39: l. *[nrg]wl* = n.d., cf. also Degen WO v 229: l. *n[r]gwl*), 240[2], 244[2], 245[2], 246[3] - ¶ subst. (?, v. supra) prob. designating temple, cf. *sgyl hykl' rb'* Hatra 107[6]: *sgyl*, the great temple; *l'bd' dy sgyl 'l ḥyyhy* Hatra 244[2]: for the work on *sgyl* for the good of his life (cf. Hatra 245[2f.]); etymology of this name diff. (v. supra), cf. also Degen JEOL xxiii 409: related to root *sgl* = to be round?? (the explanation of Aggoula MUSJ xlvii 40 (cf. also 15, 41) as "theatre" less prob. (cf. also Vattioni IH a.l. and p. 57, 74 = theatre, palace); Leemhuis JSS xxvii 52ff.: original meaning "stone" > "altar stone" > *sacrarium* (less prob. interpret.); on this word, cf. also Drijvers ActIr xvii 161 (n. 45) - Aggoula MUSJ xlvii 42, Vattioni IH a.l.: l. in Hatra 192[2] *[sgy]l* (v. also *ʾs$_1$* for context), prob. restoration :: Safar Sumer xviii 55 (div. otherwise): l. *? ʾlʾm* (without interpret.) :: Caquot Syr xli 268: l. *d/r lʾm* (without interpret.) - Vattioni IH a.l.: l. *sgl* (= *sgyl*) in Hatra 202[17] (cf. also Leemhuis JSS xxvii 53; prob. reading, less prob. interpret., cf. Teixidor Sumer xxi 87*: l. *sgl* (Sing. abs.) = property, cf. also Safar Sumer xxiv 13, Milik DFD 386: > treasure house (cf. also Degen JEOL xxiii 409) :: Caquot Syr xli 271: l. *dngl[ʾ]* (= Sing. emph. of *dngl* (= standard-bearer)); for the reading, cf. Safar Sumer xviii 63: l. *sgl* or *dngl* (without interpret.)).

sgl v. *sgyl*.

sgn$_1$ (< Akkad. *šaknu*, cf. Zimmern Fremdw 6, R.A.Bowman Pers p. 25f., Lipiński UF v 204f., ZAH i 70, Kaufman AIA 97f., 139; > Akkad. *sagānu*, cf. e.g. v.Soden Or xxxvii 265, xlvi 193, AHW s.v., CAD s.v., R.A.Bowman Pers p. 26, Lipiński UF v 205 :: Kaufman AIA 97: NeoBab. *sagānu* representing Ass pronunciation) - **OffAr** Sing. abs. *sgn* Cowl 8[13], 10[13,18], 35c 4 (= TADAE B 4.6[14]; dam. context), 47[2,7], Krael 9[19], 10[13], 12[28], Pers 93[1], 115[2] (in both Pers instances at the end of line); cstr. *sgn* Cowl 26[9,21], Del 70[1]; emph. *sgnʾ* Pers 3[2], 7[2], 11[2], 12[2], 13[2], 14[1], 15[2], ATNS 102a 3, Samar 8[12], etc., etc., *snʾ* (lapsus) Pers 124[2] - ¶ subst. m. - **1)** prefect, governor (with judicial competence): passim (cf. *sgn[ʾ] rbʾ* in Pers 2[2]; for *rbʾ* (additional), cf. R.A.Bowman Pers a.l. (this interpret. however uncert.)) - cf. the following expressions, *sgn wdyn* Cowl 8[13], 10[13,18f.]: prefect or judge (:: Cowl p. 25: or *dyn* = *dyn$_2$* (= *dn$_1$*?); *sgn wmrʾ* Cowl 47[2], Krael 9[19], 10[13]: prefect or lord (v. also *mrʾ*); *sgn wmrʾ wdyn* Krael 12[28]: prefect or lord or judge; cf. also *sgn bnšyʾ* Del 70: the governor of the B. - for the *sgn* in Elephantine, cf. e.g. Wag 208, Krael p. 36, J.J.Rabinowitz VT xi 65, Verger RCL '64, 85ff. (nn. 38, 39), RGP 183ff., Porten Arch 48f., Naveh & Shaked Or xlii 450f., Greenfield Trans iii 89, FS Rundgren 153f. - for the *sgn* in the Persepolis texts, cf. Naveh & Shaked Or xlii 448ff. (: = lower local official subordinate to the *gnzbr*; cf. also Bernard StudIr i 167, 169f.) :: Oelsner OLZ ' 75, 475: = official occupying highest position :: Delaunay CC 210, 212, 215f.: = chief of a certain number of men (in this case of the craftsmen) :: R.A.Bowman Pers p. 25ff., 32: = title of high official with priestly connotation (on these texts, cf. also Grelot RB lxxx 595, Segal BSOAS xxxv 354) - **2)** head, chief; *sgn ngryʾ* Cowl 26[9,21f.]: surveyor of the carpenters (v. *spytkn*) - Segal ATNS a.l.: l. *[s]gn* (= Sing. cstr.) in ATNS 102a 3 in the combination *[s]gn sgnʾ*

(the deputy of the gouvernor), uncert. interpret. - for this word, cf. also Saggs JThSt-NS x 84ff., Japhet VT xviii 355f., Petit JBL cvii 53ff. - cf. also *skn*$_2$.

sgn$_2$ **OffAr** Plur. abs. *sgnn* Cowl 26[10] - ¶ subst. indicating part of ship, exact meaning unknown; Cowl p. 95: it might mean a plank to keep the planks in place, but 12 cubits seems rather long for ribs; Holma Öfversigt af Finska Vetenskaps Societetens Förhandlingar '15B no. 5, 7f.: = rudder; Grelot DAE p. 289 n. v: it should be noted that a *sgn* in this text has the length of parts of the poop.

sgr **Ph** YIPH (cf. Harr 126, FR 146; cf. however Greenfield ActOr xxix 9 n. 25: or = PI ʿEL?) Impf. 3 p.pl. + suff. 3 p.pl.m. *ysgrnm* KAI 14[9,21] - ¶ verb YIPH (v. however supra) to deliver; + obj.: KAI 14[21]; + obj. + *ʾt*$_6$, *ysgrnm hʾlnm hqdšm ʾt mmlk<t>* KAI 14[19]: may the holy gods deliver them to a king ... (for the context, v. *ʾt*$_6$; cf. also Greenfield FS Albright ii 263f.) - cf. *skr*$_1$.

sd$_1$ **OffAr** Sachau Sach p. 237, 239: l. *sdn* (= Plur. abs. of *sd*$_1$ (= block of wood, log)) in RES 1792A 2, 1795A 3; improb. reading, cf. Lidzbarski Eph ii 229, 236, iii 257 n. 1: l. *swn* = n.l.

sd$_2$ **Ph** the diff. *sdy* in CIS i 91[2] poss. = Sing./Plur. + suff. 1 p.s./3 p.s.m. of subst. *sd* of unknown meaning :: Renan sub CIS i 91: *sd* = favor (Sing. + suff. 3 p.s.m.) :: Slouschz TPI p. 100f.: l. *sry* = Plur. + suff. 1 p.s. of *sr*$_3$ (= adversary) or = Plur. cstr. of *sr*$_1$ (= *šr*$_2$) :: FR 47, 235: l. *sry* = Plur. + suff. 1 p.s. of *sr*$_4$ (= *ṣr*$_2$), cf. also Harr 142.

sdd v. *ʾsr*$_1$.

sdl **Pun** Plur. abs. *sdlm* RCL '66, 201[6] - ¶ subst. of unknown meaning; Fantar RCL '66, 208f., Ferron MUSJ xcviii 60f.: = necklace or veil??, cf. however Dupont-Sommer CRAI '68, 117, 130f.: = sandal < Greek σάνδαλον / Lat. *sandalium* ("mot voyageur"?)? (for this interpret. cf. also Heltzer UF xix 434).

sdn Masson RPAE 25f.: > Greek σινδών (= linen garment) - on this word, cf. also Brown JSS xxv 13ff.

sdq$_1$ **OffAr**, cf. Frah xviii 11 (*sdkwn*; var. in FP p. 54 sub 2: *skwn*): to tear, to slitt.

sdq$_2$ (< Greek σύνδικος, cf. Cantineau Gramm 156, Rosenthal Sprache 92) - **Palm** Plur. emph. *sdqyʾ* CIS ii 3913 i 11 - ¶ subst. m. (Plur.) the Syndics (public advocates representing the state), governing body in Palmyre.

sdr **JAr** Sing. cstr. *sdr* SM 13[2] (for this prob. reading, cf. Naveh SM a.l. :: Avigad BRF iii 52f., Hüttenmeister ASI 345: l. *šdr* (= Sing. cstr. of *šdr*$_4$ (= var. of *sdr*)) - ¶ subst. office, leadership, authority; *nybnh bsdr ḥnynʾ* SM 13[2]: it was built when Ch. was in office - the same word (Plur. abs. *sdryn*, reading uncert. (= order)) also in Driv F 1a 4?

sdrh$_1$ v. *sbb$_2$*.

sdrh$_2$ JAr Fitzmyer & Harrington sub MPAT-A 1: l. *sdrh* (word of unknown meaning) in MPAT-A 1^2, cf. already Klein BJPES ii 47f. (: prob. = synagogue); Fitzmyer & Harrington sub MPAT-A 1 a.l.: *sdrh* misspelling for Sanhedrin (*snhdryn*)??, cf. however Ginsberg BJPES ii 47f.: l. *ksdryy* (= the Alexandrian; cf. also Naveh sub SM 21), cf. also Beyer ATTM 371: l. *nhwry* = n.p.

shb Pun Sing. abs. *shb* CIS i 355^2 - ¶ subst. prob. indication of occupation or function, meaning unknown; Slouschz TPI p. 262f.: poss. = goldworker; Slouschz ibid.: cf. perhaps the *[s]h[b]m* in CIS i $341^{4f.}$ (in the combination *pʿl [s]h[b]m*; cf. however CIS i sub 341: l. *sh[b]m* or *sh[r]m* (reading of *s* prob.) = word in Plur. abs. of unknown meaning).
v. *sḥb$_2$*.

shd v. *šhd$_1$*.

shyty v. *shty*.

shr$_1$ v. *sḥr$_3$*.

shr$_2$ v. *shb*.

shty (Caillat JA ccliv 467ff.: < Prakrit *se hǐ ti*, cf. however Henning BSOAS xiii 86f.: < Prakrit *sahite* (for a derivation < Prakrit, cf. also Benveniste JA ccliv 451ff.); cf. however also Bailey with Shaked JRAS '69, 122 n. 10 and with Kutscher, Naveh & Shaked Lesh xxxiv 127: < Iran. *sahyatay* (for a derivation < Iran., cf. also Humbach IPAA 15, and Hinz AISN 220: < Iran. *sahyati*)) - **OffAr** *shty* CRAI '70, 163^3, *shyty*BSOAS xiii $82^{3,4,5,6,7}$, JA ccliv $440^{1,3}$ (*[s]hyty*)'^{5} (*[s]hyty*), IPAA 11^7 (*s[h]yty*) - word of uncert. meaning; Dupont-Sommer JA ccliv 441, 462a, CRAI '70, 163, 168, Benveniste JA ccliv 451ff., Caillat JA ccliv 467ff., Hinz AISN 220: used as introduction of a translation: that is to say, this means (Caillat a.l.: thus exactly; Henning BSOAS xiii 86f.: in accordance with, composed of, connected with), cf. also (Bailey with) Kutscher, Naveh & Shaked Lesh xxxiv 127; cf. however Shaked JRAS '69, 122: does not serve to introduce a new passage but precedes or follows an Aramaic Prakrit sequence; Humbach IPAA 11,15: = verbal form with meaning "is called" (in this interpret. *sh(y)ty* is part of preceding sentence); Altheim FS Eissfeldt 30ff.: in BSOAS xiii 82 = he (namely Asoka) says.

swb v. *swr$_3$*.

swbr cf. Frah xxvi 3 (*swblʾ*): = hope.

swg Pun Rocco StudMagr vii 12, 14: l. *sg* (= Qal Imper. pl.m. of *swg* (= to bind)) in StudMagr vii 12^5 (highly uncert. reading and interpret.).
v. *ksp$_2$*.

swd$_1$ OffAr Segal ATNS a.l.: l. in ATNS 4^6 *syd* (= Qal Part. act. s.m. abs. of *swd$_1$* (= to have lordship)), uncert. reading (cf. Porten &

Yardeni sub TADAE B 8.7) and interpret. (cf. Blau Lesh xlviii/xlix 216), dam. context.

swd_2 v. *swr_3*.

swh_1 v. *swt_2*.

swh_2 **Nab** word of unknown meaning in CIS ii 994[2].

swḥ v. *sḥ*.

swy v. *$šwy_1$*.

swyd v. *swyr*.

swyh **Pun** word of uncert. meaning in KAI 76A 4 (Sing. abs. or cstr.?; cf. however Lidzbarski Eph iii 231: = Plur. of *swt_2* :: **FR** 207: = Sing. of *swyt* with ending *-īt*); = veil, curtain?, cf. CIS i sub 166, Lidzbarski Handb 328, Cooke NSI p. 125f., FR 207 (cf. also Röllig KAI a.l.: *swyt* = clothing) :: Dérenbourg JA vii/iii 223: = corner, cella, room - cf. *swt_2*.

swyr **OffAr** Sing. emph. *swyr›* Aḥiq 88 (for the reading, cf. Driver AnOr xii 55 :: Grelot RB lxviii 181: l. *swyd›* = Sing. emph. of *swyd* (= shadow), cf. idem DAE p. 435; cf. also Cowl a.l., Joüon MUSJ xviii 85f.: l. *swyd›* or *swyr›* (= lair, (the lion's) den)) - ¶ subst. hiding-place, hidden place (cf. Driver AnOr xii 55); Gressmann ATAT 457: = cavern? (on this word, cf. also Lindenberger APA 60f., 229 n. 86).

swyt v. *swyh*.

swk v. *msk_3*.

swm (< Greek σῶμα, cf. Cantineau Gramm 156, Rosenthal Sprache 92, Milik DFD 311) - **Palm** Sing. abs./cstr. *swm* Syr xiv 184[2] (v. infra); + suff. 3 p.s.m. *swmh* SBS 48[4] (for Greek par., cf. Milik DFD 310, 311f.) - ¶ subst. body, corpse; *swm nkry* Syr xiv 184[2]: the corpse of a stranger (or: a strange corpse; meaning for both interpret. the same); *‹ml bswmh* SBS 48[4]: he worked with his own body (i.e. personally).

swms›l v. *›tml*.

sws_1 cf. Frah viii 5: swallow, v. also *byt_2* (*sws br byt›* = martin).

sws_2 v. *ss_1*.

swsh v. *ssh*.

$swsy_1$ v. *ssh*.

$swsy_2$ v. *ssh*.

swsgwn **JAr** Dupont-Sommer JKF i 207, 216 n. 16: the *swsgwn* in AMB 7[10] prob. = Sing. abs. of *swsgwn* (< pers.), prob. = scarlet colour, vermillion (improb. interpret., cf. Scholem JGM 86, Naveh & Shaked AMB a.l.: = magical name).

swp_1 **Hebr** NIPH Inf. cstr. *hswp* DJD ii 45[3] - ¶ verb NIPH to run out, to be finished; *‹d hswp dgn* DJD ii 45[3]: until the grain runs out.
v. *ysp*, *‹wp_1*.

swp_2 v. *sp_2*.

swpr v. *spr_2*.

swr$_1$ **Ph** YIPH Impf. 2 p.s.m. *tsr* KAI $10^{13f.}$ (reading uncert.) - **Pun** YIPH Inf. cstr. *sr* (in the combination *lsr*; for the form, cf. FR 166, 169) CIS i 4937^3, KAI 79^7 - ¶ verb YIPH to remove; + obj., *kl ʾš lsr t ʾbn z* KAI $79^{6ff.}$: everyone who shall remove this stone (cf. also FR 268(2), and cf. on this text Krahmalkov RSO lxi 75f.), cf. also KAI $10^{13f.}$, CIS i 4937^3.
v. *ksp$_2$*, *šr$_6$*.

swr$_2$ v. *šwr$_4$*.

swr$_3$ **Pun** the *swr* in the combination *bswr* in KAI 145^4 word of unknown meaning (for this reading, cf. Krahmalkov RSF iii 187 :: Krahmalkov RSF iii 175, 187f., 192, 200 (div. otherwise): *bswr* = Sing. cstr. of *bšr$_2$* (= kin) :: e.g. Lidzbarski Eph i 46, Cooke NSI p. 151, 154: l. *swb* (cf. Février Sem vi 18: l. *swb* = Sing. abs. of *swb* (= (circle >) celestial vault; cf. also v.d.Branden RSF i 166, 168) and Röllig KAI a.l.: l. *swb* = Sing. abs. of *swb*, *bswb* = round about) :: Clermont-Ganneau RAO iii 334 (n.2): l. *swd* (= assembly, company, secret) to be connected with root *ysd* (cf. also Halévy RS ix 274, 285) :: Berger MAI xxxvi/2, 144, 157: l. *ṣwr* = n.l. (Tyre), or = Sing. abs. of *ṣr$_1$*; for the problems, cf. also Chabot sub RES 2221).

swt$_1$ (< Akkad., cf. Winckler AltorForsch ii 76f., Zimmern Fremdw 8, Kaufman AIA 38) - **OffAr** Sing. emph. *swtʾ* KAI 228A 13 (:: Aggoula Syr lxii 63f.: = Sing. of *swt$_3$* (= incense > incense altar)) - ¶ subst. f. stele.
v. *sywʿt*.

swt$_2$ (or = *swh*?)- **Ph** Sing. abs. *swt* KAI 11, 24^8 (cf. e.g. Röllig KAI a.l., Gibson SSI iii p. 5 :: Sperling UF xx 333: = Sing. abs. of *swt$_4$* (< Akkad.; = a type of groats)) - ¶ subst. garment - cf. *swyh*.

swt$_3$ v. *swt$_1$*.

swt$_4$ v. *swt$_2$*.

sz v. *zt$_3$*, *mzzh*

sḥ **OldAr** the *sḥ* in KAI 222B 42, word(?) of unknown meaning (cf. Fitzmyer AIS 72, Donner KAI a.l.); cf. also Lipiński Stud 45: *sḥ* related to root *swḥ*= to sink into the ground, or *sḥy* = to be generous??

sḥb$_1$ **Mo** QAL (cf. e.g. Gibson SSI i p. 80 :: Michaud PA 38 n. 5: = HIPH) Impf. 1 p.s. *ʾsḥb* (or rather = + suff. 3 p.pl.m.? *ʾsḥb hm*; v. *hʾ$_1$*) KAI 181^{18}; + suff. 3 p.s.m. *ʾ[s]ḥbh* KAI $181^{12f.}$ - ¶ verb QAL to drag; + obj. + *lpny*, *wʾsḥb hm lpny kmš* KAI 181^{18}: and I dragged them before K. (cf. KAI $181^{12f.}$; for a discussion of the specific meaning, cf. also Lipiński Or xl 333f., Beeston JRAS '85, 145f.).
v. *ṣḥb*.

sḥb$_2$ **Pun** Sing. abs. *sḥb* CIS i 355^2, 3327^4 - ¶ subst. indicating function or title, meaning unknown; Slouschz TPI p. 350: poss. related to *shb*; Clermont-Ganneau sub RES 1575: or rather = lapsus for *sḥr$_2$*??

sḥy v. *sḥ*.
sḥp v. *sḥr₁*.
sḥq v. *šḥq₁*.
sḥr₁ **OffAr** Cowl a.l.: l. *sḥ[rt]* (= QAL Pf. 2 p.s.m. of *sḥr* = to go about) in Aḥiq 175 (cf. already Baneth OLZ '14, 352 (n. 1): = Pf. 1 p.s. of *sḥr*); cf. however Grelot RB lxviii 192, DAE p. 446 (n. b): l. *sḥ[pt]* (= QAL Pf. 1 p.s. of *sḥp*= to destroy; and Kottsieper SAS 221: = form of *sḥp* (= to cover) cf. also Lindenberger APA 179f.) - v.Soden Or xxxv 19f., xlvi 190: > Akkad., cf. Akkad. *musaøhḫiru* (= agent, deputy), highly uncert. interpret., cf. Landsberger SVT xvi 176ff.
v. *sḥr₂*.
sḥr₂ **Ph** m. Sing. abs. *sḥr* Mem Saidah 235[2] (diff. context, cf. Teixidor Mem Saidah 236, Elayi SCA 65) - **Pun** m. Sing. abs. *sḥr* CIS i 5993[2] (= TPI 165 = TPC 55); cstr.(?) *sḥr* RES 1229[2] (= CIS i 5967 = TPC 29; for the context, cf. Chabot sub RES 1930), TPI 174; f. Sing. cstr. (v. infra) *sḥrt* KAI 92 (= CIS i 5948 = TPC 10) - ¶ subst. (or QAL Part. act. of *sḥr₁*)peddler, merchant: CIS i 5993[2]; for the combination *sḥr ʿwr*, v. *ʿwr₄*, for the combination *sḥr qnh*, v. *qnh₁*; *sḥrt hqrt* in KAI 92 = the female merchant of the town?? (cf. e.g. Clermont-Ganneau RAO v 319f., Février sub CIS i 5948, Koch TH 73ff. n. 6), cf. however Lidzbarski Eph ii 175: *sḥrt* indicating some cultic function??, cf. Röllig KAI a.l.; cf. also Ferron Mus lxxix 435ff.: = sorceress, enchantress (less prob. interpret.); Dahood Bibl lx 434: = the seller of beams (*qrt* = Plur. abs. of *qrh₂* (= beam)); cf. also Février CIS i a.l.: or *sḥrt* = Sing. abs. followed by *qrt* used as a kind of subscription of this inscription (less prob. interpret.) -
v. *sḥb₂*.
sḥr₃ **OffAr** Sing. abs. *sḥr* Pers 18[2], 48[4], 52[3], 72[3], 92[4], 95[3], 113[3], etc.; emph. *sḥrʾ* Pers 19[3] (*[s]ḥrʾ*), 43[3], 44[3], 49[4], 50[2], 73[4], 112[4] - ¶ subst. m. prob. indicating some kind of bowl, plate (cf. R.A.Bowman Pers p. 49f., 91); for the etymology, cf. Millard JRAS '73, 64: < Akkad. *siḫḫaru* (*saḫḫaru*)?? (cf. also Kaufman AIA 91); Naveh & Shaked Or xlii 455 n. 70 favour a West-Sem. origin; cf. also R.A.Bowman Pers p. 49, 68: of Sem. origin (cf. also idem ibid. p. 91); Hinz NWAP 46, AIS 220: < Iran.? :: Altheim & Stiehl ASA 19: or *sḥr* related to root *shr₁* = to be round; cf. Pers 19[3], 44[3], 49[4], etc.; cf. also *sḥr znh rb* Pers 18[2]: this large plate (cf. *sḥrʾ znh rb*: Pers 43[3f.]); *sḥr znh zʿyr* (v. *zʿr₂*) Pers 48[4f.]: this small plate.
sḥr₄ v.Soden Or xlvi 193, AHW s.v. (cf. also CAD s.v.): *sḥr₄* = tower > Akkad. *saḫḫāru* (highly uncert. interpret.).
sḥrh₁ **Pun** Sing. (or Plur., v. infra) abs. (or cstr., v. infra) *sḥrt* RCL '66, 201[5] - ¶ subst. of unknown meaning; Garbini RSO xliii 12: = Sing. cstr. of *sḥrh₁* = black marmor (poss. interpret.); Sznycer GLECS xii/xiii 6:

= Plur. of *sḥrh$_2$* (= merchandise); Ferron Mus xcviii 53ff., 61: = Plur. abs. of *sḥrh$_3$* (= trade, business); Dupont-Sommer CRAI '68, 117, 126: = Sing. abs. of *sḥrh$_3$* (= trading > collective noun "merchants"; cf. also FR 207); Mahjoubi & Fantar RCL '66, 207, 209: = Sing./Plur. abs. of *sḥrh$_4$* (= the surroundings, the vicinity, the whole > the corporation).

sḥrh$_2$ v. *sḥrh$_1$*.

sḥrh$_3$ v. *sḥrh$_1$,$_4$*.

sḥrh$_4$ **OldAr** Sing. + suff. 1 p.s. *sḥrty* KAI 224$^{7f.}$ - ¶ subst. vicinity (cf. e.g. Dupont-Sommer BMB xiii 28, Donner KAI a.l., Fitzmyer AIS 111, Ribera AO ii 148 × Gibson SSI ii p. 47, 53: = *sḥrh$_3$* (= trading relations), cf. also Lemaire & Durand IAS 129)
v. *sḥrh$_1$*.

sḥrh$_5$ v. *sḥr$_2$*.

sḥth (< Egypt., cf. Bresciani & Kamil Herm p. 402, Grelot DAE p. 161 n. e) - **OffAr** Sing. abs. *sḥth* Herm 4^{12} - ¶ subst. neighbourhood, neighbours, friends.

sṭw v. *sṭwh*.

sṭwh (< Greek στοά) - **JAr** Sing. abs. (cf. Koopmans 219, Fitzmyer & Harrington MPAT p. 352 × Kutscher AH i/2, 67, Naveh SM a.l.: = Sing. emph. of *sṭw*< Greek στοά) *sṭwh* MPAT-A 16^2 (= Frey 981, SM 17) - ¶ subst. m. colonnade (cf. e.g. Sukenik ASPG 60 n. 2, Krauss REJ lxxxix 390f., Klein SeYi 98, Frey a.l., Fitzmyer & Harrington MPAT a.l., Naveh SM a.l. × Klein ZDPV li 136: or = plastered floor? × Epstein Tarbiz i 152, Kutscher AH i/2, 67: = stone bench (cf. also Naveh EI xx 306) - cf. *ʾsṭw*.

sṭm$_1$ **Palm** the *sṭm* and *sṭmʾ* in RTP 249, 407, 480, 525, 720, 752, 997 poss. = n.p., cf. Caquot RTP p. 161, 188, cf. however Gawlikowski TP 37f.: = Sing. cstr. resp. emph. of *sṭm$_1$* (= assembly) :: du Mesnil du Buisson TMP 543ff. (cf. also ibid. 34): = Sing. cstr. resp. emph. of *sṭm$_2$* (= coronation) < Greek στέμμα.

sṭm$_2$ v. *sṭm$_1$*.

sṭr$_1$ **OffAr** Qal (?) Pf. 3 p.s.m. *sṭr* ATNS 10a 4 (?, dam. context); 1 p.pl. *sṭrn* ATNS 2^1 (for the reading, cf. Shaked Or lvi 408, Porten & Yardeni sub TADAE B 8.9 :: Segal ATNS a.l.: l. *nṭrn* (= Qal Pf. 1 p.pl. of *nṭr$_1$* (= *nṣr$_1$*); reading of the context uncert.); Imper. pl.m. *sṭrw* Driv 7^7 (cf. Whitehead JNES xxxvii 133 n. 90: reading certain, but unclear on photograph due to fold in the skin, and cf. Porten & Yardeni sub TADAE A 6.10 :: Driv p. 66: = Paʿel Imper. pl.m. of *sṭr$_2$* (= to cut) :: Segert ArchOr xxxvi 167: l. *šṭrw* = Qal Imper. pl.m. of *šṭr$_1$*); Part. pass. s.m. abs. *sṭyr* ATNS 5^8; s.f. abs. *sṭyrh* ATNS 8^3 - ¶ verb Qal (?) to mark; *sṭrw bšntʾ zyly* Driv 7^7: mark them with my mark; Part. pass. marked, inscribed; *ʾmt ... sṭyrh ʿl šmy* ATNS 8^3: the slave-girl of ... marked with my name; *sṭyr bšnytʾ* ATNS 5^8: marked with the mark (said of a slave); less prob. to combine *sṭr$_1$* with *šṭr$_1$*, cf. Kaufman AIA 101 n. 352.

sṭr$_2$ v. *sṭr$_1$*.

sṭr$_3$ v. *šṭr$_3$*.

sybw Palm Sing. abs. *sybw* Ber iii 99[6] - ¶ subst. old age - cf. *ṭlyw*.

syg v. *šg'$_3$*.

sygl JAr Plur. abs. *sygly* Syr xlv 101[16] - ¶ subst. rush, cane (on this plant, cf. Löw AP 269); *byt sygly* Syr xlv 101[16]: plot of land grown with rushes (diff. and dam. context).

syd$_1$ Hebr Sing. abs. *syd* SM 75[4] - ¶ subst. plaster, lime.

syd$_2$ v. *šyd$_2$*.

syw't Pun Sing. abs. *syw't* KAI 141[4] - ¶ subst. of unknown meaning; Février BAr '51/52, 118: = inscribed stele, monument :: Röllig KAI a.l.: = tomb??

v. *ṣyw'n*.

sym v. *šym$_1$*.

symh JAr Sing. emph., cf. PEQ '38, 238[1]: σιμαθα (for the interpret., cf. Peters OLZ '40, 218f. :: Beyer ATTM 353: = Plur. emph. :: Kirk PEQ '38, 239: = n.p.?) - ¶ subst. f. treasure (on this text, cf. also Milik LA x 154f.).

synṭr (< Lat. *senator*, cf. FR 107.4(a), 208a) - **Pun** Sing. abs. *synṭr* CIS i 3404[3] - ¶ subst. m. senator; cf. also Polselli StudMagr xii 84.

sy' Palm PA'EL Pf. 3 p.s.m. *sy'* Inv x 44[6] - **JAr** PA'EL Pf. 3 p.s.m. *syy'* MPAT-A 34[2] (= SM 69) - ¶ verb PA'EL to help; + obj.: MPAT-A 34[2f.], cf. also *sy' tgry' bkl ṣbw klh* Inv x 44[6]: he has aided the merchants in every way.

syp$_1$ JAr Sing. emph. (or + suff. 3 p.s.m.) *syph* MPAT 53[4] - ¶ subst. sword; on this word, cf. Brown Bibl lxx 212.

syp$_2$ OffAr Sing. emph. *syp'* RES 1301[6] - ¶ subst. m. indication of function or title of unknown meaning; poss. interpret.: sword-bearer (cf. Lidzbarski Eph iii 26: or = maker of swords or merchant selling swords).

sk$_1$ OffAr Sing. abs. *sk* ATNS 42b 4; cf. Nisa-c 100+91[2], 394[3] (*sk'*), cf. also GIPP 63 - ¶ subst. sum, total (cf. Harmatta with Diakonov & Livshitz PaSb ii 147 n. 38); *bsk* ATNS 42b 4: in total (prob. interpret., context however dam.) - Puech RB xci 90: this subst. (Sing. abs. *sk*) in the combination *l' sk* = "absolutely not" in At xiv 56[1] (prob. interpret., cf. already Shaked with Naveh At xiv 56 n. 6 :: Naveh At xiv a.l. (div. otherwise): l. *skl* = PA'EL Pf. 3 p.s.m. of *skl$_3$* (= to abolish; cf. also Beyer ATTM 346: = to permit) :: Cross IEJ xxxiii 245f. (div. otherwise): l. *l'yt* (= *lyš$_2$*) + *l$_5$*).

sk$_2$ v. *msk$_3$*.

sk'$_1$ Pun QAL (?) Pf. 3 p.s.m. *sk'* KAI 151[3] - ¶ verb QAL (?) to die

(?, meaning derived from context, cf. Chabot sub Punica ivE 15, Röllig KAI a.l., FR 170; Chabot ibid.: or = adj. of unknown meaning??).

sk'$_2$ v. *smy$_1$*.

skh$_1$ v. *mskh.*

skh$_2$ (< Akkad., cf. Zimmern Fremdw 35, Kaufman AIA 91 (n. 308); uncert. interpret.) - **OffAr** (?) Sing. cstr. *skt* AUSS xi 126[2] (dam. and diff. context; :: Garbini JSS xix 163f.: = Sing. abs. of *skh$_3$* (= work in the fields) :: Shea AUSS xvi 217ff.: = n.l.) - ¶ subst. tip (sc. of plough), for this poss. interpret., cf. Cross AUSS xi a.l.; on the language of the ostracon, cf. also Aufrecht sub CAI 76.

skh$_3$ v. *skh$_2$*.

skwph v. *'yskwph.*

sky v. *msk$_3$*.

skyn **OffAr** Sing. abs. *skyn* Aḥiq 104; cstr. *skyn* Aḥiq 100; cf. Frah xiv 6 (*skyn'*) - ¶ subst. knife: Aḥiq 104; *skyn pm[yn]* Aḥiq 100: prob. = a two-edged knife (cf. Baneth OLZ '14, 298, Lindenberger APA 80, 238 n. 198; on this weapon, cf. also Couroyer RB lxxxiv 70f. n. 56).

skk v. *msk$_3$*.

skl$_1$ **OffAr** ITP Impf. 2 p.s.m. *tstkl* Aḥiq 147 - ¶ verb ITP to reflect, to consider; *'l tstkl kbyr* Aḥiq 147: do not consider what is (too) grand (for you), cf. Joüon MUSJ xviii 88 (*kbyr* used as substantivated adjective) :: Ginsberg ANET 429: gaze not overmuch (*kbyr* used as adverb) :: Margolis JQR ii 441, Seidel ZAW xxxii 296f., Gressmann ATAT 461: don't be overwise (*kbyr* used as adverb; cf. Cowl p. 243: be not overcrafty; cf. also Grelot RB lxviii 189, DAE p. 443) :: Kottsieper SAS 16, 221: do not act as a fool (cf. also Lindenberger APA 147f., 262 nn. 450-452).

skl$_2$ v. *nql.*

skl$_3$ **JAr** Naveh At xiv 56ff.: l. *skl* = PA'EL Pf. 3 p.s.m. of *skl$_3$* (= to abolish) in At xiv 56[1] (uncert. reading and interpret.) :: Cross IEJ xxxiii 245f. (div. otherwise): l. *l'yt* (= *lyš$_2$*)+ *l$_5$*.
v. *sk$_1$*.

skl$_5$ (< Akkad., cf. e.g. Kaufman AIA 103, Fales AECT p. 56) - **OffAr** Sing. abs. *skl* KAI 236 Rs 2 (= AECT 49) - ¶ subst. vizier.

skl$_6$ v. *kl$_1$*.

skn$_1$ v. *škn$_1$*.

skn$_2$ **OldCan** Sing. abs. *sú-ki-na* EA 362[69]; cstr. *sú-ki-ni* EA 256[9] (on these forms, cf. Rainey EA p. 88, 99, cf. also Alt FS Pedersen 7, Mulder VT xxii 44f., Garr DGSP 31) - **Ph** Sing. abs. *skn* KAI 1[2]; cstr. *skn* KAI 31[1,2], Kition D 17 (?, heavily dam. context, cf. Amadasi Kition a.l.: or = part of n.p.?), F 6 (= RPC 72[1]; cf. however v.d.Branden BO xx 99: = Sing. abs.), EpAn ix 5[1]; Plur. abs. *snm* (lapsus for *sknm*) KAI 1[2] - **Hebr** Sing. abs./cstr. *skn* NESE ii 49 no. 8 (twice; heavily dam. context of highly uncert. interpret., cf. also Millard with Mallowan Nimrud 598, Röllig NESE ii a.l.) - **OldAr** Sing. cstr. *skn* KAI 203 (cf. prob. also Aug xi 84 no. 32) - ¶ subst. governor, prefect; *skn qrtḥdšt* KAI 31^{1,2}: the governor of Q. (cf. EpAn ix 5^1, Kition F 6 (for this text, cf. also Masson & Sznycer RPC 70ff., Dupont-Sommer RDAC '74, 87, v.d.Branden BO xx 97f.) and poss. also D 17 (v. supra)); *skn [b]yt mlkh* KAI 203: the steward of the king's house; in EA 256^9, 362^{69} indicating the commissioner of Pharao with the Canaanite vazal-kings - cf. the formula *mlk bmlkm skn bs<k>nm* KAI 1^2: a king among kings, a governor among governors (for this kind of formula, cf. Demsky EI xiv 8ff., cf. also R.Kutscher & Wilcke ZA lxviii 126f.) - prob. not < Akkad., cf. e.g. Buccellati OA ii 253f., Rainey Or xxxv 428, UF iii 171, Donner sub KAI 203, Kümmel UF i 160, v.Schuler UF ii 224ff. n. 9 (> Hitt.), Mulder VT xxii 45ff. (esp 50), cf. also Rabin SH viii 395 :: e.g. Zimmern Fremdw 40 (with reserve), Kaufman AIA 97 (n. 337): < Akkad. :: Lipiński UF v 195ff., ZAH i 70, Gibson SSI iii p. 15: < Sum. < Akkad. - cf. *sgn*$_1$.

v. *škn*$_1$.

skr$_1$ **OldAr** HAPH/APH Impf. 3 p.s.m. *yhskr* KAI 224^3, *yskr* KAI 224^3 (cf. Dupont-Sommer BMB xiii 31, Fitzmyer AIS 106, 157 (cf. also id. Or xxxix 583), Segert AAG p. 120, Hoftijzer DA p. 293 n. 19 (cf. also Barr BSOAS xxxiv 394, Stefanovic COAI 155) :: Segert ArchOr xxxii 121, Greenfield ActOr xxix 9 n. 24, Degen AAG p. 19 n. 79: = lapsus for *yhskr* (cf. also Kaufman BiOr xxxiv 94, Garr DGSP 55) :: Ben-Chayyim Lesh xxxv 252: = PA'EL Impf. 3 p.s.m. :: Silverman JAOS xciv 270: *h*, *ʾ*, *zero* orthographical variants not indicating difference in pronunciation; cf. also Donner KAI a.l., Gibson SSI ii p. 52); 2 p.s.m. + suff. 3 p.pl.m. *thskrhm* KAI 224^2 (on this form, cf. e.g. Fitzmyer AIS 105f., Degen AAG p. 70, Gibson SSI ii p. 52; interpret. of *hm* as independent per pron. less prob.); 3 p.pl.m. *yhskrn* KAI 224^3; Inf. abs. *hskr* KAI 224^2 - **OffAr** QAL Pf. 3 p.pl.m. *skrw* Cowl 27^8 - ¶ verb QAL to stop up, + obj.; *brʾ zk skrw* Cowl 27^8: they stopped up this well - HAPH/APH to deliver, to hand over: KAI 224^2 - **1)** + obj. + *byd*, *thskrhm bydy* KAI 224^2: you must surrender them into my hands - **2)** + *l*$_5$, *yhskr lbry* KAI 224^3 he must surrender (them) to my son (cf. twice ibid.), cf. Greenfield FS Fitzmyer 49 - Puech EI xx 162*ff.: the *skr* in EI xx 161*, 162* = QAL Pf. 3 p.s.m. of *skr*$_1$ (poss. interpret.; or = Sing. abs. of *skr*$_6$ (= top, lid) ?) - cf. *sgr*.

v. *skr*$_6$, *smr*$_3$, *prr*$_1$.

skr$_2$ v. *zkr*$_1$.

skr$_3$ v. *škr*$_1$.

skr$_4$ v. *zkr*$_2$, *škn*$_1$.

skr$_5$ v. *škr*$_4$.

skr$_6$ **DA** Plur. cstr. *skry* i 8 (cf. Hoftijzer DA p. 194, TUAT ii 141, Kaufman BASOR ccxxxix 73, H. & M. Weippert ZDPV xcviii 92, 103, Wesselius BiOr xliv 594, 596, Smelik HDAI 79 :: e.g. Caquot & Lemaire Syr liv 196f., Garbini Hen i 176, 185, Delcor SVT xxxii 55, McCarter BASOR ccxxxix 51, 54, Levine JAOS ci 197, H.P. Müll ZAW xciv 218, Hackett BTDA 43, 95, 132, Sasson UF xvii 288, 296, Puech FS Grelot 27: = QAL Imper. s.f. of *skr$_1$* (= to close), cf. also Rofé SB 66 and Weinfeld Shn v/vi 143; on the problem cf. also Ringgren Memorial Seeligmann 94f.) - ¶ subst. bolt; *skry šmyn* DA i 8: the bolts of heaven - for this word, cf. Kaufman AIA 91 (n. 309): prob. not < Akkad. (on this word, cf. also Berger UF ii 339f.), cf. however Barth Nominalbildung 23, Zimmern Fremdw 30.
v. *mdr$_2$*, *skr$_1$*, *smr$_3$*.

skr$_7$ v. *škr$_5$*,

skrn v. *zkrn*.

sl$_1$ v. *dl$_1$*.

sl$_2$ v. *slh$_1$*.

sl$_3$ v. *slm$_2$*.

sl$_4$ v. *slm$_2$*.

slg v. *slq$_1$*.

slh$_1$ (or **sl$_2$**?) **Hatra** Aggoula Assur a.l.: l. poss. *slt›* (= Plur. emph. of *slh$_1$*/*sl$_2$* (= basket)) in Assur 21 ii 3 or l. *ḥlt›* (= Plur. emph. of *ḥlh$_7$* (= jug)), uncert. interpret. (if reading *ḥlt›* be right, poss. = Plur. emph. of *ḥlh$_6$*?).

slh$_2$ **JAr** *slh* MPAT-A 9, 22[8], 26[10], 27[3,4], 28[2], 30[3], 33[3], 35[1], 39[4] - ¶ exclamation: *selah*; for the use, v. *›mn$_5$*.
v. *‹l$_7$*.

slwky› **Palm** e.g. Lidzbarski Eph ii 309: the *slwky›* in CIS ii 3924[4] = Sing. emph. of *slwky* < Greek συλλοχία? (= the place where soldiers were collected in companies, cf. also CIS ii a.l.), less prob. interpret., cf. Lidzbarski Handb 329, Cantineau sub Inv ix 6: = Greek Σελευκία; for this problem, cf. also Rostovtzeff Mélanges Glotz 796f., Gawlikowski Syr lx 63 n. 57.

sly **Pun** Rocco StudMagr vii 12, 14: l. *sl* in StudMagr vii 12[3] (= QAL Imper. pl.m. of *sly* (= to depreciate)), highly uncert. reading and interpret.

slyt v.Soden Or xlvi 193 (cf. idem AHW s.v. *salītu*) > Akkad. *salītu* = (fishing) net (uncert. interpret.; cf. also CAD s.v.).

slkw v. *srqwt*

slm$_1$ **Pun** Sing. cstr. *slm* CIS i 3427[3] (for the reading, cf. Dussaud CRAI '44, 392f., Février sub CIS i 5601 :: Chabot sub CIS i 3427: or l. *›lm*? (relation with *‹lm$_5$* highly uncert.)), 5601[4] - ¶ subst. castrator; *slm h‹glm* CIS i 5601[4f.]: castrator of the calves (cf. CIS i 3427[3]).

slm$_2$ **Pun** word of unknown meaning in KAI 138[5] in the combination *bkt‘b slm* (v. also *ktb$_2$*), cf. Sznycer Sem xxx 40f. :: Février Sem ii 26: = variant of *šlm$_6$* (= perfect) :: Röllig KAI a.l.: l. poss. *ṣlm* (= Sing. abs./cstr. of *ṣlm$_1$*) :: Lidzbarski Eph iii 288f.: *slm* poss. = Plur. abs. of *sl$_3$* (meaning unknown) :: Levi Della Vida RSO xxxix 309: prob. = Sing. + suff. 3 p.s.m. of *sl$_4$*= palisade or entrance, way, place :: Dussaud BAr '14, 620: = part of n.p.

slm$_3$ v. *bslq’*.

slm$_4$ v. *šlm$_2$*

slmh **Ph** Sing. (?) abs. *slmt* CIS ii 88[4] (for the difficulties of the reading, cf. Amadasi sub Kition F 1); cstr. *slmt* CIS i 88[5] (prob. reading, cf. Amadasi sub Kition F 1) - ¶ subst. stairs (cf. also v.d.Branden FS Rinaldi 66: = "entrée à gradins").
v. *bslq’*.

sl‘ **Hebr** Sing. abs. *sl‘* EI xx 256[6,7]; Plur. abs. *sl‘ym* DJD ii 30[21], *sl‘[yn]* DJD ii 46[8] (reading uncert.) - **Nab** Plur. abs. *sl‘n* CIS ii 211[5] (for the reading, cf. J 11), J 109[2,3] (= CIS ii 298; reading highly uncert., cf. RES 1187), *sl‘yn* CIS ii 198[9], 199[8], 200[7,8,9], 205[9], 206[7], 209[8], 212[8], 217[11], 224[12], J 5[9], 38[8], MPAT 64 iii 2 (*[sl]‘yn*) - **Palm** Sing. emph. *sl‘’* Sem xxxvi 89[6] (highly uncert. reading, cf. Gawlikowksi Sem xxxvi 92); Plur. abs. *sl‘n* Syr xvii 353[11], *sl‘yn* Sem xxxvi 89[4,7], Inv x 13[6] (*sl‘y[n]*, for the uncert. reading, cf. Milik DFD 147) - **JAr** Plur. abs. *sl‘yn* MPAT 43[5] (*sl‘[yn]*), 51[6], 52[8], IEJ xxxvi 206[5] (*sl[‘]yn*; diff. reading; for the context, cf. Broshi & Qimron IEJ xxxvi 210) - ¶ subst. f. certain coin; in the Nab. texts = Nab. drachme, cf. CIS ii sub 198; in the J.Ar. and Hebr. texts = tetradrachme, cf. Milik RB lxii 253, Ben-David PEQ '66, 168, '68, 145ff., '71, 109ff., '78, 28, cf. also Meshorer Proc v CJS i 84ff. (Hebrew); for the problems in the Palm. text Sem xxxvi 89, cf. Gawlikowksi Sem xxxvi 93ff. - *ksp zwzyn šb‘yn wtmnyh dy hmwn sl‘yn tš‘ ‘šrh wtql ḥd* MPAT 52[7f.]: the sum of 78 *zuzin* equivalent to 19 *selas* and one shekel (on this text, cf. also Milik Bibl xxxviii 262); *ksp zwzyn dy hmwn tmn[y]’ wsl‘yn trtn* MPAT 51[5f.]: the sum of 8 *zuzin* equivalent to two *selas* (for the reading, v. *šmn$_4$*) - for the coin system, cf. also Babelon SDB v 1358ff.

slq$_1$ **OldAr** QAL Impf. 3 p.s.m. *ysq* KAI 224[14,15,16]; 3 p.pl.m. *ysqn* KAI 222A 5, C 4 -**OffAr** QAL Pf. 3 p.s.m. *slq* HDS 9[1] (*s[l]q*; cf. Caquot HDS 15, Lipiński Stud 79, WGAV 375 × Fales AION xxviii 280ff.: = QAL Part. act. m. s. abs.); Impf. 3 p.s.m. *yslq* FUF xxxv 173[10]; Inf. *mslq* Krael 9[15], *mnsq* Krael 6[10] (*[m]nsq*),[13] (for the reading and the *scriptio anterior mnsg*, cf. Porten with Shaked Or lvi 410, Szubin & Porten BASOR cclxix 33); PA‘EL Pf. 3 p.s.m. *slq* Cowl 81[15] (cf. Grelot DAE p. 108 n. o); APH Pf. 3 p.pl.m. *’syqw* BSh 5[2] (diff. reading, cf. Naveh BSh a.l., Shn i 193); cf. Nisa-c 223b 2 (*’sqw*; cf. Diakonov &

Livshitz PaSb ii 140 (n. 16) :: Gignoux GIPP 47: *ʾsqw* = heating) - **Palm** QAL Pf. 3 p.s.m. *slq* CIS ii 3960[6], Inv x 29[4], 44[5], Syr xiv 177[5]; 3 p.s.f. *slqt* Inv x 81[4], 90[3], SBS 45[8] (*[sl]qt*; Greek par. παραγενομέν[ην]), Syr xix 74[2]; 3 p.pl.m. *slqw* CIS ii 3948[2] (Greek par. [ἀ]ναβάντε[ς]), *slq* CIS ii 3916[2], Inv x 29[3]; APH Pf. 3 p.s.m. *ʾsq* CIS ii 3936[4], Syr vii 129[4]; 3 p.pl.m. *ʾsqw* CIS ii 3913 i 5 (cf. e.g. Sachau ZDMG xxxvii 564, Cooke NSI p. 333, Teixidor Sem xxxiv 99 n. 247 × APH pass. Pf. 3 p.pl.m. (with f. subject), cf. Ben-Chayyim EI i 137 (n. 3a) :: Cantineau Gramm 90, Rosenthal Sprache 17 n. 5, 58: = APH pass. Pf. 3 p.pl.f.; Greek par. ἀνελήμφθη); APH pass. Part. s.m. abs. *msq* CIS ii 3913 i 8 - **JAr** QAL Pf. 1 p.s. *slqt* MPAT 49 i 10; 3 p.pl.f. *slqh* AMB 7[14] (for the form, cf. Scholem JGM 86, Naveh & Shaked AMB a.l. :: Dupont-Sommer JKF i 208: = QAL Part. s.m. emph., cf. also Beyer ATTM 372f.); HAPH/APH Pf. 3 p.s.m. *ʾsq* MPAT 68[5] (cf. e.g. E.Rosenthal IEJ xxiii 73, 77, Naveh Qadm vi 116, Tzaferis At vii 63, Beyer ATTM 347, 646 :: Fitzmyer & Harrington MPAT a.l.: = lapsus for *ʾsqt* = APH Pf. 1 p.s.); 1 p.s. *hsqt* IEJ xl 142[4], 144[8] - ¶ verb QAL to go, to go up; in FuF xxxv 173[10] poss. followed by n.l. - **1)** + *b*$_2$, *slq bhn ʿqly* Inv x 44[5]: O. has gone up together with them (in SbPAW '19, 1050[4] context uncert.: *b* = against??) - **2)** + *b*$_2$ + specification, *slq bhwn rš šyrʾ nšʾ* Inv x 29[4]: N. has gone up with them as leader of the caravan - **3)** + *l*$_5$ + *b*$_2$, *lrqyʿh ... slqh bsṭr krsyh ...* AMB 7[14f.]: may they rise up to the Heavens next to the Throne ... (v. *rqyʿ*; on this text, cf. also Levine with Neusner HJB v 361) - **4)** + *mn*$_5$, *ʾyš zy s[l]q mn mt ʾkdh* HDS 9[1f.]: someone who comes (v. supra) from the land of A.; *tgryʾ dy slq mn krkʾ* Inv x 29[3]: the merchants who have come from K. (cf. Inv x 90[3], SBS 45[8f.]) - **5)** + *mn*$_5$ + *l*$_5$, *wslqt mn tmn lmṣdʾ* MPAT 49 i 10: and I went up from there to M. - **6)** + *mn*$_5$ + *ʿm*$_4$ (or: + *ʿm*$_4$ + *mn*$_5$), *šyrtʾ dy slqt ʿmh mn krk* Inv x 81[4f.]: the caravan which went up with him from K. (cf. CIS ii 3916[2f.], 3948[2f.], Syr xix 74[2]) - **7)** + *ʿl*$_7$, *ysq ʿl lbk* KAI 224[14]: it (i.e. the idea) will come to your mind (cf. KAI 224[15,16]; cf. Greenfield FS Fitzmyer 50) - **8)** + *ʿm*$_4$ (with): CIS ii 3960[6f.] - PAʿEL to settle, to dismiss with payment: Cowl 81[15] (for the context, v. *ʾpn*) - APH to bring up, to lead; *ytkynt ʿl ʾsqw* Nisa-c 223b 1f.: it will be prepared (v. *kwn*$_2$) for rousing (i.e. for heating up (cf. Diakonov & Livshitz PaSb ii 140); uncert. interpret., diff. context) - **1)** + obj., *ʾsq šyrtʾ* CIS ii 3936[4]: he brought up the caravan; cf. IEJ xl 142[4]; cf. also *ʾsyqw mn ʿbwr* BSh 5[2]: they brought from the corn (for the interpret., cf. also Naveh BSh i p. 80 n. 16) - **2)** + obj. + *l*$_5$, *ʾsq ḥmrʾ ʿtyqʾ lkmryʾ* Syr vii 129[4f.]: he brought (i.e. he offered) old wine to the priests - **3)** + *b*$_2$, *bnmwsʾ ... lʾ ʾsqw* CIS ii 3913 i 4f.: they did not introduce (it) in the law (v. supra) - **4)** + *l*$_5$, *wʾsq lmtty* MPAT 68[5f.]: and he brought (back) M. (i.e. his bones) - **5)** + *ʿl*$_7$, IEJ xl 144[8] (dam. context) - APH

pass. to be brought up, to be introduced; *md‘m dy l> msq bnmws>* CIS ii 3913 i 8: anything that was not introduced in the law - > Akkad. *salāqu* = to go up, cf. v.Soden Or xxxvii 266, xlvi 194 (cf. idem AHW s.v. *salāqu* II, cf. also CAD *salāqu* B) - a form of this root (*slq*) in Assur 11 ii 4 (Aggoula Assur a.l.: = QAL Pf. 3 p.s.m., *slq bh* = he will raise him (uncert. interpret., diff. context)).
v. *qpyls*.

slq$_2$ (< Egypt., cf. Grelot RB lxxviii 528ff., DAE p. 194 n. m) - **OffAr** Sing. abs. *slq* Cowl 15^{16}, Krael 7^{18} - ¶ subst. wicker (cf. Grelot RB lxxviii 528ff., DAE p. 194 (n. m), 235, RB xcvii 273, Porten & Greenfield JEAS p. 20, 55, Delsman TUAT i 261 :: Reider JQR xliv 340: = *slq$_3$* (= well-boiled vegetables, herbs)); *pq* 1 *slq* Cowl 15^{16}: one wicker tray (for Krael 7^{18}, v. also *rmn$_2$*) - on this word, cf. also Fitzmyer FS Albright ii 157, WA 259.

slq$_3$ **OffAr** cf. Frah v 8 (*slk>*), for the reading, cf. Nyberg FP 44, 68: = beet; Zadok WO xii 200: *slq* indicating a kind of vegetable/herb > Akkad. *silqu* (= 'Mangelwurzel').
v. *slq$_2$*.

slt v. *pslh*.

sm v. *sm>*.

sm> **Hatra** Sing. abs. *sm>* 200^5 (cf. Milik DFD 408, Teixidor Sumer xxi 89*, cf. also Caquot Syr xli 270 :: Caquot ibid.: or = n.p.? :: Safar Sumer xviii 61: = Sing. emph. of *sm* (= healing, recovery)); emph. *smy>* 3^2, 56^2, 65^6 (for the reading of the context, cf. Aggoula MUSJ xlvii 29f., Vattioni IH a.l. :: Milik DFD 407: = Dual cstr.? :: Safar Sumer xi 9: = n.d.), 79^{10} (:: Altheim & Stiehl AAW iv 246, 249: = Plur. emph.), 200^3 (diff. reading, cf. Milik DFD 405f., Vattioni IH a.l. :: Safar Sumer xviii 60: l. *??qy>*, Caquot Syr xli 269f.: l. *‘qy[b]>* (= n.p.), Teixidor Sumer xxi 89*: l. poss. *lqym* = APH Impf. 3 p.s.m. of *qwm$_1$*), 201^1, 209^1, 213^4, 235^1, 338^2 (for *smy>*, v. also infra); Plur. emph. *smyt>* 52^5, 74^5, 75^2, 82^5, 151^2 (for *smyt>*, v. also infra) - ¶ subst. standard, passim (for the context of Hatra 3^2, v. *‘qb*; cf. poss. also Hatra $200^{3f.}$); *smy> dmškn>* Hatra 79^{10}: the standard of the shrine (v. however *mškn$_3$*); *smy> dy mrtn* Hatra 338^2: the standard of our lady; *smy> dy br mryn* Hatra 209^1: the standard of the son of our lords; *smy> dy bny >qlt> dy br mryn* Hatra 280: the standard of the followers (?, v. *>qlt*) of the son of our lords; the reading *smy> [d]...* in Hatra $201^{1f.}$ (cf. Aggoula MUSJ xlvii 42) highly uncert.; for the context, v. *mgn$_2$*; cf. also the following combinations, *mrn wmrtn wbr mryn >lt wsmyt> klhwn* Hatra $52^{4f.}$: our lord, our lady, the son of our lords, Allât and all the standards/*insignia* (cf. Hatra $75^{1f.}$, $82^{4f.}$, $151^{1f.}$); *mrn wgdh wšmš wmr>th wbrh wsmyt> kwlhwn* Hatra $74^{4ff.}$: our lord and his fortune (v. *gd$_1$*) and Shamash and his lady and his son and all the *insignia*/standards (v. also *mr*ʾ); *mrn wmrtn wbr mryn wsmyʾ wgndʾ dʿmh* Hatra 235[1]: our lord and our lady and the son of our lords and the standard and the fortune of his people; *rb smyʾ* Hatra 56[2]: master of the standard, holder of the standard (exact meaning of this function unknown; cf. Caquot Syr xxxii 57f., 63 :: Safar Sumer ix 248 n. 45: = keeper, guardian of the temple of Nashr (cf. also Safar Sumer ix 246 n. 40: *smyʾ* = eagle deity, *smytʾ*= his female consort)), cf. also Caquot Syr xli 269f.: the *br smyʾ* in Hatra 200[1] prob. lapsus for *rb smyʾ* (improb. interpret., cf. Teixidor Sumer xxi 88f., Milik DFD 405, Vattioni IH a.l., Abbadi PIH 11 (n. 1): *br smyʾ* = n.p. :: Safar Sumer xviii 60 (n. 66): *br smyʾ* = son of (god) *smyʾ* or = belonging to the temple of *smyʾ*); for the standards, cf. e.g. also Caquot Syr xxxii 59ff., du Mesnil du Buisson TMP 425ff., Seyrig Syr xxxvii 233ff., Hoftijzer RelAr 56f., Milik DFD 404ff., Tubach ISS 184ff.; diff. etymology, poss. influence of Greek words like σῆμα, σημεῖον, σημεία/σημαία on orig. Sem. word < root *swm*, cf. also Jastrow s.v. *symʾ* III, Caquot Syr xxxii 61 :: explicit derivation of *smʾ* <σῆμα (cf. Teixidor Sumer xxi 89*) and of *smyʾ* < σημεῖον (cf. Caquot Syr xxxii 63) or < σημεία/σημαία; on this word, cf. also du Mesnil du Buisson TMP 425f. (n. 2), Tubach ISS 190f.; cf. *smyh*.

smdh v. smr_1.

smdr **Hebr** Sing. abs. *smdr* SSI i p. 18C (for the reading, cf. Yadin Hazor ii p. 74, ad Pl. xcv, clxxi, HazorSL 190 n. 4, Gibson SSI i a.l. (cf. also Altenbauer EI x 64ff.) :: Aharoni & AmIran. Hazor ii p. 74 n. 25: l. *smrh* = n.p. or n.g. (cf. also de Vaux RB lxix 475, Diringer & Brock FS Thomas 44f.)) - ¶ subst. blossom of the vine, unripe/tender grape (cf. Yadin Hazor ii 74, HazorSL 190 n. 4), cf. also Gibson SSI i p. 19: > certain variety of wine (cf. also v.Selms JNSL iii 77); on this word, cf. also Altenbauer EI x 64ff.).

smh v. smy_1.

smy$_1$ (or **smh**??)- **OffAr** PA ʿEL Part. s.m. abs. *msmh* Aḥiq 88 - ¶ verb PA ʿEL meaning uncert., poss. interpret.: to hunt (cf. Driver AnOr xii 55, Greenfield IEJ xix 205 (n. 28: to strike), Kottsieper SAS 221 (cf. also Joüon MUSJ xviii 85, Ginsberg ANET 428: to lie in wait), cf. however Grelot RB lxviii 181 n. 9, DAE p. 435 n. f: = to scent, to find out (cf. also Lindenberger APA 60, 229 n. 82) :: Cowl a.l.: = to devour? :: Epstein ZAW xxxiii 311: = to long for, to desire :: Gressmann ATAT 457: = to wait for, poss. lapsus for *mskʾ* = PA ʿEL Part. s.m. abs. of *skʾ*$_2$ (= to wait for)) - a form (Part.) of this root prob. in Aḥiq 87: *msm[* .

smy$_2$ v. *smʾ*.

smyd **OffAr**, cf. Gignoux GIPP 63: *smyd* (= flour), abbrev. *s* in Nisa-texts.

smyh **Palm** Sing. emph. *smyt*ʾ CIS ii 3902[1] (Greek par. σίγνον) - ¶ subst. image, statue; *smyt*ʾ *dy ksp*ʾ CIS ii 3902[1], Greek par. τὸ σίγνον ἀργυροῦν - diff. etymology (v. also the remarks sub *sm*ʾ), cf. also du Mesnil du Buisson RAA xi 80 n. 6: < Greek σημαία :: Cantineau Gramm 156, Rosenthal Sprache 91: < σημεῖον :: Caquot Syr xxxii 61: or < Greek σημεῖα = Plur. of σημεῖον - Milik DFD 180: l. *smy[t]* (= Sing. cstr.) in Inv xi 6[4] (reading highly uncert., cf. Teixidor Inv xi a.l.) - cf. *sm*ʾ.

smyk$_1$ **Pun** Levi Della Vida Or xxxiii 4, 6f., 14, Amadasi IPT 132: l. poss. *[s]myk*ʾ (= Plur. cstr. of *smyk$_1$*) or l. poss. *[t]myk*ʾ (= Plur. cstr. of *tmyk*) in Trip 51[1]; meaning derived from context: account (diff. and uncert. context).

smyk$_2$ **OffAr** Sing. m. abs. *smyk* ATNS 68 i 7 - ¶ adj. (or Part. pass. of *smk$_1$*?)near (to), adjacent (to); *smyk* ʿ*l* ʾ*gm*ʾ ATNS 68 i 7: near to the marsh (dam. context).

smypr (< Greek σημειοφόρος or σημαιοφόρος, cf. J p. 217f.) - **Nab** Sing. emph. *smypr*ʾ J 60 (reading uncert., cf. RES 1173 :: CIS ii sub 268: l. *qtrwd*ʾ = Sing. emph. of *qtrwd* < Greek κιθαρῳδή = one who plays and sings to the cithara) - ¶ subst. m. standard-bearer (cf. also Negev RB lxxxiii 226f.).

smk$_1$ **OffAr** QAL Inf. *msmk* Krael 9[14] - ¶ verb QAL to prop. up; + obj.: Krael 9[14] - v.Soden Or xlvi 194: > Akkad. D-form = to support (cf. also idem AHW s.v. *samāku* D2; highly uncert. interpret., cf. also CAD s.v. *samāku* 3b).
v. *smyk$_2$*.

smk$_2$ **Nab** Sing. emph. *smk*ʾ CIS ii 350[2] - **Palm** Sing. emph. *smk*ʾ InscrP 10[1] (cf. Milik DFD 149, Gawlikowski TP 93 :: Cantineau InscrP a.l.: = Sing. emph. of *smk$_3$* (= support; i.e. base of an altar), Inv xii 45[1] (reading however highly uncert., cf. Teixidor Sem xxx 61), SBS 21, RTP 694 (*smk[*ʾ*]*), 695 (*smk[*ʾ*]*), 696, 697, 698 - ¶ subst. m. - **1)** banquet-room: InscrP 10[1], Inv xii 45[1] (v. however supra), SBS 21 - **2)** banquet: RTP 694-698 (cf. Caquot RTP p. 146f.); *gnt smk*ʾ CIS ii 350[2]: (walled) garden used for funeral banquet (v. also *gnh$_1$*) - for this word, cf. also Lipiński Stud 68ff., EI xx 132*, Gawlikowski TP 110.

smk$_3$ v. *smk$_2$*.

smksl (< Lib.??, cf. Berthier & Charlier Hofra p. 75) - **Pun** Sing. abs. *smksl* Hofra 86[3] - ¶ subst. meaning unknown, poss. indication of function or title.

sml$_1$ **Ph** m. Sing. abs. *sml* KAI 26C iv 18, 41[1], 43[2], CIS i 88[2] (= Kition F 1), 91[1], RES 1213[3], Kition A 29[2], 30[2], BMB xviii 106[1], RSF i 130[2], PW 84[1]; cstr. *sml* KAI 12[3], 26C iv 15, 19, Mus li 286[2] (v. infra),[6] (?, dam. context); Plur. abs. *smlm* KAI 40[3], CIS i 88[5] (= Kition F 1), RES 827; f. Sing. abs. *smlt* KAI 33[2] (= Kition A 1) - **Pun** Sing. cstr. *sml*

KAI 145[7] (diff. and dam. context, cf. e.g. Cooke NSI p. 154, Février Sem vi 21, Röllig KAI a.l., v.d.Branden RSF i 167, 169 :: Krahmalkov RSF iii 172f., 204 (div. otherwise): l. *sm* = QAL Imper. s.m. of *šm*ʿ$_1$) - ¶ subst. m. statue (of a man/male deity), f. statue (of a woman/female deity): passim; *mš lnʿm* (v. *mʾš*$_1$) *hsml z mš* KAI 43[1f.]: votive effigy for good fortune. This statue is my (?, v. *mʾš*$_1$) votive effigy ...; *[yt]t sml mš z bnḥšt* Mus li 286[2]: I have given this statue being a votive donation in bronze; in *sml bʿl* (KAI 12[3f.]) *sml* prob. = image, *sml bʿl* is indication of Baʿal's consort (the image of Baʿal), cf. Lidzbarski OLZ '27, 458, Röllig KAI a.l. :: Dussaud Syr vi 272f. - on this word, cf. Dohmen ZAW xcvi 263ff.
v. *dmw*, *smr*$_2$.

sml$_2$ v. *šml*$_1$.

smlh v. *sml*$_1$.

smly v. *šmly*.

smnh **OffAr** the *smnh* in LidzbAss 5[5] prob. = name of month < Akkad. :: Lipiński Stud 104f.: = eight (< Akkad.), used as name of month (on the subject, cf. also Fales sub AECT 50) - cf. *šmn*$_4$.

smr$_1$ **Ph** QAL (?, or rather = PIʿEL?, cf. v.d.Branden OA iii 259) Pf. 1 p.s. *smrt* KAI 43[13] (for this reading, cf. e.g. Clermont-Ganneau Et ii 175, Honeyman JEA xxvi 58, Röllig KAI a.l., Gibson SSI iii p. 136, 141 :: Lidzbarski Handb 329, KI sub 36, Harr 141: l. *smdt* = Sing. cstr. of *smdh* (= *ṣmdh*)), *smdt bqr* = a pair/span of oxen (cf. also Cooke NSI p. 83, 87, Friedr 47) - ¶ verb to nail; *smrt bqr* KAI 43[13]: I nailed on the wall (diff. context, v. supra and *qr*$_1$) - Dupont-Sommer JKF i 203: the *smr* in AMB 7[9] = QAL/PAʿEL Imper. s.m. of *smr*$_1$ (improb. interpret., cf. Scholem JGM 186, Naveh & Shaked AMB a.l.: = part of magical name).
v. *smr*$_2$.

smr$_2$ **Samal** Sing. abs. *smr* KAI 25[1] (:: e.g. Koopmans 17: = Sing. emph.; on the problem, cf. Dion p. 135ff., cf. however Fitzmyer CBQ xxxviii 99; :: Lipiński BiOr xxxiii 231: = orthographical variant of *smrh* (= Sing. abs.) = nail :: Swiggers Or li 252f.: = dialectal form of *sml*$_1$)- ¶ subst. of uncert. meaning; Galling BASOR cxix 16ff. (cf. already v Luschan AS v 102): = sceptre; cf. also Dupont-Sommer RHR cxxxiii 21ff., Dion p. 26, 131: = shaft? (cf. H.P.Müller ZAW xciv 224: = lance?), Sader EAS 160 (n. 25): ring :: Landsberger Samʾal 42 n. 102: = whip?? :: Gibson SSI iii p. 40: = object nailed on, nailed ornament :: Lemaire Syr lxvii 323ff.: = *smr*$_1$ (= nail, peg > amulet, talisman) :: Fales VO v 78ff.: poss. = sheath, scabbard (on this word, cf. also Kaufman AIA 152f., Caquot & Lemaire Syr liv 197).
v. *smr*$_3$.

smr$_3$ **DA** Sing. + suff. 2 p.s.f. *smrky* i 9 (cf. Hoftijzer DA a.l., TUAT ii 141, Rofé SB 66, Garbini Hen i 176, 185 :: Caquot & Lemaire Syr liv 196f.: = Sing. + suff. 2 p.s.f. of *smr*$_2$ (= shaft ?; cf. also H.P.Müller ZAW xciv 218, 224: = lance?) :: Sasson PEQ '85 102f., UF xvii 288, 291, 297f.: = darkness (less prob. etymology) :: Hackett BTDA 25, 29, 45, 94: l. *skrky* (= Sing. + suff. 2 p.s.f. of *skr*$_6$) :: Wesselius BiOr xliv 594, 596: l. *skrky* = QAL/PI ʿEL Pf. 3 p.s.m. of *skr*$_1$+ suff. 2 p.s. f. or QAL Part. act. s.m. + suff. 2 p.s. f. :: McCarter BASOR ccxxxix 51, 54, Levine JAOS ci 197, 198, Lemaire CRAI '85, 280: l. poss. *smr* (= Sing. abs. of *smr*$_4$ (= radiance)) + *ky* (for the poss. interpret. of *smr* as *smr*$_4$, cf. also H. & M. Weippert ZDPV xcviii 103, Puech BAT 356, 361, FS Grelot 17, 21f., 27)) - ¶ subst. dread; *w*ʾ*[l] smrky thby* DA i 9: do not spread the dread of you - on this word, cf. also H. & M. Weippert ZDPV xcviii 93 n. 77.

smr$_4$ v. *smr*$_3$.

smrh v. *smr*$_2$.

smš v. *šmš*$_2$.

sngr v. *srwky*.

snʾ **OffAr** Sing. emph. *sny*ʾ Aḥiq 165, 166 - ¶ subst. m. bramble (cf. also Lindenberger APA 167f.: prob. = blackberry).

snb (< Akkad., cf. Zimmern Fremdw 65, Kaufman AIA 103, cf. also Fales AECT p. 60f., VO v 77; cf. also on the etymology Rundgren JCS ix 29f.) - **Samal** Sing. cstr. *snb* KAI 215[6] (cf. Ginsberg JAOS lxii 235f. (n. 34), Dion p. 116: *w*ʾ*snb*= *w*ʾ (= variant of *w*, v. *w*$_2$)+ *snb* :: Lidzbarski Handb 329, Cooke NSI p. 176: *w*ʾ*snb* = *w* + ʾ*snb* (= variant of *snb*), cf. also e.g. Rundgren JCS ix 29, Donner KAI a.l., Dupont-Sommer AH i/2, 2, Degen ZDMG cxix 174f., Gibson SSI ii p. 83, Segert AAG p. 137, 527, Garr DGSP 47f. (on this problem, cf. also Koopmans 72)) - **OffAr** Sing. cstr. *snb* CIS ii 7a (cf. e.g. CIS ii a.l., Rundgren JCS ix 29, Kaufman AIA 103 :: Driver AnOr xii 54, Dupont-Sommer MAI xiv/2, 75: pro *snb* + worddivider l. *snby* (= *šnby*)) - ¶ subst. two thirds; *snb* ʾ*rq*ʾ CIS ii 7a: two thirds of the land; for the diff. context of KAI 215[6], v. *mšt*$_1$; cf. *šnby*.

snby v. *snb*.

snh (< Akkad., cf. Fales AECT p. 56, 137) - **OffAr** Sing. abs. *snh* CIS ii 38[1] (= Del 21; for the reading, cf. Fales sub AECT 3) - ¶ subst. deputy.

snq > Akkad. *sanāqu* (= to need, to have need), cf. v.Soden Or xxxvii 265, xlvi 194, AHW s.v. *sanāqu* II, Kaufman AIA 93 n. 316, CAD s.v. *sanāqu* B.

snqlṭyq (< Greek συγκλητικός, cf. Cantineau Gramm 156, Rosenthal Sprache 92) - **Palm** Sing. emph. *snqlṭyq*ʾ CIS ii 3944[2], Inscr P 31[1] (cf. Cantineau Inscr P a.l., Syr xii 118, Milik DFD 270 :: Cantineau sub Inv ix 28: l. *sqlṭyq*ʾ (prob. misprint)), *sqlṭyq*ʾ CIS ii 4202 - ¶ subst. m.

senator - for the instances in question, cf. Ingholt PBP 121f.

ss_1 **OldCan** Plur. abs. *sú-ú[-sí-ma]* EA 263[25] (cf. Rainey EA p. 89) - **Ph** Sing. abs. *ss* KAI 26A i 7 - **Hebr** Sing. abs. *sws*TA-H 111[5] (dam. context) - ¶ subst. m. horse; cf. also *ssh* (for the relation between ss_1 and *ssh*, cf. Driv p. 73 n. 2).
v. *ssh*.

ss_2 **OldAr** Sing. abs. *ss* KAI 222A 31 - **OffAr** Sing. emph. *ss›* Aḥiq 184, 186 - ¶ subst. f. moth; for the context of KAI 222A 31, cf. Tawil BASOR ccxxv 62; in Aḥiq 184, 186 diff. and heavily dam. context (cf. also Gressmann ATAT 462, Driver JRAS '32, 89, Lindenberger APA 183) - on this word, cf. also Masson RPAE 93f.
v. *ssh*.

ss_3 **DA** Sing. abs. *ss* i 9 - ¶ subst. f. (v. $ḥrp_1$) swift (?, cf. Hoftijzer DA a.l.; cf. also Delcor SVT xxxii 56, H. & M. Weippert ZDPV xcviii 94 (n. 80, 83)); in the comb. *ss ‹gr* a certain type of migrant bird related to the swift (Caquot & Lemaire Syr liv 198: *ss ‹gr* = sparrow).

ssh **DA** m. Sing. abs. *ssh* ii 15 (cf. Hoftijzer DA a.l. × Caquot & Lemaire Syr liv 207: = Sing. + suff. 3 p.s.m. of ss_1:: Levine JAOS ci 202: = Sing. + suff. 3 p.s.m. of ss_2;on the problems, cf. also Hackett BTDA 72f.), *]ssh* v q 1 (??, heavily dam. context) - **OldAr** f. Sing. abs. *ssyh* KAI 222A 22 - **OffAr** m. Sing. abs. *swsh*Aḥiq 38 (*[s]wsh*; cf. Milik RB lxi 594f., Driv p. 73 :: Cowl p. 230, Leand 49h: = Sing. + suff. 3 p.s.m. of ss_1),Driv 9[5], TA-Ar 1[1], 3[1], 14[1] (*sws[h]*), 15[1], 16[2], 26[1], 32 (diff. reading, heavily dam. context); Plur. abs. *swsyn*ATNS 62[2] (:: Segal ATNS a.l.: = Plur. abs. of $swsy_2$ (= horseman)), Beh 30 (Akkad. par. *sīsê*); emph. *sws›* AG 90b; cf. Frah vii 3 (*swsy›*),Paik 713 (*swsyn*), 714 (*swsy›*),GIPP 34, 64, SaSt 23 - **Nab** m. Sing. emph. *swsy›*CIS ii 890[1] (cf. also Ahlström FS Widengren 329) - **Palm** m. Sing. abs. *swsy*SBS 48[6] - ¶ subst. m. horse; f. mare; *ptkr swsh ‹m rkbh* Driv 9[2]: a sculpture of a horse with its rider (cf. *ṣlm mrkb swsy* SBS 48[6]: the sculpture of a horse rider (v. rkb_1)); *šb‹ ssyh* KAI 222A 22: seven mares (cf. on this construction Blau IOS ii 57f.: *ssyh* = non-collective noun, cf. however e.g. Dupont-Sommer Sf p. 39, Fitzmyer AIS 42, Donner KAI a.l., Degen AAG p. 104f., Gibson SSI ii p. 38).

ssṭrṭ (< Greek σηστέρτιον < Lat. *sestertium*, cf. Cantineau Gramm 157, Rosenthal Sprache 92) - **Palm** Plur. abs. *ssṭrṭyn* CIS ii 3913 ii 71 - ¶ subst. *sestertius*, sesterce - for abbrev., v. $š_{10}$.

ssyh v. *ssh*.

s‹bl **OffAr** Sing. abs. *s‹bl* Cowl 26[11,20] - ¶ subst. of unknown meaning and etym. (cf. Cowl p. 95, Grelot DAE p. 289f. n. x), indicating part of a boat.

s‹d **Samal** Qal (or Pa‹el?) Impf. 3 p.s.m. *ys‹d* KAI 214[15,21] (v. infra) - **OffAr** Qal Pf. 3 p.s.m. + suff. 1 p.s. *s‹dny* Beh 2 (*s‹dn[y]*,

Akkad. par. *is-se-dan-nu*), 5 (Akkad. par. idem), 13 (*[s]‘dny*; Akkad. par. idem), 19 (Akkad. par. idem), 28 (*[s]‘dny*; Akkad. par. idem), 41 (Akkad. par. idem), Cowl 269, 3^7 (= BIDG l. 10; Akkad. par. idem) - ¶ verb QAL (v. supra) to help, to support; + obj., *’hwrmzd s‘dn[y]* Beh 2: A. helped/supported me, cf. Beh 5, 13, 19, 28, 41, Cowl 269, 3^7 (cf. Sokoloff JAOS cix 685); *ys‘d ’brw* KAI $214^{15,21}$: he shall maintain power (cf. e.g. Gibson SSI ii p. 67, 72 (cf. also Lagrange ERS 493); uncert. interpret., diff. context, cf. Driver AnOr xii 46: he shall uphold a mighty state (cf. also Koopmans 36) :: Cooke NSI p. 162, 168: he shall grow strong (?; cf. also Donner KAI a.l.) :: Dion p. 29, 31: *ys‘d* = he will settle himself) - > Akkad. *sêdu* (= to help, to support), cf. Herzfeld API 341f., v.Soden Or xxxvii 266, xlvi 194, AHW s.v., Greenfield RAI xxv 476 - L.H.Gray AJSL xxxix 79: the *sed* in Poen 947 = nominal derivative of this root (= support)?? (:: Schroed 292, 313: *sed* = lapsus for *se* (= $š_{10}$) :: Krahmalkov Or lvii 63 (div. otherwise): l. *esde* (restored from *esed*, *ese*) = z_1), cf. however Sznycer PPP 127f. (without interpret.).

s‘n **OffAr** Segal ATNS a.l.: the *s‘nh* in ATNS 8^9 = Sing. f. abs. of *s‘n* (= endowed (< Egypt.)), less prob. interpret., prob. = n.p., cf. Porten & Yardeni sub TADAE B 5.6.

s‘r **Nab** PA‘EL (or APHel) Part. act. s.m. cstr. *ms‘r* J 301 (or = subst.(= administration)?, cf. Cantineau Nab ii 116) - ¶ verb PA‘EL (v. supra) to visit, to inspect, to occupy oneself with, to conduct affairs (?; for this interpret., cf. Jaussen & Savignac J a.l.; cf. also Negev RB lxxxiii 227).

s‘rh v. *š‘rh*.

sp_1 **Ph** Sing. abs. *sp* RES $1204^{1,5,6}$ - **Pun** Plur. abs. *spm* KAI 137^6 - ¶ subst. m. bowl, basin (for RES 1204, cf. also Cooke NSI p. 43, Ward VT xxiv 344f.); *spm šnm wzbrm šnm* KAI 137^6: two bowls and two vessels (v. *zbr_1*) - > Greek σιπύη? (cf. Masson RPAE 44f.).

sp_2 **Hebr** Sing. cstr. *swp* DJD ii 24B 14, C 12, E 9, SM 49^7; + suff. 3 p.s.m. *swpw* DJD ii 22,1-9^5 (v. infra) - **OffAr** Sing. cstr. *sp* JAOS liv 31^2 - **JAr** Sing. abs. *swp*MPAT-A 45^4, 46^5 - ¶ subst. m. end; *‘d swp ‘rb hšmṭh* DJD ii 24E 9: until the end of the eve of the Release (cf. DJD ii 24B 14, C 12); *‘l sp šnt ...* JAOS liv 31^2: at the end of the year ...; *yhy m’yt bswp byš* MPAT-A $46^{4ff.}$: may he die of an evil end (cf. MPAT-A 45^4); *lswpw* DJD ii 22,1-9^5: definitively (?; cf. also Milik DJD ii a.l.; for the context, v. also *dḥy*) - for the root, cf. Ward VT xxiv 345f. v. *ksp_2*, *lylh*.

sp_3 **OffAr** Sing. emph., cf. Warka 2 *si-ip-pa-a* - ¶ subst. threshold, doorstep: Warka 2 (cf. Dupont-Sommer RA xxxix 42 :: Landsberger AfO xii 251 n. 12: = door-hinge stone) - this subst. (Sing. emph. *sp’*) poss. also in CIS ii 3932^7 (= *praetorium*, vestibule), cf. Cantineau sub

Inv iii 22, JA ccxxii 222ff., cf. Greek par. πραιτωρίου (cf. also Chabot CRAI '41, 110ff.) :: Chabot sub CIS ii 3932: = Qal Part. act. s.m. abs. of *sp*ʾ$_2$ (= to feed; cf. already Cooke NSI p. 279, 281), for the context, cf. Cantineau JA ccxxii 222f., Chabot CRAI '41, 111f. - Zimmern Fremdw 31: < Akkad., cf. also Salonen Türen 62f.: < Akkad. < Sum. (on this last point, cf. already Zimmern a.l.), cf. however Weidhaas ZA xlv 123, Berger UF ii 335 n. 2, Kaufman AIA 92.
v. *ʾbšp*, *sbb*$_2$.

sp$_4$ v. *spr*$_3$.

spʾ$_1$ v. *ṯn*ʾ$_2$.

spʾ$_2$ v. *sp*$_3$.

spwn (< Greek par. σύμφωνος, cf. Cantineau Gramm 156, Rosenthal Sprache 92) - **Palm** CIS ii 3913 ii 96 (*spw[n]*; Greek par. [συν]εφωνήθη), 113 (Greek par. συνεφώνησεν), 144, 149 (*[s]pwn*), Inscr P 34[6] - orig. non-declinated adj., being of the same opinion, in concord, agreeing; *hww spwn* CIS ii 3913 ii 113: they have agreed (cf. CIS ii 3913 ii 96, 144, 149); *ʾqymw lh tgryʾ ... klhn spwn* Inscr P 34[5f.]: the merchants, all of them, unanimously have erected (it) for him.

spḥ v.Soden Or xlvi 194: poss. > Akkad. *sippīḫu* = uncontrolled growth (cf. also idem AHW s.v.; highly uncert. interpret., cf. also CAD s.v.: = an agricultural operation (refraining from etym.)).

spynh **OffAr** Sing. abs. *spynh* AJSL lviii 303A 5 (*[s]pynh*), Sach Pap 57 (*scriptura anterior*, cf. Ungnad ArPap sub 60); emph. *spyntʾ* Cowl 26[3,7,22], Krael 13[7]; Plur. emph. *spyntʾ* AG 5[11], ATNS 26[10,16] (or = Sing.?), AJSL lviii 303B 5; + suff. 3 p.pl.m. *sp[y]nthm* ATNS 26[1] (or = Sing.?, dam. context) - ¶ subst. f. boat (Milik Bibl xlviii 555: = greater type of boat for official use; cf. also *ʾlp*$_3$)- for *byt spyntʾ*, v. *byt*$_2$ - > Akkad. *sapīnatu*, cf. e.g. Salonen Wasserfahrzeuge 19, v.Soden Or xxxvii 265, xlvi 194, AHW s.v., CAD sv.
v. *spytkn*.

spyq **Hebr** Sing. abs. *spyq* SM 49[10] - ¶ subst. doubt; *hʿyyrwt šhn spyq* SM 49[10]: the towns which are doubtful.

spyr v. *qpr*$_1$.

spytkn **OffAr** diff. word in Cowl 26[9]; Grelot DAE p. 288 (n. p): < Egypt. *spʾt* (= district) + Iran. ending *-kn* = district official (cf. also Cowl a.l. with same type of interpret.: *spyt* = n.g., *spytkn* = man from *spyt* (cf. also Epstein ZAW xxxii 129)) :: Porten & Yardeni sub TADAE A 6.2: = whitener ? :: Herzfeld PE 281 (n. 3): = *spynt-* (= boat of Spain) with Iran. ethnic ending: = Spaniards (highly improb. interpret.) :: Sach p. 47: = *spynt-* + Iran. ending *-k*? (= naval?, ship's?) in Plur. abs. :: Epstein ZAW xxxiii 142: = Sing. + suff. 2 p.pl.m. of *spynh*.

spl **Ph** v.d.Branden BO viii 248, 261: l. *spl* in KAI 37B 8 = Sing. cstr.

of *spl* = building annex to the temple, highly uncertain interpret.

spn **OffAr** Lipiński Stud 147ff.: l. *spnw* (= QAL Imper. pl.m. of *spn* (= to care for, to respect)) in KAI 258[2] (highly uncert. interpret.; for the reading and interpret. of the diff. context, v. *ʾdr$_7$*, *ʾdrswn*).

spq$_1$ v.Soden Or xxiv 145, xxxvii 265, xlvi 194: > Akkad. *sapāqu* (= to be sufficient); cf. also idem AHW s.v.; prob. interpret. - cf. *spq$_2$*.

spq$_2$ v.Soden Or xlvi 194: > Akkad. *sapqu* (= strong, able, competent), cf. *spq$_1$*.

spr$_1$ **Hebr** QAL Imper. s.m. *spr* TA-H 3[7] - ¶ verb QAL to count; + obj., *wspr hḥṭm whlḥm* TA-H 3[6ff.]: and count the wheat and the bread - > Akkad. *sepēru* (= to write in alphabetic script), cf. CAD sv.
v. *spr$_{2,3}$*, *pr$_2$*.

spr$_2$ **Ph** Sing. abs. *spr* EpAn ix 5C 3; Plur. abs. *sprm* KAI 37A 15 (= Kition C1), RDAC '84, 103 - **Pun** Sing. abs. *spr* CIS i 154[4], 240[5], 241[4], 242[3], 273[3], 277[2], 382[4], 3749[4], 3786[4], 4881[2], RES 586[4], 1562[4], Hofra 90[2] (or cstr.?), 91[2]; cstr. *spr* CIS i 3104[3]; Plur. abs. *sprm* RES 891[4], Hofra 281[1], Punica xviii/ii 22[3] - **Amm** Sing. cstr. *spr* Syr lxiii 317 (= CAI 139) - **Hebr** Sing. abs. *spr* Vatt sig. eb. 307 (= SANSS Ar. 37 = Qedem iv 7 no. 6), 345 (= SANSS-Hebr 110 = CSOI-Hebr 51), HBTJ 9 (= IEJ xxviii 53 i), Frey 1308a, *swpr*Frey 1308b (= MPAT 99), SM 75[5] - **Mo** Sing. abs. *spr* Dir sig. 74 (= Vatt sig. eb. 74 = SANSS-Mo 1 = IS 1; cf. also Naveh BASOR clxxxiii 29 n. 24, Avigad FS Glueck 289), Vatt sig. eb. 113 (= SANSS-Mo 4 = IS 2; cf. also Naveh BASOR clxxxiii 29, Avigad FS Glueck 289) - **OffAr** Sing. abs. *spr* Aḥiq 1, 18, 35, ATNS 43a 5 (dam. context); emph. *sprʾ* Aḥiq 12 (*[s]prʾ*), 42, Cowl 26[23,28], Driv 4[4], 6[6] (*spr[ʾ]*), 7[10], 8[6], 9[3], 10[5], AG 71, CIS ii 46 (= EI viii 7* no. 7), 84, KAI 227 Rs 6, 236 Rs 6 (= AECT 49), OLZ ' 27, 1043[3], BIFAO xxxviii 58[3] (uncert. reading :: Segal Maariv iv 72: l. *k* (abbrev. of *krš$_1$*) *3*), EI viii 7* no. 6, AE '23, 42 no. 16; Plur. cstr. *spry* Cowl 2[12,14], 17[1,6] (twice, for the reading, cf. Porten RB xc 406, 413, Porten & Yardeni sub TADAE A 6.1), SSI ii 28 obv. 5 (dam. context); cf. Paik 732 (*sprʾ*), MP 5, ZDMG xcii 442B 9, Syr xxxv 331[66], xxxix 226, Nisa 455[4], 478[3], 481[5], 541[3], 542[4], 604[3], 810[2], 812[4], 813[3], etc. (in all instances: *sprʾ*; for the Nisa-instances, cf. also Diakonov & Livshitz Nisa-b p. 43, Chaumont JA cclvi 23), cf. also GIPP 63 - **Hatra** Sing. emph. *sprʾ* 35[3] (cf. Safar Sumer viii 190, Maricq Syr xxxii 275 n. 1, Degen Or xxxvi 80 (n. 4), ZDMG cxxi 125, Ingholt AH i/1, 46, i/2, 48, Milik DFD 352f., Vattioni IH a.l. :: Caquot Syr xxx 240, Donner sub KAI 249: l. *šprʾ* = Sing. emph. of *špr$_3$* (= variant of *spr$_2$*)), 215[1], 221[2], 289a, 408[9] (for the reading, cf. also Aggoula Syr lxii 282f.) - **JAr** Sing. emph. *sprʾ* MPAT 42[22] (*spr[ʾ]*), *sprh* MPAT 51[7] (for this reading, cf. Milik Bibl xxxviii 268; for the reading problems, cf. also Milik RB lxi 183, 188) - ¶ subst. (orig. QAL Part. act. of *spr$_1$*)scribe: passim; *sprʾ*

dbrmryn Hatra 35^3: the scribe of the son of our lords (cf. also Milik DFD 365); *rb sprm* KAI 37A 15: the head of the scribes, the chief clerk (cf. RDAC '84, 103, RES 891^4, Hofra 281^1, Punica xviii/ii 22^3; cf. also Kition A $30^{2f.}$ (*rb [sp]rm*; cf. also Karageorghis & Amadasi RSF i 132f.); cf. Masson & Sznycer RPC 53f., Delcor UF xi 160); for *spr hdlḥt* CIS i 3104^3, v. *dlḥh*; for *byt spr*ʾ, v. byt_2; for *spry* ʾ*wṣr*ʾ*/mdynt*ʾ, v. ʾ*wṣr*, *mdnh* - Lipiński Stud 140f.: l. *[s]pr* (= Sing. cstr.) in TH 5 obv. 4 (= AECT 57), highly uncert. reading, cf. Friedrich TH a.l.: l. *[.]q*, cf. however Degen NESE i 56 - for this word, cf. Mettinger SSO 8ff., 15ff., 19ff., 25ff. (for Elephantine, cf. also Porten Arch 51f., 60f.) - Rocco AION xxi 13f.: l. *spr* (= Sing. abs.) in GR i 61 no. 31 B 2 (= GR ii 88 no. 70^2), highly uncert. reading, cf. Guzzo Amadasi GR a.l.). v. $ḥpr_2$, spr_3.

spr_3 **Ph** Sing. abs. *spr* KAI $24^{14,15}$, EpAn ix 5C 3; cstr. *spr* KAI 50^6; + suff. 3 p.s.m. *sprh* KAI 1^2 (:: Rosenthal ANET 661: = written) - **Pun** Sing. + suff. 3 p.s.m. *spry* CIS i 6000bis 8 (= TPC 84; cf. Février BAr '51/52, 79f., sub CIS i 6000bis, Ferron StudMagr i 78 :: Lidzbarski Eph i 164f.: or = Sing. + suff. 1 p.s. (cf. Chabot sub RES 13) :: Lidzbarski Eph i 164f.: or = Sing. + suff. 1 p.s. of spr_2 (cf. also Slouschz TPI p. 183f.) :: Chabot sub RES 13 (div. otherwise): or l. *spr* = Sing. abs. of spr_2;diff. context) - **Hebr** Sing. abs. *spr* KAI $193^{5,9}$ (:: Albright ANET 322: = Sing. abs. of spr_2;for the problems of the context, v. qrʾ$_1$)^{,10,11}, Lach xviii 1; cstr. *spr* KAI 193^{19}; Plur. abs. *sprm* KAI $195^{6f.}$, 196^{14}; cstr. *spry* KAI 196^4 - **OldAr** Sing. emph. *spr*ʾ KAI 222B 8, 28, 33, C 17, 223B 18 (*spr[*ʾ*]*), C 13, $224^{4,14,17,23}$; Plur. emph. *spry*ʾ KAI 223C 2, 4 (*spr[y]*ʾ), 6f. (*spr[y]*ʾ) - **OffAr** Sing. abs. *spr* Cowl 8^{16}, 9^4, $13^{3,11}$, 28^{14}, 42^4, Krael 3^{25}, 8^4, 9^{22}, 12^{29}, 15 (cf. however Porten BiAr xlii 84f.), Herm 1^5, $5^{4,7}$, 42a 4 (dam. context), 49^4, 101^4, 177^2 (?, *spr[]*), *sp* (lapsus) Cowl 13^{12}; cstr. *spr* Cowl 5^{20}, 6^{22}, $8^{23,25,35}$, 10^{23}, 13^{21} (on the reading of the context, cf. Porten & Greenfield JEAS p. 16, Porten FS Freedman 529, Porten & Yardeni sub TADAE B 2.7 :: Cowl a.l. (div. otherwise): *bmḥsyh* (cf. also Grelot DAE p. 188) :: L.Blau with Porten Arch 335 n. 3: l. *bmḥsyh* = lapsus for *mrḥq ktb mḥsyh*), $14^{4,14}$, 20^{19} (cf. Porten Arch 255 n. 42, Porten & Greenfield JEAS p. 26, Grelot DAE p. 200 (n. j), Porten & Yardeni sub TADAE B 2.9), 25^{20}, 28^{17}, 35^4, 59, Krael 2^{17} (for this prob. reading, cf. Porten & Yardeni sub TADAE B 3.3), 4^{25}, 9^{27}, 10^7 (for a *scriptio anterior spr* in the same line, cf. Porten & Szubin JAOS cvii 231)^{,9,21}, $12^{9a,18,35}$, ATNS 16^1 (for the context, cf. Porten & Yardeni sub TADAE B 8.10), Irâq xxxiv 136 (= AECT 60), MAI xiv/ii 66^{19} (for the reading, cf. also Porten & Yardeni sub TADAE B 1.1); emph. *spr*ʾ Cowl 2^{11}, $5^{15,36}$ (*scriptio anterior*; for the reading, cf. Porten & Yardeni sub TADAE B 2.6), 6^{16}, 8^{16}, Krael $10^{7,15}$, Herm 7^4, ATNS 27^3 (or rather = Sing. emph. of spr_2?),35^5 (for the reading, cf. Porten & Yardeni sub TADAE B 4.7 :: Segal ATNS a.l.: l. *bnt*› (= n.p.)), *sprh* RSO xxxv 22^{5}, Herm $1^{12f.}$, 2^{17}, 3^{13}, 4^{12}, 5^{9}, 6^{10} (*[sp]rh*); + suff. 1 p.pl. *sprn* RES 1298A 3 (or rather = Plur. abs.?, or = Sing. + suff. 1 p.pl. or Plur. abs. of *spr*$_2$??;dam. context); Plur. cstr. *spry* ATNS 155 (?, *spry[)* - **Palm** Sing. abs. *spr* MUSJ xxxviii 106^{4} - **JAr** Sing. cstr. *spr* MPAT $40^{7,20}$ (*s[p]r*), MPAT-A 34^{5} (= SM 69); Plur. emph. *spry*› MPAT 52^{18} (cf. Milik Bibl xxxviii 259f., Beyer ATTM 322f. :: Fitzmyer & Harrington MPAT a.l.: = lapsus for *spr*› (= Sing. emph. of *spr*$_2$))- ¶ subst. m. - **1)** (art of) writing; *l*› *yd*‹ *spr* MUSJ xxxviii 106^{4}: he did not know writing (i.e. he could not write) - **2)** inscription: KAI 1^{2}, $24^{14,15}$, 222B 8, 28, 33, EpAn ix 5C 3, etc. (cf. also Hillers TC 45ff.) - **3)** letter: KAI $193^{5,9}$ (v. supra)^{,10,11,19}, $195^{6f.}$, $196^{4,14}$, Herm $1^{5,12f.}$, 2^{17}, 3^{13}, 4^{12}, $5^{4,7,19}$, 6^{10}, 7^{4} (cf. also Smelik PEQ '90, 133f.) - **4)** document, contract: Cowl 2^{11}, 3^{10}, 5^{15}, 6^{16}, 8^{16}, etc., etc. (cf. also Verger RGP 82ff., Porten & Greenfield IOS iv 25, Muffs 188f.); *spr*› ‹*lyhm* Cowl 42^{4}: a deed concerning them; *spr zy zbn bgzšt wybl l*‹*nnyh* Krael 3^{25}: the document concerning that which B. and Y. sold to A.; *spr* ›*gr*› *zy* ... Cowl 5^{20}: a deed relating to the wall (v. ›*gr*$_4$) that ...; for *spr* ›*ntw*, v. ›*ntw*; *spr* ›*srn* ATNS 16^{1} + 3^{1} (cf. Porten & Yardeni sub TADAE B 8.10): document of obligation; *spr by zy ktb* ... Krael 4^{25}: a deed concerning a house which ... wrote (cf. Krael 9^{27}, 10^{21}, $12^{9a,35}$, cf. also Cowl 8^{35}, 13^{21} (for the reading v. supra)); for *spr hmrkrny*, v. *hmrkrny*; *spr ksp* Cowl 10^{23}: document concerning silver (for the problems of the context, v. *dnt*); for *spr mwmh*, v. *mwm*›*h*; for *spr mrḥq*, v. *mrḥq*; for *spr plgn*, v. *plgn*; for *spr*› *zy qymyhm*, v. *qym*$_1$; for *spr trkyn*, v. *trk*$_2$; for *spr šlm*, v. *šlm*$_4$ - this word (Sing. abs. *spr*) poss. also in RES 1792B 6, cf. Dupont-Sommer REJ '46/47, 44 n. 18: *mlt spr* = a word as written in a document (cf. already Clermont-Ganneau RAO viii 134 (n.1), cf. however Dupont-Sommer ibid.: or = Sing. abs. of *spr*$_2$, *mlt spr* = a matter/question of a scribe (cf. also Grelot DAE p. 375), or = an official document? (uncert. interpret.)) :: Lidzbarski Eph ii 234: *spr* = n.p. (cf. also Driver AnOr xii 58: pro *spr* l. ›*spr* = n.p.) - **5)** book; *spr ḥyyh* MPAT-A 34^{5}: the book of life - Porten BiAr xliv 36, Porten & Yardeni sub TADAE A 1.1: the *spr* in KAI 266^{9} = Sing. cstr. of *spr*$_3$ (poss. interpret.) :: Dupont-Sommer Sem i 45, 53, Lipiński OLP viii 104, Donner KAI a.l.: = Sing. abs. of *spr*$_2$ :: Fitzmyer Bibl xlvi 45: = QAL Pf. 3 p.s.m. of *spr*$_1$ (cf. however idem ibid. 55) :: Meyer FS Zucker 258, Gibson SSI ii p. 114, 116, Shea BASOR ccxxiii 61: = Sing. abs. of *spr*$_4$ (= border; cf. also Koopmans 91, Horn AUSS vi 31f. (n. 14)), on this subject, cf. also Bright BiAr xii 48 n. 6 - e.g. Caquot & Lemaire Syr liv 194, Rofé SB 61, H.P.Müller ZDPV xciv 56f., Garbini Hen i 172f., Kaufman BASOR ccxxxix 73, Levine JAOS ci 196, H.P.Müller ZAW xciv 216, 218, 219, 239f., H.

& M. Weippert ZDPV xcviii 83f., Hackett BTDA 25, 27, 31, Lemaire BAT 317, Puech FS Grelot 15, 17: pro *]kr* in DA i 3 l *[s]pr* (= Sing. cstr. of *spr*$_3$) to be placed in l. 1 (heavily dam. context; poss. interpret. :: McCarter BASOR ccxxxix 51f.: l. poss. *[ʾ]mr[y]* = Plur. cstr. of *ʾmr*$_2$ (= saying); on the background, cf. also Lemaire ZDMG-Suppl vi 122) - Zimmern Fremdw 19: < Akkad. *šipru*, cf. however Muffs 207 (cf. also e.g. Kaufman AIA 29) - > Akkad. *sipru*, cf. v.Soden Or xlvi 194, AHW s.v. *sipru* II, CAD s.v. *sipru* A - on this word, cf. also Galling FS Albright ii 209ff., 217ff.
v. *sprb*, *pr*$_2$.
spr$_4$ v. *spr*$_3$.
spr$_5$ > Akkad. *sepīru*, *sepirru* (= scribe, dragoman), cf. Ebeling ZA l. 212, Lewy HUCA xxv 191, San Nicolò Or xviii 290f., xxiii 369f., v.Soden Or xxxvii 266, xlvi 194, AHW s.v. *sepīru* (cf. also Kümmel Familie 136, CAD s.v. *sepīru*).
spr$_6$ v. *qpr*$_1$.
sprb (prob. < Lyd., cf. Kahle & Sommer KlF i 38f., Donner sub KAI 260, Lipiński Stud 157f., cf. also Cook JHS xxxvii 227) - **OffAr** Sing. abs. *sprb* KAI 260[3] (v. supra :: Littmann Sardis vi/1, 27, Torrey AJSL xxxiv 192, Cuny RevEtAnc xxii 260 n. 3, 265, Cook JHS xxxvii 83, 227 (cf. also G.B.Gray with Cook ibid.): = lapsus for *sprd* (= n.g.) :: Lidzbarski ZA xxxi 127: = lapsus for *sprʾ* (= Sing. emph. of *spr*$_3$) :: Cowley Sardis vi/2, 2: l. *sgwb* (= Sing. abs.) = upright monument) - ¶ subst. poss. meaning, tomb, burial room/cave (cf. Kahle & Sommer KlF i 38f., Donner KAI a.l. (cf. Lipiński Stud 157f. (: = monument > tomb)), cf. also Cowley with Cook JHS xxxvii 227).
sprgl (prob. loanword; cf. e.g. CAD, AHW s.v. *supurgillu*; cf. also Löw AP p. 144f., 467) - cf. Frah iv 18: quince, quince-tree (cf. Nyberg FP 66).
sptryn **Nab** group of signs in J 15; without interpret.
sql v.Soden Or xxxvii 266, xlvi 194 (cf. idem AHW s.v. *saqālu* II): > Akkad. *saqālu* = to wipe, to polish (uncert. interpret.).
sqlṭyq v. *snqlṭyq*.
sr$_1$ v. *srn*, *srsr*$_2$.
sr$_2$ **OldCan** Sing. abs. *sií-ri* EA 297[12] (for this reading and interpret., cf. Rainey EA p. 89 :: Ebeling sub Knudt p. 1544: l. *zi-ri* = Sing. abs. of *zr*$_3$ (= vessel; for this reading, cf. also CAD s.v. *ziri*) :: Knudt p. 890 (n. a): l. *zi-ri* (meaning unknown) without prec. *Keil*) - **OffAr** Sing. cstr. *sr* Herm 3[6] (cf. Milik Bibl xlviii 552, 582, Grelot DAE 158 (n. e), Lipiński OLP viii 116, Swiggers AION xlii 137 :: Bresciani & Kamil Herm a.l. (div. otherwise): l. *srḥlṣh* = n.p., cf. also Gibson SSI ii p. 136) - ¶ subst. pot, vessel.
v. *srblwn*.

sr_3 v. *sd_2*.
sr_4 **Pun** Krahmalkov RSF iii 179f., 203: l. *[s]r* in Karth xii 50^2 = Sing. abs. of *sr_4* (= rebel) or l. poss. *[sr]r* = Sing. abs. of *srr_2* (= rebel) or (less prob.) l. *[ṣ]r* or *[ṣ]rr* (= Sing. abs. of resp. *$ṣr_2$* or *ṣrr* (= adversary, opponent)). Highly uncert. interpret.
v. *sd_2*.
srbyl Ebeling Frah a.l.: l. *srb[y]ly*ʾ in cf. Frah xv 12 = shirt, chemise (uncert. reading, cf. Nyberg FP 48, 85: l. *lbyly*ʾ = *l_5* + form of *bry_4* (= created (= naked?) body), highly uncert. interpret.).
srblwn **OffAr** Grelot DAE p. 131 n. g: l. this subst. (Sing. abs.) poss. in Cowl 42^9 (= trousers), related to BiblAr *srbl* (however comb. of *srbl* (= non-Sem loanword; cf. e.g. Cook Journ. Phil. xxvi 307ff., Baumgartner in KB s.v.) + *wn* less prob.) :: Cowl a.l.: l. *srblq* (= *srbl* + Iran. ending *-k*) = cloak; cf. however Sach p. 66: l. *sr[.]lṣ* (loanword of unknown meaning), cf. also Porten & Yardeni sub TADAE A 3.8: l. *srḥlṣ* (without interpret.; v. *sr_2*, *$ḥlṣ_2$*).
srblq v. *srblwn*.
srbn **Palm** Plur. abs. *srbnyn* CIS ii 3913 i 7 (Greek par. ζητήσεις) - ¶ subst. m. controversy.
$srwk_1$ v. *srk_2*.
$srwk_2$ v. *srwky*.
srwky **OffAr** Sing. emph. *srwky*ʾ KAI 260^4 - ¶ word of unknown meaning, poss. title or gentilicium, cf. e.g. Cuny RevEtAnc xxii 261, 266f., Cook JHS xxxvii 83, 228, Torrey AJSL xxxiv 188, Lidzbarski ZA xxxi 128f., Donner KAI a.l., Levine JAOS xcii 73 n. 29, Silverman JAOS xciv 271, Lipiński Stud 155, 158f. (cf. also Kahle & Sommer KlF i 55, 56 (n. 1)) :: Kahle & Sommer KlF i 55f.: or = name :: idem ibid.: or = Plur. emph. of *$srwk_2$* (= title) :: Cowley with Cook JHS xxxvii 228: l. perhaps *sngr*ʾ = Sing. emph. of *sngr* (< Greek συνήγορος = advocate); cf. also Kahle & Sommer KlF i 55f.: or l. *srwkn*ʾ (= Sing. emph. of *srwkn* (= (derivation of) name), for this reading, cf. also Driver AnOr xii 53: = the man of Seruk.
srwl **Pun** word of unknown meaning in RES 1547^3; = n.p. (cf. *srl* in CIS i 4799), or apellation? or title?
srwr v. *mrwr*.
srwšyt (< Iran., cf. Benveniste JA ccxlii 304, cf. also Driv p. 47, Rundgren VT vii 400ff., Nober VD xxxvi 103f., Grelot DAE 304 n. e, Hinz AISN 227) - **OffAr** Sing. emph. *srwšyt*ʾ Driv $3^{6,7}$ (*srwš[yt]*ʾ) - ¶ subst. corporal punishment (cf. Greenfield IrJu 8f.).
srḥ **Ph** QAL (or PIʿEL?) Impf. 3 p.s.f. + suff. 3 p.s.m. *tsrḥ[w]* KAI 10^{15} (cf. e.g. Dupont-Sommer Sem iii 36, 44, Röllig KAI a.l., Gibson SSI iii p. 94, 99 :: Dunand BMB v 74, 84f.: l. *tpr[ḥw]* = YIPH Impf. 3 p.s.f. + suff. 3 p.s.m. of *$prḥ_1$* (= to make to prosper)) - ¶ verb QAL

(or PI‘EL?) to destroy; + obj.: KAI 10[15] (cf. Dupont-Sommer Sem iii 37, 44, Röllig KAI a.l., Gibson SSI iii p. 95, 99 :: Segert JSS xvii 138: perhaps rather = to make petrifying, to make abhorrent).
v. *srs*.

srṭ **OffAr** Nyberg FP 50, 92: the *šlytwn* in Frah xix 20 prob. = form of *srṭ* (= to cut in, to scratch > to copulate (uncert. interpret.; cf. also Toll ZDMG-Suppl viii 35)), cf. also Ebeling Frah a.l.: = form of *šry*$_2$ (= to sleep with, to copulate (< Akkad. (SHAPH form of root *’ry*))).

srṭn **Hebr** Sing. abs. *srṭn* Frey 1162[4], 1806, SM 70[3] - ¶ subst. Cancer (as sign of the Zodiac).

sry cf. Frah xxvi 6 (*sly’*), 7 (*sly*): bad (cf. also GIPP 33).

srys v. *srs*.

srk$_1$ **OffAr** Altheim & Stiehl FuF xxxv 176f.: the diff. *msryk* in FuF xxxv 173[9] = APH Part. act. s.m. abs. of *srk*$_1$ (= to border (up)on); cf. also idem ASA 274: or = PA‘EL.

srk$_2$ **OffAr** diff. word in Pers 6[1], 10[1], 11[1], 12[1], 18[1], etc., etc. (in most instances in the comb. *bsrk byrt’*; in Pers 66[1], 67[1], 68[1], 137[1] (?) *bsrk* without *byrt’*), cf. *srwk*in Pers 54[1] (in the comb. *bsrwk*); for the interpret., cf. Bowman Pers 22ff., 67 (n. 35): = subst. (Sing. cstr.) = ritual (cf. also Grelot RB lxxx 596); Levine JAOS xcii 72ff.: = administration (cf. also Teixidor Syr l. 431); Segal BSOAS xxxv 354: = part of a fortress; (Kreftor with) Gershevitch Mem de Menasce 53f.: = Treasury; Delaunay CC 207ff., 215: = enclosure, walled-in room/space; cf. also Degen BiOr xxxi 125 n. 5: unexplained word of non-Semitic origin. Prob interpret.: = n.l., cf. Cameron with Bowman Pers p. 21, Bernard StudIr i 171ff., Naveh & Shaked Or xlii 447f., Teixidor Syr li 331, Degen BiOr xxxi 125, Hinz FS Nyberg 372ff., AISN 222, Lipiński Stud 156 (n. 3; cf. already Cameron with Schmidt Persepolis ii 55 n. 62).

srn **OffAr** The *srn* in KAI 271B 5, 7 prob. to be read *swn* (= n.l.), cf. RES 495, Silverman JAOS xciv 272; Donner KAI a.l.: l. *srn* = Sing. abs. (= prince) or = Sing. abs. + suff. 1 p.pl. of *sr*$_1$ (= *šr*$_2$), for this last interpret., cf. also e.g. Cooke NSI p. 204f.

srs (< Akkad., cf. Zimmern Fremdw 6, Kaufman AIA 100, 147 n. 37, 148, Fales AECT p. 138f., cf. also Lipiński ZAH i 71) - **OldAr** Plur. + suff. 1 p.s. *srsy* KAI 222B 45 (for this reading, cf. e.g. Fitzmyer AIS p. 18, 73, Lipiński Stud 52 :: Dupont-Sommer Sf p. 62, 85: l. *srḥy* = poss. QAL Part. act. pl.m. + suff. 1 p.s. of *srḥ* (= to sin); for the reading, cf. also Donner KAI a.l.), 224[5] (:: Degen AAG p. 52: = Plur. cstr.; or in both instances = Sing. + suff. 1 p.s.?) - **OffAr** Sing. abs. *srs* CIS ii 38[6] (= Del 21 = AECT 3), AJSL xlix 54 (for this reading, cf. Kaufman JAOS civ 94, AAALT 53f. :: Sprengling AJSL a.l. (div. otherwise): l. *srsy* (= Plur. cstr.)), *srys*Aḥiq 61; emph. *srs’* CIS ii 75[3] (cf. also

Naveh & Tadmor AION xviii 450f.), *srys*ʾAḥiq 63, 69; - ¶ subst. m. high court official, eunuch (for litt., cf. HAL s.v. *srys*); *rb srs* CIS ii 38[6]: great-eunuch (on this title, cf. also Tadmor FS Freedman 279ff.).
v. *srsr*$_2$.

srsr$_1$ **OffAr** PALPEL (< root *swr* or *srr*) Part. act. pl.f. abs. *msrsrn* Aḥiq 114 :: Lindenberger APA 101f., 246f. n. 288: = m. pl. (cf. on this point Muraoka JSS xxxii 188) :: Kottsieper SAS 21, 118, 216: = Plur. abs. of *msrsr* (= traitor, denunciator); = subst. < root *msr* - ¶ verb PALPEL poss. meaning: to soar, to leap, to fly up (cf. Baneth OLZ '14, 348, Driver AnOr xii 56, Grelot RB lxviii 185, DAE p. 439 n. c, Lindenberger APA 101f., 246f. n. 288); diff. context.

srsr$_2$ **Ph** Plur. abs. *srsrm* KAI 34[1,2,3] (= Kition B 45) - ¶ subst. broker, middleman (cf. e.g. Fraenkel ZA x 99f., Halévy RS iii 183f., Lidzbarski Handb 331, 366f., Cooke NSI p. 70f., Slouschz TPI p. 84, Röllig KAI a.l. :: Dérenbourg REJ xxx 118f.: *srsr* = variant of *srs*:: Nöldeke ZA ix 402: *srsrm* = Sing. cstr. of *sr*$_1$ (= variant of *šr*$_2$) + Plur. abs. *sr*$_1$); *rb srsrm* KAI 34[1,2,3]: chief of the brokers (cf. also Sznycer AEPHE '70/71, 159: = hereditary court function? (cf. also Teixidor Syr li 322)).

srq **Palm** QAL Part. pass. s.m. abs. *sryq* CIS ii 3913 ii 61 (Greek par. κενὸς); pl. abs. *sryqyn* CIS ii 3913 ii 118 (Greek par. κεναὶ) - ¶ verb QAL to empty; Part. pass. empty, unladen (said of camels): CIS ii 3913 ii 61, 118 (cf. e.g. Cooke NSI p. 326, 330, 338 :: Klíma FS Bakoš 147ff.: *sryqyn* in CIS ii 3913 ii 118 = non-pregnant (cf. however Teixidor Syr xlviii 483, cf. also idem AO i 250)).
v. *šdq*$_1$.

srqwt cf. Frah x 25 (*slkwt*ʾ) = secret (diff. word, cf. Nyberg FP 76, cf. also Schaeder with Ebeling Frah a.l. :: Ebeling Frah a.l. (on the *saklûtu* mentioned by Ebeling, cf. CAD s.v. *niṣirtu* IC).

srr$_1$ **Hebr** Sing. cstr. *srr* SM 13[2] (:: Avigad BRF iii 52f.: l. *šrr* = Sing. cstr. of *šrr*$_2$ = office; = Frey 977) - ¶ subst. prob. meaning: office (variant of *šrr*$_2$, cf. also Naveh sub SM 13); *nybnh bsrr ḥnyn*ʾ SM 13[2]: it was built during the office of Ch.

srr$_2$ v. *sr*$_4$.

srrw **JAr** Sing. abs. *srrw* AMB 7[3] - ¶ subst. f. dominion; in the comb. *srrw rbh* AMB 7[3f.]: the great dominion (diff. context; Dupont-Sommer JKF i 204f.: = certain category of superior angels (uncert. interpret.); Scholem JGM 87f.: indication of the Glory of God, that comes down to the Throne? (less prob. interpret.)).

st v. *z*$_1$.

stwn (< Iran., cf. Cook JHS xxxvii 83, Torrey AJSL xxxiv 193, Shaked with Hanson BASOR cxcii 8 n. 13, Donner KAI a.l., Lipiński Stud 156) - **OffAr** Sing. emph. *stwn*ʾ KAI 260[2,4] - ¶ subst. m. stele.

stm v. *ḥtm*$_1$.

str_1 **Palm** PA ‹EL Pf. 3 p.s.m. *str* MUSJ xxxviii 106[8] - **JAr** QAL Part. pass.f. pl. emph. *styrth* MPAT-A 22[6] (= SM 70) - ¶ verb QAL to hide; Part. pass.f. hidden thing; *ḥmy styrth* MPAT-A 22[6]: He who sees hidden things (i.e. God) - PA ‹EL exact meaning unknown; Ingholt MUSJ xxxviii 107, 114f.: = to protect (less prob. interpret.; poss. interpret. to hide, sc. a corpse (i.e. to bury)).

str_2 **OffAr** Sing. cstr. *str* Aḥiq 88, 175 - ¶ subst. secret, secret place; *bstr ›rz›* Aḥiq 175: in the secret hiding-place (v. *›rz*$_3$); *bstr swyr›* Aḥiq 88: in the secret hiding-place (v. *swyr*).
v. *štr*$_1$.

str_3 (< Greek στατήρ) - **OffAr** Plur. emph. *stry›* KAI 263 (cf. Geiger ZDMG xxi 466, Torrey ZA xxvi 92, Schaed 267, Rosenthal Forschung 24, Jansma BiOr xv 46, Donner KAI a.l., Silverman JAOS xciv 271 :: e.g. CIS ii sub 108: = Plur. emph. of *str*$_4$ (= function indication, guardian?, cf. also Cooke NSI p. 193: = commissioner?)) - ¶ subst. *stater*, cf. *›str*$_1$, *sttr*, *sttry*.

str_4 v. *str*$_3$.

sttr (< Greek στατήρ, cf. e.g. Cowl p. 131) - **OffAr** Plur. abs. *sttrn* Cowl 37[12], *s[tt]ryn* Cowl 61[8] - ¶ subst. *stater* (= two shekels), cf. *›str*$_1$, *str*$_3$, *sttry*.

sttry (< Greek στατήρ + poss. Egypt. ending *-y*, cf. Sethe NGGW '16, 114f. n. 4, cf. also Schaed 267) - **OffAr** *sttry* Cowl 29[3] (*[st]try*, cf. Sach p. 62, Porten Arch 64 (n. 13), Grelot DAE p. 86 (n. b), Porten & Yardeni sub TADAE B 4.5), 35[4,7] (*sttr[y]*), 67 ix 2, Krael 12[5,14] - ¶ subst. *stater* (= two shekels), cf. *›str*$_1$, *str*$_3$, *sttr*; *ksp š 2 hw [ks]p sttry 1* Cowl 35[3f.]: silver 2 shekels, that is the sum of 1 *stater* (cf. Cowl 35[7]); *šqln tlth hw 3 ksp ywn sttry 6* Krael 12[5]: three shekels, that is 3, in money of Greece 6 *stater*; *šqln 3 ksp ywn bmnyn sttry 6* Krael 12[14]: 3 shekels in money of Greece in number 6 *stater*; *[st]try bmnyn 7* Cowl 29[3]: *stater* in number 7 (cf. Porten Arch 64 n. 13), cf. also *mnyn*.

‹

‹$_1$ v. *‹n*$_3$; = ruin, cf. *‹y*.

‹$_2$ v. *h*$_1$, *tm*$_3$.

‹$_3$ v. *‹gl*$_1$.

‹b$_1$ **DA** Sing. + suff. 2 p.s.f. *‹bky* i 8 (:: Levine JAOS ci 197, 198, Puech FS Grelot 17, 21, 27: l. *‹b* (= Sing. abs. of *‹b*$_1$) + *ky*) - ¶ subst. cloud (cf. Hoftijzer DA a.l.).

‹b$_2$ **OffAr** Plur. abs. *‹bn* BSh 3[3] (reading of *b* less certain, cf. Naveh Shn i 193) - ¶ subst. of unknown meaning, poss. indicating a small dry measure, cf. Naveh BSh i p. 80 n. 13 - cf. also the *‹b* inscribed on a jar?, cf. however Puech Lev ix 13f.: perhaps = abbrev. for *‹(šryt) b(t)* = a tenth of a *bat*.

‹bb OffAr a form of this root (APH Imper. s.m. + suff. 3 p.s.m. *›‹bhy*) = to concentrate in RES 1299A 3??, cf. Lidzbarski Eph iii 20f. (highly uncert. interpret., dam. context).

‹bd$_1$ Ph QAL Impf. 3 p.s.m. *y‹bd* KAI 26A iii 10, C iv 11 - **Pun** QAL Pf. 3 p.pl. *‹bd›* CIS i 151[5] (for the reading, cf. Février JA ccxlvi 445 :: Guzzo Amadasi sub ICO-Sard 2: l. poss. (div. otherwise) *k‹bd* = Sing. abs. of *kbd$_2$* :: Pili BO xxii 214, 218 (div. otherwise) l.: *‹bd* = Sing. cstr. of *‹bd$_2$*); Inf. cstr. *‹bd* KAI 126[9] - **DA** QAL Impf. 3 p.s.m. *y‹bd* ii 6 (:: Hackett BTDA 26, 58, 60, 83, 96, 132: l. prob. *y‹br* = QAL Impf. 3 p.s.m. of *‹br$_1$*) - **Samal** QAL Impf. 3 p.pl.m. *y‹bdw* KAI 214[7] - **OldAr** QAL Pf. 3 p.s.m. *‹bd* Tell F 15; 3 p.pl.m. *‹bdw* KAI 223B 2; Impf. 3 p.s.m. *y‹b[d]* KAI 222C 20f.; 2 p.s.m. *[t]‹bd* KAI 224[22]; 1 p.s. *›‹bd* KAI 224[3] (for the reading, cf. e.g. Fitzmyer AIS 96, 106f., Vogt Bibl xxxix 271, Donner KAI a.l., Degen AAG p. 19 n. 80, ZDMG cxix 173, cxxi 134, Gibson SSI ii p. 46, 52, Lemaire & Durand IAS 118, 129, 144 :: Dupont-Sommer BMB xiii 31, AH i/1, 5, i/2, 5: l. *›‹br* = QAL Impf. 1 p.s. of *‹br$_1$* (= to pardon, to forgive)); 3 p.pl.m. *y‹bd[w]* KAI 222C 5 (dam. context, cf. Lemaire & Durand IAS 116, 125, 140f.: l. *y‹bd* = QAL Impf. 3 p.s.m.) - **OffAr** QAL Pf. 3 p.s.m. *‹bd* Cowl 56[2], Aḥiq 51, 198, Driv 7[3], 9[2], 12[6], Sach 76 iv 6, Sam 12, RES 438[3], KAI 262, 268[2,3], LA ix 331[1] (*[‹]bd*), SSI ii 37[2], Pers 3[3], 4[3], 5[2] (:: Naveh & Shaked Or xlii 452ff.: *‹bd* in Pers = QAL Imper. s.m. or poss. = QAL Part. pass. s.m. abs.), ATNS 8[10] (cf. Porten & Yardeni sub TADAE B 5.6; or = QAL Imper. s.m.? :: Segal ATNS a.l.: = PA‹EL Pf. 3 p.s.m.), etc., etc., *‹db* (lapsus) Pers 134[2]; 3 p.s.f. *‹bdt* KAI 269[2], IrAnt iv 109[1]; 2 p.s.m. *‹bdt* Cowl 7[6] (cf. Epstein ZAW xxxii 143 n. 3, Yaron JNES xx 128 (n. 9), Porten Arch 316, Grelot DAE p. 93 (n. c), Porten & Greenfield JEAS p. 124, Porten & Yardeni sub TADAE B 7.2 :: Cowl a.l., Joüon MUSJ xviii 62, Milik RB xlviii 566: = QAL Pf. 1 p.s.), 9[10], 71[19], ATNS 14[2], (dam. context; or = 1 p.s. or 3 p.s.f.?), Aḥiq 87 (or = 1 p.s. or 3 p.s.f.?; heavily dam. context; cf. also Kottsieper SAS 11, 19, 222: l. *‹br[t]* = QAL Pf. 3 p.s.f. of *‹br$_1$*), *‹bt* FuF xxxv 173[14] (poss. interpret.; cf. Altheim & Stiehl ibid. 177, ASA 257); 2 p.s.f. *‹bdty* Cowl 14[6]; 1 p.s. *‹bdt* Aḥiq 52, Beh 16 (Akkad. par. *e-pu-šu*), 49 (*‹bd[t]*, heavily dam. context; Akkad. par. *e-pu-šu*), Cowl p. 265[3] (cf. Greenfield & Porten BIDG p. 54), Cowl 68 v 1 (= BIDG 56 xxi 1 (Akkad. par. *e-pu-šú*)), Krael 9[22], SSI ii 28 rev. 3; 3 p.pl.m. *‹bdw* Cowl 30[13,22,27] (:: Delsman TUAT i 256: = lapsus for *t‹bd* = QAL Impf. 2 p.s.m.), 31[12,21] (cf. however Porten & Yardeni sub TADAE A 4.8: l. *‹bdn* ? = QAL Part.

act. pl.m. abs.), ATNS 126^3 (heavily dam. context), Beh 2 (Akkad. par. *i-te-ep-šu-ʾ*), 3 (Akkad. par. *i-te-ep-šu*), 4 (Akkad. par. *i-te-ep-šú*), 10 (*[ʿ]bdw*; Akkad. par. *i-te-ep-šu*), 17 (pro *mlk ʿlyhm ʿbdw* Akkad. par. *a-na ra-bu-ú ina eli-šú-nu it-tur*), 20 (Akkad. par. *i-te-ep-šu*), 29 (Akkad. par. *i-te-ep-šu*), 33 (Akkad. par. *i-te-ep-šu*), 43 (Akkad. par. *i-te-ep-šú*), FX 136^9, Pers 2^3, 13^2 (*[ʿ]bdw*), 14^2, 15^3, 95^3 (in Pers with Sing. subject (except perhaps in 95^3), diff. interpret., or rather is early symptom of ideographic writing? :: Bowman Pers p. 40ff., 66: = Qal Part. act. s.m. abs. + enclitic *w* (< Qal Pf. 3 p.s.m. of *hwy*$_1$ (cf. also Oelsner OLZ '75, 476)) :: Naveh & Shaked Or xlii 452ff.: = Qal Imper. pl.m. or perhaps = Qal Pf. 3 p.pl.m. with "neutral subject"); 3 p.pl.m. + suff. 1 p.s. *ʿbdwny* ATNS 28b 3 (:: Segal ATNS a.l.: = Paʿel Pf. 3 p.pl.m. + suff. 1 p.s.; cf. also Teixidor JAOS cv 732); 1 p.pl. *ʿbdn* Cowl 14^3; Impf. 3 p.s.m. *yʿbd* Cowl 26^{22}, 41^7, Aḥiq 21, 134, Beh 54 (*[y]ʿbd*, *yʿbd*, cf. Greenfield & Porten BIDG p. 48), Krael $7^{32,37,38,39}$, Driv 5^9, 9^2, 12^7, KAI 258^4, JRAS '29, 108^8, RSO xxxv 22^3 (*yʿb[d]*), NESE i 11^3 (cf. also Naveh & Shaked JAOS xci 381, Grelot DAE 504, Porten Or lvii 78, Porten & Yardeni sub TADAE A 3.10 :: Degen NESE i 16 (n. 10): = Qal pass. Impf. 3 p.s.m. :: Shunnar GMA 114f., CRM ii 280f., 287, Macuch JAOS xciii 59: l. *yʿbr* = Qal Impf. 3 p.s.m. of *ʿbr*$_1$), AM ii 174^5 (diff. context, cf. Altheim & Stiehl ASA 274, Suppl 96; v. also *gḥn*), Samar 2^5, 3^5; 3 p.s.f. *tʿbd* Krael $7^{33,40}$, Herm 1^7; 2 p.s.m. *tʿbd* Cowl 31^{26}, 41^6; 2 p.s.f. *tʿbdn* JRAS '29, 108^7; 1 p.s. *ʾʿbd* ATNS 90^2 (heavily dam. context); 3 p.pl.m. *yʿbdw* Cowl 26^5, Driv 5^9, *yʿbdwn* Krael 7^{34}, Driv 10^3, AJSL lviii 303A 11 (for the reading, cf. Bowman AJSL lviii 307); + suff. 3 p.s.f.(?) *yʿbdwh* Irâq xxxi 174^5 (diff. reading :: Segal Irâq a.l.: or l. *yʿtdyh* = Qal Impf. 3 p.s.m. + suff. 3 p.s.m. of *ʿtd*$_1$ (= to prepare)); 2 p.pl.m. *tʿbdwn* Cowl $38^{8,10}$, *tʿbdn* RES 1793^4 (= PSBA xxxvii 222^9; cf. Kutscher Kedem i 55, Dupont-Sommer, CRAI '45, 175, REJ '46/47, 48, Ben-Chayyim EI i 136, Grelot VT iv 378 n. 1, DAE p. 376 :: e.g. Driver AnOr xii 56: = Qal Impf. 3 p.pl.f. :: RES a.l.: = Qal Impf. 3 p.s.f. :: e.g. Segert AAG p. 308: = Qal Impf. 3 p.s.f. + suff. 1 p.s.); 2 p.pl.f. *tʿbdn* Herm 1^4; 1 p.pl. *nʿbd* Cowl 37^{16}; Imper. s.m. *ʿbd* Cowl 26^{22}, Aḥiq 52, 68, 127, Driv 13^2, ATNS $26^{11,15}$; + suff. 3 p.s.m. *ʿbdh[y]* Aḥiq 103 (cf. Lindenberger APA 85, 240 n. 224); pl.m. *ʿbdw* Driv 4^3, 7^7, 10^4, 11^3, ATNS 21^4 (cf. Naveh IEJ xxxv 211, Shaked Or lvi 409: or = Qal Pf. 3 p.pl.m.?, cf. Porten & Yardeni sub TADAE B 8.11 :: Segal ATNS a.l. (div. otherwise): l. *ʿbd* (= Sing. abs. of *ʿbd*$_2$)); Inf. *mʿbd* Cowl 26^9 (for this prob. reading, cf. Porten & Yardeni sub TADAE A 6.2)^{,10}, 27^{15}, Beh 2 (Akkad. par. *e-pe-šú*), 4 (Akkad. par. *e-peš*), 10 (Akkad. par. *e-peš*), 31 (*mʿb[d]*, cf. Greenfield & Porten BIDG p. 40f.; Akkad. par. *e-peš*), Cowl p. 269 vii 3 (= BIDG l. 9; Akkad. par. *e-pe-šú*), Driv 3^8, ATNS 31^3, 93^1 (*]mʿbd[*),

98^{9} (*m‹bd[]*), 116^{2} (*m‹bd[]*), JRAS '29, 108^{12}, FX 136^{7}; + suff. 3 p.s.m. *m‹bdh* Krael 8^{6,7,9}; Part. act. s.m. abs. *‹bd* KAI 261^{5}, Herm 1^{4,7}, 3^{4} (cf. e.g. Bresciani & Kamil Herm a.l., Gibson SSI ii p. 136 :: Milik Bibl xlviii 551, 582: = Sing. abs. of *‹bd$_2$*); s.f. abs. *‹bdh* NESE iii 34 conc. 4 (?, dam. context; cf. Degen NESE iii 36f.: or = f. Sing. abs. of *‹bd$_2$*); pl.m. abs. *‹bdn* Cowl 37^{5}, 38^{8} (for this prob. reading, cf. e.g. Grelot DAE p. 393 n. j, Porten & Greenfield JEAS p. 82, Porten & Yardeni sub TADAE A 4.3 :: Cowl a.l.: l. *‹bdw* = QAL Imper. pl.m.), Driv 7^{5,8}, AE '23, 42 no. 11^{1}; pl.f. abs. *‹bdn* Krael 5^{12}; QAL pass. Pf. 3 p.s.m. *‹byd* Cowl 6^{3} (v. also infra), 16^{5,8}, 30^{15,30}, 31^{14,29} (:: Cowl p. 302: for all Cowl-instances = QAL Part. pass. s.m. abs.; cf. however also Leand 32a: QAL Pf. pass. in Cowl 16^{5,8}, 30^{15,30}, 31^{14,29}), Driv 8^{5}, ATNS 8^{7}, 34b 2 (*[‹]byd*, dam. context; Segal ATNS a.l.: = Sing. abs. of *‹byd$_2$*), Beh 6 (cf. Greenfield & Porten BIDG p. 31 (cf. also Sokoloff JAOS cix 686) :: Kutscher PICS 140f.: = QAL Part. pass. s.m. abs. :: Cowl a.l.: = lapsus for *‹bd* (= QAL Pf. 3 p.s.m.); Akkad. par. *e-pu-uš*), KAI 279^{1} (cf. Garbini Kand 6 :: Dupont-Sommer JA ccxlvi 23, Koopmans p. 175, Altheim & Stiehl ASA 274, cf. idem GMA 346f., Donner KAI a.l.: or = QAL Part. pass. s.m. abs. (cf. also Levi Della Vida Editto 21)), SSI ii 28 obv. 6 (?, or = QAL Part. pass. s.m. abs.?, cf. Gibson SSI ii a.l.), OMRO lxviii 45^{3}, Sem xxxiii 94^{3} (= TADAE A 5.1; or = QAL Part. pass. s.m. abs.?; heavily dam. context), *‹bd* Driv 2^{3}; 1 p.s. *‹bydt* ATNS 29^{1} (dam. context, or = 3 p.s.f.? (cf. Porten & Yardeni sub TADAE B 8.1) :: Segal ATNS a.l. = form of Part. pass.); Part. pass. s.m. abs. *‹byd* Cowl 30^{18} (:: Leand 32b: = lapsus for *‹bd* (= QAL Pf. 3 p.s.m.)), 69B 4 (?, heavily dam. context), 76^{2} (?, heavily dam. context), Beh 52 (:: Leand 32b: poss. = lapsus for *‹bd* (= QAL Pf. 3 p.s.m.)), RES 1809^{2} (= HDS 165; or = QAL Part. pass. s.m. abs.?; or l. *‹byr* = passive form of *‹br$_1$*?, cf. Sznycer HDS 166); s.m. emph. *‹byd›* ATNS 83^{6} (dam. context), KAI 276^{4} (for this form, v. *nṣyḥ*); pl.m. abs. *‹bydn* SSI ii 28 rev. 2, *‹bydyn* Cowl 30^{20} (lapsus for *‹bydn* = pl.f. abs., cf. Cowl p. 117, Grelot DAE p. 411 n. z); ITP Impf. 3 p.s.m. *yt‹bd* Cowl 16^{9}, 26^{6}, 27^{9}, 33^{10}, Driv 3^{6,8}, 4^{1}, 7^{9}; 3 p.pl.m. *yt‹bdw* Cowl 73^{7}; Part. s.m. abs. *mt‹bd* Cowl 32^{11}; cf. Frah xviii 7 (*‹bydwn*), Paik 742-744 (*‹bdw*), 745, 746 (*‹bdwn*), 747-749 (*‹bd*), 751-755 (*‹bydwn*), Nisa-b 867^{3} (*‹bdt*; cf. Diakonov & Livshitz Nisa-b p. 49f., Altheim & Stiehl AAW ii 215), Syn 312^{1}, DEP 154 recto 2, BSOAS xxxiii 152^{13,15}, GIPP 19, 48f., 67, SaSt 13, cf. also Lemosín AO ii 108, Toll ZDMG-Suppl viii 35 - **Nab** QAL Pf. 3 p.s.m. *‹bd* CIS ii 158^{5}, 170^{2}, 173$^{1f.}$, 176^{2}, 190^{2}, 194^{1}, ARNA-Nab 17^{1}, 87^{2} (dam. context), 130^{1}, Lev vii 16^{1}, etc., etc.; 3 p.s.f. *‹bdt* CIS ii 211^{1}, 223^{1}, 226^{1}, RES 528^{2} (?; dam. context), BIA x 55^{4}; 3 p.pl.m. *‹bdw* CIS ii 200^{1}, 206^{10}, 213^{1}, 221^{8}, 354^{1}, RES 482^{1}, 1090^{6},

2117^{2}, RB xliv 268,2 (heavily dam. context), ADAJ xx 14^{9}, J 82 (for this reading, cf. Milik sub ARNA-Nab 111), CIS ii 198^{1}, 205^{1} (in the two last-mentioned instances with f. subject, cf. Cantineau Nab i 76f., Ben-Chayyim EI i 137), *ʿbw* (lapsus) CIS ii 207^{9}; + suff. 3 p.s.f. *ʿbdwh* RB xliii 574^{1} (for the reading, cf. Milik ADAJ xxi 144 n. 3); Impf. 3 p.s.m. *yʿbd* CIS ii 198^{7}, 199^{6}, 208^{5}, 209^{7}, 210^{7}, 212^{7}, 217^{6}, 223^{4}, 224^{10}, J 5^{8}; 3 p.s.f. *tʿbd* CIS ii 204^{4}; QAL pass. Pf. 3 p.s.m. *ʿbyd* CIS ii 221^{6}; 3 p.s.f. *ʿbydt* CIS ii 196^{8} (cf. Cantineau Nab i 75); ITP Impf. 3 p.s.m. *ytʿbd* CIS ii 350^{4} - **Palm** QAL Pf. 3 p.s.m. *ʿbd* CIS ii 3902^{1}, 3917^{2,3}, 3920^{2}, 3937^{2}, 4066^{2} (Greek par. ἀν[έθηκεν]), 4160^{1} (Greek par. κατεσκεύασεν), Inv xi 2^{2}, xii 2^{3}, 19^{1} (Greek par. ἐποί[ησ]εν), SBS 3^{1}, RIP 21^{2}, 24^{3} (Greek par. ἐπόησε), Ber ii 109^{3} (Greek par. ἐποίησεν), Syr lxii 274 ii 1 (Greek par. ἔκτισεν), etc., etc., *ʿb* (lapsus) CIS ii 4300^{3}, RIP 103c 3, *ʿb* (lapsus) CIS ii 4300^{3}; 3 p.s.f. *ʿbdt* CIS ii 3919^{2}, 3927^{2}, 3988^{1} (= RIP 128), 3994^{1}, 4010^{2} (= Inv xi 23), Inv xi 5^{2}, etc., etc.; 3 p.pl.m. *ʿbdw* CIS ii 3911^{4}, 3914^{4}, 3915^{2}, 3916^{2,6}, Inv xi 48^{1}, xii 1^{1}, SBS 19^{3}, RIP 167^{1} (for the context, cf. Gawlikowski Ber xix 74, RIP a.l.), DM ii 43 ii 2, FS Miles 50 i 1, Syr xvii 353^{4} (cf. Milik DFD 301, 303, Gawlikowski TP 57f. :: Cantineau Syr xvii 353 (div. otherwise): l. *ʿbd* = QAL Pf. 3 p.s.m.), Syr lxii 273^{1} (Greek par. ᾠκο[δό]μησαν), FS Collart 161^{1}, *ʿbd* Inv x 44^{3}, xi 74^{2}, SBS 48^{5} (cf. Milik DFD 312 :: Cantineau Syr xvii 280, Dunant SBS a.l.: = QAL Pf. 3 p.s.m.)^{,7} (Greek par. ἀνήγειρεν), Ber v 94^{5} (poss. also in CIS ii 3955^{4}, 4002^{2}, 4018^{2}, 4053^{1}, 4056^{3}, 4085^{3}, 4121, Syr xxvi 40^{1}, Inv xii 43^{2}, 46^{2}, or = QAL Pf. 3 p.s.m.?; for *ʿbdw* with Sing. subject, cf. Sadurska PBP 18); Impf. 3 p.s.m. *yʿbd* MUSJ xxxviii 106^{10}; Part. act. pl.m. cstr. *ʿbdʾ* CIS ii 3945^{4} - **Hatra** QAL (:: Aggoula Syr lxvii 411: in 40, 65, 409 = PAʿEL) Pf. 3 p.s.m. *ʿbd* 40^{1}, 61, 68^{1} (dam. context), 73, 291^{2}, 338^{1}, 409 iii 1, app. 4^{5,6}; 1 p.s. + suff. 3 p.s.f. *ʿbdyth* 72 (for this uncert. reading, cf. Milik DFD 166, Vattioni IH a.l., cf. also Caquot Syr xxxii 269 (div. otherwise): l. *ʿbd/ryt yʾ...* (without interpret.) and Safar Sumer xi 12: l. *ʿ?bd...* (without interpret.)); Part. act. s.m. abs./cstr. *ʿbd* 107^{4} (cf. Safar Sumer xviii 30, Caquot Syr xli 252f., Aggoula MUSJ xlvii 39, Vattioni IH a.l. :: Aggoula Ber xviii 98: = QAL Pf. 3 p.s.m.), *ʿbyd* 189^{3} (cf. Safar Sumer xviii 54, Milik DFD 361, Vattioni IH a.l. :: Caquot Syr xli 267: = n.p.), 229a 2 (cf. Degen WO v 232, Vattioni IH a.l. :: Safar Sumer xxi 42 n. 26: = QAL Part. pass. s.m. abs./cstr.) - **JAr** QAL Pf. 3 p.s.m. *ʿbd* MPAT-A 9^{1} (cf. Hestrin BLRF iii 63, Fitzmyer & Harrington MPAT a.l. × Naveh sub SM 3 (div. otherwise): l. *ʿbdt* = QAL Pf. 1 p.s.), 14^{1} (= SM 47), 15^{2} (= SM 18 = Frey 982), 16^{2} (= SM 17 = Frey 981), 17^{1} (= SM 7), 21 (= SM 11), 25^{2} (= SM 12 = Frey 976), 30^{1} (= SM 26), SM 40^{1}, 110, AMB 15^{13} (diff. context); + suff. 3 p.s.m./f. *ʿbdh* MPAT 145c 1 (for this diff. and uncert. reading, cf. Milik with Zayadine Syr xlvii 131,

Beyer ATTM 342; cf. however e.g. Lidzbarski Eph ii 196f.: l. *‹nyh* = n.p. :: Fitzmyer & Harrington MPAT a.l.: l. *‹nyh* = Sing. emph. of *‹ny*$_3$ (= the poor one)); 1 p.s. *‹bdt* MPAT-A 9 (cf. Naveh sub SM 3, Sokoloff Maarav i 80 :: e.g. Hestrin BRF iii 65, Fitzmyer & Harrington MPAT a.l. (div. otherwise): l. *‹bd* (= QAL Pf. 3 p.s.m.) + *h*–), Syn 269 no. 2[1] (cf. also Naveh sub SM 90 :: du Mesnil du Buisson Syr xl 308ff.: l. *‹bdh* (= Sing. abs.) = work), ZDPV xcvi 59[1]; 3 p.pl.m. *‹bdw* MPAT-A 20[1] (= SM 10), 22[10] (= SM 70), 40[2] (= SM 57; *[‹]bdw*), 42[3] (= SM 20), *‹bdwn* MPAT-A 34[3] (= SM 69), SM 30[3] (:: Fitzmyer & Harrington sub MPAT-A 36: l. *‹bdyn* = QAL Part. act. pl.m. abs., cf. Frey 987a; cf. also Hüttenmeister ASI 247, Beyer ATTM 389); Impf. 1 p.s. *›‹bd* MPAT 39[7], 53[3], 59[3], DBKP 20[42]; 2 p.pl.m. *t‹bdwn* MPAT 53[2], 54[2] (*t‹bd[wn]*; heavily dam. context); Imper. s.m. *‹bd* MPAT 55[3]; *‹ybd* MPAT 89[1] (:: Puech RB xc 484, 486, 489: l. *‹wbd* = PU‹AL Pf. 3 p.s.m. (hebraism?) :: Beyer ATTM 329, 650: l. *‹wbd* = Sing. abs. of *‹bd*$_3$; on reading and interpret., cf. also Bennett Maarav iv 252f.); Inf. *m‹bd* MPAT 52[10], MPAT-A 30[2] (= SM 26), *m‹bd›* MPAT 89[3] (cf. also Avigad IEJ xvii 104, cf. however Kutscher with Avigad ibid.: or = Ephal Inf.); Part. act. s.m. abs. *‹byd* MPAT-A 43[2] (highly uncert. text, on the problem, cf. Naveh sub SM 5, cf. also Beyer ATTM 387, 649: = QAL Part. pass. s.m. abs.); QAL pass. Pf. 3 p.s.m. *‹byd* MPAT 67[1f.] (:: Fitzmyer & Harrington MPAT p. 331: = QAL Part. pass. s.m. abs., cf. also Frey 1300 :: Puech RB xc 487 = HAPH Inf.); ITP Impf. 3 p.s.f. *tt‹bd* MPAT 53[2] - ¶ verb QAL - **1)** to make, to do, passim; cf. the final clause of Nab. tomb inscriptions mentioning the name of the mason, *ḥwrw psl› br ›ḥyw ‹bd* J 5[11]: Ch. the mason the son of A. made (it; i.e. the tomb), cf. also CIS ii 198[11f.], 201[5f.], 206[10], etc., etc. (for the instances of *‹bd* without intended object, v. sub 2) - a) + obj. - α) material result-object, *dmwt› z›t ‹bd ›l zy qdm hwtr* Tell F 15: he made this statue, he added to what was before (i.e. he made this statue more (beautiful) than it was before; cf. Akkad. par. *ṣalmu šu-a-te eli maḫ-re-e ú-šá-tir*); *›rtbrwn ‹bd ›bšwn* Pers 29[3f.]: A. made a pestle (cf. e.g. Pers 27[4f.], 37[3f.], cf. e.g. Levine JAOS xcii 77f. :: R.A.Bowman Pers p. 41ff.: *‹bd* here = to use); *‹bdw mqbrt›* RES 1090[6]: they made a tomb; *‹lt› dnh ‹bd ‹b›* CIS ii 4101[1f.]: A. made this altar; *‹bdw tr‹y› ›ln* CIS ii 3914[4]: they made these doors; *‹bd ›ksdr›* Inv xii 2[3]: he made the exedra; *‹bd hw wbnwhy mṭlt› dh w‹mwdyh* SBS 43[3f.]: he and his sons made this roof and its pillars; *[ṣ]lmy› ›ln trwyhwn ‹bd* Inv xii 83[1]: he made these two statues (cf. also *›lht›* (v. *›lh*$_1$) *d› ›sy dy ‹bdw bny* ... ADAJ xx 121[7ff.]: this goddess is Isis which the sons of ... made ...); *nṣbt ... [dy] ‹bdwh* RB xliii 574[1] (v. supra): the stela ... which they made; *gwmḥy›* ... *‹bdw* DM ii 43 ii 1f.: they made the niches; *ḥlpw ... ‹bd hdn ‹mwdh* MPAT-A 15[1f.]: Ch. made this column; *ywdn ... d‹bd hdn* *sṭwh* MPAT-A 16[1f.]: Y. who made this colonnade (v. *sṭwh*); etc., etc. - β) immaterial object, *ʿbd kl ʿbydh* Aḥiq 127: do every work; *ʾzd ʿbdw* ATNS 21[4]: made an inquiry; *tʿbd kl dy tṣbʾ* CIS ii 204[4]: she may do whatever she wants (for this type of formula, cf. Greenfield Mem Yalon 69f., Hurvitz VT xxxii 259ff.); *mndʿm bʾyš lʾ ʿbdt* KAI 269[2]: she has done nothing wrong (cf. also Grelot Sem xvii 73, Donner REAR 43); *ṣydʾ ʿbd ʾnh tnh* KAI 261[5]: I was hunting here; *ʾmt* (v. *ʾmt*) *tʿbdn psḥʾ* RES 1793[4f.]: when will you celebrate the Passover?; *ʿbdw qrb* Beh 3: they joined battle (cf. Beh 2, 10, 20, 29, 33, 43; cf. Sokoloff JAOS cix 685); *ʿbdn hm qrbʾ* AE '23, 42 no. 11[1]: they are bringing a sacrifice (dam. context); *ʾrwst ʿbt* FuF xxxv 173[14]: you acted (in) perfection (v. *ʾrwst*, *nṣyḥ*; cf. also KAI 276[3f.]); *wʿbd plṭyʾ ṣbyḥyt* Inv x 44[7]: he accomplished his career gloriously; *ʿbd ṭbtʾ* Hatra 107[4f.]: benefactory (epithet of Shamash); cf. Hatra 229a 2 (cf. also Hatra 189[3], cf. Milik DFD 361): epithet of a king; for this epithet, cf. Safar Sumer xviii 29 n. 13, Milik DFD 379, Tubach ISS 260 (n. 33); *dʿtyd mʿbd mṣwth* MPAT-A 30[2]: who will make a donation in the future; etc.; cf. also *dynʾ zy ʿbdn* Cowl 14[3]: the legal action which we took - γ) + non-resultative material object, *yʿbdw ʾrq wkrm* KAI 214[7]: they cultivated land and vineyard; *qynyʾ ʿbdʾ dhbʾ wkspʾ* CIS ii 3945[3f.]: the smiths working in gold and silver - b) + double object, *lmʿbdh ʿbd* Krael 8[7]: to enslave him (cf. Krael 8[6,9]); *prtw ... mlk ʿlyhm ʿbdw* Beh 17 (for the reading, cf. Greenfield & Porten BIDG p. 34): they made P. ... king over themselves; *wdpny ʿbdwny* ATNS 28b 3: they made me a mistreated one (i.e. they mistreated me; v. *dpny*) - c) + obj. + b_2, *mnḥh wlbw[n]h wʿlwh lʾ ʿbdw bʾgwrʾ zk* Cowl 30[21f.]: neither meal-offering, incense nor sacrifice do they offer in that temple; *ʿbdw qrb bhyw* Beh 4: they joined battle at H.; *ʿbd šlmʾ btḥwmy mdytʾ* DFD 37[3]: he established peace in the territory of the city; *mn dʿbd mṣwth bhdn ʾtrh qdyšh* MPAT-A 30[1f.]: one who has made a donation in this holy place - d) + obj. + l_5, *mh ṭb bʿyny ʾʿbd* (v. supra) *lhm* KAI 224[3]: whatever seems fitting to me I shall do to them; *bʾyš[tʾ] lʾ ʿbd lk* Aḥiq 50f.: he did you no evil; *ʿbd nšrʾ lqws* Syr xxxv 236a: He made the eagle for Q.; *krpʾ lmʿbd lkndwṣ ʾlhʾ* FX 136[7f.]: to make a sanctuary (??, v. *krp*) for the god K. (Greek par. ἱδρύσασθαι βωμὸν Βασιλεῖ Καυνίωι; :: Teixidor Syr liii 335: *ʿbd* = to adore, to serve); *ʿbdw kmrʾ lsymyn* FX 136[9]: they made S. a priest (cf. Greek par. καὶ εἵλοντο ἱερέα Σιμίαν); *ʿbd kmšhll ... mdbḥʾ dnh ... lzk b[y]t[ʾ]* LA ix 331[2ff.]: K. has made this altar for this temple; *bwlʾ wdms ʿbdw ṣlmyʾ ʾln trwyhwn lʾʿylmy* CIS ii 3930[1f.]: the Senate and the People have made these two statues for A.; *mʿrtʾ dh ... ʿbd mʿytw ... lh* CIS ii 4166[1ff.]: M. has made this hypogee for himself; *ʿbd ʾbgl ... hyklʾ lʾbgl ʾlhʾ* PNO 3b: A. has made a temple for the god A.; *dkl dʾlyšʿ ʾmr lk ʿbd lh* MPAT 55[2f.]: everything that E. says to you, do (it) for him; *ʿbdt hdh qbwrth lʾlh* ZDPV xcvi 59$^{1f.}$: I have made this tomb for I.; *qynʾ ʿlmʾ ʿybd lyswn* MPAT 89^{1}; make an everlasting lament for J. (cf. ibid. l. 3); etc., etc. (v. also *hndrz*) - α) + obj. + *lyd*, *krbr ʿbd ʾbšwn lyd dtmtr gnzbrʾ* Pers 12$^{2f.}$: K. has made a pestle at the disposal of (i.e. intended for) the treasurer D. (cf. Pers 7$^{3f.}$, 8$^{2f.}$, etc.; for these texts, cf. e.g. also Levine JAOS xcii 71, 77f., Hinz FS Nyberg 375); cf. also + obj. + *lyd* + *qdm$_3$*: *ʿbd hwn znh rb lyd bgpt ... qdm mzddt* Pers 39$^{3ff.}$: he has made this big mortar at the disposal of B. ... on the order of M. (cf. Pers 36$^{1f.}$, 47$^{3ff.}$) - β) + obj. + *lšm*, *dsgy sgy* (v. *šgʾ$_3$*) *ʾnwn* (v. *hʾ$_1$*) *ʿbdw lšmh drḥmnh* MPAT-A 22^{10}: which have done very much for the Name of the Merciful One - e) + obj. + *l$_5$* + *l$_5$*, *bt qbwrʾ dnh ʿbdw ... lhwn lyqrhwn* CIS ii 4163: they have made this tomb ... for themselves to their honour; *qbrʾ dnh ʿbd bny wʾlhšʾ ... lhwn ... lyqrhwn dy bt ʿlmʾ* CIS ii 4121: B. and E. have made this tomb ... for themselves ... to (be) their magnificent tomb (cf. however *yqr$_2$*); etc. - f) + obj. + *l$_5$* + *ʿl$_7$*, *ʿmwdʾ dnʾ ... ʿbdw ... lʾlhʾ rbʾ ... ʿl ḥyyhn* CIS ii 3911$^{2ff.}$: they made ... this pillar ... for the great god ... for their lives (cf. CIS ii 3973$^{1ff.}$, 4053^{1}, Sem xxvii 117$^{2ff.}$, etc.) - g) + obj. + *mn$_5$*, *wʿbd mṭltʾ dh ... mn kysh* SBS 40$^{6f.}$: he has made this portico ... on his costs - h) + obj. + *ʿl$_7$*, *[t]ʿbd mrmt ʿly* KAI 224^{22}: you will commit acts of treachery against me (cf. also Greenfield ActOr xxix 10); *smytʾ dy kspʾ ... ʿbd yrḥy ... ʿl ḥywhy* CIS ii 3902: Y. has made a silver statue for his life (cf. CIS ii 3993$^{1ff.}$, Inv xii 44$^{4f.}$) - i) + obj. + *ʿl$_7$* + *l$_5$*, *bt ʿlmʾ dnh ʿbd mtny ... ʿl nwrbl ʾbwhy wʿl nby ʾmh lyqrhn* CIS ii 4130$^{1f.}$: M. made this tomb ... for his father N. and for his mother N. to their honour (cf. Syr lxii 271$^{1,3f.}$) - j) + obj. + *ʿm$_4$*, *wmn byš yʿbd ʿm ptkr znh* KAI 258$^{3f.}$: and whoever will damage this relief; *dynn yʿbd ʿm yhwpdyny* Samar 3^{5}: he will enter into litigation with Y. - k) + obj. + *ʿm$_4$* + *ʿl$_7$*: *dynyn yʿbd ʿm ʾbyʿdn ʿl[* Samar 2^{5}: he will enter into litigation with A. concerning ... - l) + obj. + *qdm$_3$*, *ʿbd ʾbšwn 1 qdm mzddt* Pers 26$^{3ff.}$: he has made a pestle on the order of M. (cf. Pers 5$^{2f.}$, etc.); cf. also + obj. + *qdm$_3$* + *lyd*: Pers 94$^{3f.}$, 116$^{2ff.}$ (cf. also Delaunay CC 211, 216: *qdm* in these texts = for, at the disposal of (poss. interpret.) :: Hinz FS Nyberg 69f.: = in the presence of) - m) + *b$_2$* + obj., *wʿbd hw wlšmš ... bʾst[wʾ] dnh ʿmwdyn štʾ* CIS ii 3955$^{4f.}$: he made together with L. six columns in this portico; *ʿbd bʾlgšyʾ ḥmnʾ* CIS ii 3917^{3}: he made a chapel (with incense altar, v. *ḥmn*) in O.; *yʿbd bsṭrʾ ... ḥwlwh* MUSJ xxxviii 106^{10}: he will make his *loculi* (v. *ḥwl$_2$*) in the wall (v. *šṭr$_3$*); *lmʿbd bh kl dy yṣbwn* MPAT 52^{10}: to do there (i.e. on the site in question) whatever they want (for this type of formula, cf. Greenfield Mem Yalon 69f.); cf. also *wʿbd bslqʾ dnh ʿmwdyn šbʿʾ* CIS ii 3952^{3}: and he made seven columns in this portico (*bslqʾ* prob. pro *bbslqʾ*) - n) + *l$_5$*, *mh zy tʿbdwn lḥwr* Cowl 38^{8}: what you do for Ch. (cf.

Herm $1^{4,4f.,7}$, 3^4); *sprʾ znh zy ʾnh ʿbdt lky* Krael 9^{22}: this document which I made for you (on this text, cf. also de Boer FS Vööbus 87); *hw ʿbd lnpšh* SSI ii 37^2: he made (them) for his funerary monument (v. *npš*); *dnh qbrʾ dy ʿbd khln ... lnpšh* CIS ii 206^1: this the tomb which K. made ... for himself; *ṣlm ḥšš dy ʿbdw lh bny kmrʾ* CIS ii $3915^{1f.}$: statue of Ch. which the Bene K. made for him; *ʿltʾ dy ʿbd mlkw ... lyrḥbwl ...* MUSJ xxxviii $133^{1ff.}$: the altar which M. made ... for Y.; *dʿbd lh ʿtʿqb* AAS xxxvi/xxxvii 169 no. 10^3: what A. made for him; *ʿbd zbydʾ ... lḥywhy* Inv xi $28^{2f.}$: Z. made (it) ... for his life; etc., etc.; cf. also *klʾ lqḥw wlnpšhwm ʿbdw* Cowl 30^{13}: they took all and made (it) their own; *klʾ nḥtḥwr lqḥ ʿbd lnpšh* Driv 12^6: N. has taken everything and made it his own (for this interpret., cf. Driv p. 83, Yaron JNES xx 128, Greenfield FS Rundgren 153, cf. also Whitehead JNES xxxvii 134 (n. 101): loan translation from Iran.; cf. poss. also Cowl 7^6, v. supra) - o) + l_5 + obj., *ʿbdʾ hmt lm t ḥnt* CIS i 151^5: they made (i.e. showed) him favour (v. however supra); *ʿbd lmlkw ... ṣlm ...* RIP $161^{3f.}$: he made the statue for M. (cf. SBS $45^{10f.}$, 48^7); v. also *dyn*$_2$ - p) + l_5 + obj. + ʿl_7, *lyqr mlkʾ ... ʿbd glptʾ dnh ʾnʿm wbʿly ʿl ḥyyhwn* PNO 57: A. and B. have made this sculpture in honour of M. for their lives - q) + l_5 + b_2, *dʾ mqbrtʾ ... dy ʿbd ʿbdʿbdt ... lʾytybl ... wlʾytybl bbyt šlṭwnhm* CIS ii $196^{1ff.}$: this is the tomb ... which A. made ... for A. ... and A. in their government house; cf. also *ʿbd lh [ʾrbʿ] pḥzyʾ pḥz pḥz bt ʾlhyh ṣlm dy nḥš lyqrh* SBS 48: the four tribes made for him each tribe in his temple a bronze statue in his honour (*bt* prob. pro *bbt*) - r) + l_5 + l_5, *ʿbd ʾbgl lʾbgl ʾlhʾ lḥywh* PNO 15: A. made (it) for the god A. for his life; *lʾwrlys ... ʿbd blʿqb ... lyqrh* CIS ii $3937^{1ff.}$: B. made (it) ... for A. ... for his honour - s) + l_5 +l_5 + l_5, *ʿbd lh ... lbt ʿlmh lyqrh* CIS ii $4119^{6f.}$: he made it for himself ... to (be) his tomb for his honour - t) + l_5 + mn_5 + obj., *lbl ḥmwn ʿbdw mn kyshwn ... hyklʾ dnh* Inv xii 48^1: they made this temple for B.Ch. at their costs - u) + l_5 + ʿl_7, *mwmʾh dkʾ zy ʿbdty ly ʿl nksyʾ ʾlky* Cowl 14^6: that oath which you took to me concerning those goods; *lmrʾ ʿlmʾ ʿbd ḥyr[n] ... ʿl ḥywhy* CIS ii $3990^{1ff.}$: Ch. made (it) for the lord of the universe ... for his life (cf. Hatra $338^{1f.}$) - v) + mn_5, *ʿbd bl ḥmn wmnwt mn kys ʿtʿqb* Inv xii $43^{2f.}$: B. and M. made (it) at the expense of A. - w) + mn_5 + obj., *mnkn ʾʿbd prʿnwtʾ* MPAT 59^3: I shall exact the punishment from you (cf. MPAT 53^3) - x) + ʿl_7, *kwt tʿbd bnt ʿly* Herm 1^7: thus may Banit do to me; *lmʿbd ʿl byt mlkʾ* ATNS 31^3: to make for the house of the king (context however dam.; :: Wesselius BiOr xli 706: to add to the king's domain); *dnh kprʾ dy ʿbdw ʿnmw ... wʾrsksh ... ʿl rwmʾ wklbʾ* CIS ii $213^{1f.}$: this is the tomb which A. ... and A. have made ... for R. and K.; *ʿbd lšmšy ... ʿl ḥyy zbydʾ* Inv xi $2^{2f.}$: L. made (it) ... for the life of Z.; etc.; cf. also the foll. comb., *wʿbd ʿl bytʾ zyly* Driv 7^3: he appropiated them to my estate (said of people and objects); cf. Driv 7^{7}, 12^{7}, on the expression, cf. Driv p. 64, Whitehead JNES xxxvii 134 (n. 101, cf. however Greenfield FS Nyberg 311f.); in ATNS 14^{2} uncert. and diff. context - y) + *‘l*$_{7}$ + *l*$_{5}$, *dnh kpr› dy ‘bd mlkywn ... ‘l ḥnynw ... wlnpšh* CIS ii 201$^{1ff.}$: this the tomb that M. made ... for Ch. ... and for himself - z) + *‘m*$_{4}$ + obj., *w‘bd ‘mhwn gbwrt›* RIP 142^{2}: he did a miracle (v. *gbrh*$_{2}$) for them - aa) + *qdm*$_{3}$, *lqbl zy qdmn ‘bd qdmy* Driv 9^{2}: corresponding to that which he previously has made for me/on my order (cf. CIS ii 123^{3}) - bb) cf. also the foll. combinations - α) *‘bd wmwd› yrḥbl› ... dy ...* Inv xi 1$^{2ff.}$: Y. has made, returning thanks (sc. to the deity) ... because ... (cf. Inv xi 13$^{3f.}$, 16$^{2ff.}$, etc.); *‘bd gd› wmwd› br ḥlp›* Inv xi 15$^{2f.}$: G. the son of Ch. has made, returning thanks (lapsus??); *‘lt› dnh ‘bd wmwd› [y]rḥbwl› ...* Inv xi 20$^{3f.}$: Y. has made this altar, returning thanks; *‘bd wmwd› ‘lt› dnh ‘gylw ...* Inv xii 34$^{2f.}$: O. has made this altar, returning thanks - β) *mṭlt› dh klh ... ‘bd wqrb ‘lyš› ...* SBS 3^{1}: A. has made and offered ... this whole portico (cf. SBS 7^{1}, 21; cf. also SBS 35^{1}, Inv xii 19^{1}) - **2)** to act, to do; *bywm zy y‘b[d] kn* KAI 222C 20f.: on the day (i.e. when) he acts this way; *hn kn ‘bdw* Cowl 30^{27}: if they act thus; *kzy hwyn ‘bdn lk* Krael 5$^{12f.}$: as we were doing for you (cf. e.g. Porten & Greenfield JEAS p. 49, Grelot DAE p. 227, Porten & Yardeni sub TADAE B 3.6 :: Krael p. 181: just as we were serving thee); *‘bd lqbl zy ...* Aḥiq 68: act according to ...; *l› y‘bd kdy ‘l› ktyb* CIS ii 198^{7}: he will not act in accordance with what is written above; *y‘bd k‘yr mh dy ‘l› ktyb* CIS ii 199$^{6f.}$: he shall do otherwise than what is written above; *lqbl zy ›nh ‘bdt lk kn ›pw ‘bd ly* Aḥiq 52: according as I acted towards you, act towards me just in the same way; *gnbyt ‘bdn* Cowl 37^{5}: acting thievishly; *w›m l› kn t‘bdwn ...* MPAT 53^{2}: if you do not do so ...; etc. - **3)** to serve; for a poss. instance with this meaning, v. *‘bd*$_{2}$ - **4)** to use; *ytn› l‘bd bṣp›t* KAI 126^{9}: they gave (him) the right to use the broad purple stripe on the tunica (originally distinctive mark of a senator; cf. Lat. par. *lato clavo ... uti conce[ssit]*) - Qal pass. - **1)** to be made; *‘bydt› dy ‘l› ‘bydt* CIS ii 196$^{7f.}$: the work mentioned above (i.e. the tomb) was constructed ...; *wkpr› dnh ‘byd byrḥ ›dr* CIS ii 221$^{5f.}$: and this tomb was constructed in the month of A. - a) + obj., *zy k‘n pqyd ‘bd ḥlpwhy* Driv 2$^{2f.}$: who now has been made an officer in his place - b) + *l*$_{5}$, *k‘šq ‘byd ly* Cowl 16^{8}: a wrong was done to me (cf. also Degen GGA ’79, 44 n. 78); *b‘dn zy z› b›yšt› ‘byd ln* Cowl 30$^{17f.}$: at the time when this evil was done to us; *kwkh dnh ‘byd lgrmy ›bhtnh* MPAT 67$^{1f.}$: this sepulchral chamber was made for the bones of our fathers (cf. Cowl 16^{5}, 30^{30}, 31^{29}); cf. also *zy ›trh byb byrt› ‘byd ...* Cowl 6$^{2f.}$: whose office is in the fortress of Yeb (cf. OMRO lxviii 45^{3}; cf. Nöldeke ZA xx 146, cf. also Clermont-Ganneau RCHL ’06/2, 347 n. 2, Cowl a.l., Grelot DAE p.

174, Porten & Greenfield JEAS p. 7, Hoftijzer OMRO lxviii 46, Porten & Yardeni sub TADAE B 2.2 :: SC p. 36: *ʿbyd* = Sing. abs. of *ʿbyd$_2$* (= workman) :: Lidzbarski Eph iii 78 (n.3): = soldier :: Wag 51 (n. 3): = agricultural labourer, farmer) - 2) to happen; *kzy kznh ʿbyd* Cowl 30[15]: when this happened (cf. Cowl 31[14]); *ʿbyd zy mrʾn* KAI 279[1]: it happened that our lord ... (for the context, v. *ptytw*); cf. also ATNS 8[7] (?, dam. context) - **3)** to be faring, to be going on, *ʾyk bytʾ ʿbyd* SSI ii 28 obv. 6: how is the family faring? - **4)** to be made a slave: ATNS 29[1] (?, dam. context; or: to be engaged?, cf. Porten & Yardeni sub TADAE B 8.1) - **5)** prob. with active meaning: Beh 6 (cf. Greenfield & Porten BIDG p. 31 :: Cowl a.l.: *ʿbyd* lapsus for *ʿbd* = Qal Pf. 3 p.s.m.; cf. Akkad. par. *e-pu-uš*) - Part. pass. made; *ktwnk wlbšk ʿbydn* SSI ii 28 rev. 2: your tunic and your garment are made; *nšyʾ zyln kʾrmlh ʿbydyn* (v. supra) Cowl 30[20]: our wives are made widowlike; cf. also Part. pass. with active meaning, *hwdʿ ʾyk zy ʿbyd ʾnt* Beh 52: make known how you act (cf. Greenfield & Porten BIDG p. 47 :: Cowl a.l. (connecting otherwise): ... how it was done. You ...); - Itp - **1)** to be made; *hn ʾzd ytʿbd mn dynyʾ* Cowl 27[8f.]: if inquiries (v. *ʾzd*) are made by the judges; *kʿšq ʾl ytʿbd ly* Cowl 16[9]: let wrong not be done to me; *srwšytʾ ... ytʿbd lhm* Driv 3[6]: let the punishment be inflicted upon them (cf. Driv 3[8]; cf. also Greenfield IrJu 8f.); *wgst ptgm ytʿbd lk* Driv 4[3f.]: a punishment (v. *gst$_1$*) will be made to you (cf. Driv 7[9f.]); *mnkn prʿnwtʾ ttʿbd* MPAT 53[2]: punishment will be exacted from you; cf. also *wqn twr ʿnz mqlw [l]ʾ ytʿbd tmh* Cowl 33[10]: sheep, oxen, goats will not be offered as burnt-offering there - **2)** to happen, to be done (without logical object); *lqbl zy lqdmyn hwh mtʿbd* Cowl 32[10f.]: as formerly happened; cf. also *kdy bšṭry ... ʾnw ytʿbd wlʾ ytšnʾ* CIS ii 350[2]: according to what is in these documents of ..., it will be done and not be changed - Lipiński Stud 45: l. *ʿbd* in KAI 222B 43 (= Qal Pf. 3 p.s.m.; poss. reading, heavily dam. context) - Lemaire & Durand IAS 117, 126: l. poss. *yʿbd* (= Qal Impf. 3 p.s.m.) in KAI 223 A 11 (highly uncert. reading) - Lipiński Stud 140: l. *ʿbd* (= Qal Pf. 3 p.s.m.) in TH 5 vs. 3 (= AECT 57); *ʿbd l[s]pr ...*, he acted for the writer of ...; diff. reading, cf. Friedrich TH a.l. (: l. *ʿ.d*, Degen NESE i 56) - a form of this root also in Cowl 54[9] (*[ʿ]bdw*); for the reading cf. Porten & Yardeni sub TADAE A 3.1 recto 8 :: Cowl a.l.: l. poss. *ʿbdk* = Sing. + suff. 2 p.s.m. of *ʿbd$_2$* - Milik Syr xlv 102: l. *[ʾʿ]bydnnh* (= Aph Pf. 1 p.pl. + suff. 3 p.s.m.) in Syr xlv 101[22], heavily dam. context, improb. interpret. - Segal Irâq xxxi a.l.: l. *yʿb[d]* (= Qal Impf. 3 p.s.m.) in Irâq xxxi 174[6]? (heavily dam. context) - Milik sub ARNA-Nab 79: l. *mʿbd* (= Qal Inf.; uncert. reading) in CIS ii 200[5] (= J 30) - a form of this root prob. in NESE iii 34 conc. 3 (*tʿb[d]*), cf. also Degen NESE iii 36 - Vattioni IH a.l.: l. *ʿbdw* (= Qal Pf. 3 p.pl.m.) in Hatra 65[7] (highly uncert., reading *ʿwdw* poss., cf. Aggoula MUSJ

xlvii 30: l. *‹wdw* (= variant of *‹bdw* (= QAL Pf. 3 p.pl.m.)), cf. however Caquot Syr xxxii 266: = n.p. (cf. also Ingholt AH i/1, 46, i/2, 49, Abbadi PIH 42), cf. however also Safar Sumer xi 8 n. 27: the readings c*wdw*, *‹ydw*, *‹wrw* or *‹yrw* poss. (:: Safar ibid.: = epithet of a deity), for the reading, cf. also Milik DFD 407: readings *‹wdw*, *‹yrw*, *‹wdy*, *‹ydy* and *‹ydw* poss.) - a derivative of this root (*‹bdh*) in EI xx 306 v, heavily dam. context, uncert. interpret., cf. Naveh EI xx a.l.
v. *bny*$_1$, *br*$_1$, *dn*$_1$, *zrd*, *‹bd*$_{2,3}$, *‹byd*$_2$, *‹br*$_{1,4}$, *‹zr*$_1$, *‹rr*$_{1,2}$.

‹bd$_2$ **Ph** Sing. abs. *‹bd* KAI 26A i 15 (cf. v.d.Branden Meltô i 44, 79, Zevit JBL lxxxviii 76, Bron RIPK 68f., Gibson SSI, Pardee JNES xlii 66, iii p. 58, Lipiński SV 48 × e.g. Dupont-Sommer Oriens ii 125, O'Callaghan Or xviii 186, FR 262.3 n., Röllig KAI a.l.: = QAL Pf. 3 p.s.m. of *‹bd*$_1$ (cf. also Segert GPP p. 201: poss. = QAL Part. act. s.m. abs. of *‹bd*$_1$ (cf. also Swiggers BiOr xxxvii 339)); cstr. *‹bd* KAI 26A i 1, 31[1], 33[2f.] (*‹b[d]*; = Kition A 1), Syr liii 86, Gall 14 (= CSOI-Ph 6), Syr xxxii 42 (Ph.?; cf. also Herr sub SANSS-Ar 78, Bordreuil sub CSOI-Ar 85); + suff. 3 p.s.m. *‹bdy* KAI 52[2], EpAn ix 5[1], RES 1204[3] (for this reading cf. Teixidor Sem xxix 10f. :: Cooke NSI p. 43: l. *‹bdk*? (cf. also Chabot sub RES 1204, Catastini RSF xiii 5ff.)); + suff. 2 p.s.m. *‹bdk* DD 3[2] (= CIS i 9), 13[1], 14[2]; Plur. + suff. 3 p.s.m. *‹bdy* KAI 19[3] (v. infra), RES 1507[2] (:: e.g. Chabot RES a.l.: = Sing. + suff. 1 p.s.) - **Pun** Sing. cstr. *‹bd* CIS i 236[3], 249[4], 250[5], 251[2], 252[4], KAI 79[3f.], TPC 63[1] (cf. Sznycer Sem xxvi 86ff.), MM xvii 204 (for this prob. reading and interpret., cf. Lipiński FPI 86 :: Röllig MM xvii a.l.: l. *brk* (= part of n.p.)), etc., etc.; + suff. 2 p.s.m. *‹bdk* KAI 47[2] (or = Plur. + suff. 2 p.s.m.?, cf. also Amadasi sub ICO-Malta 1, 1bis), CIS i 3891[1f.], 4777[4f.]; + suff. 2 p.s.f. *‹bdk* KAI 82, *‹bdky* CIS i 3777[1]; Plur. + suff. 3 p.s.m. *‹bdm* KAI 71[2f.] (= ICO-Spa 12 (:: Fuentes Estañol sub CIFE 04.03: = Plur. abs.)) - **Amm** Sing. cstr. *‹bd* SANSS-Amm 1 (= Vatt sig. eb. 164 = Jackson ALIA 72 no. 18 = CAI 40), 2 (= Dir sig. 98 = Vatt sig. eb. 98 = Jackson ALIA 72 no 19 = CAI 17), 3 (= CIS ii 76 = Vatt sig. eb. 403 = CSOI-Amm 69 = Jackson ALIA 70 no. 6 = CAI 13), Vatt sig. eb. 401 (= Jackson ALIA 72 no. 17 = CAI 102; cf. Avigad BASOR ccxxv 63), CAI 129, ADAJ xxxi 196 - **Edom** Sing. cstr. *‹bd* SANSS-Edom 3 (= Vatt sig. eb. 319), 4 (= Vatt sig. eb. 119), 7 (or = Amm.?, cf. e.g. Aufrecht CAI p. 344) - **Hebr** Sing. cstr. *‹bd* KAI 193[19] (cf. e.g. Albright BASOR lxx 14, Gordon BASOR lxx 17, Röllig KAI a.l., Gibson SSI i p. 38 :: Torczyner Lach i p. 51, 60f.: l. *nkd* (= Sing. cstr. of *nkd* (= grandson)), Dir sig. 65 (= Vatt sig. eb. 65 = CSOI-Hebr 40), 67 (= Vatt sig. eb. 67 = SANSS-Hebr 4 = CSOI-Hebr 41), 68 (= Vatt sig. eb. 68 = SANSS-Hebr 1 = IS 3), 69 (= Vatt sig. eb. 69 = SANSS-Hebr 46 = IS 5), 70 (= Vatt sig. eb. 70), 71 (= Vatt sig. eb. 71), 73 (= Vatt sig. eb. 73), Mosc sig. 2 (= Vatt sig. eb. 125), 21 (= Vatt sig. eb. 141 = SANSS-Hebr 2), Vatt sig. eb. 272, 321 (= SANSS-Hebr 3 = IS 4), 356, Or xlviii 107, HBTJ 4 (*[ʿ]bd*), 5, ASB 55; + suff. 3 p.s.m. *ʿbdh* KAI 192^{5} (*[ʿ]bdh*), 200^{2}; + suff. 2 p.s.m. *ʿbdk* KAI 192$^{3f.}$, 193$^{1,5,6,7f.}$, 200^{6} (*[ʿ]bdk*; :: Vinnikov ArchOr xxxiii 547f.: = Plur. + suff. 2 p.s.m.), etc., etc.; *ʿbk* (lapsus) KAI 193^{21} - **OldAr** Sing. cstr. *ʿbd* KAI 216^{3}, CSOI-Ar 86; Plur. cstr. *ʿbdy* KAI 217^{4}; + suff. 1 p.s. (or = Sing. + suff. 1 p.s.) *ʿbdy* KAI 224^{13} - **OffAr** Sing. abs. *ʿbd* Cowl 10^{10}, 28^{4,5,17}, Aḥiq 84, Krael 6^{8}, 8^{5,7,9}, 11^{11}, ATNS 5^{1}, Samar 1^{2} (= EI xviii 8*^{2}, cf. Freedman & Andersen FS Fitzmyer 18 :: Cross EI xviii 11*: = lapsus for *ʿbdʾ* = Sing. emph.), Samar 3^{4}, 4^{2}; cstr. *ʿbd* ATNS 30a 7 (dam. context), 61a 2 (?, dam. context), LA ix 331^{2}, SANSS-Ar 12 (= CIS ii 74; for this reading, cf. e.g. Gall 129, Lemaire Sem xxviii 13f., cf. however Herr SANSS a.l.: or (div. otherwise) l. *ʿ br* (= Sing. cstr. of *br$_1$*), cf. CIS ii sub 74), 82 (= Dir sig. 66 = Vatt sig. eb. 66 = CSOI-Ar 90; or forgery?, cf. Naveh BASOR ccxxxix 76), Syr lxiii 429, IrAnt iv 113 (cf. Dupont-Sommer CRAI '64, 284, IrAnt iv 114, Naveh AION xvi 21, Teixidor Syr xliv 184, cf. however Teixidor ibid.: or = n.p. and Dupont-Sommer IrAnt iv 114: or = Qal Pf. 3 p.s.m. of *ʿbd$_1$*??; v. also *gzr$_2$*); emph. *ʿbdʾ* Cowl 28^{7,9,10}, ATNS 5^{4,7}, 50^{12}; + suff. 3 p.s.m./f. *ʿbdh* CIS ii 34^{7} (= Del 108; heavily dam. context), ATNS 9^{3}, 10a 9, 97a 2; + suff. 2 p.s.m. *ʿbdk* Cowl 30^{4}, 38^{20}, 66 ix 1, 70^{1}, Krael 13^{9}, Herm 3^{1}, 4^{13}, ATNS 195^{1} (heavily dam. context), RHR cxxx 20 conc. 1, Aeg xxxix 4 recto 1, KAI 266^{1,6} (*ʿbd[k]*)^{,8}; + suff. 2 p.s.f. *ʿbdky* Cowl 39^{1,5}; + suff. 1 p.s. *ʿbdy* ATNS 98^{6} (or = Plur. + suff. 1 p.s. or = Plur. cstr.; heavily dam. context); + suff. 2 p.pl.m. *ʿbdkm* Cowl 37^{1} (*ʿbdk[m]*), 54^{1} (highly uncert. reading; cf. Porten & Yardeni sub TADAE A 3.1 (div. otherwise): l. *ʿbd* (= Sing. cstr. or = Qal Pf. 3 p.s.m. or = Qal Imper. s.m. of *ʿbd$_1$*); heavily dam. context); + suff. 1 p.pl. *ʿbdn* ATNS 68^{5}; Plur. abs. *ʿbdn* KAI 233^{13}, ATNS 4^{5}, 45b 1 (?, or = Sing. + suff. 1 p.pl.?, dam. context), 50^{12}, Samar 9^{3}; emph. *ʿbdyʾ* ATNS 4^{4}, 44^{5}, Samar 8^{4} (*[ʿ]bdy[ʾ]*; heavily dam. context); + suff. 3 p.s.m. *ʿbdwhy* ATNS 29b i 5 (*[ʿ]bdwhy*; heavily dam. context; highly uncert. reading, cf. Porten & Yardeni sub TADAE B 8.1), 40b 4; + suff. 3 p.s.f. *ʿbdyh* Cowl 28^{3}; + suff. 2 p.s.m. *ʿbdyk* Cowl 17^{1}, 30^{1,22}, 33^{1}, 68 xii obv. 1, 82^{1}, Aḥiq 83 (for the reading, cf. also Fitzmyer CBQ xlvi 316, Muraoka JSS xxxii 187), ATNS 59^{2}; + suff. 1 p.s. *ʿbdy* ATNS 4^{1}, Samar 5^{7} (dam. context); cf. Frah xiii 1 (*ʿbdk*, *ʿbdyn*), cf. also Toll ZDMG-Suppl viii 30f., GIPP 19, 48, SaSt 13, ZDMG xcii 442A 16 - **Nab** Sing. emph. *ʿbdʾ* ARNA-Nab 130^{1} - **Palm** Plur. cstr. *ʿbdy* Inv D 40^{1} - **JAr** Sing. + suff. 3 p.s.m. *ʿbdh* AMB 3^{6} (or = Sing. emph.??) - ¶ subst. m. servant, slave, passim - *skn qrtḥdšt ʿbd ḥrm mlk ṣdnm* KAI 31^{1}: the governor of Q., the servant of Ch. the king of the Sidonians;

‹bd krtk ATNS 5^1: a Cretan slave; *lm‹bdh ‹bd* Krael 8^7: to enslave him; *dmy ‹bdy ›lk ksp kršn 15* ATNS 4^1: the value of these slaves of mine is (in) silver 15 *karš*; *‹bdy› zylh l› hnt[* ATNS 4^4: his slaves I have not released; *plgn ‹lyn ‹bdyh zy mbṭḥyh ›mn* Cowl 28^3: we have divided between us the slaves of M. our mother; *ly›znyhw ‹bd hmlk* Dir sig. 69: (on seal) belonging to Y. the servant of the king (for this title, cf. de Vaux Institutions i 184f., cf. also Riesener BZAW cxlix 150ff.; cf. also Dir sig. 70, 71, Vatt sig. eb. 319, 401, SANSS-Edom 3, 4, KAI 193^{19}, Or xlviii 107, HBTJ 4, 5); *l›dnplṭ ‹bd ‹mndb* SANSS-Amm 2: (on seal) belonging to A. the servant of A. (cf. e.g. SANSS-Amm 1, 3, ADAJ xxxi 196, SANSS-Edom 7, Dir sig. 65, 67, 73, Vatt sig. eb. 272, 321, 356, SANSS-Ar 78, 82); *›nh b[r]rkb ... mlk šm›l ‹bd tgltplysr* KAI 216$^{1ff.}$: I am B. ... the king of S. the servant (i.e. the vassal) of T.; etc. - used to indicate humility, *my ‹bdk klb ky zkr ›dny ›t [‹]bdh* KAI 192$^{3f.}$: what is your servant but a dog that my lord remembers his servant? (cf. KAI 195$^{3f.}$, 196$^{2ff.}$); *šlḥh ‹bk* (v. supra) *›l ›dny* KAI 193^{21}: your servant forwards it to my lord; *yšm‹ ›dny hšr ›t dbr ‹bdh* KAI 200$^{1f.}$: may my lord the commander listen to the word of his servant; *›l mr› mlkn pr‹h ‹bdk ›dn* KAI 266^1: to the lord of kings Pharaoh, your servant A.; *›l mr›ty šlwh ‹bdky hwš‹* Cowl 39^1: to my lady Sh. your servant H.; etc.; cf. also Loewenstamm Lesh xxxiv 148, xxxvi 316 - used to indicate the servant of a god, *l›dny lmlk‹štrt ... ›š ndr ‹bdk ‹bd›sr* DD 14$^{1f.}$: to his lord (v. *›dn*$_1$) M. ... what your servant A. vowed (cf. DD 3$^{1f.}$, 13$^{1f.}$); *‹bdy b‹l ḥmn* KAI 19^3: his servants the citizens of Ch. (cf. e.g. Cooke NSI p. 49f., Lidzbarski Handb 239, 332, KI sub 16, Eph i 335f., Röllig KAI a.l., v.d.Branden BO vii 72, Seyrig Syr xl 27f. (n. 45), Miller UF ii 182, Milik DFD 424, Gibson SSI iii p. 119f. × Röllig FS Friedrich 407: *‹bdy* = Plur. + suff. 3 p.s.f. :: Clermont-Ganneau RAO i 81, Meyer ZAW xlix 8, Dunand & Duru sub DD 4: *‹bdy* (= Sing. + suff. 3 p.s.m.) *b‹l ḥmn* = his servant(/associate) B.-Ch. :: Baldacci BiOr xl 131: *‹bdy* = Plur. cstr. ('the worshippers of B.-Ch.' or 'the worshippers of the lord of Ch.'); for the context, v. also *›l*$_1$, *ml›k*$_1$); *[lr]bt ltnt pn b‹l mš ›bn ›š ndr ‹bdky b‹lytn* CIS i 3777^1: to the lady T. the face of Ba‹a.l., the statue of stone (v. *m›š*$_1$) which your servant B. vowed; *›nk ›ztwd ... ‹bd b‹l* KAI 26A i 1f.: I am A. ... the servant of B. (cf. KAI 47^2, 82, CIS i 3891); *‹bd kmš* LA ix 331^2: servant of K.; *‹bdh d›lh šwmyh* AMB 3^6: the servant of the God of Heavens; as indication of function, *b‹l‹zr ... ‹bd ṣdmlqrt* CIS i 256$^{2ff.}$: B. ... the servant of S. (cf. CIS i 255$^{4f.}$, 4845$^{3f.}$; poss. the *‹bd ‹štrt* BAr-NS vii 262^4 to be explained in the same way, cf. Fantar ibid. 263f., cf. also Garbini StudMagr vi 31); *šmšzr ‹bd šḥr* Syr lxiii 429: S. the servant of (the god) Sh.; cf. *mqnyw ‹bd YHWH* ASB 55 (inscription on seal): M. servant of God (indication of function; on this function, cf. Cross ASB 60ff. (cf. also Avigad FS

Cross 197f., Israel Or lvii 95; cf. also SANSS-Ar 78)); cf. also *ḥmlkt ... ʿbd bt mlkʿštrt* CIS i 250[3ff.]: Ch. ... the servant of the temple of M. (cf. CIS i 247[5], 248[3f.], 249[4], 3779[5], 4834[4f.], 4835[4], etc. etc.); *ʿbd nbw ʾlhʾ* ATNS 30a 7: the servant of the god N. (dam. context) - Dupont-Sommer JA ccliv 440, 461f. (462b; cf. also Benveniste JA ccliv 450): l. *ʿbdyʾ* (= Plur. emph.) in JA ccliv 440[7] (highly uncert. reading; cf. Naveh (with Shaked) JRAS '69, 119: l. prob. *ʿwryʾ* or pro *w* l. *d/r/n* (cf. also Kutscher, Naveh & Shaked Lesh xxxiv 128f.: l *ʿwryʾ* without interpret.), cf. Shaked JRAS '69, 121: pro *lʿwryʾ* l. poss. *zʿwryʾ* (= Plur. emph. of *zʿwr* (= *zʿr₂*; = the small ones); cf. also Kutscher in Kutscher, Naveh & Shaked Lesh xxxiv 129: l. poss. *ʿwdyʾ* = variant of *ʿbdyʾ*) - v.d.Branden PO i 212: the *ʿbd* in KAI 81[7] (in *ʿbd ʾrš*) = Sing. abs. (= minister), improb. interpret., prob. = part of n.p., cf. e.g. Röllig KAI a.l) - Sanmartín Ascaso FPI a.l.: the *ʿbd* in FPI 90 no. 1.1.2 = Sing. cstr. of *ʿbd₂* (uncert. interpret.; = n.p.?).
v. *br₁*, *ʿbd₁*, *ʿbr₄*, *pḥl*.

ʿbd₃ Hatra Sing. emph. *ʿbdʾ* 244[2], 245[2], 281[7], app. 3[3] (= KAI 257; cf. e.g. du Mesnil du Buisson Syr xix 147, Caquot Syr xxx 245, Donner KAI a.l., Naveh BASOR ccxvi 11 n. 13 :: Milik DFD 333 (div. otherwise): l. *mnʿbdʾ* = Sing. emph. of *mnʿbd* (= variant of *mʿbd*) :: Ingholt YClSt xiv 135: l. *ʿwbʾ* = Sing. emph. of *ʿwb* (= kind of wooden canopy or projecting roof)) - ¶ subst. m. - **1)** construction; *mnyn 10 lʿbdʾ dy sgyl* Hatra 244[2]: 10 m. for the construction of the S. (v. *sgyl*), cf. Hatra 245[2]; *dy qryb mn ʿbdʾ hdyn lšmš ... dnrʾ 100* Hatra app. 3[2ff.]: who has offered from this construction (i.e. as a part of the expenses needed for this construction) to Sh. ... 100 *denarii* - **2)** building-site, fabric, workshop; *ʿbdʾ dy brmryn* Hatra 281[7f.]: the fabric of B. (i.e. of the temple of B.), cf. Aggoula Syr lii 182 :: Safar Sumer xxvii 5, Degen NESE iii 68, 71, AION xxvii 488f., Vattioni IH a.l.: = construction, work) - the diff. *ʿbd* CRAI '70, 163[2], IPAA 11[5] poss. = Sing. cstr. of *ʿbd₃*, *ʿbd ryq* = the doing of what is vain/senseless (cf. also Humbach IPAA p. 11, 13) or = QAL pass. Pf. 3 p.s.m./Part. pass. s.m. abs. of *ʿbd₁*? (cf. Dupont-Sommer CRAI '70 163, 165).
v. *mʿbd*, *ʿbd₁*.

ʿbdh Hebr Sing. abs. *ʿbdh* TA-H 5[14] (?, heavily dam. context) - **OffAr** Sing. abs. *ʿbydh* Cowl 21[6], Aḥiq 127, Driv 12[9] (reading *ʿbydʾ* lapsus of editor); cstr. *ʿbdt* Cowl 44 (*scriptio anterior* l. 1 (for the reading cf. Porten & Yardeni TADAE B 7.3)); emph. *ʿbydtʾ* Cowl 9[10], Driv 5[9]; + suff. 2 p.s.m. *ʿbydtk* Aḥiq 21; + suff. 3 p.pl.m. *ʿbydthm* Aḥiq 208 (:: Kottsieper SAS 23, 222: = Plur. + suff. 3 p.pl.m.) - **Nab** Sing. cstr. *ʿbydt* CIS ii 350[1]; emph. *ʿbydtʾ* CIS ii 196[7] - **Palm** Plur. abs. *ʿbydn* CIS ii 3913 i 4 - **JAr** Sing. emph. *ʾbydth* MPAT-A 14[2] (= SM 47; cf.

Hestrin IR p. 186, Naveh SM a.l.) - ¶ subst. f. - **1)** work, labour; *‘bd kl ‘bydh* Aḥiq 127: do every work (cf. Cowl 21[6]), cf. poss. also Aḥiq 208 (dam. context); *‘bydt› zyly y‘bdw* Driv 5[9]: they will perform my service (i.e. they will work for me); *‘bydtk hw y‘bd [ly]* Aḥiq 21: he shall do your work for me (i.e. he will be my servant in your place); *b‘bdt kpykn* Cowl 44[1] (*scriptio anterior*, v. supra): by the work of your hands - **2)** work, piece of work; *‘bydt› dy ‘l› ‘bydt* CIS ii 196[7]: the work mentioned above was executed; *‘bydt› zy ‘bdt* Cowl 9[10]: the work (i.e. the building) you have made (cf. however Cowl a.l.: the work which you have done, cf. also Porten & Greenfield JEAS p. 12, Grelot DAE p. 183, Porten & Yardeni sub TADAE B 2.4); *bty mqbryn ‘bydt gwḥyn* CIS ii 350[1]: burying places, a work of niches (i.e. fashioned into niches); *d‘bd ḥdh* (v. *znh*) *›bydth* (v. supra) MPAT-A 14: who made this work (i.e. a mosaic) - **3)** matter, business; *‘bydn šgyn ḥybn mks›* CIS ii 3913 i 4f.: many goods liable to taxation (cf. Greek par. πλεῖστα τῶν ὑποτελῶν); *grd› zyly ‘bydh l› ›yty lk* Driv 12[9]: my domestic staff is no concern of yours - cf. *‘ybydh*.
v. *drh*$_1$, *‘bd*$_1$.

‘bwr$_1$ v. *‘br*$_4$.

‘bwr$_2$ v. *‘br*$_4$.

‘by$_1$ v. *nbṭ*.

‘by$_2$ **OffAr** Sing. emph. *‘by›* Cowl 26[18] - ¶ subst. thickness (said of boards).

‘by$_3$ **OffAr** Plur. m. abs. *‘byn* Cowl 26[14] - ¶ adj. thick (said of textile).

‘byd$_1$ v. *‘bd*$_1$.

‘byd$_2$ **OffAr** Segal ATNS a.l.: l. this subst. (= employee, worker) in ATNS 52b 2 (*‘byd*, Sing. abs./cstr.) and 89[1] (*‘byd*, Sing. abs.) and poss. in ATNS 64b 9 (*‘byd*, Sing. abs.); uncert. interpret., in all instances diff. and dam. context (= form of *‘bd*$_1$?).
v. *‘bd*$_1$.

‘bydh v. *‘bdh*.

‘bn **Pun** QAL Part. pass. s.m. abs. *‘bn* KAI 152[2] (for this reading, cf. already Chabot **JAr** xi/vii 95: l. rather *‘bn w* :: Hoftijzer VT xi 346, Röllig KAI a.l. (div. otherwise): l. *‘bnt* = QAL Part. pass. s.f. abs. :: Février CB viii 25ff., Schedl VT xii 344f. (div. otherwise): l. *‘bnt* = OPH Pf. 3 p.s.f. of *bny*$_1$ :: Harr 73 (div. otherwise): l. *‘bnt* (= PU‘AL Pf. 2 p.s.? of *‘bn* (= *›bn*$_1$ (= to enclose in stone))) :: Chabot JA a.l.: pro *‘bn w* l. *‘bnt*); Part. pass. s.f. abs. *‘bnt* Handb 436, 8[4], Punica ivA 7[4], 8[5] (cf. Hoftijzer VT xi 346 (nn. 3, 4), Röllig KAI sub 136, for other interpret., v. supra); NIPH Pf. 3 p.s.m. *n‘bn* Punica vi 2[5] (:: Février CB viii 25ff., Hoftijzer VT xi 346 n. 3: = NIPH Pf. 3 p.s.f.); 3 p.s.f. *n‘bn‘*

KAI 171[4] (cf. Février CB viii 25ff., Hoftijzer VT xi 346 n. 3, Röllig KAI iii p. 18) - ¶ verb QAL uncert. meaning, prob. something like to bury (cf. Hoftijzer VT xi 346f.); *hnkt ʿbnt tḥt ʾbn st qbrt* Handb 436, 8[4]: here (a lady) was ..., under this stone she was buried; *hnkt qybr tḥt ʾbn st ʿbn* (v. supra) KAI 152[2]: here he is buried (?, v. *qbr*₁), under this stone he was ... (cf. Punica ivA 7[4], 8[5]) - NIPH to be ... (v. supra); *hnkt nʿbnʿ* KAI 171[4]: here she is ... (cf. Punica vi 2[4f.]) - for the contexts, v. also *hnkt* - Hoftijzer VT xi 345: l. *ʿbnt* (= QAL Part. pass.f. s. abs.) in KAI 136[2] (cf. also Röllig KAI a.l.; highly uncert. reading, drawing favours reading *ʿdrt*, cf. Février Sem v 63, MC 93f. :: Février Sem v 63, MC 93f.: *ʿdrt* = Sing. f. abs. of *ʾdr*₇ (cf. also Garbini FSR 182)).

ʿbq₁ **OffAr** QAL Imper. s.m. *ʿbq* Aḥiq 103 (cf. however Lindenberger APA 240 n. 220: or = *ʿbq*₂ used adverbially?) - ¶ verb QAL to hasten; for this root, cf. Perles OLZ '12, 54, Driv p. 74, Grelot JSS i 202ff., ii 195, Greenfield JAOS lxxxii 291 (n. 11), Rowley FS Driver 117 n. 3, Fitzmyer Gen Ap 127, Lindenberger APA 84f. - a form of this root poss. also in DA vf 2 (*mʿbq*?, cf. Hoftijzer DA p. 258 (n. 194)).

ʿbq₂ **OffAr** only in the comb. *lʿbq* Cowl 26[6,22], 42[7,8] (*[lʿ]bq*)[,13], Driv 9[3], ATNS 21[6] - ¶ original subst. (cf. Leand 61m), in the adverbial expression *lʿbq*: immediately, hastily (on the expression cf. also Dion RB lxxxix 563); cf. also (repeated): *lʿbq wlʿbq* Cowl 42[13]: immediately, immediately, cf. Porten & Yardeni sub TADAE A 3.8 :: Cowl a.l. the second *lʿbq* to be combined with next clause.
v. *ʿbq*₁.

ʿbr₁ **Ph** QAL Imper. s.f. *ʿbr* KAI 27[20] (cf. Albright BASOR lxxvi 9 (n. 30), Röllig KAI a.l., Rosenthal ANET 658, Avishur PIB 255, Baldacci BiOr xl 129, de Moor JEOL xxvii 108 (cf. also Röllig NESE ii 24: or = Inf. abs.) × Cross & Saley BASOR cxcvii 46 n. 23a: = Inf. abs. × Gibson SSI iii p. 87: = Imper. pl.m. :: Torczyner JNES vi 26: = QAL Imper. s.m. :: Caquot FS Gaster 49: = Pf. 3 p.pl. (cf. Lipiński RTAT 265) :: Garbini OA xx 285f.: = QAL Pf. 3 p.s.m. :: Dupont-Sommer RHR cxx 134f., 144: l. *ʿbd* = QAL Imper. s.m. of *ʿbd*₁ (= to act in magical sense) :: du Mesnil du Buisson FS Dussaud i 424, 431: l. *ʿbd* = QAL Pf. 3 p.s.m. of *ʿbd*₁) - **Pun** QAL Impf. 3 p.s.m. *yʿbr* Trip 51[5] (??; cf. Levi Della Vida Or xxxiii 12, 14, cf. also Amadasi IPT 134f.); Inf. cstr. *ʿbr* Trip 51[5] (??, cf. Levi della Vida Or xxxiii 12, 14) - **Hebr** QAL Impf. 3 p.s.m. *yʿbr* TA-H 5[12f.] - **Samal** HAPH Pf. 3 p.s.m. *hʿbr* KAI 215[18] - **OldAr** APH Impf. 3 p.s.m. + suff. 3 p.s.m. *yʿbrnh* KAI 224[17] (cf. e.g. Dupont-Sommer BMB xiii 34, Sf p. 147, Fitzmyer AIS 116, Donner KAI a.l., Greenfield ActOr xxix 6 n. 14, Gibson SSI ii p. 55 × Rosenthal BASOR clviii 30 n. 9, Degen AAG p. 68 (n. 54), 80: = QAL Impf. 3 p.s.m. + suff. 3 p.s.m. of *ʿbr*₂ (= to hate)) - **OffAr**

QAL Pf. 3 p.pl.m. *‘brw* Aḥiq 162 (v. however infra); Impf. 2 p.s.m. *t‘br* Aḥiq 142 (cf. e.g. Cowl a.l., Grelot RB lxviii 189, DAE p. 442 × Driver JRAS ’32, 88, Kottsieper SAS 16, 222: = QAL Impf. 2 p.s.m. of *‘br$_2$* (= to be enraged) :: Lindenberger APA 142: l. *t‘bd* (= QAL Impf. 2 p.s.m. of *‘bd$_1$*), RES 1792A 4 (*t‘b[r]*; uncert. context), B 2 (heavily dam. context); cf. Frah xxii 6, 7 (*‘blwn*), app. 8 (*bl(l)wn*; cf. Nyberg FP 99), Paik 756 (*‘blwn*), GIPP 19 - **Hatra** QAL Impf. 3 p.s.m. *l‘bwr* 74[7] (cf. Caquot Syr xxxii 270, Donner sub KAI 256, Degen NESE ii 100 (n. 7), 102, Ingholt AH i/1, 44, i/2, 48 :: Milik DFD 401ff., Vattioni IH a.l.: l. *l‘byd* = QAL Impf. 3 p.s.m. of *‘bd$_1$*) - **JAr** QAL Impf. 1 p.pl. *n‘br* AMB 15[9] - ¶ verb QAL to pass.; cf. also *bṭrm y‘br hḥdš* TA-H 5[12f.]: before the month passes - **1)** + *b$_2$*, *bḥdr ḥšk ‘br* KAI 27[19f.]: pass. from the dark chamber (v. supra; said to demon(s)); *dl‘bwr bgwph* Hatra 74[7]: who passes over his dead body (for this uncert. interpret., cf. Degen NESE ii 100 (nn. 6, 7), 102 (cf. already Caquot Syr xxxii 270) :: Donner sub KAI 256: who changes into his dead body (i.e. who dies)); *‘mm’ ‘brw bhm* Aḥiq 162: litt. peoples passed over them (exact interpret. unknown, diff. and dam. context; cf. also Kottsieper SAS 17, 222: *‘brw* = QAL Pf. 3 p.pl.m. of *‘br$_2$*: and the peoples, they (sc. the gods) fulminated against them, and Lindenberger APA 164: or l. *‘bdw* = QAL Pf. 3 p.pl.m. of *‘bd$_1$*?) - HAPH/APH - **1)** to transport; *wh‘br ’by mn dmšq l’šr* KAI 215[18]: and he transported my father (i.e. his mortal remains) from D. to A. - **2)** to let someone pass., i.e. to make him disappear, to banish him; + obj.: KAI 224[17] (v. however supra) - a form of this root in TA-H 24[6] (*]‘br[*) - a form of this root (prob. part of n.p.) in ADAJ xviii 31f. (*(l)‘br[*), cf. Zayadine ADAJ a.l. :: Teixidor Syr lii 276: l. *(l)‘bd[* - Teixidor Sem xxix 15f.: the diff. *‘br lspt* in RES 930[1] = QAL Part. act. s.m. abs. of *‘br$_1$* + *l$_5$* + Sing. abs. of *’sph* (= assembly), *rb ‘br lspt* = the acting *rb* of the assembly - Garbini with Hölbi AGPPS i 134f.: the *‘br* in ibid. 134 = QAL Imper. s.m. (uncert. interpret.) - Février BAr ’51/52, 76, sub CIS i 6000bis 5 (= TPC 84): the *‘br* in line 5 = PI‘EL(?) Pf. 3 p.s.m. (= to do ?), highly uncert. interpret. (:: e.g. Ferron StudMagr i 77f.: l. *‘bd* = QAL Pf. 3 p.s.m. of *‘bd$_1$*; cf. also Lidzbarski Eph i 167f.).

v. *blr*, *‘bd$_1$*, *‘br$_3$*.

‘br$_2$ v. *‘br$_1$*.

‘br$_3$ **Pun** Röllig sub KAI 162 (cf. FR 112.2); the diff. *‘brtm* in KAI 162[4] poss. = PI‘EL Pf. 2 p.s.m. + suff. 3 p.s.f. of *‘br$_3$* (= to beget), cf. also Février AIPHOS xiii 164, 170: = Pf. 3 p.s.f. + suff. 3 p.s.f.., v.d.Branden BO xiv 199: = Pf. 2 p.pl.m. of *‘br$_1$*.

‘br$_4$ **Pun** Sing. abs. *‘b‘r* FPI 91 no. 1.2 - **Hebr** Sing. abs. *‘br* TA-H 31[10] (dam. context; cf. also Pardee HAHL 66) - **OffAr** Sing. abs.

ʿ*bwr* Cowl 14[4], 20[6,12], 24[39] (*[ʿ]bwr*), 42[11] (for this poss. reading, cf. Porten & Yardeni sub TADAE A 3.8 :: Cowl a.l.: l. poss. *kndr* = k_1 + Sing. abs. of *ndr*$_3$ (= subst. of unknown meaning)), Krael 11[11,15] (ʿ*bwr[*; dam. context), Driv F iii 16[2] (heavily dam. context), NESE i 11[4,5], ʿ*br* Herm 2[14] (cf. e.g. Milik Bibl xlviii 551, 582, Grelot DAE p. 155 (n. g), Gibson SSI ii p. 133, 135, Porten & Greenfield JEAS p. 154, Porten & Yardeni sub TADAE A 2.2 :: Bresciani & Kamil Herm p. 384f., 426: l. ʿ*bd* = Sing. abs. of ʿ*bd*$_2$, cf. also Kutscher IOS i 119), ATNS 19[7], 20[4] (:: Segal ATNS a.l.: in both instances = Qal Part. act. s.m. cstr. of ʿ*bd*$_1$); cstr. ʿ*bwr* Driv 12[6], BSh 5[2], 6[3] (in both BSh instances ʿ*bwr[)*; emph. ʿ*bwr*ʾ Cowl 2[9,17], 3[12], 45[5], Krael 16A 1, Driv 12[6], NESE i 11[6] (ʿ*bw[r*ʾ*]*; for the reading, cf. also Porten Or lvii 78, 80, Porten & Yardeni sub TADAE A 3.10), iii 48[7,11], RES '41-45, 67 conc. 4 (cf. Milik Bibl xlviii 555, Grelot DAE p. 136 (n. b), Degen NESE i 17 n. 11 :: Dupont-Sommer RES '41-45, 67, 73 (n. 3): = Sing. emph. of ʿ*bwr*$_2$ (= ferryman or carrier); cf. also Porten Arch 276) - ¶ subst. m. - **1)** crop; ʿ*bwr* ʾ*rqt*ʾ Driv 12[6]: the crop from the fields (for the context, v. also ʾ*rṣ*$_1$; cf. ʿ*bwr*ʾ in Driv 12[6]) - **2)** grain, passim - this word (Sing. abs.) poss. also in TA-H 111[6] (cf. Rainey TA a.l.) - Degen NESE i 11, 17, Naveh & Shaked JAOS xci 379, 381: l. *[*ʿ*b]wr* (= Sing. abs.) in NESE i 11[5] (cf. also Degen NESE i a.l., Grelot DAE p. 504) :: Macuch JAOS xciii 60: l. *t*ʾ*br* - Degen NESE i 11, 19: l. ʿ*b[wr*ʾ*]* (= Sing. emph.) in NESE i 11[6], cf. however Naveh & Shaked JAOS xci 379: l. ʿ*b[wr šgy*ʾ*]* (= Sing. abs.) - for this word, cf. also Kaufman AIA 47 (n. 77) - cf. ʿ*br*ʾ.
v. ʿ*br*$_7$.

ʿbr$_5$ v.Soden Or xxxv 8, xlvi 185 (cf. also idem AHW s.v. *Eber nāri*): > Akkad. in the comb. *eber nāri* (< ʿ*br* (= Sing. cstr. of ʿ*br*$_5$ (= far side)) *nhr*ʾ (= Sing. emph. of *nhr*$_2$ (= river)) - cf. also ʿ*br nhr*ʾ as geographical indication in Aug xi 74 no. 42 (ʿ*br nhr*ʾ *wḥlk* (= Cilicia)) - Teixidor Syr lvi 381f.: this word (Sing. cstr. ʿ*br*) poss. in RES 930[1] (uncert. interpret., cf. RES 930 for older litt.).

ʿbr$_6$ v. ʿ*dr*$_3$.

ʿbr$_7$ **Ph** only in the comb. *b*ʿ*br* KAI 26A i 8, ii 6,12, iii 11, C iv 12 - ¶ original subst. in the prep. expression *b*ʿ*br*: thanks to, by the grace of - the same word as ʿ*br*$_4$?, cf. also HAL s.v. ʿ*bwr*/ʿ*br* (and litt. quoted there).

ʿbrʾ **Pun** Dussaud BAr '17, 167, Février Sem ii 27: the diff. ʿ*br*ʾ in KAI 138[3] = Sing. abs. of ʿ*brh* (= cereals, grain), cf. also Röllig KAI a.l., Sznycer Sem xxx 39; cf. ʿ*br*$_4$.

ʿbrh v. ʿ*br*ʾ.

ʿbrny **OffAr** Segal ATNS a.l.: l. *ʿbrny* (= adj. Sing. m. abs. (= of a tanner)) in ATNS 26[4] (highly uncert. reading and interpret. (cf. Shaked Or lvi 409)).

ʿg **Ph** Sing. abs. *ʿg* MUSJ xlv 262[2] (uncert. interpret., diff. context, cf. Teixidor Syr xlix 431; :: Cross IEJ xxix 41f. (div. otherwise): l. *ʿgzt* = Plur. f. abs. of *ʿgz* (= decrepit, mouldering; for this reading, cf. Garr DGSP 122) :: Garbini AION xxiv 412, FSR 58f. n. 4 (div. otherwise): l. *hʿdyt* = Hoph Pf. 1 p.s. of *ʿ*dy_1 (= to be robbed) :: v.d.Branden RSF ii 142f. (div. otherwise): l. *ʿpyt* = Qal Part. pass.f. pl. abs. of *ʿ*py_2 (= to envelop)) - ¶ subst. (?, v. supra) of unknown meaning; Schiffmann RSF iv 172, 174f.: = noise, crying (syntactical context interpret. improb.) :: Starcky MUSJ xlv 264ff., Röllig NESE ii 4ff.: = nd.

ʿgh v. *ʿgʿ*.

ʿgz v. *ʿg*.

ʿgl_1 **Pun** Sing. abs. *ʿgl* KAI 69[5]; Plur. abs. *ʿglm* CIS i 5601[5], *glm* (in *hglm* = *h* (= article) + *ʿglm*) CIS i 3427[3] (cf. Dussaud CRAI '44, 392f.) - **OldAr** Sing. abs. *ʿgl* KAI 222A 23, Tell F 21 (Akkad. par. *mu-ri*); emph. *ʿglʾ* KAI 222A 40 - ¶ subst. calf; for the context of CIS i 3427, 5601, v. slm_1 - Seyrig sub RTP 161: thc *ʿ* in RTP 161 poss. = abbrev. of *ʿglʾ* (= Sing. emph. of *ʿ*gl_1; cf. also Teixidor PP 51), cf. however Milik DFD 156: = numerical sign (5).

ʿgl_2 **Hatra** Sing. emph. *ʿglʾ* 344[6] - ¶ subst. poss. meaning: crushing roller, cf. Aggoula Syr lxiv 94, lxv 210, cf. also *ʿ*glh_2.

ʿglh_1 **Ph** Plur. abs. *ʿglt* RES 1207[2] (= Kition B 46) - **Pun** Plur.(/Sing.) cstr. *ʿglt* CIS i 346[3] (v. infra) - ¶ subst. chariot; *ʾš ndr mgn ... ʿglt ʿṣ* CIS i 346[2f.]: which M. donated ... a wooden chariot (cf. Slouschz TPI p. 296), or *ʿglt ʿṣ* = lapsus for *pʿl ʿglt ʿṣ* (= maker of wooden chariots; cf. CIS i sub 346)? - for RES 1207, v. $ḥrš_4$.

ʿglh_2 **Hatra** Sing. emph. *ʿgltʾ* 344[12] - ¶ subst. poss. meaning: crushing roller, cf. Aggoula Syr lxiv 94, lxv 210, cf. also *ʿ*gl_2.

ʿgʿ **Pun** Dussaud BAr '14, 620, '17, 167, Février Sem ii 27: the diff. *ʿgʿ* in KAI 138[4] = Sing. abs. of *ʿgh* (= cake), cf. Röllig KAI a.l., cf. also Sznycer Sem xxx 39, 41 :: Lidzbarski Eph iii 289: = part of n.p. (*šʿgʿš*).

ʿgr **DA** Sing. abs. *ʿgr* i 9 - ¶ subst. indicating certain kind of bird, v. ss_3 - on this word, v. also Masson RPAE 73.

ʿd_1 **OldAr** Plur. abs. *ʿdn* KAI 222B 24, 41 (cf. however Lipiński Stud 43f.: = Sing. cstr. of *ʿdn*; heavily dam. context); cstr. *ʿdy* KAI 222A 1, 2, 3, 4, 13, B 1, 4 , 5, 6; emph. *ʿdyʾ* KAI 222A 7, B 7, 11, 23, 24, 33, 38, 223B 2, 18 (*[ʿ]dyʾ*), 224[4,7,9,14](*[ʿ]dyʾ*)[,17,19,20,23,27] - ¶ subst. Plur. treaty, treaty-stipulations, passim; *ʿdy brgʾyh ... ʿm mtʿʾl ...*

KAI 222A 1: the treaty of B. with M. (cf. KAI 222A 2, B 1); *ʿdy bʿly ktk ʿm ʿdy bʿly ʾrpd* KAI 222A 4: treaty-stipulations concerning the aristocracy (?, v. *bʿ*l_2) of K. together with those concerning the aristocracy of A. (cf. KAI 222B 4); *ʿdy ʾlhy ktk ʿm ʿdy ʾ[lhy ʾrpd]* KAI 222B 5: treaty-stipulations guaranteed by the gods of K. together with those guaranteed by the gods of A.; *ʾlhy ʿdyʾ zy bsprʾ znh* KAI 222B 33: the gods who are guarantors of the treaty contained in this inscription (cf. KAI 222B 23, 224[4,14,17,23]); *ʿdy ʾlhn hm zy šmw ʾlhn* KAI 222B 6: this is the divine treaty which gods have concluded; *gbr ʿdn* KAI 222B 24: an ally (v. also *gbr*$_2$) - for this word (root, relation to Akkad. *adê* (either loan from Akkad. or loan into Akkad.)), cf. e.g. Cantineau RA xxviii 168, Dupont-Sommer Sf p. 19f., Fitzmyer AIS 23f., Thompson JSS x 235ff., Volkwein BZ xiii 32ff., Cross CMHE 267, Kaufman AIA 33, 142, Gibson SSI ii p. 34, Parnas Shn i 239ff., Veijola UF viii 347f., McCarthy TaC 142f., Pardee JNES xxxvii 196, Hillers JAOS c 178, Tadmor RAI xxv 455ff., Lemaire & Durand IAS 24ff., 91ff., Watanabe AVTA 6ff., Krebernik ZA lxxiv 159, v.Soden SEL ii 139, Fales RA lxxx 90f., Couroyer RB xcv 325ff. - Lemaire & Durand IAS 117, 128, 142: l. *ʿdn* (= Plur. abs.) in KAI 223B 19 (cf. already Lipiński Stud 54; poss. reading and interpret.).
v. *ṭby*$_3$.

ʿd$_2$ **Hebr** Sing. abs. *ʿd* EI ix 26* (?, or Edom./Amm.?, cf. Naveh BASOR cciii 32 (n. 40), cf. also Garbini JSS xix 166f.: = Amm. (cf. also Aufrecht sub CAI 66); on this text on seal, cf. also Cross EI ix a.l.; :: Becking UF xviii 446: = Sing. abs. of *ʿd*$_3$ (= messenger) :: Garbini JSS xix 166f.: = n.p.), DJD ii 40[3], 42[11,12], EI xx 256[15] (diff. reading); in J.Ar. context DJD ii 40 i 3, MPAT 39[12], 42[26] (*ʿ[d]*), 51[18] - ¶ subst. witness (apart from EI ix 26*, where Cross transl. "notary" (cf. also Naveh sub SM 77, FS Loewenstamm ii 303ff.), poss. interpret.); used after names of witnesses on contracts (in DJD ii 40, MPAT 39, 42, 51 par. with Aramaic *šhd*).
v. *yd*, *ʿd*$_7$.

ʿd$_3$ v. *ʿd*$_2$.

ʿd$_4$ **Palm** Sing. abs. *ʿd* RTP 252 - ¶ subst. prob. meaning feast (cf. Caquot RTP p. 147, cf. also Milik DFD 157).

ʿd$_5$ **Hebr** Sing. abs. *ʿd* AMB 4[12] - ¶ subst. future time; *lʿwlm wʿd* AMB 4[12]: for ever and ever.

ʿd$_6$ v. *ʿd*$_7$, *ʿwd*$_5$, *pʿm*$_2$.

ʿd$_7$ cf. *ʿdy* in MPAT 62[12] (= DBKP 27); cf. poss. *ed* (variant *aed*) in Poen 932 (v. *hn*$_3$); cf. Frah xxv 14, Paik 757, Syr xxxv 317[42], GIPP 19, 27, 56, SaSt 13 - ¶ 1) prep. - a) loc., to, unto; *lmmṣʾ šmš wʿd mbʿy* KAI 26A i 4f.: from the rising of the sun to its setting (cf. KAI

26A ii 2f.); *[m]n bq‘t w‘d ktk* KAI 222B 10: from theValley to K.; *mn mdynh ‘d mdynh* Driv 6[5]: from province to province; *‘d tnh tḥwm d(?)* ... SSI ii 34[1]: to here extends the boundary of D.; *mn ’r‘’ w‘d ‘l’* Cowl 5[5]: from the ground upwards (litt.: from the ground to the top); *sṭr’ dnh mdnḥy’ dy m‘rt’ ... ‘d nyq’ dy qym’ lqblh* Syr xix 156[1f.]: this eastern wall of the hypogee ... up to the *Nike* who is placed before it; *ndšwhy ‘d ’r‘’* Cowl 30[9]: they destroyed it to the ground (cf. Cowl 31[8]); etc. (for *‘d ’ykn*, v. *’ykn*); cf. also the foll. expressions - α) *[mn?] ’drnm w‘d ṣ‘rnm* KAI 81[4f.]: (from) their large ones to their small ones (i.e. in their totality; cf. also KAI 65[2]; v. *’dr*$_7$) - β) *mn ḥm ‘d ḥwṭ* Cowl 15[25]: from straw to string (i.e. totally; v. also *ḥm*$_3$; cf. Cowl 15[28], Krael 2[8f.,10]) - and cf. the combination *‘d*$_7$ + *l*$_5$, *wtṣbyth klh ‘d l‘l* Inv xii 19[1] (= Inv iii 2): and its whole ornamentation unto the top; *‘d lpnh* RES 1372: unto P. - b) temp., to, until; *mbq‘ hšḥrt ‘d hṣhrm* KAI 181[15]: from the break of dawn until noon; *‘d ‘lm* KAI 43[12]: forever (cf. KAI 78[1], 224[25], DA 1[9], Cowl 8[11], CIS ii 206[2], 4114[6], etc., etc.); *mn hšlšh ‘šr lḥdš ‘d hšmnh ‘šr lḥdš* TA-H 8[2ff.] (cf. MPAT 62[12f.]); *‘d hššh lḥdš* TA-H 7[4f.]: up to the 6th of the month; *mn ywm’ znh w‘d ‘lm* Cowl 8[9]: from this day forever (cf. Cowl 14[6f.], Krael 2[4], etc.); *mn ywm’ znh ‘d ‘lm* Krael 7[4]: from this day forever (cf. Krael 4[4f.], 10[8], J 38[5]); *mn yrḥ tmwz ... w‘d znh ywm’* Cowl 30[2]: since the month of T. ... till this day; *mn zy ḥnnyh bmṣryn ‘d k‘n* Cowl 38[7]: from the time that Ch. was in Egypt till now; *‘d mḥr* Sach 76 i B 6: till tomorrow; *mn h‘ṣrt ‘d hḥnwkh* SM 49[3]: from the Concluding Feast to the feast of Chanukka; etc.; cf. *]l’ dy zbynt ‘d zm[n’] dnh* MPAT 39[5f.]: if I have not paid (?, uncert. interpret., cf. also Milik DJD ii p. 103) by that time ...; *l’ ‘d zmn’ ybyl lhm* ATNS 2[4]: not by the appointed time was he brought to them; *w’šlmn lky ‘d 30 lprmty* Cowl 35[5f.]: I will pay you in full by the 30th of P. (cf. Cowl 11[8]; for the diff. text Cowl 81[138], cf. Grelot DAE p. 118 (n. d)) - cf. the diff. expression *w‘d ḥyyn* RES 2023 (= CIS ii 163): as long as he lives (??; cf. Cantineau Nab ii 127; :: Milik RB lxvi 558: *w‘d ḥyyn bšlm* = and moreover (*‘d* = *‘d*$_6$(= *‘wd*$_5$)) a life in peace :: Littmann PAES p. 77: those who are still (*‘d* = *‘d*$_6$) alive :: Lidzbarski ZS i 89f.: until a life in peace (reference to a beatific life after death) - the diff. *‘d l’ty* CIS i 6000bis 5 = till his exhaustion (??, v. *l’y*) - cf. the foll. comb. - α) *‘d*$_7$ + *l*$_5$, *‘[d] lywmn ’ḥrnn* Aḥiq 52: until other days - for *‘d ’ḥrn*, v. *’ḥrn* - c) temp., during; *w‘d mwtk nsbl lzkwr* Krael 5[12]: when you are dead (i.e. at your death) we will provide for Z. (cf. Porten & Greenfield JEAS p. 49, Porten & Yardeni sub TADAE B 3.6; or rather (combining otherwise): *’nḥn yplḥnk* (v. *plḥ*) ... *bḥyyk w‘d mwtk* Krael 5[11f.]: we will serve you ... during your lifetime even until your death, cf. Krael a.l., Grelot DAE p. 226) - **2)** conj., until; *‘d ’hk ’nh* KAI 224[6]: until I come; *‘d ptgm’ y’m[r]* ATNS 1[2]: until he speaks

the word; *ʿd ymṭʾ mṣryn* Driv 6[5]: until he reaches Egypt (cf. NESE i 11[8]); *ʿd šzbwny* Cowl 38[5]: until they got me freed; etc. - > final sense, so that; *whndrzʾ ʿbdw lpqydʾ z[y]ly ʿd mndt [bgyʾ zyly yhy]th* Driv 11[3]: instruct my officer to bring me the rent on my domains (v. infra) - cf. the foll. combinations - α) *zy* + *ʿd, hn kn tʿbd zy ʿd ʾgwrʾ zk yt[bnh]* Cowl 31[26]: if you do so in order that this temple may be rebuilt (// *ʿd zy* in Cowl 30[27] :: Cowl p. 122, Leand 63j: *zy ʿd* lapsus for *ʿd zy*, cf. also Driv p. 76); *hndrz yʿbdwn lḥtwbsty ... zy ʿd mndt bgyʾ ʾlk yhnpq* Driv 10[3]: they will instruct Ch. ... that he may collect the rent on these domains (cf. Driv 10[4] :: Driv p. 76: *zy ʿd* = imitation of Bab. *kî adi* or *kî adî/ê* "that surely"; :: Driv p. 80: the *ʿd* in Driv 11[3] = asyndetic counterpart of *zy ʿd* (cf. Driv 10[3,4]), cf. also Milik RB lxi 595) - β) *ʿd* + *lʾ*$_1$ = not yet; *ʿd lʾ ʾzlt* IEJ xl 142[1]: before I went (cf. IEJ xl 142[3]) - Caquot FS Gaster 48: l. prob. *ʿd ʿlm* in KAI 27[13f.] (cf. also Garbini OA xx 283f., Sperling HUCA liii 3, 8, Gibson SSI iii p. 82, 86) = forever (cf. Sperling HUCA liii 3, 8 :: Gibson SSI iii p. 83, 86: *ʿd* = Plur. cstr. of *ʿd*$_2$, cf. also Caquot FS Gaster 48, Lipiński RTAT 265 (n. 92), Garbini OA xx 283f.) :: du Mesnil du Buisson FS Dussaud 422, 424, 428: l. . *ʿlm* (= universe) or l. *[l]ʿlm* = forever (for this last interpret., cf. e.g. Dupont-Sommer RHR cxx 134, 141, Gaster Or xi 44, 66, Avishur PIB 248, 253, de Moor JEOL xxvii 108 :: Cross & Saley BASOR cxcvii 44f.: l. *ʿlm* (combined with prec. *ʾrṣ* = ancient earth; cf. also Baldacci BiOr xl 128) :: Röllig NESE ii 18, 23: l. *ʿlm* (combined with prec. *ʾlt šmm wʾrṣ* = eternal covenant (v. *ʾlh*$_2$) of heaven and earth)) - for KAI 68[5], v. *pʿm*$_2$.
v. *ʾdm*$_1$, *dbr*$_3$, *hn*$_3$, *mzzh*, *ʿdm*$_2$, *ʿwd*$_5$, *pʿm*$_2$.

ʿdb **OffAr** Sing. + suff. 2 p.s.m. *ʿdbk* Aḥiq 136 - ¶ subst. lot; *[ʾl tmʾs] zy bʿbdk* Aḥiq 136: do not despise which is in your lot (cf. however, for the restoration of the context, Lindenberger APA 133).
v. *ʿdw*.

ʿdbr v. *dbr*$_3$.

ʿdd$_1$ v. *ʿrr*$_2$.

ʿdd$_2$ **OldAr** Plur. abs. *ʿddn* KAI 202A 12 (for the reading, cf. e.g. Donner KAI a.l., Dupont-Sommer AH i/1, 2, i/2, 5, Degen Lesh xxxii 409ff., AAG p. 6 (n. 31), 47, 52, Gibson SSI ii p. 8, 15 :: Uffenheimer Lesh xxx 163ff.: l. *ʿrrn* = Plur. abs. of *ʿrr*$_3$ (= awakener) :: Pognon ISS 167 n. 1: = lapsus for *ʿdrn* (= Plur. abs. of *ʿdr*$_3$ or = Qal Part. act. pl.m. abs. of *ʿdr*$_1$ (= *ʿzr*$_1$))??) - ¶ subst. (or Qal Part. act. of a verb *ʿdd*, cf. Garb 254f., Degen AAG p. 73, GGA '79, 34) messenger, herald (for this interpret., cf. Ginsberg EI v 62*: < root *ʿdd* = to send (cf. also Ross HThR lxiii 4ff., Gibson SSI ii p. 9, 15, Becking UF xviii 446), cf. also Thompson JSS x 232f.: < root *ʿdd* = to recount, cf. also Fuhs

HZH 47f. (n. 220) :: e.g. Halévy RS xvi 363, Koopmans 27, Donner KAI a.l., Zobel VT xxi 97: = oracle priest diviner < root *‘dd* = to count (cf. also Lidzbarski Eph iii 8, 10) :: Grimme OLZ ’09, 16: = soothsayer < root *‘dd* = to make incisions :: Sanmartín UF xii 346: official or priest competent to conclude a treaty); on this word, cf. also Greenfield Proc v CJS i 175f. (n. 11), FS Cross 73.

‘dd$_3$ **OffAr** Sing. + suff. 3 p.s.m. *‘ddh* Aḥiq 99 (for this poss. reading and interpret., cf. Grelot RB lxviii 183 (cf. also DAE p. 437) :: Ginsberg ANET 428 (n. 5): = Sing. abs. of *‘ddh* (= number) :: Cowl p. 223, 237, Gressmann ATAT 458, Lindenberger APA 77f., 237 n. 185: l. *‘drh* = Sing. + suff. 3 p.s.m. of *‘dr$_3$*) - ¶ subst. time (v. however supra).

‘ddh v. *‘dd$_3$*.

‘dh$_1$ **OffAr** Sing. abs. *‘dh* Cowl 15^{22,26}, Krael 2^7, 7^{21} (cf. e.g. Cowl a.l., Kutscher JAOS lxxiv 234, Reider JQR xliv 340, Volterra SOLDV ii 598, Yaron JSS iii 14ff., Ginsberg JNES xviii 148, ANET 223, Verger RCL ’64, 77f., RGP 117f., Porten Arch 210 n. 38, Fitzmyer FS Albright ii 161f., WA 263 :: Krael p. 147f. (div. otherwise): l. *b‘dh* =*b‘d$_2$* (= on account of) + suff. 3 p.s.f. :: Driver PEQ ’55, 92 (div. otherwise): l. *b‘dh* = *b‘d$_2$* (= behind) + suff. 3 p.s.f.) - ¶ subst. community, assembly; *b‘dh* Cowl 15^{22,26}, Krael 2^7, 7^{21}: in the community (i.e. publicly, cf. e.g. Yaron Law 54f., Verger OA iii 53, RCL ’64, 77f. (n. 13), Porten Arch 210 n. 38, Grelot DAE p. 195 n. r, cf. also Ginsberg ANET 223, Greenfield SVT xxxii 121, 124 :: Funk JJLG vii 378f., xvi 127: assembly serving here as a court (cf. also Volterra SOLDV ii 598) :: EM iii 428: *‘dh* = specific number of persons with a legal function) - the derivation of *‘dh* from can dialect (cf. e.g. Cowl p. 49, Kutscher JAOS lxxiv 234, Ginsberg JNES xviii 148 n. 16) highly uncert. - Cowl sub 82: l. *‘d[t›]* (= Sing. emph.) in Cowl 82^5 (*r›šy ‘dt›* = the heads of the congregation). v. *m‘rh*.

‘dh$_2$ **OffAr** cf. Nisa-c 287^{5,11} (*‘dt›*; :: Diakonov & Livshitz PaSb ii 145 n. 34: = Sing. emph. of *‘dt$_1$* (= time)) - **Palm** Sing. emph. *‘dt›* CIS ii 3913 ii 54, 107 - ¶ subst. custom, habit; *hyk ‘dt›* CIS ii 3913 ii 54, 107: according to custom (cf. Greek parallels: ἐκ συνηθείας and συνηθείᾳ), cf. also *›yk ‘dt›* Nisa-c 287^5: prob. = as usual (:: Gignoux GIPP 49: = time?).

‘dh$_3$ v.d.Branden BO xii 215, 218: l. *‘dt* = Sing. abs. (= sum) in KAI 50^4, highly uncert. reading and interpret.

‘dw **Nab** Sing. emph. *‘dw›* MPAT 64 i 2, 3, 10, 11, iii 4, 6 - ¶ subst. of unknown meaning only in the comb. *šṭr ‘dw›*; Starcky RB lxi 168: *‘dw* = variant of *‘db* (= lot, part), *šṭr ‘dw›* = writ of partition :: J.J.Rabinowitz BASOR cxxxix 12: *šṭr ‘dw›* = act of seizure (cf. also Fitzmyer & Harrington MPAT a.l., Muffs 37 n. 2).

ʿ**dy**$_1$ **OffAr** QAL Part. act. s.m. abs. *ʿdh* SSI ii 37[4]; HAPH Pf. 1 p.s. *hʿdyt* Aḥiq 50, *hʿdt* Cowl 15[35]; 3 p.pl.m. *hʿdyw* AG 5[3]; Impf. 2 p.s.m. *thʿdy* Aḥiq 146 (on the reading, cf. Kottsieper SAS 171); 3 p.pl.m. *yhʿdw* Cowl 30[6], 31[6]; Inf. *hʿdyh* Krael 10[13]; ITP Pf. 3 p.s.m. *ʾtʿdy* Driv F v 1[3]; cf. Paik 758 (*ʿdytn*), GIPP 19, SaSt 13 - ¶ verb QAL to pass.; + obj.: SSI ii 37[3f.] (for the context, v. *ʾrḥ*$_2$) - HAPH to remove, to take away, passim - **1)** + obj. + *mn*$_5$, *whn hʿdt hmw mnh* Cowl 15[35f.]: and if I take them away from her; *ʾgwrʾ zy yhw ... yhʿdw mn tmh* Cowl 30[6]: let them remove the temple of Y. from there (i.e. let them destroy it) - **2)** + obj. + *mn qdm*, *lhʿdyh bytʾ znh mn qdmyky* Krael 10[13]: to take away this house from you (on the context, cf. Porten & Szubin JAOS cvii 237) - **3)** + obj. + *qdm*$_3$, *hʿdyt ḥṭʾyk qdmwhy* Aḥiq 50: I took away your offences before him (i.e. I exculpated you before him) - **4)** + *mn*$_5$ + obj., *ʾl thʿdy mnk ḥkmtʾ* Aḥiq 146: do not remove wisdom from yourself - ITP to be removed; + *mn*$_5$ + *byn*$_2$, *ʾtʿdy mn byn bgyʾ* Driv F v 1[3]: (prob. meaning) it is removed from the domains (for the context, cf. also Porten & Yardeni sub TADAE A 6.6) - Bron & Lemaire RA lxxxiii 38f.: l. *ʿdh* (= QAL Inf.) in MDAIA ciii 62 (poss. reading and interpret.; cf. also Ephʿal & Naveh IEJ xxxix 193 ff) :: Kyrieleis & Röllig MDAIA ciii 65f.: l. *tʿrh* = Sing. + suff. 3 p.s.m. of *tʿr* (= cover of forehead, sc. of a horse).
v. *dn*$_1$, *ḥky*, *ʿg*, *ʿly*$_1$.

ʿ**dy**$_2$ v.Soden Or xlvi 189, 196: *ʿdy*$_2$ (PAʿEL) = to make pregnant > Akkad. *uddû* (cf. also idem AHW s.v. *uddû* III), PAʿEL Part. pass. > Akkad. *mādiyā* (cf. also Or xxxv 15, AHW s.v.), cf. however CAD s.v. *mādiya*; uncert. interpret.

ʿ**dy**$_3$ **Ph** v.d.Branden OA iii 248, 259: l. *ʿ[d]y* (= Sing. abs.) = ornamentation in KAI 43[14] (highly uncert. reading, cf. Honeyman JEA xxvi 57, 64: 4 letters of uncert. reading pro *hʿ[d]y* (reading proposed by v.d.Branden), Gibson SSI iii p. 141: beginning of line lost).

ʿ**dy**$_4$ v. *ʿd*$_7$.

ʿ**dyy** v. *ʿdyn*$_1$, *ʿny*$_3$.

ʿ**dyn**$_1$ **Nab** Sing. m. abs. *ʿdyn* CIS ii 219[3] (for the reading, cf. Guidi RB xix 423, cf. also Lidzbarski Eph iii 269, cf. however J sub 4: l. *ʿdyn[ʾ]* = Sing. m. emph. :: CIS ii sub 219: l. *ʿdyy* = Sing. m. abs. of *ʿdyy* (= strange, foreign)) - ¶ adj. strange.

ʿ**dyn**$_2$ v. *znh*.

ʿ**dyt** **Nab** Zayadine ADAJ xxvi 367: the *ʿdytʾ* in ADAJ xxvi 366[3] = Sing. emph. of *ʿdyt* (= ornament), dam. context of uncert. interpret.

ʿ**dm**$_1$ v. *ʿṭm*.

ʿ**dm**$_2$ **Hatra**, cf. Assur 27e 2 - ¶ prep. (< *ʿd*$_7$ + *mʾ* (= *mh*)) until; *mn* *ywm ... ʿdmʾ lywm ...* Assur 27e 1f.: from the day ... until the day ...

ʿdn$_1$ OldAr PAʿEL Part. act. s.m. abs. *mʿdn* Tell F 4 (Akkad. par. *mu-ṭa-ḫi-du*) - ¶ verb PAʿEL to make prosperous; *mʿdn mt kln* Tell F 4f.: he who lets all countries prosper (epithet of a deity; cf. also Greenfield FS Duchesne-Guillemin 220f.).

ʿdn$_2$ OffAr Sing. abs. *ʿdn* Cowl 17^2, $26^{3,9}$, 28^{13} (*[ʿ]dn*), $30^{2,3,17}$ (or = Sing. cstr.?, cf. Degen GGA '79, 43)^{,26}, $31^{2,3}$, 37^2, 39^1, 40^1, 56^1, 57^9 (?, heavily dam. context), Aḥiq 49 (*ʿd[n]*), Krael 13^1, RES 1300^3, NESE i 11^1, iii 48 conv. 4, RSO xxxii 403^2, ASAE xxxix 340; emph. *ʿdnʾ* ATNS 79^2, Aḥiq 70, KAI 270A 3; cf. Frah xxvii 9 (*ʿdnʾ*), GIPP 19, SaSt 13 - ¶ subst. m. time, passim; *bkl ʿdn* Cowl 30^2: every time, always (cf. Cowl 17^2, $30^{3,26}$, $31^{2,3}$, 37^2, 39^1, 40^1, 56^1, Krael 13^1, RES 1300^3, NESE i 11^1, iii 48 conv. 4, RSO xxxii 403^2 (cf. prob. also ASAE xxxix 340); *bʿdn zy ...* Cowl 30^{17}: at the time that ...; *bzk ʿdnʾ* Aḥiq 70: at that time (cf. ATNS 79^2); *lʿd[n ʾ]ḥrn wlywmn ʾḥrnn šgyʾn* Aḥiq 49f.: in after time and many days after; *kzy [ʿ]dn yhwh nplg hmw* Cowl 28^{13}: when it is time we will divide them (cf. Cowl $26^{3,9}$) - Segal ATNS a.l.: l. *ʿdnyk[* = Plur. + suff. 2 p.s.m. in ATNS 28a fragment i (heavily dam. context, uncert. interpret.).
v. *ʿd$_1$*, *ʿdn$_3$*, *ʿlm$_4$*.

ʿdn$_3$ Hatra Sing. emph. *ʿdnʾ* 413 ii 1, app. $4^{2,7}$ (v. infra) - ¶ subst. of unknown meaning, prob. indicating an object with cultic function, or part of some religious fabric (cf. Caquot Syr xl 12, cf. also Aggoula MUSJ xlvii 46 :: Aggoula ibid.: related to *ʿdn$_2$*); Milik DFD 395, 397f.: = chapel? (cf. Teixidor Syr l. 409); Safar Sumer xvii 38 n. 87, 40: = garden, park (cf. also Caquot Syr xl 13, Teixidor Syr xli 273, 276); Tubach ISS 399 (n. 690): poss. = votive offering (less prob. interpret.) or = relief :: Safar ibid.: < Sum. :: Aggoula Sem xxvii 138ff., Syr lxvii 416: = stopping place, caravanserai (= form of *ʿdn$_2$*); cf. also Altheim & Stiehl AAW v/1, 80f. (= Plur. emph.).

ʿdr$_1$ v. *ʿdd$_2$*, *ʿdr$_3$*, *ʿzr$_1$*.

ʿdr$_2$ OffAr QAL (or PAʿEL?) Impf. 3 p.pl.m. *yʿdrn* ASAE xlviii 112B 3 - ¶ verb QAL (or PAʿEL?) to pick, to clean, to weed (?, diff. context) - this root also in the form *mʿdr* Krael 7^8?? in the combination *lbš 1 mʿdr ḥdt*, Krael a.l.: = PAʿEL (or APH) Part.: = hacked > flounced or damaged (last interpret. improb.) or l. *mʿdd* (without interpret.); Reider JQR xliv 340: *lbš mʿdr* = a stripped garment, i.e. a short and sleeveless garment; Porten & Greenfield JEAS p. 52, Porten & Yardeni sub TADAE B 3.8: a fringed garment :: Körner with Porten Arch 88 n. 133: *mʿdr* = variant of *mqdr* (= dark, black).

ʿdr$_3$ OffAr Sing. + suff. 3 p.s.m. *ʿdrh* Aḥiq 126 (× Kottsieper SAS 15, 223:= QAL Part. act. s.m. + suff. 3 p.s.m. of *ʿdr$_1$* (=*ʿzr$_1$*)), 167 (::

Kottsieper SAS 10, 17, 222: l. *‘brh* = Sing. + suff. 3 p.s.m. of *‘br*$_6$ (= wrath); the interpret. proposed by Kottsieper for Aḥiq 126 is also poss. here) - ¶ subst. help, assistance; *b‘drh* Aḥiq 126, 167: to his help (for Aḥiq 167, v. *ntḥ*$_1$; for Aḥiq 126, v. supra).
v. *‘dd*$_{2,3}$.

‘dr$_4$ Ph Sing. abs. *‘dr* KAI 24^{11} - ¶ subst. flock - Ar. > Akkad. *ḫadiru*, cf. v.Soden Or xxxv 9, xlvi 187, AHW s.v., cf. also CAD sv.

‘drw v. *‘zr*$_1$.

‘dry Hatra Sing. abs. *‘dry* 410^2 (for this poss. reading and interpret., cf. Aggoula Syr lxvii 414 :: As-Salihi Sumer xlv 103: l. *gd dy*) - ¶ subst. helper: Hatra 410^2 (v. supra).

‘drn Hatra Sing. emph. *‘drn’* Ibr 20^1 - ¶ subst. help.

‘dt$_1$ v. *‘dh*$_2$.

‘dt$_2$ v. *‘ph*$_1$.

‘wb v. *‘bd*$_3$.

‘wbd v. *‘bd*$_1$.

‘wd$_1$ Hebr HIPH Inf. cstr. *h‘yd* TA-H 24^{18}; Part. s.m. abs. *m‘yd* DJD ii 42^{13}, 43^3 - ¶ verb HIPH - **1)** to testify; + *b*$_2$, *šlḥty lh‘yd bkm hym* TA-H $24^{18f.}$: I have sent a message to warn you today (cf. Dion with Pardee HAHL 61 :: Dahood Or xlvi 331: these words to be combined with following ones); Part. testifier: DJD ii 42^{13} (following the last signature under a contract, prob. the man who testifies concerning the correctness of the preceding signatures, cf. Lehmann & Stern VT iii 395, cf. also Ginsberg BASOR cxxxi 27, Yeivin At i 101, Milik DJD ii a.l., Pardee JBL xcvii 341, HAHL 126 (cf. also Sonne PAAJR xxiii 94)) - **2)** to take as a witness; *m‘yd ’ny ‘ly tšmyn* DJD ii 43^3: I take the Heavens as witness against myself - for the root, cf. also e.g. Veijola UF viii 343ff.
v. *yd*, *‘wr*$_1$.

‘wd$_2$ Palm APH Part. s.m. abs. *m‘yd* CIS ii 3973^{10}; s.m. emph. *m‘yd’* CIS ii 4207 (for this diff. reading, cf. CIS ii a.l., Milik DFD 183, cf. however Cantineau sub Inv iv 1b: l. *‘lm’* = Sing. emph. of *‘lm*$_4$) - ¶ verb APH prob. meaning to visit regularly: CIS ii 4207 (v. supra); + obj., *kl m‘yd ‘lwt’ ’ln* CIS ii $3973^{9f.}$: everyone who visits these altars.

‘wd$_3$ v. *hn*$_3$.

‘wd$_4$ Hebr Sing. cstr. *‘wd* TA-H 1^5, 5^3 - ¶ subst. what remains, what is left, surplus; *m‘wd hqmḥ* TA-H 1^5: from the surplus of the flour (cf. TA-H 5^3); cf. also Brock & Diringer FS Thomas 43 - cf. also *‘wd*$_5$.

‘wd$_5$ Ph *‘d* KAI 14^{18}, RES 1204^2 (?, v. infra) - **Pun** prob. prec. by *b*$_2$ and + suff. 1 p.s. in Poen 939: *bodi* (cf. e.g. Sznycer PPP 105, FR 248b, J.J.Glück & Maurach Semitics ii 113f. :: Schroed 290, 292, 314: = *b‘dy*

(= variant of *bʿ*d_2), cf. also L.H.Gray AJSL xxxix 78), and prec. by b_2 in Poen 949: *bode* (cf. Sznycer PPP 129 :: e.g. FR 248b: = poss. prec. by b_2 and + suff. 1 p.s. :: Schroed 292, 314f.: = *bʿdy* (= variant of *bʿ*d_2), cf. also L.H.Gray AJSL xxxix 78) - **Hebr** *ʿwd* KAI 189[1,2], TA-H 2[7], 21[8] (*ʿwd[)* - **OffAr** *ʿwd* Cowl 34[7], *ʿd* Cowl 28[13], 34[7], Krael 11[8], Herm 2[12] - **Nab** *ʿd* J 18B (for the reading, cf. Milik & Starcky sub ARNA-Nab 90) - ¶ adv. (prob. the same word as *ʿwd*$_4$), still, moreover; *wʿd ytn ln ʾdn mlkm* KAI 14[18]: furthermore, the lord of kings gave us ... (:: Avishur PIB 197f.: clause quoted, out of context, from a palace archive (cf. also Faber JAOS cvi 428f.)); *wʾm ʿwd ḥmṣ* TA-H 2[7]: and if there is yet vinegar; cf. also *ʿwd* in Cowl 34[7]; cf. also *wʿd ksp 1070* RES 1204[2]: and moreover 1070 (shekels??) silver (??, uncert. and dam. context, cf. also Catastini RSF xiii 7; or = *ʿd*$_7$??; for another less prob. reading and interpret. of the context, cf. Teixidor Sem xxix 10f., v. also *ksp*$_2$); for *ʿd pʿmt* KAI 68[5], v. *pʿm*$_2$ - **1)** prec. by prep. b_2, *bʿwd šlš ʾmt lhnq[b]* KAI 189[2]: when there were still three cubits to be cut through (cf. KAI 189[1], and also Poen 939, 949 (v. supra)) - **2)** prec. by *lʾ*$_1$ (or l_2) - a) not yet, *tbʾ šmh ʾmhm ... wlylw brh zy lʾ ʿd nplg ʿlyn* Cowl 28[12f.]: T. their mother ... and her son L. whom we will not yet divide between us (cf. Hayes & Hoftijzer VT xx 103 (cf. also Cowl a.l., Grelot DAE p. 206, Porten & Yardeni sub TADAE B 2.11) :: Porten & Greenfield JEAS p. 30: we have not yet divided); *wlʿd ʾškḥ ʾš lmwšrthm* Herm 2[12f.]: I cannot yet find a man to deliver them (cf. Hayes & Hoftijzer VT xx 103 (cf. also Bresciani & Kamil Herm a.l., Gibson SSI ii p. 133 :: Milik Bibl xlviii 582, Porten & Greenfield JEAS p. 154, Porten & Yardeni sub TADAE A 2.2: I have not yet found ...); *whn mytt wlʿd šlmt ... kspʾ zylk* Krael 11[8]: and if I die and I have not yet paid ... your silver - b) no further; *ʿwd ṭʿm lʾ ʿd yhwy lhn tnh* Cowl 34[7]: and moreover they will have no further authority (?, v. *ṭʿm*$_2$) - the diff. *ʿd* in KAI 214[17] poss. = *ʿd*$_6$ (= *ʿwd*$_5$), cf. e.g. Halévy RS i 153, 166 ('again'), ii 57, Lidzbarski Handb 337, Cooke NSI p. 162, 168, Donner KAI a.l., Gibson SSI ii p. 73, cf. however e.g. Dion p. 318, 500: = *ʿd*$_7$, cf. also Koopmans 36.

v. *yḥd*$_2$, *kn*$_4$, *ʿrkw*, *pʿm*$_2$.

ʿwz v. *yd*.

ʿwy v. *ʿt*$_1$.

ʿwyh **Nab** Word of unknown meaning in CIS ii 200 (= J 30 = ARNA-Nab 79).

ʿwyl **OffAr** Sing. abs. *ʿwyl* Aḥiq 216 - ¶ subst. child, boy (?, heavily dam. context, diff. interpret., cf. also Lindenberger APA 215 (cf. also Kottsieper SAS 23, 223: = scoundrel)).

ʿwyr **OffAr** Sing. m. abs. *ʿwyr* ATNS 21[5] (for this prob. reading, cf.

Porten & Yardeni sub TADAE B 8.11 :: Segal ATNS a.l.: l. *ʿryb* = variant form of *ʿrb$_7$* (Sing. abs.; = security, guarantor)); cstr. *ʿwyr* Aḥiq 213 - ¶ adj. blind; *ʿwyr ʿynyn* Aḥiq 213: blind in the eyes - Michałowski sub FP ii 19: l*ʿwyr*ʾ (= Sing. m. emph.) in RIP 209 (less prob. interpret., cf. Gawlikowski sub RIP 209: l. *ʿwydʾ* = n.p.) - cf. *ʿwr$_5$*.

ʿwl v. *ʿll$_1$*.

ʿwlm v. *ʿlm$_4$*.

ʿwn v. *hwy$_1$*.

ʿwnh **Palm** Sing. emph. (or Plur. emph.?, cf. Milik DFD 284) *ʿwntʾ* RTP 37-39, 40 (*[ʿw]ntʾ*) - ¶ subst. division for duty of priests (for this interpret., cf. Milik DFD 283f., Gawlikowski Sem xxiii 118f. :: Caquot RTP p. 147: = certain type of religious confraternity dedicated to a special god, brotherhood of diviners??, cf. also du Mesnil du Buisson TMP 443 n. 3); cf. the foll. combinations: *hyklʾ wrbny ʿwntʾ dy bl* RTP 37: the temple and the leaders of the *ʿwntʾ* of B. (cf. *rbny ʿwntʾ* RTP 38), *ʿwntʾ ršʾ* RTP 39: the *ʿwntʾ*, the leaders (v. *rʾš$_1$*); *ʾḥydy* (v. *ʾḥz*) *[ʿw]ntʾ* RTP 40: the functionaries of the *ʿwntʾ* - Milik DFD 92: ουνθα in RB xli 578, no. 129^5 = Sing. emph. of *ʿwnh* (diff. reading, cf. also Dunand RB a.l.: l. οὐνόα) - Milik DFD 145: the εωνθασ in Syr xiv 276^4 = Sing. emph. of *ʿwnh* - Milik DFD 285: the *ʿntʾ* in RIP 206^{2,3} = Sing. emph. of *ʿnh$_1$* (= variant of *ʿwnh*; uncert. interpret., heavily dam. context, cf. also Gawlikowski RIP a.l. (cf. du Mesnil du Buisson BiOr xx 175: *ʿntʾ* = n.l.?)).
v. *pnyh*.

ʿwp$_1$ **Ph** Qal Imper. s.m. *ʿp* KAI 27^{28} (for this reading and interpret., cf. Cross & Saley BASOR cxcvii 47 (n. 36), Gibson SSI iii p. 82, 88, de Moor JEOL xxvii 108 (cf. also Avishur PIB 248, 255f.: or = Qal Imper. s.f. :: Caquot FS Gaster 51 :: Lipiński RTAT 266: *ʿp* = Qal Pf. 3 p.pl. :: Garbini OA xx 286: *ʿp* = Qal Pf. 3 p.s.m. :: Baldacci BiOr xl 129: *ʿp* = Qal Part. act. (= flying one); cf. however Röllig NESE ii 19, 26: l. *sp* = Qal Imper. s.m. of *swp$_1$* :: v.d.Branden BiOr xxxiii 13 (div. otherwise): l. in 27f. *ssm* (= *nomen demonis*) *y* ...) - ¶ verb Qal to fly, to fly away: KAI 27^{28} - Dupont-Sommer Sf p. 82: l. *yʿpn* (= Qal Impf. 3 p.pl.m.) in KAI 222B 33? or l. perhaps *yhkn* (= Qal Impf. 3 p.pl.m. of *hlk$_1$*), cf. also Donner KAI a.l., cf. however also Lipiński Stud 39: l. *yʿpn* (= Qal Impf. 3 p.pl.m. of *yʿp* (= to grow weary)) and Lemaire & Durand IAS 115, 124, 139: l. poss. *yṭpn* (= Qal Impf. 3 p.pl.m. of *ṭpp* (= to join)).
v. *ʿt$_1$*.

ʿwp$_2$ v. *ʿyp*.

ʿwṣ **DA** ITP Impf. 3 p.s.m. *ytʿṣ* ii 9 (on the form, cf. also Hackett BTDA 64, 97 :: Garr DGSP 133f.: not < root *ʿwṣ*) - ¶ verb ITP to take counsel with; + b_2, *bk lytʿṣ* DA ii 9: one will not take counsel with you (i.e. will not seek your advise); for the context, cf. also Weinfeld Shn v/vi 144.
v. *ʿṣh*, *pṣy*.

ʿwr$_1$ **OldAr** QAL pass. Impf. 3 p.s.m. *yʿr* KAI 222A 39 (cf. Cantineau RA xxviii 174, Bauer AfO viii 16, Degen AAG p. 75 (n. 75) × e.g. Dupont-Sommer Sf p. 57, Fitzmyer AIS 56, 157, Donner KAI a.l., Gibson SSI ii p. 42: = HOPH Impf. 3 p.s.m.) - ¶ verb QAL pass. (v. supra) to be blinded - Dupont-Sommer Sf p. 108: the diff. *yʿwrn* in KAI 223B 4 poss. = PU ʿAL Impf. 3 p.pl.m. of *ʿwr$_1$* (= to be blinded; cf. Koopmans 59, Segert AAG p. 290, cf. also idem ArchOr xxxii 125, Garr DGSP 133), cf. however Dupont-Sommer ibid.: or = QAL Impf. 3 p.pl.m. of *ʿwr$_2$* (= to be awake, to be watchful; cf. Koopmans 60, Donner KAI a.l. (cf. idem BiOr xxvii 248), Fitzmyer AIS 81, 86f., 145, Gibson SSI ii p. 42 (cf. also Garbini AION xix 13, Stefanovic COAI 145, 264); cf. also Degen AAG p. 28, 76 (n. 76): = PU ʿAL Impf. 3 p.pl.m. of *ʿwr$_2$* (= to be awakened) or = QAL Impf. 3 p.pl.m. of *ʿwr$_2$*); for the other poss. reading, cf. Dupont-Sommer Sf p. 108: l. *yʿwdn* (< root *ʿwd$_1$*), cf. Thompson JSS x 238f. : = PA ʿEL Impf. 3 p.pl.m. of *ʿwd$_1$* (= to make a treaty, to be under treaty obligations), cf. also Lipiński Stud 45f., BiOr xxxiii 234: = PA ʿEL Impf. 3 p.pl.m. of *ʿwd$_1$* (= to bear witness), cf. also Sader EAS 133 (n. 53; cf. however idem ibid. 125: l. *yʿwrn*); cf. also Lemaire & Durand IAS 95 (n. 18), 117, 127, 141.

ʿwr$_2$ **Pun** Vattioni AION xvi 47: the *ir* in IRT 886a 7 (for the text, cf. OA ii 81) is form of this root (with causal meaning: to erect), imposs. interpret., *ir* = part of n.p. (*yriraban*), cf. Levi Della Vida OA ii 82, 94, cf. also Vattioni Aug xvi 545 - Vattioni Aug xvi 546, 548: the *ir* in IRT 886k, 886s 11 and the *yr* in IRT 886e 7 = form of *ʿwr$_2$* (or in 886e 7 poss. = part of n.p.), improb. interpret.
v. *ʿwr$_1$*, *ʿrb$_2$*.

ʿwr$_3$ v. *ʿrr$_2$*.

ʿwr$_4$ **Pun** Sing. abs. *ʿwr* TPI 174 - ¶ subst. of unknown meaning in the comb. *sḥr ʿwr* = merchant of ... (= hide??, cf. however Slouschz TPI a.l.) :: Slouschz TPI a.l.: perhaps = Sing. m. abs. of *ʿwr$_5$* (= blind) or = n.l.

ʿwr$_5$ (= blind), v. *ʿwyr*, *ʿwr$_4$*.

ʿwr$_6$ v. *ʿbd$_2$*.

ʿwšrw v. *ʿnwšw*.

ʿwt v. *ʿt$_1$*.

ʿwtr cf. Frah xxvii 11 (*ʿwtl*ʾ): = opulence > summer (cf. Nyberg FP 56, 107 :: Ebeling Frah a.l.: l. *ttr*ʾ, form of *ttr* = summer (< root *ytr*).

ʿz$_1$ **Ph** Sing. abs. *ʿz* KAI 26A iii 4, 6, C iii 18, iv 1 - ¶ subst. m. force, strength (on the meaning, cf. also Barré Maarav iii 187f.); in all instances in the comb. *ʿz ʾdr*, powerful strength (:: Barré Maarav iii 183: *ʾdr* not specially related to *ʿz*).
v. *yd*, *mʿz*.

ʿz$_2$ v. *ʿnz*.

ʿz$_3$ **Ph** Plur. f. abs. *ʿzt* KAI 26A i 13f., 18 - ¶ adj. strong, mighty; *ḥmyt ʿzt* KAI 26A i 13f.: strong fortresses; *ʾrṣt ʿzt* KAI 26A i 18: mighty countries - Rocco StudMagr vii a.l.: l. *ʿz* (= Plur. m. cstr.) in StudMagr vii 12[1] (uncert. reading and interpret.).
v. *zt*$_3$, *yyn*.

ʿzz$_1$ **OldAr** Qal (cf. e.g. Fitzmyer AIS 89, Donner KAI a.l., Degen AAG p. 72 :: Dupont-Sommer Sf p. 147 : = Aph) Impf. 3 p.s.m. *yʿz* KAI 223B 20 (heavily dam. context); Paʿel Impf. 3 p.s.m. *yʿzz* KAI 222B 44 (dam. context) - ¶ verb Qal (v. supra) to be strong; *zy yʿz mnk* KAI 223B 20: who is stronger than you - Paʿel to strengthen; + obj.: KAI 222B 44.

ʿzz$_2$ **Pun** Sing. m. abs. *ʿzz* KAI 71[1] (v. however infra) - **OffAr** Sing. m. abs. *ʿzyz* Aḥiq 99, 100, 143 - ¶ adj. strong; *zy ʾṣy[l] wʿzyz mnk* Aḥiq 143: who is nobler (?, v. *ʾṣyl*) and stronger than you are (dam. context); *rkyk mmll mlk šrq wʿzyz hw mn skyn pm[yn]* Aḥiq 100: soft is the word of a king (yet) it is sharper and stronger than a two-edged knife; *ʿzyz ʾrb pm mn ʾrb mlḥm* Aḥiq 99: the ambush of the mouth is stronger than the ambush of war (v. *ʾrb*) - the expression *lʾdn lʿzz mlkʿštrt* KAI 71[1f.] poss. = to the lord to the powerful one M. (cf. Solá-Solé Sef xxi 250f., Röllig KAI a.l., Amadasi sub ICO-Spa 12; or rather *ʿzz* in this text = n.d.?).

ʿzy **Palm** Milik DFD 189f.: the *ʿzy* in RTP 707 (*ʿz[y]*), 708 is subst. (Sing. cstr.) = as much as possible (*ʿzy ḥmr*ʾ RTP 708: as much wine as one can drink), highly uncert. interpret. (cf. Starcky RTP a.l., Caquot RTP p. 164: *ʿzy* = n.p. (cf. also Stark PNPI 44)).

ʿzyz v. *ʿzz*$_2$.

ʿzkh v. *ʿzqh*.

ʿzl **OffAr** Plur. cstr. *ʿzly* Cowl 26[13,20] - ¶ subst. word of unknown meaning, poss. something woven; *ʿzly ktn ʿbyn kršn mʾh wtmnyn* Cowl 26[13f.]: sails (??) of linen, thick ones of 180 *karsh* (cf. Grelot DAE p. 291; cf. also Cowl a.l.: or = nets?); cf. *ʿzly ktn*ʾ ... *bmtqlt prs* Cowl 26[20f.]: sails (??) of linen ... according to the Persian (i.e. official) weight, cf. also Grelot DAE p. 293 n. u (: the sails (??) weighing 19.5 kg)); cf.

however Porten & Yardeni sub TADAE A 6.2: = cloth.

ʿzq **Palm** Milik DFD 233: l. *ʿzq* (= Sing. cstr.) in the combination *ʿzq b[ytʾ]* (indicating some type of circular construction) in Inv viii 71[2] (cf. however Cantineau Syr xiv 191 (div. otherwise): l. *ʿzqb* = perhaps n.p.?).

ʿzqh **OffAr** Sing. abs. *ʿzqh* Aḥiq 19; cstr. *ʿzqt* Sem xxxviii 94[6] (= TADAE A 5.1); + suff. 3 p.s.m. *ʿzqth* Aḥiq 3; *ʿzktyh* RES 1300[7] (?; cf. Grelot DAE p. 144; or = Plur. + suff. 3 p.s.m.?, cf. Lidzbarski Eph iii 24, Chabot RES a.l.; diff. context) - ¶ subst. seal, signet-ring - v.Soden AfO xx 155, Or xxxv 12, xlvi 188: > Akkad. *iz/ṣ/šqātu* = fetter, cuff (cf. also Degen Or xliv 124, Kaufman AIA 60f. (n. 142), cf. however CAD s.v. *iṣ qātī* (: not related to *ʿzqh*) :: Zimmern Fremdw 35: *ʿzqh* < Akkad. (for this interpret., cf. also e.g. Baumgartner KBL s.v. *ʿzqh*)).

ʿzr$_1$ **Ph** QAL Part. act. pl.m. + suff. 3 p.pl.m. *ʿzrnm* CIS i 91[2] (for this interpret., cf. CIS i a.l., Slouschz TPI p. 101; dam. and highly uncert. context) - **Pun** QAL Pf. 3 p.s.m. *ʿzr* KAI 147[4] (dam. context; uncert. interpret.); + suff. 3 p.s.m. *ʿzrʾ* Punica xviii/ii 92[4] - **OffAr** QAL Imper. s.m. *ʿzwr* Cowl 71[23] (uncert. context, cf. Leand 32a, 34c); Part. act. s.m. + suff. 2 p.s.m. *ʿzrk* KAI 233[13] (for the reading, cf. Lidzbarski ZA xxxi 195, R.A.Bowman UMS xx 281, Dupont-Sommer Syr xxiv 44; for this interpret., cf. e.g. Donner KAI a.l., Gibson SSI ii p. 109, cf. however Altheim & Stiehl AAW i 225: = Sing. + suff. 2 p.s.m. of *ʿzr$_2$*) - **Palm** QAL Pf. 3 p.s.m. *ʿdr* RTP 722 (cf. however du Mesnil du Buisson TMP 216: l. rather *ʿbd* = QAL Pf. 3 p.s.m. of *ʿbd$_1$*), Syr xii 122[4] (= Inv ix 11), xlviii 413[2] (heavily dam. context); + suff. 3 p.s.m. *ʿdrh* Syr xix 75 ii 4; + suff. 3 p.s.f. *ʿdrh* CIS ii 3928[3], Syr xix 74[4]; + suff. 3 p.pl.m. *ʿdrnwn* CIS ii 3916[4], 3963[3] (*ʿdrn[wn]*), Inv x 124[5], *ʿdrnn* Syr xix 75 i 4; Part. act. pl.m. abs. *ʿdryn* Syr xiv 179[2] (uncert. interpret., cf. also Rosenthal Sprache 62 n. 1) - **Hatra** QAL Pf. 1 p.s. *ʿdryt* 107[3] (for this reading, cf. Milik DFD 377f., Aggoula MUSJ xlvii 39, Vattioni IH a.l., cf. also As-Saliḥi Sumer xxxi 77*, Drijvers SV 408, Tubach ISS 259 (n. 27) :: Altheim AAW iv 256: l. *ʿdrw* (= QAL Pf. 3 p.pl.m.) :: Caquot Syr xli 252f.: l. *ʿdrw[tʾ]* = Sing. emph. of *ʿdrw* (= help) :: Safar Sumer xviii 29 (n. 11): l. *ʿdrw[t]* = Sing. abs. of *ʿdrw* (= help > assisting troops/soldiers) :: Aggoula Ber xviii 97f.: l. *ʿdry* = part of name of clan/tribe/family) - ¶ verb QAL to help, passim - **1)** + obj.: Punica xviii/ii 92[4], CIS ii 3928[3]; cf. *wʿdr bnynʾ dy h[y]klʾ* Syr xii 122[4f.]: he has assisted in the construction of the temple - **2)** + obj. + *b$_2$*, *ʿdrh bkrk myšn* Syr xix 75 ii 4: he helped him in K.-M.; *wʿdrnn bkl ṣbw* Syr xix 75 i 4: he helped them in everything (cf. CIS ii 3916[4], Inv x 124[5], Syr xix 74[4]) - **3)** + *b$_2$*, *ʿdr bh* RTP 722: he helped therein (v. however supra) - **4)** + *l$_5$*, *ʿdryt lšmš* Hatra 107[3f.]: I assisted Sh. -

Part. act. helper: KAI 233[13] (v. however supra), cf. possibly CIS i 91[2] (v. however supra).
v. *ʾzr*$_4$, *ʾzrh*$_1$, *ʿdd*$_2$, *ʿdr*$_3$, *ʿzr*$_2$.

ʿzr$_2$ **Pun** Sing. abs. *ʿzr* CIS i 6000bis 3 (= TPC 84; cf. e.g. Février BAr '51/52, 75, CIS i a.l., Ferron StudMagr i 72 (or = rather QAL Part. act. s.m. abs. of *ʿzr*$_1$?) :: Slouschz TPI p. 180f.: = n.d.) - ¶ subst. m. help; *mṣbt lʿzr yšr* CIS i 6000bis 3: memorial stele for the right help (diff. context, cf. Février CIS i a.l., cf. also Ferron StudMagr i 72, 78: > ... for a correct patron; poss. interpret.).
v. *ʿzr*$_1$.

ʿzr$_3$ **Pun** Plur. abs. *ʿzrm* KAI 120[3], 121[2], 126[2] - ¶ subst. of uncert. meaning in the combination *ʾdr ʿzrm* (in KAI 121, 126 Lat. par. *praefectus sacrorum*); Levi Della Vida AfrIt vi 107, FS Friedrich 305f., 312f. n. 33 (cf. also Friedrich FS Eissfeldt 123, Jongeling SV 412, 415): *ʿzr* (to be related to Hebr. *ʿzrh*) = inner court of temple (cf. also Tsevat UF xviii 347), *ʿzrm* = ritual performed in this court; cf. however Février RA xlii 85ff.: *ʿzr* = (young man >) special type of sacrificer (cf. also H.P.Müller UF i 90f., Amadasi IPT 53); Dijkstra & de Moor UF vii 172: *ʿzr* = sacrifice (proposed etymology improb.); for the title *ʾdr ʿzrm*, cf. also Teixidor Syr lii 265f.: = leader of the ritual ("chef de culte"), cf. also Huss 543 (n. 336); on this word cf. also Loewenstamm Tarbiz xxv 472.

ʿzrh v. *mʿzrh*.

ʿṭh v. *ʿṣh*.

ʿṭy **OffAr** QAL Part. act. pl.m. abs. *ʿṭyn* RES 1785A 3 - ¶ verb QAL to cover; for this highly uncert. interpret., cf. Lidzbarski Eph i 325.
v. *ʿṭm*.

ʿṭyq v. *ʿtq*.

ʿṭm **DA** word of uncert. meaning in i 9; Hoftijzer DA a.l. and p. 284: poss. = adj. Sing. m. abs. (= heavy, mighty, said of darkness, highly uncert. interpret., cf. also Naveh IEJ xxix 136, Greenfield JSS xxv 251); Dijkstra GTT xc 163 (n. 18): = clear (said of night); H. & M. Weippert ZDPV xcviii 92f., 103: = Sing. abs. of noun *ʿṭm* (= darkness)? (cf. also Sasson PEQ '85, 102f., UF xvii 288, 290, 296f.: = impenetrable gloom (proposed etym. improb.), Puech BAT 356, 361, FS Grelot 22, 27: = obscurity, darkness (proposed etym. less prob.); Rofé SB 66 (n. 28): = PIʿEL Imper. + suff. 3 p.pl.m. of *ʿṭy* :: e.g. Caquot & Lemaire Syr liv 196, 197f.: l. *ʿdm*$_1$ (= Sing. abs.) = darkness :: Garbini Hen i 176, 185: l. *ʿdm*$_1$ (Sing. abs.) = nothingness, absence :: McCarter BASOR ccxxxix 51, 54, 59 n. 2, Hackett BTDA 25, 29, 44: l. prob. *ʿlm* = Sing. abs. of *ʿlm*$_4$ (cf. also Garr DGSP 27) :: Levine JAOS ci 197: l. *ʿlm*

= Sing. abs. of *ʿlm*$_8$ (= concealment) - on this word, cf. also H. & M. Weippert ZDPV xcviii 93 n. 77.

ʿṭp v. *ʿṭph*.

ʿṭph **Pun** Sing. abs. *ʿṭpt* CIS i 6051[1] (cf. Lidzbarski Eph iii 55f., Clermont-Ganneau RAO viii 95f. :: Février sub CIS i 6051: prob. = QAL Part. pass. s.f. abs. of *ʿṭp* (= to cover)) - ¶ subst. covering (v. supra): CIS i 6051[1] (heavily dam. context).

ʿṭr$_1$ **Ph** QAL Inf. cstr. *ʿṭr* KAI 60[1] - ¶ verb QAL to crown; *lʿṭr ʾyt šmʿbʿl* ... *ʿṭrt ḥrṣ* KAI 60[1ff.]: to crown Sh. ... with a golden crown.

ʿṭr$_2$ **Pun** Sing. abs. *[ʿ]ṭr* CIS i 6000bis 6 (= TPC 84; for the reading, cf. e.g. Février BAr '51/52, 77f., CIS i a.l., Ferron StudMagr i 77 :: Lidzbarski Eph i 166f., 169: l. *[š]ṭr* = QAL Pf. 3 p.pl.m. of *šṭr*$_1$) - ¶ subst. gable; *brʾ[š ʿ]ṭr* CIS i 6000bis 6: on the top of the gable.

ʿṭrt **Ph** Sing. cstr. *ʿṭrt* KAI 60[3] (or abs.?, cf. FR 309) - **Pun** Sing. abs. *ʿṭrt* KAI 165[6] , Karth xii 53 iii 1; Sing. or Plur. abs. *ʿṭrt* KAI 145[3] (v. infra) - ¶ subst. f. - **1)** crown, wreath: KAI 60[3] (for the context, v. *ʿṭr*$_1$); *tsdt dl ʿṭrt wdl šm tʿṣmt* KAI 165[5f.]: T. ... provided with a wreath (or wreaths?, cf. Chabot sub Punica xvi 1) and with a glorious name (otherwise unknown honorific titles) - **2)** part of building or construction, exact meaning unknown: KAI 145[3]; Février Sem vi 17f., 20: *ʿṭrt ʾdrʾt* = magnificent gables (cf. also Clermont-Ganneau RAO iii 28f.: *ʿṭrt* = cornice), cf. v.d.Branden RSF i 166, 168; Krahmalkov RSF iii 188, 190f.: *ʿṭrt ʾdrʾt* (= Sing.) = the great lintel :: Lidzbarski Eph i 48f.: *ʿṭrt* (= Sing. cstr.) *ʾdrʾt* (= Plur. abs.) = a crown of splendid monuments (cf. FR 307); the same meaning also in Karth xii 53 iii 1 (cf. Février & Fantar Karth xii a.l.: = gable or cornice; Krahmalkov RSF iii 184 (n. 53): = lintel :: v.d. Branden RSF v 61: here = splendour, prosperity).

ʿy **Mo** Plur. abs. *ʿyn* KAI 181[27] - ¶ subst. ruin.
v. *ʿyn*$_2$, cf. *ʿ*$_1$.

ʿybydh **JAr** Sing. emph. *ʿybyth* SM 88[6] (= Syn D A 6; for this reading, cf. Naveh SM a.l.; cf. however Torrey Syn D p. 263f.: l. *ʿybydh* with secondary marks across the head of *dalet* making it resemble a *taw* (i.e. corrected to *t*?) - ¶ subst. work - Naveh sub SM 89: l. in SM 89b 4 (= Syn D C 1c) *ʿybydth*? (= Sing. emph.; highly uncert. reading; cf. however Torrey Syn D p. 268: l. *mlʾktyh* (= Sing. + suff. 3 p.s.m. of *mlʾkh*$_1$) + *kh[* (= *kh[nyʾ]* (= Plur. emph. of *khn*$_1$)) - cf. *ʿbdh*.

ʿyd **Palm** Sing. emph. *ʿydʾ* CIS ii 3913 i 5 (Greek par. συνηθείας), 6 (Greek par. συνηθείᾳ), 9 (Greek par. συνηθείας), ii 136 - ¶ subst. custom; *mn ʿydʾ* CIS ii 3913 i 5, 9: by custom; *bnmwsʾ wbʿydʾ* CIS ii 3913 i 6: by law and by custom; *hyk ʿydʾ* CIS ii 3913 ii 136: according to

custom.
v. *zʿr₂*.

ʿydw **Palm** Milik DFD 183: l. in Ber iii 99[5] *ʿydwth* (= Sing. + suff. 3 p.s.m. of *ʿydw* (= frequent visit, sc. of sanctuary or cultic feast)), uncert. reading and interpret., dam. context; cf. also Ingholt Ber iii 103: l. *ʿyrwth* (= Sing. + suff. 3 p.s.m. of *ʿyrw* (= splendour) or Sing. + suff. 3 p.s.f. of *ʿyrw* (= vigilance)).

ʿydls (< Lat. *aedilis*, cf. Février RevEtAnc lv 358, Friedrich Or xxiv 157) - **Pun** Sing. abs. *ʿydls* KAI 125 (dam. context) - ¶ subst. aedilis.

ʿylm v. *ʿlym*.

ʿym v. *ḥy₁*.

ʿyn₁ v. *ʿyn₂,₃*.

ʿyn₂ **OldCan** Dual + suff. 1 p.s. *ḫe-na-ia* EA 144[17] (cf. Sivan GAG 127, 206, Kossmann JEOL xxx 45) - **Ph** Sing. abs. *ʿn* Syr xlviii 396[2,4], 403[5] (cf. e.g. Gaster BASOR ccix 19, 25, Röllig NESE ii 29, 34, Liverani RSF ii 37, Lipiński RSF ii 53f., v.d.Branden BiOr xxxiii 13, xxxvi 202, Gibson SSI iii p. 90, 92, de Moor JEOL xxvii 111 :: Caquot Syr xlviii 403, 406, Avishur PIB 266f., 271, UF x 32, 36: = Sing. cstr. (v. *tm₁*) :: Cross CBQ xxxvi 488f. (div. otherwise): l. *tʿn* = QAL Impf. 3 p.s.f. of *ʿyn₁* (= to see) :: Garbini OA xx 291f. (div. otherwise): l. *tʿn* = Sing. abs. of *tʿn* (= perdition) :: Teixidor AO i 108: l. *ʿnm* or *bnm* (without interpret.)); cstr. *ʿn* KAI 14[17], BMB xviii 106 ii, MUSJ xlix 493[2]; Dual cstr. *ʿn* KAI 10[10], 48[4], 60[5] - **DA** Sing. abs. or cstr. *ʿyn* i 18 (??, heavily dam. context; *ʿyn[*; cf. Lemaire CRAI ’85, 281: poss. = Plur. abs. of *ʿy*) - **Samal** Sing. + suff. 2 p.s.m. *ʿynk* KAI 214[32]; + suff. 1 p.s. *ʿyny* KAI 214[30] - **OldAr** Dual + suff. 1 p.s. *ʿyny* KAI 224[3]; + suff. 2 p.pl.m. *ʿynykm* KAI 222A 13 - **OffAr** Dual abs. *ʿynyn* Aḥiq 213, 215 (dam. context); cstr. *ʿyny* Aḥiq 124, RES 1789; + suff. 3 p.s.m. *ʿynwhy* Cowl 41[7]; + suff. 1 p.s. *ʿyny* Aḥiq 169, KAI 226[5]; cf. Frah x 13 (*ʾynh*), xxv 46 (in comb. *lʿyn*), Paik 594 (in comb. *lʿyny*), GIPP 26, SaSt 21 - **Nab** Sing. cstr. *ʿyn* RB xlvi 405[2] (:: Savignac RB xlvi a.l.: poss. = part of compound n.d.; v. *rʾš₁*) - **Palm** Sing. abs. *ʿyn* RIP 126[2], 127[8]; emph. *ʿynʾ* CIS ii 3976[1], 4064[6], 4065[4], RTP 722, Inv xii 44[1], Inv D 33[2], RIP 127[1,3]; Plur. abs. *ʿynn* CIS ii 3913 ii 58 (Greek par. πηγῶν); emph. *ʿyntʾ* CIS ii 3913 ii 1, 63 - **JAr** Sing. cstr. *ʿyn* AMB 1[16,17] (in both instances diff. context), 13[6], *ʿyyn* AMB 14[2]; emph. *ʿynh* AMB 2[2]; Dual + suff. 3 p.s.m. *ʿynwh* MPAT-A 22[5] (= SM 70[13]), *[ʿ]ynwy* AMB 5[5] - ¶ subst. f. (in KAI 214[30] however m., cf. also Lipiński VT xx 26 (n. 2)) - 1) eye: EA 144[17], KAI 226[5], Aḥiq 213, 215; cf. also *qm ʿyny ʾw dlḥ* KAI 214[30]: my eye is dim (v. *qwm₁*) or troubled (v. *dlḥ₁*), diff. context; *wtlʿy ʿynk* KAI 214[32]: your eye will be weary; *pqḥw ʿynykm lḥzyh ʿdy br ...* KAI 222A 13: open your eyes to behold the

treaty of B.; *ʿyny zy nṭlt ʿlyk wlbby zy yhbt lk* Aḥiq 169: my eyes which I lifted up on you (indicating the sympathy shown for someone) and my heart which I gave you (v. also *lbb$_2$*); *hn ʿyny ʾlhn ʿl ʾn[šʾ]* ... Aḥiq 124: if the eyes of the gods are over men (sc. nobody will escape their scrutiny); *dyn dʿynwh mšwṭṭn bkl ʾrʿʾ wḥmy styrth* MPAT-A 22[5f.]: the Judge whose eyes range over all the earth and who sees hidden things; *ʿynh byšth* AMB 2[2f.]: the evil eye (cf. also AMB 13[6], 14[2]) - cf. also - a) prec. by prep. *b$_2$*, *mh ṭb bʿyny* KAI 224[3]: what is good in my eyes (i.e. what seems fitting to me) - b) prec. by prep. *l$_5$*, *ḥn lʿn ʾlnm wlʿn ʿm ʾrṣ z* KAI 10[10f.]: favour in the eyes of the gods and the eyes of the people of this land (cf. KAI 48[4]); *lʿynwhy* Cowl 41[7]: before his eyes (i.e. in his presence); the meaning of RES 1789 obscure; for a comparable expression without prec. *l$_5$*, cf. *wyṭnʾy* ... *ʿn ʾš* KAI 60[5]: and they will set it up ... before the eyes of men (i.e. in public) - c) prec. by *mn$_5$* in diff. context AMB 1[16f.] (cf. also Naveh & Shaked AMB a.l.); for the combination of *ʿyn* + *ʾl* in transcribed names, cf. Milik DFD 346 - **2)** source: KAI 14[17], BMB xviii 106 ii (cf. Elayi SCA 62), MUSJ xlix 493[2] and passim in Nab. and Palm. texts; *ʿyntʾ dy myʾ* CIS ii 3913 ii 1, 63: wells of water (cf. also CIS ii 3913 ii 58) - a second instance of this word also in Syr xlviii 403[5], cf. Caquot Syr xlviii 403, 404f., Gibson SSI iii p. 90, 92: l. *ʿn* = Sing. cstr., cf. however Gaster BASOR ccix 19, 26, Avishur PIB 266, 267, 271, UF x 32, 26: l. *ʿn* (= Sing. abs.), or div. otherwise l. *ʿny*, cf. Röllig NESE ii 29, 34, Garbini OA xx 291f., de Moor JEOL xxvii 111 (: = Sing. + suff. 1 p.s.), Lipiński RSF ii 53f. (: = Sing. + suff. 3 p.s.m., cf. also Cross CBQ xxxvi 488f.), v.d. Branden BiOr xxxiii 13 (: = Dual + suff. 3 p.s.m.); cf. also Garbini OA xx 292 - this word poss. also in Syr xlviii 403[6]: *ʿnk* (= Sing. + suff. 2 p.s.m.), cf. Caquot Syr xlviii a.l., Gaster BASOR ccix 19, 26, Lipiński RSF ii 52f., Garbini OA xx 292, de Moor JEOL xxvii 111 (n. 23) (cf. also Avishur PIB 267: or = Dual + suff. 2 p.s.m., cf. also idem UF x 32, 36), on the diff. reading of this word, cf. also Röllig NESE ii 34 :: Cross CBQ xxxvi 487ff. (n. 32, div. otherwise): l. *mʿnn* = L-form Part. s.m. abs. of *ʿnn$_1$* (= to chant a spell) or = lapsus for *mʿnnm* = L-form Part. pl.m. abs. of *ʿnn$_1$*? - Rocco StudMagr vii a.l.: l. *ʿn* (= Sing. abs. of *ʿyn$_2$* (= depth of the sea)) in StudMagr vii 12[3] (highly uncert. interpret.) - for *gl ʿn*, v. *gly*, for *rb ʿ(y)n*, v. *rb$_2$*, for *rbnwt ʿynʾ*, v. *rbnw*, for *mṣbʾ dy ʿynʾ/mṣb ʿynʾ*, v. *mṣb*.
v. *ʾzn$_2$*, *byn$_1$*, *bnh$_1$*, *ḥzy$_1$*, *ʿyn$_3$*, *ʿynyn*, *ʿny$_1$*, *pnh$_1$*, *qmt$_1$*.

ʿyn$_3$ **Ph** Sing. abs. *ʿyn* Syr xlviii 403[2] (cf. Caquot Syr xlviii 404, Röllig NESE ii 29, 32, cf. however Gaster BASOR ccix 19, 24, Lipiński RSF ii 53, Gibson SSI iii p. 90f., Cross CBQ xxxvi 488f., de Moor JEOL xxvii 111 (n. 22): = QAL Part. act. s.m. abs. of *ʿyn$_1$* (= one who casts an evil eye) :: Garbini OA xx 290, 292: = Sing. abs. of *ʿyn$_2$* (=evil eye) :: Avishur PIB 267, 270f., UF x 32, 35: l. *ʿn* = Sing. abs. of *ʿyn$_2$*) - ¶ subst. (v. however supra) one who casts an evil eye, sorcerer (for the litt., v. supra, cf. also Ceresko JLNS 201 :: v.d.Branden BiOr xxxiii 13: = spirit of the evil eye); uncert. interpret.

ʿynyn OffAr Sing. cstr. *ʿynyn* Cowl 26^{22} (lapsus for *ʿnyn*??, cf. Leand 43m'''', cf. Cowl p. 97 :: Porten & Yardeni sub TADAE A 6.2: = Dual + suff. 1 p.pl. of *ʿyn$_2$*) - ¶ subst. only in the combination *lʿynyn*, for the purpose of (for the context, v. also *ʾwpšr*).

ʿyp Palm the diff. *ʿyph* in RIP 199^6 poss. = QAL Part. pass. s.f. abs. of *ʿwp$_2$* (= to redouble), cf. Gawlikowski Sem xxiii 116 (cf. also idem RIP a.l.), cf. however Milik DFD 286f. (div. otherwise): pro ʿ (Gawlikowski RIP a.l., Sem xxiii 116: = sign for 5) *ʿyph* l. *zʿyph* (= Sing. f. abs. of *zʿyp* (= subjected to the rage/wrath, sc. of a deity); or = QAL Part. pass. s.f. abs. of *zʿp* (= to be angry?)).

ʿyprwr Hebr Sing. abs. *]ʿyprwr* DJD ii 24L 5 (heavily dam. context) - ¶ subst. (?) of unknown meaning, cf. Milik DJD ii a.l.

ʿyr$_1$ (< Arab., cf. Cantineau Nab i 68, O'Connor JNES xlv 217f., 220) - **Nab** PAʿEL Impf. 3 p.s.m. *yʿyr* CIS ii 206^8, 212^7, 217^{10}, J 17^9 (or l. rather *yqbr* (= QAL Impf. 3 p.s.m. of *qbr$_1$*)?, cf. Chabot sub RES 1175); Impf. 3 p.pl.m. *yʿyrwn* J 12^7 (= CIS ii 205) - ¶ verb PAʿEL to change: CIS ii 212^7 - **1)** + obj.: J 17^9 (v. however supra) - **2)** + *mn$_5$*, *yʿyr mn kl dy ʿlʾ* CIS ii 217^{10}: he will change anything which is (written) above (cf. CIS ii 206$^{8f.}$) - **3)** + *mn$_5$* + *l$_5$*, *wlʾ yʿyrwn mn wgrʾ dnh lʾnwš klh* J 12$^{7f.}$: they will not change anything from this rock tomb for anyone whomsoever - on this root, cf. also Greenfield Mem Yalon 82.

ʿyr$_2$ v. *ʿr$_1$*.

ʿyr$_3$ (< Arab., cf. Cantineau Nab 66, O'Connor JNES xlv 217f., 220f.) - **Nab** m. Sing. abs. *ʿyr* CIS ii 199^5; cstr. *ʿyr* CIS ii 198^6, 199^6, 208^5, 209^7, 210^7, 217^6, 223^4, 224^{11}, J 5^8, BASOR cclxiii 78^3; + suff. 3 p.s.f. *ʿyrh* CIS ii 209^6 (:: Cantineau Nab ii 129: = + suff. 3 p.s.m.) - ¶ substantivated adj., another: CIS ii 199^5; *mn yqbr bh ʿyr kmkm wbrth* CIS ii 198^6: whoever shall bury in it any other than K. and her daughter; *yktb mwhbh ʾw ʿyrh* CIS ii 209^6: he will write a (deed of) gift or anything else - prec. by prep. *k$_1$*, *yʿbd kʿyr dnh* CIS ii 209^7: he will do otherwise than this; *yʿbd kʿyr mh dy ʿlʾ ktyb* CIS ii 199$^{6f.}$: he will do otherwise than is written above; *ʿbd kʿyr kl dy ʿlʾ ktyb* BASOR cclxiii 78^3: he did otherwise than all that is written above; *yʿbd kʿyr dy ʿlʾ* CIS ii 208^5: he will do otherwise than (is written) above (cf. also CIS ii 210^7, 217$^{6f.}$, 223^4, 224$^{10f.}$, J 5^8).

‘yr$_4$ v. *‘yry*.

‘yrw v. *‘ydw*.

‘yry **JAr** Naveh sub SM 34: the *‘yry’* in MPAT-A 28[4] (= SM 34) = Plur. m. emph. of *‘yry* (= nisbe adj. < *‘yr$_2$*) = townspeople? (cf. also Klein SeYi 46, Hüttenmeister 157f.), cf. however Sukenik JPOS xv 145, ASH 55, Beyer ATTM 385, 655: = Plur. emph. of *‘yr$_4$* (= the wakeful; i.e. those who experienced an inward urge); cf. also Fitzmyer & Harrington MPAT p. 265, 292, 352: = Plur. emph. of *‘yr$_4$* (= the guardians, i.e. overseers of the synagogue or secular authorities?), Frey sub 858: ‘les hommes attentifs’, cf. also Klein SeYi 46.

‘yšrh **JAr** Milik Syr xlv 101: l. poss. *[‘]yšrh[* in l. 13 = Sing. abs. (= tithing, decimation; heavily dam. context; diff. interpret.).

‘kb **JAr** Pa‘el Impf. 2 p.s.f. *t‘kbyn* AMB 3[15,16] - ¶ verb Pa‘el to detain; + *‘l$_7$*: *l’ t‘kbyn ‘lwy* AMB 3[15]: do not detain him - the form *t‘kb* in DBKP 17[42] of diff. interpret.; Greenfield DBKP a.l.: poss. = pass. Impf. 3 p.s.f. (= to be withheld?) or = lapsus for *’‘kb* = Qal/Pa‘el Impf. 1 p.s. (= to withhold)??

‘kn$_1$ v. *khn$_1$*.

‘kn$_2$ v. *’bn$_2$*.

‘ksndr‘ v. *’ksdr*.

‘kr **Pun** Qal Inf. cstr. *‘kr* CIS i 5510[3] - ¶ verb Qal to destroy - Milik sub DJD ii 72: the diff. *‘kyr* in MPAT 49 i 4 (= DJD ii 72) = Qal Pf. (prob. misprint for Part.) pass. of *‘kr* (= to trouble > to stir (flour with water), to hydrate (improb. interpret., cf. also Beyer ATTM 318, 655: = troubled, sad)).
v. *bkr$_1$*.

‘l$_1$ **OffAr** Sing. abs. *‘l* Cowl 25[8], 35[8], 43[10], Krael 3[18], 10[11,16], 11[5,7-11], 12[29]; emph. (cf. Kottsieper SAS 81 :: e.g. BL 55b, 68o, Leand 47b, Joüon MUSJ xviii 50, Bibl xv 399, Segert AAG p. 103: + (orig.) acc. ending; cf. however Degen GGA ’79, 22: -’ = adv. ending) *‘l’* Cowl 3[20], 5[5,10,11,13], 25[6], 48[2], Aḥiq 114, Krael 6[11]([*‘*]*l’*; for this poss. reading, cf. Szubin & Porten BASOR cclxix 39f., Porten & Yardeni sub TADAE B 3.7),[13], 8[4], RES 492B 4, CRAI ’70, 163[3bis] (diff. context, cf. Dupont-Sommer ibid. 169); cf. Frah xxv 2 (in *l’l’*), GIPP 26, SaSt 21 - **Nab** Sing. emph. *‘l’* (v. supra) CIS ii 182[2], 196[2,8], 197[8], 198[7], 199[5,6], DBKP 22[34], etc. (cf. also the variant *‘ly* in J 17[9] (for the diff. reading of the context, cf. however Chabot sub RES 1175)) - **Palm** Sing. abs. *‘l* CIS ii 3911[3], 3913 ii 68, 142, 4190[5], Inscr P 47[1] (= Inv xii 19), Inv xii 48[2], 49[5], RIP 21[3], 25[11] - **JAr** Sing. abs. *‘l* MPAT 61[24] (cf. Yadin & Greenfield sub DBKP 15 :: Fitzmyer & Harrington MPAT a.l.: = *‘l$_7$*), DBKP 17[42], 18[69, 71], 19[28], 20[41,42], MPAT-A 17[1] (= SM 7); emph. (v. supra)

ʿlʾ MPAT 42[18] (*ʿl[ʾ]*, heavily dam. context), 44 xiii 2 (*ʿl[ʾ]*), 45[8], 49 i 6, 52[9], 61[25] - ¶ subst. height, that which is situated on high; occurring in the foll. expressions - **1)** *ʿl* above: DBKP 20[41]; *kl dy ʿl ktb* MPAT 61[24]: all that is written above (v. supra; cf. also DBKP 17[42], 18[69], 19[28], 20[42]) - **2)** *ʿlʾ* - a) above, upwards; *lmnsq ʿlʾ* Krael 6[13]: to ascend (above) - b) above; *lhn lmn dy ʿlʾ ktyb* CIS ii 197[8]: except those who are written (i.e. mentioned) above; *kdy ʿlʾ ktyb* MPAT 61[25] (= DBKP 15): as it is written above (cf. CIS ii 198[7], 199[5], DBKP 22[34], etc.); > mentioned above; *rwḥw dnh dy ʿlʾ* CIS ii 182[2]: this R. mentioned above; *ʿbydtʾ dy ʿlʾ* CIS ii 196[8]: the work just mentioned; *kl dy ʿlʾ* CIS ii 206[8f.]: everything which is mentioned above - c) followed by prep. *mn₅*: above; *yktbw ʿl drʿh ʿlʾ mn ktbtʾ* RES 492B 4: they will inscribe it on her arm above the inscription; *dʾ mqbrtʾ wnpšʾ dy ʿlʾ mnh* Syr xxxv 244[1f.]: these are the tomb and the monument that is upon it (cf. CIS ii 196[1f.]) - **3)** *lʿl*: Frah xxv 2 (up, upwards) - a) prec. by prep. *mn₅*: above; *hyk ktyb mn lʿl* CIS ii 3913 ii 68: as it is written above (cf. CIS ii 3913 ii 142, RIP 25[11]); *ʾmh dy ʾqmt dh dy mn lʿl* CIS ii 4190[3ff.]: the mother of this A. mentioned above - b) followed by prep. *mn₅*: above, upon; *wtṭlylʾ dy lʿl mnh* CIS ii 3911[3f.]: and the roof that is upon (i.e. over) it; *bt ʿlmʾ dnh wbnynʾ dy lʿl mnh* RIP 21[2f.]: this tomb and the construction (built) upon it (cf. also Inv xii 48[2], 49[5]) - c) prec. by prep. *ʿd₇*: up to the top; *wtṣbyth klh ʿd lʿl* Inscr P 47[1] (= Inv xii 19): and all its ornamentation up to the top - **4)** *lʿlʾ* - a) prec. by prep. *mn₅*, above: MPAT 42[18] (heavily dam. context) - b) followed by the prep. *mn₅*: above; *msrsrn lʿlʾ mnh* Aḥiq 114: flying away above him - **5)** *mn ʿl*: above; *bytʾ zy tḥwmwhy ktybn mn ʿl* Cowl 25[8]: the house the boundaries of which are described above; *[ywmʾ] znh zy mn ʿl ktyb* Cowl 35[8]: the day which is mentioned above; *ʾbgrnʾ zy mn ʿl kty[b]* Krael 11[7]: the fine mentioned above (v. also *ʾbgrn*); cf. Cowl 43[10], Krael 3[17f.], 10[11], 11[5], etc. - **6)** *mn ʿlʾ*: above; *kspʾ zy ktyb mn ʿlʾ* Cowl 5[10]: the silver mentioned above (cf. Cowl 3[20], 5[13], 48[2]); *btḥtyh wmn ʿlʾ kwyn ptyḥn tmh* Cowl 25[6]: at the south side there are open windows upon high (v. also *w₂*, *ptḥ₁*, *tḥtyh*); *zbnyh zy mn ʿlʾ* MPAT 45[8]: the above mentioned buyers (cf. MPAT 52[9]); *kl qbl zy mn ʿlʾ kt[yb]* MPAT 49 i 6: according to what is writen above (cf. prob. also *kl dy mʿl[ʾ]* MPAT 44 xiii 2: all that is above ... (heavily dam. context) - **7)** *ʿd ʿlʾ*, upwards, up to the top; *mn ʾrʿʾ wʿd ʿlʾ* Cowl 5[5]: from the ground up to the top (cf. Cowl 5[11]) - **8)** *ʿl mn*, above: MPAT-A 17[1], J 17[9] (v. however supra).
v. *brḥ₁*, *mʿl₂*, *ʿl₇*, *ʿlʾ*, *ptḥ₁*.

ʿl₂ **OldCan** Sing. cstr. *ḫu-ul-lu* EA 296[38] - ¶ subst. yoke.

ʿl₃ **OldAr** Sing. abs. *ʿl* KAI 222A 22 - ¶ subst. m. foal.

ʿl_4 **Pun** Plur. abs. *ʿlm* KAI 81[3] (cf. CIS i a.l., Clermont-Ganneau RAO iii 9f., 337 n.2; or = Sing. abs. of *ʿlm*$_7$ (= stairs?); cf. Röllig KAI a.l.) - ¶ subst. Plur. (v. however supra) stairs (uncert. interpret.) :: v.d Branden PO i 208f.: = Sing. (= high column).

ʿl_5 **DA** Sing. cstr. *ʿl* ii 13 (diff. context; cf. e.g. Hoftijzer DA a.l., cf. also Levine JAOS ci 200, H.P.Müller ZAW xciv 219, 236 :: e.g. Caquot & Lemaire Syr liv 296, Garbini Hen i 186, Delcor SVT xxxii 62: = *ʿl*$_7$) - ¶ subst. embryo, foetus; *ʿl rḥm* DA ii 13: the foetus in the womb (cf. however Hackett BTDA 30, 70: = a newborn child).
v. *ʾš*$_1$, *mlk*$_5$.

ʿl_6 **Mo** Lipiński Or xl 340: the *ʿl* in KAI 181[33] = Sing. abs. of *ʿl*$_6$ (= *ʿwl* (= injustice)), highly uncert. interpret. (cf. e.g. Gibson SSI i p. 77: *ʿl* = *ʿl*$_7$ :: e.g. Cooke NSI p. 14: = part of n.l.).

ʿl_7 prep. (cf. allomorph *ʿly* in CIS ii 4018[5] (Palm.)). For forms with pron. suff., cf. e.g. - a) **Ph/Pun** + suff. 3 p.s.m. *ʿly* KAI 24[8]; + suff. 2 p.s.m. *ʿlk* KAI 3[5]; + suff. 1 p.s. *ʿly* KAI 3[6], 24[7]; + suff. 3 p.pl.m. *ʿlhm* KAI 10[6], *ʿlnm* CIS i 3920[4] - b) **Hebr** + suff. 3 p.s.m. *ʿlyw* DJD ii 30[3,4,15,19], 46[9]; + suff. 2 p.s.f. *ʿlyk* AMB 1[23]; + suff. 1 p.s. *ʿly* DJD ii 24C 18, 43[3] - c) **Samal** + suff. 3 p.s.m. *ʿlyh* KAI 214[34] - d) **OldAr** + suff. 3 p.s.f. *ʿly[h]* KAI 224[9]; + suff. 2 p.s.m. *ʿlyk* KAI 202A 15; + suff. 1 p.s. *ʿly* KAI 202A 4, 222B 26 - e) **OffAr** + suff. 3 p.s.m. *ʿlwhy* Cowl 42[6], Aḥiq 54, NESE i 11[7], RSO xxxv 22[4] (for this reading, cf. Porten FS Bresciani 434, Porten & Yardeni sub TADAE A 3.4, Lipiński Or lvii 435 :: Bresciani RSO xxxv 23: l. *ʿl* (= *ʿl*$_7$) *pmy* (= Sing. + suff. 1 p.s. of *pm*$_1$), cf. also Fitzmyer JNES xxi 22, Naveh AION xvi 29); + suff. 3 p.s.f. *ʿlyh* Cowl 8[24]; + suff. 2 p.s.m. *ʿlyk* Cowl 5[3], 6[5], Krael 7[3] (*ʿly[k]*; for the reading, cf. Porten GCAV 247, Porten & Yardeni sub TADAE B 3.8 :: Krael a.l. (div. otherwise): l. *ʿl*)[,8], 14[3] (cf. also Porten GCAV 255), Driv 12[5]; + suff. 2 p.s.f. *ʿlyky* Cowl 8[13,15], Krael 5[7,10], Herm 1[9]; + suff. 1 p.s. *ʿly* Cowl 7[7], Krael 1[4], Driv 1[3], ATNS 14[3], 82b 1 (heavily dam. context); + suff. 3 p.pl.m. *ʿlyhm* Cowl 14[5,8], *ʿlyhwm* Cowl 30[24], *ʿlyhn* Herm 2[10] (:: Bresciani & Kamil Herm a.l., Segert AAG p. 230: = + suff. 3 p.pl.f.); + suff. 2 p.pl.m. *ʿlykm* Cowl 38[5,9], Driv 7[5], ATNS 18[6], *ʿlykwm* NESE iii 48 conc. 14; + suff. 1 p.pl. *ʿlyn* Cowl 26[2], Krael 13[7], ATNS 6[5], NESE i 11[6]; - f) **Nab** + suff. 3 p.s.m. *ʿlwhy* CIS ii 197[7], 217[7], 224[11], BASOR cclxiii 78[3]; + suff. 2 p.s.m. *ʿlyk* MPAT 64 ii 2; + suff. 3 p.pl.m. *ʿlyhm* CIS ii 226[3] - g) **Palm** + suff. 3 p.s.m. *ʿlwhy* CIS ii 3956[4], 4109A 3, 4218[3]; + suff. 3 p.s.f. *ʿlwh* MUSJ xxxviii 106[9]; + suff. 3 p.pl.m. *ʿlyhwn* MUSJ xxxviii 106[11] - h) **Hatra** + suff. 3 p.s.m. *ʿlwhy* 74[8] (for this reading, cf. Milik DFD 401 (v. infra) :: Caquot Syr xxxii 270, Donner KAI sub 256, Ingholt AH i/1, 44: l. *ʿlyh* (= + suff. 3 p.s.m.)); + suff. 3 p.pl.m./f. *ʿlyhw/yn*, cf. Assur 11 ii

3 - i) **JAr** + suff. 3 p.s.m. *ʿlwy* MPAT 53[4], MPAT-A 46[4] (:: Avigad IEJ iv 95: l. *ʿlyw*, cf. also Fitzmyer & Harrington MPAT p. 352), AMB 3[15,16], *ʿlwh* AMB 1[19]; + suff. 3 p.s.f. (or m.?) *ʿlh* MPAT 44 i 3 (heavily dam. context); + suff. 3 p.s.f. *ʿlh* MPAT-A 51[10] (for this reading and interpret., cf. Hestrin IR sub 174 :: Driver ADAJ ii 64: l. *slh* = forever :: Sukenik Kedem ii 86: l. *ʿlt* (cf. Fitzmyer & Harrington MPAT p. 272f., 352: = QAL Pf. 3 p.s.f. of *ʿll*$_1$; Wacholder HUCA xliv 181: = Sing. abs. of *ʿlh*$_2$) :: de Boer JEOL xiv 118: l. *nwlh* = the disgraced one (= f. Sing. abs.?)); + suff. 2 p.s.f. *ʿly[k]* MPAT 42[13]; + suff. 1 p.s. *ʿly* MPAT 51[10]; + suff. 3 p.pl.m. *ʿlyhwn* MPAT 67[4] - cf. also the foll. transcriptions: - **1)** *aly*: Poen 939 - **2)** *al*: Warka 4, 29; cf. Frah xxiv 13 (*ʿlh*), xxv 33 (*ʿl*), Paik 581, 762, 763 (*ʿlh*), 761 (*ʿl*), 764 (*ʿly*), 765 (*ʿlyn*), 766 (*lʿḥw*), 767 (*ʿl* in comb.), Nisa 18[7], 19[5], 23[4], 24[3], 26[7], 27[3], 28[2], 30[4], 31[5] (*ʿl*), etc., Sogd R 43 (?), Ve 122, Syr xxxv 317[42], Syn 301[4], 305[4], 307[2], 315 i 1, DEP 153[1], 154 recto 5, Chw Ir 57, GH iv 79f., BSOAS xxxiii 152[18] (*mn ʿlh*), GIPP 19, 49, SaSt 14, cf. also Toll ZDMG-Suppl viii 40 - ¶ prep. (on this prep., cf. also Pennacchietti AION xxiv 182ff.) - **1)** loc. - a) on; *mʾš hnḥšt ʿl mʾknʾ* KAI 119[4]: the bronze statue on its piedestal (v. *mʾš*$_1$); *mṣbt ʾz ʾš yṭnʾ ʾrš ... ʿl mškb nḥtnm* KAI 34[1,5]: this stele is it which A. has erected ... on the tomb where they rest; *wyšb ʾnk ʿl ksʾ ʾby* KAI 26A i 11: and I set him on his father's throne (v. *ʾb*$_1$, *yšb*$_1$); *wšt šm ʿly* KAI 26A iii 16: and he will put his name on it; *wysk ʿl ʾrpd [ʾbny b]rd* KAI 222A 26f.: and let him pour out upon A. hailstones; *wymḥʾ ʿl ʾpyh* KAI 222A 42: one strikes (her) on her face (v. *mḥʾ*); *šlw ʿl ʾšrkm* KAI 224[5]: stay quietly in your place; *kl zy ʾyty lh ʿl ʾnpy ʾrʿʾ* Cowl 15[19]: everything he owns on the face of the earth; *šnyth ʿl ydh* Krael 5[3]: a mark is on her hand; *yktbwn ʿl drʿh* RES 492B 4: they will mark her on her arm; *lktwb ʿlwhy* (for this reading, cf. Milik DFD 401, Vattioni IH a.l. :: idem ibid.: *ʿlwhy* prec. by *l*$_5$ :: Caquot Syr xxxii 270: l. *ʿlyh* (cf. also Donner KAI sub 256, Ingholt AH i/1, 44)) *mdʿn* (v. *mdʿm*) Hatra 74[7f.]: he will write something on it; *wmnḥtʾ wlbwntʾ yqrbwn ʿl mdbḥʾ zk* Cowl 32[9f.]: they will offer a meal-offering and frankincense on this altar; *lbšʾ zy ʿlyk* RHR cxxx 20 conc. 4f.: the garment you wear; *ytʾlp ʿlwhy ktb klh* CIS ii 197[7]: he will compose on it any text whatever (v. *ʾlp*$_1$); *lmqmw ʿlwhy [ṣlm]yn trn* CIS ii 3956[4f.]: to place thereon two statues; *dy lʾ ytptḥ ʿlyhm* CIS ii 226[2f.]: that it (i.e. the tomb) may not be opened above them (cf. CIS ii 4218[3], Frey 1300[4] (= MPAT 67; :: Fitzmyer & Harrington MPAT a.l.: (it is) not (permitted) to open them)); *šhdyʾ zy ʿl sprʾ znh* Cowl 11[16]: the witnesses who are mentioned on this document; *nksyʾ zy ʿl spr ʾntwtky* Cowl 35[4f.]: the goods which are mentioned in your marriage deed (cf. EI xx 256[12]); cf. also *dbr lʿnh ʿl lšn* DA ii 17: an iniquitous word on (your) tongue (v. *dbr*$_3$, *lʿnh*$_2$); *šlwm*

ʿl mškbh Frey 1536²: peace be on her resting-place; *ʿl myṭbʾ ršʾ hšlky* KAI 172²: on (i.e. with) the approbation of the senate of Sulcis (v. *myṭb*); *ʿlyky mtkl ʾnh* Herm 7²: I am relying on you; *wʿl ʿṭth wmlwhy ḥyl [ʾtw]r klʾ hww* Aḥiq 60f.: by his counsel and words the whole army of A. was guided; *ktb hwšʿ ʿl pm ʾḥyʾb* Cowl 2¹⁸: H. has written (it) according to the instructions of A. (v. *pm_1*) - used metaphorically: α) with the meaning "incumbent upon"; *ʾt ly ʿlyk ksp* Cowl 49²: I have against you a claim of silver; *ʿmrh zy ʿl mky* Herm 2⁹: the wool which is owed by M. (:: Donner FS Albright ii 84: which belongs to M.); *8 šql[n] ksp zy blšy ʿl blzr* LidzbAss v 1ff. (= AECT 50): 8 shekel silver of B. incumbent upon B. (i.e. which he has to repay); *šʿrn zy br mlkʾ ʿl nbzrdn* CIS ii 39¹ᶠ· (= Del 23; for the reading, cf. Fales sub AECT 9): wheat of the son of the king (i.e. from him) incumbent upon N. (i.e. what N. has to repay); *mrbyth zy yštʾr ʿly* Cowl 11⁹: the interest on it, which remains from me; *ʿl kl ʾnwš ... dy lʾ yzbn* CIS ii 206³ᶠ·: it is incumbent upon everyone that he will not sell; *wqm ʿl wʾlt wbnyh ... dy ytqbrwn yth* CIS ii 212⁵ᶠ·: it is incumbent upon W. and her sons to bury him; *wʾyty ʿlwhy ḥṭyʾh ldwšrʾ* CIS ii 224¹¹ᶠ·: he owes D. a fine; etc. - β) with the meaning "exerting authority over"; *ʾby mlk ʿl mʾb* KAI 181²: my father reigned over Moab; *pʿltn hrbt bʿlt gbl mmlkt ʿl gbl* KAI 10²: the lady the mistress of G. has made me king over G.; *wtʾrk ymw wšntw ʿl gbl* KAI 10⁹: may she prolong his days and years (sc. of his reign) over G.; *ʾšr ʿl hms* IEJ xxx 171²ᶠ·: who is over the corvee; *ʾš ʿl ʾšrt* IEJ xxxv 83²: the overseer of the shrine(s); *ʿšrt hʾšm ʾš ʿl mqdšm* KAI 80¹: the *decemviri* who are over the sanctuaries (cf. Huss 543); *šlšm hʾš ʾš ʿl hmšʾ[tt]* CIS i 3917¹: the thirty men who are over the payments (cf. also Huss 543; cf. KAI 37A 6); *ṭnʾm ʿl hmlkt z* RCL '66, 201³: appointed over this work (v. also *$ṭnʾ_1$*); *knʾ ʿl mlkt hbnʾ* KAI 137²: they were set over the construction work; *byknʾ zy ʿl gngnyʾ* ... ATNS 40¹: B. who is over the gardeners; *wgbr ʾḥrn lʾ šlyṭ ʿlyky* Krael 5⁹ᶠ·: another man will have no authority over you; *dy ʿl qšṭʾ* Inv D 19²: one who is over the archers; *hwʾ rb ʿyn ʿl ʾpqʾ* RIP 126²ᶠ·: he was the overseer of the source with authority over E.; etc.; cf. also *ʾš ʿl knṣwlʿt* Karth xii 50¹: who was charged with the consulship (for the context, v. *knṣwlʿt*) - γ) used in comparison; *wbrk bʿl kr[n]tryš ʾyt ʾztwd ḥym ... ʿl kl mlk* KAI 26A iii 2ff.: may B.K. bless A. with life ... above every king (:: Barré Maarav iii 183: *ʿl kl mlk* specially related to preceding *ʾdr*; cf. KAI 26A iii 4ff.); *wḥnʾh mrʾh mlk ʾšwr ʿl mlky* KAI 215¹²: his lord the king of A. placed him above kings ... - δ) with additive meaning; *wpʿl ʾnk ss ʿl ss wmgn ʿl mgn wmḥnt ʿl mḥnt* KAI 26A i 6f.: and I acquired horse upon horse and shield upon shield and army upon army (cf. prob. KAI 222B 30 (cf. e.g. Greenfield JSS xi 103ff.; for the context, v. *rby_1*); *ʿl spr ʾntwth* Krael 12¹⁸: above (i.e.

more than is mentioned in) her marriage contract (cf. Yaron JSS xiii 210 :: Krael a.l.: = (what is written) upon her ..., cf. poss. also Krael 10[7f.] (cf. Yaron JSS xiii 210)) - ε) used in local-separative context; *nḥt tbrḥ ʿl gbl* KAI 1[2]: may peace flee from G. (cf. e.g. Dupont-Sommer Sem iii 43 (n. 7), Driver WO i 413, JSS ix 349, Dahood Bibl xlvii 265 (n. 1)) - b) with, at; *ttb ʿl mwznʾ* Cowl 15[23f.]: she will sit down at the scales (v. *yšb*$_1$); *ʿmwdʾ dy ʿl bbʾ rbʾ* Syr xvii 274[3]: the column at the great gate (cf. SBS 24[3f.]); *plgn ʿlyn ʿbdyh* Cowl 28[3]: we have divided between us her slaves (cf. Cowl 28[13f.]); *glyn ʾnpyn ʿl ʾršm* Cowl 37[8]: we have revealed our face before A. (v. however *gly*); *ʿl ymynʾ* CIS ii 4172[2]: to the right; *ʿl smlk* CIS ii 4204[1]: to your left (cf. CIS ii 4174[5], 4199[4,7], Ber v 106[3], Inv xii 14[2] (= RIP 51), etc.); for *ʿl pn*, v. *pnh*$_1$ - **2)** directional, to - a) litterally; *ṣwk ḥnnyhw ʿl bʾr šbʿ* TA-H 3[3f.]: Ch. has commanded you to B.Sh. (cf. Aharoni TA-H a.l., Levine Shn iii 289, Dahood Or xlvi 330f., Pardee UF x 300, HAHL 35, cf. however Lemaire IH i 163f., Or lii 446: *ʿl* = Qal Imper. s.m. of *ʿly*$_1$ (prob. interpret.; cf. also Hospers SV 103f.)); *ʾzl ʿl mlkʾ* Cowl 27[3]: he went to the king; *ʾgrt šlḥ ʿl npyn brh* Cowl 30[7]: he sent a letter to his son N.; *ʿyny zy nṭlt ʿlyk* Aḥiq 169: my eyes which I lifted up unto you; *ḫa-al-li-tú al pi-la-nu* Warka 29: I entered at someone's; *kḥsn ʾtw ʿl bytʾ zyly* ATNS 30a 4: by force they came to my house (cf. Porten & Yardeni sub TADAE B 8.4); *ʾtyt ʿlyk* Cowl 5[3]: I came to you; *kzy ʾgrtʾ zʾ [t]mṭʾ ʿlyk* Cowl 42[6]: when this letter reaches you; *yhbt ʿl ps[mš]k* Driv 12[1f.]: (the letter) was given to P.; *ybltwn ʿl btyn* NESE i 11[5f.]: you have brought (it) to our houses; *šlḥy ʿl tby* Herm 2[6f.]: send (a message) to T.; *mn ʾršm ʿl ʾrtwnt* Driv 3[1]: (letter) from A. to A.; *ʿl mrʾy psmy ʿbdk mkbnt* Herm 3[1]: to my lord P. (a letter from) your servant M. (on this and comparable formulae, cf. Fitzmyer JBL xciii 213); *ʿl ḥgy* RES 1295[1]: (letter) to Ch.; etc. (for *ʿl* in the address of a letter cf. also Whitehead JNES xxxvii 135); cf. also, *whn ysq lbbk wtšʾ ʿl šptyk lhmtty* KAI 224[14f.]: if (the idea) comes to your mind and you raise to your lips (you shall express yourself with the intention) to kill me; *[kl m]lh [zy] tʾth ʿl blk* Aḥiq 96f.: everything that enters into your mind; *mwmʾh mṭʾh ʿlyky* Cowl 14[4f.]: an oath has come to you (i.e. has been imposed upon you; cf. Cowl 7[6f.]); *mll ʿl pṭnpḥtp* Cowl 69A 2: he spoke to P.; *ʾšr yspty ʿl hʾrṣ* KAI 181[29]: which I annexed to the land; *yhwspwn ʿl ʿqyʾ* Cowl 26[18]: they shall add to the planks; *kspʾ zy ʾtwsp ʿl mks pṭʾsy* ATNS 19[4]: the silver which is added to the tax of P.; *wʿbdw ʿl bytʾ zyly* Driv 7[7]: they appropiated (it) to my estate; *ḥzy ʿl ynqyʾ* PSBA '15, 222[2f.] (= RES 1793[8f.]): look after the children (cf. Cowl 41[6], Herm 1[11f.], 7[2f.]) - b) used as so-called *ʿl* comm., for, to, in the interest of; *wyntn lky wʿl bnyky ʾbygrn* Krael 10[13f.]: and he will give (i.e. pay) to you and your sons a fine (v. *ʾbgrn*; cf. however Yaron

JSS xiii 211: *ʿl* mistakenly corrected from *l*); *ʿl ʿlyk* Cowl 15[5]: it (i.e. the price) came to you (i.e. has been received by you), cf. Cowl 15[15]; *kzy ʿbd ʾnh lḥrwṣ kwt tʿbd bnt ʿly* Herm 1[7]: as much as I am doing for Ch., so may B. do for me; *dy hw bnh ʿl bʿl šmyn* CIS ii 163C: what he built for B.Sh.; *dnh kprʾ dy ʿbd mlkywn ... ʿl ḥnynw ... ʾbwhy wlnpšh* CIS ii 201[1ff.]: this is the tomb that M. made for Ch. his father and for himself; *bt ʿlmʾ dnh ʿbd mtny ... ʿl nwrbl ʾbwhy wʿl nby ʾmh* CIS ii 4130[1f.]: M. made this tomb for his father N. and his mother N. (the *ʿl* in this type of funerary texts (cf. CIS ii 201, 4130, etc.) prob. used in connnection with deceased persons (orig. local meaning: to construct a tomb over someone?) as against *l* used in connection with persons still alive at the moment of the building of the tomb); *wlʾ ʾḥ[y]s npšh ʿl mdyth* DFD 37[3f.]: and he did not spare himself (v. *ḥws*) for his town (i.e. in favour of his town); *ʾš ndr ʿbdʾšmn ʿl bny* CIS i 8[3]: what A. has vowed on behalf of his son(s) (cf. CIS i 15[2], Kition A 30[3]); *ndr mtnybʿl lbʿl ʿmn ʿl ḥtmlkt* Hofra 122[1f.]: vow of M. (or M. has vowed?) to B. on behalf of Ch.; *ʿl šlmʾ dy mtm[ky]n [l]k[l ʿ]l[mʾ* BIA x 55[4]: for the well-being of the rulers of the whole world (beginning of an inscription; Greek par.: ὑπὲρ αἰωνίου διαμονῆς κρατήσεως τῶν ... and ἐπὶ νείκῃ καὶ αἰωνίῳ διαμονῇ ...); *[dnh] msgdʾ dy qrb [y]mlk ... ldwšrʾ ... ʿl šlmh wšlm bnwhy* RES 676[1ff.]: this is the stele (v. *msgd*) which Y. has dedicated to D. for his own welfare and that of his children; *dnh ṣlmʾ dy ʿbdt ʾlhʾ dy ʿbdw bny ḥnynw ... ʿl ḥyy ḥrtt mlk nbṭw* CIS ii 354[1f.]: this is the statue of the god O. that the *Benay Ch.* made ... for the benefit of the life (i.e. for the welfare) of Ch. the king of N.; *[t]rtn ʿlwtʾ ʾln ʿbd ʿbydw ... lšyʿʾlqwm ʾlhʾ ... ʿl ḥywhy* CIS ii 3973[1,4f.]: O. has made these two altars for the god Sh. for the benefit of his life (i.e. for his welfare); *ʿbd šqy ... br zbdbwl ʿl ḥyyhwn* Inv xii 46[2f.]: Sh. ... (and ...) the son of Z. made it for the benefit of their lives (i.e. for their welfare; cf. Greek par.]ζαδβωλου ὑπὲρ[; v. also *ḥy*₁); *[l]bryk šmh [lʿ]lmʾ ʿbd zbyd[ʾ] ... ʿl byth* CIS ii 3997[1f.]: Z. made (it) for the one whose name is blessed forever ... for the benefit of his family; *ʿl npšh* MPAT 51[16]: for herself (after the name of an interested party signing a document; v. also *npš*); *ʾt ... ʿlyky* Herm 1[9]: you have ... (v. also *ʿrb*₅); etc.; - c) cf. also the foll. combination with metaphorical use of *ʿl*, *[wʿṭtʾ hʾ] ṭybt ʿl knwth* Aḥiq 67: and this counsel seemed good to (i.e. pleased) his companions; *hn ʿl mrʾn ṭb* Cowl 30[23]: if it seems good to our lord (cf. Cowl 31[22]; v. also *ṭb*₂); *whn ʾšbqn ʿl lbbk* Aḥiq 82: if I leave you to your own heart - **4)** temp. - a) during, at; *ʿl šny ḥrtt mlk nbṭw* CIS ii 196[6f.]: during the (regnal) years of Ch. the king of N.; *ʿl ywmwhy* (reading uncert.) *ktb* CIS ii 224[5]: during his life he wrote ...; *ʿl sp šnt ...* JAOS liv 31[2]: at the end of the year ...; *ʿl šttʾ bṭbt* Hatra 49[4]: on the sixth of (the month) T. (cf. Safar Sumer ix 245, Vattioni IH a.l., cf. also Milik Syr xliv 297) - b) until; *ʿl ʿlm* J 169: forever (for the reading, however, cf. Chabot sub RES 1130); *ʿl ʿlm ʿlm* BSOAS xvi 223,72[2]: for ever and ever; *ʿl ʾḥrn* Cowl 38[4]: afterwards (v. also *ʾḥrn*) - **5)** causal; *ʿl ky hmzrʾ* ... Karth xii 53[2]: because the *mizraḥ* ...; *ʿl zk ʾnh šwyt lk* ... KAI 264[7]: because of that I have made you ...; *wʿl hnn shd lh ʾlhʾ* Inv x 115[2]: and therefore the god has declared about him ...; *ʿl kn yqrʾwn* Aḥiq 117: therefore they call; etc.; for *ʿl ky*, v. *ky*, for *ʿl zy*, v. *zy* - **6)** with the meaning "concerning", *šlḥ ʾdny ʿl dbr byt hrpd* KAI 194[4f.]: my lord has sent a message concerning B.H.; *wltršh ly ʿly[h]* KAI 224[9]: you shall not overrule me in this respect; *spr mrḥq 1 zy drgmn ... ktb ly ʿl ʾrqʾ zk* Cowl 8[23f.]: an act of renunciation which D. wrote for me concerning this land; *hwṭbt lbby ʿl ʾrqʾ zk* Cowl 6[11f.]: you have satisfied my mind about this land; *wtktb ly nbz ʿl kl ksp* Cowl 11[6f.]: you shall write me a receipt for all the silver; *wʿl zhb ʿl znh šlḥn* ... Cowl 30[28f.]: and concerning the gold, on that point we have sent (a message) ... (cf. e.g. Cowl a.l., Grelot DAE p. 412 n. g :: e.g. Ginsberg ANET 492, Porten Arch 111 (n. 20), Porten & Greenfield JEAS p. 92, Porten & Yardeni sub TADAE A 4.7: first *ʿl* is anticipatory dittography); *ʾgrt ʾršm zy hytyw ʿl psmšk ʿl ḥlkyʾ* Driv 12[4]: the letter of A. that they brought to P., concerning the Cilicians; *wtštʾl ʿl znh* Driv 12[8]: you will be called to account on this matter; *qdmn šlḥt ʿlykm ʿl znh* Driv 7[5]: I have sent you a letter concerning this matter previously; *dyn lʾ ʾyty ly ʿmhm ʿl znh ṭʿm[ʾ]* ATNS 2[2]: I do not have a suit with them about this matter (for the reading, cf. Porten & Yardeni sub TADAE B 8.9); *lʾ ʾkhl ʾnh ʿnnyh ʾršnky ʿl dbrh dyn* Krael 4[12f.]: I A. will not be able to start a suit against you on account of that; *lh šʾl ʿl ḥrwṣ* Herm 1[6]: he even does not ask about Ch. (cf. poss. also KAI 271A 4, 6, dam. context); *[hw]dʿw lʾrmtydt ʿlwhy* NESE i 11[7]: inform A. about it; *ʾmrt lʾšyn ʿl ksp mrzḥʾ* RES 1295[1ff.]: I spoke to A. about the funds of the confraternity (v. *mrzḥ*); *wmṭl kwt zbnyn šgyn ʿl ṣbwtʾ ʾln srbnyn hww* CIS ii 3913 i 6f.: and on this account many times about these matters disputes arose (cf. Greek par. συνέβαινεν δὲ πλειστάκις περὶ τούτου ζητήσεις γείνεσθ[αι]); *ʿl mlḥʾ qšṭ[ʾ ʾ]tḥzy ly dy* CIS ii 3913 ii 130f.: concerning the salt it seemed correct to me that ...; etc.; for *ḥqq ʿl*, v. *ḥqq₁* - **7)** with hostile meaning, against; *wškr ʾnk ʿly mlk ʾšr* KAI 24[7f.]: and I hired against him the king of A.; *[whn t]ʿbd mrmt ʿly* ... KAI 224[22]: and if you commit acts of treachery against me; *whwḥd ʿly brhdd ... ʿšr mlkn* KAI 202A 4f.: B. gathered against me (organized an alliance against me of) ten kings; *mḥʾw ʿlyk mṣr* KAI 202A 15: they have forced a siege upon you; *qbylh šlḥ ʿlyk* Driv 12[5]: he has sent a complaint against you; *zk sprʾ zy yhnpqwn ʿlyky kdb yhwh* Cowl 8[16f.]: such a document which they produce against you, will be forged; *wz[y] yqwm ʿl mpṭḥyh ltrkwth mn byth* Cowl 15[29f.]: and whoever should rise up against M. to drive her from his house; *‛bdh ... mll ‛l pn›* ATNS 9[3]: his slave spoke against P. (cf. also Porten & Yardeni sub TADAE B 8.6); *lmh hw yḥbl mt› ‛lyn* Aḥiq 36: why should he corrupt the land against us; *›srḥ›dn mlk› ḥmr ‛lyk* Aḥiq 47: king A. became angry with you; *w›qbl ‛lyhn* Herm 2[10]: I will lodge a complaint against them; *mn ‛l mn yšb* Sem xxiii 95 verso 4: who will turn himself against the other (v. mn_4); cf. also *wl› m‛l wl[›] mpq ‛ly* MPAT 51[10]: there is no entrance nor egress (i.e. no right of way) against my will; *›l thrkb ḥṭk lṣdyq lmh ›lhy› ysgh b‛drh wyhtybnhy ‛lyk* Aḥiq 126: shoot not your arrow at a righteous man, lest God come to his help and turn it back against you; for Cowl 50[4], SbPAW '19, 1050[3], RIP 199[14], v. $b‛y_1$; for *›ḥz ‛l*, v. *›ḥz*; for *bgn ‛l*, v. bgn_2; for poss. *‛l* in BASOR cxciii 8[2], v. sbb_1 - **8)** combined with other prep. - a) l_5 + $‛l_7$, *lmrḥ l‛lwh ‛l rbw‛t›* MUSJ xxxviii 106[9]: to enlarge his recess with respect to it (i.e. as far as it (i.e. his share) is concerned);*yrḥ l‛lyhwn bh bšṭr›* MUSJ xxxviii 106[11f]: he will enlarge the wall with respect to them (i.e. by means of them, sc. the materials just mentioned in the text) - b) mn_5 + $‛l_7$, *mn ‛l ṭ‛m›* CIS ii 161 ii 2: because of a decision (cf. J 255, RES 624 (= CIS ii 466); for the special context, v. $ṭ‛m_2$) - the diff. *‛lh* in Krael 12[21] = $‛l_7$ + suff. 3 p.s.m.??, cf. however Krael a.l.: = variant of *‛l›* (= Sing. emph. of $‛l_1$) = above (cf. also Grelot DAE p. 259, Porten & Greenfield JEAS p. 71; reading *‛lh* however improb., cf. Porten & Yardeni sub TADAE B 3.12: l. *zy lh*) - the *‛lh* in AJSL lviii 302A 2 poss. = $‛l_7$ + suff. 3 p.s.m. :: Bowman AJSL lviii 306: poss. = Qal Pf. 3 p.s.m. of $‛ly_1$ - Henning AM a.l.: l. *‛lyh* (= *‛l* + suff. 3 p.s.) in AM ii 174[5] (cf. also Bivar & Shaked BSOAS xxvii 288f.), cf. however Altheim & Stiehl Suppl 94: l. *‛lh* (= *‛l* + suff. 3 p.s.m.).

v. *›ḥrn*, $›l_6$, $›ln_1$, dbr_3, $yš‛_1$, *lk*, mll_1, $‛l_{1, 5, 6}$, *‛l›*, $‛lh_5$, $‛ly_{1,2}$, $‛lm_4$, $‛m_4$.

‛l› **OffAr** Cowl 13[3,10], 28[9], Krael 8[4], ATNS 1[2], 8[11] (for this reading, cf. Porten & Yardeni sub TADAE B 5.6 :: Segal ATNS a.l.: l. *l›* (= $l›_1$)), 21[6] - **Nab** IEJ xxix 112[3] (interpret. of context highly uncert.) - **Palm** Syr xvii 271[3] (for this poss. interpret., cf. Gawlikowski Syr li 98 :: Milik DFD 291f.: = $‛l_7$ + suff. 3 p.s.) - ¶ adv. (orig. prob. = $‛l_1$ + emph. ending, cf. also Gawlikowski Syr li 98 :: Joüon MUSJ xviii 47: = $‛l_7$ + ending *-ā* :: Leand 61i: = $‛l_1$ + acc. ending; cf. also Cantineau Syr xvii 272: = adv.) about it, concerning it; *wspr ktb ly ‛l›* Cowl 13[3]: and he wrote a document for me about it (cf. Cowl 13[9f], Krael 8[4]); *hn ršynk dyn› ‛l›* Cowl 28[9]: if we bring a suit against you in this matter; *ptgm› l› ›mr ... ‛l›* ATNS 1[2]: he did not make a statement ... about it; Syr xvii 271[3] heavily dam. context - for KAI 224[9], v. $ršy_1$.

‛lb **OldAr** Sing. abs. *‛lb* KAI 223C 10 - ¶ subst. oppression, humiliation; *blḥṣ ʿlb* KAI 223C 10: by crushing torment.

ʿlh$_1$ **Palm** Sing. emph. *ʿltʾ* CIS ii 3903[1], 3975[2], 3980[1], 4008[1], Inv xi 9[2], xii 30[1], SBS 23[1], RIP 138[2], etc., etc., *ʿlth* MUSJ xlii 177[7], *ʿlt* DM ii 39 iv 2 (lapsus); Plur. emph. *ʿlwtʾ* CIS ii 3973[1,10], 4002[2] (*ʿlw[t]ʾ*), SBS 24[1,3], DFD 162 ii 1 (*[ʿ]lwtʾ*), MUSJ xxviii 52[2], Syr xix 78[4] - ¶ subst. f. (but in CIS ii 4013[3], 4014[2f], 4029[2], 4053[1], 4101[1], PNO 14[1], 37[1], 72[1], Inv xi 20[3], xii 34[2], Syr xiv 189[3], AAS iii 156[2], vii 96[6] combined with dem. pronoun m., cf. also Inv xi 32[2]; cf. Cantineau Gramm 145, Rosenthal Sprache 50) altar.
v. *bʿl$_2$*, *mṭlh.*

ʿlh$_2$ **Pun** Sing. abs. *ʿlt* KAI 159[8] (cf. e.g. Cooke NSI p. 144, 146, Röllig KAI a.l. :: Février RHR cxliii 17, JA ccxliii 50, ccxlviii 170 (div. otherwise): pro *ʿlt ʾw* l. *ʿltʾ* (= Sing. + suff. 3 p.s.m.) + *w*) - ¶ subst. burnt-offering - Vattioni Aug xvi 551: the *uleh* in IRT 892[5] = Sing. abs. of *ʿlh$_2$* (improb. interpret.) - cf. *ʿlwh.*
v. *ʿl$_7$*, *ʿlt.*

ʿlh$_3$ v. *bʿl$_2$*.

ʿlh$_4$ **Ph** The diff. *ʿlt* in RES 1508 word of uncert. meaning poss. to be connected with the *ʿlt* in CIS i 5980[1] (v. infra); Euting with Spiegelberg Dem Denkm i 90, Lidzbarski Eph iii 124f. = prep. *ʿlt* (followed by n.p.); Février Sem v 60: = subst. Sing. cstr. (= gleaning; less prob. interpret.) - **Pun** The diff. *ʿlt* in CIS i 5980[1] (= TPC 42) word of uncert. meaning; Ferron CT xix 225ff.: = Sing. cstr. of *ʿlh* (= burnt remains; uncert. interpret.); or = prep. *ʿlt*? (cf. Bénichou-Safar TPC p. 199ff.), cf. however Février sub CIS i 5980 (cf. also e.g. Lidzbarski Eph iii 286, Chabot sub RES 1569, Février Sem v 60): = Sing. cstr. of *ʿlh* (= cover, lid).
v. *ʿlt.*

ʿlh$_5$ **OldAr** The diff. *ʿlh* in KAI 222A 32 poss. = form of *ʿlh$_5$* (= leaf, foliage); cf. Rosenthal ANET 660, Gibson SSI ii p. 31, 40f.: = Sing. abs. (cf. Lemaire & Durand IAS 134; cf. also Hoftijzer DA p. 256 (n. 188): = Sing. cstr.) :: Dupont-Sommer Sf p. 20, 47, Koopmans 52, Fitzmyer AIS 15, 49, 161, Donner KAI a.l., Hillers TC 55, Lipiński Stud 40, Rössler TUAT i 181: = *ʿl$_7$* + suff. 3 p.s.f. :: Cantineau RA xxviii 172f.: l. *[y]ʿlh* = Qal Impf. 3 p.s.m. of *ʿly$_1$*.

ʿlh$_6$ v.Soden Or xxxv 9, xlvi 187, AHW s.v.: the Akkad. *ḫallatu* (= kind of dues of tax) derived from Aramaic < root *ʿll$_1$* (improb. interpret.); Feuchtwang ZA vi 438: < root *ḥll* (comb. with jewish Aramaic *ḥltʾ* improb.; cf. also CAD s.v. *øhallatu* A).

ʿlwh **OffAr** Sing. abs. *ʿlwh* Cowl 30[21,28], 31[21,27]; emph. *ʿlwtʾ* Cowl 30[25], 31[25] - ¶ subst. burnt-offering - cf. *ʿlh$_2$* - the same word also as *scriptio anterior* in Cowl 32^{9}??, cf. Porten BiAr xlii 99.

ʿlwy **OffAr** *ʿlwy* Cowl 5^{6,9}, ATNS 10a 5; + suff. 3 p.s.f. *ʿlwyh* Cowl 5^{11} - ¶ prep. (cf. Leand 62n, Segert AAG p. 231) - a) prob. meaning in Cowl 5: against (cf. Porten Arch 239, cf. however Cowl a.l., Grelot DAE p. 172, Porten & Greenfield JEAS p. 4f., Porten & Yardeni sub TADAE B 2.1: = upon, cf. also Porten Arch 239: or = upon); *lmbnh ʿlwyh ʿd ʿlʾ* Cowl 5^{11}: to build against it (i.e. the wall) up to the top - b) prob. meaning in ATNS 10a 5: above; *ʿlwy šnytʾ* = above the mark.

ʿly$_1$ **Ph** QAL Pf. 3 p.s.m. *ʿly* KAI 1^{2} (cf. e.g. Albright JAOS lxvii 155 n. 20, FR 63b, 174, 176b, Röllig KAI a.l., Gibson SSI iii p. 14f. :: e.g. Dussaud Syr v 139, Vincent RB xxxiv 185 (cf. also Garbini RSO xxxiv 52 n. 2), Yeivin Lesh xxxvi 248f.: *ʿly* = *ʿly$_3$* (= variant of *ʿl$_7$*); cf. also Levi Della Vida RSO xxxix 301); 1 p.s. *ʿlt* CIS i 113^{1} (dam. context) - **Pun** QAL Pf. 3 p.s.m. *ʿlʾ* KAI 124^{3} (v. infra); Part. act. pl.m. abs. *ʿlm* CIS i 170^{2,3} (cf. v.d.Branden GP p. 106 :: Harr 133: = PIʿEL Pf. 3 p.pl. + suff. 3 p.pl.m.); YIPH/HIPH (cf. Février RHR cxliii 17f., cf. also Naveh IEJ xxviii 206) Pf. 3 p.s.m. *hʿlʾ* KAI 159^{8} (cf. e.g. Lidzbarski Handb 341, Cooke NSI p. 146, Röllig KAI a.l., FR 174, v.d.Branden GP p. 107, Segert GPP p. 153, cf. however Février RHR cxliii 17, JA ccxlviii 170: = Pf. 3 p.pl.) - **Hebr** QAL 1 p.s. *ʿlty* DJD ii 42^{5,7} (cf. e.g. Milik DJD ii a.l., cf. also de Vaux RB lx 270, 272, I.Rabinowitz BASOR cxxxi 21ff., Ginsberg ibid. 26, Lehmann & Stern VT iii 392, Bardtke ThLZ lxxix 300 :: Yeivin At i 98f.: l. in l. 5 *ʾz bʿlyh* (= *ʾz$_2$* + Sing. + suff. 3 p.s.f. of *bʿl$_2$*)); Part. act. pl.m. cstr. *ʿwly* SM 49^{13}; HIPH Impf. 3 p.s.m. + suff. 3 p.s.m. *yʿlhw* KAI 194^{7} - ¶ verb QAL - **1)** to go up; *lʾ ʿlty ʾṣlk* DJD ii 42^{7}: I did not ascend to you - a) + subst./name (without prep.), *ʿly gbl* KAI 1^{2}: he marches to G. (cf. e.g. Vinnikov VDI '52(4), 144, Röllig KAI a.l., Dahood Bibl lix 178, Gibson SSI iii p. 14f., Baldacci BiOr xl 125 :: Gevirtz VT xi 147 (n. 1): he arises in G., or: he comes to G. :: Albright JAOS lxvii 155: l. *ʿly* < *ʿl*> *gbl*); *ʿwly bbl* SM 49^{13}: those who go to B. (cf. however Naveh ASR 152: that returned from B.) - b) with metaphorical meaning; *ʾš ʿlʾ bbn mʾt mʿqr ... bktbt dbrʾ hbt* KAI 124$^{3f.}$: who came up as (i.e. who became) the adoptive son of M. ... by testament (cf. Amadasi IPT 65 (cf. however Février GLECS '52, 12), v. *dbr$_3$*; cf. Lat. par. *macri f(ilius) ... testamento adoptatus*; cf. Levi Della Vida RCL '49, 400, 402, 404, Röllig KAI a.l. (cf. also v.d.Branden PO i 437) :: Février GLECS vi 12: pro *ʿlʾ bbn* l. *ʿl* (= *ʿl$_7$*) + *ʾbbn* (= nomen verbale < YIPH of *bbn* (= to adopt; < *b$_2$* + *bn$_1$*), highly improb. interpret.) - **2)** to be offered (said of sacrifice) + *ʿlt* (= upon (sc. upon the altar)): CIS i 170^{2,3} - YIPH/HIPH - **1)** to make go up, to take; + obj., *lqḥh šmʿyhw wyʿlhw hʿyrh* KAI 194$^{6f.}$: Sh. has made him a prisoner and took him to the

town (for the transl., cf. however Lipiński BiOr xxxv 287) - **2)** to offer (sc. as a burnt-offering); + obj. + b_2, *ʾš hʿlʾ ... ʿlt ʾw m[n]ḥt bmqdš* KAI 159[8]: who brings (v. supra) a burnt-offering or meal-offering in the sanctuary - Grelot RB lxviii 185, DAE p. 439, Lindenberger APA 102, 247 n. 291: l. *mʿ[l]h* = APH Part. s.m. abs./cstr. of *ʿly*$_1$ (= to exalt) in Aḥiq 114 (highly uncert. interpret.), cf. however Gressmann ATAT 459: l. *mʿ[l]h* = Sing. cstr. of *mʿlh* (= entrance; for this reading, cf. also Cowl a.l.), cf. also Ginsberg ANET 429 (n. 16): l. *mʿ[n]h* = Sing. cstr. of *mʿnh* (= utterance) and Baneth OLZ '14, 348: l. *mʿ[d]h* = APH Part. s.m. abs./cstr. of *ʿdy*$_1$ :: Epstein ZAW xxxiii 230: l. *mʿ[g]h* = Sing. cstr. of *mʿgh* (= crying out, shouting) :: Kottsieper SAS 21, 216: l. *mʿ[sh]* = QAL/PAʿEL Pf. 3 p.s.m. (or Part. act. s.m.) + suff. 3 p.s.m. of *mʿs* (= to wreck, to ruin) - Livingstone Atlal vii 109f.: the *hʿly* in Atlal vii 109[3] = HAPH Pf. 3 p.s.m. of *ʿly*$_1$ (cf. also Cross CBQ xlviii 392; improb. interpret., cf. also Beyer & Livingstone ZDMG cxxxvii 286f.: = n.p., Aggoula Syr lxii 66f.: = n.l.) - O'Connor JNES xlv 226f.: the diff. *ʾʿly* in J 17[9] (for the reading *wʾʿly*, cf. already Chabot CRAI '08, 270ff., J p. 481, Milik sub ARNA-Nab 91 :: J p. 172, 176: l. *dʾ ʿly* (= *ʿly*$_3$)) = APH Pf. 3 p.s.m. of *ʿly*$_1$ (= to exhume; highly uncert. interpret.); for the problems cf. also Chabot CRAI '08 a.l. - v.d.Branden BO xii 215, 218: the *ʾʿl* in KAI 50[4] = YIPH Impf. 1 p.s., poss. interpret.
v. *lḥ*$_1$, *mʿl*$_1$, *ʿl*$_7$, *ʿlh*$_5$, *ʿll*$_1$.

ʿly₂ **OldAr** Sing. m. cstr. *ʿly* KAI 222A 6 (cf. e.g. Dupont-Sommer Sf p. 148, Fitzmyer AIS 154, Degen AAG p. 88 :: Na'aman WO ix 226: = *ʿly*$_3$ (= variant of *ʿl*$_7$) - **Nab** Sing. f. emph. *ʿlytʾ* CIS ii 164[3] - **Hatra** Sing. m. emph. *ʿlyʾ* 107[5] - ¶ adj. high; *hw bnh byrtʾ ʿlytʾ* CIS ii 164[3]: he has built the high temple; for Hatra 107[5], v. *ḥdy*$_3$ - substantivated: what is upon high; *kl ʿly ʾrm wtḥth* KAI 222A 6: the whole of upper and lower Aram (cf. also Levine FS Morton Smith 50, Lemaire & Durand IAS 131) - this word (Sing. m. emph. *ʿlyyh*, Sing. f. emph. *ʿlyyth*) resp. in SM 49[16,22] and SM 49[12,27] in nn. ll., *trngwlh ʿlyyh* (SM 49[16], cf. 49[22]): upper T., *ḥnwth ʿlyyth* SM 49[12]: upper Ch. (v. also *ʾrʿʾ*), *blʿm ʿlyyth* SM 49[27]: upper B.

ʿly₃ v. *ʿl*$_7$, *ʿly*$_{1,2}$.

ʿlyh **OldAr** Sing. + suff. 3 p.s.m. *[ʿ]lyth* KAI 222C 24 - **OffAr** Sing. abs. *ʿlyh* Cowl 5[4,5], 6[11], 8[4,5], 13[13], 25[5], 65 xvii, Krael 3[7], 4[6,9], 12[16], *ʿlyʾ* Krael 9[6,9], 10[5], 12[8], 13[5]; emph. *ʿlytʾ* Driv 2[3], 5[6] - **Palm** Sing. emph. *ʿlytʾ* CIS ii 4211[2] (*ʿly[tʾ]*; Greek par. ἀναγαί[ῳ]), 4212[1] - **JAr** Sing. emph. *ʿlyth* IEJ xxxvi 206[2] - ¶ subst. - **1)** what is upon high; *wyšmw tḥtyth [lʿ]lyth* KAI 222C 23f.: may they make its lower part its upper part (said of a house that is to be overturned; cf. also Levine FS

Morton Smith 53 n. 58); cf. also *bʿly[tʾ dy] qbrʾ dnh* CIS ii 4211[2]: in the upper floor of this tomb (cf. Greek par. ἐν τῷ ἀναγαί[ῳ τοῦ δ]ε τοῦ μνημείο[υ]; cf. also CIS ii 4212[1]; cf. also Milik DFD 384f.) - **2)** upper chamber: IEJ xxxvi 206[2] - in spec geographical context: - **1)** *bgyʾ zyly zy bʿlytʾ wtḥtytʾ* Driv 5[5f.]: my domains which are in the upper part and the lower part (i.e. in Upper and Löwer Egypt; cf. also Driv 2[3], cf. also Levine FS Morton Smith 52) - **2)** in Elephantine papyri "upper end" indicating the North (cf. Krael p. 79f., Ginsberg JAOS lxxiv 154, Porten JAOS lxxxi 39, Arch 308ff., Fitzmyer AIS 31, Levine FS Morton Smith 49ff., cf. however Couroyer RB lxviii 526ff., lxix 155, lxxv 80f., BiOr xxvii 251f., Ayad JACA 189ff. (cf. also Grelot DAE p. 176f. (n. e)): *ʿlyh* indicating the South) - a) *ʿlyh* Cowl 25[5]: at the upper end - b) *ʿlyh lh* Cowl 8[5], 13[13], Krael 4[9], 12[9], *ʿlyʾ lh* Krael 9[9], 10[5]: at its upper end - c) *lʿlyh* Cowl 5[4,5]: at the upper end - d) *lʿlyh lh* Cowl 6[11], Krael 3[7f.]: at its upper end - e) *mn ʿlyh ltḥtyʾ* Krael 12[16], *mn ʿlyh ʿd tḥtyh* Krael 4[6]: from the upper end to the lower end; *mn tḥtyh lʿlyh* Cowl 8[4], *mn tḥtyʾ lʿlyʾ* Krael 9[6], 12[8]: from the lower end to the upper end.

ʿlyl **Palm** the comb. of signs *]ʿlyl* in Syr xvii 271[10] unexplained (heavily dam. context), cf. Cantineau Syr xvii 274: the second *l* poss. = l_5 (cf. also Milik DFD 289) :: Gawlikowski Syr li 99f. (div. otherwise): l. *ʿ]lylnw* = Aph Pf. 3 p.s.m. + suff. 3 p.pl.m. of *ʿll*$_1$ (for the context, v. also *nwr*$_3$).

ʿlylh **JAr** the *ʿlylt[* in Syr xlv 101[15] poss. = form of *ʿlylh* (= harvest), heavily dam. context.

ʿlylw v. *mll*$_1$.

ʿlym m **OldAr** Sing. abs. *ʿlym* KAI 222A 22, Tell F 21 (Akkad. par. *māru*) - **OffAr** Sing. abs. *ʿlym* Cowl 77[2], Aḥiq 83, Driv 8[1,5], ATNS 68 ii 5; cstr. *ʿlym* Cowl 17[7] (dam. context), 38[8], 83[30] (dam. context), Del 83[2]; emph. *ʿlymʾ* Aḥiq 63, Krael 8[3] (*ʿlym[ʾ]*, diff. reading), Driv 2[2], 9[1] (*ʿlym[ʾ]*), F vii 1[1] (for the context, cf. Porten & Yardeni sub TADAE A 6.3), AE '23, 40 no. 2[3] ; + suff. 1 p.s. *ʿylmy* Beh 7 (prob. lapsus for *ʿlymy*, cf. Cowl a.l., Greenfield & Porten BIDG p. 31; Akkad. par. *qal-la-a*); Plur. abs. *ʿlymn* Driv 6[4]; cstr. *ʿlymy* Cowl 38[4], Sem xxxiii 94[5] (for this poss. reading, cf. Porten & Yardeni sub TADAE A 5.1; cf. however Porten Sem xxxiii 94, 98: l. poss. *šlymy* without interpret. :: Sznycer HDS 163 (div. otherwise): l. *yšʾl* (= Qal Impf. 1 p.s. of *šʾl*$_1$) *my* (without interpret.); emph. *ʿlymyʾ* Cowl 28[13], 41[6] - **Nab** Sing. abs. *ʿlym* CIS ii 1140[2]; cstr. *ʿlym* CIS ii 376 + 377 (cf. Milik & Starcky ADAJ xx 125 n. 41), J 53 (= ARNA-Nab 55), 85[1], 257, RES 1406, ADAJ xx 124, 129[2], cf. also a new instance in ADAJ xx 125 n. 41; emph. *ʿlymʾ* CIS ii 2106; + suff. 3 p.s.m. *ʿlymh* CIS ii 790[3]; Plur. cstr. *ʿlymy* CIS ii 235A 1 (= J 57; for the reading, cf. Chabot sub RES 1160), RES

837A (for the reading, cf. Milik & Starcky ADAJ xx 125 n. 41), RB xlii 411[3], 415[3] - **Palm** Sing. abs. *ʿlm* CIS ii 3913 ii 4, 5, 86; + suff. 3 p.s.m. *ʿlymh* CIS ii 4115bis 6 (for this reading, cf. CIS ii a.l., Cantineau sub Inv iv 18b, cf. however Ingholt MUSJ xlvi 193: l. prob. *glydh* (= Sing. + suff. 3 p.s.m. of *glyd*, v. *glyd*); Plur. abs. *ʿly[m]yn* CIS ii 3913 ii 6; emph. *ʿlymyʾ* CIS ii 3913 ii 2 - f. **OffAr** Sing. abs. *ʿlym[h]* AG 87b 19; Plur. + suff. 3 p.s.m. *ʿlymth* RES 492B 6 (cf. e.g. Halévy RS xii 64, 66, Lidzbarski Eph ii 240f. × Grelot DAE p. 141: = Sing. emph. :: Sayce PSBA xxv 315: derivative of root *ʿlm* (= to be hidden)) - **Nab** Sing. cstr. *ʿlymt* CIS ii 432[1], 443 (for this reading, cf. Milik & Starcky ADAJ xx 125 n. 41) - **Palm** Sing. + suff. 3 p.s.m. *ʿlmth* CIS ii 4540[4]; Plur. emph. *ʿlymtʾ* CIS ii 3913 ii 125, 126 - ¶ subst. - **1)** m. child (not yet weaned): KAI 222A 22, Tell F 21 - **2)** m. slave, f. slave-girl: Cowl 28[13], 38[4,8], Aḥiq 63, Beh 7, Driv 2[2], 6[3], AG 87b 19, RES 492B 6, 1406, J 85[1], CIS ii 376 + 377 (v. supra), 443 (v. supra), 790[3], 3913 ii 2, 4, 4540[4], etc.; cf. also *ʿlym ʾlʿzʾ* ADAJ xx 124: the servant of (the goddess) Al-Uzza (cf. also Díez Merino LA xix 275); for *ʿlm wṭrn*, v. *wṭrn* - **3)** f prostitute: CIS ii 3913 ii 125, 126 (:: e.g. Cooke NSI p. 330: = female slave) - Milik ADAJ xxi 144 n. 3: l. *[ʿ]lymy* = Plur. cstr. in RB xliii 574[3] (uncert. reading) - for this word, cf. e.g. Cantineau Gramm 48, Segert AAG p. 151, Milik & Starcky ADAJ xx 125 n. 40, Hopkins BSOAS xl 141, cf. also Hoftijzer DA p. 221f. n. 104 - cf. also *ʿlm*$_5$.

ʿlymh v. *ʿlym*.

ʿlyn **Hebr** Plur. abs. *ʿlynm* TA-H 25[3] - ¶ adj. upper; *[m]ʿnym tḥtnm* ... *mʿlynm* TA-H 25[2f]: from lower Anim ..., from upper (sc. Anim).

ʿll$_1$ **DA** Qal Impf. 3 p.s.m. *yʿl* i 6, ii 7 (for both instances, cf. Hoftijzer DA a.l., TUAT ii 145f., McCarter BASOR ccxxxix 51, 53, Levine JAOS ci 200, Garr DGSP 138, Weinfeld Shn v/vi 144f., 146 :: Hackett BTDA 29f., 37, 60f., 98, 132: = Qal Impf. 3 p.s.m. of *ʿly*$_1$ (cf. also Wesselius BiOr xliv 594, 598) :: Caquot & Lemaire Syr liv 203, Garbini Hen i 185: in ii 7 = Sing. cstr. of *yʿl*$_2$ (= service, usefulness), cf. also Rofé SB 68, Ringgren Mem Seeligmann 94 :: H.P. Müll ZAW xciv 219, 232f.: = Qal Impf. 3 p.s.m. of *yʿl*$_1$ (= to avail)) - **OldAr** Qal Impf. 3 p.s.m. *yʿl* KAI 222B 35; Part. act. s.m. abs./cstr. *ʿll* KAI 222A 6 (for this prob. word division, cf. e.g. Koopmans 45, BiOr xvii 51, Fitzmyer AIS 12, 32, Degen AAG p. 9, 73, Gibson SSI ii p. 28, 36 :: Dupont-Sommer Sf p. 17, 148 (div. otherwise): l. *ʿl* (= Qal Part. act. s.m. abs.) + *l*$_5$) - **OffAr** Qal Pf. 3 p.s.m. *ʿl* Cowl 15[5,15], 30[13], Krael 7[5], HDS 9[5], Irâq xxxi 173[5] (cf. Teixidor Syr xlvii 373, cf. however Segal Irâq xxxi a.l.: = Qal Imper. s.m.), FuF xxxv 173[6] (diff. context); 1 p.s. *ʿlt* Cowl 7[8], cf. Warka 4, 29: *ḫa-al-li-tú* (for this form, cf. Garbini HDS

30ff., Segert AAG p. 133); 3 p.pl.m. *ʿlw* Cowl 16^{6}, 30^{9}, 31^{8}, 34^{6}; Impf. 2 p.s.m. *tnʿl* Krael 12^{22}; 1 p.s. *ʾʿl* RES 1792A 2, Irâq xxxi 173^{6}; Inf. *mnʿl* Driv 5^{5*} (reading however highly uncert., cf. Porten & Yardeni sub TADAE A 6.7)^{,7}; Part. act. s.m. abs. *ʿʾl* RES 1785F 2 (?, uncert. context); HAPH/APH Pf. 3 p.s.f. *hnʿlt* Cowl $15^{6,7,24,27}$ (for all instances in Cowl 15, cf. e.g. Krael p. 146, Fitzmyer FS Albright ii 141ff., WA 246ff., Grelot DAE p. 195, Muffs 58, Porten & Greenfield JEAS p. 23, Porten & Yardeni sub TADAE B 2.6, Delsman TUAT i 261 :: Cowl a.l.: = Pf. 1 p.s.), Krael $2^{4,8,10,16}$, $7^{5,22}$; 3 p.pl.m. *yhnʿlw* Cowl 42^{12} (for this uncert. reading, cf. also Grelot DAE p. 131, cf. however Porten & Yardeni sub TADAE A 3.8: l. prob. *yhnʿln* = HAPH Impf. 3 p.pl.m.); Imper. pl.m. *hnʿlw* Driv 7^{7}, Cowl 21^{9} (*[h]nʿlw*; for the reading cf. Porten & Yardeni sub TADAE A 4.1); cf. Nisa 18^{7}, 19^{4}, 20^{4}, 21^{4}, 22^{4}, 23^{4}, 24^{3}, 28^{3}, 30^{4}, etc. (*hnʿl*), Nisa 297^{6}, 506^{2}, 670^{4}, 852^{3}, etc. (*hnʿlw*), cf. GIPP 54, SaSt 15 - **Palm** QAL Part. act. s.m. abs. *ʿll* CIS ii 3913 ii 115 (cf. Greek par. φέρεται), $4199^{5,7}$; APH Impf. 3 p.s.m. *yʿl* Syr xiv 184^{2}; Part. s.m. abs./cstr. *mʿl* CIS ii 3913 ii 80, 85, *[m]ʾʿl* CIS ii 3913 ii 112 (v. infra; for the form, cf. Rosenthal Sprache 29); s.m. emph. *mʾʿlʾ* CIS ii 3913 ii 149; pl.m. cstr. *mʿly* CIS ii 3913 ii 2; ITTAPH Impf. 3 p.s.m. *[y]tʾʿl* CIS ii 3913 ii 19, 56 (Greek par. εἰσκομιζόν[των]; cf. Rosenthal Sprache 29), *ytʾyʿl* CIS ii 3913 ii 61 (cf. Greek par. εἰσαχθῇ; diff. form, lapsus?, cf. Rosenthal Sprache 34; cf. however Cooke NSI p. 338); Part. s.m. abs. *mtʾʿl* CIS ii 3913 ii 14; s.f. abs. *mtʾʿlʾ* CIS ii 3913 ii 145 (*[m]tʾʿlʾ*), 146 (*[mt]ʾʿlʾ*), 147, *mʾʿlʾ* (lapsus) CIS ii 3913 ii 149; pl.m. abs. *mtʾʿlyn* CIS ii 3913 ii 2, 119 (Greek par. εἰσάγωνται) - **Hatra** QAL Impf. 3 p.s.m. *lʿwl* 29^{5} (cf. Ingholt AH i/2, 49, Milik DFD 214, 359, Hillers BASOR ccvii 55, Teixidor Syr l. 436, Degen NESE ii 100, Vattioni IH a.l. (cf. also Caquot GLECS ix 88) :: Safar Sumer viii 185f. (n. 10): = QAL Impf. 3 p.s.m. of *ʿwl* (= to tres pass., to fall into sin (cf. also Caquot Syr xxx 235f., Donner sub KAI 247: < *ʿwl* = to penetrate)) - **JAr** QAL Pf. 3 p.s.m. *ʿl* AMB 15^{10}; 3 p.pl.m. *ʿlw* RB xci 382 (context however diff. and uncert.; for the problems, cf. also Patrich RB xcii 272, cf. also id. EI xviii 159); Impf. 3 p.s.m. *lyʿwl* Syr xlv 101^{18} (dam. and diff. context); Part. act. s.m. abs. *ʿlʾ* AMB 11^{5} (diff. context); APH Inf. *mʿlh* At xiv 56^{1} (cf. Puech RB xci 91f. :: Shaked with Naveh At xiv 56 n. 6: = QAL Inf. + obj. suff. 3 p.s. (= to enter it) :: Naveh At xiv a.l.: + subj. suff. 3 p.s.m. (his entering) :: Beyer ATTM 346, 658: = Sing. emph. of *mʿl*$_1$) - ¶ verb QAL to enter: KAI 222B 35, CIS ii $4199^{5,7}$, cf. *ʾnš dlypwq wlyʿwl* Syr xlv 101^{18}: someone who will go out or enter (v. supra); cf. Krael 12^{22} (for the clause division, cf. Yaron RIDA v 307, JSS xviii 277, Porten & Greenfield JEAS p. 71, Porten & Yardeni sub TADAE B 3.12 :: Krael a.l., Grelot DAE p. 259: combine with foll. *bytʾ*) - **1)** + subst./name (without prep.), *byt lyʿl hlk* DA ii 7: a traveller will not enter a house (v. supra); *ʾʿl swn ymʾ* RES 1792A 2f.: today I will come to S. (cf. also FuF xxxv 173[6]); cf. also *kl ʿll. byt mlk* KAI 222A 6: everyone who enters the palace (poss. indicating every "legitimate successor", cf. Kaufman AIA 153, Na'aman WO ix 225f. (cf. already McCarthy Treaty 189: who may take over the rulership), cf. however Friedrich & Landsberger ZA xli 314: poss. = nomads as subjects of the king (cf. also Donner KAI a.l.) and Dupont-Sommer Sf p. 29: chiefs of small principalities (cf. also Donner KAI a.l.) :: Driver AfO viii 203: regular attendant at the court, courtier (cf. Sacchi RCL '61, 190 n. 45) :: Rosenthal ANET 659, Lipiński Stud 25: anybody entering the royal palace) - **2)** + *ʾl_6*, *wyʿl ʿmh ʾlwh* DA i 6: his people came in to him (for reading and interpret., v. also *ʾl_6*, *ʿm_2*) - **3)** + *b_2*, *bbytk [lʾ] ʿlt* Cowl 7[8]: I did not enter your house; *ʿlw bʾgwrʾ zk* Cowl 30[9]: they entered this temple (cf. Cowl 31[8]); *lʾ šnṣyw lmnʿl bbyrtʾ* Driv 5[7]: they did not succeed in entering the fortress; *btyʾ zy ʿlw bhn byb* Cowl 34[6]: the houses which they had entered in Yeb; cf. HDS 9[5], AMB 11[5] (diff. context); in Cowl 7, 30/31, 34 indicating forced entry, cf. Porten Or lvi 91 (this meaning less prob. in Driv 5[7] :: Porten Or lvi 91) - **4)** + *l_5*, *ʿlw lswn* Cowl 16[6]: they went up to S.; *kzy knbwzy ʿl lmṣryn* Cowl 30[13]: when K. came into Egypt; cf. also *kl dy ʿll. lḥšbn tgrʾ* CIS ii 3913 ii 115: everything that comes into the market (v. *ḥšbn₁*); cf. AMB 15[9] (dam. context) - **5)** + *mn_5*, *dlʿwl mhkʾ* Hatra 29[5]: whoever proceeds from here (i.e. past this point; for the context, v. *mšn*) - **6)** + *ʿl_7*, *ḫa-al-li-tú al ba-a-a* Warka 4: I entered the house; *ḫa-al-li-tú al pi-la-nu* Warka 29: I entered at someone's; cf. also *ʿl ʿlyk* Cowl 15[5]: it came to you (i.e. you have accepted the payment, cf. Cowl 15[15], Krael 7[5]; for this expression, cf. Muffs p. 52f. (n. 1), 173 n. 4, cf. also idem JANES v 287ff.) - **7)** + *ʿm_4*: AMB 15[10] (dam. context) - HAPH/APH to make to enter, to import, to bring - **1)** + obj., *mʿly ʿlymyʾ* CIS ii 3913 ii 2: those who import slaves - **2)** + obj. + *l_5*, *mn dy mʿl rglyn ltdmr* CIS ii 3913 ii 80: who imports slaves in T. - **3)** + obj. + *qdm_3*, *yhnʿlw hmw ... qdm [ʾršm]* Cowl 42[12]: they wil bring them ... before A. - **4)** + *b_2*, *kl zy hnʿlt bbyth* Krael 7[22]: everything she brought into his house; *whnʿlw btrbṣʾ zyly* Driv 7[7]: and bring (them) into my court; cf. Cowl 21[9] (v. supra) - **5)** + *byd*, *kl zy hnʿlt bydh* Cowl 15[24f]: everything she brought in personally (cf. Cowl 15[27f], Krael 2[8,10]; v. supra for Cowl 15) - **6)** + *l_5* + obj., *dy yʿl ltnn swm nkry* Syr xiv 184[2]: whoever will bring in here the corpse of a stranger (v. *swm*) - **7)** + *l_5* + *byd* + obj., *hnʿlt ly ... tmt bydh lbš 1* Krael 2[4]: T. has brought in to me personally one garment (cf. Cowl 15[6,7], Krael 2[16]; v. supra for Cowl 15) - **8)** + *l_5* + *l_5* + obj., *hnʿlt ly yhwyšmʿ ... lbyty tkwnh zy ksp* Krael 7[5f]: Y. has brought in to me ... to my house money in silver - 9) + *mn_5*, *mn dy ... [m]ʾʿl mn qryʾ* CIS ii 3913 ii 112: whoever ... imports from the villages

- ITTAPH to be brought in, to be imported: CIS ii 3913 ii 14, 19, 56, 61, 145, 146 - **1)** + *br mn*, v. br_3 - **2)** + l_5, *‘lymy’ dy mt’‘lyn ltdmr* CIS ii 3913 ii 2: slaves who are imported into T. (cf. CIS ii 3913 ii 147) - the *w‘l* in KAI 271A 1 (for the reading, cf. e.g. Cowley PSBA xxv 313, Lidzbarski Eph ii 242, Ungnad ArPap p. 115, Degen NESE i 28 :: CIS ii sub 138, Donner KAI a.l.: l. *p‘l* = QAL Pf. 3 p.s.m. of *p‘*l_1) prob. = *w* + QAL Pf. 3 p.s.m. of *‘l*l_1 (cf. Degen NESE i 30, 33) - CIS ii sub 43, Delaporte sub Del 26: l. *y‘l* (= APH Impf. 3 p.s.m. of *‘l*l_1) in CIS ii 43[5] (highly uncert. reading, cf. also Fales sub AECT 13: l. *-y 30?*) - Bergman JNES xxvii 69f.: the forms of QAL and HAPH/APH with *-n-* preceding the *‘* < secondary root *n‘*l_3 (< *‘l*l_1), cf. however e.g. Leand 6i, Spitaler IF lxi 264f., Segert AAG p. 112f., 283 - QAL Inf. *mn‘l* > Akkad. *manḫālu/manḫallu*, cf. v.Soden Or xxxv 6, xlvi 190, AHW s.v. (cf. also CAD s.v.) - v.Soden Or xxxv 6, xlvi 190: the *ta-a-la* in YOS vi 188[18,26] < Ar. *‘l*l_1 (cf. also San Nicolò & Petschow in BR 6,3; improb. interpret., cf. also Greenfield MSN ii 479 n. 4: = scribal error for *tallak*; cf. also Zadok WO xii 199) - Segal ATNS a.l.: l. *y‘lw* (= QAL Impf. 3 p.pl.m.) in ATNS 28b 2 (improb. interpret., cf. Porten & Yardeni sub TADAE B 8.4: = n.p.) - Harmatta ActAntHung vii 347, 383: the *‘l[* in Cowl 81[12] prob. = QAL Pf. 3 p.s.m. of *‘l*l_1 (uncert. and dam. context) - Aggoula Assur a.l.: the *‘l* in Assur 30 = QAL Pf. 3 p.s.m. of *‘l*l_1 (heavily dam. context, highly uncert. interpret.).
v. *m‘*l_1, *n‘*l_1, *‘*l_7, *‘lh*$_6$, *‘lyl*, *‘l*l_3, *‘ln*$_3$.

‘ll₂ v. *myll*.

‘ll₃ **OffAr** Segal ATNS a.l.: the *‘ll* in ATNS 46[3,5] = Sing. abs. of *‘l*l_3 (= produce), context however diff. and dam. (cf. Shaked Or lvi 410: in l. 3 *‘ll* = QAL Part. act. s.m. abs. of *‘l*l_1).

‘llh **OffAr** Plur. abs./cstr. *‘llt* BASOR cclxiv 48 no. 6[1] - **Nab** Sing. cstr. *‘llt* DBKP 22[31,34] (diff. and dam. context, or = Plur.?) - ¶ subst. produce; *‘llt gny tmyry’* DBKP 22[31]: the produce of the Palm. orchards; Plur. gleanings: BASOR cclxiv 48 no. 6[1] (interpret. and reading of context however highly uncertain).

‘lln v. *’rn*$_2$.

‘lm₁ **Pun** L.H.Gray AJSL xxxix 78: the *italme* in Poen 941 = HITP Pf. 3 p.pl. of *‘lm*$_1$ (= to reach maturity); highly uncert. interpret., cf. also Schroed 290f.: l. *isal e...*, *isal* = QAL Impf. 1 p.s. of *š’*l_1; Sznycer PPP 120ff. gives no interpret.

‘lm₂ **JAr** QAL Part. act. s.m. emph. *‘lm’* MPAT 89[1,3] (v. infra; :: Fitzmyer & Harrington MPAT a.l.: = Sing. emph. of *‘lm*$_4$) - ¶ verb to be strong; in the comb. *qyn’ ‘lm’* MPAT 89[1,3]: a powerful lament (cf. Avigad IEJ xvii 103, 105) - a form of this root also in DA ii 32?? (cf. Hoftijzer DA a.l.): *‘lm*.

ʿ**lm**$_3$ v. *ʿwd*$_2$, *ʿlym*.

ʿ**lm**$_4$ **Ph** Sing. abs. *ʿlm* KAI 1^{1}, 14^{20} (*ʿl[m]*)^{,22}, 18^{8}, 19^{11}, 26A iii 19, iv 2, C v 6, 27^{10} (v. infra)^{,14}, 34^{5} (= Kition B 1), 35^{2} (= Kition B 45), 43^{12}, DD 9^{3}; cf. also in Greek ουλωμος, cf. FR 78a, 79b, 198a - **Pun** Sing. abs. *ʿlm* CIS i 124^{1}, 6000bis 6 (*ʿl[m]*), KAI 78^{1}, *ʾlm* KAI 165^{8}, *ʾwlm* KAI 128^{2}, Punica xvi 2^{4} (for the reading, cf. Chabot Punica a.l., Levi Della Vida RCL '49, 410), Rev Arch ii/xxxi 176^{3} (:: Dérenbourg ibid. 176, 179 (div. otherwise): l. *ʾwlmm* = Plur. abs.) - **Hebr** Sing. abs. *ʿlm* DJD ii 22,1-9^{5,6}, *ʿwlm* Frey 569^{6}, 571^{2}, 661^{4}, 668^{3}, 1175, 1536^{3}, SM 49^{5,23}, 76^{4} (*ʿwl[m]*), IEJ iv 98^{1}, AMB 4^{12}, 15^{24}, *ʿwm* (lapsus) IEJ iv 99, DJD ii 30^{6,7,25}; Plur. abs. *ʿwlmym* AMB 3^{2} - **Mo** Sing. abs. *ʿlm* KAI 181^{7,10} - **DA** Sing. abs. *ʿlm* i 9; Plur. abs. *ʿlmn* ii 6 (cf. Hoftijzer DA a.l., TUAT ii 145 :: Caquot & Lemaire Syr liv 203, Rofé SB 68f., Garbini Hen i 185: = Plur. abs. of *ʿlm*$_5$ :: Rofé SB 68f.: or = Plur. abs. of *ʿlm*$_6$; on the subject, cf. also Delcor SVT xxxii 61); + suff. 2 p.s.m. *ʿlmyk* ii 11 (cf. e.g. Hoftijzer DA a.l., TUAT ii 146, Hackett BTDA 30, 67 :: e.g. Caquot & Lemaire Syr liv 205, Rofé SB 68f., Ringgren Mem Seeligmann 94: = Plur. + suff. 2 p.s.m. of *ʿlm*$_6$ (cf. also Delcor SVT xxxii 62) :: Garbini Hen i 186: = Plur. + suff. 2 p.s.m. of *ʿlm*$_5$) - **OldAr** Sing. abs. *ʿlm* KAI 224^{24,25} - **OffAr** Sing. abs. *ʿlm* Cowl 8^{9,11}, 13^{16}, 14^{7}, Krael 2^{4}, 4^{5}, ATNS 8^{6} (for this uncert. reading, cf. Shaked Or lvi 409, Porten & Yardeni sub TADAE B 5.6 :: Segal ATNS a.l.: l. *šlm* (= Sing. cstr. of *šlm*$_2$), etc.; emph. *ʿlmʾ* Samar 1^{4} (= EI xviii 8*), 2^{4}, 3^{4} (*[ʿ]lmʾ*), 5^{5}, 6^{4}; Plur. abs. *ʿlmn* Krael 3^{11}, 12^{23}; cf. Frah xxvii 14 (*lʿlmn*), Syn 315 i 2, GIPP 56 - **Nab** Sing. abs. *ʿlm* CIS ii 199^{4}, 206^{5}, 209^{3}, 212^{4,5}, ARNA-Nab 16^{2}, ADAJ xxi 144^{3} (*ʿ[l]m*; dam. context); cstr. *ʿlm* CIS ii 197^{9}, 1841, 2160^{2}, BSOAS xvi 223,72^{2}; emph. *ʿlmʾ* J 11^{4} (= CIS ii 211), 17^{7}, IEJ xxi 50^{1}; Plur. abs. *ʿlmn* CIS ii 1841, 2160^{2} (*ʿlm[n]*), *ʿlmyn* CIS ii 197^{9} - **Palm** Sing. abs. *ʿlm* CIS ii 4024^{1} (or l. *ʿlm[ʾ]* (= Sing. emph.)??), 4087^{2}, PNO 2ter 8, Inv xii 17^{5} (= RIP 105), 26, RIP 24^{6}; emph. *ʿlmʾ* CIS ii 3912^{1}, 3927^{3}, 3986^{1}, 3989^{1}, 3990^{1}, 3993^{2} (:: Chabot sub CIS ii 3993: l. *rmnʾ* (= lapsus for *rḥmnʾ* (= Sing. m. emph. of *rḥmn*)) :: Cantineau Syr xiv 192: l. *ʿdnʾ* (= Sing. emph. of *ʿdn*$_2$ (= time), cf. Díez Merino LA xxi 136: = fortune)), etc., etc., *lʿmʾ* (lapsus) Inv xi 22^{2}, *ʿlʾ* (lapsus) RIP 119^{1f}; + suff. 3 p.s.m. *ʿlmh* CIS ii 4119^{7} - **Hatra** Sing. abs. *ʿlm* 79^{12,14}, 184^{2}, 230^{4}, 297^{2}, 408^{7}, app. 3^{4}, cf. Assur 15d 3, 25g 6, 28a 4 (*[ʿ]lm*), etc.; emph. *ʿlmʾ*, cf. Assur 27k 2; Plur. abs. *ʿlmyn*, cf. Assur 17 i 6 (*[ʿ]lmyn*), 28c 3, 32j 5 (*[ʿ]lm[y]n*) - **JAr** Sing. abs. *ʿlm* MPAT 41^{4}, 45^{6}, 51^{6,11,12,13}, 52^{9,10}, 71^{3} (*ʿl[m]*), IEJ xxxvi 206^{5}; emph. *ʿlmʾ* MPAT 41^{7}, Frey 1415^{1}, 1418^{1}, *ʿlmh* MPAT-A 26^{9} (= SM 32), 27^{4} (*ʿlm[h]*; = SM 33), 28^{2,3} (= SM 34), 34^{3} (= SM 69), SM 82, 88^{20} (= Syn B 5; heavily dam. context), 107 (*‹lm[h]*; for the reading, cf. Naveh SM a.l.); Plur. emph. *‹lm[yh]* AMB 3[1] - **Waw** Sing. emph. *‹lm›* AMB 6[5f.,6f] - ¶ subst. - **1)** indetermined span of time, eternity: passim; *›lt ‹lm* KAI 27[9f]: an everlasting covenant (:: Cross & Saley BASOR cxcvii 44f. (n. 15): *‹lm* = the eternal one; for the context, v. also *›lh$_2$*); *lyqrhn dy ‹lm›* CIS ii 4122[3f]: to their everlasting honour (cf. CIS ii 4130[3], 4172[3], Ber ii 76[2], 77[2], 85[13f], 86[17], RIP 24[6], etc.; v. *yqr$_2$*); *ldkrnh dy ‹lm›* DFD 163[6]: for his everlasting memory (cf. Greek par. μνήμης χάριν); *lh wlbnwhy wlbny bnwhy dy ‹lm›* RB xxxix 523[1f]: for him and his sons and the sons of his sons forever; *šmš ‹lm* KAI 26A iii 19: the eternal sun (cf. also Cross HThR lv 237); *ḥyy ‹wlm* Frey 1536[3]: eternal life (cf. e.g. Frey 569[5]); *mškby ‹lmyk* DA ii 11: your everlasting lying down (i.e. your eternal sleep; v. *mškb$_1$*, v. supra); for *byt/bt ‹lm(›)*, v. *byt$_2$*; for *byt ‹lmn*, v. *byt$_2$*; for *›bd ‹lm*, v. *›bd$_2$*; used adverbially?: *dkyr ‹lm bṭb ‹mrw* CIS ii 788[1f]: may A. be remembered forever in good (or lapsus?) - cf. the foll. comb. with prep., cf. - a) prec. by prep. *b$_2$*, for an eventual instance, v. *šyt$_1$* - b) prec. by prep. *l$_5$*: = forever: passim; *šm ›ztwd ykn l‹lm* KAI 26A iv 2: may the name of A. last forever ...; *›nk ... mṣbt ... yṭn›t ‹l mškb nḥty l‹lm* KAI 35[1f]: I set up a stele over the tomb in which I rest, forever; *z mṣbt ... ›š ṭn› ...‹zb‹l l‹lm* DD 9: this is the stele which O. has erected forever; *bl› ršwt šl‹lm* DJD 22,1-9[5]: without any authority forever (cf. ibid. l. 6); *bnwhy mn ›ḥrwhy l‹lm›* Samar 1[4] (= EI xviii 8*): his sons after him in perpetuity; *dkyr bṭb l‹lm ‹wdw* CIS ii 820[1]: may A. be remembered forever in good (v. also *zkr$_1$*); *šlm zyd›lhy l‹lm* CIS ii 302[1]: the well-being of Z. be forever (cf. *šlm wdkyr zydw ... bṭb l‹lm* ARNA-Nab 67); *šlwm ‹l yšrwn l‹wlm* Frey 1175: peace on Y. forever; *dnh kpr› dy lmgyrw ... dy ytqbrwn bh l‹lm* J 22[1ff]: this is the tomb of M. ... so that they will be buried therein forever; *yhw› kpr› hw lw›lt wlbnyh ... qym l‹lm* CIS ii 212[4f]: this tomb shall be for W. and her sons ... a definite property forever; *wl› ršyn w›lt wbnyh dy ... yktbwn bkpr› hw ktb klh ... l‹lm* CIS ii 212[3f]: W. and her sons shall not be allowed to ... write in respect of this tomb any deed ... forever; *wl› ytptḥ ‹lyhm l‹lm* CIS ii 226[2f]: that it will not be opened over them forever; *lyqrhwn l‹lm›* CIS ii 4164: to their everlasting honour (v. also *yqr$_2$*); *lbryk šmh l‹lm›* CIS ii 3992[1], 3994[2], 3995[1], etc., etc.: for the one whose name is blessed forever (cf. also CIS ii 4024[1], 4087[2]: ... *l‹lm*; cf. also Díez Merino LA xxi 103f.); *ṣlm› dnh dy ›ḥply ... dy ‹bdt lh bwl› ... l‹lm›* CIS ii 3927[1f]: this is the statue of A. that the Senate ... made for him ... forever; *qbr› dnh dy kytwt ... dy ‹bd lh wlbnwhy l‹lm›* CIS ii 4115[1,3]: this is the tomb of K. ... that he made for himself and his sons forever; *l› ypthh ›nš l‹lm* RIP 105[4f] (= Inv xii 17): that no one opens it forever; *dkyrn l‹lm bhṭr› ...* Hatra 79[14]: that they may be remembered forever in Hatra (v. *zkr$_1$*); *dkyr ‹qyb›sr qdm mrtn l‹lm›* Assur 27k 2: may A.

be remembered before our lady forever (v. *zkr*$_1$); *dlʿlm lʾ ldbrhn wʾnš mn bnʾ ddhwn bqṭyrʾ mʿnʾ* ... Hatra 79[12f]: that M. will not lead them or anyone from their descendants into oppression; *lʿlm ršy ʾlʿzr bzbn bth dk* MPAT 51[6f]: forever E. is given authority by the purchase of this house ... (cf. Milik RB lxi 183, Puech RQ ix 215 × Abramson & Ginsberg BASOR cxxxvi 19, Birnbaum PEQ lxxxix 131, Fitzmyer & Harrington MPAT a.l.: comb. *lʿlm* with prec. *dmyn gmryn* = the full price forever; cf. also MPAT 52[9], IEJ xxxvi 206[5]); *yrthn mn ywmʾ dnh wlʿlm* MPAT 52[10]: their heirs from this day and forever; *wlʾ lmptḥ lʿl[m]* MPAT 71[2f]: not to be opened forever; etc., etc.; cf. also *lʿlmyn* Assur 28c 3, *lʿlm ʿlmn* CIS ii 1841, 2160[2], *lʿlm ʿlmyn* CIS ii 197[9] and Frah xxvii 14 (*lʿlmn*); for *lymt ʿlmyn*, v. *ywm*; the diff. *wlʿlm* in MPAT 51[13] poss. lapsus for *mn y(w)mʾ dnh wlʿlm* (cf. e.g. Milik RB lxi 188, Abramson & Ginsberg BASOR cxxxvi 17f., Birnbaum PEQ lxxxix 127, 131, Puech RQ ix 220); cf. also *lʿwlm wʿd* in AMB 4[12]: for ever and ever, and *lʿ[l]m l[ʿ]lm[yn]* in ADAJ xxi 144[3] (??, heavily dam. context) - c) prec. by prep. *mn*$_5$, *mʿlm* KAI 181[10]: from of old; *lʾ ḥṭʾ mʿwlm* Frey 668[3]: he has never sinned - d) prec. by prep. *ʿd*$_7$ = forever, *yrḥ md yrḥ ʿd ʿlm kqdm* KAI 43[12]: month by month forever as aforetime; *ybrky wyšmʿ ql ʿd ʿlm* KAI 78[1]: they may bless him and hear his voice forever; *wʾl thgy ʿd ʿlm* DA i 9: and will never say ... (v. *hgy*); *wšbt tlʾym l[brgʾy]h* (reading of *h* uncert.) *lbrh lbr brh wlʿqrh ʿd ʿlm* KAI 224[25]: T. has returned to ... (v. supra) and to his son, the son of his son and his descendants forever; *dylky hw ʿd ʿlm* Cowl 13[16]: it is yours forever; *mn ywmʾ znh wʿd ʿlm* Cowl 8[9]: from this day and forever (cf. Cowl 14[6f], 15[4], Krael 2[4], 4[4f], J 38[4], etc.); *dnh qbrʾ dy ʿbd khln ... lnpšh wyldh wʾḥrh ... ʿd ʿlm* CIS ii 206[1f]: this is the tomb which K. made ... for himself, his children and his posterity ... forever; *ʿl kl ʾnwš ... dy lʾ ... yktb bqbrʾ dnh ktb klh ʿd ʿlm* CIS ii 206[3ff]: it is incumbent upon everyone ... not to ... write with respect to this tomb any document whatsoever forever; *wlʾ ytqbr bqbrʾ dnh ʾnwš klh lhn mn dy ktyb lh tnʾ mqbr ... ʿd ʿlm* CIS ii 350[5]: nobody shall be buried at all in this tomb forever, unless he has a written document of burial; *dkyr bṭb wšlm šʿdw ʿd ʿlm* CIS ii 2072[1f.,4]: that Sh. be remembered in good and well-being forever (v. *zkr*$_1$); *šlm NP ʿd ʿlm* BIA x 59 no. 8: peace to NP forever; *lyqrhn ʿd ʿlmʾ* CIS ii 4123bis 4: for their everlasting honour; *lʾ yptḥ ʿlwhy gwmḥʾ dnh ʿd ʿlmʾ* CIS ii 4218[3f]: let no one open this niche over him forever; *bkl šnʾ ʿd ʿlmʾ* Syr xvii 274[4]: every year and forever; etc.; cf. also the expression *mn ywmʾ znh wʿd ʿlmn* Krael 3[11], 12[23], cf. also *ʿlm ʿd ʿlm* ARNA-Nab 16[2] - e) prec. by prep. *ʿl*$_7$ = forever, *dkyr hnwmʾ ... bṭb ʿl ʿlm* J 169[1f]: that H. be remembered in good forever (cf. however Chabot sub RES 1130: pro *ʿl ʿlm* l. *lʿlm* or *ʿd ʿlm*); *šlm plṭʾl ... ʿl ʿlm ʿlm* BSOAS xvi 223,72: may peace be (on) P. ... for ever

and ever (reading however uncert.); cf. poss. also ATNS 8^6 (reading however uncert., dam. context, Yardeni with Shaked Or lvi 409: *ʿl ʿlm* changed in *ʿd ʿlm*, cf. also Porten & Yardeni sub TADAE B 5.6; v. supra) - **2)** world, universe: AMB 3^2, 6$^{5f.,6f.}$; *mrʾ ʿlmʾ* CIS ii 3912^1, 3986^1, 3989^1 (= Inv vi 9 = RIP 131), SBS 25^1, etc.: the lord of the world (for this title, v. *mrʾ*); *mlk ʿlmh* MPAT-A 26^9, 27^4, 28^{2,3} (cf. also *mlkyh dʿlmh* MPAT-A 34^3, *mlk hʿwlm* AMB 15^{24}, *mlk ʿlm[yh]* AMB 3^1) the King of the Universe (epithet of God); *myʾ wʿlmʾ* AMB 6$^{5f.}$: the water and the world (cf. Dupont-Sommer Waw p. 17f., cf. also AMB 6^{6f}); *hʿwlm hbʾ* Frey 661^4: the future world.
v. *ʾl$_1$*, *ʾmn$_3$*, *mn$_4$*, *ʿd$_7$*, *ʿwd$_2$*, *ʿṭm*, *ʿlm$_2$*, $_{5,6}$, *ṣlm$_2$*, *qwm$_1$*, *šyt$_1$*.

ʿlm$_5$ m. **Pun** Sznycer PPP 128: the *alem* in Poen 948 poss. = Sing. abs./cstr. of *ʿlm$_5$* (poss. interpret., cf. however Schroed 292: = *hlm$_2$*, cf. also L.H.Gray AJSL xxxix 78) - f. **Ph** Sing. abs. *ʿlmt* KAI 24^8; Plur. abs. *ʿlmt* KAI 37B 9 (= Kition C 1; twice, cf. however Segert JSS xvii 138: the first *ʿlmt* = Sing. abs.) - **DA** m. Sing. abs. *ʿlmh* ii 4 (diff. and dam. context; cf. e.g. Hoftijzer DA p. 180, 221f. n. 104, Caquot & Lemaire Syr liv 202, Rofé SB 68, Garbini Hen i 185, Ringgren Mem Seeligmann 97, McCarter with Hackett BTDA 79, Puech RB xciii 286, cf. however Hoftijzer DA a.l.: or = Sing. + suff. 3 p.s.m./f. of *ʿlm$_4$*? :: Hackett BTDA 29, 56, 94, 133: = m. Sing. + suff. 3 p.s.m. of *ʿlm$_5$*?) - ¶ subst. m.) man: Poen 948 (v. however supra) - f) girl, young woman, *ʿlmt ytn bš wgbr bswt* KAI 24^8: they gave a maid for the price of a sheep and the man for the price of a garment (v. however *ytn$_1$*); for the diff. *lʿlmt wlʿlmt 22* ... In KAI 37B 9 (*ʿlmt* in both instances the same word?), cf. Peckham Or xxxvii 306, 323 (n. 9), Masson & Sznycer RPČ 64f., Amadasi sub Kition C 1, Healy BASOR ccxvi 57, Delcor UF xi 162f., Gibson SSI iii p. 127, 131 - the diff. *ʿlm* in RCL '66, 201^7 to be connected to *ʿlm$_5$*??, cf. however Dupont-Sommer CRAI '68, 117, 132 (div. otherwise): l. *ʿl$_7$* + *mnm* (= Plur./Dual abs. of *mnh$_2$*) :: Milik DFD 292 (div. otherwise): l. *ʿl$_7$* + *mnm* (= whatever) - cf. also *ʿlym*.
v. *byt$_2$*, *slm$_1$*, *ʿlm$_4$*.

ʿlm$_6$ **Samal** Plur. + suff. 1 p.s. *ʿlmy* KAI 214^1 (cf. Cooke NSI p. 164f., Poeb 43, Dupont-Sommer Ar 110, Degen ZDMG cxxi 132, Tawil Or xliii 42f., Dahood Or xlv 382, Gibson SSI ii p. 65, 70, Dion p. 26, 131, 152, Sader EAS 163 n. 29 :: Nöldeke ZDMG xlvii 98 (with reserve), Donner KAI a.l.: = Sing. + suff. 1 p.s. of *ʿlm$_4$*) - ¶ subst. Plur. youth; *bʿlmy* KAI 214^1: in/since my childhood (for the context, cf. Tawil Or xliii 42f.).
v. *ʿlm$_4$*.

ʿlm$_7$ v. *ʿl$_4$*.

ʿlm$_8$ v. *ʿṭm*.

ʿlmh v. *ʿlm*$_5$.

ʿlmt v. *ywm*.

ʿln$_1$ v. *ʾln*$_1$.

ʿln$_2$ v.Soden Or xxxv 14, xlvi 189: *ʿln* (= what is above) prec. by *l*$_5$ > Akkad. *lālēnu*, *lālennu* (above; cf. also idem AHW s.v. and CAD s.v. *lalēnu*).

ʿln$_3$ **OffAr** Word of unknown meaning in Cowl 73[1] (dam. context). CIS ii sub 147: = QAL Part. act. pl.m. abs. of *ʿll*$_1$ or l. *[h]ʿln* (= HAPH Pf. 1 p.pl. of *ʿll*$_1$)?, cf. however *ʿlnh* word of unknown meaning in Cowl 78[1], Cowl p. 188 = accounts (meaning derived from context); reading of both *ʿln* and *ʿlnh* uncert.

ʿlnh v. *ʿln*$_3$.

ʿlʿ **OffAr** Plur. cstr. *ʿlʿy* Aḥiq 106; cf. Frah x 4 (*ʿlktʾ* (= Plur.), cf. Nyberg FP 45, 74 :: Ebeling Frah a.l.: l. *ʿrktʾ* (= bone), to be compared to Akkad. *ariktu*) - ¶ subst. rib.

ʿlṣ$_1$ **Pun** QAL Pf. 3 p.s.m. *ʿlṣ* KAI 89[5] (= CIS i 6068); 3 p.s.f. *ʿlṣʾ* KAI 89[4] (for this interpret., cf. e.g. Cooke NSI p. 136, Février sub CIS i 6068 × FR 131: = QAL Pf. 3 p.pl.; cf. also Levi Della Vida RSO xiv 312f., Röllig KAI a.l.: = 3 p.s.f. or 3 p.pl.; :: Halévy RS ix 264, Lidzbarski Eph i 33f., 176, Chabot sub RES 1590, Slouschz TPI p. 201f.: = resp. QAL Pf. 3 p.s.m. and 3 p.s.f. of *ʿlṣ*$_2$ (= *ʾlṣ* (= to oppress, to torment) cf. also Lidzbarski sub KI 85, Clermont-Ganneau RAO iv 95f.) :: v.d.Branden MUSJ xlv 311, 315: = *ʾlṣ* (= to cast lots)) - ¶ verb QAL to rejoice, to exult + *ʿlt* (over), cf. Cooke NSI p. 136, Levi Della Vida RSO xiv 312f., Röllig KAI a.l., FR 131, Février sub CIS i 6068.

ʿlṣ$_2$ v. *ʿlṣ*$_1$.

ʿlq v. *ḥlt*$_2$.

ʿlš **Pun** word of unknown meaning in CIS i 5510[10] (cf. Février CIS i a.l.); cf. Février BAr '46/49, 172: = QAL Inf. abs. of *ʿlš* used adverbially (= persistently); Garbini RSO xlii 10ff.: *ʿlš* = subst. Sing. abs. indicating certain kind of sacrifice (less prob. etymology; cf. also idem FSR 199) :: Krahmalkov RSF ii 173, 175 (n. 10): = n.p. :: v.d.Branden RSF v 141f., BiOr xxxvi 203: = n.l.

ʿlt **Ph** KAI 9A 2, B 4, 10[11,12,14], 14[6,7,10,20], 43[13] (cf. e.g. Honeyman JEA xxvi 58, v.d.Branden OA iii 249, 259, Röllig KAI a.l., Gibson SSI iii p. 137, 141 :: Lipiński RTAT 251: = Plur. cstr. of *ʿlh*$_2$), 60[5,6], MUSJ xlv 262[2] (*[ʿ]lt*); + suff. 3 p.s.m. *ʿlty* KAI 60[4]; + suff. 1 p.s. *ʿlty* KAI 13[4] (cf. e.g. Röllig KAI a.l., Gibson SSI iii p. 103f. :: Baldacci BiOr xl 130: + suff. 3 p.s.m. (cf. also Rosenthal ANET 662)),[6,7], 14[20,21] - **Pun** KAI 69[3], 76A 4, B 8, 81[4], 137[4,6], 159[5], CIS i 170[2,3]; + suff. 3 p.s.m. *ʿlty* CIS

i 5510[6], 6000bis 7 (= TPC 84); + suff. 1 p.s. *ʿlty* KAI 89[4,5] - ¶ subst. used as prep. (cf. FR 250, 254III) - **1)** loc. - a) on, upon; *kl ʾdm ʾl ypth ʿlty* KAI 14[20]: let none open up (what is) over me (cf. KAI 13[3f.,5f.,6f]), cf. *kl ʾdm ʾš ypth ʿlt mškb z* KAI 14[7]: anyone who opens up (what is) over this resting-place (for these instances, cf. however Février Sem v 60f.: *ʿlt(y)* = Sing. cstr./+ suff. 1 p.s. of *ʿlh₄* (= cover, lid) :: Silverman JAOS xciv 268: or = nominalized prep. :: Faber JAOS cvi 426 n. 9: = object marker?); *ʾš bl ʿlm ʿlt mzbh* CIS i 170[2]: which are not offered upon the altar; *lktb hʾdmm ... ʿlt mṣbt* KAI 60[4f]: that the men should write ... on a stele - used metaphorically, *kl ʾš ʿlty mšrt* KAI 60[3f]: all that was incumbent upon him by way of service; ... *wʾyspn ʿlt mqdšm* KAI 159[5]: ... and A. were over the sanctuaries; cf. also the expression *ʿlt pn* in *ykn ʿlt pn hmšʾt z š[ʾr]* KAI 69[3]: they shall have besides this payment flesh - b) with, at; *lšt ʿlt hhdrt* KAI 76B 8: to place (it) near the chamber (sc. in the sanctuary; v. *hdrh* :: Février Sem v 59: to place (it) in ...) - **2)** directional, to into - a) litterally, *bʾ hʾlnm ʾl ʿlt hmqdšm ʾl* KAI 137[4f]: these gods came to these sanctuaries; *ʾš ybʾ ʿlt hhrz š mqdšm ʾl* KAI 81[4]: who will come (v. *bwʾ*) to the ... (v. *hrz₁*) of these sanctuaries; *wʾl yʿmsn bmškb z ʿlt mškb šny* KAI 14[5f]: let no one carry me away from this resting-place to another one; cf. *wyspnnm ʿlt gbl ʾrṣ* KAI 14[19f]: we added them to the territory of the country; cf. also *kl ʾdm ʾš ysp lpʿl mlʾkt ʿlt mzbh zn* KAI 10[11f]: whoever may do further work on this altar (cf. poss. CIS i 5510[6]) - b) used as so-called *ʿlt* comm., for, to; *npʿl nbl nskt ʾrbʿ ʿlt mqdšm ʾl* KAI 137[5f]: four vessels of cast metal have been made for these sanctuaries; cf. also *ʿlt mṣbt z yšʾn bksp ʾlm bʿl ṣdn drkmnm 20* KAI 60[6]: for this stele the citizens of S. shall draw 20 *d.* from the temple treasury (cf. e.g. Cooke NSI p. 94, 99, Chabot sub RES 1215, Gibson SSI iii p. 149, 151 :: Röllig KAI a.l. (div. otherwise): l. *ʿrb ʿlt mṣbt z* = a guarantee for this stele; cf. also Lidzbarski sub KI 52) - **3)** with hostile sense?, *kl ʾdm ʾš ʿlṣ ʿlty* KAI 89[5]: whoever exulted over me (cf. KAI 89[4]; v. also *ʿlṣ₁*) - v.d.Branden BO xii 215, 218: this preposition also in KAI 50[4] - Catastini RSF xiii 6: the *ʿlt* in RES 1204[1] = this preposition.
v. *l₅*, *ʿlh₄*, *tmk*, *tʿlh*.

ʿm₁ **Ph** Sing. abs. *ʿm* KAI 26A iii 7, C iv 7; cstr. *ʿm* KAI 10[10], 18[5], 19[8], 43[5], 60[1] - **Pun** Sing. abs. *ʿm* KAI 126[5,6], CIS i 272[5]; cstr. *ʿm* KAI 62[1,8], 68[1], 71[3], 86[4], 99[5], 119[4], 126[7], 170[3], 173[1], CIS i 265[3], 266[3], 267[4], 269[5], 270[3], 271[4], 290[6], 291[5], 3707[4], 4908[5], 4909[4f] (*[ʿ]m*), 5606[4], Trip 35, 41[2], Müll ii 75, CHC 585 no. 7-12, Antas p. 61[1], 65[4], 86 (heavily dam. context), etc., *hm* Müll ii 28 (??, uncert. interpret.), *m* (in *bm* = *b₂* + variant of *ʿm*) Antas p. 51[2]; + suff. 3 p.s.m./f. *ʿmʾ* KAI 145[3] (cf. e.g. Cooke NSI p. 152, 154, Février Sem vi 20, Röllig KAI a.l., v.d.Branden RSF i 166, 168, Sznycer Sem xxii 38 × Krahmalkov RSF iii 188, 191 (div. otherwise): l. *ʿm* (= Sing. abs.) + *ʾ* (= article)) - **Mo** Sing. abs. *ʿm* KAI 181[11,24] - **Hebr** Sing. abs. *ʿm* DJD ii 47[3] (?, heavily dam. context); + suff. 3 p.s.m. *ʿmw* Frey 973[2] (= SM 3) - **OldAr** Sing. emph. *ʿmʾ* KAI 224[5,13]; + suff. 3 p.s.m. *ʿmh* KAI 223B 3; + suff. 3 p.s.f. *ʿmh* KAI 222A 29, 30, B 5, 11; + suff. 1 p.s. *ʿmy* KAI 224[21]; + suff. 3 p.pl.m. *ʿmhm* KAI 223C 16; Plur. emph. *ʿmyʾ* KAI 224[10] (cf. e.g. Dupont-Sommer BMB xiii 27, 33, Degen AAG p. 21, Lemaire & Durand IAS 119, 145, cf. however Gibson SSI ii p. 48, 54: l. *ʿm[my]ʾ*) - **OffAr** Plur. emph. *ʿmmʾ* Aḥiq 94, 162 (for this form, cf. Leand 52d, Kaufman AIA 127f. (n. 58), Degen GGA '79, 29 (n. 57), Lindenberger APA 68f., 285, 300 n. 22, cf. however Kottsieper SAS 118ff., 224: = Sing. emph. of *ʿmm* (= world population, mankind)) - **Nab** Sing. + suff. 3 p.s.m. *ʿmh* CIS ii 182[3], 183[4], 196[7], 197[5], 198[3], IEJ xxi 50[6], etc., etc. - **Hatra** Sing. + suff. 3 p.s.m. *ʿmh* 235[1] (:: Aggoula MUSJ xlvii 12, Vattioni IH a.l.: l. *ʿmʾ* (= Sing. emph.) × Safar Sumer xxiv 11 (n. 12), Degen JEOL xxiii 406: *ʿmh* = *ʿm₄* + suff. 3 p.s.m.) - **JAr** Sing. emph. *ʿmh* MPAT-A 22[8] (= SM 70[16]); Plur. emph. *ʿmmyh* MPAT-A 22[3,5] (= SM 70[11,13]) - ¶ subst. m. people, passim (:: Good SHP 27ff.: *ʿm* in KAI 224 may indicate both group or individual belonging to group); *ḥn lʿn ʾlnm wlʿn ʿm ʾrṣ z* KAI 10[10]: favour in the sight of the gods and in the sight of the people of this land; *hqrt z ... wʿm z ʾš yšb bn* KAI 26A iii 7f.: this town and this people who dwell therein (cf. KAI 26C iv 6ff.); *ʿmʾ yšb ʾdmt* KAI 145[3]: its people that lives in the land (v. supra, v. *ʾdmh*); *wʾl yštmʿ ql knr bʾrpd wbʿmh* KAI 222A 29: let not the sound of the lyre be heard in A. and among its people (for the context, cf. also Lipiński Stud 29; cf. also KAI 222B 5); *ḥd ʿmʾ zy bydy* KAI 224[5]: any of the people who is under my control (or: any people??, cf. KAI 224[10]; cf. KAI 224[13]); *bnʾ ʿm* KAI 126[5,6]: compatriots (Lat. par. *civium*; for the context, v. *ḥbb₁*); *rḥm ʿmh* CIS ii 196[7], 197[5], etc., etc.: who loves his people (epithet of king Haretat IV of the Nabateans); *dy ʾḥyy wšyzb ʿmh* RES 83[9ff]: who vivifies and saves his people (epithet of Rabel II king of the Nabateans; passim); *mrn wmrtn wbr mryn wsmyʾ wgndʾ dʿmh qdmykwn šlmn ...* Hatra 235[1]: our lord, our lady and the son of our lords and the standards and the fortune of his people, before you Sh. ...; *ʿmw yšrʾl* Frey 973[2] (= SM 3): His people Israel (cf. also MPAT-A 22[8] (= SM 70[16])) - used with specialized meanings, *ʿmmyh* MPAT-A 22[3,5] (= SM 70[11,13]): the gentiles; cf. the instances where *ʿm* designates those who officially represent the people of a town/country (i.e. the assembly; cf. Moscati RSO xliii 1ff.; cf. however Garbini AION xxix 323ff.: rather = religious community); *lpny ʾdrʾ ʾlpqy wʿm ʾlpq[y]* KAI 126[7]: before the notables of Lepcis and the people of Lepcis (cf. Lat. par. *ordo et populus*; cf. also Sznycer Sem xxv 66f.; cf. also KAI

119[4]); *kl ʿm bytʿn* KAI 173[1]: the whole people of Bitia (cf. Sznycer Sem xxv 51f., 67); *pʿl wḥdš ʿm gwl* KAI 62[1]: the people of G. has made and restaured ...; *ʿm ʾgdr* KAI 71[3]: the people of A. (cf. Sznycer Sem xxv 54ff.); cf. the comb. *lmyʿs.m. ʿm ...* (and variants), v. *myʿms*; cf. the comb. *ʾš bʿm ...* (= a member of the assembly of ...; cf. Sznycer Sem xxv 60ff.), e.g. *[ḥ]nbʿl ... ʾš bʿm ybšm* CIS i 266[2ff.]: H. ... member of the assembly of Ibiza (cf. KAI 86[4] (cf. Sznycer Sem xxv 61 n. 2), 99[5], 170[3], CIS i 265[3], 266[3], 267[4], 3707[4], 5606[4], Trip 35, 41[2], Antas p. 51[2], 61[1], 65[4]; cf. also the following texts from Sousse: RevAfr. lxxxviii 37[5], 38[3], 39[2], 40[2] (for the reading, cf. Jongeling VO vi 253); used in dating (cf. Sznycer Sem xxv 53ff.), *bšt 180 lʾdn mlkm 143 št lʿm ṣr* KAI 18[4ff.]: in the year 180 of the lord of kings (i.e. the Seleucid era), (i.e.) the year 143 of the people of Tyre; *bšnt 11 lʾdn mlkm ptlmyš ... ʾš hmt lʿm lpš* (for this reading, cf. Masson & Sznycer RPC 99) *šnt 33* KAI 43[4f.]: in the year 11 of the lord of kings P. ... that is of the people of L. the year 33; *bym 4 lmrzḥ bšt 14 lʿm ṣdn* KAI 60[1]: on the fourth day of the feast (v. *mrzḥ*) in the year 14 of the people of S. (cf. KAI 19[8]; poss. KAI 62[8] (cf. e.g. Sznycer Sem xxv 54)); for a related meaning of *ʿm*, cf. prob. also *ʿm (h)mḥnt* Müll ii 75 (text on coins minted by Carthage in Sicily; cf. also CHC 585 no. 7-12): the people of the camp (i.e. those having authority over the camp; cf. Huss 477 n. 24, 492f.: 'Heeresversammlung', cf. also Müll 81, Acquaro RIN lxxvi 80, Heltzer UF xix 434) - for this word in Ph., cf. also Kutler JANES xiv 72f.; for this word in epigraphic material, cf. Good SHP 22ff. - Puech RB lxxxviii 547ff., 561: the *ʿmʾ* in KAI 232 = Sing. emph. of ʿm_1 (= troop, band; less prob. interpret., cf. e.g. Röllig KAI a.l., Gibson SSI ii p. 5, Bron & Lemaire RA lxxxiii 37: = n.p.) - this word also in Sem xxv 44 (Hebr.; *lʿm*)??, cf. however Lemaire Sem xxv 45f.: = n.p. (cf. also Teixidor Syr liii 326) - for KAI 43[10], v. *qmt*$_1$.
v. *bn*$_1$, *lʿnh*$_2$, *mšʿrt*, ʿm_2.

ʿm_2 **Nab** Sing. cstr. *ʿm* CIS ii 182[2]; + suff. 3 p.pl.m. *ʿmhm* CIS ii 354[2] - ¶ subst. m. great-grandfather: CIS 182[2], 354[2] (for this interpret., cf. Clermont-Ganneau RAO ii 372ff., Milik Syr xxxv 228, Good SHP 26, cf. however Cooke NSI p. 245: = ancestor, kinsman) - Hoftijzer DA a.l., Garbini Hen i 175, Delcor SVT xxxii 54, H.P. Müll ZAW xciv 218, Puech BAT 356, 361: l. this noun (Sing. + suff. 3 p.s.m. *ʿmh*) = paternal uncle in DA i 6 (improb. interpret.; cf. also e.g. Caquot & Lemaire Syr liv 194, McCarter BASOR ccxxxix 51, 53, Levine JAOS ci 196, 198, H. & M. Weippert ZDPV xcviii 87, 103, Dijkstra GTT xc 169 n. 40: = ʿm_4 + suff. 3 p.s.m., Weinfeld Shn v/vi 142, 146, Good SHP 25, Puech RB xcii 308, Hackett BTDA 37, Lemaire BAT 318, Sasson UF xvii 287, 294, Wesselius BiOr xliv 594 (cf. also Puech FS Grelot 20,

27): = *ʿm$_1$* + suff. 3 p.s.m. (prob. interpret.)).

ʿm$_3$ v. *ʾl$_1$*.

ʿm$_4$ **Hebr** TA-H 3^4; + suff. 1 p.s. *ʿmy* EI xx 256^4 - **Samal** KAI 214^{15,17,22}; + suff. 2 p.s.m. *ʿmk* KAI 214^{17}; + suff. 1 p.s. *ʿmy* KAI 214^{2,3} - **OldAr** KAI 217^{4,5}, 222A 1, 2, 3, 4, 5, B 1, 2, 3, 4, 5, 11; + suff. 2 p.s.m. *ʿmk* KAI 202A 14, 222B 43 (for the context, cf. also Lipiński Stud 45); + suff. 1 p.s. *ʿmy* KAI 202A 3, 222B 33 - **OffAr** KAI 226^7, 233^{3,7}, 258^4, Cowl 1^4, 26^4, 27^4, Krael 7^{26}, Driv 8^4, 9^2, Aḥiq 49, 104, Beh 19 (Akkad. par. *itti*), AG 26^{2,3}, etc., etc.; + suff. 3 p.s.m. *ʿmh* Driv 5^8, 6^4, F iia 1-2^2 (dam. context), Aḥiq 37, 39, 40, 56, 107, 154 (cf. however Grelot DAE p. 444 (n. h): l. *ʿmh[wn]* = + suff. 3 p.pl.m.; dam. context; cf. also Puech RB xcv 591: l. perhaps *ʿmhm* (= + suff. 3 p.pl.m.)), 164, 197 (heavily dam. context; Kottsieper SAS 22, 224: or = Sing. abs. of *ʿmh$_3$* (= darkness)??), AE '23, 40 no. 2^{3,8} (diff. context); + suff. 2 p.s.m. *ʿmk* Cowl 42^4, NESE i 11^8, Samar 1^7 (= EI xviii 8*); + suff. 2 p.s.f. *ʿmky* Cowl 68 ii obv. 3; + suff. 1 p.s. *ʿmy* KAI 226^6, 233^2, Beh 26 (Akkad. par. *it-ti-iá*), 59 (Akkad. par. *it-ti-ia*), AG 90, MAI xiv/2, 66^4; + suff. 3 p.pl.m. *ʿmhwn* NESE iii 48^{11}; cf. GIPP 49 - **Nab** IEJ xxix 112^4 (diff. context); + suff. 3 p.s.m. *ʿmh* CIS ii 198^7, 199^7, 205^9, 206^7, 208^6, 209^8, etc.; + suff. 1 p.s. *ʿmy* MPAT 64 i 10 - **Palm** CIS ii 3913 i 9 (Greek par. μετὰ), SBS 48^7, Syr xix 74^3, xl 33^3, Inv x 112^4; + suff. 3 p.s.m. *ʿmh* CIS ii 3916^3, 3933^4, 3948^3, 3959^5 (= SBS 44), Inv x 81^4, 124^3; + suff. 3 p.pl.m. *ʿmhwn* CIS ii 3960^7, RIP 142^2, Syr xlviii 413^4 (heavily dam. context) - Hatra 79^1 (cf. Safar Sumer xvii 12 n. 3, 16, Caquot Syr xl 3, 6, Teixidor Syr xli 280, Ingholt AH i/2, 49 :: Caquot Syr xxxii 272 (div. otherwise): l. *ʿmʾlhʾ* = n.p.) - **JAr** MPAT 42^{10}, MPAT-A 16^4; + suff. 3 p.s.m. *ʿmh* MPAT 55^4; + suff. 2 p.s.f. *[ʿ]mk* MPAT 42^{12}; + suff. 1 p.s. *ʿmy* MPAT 39^3, 51^{5,10}; + suff. 3 p.pl.m. *ʿmhn* MPAT 60^2; + suff. 2 p.pl.m. *ʿmkwn* MPAT 58^2 - ¶ prep. (for this prep., cf. Pennacchietti AION xxiv 182ff.) - **1)** with, together with, in combination with; *[tʾk]l nbš pnmw ʿmk* KAI 214^{17}: may the soul of P. eat with you (v. *npš*); *ʿdy brgʾyh ... ʿm mtʿʾl* KAI 222A 1: the treaty of B. with M. (cf. KAI 222A 2, 3, B 1, 2, etc.); *wtb bgw ʿm ʾnttk* Cowl 9^6: dwell on it with your wife; *hmwnyt ʿm wydrng* Cowl 27^4, 30^5: in agreement with W.; *npyn dbr mṣryʾ ʿm ḥylʾ ʾḥrnn* Cowl 30^8: N. led out the Egyptians with the other forces; *ʾbd ʿm nšy [byth]* Driv 8^4: he perished together with the women of his house; *ʾrmpy ʿm ḥylʾ zy lydh lʾ mštmʿn ly* Driv 4^1: A. with the troop which is under him do not obey me; *ʿlymn zyly zy ʾzln ʿmh mṣryn* Driv 6^4: my servants who are going with him to Egypt; *wyʿbd ptkr swsh ʿm rkbh* Driv 9^2: and he may execute a sculpture of a horse with its rider (cf. Pers 103$^{2f.}$, etc.); *ʾnḥnh ʿm nšyn ... šqqn lbšn hwyn* Cowl 30^{15}: we with our wives ... were clothed in sackcloth; *ʾth ʿm ʾḥwh* Syr xli 285[3]: he has come with his brother (cf. MPAT 58[2]); *wtplg ʿmy* MAI xiv/2, 66[4]: you must share with me; *dy nḥt ʿmh lʾlgšyʾ* CIS ii 3933[4]: who descended with him to A.; *dy slqt mn krk ʾspsnʾ ʿm ʾbgr* Syr xix 74[2f]: who went up from K.A. with A.; *wršh lʾ ʾyty lk {lk} ʿmy bgw drkh dk* MPAT 51[5]: you have no authority inside the courtyard together with me (i.e. I alone have authority; cf. MPAT 51[9f]); *try ḥmryn dy tšlḥ ʿmhn tr* (v. *tryn*) *gbryn* MPAT 60[1f]: two donkeys with which you must send two men; *yhy lh ḥwlq ʿm ṣdyqyh* Frey 981[3f] (= MPAT-A 16): that his share will be with the righteous ones; etc.; cf. *ṣwk ḥnnyhw ʿl bʾr šbʿ ʿm mšʾ ṣmd ḥmrm* TA-H 3[3ff]: Ch. has commanded you to B.Sh. with two packed donkeys (v. *mšʾ*); *brh yʾth ʿly bbʾl ʿm mndtʾ* Driv 11[5]: his son shall come to me in B. with the rent; *wyʾth ʿm gnzʾ* Driv 10[5]: he will come with the treasure; *wtnpq mnh ʿm šʾrt* Krael 7[26]: and she will leave him with the rest; *ʾtw lbyrt yb ʿm tlyhm* Cowl 30[8]: they came to the fortress of Y. with their weapons; *lmh yšpṭwn ʿqn ʿm ʾšh bšr ʿm skyn* Aḥiq 104: why should wood strive with fire, flesh with a knife?; *dyn lʾ ʾyty ly ʿmhm* ATNS 2[2]: I have no suit with them (for the reading and interpret., cf. Porten & Yardeni sub TADAE B 8.9); *wlkmryʾ plgʾ ʾḥrnʾ ʿm ʾkltʾ* BASOR cclxiii 78[2]: and to the priests is assigned the other portion together with the food (cf. Jones BASOR cclxxv 43 :: Hammond, Johnson & Jones BASOR cclxiii 78: *ʿm* used here as subordinating conjunction (with/on the condition that)); *wktb ʿm nmwsʾ qdmyʾ bgllʾ* CIS ii 3913 i 9: it will be written (v. *ktb*$_1$) down with the former law on the stele ...; for *ʿm yqrʾ*... in SBS 48[7], v. *yqr*$_2$ - **2)** with, near; *wlšmw ʿmy mʾn ksp* KAI 226[6f]: they have not laid with me any vessel of silver; *gbryʾ ʾlk tryn zy ʿmh* Aḥiq 56: those two men who were with him; *ʿmh hww* Driv 9[8]: they were with him; *yzkr nbš pnmw ʿm [h]d[d]* KAI 214[17f]: let him remember the soul of P. (who is) with H. (v. *zkr*$_1$; for the context, v. *ʿwd*$_5$); *zkyʾ dgndh ʿm ʾlhʾ* Hatra 79[1f]: the victorious one whose fortune is with the gods (cf. Aggoula MUSJ xlvii 30 (: not necessarily a deceased one, cf. also Bikerman IS 97 :: Ingholt AH i/2, 49), cf. also Safar Sumer xvii 16 n. 34, Caquot Syr xl 3, 6, Teixidor Syr xli 280 n. 2); *ḥṣdyʾ ʾln dy hww ʿm ʾbgr* Syr xl 33[2f]: those reapers who have been with A.; for *ntyrh ʿmhwn* in NESE iii 48, v. *ntyrh*; cf. also the foll. instances, *ṣḥʾ wḥwr ʿlymy ʿnny ʾštdrw ʿm wydrng* Cowl 38[4]: S. and Ch. servants of A. interceded with W.; *whtšdr ʿmh* MPAT 55[3f]: intercede with him (cf. Kutscher Lesh xxv 122f. :: Yadin IEJ xi 43, Fitzmyer & Harrington MPAT a.l.: help him, make an effort for him; dam. context); *qmw ʿmy ʾlhw* KAI 214[2]: the gods stood with me (v. *ʾlh*$_1$); *[gbr]yʾ zy qdmn ʿmy hww* Beh 59: the men who previously stood on my side (v. *qdm*$_2$); *zy ʾl ʿmh* Aḥiq 107, 154: with whom God is (v. *ʾl*$_1$; cf. also Aḥiq 161 (for the reading of the

context, cf. Lindenberger APA 163, 267 nn. 495-496)); *[hn lʾ y]štmr* (v. *šmr₁*) *ʾyš ʿm ʾlhn* Aḥiq 160: if a man abide not by the gods; *mnyh ʿmy ... ksp ...* MPAT 39[3f]: there is counted out with me (i.e. to me) ... silver ...; *wlh ytqbr ʿmh bʾrnh dnh kwl ʾnš* EI xx 161*: and no one may be buried with him in this sarcophagus - **3)** with, towards, with regard to, *ṣdq ʾnh ʿm[...* KAI 217[5]: I have been loyal towards (cf. poss. also Aḥiq 173 (dam. context)); *tmh hwyt msbl lk kʾyš ʿm ʾḥwhy* Aḥiq 48f.: there I supported you like a man (deals) with his brother; *ʾnt kl[k] kbn ʿm zy ngʿ bk* Aḥiq 166: (said to the bramble) you are all thorns to him who touches you; cf. also *wmn byš yʿbd ʿm ptkr znh* KAI 258[3f]: and whoever does damage to this sculpture; *wʿbd ʿmhwn gbwrtʾ* RIP 142[2]: and he (sc. the god) did mighty deeds to them (v. also *gbrh₂*) - **4)** with, incumbent upon; *pʾyty ʿmh ldwšrʾ ...šmdyn 5* CIS ii 198[7f]: he owes D. ... (a sum of 5 *sh.*; *pʾyty ʿmh lʾsrtgʾ ... slʿyn ʾlp* J 38[7]: he owes the commander ... 1000 *selac* (cf. CIS ii 199[7], 205[9], 206[7], 209[7f], etc.); *mh dy lk ʿmy* MPAT 64 i 10: what I owe you; *ʿmy ... ksp zwzyn ʾrbʿh* EI xx 256[5f.]: I owe a sum of 4 *zwz* - **5)** the meaning of *ʿm* in CRAI '70, 163[4], IPAA 11[9] uncert. (diff. context), Dupont-Sommer CRAI '70, 169: or = together with, or with temporal meaning: in the time of, Humbach IPAA a.l.: = according to - Milik RN vi/iv 56 n. 2, Syr xliv 297: l. *ʿm* in Hatra 49[3] (prob. reading) :: Safar Sumer ix 245, Caquot Syr xxxii 54, Vattioni IH a.l.: l. *ʿl* (= *ʿl₇*) - Février Sem vi 17: *pʿmʾ* in Punica xviii/i 15[4], CB viii 31 = *p₁* + *ʿm₄* + suff. 3 p.s.m./f. (improb. interpret., cf. Jongeling NINPI 190: = part of n.p. *nʿmtpʿmʾ*) - Vattioni Aug xvi 551: the second *im* in IRT 892[5]: = *ʿm₄* (highly improb. interpret.).
v. *ydʿ₁*, *ʿm₁, ₂*, *ʿmd₁*.

ʿmd₁ Edom a verbal form of this root prob. in TeAv xii 97[4] (QAL/PIʿEL Pf. 3 p.s.m.), word of uncert. meaning; Israel RivBib xxxv 341: l. *ʿmd* (= he has placed) or l. *ʿmr* (= QAL Pf. 3 p.s.m. of *ʿmr₂* (= to measure)), Beit-Arieh & Cresson TeAv xii 97f.: l. prob. *ʿmd* = PIʿEL Pf. 3 p.s.m. (= to prepare, arrange, allocate), uncert. interpret., cf. however also Misgav IEJ xl 216: *ʿmd* = ʿmd₃ (= variant form of *ʿm₄* (uncert. interpret.)).
v. *šmr₁*.

ʿmd₂ Ph Plur. + suff. 3 p.s.f. *ʿmdh* KAI 10[6] - **Pun** Plur. abs. *ʿmdm* KAI 124[1], Mus xxxvii 163[2] (?, dam. context) - **OffAr** Plur. emph. *ʿmwdyʾ* Cowl 30[9], 31[8] - **Palm** Sing. emph. *ʿmdʾ* SBS 20[3], *ʿmwdʾ* CIS ii 3911[2], 3956[4], 3966[7] (= RIP 156[16] = Inv ii 1), Syr xvii 274[3], SBS 11[2], Inv xi 79[3] (*ʿmwd[ʾ]*), xii 22[4], DFD 162[4]; Plur. abs. *ʿmwdyn* CIS ii 3952[3], 3955[5]; emph. *ʿmwdyʾ* CIS ii 3983[1] (= SBS 13 = Inv i 4), 3984[1], SBS 10[3], 14[1], 16[1], 17[1] (*[ʿ]mwdyʾ*), 18[1], 19[1]; + suff. 3 p.s.f. *ʿmwdyh* SBS 1a 1, 1b 1 (= Inscr P 30), 3[1], 7[1], 9[1], 43[4], Syr xii 130[2], xvii 274[1] -

JAr Sing. emph. *ʿmwdʾ* MPAT-A 12^5 (= Frey 1195 = SM 71), *ʿmwdh* MPAT-A 15^2 (= Frey 982 = SM 18), SM 40^2; Plur. abs. *ʿmwdyn* AMB 9^7; emph. *ʿmwdyh* MPAT-A 17^1 (= SM 7) - ¶ subst. m. (cf. however Inv xi 79^3: *dʾ ʿmwd[ʾ]*, v. also *znh*) column, passim; *qrbw ... ʿmwdyʾ ʾln tryhwn* SBS 10^{2ff}: they have offered ... these two columns; *mṭltʾ dh klh ʿmwdyh wšryth ... qrb* SBS 1a 1: this complete portico its columns and its entablature he offered - the *ʿmwdʾ* in Inscr P 31^6 prob. = Plur. emph. (cf. Rosenthal Sprache 76, du Mesnil du Buisson RES '45, 80, Gawlikowski Syr xlviii 414 n. 3, 415, TP 76, 79f., Milik DFD 277 :: Cantineau Inscr P a.l. and sub Inv ix 28: l. *ʿmwrʾ* = Plur. emph. of *ʿmwr* (= one habitating (sc. the temple); cf. also Aggoula Sem xxxii 111, 115) or l. *ʿmwdʾ* = Plur. emph. of *ʿmwd*$_2$ (= one who makes ritual purifications); the *ʿmwrʾ* in Inscr P 31^8 poss. = Plur. emph. of *ʿmwr*, cf. Cantineau Inscr P a.l. and sub Inv ix 28 (v. supra), cf. also Milik DFD 277 (or = habitation), Rosenthal with Cantineau Syr xix 170: = traveller (or preferably = client, cf. PS 2920?), cf. however Cantineau (v. supra) and Rosenthal Sprache 76, du Mesnil du Buisson RES '45, 80, Gawlikowski Syr xlviii 414 n. 3, 415, TP 76, 79f.: l. *ʿmwdʾ* = Plur. emph. of *ʿmd*$_2$ :: Aggoula Sem xxxii 111, 115: = Plur. emph. of *ʿmwd*$_3$ (= bather) - Dupont-Sommer JKF i 46: the *ʿm dšpqʾ* in JKF i 46^2 prob. = lapsus for *ʿmd špqʾ*, *ʿmd* being *ʿmd*$_2$ (highly uncert. interpret.) - Dupont-Sommer JKF i 46: l. *[ʿ]mwd* (= Sing. cstr.) in JKF i 46^1? (uncert. interpret.).
v. *mʿmd*.

ʿ$\mathbf{md_3}$ v. *ʿmd*$_1$.

ʿ$\mathbf{mh_1}$ v. *ʾlmh* , *ʾmh*$_2$, *pʿm*$_2$.

ʿ$\mathbf{mh_2}$ **Hebr** Sing. cstr. *ʿmt* DJD ii 24C 18, D 19 (*[ʿ]mt*), $30^{6,24}$ - ¶ subst. juxtaposition; in the comb. *lʿmt*, *lʿmt kkh* DJD ii 24C 18f., D 19, $30^{6,24f}$: according to its terms (sc. of the document).
v. *ʾl*$_1$, *ʾlmh*.

ʿ$\mathbf{mh_3}$ v. *ʿm*$_4$.

ʿ$\mathbf{mwd_1}$ v. *ʿmd*$_2$.

ʿ$\mathbf{mwd_2}$ v. *ʿmd*$_2$.

ʿ$\mathbf{mwd_3}$ v. *ʿmd*$_2$.

ʿmwq **Hebr** Sing. abs. *ʿmwq* DJD ii 24F 11 (heavily dam. context) - ¶ subst. depth.

ʿmwr v. *ʿmd*$_2$.

ʿmydh **Hebr** Sing. + suff. 3 p.pl.f. *ʿmydt[n]* IEJ vii 239^8 - ¶ subst. resurrection.

ʿmyr **OffAr** Sing. abs. *ʿmyr* Driv 6^4 - ¶ subst. fodder.

ʿ$\mathbf{ml_1}$ **OldAr** QAL Pf. 3 p.s.m. *ʿml* KAI 216^{7f} (for the reading, cf. Degen

ZDMG cxxi 124; cf. e.g. Degen AAG p. 68, cf. however Landsberger Samʾal 71 n. 187: = QAL Part. act. s.m. abs.; cf. also Cooke NSI p. 183, Donner KAI a.l.) - **OffAr** QAL Pf. 2 p.s.m. *ʿmlt* Cowl 40[2]; APH Impf. 3 p.s.m. *yʿml* SSI ii 37[4] (cf. Delcor Mus lxxx 311, Altheim & Stiehl AAW v/1, 74, Gibson SSI ii p. 158 :: Dupont-Sommer CRAI '66, 47, 54, Cross BASOR clxxxiv 9 (n. 22): = QAL Impf. 3 p.s.m. (resp.: = to suffer harm and to disturb) - **Palm** QAL Pf. 3 p.s.m. *ʿml* SBS 48[4] - **JAr** QAL Pf. 3 p.pl.m. *ʿmlw* Syn D A 11, 13 (= SM 88) - ¶ verb QAL to take trouble, to toil, to exert oneself; *šmʿt kʿmlʾ zy ʿmlt* Cowl 40[2]: I have heard of the trouble that you took; *wʿml bswmh* SBS 48[4]: he worked with his own body (i.e. personally); cf. Syn D A 11, 13 (dam. context); cf. also *wbyt ʾby ʿml mn kl* KAI 216[7f]: my father's house laboured more than all (others; cf. e.g. Cooke NSI p. 181, 183, Donner KAI a.l., Gibson SSI ii p. 90f., cf. also Dahood Bibl xlvii 269, Weinfeld JAOS xc 187 n. 21, Sader EAS 170 (n. 48), Stefanovic COAI 189, 192, 285 :: Rosenthal ANET 655 (n. 1): the house of my father has profited more than anybody else (cf. Greenfield Bibl l 101; cf. also Poeb 50 (n. 3): the house of my father has gained more ...) :: Landsberger Samʾal 71: the *ʿml* (= QAL Part. act.) = exerting oneself > wretched; cf. also Koopmans p. 77) - APH to harm, to disturb; *ʾyš ʾl yʿml* SSI ii 37[4]: let no one disturb (sc. me or the tomb).

ʿml₂ **OldAr** Sing. abs. *ʿml* KAI 222A 26 - **OffAr** Sing. emph. *ʿmlʾ* Cowl 40[2] - **JAr** Sing. emph. *ʿmlh* MPAT-A 28[2] (or = + suff. 3 p.s.m.?, cf. e.g. Sukenik JPOS xv 144, Frey sub 858, Naveh sub SM 34 :: Fitzmyer & Harrington MPAT a.l.: = + suff. 3 p.s.m./f.),[3] (or = + suff. 3 p.s.f.?, cf. e.g. Sukenik JPOS xv 144, Fitzmyer & Harrington MPAT a.l., Naveh sub SM 34); + suff. 3 p.s.m. *ʿmlh* MPAT-A 39[3] (for the reading, cf. Naveh sub SM 42 :: Ben-Dov Qadm vi 61, Fitzmyer & Harrington MPAT a.l.: l. *ʿmly* = Sing. + suff. 1 p.s. (cf. also Hüttenmeister ASI 274)); + suff. 3 p.pl.m. *ʿmlhwn* MPAT-A 26[10] (= SM 32), 27[3] (*ʿmlh[wn]*),[4] (= SM 33) - ¶ subst. - **1)** effort, trouble; *šmʿt kʿmlʾ zy ʿmlt* Cowl 40[2]: I have heard of the trouble that you took (cf. also Dion RB lxxxix 556); *mlk ʿlmh ytn brkth bʿmlhwn* MPAT-A 26[9f.]: may the King of the Universe set His blessing on their exertions (cf. MPAT-A 27[2f.,4], 28[2,3]); *dškn* (v. *škn₁*) *skwpth mn drḥmnh* (v. *rḥmn*) *wmn ʿmlh* (v. supra) MPAT-A 39[1ff.]: who established this lintel out of what belongs to the Merciful One and out of his own effort - **2)** trouble, affliction; *kl mh lḥyh bʾrq wbšmyn wkl mh ʿml* KAI 222A 26: all manner of evil in earth and heaven and all manner of trouble - Lipiński Stud 40f.: l. *[ʿ]mlh* (= Sing. + suff. 3 p.s.m.) in KAI 222B 36 (uncert. interpret., dam. context).

ʿmm v. *ʿm₁*.

ʿms **Ph** QAL Impf. 3 p.s.m. + suff. 1 p.s. *yʿmsn* KAI 14[5f.,7,21] - **Pun** NIPH Impf. 3 p.s.m. *yʿms* KAI 69[13], 74[8] (cf. CIS i sub 165, Cooke NSI p. 121, Lagrange ERS 470, Dussaud Orig 321 (cf. also Lidzbarksi Handb 343) × Röllig KAI a.l. (cf. KAI iii p. 19 s.v. *ʿms*): = QAL Impf. 3 p.pl. (cf. also FR 141a)) - ¶ verb QAL to carry; *wʾl yʿmsn bmškb z ʿlt mškb šny* KAI 14[5f.]: let nobody carry me away from this resting place to another one (cf. KAI 14[7f.,21]) - NIPH (v. however supra) to be brought/carried; for the context of KAI 69[13], 74[8], v. *pnt* (cf. also Février CB viii 41, 43: in KAI 69[13], 74[8] = to be presented) - Vattioni Aug xvi 543: the *oms* in IRT 877[7f] to be derived from this root (highly uncert. interpret.).
v. *myʿms.*

ʿmṣ **JAr** PAʿEL Impf. 2 p.s.m. *tʿmyṣ* Syr xlv 101[20] - ¶ verb PAʿEL to close; *lʾ tʿmyṣ mynh ʿy[nyk]* Syr xlv 101[20]: you must not close your eyes on him (heavily dam., uncert. context).

ʿmṣmṣm **Nab** Naveh with Negev EI x 181: the diff. *ʿmṣmṣm* in EI x 181, no. 5: poss. = magic formula.

ʿmq$_1$ **OldAr** HAPH Pf. 3 p.pl.m. *hʿmqw* KAI 202A 10 - **JAr** APH Inf. *mʿmqh* IEJ xxxvi 206[5] (for the form, cf. also Broshi & Qimron IEJ xxxvi 213) - ¶ verb HAPH to make deep; *hʿmqw ḥrṣ mn ḥr[ṣh]* KAI 202A 10: they dug a moat deeper than its moat (sc. of the town; cf. Greenfield Proc v CJS i 178 n. 15, 191) - for the dam. context of IEJ xxxvi 206[5], cf. also Broshi & Qimron IEJ xxxvi 211.
v. *mʿmq.*

ʿmq$_2$ **Ph** Sing. cstr. *ʿmq* KAI 26A i 4, ii 2, 8f., 14, 15 - **Pun** Sing. abs. *ʿmq* KAI 145[8]; cstr. *ʿmq* RCL '66, 201[5] - **Hebr** Sing. cstr. *ʿmq* KAI 190[2] (for this reading, cf. e.g. Gibson SSI i p. 25)[,3] (for both instances, v. infra) - ¶ subst. plain, valley; *ʾrṣ ʿmq ʾdn* KAI 26A i 4: the land of the plain of A. (cf. KAI 26A ii 15f.); *gbl ʿmq ʾdn* KAI 26A ii 2: the territory of the plain of A. (cf. also KAI 26A ii 8f., 14); *yrd bʿmq* KAI 145[8]: descending in the valley (for the context, v. *yrd*); *ʿmq qrt* RCL '66, 201[5]: down-town, lower town (cf. Mahjoubi & Fantar RCL '66, 207f. (n. 32), Dupont-Sommer CRAI '68, 119 :: Ferron Mus xcviii 57ff., 61: indication of higher part of the city) - *bʿmq* ... KAI 190[2,3]: in the valley of ... (for this interpret., cf. e.g. Albright JPOS vi 92, Dir p. 74, 77, Torczyner BJPES vii 8, Mosc p. 46, Milik RB lxvi 550ff., Röllig KAI a.l., Gibson SSI p. 26, Hestrin IR p. 62*, 140, Lemaire IH i 239, 242 :: Sukenik BJPES xiii 115ff., Kutscher SY 173, Degen ZDMG cxxi 130: = b_1 (= variant of bn_1) + part of n.p.) - Kyrieleis & Röllig MDAIA ciii 65: the *ʿmq* in MDAIA ciii 62 = Sing. cstr. of *ʿmq$_2$* (less prob. interpret.), cf. also Bron & Lemaire RA lxxxiii 38, Ephʿal & Naveh IEJ xxxix 193, 195f.: = n.g. (interpret. of context however uncert.).

ʿmqh **Pun** Levi Della Vida Or xxxiii 11, 14, Amadasi IPT 134: the *ʿmqt* in Trip 51[4] = Sing. abs. of *ʿmqh* (= valley); *ʿmqt šhtʿmʾr* = the valley of the palm-tree (diff. context, uncert. interpret.).

ʿmr$_1$ **Nab** QAL Part. s.m. abs. *ʿmr* CIS ii 1205[2] (:: Cantineau Nab ii 133: = QAL Pf. 3 p.s.m. :: Levinson AIN 200: or = Sing. abs. of *ʿmr$_4$*) - **Hatra** QAL Pf. 3 p.s.m. (or Part. s.m. abs.) 336[7], 343[4] - ¶ verb QAL to inhabit + *b$_2$*; *ʿbdʾlgʾ ... dy ʿmr bʾylt* CIS ii 1205[1ff]: A. ... who lives in A.; *kwl dy ʿmr bḥṭrʾ* Hatra 343[4]: everyone who resides in Hatra (cf. Hatra 336[7]).

ʿmr$_2$ **JAr** QAL (or PAʿEL?) Impf. 3 p.pl.m. *yʿmrn* MPAT 60[2] - ¶ verb QAL (or PAʿEL?) to pack, to load (?; for this interpret., cf. Yadin IEJ xi 48, Fitzmyer & Harrington MPAT a.l., cf. however v. Bekkum SV 123: to gather in the crops, to harvest).
v. *ʿmd$_1$*

ʿmr$_3$ **Hebr** PIʿEL(?) Imper. s.m. *ʿmr* DJD ii 46[9]; Inf. cstr. + suff. 2 p.s.m. *ʿmrk* DJD ii 46[2] - ¶ verb PIʿEL(?) uncert. meaning; Milik DJD ii a.l.: = to insist (cf. however Pardee HAHL 136).

ʿmr$_4$ **Palm** Sing. + suff. 3 p.s.m. *ʿmrh* CIS ii 3932[6] - ¶ subst. life, career; *wdbr ʿmrh škytyt* CIS ii 3932[6]: he led his life in an honourable way (cf. Greek par. καὶ καλῶς πολειτευσάμενον) - Altheim & Stiehl AAW v/1, 74f.: l. *ʿmrʾ* (= Sing. emph. of *ʿmr$_4$*) in NESE ii 87[1] (improb. reading, cf. Segal Irâq xxxi 171f., Degen NESE ii 85, 87: l. *smrṣ* = part of n.p. (cf. also Texidor Syr xlvii 373: l. prob. *smrʾ* = part of n.p.).
v. *ʿmr$_1$*.

ʿmr$_5$ v. *mrʾ*.

ʿmr$_6$ **OffAr** Sing. abs. *ʿmr* ASAE xlviii 112 conv. 4 - ¶ subst. indicating dry measure of capacity; for the context of ASAE xlviii 112 conv. 4, cf. Dupont-Sommer ASAE xlviii 116, Porten Arch 277 - for this measure, cf. Barrois ii 248ff., Trinquet SDB v 1222ff., de Vaux IAT i 305f., cf. also EM iv 853ff., Lipiński Stud 88.

ʿmr$_7$ **OffAr** Sing. abs. *ʿmr* Cowl 15[7,10], Krael 2[4], Herm 2[7,16], 6[5], *qmr* Cowl 20[5], 36[3], 42[9], Krael 7[6,7,9] (for the reading, cf. Porten & Yardeni sub TADAE B 3.8 *qm[r]*),[13], ATNS 44 i 7; emph. *ʿmrʾ* Sach 76 i A 4, *ʿmrh* Herm 2[9], *qmrʾ* Sach 76 v 3 (diff. context) - **Palm** Sing. emph. *ʿmrʾ* CIS ii 3913 ii 93 (Greek par. ἐρίων), 94, 96 - ¶ subst. (f. in Palm.) wool; for the context interpret. of Sach 76 i A 4, cf. Lidzbarski Eph iii 256, Greenfield Or xxix 100.
v. *ṣmd$_1$*.

ʿn$_1$ v. *ʿyn$_2$*.

ʿn$_2$ v. *ṣʾn*.

ʿn_3 **Pun** Février & Fantar Karth xii 53: the *ʿn* in Karth xii 53[1] prob. = noun Sing. abs. (= architectural term; in the context portico, porch or colonnade would be fitting), poss. interpret. :: v.d.Branden RSF v 57, 61: *ʿn* = Sing. abs. of *ḥn_1* (= benevolence) :: Krahmalkov RSF iii 178, 184, 203 (div. otherwise): l. *ʿ* (= Sing. abs. of ʿ$_1$ (= ruin)) +*n* (v. *nšl$_1$*).

ʿnb **OffAr** Plur. emph. *ʿnbyʾ* Cowl 81[1], cf. Frah v 2 (*ʾnbh*), Nisa-b 812[1] (*ʿnbyn*), cf. also GIPP 49 - ¶ subst. - **1)** grape: Frah v 2 - **2)** Plur. produce in general: Cowl 81[1]; in Nisa-b 812[1] prob. some produce of the vine.

ʿnbh **Pun** Schroed 311: l. *onobuth* in Poen 945 (= Plur. abs. of *ʿnbh*), poss. = duty (cf. also L.H.Gray AJSL xxxix 77ff., cf. however e.g. Sznycer PPP 113: reading of Studemund *onobunt/e/ph* (var. readings *ono but ...* and *ono buth*; cf. also Sznycer PPP 127: interpret. imposs.).

ʿnh_1 v. *ʿwnh*, *ʿntw*.

ʿnh_2 **OldAr** Sing. m. abs. *ʿnh* KAI 202A 2 (v. infra) - ¶ adj. prob. meaning: humble, in the comb. *ʾš ʿnh ʾnh*: I am a humble man (cf. e.g. Nöldeke ZA xxi 381, Garb 253f., Rosenthal ANET 655, Donner KAI a.l., Tawil Or xliii 51ff., Segert AAG p. 319, Teixidor Syr liv 271 (cf. also Degen AAG p. 39, 77, Briend TPOA 96), cf. also Ronzevalle MUSJ iii 110* n. 5, Gibson SSI ii p. 9, 12f., Stefanovic COAI 130ff., 239, de Moor UF xx 161: > pious (cf. also Greenfield Proc v CJS i 178f.; cf. however Teixidor Syr liv 271f.) :: e.g. Grimme OLZ '09, 14, Jepsen MiOr xv 1f.: = a man of humble origin (cf. also Dupont-Sommer Ar 46f., AH i/1, 1 n. 2, Delsman TUAT i 626; cf. however Teixidor Syr xlviii 478f.) :: Lidzbarski Eph iii 6 (: or l. *ʿkh*??), Gressmann ATAT 443, Black DOTT 246, 248, Lewy Or xxi 415 n. 6, Ross HThR lxiii 22ff., Millard Sem xxxix 47ff.: I am a man of A. (= n.l.; cf. however Teixidor Syr xlviii 478) :: Lipiński Stud 22: I am an oppressed man :: Sader EAS 208 (n. 27): I am a conqueror (*ʿnh* = QAL Part. act. s.m. abs. of *ʿny$_2$*) :: Torrey JAOS xxxv 357: *ʾš* = *ʾš$_4$* (= rel. pron.) + *ʿnh* (= QAL Part. pass. s.m. abs. of *ʿny$_2$* (= being in distress)) :: Albright JPOS vi 87: *ʾš* = *ʾš$_4$* (= rel. pron.) + *ʿnh* (= QAL Part. act. s.m. abs. of *ʿny$_1$* (= to speak; cf. also Donner KAI a.l.)) :: Pognon ISS 159: *ʾš* (= Sing. abs. of *ʾš$_1$* (= to everyone)) *ʿnh* (= QAL Part. act. s.m. abs. of *ʿny$_1$* (= to speak))) - cf. *ʿny$_3$* sub *ʿbd$_1$*.

ʿnw v. *bʿnw*.

ʿnwh **OffAr** Sing. abs. *ʿnwh* Aḥiq 105 - ¶ subst. prob. meaning: humiliation, cf. Joüon MUSJ xviii 14 :: e.g. Cowl a.l., Ginsberg ANET 429, Grelot DAE p. 438, Lindenberger APA 89f., 243 n. 254: = poverty (cf. also Kottsieper SAS 20, 224: = misery, low position).

ʿnwn cf. Frah xiv 15 (cf. Nyberg FP 47, 83) :: Ebeling Frah a.l.: l. *ʿnn* (= someone).

ʿnwšw **Palm** Sing. cstr. *ʿnwšwt* CIS ii 3994B 3, *ʿnwšt* CIS ii 3994A 3, C 3 (Greek par. for CIS ii 3994: ἀργυροταμιῶν); emph. *ʿnwštʾ* Inv ix 12[3], MUSJ xxviii 56 (*ʿnwš[tʾ]*), RTP 8, 36 (*ʿnwš[t]ʾ*) - ¶ subst. - **1)** Treasury; *ʾnwš ʿnwštʾ* Inv ix 12[3]: the treasurers (Greek par. οἱ ἀργυροτομίαι); *ʿnwš[t]ʾ dy bl* RTP 36: the Treasury of Bel; *mn ksp ʿnwš[tʾ]* MUSJ xxviii 56: at the expense of the Treasury (cf. RTP 8) - **2)** financial administration, quaestorship; *bʿnwšt zbyd[ʾ]* CIS ii 3994A 3: under the quaestorship of Z. (cf. CIS ii 3994B 3, C 3) - this word Sing. emph. (*ʿnš[tʾ]*) poss. also in Inv vi 11b 2 (= RIP 132B), cf. Cantineau sub Inv vi 11 (dam. context) :: Milik DFD 287: l. *ʿwšrw*? (= Pu ʿal Pf. 3 p.pl.m. of *ʿšr₁* (= to be tithed)) :: Gawlikowski sub RIP 132: or l. rather *ʿnšw[hy]* = Plur. + suff. 3 p.s.m. of *ʿnš₂*.

ʿnz **Pun** Sing. cstr. *ʿz* CIS i 3915[2], KAI 69[7]; Plur. abs. *ʿzm* KAI 74[4] - **OffAr** Sing. abs. *ʿnz* Cowl 33[10], JRAS '29, 108[10], RES 1300[5]; emph. *ʿnzʾ* Aḥiq 118, 119; cf. Frah vii 11, 12 (*ʾz*), cf. Toll ZDMG-Suppl viii 30 - **Palm** Sing. abs. *ʿz* CIS ii 3913 ii 18 (*ʿ[z]*), 22 (*[ʿ]z*), 24, 26, 29, 31, 98 - ¶ subst. f. goat, passim; *bzqyn trt[n dy] ʿz* CIS ii 3913 ii 31: in two goat-skins (cf. Greek par. [ἐν] ἀ[σ]κοῖς δυσὶ αἰγείοις; cf. also CIS ii 3913 ii 18, 23f., 26, 29, 98) - in KAI 69[7], CIS i 3915[2] poss. indicating he-goat, cf. Dussaud Orig 140, Capuzzi StudMagr ii 51 (cf. Lagrange ERS 474: *ʿz* = she-goat or used to indicate goat in general).

ʿny₁ **Pun** Qal Inf. cstr. *ʿnt* Karth xii 53[3] (for the reading, cf. Février & Fantar Karth xii a.l.; for this uncert. interpret., cf. Krahmalkov RSF iii 178f., 185, 203) - **Hebr** Qal Impf. 3 p.pl.m. *yʿnw* KAI 200[10,11] (cf. e.g. Gibson SSI i p. 29f., Pardee Maarav i 49 :: Michaud VT x 454: l. *yʾnw* = Qal Impf. 3 p.pl.m. of *ʾny₁* (= to be grieved about), or l. *yzmw* = Qal Impf. 3 p.pl.m. of *zmm* (= to plot against); v. infra) - **DA** Qal Impf. 3 p.s.m. *yʿnh* i 10 (cf. e.g. Hoftijzer DA a.l., Caquot & Lemaire Syr liv 198f., McCarter BASOR ccxxxix 51, 54f., Hackett BTDA 29, 47, 98, 133, Puech FS Grelot 28 :: Garbini Hen i 177f., 185: = Sing. abs. of *yʿnh* (= ostrich), cf. also Delcor SVT xxxii 56f., H. & M. Weippert ZDPV xclviii 95, 103, Lemaire BAT 318, CRAI '85, 280 :: H.P. Müll ZAW xciv 218, 225f.: = Qal Impf. 3 p.s.m. of *ʿny₂* (= to lower oneself, to be miserable)) - **OldAr** Qal Impf. 3 p.s.m. + suff. 1 p.s. *yʿnny* KAI 202A 11 - **OffAr** Qal Pf. 3 p.s.m. *ʿnh* Cowl 71[11], Aḥiq 110, 118, AE '23, 41 no. 8[7]; 1 p.s. *ʿnyt* Aḥiq 14, 45; 3 p.pl.m. *ʿnw* Aḥiq 121; Impf. 3 p.s.m. *yʿny* Cowl 71[32] (dam. context); cf. Paik 768 (*ʿnʿy*; ?), GIPP 49 - **Palm** Qal Pf. 3 p.s.m. *ʿnh* CIS ii 4022[3] (for this interpret., cf. also PNO 73 :: Cantineau Gramm 74: = Qal Pf. 3 p.s.m. + suff. 3 p.s.m.; cf. also Rosenthal Sprache 21f.), *ʿnʾ* RIP 121[4], *ʿn* Inv xi 1[7] (v. infra);

+ suff. 3 p.s.m. *ʿ[ny]hy* CIS ii 4046[7], *ʿnyh* CIS ii 4011[5], 4034[5], 4051[6], PNO 72[6], Inv xi 16[5], 19[5], 26[3], RIP 120[5], *ʿny* CIS ii 4038[4], 4092[3], RIP 114[5], *ʿnh* CIS ii 4074 (cf. Cantineau Gramm 74, Rosenthal Sprache 71; or rather is QAL Pf. 3 p.s.m.?, cf. *ʿnh* in CIS ii 4022[3] and *ʿnʾ* in RIP 121[4]), *ʿynh* Inv xi 11[8] (prob. lapsus for *ʿnyh*, cf. Teixidor Inv xi a.l. :: Milik DFD 104, Aggoula Sem xxix 110f.: = Sing. + suff. 3 p.s.m. of *ʿyn$_2$*); + suff. 3 p.s.f. *ʿnh* CIS ii 4020A 3(*ʿ[n]h*), 4067[3], 4083[4]; + suff. 1 p.pl. *ʿnn* CIS ii 4048[6], RIP 119[8]; + suff. 3 p.pl. *ʿnnwn* CIS ii 4053[7], 4100[4], Inv xi 1[6] (v. infra), *[ʿn]nn* CIS ii 4085[6] (?); Impf. 3 p.s.m. + suff. 3 p.s.f. *yʿnnh* Ber iii 99[4] - **JAr** QAL Part. act. s.m. abs. *ʿn[h]* MPAT 49 ii 2 (diff. reading, heavily dam. context, cf. also Milik sub DJD ii 72) - ¶ verb QAL - **1)** to answer: Cowl 71[11,32], Aḥiq 14, 45, 110, 118, 121; cf. *ʿnyt wʾmrt* Aḥiq 45: I answered and said (cf. Aḥiq 110, 118, 121, AE '23, 41 no. 8[7]) - **2)** to grant, to answer someone's prayer: RIP 121[4], CIS ii 4022[3]; + obj.: KAI 202A 11 (cf. also Greenfield Proc v CJS i 181ff., Ross HThR lxiii 3f.), CIS ii 4011[5], 4020A 3, 4034[5], 4038[4], Inv xi 16[5], 19[5], etc.; cf. also *ʿnnwn ʿnlhwn* Inv xi 1[6f]: he heard their prayer, (yes) he did (or lapsus?); + obj. + *b$_2$*, *ʿnnwn brwḥʾ* CIS ii 4100[4f]: he answered them by (giving them) relief (cf. RIP 119[8]) - **3)** to testify; *kl ʾḥy yʿnw ly* KAI 200[10]: all my colleagues will testify on my behalf (cf. KAI 200[11]) - **4)** to resound; *q[l] rḥ[m]n yʿnh* DA i 10: the voice of the vultures will resound (cf. Hoftijzer DA p. 201f., 299 :: Caquot & Lemaire Syr liv 199, Smelik HDAI 79: he will answer (the contumely of the eagle and) the voice of the vultures, or *ʿny* here = to chant; cf. also Weinfeld Shn v/vi 145) - Kottsieper SAS 23, 225: the *ʿnt* in Aḥiq 210: = QAL Pf. 3 p.s.f. of *ʿny$_1$* (poss. interpret.; diff. and dam. context; cf. also Puech RB xcv 591) - Milik DFD 294: l. *ʿnyh* (= QAL Pf. 3 p.s.m. + suff. 3 p.s.m.) in Inv xi 35[4] (uncert. reading).
v. *bnh$_1$*, *ḥzy$_1$*, *lʿnh$_2$*, *ʿnh$_2$*.

ʿny$_2$ **Ph** PIʿEL Pf. 3 p.s.m. *ʿn* KAI 26A i 18 (cf. FR 267b also for litt.; interpret. as Inf. (abs.) less prob.); 3 p.pl.m. *ʿn* KAI 26A i 19 (× Garr DGSP 142: = QAL Inf. abs. :: FR 174: = PIʿEL Pf. 3 p.s.m.); 1 p.s. + suff. 3 p.pl.m. *ʿntnm* KAI 26A i 20 - **Mo** PIʿEL Impf. 3 p.s.m. *yʿnw* KAI 181[5]; 1 p.s. *ʾʿnw* KAI 181[6] (:: Dahood FS Horn 431f.: both forms + *waw emphaticum*; on the Moab. forms, cf. Garr DGSP 143, Jackson & Dearman SMIM 106 (n. 53)) - **JAr** PAʿEL Part. pass. s.m. emph. *mʿnyh* MPAT 68[3] - ¶ verb PIʿEL/PAʿEL to oppress, to subdue; *wʿn ʾnk ʾrṣt ʿzt ... ʾš bl ʿn kl hmlkm ʾš kn lpny wʾnk ʾztwd ʿntnm* KAI 26A i 18ff.: I subdued (i.e. conquered) strong lands ... which none of the kings who were before me had been able to subdue, but I A. subdued them (:: Swiggers BiOr xxxvii 339: the pron. suff. in *ʿntnm* poss. also referring to *ʾšm rʿm* in l. 15); *wyʿnw ʾt mʾb ymm rbm* KAI 181[5]: and

he had oppressed Moab during a long time (cf. KAI 181[6]) - Part. pass. oppressed: MPAT 68[3].
v. *ʿnh$_2$*, *ʿny$_1$*.

ʿny$_3$ **Hebr** Plur. abs. *ʿnyʾyn* DJD ii 46[5] - ¶ subst. poor one - the diff. *ʿnyʾ* in CIS ii 964[3] (Nab.) poss. = Plur. cstr. of *ʿny$_3$*, *ʿnyʾ ʾrʿʾ* = the poor ones of the land (cf. Clermont-Ganneau with Berger Revue Critique xxvi 492f., RAO iv 187ff., Díez Merino LA xix 278 (cf. also Cantineau Nab i 93) :: Chabot sub RES 2019: prob. = tribal name :: Lagrange RB xi 138: = lapsus for *ʿynʾ* (Plur. cstr. of *ʿyn$_2$* (= source)) :: Lidzbarski Eph i 339: l. *ʿdyyʾ*? = the strangers, foreigners (= Plur. emph. of *ʿdyy*) :: Euting SinInschr. sub 463: l. *ʿ[rb]yʾ* = Plur. emph. of *ʿrby* (= Arab)? - cf. *ʿnh$_2$*.
v. *ʿbd$_1$*, *ʿnyh*.

ʿnyd v. *ʾs$_2$*.

ʿnyh **DA** Sing. abs. *ʿnyh* i 13 (cf. Hoftijzer DA a.l., Rofé SB 67 (n. 33), H.P.Müller ZAW xciv 218, 228, Malamat FS Cross 41,50 n. 21 (cf. also Weinfeld Shn v/vi 145) × e.g. Caquot & Lemaire Syr liv 200, Garbini Hen i 185, Delcor SVT xxxii 58, McCarter BASOR ccxxxix 51, 56, H. & M. Weippert ZDPV xcviii 98, 103, Hackett BTDA 29, 51f., 133, Sasson UF xvii 288, 302 (n. 42), Smelik HDAI 79: = f. Sing. abs. of *ʿny$_3$* (= the poor woman) :: Levine JAOS ci 197, 199: = oracle) - ¶ subst. female oracle priest (v. however supra; cf.also Weinfeld Shn v/vi 145: the answering woman (with an elegy, in the context of burial rites)); on this word, cf. also Ringgren Mem Seeligmann 96.

ʿnyn v. *ʿynyn*.

ʿnn$_1$ v. *ʿyn$_2$*.

ʿnn$_2$ v. *byn$_1$*.

ʿnn$_3$ v. *ʿnwn*.

ʿnq > Akkad. *unqu* = neck, cf. v.Soden Or xxxvii 269, xlvi 196, AHW s.v. *unqu* II.

ʿnš$_1$ **Pun** Qal Pf. 3 p.pl. *ʿnš* RCL '66, 201[7]; Niph Pf. 3 p.s.m. *nʿnš* KAI 69[20] - **Palm** Aph Pf. 1 p.s. *ʾʿnšt* Syr xvii 271[3] (uncert. interpret., heavily dam. context; cf. Cantineau Syr xvii 273, Gawlikowski Syr li 98; cf. however Milik DFD 291f., 296 (div. otherwise): = Ph. forms in Palm. script, l. *ʾʿnš* (= Qal/Yiph Impf. 1 p.s.) + *t$_1$* (= variant of *ʾyt$_3$*) ; against Milik, cf. Lipiński BiOr xxxiii 233) - ¶ verb Qal to exact a fine; *wʿnš hmḥšbm ... ʾyt hʾdm* RCL '66,201[7]: the quaestores will exact a fine of the man ... - Niph to be punished, to be fined: KAI 69[20] - Aph (v. however supra) to let (someone) be fined: Syr xvii 271[3].
v. *šty$_2$*.

ʿnš$_2$ **Pun** Plur. abs. *ʿnšm* KAI 130[2,5] - ¶ subst. fine; in KAI 130[2,5] poss.

> contribution (cf. also Levi Della Vida Lib ii 13, 15, Amadasi IPT 44); *dnʿryʾ šmnm ... lmbʿnšm* KAI 130[2]: eighty *denarii* ... according to the fines (or: contributions), cf. Levi Della Vida Lib ii 13, 15, FR 253; or rather = eighty *d.* ... from the fines (or: contributions)?, cf. Jongeling SV 413.
v. *ʿnwšw.*

ʿnš$_3$ Pun Sanmartín Ascaso FPI a.l.: the *ʿnš* in FPI 90 no. 1.1.3 = Sing. m. abs. of *ʿnš$_3$* (= humble) used adverbially (highly uncert. interpret.; = n.p.?).

ʿnšw v. *ʿnwšw.*

ʿntw JAr the diff. *ʿntw* in Syr xlv 101[14] unexplained; Milik Syr xlv a.l.: poss. = Sing. + suff. 3 p.s.m. of *ʿnh$_1$* (= time), highly uncert. interpret.

ʿs OffAr cf. Frah v 1 (*ʾs*) , Nisa-b 1704[1,2,4] (*ʿs*; v. infra) - ¶ subst. must, young wine; :: Diakonov & Livshitz Nisa-b p. 38, Sznycer Sem xii 125: in Nisa-b 1704[1,2,4] = abbrev. of *ʿsys.*

ʿsy v. *ʿšy.*

ʿsys OffAr Ebeling Frah a.l.: l. *ʾsys* (= must, young wine) in Frah v 4 (highly uncert. reading and interpret., cf.also Nyberg FP 43, 68: l. *hsyh* (= Iran. word)).
v. *ʿs.*

ʿsr$_1$ Hebr HITP Part. pl.m. abs. *mtʿsryn* SM 49[19,21,22], *mtʾsryn* SM 49[1] - ¶ verb HITP to subject to tithing.

ʿsr$_2$ v. *ʿtr$_2$.*

ʿsr$_3$ v. *ʿšr$_5$.*

ʿsrh v. *ʿšr$_5$.*

ʿsryn v. *ʿšr$_5$, ʿšrm.*

ʿsrm v. *ʿšrm.*

ʿst v. *mlk$_5$.*

ʿph$_1$ Ph Sing. cstr. *ʿpt* KAI 10[5] (for this reading, cf. e.g. Dunand BMB v 77f., Dupont-Sommer Sem iii 39, Röllig KAI a.l., Gibson SSI iii p. 94, 97 :: e.g. Cooke NSI p. 23 (< Egypt., = uraeus), CIS i sub 1 (= uraeus), Lidzbarski Handb 346 (without interpret.), sub KI 5 (: = skin, hide, v. *ʿrh$_1$*; cf. Slouschz TPI p. 12: = skins): l. rather *ʿrt* :: v.d.Branden BMB xiii 88: l. *ʿdt* = Sing. abs. of *ʿdt$_2$* (= ornament, decoration); cf. also Yeivin IEJ xxiv 18f., Dalley Irâq xlviii 92) - ¶ subst. poss. meaning: winged disk, cf. Dunand BMB v 77f., Dupont-Sommer Sem iii 39, Röllig KAI a.l., Gibson SSI iii p. 95, 97 (cf. also Ockinga WO xii 71, Butterweck TUAT ii 587).

ʿph$_2$ v. *ʿt$_1$.*

ʿpy_1 **OffAr** QAL Impf. 1 p.s. *ʾʿph* Aḥiq 140 (:: Lindenberger APA 136, 139 (cf. also ibid. 261 nn. 437-438, 279): = lapsus for *ʾpʿh* = QAL Impf. 3 p.s.m. of *pʿy* (= to protest, to complain)) - ¶ verb QAL poss. meaning, to strive, to do one's utmost, cf. Strack ZDMG lxv 833, Cowl a.l., Grelot DAE p. 442 (cf. also Grelot RB lxviii 189: cf. the roots *yʿp* and *ʿyp* both = to do one's utmost; cf. Kottsieper SAS 16, 225: to be successful) :: Seidel ZAW xxxii 296: = to stay unharmed.

ʿpy_2 v. *ʿg*.

ʿpl **Mo** Sing. abs. *ʿpl* KAI 181[22] - ¶ subst. (height, hillock >) acropolis.

ʿps v. *ʿpṣ*.

ʿpṣ **Pun** QAL Pf. 3 p.s.f. *ʿpṣʾ* (or l. *ʿpsʾ*?) RES 303[1] (for the reading and division of words, cf. Clermont-Ganneau RAO v 105f. :: Slouschz sub TPI 240 (div. otherwise): l. *bʿrk* (= Sing. abs. of *brkh*$_1$) + *pṣʾ* (= QAL Pf. 3 p.s.m. of *pṣy* (= to open, sc. the mouth)), cf. also Berger sub RES 303) - ¶ verb QAL uncert. meaning; Clermont-Ganneau RAO v 107: poss. = to take pleasure in // *ḥpṣ*$_2$; *ʿpṣ/sʾ ʾt ndr* = she fulfilled her vow with pleasure.

ʿpr_1 **OldCan** Sing. abs. *a-pa-ru* EA 141[4], 364[8], *ḫa-pa-ru* EA 143[11] - **Hebr** Sing. abs. *ʿpr* DJD ii 24A 8, B 7, C 7, 9, D 11, E 6, 8, F 6, 9 - **OffAr** Plur. cstr. *ʿpry* Del 99 (reading of *yod* highly uncert., cf. also Lidzbarski Eph ii 202f.); cf. Frah ii 3 (*ʾplyʾ*, *ʾplʾ*) - ¶ subst. - **1)** dust; Plur. (v. however supra) ruins - **2)** plot, terrain: DJD ii 24 passim - on this word, cf. also Rainey TeAv i 77ff. - Vattioni Aug xvi 543: the *apero* in IRT 877[5f] poss. = Sing. + suff. 3 p.s. (highly uncert. interpret.).
v. *bny*$_1$.

ʿpr_2 **Hatra** the *ʿprʾ* (in *dʿprʾ*) Hatra 202[1] poss. = subst. Sing. emph. Safar Sumer xviii 62 (n. 72): poss. = sweeper (cf. also Milik DFD 387: = indication of function).

ʿpr_3 **OffAr** Plur. abs. *ʿprn* ATNS 99[2] - ¶ subst. young stag/gazelle, roe; *mšky ʿprn* ATNS 99[2]: hides of young stags (v. supra).

ʿprh **Pun** Sing. abs. *ʿprt* KAI 89[6] (= CIS i 6068) - ¶ subst. plumb.

ʿṣ **Pun** Sing. abs. *ʿṣ* CIS i 346[3] - **Hebr** Sing. abs. *ʿṣ* DJD ii 30[18] - **OffAr** Sing. abs. *ʿq* Cowl 20[5], Krael 7[19], cf. Warka 2: *aḫ-ḫu*? (cf. Gordon AfO xii 107, 111 (n. 24) :: Dupont-Sommer RA xxxix 42: cf. Akkad. *aḫu* = hunting net); emph. *ʿqʾ* ATNS 14[2] (diff. reading, cf. also Garbini RSO lxi 212), Sem xxi 85 conv. 1; Plur. abs. *ʿqn* ATNS 41[5], Aḥiq 104, 125, *ʿqhn* Cowl 30[11], 31[10] (cf. Joüon MUSJ xviii 53f.; but not with f. ending, cf. Segal sub ATNS 40 :: Cowl p. 116: = lapsus), *ʿṣn* RES 1299B 3 (??, uncert. reading, dam. context); cstr. *ʿqy* Cowl 26[10,12,13,14,17,20], *ʿqhy* ATNS 40[4]; emph. *ʿqyʾ* Cowl 26[18] - **Nab** Sing. abs. *ʾʿ* IEJ xxix 112[9] (diff. context) - ¶ subst. m. - **1)** wood: Sem xxi 85 conv. 1 - a) Sing.

used as indication of material from which something is made; *mʾny ʿq* Cowl 20[5]: vessels of wood (cf. Krael 7[19]; for CIS i 346[3], v. also *ʿglh₁*) - **2)** piece of wood, plank; *lmh yšpṭwn ʿqn ʿm ʾšh* Aḥiq 104: why should pieces of wood strive with fire; for Aḥiq 125, v. *ṣlḥ₁*; in Cowl 26[10,12,13,14,17,18,20] indicating planks used in shipbuilding; *ʿqhn zy ʾrz* Cowl 31[10]: planks of cedarwood (cf. Cowl 30[11]); *ʿqhy ʾšh* ATNS 40[4]: pieces of fire-wood; cf. also RES 1299B 3?? - **3)** tree: DJD ii 30[18] (used in collective sense) - Garbini with Bisi AION xix 557: l. *ʿṣʿt* (= Plur. abs.) in AION xix 556[1] (highly uncert. interpret., cf. also Bisi a.l. (div. otherwise): l. *ʿṣʿ* = wood(en) or Bisi ibid. n. 8 (div. otherwise): l. *ʿṣʿr* (= variant of *ʿšr₅*; improb. interpret.)).

ʿṣʾl v. *ʾṣl₂*.

ʿṣb **OffAr** (Segal Maarav iv 72: = Palm.) Aimé-Giron BIFAO xxxviii a.l.: l. *ʿṣb* (Sing. abs. = idol) in BIFAO xxxviii 38[3] (uncert. interpret.) :: Segal Maarav iv 71 (div. otherwise): l. *ʾtšm* = ITP Pf. 3 p.s.m. of *šym₁*.

ʿṣd **Hebr** Sing. cstr. *ʿṣd* KAI 182[3] - ¶ subst. cutting; for the expression *ʿṣd pšt* KAI 182[3], v. *pšt₁*.

ʿṣh **DA** Sing. abs. *ʿṣh* ii 9 (cf. Hoftijzer DA a.l., Garbini Hen i 182f., 186 :: Caquot & Lemaire Syr liv 204: = QAL Inf. abs. of *ʿwṣ*) - **OffAr** Sing. abs. *ʿṭh* Aḥiq 57; emph. *ʿṭtʾ* Aḥiq 42, 57; + suff. 3 p.s.m. *ʿṭth* Aḥiq 28, 43, 55, 60; + suff. 1 p.s. *ʿṭty* Aḥiq 53 - ¶ subst. counsel - for the context of DA ii 9, cf. Weinfeld Shn v/vi 144.

ʿṣy **Hatra** QAL (v. infra) Impf. 3 p.s.m. *lʿṣʾ* 247[2] - ¶ verb QAL to remove, to erase?, cf. Safar Sumer xxiv 19 (n. 34; cf. also Aggoula MUSJ xlvii 17: to scrape), cf. however Degen JEOL xxiii 413: poss. = QAL (= to force, to compel, etc.) or = PAʿEL (= to refuse, to resist, to scrape up), cf. also idem NESE ii 101; + obj. (or + *l₅*, v. *lbyn*).

ʿṣm₁ **Ph** Plur. + suff. 1 p.s. *ʿṣmy* KAI 9A 5, MUSJ xlv 262[2] - **Pun** Plur. abs. *ʿṣmm* RES 906[1], 949[2], 950D 1f., 951, BAr '14, 345b 1 (*ʿṣ[mm]*; poss. interpret.); cstr. *ʿṣmʾ* RES 593[1] (= 892), 937[1]; + suff. 3 p.s.m. *ʿṣmty* CIS i 6000bis 7 (= TPC 84; v. *kbdh*); + suff. 3 p.s.f. *ʿṣmyʿ* Punica xiv 3[4f] (uncert. interpret., diff. context), *ʿṣmy* CIS i 6000bis 4 (= TPC 84; cf. e.g. Février BAr '51/52, 75, sub CIS i 6000bis, Ferron StudMagr i 78 :: e.g. Lidzbarski Eph i 165f.: + suff. 1 p.s.) - **Hebr** Sing. + suff. 3 p.s.f. *ʿṣmh* SM 49[2,14]; Plur. cstr. *ʿṣmt* Frey 1395[1] (reading uncert.) - ¶ subst. - **1)** bone; *byt hʿṣmt* Frey 1395[1] (v. supra): ossuary; for *mʿšn (š)ʿṣmm*, v. *mʿšn*; *[m]ḥsp šʿṣ[mm]* BAr '14, 345b 1: poss. = urn for the bones ... (v. *mḥsp*) - **2)** self; *rʾš my gyʾtw wgyʾtw ʿṣmh* SM 49[14]: the head of the brook of G. and G. itself; for SM 49[2], v. *ʾgd₁* - this word poss. also in DA viic 3 (heavily dam. context), cf. also Hoftijzer DA p. 260, 284.

ʿṣm$_2$ **Ph** Plur. f. abs. *ʿṣmt* KAI 14[19] (cf. e.g. Lipiński RSF ii 59 × Plur. abs. of *ʿṣmh* (= mighty deed)) - ¶ adj. mighty; f. substantivated: mighty/striking deed (for the context, v. also *mdh$_1$*).

ʿṣmh v. *ʿṣm$_2$*.

ʿṣʿ v. *ʿṣ*.

ʿṣʿr v. *ʿṣ*.

ʿṣr **OldCan** QAL Pf. pass. 3 p.s.m. *ḫa-ṣí-ri* EA 138[130] (prob. interpret., cf. Rec Dhorme 423) - ¶ QAL pass. to be retained - Lemaire & Vernus Or xlix a.l.: l. poss. *tʿṣr* in Or xlix 342 i 2, 3 (*t[ʿṣ]r*) = QAL Impf. 2 p.s.m. (= to close), highly uncert. reading, diff. interpret.
v. *mʿṣrh*.

ʿṣrt **Hebr** Sing. abs. *ʿṣrt* SM 49[3] - ¶ subst. gathering; in SM 49[3] indication of the Concluding Feast (of Sukkoth).

ʿq$_1$ v. *ʿṣ*.

ʿq$_2$ **Palm** Sing. emph. *ʿqʾ* CIS ii 4100[4], RIP 119[7] - ¶ subst. anguish, distress; *qrw lh bʿqʾ* RIP 119[7]: they invoked him (sc. the deity), when they found themselves in distress (cf. CIS ii 4100[3f]); cf. *qq$_1$*.

ʿqb$_1$ **Pun** Rocco AION xxiv 476, 478: l. *ʿqbm* (= QAL Imper. s.m. + suff. 3 p.pl.m. of *ʿqb$_1$* (= to pursue)) in GR ii 36 no. 20[3] (highly uncert. reading and interpret., cf. Polselli GR a.l.).
v. *ʿqb$_3$*.

ʿqb$_2$ **OffAr** Sing. abs. *ʿqb* KAI 233[11]; cf. Frah x 5 (*ʾkbyʾ*) - ¶ subst. heel; in the expression *mn ʿqb* KAI 233[11]: (poss. meaning) immediately (cf. Lidzbarski AUA p. 12, Dupont-Sommer Syr xxiv 42, cf. also Donner KAI a.l., Gibson SSI ii p. 105, 108 × R.A.Bowman UMS xx 277, 280: *ʿqb* = n.l. :: Lidzbarski ZA xxxi 200: *mn ʿqb* = because).

ʿqb$_3$ **Hatra** Sing. + suff. 3 p.s.m. *ʿqbh* 335[4] (v. infra) - ¶ subst. successor: Hatra 335[4] (?, dam. context), cf. e.g. Al-Salihi Sumer xxxi 188, Aggoula Sem xxvii 135, Syr lxiii 359, Vattioni IH a.l. (cf. also Degen NESE iii 111: = QAL Part. act. s.m. + suff. 3 p.s.m. of *ʿqb$_1$*) - Al-Najafi Sumer xxxix 184 (n. 12): l. *ʿqb* (= Sing. cstr.) in Hatra 360, cf. however Aggoula Syr lxiii 359: *ʿqb* = n.p. (prob. interpret.) - As-Salihi Sumer xlv 102f.: l. *ʿqbh* = Sing. + suff. 3 p.s.m., cf. however Aggoula Syr lxvii 411: l. *ʿqbʾ* = n.p. (prob. interpret.).

ʿqb$_4$ **Ph** Sing. abs. *ʿqb* KAI 37B 1 - ¶ subst. prob. meaning: reward (cf. Peckham Or xxxvii 306, 318 (n. 2), cf. also v.d.Branden BO viii 249, Amadasi sub Kition C 1; cf. Gibson SSI iii p. 127, 130: = audit) :: Cooke NSI p. 69 (cf. Röllig KAI a.l.): = continuation? :: Segert JSS xvii 138: = end? (cf. also Levi Della Vida RSO xxxix 302) :: Healy BASOR ccxvi 53, 56: = n.p.; on the subject cf. also Delcor UF xi 148f.

ʿqb$_5$ v.Soden Or xxxv 6, xlvi 184: > Akkad. *aqqabu* (= rest, remainder), highly uncert. interpret., cf. also v.Soden AHW s.v. and CAD sv.

‘qb_6 v.Soden Or xxxv 11, xlvi 188: > Akkad. *e/iqbu* = what succeeds, follows/rest, remainder (cf. also idem AHW s.vv.), highly uncert. interpret., cf. also CAD s.v. *eqbu, iqbû.*

‘qb_7 **Hatra** Pirenne GLECS vii 112ff.: the *‘qb’* in 3^2 = Sing. emph. of *‘*qb_7 (= end), *bt ‘qb’* = final/eternal resting-place (with positive undertones), cf. also v.d.Branden Mašr liv 223: *bt ‘qb’* = tomb. Improb. interpret., *‘qb’* = n.p., cf. e.g. Ingholt PSH 24, Caquot Syr xxxii 62f., Vattioni IH a.l.; cf. also the par. *[bt] ‘qyb’* in 200^{3f} (cf. e.g. Milik DFD 405f.).

‘qg v. *‘*qr_2.

‘qdh v. *‘qrh.*

‘qh **OldAr** Sing. abs. *‘qh* KAI 222A 33 - ¶ subst. magpie (cf. e.g. Dupont-Sommer Sf p. 48).

‘ql_1 v. *gqwl.*

‘ql_2 **Ph** Plur. abs. *‘qlm* BIFAO xxxviii 3^8 - ¶ subst. of unknown meaning, poss. = some fruit, vegetable or spice (cf. also Aimé-Giron BIFAO xxxviii 8).

‘qly **Palm** word of unknown meaning in the comb. *‘qly dy* (Inv x 44^5), poss. meaning: because?? (cf. however Cantineau Gramm 140, 146: = apart from?). The comparison with Arab. *caql-* (cf. Starcky sub Inv x 44) less prob.

‘qm **Ph** word of unknown meaning on amphora (Ber xxv 160), indicating its contents??, cf. however Bordreuil Ber xxv 160f.: prob. = nl.

‘qp **OffAr** QAL Impf. 3 p.s.m. *y‘qp* Cowl 11^8 - ¶ verb QAL prob. meaning: to be doubled, cf. Cowl p. 35, Lidzbarski Eph ii 226, Greenfield JAOS lxxxii 291 n. 14, Grelot DAE p. 80 (n. e), Porten Arch 78, Porten & Greenfield JEAS p. 108, Muffs p. 184f., Yaron RB lxxvii 415, Porten & Yardeni sub TADAE B 4.2; for the etymology, cf. also Barth RS xv 524, Stol BMS 24 n. 17, Lipiński Or lix 553f. (the remarks of Driver JRAS ’32, 77 less prob.). On the interpret. of the diff. context of Cowl 11^8, cf. Yaron Law 95; :: Clermont-Ganneau RAO vi 152: = to be included, to be accumulated :: Halévy RS xi 257f.: to be overcharged - on this root, cf. also Blau PC 47f. n. 8.

‘qr_1 **JAr** QAL Impf. 3 p.s.m. *y‘qwr* MPAT-A 22^7 (= SM 70^{15}); 2 p.pl.m. *t‘qrw* AMB 11^9 (*]t‘qrw*; ?); ITP Impf. 2 p.pl.m. *tt‘qrwn* AMB 11^4 - ¶ verb QAL to uproot; *wy‘qwr ytyh mn tḥwt šwmyh* MPAT-A 22^7: and may He uproot him from beneath the heavens; cf. also AMB 11^9 (v. however supra) - ITP to be uprooted, to be coerced to depart; + *mn*$_5$

(= from): AMB 11[4] - Patrich & Rubin RB xci 382, Patrich RB xcii 271f. (cf. also Patrich EI xviii 189): a form of this root (*ʾtʿqr* = ITP Pf. 3 p.s.m. (= to be removed, to be abducted)) in RB xci a.l. (diff. and uncert. context).

ʿqr₂ OldAr Sing. cstr. *ʿqr* KAI 222A 3, 15, B 2, 224[3]; + suff. 3 p.s.m. *ʿqrh* KAI 222A 25, 41, 223B 6, C 15, 224[25], *ʿqgh* (lapsus, cf. Puech RB lxxxix 584, Lemaire & Durand IAS 145 :: e.g. Dupont-Sommer Sf p. 27, Donner KAI a.l., Degen AAG p. 21, Gibson SSI ii p. 48: l. *ʿqrh*); + suff. 2 p.s.m. *ʿqrk* KAI 224[1,3,12,15]; + suff. 1 p.s. *ʿqry* KAI 222B 25, 32f. (*ʿqr[y]*), 224[1,3,11,12,16,21] (*[ʿ]qry*),[22] (*ʿqr[y]*),[26] - ¶ subst. root; in KAI 222-224 with spec meaning: descendance - this subst. (Sing. cstr. *ʿqr*) poss. also in CIS ii 4173[2], 4174[5], but its meaning in these contexts obscure (cf. also CIS ii sub 4172) - Dupont-Sommer JKF i 203: the *ʿqr* in AMB 7[9] = Sing. abs. of *ʿqr₂* (= root); improb. interpret., cf. Scholem JGM 186, Naveh & Shaked AMB p. 71, 74: = part of magical name).

ʿqrb OldAr Sing. abs. *ʿqrb* KAI 222A 31 - **OffAr** Sing. emph. *ʿqrbʾ* Aḥiq 85 - **JAr** Sing. abs. *ʿqrb* Frey 1162[8] (= SM 45), SM 70[4] - ¶ subst. scorpion: KAI 222A 31, Aḥiq 85; as a sign of the Zodiac: Frey 1162[8], SM 70[4].

ʿqrh Ph Plur. cstr. *ʿqrt* KAI 26A i 6 - ¶ subst. prob. meaning: granary, storehouse (cf. e.g. Dupont-Sommer RA xlii 170, Bossert Oriens i 184f., Röllig KAI a.l., Dahood Bibl xlvii 270, Bron RIPK 45f., Gibson SSI iii p. 47, 57; cf. Lipiński SV 48, 50 n. b: storage room; cf. also Marcus & Gelb JNES viii 118: = building :: Lipiński RSF ii 47, RTAT 258 (n. 64), Stud 80 n. 2, 98, OLZ '82, 458 (cf. also v.d.Branden BiOr xxxvi 203): = temple (< Akkad. *ekurru*) :: O'Callaghan Or xviii 185: = foundation :: Obermann Conn xxxviii 18: = land, country-side, *ʿqrt* being Sing. abs., the context being *ʿqrt* <*ʾ*>*p ʿr* = alike country and town (cf. however Pedersen ActOr xxi 50) :: v.d. Branden Meltô i 36f., 79: = Plur. abs. (= dry land) :: Alt WO i 280: or l. *ʿqdt* = Plur. cstr. of *ʿqdh* (= vault)).

ʿr₁ Ph Sing. abs. *ʿr* KAI 37A 7 (for this interpret., cf. e.g. Slouschz TPI p. 77, 372, Peckham Or xxxvii 306, 311 (n. 2), Healy BASOR ccxvi 53, 55, Amadasi sub Kition C 1, Masson & Sznycer RPC 27, 42f., Gibson SSI iii p. 125, 128 :: (Dérenbourg with) CIS i 86 (div. otherwise): l. *bʿr* poss. = QAL Part. act. s.m. abs. of *bʿr₂* (= to kindle; cf. Röllig KAI a.l.: = PIʿEL form of *bʿr₂* (= to keep up, sc. a fire), cf. also Slouschz TPI p. 78)); cstr. *ʿr* CIS i 113[1,2] (dam. context) - **Hebr** Sing. abs. *ʿr* Vatt sig. eb. 394 (= HBTJ 10), 402, *ʿyr* TA-H 24[17]; + loc. ending *ʿyrh* KAI 194[7], Lach xviii 2 (diff. reading, dam. context); Plur. abs. *ʿyyrwt* SM 49[9,10,11,26] - ¶ subst. town: TA-H 24[17], SM 49[10]; *hʿyyrwt hʾswrwt*

SM 49^9 (cf. SM 49^{11}): the forbidden towns; for *hʿyyrwt hmwrwt* SM 49^{26f}, v. *ntr₁*; the *ʿyrh* in KAI 194^7 (and Lach xviii 2??) indication of Jerusalem? (cf. e.g. Thomas PEQ '46, 88f., Conrad TUAT i 623); for *šr hʿr* Vatt sig. eb. 394, 402, v. *šr₂*; for the *ʿr* in KAI 37A 7 of diff. interpret., cf. Peckham Or xxxvii 311 (n. 2): = temple quarter (cf. also Amadasi sub Kition C 1, Masson & Sznycer RPC 27, 42f., Gibson SSI iii p. 128), Healy BASOR ccxvi 53, 55: = citadel (v. also supra) - on this word, cf. also Zimmermann SFAV 582ff., Dreyer FS v Selms 20ff.
v. *hr*, *ʿqrh*, *ʿrb₂*.

ʿr₂ v. *ʿrh₁*.

ʿr₃ **OldAr** Lemaire & Durand IAS 114, 135: l. prob. *ʿr* (= Sing. abs. of *ʿr₃* (= bearded vulture)) in KAI 222A 33.

ʿr₄ **Ph** Liverani RSF iii 39f.: the *ʿr* in Kition D 21^1 poss. = juniper (cf. also Amadasi sub Kition D 21) :: Coote BASOR ccxx 47f., 49 (div. otherwise): l. *ʿrz* (= QAL Imper. s.m. of *ʿrz* (= to prod)); the same word also in Kition D $21^{3,4}$ (cf. Amadasi sub Kition D 21 :: Coote BASOR ccxx 47f., 49 (div. otherwise): l. *ʿrz* (= QAL Imper. s.m. of *ʿrz* (= to prod))), v. also *mlš₁*.

ʿrb₁ **Pun** QAL Inf. cstr. *ʿrb* KAI 119^7 (cf. Levi Della Vida RCL '55, 561, Röllig KAI a.l. × Levi Della Vida RCL '55, 561, Février RA l. 188f.: = Sing. cstr. of *ʿrb₅*, cf. also Amadasi IPT 81) - **Nab** PAʿEL Pf. 2 p.s.m. *ʿrbt* MPAT 64 i 11 (for this reading, cf. Fitzmyer & Harrington MPAT a.l. :: Starcky RB lxi 164, 174: l. *ʿrpt* = variant of *ʿrbt*) - ¶ verb QAL to guarantee (for KAI 119^7, v. supra); Février JA ccxxxvii 89f.: l. *ʿrb* in KAI 153^5 (= QAL Inf. cstr. of *ʿrb₁* or rather = QAL Part. act. s.m. abs. of *ʿrb₁*??), highly uncert. reading and interpret., cf. also Röllig sub KAI 153: l. *ʿ--* - PAʿEL to take in guarantee: MPAT 64 i 11 - Naveh IEJ xxix 113, 116: the *ʿrb* in IEJ xxix 112^3 prob. = form of this root (guarantor); very diff. context - on this root, cf. Ben-Chayyim Lesh xliv 85ff.
v. *ʿrb₅*, *ʿšy*.

ʿrb₂ **Amm** the diff. *mʿrb* in BASOR cxciii 8^3 poss. = PIʿEL Part. s.m. of *ʿrb₂* (= to enter; cf. Puech & Rofé RB lxxx 534, 536 (n. 14), Fulco BASOR ccxxx 41f.; or = HIPH? (= to cause to enter), cf. Jackson ALIA 17, 26, Smelik HDAI 84) :: v.Selms BiOr xxxii 8: poss. = PUʿAL Part. s.m. of *ʿrb₂* (for a pass. interpret., cf. also Sivan UF xiv 231f., Aufrecht sub CAI 59) :: Horn BASOR cxciii 8, 10: poss. = Sing. of *mʿrb₁* (cf. also Shea PEQ '79, 18) :: Garbini AION xx 254, 256: = Sing. of *mʿrb₅* (= squared stone; cf. also v.Selms BiOr xxxii 8: poss. = concrete feature of the building or its surroundings) :: Shea PEQ '81, 105f.: *mʿrb* = *m₁₂* + Sing. abs. of *ʿrb₁₀* (= desert) :: Cross BASOR cxciii 17f.: l. *mʿr* (= HIPH Part. s.m. of *ʿwr₂* (= to incite)) + *b* (= *b₂*;

cf. R.Kutscher Qadm v 27f., Dion RB lxxxii 32 (n. 52), Sasson PEQ '79, 120f.; for this reading, cf. also Horn BASOR cxciii 10f. n. 20) :: Cross BASOR cxciii 18 n. 9: or *mʿr* = *mn*$_5$ + Sing. of *ʿr*$_1$ :: Albright BASOR cxcviii 38f.: l. *mʿrk[t]* = Plur. of *mʿrkh* (= battle position); cf. also Puech RB xcii 289.

ʿrb$_3$ Hebr/JAr a derivative of *ʿrb*$_3$ (= to mix): *mʿrb* poss. in Mas 550 :: Yadin & Naveh Mas a.l.: or = Sing. abs. of *mʿrb*$_1$?? (on the reading problems, cf. Yadin & Naveh ibid.).
v. *mʿrb*$_2$.

ʿrb$_4$ Ph QAL Part. act. pl.f. abs. *ʿrbt* IEJ xxxii 120 (v. infra) - ¶ verb QAL to bring, to offer; *qbʿm ʾnḥn ʿrbt lmrzḥ šmš* IEJ xxxii 120: we offer cups to the *mrzḥ* (v. s.v.) of Sh. (for this interpret., cf. Avigad & Greenfield IEJ xxxii 124f.; cf. however Amadasi Guzzo SEL iv 123f.: *ʿrbt* = Plur. abs. of *ʿrbh*$_3$ (= valued gift; cf. also Catastini FS Bresciani 112) or = QAL Part. act. f. pl. abs. of *ʿrb*$_4$ (= to please, to be valued); cf. also Lemaire SEL vi 100)

ʿrb$_5$ Ph Sing. abs. *ʿrb* KAI 60[6] (× = QAL Part. act. s.m. abs. of *ʿrb*$_1$, cf. e.g. Cooke NSI p. 99, Gibson SSI iii p. 151; or = form of *ʿrb*$_7$ (= guarantor? :: Donner FS Albright ii 80: = 'Zahlungspflichtiger') - **Hebr** Plur. abs. *ʿrbym* DJD ii 30[5,24] - **OffAr** Sing. abs. *ʿrb* Herm i 9 (cf. Bresciani & Kamil Herm a.l., Hayes & Hoftijzer VT xx 101f., Kutscher IOS i 110, Gibson SSI ii p. 130f., Hoftijzer SV 109 :: Porten & Greenfield ZAW lxxx 226, 228, JAOS lxxxix 153f., JEAS p. 152, Porten & Yardeni sub TADAE A 2.3: = guarantor (= *ʿrb*$_7$ or QAL Part. act. of *ʿrb*$_1$; cf. also Grelot DAE p. 152 (n. k), Segal sub ATNS 29) :: Milik Bibl xlviii 550 (n. 2), 581, 616: = Sing. abs. of *ʿrb*$_6$ (= gift :: Donner FS Albright ii 82: poss. = 'Pfandschuld')); emph. *ʿrbʾ* CIS ii 65[1] (= Del 101; :: Brockelmann OLZ '42, 370: l. *grbʾ* = Sing. emph. of *grb*$_2$ (= source)) - **Palm** Sing. emph. *ʿrbʾ* Ber v 133[4] (v. infra) - **JAr** Sing. abs. *ʿrb* MPAT 47 ii 10, 51[11]; emph. *ʿrbʾ* MPAT 48[4], *ʿrbh* MPAT 45[4]; Plur. abs. *ʿr[byn]* MPAT 41[12] - ¶ subst. security, pledge, surety; for the comb. of *ʾḥry*$_1$ + *ʿrb*$_5$, v. *ʾḥry*$_1$; *lknt gw ʿrb* KAI 60[5f]: to appoint the community as a surety (for the context, v. *ʿlt*); *ʿrbʾ zy qdm kyšwš* CIS ii 65[1f]: pledge which is before K. (i.e. given to K. as a security for rent which still has to be paid); *hn ʾt ʿrb ʿlyky* Herm i 9: if you have something which can serve as a pledge (cf. Hayes & Hoftijzer VT xx 101f., Gibson SSI ii p. 130f., Hoftijzer SV 109); *ʿrbʾ dy qdm mʿrtʾ* Ber v 133[4ff]: the pledge before the tomb (i.e. poss. a pledge which serves as a security for the preservation of the tomb; for the context, v. also *qdm*$_3$) - Vattioni Aug x 501, 531: l. poss. *[ʿ]rbʾ* = Sing. emph. of *ʿrb*$_5$ in CIS ii 35[2] (= Del 31) - > Copt. APHB, cf. e.g. Stricker ActOr xv 7.
v. *ʿrb*$_1$, *ʿšy*.

ʿ**rb**$_6$ v. *ʿrb*$_5$.

ʿ**rb**$_7$ **OffAr** the diff. *ʿrby*ʾ in ATNS 29 ii 6 poss. = Plur. emph. of *ʿrb*$_7$ (= guarantor, surety), cf. Segal ATNS a.l., Porten & Yardeni sub TADAE B 8.1 (:: Porten & Yardeni TADAE a.l.: or = Plur. emph. of *ʿrby* (= Arab)? (cf. Segal ATNS a.l.)).
v. *ʿwyr*, *ʿrb*$_5$.

ʿ**rb**$_8$ **Hebr** Sing. abs. *ʿrb* Lach xviii 1; cstr. *ʿrb* DJD ii 24B 14, C 12, D 14, E 9 - ¶ subst. - **1)** evening; *ʿd hʿrb* Lach xviii 1 : until the evening (dam. context; for this text, cf. also Gibson SSI i p. 48, Lemaire IH i 132) - **2)** eve: DJD ii 24B 14, C 12, D 14, E 9 (for the context, v. *sp*$_2$) - Driver JRAS '32, 89: the *ʿrb[* in Aḥiq 184: prob. = Sing. emph. (*ʿrb[ʾ]*) of *ʿrb*$_8$ (poss. interpret., heavily dam. context, cf. also Lindenberger APA 183, 272 n. 546 :: Kottsieper SAS 11, 18, 225: l. *ʿrb[t]* or *ʿrb[tʾ]* = Sing. cstr. or emph. of *ʿrbh*$_1$ (= willow) ?).

ʿ**rb**$_9$ v. *rʾrb*.

ʿ**rb**$_{10}$ v. *ʿrb*$_2$.

ʿ**rbh**$_1$ **JAr** Plur. abs. *ʿrbyn* MPAT 60[4] - ¶ subst. willow branch; *hdsyn* (v. *hds*) *wʿrbyn* MPAT 60[4]: myrtle and willow branches.
v. *ʿrb*$_8$.

ʿ**rbh**$_2$ **Pun** v.d.Branden RSF v 56, 60: l. *ʿrbt* in Karth xii 51[3] (= Sing. abs. (= desolation)), *ql ʿrbt* = the voice of desolation; highly uncert. interpret., cf. also Février & Fantar Karth xii 51: l. *qlʿrnt* without interpret.; Krahmalkov RSF iii 177f., 182, 203f.: l. *qlʿ* (= Sing. + suff. 3 p.s.m. of *ql*$_1$) + *rnt* (= Sing. abs. of *rnh* (= shout > proclamation)), improb. interpret.).

ʿ**rbh**$_3$ v. *ʿrb*$_4$.

ʿ**rbl** cf. Frah app. 21; Nyberg FP 100: the *ʿlplwn* in Frah app. 21 poss. = form of *ʿrbl* (= to sift, to riddle; cf. Ebeling Frah a.l.).

ʿ**rbn** **OffAr** Sing. abs. *ʿrbn* Cowl 10[9,13,17], 35[11] (for the reading, cf. Porten JNES xlviii 166, Porten & Yardeni sub TADAE B 4.6), 42[5], 68 x obv. 3; + suff. 1 p.s. *ʿrbny* Krael 11[10] (for this reading, cf. e.g. Ginsberg JNES xviii 148f., Yaron JNES xx 127, Grelot DAE p. 253, Porten & Greenfield JEAS p. 66, Porten & Yardeni sub TADAE B 3.13 :: Krael a.l. (div. otherwise): l. *bʿd* (= *bʿd*$_2$ (= over)) + *bny* (= Plur. + suff. 1 p.s. of *br*$_1$)) - ¶ subst. security, surety, pledge: passim; *ʿrbny* Krael 11[10]: my attachable property (that can serve as a pledge) - > Greek ἀρραβών > Lat. *arr(h)abo*, cf. also Cohen GLECS viii 13ff., Yoyotte GLECS viii 24, Masson RPAE 30f., Freedman JANES xix 26.
v. *grwb*.

ʿ**rg** **Palm** Aggoula Sem xxix 112: the *ʿrgʾ* in Inv xi 20[5] = Sing. emph. of *ʿrg* used as epithet (the lame, the limping), poss. interpret.

ʿrd$_1$ **OffAr** Sing. emph. *ʿrdʾ* Aḥiq 204 (for the reading of the last dam. sign, cf. Epstein ZAW xxxiii 233, Baneth OLZ '14, 353, Puech RB xcv 591 :: Cowl p. 219, Lindenberger APA 203: l. *ʿrdh* = Sing. emph.) - ¶ subst. wild ass - > Akkad. *ḫarādu*, cf. CAD s.v. *ḫarādu* A, v.Soden AHW s.v. *ḫarādu* II, Or xxxv 10, xlvi 187.
v. *ʿrd$_2$*.

ʿrd$_2$ **Palm** Plur. abs. *ʿrdyn* Syr xiv 179[2] (for this poss. reading, cf. Milik Syr xliv 295 n. 1) - ¶ subst. poss. indicating military engine (for discharging large stones), catapult; identical with *ʿrd$_1$*? (loan transl.?: cf. Greek ὄναγρος, Lat. *onager* both = wild ass and catapult).

ʿrh$_1$ **Pun** Sing. abs. *ʿrt* KAI 69[4,6,8,10], 74[3,5] (or = Plur. abs. of *ʿr$_2$* (= hide?)); plur cstr. *ʿrt* KAI 74[4] - ¶ subst. hide.
v. *ʿph*.

ʿrh$_2$ **OffAr** word of uncert. meaning in RES 1300[6], Lidzbarski Eph iii 24: = adj. Sing. m. cstr. (= naked, stripped) > lacking, devoid of, without (cf. also Grelot DAE p. 144).

ʿrwbh **OffAr** Sing. abs. *[ʿ]rwbh* Sach 76 i B 7 (for this prob. reading, cf. Porten Arch 277) - **JAr** Sing. cstr. *ʿrwbt* IEJ xl 135[1,6], 140[1] (on the reading in these instances, cf. Yardeni IEJ xl 137) - ¶ subst. sixth day of the week, Eve of the Sabbath; this word (Sing. abs. *ʿrwbh*) prob. also in unpubl. ostracon (Clermont-Ganneau no. 204), cf. Dupont-Sommer MAI xv/1, 69, 71 n. 1; *ʿrwbt šbtʾ* IEJ xl 135[1,6], 140[1]: the Eve of the Shabbat.

ʿrz v. *ʿr$_4$*.

ʿry$_1$ **Ph** PI ʿEL Impf. 3 p.s.m. *yʿr* KAI 14[21] - ¶ verb PI ʿEL to strip of; + *ʿlt, wʾl yʿr ʿlty* KAI 14[21]: let none strip me of what is on me.
v. *nʿr$_4$*.

ʿry$_2$ **OffAr** Sing. f. abs. *ʿryh* Aḥiq 118 - ¶ adj. cold; *hy ʿryh* Aḥiq 118: she (i.e. the goat) was cold (for this interpret., cf. already Grimme OLZ '11, 534, cf. also Lindenberger APA 108 :: Sach p. 167, Rosenthal AH i/2, 13, Kottsieper SAS 21, 225: = naked).

ʿryb v. *ʿwyr*.

ʿryh **Hebr** Sing. abs. *ʿryh* AMB 4[29] - **JAr** Sing. emph. *ʿryth* AMB 2[2,8,12], 3[22], *ʾwryth* AMB 9[1] (on this form, cf. Naveh & Shaked AMB a.l.) - ¶ subst. shiver; *ʾšth wʿryth* AMB 2[2]: the fever and the shiver (cf. AMB 2[8,12], 3[22], 9[1]; cf. also AMB 4[29]); on this word, cf. Naveh AAALT 85ff., Naveh & Shaked sub AMB 2[2].

ʿrk$_1$ **OffAr** QAL(?) Impf. 3 p.s.m. + suff. 3 p.s.f. *yʿrkh* RES 492B 2 - ¶ verb QAL(?) to prepare, to arrange, to evaluate; for the diff. context of RES 492B 2, cf. also Grelot DAE p. 140 n. o.

ʿrk$_2$ **Pun** Sing. + suff. 3 p.pl. *ʿrkʾm* KAI 119[5] (cf. Levi Della Vida

RCL '55, 552, 559 × Février RA l 187, Röllig KAI a.l. (div. otherwise): l. *ʿrkʾ* = Plur. cstr.; cf. also Amadasi IPT 79) - ¶ subst. evaluation: KAI 119[5] (obscure context).
v. *ʿrkh$_1$*.

ʿrk$_3$ v. *brk$_1$*.

ʿrkh$_1$ **Ph** Sing. abs. *ʿrkt* RES 367 i 2 (cf. Delavault & Lemaire RB lxxxiii 569ff., cf. however also Lidzbarski Eph i 285ff.: = fraud) - **Pun** Sing. abs. *ʿrkt* KAI 62[4] (or = Plur.?, cf. CIS i sub 132, Février RA xlii 83, cf. also Gianto Bibl lxviii 400: = Plur. abs. of *ʿrk$_2$*), 130[5] - ¶ subst. estimate, valuation :: Teixidor Syr lvi 383: in RES 367 i 2: = Treasury or other type of corporation?; *[n]ṣb mlk ʾš ndr wytn hʿrkt ʾš ʿbdʾ bn ʿbdʾs lʾdnnm ...* RES 367 i 1f. (v. however supra): a stela commemorating a *mlk*-sacrifice (v. *mlk$_5$*) which vowed and gave the men of A. ... to their lord (as their) personal contribution (cf. Gianto Bibl lxviii 399: the second *ʾš* = Plur. m. cstr. of *ʾš$_1$* (cf. also Teixidor Syr lvi 383) :: Delavault & Lemaire RB lxxxiii 575f.: the second *ʾš* to be taken as Sing. abs. of *ʾš$_1$*, sentence structure however abnormal :: Teixidor Syr lvi 383: *ʿrkt* = subject of *ytn*); *yšbm ʾrbʿ pʿlʾ bʿnšm ʿrkt ʾš ʿl hmḥzm* KAI 130[5]: they made four seats from the fines (v. also *ʿnš$_2$*) (according to) the account which (is deposited) with the *aediles* (cf. e.g. Levi Della Vida Lib iii 14f., Jongeling SV 413f. (n. e), Gianto Bibl lxviii 400 :: Delavault & Lemaire RB lxxxiii 577 (n. 30): *ʾš* = *ʾš$_1$* (Sing. abs.)); *bʿt r ʾdr ʿrkt ʾrš bn ...* KAI 62[4]: during the term of office (v. *r$_1$*) of the chief of the tax(es) assessments A. the son of ... (cf. CIS i sub 132, Février RA xlii 83f., cf. also Röllig KAI a.l., Amadasi ICO sub Malta 6, Bondi SCO xxvi 299: comparable to *censor* (cf. Delavault & Lemaire RB lxxxiii 576: = treasurer) :: Dahood Or xxxviii 159: = superintendant of buildings (*ʿrkt* = Plur. abs. of *ʿrkh$_2$* (= building)) :: Cooke NSI p. 105f.: *ʾdr ʿrkt* = noble worth ? (cf. also Slouschz TPI p. 129) :: Slouschz ibid.: *ʾdr* (= Sing. cstr. of *ʾdr$_5$* (= preparation)) + *ʿrkt* (= Plur. abs. of *ʿrkh$_1$* (= arrangement)); on this text, cf. also Levi Della Vida RSO xxxix 303).
v. *ʿrph*.

ʿrkh$_2$ v. *ʿrkh$_1$*, *ʿrkw*.

ʿrkh$_3$ v. *ʿlʿ*.

ʿrkw (or **ʿrkh**?) **Nab** Plur. (?) emph. *ʿrkwtʾ* CIS ii 350[2] - ¶ subst. exact meaning unknown, poss. = portico (cf. also Cooke NSI p. 241f.: prob. = rows (of pillars), arcade); Dahood Bibl l 355: = buildings (cf. Teixidor Syr xlviii 459) :: Milik RB lxvi 556, 558 (div. otherwise): l. *ʿd* (= *ʿd$_6$* (= *ʿwd$_5$*)) + *kwtʾ* (= Plur. emph. of *kwh* (= window, in the context poss. = entry) = and also the apertures).

ʿrs v. *ʿrš*.

ʿrsh v. *qryh*.

ʿrʿ v. *ʿrq₄*.

ʿrp v. *ʿrb₁*.

ʿrph **Ph** Sing. abs. *ʿrpt* KAI 10[6,12] (:: CIS i sub 1: l. *ʿrkt* = Sing. cstr. of *ʿrkh₁*); cstr. *ʿrpt* KAI 19[1] (= DD 4), 60[5] - **Pun** Sing. abs. *ʿrpt* KAI 129[2]; Plur. abs. *ʿrpʾt* KAI 122[2] (the same word *[ʿ]rpʾt* (reading uncert.) poss. also in KAI 118[1], cf. Levi Della Vida PBR xix 66, Röllig KAI a.l., cf. also Amadasi IPT 110: l. *ʿrpʾt* = Plur. abs.) - ¶ subst. f. portico (for KAI 122[2], cf. also Amadasi IPT 56f.) - Rocco AION xix 413f.: l. *ʿrpʾ* (= Sing. abs.) in GR i 49[1] (improb. reading, cf. Guzzo Amadasi GR a.l. (div. otherwise): l. *šdrpʾ* (= n.d.), cf. also idem GR ii p. 55).

ʿrpl v. *ʿrbl*.

ʿrpn **Palm** Sing. abs. *ʿ[r]pn* CIS ii 3913 ii 107 - ¶ subst. small coin; *hyk ʿdtʾ ʿ[r]pn yhʾ gbʾ* CIS ii 3913 ii 106f.: according to custom he must levy in small coin (Greek par. συνηθείαι ... πρὸς κέρμα πράξει), cf. also Teixidor Sem xxxiv 81f.

ʿrṣ₁ **Pun** Garbini AION xxv 262, 264: l. *ʿrṣ* (= form of root *ḥrṣ₁* (= to stabilize)) in Karth x 133[4] (highly uncert. reading (for this reading, cf. also Février Karth x 133f.: *ʿrṣ* = Sing. m. abs. of *ʿrṣ₂* (= violent, mighty > tyrannical master, oppressor > master), less prob. interpret.); cf. however Fantar Sem xxv 72f.: l. *ʿwʾ* = QAL Pf. 3 p.s.m. of *ḥwy₂*, highly uncert. reading).

ʿrṣ₂ v. *ʿrṣ₁*, *šʿbṣ*.

ʿrq₁ **OffAr** QAL Imper. s.f. *ʿrqy* Sem ii 31 conc. 2 (cf. Rosenthal AH i/2, 13, Milik RB xlviii 555, 616, Porten Arch 126, Grelot RB lxxiv 586, DAE p. 370 (n. d) :: Dupont-Sommer Sem ii 32f., MAI xv/1, 72 n. 4: = QAL (?) Imper. s.f. of *ʿrq₂* (= to attach, to bind)) - ¶ verb QAL to meet; *ʿrqy ʾlpʾ mḥr* Sem ii 31 conc. 2: meet the boat tomorrow (v. also *ʾlp₃* and v. supra).

ʿrq₂ v. *ʿrq₁*.

ʿrq₃ v. *qrq₁*.

ʿrq₄ **OffAr** Sing. + suff. 3 p.s.m. *ʿrqh* Beh 4 (*ʿrq[h]*, Akkad. par. of *lʿrqh*, *a-na tar-ṣi*), 10 (Akkad. par. idem), 31 (*ʿr[q]h*, Akkad. par. idem), *ʿrʿh* Cowl p. 269, 3[6] (= BIDG l. 9; Akkad. par. idem) - ¶ subst. meeting; *ʾzlw lʿrq[h]* Beh 4: they went against him (cf. Beh 10, 31) - cf. Greenfield FS Rundgren 152.

v. *qrq₁*.

ʿrr₁ **OffAr** PAʿEL Imper. s.f. *ʿrry* Cowl 8[27] (poss. reading :: Cowl a.l.: l. *ʿwry* = QAL Imper. s.f. (cf. also e.g. SC sub D, Leand 41 b, c, Muffs 182f. n. 6, 188 n.) :: Porten & Greenfield JEAS p. 10, Porten & Yardeni sub TADAE B 2.3: l. *‘[b]dy* = QAL Imper. s.f. of *‘bd₁*) - ¶ verb PA‘EL (v. supra) to incite, to stir up; *dyn ‘rry ‘mh* Cowl 8[27]: start a process with him.

‘rr₂ **OldAr** PU‘AL Impf. 3 p.pl.f. *y‘rrn* KAI 222A 41 (cf. Degen AAG p. 12 n. 57, 73, Huehnergard ZDMG cxxxvii 276 n. 37 :: e.g. Fitzmyer AIS 14, 57, 156, Donner KAI a.l., Gibson SSI ii p. 42: = QAL pass. Impf. 3 p.pl.f.; for this reading, cf. already Bauer AfO viii 10 :: Lipiński BiOr xxxiii 234: = PU‘AL Impf. 3 p.pl.f. of *‘wr₃* (= variant of *‘rr₂*) :: Dupont-Sommer Sf p. 18, 58f., 147: l. *y‘bdn* = QAL Impf. 3 p.pl.f. of *‘bd₁* (= to serve as a slave) :: Epstein Kedem i 42: l. *y‘ddn* = PAL Impf. 3 p.pl.f. of *‘dd₁* (= to weep)) - ¶ verb PU‘AL to be denudated, to be stripped. For the context of KAI 222A 40f., cf. also Hillers TC p. 58f.

‘rr₃ v. *‘dd₂*.

‘rr₄ > Akkad. *ḫarāra* = contestation, cf. CAD s.v., v.Soden AHW s.v., Or xxxv 10, xlvi 187, cf. however Greenfield RAI xxv 473.

‘rš **OffAr**, cf. Frah ii 13 (*’lšy’*), Paik 152 (*’lš’*), GIPP 15, SaSt 13 - **Palm** Sing. emph. *‘rš’* CIS ii 3912[2] (Greek par. κλίνη[ν]), *‘rs’* Ber ii 102 ii 4 - ¶ subst. couch; in CIS ii 3912[2] couch in temple of Ba‘al-Shemin; in Ber ii 102 ii 4 a couch in a grave (for this text, cf. also Ingholt MUSJ xlvi 182f.).

‘š₁ v. *mlk₅*, *‘šy*.

‘š₂ **Mo** Lipiński Or xl 340: the *‘š[* in KAI 181[33] = Sing. abs. of *‘š₂* (= moth). Highly uncert. interpret., heavily dam. context.

‘š₃ Hatra Aggoula Assur a.l.: l. *‘š’* (= Sing. emph. of *‘š₃* (= rush)) in Assur 21 ii 2 (highly uncert. interpret., diff. context).

‘š₄ v. *‘šy*, *š₁₀*.

‘šb **Palm** Plur. abs. *‘šb[y]’* CIS ii 3913 ii 123 - ¶ subst. herb.
v. *pḥd₂*.

‘šy **Mo** QAL Pf. 1 p.s. *‘šty* KAI 181[23,26], BASOR clxxii 7[3]; Impf. 1 p.s. *’‘š* KAI 181[3,9]; Imper. pl.m. *‘šw* KAI 181[24] - **Hebr** QAL Pf. 3 p.s.m. *‘šh* KAI 194[3], TA-H 21[3], SM 75[2], 80, Frey 974 (= SM 1), 978 (= SM 14); 1 p.s. *‘st[y]* DJD ii 43[6] (cf. e.g. Milik RB lx 277, 292 :: Yeivin At i 106: l. *‘syt[y]* = QAL Pf. 1 p.s. :: Sonne PAAJR xxiii 100: l. *‘st[m]* = QAL Pf. 2 p.pl.m.); 3 p.pl. *‘šw* SM 76[2]; Impf. 1 p.s. *’‘š[h]* DJD ii 7 iii 2 (heavily dam. context); 2 p.pl.m. *t‘šw* KAI 196[9,11] (*[t]‘šw*, cf. e.g. Ginsberg BASOR lxxi 27, Albright BASOR lxxiii 20, Röllig KAI a.l., Gibson SSI i p. 45f.; for the reading, cf. also Diringer Lach iii p. 334, cf. however Torczyner Lach i p. 117, Lemaire IH i 121); 1 p.pl. *n‘šh* KAI 197[8] (cf. e.g. Albright BASOR lxxxii 23, Diringer Lach iii p. 335, Michaud Syr xxxiv 53f., Röllig KAI a.l., Gibson SSI i p. 47, Lemaire

IH i 127 :: e.g. Torczyner Lach i p. 136: = NIPH Pf. 3 p.s.m.); Inf. cstr. *ʿšt* KAI 198[1], TA-H 1[8], *ʿšwt* DJD ii 30[23]; Part. act. s.m. abs. *ʿwsh* DJD ii 24B 11, C 10, D 10 (heavily dam. context) - ¶ verb QAL to make, to do, to act: passim - **1)** + obj., *šʿšh hpsypws hzh* SM 75[2f.]: who has made this mosaic (cf. Lach xiii 1, SM 80, Frey 974 (= SM 1), 978 (= SM 14)) - **2)** + obj. + *b$_2$*, *wʾnk ʿšty hmslt bʾrnn* KAI 181[26]: and I made the highway alongside (the river) A. (v. *b$_2$*), cf. KAI 181[23] - **3)** + obj. + *l$_5$* + *b$_2$*, *wʾʿš hbmt zʾt lkmš bqrḥh* KAI 181[3]: and I built this high place for K. in Q. - **4)** + *b$_2$* + obj., *wʾʿš bh hʾšwḥ* KAI 181[9]: and I built therein the water reservoir (v. *ʾšwḥ*); *lʿšwt bw kl š tḥpṣ* DJD ii 30[23]: to do there all you want (for this type of formula, cf. Hurvitz VT xxxii 259ff.) - **5)** + *l$_5$* + obj., *lʿšt lhm lḥm* TA-H 1[8f.]: to make for them bread (for the context, cf. also Aharoni TA a.l., Pardee UF x 296) - **6)** + *l$_5$* + obj. + *b$_2$*, *wʾmr lkl hʿm ʿšw lkm ʾš br bbyth* KAI 181[24f.]: and I said to all the people: each of you make for yourselves a cistern in his house - **7)** + *k$_1$*, *lmh tʿšw kzʾt* KAI 196[9f.]: why do you behave like this; *kkl ʾšr šlḥ ʾdny kn ʿšh ʿbdk* KAI 194[2f.]: in accordance with all the instructions that my lord has sent, so has your servant acted - **8)** + *l$_5$*, *ʾny ntn t kblym brglkm kmh šʿšt[y] lbn ʾplwl* DJD ii 43[6f.]: I will put fetters on your feet just as I did to B.A. - Février CB vi 23f., sub CIS i 5866: the *ʿš* in CIS i 5866[2]: = QAL Pf. 3 p.s.f. of *ʿšy* (improb. interpret.; interpret. as *ʿš$_4$* (= *š$_{10}$*) also less prob.; or *ʿš$_1$* = variant of *ʾš$_1$* (Sing. cstr.)??, v. also *mlk$_5$*) - Clermont-Ganneau RAO vi 387: l. QAL Part. act. pl.m. abs. *ʿšym* in RES 679[3]??, cf. however Février JA ccxxxvii 90f.: l. rather *ʿrbym* (= QAL Part. act. pl.m. abs. of *ʿrb$_1$* or = Plur. abs. of *ʿrb$_5$*)?? - the *lʿšt* in SANSS-Amm 36 = *l$_5$* + QAL Inf. cstr.??, cf. however Avigad IEJ xvi 248f.: = *l$_5$* + abbrev. of n.d. *ʿštrt*, Ph. text (less prob. interpret.).

ʿšyq **Pun** Levi Della Vida Or xxxiii 4, 9f., 13f. Amadasi IPT 134: the *ʿšyq* in Trip 51[3] = Sing. m. abs. (= suppressing > victorious, outdoing (sc. his competitors)); uncert. interpret.

ʿšyr **JAr** Milik Syr xlv 101: l. poss. *[ʿ]šyry[n]* in ibid. l. 13 = Plur. abs., meaning: tithes (heavily dam. context, diff. interpret.).

ʿšyry v. *ʿšry*.

ʿšk **OffAr** Sing. cstr. *ʿšk* ATNS 6[4] (uncert. reading, cf. Porten & Yardeni sub TADAE B 8.12), 48[2,3]; Plur. cstr. *ʿškt* ATNS 48[7] (dam. context) - ¶ subst. prob. meaning portion of land or property assigned by lot, estate, domain; Segal sub ATNS 6: poss. to be related to Akkad. *isqu* (cf. also Zadok WO xvi 174) :: Ullendorff JRAS '85, 69f.: or to be related to *ʿšq$_3$*?, or to *ʿšq$_4$* (= business, affair)? - a form of this word prob. also to be restored in ATNS 48[1] (*ʿš[]*).

ʿšn$_1$ **Hebr** QAL Part. pass. s.m. abs. *ʿšn* TeAv v 83 (cf. e.g. Demsky

TeAv vi 163, cf. also Ussishkin TeAv v 83f.: or *‘šn* = n.l.??; cf. also Greenfield with Ussishkin TeAv v 83f.: = m. Sing. abs. of *‘šn$_3$* (= adj. denoting some characteristic of wine)) - ¶ verb QAL to smoke; *yyn ‘šn* TeAv v 83: smoked wine (cf. however supra).
v. *m‘šn*.

‘šn$_2$ v.Soden with v.Weiher SbTU ii p. 120: > Akkad. *ḫuš(i)nu* = force.

‘šn$_3$ v. *‘šn$_1$*.

‘šq$_1$ **OldAr** QAL Impf. 2 p.s.m. + suff. 1 p.s. *t‘šqny* KAI 224[20] - **OffAr** QAL Impf. 2 p.s.m. *t‘šq* KAI 226[8] - ¶ verb QAL to do wrong: KAI 226[8]; + obj., *[’]l t‘šqny* KAI 224[20]: do not speak ill of me (for this interpret., cf. Gibson SSI ii p. 49, 55, cf. however e.g. Dupont-Sommer Sf p. 131, 148: to wrong someone, Fitzmyer AIS 101, 117, Lipiński Stud 57: to hinder (cf. also Degen AAG p. 68), Donner KAI a.l.: to intercede by force, Lemaire & Durand IAS 146: or = QAL Impf. 2 p.s.m. + suff. 1 p.s. of *‘šq$_2$* (= to dispute with, to quarrel with)) - a derivative of this root also in DA ii 18 (*]‘šq[*)?? (cf. Hoftijzer DA a.l.; heavily dam. context).

‘šq$_2$ v. *‘šq$_1$*.

‘šq$_3$ **OffAr** Sing. abs. *‘šq* Cowl 16[5,8,9] - ¶ subst. m. wrong; *k‘šq ‘byd ly* Cowl 16[8]: a wrong was done to me (cf. Cowl 16[5,9]).
v. *‘šk*, *‘št$_1$*.

‘šq$_4$ v. *‘šk*.

‘šr$_1$ **Hebr** PU‘AL Part. s.f. abs.(?) *m‘šrt* DJD ii 24B 17, *m‘srt* DJD ii 24C 16 (on the form, cf. Milik DJD ii p. 128) - ¶ verb PU‘AL to be tithed.
v. *‘nwšw*, *‘šr$_2$*.

‘šr$_2$ **Ph** Sing. cstr. *‘šr* Sar 1[1] (= IEJ xxxv 129A), TA 181 (= IEJ xxxv 129B), IEJ xxxv 129C (= GHPO 301A), D (= GHPO 301f. B), GHPO 302C (= Syr lxv 440 ii 6) - ¶ subst. tithe, cf. Greenfield IEJ xxxv 133 :: Bordreuil TA 181ff.: = PI‘EL Inf. cstr. of *‘šr$_1$* (= to tithe), cf. also Bordreuil GHPO 301 :: Teixidor Sar 98f.: poss. = Sing. cstr. of *‘šr$_5$* (= the (council of) ten).

‘šr$_3$ v. *‘šr$_5$*.

‘šr$_4$ **Hebr** Lemaire RB lxxxiv 599f., Miller SVT xxxii 315 (n. 9), 317, Zevit BASOR cclv 40, 43, Hadley VT xxxvii 51ff., O'Connor VT xxxvii 224, Margalit VT xxxix 373f., Conrad TUAT ii 557: l. *h‘šr* (= *h$_1$* + Sing. m. abs. of *‘šr$_4$* (= rich (one)) in HUCA xl/xli 159[1] (poss. reading and interpret.) :: Avigad with Dever HUCA xl/xli 160 n. 39, Cross ibid., Naveh BASOR ccxxxv 28, Mittmann ZDPV xcvii 141f., Angerstorfer BN xvii 9 (n. 13): l. *hšr* = *h$_1$* + Sing. abs. of *šr$_2$* (on this reading, cf. also Spronk BAAI 308 n.1; cf. further Mittmann ZDPV xcvii a.l.:

or rather *šr* = QAL Part. act. s.m. abs. of *šyr*$_1$, cf. also Cross a.l.) :: Garbini AION xxviii 191, 193: l. *hqšr* = HOPH Pf. 3 p.s.m. of *qšr*$_1$ (= to be connected; cf. also Catastini Hen vi 133) :: Dever HUCA xl/xli 159f.: l. *hqšb* = HIPH Imper. s.m. of *qšb*$_1$ (= to be careful) :: Shea VT xl 110f.: l. *ʾšr* (= *ʾšr*$_7$).

ʿšr$_5$ Ph m. *ʿsr* KAI 14[1]; f. *ʿšrt* Mus li 286[2] - **Pun** m. *ʿsr* KAI 101[1],111[2], 112[3], 120[1], 136[4], 137[5], 144[3], Hofra 64[3], Punica xii 18b 2, 29[3], xiv 5[2], xx 4[3] (*ʿs[r]* :: Chabot Punica a.l.: l. *ʿṣʿ[r]* or *ʿṣ[r]*), *ʿsʿr* Punica xii 32[3], *ʾsr* RES 336[4], Trip 51[2]; f. *ʿšrt* KAI 69[3], 80[1] - **Hebr** m. *ʿšr* TA-H 8[3,4], DJD 29[9], SM 106[13]; f. *ʿšrh* Frey 622[3] - **OldAr** m. *ʿšr* KAI 202A 5 - **OffAr** m. *ʿšr* CIS ii 1b; f. abs. *ʿšrh* Cowl 8[14], 20[15], 26[10,11,16,17], 28[11]; emph. (:: Degen GGA '79, 29: emph. = specialized form) *ʿšrtʾ* Cowl 6[15], 8[14,21], 9[15], Krael 3[16], 7[17], 8[8], *[ʿ]šrth* Krael 16G 2 (?, dam. context); cf. Frah xxix 10 (*ʾsl(y)ʾ*) - **Nab** m. *ʿšr* CIS ii 182[3], 199[9], 200[10], 201[4], 221[6], on coins, cf. Meshorer NC no. 30; f. *ʿšrh* J 22[4] (:: J a.l.: l. *ʿšr*) - **Palm** m. *ʿšr* CIS ii 3913 ii 70, *ʾʿšr* RTP 997 (??, highly uncert. interpret., cf. also Caquot RTP p. 147f.); f. abs. *ʿšrh* Sem xxxvi 89[6], *ʿšrʾ* Ber v 104[1]; emph. *ʿšrtʾ* CIS ii 3913 i 7, 10; cstr. *ʿšrt* Syr xvii 271[11,12] (poss. interpret., heavily dam. context, cf. Cantineau Syr xvii a.l., Gawlikowski Syr li 100 (cf. however Milik DFD 299: *ʿšrt* indication of the δεκάπρωτοι, highly uncert. interpret.)) - **Hatra** f. emph. *ʿšrtʾ* 207[3] (for the reading, cf. Aggoula Sem xxii 53, Vattioni IH a.l. (*ʿšrt* prob. = misprint repeated on p. 117)) - **JAr** m. abs. *ʿšrh* Mas 575[5], 583[4] (*[ʿ]šrh*); f. abs. *ʿšrh* MPAT 52[8], Syr xlv 101[2] (heavily dam. context); *ʿsrh* MPAT 51[1] (for this diff. reading, cf. Birnbaum PEQ '57, 121, 130, Puech RQ ix 214f., Beyer ATTM 520, 665 :: Milik RB lxi 183, Bibl xxxviii 264, Fitzmyer & Harrington MPAT a.l.: l. *ʿsry[n]* :: Abramson & Ginsberg BASOR cxxxvi 17: l. *ʿšry[n]*) - ¶ cardinal number, ten: passim; for a m. noun with a m. form of *ʿšr*$_5$, cf. prob. *ʿsr kkrʾ* (or: *kkrm*, v. *kkr*) Trip 51[2]: ten talents (cf. Levi Della Vida Or xxxiii 8, Amadasi IPT 133, FR 312b); cf. also the foll. chronological indications, *bšnt ʿsr wʾrbʿ* KAI 14[1]: in the fourteenth year; *bym ʿšrt wšlšt* Mus li 286[2]: on the thirteenth day; *bšt ʿsr* KAI 101[1]: in the tenth year (v. supra); *bʿsr wšbʿ lyrḥ* KAI 137[5]: on the seventeenth of the month; *bʿsr wʾḥd lmlkm* Hofra 64[3]: in the eleventh (year) of his reign; *hšlšh ʿšr lḥdš* TA-H 8[2f]: the thirteenth of the month (cf. TA-H 8[3f], cf. also DJD ii 29[9]); *šnt ʿšr wtlt lḥrtt* CIS ii 199[9]: the thirteenth year of Ch.; *bywm ʿšrh wšbʿh* J 22[4]: on the seventeenth day; cf. also - **1)** f. emph. in Cowl 6[15], 8[14,21], 9[15], Krael 3[16], 7[17], 8[8], 16G 2 (??): = ten shekels, coin of the worth of ten shekels (for the context, v. *rbʿ*); cf. also *ksp ʿšrt* KAI 69[3]: ten shekels silver - **2)** *ʿšrt hʾšm ʾš ʿl hmqdšm* KAI 80[1]: the *decemviri* who are over the sanctuaries (cf. the *decemviros sacrorum* in

Liv iii 10, etc., cf. (Dahood with) Vattioni AION xvii 158 (n. 12) - **3)** *ʾtḥzy lbwlʾ dy ʾrkwnyʾ ʾln wlʿšrtʾ* ... CIS ii 3913 i 7: it seemed good to the counsel of these archons and the Ten (cf. Greek par. δεδόχθαι τοὺς ἐνεστῶτας καὶ δεκαπρώτους; cf. CIS ii 3913 i 10), on this councel of ten (the chief municipal authority of the city), cf. also Vattioni AION xvii 159 (cf. also Teixidor AO i 238f. (n. 7), Sem xxxiv 63) - **4)** *ʿbnʾ ʾrdklʾ wḥbryhy bnʾ ʿšrtʾ* Hatra 207^{1ff}: A. the architect and his colleagues the members of the Ten (Aggoula Sem xxii 53ff.: *ʿšrtʾ* = team of ten fellow-workers without religious connotations) - for *ʿšr*$_5$, cf. also Blau Lesh xxxii 267f. - this word (*ʿšr*) poss. also in BiAr xlii 170^2 (or = form of *ʿšr*$_3$ (= riches), diff. and dam. context).
v. *ʿṣ*, *ʿšr*$_2$, *šrḥ*.

ʿšrh v. *ʿšr*$_5$.

ʿšry Hebr m. Sing. abs. *ʿšry* TA-H $7^{3,7f}$, *ʿšyry* Mas 588; f. abs. *ʿšrt* KAI 183^1, 184^{1f}, 186^1, 187^1, etc., etc. - ¶ ordinal number, tenth: passim; interpret. of TA-H $7^{3,7f}$ diff. (Aharoni TA a.l., Pardee UF x 305, v Dyke Parunak BASOR ccxxx 26: = indication of the 10th month).

ʿšryn v. *ʿšrm*.

ʿšrm Pun *ʿsrm* KAI 141^3, 158^3, Punica iv 7^{3f}, vi 2^4, xi 13^{1f} (:: Chabot Punica a.l.: l. *ʿšrm*), Hofra 59^3 (reading uncert.), *ʾsrm* KAI 135^4, 169^{3f}, *hsrm* KAI 148^2 (for this reading, cf. also Chabot sub Punica ivE 8 :: Lidzbarski Eph ii 65: l. *ḥṣrm*), cf. IRT 826^4: *esrim* (cf. Friedrich ZDMG cvii 297, Levi Della Vida OA ii 84, 91, FR 242, 243, Krahmalkov JSS xvii 72f., Vattioni Aug xvi 539), IRT 827^2: *ysrim* (cf. Levi Della Vida OA ii 85, 91, FR 242, Krahmalkov JSS xvii 72, Vattioni AION xvi 48, Aug xvi 539 :: Vattioni AION xvi 48: or = Sing. + suff. 3 p.s.m. of *ʾšr*$_4$) - **Hebr** *ʿšrym* IEJ vii 239^3, DJD ii $30^{8,21}$, *ʿšryn* DJD ii 24B 1, D 1, F 1, *[ʿ]sryn* EI xx 256^1 - **OffAr** *ʿšrn* Cowl 6^{14}, $26^{11,13,16}$, Krael 7^{32}, 11^7 - **Nab** *ʿšryn* CIS ii 183^3, 202^4, 223^5, 333^5, RES 471^3, J 38^9, MPAT 64 i 1 (*ʿšry[n]*), iii 3 (*[ʿ]šryn*), IEJ xiii 119^4, xxi 50^5 - **Palm** *ʿšryn* MUSJ xxxviii 106^1, Sem xxxvi 89^6, *ʿsryn* CIS ii 4172^2, RB xxxix 548^4, DM ii 43 ii 2 - **JAr** *ʿšryn* Mas 561^2, 576, MPAT 50e 1, 62^{13} (= DBKP 27), *ʿsryn* MPAT 39^4 (*ʿs[ry]n*, cf. however Beyer ATTM 307: l. prob. *ʿš[r]yn*; on the reading, cf. also Bennett Maarav iv 255) - ¶ cardinal number, twenty: passim; cf. e.g. *slʿym ʿšrym wštym* DJD ii 30^{21}: twenty-two *selac*; *ksp kršn 20 hw ʿšryn bʾbny mlkʾ* Cowl 6^{14f}: silver 20 *karš* (i.e. twenty) according to the royal weight; *ʾmn ʿšrn* Cowl 26^{13}: twenty cubits (cf. also Cowl 26^{16}, Krael 7^{32}); *byn ywmn 20 hw ʿšrn* Krael 11^7: within 20 days (i.e. twenty); *ʿwh šʿnt ʿsrm wʾd* KAI 158^{2f}: he lived twenty-one years (cf. KAI 135^{3f}, 169^{2ff}); *bt šʿnt hsrm wšbʿ* KAI 148^{2f}: aged twenty-seven years (cf. IEJ vii 239^{3f}); for *bal ysrim* in IRT 827^2, v. *bʿl*$_2$; cf. also the foll. chronological indications,

bšt ‘srm w’ḥt lmlkm KAI 141^{3f}: in the twenty-first year of his reign; *bšnt ‘šryn w’rb‘ lḥrtt* CIS ii 202^{3f}: in the twenty-fourth year of Ch.; *byrḥ ’lwl šnt ḥmš m’h w‘šryn wḥmš* MUSJ xxxviii 106^{1}: in the month E. (in) the year five hundred and twenty-five (cf. CIS ii 183^{2f}, 223^{5}, RES 471^{3}, J 38^{9}, IEJ xxi 50^{5}, MPAT 62^{13} (= DBKP 27)).
v. *‘šr*$_5$.

‘šrn v. *‘šrm.*

‘št$_1$ **OldAr** QAL Impf. 2 p.s.m. *t‘št* KAI 223B 5 - **OffAr** QAL Pf. 3 p.s.m. *‘št* Aḥiq 25; 1 p.s. *‘štt* Krael 5^{3}, 9^{2}; Part. act. s.m. abs. *‘št* Aḥiq 68 (*‘št[*; × Leand 32a: = QAL Pf. 2 p.s.m.; on the problem, cf. Hopkins BSOAS xl 142, Degen GGA ’79, 22f.; :: Segert AAG p. 114: = QAL Pf. 1 p.s.); ITP Pf. 3 p.pl.m. *’t‘štw* FX 136^{6} (v. infra); Impf. 3 p.s.m. *yt‘št* Driv F iii 13^{1}; Imper. s.m. *’t‘št* Cowl 30^{23}, Driv 8^{3}; Part. pl.m. abs. *mt‘štn* AE ’23, 42 no. 11^{2} (dam. context) - ¶ verb QAL to think, to consider; *‘bd lqbl zy ’nt ‘št[* Aḥiq 68: do according as you think (v. supra) - **1)** + *b*$_2$, *t‘št blbb[k]* KAI 223B 5: you will consider in your heart (cf. e.g. Fitzmyer AIS 81, 87, Donner KAI a.l., Lipiński Stud 54 :: Greenfield ActOr xxix 6, FS Fitzmyer 50: you will plot (against ...)) - **2)** + *l*$_5$, *‘štt lky bḥyy* Krael 5^{3}: I thought of you during my lifetime (cf. Muffs p. 25f., 134f., 185, Yaron RB lxxvii 415), cf. Krael 9^{2} - **3)** + *‘l*$_7$, *‘št ‘l[y b’yšt’]* Aḥiq 25: he thought wrong (i.e. he conspired) against me - ITP to think - **1)** + *l*$_5$, *’t‘št ly* Driv 8^{3}: bear me in mind (cf. Driv F iii 13^{1}) - **2)** + *l*$_5$ + Inf., *’t‘štw ... krp’ lm‘bd* FX 136^{6f}: they have planned ... to make an altar (??, v. *krp*; Greek par. ἔδοξε ... ἱδρύσασθαι βωμὸν; :: Garbini SMEA xviii 270: they have decided ... :: Teixidor Syr lii 288: they have decreed ...; cf. also Frei BiOr xxxviii 366f.) - **3)** + *‘l*$_7$ + *l*$_5$ + Inf., *’t‘št ‘l ’gwr’ zk lmbnh* Cowl 30^{23}: take thought of that temple to build it (:: Teixidor Syr lii 288: issue a decree ...; on the formula, cf. Dion RB lxxxix 551f.) - Porten EI xiv 169 (cf. also Porten & Greenfield JEAS p. 88): l. *‘š[t]* = QAL Imper. s.m. in Cowl 27^{19} (dam. context, cf. however Cowl a.l., Grelot DAE p. 404 (n. r): l. *‘š[q’]* = Sing. emph. of *‘šq*$_3$) - a form of this root prob. also in ATNS 7^{3} (*]‘št*).

‘št$_2$ v. *mlk*$_5$.

‘št$_3$ v. *‘št’*.

‘št’ **OffAr** Cowl 8^{5}, 9^{5}, Krael 4^{7}, 6^{4}, $9^{6,7}$, $12^{7,8,16}$ (on the interpret. and etymology of this word, cf. Kaufman AIA 60 (n. 139)) - ¶ word of uncert. meaning (= subst. Sing. emph.?) only in the comb. *b‘št’*; Nöldeke ZA xx 145 (n. 4): = measuring rod (cf. also SC 38, Cowl sub 8 and 9, Grelot DAE p. 178 (and elsewhere), Porten & Greenfield JEAS p. 9 (and elsewhere), Porten & Yardeni sub TADAE B 2.3 (and elsewhere)), cf. however Jampel MGWJ li 624, Peiser OLZ ’07, 625f.,

Krael p. 173, Cecchini Or l. 109 n. 21: = cardinal number one (less prob. interpret.).

‘štr **DA** e.g. Caquot & Lemaire Syr liv 201f., McCarter BASOR ccxxxix 52, 56, Hackett BTDA 41, 94, 133: the *‘štr* in i 16 = subst. Sing. abs. (= abundance (sc. of small cattle)), improb. interpret., cf. Hoftijzer DA p. 273f., TUAT ii 144f., Rofé SB 65f., H.P.Müller ZDPV xciv 64f. (n. 48), Garbini Hen i 181, 185, Hvidberg-Hansen TNT ii 153 n. 73, Delcor SVT xxxii 59, H. & M. Weippert ZDPV xcviii 100f., Smelik HDAI 82: = n.d., v. also *šgr*.

‘štrny v. *mtrḥ*.

‘t$_1$ **Ph** Sing. cstr. *‘t* KAI 26A iii 2, C iv 5; + suff. 1 p.s. *‘ty* KAI 14[3,12] - **Pun** Sing. abs. *‘t* Karth xii 52[3], (for this interpret., cf. Krahmalkov RSF iii 178, 184, 203; diff. context; :: Février & Fantar Karth xii 52, 57, v.d.Branden RSF v 57, 61 (div. otherwise): l. *b‘t* = Sing. cstr. of *b‘h* (= tax, contribution)); cstr. *‘t* KAI 62[4], 69[1], CIS i 170[1], 3919[4], Punica ivA 1[3], 5[2] (cf. e.g. Jongeling VO vi 249f. for both Punica texts :: Chabot Punica a.l. (div. otherwise): l. *‘tr* (without interpret.)), Karth xii 48[3], RCL ’66, 201[2],Trip 51[2] (cf. Levi Della Vida Or xxxiii 9; uncert. interpret.); cf. Poen 934: *byth* = b_2 + Sing. abs./cstr. of *‘t$_1$*, for the context, v. *ywm* - **Hebr** Sing. abs. *‘t* KAI 196[2] - ¶ subst. (in KAI 196[2] m!) time: passim; *b‘t qṣr* KAI 26A iii 2: in the time of the harvest (cf. KAI 26C iv 5); *bl ‘ty* KAI 14[3,12]: before my time; cf. also the foll. comb. *‘t r* (KAI 62[4], 69[1] (*‘t [r]*), CIS i 170[1], 3919[4], Punica ivA 1[3], 5[2], Karth xii 48[3], RCL ’66, 201[2]) prob. = in the time of ... (followed by abbrev. derived from derivative from root *rbb*; v. *r$_1$*); *h‘t hzh* KAI 196[2]: this moment, at this time (for the context, v. *r’y*, *šlm$_2$*) - Lipiński RTAT 265 (n. 87): *‘t’* in KAI 27[1] = form of *‘t$_1$*, *l‘t’* = for the right moment (improb. interpret., *‘t’* prob. = n.d. f. (cf. e.g. du Mesnil du Buisson FS Dussaud 424f., Dupont-Sommer RHR cxx 134f., 146ff., Zevit IEJ xxvii 111ff., Gibson SSI iii p. 83f.) :: Albright BASOR lxxvi 7 (n. 6): l. *‘pt’* = Ar. Qal Part. act. s.f. emph. of *‘wp$_1$* (= Flying One; cf. Gaster Or xi 44ff., JNES vi 186, cf. also Rosenthal ANET 658, Tsevat UF xi 762, Butterweck TUAT ii 436) :: Torczyner JNES vi 19, 28: l. *‘pt’* = Ar. Plur. emph. of *‘ph$_2$* (= gloom, darkness, *‘pt’* = female demons of darkness) :: Baldacci BiOr xl 127: l. *‘p’* = Qal Part. act. s.f. abs. of *‘wp$_1$* :: e.g. Röllig KAI a.l., de Moor JEOL xxvii 108: l. *‘t’* = lapsus for *‘pt’* = Ar. Qal Part. act. s.f. emph. of *‘wp$_1$* (cf. also Röllig NESE ii 19f., Avishur PIB 248f.) :: Cross & Saley BASOR cxcvii 44f., Sperling HUCA liii 3f.: *‘t’* = lapsus for *‘pt’* = Ar. Qal Part. act. pl.f. emph. of *‘wp$_1$* (cf. also Caquot FS Gaster 46f., Garbini OA xx 280, 283: l. *‘<p>t’* = Sing. or Plur.) :: Garbini OA xx 280: or *‘t’* = Sing./Plur. form with Ar. ending of root *‘wy/ ‘wt* (= either to bend, to twist or

to deceive, to overthrow)) - Levi Della Vida Or xxxiii 12: l. *[ʿ]t* in Trip 51^5 (uncert. interpret.).
v. *ḥyh₁*, *ywm*, *ʿt₂*.

ʿt₂ **Hebr** KAI 192^3, $194^{1,2}$, Lach viii 2, DJD ii 17A 2, TA-H 1^2, 2^1, 3^1, 5^{1f}, 7^{1f}, 8^1, 10^1, 11^2, 16^3, 17^1, 18^3, 21^3, 40^4 - **Amm** *ʿt* BASOR cclxiv $47^{2,4}$ (= CAI 144) - **Edom** *ʿt* TeAv xii 97^3 - ¶ adv. (originally form of *ʿt₁*) now, at this moment (for the orthography, cf. e.g. CF 52f., Freedman IEJ xix 52, v.Dyke Parunak BASOR ccxxx 26, Pardee UF x 292f.); *wʿt* (passim) used as introduction of the factual contexts of a letter following the destination and/or greeting formula (cf. Dion RB lxxxix 541, 546); introducing new subject: TeAv xii 97^3; for *ʿt kym*, v. *ywm* - in DJD ii 22,1-9^9: l. prob. *ʿt[h]* (heavily dam. context).

ʿtd₁ **OffAr** Pa ʿel Pf. 3 p.s.m. *ʿtyd* BSOAS xxvii 272 iv 2 (cf. Bivar & Shaked BSOAS xxvii a.l., Altheim & Stiehl AAW iii 70, Sznycer JA '65, 7 :: Teixidor Syr xliv 183: = Qal pass. Pf. 3 p.pl.m.); Imper. s.m. *ʿtd* Cowl 9^5 (v. infra) - **Nab** Pa ʿel Pf. 3 p.s.m. *ʿtyd* Syr xxxv 250b 1 (:: Milik Syr xxxv 250f., Teixidor Syr xliv 183: = Qal pass. Pf. 3 p.s.m.) - ¶ verb Pa ʿel to prepare, to arrange, to erect; *ṣlmyʾ ʾlh zy ʿtyd šptw* BSOAS xxvii 272 iv 1ff.: these are statues which Sh. prepared; *lšbʿ ... ʿtyd šnt ...* Syr xxxv 250b: belonging to Sh. ..., he arranged (it) in the year ... (poss. interpret.); *ʾrqʾ zk bny wʿtd bh myth wtb bgw* Cowl 9^{5f}: build on this plot and arrange in it ... and live thereon (for *ʿtd*, cf. Peiser OLZ '07, 626, Nöldeke ZA xx 146, Grelot DAE p. 182 (n. a) :: Cowl a.l.: = Imper. s.m. of root *ʿtd₂* (= to rear (cattle)?; against this solution, cf. Ribera i Florit AO v 147 (n. 6)) :: Krael p. 60 n. 25, Porten Arch 242 n. 14: = Pa ʿel Imper. s.m. of *ʿtr₁* (= to enrich); *bhmyth* prob. to be split up in *bh* (= *b₂*+ suff. 2 p.s.f.) + *myth* (= word of unknown meaning, Grelot DAE p. 182 (n. a): = subst. < Egypt. (Sing. + suff. 3 p.s.m.) = exit (highly uncert. interpret.); for this division of words, cf. Nöldeke ZA xx 146; cf. also Porten & Yardeni sub TADAE B 2.4: enrich it? or: prepare in it her house?) :: Peiser OLZ '07, 626: *bhmyth* = *b₂* + Plur. + suff. 3 p.s.m. of *hmyh* (= unattested word, poss. meaning: arrangement), cf. also Krael p. 60 n. 25: *hmyh* = neglected condition :: Milik RB lxi 249: l. *bhm yth* (= *yt* + suff. 3 p.s.m. (= of his)) :: e.g. Cowl a.l.: l. *bhmyth* = Sing./Plur. + suff. 3 p.s.m. of *bhmh* (= cattle)) - Harmatta ActAntHung vii 370: l. poss. *ʿtyd* in Cowl 81^{109} (= Qal Part. pass. s.m. abs.) = ready (uncert. reading, cf. Cowl a.l.: l. *(l)ʿtyk* (without interpret.)).
v. *ʿbd₁*.

ʿtd₂ v. *ʿtd₁*.

ʿth v. *ʿt₂*.

ʿtyd **JAr** Sing. m. abs. *ʿtyd* MPAT-A 30^2 (= SM 26) - ¶ adj. destined;

+ inf. used to indicate future tense: MPAT-A 30^2 (on this word, cf. also Ribera i Florit AO v 146ff.).

ʿtyq v. *ʿtq*.

ʿtyr **OffAr** Sing. m. emph. *ʿtyrʾ* Aḥiq 207 - ¶ adj. rich; in Aḥiq 207 subst. adj.: the rich one.

ʿtq **OffAr** Sing. m. abs. *ʿtq* Cowl 13^{12}, *ʿtyq* Cowl 8^{16}, *ʿṭyq* Krael 9^{22}, 10^{15}; emph. *ʿtyqʾ* Cowl 13^6, *ʿṭyqʾ* Krael 12^{31}; cf. Nisa 42^3, 190^4, 417^3, 418^3, 438^2, 442^3, 443^4, 445^2, 446^2, etc. (*ʿṭyq*), cf. also GIPP 49 - **Palm** Sing. m. emph. *ʿtyqʾ* Syr vii 129^4, JSS xxxiii 171^1; Plur. abs. *ʿtyqyn* CIS ii 3948^4; emph. *ʿtyqʾ* CIS ii 3958^3 (cf. however Dunant sub SBS 49: l. *[ʿ]tyqʾ*) - ¶ adj. old; said of a document: Cowl 13^6, Krael 12^{31}, cf. also *spr ḥdt wʿtyq* Cowl 8^{16} (cf. Cowl 13^{12}, Krael 9^{22}, 10^{15}): a new and an old document; poss. said of foundations in CIS ii 3958^3 (dam. context); said of wine and vinegar: Syr vii 129^4; cf. also *dnryn dy dhb ʿtyqyn* CIS ii 3948^{3f} (cf. Greek par. χρυσᾶ παλαιὰ δηνάρι[α]): old gold *denarii* (i.e. prob. *denarii* of old weight; cf. e.g. Cantineau sub Inv iii 28, Buttrey Ber xiv 117ff.) - for the alternation *t/ṭ*, cf. e.g. Altheim & Stiehl AAW ii 219f., Segert AAG p. 108.

ʿ$\mathbf{tr}_1$ v. *ktb*$_1$, *ʿtd*$_1$.

ʿ$\mathbf{tr}_2$ **OldAr** Sing. abs. *ʿsr* Tell F 2 (Akkad. par. *nuḫše*) - **OffAr** Sing. abs. *ʿtr* FuF xxxv 173^{12} (diff. context); Sing. (or rather Plur.?, cf. Leand 43t') + suff. 1 p.s. *ʿtry* Aḥiq 207 - ¶ subst. riches; for the context of Aḥiq 207, cf. also Lindenberger APA 207.

ʿ$\mathbf{tr}_3$ v. *ʿt*$_1$, *r*$_1$.

P

$\mathbf{p}_1$ **Samal** *p* KAI $214^{3,13,14,30,31}$, 215^{12} (cf. Ginsberg JAOS lxii 236 n. 36, Landsberger Samʾal 69 (n. 179), Koopmans 74, Dion p. 39, 172, 214, Gibson SSI ii p. 81, 84, Sader EAS 168 (n. 45): l. p_1 + *ḥy*$_2$ (v. *ḥy*$_2$) :: e.g. Cooke NSI p. 174, 178 (div. otherwise): l. *pḥy* = Plur. abs. of *pḥh* :: D.H.Müller WZKM vii 39, 47f., 126, 136, Dupont-Sommer AH i/2, 6 (div. otherwise): l. *pḥy* (= Plur. cstr. of *pḥh*) :: Donner KAI a.l. (div. otherwise): l. *pḥy* (= Plur. cstr. of *pḥ*$_1$ (variant of *pḥh*) :: Halévy RS i 231f., 241, 247, ii 58 (div. otherwise): l. *pḥy* (= Qal Pf. 3 p.s.m. of *pḥy* (= to be a governor)); cf. also Lidzbarski Handb 350), *pʾ* (Garbini HDS 29: = allomorph of p_1) KAI $214^{17,33}$, 215^{22} (cf. e.g. D.H.Müller WZKM vii 136, Lidzbarski Handb 349, Koopmans 36, Friedr 41*, Garb 264, Donner sub KAI 214^{17}, Friedrich FS Landsberger 428, Lambdin FS Albright ii 323 n. 14, Dion p. 61f., 173, Gibson SSI ii p. 62, Stefanovic COAI 169 :: Halévy RS i 153, 240f., ii 58: in 214^{17},

215^{22} = p'_3 (= variant of *ph*), RS i 164f.: in 214^{33} = Sing. cstr. of py_1 :: Sachau with v. Luschan AS i 78, 81: = Sing. cstr. of p'_2 (= possession)?? (cf. also Rosenthal JBL xcv 154: *p'* prob. related to Hebr. *pō* (= here); on the problem, cf. also Andersen & Freedman FS Fitzmyer 11)), *py* KAI 215^{11} (cf. e.g. Cooke NSI p. 177f., Ginsberg JAOS lxii 235 n. 32, Koopmans 74, Garb 264, Garbini Bibl xxxviii 422, Donner KAI a.l., Dupont-Sommer AH i/2, 6, Dion p. 110f.: = variant form of p_1? (cf. also Stefanovic COAI 169) × Lidzbarski Handb 443: l. *py'ḥz* (pro *py. 'ḥz*) = p_1 + QAL Impf. 3 p.s.m. of *'ḥz* (cf. Gibson SSI ii p. 84, cf. also Altheim & Stiehl AAW i 225 :: Sachau with v. Luschan AS i 75, 80, D.H.Müller WZKM vii 39, 136: = Sing. abs. of py_1? :: Halévy RS i 219, 231, ii 58: = lapsus for *ky*)) - **OldAr** *p* KAI 216^{18}, 223B 4, 6 - **OffAr** *p* MAI xiv/2, 66^6, JAOS liv $31^{3,4}$ - **Nab** (Brockelmann OLZ xxxvii 690, Altheim & Stiehl AAW i 191, Diem ZDMG cxxiii 228 n. 11, Segert AAG p. 357: < Arab., cf. also Diem Or xlix 73, cf. however Cantineau Nab i 103: poss. = Aramaic) *p* CIS ii $198^{7,10}$, 199^7, 202^3, $205^{5,9}$, $206^{6,7}$, 208^5, 209^7, 210^7, 211^4, 212^8, 213^3, $217^{7,11}$, 350^4, J 2^4, 5^9, $30^{4,5}$ (= CIS ii 200), 38^7, 246, BSOAS xv $10,19^2$, $15,44^2$, BASOR cclxiii 78^2 - **Palm** *p* RB xxxix 542^3 (reading uncert.) - ¶ conjunction (v. however infra) and: passim (on this conjunction, cf. Garbini Bibl xxxviii 419f., AION xxi 245ff., Degen AAG p. 63 n. 49, Dion p. 173f., 455 nn. 6-13, Levinson NAI 58f., Garr DGSP 114f., 157 n. 231); used to introduce the main clause after a preceding hypotactic clause, *mn dy l' y'bd kdy 'l' ktyb p'yty 'mh* ... CIS ii 198^7: anyone who shall not do according to what is written above, he shall be charged ... (cf. CIS ii 199^{8f}, 206^{6f}, 208^{5f}, 209^{7f}, 210^{6f}, 211^{3f}, 212^{7f}, $217^{6f.,10f}$, J 5^{8f}, 38^7); with the meaning "namely" in RB xxxix 542^3?? (v. however supra) - the *p'* in KAI 214^{33} prob. not used to introduce a new clause (cf. e.g. Cooke NSI p. 163, 171, Gibson SSI ii p. 69: = also).
v. $'p_2$, npq_1, $'m_4$, *pḥnt*, *plb*.

p_2 **Pun** Levi Della Vida OA ii 86 n. 44: the diff. *fo* in IRT 894^7 = name of letter *p* as numerical sign 80 (highly improb. interpret.).

p_3 **OffAr** obscure abbrev. in Cowl $63^{2,3,5}$.

p_4 **Ph** abbrev. in CIS i 87^2 (uncert. reading, cf. also Amadasi sub Kition C2: l. poss. *k*(= unknown abbrev.)), exact meaning unknown; prob. indicating some sort of coin (= p'_1?) :: Slouschz TPI p. 83: = small coin, *p(rwṭh)* :: Lane BASOR clxiv 21f.: = abbrev. of *pym*.

p_5 (= py_1) v. plk_1.

p_6 v. plg_3.

p_7 v. prs_2.

p_8 v. *pḥnt*.

p'_1 **Ph** Sing. abs. *p'* KAI 37A 16, B 10 - ¶ subst. indicating small coin/weight (cf. e.g. Amadasi Kition p. 108, Gibson SSI iii p. 126 ::

Lane BASOR clxiv 22: = abbrev. of *pym*); cf. Manfredi RSO lxi 83: = obol?

v. p_4, qp'_1.

p'₂ v. p_1.

p'₃ v. p_1.

p'₄ v. p_1.

p'dy (< Lat. *podium*, cf. Lat. par. *podi(um)*; cf. FR 107,4b, 208c) - **Pun** Sing. abs. *p'dy* KAI 126[10] - ¶ subst. elevated place, podium; *mzbḥ wp'dy p'l* KAI 126[10f]: he made an altar and a podium (cf. Lat. par. *podi(um) et aram ... f(acienda) c(uravit)*; on this word, cf. also Amadasi Guzzo StudMagr xi 34.

p'r **Hebr** PI'EL Part.s.m. abs. *mp'r* AMB 4[3] - **JAr** PA'EL Part. pass. s.m. emph. *m'rh* AMB 7[16] (lapsus for *mp'rh*, cf. Naveh & Shaked AMB a.l. (cf. also Scholem JGM 86, 90) :: Dupont-Sommer JKF i 203, 208: = m_{12} (= mn_5) + *'rh* (= Sing. emph. of $'r_1$ = light):: Beyer ATTM 372f.: l. *m'rh* trnsl.: the Lord (= Sing. emph. of *mr'* ?) - ¶ verb PI'EL to glorify, to adorn; *rmy'l mp'r yh* AMB 4[3]: R. glorifies Y. - PA'EL Part. pass. glorified, praised: AMB 7[16].

p'rt **Pun** Solá-Solé Sef xv 43f.: l. in ICO-Spa 1 *p'rt* (Sing. abs.) = the one who wears the crown (highly uncert. reading and interpret., cf. Guzzo Amadasi ICO-Spa a.l.: l. *b'rt* (= n.p.), Fuentes Estañol sub CIFE 04.02 (div. otherwise): l. *'dt* (= Sing. abs. of *'dt* (= f. form of $'dn_1$)).

pb'wn v. *pg'wn*.

pg **Hebr** the diff. *pg* in At ix-x 201[2] prob. to be interpreted as two abbreviations: *p* of plg_3, *g* of grb_1(cf. Naveh At ix-x a.l., cf. also Teixidor Syr l. 429).

pgdh v.Soden Or xxxvii 263, xlvi 192 (cf. idem AHW s.v.): > Akkad. *pugūdātu* = bridle (improb. interpret., cf. Greenfield & Shaked ZDMG cxxii 42f. n. 35, Kaufman AIA 79: Aramaic *pgdh* < Akkad., cf. already Jensen with Brockelmann LS 555b).

pg'₁ **Ph** PI'EL Impf. 3 p.s.m. *ypg['*] Kition D 21[1] (cf. Dupont-Sommer MAIBL xliv 281, Puech RSF iv 13, Liverani RSF ii 39, Amadasi sub Kition D 21 :: Coote BASOR ccxx 47: *ypg* (= QAL Impf. 3 p.s.m. of *pwg* (= to slump)) :: Teixidor Syr xlix 434: or = non-Semitic text?, v. also infra) - **Pun** PI'EL Pf. 3 p.s.m. *pg'* Punica xi 35 c 2 (:: Roschinski TUAT ii 619 = Sing. abs. of pg'_2 (= fulfilment)), *pyg'* Punica ix 9[2] (for this interpret., cf. Février JA cclv 61f., Garbini BO xx 111 :: Chabot Punica a.l.: = part of n.p.), xiv 7[1] (reading of *g* uncert.), MAIBL xvi 411[2] (cf. Garbini StudMagr x 9 :: Fantar MAIBL xvi a.l.: = n.p.; interpret. of context uncert.), *pg* Punica xi 38[3] (cf. e.g. Chabot Punica a.l., Garbini BO xx 110, or = 3 p.s.f.?, cf. Février JA '55, 60, cf. also Jongeling NINPI 149f.) - **OffAr** QAL Pf. 3 p.s.m. *pg'* Aḥiq 118 - ¶

verb QAL + *l*$_5$, to meet someone: Aḥiq 118 - PI‘EL meaning uncert.: to fulfill? (cf. also Garbini BO xx 113: = to sacrifice (factitive of to meet)), *wpg ’t nd‘rm* Punica xi 38[3]: and he fulfilled his vow (v. *ndr*$_2$, v. also supra), cf. Punica xiv 7[1], MAIBL xvi 411[2] (for this interpret., cf. Chabot sub Punica xi 35c; v. also *ṣd* for MAIBL xvi 411[2]); *pg‘ ’šrm h’š* Punica xi 35c: he offered a *’šrm h’š* (v. *mlk*$_5$), cf. however Dussaud CRAI ’46, 379 n. 3, Février JA cclv 61f.: = (to hit >) to sacrifice; the meaning ‘to offer’ probably also in Kition D 21[1] (cf. Liverani RSF iii 39, Amadasi sub Kition D 21 :: Dupont-Sommer MAIBL xliv 281: = to supplicate (cf. also Puech RSF iii 13)) - Garbini Malta ’65, 54: the *mpg‘* in ICO-Malta 31[4] = PI‘EL Part. s.m. (diff. and dam. context) - Garbini BO xx 112: the *pyg’* in Teb. 411[2] = PI‘EL Pf. 3 p.s.m.
v. *pwq*$_1$.

pg‘$_2$ **Hebr** Sing. abs. *pg‘* AMB 1[4], *pg* AMB 4[28] (lapsus) - **OffAr** Sing. + suff. 3 p.pl.m. *pg‘hm* Aḥiq 89 - ¶ subst. - **1)** meeting, contact: Aḥiq 89 (:: Kottsieper SAS 19, 226: = fate) - **2)** affliction: AMB 1[4], 4[28].
v. *pg‘*$_1$.

pg‘wn **Nab** Sing. abs. *pg‘wn* MPAT 64 i 10; emph. *pg‘wn’* MPAT 64 i 10, 11 (for the reading, cf. Fitzmyer & Harrington MPAT a.l. (cf. also Starcky RB lxi 164, 174: l. *pb‘wn* or *pg‘wn* :: J.J.Rabinowitz BASOR cxxxix 13: l. *pr‘wn(’)* in all instances (= payment)) - ¶ subst. m. meaning uncert. (diff. context), poss. = agreement (cf. Fitzmyer & Harrington MPAT a.l.); *w’qrb mh dy lk ‘my mn pg‘wn ḥqq wtḥšb bty bpg‘wn’* MPAT 64 i 10: and I will present what is due to you from my side as result of a detailed agreement and you will give an evaluation of my house in the agreement (cf. MPAT 64 i 11).

pgr$_1$ **DA** the *tpgr[* in DA v c 3 poss. = PA‘EL Impf. 3 p.s.m. of *pgr*$_1$ (= to be weak, to faint (cf. Hoftijzer DA a.l.), cf. however Puech FS Grelot 17, 24, 28: l. *mtpgr* = ITP Part. s.m. abs. (= exhausted).

pgr$_2$ **OldAr** Sing. abs. *pgr* KAI 222B 30, 223B 11; cstr. *pgr* KAI 222B 30, 223B 11 (?, in all instances diff. and dam. context; for the context, cf. also Lipiński Stud 54) - **OffAr** Sing. + suff. 3 p.s.m. *pgrh* Cowl 71[31] (reading uncert.; CIS ii sub 145D 7: l. *[yb]rkwn* = PA‘EL Impf. 3 p.pl.m. of *brk*$_1$), Aḥiq 63 - **Palm** Plur. abs. *pgryn* CIS ii 3913 ii 108 (Greek par. νεκριμαῖα) - **JAr** Sing. + suff. 3 p.s.f.. *pgrh* AMB 2[9] (or = Sing. emph.??) - ¶ subst. m. - **1)** body (of living person), *g‘wrw ’šth w‘ryth mn pgrh dy’yth* AMB 2[8f.]: drive out the fever and the shiver ... from the body of Y. - 2) mortal remains, dead body, carrion; said of human beings: KAI 222B 30, 223B 11, Cowl 71[31] (v. however supra), Aḥiq 63; said of animals: CIS ii 3913 ii 108 (cf. e.g. Cooke NSI p. 339) - Lemaire & Durand IAS 117, 127: l. poss. *[p]gry* (= Sing. + suff. 1 p.s.) at the beginning of KAI 223B 11 (poss. restoration).

pgr$_3$ v. *wgr*.

pgrh v. *gnh*$_1$.

pgš **Hebr** the diff. *pgš* in TA-H 37[2] (heavily dam. context) poss. = derivation of root *pgš* (= to meet).

pgt **OffAr** word of unknown meaning and uncert. reading in PF 1791.

pdḥš **Hatra** Caquot Syr xli 256f.: l. *ʿwd* (= n.p.) *pdḥšʾ* (= Sing. emph. of *pdḥš* (= variant of *bṭḥš*?))in Hatra 127 (for this reading and division of words, cf. also Abbadi PIH 42; cf. however Safar Sumer xviii 37 (div. otherwise): l. *ʿwdp dḥšʾ* (= n.p.) :: Vattioni IH a.l.: l. *ʿbd pdḥšʾ* (= n.p.), cf. *bṭḥš*, *pyṭḥš*.

pdy **OffAr** QAL Pf. 1 p.s. *pdt* Herm ii 5 (cf. Swiggers AION xli 146, Wesselius FS Lebram 11, Lipiński Or lvii 435, Hoftijzer SEL vi 117 :: Donner FS Albright ii 84: = QAL Pf. 3 p.s.f. :: Bresciani & Kamil Herm p. 385, 387, 426: = QAL Pf. 3 p.s.f. of *pry*$_1$ (= to bear fruit > to bear interest) :: Porten & Greenfield ZAW lxxx 222 (div. otherwise): l. *wprt*= subst. (Sing. abs.) of unknown meaning, poss. < Egypt. (cf. also Gibson SSI ii p. 134) :: Milik Bibl xlviii 551, 582 (div. otherwise): l. *wpdt*(< pers.?) = on interest (cf. also Grelot DAE p. 154 n. a: l. *wpd/rt* = on interest) :: Kutscher IOS i 119 (div. otherwise): l. *wprt*(< root *wpr*) = completely?; cf. also Porten & Yardeni sub TADAE A 2.2: as a *wpdt/wprt*) - ¶ verb QAL to ransom, to redeem; *wpdt lbntsr* Herm ii 5: and I have ransomed B. (cf. Wesselius FS Lebram 11, Hoftijzer SEL vi 117 :: Swiggers AION xli 146: and I paid for B.; cf. also Lipiński Or lvii 435).
v. *pdn*$_1$.

pdypt v. *prypt*.

pdn$_1$ **OffAr** (?) Sing. emph. *pd[nʾ]* AUSS xi 126[2] (diff. and dam. context; :: Garbini JSS xix 163f.: l. *pd[y]* = QAL Pf. 3 p.s.m. of *pdy* (= to pay) :: Shea AUSS xvi 217ff.: l. *pd[n]* = Sing. abs. of *pdn*$_2$ (= way, route)) - ¶ subst. plough (for the interpret., cf. Cross AUSS xi a.l.; on the language of the ostracon, cf. also Aufrecht sub CAI 76).
v. *pr*$_3$.

pdn$_2$ v. *pdn*$_1$.

ph **Pun**, cf. Poen 932: *pho* - **Hebr** *ph* KAI 191B 1 (reading uncert.), Frey 621[1], 622[1], 630b 1, 634[1] - ¶ adv. here - cf. also Garbini AION xxi 245ff.
v. *p*$_1$.

phn v. *khn*$_1$.

pwd **Ph** Albright JAOS lxvii 156 n. 30, Gibson SSI iii p. 117: the *ypd* in KAI 2[2] = QAL Pass Impf. 3 p.s.m. of *pwd* (= to suffer), *hn ypd lk* = behold you shall come to grief (cf. also Röllig KAI a.l.: *ypd* = QAL Impf. 3 p.s.m. of *pyd* (= intransitive verb, to come to grief; cf. also Baldacci BiOr xl 125)), cf. also Cecchini UF xiii 28: will cause grief :: Vincent RB xxxiv 189 n. 1 (div. otherwise): l. *hnypd* = HINPAʿAL Imper. s.m.

of *ypd*(= to take care) :: Dussaud Syr v 143 (div. otherwise): l. *hny bdlk* (*hny* = variant of *hnh* (= hn_3), *bdlk* = Sing. + suff. 2 p.s.m. of *bdl*(= loss)) :: Torrey JAOS xlv 278: l. *hn* (= Sing. abs. of hn_2(= power, strength))*ybd* (= QAL Impf. 3 p.s.m. of bdd_3 (= to fail) ?) *lk* ?

pwg v. *pg*ʿ$_1$.

pwl **Hebr** Sing. abs. *pwl* SM 49[2,20] - **OffAr** Sing. abs. *pwl* ASAE xlviii 112 conv. 5 - ¶ subst. bean (cf. Dupont-Sommer ASAE xlviii 116, cf. also Porten Arch 84, 277); in the comb. *pwl plḥ* ASAE xlviii 112 conv. 5f. (diff. reading): split beans (?; *plḥ* = QAL Part. pass. s.m. abs. of *plḥ*$_2$ (= to split), cf. Dupont-Sommer ibid.); *pwl hmṣry* SM 49[2,20]: the Egyptian bean (*colocasia*) - on this word, cf. Borowski AIAI 97f.
v. *pl.*

pwm v. pm_1.

pwn Nyberg MP ii 154f.: the ideogram *pwn* (cf. e.g. Gignoux GIPP 32f., cf. also BSOAS xxxiii 152[6,8,9]) poss. = *p* (= b_2) + ending *-wn* - this ideogram also Frah xxviii 15, 23, 31 - on this ideogram, cf. also Back SaSt 21, Lemosín AO ii 265f., cf. also GIPP 32f.

pws **Pun** Vattioni Aug xvi 546: the *pvs* in IRT 886s 11 poss. = Sing. abs. of *pws* (= tomb; < Sem. root? or < Lat. *fossa*?); improb. interpret., diff. context.

pwṣ v. *pṣy*, *pṣṣ*.

pwq$_1$ **Ph** YIPH Impf. 2 p.s.m. *tpq* KAI 13[3] (cf. e.g. Hoffmann Ueber einige phön. Inschr. 157f., Harr 136, FR 166 :: Röllig KAI iii p. 20: = QAL (cf. also Gibson SSI iii p. 103f.) :: e.g. Cooke NSI p. 28: or = YIPH Impf. 2 p.s.m. of *pwq*$_2$ (= to bring forth, to fetch out // Ar. *npq*) :: FR 152: = YIPH Impf. 2 p.s.m. of *npq*$_1$:: Lidzbarski Eph ii 136: = QAL Impf. 2 p.s.m. of *pqy* (= *pg*ʿ$_1$));1 p.s. ʾ*pq* KAI 50[3] (+ deprecative particle n_3, v. *n*ʾ; cf. Dupont-Sommer PEQ '49, 53, 55, FR 166 (cf. also Röllig KAI a.l., CISFP i 383, Pardee HAHL 167, cf. also v.d.Branden GP p. 98, BO xii 215,217) :: Krahmalkov BASOR ccxxiii 78: < root *ypq*$_2$ (= to send back, to return; cf. also Dietrich & Loretz UF xix 405 n. 4) :: Aimé-Giron ASAE xl 439, 443: = HIPH Pf. 3 p.s.m. + suff. 1 p.s.? of *pwq*$_1$) - ¶ verb YIPH to find, to obtain, to encounter; + obj.: KAI 13[3], 50[3].
v. *pqh.*

pwq$_2$ v. *pwq*$_1$.

pwrzyl v. *przl.*

pwš **Pun** Roschinski TUAT ii 619: the *ypš* in Punica xi 35 c 2 = YIPH Impf. 3 p.s.m. of *pwš* (= to complete), highly uncert. interpret.
v. *pšš.*

pwšnby v. *šbny.*

pwt v. *mpt.*

pzgrb v. *pšgrb.*

pzgryb v. *pšgrb*.
pḥ$_1$ v. *p$_1$*.
pḥ$_2$ **Ph** Puech Sem xxix 30: l. poss. *pḥ* (= Sing. abs.; = metal plate) in RES 1209B (uncert. interpret. and reading, cf. also Masson & Sznycer RCP 109).
pḥ$_3$ v. *pḥz$_2$*.
pḥʾ v. *pḥh*.
pḥd$_1$ v. *pḥz$_2$*, *pḥr$_1$*.
pḥd$_2$ **DA** Hoftijzer DA a.l.: l. *[p]ḥd* (= Sing. abs.) = fear in i 12 (poss. interpret.; cf. Sasson UF xvii 288, 300 (n. 37), cf. also H.P.Müller ZAW xciv 218, 226f.: = Sing. cstr.) :: e.g. Caquot & Lemaire Syr liv 199f.: l. *[y]ḥd$_2$*(= together; cf. Levine JAOS ci 197, 199, Puech BAT 356, 359, 362, FS Grelot 17, 23, 28 (cf. however idem ibid. 23 n. 45)) or *[ʾ]ḥd* (= *ʾḥd$_4$*) :: H. & M. Weippert ZDPV xcviii 83, 96f. 103: l. *[ʿ]šb* = Sing. abs. of *ʿšb*(= grass); *ʾklw [p]ḥd* i 11f.: eat fear (i.e. be afraid; ?), cf. also Hoftijzer DA a.l. for parallels - on the problems of DA i 12, cf. also Garbini Hen i 179.
pḥh (< Akkad., cf. Zimmern Fremdw 6, Kaufman AIA 82; cf. also Lipiński ZAH i 71) - **Hebr** Sing. abs. *pḥh* on coins, cf. IEJ xxi 158f. no. 2, 3 (*pḥ[h]*; Rahmani IEJ xxi 159f.: l. also *pḥh* in AJC no. 2 (cf. also Teixidor Syr l. 413, Kindler IEJ xxiv 76, cf. however Sukenik JPOS xiv 181, Reifenberg AJC a.l. (div. otherwise): l. *yhd* (= n.g.)); cstr. *pḥt* Vatt sig. eb. 408 - **OffAr** Sing. abs. *pḥh* KAI 266^{9}; cstr. *pḥt* Cowl 30^{1,29}, Samar 7^{17}, 8^{10}; emph. *pḥtʾ* Beh 18 (for the reading, cf. Greenfield & Porten BIDG 34f.; Akkad. par. *paḫātu*); cf. Nisa 28^{2}, 61^{3}, 69^{1}, 75^{3}, 76^{4}, 77^{2}, 88^{4}, 90^{2}, 135^{3}, etc., cf. also GIPP 60 - ¶ subst. m. governor passim (for the use of *pḥh* as ideogram for satrap, cf. Diakonov & Livshitz PaSb ii 142f. :: Garbini AION xv 339: or preferably = high official); *pḥt yhwd* Cowl 30^{29}: the governor of Y.; *pḥt šmryn* Cowl 30^{1}, Samar 7^{17}, 8^{10}: the governor of Sh. (cf. Vatt sig. eb. 408) - Mazar with Rainey PEQ '67, 40 n. 84: the *pḥʾ* in Sam 5 poss. = Sing. abs./cstr. of *pḥʾ* (= variant of *pḥh*), less prob. interpret., cf. e.g. Sukenik Sam a.l.: prob. = (part of) n.p. - on this word, cf. also Japhet VT xviii 356f., Chaumont JA cclvi 28 n. 45, Wilson NWL 12ff., Petit JBL cvii 53ff., Lemaire Trans iii 35ff., Lipiński Trans iii 96f.
v. *ṭlpḥt*, *p$_1$*, *pḥw$_1$*, *pḥr$_2$*, *tlpḥt*.
pḥw$_1$ **OffAr** Sing. emph. *pḥwtʾ* SSI ii 28 obv. 4 (cf. Avigad Qedem iv 6 n. 5 :: Bresciani RSO xxxv 13f., Fitzmyer JNES xxi 16, 19, WA 220, 223, Naveh AION xvi 26, 28, Gibson SSI ii a.l., Porten FS Bresciani 432, Porten & Yardeni sub TADAE A 3.3: = Plur. emph. of *pḥh*(= governors, cf. Fitzmyer ibid.; = officials (general term), cf. Naveh ibid., Gibson ibid.; = treasury officials, cf. Bresciani ibid.; :: Lipiński Or lvii 435f., Trans i 108 = Plur. emph. of *pḥw$_2$* = indication of certain official

'plugger') - ¶ subst. the office of the *pḥh*, prefecture.

pḥw₂ v. *pḥw₁*, *pḥr₂*

pḥwz v. *pḥz₂*.

pḥz₁ > Akkad. *paḫāzu* (= to act insolently), cf. v.Soden Or xxxvii 262, xlvi 191, cf. also idem AHW s.v. (cf. also *pḥz₅*).
v. *pḥz₂,₅*.

pḥz₂ **DA** Plur. cstr. *pḥzy* ii 8 (cf. Hoftijzer DA a.l., id. TUAT ii 145f. :: Caquot & Lemaire Syr liv 204: = Plur. cstr. of *pḥz₅* (= insolent; cf. also Ringgren Memorial Seeligmann 94, Dahood Bibl lxii 126) :: Levine JAOS ci 200f., H.P.Müller ZAW xciv 219, 233 (nn. 127-129): = Plur. abs. of *pḥz₃* (= recklessness, instability) :: Rofé SB 68, BAT 366: = Plur. cstr. of *pḥz₄* (= testicle (cf. also Greenfield JSS xxv 252; cf. also Lemaire CRAI '85, 276: hip, Weinfeld Shn v/vi 146: desire)) :: Kaufman BASOR ccxxxix 73: l. *mḥzy* = Sing. cstr. of *mḥzy₄*(= sight) :: (Cross with) Hackett BTDA 30, 62f., 97, 133: = QAL Part. act. pl.m. cstr. of *pḥz₁*(= to rise impulsively, to rise, cf. also McCarter with Hackett BTDA 83)? :: McCarter BASOR ccxxxix 59 n. 3: l. *pḥ.zy* (= Sing. abs. of *pḥ₃*(= bird-trap) + *zy*, cf. however Hackett Or liii 60)) - **Palm** (poss. < Arab., cf. Cantineau Gramm 41, 150f., Rosenthal Sprache 24, 94f., Hillers JBL xci 91, Hoftijzer DA p. 227 n. 121, Diem Or xlix 71; cf. also Blau PC 46 n. 2) Sing. abs. *pḥz* SBS 48[8]; cstr. *pḥd*CIS ii 3978[6], 4113[5], 4114[4], 4115[2], 4116[3], 4119[5], Inscr P 41[1], Inv x 145[?], xi 100[4], SBS 11[5], 38[3], Syr xii 126[2], xiv 191[4], xix 78[3], xxvi 45 ii 2, xxvii 138[5], *pḥz* RB xxxix 530[4], Inv x 42 (dam. context), *pḥwz* RB xxxix 523[1] (on this form, cf. Littmann with Cantineau sub Inv vii 5, Cantineau Gramm 41); + suff. 3 p.s.m. *pḥzh* AAS xxxvi/xxxvii 165 no. 3[3]; Plur. emph. *pḥzyʾ* Inv x 44[3], SBS 48[8] (Greek par. φυλαὶ), *pḥzʾ* DFD 37[5] (Greek par. φυλαὶ, cf. Syr xiii 279[13]) - ¶ subst. f. clan, tribe, passim; *pḥzy bny ʾš* DA ii 8: the clans/tribes of mankind (v. supra); *pḥzh dy mtbwl* AAS xxxvi/xxxvii 165 no. 3[3]: the tribe of M.; *ʾrbʿ pḥzyʾ* Inv x 44[3]: the four tribes (Greek par. τέσσαρες φυλαὶ, cf. Syr xiii 289[2]; also in SBS 48[7f.], cf. Greek par. τέσσαρες φυλαὶ, cf. also τέσσαρες φυλαὶ in Syr xiii 279[13]), these four tribes forming together the city of Palmyra, each with its own sanctuary (on this subject, cf. Schlumberger Syr xlviii 121ff. (cf. also v.Berchem PBP 170f., Lipiński VT xxiv 50f.), on the historical development, cf. Gawlikowski TP 26ff., 45ff. (on the tribes, cf. also Garbini AION xviii 74ff., Díez Merino LA xxi 81f., Milik DFD 16ff.)) - Milik DFD 310: l. *pḥz[yʾ]* (= Plur. emph. of *pḥz₂*) in SBS 48[9] (heavily dam. context, diff. reading) - the *p* in Syr xiv 186[2] prob. lapsus for *pḥd*(Sing. cstr.), cf. Cantineau Syr xiv 187 - Hoftijzer DA a.l.: l. poss. *[p]ḥzn* (= Plur. abs. of *pḥz₂*) in DA ii 16 (highly uncertain reading, dam. context, cf. also Hackett BTDA 73: l. poss. *ḥzn* = Sing. abs. of *ḥzn* :: Levine JAOS ci 200: l. *ḥzn* = QAL Part. act. pl.m.

abs. of *ḥzy*$_1$) - on the etymology, cf. also Grabbe CPTJ 122ff. - Fiema BASOR cclxiii 83: l. *bny* (= Plur. cstr. of *br*$_1$) *pyḥd/r*› (= Sing. emph.; indication of professional/social group) in Inv ix 5[4], to be related with *pḥz*$_2$??
v. *pḥr*$_1$.

pḥz$_3$ v. *pḥz*$_2$.

pḥz$_4$ v. *pḥz*$_2$.

pḥz$_5$ > Akkad. *paḫḫuzu* (= insolent), cf. v.Soden Or xxxvii 262, xlvi 191, cf. also *pāḫizu* (= insolent one), cf. v.Soden ibid. (= Qal Part. act. of *pḥz*$_1$?).
v. *pḥz*$_2$.

pḥṭmwny <Egypt., cf. Couroyer with Grelot DAE p. 290 n. d, RB lxxviii 527) - **OffAr** Sing. abs. *pḥṭmwny* Cowl 26[12] - ¶ subst. mooring post (sc. on the ship), cf. also Porten & Yardeni sub TADAE A6.2.

pḥy v. *p*$_1$.

pḥl cf. Frah ix 9 (*bḥl*;< Akkad. *puḫālu* = vigorous male animal), in the comb. *bḥl br byt*› = huge strong elephant (v. also *byt*$_2$), cf. however Nyberg FP 44, 74: l. ‹*bd br byt*› = servant member of the house.

pḥlm **Pun** word of unknown meaning in CIS i 226[3]; Slouschz TPI p. 327: = nl.

pḥlṣ **OffAr** Plur. abs. *pḥlṣn* Lesh xxxvii 270[1] - ¶ subst. indicating some measure (used to describe a certain amount of straw), cf. Naveh Lesh xxxvii 271.

pḥmt **Pun** word of unknown meaning in BAr '16, ccxiv: *-š* ›*bn pḥmt*= of coal (cf. Renault BAr a.l., less prob. interpret.), or (div. otherwise): l. *-š*› *bn pḥmt* = *-š*› son of P. (cf. Vassel BAr '16, ccxv; second interpret. prob.).

pḥnt **Pun** word of unknown meaning in KAI 145[2], prob. = subst. indicating part of building (Sing./Plur. cstr.) or = apposition to preceding *ḥṣrt*? :: Lidzbarski Eph i 48, Cooke NSI p. 152f., Röllig KAI a.l., Sznycer Sem xxii 40 (div. otherwise): = *p*$_8$(variant of ›*p*$_2$) + *ḥnt* (Sing. cstr. of *ḥnt*$_2$= vaulted room used as store(room)) :: Février Sem vi 16f. (div. otherwise): = *p*$_1$ + *ḥnt* (= Sing. cstr. of *ḥnt*$_2$,v. supra) :: Halévy RS ix 270, v.d.Branden RSF i 166f., BiOr xxxvi 203, Krahmalkov RSF iii 190, 203: = orthographical variant of *pnt*).

pḥstmḥ v. *ḥstmḥ*.

pḥṣ **Ph** Qal Part. act. s.f. abs. *pḥṣt* KAI 27[21] (for the reading, cf. Albright BASOR lxxvi 9 n. 34, Gaster Or xi 44, 48f., JNES vi 187 (cf. also Cross & Saley BASOR cxcvii 46 (n. 27), Röllig NESE ii 19, 25: l. *lpḥṣt* (= *l*$_3$(= oh) + *pḥṣt*) :: du Mesnil du Buisson FS Dussaud 432, Röllig KAI a.l., FR 139, Avishur PIB 248, de Moor JEOL xxvii 108: l. *mḥṣt* = Qal Part. act. s.f. abs. of *mḥṣ*$_1$(cf. also Botterweck TUAT ii 437) :: Baldacci BiOr xl 129: l. *lḥṣt* = Qal Part. act. s.f. abs. of *lḥṣ*$_1$(= to oppress, to vex) :: Dupont-Sommer RHR cxx 134f., 144f.: l. *ḥṣt* = Plur. abs. of *ḥṣ*$_2$(cf. also Caquot FS Gaster 50, Garbini OA xx 286) :: v.d.Branden BiOr xxxiii 12f.: l. *[wb]ḥṣr* = *w*$_2$ + *b*$_2$ + Sing. abs. of *ḥṣr*$_4$ :: v.d.Branden BO iii 47: l. *ḥṣt* (= Sing. abs. of *ḥṣt* (= half, h.l sc. of the night)) :: Gibson SSI iii p. 83, 87: l. *lḥṣt* = *l*$_5$ + Plur. abs. of *ḥṣ*$_2$(= to the outside; cf. also Lipiński RTAT 266) :: Torczyner JNES vi 26, 29: l. *rḥṣt* (= QAL Pf. 2 p.s.m. of *rḥṣ*$_1$)) - ¶ verb QAL to break, to crush (sc. bones), cf. Albright BASOR lxxvi 9 n. 34; *pḥṣt* (= bone breaker) epithet of a female demon (v. also supra).

pḥr₁ (prob. < Akkad., cf. Zimmern Fremdw 46, Kaufman AIA 83 (n. 268)) - **Palm** Plur. cstr. *pḥry* RTP 24; emph. *pḥry*ʾ RTP 304 (for this prob. interpret. in both instances, cf. Gawlikowski TP 31 n. 15, cf. however du Mesnil du Buisson TMP 629: l. *pḥdy* in RTP 24 (= Plur. cstr. of *pḥd*$_1$(= tribe, = *pḥz*$_2$)) and Caquot RTP a.l.: l. *pḥdy*ʾ in RTP 304 (= Plur. emph. of *pḥd*$_1$(= tribe, = *pḥz*$_2$), cf. also du Mesnil du Buisson TMP 444, 453, 789 n. 1, cf. however idem ibid. 286: l. *pḥry*ʾ) :: Caquot RTP a.l.: l. *kmry* (= Plur. cstr. of *kmr*$_2$)in RTP 24) - **Hatra** Sing. emph. *pḥr*ʾ 282, 283[1] (cf. Safar Sumer xxvii 5f., Caquot Syr lii 183f., Vattioni IH a.l. (v. also infra)) :: Degen NESE iii 72ff.: l. prob. *pḥr*ʾ (= Plur. emph. of *pḥr*$_2$) or l. *pḥd*ʾ (= Sing. emph. of *pḥd*$_1$ (= clan, *pḥz*$_2$)) :: v.d.Branden BiOr xxxvi 341: = Sing. emph. of *pḥr*$_3$ (= pottery)) - ¶ subst. assembly, banquet; *pḥr*ʾ *dy* ʿ*bdsy*ʾ Hatra 283[1]: the assembly of A. (prob. religious assembly); *hd*ʾ *dkt*ʾ *wlpḥr*ʾ *dy brmryn* Hatra 282[1]: this is the offertory-box for the assembly of B.M. (cf. Vattioni IH a.l. (or = Plur. emph. = banquets?), cf. also Teixidor Sem xxx 66: = symposium, Safar Sumer xxvii 5f.: = place of banquet in both Hatra instances :: Caquot Syr lii 183f., Aggoula Syr lxv 204: = restaurant, tavern in both Hatra instances); *pḥry bl* RTP 24: the banquets of B. (cf. Gawlikowski TP 31 n. 15); *mšmšmy pḥry*ʾ RTP 304: the servants of the banquets (cf. Gawlikowski ibid.).
v. *pḥr*$_2$.

pḥr₂ (< Akkad., cf. Zimmern Fremdw 26, Kaufman AIA 79) - **OffAr** Sing. emph. *pḥr*ʾ Qedem iv 22 no. 7, 8, 9 (for the reading, cf. Cross EI ix 24*ff., Naveh DAS 61, Proc v CJS i 99f. (Hebr.), Lemaire RB lxxix 253, Kaufman AIA 82 n. 263, Bianchi OA xxviii 37 × Aharoni IEJ ix 273f., x 262, xi 194, RB lxix 403, RR p. 21f., (Yeivin with) Aharoni BiAr xxiv 110f., Garbini OA i 139, Galling Studien 182f., Weippert ZDPV lxxx 175f., Porten Arch 290 (n. 24), Avigad Qedem iv a.l., Naʾaman BASOR cclxi 16: l. *pḥw*ʾ = Sing. emph. of *pḥh*,for this interpret., cf. also Kutscher Tarbiz xxx 112ff., Greenfield JNES xli 229, and cf. Lemaire Trans iii 34f.), Qedem iv 6 no. 5 (for the reading, cf. Vattioni sub sig. eb. 306 :: Avigad Qedem iv a.l., Herr sub SANSS-Ar 36: l. *pḥw*ʾ (v. supra)), Qedem iv 11 no. 14 (*pḥ[r*ʾ*]*, for the reading, cf. Vattioni sub

sig. eb. 315 :: Avigad Qedem iv a.l.: l. *pḥ[w᾽]*, cf. also Meyers EI xviii 33*ff.; for the readings *pḥr᾽/pḥw᾽*, cf. also Coote BASOR ccxxvii 76) :: Lipiński Or lvii 435f., Trans i 107ff.: in all instances l. *pḥw᾽* = Sing. emph. of *pḥw*$_2$(for the choice between "potter" and "governor", cf. also Smelik HDAI 134f.) - cf. also the dam. text on a storage-jar *]pḥr* At vii 84 (for the reading, cf. Dothan & Freedman ibid. 84f. (= Sing. abs. of *pḥr*$_1$?)) - for *pḥr᾽/pḥw᾽*, see further also IEJ xxix 246 - ¶ subst. potter - Aggoula Assur a.l.: l. *pḥ[r᾽]* (= Sing. emph. of *pḥr*$_2$) in Assur 42[2] (heavily dam. context).
v. *pḥr*$_1$, *prḥ*$_2$.

pḥr$_3$ v. *pḥr*$_1$.

pḥšpt (< Iran., cf. Justi IN 104f., Hinz AISN 177) - **OffAr** (or Iran. in Aramaic script?) Sing. abs. *pḥšp[t]* on coin (cf. Justi IN 104) - ¶ subst. head of district.

pḥt v. *nḥt*$_3$.

pṭm$_1$ **Palm** Pa ᶜel Pf. 3 p.s.m. *pṭm* Inv vi 4[3] (?, dam. context) - ¶ verb Pa ᶜel to fatten - Henning BSOAS xiii 82, Kutscher, Naveh & Shaked Lesh xxxiv 127: restore prob. *ḥyw]t᾽* (= Sing./Plur. emph. of *ḥywh*,or Plur. emph. of *ḥyh*$_2$)*pṭ[ymt᾽]* (= Qal Part. pass.f. s./pl. emph. of *pṭm*$_1$ in BSOAS xiii 82[1] (poss. interpret.).

pṭm$_2$ **Palm** Sing. emph. *[p]ṭm᾽* Inv vi 4[2] (?, dam. context) - ¶ subst. fat(tened) animal.

pṭply (< Greek παντοπωλεῖον) - **Palm** Sing. abs. (?, dam. context) *pṭply* CIS ii 3913 ii 53 (Greek par. παντοπωλ[εί]ων) - ¶ subst. general market, bazaar.

pṭr$_1$ **Hebr** Niph Pf. 3 p.s.f. *npṭrh* Frey 634[8]; Impf. 3 p.s.m. *ypṭr* DJD ii 46[9] - **OffAr** Qal (?) Impf. 3 p.pl.m. *ypṭrw[n]* Krael 13[7] (cf. Krael a.l., cf. however Porten & Yardeni sub TADAE A3.9: l. *ypṭrwn[ny]* = Qal Impf. 3 p.pl.m. + suff. 1 p.s., dam. context); Part. pass.m. pl. abs. *pṭyrn* ATNS 52a 6 (uncert. reading, diff. context); pl.f. + suff. 2 p.s.m. *pṭrtk* ATNS 52b ii 7; Itp Impf. 2 p.pl.m. *ttpṭrn* SSI ii 28 rev. 6 - ¶ verb Qal to free, to dismiss, to let go, to release (exact meaning in Krael 13[7] unknown, heavily dam. context), for the context of Krael 13[7], cf. Milik RB lxi 251; Part. pass. freed, released, *pṭrtk* ATNS 52b ii 7: your freedwomen - Niph to be discarded, *šypṭr bw mhw[* DJD ii 46[9]: that whatever ... will be discarded from him (uncert. interpret., diff. and dam. context, cf. also Pardee HAHL 136); to die: Frey 634[8] - Itp to be released, to be dismissed: SSI ii 28 rev. 6 (dam. context, exact meaning uncert.; Gibson SSI ii p. 145, 147: prob. = to be given leave, to be allowed home) - Milik sub DJD ii 21: l. in MPAT 42[9]: *᾽pṭ[rnk]* (= Qal/Pa ᶜel Impf. 1 p.s. + suff. 2 p.s.f. (= to divorce)), diff. reading, heavily dam. context.

pṭr$_2$ **JAr** Beyer ATTM 308, 667: l. poss. *pṭrn* = Plur. abs. of *pṭr*$_2$ (=

loss) in MPAT 40^9 (dam. text, diff. and uncert. reading).

pṭrh$_1$ **Ph** Sing. cstr. *pṭrt* KAI 49^{34} - ¶ subst. of unknown meaning; Lidzbarski Eph iii 109f., Röllig KAI a.l.: state of freedman?, *bpṭrt* *ʿbdmlqrt* (this reading preferable to *ʿbdmnqrt*) KAI 49^{34}: being the freedman of A.? (cf. also Harr 137); Slouschz TPI p. 57: = departure from this world, death; for other interpret., cf. CIS i sub 102.
v. *pṭrh$_2$*.

pṭrh$_2$ **Palm** Milik DFD 61f.: the *pṭrtʾ* (in the comb. *bny pṭrtʾ*) in Syr xvii 348^4 = Plur. emph. of *pṭrh$_2$* (= guard of the necropolis; f. used for males), improb. interpret.; Gawlikowski TP 34: *pṭrtʾ* (in the comb. *bny pṭrtʾ*) in RIP 154^1 poss. = Sing. emph. of *pṭrh$_1$*, *bny pṭrtʾ* = liberated ones, exempt ones (indication of the priests of the anonymous god?), highly uncert. interpret.; Cantineau Syr xvii 348: *bny pṭrtʾ* indication of clan (cf. also Gawlikowski TP 34).

py$_1$ **Ph** Sing. + suff. 3 p.s.m./f. *py* KAI 27^{16} (cf. Albright BASOR lxxvi 9 (n. 26), cf. also Gibson SSI iii 86f.: = suff. 3 p.s.m. or 3 p.s.f.??; FR 240,15: = suff. 3 p.s.m. (cf. also Röllig KAI a.l., NESE ii 48, Cross & Saley BASOR cxcvii 45, de Moor JEOL xxvii 108); du Mesnil du Buisson FS Dussaud 424, 430: = suff. 3 p.s.f. (cf. also Gaster Or xi 62, JNES vi 187, Caquot FS Gaster 48f., Avishur PIB 248, 253, Sperling HUCA liii 4, 9) :: Dupont-Sommer RHR cxx 142, Torczyner JNES vi 25, 29: + suff. 1 p.s. :: Garbini OA xx 284, 286: = Sing. abs.); + suff. 1 p.s. *py* KAI 11 - **Pun** Sing. cstr. *py* KAI 69^{18}, 79^9, 119^5, 126^8; + suff. 1 p.s. *py* KAI 79^8 - **Hebr** Sing. + suff. 3 p.s.f. *pyh* AMB 4^{19} (diff. context) - ¶ subst. m. - **1)** mouth: KAI 11; for KAI 27^{16} v. *rtm$_1$* - **2)** prec. by prep. *by$_2$*, v. *by$_2$* - **3)** prec. by prep. *l$_5$*, v. *l$_5$* - Michaud Syr xxxiv 55, PA 96: l. *bpy* in Lach xvi 4 (=*b$_2$* + Sing. cstr. of *py$_1$*), cf. however Torczyner Lach i a.l., Diringer Lach iii p. 337, Lemaire IH i 131: l. *bny* (both readings poss., heavily dam. context).
v. *p$_{1,5}$*, *pym*, *plk$_1$*.

py$_2$ **Nab** Naveh IEJ xxix 113, 117: the *pyʾ* in IEJ xxix 112^4 = Sing. emph. of *py$_2$* (= accomplishment of vow), < Arab. (highly uncert. interpret.).

py$_3$ (< Arab., cf. Cantineau Nab. ii 172, Altheim & Stiehl AAW i 191, Diem ZDMG cxxiii 228 (n. 11), Or l. 368, Garbini HDS 36, cf. also O'Connor JNES xlv 225) - **Nab** *py* J 17^4 - ¶ prep. in, at, *hlkt py ʾl hgrw* J 17^4: she died in A.H.

py$_4$ v. *p$_1$*.

py$_5$ **JAr** word in AMB 4^1 of uncert. interpret.; Naveh & Shaked AMB a.l.: *py* = dittography for following *ptgmʾ* ?? (highly uncertain interpret.).

pygʾ v. *pgʿ$_1$*, *prh$_1$*.

pyd v. *pwd*.

pyṭḥš **OffAr** Sing. abs. *pyṭḥš* FuF xxxv 173[5] (*pyṭ[ḥ]š*); cstr. *pyṭḥš* FuF xxxv 173[2] (:: Altheim & Stiehl FuF xxxv 175: = Sing. abs., cf. also idem ASA 250) - ¶ subst. designation of high official, variant of *bṭḥš*(v. s.v.); cf. *pdḥš.*

pyl v. $p^{c}l_2$, cf. *pyly.*

pyly (< Greek πύλαι) - **Hebr** Sing. abs. *pyly* SM 49[6,7,8] - ¶ subst. gate - cf. *pyl* sub $p^{c}l_2$.

pylkh **Hebr/JAr** Yadin & Naveh Mas a.l.: the *pylk[h]* in Mas 642 = spinning (uncert. interpret.).

pym **Hebr** Sing. abs. *pym* Dir pes. 11-13 (for the problems of Dir pes. 11, cf. Dir p. 274 n. 1), 14 (*py[m]*), Mosc pes. 5-7, Sem xxvi 35 no. 5, 6, 43 no. 27, 28, Sem xxxii 19, PEQ '65, 129 (2 examples), HUCA xl/xli 180 (1 example), RB lxxxii 89 (1 example), IEJ xxviii 216f., xxxii 251; for a list of published and unpublished *pym* weights, cf. Ben-David UF xi 37, cf. also IEJ xxxi 244a - ¶ subst. certain weight (the *pym* weights ranging from around 7.15 gr. to around 8.60gr.); prob. = 2/3 of a light shekel. On this weight, cf. Dir p. 275ff., Mosc p. 99, de Vaux IAT i 312, Barrois ii 256f., Wambacq VD xxix 348, Trinquet SDB v 1247, Enc Miqr iv 869ff., Pritchard HISG 30, Sarfatti Tarbiz xxviii 4f., Lane BASOR clxiv 21ff. (v. however p_4, $p^{\prime}_1$), Scott PEQ '65, 135ff., Diringer & Brock FS Thomas 40, Dever HUCA xl/xli 182, Couroyer RB lxxviii 452 n. 1, Lemaire & Vernus Sem xxviii 56, Ben-David UF xi 35ff., Pardee AUSS xvii 63 (n. 11), Zevit MLAHE 22f. (n. 32) - *pym* (orig.) = Dual? of py_1?,cf. e.g. Clermont-Ganneau RAO viii 105ff., Barrois RB xli 67ff., Barrois ii 256f., Albright with Speiser OBS 159 n., Couroyer RB lxxviii 452 n. 1, cf. also Ben-David UF xi 36f., HAL s.v. (cf. already Speiser OBS 156ff.), Sarfatti Maarav iii 73f.

v. p_4, $p^{\prime}_1$.

pyn v. *᾽ḥšyn.*

pynk (< Greek πίναξ) - **OffAr** Sing. abs. *pynk* RES 1300[8] - ¶ subst. plate.

pys **OffAr** Cowl a.l.: the *pysn* in Cowl 37[9] prob. = PAᶜEL Pf. 3 p.s.m. + suff. 1 p.pl. of *pys* (= to appease), incorrect interpret., *pysn* = n.p. (cf. e.g. Grelot DAE p. 389, 485, Porten & Greenfield JEAS p. 81, Porten & Yardeni sub TADAE A4.2) - v. *pṣy.*

pyṣ v. *pṣy.*

pyq v. *pq.*

pyq᾽ **Pun** Février JA ccxlvii 86f.: l. *pyq᾽* (< Greek ἱππικός; Sing. abs. = horseman, *equester*) in KAI 153[3] in the diff. comb. of signs ... *bn ᾽šṭ᾽rny pyq᾽ bšdlbym* (= the son of O. the *equester* in the land of the Libyans; for the land of the Libyans, cf. also Clermont-Ganneau with Chabot sub Punica xxv 3 (= JA xi/xi 285f. n. 3); or = the son of A. the *rnypyq᾽* (unknown title) in the land of ..., cf. Clermont-Ganneau l.c.; cf. also Alvarez Delgado ILC 237 (div. otherwise): l. *pyq›d šd lbym* = the prefect (Sing. cstr.) of the land of the L. (poss. interpret.). v.*hpq, hpqws, ḥpqws.*

pyq›d v. *pyq›*.

pyrk v. *ptk.*

pyt v. *mpt.*

pytr‹ v. *ṭbḥ*, ptr_2.

pkmt **Hebr** word of uncert. reading and unknown meaning on storage jar in TeAv v 87[2] (Ussishkin TeAv a.l.: or l. *pknt*?).

pknt v. *pkmt.*

pkr > Akkad. *pakāru* (= to fetter), cf. v.Soden Or xxxvii 262, xlvi 191 (cf. also idem AHW s.v.).

pkš **Ph** Plur. abs. *pkšt* EI xviii 117[3f.] (= IEJ xxxv 83[3f.]) - ¶ subst. of uncert. meaning indicating a certain type of object; Dothan EI xviii 118, IEJ xxxv 87: < Greek πύξος, πυξίς (= box).

pl **Pun** Sing. abs. *pl* CIS i 3885[2] - ¶ subst. of uncert. meaning, in the combination *mkr hpl*, CIS i a.l. = ivory, Slouschz TPI p. 349 (cf. Heltzer UF xix 435): = bean (cf. *pwl*).

pl›₁ **OffAr** Dupont-Sommer RA xxxix 51: the *ip-li-e* in Warka 26 = QAL Impf. 1 p.s. of *pl›₁* (uncert. interpret.) = to scrutinize, to scan :: Gordon AfO xii 107f., 116: l. *íb-li-e* (= Plur. cstr. or Sing. + suff. 3 p.s.m. of *›bl₂* (= Trouble)); on the context, cf. also Landsberger AfO xii 254 n. 29 - > Akkad. *palû* = to search, cf. v.Soden Or xxxvii 262, xlvi 191, AHW s.v. *palû* III.

pl›₂ **Pun** the diff. *pal* in Poen 1017 poss. = nominal derivative of root *pl›₂* (= to be miraculous, to be magnificent), cf. L.H.Gray AJSL xxxix 82, Sznycer PPP 143f.: = Sing. abs. (cf. also Schroed 296), J.J.Glück & Maurach Semitics ii 122: = Sing. cstr.

pl›w cf. Frah viii 1 (*pl‹wt*) = wonder.

plb **Ph** Difficult group of signs in Kition D 21[1]; Amadasi sub Kition D 21: poss. = p_1 (:: Liverani RSF iii 39 (div. otherwise): l. poss. *z›* (= *z›₁*) + *lb* (= QAL Perf 3 p.s.m. of *lbb* (= to form, to bake); cf. also Liverani RSF iii 39) :: Dupont-Sommer MAIBL xliv 281, 292ff.: l. *glb* (= QAL Pf. 3 p.s.m. of *glb₁* (= to shave)), cf. also Puech RSF iv 12f. :: Coote BASOR ccxx 47, 49: l. *klb* (Sing. abs. of *klb₁* (= dog), contemptuous indication of a demon) :: Teixidor Syr xlix 434: non-semitic text?) - ¶ verb QAL to shave: Kition D 21[1] (for the context, cf. also Puech RSF iv 18ff., v. however supra)

plg₁ **OffAr** QAL (or PA‹EL?, cf. Leand 23d) Pf. 1 p.pl. *plgn* Cowl 28[3]; Impf. 2 p.s.m. *tplg* MAI xiv/2, 66[4]; 1 p.pl. *nplg* Cowl 28[13], MAI xiv/2, 66[6] - **Palm** QAL (or PA‹EL?) Pf. 3 p.pl.m. *plg* Ber v 125[9] (:: Ingholt Ber v 133: = QAL Pf. 3 p.pl.m. of *plg₂* (= to be in the middle)) - ¶ verb QAL (or PA‹EL?) to divide; *gwmḥyn tlt› dy plg bnyhwn* Ber v

125[8f]: three niches which they (i.e. the two buyers) have divided among them - **1)** + obj.: MAI xiv/2, 66[5f] - **2)** + obj. + *ʿl*$_7$, *nplg hmw ʿlyn* Cowl 28[13f]: we will divide them between us - **3)** + *ʿl*$_7$ + obj., *plgn ʿlyn ʿbdyh* Cowl 28[3]: we have divided between us her slaves - **4)** + *ʿm*$_4$, *wtplg ʿmy bšnn 8 ḥmr qbl ḥmr* MAI xiv/2, 66[4f]: and you will share with me in the eighth year *ḥomer* for *ḥomer* (i.e. each fifty procent of the yield).
v. *plg*$_{5,6}$.

plg$_2$ v. *plg*$_1$.

plg$_3$ **Hebr** Sing. cstr. *plg* Mosc pes. 1 (or = Ph.?, cf. Delavault & Lemaire RSF vii 32, Bron & Lemaire CISFP i 767f.) - **OffAr** Sing. abs. *plg* Cowl 79[3], 81[86] (on the text, cf. Harmatta ActAntHung vii 368), Krael 2[5] (for the context, cf. Yaron JSS xiii 207)[,7], 9[6], FX 136[14]; cstr. *plg* Cowl 1[2,3], 9[11], 71[33] (reading and context uncert.), Krael 2[6], 4[3,6], 6[13], 9[4,7,15], *scriptio anterior* in Krael 2[11](cf. Krael a.l., Hoftijzer & Pestman BiOr xix 216, Porten & Yardeni sub TADAE B3.3)[,12] (*scriptio anterior*; cf. Yaron JNES xx 129f., Porten & Yardeni sub TADAE B3.3); emph. *plgʾ* Cowl 9[11,12], Krael 6[12], 9[14]; + suff. 3 p.s.m. *plgh* Cowl 74[1], Krael 9[8]; + suff. 3 p.s.f. *plgh* Cowl 44[6,8]; cf. Frah xxx 39 (*prg*), Paik 814 (*plg*), GIPP 60 - **Nab** Sing. emph. *plgʾ* J 33[5] (= CIS ii 215), BASOR cclxiii 78[2] - **Palm** Sing. abs. *plg* RTP 39, 284, 526, 569, 694-701, 702 (*p[l]g*), MUSJ xxxviii 106[7]; cstr. *plg* RTP 564, 703, 704, 705(?) (:: Lipiński EI xx 131*: in the RTP instances = Sing. abs. of *plg*$_7$ (= part, portion)); emph. *plgʾ* RB xxxix 538[2], Inscr P 33[2,3] (= Inv xii 21?), FS Miles 38[1]; + suff. 3 p.s.m. *plgh* MUSJ xxxviii 106[8]; + suff. 3 p.s.f. *plgh* CIS ii 4206[2] (v. infra), 4227[3] - **JAr** Sing. + suff. 3 p.s.f. *plgh* SM 49[29] - ¶ subst. m. half: Cowl 1[2,3], 9[11], Krael 2[6], 4[3], etc.; cf. *plg drgʾ wbyt prsʾ plgh* Krael 9[7f]: half the stairs and half the *byt prsʾ* (v. *prs*$_3$); *whʾ mšḥt bytʾ zk zy ʾnh ... yhbt lky ... mn plg try rbtʾ wtwnh* Krael 4[5f]: and behold the measurements of that house which I ... gave to you ... to wit the half of the great *try* (v. *try*$_1$) and the chamber (cf. Hoftijzer VT ix 314f. :: Krael a.l., Porten & Greenfield JEAS p. 45, Porten & Yardeni sub TADAE B3.5: ... *mn plg* ... = from half of ...; v. *mn*$_5$); *mnth plgh dqbrʾ* CIS ii 4206[2]: the half of his part of the tomb (:: CIS ii a.l.: ... half of the tomb), cf. MUSJ xxxviii 106[7,8]; *mʿrtʾ dnh ... plgʾ wplgʾ dy bt mtry wdy bt ʾylyd* FS Miles 38[1]: this hypogeum belongs half-and-half to B.M. and to B.E. (i.e. each of them possesses half of it); cf. also *ḥlrn 7 plg* Krael 2[5]: seven and a half *ḥallur* (cf. Krael 2[7]); *ʾmn 9 wplg* Cowl 79[3]: nine and a half cubit (cf. Krael 9[6], cf. also FX 136[14]); *mkl wplg* RTP 39: one and a half *mkl* (v. *mkl*$_1$; cf. RTP 284, 694-702); *plg mkl* RTP 564, 703, 704: a half *mkl*; *plg* RTP 526, 569: prob. = a half *mkl* (:: Milik DFD 187f.: = half a *denarius*); *plg rbʿt* Mosc pes. 1 (v. *rbʿy*): an eighth part (sc. of a shekel × Scott BASOR clxxiii 55: l.

plg rbʿ = a fourth part (sc. of a shekel); *plg* Cowl 81[86]: a half (*kʾ*; v. *kʾ*1), cf. Driver JRAS '32, 84f. - abbrev. *p*: Cowl 81[3](on the context, cf. Harmatta ActAntHung vii 341f.),[62,70,71,79,81,87,94,96-98,107,126] (cf. Driver JRAS '32, 84f.), ATNS 127a 1, 2, BSh 3[2], 10, 27[2], 37[3] (context however dam.: *p[)*, BIFAO xxxviii 58[2,3,5](:: Segal Maarav iv 72: there is no sign),[6], IEJ xxxv 19[3] (dam. context), Mas 426[2], 591, 592 - Krael a.l.: l. prob. *plgh* (= Sing. + suff. 3 p.s.m.) in Krael 6[12] (cf. e.g. Grelot DAE p. 231, Porten & Greenfield JEAS p. 50), less prob. reading, cf. Szubin & Porten BASOR cclxix 39: l. *plṭyh* (= n.p.), cf. also Porten & Yardeni sub TADAE B3.7.
v. *pg*, *plg*6, *prʿʿ*.

plg4 (< Akkad, cf. Kaufman AIA 79 (n. 250), cf. also Aro ZDMG cxiii 478, Fronzaroli RCL '68, 273) - **OffAr** Sing. emph. *plgʾ* (for the reading of the photograph in Koldewey WB 80 (Abb. 52), cf. Driver PEQ '45, 12 (poss. reading)) - ¶ subst. canal (v. supra).

plg5 **Ph** Sing. cstr. *plg* KAI 18[3] - ¶ subst. of uncert. meaning; e.g. CIS i a.l., Cooke NSI p. 46, Lidzbarski KI sub 12, Harr 137, Röllig KAI a.l., v.d.Branden GP p. 7: = district (cf. also Kaufman AIA 83 (n. 265): < Akkad. *pilku*, cf. also Cooke NSI a.l., Lidzbarski KI a.l., v.d.Branden GP a.l., cf. however Röllig KAI a.l., BiOr xxvii 377: of uncert. etymology), for the context, cf. Meyer ZAW xlix 4ff.; cf. however also Dunand & Duru sub DD 1: poss. = family, clan (< root *plg*1); or *plg* = title?, cf. *plg*6.

plg6 **OffAr** Sing. abs. *plg* Pers 17[3], 22[2] (*pl[g]*), 31[2], 32[3], 47[3], 48[4], 63[2], 81[2], 83[2], 87[3], 88[2], 118[3], 130[2] - ¶ subst. prob. title, exact meaning unknown; = commander of an army unity? (cf. Bowman Pers p. 34, 66f., 90, Teixidor Syr li 331f., Grelot RB lxxx 595 (cf. also Millard JRAS '73, 63) :: Hinz FS Nyberg 378f.: *plg* = *plg*3(= share, portion) :: Naveh & Shaked Or xlii 452f. n. 54, 454f. (n. 63): *plg* = either *plg*3(Sing. abs., cf. Hinz FS Nyberg 378f.) used adverbially or QAL (or PA ʿEL?) Pf. 3 p.s.m. of *plg*1(or QAL (or PA ʿEL?) Imper. s.m. of *plg*1):: Delaunay CC 203f., 217: = QAL Part. pass. s.m. abs. of *plg*1 (= separated, set apart)) - *ʾlp plg* in Pers 118[3] prob. = a comb. of two titles both Sing. abs., cf. however Bowman Pers p. 34, 67: *plg* = military unit (v. *ʾlp*4) - v. *plg*5.

plg7 v. *plg*3.

plg8 **OffAr**, cf. Frah i 13 (*prg*, cf. Nyberg FP 61) = half-splendour ("the lesser shine", "the half-moon")? :: Ebeling Frah a.l.: l. *prq* = *brq*.

plgh1 **OffAr** Sing. + suff. 3 p.s.m. *plgth* RES 1367[3] (= CIS ii 129), 1372B 2 (for the reading in both instances, cf. Dupont-Sommer AEPHE '66/67, 119, cf. also Grelot DAE p. 339 nn. c, d :: RES a.l.: l. *plwth* = Sing. + suff. 3 p.s.m. of *plwt* (subst. of uncert. meaning, Lidzbarski

Eph iii 105: = fellow, servant, pupil?)) - ¶ subst. concubine.

plgh₂ v. *rbʿy*.

plgw **Palm** Sing. cstr. *plgwt* CIS ii 3913 ii 130 (dam. context), RB xxxix 548^4 (*p[l]gwt*), Inv viii 81^3 (dam. context), RIP 24^6, Syr xvii 268^4, xix 154^3 (dam. context) - **JAr** Sing. abs. *plgw* MPAT-A 22^2; cstr. *plgwt* MPAT-A 29^3 - ¶ subst. - **1)** half, passim; *plgwt mʿrtʾ* RIP 24^6: half the tomb; *plgwt [dy]nr* MPAT-A 29^{3f}: half a *denarius* - **2)** discord, *kl mn dyhyb plgw bn gbr lḥbryh* MPAT-A 22^2: everyone who sets discord between a man and his fellow.

plgn **OffAr** Sing. abs. *plgn* MAI xiv/2, 66^3; cstr. *plgn* Cowl 28^{17}; + suff. 1 p.pl. *plgnn* Cowl 28^{14} - ¶ subst. sharing, partition; *spr plgnn* Cowl 28^{14}: a deed of our partition; *spr plgn ʿbd pṭwsyry* Cowl 28^{17}: a deed of division by which the slave P. is assigned (sc. to a certain party); the text MAI xiv/2, 66^3 dam., of uncert. reading and diff., Dupont-Sommer MAI xiv/2, 72: l. *wlplgn*, Bauer & Meissner SbPAW '36, 415, 423: l. *[ʿ]l plgn* = "auf Teilpacht".

plhdrw (< Greek πρόεδρος + suff. *-ū*, cf. also Cooke NSI p. 332) - **Palm** Sing. emph. *plhdrwtʾ* CIS ii 3913 i 1 (Greek par. προέδρου) - ¶ subst. office of *proedros*, presidency, *bplhdrwtʾ dy bwnʾ* CIS ii 3913 i 1: during the presidency of B. (cf. Greek par. ἐπὶ Βωννέους ... προέδρου).

plwt v. *plgh₁*.

plz **Palm** Sing. emph. *plzʾ* CIS ii 3914^4 - ¶ subst. brass.

plḥ₁ **OffAr** QAL Impf. 1 p.pl. + suff. 2 p.s.m. *yplḥnk* (prob. lapsus for *nplḥnk*) Krael 5^{11}; Inf. *mplḥ* Aḥiq 17; Part. act. s.f. abs. *plḥh* KAI 269^4; cf. Frah xviii 5 (cf. Nyberg FP 49, 88 :: Ebeling Frah a.l.: l. *prʾwn*, *(y)prʾwn* = form of *prʾ₁* (= to tread, to walk)); cf. SbPAW '33, 132 - **Palm** QAL Part. act. s.m. emph. *plḥʾ* CIS ii 3944^4 - **Hatra** QAL Part. act. s.m. cstr. *plḥ* 21^2, 412 ii 5; emph. *plḥʾ* Ibr 14^2; f. pl. emph. *plḥtʾ*, cf. Assur 21 ii 2 (or = f. Plur. emph. of *plḥ₃* (= workman)) - ¶ verb QAL - **1)** to serve - a) + obj., *ʾnḥn yplḥnk* (v. supra) *zy ysbl br wbrh* Krael 5^{11}: we will serve you as a son or a daughter would provide ... (Grelot DAE p. 226 n. i: *zy* lapsus for *kzy* by haplography, cf. also Krael a.l. (uncert. emendation)) - b) + *b₂*, *lʾ ʾkhl lmplḥ bbb hyklʾ* Aḥiq 17: I cannot serve in the gate of the palace - **2)** to serve a god > to adore; *plḥ ʾlhʾ* Hatra 21^2: a servant of the gods (v. *ʾlh₁*; cf. Tawil Or xliii 54), cf. Hatra 412^5; cf. SbPAW '19, 1044^2; cf. poss. also *hwy plḥh nmʿty* KAI 269^4: be a servant of N. (v. *nmʿty*; cf. however (Quaegebeur with) Lipiński OLP viii 113ff.: do attend on the righteous ones, v. also *nmʿty*) - **3)** to serve (sc. in the army), Part. act., soldier: CIS ii 3944^4 (cf. Cantineau Gramm 159), Ibr 14^2 (cf. however Segal JSS xxxi 78: = workman) - **4)** Part. f. (v. however supra), working woman: Assur 21 ii 2 (context however diff. and uncert.) - a form of this root in KAI 214^4: *plḥ[* (dam. context).

v. *plḥh.*

plḥ$_2$ v. *pwl.*

plḥ$_3$ v. *plḥ$_1$*.

plḥh **Hatra** Sing. emph. *plḥt>* 409 iii 5 (:: as-Salihi Sumer xlv 103 (n. 38): = QAL Part. Sing. f. emph. of *plḥ$_1$*) - ¶ subst. service: Hatra 409 iii 5.

plḥn v. *plḥnh.*

plḥnh **Nab** word of unknown meaning in CIS ii 340; Levinson NAI 203: = Sing. emph. of *plḥn*(= worship).

plṭ **Samal** PA<EL Pf. 3 p.pl.m. + suff. 3 p.s.m. *plṭwh* KAI 215[2] - **JAr** PA<EL Inf. *plṭ>* AMB 13[4] (prob. reading) - ¶ verb PA<EL to deliver, to save; + obj. + *mn$_5$* (= from), *plṭwh >lh y>dy mn šḥth* KAI 215[3]: the gods of Y. delivered him from destruction; *[l]plṭ> yth mn [m]zqyn* AMB 13[4f]: to save her from evil-doers.

v. *lyṭ>*, *mplṭ.*

plṭy$_1$ (< Greek πλατεῖα) - **Palm** Sing. emph. *plṭy>* Ber ii 84[1], 85[7] - ¶ subst. street; in Ber ii 84[1], 85[7] part of a tomb construction (// with *šqq* in CIS ii 4199[3,7], cf. Ingholt Ber ii 84); prob. = identical with *exedra* (cf. also Ingholt FS Miles 48 (n. 59)) :: Bauer with Ingholt Ber iii 126: = part of the tomb construction outside the *exedras.*

plṭy$_2$ (< Greek πολιτεία) - **Palm** Sing. emph. *plṭy>* Inv x 44[7] - ¶ subst. tenure of public office.

plṭy$_3$ **Hatra** Plur. emph. *plṭy>* Ibr 21[4] (cf. Aggoula Syr lxiv 227) - ¶ substantivated adj. traveller: Ibr 21[4].

ply v. *wly$_2$*.

plk$_1$ **Ph** Plur. abs. *plkm* KAI 26A ii 6 - ¶ subst. spindle (for KAI 26A ii 6, cf. also Kaufman AIA 82f. (n. 265)); *dl plkm* KAI 26A ii 6: with spindles (cf. Röllig KAI a.l., Ginsberg FS Gaster 145f. n. 61, Bron RIPK 84, Avishur PIB 224, 231, Gibson SSI iii p. 49, 59, Lipiński SV 48 (cf. also Starcky MUSJ xlv 262, Greenfield EI xiv 75ff., H.P.Müller TUAT i 642f.; on the use of a plural, cf. also Amadasi RSO xlv 206) :: Rosenthal ANET 654 n. 4, v.Selms JNSL i 53f.: = work (= Sing. cstr. of *dl$_2$* (= work))with spindles :: Friedrich FuF '48, 78: = fibrous material (= Sing. cstr. of *dl$_4$*)of spindles :: Swiggers UF xii 440: she prepared (rolled up; = QAL Pf. 3 p.s.f. of *dwl, dll*)the spindles :: Lipiński RSF ii 48, RTAT 259 (n. 66; div. otherwise): l. *ydl* (= YIPH Pf. 3 p.s.f. of *dwl*(= to spin)) + *plkm* (cf. Swiggers BiOr xxxix 339) :: Honeyman Mus lxi 52, 55, Marcus & Gelb JNES viii 119, O'Callaghan Or xviii 177, Leveen & Moss JJS i 191: = the poor (= Plur. cstr. of *dl$_3$*)of the provinces/regions (= Plur. abs. of *plk$_2$* (= province)) :: Dupont-Sommer RA xlii 172: = together (= *dl$_6$* used adverbially) the districts :: v.d.Branden BMB xiii 92f.: = wandering through (= QAL Part. act. s.m. abs. of *dwl*)the provinces :: Pedersen ActOr xxi 40, 46, 52f. (div.

otherwise: l. *ydl plkm*): that kept in obedience (= YIPH Pf. 3 p.pl. of *dll*)the provinces :: Leveen & Moss Irâq x 65: l. *b[k]l plkm* = in all (= b_2 + Sing. cstr. of kl_1) the regions :: Obermann JAOS Suppl ix 24, 39: on (*dl* = ‘l_7) the highways (cf. however Obermann Conn xxxviii 24f. (n. 45), 40: *dl* poss. = Plur. cstr. of dl_5(= highway) *plkm* (Plur. abs. of plk_2 (= province) ??) :: Gordon JNES viii 110, 114 (div. otherwise: l. *yd lp lkm*): hand (Sing. abs. of *yd*)to mouth (= l_5 + Sing. abs. of p_5 (= py_1)for you (= l_5 + suff. 2 p.pl.m.), i.e. without scandal :: Gordon JQR xxxix 46: *dl plkm* = without molesters.

plk$_2$ v. *plk$_1$*.

pln **OffAr** m. Sing. abs., cf. Warka 14, 22, 29: *pi-la-nu* (cf. also Garbini HDS 31); f. Sing. abs., cf. Warka 22: *pi-la-*ʾ (for this form, cf. Gordon AfO xii 106 n. 5, 113, cf. also Kaufman JAOS civ 89; for the context, cf. Gordon AfO xii 109) - ¶ subst. m./f. a certain one, someone - Ebeling Frah a.l.: l. this word (*pln*) in Frah xi 2 (improb. interpret., cf. Nyberg FP 78: l. Iran. word here).

plny **OffAr** Shaked Or lvi 410: the *plnyh* in ATNS 41[8] poss. = f. Sing. abs. of *plny* (= a certain person, such-and-such), highly uncert. interpret. (cf. Segal ATNS a.l.: *plnyh* = n.p., cf. also Zadok WO xvi 175).

pls **Ph** Sing. abs. *pls* CIS i 40[1] (= Kition E 2; ?, dam. context :: CIS i a.l.: = part of n.p.; uncert. reading, cf. Amadasi sub ICO-Sard 31: l. *pns* ?? (without interpret.) - **Pun** Sing. abs. *pls* KAI 81[9], CIS i 356[2f] (*pl[s]*, dam. context), RES 1593[6] (for the reading, cf. Lidzbarski Eph i 174), RCL ’66, 201[4] - ¶ subst. m. indication of function, exact meaning unknown: leveller (cf. Röllig sub KAI 81), cf. Harr 137: leveller, engineer (for the meaning “engineer”, cf. also Dupont-Sommer CRAI ’68, 117, 125: = engineer (orig. surveyor of roads), contractor, Ferron Mus xcviii 52, 61: engineer whose task it is to level the terrain to enable the construction of the street, v.d.Branden PO i 214: ‘cantonnier’, and already Slouschz TPI p. 87); Cooke NSI p. 127, 130: surveyor; for a discussion, cf. Mahjoubi & Fantar RCL ’66, 206f., Garbini Monte Sirai ii p. 85.

pltʾ **Pun** the diff. *plt*ʾ in KAI 145[7] poss. = n.p. (< Lat.), cf. Février Sem vi 21, cf. however Krahmalkov RSF iii 189, 193, 203: = Sing. + suff. 3 p.s.m. of *p*‘*lh*; v.d.Branden RSF i 166, 169: = QAL Pf. 1 p.s. + suff. 3 p.s.m. of *p*‘*l_1*; or div. otherwise l. *mplt*ʾ (= Sing. + suff. 3 p.s.m. of *mplh*? (highly uncert. context).

plty **Pun** Sing. abs. *plty* RES 1550[2f] (:: Lidzbarski Handb 352, 433: l. *pnty*) - ¶ subst. indication of function (??, uncert. interpret., rather = *gentilicium*?, cf. also Lidzbarski Handb 352 (v. supra), Schult ZDPV lxxxi 76ff., Bertrandy & Sznycer SPC sub 28).

pm$_1$ **Samal** Sing. abs. *pm* KAI 214[29]; cstr. *pm* KAI 214[30] - **OldAr**

Sing. cstr. *pm* KAI 222A 30f. (*[p]m*), 31, 223A 9; + suff. 3 p.s.m. *pmh* Tell F 10 (Akkad. par. *pi-ia*), 14 (Akkad. par. *pi-šú*) - **OffAr** Sing. abs. *pm* Aḥiq 99, Krael $7^{8,10}$, 12^{11}, 14a; cstr. *pm* Cowl 2^{18}, 5^{15}, 6^{17}, ATNS 3^{6} (cf. Porten & Yardeni sub TADAE B8.10 :: Segal ATNS a.l. (div. otherwise): l. *pmh* (= Sing. + suff. 3 p.s.m.), Aḥiq 123, Krael 1^{10}, 3^{22b}, 4^{22}, MAI xiv/2, 18, etc., etc.; + suff. 3 p.s.m. *pmh* Aḥiq 114, cf. Warka 21, 34: *pu-um-mi-e*, Warka 32: *pu-um[-mi-e]*; + suff. 2 p.s.m. *pmk* Aḥiq 97, 98, 99; + suff. 1 p.s. *pmy* KAI 226^{4}, Aḥiq 155 (dam. context); + suff. 3 p.pl.m. *pmhm* Aḥiq 124; Dual abs. *pm[yn]* Aḥiq 100; cf. Frah x 18 (*pwmh*) - **Nab** Sing. cstr. *pwm*DBKP 22^{34} - ¶ subst. m. - **1)** mouth: passim; said of animals: KAI 222A 30f., 31, 223A 9; for Tell F 10, 14, v. *ʾmrh*; for Aḥiq 99, v. *ʾrb*; for Aḥiq 156, v. *ʾpk* - a) prec. by prep. *k*$_1$ - α) *kpm* + indication of person, according to the instruction of (cf. Joüon MUSJ xviii 59, cf. also Grelot DAE p. 173 a.e., Porten & Yardeni sub TADAE B 2.1 a.e. :: Cowl p. 15 a.e., Yaron Law 15, Porten & Greenfield JEAS p. 4 a.e., Verger RGP 94: at the dictation of): Cowl 5^{15}, 6^{17}, 8^{28}, Krael 1^{10}, 3^{22b}, 4^{22f}, ATNS 3^{6} (v. supra), etc., etc. - β) *kpm ḥd* Krael 12^{11}: unanimously (cf. Couroyer RB lxi 559) - b) prec. by prep. *ʿl*$_7$, *ʿl pm* + indication of person, according to the instruction of, by order of: MAI xiv/2, 66^{18} (for this text, cf. also Yaron JSS ii 43), DBKP 22^{34}; in Cowl 11^{16} with the meaning "at the declaration of"?, cf. Joüon MUSJ xviii 59f., Grelot DAE p. 80, cf. however Cowl p. 35, Leand 62 n', Yaron JSS ii 41, Porten & Greenfield JEAS p. 108: in presence of; in Cowl 2^{18} with the meaning "at the declaration of"?, cf. Joüon MUSJ xviii 60, Grelot DAE p. 269 (:: Cowl a.l.: at the dictation of), cf. however Yaron JSS ii 41ff.: in presence of - **2)** prob. edge, hem (sc. of garment), *pšk 1 lpm 1* Krael 7^{8}: a handbreadth on each edge (cf. Krael 7^{10}, 14a - **3)** sharp (of a sword, knife), *skyn pm[yn]* Aḥiq 100 (prob. meaning): a two-edged knife (v. *skyn*) - **4)** this word also in the comb. *pm ṭb* in MAI xiv/2, 66^{15}? (for this reading, cf. Torrey JAOS lviii 394f., Dupont-Sommer MAI xiv/2, 84 × Bauer & Meissner SbPAW '36, 421, Koopmans sub 19, Porten & Yardeni sub TADAE B1.1: l. *pmṭn* or *pmṭz*?, without interpret.), uncert. meaning, caution?? (cf. Dupont-Sommer MAI xiv/2 a.l.; Torrey JAOS lviii 395: accord); on the word and its reading, cf. also Grelot DAE p. 74 nn. l, o.

v. *ʾpm*, *ʿl*$_7$, *ptḥ*$_1$.

pm$_2$ v. *ʾpm*.

pmhn **OffAr** Grelot DAE p. 374 (n. d): the *pmhn* in RES 1792A 2 = subst. Sing. abs. (< Egypt.) = milk jug (or rather < Egypt. = chest??), cf. however Chabot sub RES 1792: = n.p. (cf. also Lidzbarski Eph ii 232, Vincent Rel 266).

pmṭb v. *pm*$_1$.

pmṭz v. *pm$_1$*.
pmṭn v. *pm$_1$*.
pn$_1$ **Pun** Levi Della Vida Mem Brockelmann 129f.: l. subst. of uncert. interpret. Sing. abs. *pn* or *pt* in Trip 52^5; Amadasi-Guzzo FS Delcor 11f., IPT 100ff.: prob. = sundial (< root *pny*).
pn$_2$ v. *ʾḥšyn*.
pn$_3$ **Hebr** TA-H $24^{16,20}$ - ¶ conj. lest; *whbqydm ʿl yd ʾlyšʿ ... pn yqrh ʾt hʿyr dbr* TA-H 24^{14ff}: and he must hand them over to E. ... lest anything should happen to the city (cf. TA-H 24^{19f}) - for this word, cf. Margain Sem xxviii 85ff.
pnh$_1$ **Ph** Plur. abs. *pnm* KAI 26A ii 4; cstr. *pn* KAI 4^7, $10^{5,16}$, $24^{9,11}$, 43^7, 51 rs 2, 3 (dam. context), 60^8, Mus li 286^2; + suff. 3 p.s.m. *pny* EpAn ix 5^9; + suff. 1 p.s. *pny* KAI 11, 26A i 19 - **Pun** Plur. cstr. *pn* KAI $69^{3,6,10}$, 78^2, $79^{1,10}$, 81^3, 85^1, 86^1, 88^1, 137^1, etc., etc., *pʿn* KAI 102^2, 105^1, CIS i 188^1, 446^1, 624^2, 853^1, 910^1, 922^1, RES 1560^2 (for this reading, cf. Bertrandy & Sznycer sub SPC 47 :: Chabot sub RES 1560: l. *pn*), Punica xviii/ii 82^2, Hofra 133^2, 274, etc., etc., *pnʾ* KAI 164^1, CIS i 200^1, 239^2, 518^2, 658^1, 730^1, 850^1, RES 1537^2, Hofra 16^2, etc., etc., *pʿnʾ* CIS i 1125^1, 2155^1, Punica xviii/i 31^2, xviii/ii 86^2, Hofra 4^2, 21^1, 80^2, RES 332^1, etc., etc., *pnʿ* KAI 97^1, CIS i 992^1, 1834^2, 2005^1, 3363^1 (cf. also KAI 94^1 *pnʿʿl*, lapsus for *pnʿ bʿl*, cf. CIS i sub 2992, Röllig KAI a.l., or rather = lapsus for *pn bʿl*?; CIS i 1513^1: *pnʿl* lapsus for *pnʿ bʿl* or rather lapsus for *pn bʿl* or *pn bl*?; CIS i 5327^2: *pnʿbl* lapsus for *pnʿ bʿl*? or rather lapsus for *pn bʿl*?, cf. CIS i a.l.), *pʿnʾ* Trip 51^6, *bn*(cf. FR 40) CIS i 903^1, 2118^1, 3175^1, 3263^1, 5086^2, 5214^1, *b[n]ʾ* CIS i $3913^{2f.}$, *pny* KAI 126^7 (v. however infra), *pb* (lapsus) CIS i 5929^1, *pʿ* (lapsus) Hofra 172^2 (cf. CIS i 787^1), *pl* CIS i 644^2 (the *l* partly looking like *l*, partly like *n*), *nn* (lapsus) CIS i $610^{1f.}$, 2461^1, *tn* (lapsus) CIS i 716^2, *p* (lapsus) CIS i 3249^1, Punica xviii/i 29 (= NP 91), *n* (lapsus) CIS i 891^1, 3839^1, *pʾ* (lapsus) CIS i 4373^1, cf. KAI 175^2: φανε (cf. FR 89.2a), Hill lix no. 129: φανη (cf. FR 89.2a), KAI 176^2: φενη (cf. Friedrich ZDMG cvii 286, FR 89.2a; for the Greek transcriptions, cf. also Hvidberg-Hansen TNT ii 11ff. nn. 50, 76-78, 82; cf. also *Benefal* in Dessau 4341, Milik with Starcky SOLDV ii 528: = lapsus for *Fenebal* = *pn bʿl*, cf. also du Mesnil du Buisson TMP 199, Yadin FS Glueck 229 n. 92); + suff. 3 p.s.m. *pny* KAI 78^5, *pʿny* KAI 173^1 (?, dam. context), *pʿnyʿ* Trip 35 (?, dam. context) - **Mo** Plur. cstr. *pny* KAI $181^{13,18}$; + suff. 1 p.s. *pny* KAI 181^{19} - **Hebr** Plur. abs. *pnym* SM 49^9, AMB 4^{12}; cstr. *pny* KAI 200^5, Frey 634^5, SM 49^2; + suff. 3 p.s.m. *pnyw* DJD ii 44^5 (:: Pardee HAHL 133: = metathesis for *pnwy* (= QAL Part. pass. s.m. of *pny*)= empty); + suff. 2 p.s.m. *pnyk* TA-H 7^6, AMB 1^2, 15^{25}, *pnk* DJD ii $30^{6,24}$ - **OffAr**, cf. Frah xx 8 (*lpnmh*), Paik 817, 818 (*pnh*), 878 (*pʿn*), GIPP 52, 60 - ¶ subst. Plur. - **1)** face: passim; cf. the epithet

of the goddess Tanit in punic votive texts *pn b‘l*, face of Ba‘al (cf. e.g. KAI 78[2], 79[1,10f.], 85[1], CIS i 181[1], 182[1], 183[1], etc., etc.), on this epithet, cf. e.g. Hvidberg-Hansen TNT i 15ff., 46f., 104f., 119, 138, Garbini FSR 177, Ferron Mus xcix 16f., 30f., cf. also García de la Fuente Aug viii 501, du Mesnil du Buisson BiOr xviii 110 (less prob. interpret.); cf. also *my bl ḥz pn š* KAI 24[11]: who had never seen the face of a sheep; *mš pn ʾby* KAI 43[7]: a statue representing my father (cf. e.g. Honeyman JEA xxvi 50, Röllig KAI a.l., cf. however Lipiński RTAT 251, Gibson SSI iii p. 137: an effigy of the face of my father (cf. also v.d.Branden BMB xiii 93, OA iii 256, cf. already Bruston EPIS 43)) :: e.g. Cooke NSI p. 85 (div. otherwise): l. *mšpn* (= Sing. cstr. of *mšpn*),cf. also Lidzbarski Handb 381, Eph ii 189, KI sub 36 - used prepositionally, *pny mbʾ šmš* KAI 78[5]: before him is the West; *wtmṣʾ pny ʾl ḥnynh* Frey 634[5f.]: may she find grace with God - prec. by prep. - a) prec. by *ʾt*$_6$, *ʾt pn* = in the presence of; *[yt]t sml mš z ... ʾt pn ʾdny* Mus li 286[2]: I placed this statue being a votive donation (v. *sml*$_1$) ... before my lord; *ʾdmm ʾš p‘l mšrt ʾt pn gw* KAI 60[7f.]: the men who have rendered service before the community (cf. KAI 10[16], for this text cf. also Baldacci BiOr xl 130) - b) prec. by prep. *b*$_2$, v. *ʾgd*$_1$ - c) prec. by *l*$_5$ - α) in abs. state, *lpnm* = formerly: KAI 26A ii 4, cf. also SM 49[9] - β) in construct state with local meaning, before, in the presence of: EpAn ix 5[9], Frah xx 8; *wʾsḥb hm lpny kmš ...* KAI 181[18]: and I dragged them before K. (cf. KAI 181[12f.]); *lpn hmlkm hlpnym ytlnn mškbm km klbm* KAI 24[8f.]: in the presence of (?) of the former kings the M. used to spend the night (v. *lyn*$_1$) like dogs; *lpny ʾdrʾ ʾlpqy* KAI 126[7]: in the presence of the notables of L. (:: Amadasi IPT 66, 68: *lpny* = Sing. + suff. 3 p.s.m. of *lpn* (used adverbially = for the first time, cf. also Levi Della Vida RCL '49, 406)); cf. also *[w]ktbth lpnyk* TA-H 7[5f.]: and you must make an official note for yourself (for the context, cf. also Pardee UF x 305f.; v. also *ktb*$_1$; :: Levine Shn iii 288: make a note on the reverse side of the ostracon) - γ) in construct state with the meaning "in the sight of, in the appraisal of", *mlk ṣdq ... lpn ʾl gbl* KAI 4[6f.]: a rightful king ... in the sight of the gods of G. - δ) in construct state with temporal meaning, before, *kl hmlkm ʾš kn lpny* KAI 26A i 19: all the kings who were before me (cf. KAI 11); for KAI 200[5], v. *šbt*$_1$ - ε) for DJD ii 30[6,24], v. *mrq*$_1$ - d) prec. by prep. *mn*$_5$, *wygršh kmš mpny* KAI 181[19]: K. drove him out before me; cf. also prec. by *mn*$_5$ and *l*$_5$, *mlpnyk* AMB 15[25]: from your presence - e) prec. by prep. *‘l*$_7$, before, *‘l pn hmqdš[m ʾl]* KAI 81[3]: before these sanctuaries (cf. KAI 10[5], 173[1], Trip 35, cf. also *ʾdmm hmt bḥym ‘l pn šmš* CIS i 5510[5]: these men during their lives in the presence of the sun; cf. KAI 51 rs 2 (dam. context) - f) prec. by prep. *‘lt*, over and above, *‘lt pn hmšʾt z* KAI 69[3]: over and above (i.e. besides) this payment (cf. KAI 69[5f.] (*[‘l]t*)) - Milik DJD ii sub 44:

ttqn lhn mqwm pnyw in DJD ii 44[4f.] = you must prepare for them a place of his presence (i.e. for everyone a place to stay as a guest; uncert. interpret., diff. context) - **2)** east: AMB 4[12] - Albright BASOR lxxvi 8: l. *pn* in KAI 27[15]? (= Plur. cstr. of *pnh*$_1$; cf. Röllig KAI a.l., cf. also Dupont-Sommer RHR cxx 134, 141: l. *[-t kl* (= Sing. cstr. of *kl*$_1$)*p]n*), cf. however Gaster Or xi 44, 61: l. *[ʾ]dn* (= Sing. cstr. of *ʾdn*$_1$, cf. also Cross & Saley BASOR cxcvii 44 (n. 11), Röllig NESE ii 18, 23, Avishur PIB 248, 253), cf. also Caquot FS Gaster 48: l. *[ʾdn* (= Sing. cstr. of *ʾdn*$_1$) *k]l* (= Sing. cstr. of *kl*$_1$;cf. also Lipiński RTAT 265, Gibson SSI iii p. 82, 86) :: du Mesnil du Buisson FS Dussaud 422, 428: l *[-t kl* (= Sing. cstr. of *kl*$_1$) *ʿ]n* (= Sing. cstr. of *ʿyn*$_2$)or l. *[-t kl hm]n* (= Sing. cstr. of *hmn*$_2$(= multitude)) :: Torczyner JNES vi 23f., 28: l. *t[ḥt]* - cf. also *pʾn* of uncert. reading in CIS i 2926[1] - Puech Sem xxix 20f., 24: l. *lpny* (= *l*$_5$ + Plur. + suff. 3 p.s.m.?) in KAI 30[7] (poss. reading, diff. and dam. context) - Segal ATNS a.l., and p. 212: the *pnh* in ATNS 26[3,6] = Sing. abs. (the face, what is before someone > forward direction), improb. interpret., *pnh* prob. = n.l. (cf. also Shaked Or lvi 409 and cf. Porten & Yardeni sub TADAE A 5.5 l. 6; also :: Teixidor JAOS cv 732: = opposite side) - Lidzbarski Eph iii 106: the *pnh* in RES 1367[4], 1372B 2 = lapsus for *pnwh* (= Plur. + suff. 3 p.s.m.; cf. Grelot DAE p. 339 n. d: or l. *tnh*??), improb. interpret., *pnh* prob. = n.l. - v.d.Branden BO xii 215, 218: a form of this word possibly also in KAI 50[4].
v. *lpny*, *pp*$_2$.

pnh$_2$ v. *pnt*.

pny **OldAr** Qal Impf. 2 p.pl.m. *tpnw* KAI 224[7] - **Palm** Qal Part. pass. s.m. abs. *pnʾ* CIS ii 4172[1] (cf. Rosenthal Sprache 69, Bauer Ber iii 127 :: Chabot sub CIS ii 4172: = Qal Part. act.); m. pl. abs. *pnn* CIS ii 4172[2] (cf. Rosenthal Sprache 69, Bauer Ber iii 127 :: Cantineau Gramm 77, Chabot sub CIS ii 4172: = Qal Part. act.), Ber ii 104[5] (cf. Bauer Ber iii 127 :: Ingholt Ber ii 104, 106: = Qal Part. act.) - ¶ verb Qal to return, *ʾl tpnw bʾšrh* KAI 224[7]: do not return to his region (cf. Fitzmyer AIS 110f., cf. also Dupont-Sommer BMB xiii 28, Donner KAI a.l., Lemaire & Durand IAS 129, Sader EAS 134 × Rosenthal BASOR clviii 29 (n. 7), ANET 660: pay no attention to him (*bʾšr* = older variant of *btr*;cf. Greenfield ActOr xxix 7, FS Fitzmyer 50; cf. also Gibson SSI ii p. 47, 53) :: Koopmans 64: > do not take his side) - **2)** to empty; Part. pass. (v. supra), empty (in Palm. sepulchral texts CIS ii 4172[1,2], Ber ii 104[5] with special meaning: not (yet) used for burying); *ʾksdrʾ dy hw pnʾ lymynʾ* CIS ii 4172[1f.]: the exedra which is empty on the right side (cf. Ber ii 104[4f.]); *gwmḥyn pnn* CIS ii 4172[2]: empty niches - Beyer & Livingstone ZDMG cxxxvii 291: l. *pny* (= Qal Part. act. s.m. cstr.) in Atlal vii 105[1] (= someone who has attached himself (sc. to a certain tribe/clan, "Schutzbefohlener"); uncert. reading and

interpret.).
v. *pn_1*, *pnh_1*, *pnn_1*, *šzb*.

pnyh Palm Plur. abs. *pnyn* Ber v 95[6] - ¶ subst. f. meaning uncert. Ingholt Ber v 96: = locus, stretch (cf. also Milik DFD 3; cf. also Gawlikowski MFP 214: = part?) - the same word also in Inv xi 80[5]? (cf. Milik DFD 2ff.: l. *pnt*ʾ (= Sing. emph.), cf. also Gawlikowski Syr xlvii 324, Sem xxiii 119 n. 7 :: Teixidor Inv a.l.: l. poss. *[ʿw]ntʾ* = Sing. emph. of *ʿwnh*).

pnymy Hebr Sing. f. abs. *pnymyt* IEJ vii 241[1] - ¶ adj. internal, inner (said of a sarcophagus).

pnkn Hatra group of letters (for the reading, cf. Caquot Syr xli 271, Vattioni IH a.l.) resting of l. 6 of Hatra 203.

pnn_1 Pun Sznycer PPP 144: the diff. *muphonnim* (var. *muphonnium*) = YOPH Part. m. pl. abs. of *pnn_1* (related to *pny*)= to return :: Schroed 318: or = POʿAL Part. pl.m. abs. of *pny* :: L.H.Gray AJSL xxxix 82: = POL Part. pl.m. abs. of *pnn_2* (= to weaken), Part. = imbeciles; cf. also J.J.Glück & Maurach Semitics ii 123: = HOPH Part. pl.m. abs. of *pny*(= the opposite).

pnn_2 v. *pnn_1*.

pns v. *pls*.

pnqrym Nab unexplained word in CIS ii 3074[2], 3199[3], prob. = n.l. or tribal name (cf. also Cantineau Nab ii 136).

pnt Pun *pnt* KAI 69[13], *bnt*KAI 74[8] (cf. FR 40) - ¶ subst. (Sing. or Plur.) used as prep., before: *ṣwʿt ʾš yʿs.m. pnt ʾlm* KAI 69[13]: a *ṣwʿt*-offering (v. *ṣwʿt*) which will bc brought (v. however *ʿms*) before the gods (for this interpret. of *pnt*, cf. e.g. CIS i sub 165, Cooke NSI p. 114, 121, Röllig KAI a.l., FR 40, 250, Capuzzi StudMagr ii 68, cf. also v.d.Branden GP p. 117, Segert GPP p. 163) or rather = the *ṣwʿt*-offering which will be carried to the pinnacle(s) of the temple (*pnt* = Sing. or Plur. cstr. of *pnh_2*)?
v. *ʾp_2*, *pḥnt*, *tm_3*.

ps_1 Nab Sing. cstr. *ps* MPAT 64 iii 2 - ¶ subst. part, portion; *kps rʾš* MPAT 64 iii 2: as part of the principal (:: Fitzmyer & Harrington MPAT p. 324 s.v. *kps*: *kps* = interest) - for *ps šrt*, v. *psšrt*.
v. *dḥšpṭ*.

ps_2 Pun Sing. abs. *ps* KAI 69[18,20], 74[11], 75[6], CIS i 6000bis 8 (= TPC 84), *pʿs* KAI 165[2] - ¶ subst. tablet (on this word, cf. Bénichou-Safar TPC p. 193ff.); Février Sem xi 7f.: l. *pʿs* (= Sing. cstr.) in KAI 166[4] (highly uncert. reading and interpret.; cf. Chabot sub Punica xi 7: l. *pʿš* without interpret. :: Lidzbarski Handb 438 (div. otherwise): l. *(b)n ʿš(mnltm)* = n.p., cf. idem ibid. 346 (cf. also Röllig KAI a.l.), cf. however Jongeling NINPI 198) - the diff. *ps* in CIS i 226[2] (= TPI 525) poss. = part of n.p. which however remains unexplained (cf. Benz PNP p. 392).

ps$_3$ v. *prs*$_2$.
psg **OffAr** word of highly uncert. meaning in ATNS vii 2; Segal ATNS a.l.: *psg* prob. = dialectal variant of *psq*$_1$ (= derivative of root *psq* (= to break, to divide)).
psd **Hebr** NIPH Pf. 3 p.s.m. *npsd* DJD ii 24B 12 (uncert. reading; Milik Milik DJD ii a.l.: or l. *npsq* = NIPH Pf. 3 p.s.m. of *psq*$_1$) - ¶ verb NIPH to lose + *›t*$_6$: DJD ii 24B 12 - Segal ATNS a.l.: l. *ypsyd* in ATNS 85^2 (= APH Impf. 3 p.s.m. (highly uncert. interpret., dam. context)).
v. *psq*$_1$.
pswl **Hebr** Plur. f. abs. *psw[l]wt* Mas 454^2 - **JAr** Sing. *pswl›* Mas 455 - ¶ adj. 1) unfit, disqualified; *hkdyn h›<l>h psw[l]wt* Mas 454: these jars are disqualified - **2)** substantivated adj. what is disqualified: Mas 455.
psḥ$_1$ **OffAr** Sing. emph. *psḥ›* RES 1792A 5, 1793$^{4f.}$ (=PSBA '15, 222$^{9f.}$) - ¶ subst. feast of Pesach; for RES 1792A 5, cf. Clermont-Ganneau RAO viii 133f., Dupont-Sommer REJ cvii 45f., Grelot DAE p. 375 :: Lidzbarski Eph ii 232: or = Sing. emph. of *psḥ*$_2$ (= ford); for RES 1793, cf. e.g. Grelot DAE p. 376 - for Pesach in Elephantine, cf. Wag 152f., Vincent Rel 711f., Dupont-Sommer REJ cvii 39ff., Grelot VT iv 349ff., v 250ff., xvii 114ff., 201ff., Porten Arch 122ff.
psḥ$_2$ v. *psḥ*$_1$.
psḥmṣnwty (< Egypt., cf. Zauzich Ench xiii 116; cf. also Segal sub ATNS 6, Porten & Yardeni sub TADAE B8.12) - **OffAr** Sing. abs. *psḥmṣnwty* ATNS 6^4 - ¶ subst. the scribe of the divine book.
psṭy **Pun** Vattioni AION xvi 42: *fositio* in IRT 865 (punic text in Lat. characters) = position (< Lat. *positio*), cf. also Vattioni Aug xvi 541: l. *positio* with same explanation (highly uncert. interpret.).
psy v. *bzq*$_1$, *pšt*$_1$.
psylh v. *pslh*.
psypws v. *psyps*.
psyps (< Greek ψῆφος) - **Hebr** Sing. abs. *psypws* SM 75^3 - **JAr** Sing. emph. *psypsh* MPAT-A 2^2 (= SM 58 = Frey 1197), 34^4 (= SM 69), *[psy]pwsh* MPAT-A 11^1 (for this reading, cf. Naveh sub SM 43; = Frey 1165) - ¶ subst. m. mosaic, cf. *psp*.
psl$_1$ **Nab** QAL (or PA ‹EL?) Pf. 3 p.s.m. *pšl* RES 2030 (for the orthography, cf. Cantineau Nab i 43, Diem Or xlix 76f.; heavily dam. context) - **Palm** QAL (or PA ‹EL?) Pf. 3 p.s.m. *p[s]l* ARNA-Palm 1^6 - ¶ verb QAL (or PA ‹EL?) to sculpt.
v. *psl*$_2$, *pslh*, *psq*$_1$.
psl$_2$ **Nab** Sing. emph. *psl›* CIS ii 201^5, 208^9, 212^{10}, 213^9, 220^4, 229, 230, J 5^{11}, 12^{12} (= CIS ii 205), 62, 71 (for this text, cf. Milik sub ARNA-Nab 104), 76, 125 (for this reading, cf. Milik sub ARNA-Nab 62), 141, 171, ARNA-Nab 109^2(cf. Milik a.l. for the relation of this text

to parallel ones), RB xliii 577 ii; Plur. emph. *psly*ʾ CIS ii 206[10], 207[8], 209[10], 221[8], J 30[10] (= CIS ii 210), RB xlii 415[2] - ¶ subst. m. (or = QAL Part. act. m. of *psl*$_1$?)sculptor (cf. also Schmidt-Collinet Ber xxxi 95ff. for the sculptors mentioned in Nab. texts).
v. *ml*ʾ$_5$.

pslh **Pun** Sing. abs. *pslt* KAI 78[4] (or rather = QAL Part. pass. s.f. abs. of *psl*$_1$,cf. FR 139, Ferjaoui Sem xxxviii 114f.); Sing. or Plur. abs. *pslt* KAI 65[1] (for this word division and reading, cf. Chabot sub Punica xiii, Amadasi sub ICO-Sard 36, Schiffmann RSF iv 50f. :: Lidzbarski Eph iii 284 (div. otherwise): l. *mbn* (= Plur. cstr. of *mbn* (= building) *slt* (word of unknown meaning)??, cf. also Röllig KAI a.l.) - **OffAr** Sing. abs. *pslh* Cowl 31[9], *psylh* Cowl 30[10] - ¶ subst. (or adj.? in KAI 78[4], cf. Röllig KAI a.l.; v. also supra) hewn stone, passim; *mnṣbt pslt* KAI 78[4]: a stele of hewn stone; *bnyn psylh* Cowl 30[10]: a building of hewn stone (v. also *bnyn*; cf. Cowl 31[9]); on this word, cf. also Bonnet SEL vii 121.

pss v. *psq*$_1$.

psp (< Greek ψῆφος) - **JAr** Sing. emph. *psph* MPAT-A 40[2] (for this interpret., cf. Yeivin BRF iii 38, Naveh sub SM 57 :: Fitzmyer & Harrington MPAT a.l., Hüttenmeister ASI 305: = lapsus for *pspsh* = Sing. emph. of *psps* variant of *psyps*) - ¶ subst. m. mosaic; cf. *psyps*.

psps v. *psp*.

psq$_1$ **OffAr** QAL Pf. 3 p.pl.m. *psqw* AM ii 174[1]; cf. Frah xviii 9 (*pskwn*) - **JAr** QAL Pf. 3 p.s.m. *[p]sq* MPAT-A 32[2] (= SM 39 = Frey 885) - ¶ verb QAL - **1)** to cut (cf. also Altheim & Stiehl ASA 275: or = PAʿEL?); + obj. (image): AM ii 174[1] - **2)** to pledge: MPAT-A 32[2] - Milik RB lx 277, 286: l. *wps[q]* = *w* + QAL Imper. s.m. (= to leave off from (*mn*$_5$)) in DJD ii 43[4] (poss. interpret.; cf. also Vogt Bibl xxxiv 421: = PIʿEL/HIPH Imper. s.m.) :: J.J.Rabinowitz RB lxi 191f.: l. *wps[d]* = *w* + QAL Pf. 3 p.s.m. of *psd* (= to be missing; cf. also Pardee HAHL 130) :: Habermann Ha-arez 18-9-'53 (quoted RB lxi 192): l. *wps[d]* = *w* + QAL Imper. s.m. of *psd* (= to destroy) :: Cross RB lxiii 46ff.: l. *yps[d]* = QAL/HIPH Impf. 3 p.s.m. of *psd* (= to cause trouble; cf. ibid. p. 47 n. 5) :: Milik DJD ii a.l.: l. *yps[d]* = NIPH Impf. 3 p.s.m. of *psd* (= to be ill-treated; cf. Ginsberg BASOR cxxxi 25) :: Ginsberg BASOR cxxxi 25: or l. *yps[l]* = NIPH Impf. 3 p.s.m. of *psl*$_1$(= to be harmed) :: Vogt Bibl xxxiv 421: or l. *wps[w]* = *w* + QAL Imper. pl.m. of *pss*(= to leave off; cf. also Bardtke ThLZ lxxix 295) :: Teicher JJS iv 133f.: l. *yps[s]* (cf. ibid. p. 134 n. 1) = QAL/NIPH Impf. 3 p.s.m. of *pss*(= to keep apart from) :: Birnbaum PEQ '54, 25ff., 32: l. *ypq[d]* = NIPH Impf. 3 p.s.m. of *pqd*$_1$ (= to be missing).
v. *psg*, *psd*.

psq$_2$ v. *pšq*.

psq₃ v. *psqh*.

psqh **JAr** Sing. + suff. 3 p.pl.m. *psqtwn* MPAT-A 32[2] (= SM 39 = Frey 885; for this reading, cf. Naveh SM a.l. × Avi-Yonah QDAP iii 129f., Vincent RB xliii 468, Frey sub 885, Hüttenmeister ASI 183f.: l. *psqth* = Sing. + suff. 3 p.s.m. :: Beyer ATTM 386: l. *psqhwn* = Sing. + suff. 3 p.pl.m. of *psq*₃(= gift) :: Fitzmyer & Harrington MPAT a.l.: l. *psqth* = Sing. emph.) - ¶ subst. donation.

psqws ((< Greek φίσκος) < Lat. *fiscus*) - **Palm** Sing. abs. *psqws* Syr xiv 184[2] - ¶ subst. public revenues.

psšrt **OffAr** diff. word in Krael 10[7,9], 12[9,18]. Poss. < Egypt., cf. (Couroyer with) Grelot DAE p. 249 n. g: = dem. pronoun + suff. and *šrt.t* (= dowry), cf. however Hinz AISN 184: < Iran. = after-gift, cf. also Porten & Szubin JAOS cvii 234 (n. 5), Porten & Yardeni sub TADAE B 3.11 a.e. :: Krael p. 253 (div. otherwise): l. *ps* (= Sing. cstr. of *ps*₁)*šrt* (< root *š›r*₁), *ps šrt* = remainder portion, or *šrt* < root *šrw*, *ps šrt* = sustenance portion (for this division of words, cf. e.g. Reider JQR xliv 340, J.J.Rabinowitz Law 163, Porten Arch 226, Porten & Greenfield JEAS p. 62; for the context of Krael 10[7], cf. also Yaron JSS xiii 209f.).

p‹y v. *b‹y*₁, *‹py*₁.

p‹y› **Pun** Sing. abs. *p‹y›* RES 951 (reading uncertain) - ¶ subst. of unknown meaning, poss. indication of function.

p‹l₁ **Ph** Qal Pf. 3 p.s.m. *p‹l* KAI 1[1], 6[1], 24[3,4], 26A iii 15, C iv 19, 60[3,7], RSF vii 18[2], RES 1204[5] (or = 3 p.pl.?), 1207[2] (= Kition B 46), 1214[1], PW 84[1f] (cf. also KAI 10[3,6], 26A i 6f., 10, cf. FR 174, 267b, also for litt. (cf. also Chiera Hen x 134), interpret. as Inf. (abs.; cf. also Amadasi Guzzo VO iii 89f., Gai Or li 254f.) less prob.); + suff. 1 p.s. *p‹ln* KAI 26A i 3, 12; 3 p.s.f. *p‹l* KAI 10[8]; + suff. 1 p.s. *p‹ltn* KAI 10[2]; 1 p.s. *p‹lt* KAI 9A 1, 2 (*p‹l[t]*), 12[1], 14[19], 18[4] (:: Rosenthal JAOS lxxii 173: or = Sing. abs. of *p‹lh*?, cf. also Levi Della Vida RSO xxxix 302) , 24[4], 43[13] (also in RES 921[2]??, dam. context); 3 p.pl. *p‹l* KAI 24[5], 37A 14 (= Kition C 12); Impf. 3 p.s.m. *yp‹l* KAI 26A iii 16; 1 p.s. *›p‹l* KAI 26C iv 17; 3 p.pl. + suff. 2 p.s.f. *yp‹lk* KAI 50[3]; Inf. cstr. *p‹l* KAI 10[11]; Part. act. s.m. cstr. *p‹l* KAI 19[6], CIS i 45 (= Kition B 36); pl.m. abs. *p‹lm* KAI 37 A 13 (= Kition C 12 :: v.d.Branden RSF v 62: = Plur. abs. of *p‹l*₃ (= salary)), CIS i 87[2,4] (dam. context; = Kition C 1); Niph Pf. 3 p.s.m. *np‹l* RES 1204[1] - **Pun** Qal Pf. 3 p.s.m. *p‹l* KAI 62[1], 72B 1, 83[1], 96[1] (cf. e.g. Lidzbarski Eph ii 57, Röllig KAI a.l., Février sub CIS i 5523; or = 3 p.pl.?, dam. context), 121[2], 126[11], 161[11] (dam. context), 173[1], 277[2], CIS i 151[2] (= ICO-Sard-NPu 2), 5684[2], Trip 2[1], 18[1] (:: Levi Della Vida Lib iii/ii 20: rather = Part. act. s.m. abs.), RCL '66, 201[1], NP 130[2], Punica xi 33[1], *pl* ICO-Spa-NPu 2 (this form also in CB viii 31[3]?, diff. reading), cf. IRT 828[1] (cf. Levi Della Vida OA ii 78f., Vattioni

Aug xvi 538 :: Vattioni AION xvi 48 (div. otherwise): l. *[mu]fel* = pass. form of *pʿ*l_1),[3] (cf. Levi Della Vida OA ii 78, Vattioni AION xvi 49, Aug xvi 538), 873 (cf. Levi Della Vida OA ii 79, Vattioni Aug xvi 542, Polselli OAC xiii 237 :: Vattioni AION xvi 45: = Impf. pass. form of *pʿ*l_1), 877[2] (cf. Levi Della Vida OA ii 87, cf. however Vattioni Aug xvi 543 (div. otherwise): l. *felthi* = QAL Pf. 1 p.s.), 901[2,4] (cf. Levi Della Vida OA ii 79), OA ii 83[1], Poen 935 (cf. Sznycer PPP 81ff., J.J.Glück & Maurach Semitics ii 108f. :: Schroed 290, 311 (div. otherwise): l. *thyfel* = QAL Impf. 2 p.s.m. (cf. also L.H.Gray AJSL xxxix 77f., FR 31b, 38, 133, 263.2), 944 (*tefet* lapsus for *ke* (= *ky*) *fel*?, cf. variant text *tefel*, on the context, cf. Sznycer PPP 81f., 127, cf. however L.H.Gray AJSL xxxix 76f.: pro *tefet* l. *tefel* = QAL Impf. 2 p.s.m. (cf. also Schroed 291, 311)): *fel*; + suff. 3 p.s.m. *pʿlʾ* Trip 8[2], 73, KAI 132[2], cf. OA ii 83[5] (prob. interpret., cf. Levi Della Vida OA ii a.l., Vattioni AION xvi 40f., Aug xvi 539, cf. also Friedrich ZDMG cvii 297, Sznycer GLECS x 102; cf. also Polselli StudMagr xi 41): *felo*; + suff. 3 p.s.m. *pʿlm* Trip 38[1] (cf. also FR 112,2); 3 p.s.f. *pʿl* RES 1226[2] (= CIS i 5945 = TPC 7), cf. IRT 901[2,4]: *fela* (cf. Krahmalkov JSS xxiv 26, cf. also Vattioni Aug xvi 552, Polselli StudMagr xi 39 :: Vattioni AION xvi 50 (div. otherwise): l. *mufela* = *fel* prec. by pass. prefix and followed by suff. 3 p.s.m.); 3 p.pl. *pʿl* KAI 80[1], 137[1], ICO-Spa 16[1], *pʿlʾ* KAI 130[5], Trip 39[1], *phlʾ* KAI 142[4], cf. IRT 889[2] (= KAI 179), 906[1], IRTS 24[2], PBR xxviii 53.5[10] (diff. context, cf. Levi Della Vida OA ii 88, cf. also Vattioni Aug xvi 550): *felu*; 1 p.pl. *pʿln* KAI 145[11] (cf. e.g. Cooke NSI p. 155, Février Sem vi 25f., Röllig KAI a.l., Krahmalkov RSF iii 197, 203 :: Chabot sub RES 2221: l. *pʿlt* = Sing. cstr. of *pʿlh*); Inf. cstr. *pʿl* KAI 124[4], cf. Poen 935: *ful* (in *liful*), 945: *ful* (in *luful*, var. *lueui*); Part. act. s.m. abs. *pʿl* CIS i 3284[4]; s.m. cstr. *pʿl* KAI 120[2] (v. *šḥ*$_2$), CIS i 336[3] (for the dam. context cf. also RES sub 1935), 337[4], 338[3], 339[4], 340, 341[4], 342[4], 4882[2] (dam. context), 5952[2] (= TPC 14), Punica xi 14[4f.] (cf. also Février sub CIS i 5952), Hofra 100[3], 101[3]; pl.m. cstr. *pʿl* RCL '66, 201[6]; NIPH Pf. 3 p.s.m. *npʿl* Karth xii 51 ii 1 (diff. context; cf. Février & Fantar Karth xii 51 :: Krahmalkov RSF iii 178, 182, 202: = QAL Part. s.m. abs. of *npl*$_1$ :: v.d.Branden RSF v 60: = NIPH Part. s.m. abs. of *npl*$_1$); 3 p.s.f. *nplʿ* Trip 38[5] (:: Levi Della Vida LibAnt i 59: *nplʿ* = lapsus for *npʿl*), *npʿlʾ* Trip 40[1]; 3 p.pl. *npʿl* KAI 137[5], *npʿlʾ* KAI 130[1] - ¶ verb QAL to make, to construct, passim; said of a statue (KAI 6[1]), altar (KAI 173[1]), sanctuary (KAI 137[1]), stela (Trip 39[1], IRT 873[1f.], cf. also IRT 828[1]), a seat (?, ICO-Spa 16[1]), grave/tomb (RES 1226[2]), a gate (KAI 26A iii 15), gate with doors (KAI 18[3f.]); to accomplish (mighty deeds): KAI 14[19]; cf. *bl pʿl* KAI 24[3,4]: he accomplished nothing (:: Landsberger Samʾal 51: he did not do (it), cf. also Sperling UF xx 325f.); for KAI 124[4], v. *kʿs*$_1$ - **1)** + obj.: statue (KAI 26C iv 17f.), stela (IRT 906[1f.]), altar and *podium* (KAI 126[10f.]; for this text, v. *pʾdy*), basin (RES 1204[5]), columns (KAI 37A 14), seats (KAI 130[1]); *felu centeinari* IRT 889[2] (= KAI 179): they made the *limes*-fortress; *pʿl mlkt* Trip 18[1]: he did the work (cf. KAI 10[11]); *mʾš pʿlt bl pʿl hlpnyhm* KAI 24[4f.]: what I did, those (who reigned) before them did not do (on the context, cf. Ishida SVT xxxvi 149f.); *wpʿl ʾyt kl ʾš ʿlty mšrt* KAI 60[3f.]: and he did all that was required of him by way of service; *pʿl nʿm* KAI 19[6]: the beneficent (epithet of the Ptolemaic king, cf. Greek εὐεργέτης); cf. *wmlʾ ʾnk ʿqrt pʿr wpʿl ʾnk ss ʿl ss wmgn ʿl mgn* KAI 26A i 6f.: and I filled the storehouses (v. *ʿqrh*) of P. and acquired horse upon horse and shield upon shield (cf. Dahood Bibl xliii 351, xliv 70, Greenfield FS Nyberg 314f., Gibson SSI iii p. 47, 57, Lipiński SV 48, Pardee JNES xlii 65f., cf. e.g. also Rosenthal ANET 653, Röllig KAI a.l.: ... I added horse to horse ...); cf. also the foll. comb. *pth̠ wpʿl ʾyt hḥṣ z* RCL '66, 201[1]: he opened and made this street (v. also *ḥṣ*$_2$); for Poen 935, cf. Sznycer PPP 81ff.: l. *fel yth chil ys chon chem liful*: he did everything which he had to do thus (v. *kn*$_3$), i.e. he died - **2)** + double object, *pʿltn hrbt bʿlt gbl mmlkt ʿl gbl* KAI 10[2]: the lady, the mistress of G. made me ruler over G.; cf. *ypʿlk šlm* KAI 50[3]: may they (sc. the gods) keep you in good health - **3)** + obj. + *ʾt pn*, *ʾdmm ʾš pʿl mšrt ʾt pn gw* KAI 60[7f.]: the men who have rendered service before the community - **4)** + obj. + *l*$_5$, *hḥnwṭm ʾl pʿlt ʾnk ... lʾdnn* KAI 12[1ff.]: I made these molten images (?, v. *ḥnwṭ*) for our lord, cf. PW 84[1ff.], Trip 38[1ff.] - **5)** + obj. + *l*$_5$ + *l*$_5$, *pʿln bʿl ldnnym lʾb wlʾm* KAI 26A i 3: B. made me for the D. a father and a mother - **6)** + *l*$_5$, *ʾrn z pʿl ... lʾḥrm ʾbh* KAI 1[1]: the sarcophagus which he made for his father A. (cf. KAI 10[6f.], RES 1214[1f.], Trip 2[1f.], Punica xi 36[1]); cf. also *wypʿl lšʿr zr* KAI 26A iii 16: and he will make it into another gate (cf. e.g. O'Callaghan Or xviii 181, Gordon JNES viii 111, Pedersen ActOr xxi 40, Lipiński RTAT 260, OLZ '82, 459, Del Olmo Lete AO i 289, Puech RB lxxxviii 98 (cf. also Garbini AION xli 158, Pardee JNES xlvi 142), cf. however Ginsberg JANES v 140 (n. 36), Gibson SSI iii p. 51, 63: *l* = *l*$_5$ + suff. 3 p.s.f. = for it (sc. the city) and cf. Pardee JNES xlvi 142; or *l* = *l*$_5$ + suff. 3 p.s.m. = for himself (sc. the subject of the clause)? :: e.g. Dunand BMB viii 28, 32, Dupont-Sommer RA xlii 167, 175, Bron RIPK 117: *wypʿl lšʿr* = lapsus for *wypʿl šʿr* :: e.g. Alt WO i 275, 284, Marcus & Gelb JNES viii 118: he shall do something strange to the gate) - **7)** + *l*$_5$ + obj., *wpʿl ʾnk lšrš ʾdny nʿm* KAI 26A i 10: and I acted kindly to the scion of my lord (cf. KAI 10[8]) - **8)** + *ʿl*$_7$, *glbm pʿlm ʿl mlʾkt* KAI 37A 13: the barbers performing their duties for cultic purposes - **9)** + *ʿlt*: KAI 43[13] (poss. instance, dam. context, v. *ʿlt*, cf. also KAI 10[11]) - **10)** for KAI 26A i 12, *bʾbt pʿln kl mlk*, every king considered me his father (for the problems of *ʾbt*, v. *ʾbt*; cf. e.g. O'Callaghan Or

xviii 177, 185, Rosenthal ANET 654, Röllig KAI a.l., Bron RIPK 61f., Paul Maarav ii 181, Gibson SSI iii p. 49, 58 :: Dunand BMB viii 26, 30: all kings acted as fathers towards me :: Swiggers BiOr xxxvii 339: *bʾbt* = among the fathers :: Lipiński RSF ii 48, RTAT 258 (n. 65), OLZ '82, 459: every king put me among the fathers (i.e. the counsellors, the wise ones)) - **11)** Part. act., manufacturer, *grs bn ʾdnblʿ ʾpʿl* CIS i $3284^{3f.}$: G. the son of A. the manufacturer; *pʿl hmgrdm* CIS i $338^{3f.}$: the manufacturer of scrapers; *pʿl sdlm* RCL '66, 201^{6}: the manufacturer of veils (??, v. *sdl*), cf. CIS i 337^{4}, 339^{4}, etc. - **12)** cf. the following comb., *pʿl wʾyqdš* KAI 121^{2}: he made and consecrated; *pʿl wḥdš* KAI 62^{1}: he made and renewed (cf. *ḥdš wpʿl* KAI 80^{1}: he renewed and made (cf. JA xi/xvii 190^{1})); *pʿl wndr wḥdš* KAI 72B 1: he made, vowed and renewed - NIPH to be made: RES 1204^{1} (said of a basin), KAI $137^{5f.}$ (said of vessels of cast metal; + *ʿlt* (for)), Trip 40^{1} (said of a stela), Trip 38^{5} (diff. context, said of a tomb??); *npʿlʾ šš hyšbm ʾlʾ* KAI 130^{1}: these six seats were made - v.d.Branden OA iii 248, 257, Gibson SSI iii p. 136, 140: l. *pʿlt* in KAI 43^{10} (= QAL Pf. 1 p.s.), for the reading, cf. already Clermont-Ganneau Et ii 164 :: Clermont-Ganneau ibid.: = QAL Part. act. pl.f. cstr. :: Cooke NSI p. 83, 85 (div. otherwise): l. *mnʿlt* (cf. also Röllig KAI a.l.; without interpret.) :: Honeyman JEA xxvi 57f., 63 (div. otherwise): l. *ymn* (v. *mny*) *ʿl* (= *ʿl*$_7$); for the context, v. also *qmt* - Vattioni Aug xvi 541f.: the diff. *mufelyn* in IRT 865 = *mh*$_2$ + form of *pʿl*$_1$ (he made it or which they made) :: Vattioni AION xvi 42: *mufelyn* = form of *pʿl*$_1$ + suff. 3 p.s.m., he had it made - a form of this root *pʿl[* in CIS i 145^{2} - Vattioni Aug xvi 538: the diff. *fela* in IRT $826^{1f.,3}$ = QAL Pf. 3 p.s.f. of *pʿl*$_1$ (poss. interpret., cf. however idem ibid.: or = Pf. 3 p.s.m. + suff. 3 p.s.m.) :: Krahmalkov JSS xvii 73 (div. otherwise): the *fel* in l. 3 = QAL Pf. 3 p.s.m. :: Levi Della Vida OA ii 84: *fela* in both instances = part of n.p. (v. also *ʾḥ*$_1$) - Greenstein JANES viii 50: the *pʿl* (= QAL Pf. 3 p.s.m.) in Sar 6^{1} is Ph. (:: Owen Sar p. 102ff.: *pʿl* = Sing. cstr. of *pʿl*$_2$ (= work) - CIS ii sub 138, Cooke NSI p. 203f., Donner KAI a.l.: l. *pʿl* (= QAL Pf. 3 p.s.m.) in KAI 271A 1 (less prob. reading, cf. Lidzbarski Eph ii 242: l. *wʿl* = *w*$_2$ + *ʿl*$_7$).
v. *bʿl*$_2$, *ypʿ*$_2$, *mh*$_2$, *mypʿl*, *ʿll*$_1$, *pltʾ*, *pʿlh*.

pʿl$_2$ **JAr** Sing. + suff. 3 p.s.m. *pʿlh* MPAT-A 16^{3} (= SM 17 = Frey 981; v. infra), 56^{3} (*pʿl[h]*; = SM 74; or l. *pʿl[hwn]* = Sing. + suff. 3 p.pl.m., cf. Fitzmyer & Harrington MPAT a.l.) - ¶ subst. possessions, property; *dʿbd hdn ... mpʿlh* MPAT-A $16^{2f.}$: who made this ... from his own resources (for this reading and interpret., cf. Naveh Lesh xxxviii 296f., SM sub 17, Beyer ATTM 383, 669 (for the reading, cf. already Marmorstein PEQ '27, 52, Klein ZDPV li 136; cf. also Fitzmyer & Harrington: *mpʿlh* = with his own skill, less prob. transl.) :: Sukenik ASPG 60 n. 2: pro *mpʿlh* l. *bpʿlh* = *b*$_2$ + Sing. + suff. 3 p.s.m. of *pʿl*$_2$

(= reward), *bp‘lh* being the first word of the foll. clause (cf. Galling TGI (1), 82 (n. k), cf. also Owen with Goodenough JS i 198 (nn. 146, 147); cf. Kutscher AH i/1, 70, i/2, 70: l. *bp‘lh* = b_2 + Sing. + suff. 3 p.s.m. of *p‘l*$_2$ (= property?)) :: Sukenik Tarbiz i 148ff., Frey sub 981: l. *dpylh* = d_3 + *pylh* (= Sing. emph. of *pyl*(= gate)) :: Krauss REJ lxxxix 390 (div. otherwise): l. *šb‘* (= *šb‘*$_6$) *l* ...); *dyhb* ... *mn p‘l[h]* (v. supra) MPAT-A 56[2]: who gave ... from his resources.
v. *p‘l*$_1$.

p ‘l$_3$ v. *p‘l*$_1$.

p ‘lh **Pun** Sing. abs. *p‘lt* KAI 123[5] (or = Plur. abs.?, cf. Röllig KAI a.l.) - **DA** Plur. cstr. *p‘lt* i 7 - ¶ subst. f. work, act; *wlkw r’w p‘lt ’lhn* DA i 7: come and see the deeds of the gods (for reading and context, cf. Hoftijzer DA a.l., Delcor SVT xxxii 54f., H.P.Müller ZAW xciv 221f.); for the context of KAI 123[5], v. *yšr*$_1$ - Levi Della Vida OrAnt iv 59f.: the diff. *fillyth* in PBSR xxii 115f[3] prob. = Sing. cstr. of *p‘lh* (cf. also Vattioni Aug xvi 452; uncert. interpret., cf. also FR 204a; poss. = Sing. cstr. of *p‘lyh*?) :: Vattioni Aug xvi 452: or = QAL Pf. 3 p.s.f. of *p‘l*$_1$?
v. *mplh, plt’, p‘l*$_1$.

p ‘lyh **Pun** Sing. cstr., cf. KAI 178: *felioth* (cf. Levi Della Vida OA ii 70 n. 16, Röllig sub KAI 178, FR 204a, 227b, Polselli OAC xiii 238 (cf. also Vattioni AION xvi 41 n. 34) :: Levi Della Vida Lib iii/ii 19, Friedrich ZDMG cvii 296: = Plur. cstr. (cf. also FR 228: or = Plur.?) - ¶ subst. work; *felioth iadem sy rogate* KAI 178: the handiwork of R. (v. also *yd*).
v. *p‘lh*.

p ‘m$_1$ v. *p‘m*$_2$.

p ‘m$_2$ **Ph** Sing. abs. *p‘m* KAI 27[20] (v. infra); Dual cstr. *p‘m* KAI 18[7]; + suff. 1 p.s. *p‘my* KAI 26A i 16f. - **Pun** Sing. abs. *p‘m* Trip 41[1]; Plur. abs. *p‘mm* KAI 69[4,6] (*p‘[mm]*)[,8,10], 80[1] (v. infra), *p‘mt* KAI 68[5] (v. infra), *p‘m’t* KAI 120[1] (ter; or = Plur. abs. of *p‘mh*?) - ¶ subst. - 1) foot, *lkny ly lskr lšm n‘m tḥt p‘m ’dny* KAI 18[6f.]: that it may be to me a memorial and a good name under the feet of my lord; *w’nk ’ztwd štnm tḥt p‘my* KAI 26A i 16f.: and I A. placed them under my feet (i.e. I subjugated them); indication of animal foot: KAI 69[4,6,8,10]; indication of the legs of a slaughtering table, *hmzbḥ z dl p‘mm* KAI 80[1]: this slaughtering table with legs (v. *dl*$_6$), for this interpret., cf. Röllig KAI a.l. (for the transl. of *p‘mm* as feet, legs, cf. also Lidzbarski sub KI 68, Slouschz TPI p. 162f.) :: CIS i sub 175, Cooke NSI p. 130, Harr 138: *p‘mm* = stairs, steps (v. *dl*$_6$) :: Mulder FS Fensham 180: *p‘m* here = measure of length, foot :: (Hoffmann with) Lidzbarski Eph i 22 n. 1: *p‘mm* = Dual abs. (= for the second time, twice); > base, cf. Levi Della Vida RCL ’63, 465: *’yb’ t hp‘m* Trip 41[1] = he added the base (to the temple), cf. however also Amadasi IPT 83f.: = he

offerred the base (to the temple), or he went his step (to the temple) - **2)** time, turn, *rb mḥnt p‘m’t ‘sr w’ḥt wmynkd p‘m’t ‘sr w’rb‘* KAI 120[1]: consul for the eleventh time, *imperator* for the fourteenth time (cf. Lat. par. *cos xi imp xii*); cf. prob. also *p‘m p‘m* KAI 27[20]: now!, now! (cf. e.g. Albright BASOR lxxvi 9 n. 32, Gaster Or xi 44, 67, JNES vi 187, Cross & Saley BASOR cxcvii 46, cf. also Rosenthal ANET 658 (: time and again; cf. also de Moor JEOL xxvii 108), cf. however Baldacci BiOr xl 129: = immediately) :: v.d.Branden BO iii 47: step by step (cf. also Röllig KAI a.l., NESE ii 19, Lipiński RTAT 265, Garbini OA xx 286) :: Dupont-Sommer RHR cxx 144: prob. = Qal Inf. abs. of *p‘m*$_1$(= to press, to chase) + Qal Imper. s.m. of *p‘m*$_1$:: du Mesnil du Buisson FS Dussaud 431: = n.d. :: Torczyner JNES vi 26, 29: *p‘m*^{1} = Sing. abs. of *p‘m*$_3$ (= terror, trouble), *p‘m*^{2} = Sing. cstr. of *p‘m*$_3$ - the diff. *‘d p‘mt* KAI 68[5] poss. = until times (i.e. several times) = *‘d*$_7$ + Plur. abs. (cf. Amadasi sub ICO-Sard 34) :: Röllig sub KAI 68: *‘d* = *‘d*$_6$(= variant of *‘wd*$_5$)+ Plur. abs.: yet once (cf. also FR 247, 248b: *p‘mt* = Sing. abs. of *p‘mh*??, cf. also Lidzbarski Eph iii 282) :: Guidi with Chabot sub Punica i: l. *‘d* (= *‘d*$_4$) *b‘mt* (= *b*$_2$ + Sing. abs. of *‘mh*$_1$(= congregation)), cf. also Chabot sub RES 1216 (for *p‘mt* as Plur., cf. also Silverman JAOS xciv 269).
v. *yd‘*$_1$, *ksp*$_2$.

p‘m$_3$ v. *p‘m*$_2$.

p‘mh v. *p‘m*$_2$.

p‘ps **OffAr** Sing. abs. *p‘ps* Cowl 42[9] (for the reading, cf. e.g. Cowl p. 144 :: Ungnad sub ArPap 27: l. *p‘qs*) - ¶ subst. of unknown meaning, prob. indicating some type of cloak or garment (cf. Cowl a.l.); Grelot DAE p. 131: = *p* (< Egypt. article) + *‘ps* (< Egypt.; unidentified).

p‘qs v. *p‘ps*.

p‘r$_1$ **Ph** v.d.Branden Meltô i 36ff., 80: the *p‘r* in KAI 26 A i 6 = Sing. abs. of *p‘r*$_1$ (= irrigation system), improb. interpret., cf. e.g. Röllig KAI a.l., Gibson SSI iii p. 57: = n.l.

p‘r$_2$ **Pun** Lidzbarski Eph iii 60: the diff. *šp‘r* in KAI 118[1] = *š*$_{10}$ + *p‘r* (Sing. abs.) = clay (cf. Tomback CSL 270), or = marmor? (*marmor Parium*??, cf. also Röllig KAI a.l.), less prob. interpret. (cf. Amadasi IPT 110, cf. also Février Sem vi 29, Jongeling NINPI 80 : *šp‘r* = n.d., prob. interpret.) :: Levi Della Vida PBR xix 67: or *šp‘r* = Sing. m. abs. of *špr*$_4$ (= beautiful).

p‘r‘r (< Egypt., *p* (article) + *‘r‘r*, cf. Couroyer RB lxix 626, Grelot DAE p. 290 n. e, cf. also Porten & Yardeni sub TADAE A 6.2) - **OffAr** Sing. abs. *p‘r‘r* Cowl 26[12] - ¶ subst. prow, bow (of ship), cf. Grelot DAE p. 290 n. e.

p‘š v. *ps*$_2$.

pp$_1$ **Hatra** Sing. emph. *pp’* 9[1] (for the reading, cf. Altheim & Stiehl

AAW ii 195f., Vattioni IH a.l.) - ¶ subst. father, grandfather (?, cf. Altheim & Stiehl ibid.; or id. ibid.: or = n.p.?).

pp$_2$ **Ph** Sing. cstr. *pp* KAI 1[2] - ¶ subst. edge (of knife, etc.); *lpp* ... KAI 1[2]: with the sharp edge of ... (cf. Donner WZKMU '53/54, 157 n. 16 (cf. Röllig KAI a.l., Galling TGI 49 (n. 4), Gibson SSI iii p. 16; cf. already Dussaud Syr v 141, vi 107)) :: Albright JAOS lxvii 156 n. 27 (div. otherwise): *lpp* = QAL Part. s.m. cstr. of *lpp* (= to continue his way; for other derivations of the *lpp*, cf. e.g. Vincent RB xxxiv 184, 188, Torrey JAOS xlv 274, v.d.Branden BO xv 203, Mašr liv 735) :: Healy CISFP i 664: = derivative of root *lpp*(= to join)?? × Aimé-Giron ASAE xlii 316, Vinnikov VDI xlii 146, Teixidor Syr lxiv 139f.: pro *lpp* l. *lpn* = l_5 + Plur. cstr. of pnh_1).

ppyr v. *ppr*.

ppl cf. Frah x 40 (*ppl*ʾ, *ppl*; = dress reaching to the knees, cf. Nyberg FP 78 :: Ebeling Frah a.l.: poss. related to Akkad. *pappaltu* = *semen virile*).

ppr cf. Frah xv 2 (*ppy*ʾ, cf. Nyberg FP 84: abbrev. for *ppyr*ʾ):reed pen.

pṣʾ v. *ʿpṣ*, *pṣl*.

pṣy **Hebr** a form of this root in DJD ii 42[6]?: *hpṣtyk* (= HIPH Pf. 1 p.s. + suff. 2 p.s.m. (HIPH of *pṣy* = to account for, cf. Milik DJD ii a.l. (uncert. interpret.), cf. already idem Bibl xxxviii 263), cf. however - **1)** Birnbaum PEQ '55, 26f.: = HIPH Pf. 1 p.s. + suff. 2 p.s.m. of *pṣy* (= to cause to compensate, to arrange compensation) - **2)** Ginsberg BASOR cxxxi 26 (n. 15): = HIPH Pf. 1 p.s. + suff. 2 p.s.m. of *pyṣ*(var. of *pys*)= to satisfy (cf. also Sonne PAAJR xxiii 91f., Yaron BASOR cl 26f.) - **3)** de Vaux RB lx 270, 272, J.J.Rabinowitz Bibl xxxv 198, 200: = HIPH Pf. 1 p.s. + suff. 2 p.s.m. of *pṣy* (= to rid (someone) of, to save (someone)) - 4) Pardee HAHL 124f.: = HIPH Pf. 1 p.s. + suff. 2 p.s.m. of *pṣy* = to declare free from obligation :: I.Rabinowitz BASOR cxxxi 23: l. *hʿṣtyk* = HIPH Pf. 1 p.s. of *yʿṣ*, *ʿwṣ*:: Lehmann & Stern VT iii 393: l. *hpṣrtk* = HIPH Pf. 1 p.s. + suff. 2 p.s.m. of *pṣr* (= to insist, to press (someone)) :: Bardtke ThLZ lxxix 302: l. *hpṣyrk* = HIPH Inf. cstr. + suff. 2 p.s.m. of *pṣr*, with preceding *k* (pro *w*) = according to your stern commandment :: Yeivin At i 99f.: l. *lhpṣywk* (*l* pro *w*) hybrid Hebr./Ar. construction = l_5 + HIPH Inf. + suff. 2 p.s.m. of *pṣy* (= to relieve someone of legal importunities) - the *whpṣ* in DJD ii 42[5] prob. = wrong start of the first word of l. 6, cf. de Vaux RB lx 272, Birnbaum PEQ '55, 25, Lehmann & Stern VT iii 393, Ginsberg BASOR cxxxi 26 n. 13, Sonne PAAJR xxiii 91, Yeivin At i 98, Milik DJD ii a.l., Pardee HAHL 124 :: I.Rabinowitz BASOR cxxxi 23: = *w* + HIPH Imper. s.m. of *pwṣ*(= to disperse) :: Bardtke ThLZ lxxix 302: = *w* + HIPH Inf. abs. of *pwṣ* - **Hatra** Aggoula Assur a.l.: l. *lpṣyhy* = PAʿEL Impf. 3 p.s.m. + suff. 3 p.s.m. (= to rescue) in Assur 15d 2 (diff. and dam. context) ::

Milik DFD 350 (div. otherwise): l. poss. *nṣwḥn/nṣyḥn* = Sing. m. abs. of *nṣwḥn/nṣyḥn* (= triumphant) - this root also in AG 40^2 (*pṣn*)?? v. *ḥpṣ*$_3$, *ʿpṣ*, *pṣl*.

pṣym v. *pṣm*.

pṣl **OffAr** QAL (or PA ʿEL?) Pf. 1 p.pl. *pṣln* Krael $3^{20,22a}$; Impf. 1 p.pl. *npṣl* Krael 3^{20} (:: J.J.Rabinowitz Bibl xxxv 201f.: pro *pṣln* and *npṣl* l. resp. *nṣln* and *nnṣl* < root *nṣl* = to save :: id. Law 148 n. 23, VT xi 70: (if the reading *npṣl* is correct) < root *pṣl* = contamination of *nṣl* and *pṣʾ* :: Kutscher JAOS lxxiv 240: < *pṣl* = contamination of *pṣy*+*l*$_5$; on the poss. connection of *pṣy* and *pṣl*, cf. Kaufman AIA 84f.) - ¶ verb QAL (or PA ʿEL?) prob. meaning to clear a claim (cf. Yaron BiOr xv 20, Law 90, cf. also Kutscher JAOS lxxiv 240, 247 n. 131, Porten & Greenfield JEAS p. 42, Porten & Szubin JNES xli 126f.) :: Grelot DAE p. 219: to recover :: Reider JQR xliv 339: to compensate) - a form of this root (*ʾpṣl* = QAL (or PA ʿEL) Impf. 1 p.s.) prob. to be read in Krael 1^9 (cf. Porten & Yardeni sub TADAE B 3.2, cf. also Porten & Greenfield JEAS p. 36).

pṣm **JAr** the *pṣ[* in MPAT-A 17^2 (= SM 7) prob. to be completed to *pṣ[ymyh]* = Plur. emph. of *pṣm/pṣym*(= beam), cf. Urman IEJ xxii 17, Fitzmyer & Harrington MPAT a.l., Naveh SM a.l.

pṣṣ (< Arab., cf. Cantineau Nab ii 172, Diem Or xlix 83f., O'Connor JNES xlv 217f., 220) - **Nab** ITP Impf. 3 p.s.m. *ytpṣṣ* CIS ii 350^5 - ¶ verb ITP prob. meaning to be divided (cf. Milik RB lxvi 560) :: CIS ii sub 350: to be violated, to be transgressed (:: Levinson NAI 204: = to be opened) :: Cooke NSI p. 241, 243: to be separated, to be withdrawn; *wlʾ ytšnʾ wlʾ ytpṣṣ mn kl dy bhm* CIS ii $350^{4f.}$: it may not be changed nor divided in disaccord with what is (stated) in them - Rocco AION xxiv 475, 478: l. *pṣṣ* in GR ii 36 no. 20^1 = POL/PI ʿEL Imper. s.m. of*pṣṣ* (= to break down, to smash) or = POL Imper. s.m. of *pwṣ* (=to disperse, to scatter), highly uncert. reading, cf. Polselli GR a.l. v. *ḥpṣ*$_1$.

pṣr v. *pṣy*.

pq **OffAr** Sing. abs. *pq* Cowl 15^{16}, *pyq* Krael 2^6, 7^{18} - ¶ subst. tray (cf. Grelot RB lxxviii 529f., DAE p. 194 (n. m), Porten & Greenfield JEAS p. 20, 39, 55, Delsman TUAT i 261, Porten & Yardeni sub TADAE B 2.6 ea :: Driver JRAS '32, 78: bowl :: Epstein JJLG vi 366 n. 3: jar, jug (cf. also Reider JQR xliv 339f.) :: Fitzmyer FS Albright ii 157, WA 259: related to Hebr. *pīqāh* = spindle-whorl?; < Egypt., cf. Grelot RB lxxviii 529f., DAE p. 194 (n. m) :: Driver JRAS '32, 78: = Akkad. *paqqu* :: Scheftelowitz SUBH i 15: < Iran. (cf. also Epstein JJLG vi 366 n. 3, Reider JQR xliv 339f., cf. however Schaed 267 n. 1, Krael p. 147) :: Epstein JJLG vi 366 n. 3 (cf. also Reider JQR xliv 339f.): related to Ar. *bwq* and Hebr. *pk*, *bqbq*.

pqd$_1$ **Ph** QAL Inf. cstr. *pqd* CIS i 88^{4,5} (cf. also v.d.Branden FS Rinaldi 65 × CIS i sub 88, Amadasi sub Kition F 1: = QAL Pf. 3 p.s.m. in l. 4 and QAL Pf. 3 p.pl.m. in l. 5 × FR 131 = QAL Pf. 3 p.s.m. in both instances :: Harr 138: or = QAL Part. act. s.m. cstr.; cf. also Cooke NSI p. 74f.); YOPH (?, cf. also e.g. FR 148) Pf. 3 p.s.m. *ypqd* CIS i 88^4 (:: Cooke NSI p. 75: = Pf. 3 p.pl. :: Harr 138: = YIPH Pf. 3 p.s.m.?, uncert. reading, cf. Amadasi sub Kition F 1); 3 p.pl. *[yp]qd* CIS i 88^5 (cf. e.g. Cooke NSI p. 75 :: Harr 138: = YIPH Pf. 3 p.s.m.? :: v.d.Branden FS Rinaldi 67ff.: = QAL Impf. 3 p.s.m.; for the reading, cf. also Amadasi sub Kition F 1) - **Hebr** QAL Pf. 1 p.s. *pqdty* DJD ii 44^8; HIPH Pf. 3 p.s.m. + suff. 3 p.pl.m. *hbqydm* TA-H 14$^{14f.}$ (for this form, cf. Aharoni BASOR cxcvii 20 nn. 12, 13, TA-H a.l., cf. also Dahood Bibl l 74f., Heltzer AION xxi 195, Lemaire Sem xxiii 15f., Pardee UF x 321f. (n. 136), JNES xliv 70, Zevit MLAHE 28, Sarfatti Maarav iii 69ff.) - **OffAr** QAL Pf. 3 p.s.m. *pqd* KAI 233^{17} (*pqd[*); Impf. 3 p.s.m. *ypqd* Aḥiq 192; Part. pass.m. s. abs. *pqyd* Aḥiq 103 (for the context, cf. e.g. Lindenberger APA 84, 240 n. 218); HOPH 3 p.pl.m. *hpqdw* Cowl 20^7 (for this reading, cf. Lidzbarski Eph iii 80, the reading of the *h* uncert.) - ¶ verb QAL - **1)** to command: KAI 233^{17} (dam. context) - a) + *ʾt*$_6$, *wpqdty t my š ytn ...* DJD ii 44$^{8f.}$: and I ordered anyone who will give ... - b) + *l*$_5$, *hn ypqd lk mrʾk myn lmnṭr* Aḥiq 192: if your lord entrusts to you water to keep ...; *hn pqyd lk* Aḥiq 103: if something is commanded you - **2)** to survey, *pqd hmpqd z ... ʾš ypqd ʾ[dn]š[mš]* CIS i 88^4: the surveyance of this *mpqd* (v. *mpqd*$_1$) it is with which A. has been charged (cf. CIS i 88^5) - HIPH to hand over (to), *wšlḥtm ʾtm ... [by]d mlkyhw ... whbqydm ʿl yd ʾlyšʿ* TA-H 24$^{13ff.}$: you shall send them through M. ... and he shall hand them over to E. - HOPH/YOPH - **1)** to be charged: CIS i 88^{4,5} (v. supra) - **2)** to be put in deposit, *ʾyty zy bpq[dwn] hpqdw* Cowl 20^7: it is a fact that they were put in deposit (the clause division of Cowl a.l. less prob.) - a YOPH (or PU ʿAL) Part. s.m. abs. (*mpqd*) in KAI 119^3 (?; indication of function?), cf. Février RA l. 186: = someone charged, commissioner (cf. also Röllig KAI a.l., Levi Della Vida RSO xxxix 307, Amadasi IPT 77, 161) :: Levi Della Vida RCL '55, 553, 557: l. *npqd* = NIPH Pf. 3 p.s.m. (= the commission was given) - Altheim & Stiehl FuF xxxv a.l., ASA 244, 275: the *pqd* in FuF xxxv 173^{12} = QAL Pf. 3 p.s.m. (= to pursue; highly uncert. interpret. and context).

v. *ʾlp*$_3$, *ʾnth*$_2$, *nqy*$_1$, *psq*$_1$.

pqd$_2$ **OldAr** Plur. + suff. 1 p.s. (or = Sing. + suff. 1 p.s.?) *pqdy* KAI 224^{4,10} (*[p]qdy*)^{,13} - **OffAr** Sing. abs. *pqyd* Cowl 37^6, Driv 2^2 (*pq[yd]*)^{,3} 6^5, FS Driver 54 conc. 2 (dam. context); cstr. *pqyd* Driv 10^4, F ii A 13^2, B 1^1, RES 248A 1 (for the reading of the context, cf. Porten & Yardeni sub TADAE A 5.5), ATNS 64b 9, 15 (for l. 9 :: Segal ATNS a.l.: or =

n.p.), 85[3] (or = abs.?, dam. context); emph. *pqydʾ* Driv 1[2] (*pqy[dʾ]*), 2[4*], 4[1], 6[1], 7[1*], 8[1*], 9[1*](*pqyd[ʾ]*), 10[1*,2,3], 11[2,3,4], 12[1]; Plur. emph. *pqydyʾ* Driv 7[3,7]; cf. Frah xii 13 (*pkytʾ*, cf. Nyberg FP 81, cf. already Schaeder with Ebeling Frah a.l. :: Ebeling ibid.: cf. Akkad. *piqittu* (= supervision > supervisor) - ¶ subst. officer, magistrate: passim; for the precise connotation of this word in **OffAr** texts, cf. Krael p. 33f., Verger RCL '64, 81 (nn. 20, 22), RGP 69, Porten Arch 54f. (n. 102) - on this word, cf. Kaufman AIA 79f. (n. 251) - Driv a.l.: l. prob. *pqy[dʾ]* = Sing. emph. in Driv 1[2] (reading however highly uncert., cf. Porten & Yardeni sub TADAE A 6.5.
v. *mpqd₂*, *pqr*.

pqdwn **OffAr**, cf. Frah xvii 4 (*pkdwn*), GIPP 31, SaSt 21 cf. Toll ZDMG-Suppl viii 34 - **Nab** Sing. cstr. *pqdwn* CIS ii 350[4] - **JAr** Sing. abs. *pqdwn* DBKP 17[41]; emph. *pqdnh* DBKP 17[42] - ¶ subst. - **1)** judgement, punishment: Frah xvii 4 - **2)** responsability, task (cf. Milik RB lxvi 560), *ppqdwn dwšrʾ ... dy ... ytʿbd* CIS ii 350[4]: it is the responsability of D. that it will be done (:: CIS ii sub 350, Cooke NSI p. 241, 243, Cantineau Nab ii 137: *pqdwn* here = order) - **3)** deposit, *lḥšbn pqdwn* DBKP 17[41]: on account of deposit (cf. Greek par. εἰς λόγον παραθήκης), *knmwš pqdnh* DBKP 17[42]: according to the law of deposit - this word (Sing. abs.; *pq[dn]*) prob. to be restored in Cowl 20[7] (= deposit), cf. Porten & Greenfield JEAS p. 24, Porten & Yardeni sub TADAE B 2.9 (cf. also Grelot DAE p. 198) :: Cowl a.l.: restore *pq[dwn]*.

pqdn v. *pqdwn*.

pqh **Ph** Sing. abs. *pqt* KAI 43[15] - ¶ subst. poss. meaning profit (cf. Gibson SSI iii p. 137, 141: < *pwq₁*; cf. also Honeyman JEA xxvi 58: = advantage and cf. also Cooke NSI p. 88: = profit < *npq₁*? (derivation less prob.) :: v.d.Branden OA iii 259, BiOr xxxvi 203: = greatness, magnificence < *pwq₁* :: Lidzbarski sub KI 36, Röllig KAI a.l.: = deliverance < *npq₁* (cf. also Silverman JAOS xciv 268) :: Lipiński RTAT 251 (n. 36): = official authority < Akkad. *piqittu*).

pqḥ₁ **OldAr** Qal Imper. pl.m. *pqḥw* KAI 222A 13 - ¶ verb Qal to open; + obj., *pqḥw ʿynykm lḥzyh* KAI 222A 13: open your eyes to see ... (cf. also Watanabe AVTA 197, Greenfield FS Fitzmyer 50) - Albright BASOR lxxxii 19: the diff. *hpqḥ* in KAI 193[4] = Hiph Pf. 3 p.s.m. of *pqḥ₁* (= to open), cf. e.g. also Albright ANET 322, Röllig KAI a.l., cf. however de Vaux RB xlviii 191: = Hiph Imper. s.m. of *pqḥ₁* (cf. Pardee HAHL 85) or l. *-h pqḥ* (= Qal Imper. s.m. (cf. also Michaud PA 97, Lemaire IH i 100, 102), cf. also Lipiński OLP viii 89f., BiOr xxxv 287: *hpqḥ* = *h₂* + Qal Pf. 3 p.s.m. of *pqḥ₁* × Reider JQR xxix 234: *hpqḥ* = *h₁* + Sing. abs. of *pqḥ₂* (= overseer, supervisor), cf. also Albright BASOR lxiii 37, Gibson SSI i p. 39 (cf. also Dussaud Syr xix 264: = commander of the life guard, policeman, spy) :: Torczyner Lach i p. 53,

65f.: = h_1 + Sing. abs. of *pqḥ*$_3$ (= open-eyed, the open-eyed one = the prophet) :: Albright BASOR lxi 13: *hpqḥ* = h_1 + QAL Part. act. s.m. abs. of *pqḥ*$_1$ (= inspector), cf. Cassuto RSO xvi 393, Chapira RES '45, 114; for the interpret. as QAL Part., cf. also Ginsberg BASOR lxxi 25 :: Albright BASOR lxxiii 17f.: l. *hpqḥ[t]* = HIPH Pf. 2 p.s.m. of *pqḥ*$_1$ :: Albright BASOR lxx 13: = n.p. (cf. Elliger PJB '38, 48 n. 1)); for the context of KAI 193[4], v. also *ʾzn*$_2$.

pqḥ$_2$ v. *pqḥ*$_1$.

pqḥ$_3$ v. *pqḥ*$_1$.

pqy v. *pwq*$_1$.

pqyd v. *pqd*$_2$.

pql **OffAr** Dupont-Sommer Sem xiv 72: l. ibid. conv. 3 *]pql* (reading of *p* uncert.), *pql* (= Sing. abs.) = linseed? (uncert. interpret.).

pqq v. *prr*$_1$.

pqr **Ph** Kornfeld Abydos sub 14: the *pqr* in RES 1535[1] (= KAI 49, 45) = Sing. abs. of *pqr* (= supervisor, inspector)?; highly uncert. interpret.: l. perhaps *pqd* (= Sing. abs. of *pqd*$_2$)??,cf. also Kornfeld Abydos a.l.

pqt$_1$ (< Akkad., cf. Kaufman AIA 43, cf. also Caquot HDS 14, Dion Bibl lv 402, Lipiński Stud 81, ActAntHung xxii 376, WGAV 376, Fales AION xxviii 276 n. 15 and cf. Millard JSS xxi 176) - **OffAr** Sing. cstr. *pqt* HDS 9[4]; emph. *pqtʾ* HDS 9[7] - ¶ subst. administration; *bʿl pqt mlkʾ* HDS 9[4f.]: royal superintendant (on this function, cf. the litt. mentioned supra and cf. Caquot HDS 16), cf. HDS 9[6f.].

pqt$_2$ v. *pqh*.

pr$_1$ v. *pry*$_2$.

pr$_2$ **DA** Sing. abs. *pr* ii 17 (:: H.P.Müller ZAW xciv 219, 237: = Sing. cstr.) - ¶ subst. poss. meaning foolishness, silliness (cf. Hoftijzer DA a.l. :: H.P.Müller ZAW xciv 219, 237: = confusion :: Caquot & Lemaire Syr liv 207, H.Weippert LJPM 95 n. 54: pro *wpr* l. *spr* (= Sing. cstr. of *spr*$_3$(= formula)), cf. also Rofé SB 63, McCarter BASOR ccxxxix 59 n. 1, Ringgren Memorial Seeligmann 95, Hackett BTDA 30, 73, 132 :: Levine JAOS ci 201: pro *wpr* l. *spr* = PAʿEL Inf. of *spr*$_1$:: Garbini Hen i 184, 186: l. *spr* = QAL Imper. s.m. of *spr*$_1$(= to write)? :: Lemaire CRAI '85, 277: l. *spr*$_3$= (art of) writing, for the reading *spr*, cf. also Weinfeld Shn v/vi 147); *ldʿt wpr* DA ii 17: foolishness and silliness (for *ldʿt* being l_2 (= *lʾ*$_1$) + QAL Inf. cstr. (subst.) of *ydʿ*$_1$, cf. Hoftijzer DA a.l. :: Caquot & Lemaire Syr liv 207, Garbini Hen i 184, 186, Levine JAOS ci 201: = l_5 + QAL Inf. of *ydʿ*$_1$; cf. also Dijkstra GTT xc 165 (n. 28) = take heed).

pr$_3$ (or *prh*$_3$?) **OffAr** Plur. abs. *prn* Aḥiq 112 - ¶ subst. Plur. bran (for this interpret., cf. Smend ThLZ xxxvii 391, Halévy RS xx 57, Epstein ZAW xxxii 135, Nöldeke AGWG xiv/4, 14, Leand 43q, Ginsberg ANET 429, Grelot RB lxviii 185, DAE p. 439, Lindenberger APA 99,

Kottsieper SAS 109f., 226 :: Cowl p. 239: = crumbs :: Sach 161, Grimme OLZ '11, 533: l. *pdn* (= Sing. abs. of pdn_1)).

pr>₁ v. *plḥ₁*.

pr>₂ **OffAr** word of unknown meaning and uncert. reading in Cowl 42[7] (*pr>* = Sing. emph.?), cf. also Porten & Yardeni sub TADAE A 3.8: l. *pd/r>* (without interpret.).

prb **Pun** word of unknown meaning in KAI 130[1]: prob. = indication of function or name of clan or tribe (:: Levi Della Vida Lib iii/ii 12: poss. = lapsus for rb_2?, cf. also Röllig KAI a.l., cf. however Levi Della Vida IRT p. 12, IPT 43 n. 4); in the comb. *>rš* (= n.p.) ***hprb*** KAI 130[1] (cf. also Jongeling NINPI 164 (div. otherwise): ***hprb*** poss. = name of tribe).

prbd v. *prbr*.

prbst (< Iran., cf. litt. mentioned infra) - **OffAr** *prbst* KAI 279[5] (indeclinable word) - ¶ adj.(?) poss. meaning: tied around (*zy prbst* = those who are bound), cf. Altheim & Stiehl GH i 404, EW ix 196, x 258 n. 21, ASA 26f. n. 103, 275 × Benveniste JA ccxlvi 41f.: intemperate (interpret. based on Greek par. ἀκρατεῖς), cf. also Kutscher, Naveh & Shaked Lesh xxxiv 134, Rosenthal EI xiv 97*; for this word, cf. also Nober VD xxxvii 373, Levi Della Vida Editto 26, 34, Schwarzschild JAOS lxxx 156, Donner KAI a.l., Garbini Kand 11ff., Altheim & Stiehl GMA 349 n. 21, 350.

prbsty (< Iran., cf. litt. mentioned s.v. *prbst*) - **OffAr** *prbsty* KAI 279[6] - ¶ subst. poss. meaning: ties (cf. Altheim & Stiehl GH i 404, EW ix 196) × Benveniste JA ccxlvi 41f.: intemperance (interpret. based on Greek par. ἀκρασίας), for further discussion, v. litt. mentioned sub *prbst*.

prbr (< Iran., cf. e.g. D.H.Müller WZKM viii 97, Schaed 97, 295, Donner KAI a.l., Lipiński Stud 156f., Hinz AISN 179, HAL s.v. *prbr*, cf. also Hübschmann Studien 39f. :: Cowley with Cook JHS xxxvii 226f., CRAI '21, 10: < Greek περίβολος? :: Andreas with Littmann Sardis 26: l. *prbd*< Iran. = court, place; cf. also Lidzbarski ZA xxxi 124, Kahle & Sommer KlF i 34ff.; for etymology, cf. also J.Ar. and Rabb. Hebr. *prwwr* and class Hebr. *prbr* and *prwr*) - **OffAr** Sing. abs. *prbr* KAI 260[3,5]; + suff. 3 p.s.m. *prbrh* KAI 260[3] - ¶ subst. prob. meaning precinct, entrance corridor (v. litt. mentioned supra); *prbr zy ‘l sprb* KAI 260[3]: the precinct connected with the tomb (v. *sprb*).

prg cf. Frah iv 1 (*p* = abbrev. for *prg>*): = millet, cf. Nyberg FP 65.

prgmṭt (< Greek πραγματευτής) - **Palm** Sing. emph. *prgmṭt>* Inv x 113[3f.] - ¶ subst. agent, representative (in Inv x 113 of a publican).

prh₁ **Hebr** Sing. abs. *prh* DJD ii 42[3] - ¶ subst. f. cow - Février JA cclv 61f.: the *prh* in Punica ix 9[1]: = Sing. abs. of prh_1 (= heifer), less prob. interpret., cf. also Chabot sub Punica ix 9 a.l. (div. otherwise):

l. *prhpyg›* poss. = n.p. < Lat. (cf. however *pg*‘$_1$); *prh* prob. = n.p.; cf. also Garbini BO xx 111.
v. *prh*$_2$.

prh$_2$ **Hatra** Sing. emph. *prt›* 245[2] (for this poss. interpret., cf. Degen JEOL xxiii 412 :: Aggoula MUSJ xlvii 15f.: = Sing. emph. of *prh*$_1$(= ewe of sheep; cf. also Vattioni IH a.l.) :: Safar Sumer xxiv 18: *prt›* = Parthian (gold) :: Vattioni IH a.l.: or *prt›* pro *prṭ›* (without interpret.) - ¶ subst. portion (v. supra); *›s 8 mn prt› ḥd›* (v. *›ḥd*$_4$) Hatra 245[2]: 8 *as* (v. *›s*$_1$) being a portion ... (poss. interpret.; *mn* interpreted as *mn*$_5$ of identification).

prh$_3$ v. *pr*$_3$.

prwṭ **Hebr** Plur. m. abs. *prwṭyn* Mas 450[2] (*pr[w]ṭyn*), 452[3] - ¶ adj. first-class; in Mas 450[2], 452[3], referring to first-class wine or oil; Naveh sub Mas 449-452: the diff. *krwṭyn* in Mas 449[1] poss. = lapsus for *prwṭyn* (poss. interpret.) :: Yadin sub Mas 449-452: = variant of *qrwtym* = (n.l.).

prwṭh v. *p*$_4$.

prwk **JAr** Milik Syr xlv 101f.: l. *[p]rwkh* (= Sing. emph. or Sing. + suff. 3 p.s.m.) of *prwk* (= wheat flour) in Syr xlv 101[21] (dam. context); *prwkh dlḥm›* Syr xlv 101[21]: fine wheaten bread > gruel (highly uncert. interpret.).

przl (derivation unknown, v. *brzl*) - **OffAr** Sing. abs. *przl* Cowl 10[10], 14[4], 20[5], 26[12], 35[12] (*pr[z]l*, cf. Porten & Yardeni sub TADAE B 4.6; cf. also Porten JNES xlviii 166), Krael 11[11] - **JAr** Sing. abs. *pwrzyl* AMB 11[7]; emph. *przl[h]* AMB 15[5] - ¶ subst. iron; *nḥš wprzl* Krael 11[11]: bronze and iron (cf. Cowl 14[4], 20[5], 26[12]); *ksp wdhb nḥš wprzl* Cowl 10[9f.]: silver and gold, bronze and iron.

prḥ$_1$ v. *srḥ*.

prḥ$_2$ **OffAr** Cross EI ix 26: the *prḥ›* on 4 stamp impressions from Ramat Raḥel = lapsus for *pḥr›* (= Sing. emph. of *pḥr*$_2$,v. also *pḥr*$_2$),cf. also Naveh Proc v CJS i 99 (Hebr.).

prḥ$_3$ Ebeling AfO xvi 215, v.Soden Or xxxvii 263, xlvi 192: = flower, bloom > Akkad. in comb. *puruḫ libnu* (an aromatic essence; cf. also v.Soden AHW s.v.).

prṭ **Pun** the diff. *hprṭ* in KAI 172[2] prob. = *h*$_1$ + Qal Part. act. s.m. abs. of a root *prṭ* (= to take care of, to cause to be done; cf. Lat. par. *quei fac(iendam) coeravit*); uncert. etymology, cf. Friedrich AfO x 82f., FS Eissfeldt 122 n. 32, Levi Della Vida RCL '49, 403 n. 1, cf. however Levi Della Vida RSO xxxix 310: *prṭ* = to divide > to decide (cf. also Amadasi sub ICO-Sard-NPu 5).

pry$_1$ v. *pdy*.

pry$_2$ **Ph** Sing. abs. *pr* KAI 14[12] (v. infra); cstr. *pr* KAI 43[3,6] (v. infra) - **Pun** Sing. abs. *pry* Trip 51[6] (diff. context, cf. Levi Della Vida Or xxxiii a.l., Amadasi IPT 135), *pr* KAI 76B 2 - **Hebr** Plur. abs. *pyrwt* SM 49[1,18,22] - ¶ subst. m. - **1)** fruit: Trip 51[6] (v. supra), SM 49[1,18,22]; *pr y'* KAI 76B 2: good (fine) fruit; prob. > descendant, *pr krml* KAI 43[3,6]: fruit/descendant of Karmel (cf. Gibson SSI iii p. 138 (cf. also Lipiński RTAT 250 n. 23), cf. also v.d.Branden OA iii 251: = originating from the Karmel (cf. already Honeyman JEA xxvi 62 (n. 3)) :: Clermont-Ganneau Et ii 160 (div. otherwise): *prkrml* = indication of function (cf. also Lidzbarski sub KI 36: = indication of function or surname) :: Honeyman JEA xxvi 58, 61 (n. 11), 62 (nn. 1-5): or l. *prkdml* = transcription of Greek προεχ(εῖς) (τοῦ) δήμου (= prominent among the people, leading citizens, used as honorific title) - **2)** branches: KAI 14[12] (cf. Ginsberg FS Driver 72ff. (cf. also Greenfield JAOS lxxxv 257, Hoftijzer BiOr xxiv 29) × e.g. CIS i sub 3, Lidzbarski Handb 354, Cooke NSI p. 31, 36, Röllig KAI a.l., Gibson SSI iii p. 107, 111, Butterweck TUAT ii 592: = fruit) - on this word, cf. also Conti RESL 114f.

v. nss_1.

pryd v.Soden Or xxxvii 262, xlvi 191: Akkad. *parīdu* (indicating a certain commodity) poss. = Ar. *pryd* (= jujube berry or material consisting of small particles), cf. also v.Soden AHW sv.

pryk v. prk_2.

prys v. prs_2.

prypt **OffAr** word of uncert. reading and meaning in Krael 12[11] (*prypt* or *pdypt*?)prob. = subst. Sing. abs. (prob. non-semitic origin). Yaron HUCA xxviii 49f.: l. *pdypt*(< παιδευτή) = who has been brought up by ... (cf. J.Ar. *qqw pdypty* < Greek κακο-παίδευτοι = badly brought up), less prob. interpret.; Eilers AfO xvii 333: < Iran.? = equal/of equal rank, cf. also Grelot DAE p. 257 (n. j); Porten & Yardeni sub TADAE B 3.12: = main-beloved?; Erichsen with Krael p. 277: related to Egypt. (demotic) *pr-ip.t* = workhouse and indicating a slave (improb. interpret.; cf. also Kutscher JAOS lxxiv 237f., J.J.Rabinowitz Law 36f.); Ginsberg JAOS lxxiv 161: *prypt* = something like "freed woman" (:: Ginsberg ibid.: the *brt ptw* in l. 3 = lapsus (through mishearing) for *prypt*, cf. however *brt ptw* in l. 33) :: J.J.Rabinowitz Bibl xxxix 78, Law 36f.: *prypt* < Greek θρεπτή = female slave bred in the house - on this word, cf. Porten Arch 231, Porten & Greenfield JEAS p. 68: without interpret. - Segal ATNS a.l.: the same word poss. in ATNS 85[4]: *pryp[t]* (heavily dam. context).

pryṣ **OffAr** Sing. abs. *pr[yṣ]* Aḥiq 84 (for this reading, cf. e.g. Cowl a.l. :: Epstein ZAW xxxiii 228: l. *pry[r]* = Sing. abs. of *pry[r]* (= fugitive)) - ¶ adj. licentious, impudent (cf. e.g. Cowl a.l., cf. also Kottsieper SAS 19, 226f.: violent) :: Grelot RB lxviii 180f., DAE p. 435: = runaway (cf. also Ginsberg ANET 428, Lindenberger APA 55, 227 n. 65).

pryr v. *pryṣ*.

pryš v. *$prš_1$*.

prk_1 **OffAr** QAL (cf. Donner KAI iii p. 40; or PA ‘EL?) Impf. 3 p.s.m. *yprk* KAI 260[6] - ¶ verb QAL (or PA ‘EL?) to break, to damage (for KAI 260[6], cf. also Lipiński Stud 161); + obj.: KAI 260[6].

prk_2 (< Akkad., cf. Zimmern Fremdw 68, Altheim & Stiehl AAW v/1 80, Kaufman AIA 80, 150) - **Hatra** Sing. emph. *prk›* 42[1] (diff. reading, cf. Safar Sumer viii 195) 288a 8, 340[1], 409 iii 1, app. 4[3] (cf. also Assur 9[2]), *pryk›* 40[1] - ¶ subst. (incense) altar: passim (:: Tubach ISS 399 (n. 691): or = chapel, sanctuary?); *prk› dy nbw* Hatra 340[1f.]: the altar of N.; *‹dn› wprk› dmrlh›* Hatra app. 4[2f.]: the *‹dn* (v. *$‹dn_3$*) and the altar of M.; *›qmt prk› lgd›* Hatra 288a 7f.: I have erected the altar for G. - on this word, cf. also Aggoula sub Assur 9.

prk_3 **Ph** Plur. abs. *prkm* KAI 37A 6 (for this reading, cf. e.g. CIS i sub 86, Lidzbarski Handb 354, Cooke NSI p. 65, 67, Röllig KAI a.l., Masson & Sznycer RPC 26, 38, Gibson SSI iii p. 124, 127 :: Peckham Or xxxvii 310 (n. 4): l. *drkm* = QAL Part. act. pl.m. abs. of *drk_1*(= marcher, marshall, cf. Amadasi sub Kition C_1, cf. also Teixidor Syr xlvi 338, l. 423f., Healy BASOR ccxvi 53, 55, Puech Sem xxix 31, cf. also Teixidor Syr lvi 149) - ¶ subst. indication of certain cultic function; Dérenbourg with CIS i 86, Lidzbarski Handb 354, sub KI 29, Cooke NSI p. 67, Delcor UF xi 152f., FS Cazelles 120: poss. = one who has charge of the temple-curtains (cf. Hebrew *prkt*) × Masson & Sznycer RPC 27, 38ff., Gibson SSI iii p. 127: = janitor (cf. Akkad. *parāku*; cf. already Röllig KAI a.l.).
v. *prmn*.

prk_4 v. *bz_1*.

prk_5 v. *bz_1*.

prk_6 v. *bz_1*.

prk_7 v. *prmn*.

prkdml v. *pry_2*.

prkh v.Soden Or xlvi 191f.: > Akkad. *paruktu* (= sail), cf. also idem AHW s. v. (uncert. interpret.).

$prkn_1$ v. *prtn*.

$prkn_2$ **OffAr** the *prkn* passim in Pers (4[1], 5[1], 9[1], 13[1], 14[1], etc., etc.) prob. = n.l., cf. Bernard StudIr i 169, 171ff., 176, Naveh & Shaked Or xlii 446f., Teixidor Syr li 331, Degen BiOr xxxi 125 (n. 5), Lipiński Stud 156 (n. 3), Hinz FS Nyberg 372ff., 384, AISN 179f. (cf. already Cameron with Schmidt Persepolis ii 55 n. 62) :: Gershwitch Mem de Menasce 53: = Sing. cstr. of *$prkn_3$* (prob. = basement-room) :: Segal BSOAS xxxv 354: = Sing. cstr. of *$prkn_4$* (= shrine, cell)? (cf. Delaunay with Teixidor Syr l. 431, cf. also Delaunay CC 205ff., 209, 215: prob. = palace-room (or: = cella??)) :: Levine JAOS xcii 75f.: = non-Semitic word denoting a place or agency within the fortress or poss.

administrative term :: Bowman Pers p. 20ff., 67: = (haoma) crushing ceremony (cf. also Grelot RB lxxx 596).

prkn$_3$ *prkn$_2$*.

prkn$_4$ *prkn$_2$*.

prks (prob. < Egypt., cf. Grelot RB lxxviii 526ff., 532, DAE p. 194 n. o) - **OffAr** Sing. abs. *prks* Cowl 15^{16} - ¶ subst. prob. meaning cosmetic box (cf. Grelot RB lxxviii 526ff., 532, cf. already Cowl a.l., cf. also Porten & Greenfield JEAS p. 20, Porten & Yardeni sub TADAE B 2.6, Delsman TUAT i 261 :: Nöldeke ZA xx 148: = basket, tray).

prkrml v. *pry$_2$*.

prmn **Ph** the *prmn* in KAI 37A 11 (for this reading, cf. Peckham Or xxxvii 305, 315, Amadasi sub Kition C 1, Masson & Sznycer RPC 26, 49, Healy BASOR ccxvi 53, 55f., Gibson SSI iii p. 124) poss. = n.p. (cf. Peckham Or xxxvii 305, 315, Amadasi sub Kition C$_1$; cf. however Gibson SSI iii p. 129: or = indication of profession or word indicating baked article) :: CIS i sub 86, Lidzbarski Handb 354, KI sub 29, Cooke NSI p. 65, 67, Röllig KAI a.l.: l. *prkm* = Plur. abs. of *prk$_3$* :: v.d.Branden BO viii 247, 254f.: l. *prkm* = Plur. abs. of *prk$_7$* indicating cooked food.

prmndr v. *prmnkr*.

prmnkr (< Iran., cf. Schaed 265, Herzfeld API 147, 155) - **OffAr** Plur. emph. *prmnkry*ʾ Cowl 26^4 (*prmnkr[y*ʾ*]*)^{,8} (for this reading in both instances, cf. Grelot Sem xx 27 n. 1, DAE p. 286 n. g :: Sach p. 44, 46, Eilers Beamtennamen 122f.: l. *prmndry*ʾ < Iran. = Plur. emph. of prmndr= commander), AJSL lviii 302A 1 (*pr[m]nkry*ʾ) - ¶ subst. engineer (for this interpret., cf. Herzfeld API 147, 155, Grelot Sem xx 27, DAE p. 286f. (n. g), cf. poss. also Porten Arch 58f., Porten & Yardeni sub TADAE A 6.2: = foreman :: Schaed 265: indication of administrative title (cf. also Cowl a.l.: commander, Bowman AJSL lviii 306: supply officer? (cf. also Porten Arch 46f., 56 n. 108))).

prn (< Greek φερνή, cf. Katzoff IEJ xxxvii 239, Greenfield IEJ xxxvii 250, DBKP p. 143) - **JAr** Sing. cstr. *prn* DBKP 18^{71} - ¶ subst. dowry.

prnʾ**yn** (< Greek προνάιον) - **Palm** Sing. abs. *prn*ʾ*[yn]* CIS ii 3959^6 (= SBS 44; Greek par. π[ρο]ναίῳ), *[p]rnyn* CIS ii 3985^2 (= Inv vi 1 = RIP 152), JSS xxxiii 171^3 - ¶ subst. front hall of a temple.

prnws v. *prnwš*.

prnwš (< Iran., v. infra) - **OffAr** Sing. abs. *prnwš* KAI 276^8 - ¶ diff. word in KAI 276^8, prob. to be compared to foll. words of Iran. origin in Syriac: *prnwš* = worn out with age, decrepit old man, *prnwšy* = senile, *prnwšw* = decrepitude, extreme old age (cf. Henning with Altheim, Junker & Stiehl AIPHOS ix 3 n. 1, Frye Mem Herzfeld 94, Grelot Sem viii 17f., Benveniste Titres 80, cf. also Kutscher & Naveh Lesh xxxiv 313), prob. meaning: old age, *m*ʾ *zy prnwš l*ʾ *gmyr whkyn* *ṭb wšpyr yhwh* KAI 276[7f.], prob. transl.: because she did not reach full age and she was so good and pleasant that ... (*gmyr*, *ṭb*, *špyr*, *yhwh* m. forms used for f. subject), cf. Frye Mem Herzfeld 91 (for this transl., cf. also Grelot Sem viii 17f. :: Grelot ibid.: *gmyr*, *ṭb*, *špyr* = Sing. f. abs.) :: Bailey JRAS '43, 2f., Metzger JNES xv 20, 24: (her) who was not of full age, incomplete and so good and ... (taking *prnwš* as adj. "not of full age" :: Kutscher & Naveh Lesh xxxiv 310, 313: because her old age was not completed and she was so good and ... (taking *prnwš* (= old age) as subject of *gmyr*) :: Donner KAI a.l.: that her life (= variant of *prnws* (= subsistence, life)) remained incomplete. And she was so excellent and ... (taking *prnwš* as subject of *gmyr*) :: Altheim & Stiehl Suppl 81f., EW x 251f., ASA 45f., 221, 247, 267, 268, 272, 275: what is incomplete toward a (good) life and so beautiful and good was it (sc. the *prnwš*) that ... (*prnwš* = variant of *prnws* (= Sing. abs.) = subsistence, life; cf. also idem Das erste Auftreten der Hunnen 58, AAW i 656f.)), cf. Nyberg Eranos xliv 235, 240: when her life was not completed; cf. also Altheim GH i 266f.

prnyn v. *prnʾyn*.

$prns_1$ **Palm** QAL Pf. 3 p.s.m. *prns* CIS ii 3915[3] - ¶ verb QAL to support (for the context, v. *br_3*).

$prns_2$ **Hebr** Sing. + suff. 3 p.s.m., on weights of the second revolt: IEJ xl 61, 62 (*prn[šw]*; cf. also Kloner ibid. 62ff., EI xx 347f.); Plur. abs. *prnsyn* DJD ii 42[1] (for the reading, cf. Lehmann & Stern VT iii 392, Birnbaum PEQ '55, 22, I.Rabinowitz BASOR cxxxi 22, Bardtke ThLZ lxxix 301, Milik DJD ii a.l. :: de Vaux RB lx 270: l. *prnšyn*) - **JAr** Sing. emph. *prnsh* MPAT-A 4[2] (for the reading, cf. Naveh sub SM 63 :: Vincent & Carrière RB xxx 587, Frey sub 1202, Fitzmyer & Harrington MPAT a.l.: l. *prns[h]*) - ¶ subst. administrator (on this word, cf. also Vattioni Aug ix 472f.).

prnš v. *$prns_2$*.

prs_1 **Palm** QAL Part. pass. s.m. abs. *prys* RIP 145[3] - ¶ verb QAL to extend (oneself); *dkl ʾḥyd wʿl kl prys* RIP 145[3]: who is all-powerful and extends himself over everything (for the context, v. also *ʾḥz*) - v.Soden Or xxxvii 262, xlvi 191: > Akkad. used in Dt = to disperse (sc. in skirmishing order), cf. idem AHW s.v. *parāsu* II (uncert. interpret.; rather to be interpreted as derivative of *parāsu* I; cf. also Stolper ZA lxviii 264 n. 9) - Rocco AION xxiv 476, 479: l. *prs* = QAL Imper. s.m. of *prs_1* (= to scatter) in GR ii 36 nr. 20[5] (highly uncert. interpret., cf. Polselli GR ii a.l.).

v. *sgd_1*.

prs_2 **Ph** Sing. abs. *prs* Mus li 286[4] - **Hebr** Sing. abs. *prs* on weight: IEJ xl 67 - **Samal** Sing. abs. *prs* KAI 215[6] - **OldAr** Sing. abs. *prys*Tell F 19 - **OffAr** Sing. abs. *prs* Cowl 45[8], RES 492A 3, 1784, MAI xiv/2,

66[5] (*pr[s]*, *[p]rs*), Herm 1[8], SSI ii 28 obv. 3, *prš* CIS ii 10; cstr. *prs* RES 496[3]; + suff. 1 p.s. *prsy* Cowl 11[6]; + suff. 2 p.pl.m. *prskn* SSI ii 28 obv. 4, 6 (*[p]rskn*); + suff. 1 p.pl. *prsn* Cowl 2[16]; Plur. abs. *prsn* Krael 11[3] - ¶ subst. - **1)** portion (> payment, salary); *prsy zy yn[t]nwn ly mn ʾwṣrʾ* Cowl 11[6]: my portion (i.e. my payment) that they will give me from the Treasury (cf. Cowl 2[16], SSI ii 28 obv. 3, 4, RES 492A 3); *yhb lhn prs* Herm 1[8]: he has offered them a salary (v. also *yhb*); *prs mšḥʾ* RES 496[3]: a quantity of oil (?, uncert. context) - **2)** half a measure - a) half a *mina*; *ksp prs 1 š 5* RES 1784: silver one *prs* (and) 5 shekel (cf. Akkad. par. *1/2 ma-na 5 šiqlu piṣu-u*), cf. CIS ii 10, cf. also Mus li 286[4] (cf. Honeyman ibid. 293), KAI 215[6] (cf. e.g. Cooke NSI p. 176, Gibson SSI ii p. 83 :: Eissfeldt ZAW lxiii 111: half (or portion) of grain measure (cf. also Kaufman AIA 80, Younger JANES xviii 98; on this problem cf. also Porten Arch 71f.); cf. poss. also Cowl 45[8] (cf. also Grelot DAE p. 97, Porten RB xc 568f., Porten & Yardeni sub TADAE B 7.1 :: Cowl a.l.: *prs* here = portion; cf. also Krael p. 262), cf. poss. also IEJ xl 67 (cf. Kloner IEJ a.l., EI xx 348) - b) half an *ardab*, *kntn prsn 2 sʾn. 2* Krael 11[3]: emmer two *peras* two *seah* (cf. Krael p. 261f.; ?) - c) half a *ḥomer*: MAI xiv/2, 66[5] (cf. Bauer & Meissner SbPAW '36, 418, Dupont-Sommer MAI xiv/2, 73); on b) and c), cf. also Porten Arch 71f.; cf. also *prys* Tell F 19: half a measure (cf. also Zadok TeAv ix 119, Kaufman Maarav iii 155 n. 48, 169, JAOS civ 572, Porten RB xc 569 n. 16, Greenfield & Shaffer RB xcii 53 (cf. also idem Shn v/vi 124), Delsman TUAT i 637, cf. however Abou-Assaf, Bordreuil & Millard Tell F p. 35: *prys* poss. = a third of a measure :: Muraoka AN xxii 83: = half (as much)) - for *šp* = *šʿrn prsn*, cf. BSh 39[3,4], Krael 17[3] (for this interpret., cf. Naveh TeAv vi 189 :: Krael a.l.: *šp* = measure of length), Cowl 63[2] (cf. Porten Arch 71f. :: Cowl: *š* = abbrev. for *šqln*); cf. also *kp* in Krael 11[4] = *kntn prsn* (v. *knt₂*) - the *ps*(uncert. reading) in Mus li 286[4] = lapsus for *prs*??, cf. Honeyman Mus li 293 - on the etymology of this word, cf. Kaufman AIA 80 :: Zimmern Fremdw 21: *prs₂* = half a *mina* < Akkad.
v. *ptprs*.

prs₃ **OffAr** word (Sing. emph. *prsʾ*) of unknown meaning in the comb. *byt prsʾ* Krael 9[4,7f.], probably indicating a room under the staircase, cf. Couroyer RB lxi 554ff. (cf. also Porten Arch 98, Grelot DAE p. 243 (n. c) :: Reider JQR xliv 340: cf. J.Ar. *byt prsʾ* = an area of a square *peras* (cf. also Porten & Greenfield JEAS p. 59, Porten & Yardeni sub TADAE B 3.10: = *peras*-sized storage area).
v. *prsy*.

prsd (< Greek παραστάς) cf. Aggoula Syr lxvii 408 :: As-Salihi Sumer xlv 102 (n. 24) < Greek προστάς = 'Vorhalle') - **Hatra** Sing. emph. *prsdʾ* 408[2] - ¶ subst. column: Hatra 408[2] (v. supra).

prsy **OffAr** Plur. abs. *prsyn* Krael 7^{20} (cf. Grelot RB lxxviii 535f., DAE p. 235 (n. y), Porten & Greenfield JEAS p. 55, Degen GGA '79, 28 :: Krael p. 214: = Dual abs. of *prs*$_3$?(cf. also Segert AAG p. 185)) - ¶ adj. Persian.

prsyq v. *prʿʿ*.

prʿ$_1$ **Hebr** QAL Impf. 1 p.s. + suff. 2 p.s.m. *ʾprk* EI xx 256^8 (on orthography and form, cf. Broshi & Qimron EI xx 258f.) - **OffAr** Part. pass. s.m. abs. *pryʿ* Del 69^2, 79^2 (= AM 110), 80^3, 84^3, 100^1 - **Nab** QAL Impf. 3 p.s.m. *yprʿ* BASOR cclxiii 78^3 - **Palm** QAL Pf. 3 p.s.m. *prʿ* CIS ii 3913 ii 149; Impf. 3 p.s.m. *yprʿ* CIS ii 3913 ii 71 (*[y]prʿ*), 82, 83, 88, RIP 199^8; Part. act. s.m. abs. *prʿ* CIS ii 3913 ii 80, 129; s.f. abs. *prʿʾ* CIS ii 3913 ii 94, 97 (v. infra) - **JAr** QAL Impf. 1 p.s. + suff. 2 p.s.m. *ʾprwʿnk* MPAT 39^6 - ¶ verb QAL to pay - **1)** + obj., *yprʿ d 9* CIS ii 3913 ii 88 : he will pay 9 *denarii* (cf. CIS ii 3913 ii 83 (dam. context)); *prʿ mksʾ* CIS ii 3913 ii 149: he has paid the tax; cf. also *pyprʿ mh dy yštkḥ[..* BASOR cclxiii 78^3: and he will pay what is found (for this interpret., cf. Jones BASOR cclxxv 43) - **2)** + obj. + *b*$_2$, *ʾprwʿnk bḥmš* MPAT 39^6: I will reimburse you with a fifth part (sc. as interest); cf. *ʾprk bkl zmn* EI xx 256^8: I will repay you at any moment ... - **3)** + obj. + *l*$_5$, *lʾ ʿmrʾ ʾyṭlyq[ʾ t]hwʾ prʿʾ [mk]s[ʾ] lmpqʾ* (lapsus for *lmpqnʾ*, v. *mpqn*) CIS ii 3913 ii 96f.: Italian wool is not liable to taxation when exported (cf. Greek par. [ἐρίων ἰτ]αλικῶν ἐξαγ[ομένω]ν πράσσειν ὕστ[ερον ὡς συν]εφωνήθη μ[ὴ ἀπὸ τ]ούτων ἐξαγο[μένων τὸ τέλος δί]δοσθαι), cf. CIS ii 3913 ii 94f. - **4)** + *b*$_2$, *wyhwʾ prʿ ṣlm bplgwt [ṭʿw]n* CIS ii 3913 ii 129f.: a statue will pay as half a load (i.e. a statue will be liable to the same tax as half a load); cf. also RIP 199^8 (dam. context; cf. also Milik DFD 287, Gawlikowski RIP a.l., Sem xxiii 116f.) - **5)** + *l*$_5$: CIS ii 3913 ii 80 - 6) + *l*$_5$ + obj., *[m]pq yprʿ lmk[s d] 12* CIS ii 3913 ii 82: the one who exports shall pay 12 *denarii* to the tax-collector; *[y]prʿ lkl mdʾ ... ssṭrṭyn [tr]n* CIS ii 3913 ii 71: he will pay for every *modius* ... two *sestertii* - Part. pass.: paid; *šṭr bnḥ [z]y ksp š [2]4 zy šnt [4] pryʿ* Del 80: document concerning the "gift" (v. *bnḥ*) of 24 shekel silver for the fourth year, paid (cf. Del 84); *šṭr bnḥ zy ksp hlkʾ zy pryʿ zy šnt 3 dryhwš* Del 79 (= AM 110): document concerning the "gift" (v. *bnḥ*) of the silver of the tax that is paid, of the third year of D. (cf. Del 69, 100) - Cowl sub 17: l. *nprʿ* (= QAL Impf. 1 p.pl.) in l. 6, highly uncert. reading, heavily dam. context, cf. Porten RB xc 413, Porten & Yardeni sub TADAE A 6.1: *nprʿ* prob. part of n.g.

v. *prʿ*$_2$.

prʿ$_2$ **OffAr** the *prʿy* in Sem ii 31 conc. 6 (for the reading, cf. Rosenthal AH i/1, 13) poss. = Plur. + suff. 1 p.s. of *prʿ*$_2$ (= payment, due), cf. however Rosenthal AH i/2, 13, Grelot DAE p. 370 (n. h): = QAL Imper. s.f. of *prʿ*$_1$:: Dupont-Sommer Sem ii 31, 36: l. *kbʿy* = Plur. +

suff. 1 p.s. of *kb'* (= bonnet) :: Levine JAOS lxxxiv 20: l. *kb'y* = k_1 + QAL Part. act. s.m. cstr. of *b'*y_1(= as (he) requires).

pr'h (< Egypt.) - **OffAr** KAI 266[1,3,6] - ¶ indication of Egypt. king; *'l mr' mlkn pr'h* KAI 266[1]: to the lord of kings Pharao (cf. KAI 266[6]) -

pr'wn v. *pg'wn*.

pr'n **Hebr** Sing. abs. *pr'n* DJD ii 22[2] - ¶ subst. payment: DJD ii 22[2] (diff. and dam. context); Rosenthal AH i/1, 13, i/2, 13, Grelot DAE p. 370 (n. h): l. *pr'n* = Sing. cstr. (= payment) in Sem ii 31 conc. 6 (less prob. reading, cf. also Dupont-Sommer Sem ii 31f., 36, Levine JAOS lxxxiv 20: l. *pd'* = n.p. (reading of *'* uncert.).

pr'nw **JAr** Sing. emph. *pr'nwt'* MPAT 53[2], 59[3]; + suff. 3 p.s.m. *pr'nwth[* MPAT 53[3] (or = Sing. emph.?) - ¶ subst. f. punishment, *mnkn pr'nwt' tt'bd* MPAT 53[2]: punishment will be exacted from you (cf. MPAT 53[3], 59[3]).

pr'' The *pr''* in Frah iv 22 (equated with *ālūδ*) prob. = peach; Ebeling Frah a.l.: *pr''* = abbrev. of *prsyq'*(uncert. interpret., cf. plantname *pr'*, cf. Löw AP 319f.), cf. however Nyberg FP 43, 67: l. *prg* = *plg*$_3$.

prp Ebeling Frah a.l.: l. *prpwn* in Frah xviii 14 = form of *prp* (= to irrigate) < *prp'* = to rinse (cf. Syriac), improb. reading and interpret., cf. Nyberg FP 49, 89: l. Iran. word.

prp' v. *prp*.

prṣ **Pun** Plur. abs. *prṣm* Trip 51[5] - ¶ subst. of uncert. meaning. Poss indicating a coin (cf. Levi Della Vida Or xxxiii 12, 14, Amadasi IPT 134).

prq$_1$ **OldAr** QAL Impf. 3 p.s.m. *[y]prq* KAI 222B 34 (for this reading, cf. Degen AAG p. 15, Kaufman BiOr xxxiv 95, Lemaire & Durand IAS 115, 124, 139 :: Dupont-Sommer Sf p. 62, 82f., 148: l. *]prq* = QAL Inf. cstr. (cf. also Fitzmyer AIS 18f., 79, Donner KAI a.l., Lipiński Stud 39) - **JAr** QAL Imper. s. m. *prq* AMB 6[13] (cf. Gordon Or xviii 336, 338f., Naveh & Shaked AMB a.l. :: Dupont-Sommer Waw p. 11, 21, 26: = Sing. cstr. of *prq*$_3$ (= part, section); s.f. *prqy* AMB 6[9] (cf. Naveh & Shaked AMB a.l. :: Gordon Or xviii 336, 338f.: l. *prq* {!} = QAL Imper. s.m. :: Dupont-Sommer Waw p. 11, 21, 26: l. *prqy* = Plur. cstr. of *prq*$_3$ (= part, section) - ¶ verb QAL - **1)** to cut off: KAI 222B 34 (sc. the water supply?, cf. Lipiński Stud 39), cf. however Dupont-Sommer Sf p. 83, Fitzmyer AIS 19, Donner KAI a.l., Degen AAG p. 37 - **2)** to loosen (sc. a demon): AMB 6[9,13]; *prqy ṭrpsdk* AMB 6[9]: loosen *ṭrps-dk* (name of demon), cf. Naveh & Shaked AMB a.l. :: Gordon Or xviii 336, 339, 341: *ṭrps* = Sing. abs. of *ṭrps*(= sheet) + *dk* (= *zk*$_2$):: Dupont-Sommer Waw 11, 21f.: *ṭrps*(< Greek τρόπος = way, manner) + *dk* = *zk*$_2$, *prqy ṭrps dk* = the sections of this manner = these sections.

prq$_2$ **Nab** QAL Impf. 1 p.s. *'prq* MPAT 64 i 10 - ¶ verb QAL to redeem; + *mn*$_5$ + obj.: MPAT 64 i 10.

prq3 v. *prq1*.
prq4 v.Soden Or xxxvii 263, xlvi 192, AHW s.v. *pirqu* II : > Akkad. *pirqu*, *pišqu* = redemption (sc. from slavery).
prr1 **DA** APH Impf. 2 p.s.f. *tpry* i 8 (for the reading, cf. Rofé SB 61, 66; for the interpret., cf. H. & M. Weippert ZDPV xcviii 92, 103, Hoftijzer TUAT ii 141, Dijkstra GTT xc 163 (n. 17) :: e.g. Caquot & Lemaire Syr liv 196f., Garbini Hen i 176, 185, Delcor SVT xxxii 55, McCarter BASOR ccxxxix 51, 54, Levine JAOS ci 197, Hackett BTDA 43, 95, 135, Garr DGSP 181, Puech FS Grelot 21, 27, Weinfeld Shn v/vi 143: = QAL Imper. s.f. of *tpr* (= to sew) :: H.P.Müller ZAW xciv 218, 224 n. 60: QAL Imper. s.f. of *tpr* (= to cover)? :: Hoftijzer DA a.l. (div. otherwise): l. *[y]ḥtp* (= PA ʿEL Impf. 3 p.s.m. of *ḥtp*(= to break)) + *ry* (= Sing. abs. of *ry* (= abundant rain); cf. also Dahood Bibl lxii 125) :: Sasson UF xvii 288, 290, 296: l. *[ytk]* (= QAL Impf. 3 p.s.m. of *ntk1*= to fall down) *ry* (= Sing. abs. of *ry*, v. supra) :: Knauf ZAH iii 16: l. *tpqy* (= QAL Impf. 2 p.s.f. of *pqq*(= to break)) :: Wesselius BiOr xliv 594, 596: l. *[ts]tkry* = HITP 2 p.s.f. of *skr1*(= to be closed, to be locked up)) - ¶ verb APH to break: DA i 8.
prr2 v. *brk1*.
prš1 **Hebr** QAL Part. pass. s.m. abs. *prwš* AMB 3[3] - **OffAr** QAL Inf. *mprš* RES 1792B 7; Part. pass. s.f. abs. *pryšh* Aḥiq 208 (reading uncert.; cf. however Lindenberger APA 274 n. 565; cf. Kottsieper SAS 23, 227: = Plur. f. abs. of *pryš*(= adj. different)); pl.m. abs. *pryšn* Cowl 27[10] (cf. Grelot DAE p. 403 n. k × Nöldeke ZA xx 141 n. 1, Leand 33a: = QAL Pf. pass. 1 p.pl.); PA ʿEL Part. pass. s.m. abs. *mprš* Cowl 17[3] (cf. Leand 33f., Porten RB xc 411 × Grelot DAE p. 282: = Sing. abs./cstr. of *mprš*(= repartition)); cf. Frah xviii 8 (*plšwn*) - **Nab** QAL Part. act. s.m. abs. *prš* J 2[4] - ¶ verb QAL - **1)** to divide, to separate, *prš lylyʾ mn ymmʾ* J 2[4]: the one who separates the night from the day - a) Part. pass. = different from, *ky ʿbydthm pryšh* Aḥiq 208: for their work is different (dam. context; cf. Lindenberger APA 209) - > innocent?, *pryšn ʾnḥnh [mn]* Cowl 27[10f.]: we are innocent of (cf. Cowl a.l., cf. also Grelot DAE p. 403 (n. k), cf. however Porten & Greenfield JEAS p. 86, Porten & Yardeni sub TADAE A 4.5: we are separated) - **2)** to explain, *lmprš ly mltʾ* RES 1792B 7f.: to explain the matter to me (cf. Lidzbarski Eph ii 234, Dupont-Sommer REJ cvii 44 n. 17, Grelot DAE p. 375, cf. also Porten Arch 58); *rwz prwš* AMB 3[3]: distinct mystery; cf. Frah xviii 8 - PA ʿEL Part. pass. exactly, plainly: Cowl 17[3] (cf. Sach p. 35, cf. also Cowl a.l., Porten RB xc 407, 411f.: or = separately? (cf. Porten & Yardeni sub TADAE A 6.1); cf. also Asmussen ArchOr lvi 343f.: *mprš zn zn* = explained (translated) item by item; v. also supra) - a form of this root (*pršt*) in ATNS xxii 1, 2, Segal ATNS a.l.: = QAL Pf. 1 p.s.m. (= to set aside)?

v. *mh*₂.

prš₂ **OldAr** Sing. abs. *prš* KAI 202B 2 (v. infra × Halévy RS xvi 366, Lidzbarski Eph iii 11, Black DOTT 247, Gibson SSI ii p. 11, 16: = Sing. abs. of *prš*₃ (= horse) :: Lipiński Stud 23: = turn-out (form of *prš*₃?) - **OffAr** Sing. abs. *prš* TA-Ar 11¹ (dam. context); Plur. cstr. *pršy* TA-Ar 7¹; emph. *pršy*ʾ TA-Ar 8¹; cf. Frah xiv 1 (*pršy*ʾ, *plšy*ʾ), Paik 858 (*plšy*ʾ), GIPP 31, 32, SaSt 21 - **Nab** Sing. emph. *prš*ʾ J 227; Plur. emph. *pršy*ʾ HDS 151², J 246 - **Palm** Sing. abs. *prš* CIS ii 3973² (here Arabic title?, cf. Teixidor Sem xxxiv 24); Plur. emph. *pršy*ʾ SBS 51³ - ¶ subst. m. horseman, cavalry-man; *pršy* ʾ*lyšyb* TA-Ar 7¹: the horsemen of E. (i.e. commanded by E.), cf. also TA-Ar 8¹, 11¹; *rb pršy*ʾ HDS 151²: the commander of the horsemen (cf. Starcky HDS 152, 155, 157ff.); cf. also J 227, 246 (cf. also Starcky HDS 158f., Negev RB lxxxiii 227); *pršy*ʾ *b*ʾ*br[*ʾ*] dy gml*ʾ *w*ʿ*n*ʾ SBS 51³ᶠ·: the cavalry-men of the wing of G. and A. (cf. CIS ii 3973²) - in KAI 202B 2 poss. used collectively: cavalry (cf. e.g. Dupont-Sommer AH i/2, 6, Gibson SSI ii p. 16).

prš₃ v. *prš*₂.

prš₄ v. *prs*₂.

prš₅ v. *pršh*.

pršh **Pun**, cf. Poen 1010: *phursa* = Sing. abs. of *pršh* (= meaning), cf. Schroed 295, Sznycer PPP 142 or = Sing. + suff. 3 p.s.f. of *prš*₅(= meaning)?; for other interpret., v. *mh*₂.

prt v. *npr*₂.

prtk (< Iran.?) - **OffAr** Plur. emph. *prtky*ʾ Cowl 16⁷ (for this reading, cf. Porten Arch 47, Grelot DAE p. 134 n. j, Porten & Yardeni sub TADAE A 5.2, cf. already Seidl with Epstein ZAW xxxiii 138 n. 3, cf. also Eilers Beamtennamen 119 :: Cowl a.l.: l. *dtky*ʾ = Plur. emph. of *dtk*(< Iran.?; = assessor, lawyer, cf. also Eilers Beamtennamen 42, Hinz AISN 85) - ¶ subst. indicating function, meaning unknown; Grelot DAE p. 134: = assessor?

prtn Ebeling Frah a.l.: l. *prtn* in Frah xviii 5 = lapsus for *prkn*₁(= oppression), improb. interpret., cf. Nyberg FP 48, 78: l. Iran. word.

prtr (< Iran., cf. Sims-Williams BSOAS xliv 5, Greenfield & Porten BIDG p. 49 :: Cowl a.l.: = n.p.?) - **OffAr** *prtr* Beh 53 - ¶ adv. openly, aloud.

prtrk (< Iran., cf. e.g. Schaed 267, Hinz AISN 98f. :: J.J.Rabinowitz Bibl xxxix 78, 80f., Law 537: < Greek πρώταρχος) - **OffAr** Sing. abs. *prtrk* Cowl 20⁴, 27⁴, 30⁵; emph. *prtrk*ʾ Cowl 31⁵, on coins from Iran, cf. Hill clxiv-clxx, 195ff., for the reading, cf. also Henning Ir 25 n. 1, Altheim & Stiehl GMA 504 - ¶ subst. indication of function, prob. governor (cf. e.g. Porten Arch 44 n. 62, Frye Heritage 282 n. 91, BAG 90f., cf. also Altheim & Stiehl GMA 504, Greenfield Trans iii 89); *prtrk*ʾ *zy* ʾ*lhy*ʾ on iranian coins (v. supra): the governor of the gods (title of iranian kings; for this title, cf. also Henning Ir 25 (n. 1)) - the diff. *rmndyn prtrk wydrng rb ḥyl*ʾ Cowl $20^{4f.}$ lapsus for *rmndyn prtrk wwydrng rb ḥyl*ʾ, cf. Pritsch ZA xxv 350, Cowl p. 59, Grelot DAE 198 (nn. b, c), Porten & Greenfield JEAS p. 24f. :: J.J.Rabinowitz Bibl xxxix 81: l. *d* (= d_3 (= *zy*)) *mn* (= mn_5) *dyn* (= Sing. abs. of dn_1 (= court)) *prtrk* = the chief magistrate of the court (v. also dn_1).

pš v. *dhšpṭ*.

pšgrb (< Iran., cf. Maricq Syr xxxii 275f., CO 3f., 15, Altheim GH iv 39 n. 6, Benveniste Titres 58ff., cf. also Widengren ISK 28 n. 102) - **Hatra** Sing. emph. *pšgrb*ʾ 28^2, *pzgryb*ʾ36^4 (Altheim & Stiehl AAW iv 262: reading uncert., cf. however id. GMA 516), *pšgryb*ʾ 287^6, 367, 368 (*pšghryb[*ʾ*]*), *pšgry*ʾ 195^3 - ¶ subst. prob. meaning high official, viceroy, cf. Benveniste Titres 64f., in Hatr.ean texts used for ʿ*bdsmy*ʾ son of king Sanatruq; Maricq Syr xxxii 275ff.: = crown-prince (cf. also Vattioni IH a.l., Milik DFD 363f., Altheim & Stiehl AAW ii 245, GMA 516ff., Degen NESE iii 78, Tubach ISS 248 (n. 60) - Milik DFD 363f.: l. *p[zg]rb*ʾ(= Sing. emph.) in Hatra 33 (uncert. reading).

pšgry v. *pšgrb*.

pšṭ v. *pšyṭ*, *šwṭ*.

pšyṭ **JAr** Sing. m. abs. *pšyṭ* MPAT 51^{14} (or = Qal Part. pass. s.m. abs. of *pšṭ*(= to straighten); for the reading, cf. also Birnbaum PEQ '57, 116, 120) - ¶ adj. straightened, not folded, simple, said of a document (cf. J.J.Rabinowitz BASOR cxxxvi 16, Birnbaum PEQ '57, 127, Puech RQ ix 215 :: Milik RB lxi 188, Beyer ATTM 320, 672: = simple, i.e. written only once, not duplicated.

pšyl **Nab** this subst. (Sing. abs.) = sculpture in RES 2030?? (reading highly uncert.).

pšk **OffAr** Sing. abs. *pšk* Cowl 8^4, 9^4, 26^{19}, Krael 7^8; Plur. abs. *pškn* Cowl 8^0 (for the reading, cf. Porten & Yardeni sub TADAE B 2.3), $26^{10,15,18,19,20}$, 36^1 (for this poss. reading cf. Porten & Yardeni sub TADAE B 6.2, Porten AN xxvii 90, 93)^{,2}, 79^2 (*p[š]kn*)^{,4} (*pš[kn]*), Krael 7^6 - ¶ subst. m. hand-breadth; > Akkad. *pušku*, cf. v.Soden Or xxxvii 263, xlvi 192, AHW sv.

pšl v. *psl*$_1$.

pšq **Palm** Paʿel Pf. 3 p.s.m. *pšq* CIS ii 3913 ii 104 (cf. Greek par. διασαφήσαντος); 1 p.s. *pšqt* CIS ii 3913 ii 125 - **Hatra** Qal Pf. 3 p.pl.m. *psqw* 336^8, 342^1, 344^3, *psq* 343^4 - ¶ verb Qal to decide, Hatra 336^8, 342^1, 344^3 - Paʿel to explain; *mks*ʾ *dy* ʿ*lymt*ʾ ... *pšqt* CIS ii 3913 ii 125: the tax on the prostitutes .... I have explained; *b*ʾ*grt*ʾ *dy ktb lsṭṭyls pšq dy* ... CIS ii 3913 ii 104: in the letter which he wrote to S. he has explained that ...

pšr$_1$ **OffAr** Haph Pf. 3 p.s.m. *hpšr* Cowl 63^{14} - **Nab** Qal Part. act. pl.f. emph. *pšrt*ʾ IEJ xxix 112^5 (v. infra); Aph Imper. s.m. ʾ*pšr* IEJ xxix

112[8] (cf. Naveh IEJ xxix 113, 119; diff. context) - **JAr** PA ‘EL Impf. 1 p.s. *ʾpšr* MPAT 39[6] (cf. Fitzmyer & Harrington MPAT a.l. :: Milik sub DJD ii 18: = ITP Pf. 3 p.s.m.) - ¶ verb QAL to melt, to dissolve, to annul a charm; Part. act. f. disenchantress: IEJ xxix 112[5] (cf. Naveh IEJ xxix 113, 117f.; very diff. context) - PA ‘EL to settle: MPAT 39[6] - HAPH/APH to cause a charm to be annulled: IEJ xxix 112[8] (v. however supra); in Cowl 63[14] meaning uncert., heavily dam. context: to settle an obligation, to pay?? (cf. Cowl p. 168) - Noth with Galling ZDPV lxiv 196 n. 1: l. *mpšr* in Gall 160 = APH/PA ‘EL Part.s.m. abs. of *pšr*$_1$ (= interpreter of dreams), reading and interpret. uncert., cf. Driver RSO xxxii 55 (div. otherwise): l. *ṣmdšr* = n.p. - a form of this root poss. in Aḥiq 194 (*ypšr*)?, for this diff. reading, cf. Cowl a.l., Puech RB xcv 591 (Lindenberger APA 192: l. poss. *ynšr* (without interpret.)).

pšr$_2$ **Nab** Naveh IEJ xxix 113: the *pšr* in IEJ xxix 112[9] = Sing. abs. of *pšr*$_2$ (= counter-charm), very diff. context, uncert. interpret.

pšš **Samal** QAL (or PA ‘EL) Pf. 3 p.s.m. *pšš* KAI 215[8] - ¶ verb QAL (or PA ‘EL) meaning unknown; Lagrange ERS 497: to open without a key (cf. Arab. *fašša*, cf. also Rosenthal JBL xcv 154, Zevit UF xiii 196); Donner KAI a.l.: = to destroy (cf. Akkad. *pasāsu*, cf. also Lipiński BiOr xxxiii 232, OLP viii 102: = PA ‘EL < Akkad. *pasāsu*) :: Gibson SSI ii p. 79, 83: = PA ‘EL to abolish (related to root *pwš*):: D.H.Müller WZKM vii 39, 46, 136: = to search (cf. J.Ar. *pšpš*), cf. also Dion p. 38, 89f.: = to inspect (related to root *mšš*??), cf.also Delsman TUAT i 629 :: Koopmans 73: = to open, cf. Ar. *pss*.

pšt$_1$ **Ph**, cf. Diosc ii 103 (cf. Löw AP 406): (ζερα)φοιστ (variant ζεραφοις) - **Pun** Sing. abs. *pšt* CIS i 4874[2] - **Hebr** Sing. abs. *pšt* KAI 182[3] - ¶ subst. flax; *‘ṣd pšt* KAI 182[3]: the cutting of the flax (cf. e.g. Röllig KAI a.l., H.P.Müller UF ii 229ff., Conrad TUAT i 247 (cf. also Smelik HDAI 27) :: Ginsberg ArchOr viii 146f.: the pulling out of flax (with a mattock), cf. Albright BASOR xcii 22 (n. 33): the hoeing up of flax (cf. already Dalman PEQ '09, 118), cf. also Gibson SSI i p. 2f. :: Lipiński OLP viii 83f.: the cutting with a hatchet (*pšt* = Sing. abs. of *pšt*$_2$ (= hatchet)) :: Talmon Lesh xxv 199f., JAOS xciii 178, 185f.: the green-fodder cropping :: Borowski AIAI 34ff.: < root *psy* (= to spread), subst. *pšt* = weeds, grasses and other plants which grew wild in the fields (cf. also ibid. 98f., 136, 162), *‘ṣd* = hoeing (for *‘ṣd*,cf. also Finkelstein BASOR xciv 28f., for *pšt*, cf. also Tångberg VT xxvii 222f.). v. *mgšh*.

pšt$_2$ v. *pšt*$_1$.

pt$_1$ **Hebr** Sing. cstr. *pt* SM 49[5,22] - **OffAr** Sing. emph. *ptʾ* RCL '62, 259 i 1 (written above the line; v. infra) - ¶ subst. Bresciani RCL '62, 261: in RCL '62, 259 i 1 = (round) bread (cf. also Naveh AION xvi 35f.); highly uncert. interpret. (or = Sing. abs. of *ptʾ*$_2$ of unknown meaning?, or combined with prec. *w*, *wpt*› = Sing. emph. of *wpt*of unknown meaning??) - for *pt ḥlh* in SM 49[5,22] v. *ḥlh*$_4$.

pt$_2$ *pn*$_1$.

pt›$_1$ **Pun** Sing. abs. *pt*› CIS i 357[5] (v. also infra) - ¶ subst. (or QAL Part. act. s.m. abs.?) indicating title or function, exact meaning unknown, cf. e.g. Slouschz TPI p. 256: < root *ptt*$_1$ = to cut? or < root *ptḥ*$_2$ = to cut, to carve, to chisel?

pt›$_2$ v. *pt*$_1$.

ptgm (< Iran., cf. e.g. Driv p. 50, Hinz AISN 186, cf. also Vogt Lex s.v., Degen Or xliv 124) - **OffAr** Sing. abs. *ptgm* Driv 4[3], 7[9]; emph. *ptgm*› ATNS 1[2,3] - **JAr** Sing. emph. *ptgm*› AMB 4[1] - ¶ subst. word; *ptgm*› *l*› ›*mr* ATNS 1[2]: he did not make a statement (cf. ATNS 1[3]); in the Driv texts only in the expression *gst ptgm* prob. = punishment (v. *gst*$_1$).

ptwm **OffAr** word of unknown meaning in Cowl 68 iii obv. 5 (heavily dam. context).

ptwr$_1$ **Nab** Sing. emph. *ptwr*› CIS ii 201[1], RB xliv 215[4], lxxiii 237[4] - ¶ subst. prob. meaning "diviner" (cf. Starcky RB lxiv 210, Starcky & Strugnell RB lxxiii 237, 242, Negev RB lxxxiii 25f., Delcor Sem xxxii 90 (cf. also Yaure JBL lxxix 312 n. 26: = interpreter of dreams), cf. however Negev ibid.: or = Sing. emph. of *ptwr*$_4$ (= paymaster (of the army))? (cf. also Clermont-Ganneau RAO vii 248 n. 2: = military title? (cf. also Chabot sub RES 1289B)) :: Nöldeke with Euting Nab Inschrift p. 36: = nickname? (cf. also CIS ii sub 201)).
v. *hymn*, *ptr*$_2$.

ptwr$_2$ **Nab** Sing. abs. (or cstr.) *ptwr* MPAT 64 ii 8 - ¶ subst. of unknown meaning (diff. and dam. context); Starcky RB lxi 177: prob. = amicable settlement, settlement by agreement.

ptwr$_3$ v. *ptr*$_1$.

ptwr$_4$ v. *ptwr*$_1$.

pṭḥ$_1$ **Ph** QAL Impf. 3 p.s.m. *ypth* KAI 14[4,7,10,20]; 2 p.s.m. *tpth* KAI 13[3f.,5f.,7]; Inf. abs. *pth* KAI 13[6f.] - **Pun** QAL Pf. 3 p.s.m. *pth* RCL '66, 201[1]; 3 p.pl. *pth*› Trip 51[1] (diff. and uncert. context, cf. also Amadasi IPT 132); Inf. cstr. *pth* KAI 70[4] - **Hebr** QAL Impf. 3 p.s.m. *ypth* KAI 191B 3 (for the reading, cf. e.g. Avigad IEJ iii 143, Gibson SSI i p. 24 :: Röllig KAI a.l.: l. *pth* (= QAL Pf. 3 p.s.m.)?); Part. pass. s.m. abs. *ptwh* IEJ xxxvi 206b2 - **OldAr** QAL Part. pass. s.f. abs. *pthh* KAI 224[8f.] (cf. e.g. Dupont-Sommer BMB xiii 32, Fitzmyer AIS 112, 156, Donner KAI a.l., Degen AAG p. 69, GGA '79, 46, Gibson SSI ii p. 54, Lemaire & Durand IAS 129, Rössler TUAT i 187, cf. however Dupont-Sommer BMB xiii 32: or = QAL Imper. s.m. + ending -*h*?? (poss. interpret.)) - **OffAr** QAL Inf. *mpth* Cowl 5[14]; Part. act. s.m. abs. *pth* Krael 9[13]; pass. s.m. abs. *ptyh* Krael 12[21]; m. (or f.?) pl. abs. *ptyhn* Cowl 25[6] -

Nab QAL Impf. 3 p.s.m. + suff. 3 p.s.m. *ypthh* J 17[8] (= CIS ii 271 :: RES sub 1148: = lapsus for *ypth*; on the form, cf. O'Connor JNES xlv 223); ITP Impf. 3 p.s.m. *ytpth* CIS ii 226[2], J 11[3] (= CIS ii 211), IEJ xii 174[4] (heavily dam. context) - **Palm** QAL Pf. 3 p.s.m. + suff. 3 p.s.m. *pthh* SBS 60[5]; Impf. 3 p.s.m. *ypth* CIS ii 4218[3], Inv viii 86[2]; + suff. 3 p.s.m. *ypthh* RIP 105[4] (:: Bounni & Teixidor sub Inv xii 17: l. *ypth*ʾ), *ypthyhy* CIS ii 4218[6] (on this form, cf. Cantineau Gramm 71, Rosenthal Sprache 71); Part. pass. s.m. abs. *ptyh* RB xxxix 526B 3, SBS 60[2]; s.f. abs. *ptyh*ʾ RB xxxix 548[6] - **JAr** QAL Pf. 3 p.s.m. *pth* AMB 15[14]; 3 p.s.f. *ptht* AMB 15[10]; Impf. 3 p.s.m. *ypth* MPAT-A 45[1], 46[4], 47[1] (dam. context); 2 p.s.m. + suff. 3 p.s.m. *tpthnh* MPAT 51[4]; Inf. *mpth* MPAT 67[4] (= Frey 1300), 70[4] (against the authenticity of this text, cf. however Garbini OA xxiv 67ff.), 71[2f.] (= Frey 1334), 95b 1 (= Frey 1359); Part. pass. s.m. abs. *ptyh* MPAT 51[4], IEJ xxxvi 206[2]; s.f. abs. *ptyh[h]* IEJ xxxvi 206[2] (diff. reading, dam. context) - ¶ verb QAL to open - **1)** with transitive meaning, passim, cf. also *wlʾ lmpth* (inscription on tomb) MPAT 70[4]: not to be opened (cf. MPAT 71[2f.], 95b 1); *pth wpʿl ʾyt hhs z* RCL '66, 201[1]: they opened and made this street (v. *hs*2; on the context, cf. also Ferron Mus xcviii 49f.) - a) + obj. - α) said of tomb constructions, *qnmy ʾt ... ʾl ypth ʾyt mškb z* KAI 14[4]: whoever you are ... let no one open this ultimate resting place (cf. KAI 191[3], J 17[8], CIS ii 4218[6], RIP 105[4]); *pthh wʾbrh* SBS 60[5]: he opened it (sc. the tomb) and purified it (v. *brr*) - β) said of a gate, *wʾnt šlyt lmpth trʿʾ zk* Cowl 5[14]: and you have the right to open this gate - b) + obj. + *l*5, *tpthnh lgh btk* MPAT 51[4]: you will open it into your house (i.e. make an opening in the house (sc. to go through) into ...), for the context, v. also *gw*2 - c) + obj. + *ʿl*7, *kl mn dypth hdh qbwrth ʿl ... mn dbgwh* MPAT-A 45[1ff.]: everyone who will open this grave on the one who is within it (sc. in the tomb) - d) +*l*5, *ptht lhwn* AMB 15[10]: she opened for them - e) + *ʿl*7, *wlʾ lmpth ʿlyhwn* MPAT 67[4]: (said of a tomb) not to be opened on them (cf. MPAT-A 46[4]) - f) + *ʿl*7 + obj., *lʾ ypth ʿlwhy gwmhʾ dnh* CIS ii 4218[3f.]: let no one open this niche over him - g) + *ʿlt* (v. s.v.), *wkl ʾdm ʾl ypth ʿlty* KAI 14[20]: let no one open up (what is) over me (cf. KAI 13[3f.,5f.,6f.]); *kl ʾdm ʾš ypth ʿlt mškb z* KAI 14[7]: anyone who opens up (what is) over this resting-place (cf. KAI 14[10]) - h) Part. pass.: open(ed), *kwyn ptyhn* Cowl 25[6]: open windows (i.e. bay windows looking out over the ground outside the *byt*; cf. e.g. Cowl a.l., Hoftijzer VT ix 316 n. 2); *ptyh qbrʾ dnh* SBS 60[2]: this tomb has been opened (on the background, cf. Dunant SBS a.l., Garbini OA xiv 178) - α) + *l*5, *bth dyly dy ptyh spn lgh drty* MPAT 51[3f.]: my house which opens at the north side into my courtyard (cf. also IEJ xxxvi 206[2], 206b 2; *wtrʿʾ zylh ptyh lšwq mlkʾ* Krael 12[21]: and the gateway thereof opens towards the royal street (for the reading of

zylh cf. Porten & Yardeni sub TADAE B 3.12 :: e.g. Krael a.l., Grelot DAE p. 259, Porten & Greenfield JEAS p. 71: l. *ʿlh* (= variant of *ʿlʾ*, Sing. emph. of *ʿl_1*)); *ʾblʾ ... ptyḥʾ lʾpʾ mdnḥʾ* RB xxxix 548[6]: the hall (sc. of the tomb construction) opens towards the East (cf. RB xxxix 526B 3), cf. also *ptḥh ly ʾrḥʾ* KAI 224[8f.]: the road shall be open to me (v. also supra) - **2)** with intransitive meaning, *dš ḥd ... ʾḥd wptḥ* Krael 9[13]: one door ... closing and opening (exact meaning of the formula unknown) - ITP - **1)** to be opened, *wlʾ ytptḥ ʿlyhm* CIS ii 226[2f.]: it is not to be opened over them (sc. the niche) - **2)** to open for oneself + obj. (niche): J 11[3] - a form of this root in the diff. text KAI 27[22f.] (highly uncert. interpret.), Cross & Saley BASOR cxcvii 46f. (nn. 29, 30, 31, 37): l. *ʾl yptḥ ly* = *ʾl_3* + NIPH Impf. 3 p.s.m. of *pth_1* + *l_5* + suff. 3 p.s.m. (let it not be opened to him; cf. Garr DGSP 52f., 118); Avishur PIB 248: l. *lyptḥ ly* = *l_2* + QAL Impf. 3 p.s.m. of *pth_1* + *l_5* + suff. 3 p.s.f. (let he not open for her); Röllig NESE ii 19, 25f.: l. *ʾl yptḥ ly* = *ʾl_3* + QAL Impf. 3 p.s.m. of *pth_1* + *l_5* + suff. 3 p.s.m. (one may not open for him; cf. also de Moor JEOL xxvii 108); Caquot FS Gaster 50f., Garbini OA xx 286: l. *lptḥy* = *l_5* + Sing. + suff. 3 p.s.m. of *pth_3* (at his door), cf. also v.d.Branden BO iii 43, 47; Lipiński RTAT 266, Gibson SSI iii p. 82f.: l. *lptḥy* = *l_5* + Sing. + suff. 1 p.s. of *pth_3* (at my door) :: Torczyner JNES vi 26f., 29: l. *ly ptḥy* = *l_5* + suff. 1 p.s. + QAL Imper. s.f. of *pth_1* (open for me), cf. also du Mesnil du Buisson FS Dussaud 424f.: > make me fecund :: Albright BASOR lxxvi 9f. (n. 36), Gaster Or xi 44, Röllig KAI a.l.: l. *lyptḥ rḥ[my]* = *l_1*+ NIPH Impf. 3 p.s.m. of *pth_1* + Sing. + suff. 3 p.s.f. of *rhm_5* (may her womb be opened; cf. also Röllig KAI a.l.: *l* = *lw*) :: v.d.Branden BiOr xxxiii 13: l. *ly ptḥy* = *l_5* +suff. 3 p.s.m. + Sing. + suff. 3 p.s.m. of *pth_3* (for him his opening/aperture) :: Rosenthal ANET 658: may his [mouth] not open, based on reading *lyptḥ [p]my* (= Sing. + suff. 3 p.s.m. of *pm_1*) - a form of this root (*]ptḥ*) in DA v d 4 (heavily dam. context (Puech FS Grelot 25,28: = QAL Pf. 3 p.s.m.)) - Ussishkin BiAr xxxiii 44: l. *yp[tḥ]* (= QAL Impf. 3 p.s.m.) in Mosc var. B 2[2] (prob. restoration).
v. *mptḥ*, *pth_2*.

pṭḥ2 v.d.Branden RSF i 166, 171: the *nptḥt* in KAI 145[10] = NIPH Part. pl.f. abs. of *pth_2* (= to engrave, to chisel) = chiseled objects, carved objects (poss. interpret.), cf. also Février Sem vi 26, Röllig KAI a.l., Bonnet SEL vii 116: *nptḥt* = Sing. abs. of *nptḥh*(= the chiseling, chisel-work); for the reading, cf. already Clermont-Ganneau RAO iii 340 :: Krahmalkov RSF iii 188f., 197, 203: *nptḥt* = NIPH Part. pl.f. abs. of *pth_1*(= to be thrown open, said of an army camp) :: e.g. Cooke NSI p. 151: l. *nktḥt* without interpret. - **OffAr** Driver JRAS '32, 86: the *ptḥn* in Cowl 81[110] poss. = QAL Part. pass.m. pl. abs. of *pth_2* (= carved; poss. interpret.), cf. however Grelot DAE p. 116: poss. = QAL Part.

pass.m. pl. abs. of *ptḥ*$_1$(cf. also Cowl a.l.) :: Harmatta ActAntHung vii 370f.: = Plur. abs. of *ptḥ*$_3$ (= curtain before a door) - a form of this root (Hitp Impf. 3 p.s.m. ?) *ytptḥ[* in EI xii 147^4 (= AAW v/1, 310^4) - for the root, cf. Collini SEL vi 23f.
v. *pt*ʾ$_1$.

ptḥ$_3$ Ph Sing. abs. (cf. Gibson SSI iii p. 96) *ptḥ* KAI 10^{4,5}; + suff. 1 p.s. *ptḥy* KAI 10^5 (for the Ph. instances, cf. e.g. Dussaud Syr xxv 331, Mél Dérenbourg 152f., Dupont-Sommer Sem iii 39, Gibson SSI iii p. 95, 97 :: Halévy JA vii/viii 181f., 186, Bonnet SEL vii 116: = *ptḥ*$_4$ (= chisel work, carved work), cf. e.g. CIS i sub 1, Lidzbarski Handb 355 (?), Cooke NSI p. 18, 22f., Harr 139, Röllig KAI a.l. (?), Rosenthal ANET 656, Garbini AION xxvii 406 :: Ockinga WO xii 70f.: the *ptḥ* in ll. 4, 5 = *ptḥ*$_3$, the *ptḥy* in l. 5 = form of *ptḥ*$_4$ (= inscription) :: Baldacci BiOr xl 130, UF xvii 399f.: the *ptḥ* in ll. 4, 5 = *ptḥ*$_4$, the *ptḥy* in l. 5 = form of *ptḥ*$_3$ :: Clermont-Ganneau Et i 16f.: in all instances = *ptḥ*$_4$ > statue) - **Pun** Sing. abs. *ptḥ* Trip 35 - ¶ subst. m. door, gateway: KAI 10^{4,5} (v. supra; for the context, v. also *ḥrṣ*$_5$), Trip 35.
v. *ptḥ*$_{1,2}$.

ptḥ$_4$ v. *ptḥ*$_3$.

pty$_1$ v. *yrt*$_2$.

pty$_2$ v. *mpt*.

pty$_3$ OffAr Sing. abs. *pty* Cowl 8^4, 79^{2,3,4}, Krael 4^7 (v. infra), 7^6, 12^{8,16}, Pers 43^4, 114^3 (cf. Naveh & Shaked Or xlii 455f., Degen BiOr xxxi 126 :: Bowman Pers p. 63: = Sing. cstr. of *pty*$_4$ (= value)); emph. *pty*ʾ Cowl 26^{18,19} (:: Naveh & Shaked Or xlii 456 (div. otherwise): l. *pty* = Sing. abs.; v. also *ṣb*ʿ$_2$)^{,20} - ¶ subst. breadth, width - a) said of a house: Cowl 8^4, Krael 4^7, 12^{8,16} - b) said of boards/planks: Cowl 26^{18}, 79^{2,3,4} - c) said of a garment: Krael 7^6 - d) of a plate: Pers 43^4 - e) of a mortar: Pers 114^3 - f) of unknown objects: Cowl 26^{19,20} - in Krael 4$^{6f.}$ l. *mn ʿlyh ʿd tḥtyh ʾmn bʿštʾ 11 bpty* {*ʾmn*} *mn mwʿh ʿd mʿrb ʾmn bʿštʾ 7 k 1* (cf. also Grelot DAE p. 222 :: Krael p. 169, Ginsberg JAOS lxxiv 158: *bpty ʾmn* = in the width of cubits (cf. also Porten & Greenfield JEAS p. 49: = cubits in width)): from the North to the South 11 cubits *bʿštʾ* (v. *ʿštʾ*), from East to West 7 cubits 1 *k bʿštʾ*.

pty$_4$ v. *pty*$_3$.

ptybrt v. *ḥy*$_1$.

ptyzbt (< Iran., cf. e.g. Benveniste JA ccxlvi 40f.) - **OffAr** KAI 279^5 - ¶ adj. (indeclined) refraining from, eschewing (cf. Garbini Kand 11, 18 (cf. also Nober VD xxxvii 372f., Schwarzschild JAOS lxxx 156); transl. as "prohibited" (cf. Benveniste JA ccxlvi 40f., cf. also Dupont-Sommer ibid. 29, Altheim & Stiehl EW ix 196, ASA 275, Donner KAI a.l., Hinz AISN 190) less apt :: Benveniste JA ccxlvi 40: or l. *ptyzrt* (< Iran.) = afflicted, tormented; cf. also πέπαυνται in the Greek par. text; on *ptyzbt*,

cf. also Kutscher, Naveh & Shaked Lesh xxxiv 134).
ptyzrt v. *ptyzbt*.
ptysty v. *ptystykn*ʾ.
ptystyknʾ (< Iran., for *ptysty*, cf. Benveniste JA ccliv 449, Dupont-Sommer JA ccliv 458, Hinz AISN 190, for *kn*ʾ(and problems involved), cf. Shaked JRAS '69, 121, Kutscher, Naveh & Shaked Lesh xxxiv 128f. :: Benveniste JA ccliv 449f.: *kn*ʾ prob. < Ar., cf. Dupont-Sommer ibid. 458: *kn*ʾ poss. = subst. or adj. s.m. emph. (related to kn_3) = right, just, what is right/just) - **OffAr** Sing. abs. *ptystykn*ʾ JA ccliv $440^{4,5}$ - ¶ subst. obedience (v. *hwptysty*);*wyhwtrwn bptystykn*ʾ JA ccliv 440^4: they will grow in obedience (for the context, v. ytr_1).
ptyprs v. *ptp*, *ptprs*.
ptyš **OffAr** Segal ATNS a.l.: l. prob. *ptyš* in ATNS 5^5 (*ptyš[)*, < Iran., prob. part of word of uncert. meaning (reading of *š* however highly uncert.).
ptytw (< Iran., cf. Benveniste JA ccxlvi 36f., Hinz AISN 189, v. also infra) - **OffAr** Sing. abs. *ptytw* KAI 279^1 (:: Köbert with Nober VD xxxvii 371: pro *ptytw* ʿ*byd* l. *ptyt w*ʿ*bd* (Nober ibid.: *ptyt* = QAL pass. Pf. 3 p.pl.f. of ptt_2 (= to cut, to decide)?, ptt_2 being variant of *btt*or l. *ptytw* = QAL pass. 3 p.pl.f. of ptt_2) - ¶ subst. of unknown meaning, poss. = duration (cf. Benveniste JA ccxlvi 37, cf. also Kutscher, Naveh & Shaked Lesh xxxiv 131, Rosenthal EI xiv 97*f, cf. Greek par. πληρη[θέντ]ων) :: Levi Della Vida Editto 20: *ptytw* < Iran. = expiation (cf. Altheim GH ii 168f., Altheim & Stiehl GH i 398f., 407, EW ix 193f., x 243f., ASA 23f., 275, GMA 344ff., Donner KAI a.l., Garbini Kand 3ff., 18, 20, Teixidor Syr xlvi 347, Humbach IPAA p. 16) - cf. *ptyty*. v. *ptstw*.
ptyty **OffAr** word of unknown meaning in IPAA 12^{10}, *ptyty* (for this reading, cf. Davary IPAA 15); Humbach IPAA 12, 15f., Hinz AISN 189: < Iran. = expiation (highly uncert. interpret., diff. context) - cf. *ptytw*.
ptyk v. *ptk*.
ptk **OffAr** QAL Part. pass. s.m. abs. *ptyk* Pers 9^3 (*pt[y]k*), 13^3 (*[p]tyk*), 14^3, 17^5 (for the reading and interpret., cf. Naveh & Shaked Or xlii 456 :: Bowman Pers p. 22, 48, 67 and a.l.: l. *pyrk*(= Sing. abs.) = crushing, cf. also Levine JAOS xcii 75 n. 40: the reading *pyrk* in Pers 17^5 ascertained) - ¶ verb QAL Part. pass.: mixed, varied, diverse, adorned (cf. Naveh & Shaked Or xlii 456 (n. 78)), uncert. interpret., diff. context.
ptkr (< Iran., cf. Driv p. 72f., cf. also Telegdi JA ccxxvi 253f., Brown Bibl lxx 202f.) - **OffAr** Sing. abs. *ptkr* KAI $258^{1,4}$; cstr. *ptkr* Driv 9^2; Plur. abs. *ptkrn* Driv $9^{2,3}$ - ¶ subst. m. relief, sculpture; in KAI $258^{1,4}$ clearly indicating bas-relief (cf. Cross BASOR clxxxiv 10, Teixidor Syr liii 310); *ptkr swsh* Driv 9^2: sculpture (or relief?) of a horse.
ptkrkr (< Iran., cf. Driv p. 72, Hinz AISN 187) - **OffAr** Sing. abs.

ptkrkr Driv 9[1] - ¶ subst. m. sculptor.

ptstw (< Iran., cf. Driv p. 87, Hinz AISN 188) - **OffAr** Sing. (m.) abs. *pt[s]tw* Driv 13[4] (reading uncert.; for this reading, cf. also Benveniste JA ccxlii 299 n. 4) - ¶ adj. praiseworthy (cf. Driv p. 87); *ʾnt šgyʾ ptstw ly* Driv 13[4]: you have earned my praise (cf. also Grelot DAE p. 327 (n. d), Porten & Yardeni sub TADAE A 6.16) :: Altheim GH ii 167f., Altheim & Stiehl EW x 243, ASA 22f., GMA 344f.: *ptstw* (< Iran.) = obedience, *ʾnt šgyʾ ptstw* = you (were) obedient in manifold ways :: Driv[1] p. 35f.: l. *ptytw*(< Iran.) = satisfaction, *ʾnt šgyʾ ptytw ly* = you have completely satisfied me (cf. also Eilers AfO xvii 333; cf. however against reading *ptytw* Benveniste JA ccxlii 299, de Menasce BiOr xi 162).

ptp (< Iran., cf. Eilers Beamtennamen 70ff., AfO xvii 331, 333, de Menasce BiOr xi 162, Krael p. 263, Driv p. 61, Henning Ir 113, Diakonov & Livshitz Nisa-b p. 40, Altheim & Stiehl AAW iv 22ff., Hinz AISN 193 :: Lidzbarski Eph iii 250: = shortening of *ptyprs* (cf. also Rowley AramOT 138 n. 7); cf. however Benveniste JA ccxlii 300: derivation uncert.) - **OffAr** Sing. abs. *ptp* Cowl 24[42], Driv 6[2] (*[p]tp*, uncert. reading),[4,6], PF 857 (*p[tp]*), 858[2], 1587[2]; cstr. *[p]tp* PF 855[3]; emph. *ptpʾ* Cowl 24[39], 43[8,10] (*pt[pʾ]*), Krael 11[4], Driv 6[5], 9[1], Or lvii 43 i (heavily dam. context); + suff. 3 p.s.m. *ptph* PF 2059[2]; cf. Nisa-b 2067[2], cf. also GIPP 61 - ¶ subst. m. ration, portion, provision; *ytntn ly ptpʾ mn byt mlkʾ* Krael 11[5f.]: the ration will be given me from the royal treasury (cf. Krael 11[4], Cowl 43[8], Driv 6[2], cf. also Driv 6[4,6], 9[1]); *ptpʾ znh hbw lhm mn pqyd ʿl pqyd lqbl ʾdwnʾ zy mn mdynh ʿd mdynh ʿd ymṭʾ mṣryn* Driv 6[5]: give them these provisions, each officer of you in turn, in accordance with (the stages of) the journey from province to province until he reaches Egypt; *ptp lnqry gll* PF 1587[2]: rations for the diggers of stone (v. *nqr₁*).

ptprs (< Iran., cf. Eilers Beamtennamen 24ff., Cardascia AM 21, Porten Arch 53, Grelot DAE p. 388 (n. d), Hinz AISN 186) - **OffAr** Sing. abs. *ptyprs* Cowl 37[3]; emph. *ptprsʾ* Cowl 37[12]; Plur. abs. *ptyprsn* Cowl 37[3] - ¶ subst. indicating function, exact meaning unknown, prob. = examiner, inquisitor, investigator, cf. Cardascia AM 21, Porten Arch 53f., Porten & Greenfield JEAS p. 80f., Grelot DAE p. 388 (n. d), cf. also Eilers Beamtennamen 23ff., Driver JRAS '32, 80, Porten & Yardeni sub TADAE A4.2 (cf. Hinz AISN 186: = provost-sergeant) :: Cowl a.l.: < Iran. = payment (cf. also Lidzbarski Eph iii 250: = payment < Iran. *pty* + Ar. *prs₂*;cf. also Schaed 267, Geiger WZKM xliv 60f.).
v. *ptp*.

ptr₁ **OffAr** Sing. abs. *ptwr* NESE iii 31[1] (or cstr.?, heavily dam. context; = Or lvii 43 ii 1), cf. Warka 5: *pa-tu-ú-ri*, Warka 8: *pa-tu-ú-ru*; emph. *ptwrʾ* Cowl 83[21] (v. infra) - **Hatra** Sing. emph. *ptrʾ* 62[1], *ptwrʾ*

68[1], 290[2] (v. however *hymn*) - ¶ subst. m. - **1)** tablet; *pa-tu-ú-ri a-si-ir li-iš-šá-an* Warka 5: the tablet that binds the tongue (v. *'sr*$_1$), cf. Warka 8 - **2)** altar-table (cf. Degen NESE iii 86, Aggoula Syr lxv 207): Hatra 62[1], 68[1], 290[2] (for this text, v. also *hymn*) - **3)** *b'ly ptwr'* Cowl 83[21]: the lords of the table (?), exact meaning unknown (diff. context), Cowl a.l.: *ptwr'* here = table of money-changer?, *b'ly ptwr'* = money-lenders (uncert. interpret.) - for etymology, cf. Kaufman AIA 81f. :: Zimmern Fremdw 33, Teixidor Sem xxx 64 (n. 3): < Akkad. *paššuru* (cf.also Blau PC 51f.).

ptr$_2$ **Pun** Sing. abs. *ptr* RES 1535[2] - ¶ subst. m. meaning unknown, prob. indicating title or function (related to *ptwr*$_1$??, cf. however Chabot sub Punica xv n. 2); the same word also in the title/function indication *pytr'* (Sing. abs. Punica xv 2[3], 3[2], 4[2] (cf. Chabot sub RES 1535 and sub Punica xv 2))??

v. *ṭbḥ*.

ptt$_1$ **Hebr** QAL Impf. 3 p.s.m. *ypt* NESE ii 45[1] (for this interpret., cf. Gibson SSI i p. 19f., Röllig NESE ii a.l. :: Lemaire Sem xxvi 69: = Sing. f. cstr. of *yph*(= beautiful)) - ¶ verb QAL to break: NESE ii 45[1] .

v. *yrt*$_2$, *pt'*$_1$.

ptt$_2$ v. *ptytw*.

Ṣ

ṣ'n **OldCan** Sing. abs. *ṣú-ú-nu* EA 263[12] (cf. Rainey EA p. 91, Sivan GAG 30, 38, 270, Huehnergard JAOS cvii 718) - **Ph** Sing. abs. *ṣ'n* KAI 26A iii 9, C iv 9 - **Mo** Sing. cstr. *ṣ'n* KAI 181[31] (dam. context; cf. also Beeston JRAS '85, 148) - **Amm** Sing. abs. *ṣ'n* AUSS xiii 2[2,7,10] (= CAI 80) - **OffAr** Sing. abs. *qn* Cowl 33[10], JRAS '29, 108[3]; cstr. *qn* ATNS 52a 12, b 14, 67a 1 (uncert. reading, dam. context); emph. *qn'* Del 71, JRAS '29, 108[4]; cf. Frah vii 7 (*kyn'*), cf. also GIPP 62 - **Palm** Sing. abs. *'n* CIS ii 3913 ii 149; emph. *'n'* CIS ii 3913 ii 145 - ¶ subst. small cattle, sheep: passim; *ṣ'n 8* AUSS xiii 2[2]: 8 sheep (cf. also AUSS xiii 2[7,10]) - Lipiński Stud 43f.: l. *ṣn* in KAI 222B 40 (= Sing. abs.), improb. interpret. (cf. Millard JSS xxi 175; cf. also Lemaire & Durand IAS 115, 125: pro *ṣn* l. *wl* (= *w*$_2$ + *l*$_2$ (= *l'*$_1$); highly uncert. reading)) - Gawlikowski TP 49f.: reflection of *'n'* (= Sing. emph.) in the n.d. Βωρροαωνου (= *bwl rw' 'n'*? = B. the shepherd of small cattle), highly uncert. interpret., cf. e.g. Milik DFD 48: = *bwl rw'wn* (= *qutlân*-form of root *r'y* (= to please, to love)) :: de Vaux RB xlviii 157 n. 2: poss. = *bôl rô'en* (< root *r'n*) = 'Bôl-le-Verdoyant'.

v. *kr*$_2$, *qrb*$_7$.

ṣb v. *ṣb'$_6$*.
ṣb'$_1$ v. *ṣby$_1$*.
ṣb'$_2$ v. *ṣb'$_3$*.
ṣb'$_3$ **Hebr** Sing. abs. *ṣb'* KAI 193[14]; Plur. abs. *ṣb'wt* AMB 12[24] - ¶ subst. army; *šr hṣb'* KAI 193[14]: the commander of the army (v. also *šr$_2$*); *'l ṣb'wt* AMB 12[24]: God of Hosts - Cross BASOR ccviii 15f.: l. in KAI 46[4f.]: *šlm* (= QAL Pf. 3 p.s.m. of *šlm$_1$*) *ṣb'* (= Sing. + suff. 3 p.s.m. of *ṣb'$_3$*) *mlktn* (= n.p.) = his army is at peace: Milkaton ... (cf. Peckham Or xli 459, 464f.: his forces found refuge; Milkûtôn ...; cf. Ahlström JNES xlv 312: l. *ṣb'* = Sing. cstr. of *ṣb'$_3$*: the army of M.), uncert. interpret., cf. - a) Cross CMHE 220 n. 5: l. *šlm* (= PI'EL Pf. 3 p.s.m. of *šlm$_1$*) *h'* (= *h'$_1$*) *šlm* (= PI'EL Pf. 3 p.s.m. of *šlm$_1$*) *ṣb'* (= Sing. + suff. 3 p.s.m.) *mlk<y>tn* (= n.p.) = M. and his army made peace (less prob. interpret.) - b) Bunnens EPM 34ff.: = *šlm* (= QAL Pf. 3 p.s.m.) *ṣb'* (= Sing. cstr. of *ṣb'$_3$*) *mlkt* (= Sing. abs. of *mlkt*(= kingship)) = may the royal army be at peace, or: the royal army is safe, less prob. interpret. - c) Lipiński BiOr xlv 63: *šlm ṣb'* (= Sing. cstr. of *ṣb'$_3$*) *mlkt* (= lapsus for *mlk* (= Sing. cstr. of *mlk$_3$*)) *kt* = safe is the crew of the king of K. - d) Février RA xliv 124ff.: l. *šlm* (= PI'EL Pf. 3 p.s.m. of *šlm$_1$*) *ṣb'* (= Sing. cstr. of *ṣb'$_4$* (= task)) *mlkt* (= Sing. abs. of *ml'kh$_1$*):he has completed the task of the work (cf. v.d.Branden Mašr lvi 286, 289f.: he has completed the whole of the work, cf. also Ferron RSO xli 285, 287f.: l. *šlm* (= m. Sing. abs. of *šlm$_7$*) *ṣb' mlkt* = may be preserved the work of the masonry) - e) Albright BASOR lxxxiii 19 (div. otherwise): l. *h'š* (= *h* + Sing. abs. of *'š$_1$*) *l[' (= l'$_1$)* ... *bn* (= *bn$_5$* (= *byn$_2$*)) *]mṣb'* (= HIPH Part. of *ṣb'$_2$*)*m[mm]lkt* (= Sing. abs. of *mmlkh*)= man who has n[ot .....] commander of a ... king (for this prob. description of the state of preservation of the text, cf. Albright BASOR clxxxix 55; cf. also Silverman JAOS xciv 269: l. ... *mṣb' mlkt* = commander (or) king, improb. interpret.) :: Delcor Syr xlv 331, 346ff.: l. *šlmṣb'* (= *šlm* (= QAL Pf. 3 p.s.f. of *šlm$_1$*) + *mṣb'* (with haplography; = Sing. + suff. 3 p.s.m. of *mṣb*))*mlktn* (= n.p.) = his stele. Milkaton ... :: Dupont-Sommer CRAI '48, 15ff. (cf. id. JA cclii 300, Röllig KAI a.l.): l. *šlm* (= Sing. abs. of *šlm$_2$*) *ṣr* (= n.l.) *'m* (= Sing. abs. of *'m$_1$*) *lkt* (= *l$_5$* + n.l.) = may Tyre the mother of Kition be prosperity (i.e may she prosper; cf. also Hvidberg-Hansen TNT ii 55 n. 50: l. *ṣr 'm* (= Sing. cstr.) / *kt*) :: Cooke NSI p. 110f. (div. otherwise): l. *'š* (= *'š$_4$*) *lnṣb'* (= *l$_5$* + QAL Inf. cstr. + suff. 3 p.s.f. of *nṣb$_1$*)*mlktn* (= n.p.) = which (was required) for setting it up. Milkaton ... (cf. Lidzbarski Handb 325, 427, CIS i sub 144; cf. also Slouschz TPI p. 136f.: or *lnṣb'* = *l$_5$* + Sing. + suff. 3 p.s. of *nṣb$_6$* (= prefect)); on the text, cf. also Gibson SSI iii p. 27 - Vattioni Aug xvi 547: a form of this subst. poss. in IRT 886f. 8 (and 9?), improb. interpret. - Szemerényi FS

Gordon ii 223ff.: Westsemitic *ṣb'* (Plur. *ṣb't*) > Iran. (highly uncert. interpret.).
v. *'t*$_1$, *ṣb'*$_6$.

ṣb'$_4$ v. *ṣb'*$_3$.

ṣb'$_5$ v. *ṣbw*.

ṣb'$_6$ **Pun** the diff. *ṣb'* in CIS i 197[5] = subst. *ṣb*(of unknown meaning) + suff. 3 p.s.m.??, cf. however Slouschz TPI p. 327: = Sing. + suff. 3 p.s.m. of *ṣb'*$_3$;or = Sing. abs. of *ṣb'*$_3$??

ṣbh **OldAr** word of unknown meaning in KAI 205-208 (for some other texts, cf. Ingholt Hama p. 116); poss. = verbal form :: Ingholt Hama 116 n. 4 (cf. 117 n. 5): poss. = title < Hitt. (cf. also Donner KAI a.l.; cf. however Degen ZDMG cxxi 132) :: Dupont-Sommer Ar 30 n. 13: = n.g. (cf. also Gibson SSI ii p. 18) :: Otzen ZAW c Suppl 234ff.: = QAL Part. act. s.m. abs. of *ṣby*$_1$; on the subject, cf. also Noth ZDPV lxiv 109 n. 2.

ṣbw **OffAr** Sing. abs. *ṣbw* Sem xxxiii 94[3] (for the reading, cf. Porten Sem xxxiii 94, 97, Porten & Yardeni sub TADAE A 5.1 :: Sznycer HDS 168, 171f.: l. prob. *ḥbr* = Sing. abs. of *ḥbr*$_3$(= association)); cstr. *ṣbwt* Driv 4[2], RES 1785A 4; emph. *ṣbwt'* ATNS 21[3] (or = Plur. emph.?, dam. context); + suff. 1 p.s. *ṣbwty* NESE iii 34 conv. 1 (dam. context; for the reading, cf. Degen NESE iii 38); cf. Frah xvi 8 (*ṣbw*, *ṣpw* :: Ebeling Frah a.l. : l. poss. *ṣbn/ṣpn* = *ṣpn*$_3$ (= treasure)), Paik 888 (*ṣbw*), GIPP 21, 50, SaSt 23 - **Palm** Sing. abs. *ṣbw* CIS ii 3915[4] (*[ṣ]bw*), 3917[5], 3930[4], Syr xix 75 i 4, Inv x 44[6], 77[3], 107[4], 111[4], 112[6], Inscr P 34[7], *ṣb'* Inv xii 35[4], *ḥbw* (lapsus) CIS ii 3916[4], *ṣbk* (lapsus) Syr xix 74[4]; cstr. *ṣbwt* Inv xii 49[8] (cf. Dupont-Sommer CRAI '66, 189f., cf. also Bounni & Teixidor Inv xii a.l. :: du Mesnil du Buisson CRAI '66, 172: = Sing. cstr. of *ṣbwt* (= *ṣbt*$_3$ (= ornamentation)); × = Plur. cstr. (cf. Bounni & Teixidor Inv xii a.l.)); Plur. emph. *ṣbwt'* CIS ii 3913 i 6 - **JAr** Plur. + suff. 3 p.s.m. *ṣbwtyh* MPAT-A 22[4] - ¶ subst. f. - **1)** longing, desire: RES 1785A 4; cf. prob. also Sem xxxiii 94[3] - **2)** affair, thing (for this meaning. cf. Driv p. 49); *'rmpy 'm ḥyl' ... l' mštm'n ly bṣbwt byt' mr'y* Driv 4[1f.]: A. and the troop ... do not obey me in the affair of my lord; *'ršm kn 'mr ṣbwt byt' zyly ... zky 'štm'w lh* Driv 4[2f.]: A. says thus: as to this affair of my estate ... obey him; *'l ṣbwt' 'ln srbnyn hww* CIS ii 3913 i 6f.: about these matters disputes arose (cf. Greek par. περὶ τούτου ζητήσεις γείνεσθ[αι]) *wsy' tgry' bkl ṣbw* Inv x 44[6]: he aided the merchants in everything (cf. CIS ii 1915[3f.], 3916[4], 3917[5], 3930[4], Syr xix 74[4], Inv xii 35[4], etc.); *wtrṣw ṣbwt bt'* Inv xii 49[8]: they have arranged/settled the affair(s) of the temple; for Inscr. P 34[7], v. *npl*$_1$ - **3)** good, possession; *ṣbwtyh dḥbryh* MPAT-A 22[4]: the goods of his fellow - the same word also in *bṣbw* (dam. context) in Cowl 54[13]?? (improb. reading & interpret., cf. e.g. Porten & Yardeni sub TADAE

A 3.1: l. *b'bṭ* = *b$_2$* + n.l.).
v. *sby$_1$*.

ṣbwt v. *ṣbw*.

ṣby$_1$ **OffAr** QAL Pf. 3 p.s.m. *ṣby* NESE i 11[3] (cf. Degen NESE i 16, Or xliv 124 × Degen NESE i 16: or = QAL Part. act. s.m. abs.? (cf. also Naveh & Shaked JAOS xci 380f.) × Naveh & Shaked JAOS xci 380f., Porten & Yardeni sub TADAE A 3.10: or = QAL Part. pass. s.m. abs. (cf. also Grelot DAE p. 504 n. g) :: Shunnar GMA 14f. : l. *ḥby* = Sing. + suff. 1 p.s. of *ḥb$_2$*(= grain; cf. also Macuch JAOS xciii 59, Shunnar CRM ii 280, 287; on the form *ṣby*, cf. Porten Or lvii 79)); 3 p.s.f. *ṣbyt* Cowl 15[25,29], Krael 6[15] (for the reading *npšy ṣbyt*, cf. Milik RB lxi 250, Grelot DAE p. 231 n. t, Porten & Greenfield JEAS p. 50, Porten & Yardeni sub TADAE B 3.7 :: Krael a.l.: l. *npš 'ḥryt* (f. Sing. abs. of *'ḥry$_3$*= other), cf. also Muffs 38, Porten Arch 226); 2 p.s.m. *ṣbyt* Cowl 4[4] (dam. context), 28[7,12], Krael 3[12,14,15,16]; 1 p.s. *ṣbyt* Cowl 18[2], Krael 7[41]; 3 p.pl.m. *ṣbw* Cowl 38[6] (cf. Cowl a.l. (cf. also Joüon MUSJ xviii 5) :: Grelot DAE p. 393, Porten & Greenfield JEAS p. 83, Dion RB lxxxix 567, Porten & Yardeni, sub TADAE A 4.3: = Sing. abs. of *ṣbw*); Impf. 2 p.s.m. *tṣbh* Herm 3[7]; 2 p.s.f. *tṣbyn* Cowl 13[16]; Part. act. s.m. abs. *ṣbh* Aḥiq 149; pl.m. abs. *ṣbyn* NESE iii 48[7]; cf. Frah xviii 2 (*yṣbhn*), Paik 508, 509 (*yṣbh*), cf. also Toll ZDMG-Suppl viii 33f., 37 - **Nab** QAL Impf. 3 p.s.m. *yṣb'* CIS ii 207[5], J 5[7]; 3 p.s.f. *tṣb'* CIS ii 204[4] - **Palm** QAL Pf. 3 p.s.m. *ṣb'* MUSJ xxxviii 106[9] (or = QAL Part. act. s.m. abs.?, cf. Ingholt MUSJ xxxviii 116); Impf. 3 p.s.m. *yṣb'* CIS ii 3913 ii 149, RB xxxix 539[2,4]; Part. act. pl.m. abs. *ṣbyn* Ber v 95[9] - **JAr** QAL Impf. 3 p.s.f. *tṣb'* DBKP 17[41]; 2 p.s.f. *tṣbyn* MPAT 40[7,19]; 3 p.pl.m. *yṣbwn* MPAT 52[10]; Part. act. s.m. abs., cf. PEQ '38, 238[2]: σαβη (cf. Peters OLZ '40, 218f., Beyer ATTM 353; cf. also Milik LA x 154f.) - ¶ verb QAL to want, to long for: passim; *ḥzw 'lyhm mh ṣbw* Cowl 38[5f.]: look after them in what they want (v. supra); *kl zy tṣbh šlḥ ly* Herm 3[7]: inform me about everything you want; *thk lk 'n zy ṣbyt* Cowl 15[28f.]: she may go where she wants (cf. Cowl 15[25]); *wzy ṣby* (v. supra) *y'bd lh* NESE i 11[3]: let one do for him what he wants; *yqbr mn dy yṣb'* CIS ii 207[5]: he may bury whomever he wants (cf. J 5[7]); *dy t'bd kl dy tṣb'* CIS ii 204[4]: that she do whatever she wants (cf. Greenfield Mem Yalon 69f.); *dy mn dy yṣb' yḥpr* RB xxxix 539[2]: that anyone who wants may dig (cf. RB xxxix 539[3f.]); *lmn zy tṣbyn hbhy* Cowl 13[16]: give it to whom you want (cf. Cowl 28[7,12], Krael 3[12,14,15,16]; for this and par. expressions, cf. Szubin & Porten BASOR cclii 36ff.); *lmhy 'nt' lkwl gbr yhwdy dy tṣbyn* MPAT 40[18f.]: to become the wife of any Jewish man you want (cf. MPAT 40[6f.]); *dy yhwn ḥpryn ... hyk dy ṣbyn* Ber v 95[9]: that they dig ... as they want; *bkl zmn dy tṣb'* DBKP 17[41]: at any time that she will desire - a) + obj., *'n ṣb' dy y'bd* MUSJ xxxviii 106[9f.]:

if he wants to make; cf. also *ṣbyt ʾhnṣl hm* Cowl 18[2f.]: I want to take them away (cf. Krael 7[41f.]); *npšy ṣbyt ʾhnṣl mnky* Krael 6[15]: I myself want to take (it) from you (v. supra) - b) + l_5 + Inf., *whyn lʾ ṣbyn lmʾth* NESE iii 48[7f.]: if they do not want to come.
v. *ṣbh*, *ṣbt$_3$*, *ṣdq$_3$*.

ṣby$_2$ v. *bʿy$_1$*.

ṣby$_3$ **OldAr** Sing. abs. *ṣby* KAI 222A 33 - ¶ subst. gazelle (for KAI 222A 33, cf. also Greenfield JSS xi 99 n. 2, Hoftijzer DA p. 207).

ṣbyt (< Akkad., cf. Cowl a.l., Claassen AION xxi 297f.) - **OffAr** Sing. cstr. *[ṣb]yt* Aḥiq 3 (poss. interpret., cf. however Kaufman AIA 96; for this reading, cf. Cowl a.l. :: Perles OLZ '11, 500: l. *[ṣb]t* = Sing. cstr. of *ṣbt$_2$* (= *ṣbyt*) :: Epstein OLZ '16, 204: l. *[rb]* (= Sing. cstr. of *rb$_1$*) + *byt* (= Sing. cstr. of *byt$_2$*)) - ¶ subst. bearer (sc. of seal); cf. Aḥiq 19 (*[ṣby]t*, poss. interpret., cf. also Grelot DAE p. 433, 448); on the title *[ṣb]yt ʿzqth/[ṣby]t ʿzqh* (= seal bearer), cf. Greenfield JAOS lxxxii 297ff., cf. also Vattioni Aug x 280.

ṣbn v. *ṣbw*.

ṣbʿ$_1$ **OffAr** QAL Part. pass. s.m. abs. *ṣbʿ* Cowl 15 [8], Krael 7[8], 14a (dam. context :: Krael p. 210: = Sing. abs. of *ṣbʿ$_3$* (= dye), cf. also Fitzmyer FS Albright ii 153, WA 256), *ṣbyʿ* Cowl 42[9] (for this reading, cf. Porten & Yardeni sub TADAE A 3.8 :: e.g. Cowl a.l.: l. *ṣbʿ*) - ¶ verb QAL to dye; Part. pass. dyed; for the expression *ṣbʿ ydyn* (Cowl 15[8], Krael 7[8], 14a), v. *yd*.

ṣbʿ$_2$ **OffAr** Sing. abs. *ṣbʿ* Cowl 26[20]; Plur. abs. *ṣbʿn* Cowl 26[16,18,19] (:: Naveh & Shaked Or xlii 456 (div. otherwise): l. *ʾṣbʿn* = Plur. abs. of *ʾṣbʿ*;v. also *pty$_3$*), Krael 7[10] - ¶ subst. certain measure of length, finger.
v. *ʾwṣtph*, *ʾṣbʿ*.

ṣbʿ$_3$ v. *ṣbʿ$_1$*.

ṣbr cf. Frah xviii 18 (*ṣblwn*): to gather, to collect - a form of this root also in BiAr xlii 170[1] (*ṣbr*), diff. and dam. context - on this root, cf. also Blau PC 61.

ṣbt$_1$ **Palm** PAʿEL Pf. 3 p.s.m. *ṣbt* CIS ii 4199[10], Inscr P 40[1]; 3 p.pl.m. *ṣbt* CIS ii 4173[3]; Part. act. s.m. + suff. 3 p.s.f. *mṣbth* Syr xiv 175[2] (cf. Cantineau Syr xiv 176, Gawlikowski TP 71 (prob. Greek par. κ[οσμητ]ήν)) - ¶ verb PAʿEL to decorate: CIS ii 4199[8ff.] (said of an exedra), Inscr P 40[1] (said of a hypogee); *mṣbth bbnyny [ʾ]l[hyʾ]* Syr xiv 175[2]: its decorator (sc. of the senate or the town, v. also supra) in the temples of the gods (v. also *bnyn* :: du Mesnil du Buisson Syr xl 313: sculptor making bas-relies.f. ....; cf. also Greek par., v. supra); + obj. (hypogee): CIS ii 4173[3] - for the PAʿEL of *ṣbt$_1$* (= to decorate, to ornament, etc.), cf. Kaufman AIA 95f.: loan from Akkad. less prob. (cf. however Greenfield JAOS lxxxii 293ff.) - Lidzbarski Eph ii 253f.: l. *ṣbt* (= PAʿEL Pf. 3 p.s.m. of *ṣbt$_1$*) in RES 2126[3] (= RES 468)??, reading highly uncert.

ṣbt$_2$ v. *ṣbyt*.

ṣbt$_3$ **OffAr** Plur. + suff. 1 p.s. *ṣbty* KAI 270B 1 (cf. Gibson SSI ii p. 124 :: Levine JAOS lxxxiv 20f.: = Plur. + suff. 1 p.s. of *ṣbt$_4$* (= bundle (of grain)) :: CIS ii sub 137, Cooke NSI p. 203: = Plur. cstr. of *ṣbt$_3$* (cf. also Koopmans p. 170, Donner KAI a.l.) :: Hoffmann ZA xi 223: = Plur. cstr. of *ṣbt$_4$* (= bundle) :: Dupont-Sommer ASAE xlviii 126, Grelot DAE p. 138 (n. e): = QAL Pf. 2 p.s.f. of *ṣby$_1$*) - ¶ subst. valuable; *k‘n hn ṣbty kl tzbnyhmw* KAI 137B 1f.: now, if you will sell all my valuables ... - Kaufman AIA 96: > Akkad. *ṣibtu* (= garment for cult statues)?, cf. however v.Soden AHW s.v. *ṣibtu* III.
v. *ṣbw*.

ṣbt$_4$ v. *ṣbt$_3$*.

ṣbt$_5$ v.Soden Or xlvi 194: = (pair of) tongues > Akkad. *ṣibtā/ētu* = fetters (cf. however id. AHW s.v.), highly uncert. interpret.

ṣbt$_6$ Kaufman AIA 96: > Akkad. *ṣubbutu* (var. *ṣabbutu*) = collected, connected, arrested? uncert. interpret.

ṣd$_1$ **Pun** Sing. abs. *ṣd* KAI 69[12], 74[9] - ¶ subst. word of uncert. meaning in the comb. *zbḥ ṣd* (KAI 69[12], 74[9]); Dussaud Orig 152: = offering of food > flour, bread; Lagrange ERS 470, 474f.: = sacrifice of game (cf. Lidzbarski Handb 358, cf. also Rosenthal ANET 657: = hunt offering); on the subject, cf. e.g. also CIS i sub 165, Cooke NSI p. 114, 120, Lidzbarski sub KI 63, Röllig KAI a.l., Loewenstamm CSBA 422, Amadasi Guzzo SSMA 114f. - Garbini StudMagr x 9: l. poss. *ṣd* in Teb. 411[2] (= Sing. abs. (= game)) :: Garbini ibid.: or l. *ṣy* (= Sing. abs. (= sheep)) :: Fantar Teb. 411f.: l. prob. *bn* (= Sing. cstr. of *bn$_1$*) - cf. *ṣyd$_1$*.

ṣd$_2$ **Pun** Sing. abs. *ṣd* KAI 130[2]; + suff. 3 p.s.m. *ṣd›* KAI 78[6] - **OffAr** Sing. cstr. *ṣd* ATNS 26[3,6]; cf. Frah xxv 37 (in the comb. *lṣd* (cf. Nyberg FP 55, 104 :: Ebeling Frah a.l.: l. *lṣt*)), Paik 596 (in the comb. *lṣd*), 597 (in the comb. *lṣdw*), SaSt 22, BSOAS xxxiii 152[11] - ¶ subst. side, back - **1)** prec. by prep. *b$_2$*, *›š bṣd ‘l hmḥzm* KAI 130[2f.]: which is set aside with the *aediles* (prob. said of money administrated by the *aediles*, cf. e.g. Levi Della Vida Lib iii/ii 13, v.Selms UF ii 256 n. 14 :: Delavault & Lemaire RB lxxxiii 577 n. 30: *bṣd* = voluntarily), for the context, v. also *‘nš$_2$* - **2)** prec. by prep. *l$_5$*, *lmnpq lṣd pnh* ATNS 26[3]: to go forth in the direction of P. (cf. Shaked Or lvi 409; v. *pnh$_1$*) - **3)** used prepositionally, *pny mb› hšmš wṣd› mṣ› hšmš* KAI 78[5f.]: before him is the west and behind him is the east (cf. also v.Selms UF ii 255f.) - Levi Della Vida IRT p. 12: this word poss. also in *ṣdšmr* (KAI 130[6]) = function indication?: assistant inspector (or rather = n.p.?, cf. Levi Della Vida Lib iii/ii 15, cf. also Jongeling NINPI 48, 201) - Vattioni AION xvi 50ff.: *bsdi* in IRT 906[5] = *b$_2$* + *ṣdy* (= Sing. + suff. 3 p.s.m. of *ṣd$_2$*), cf. also Vattioni Aug xvi 550: *ṣdy* = Sing. + suff. 1 p.s. (highly uncert. interpret., cf. also Levi Della Vida OA ii 74: without interpret.). v. *nd*, *ṣdq₂*.

ṣd₃ v. *ṣdqh.*

ṣdʾ₁ **OffAr** diff. word in KAI 233[12] (in the comb. *hṣdʾ;h* prob. = *h₂*).Poss. interpret.: what is solid, what is true (related to root *yṣd*= to be firm??, cf. e.g. Torrey JAOS xliii 231f., BL 371, Dupont-Sommer Syr xxiv 42f.); *hṣdʾ hny mlyʾ ʾlh* KAI 233[12]: are these words true? (cf. also R.A.Bowman UMS xx 280) for the interpretations/etymologies, cf. Baumgartner ZAW xlv 89.

ṣdʾ₂ v. *kṣr₃*.

ṣdh₁ **OldAr** Sing. abs. *ṣdh* KAI 222A 33 - ¶ subst. owl (cf. also Fitzmyer AIS 50); for the context of KAI 222A 33, cf. Hillers TC 44f. v. *ṣrh₂*.

ṣdh₃ v. *ṣdq₂*.

ṣdwq v. *zkrwt₁*.

ṣdy v. *ṣdq₂*.

ṣdyḥ v. *ṣryḥ₂*.

ṣdyq v. *ṣdq₃*.

ṣdn **Pun** word of unknown meaning in the foll. expressions in votive inscriptions (following the name of the donator of the votive offering), *ʾš ṣdn bd ʾdny bd ʾšmnytn ʿm qrtḥdšt* CIS i 269[3ff.]; *[ʾš] ṣdn bd bʿlḥnʾ bn ḥm[lk] lmyʿms ʿm qrtḥdšt* CIS i 270; *ʾš ṣdn bd ʾdny b[d ʿbdm]lqrt bn ʾšmn[ytn lmy]ʿms ʿm* CIS i 272[3ff.]; *ʾš ṣdn lmyʿms* CIS i 273[4] (uncert. whether the donator is male or female); *ʾš ṣdn bd bnʾ lmyʿms* CIS i 275[4f.]; *[ʾš] ṣdn bd ʾdnm bd ʾ[dn]bʿl bn bʿlḥnʾ* CIS i 276; *ʾš ṣdn* CIS i 277[3]; *[ʾ]š ṣdn b[d ...]* CIS i 278[3f.]; *[ʾš] ṣdn bd ʾ[dny bd] bʿlḥnʾ* CIS i 279[3ff.] (following the name of a woman); *ʾ[š ṣd]n bd ʾdny bd ḥm[l]kt* CIS i 280[3ff.] (following the name of a woman); *ʾš ṣdn ʿ[...* CIS i 281[3f.] (following the name of a woman); *ʾš ṣdn bd mgn bn mlqrtḥlṣ bn ʿbdmlkt* CIS i 282[3ff.]; *[ʾš] ṣdn bd ʿbdmlqrt bn ʿbd[ʾš]mn* CIS i 283[2ff.]; *ʾš ṣdn bd mlk[y]tn bn bʿlḥnʾ* CIS i 284[4f]; *ʾš ṣdn bd [ʿbdm]lqrt bn bdʿš[trt]* CIS i 285[3ff.]; *ʾš ṣdn bd [...] bn ʿbdʾšmn* CIS i 286[3f.]; *ʾš [ṣd]n bn* (lapsus pro *bd*?) *špṭ bn šḥrb[ʿ]l* CIS i 287; *[ʾš] ṣdn bd ʾdny bd bdmlqrt* CIS i 289[4ff.]; *[ʾš] ṣdn bd [...* CIS i 290[4f.]; *ʾš ṣdn bd [b]dʿštrt bn špṭ* CIS i 2998[2f.]; *ʾš ṣdn bd ʾdnm bd mlkytn bn ytnbʿl bn mlkytn* CIS i 4901[3f.]; *ʾš ṣdn bd ʾdnm bd ʿbds* CIS i 4902[4f.]; *ʾš ṣdn bd ʾdnm bd ʿbdʾšmn bn ʾrš* CIS i 4903[3f.]; *ʾš ṣdn bd ʾdnm bd bʿlḥnʾ bn šṭldšn* CIS i 4904[2f.]; *ʾš ṣdn ʾdny bd ḥmlkt* CIS i 4905[4f.]; *ʾš ṣdn bd grʿštrt bn ḥnʾ* CIS i 4906[5ff.]; *ʾš ṣdn bn* (diff. reading, lapsus for *bd*?, or l. *bd*?) *ʿbdmlqrt bn bdʿštrt* CIS i 4907[4f.]; *ʾš ṣdn lmʾʿmsʾ ʿm qrtḥdšt* CIS i 4908[4f.]; cf. also *ʿbdmlqrt ... ʾš ṣdn ʿbdmlqrt* RES 906[1]; *ʿkbr hbnʾ ʾš ṣdn klm* KAI 65[11]; *ʾbn ʾš ṭʿnʿ lpʾlyks hṣydn šbʿlšmʿ* Punica xiv 2; *hṣdn šmʿrkʾ* Punica xv 1[4]; *h[s]dn š dʿbr* Punica xi 8[2f.] (for this reading, cf. Jongeling NINPI 8); the same

word also in *b'nṣdn ḥnm by ksp* CIS i 5522[4]? - CIS i sub 269, Harr 79: *'š ṣdn* = man of Sidon, Sidonian, cf. also Slouschz TPI p. 251, Röllig KAI a.l. (cf. Heltzer UF xix 435: *'š ṣdn* originally = man from Sidon, later used for people who where not from Sidon as indication of a certain legal status (cf. also idem OA xxiv 80f.) explanation of *'š* as *'š*$_1$ however diff., cf. *'š ṣdn* following the name of a woman: CIS i 279-281, cf. already Lidzbarski Handb 134 n. 4, CIS i sub 2998; Chabot sub Punica xv 1: *'š ṣdn* = freedman (< Sidonian; cf. also Huss 497ff.), invariable expression for both males and females (cf. also Chabot ibid.: *ṣdn/ṣydn* in *hṣ(y)dn* in Punica xiv 2, xv 1 = freedman (both *'š ṣdn* and *ṣdn* as distinguished from *ṣdny* = from Sidon), for *'s*, cf. however supra; Février Sem iv 14f.: *ṣdn* = copper, *'š ṣdn* = man of copper > freedman (for this meaning, cf. also Sznycer Sem xxv 56 n. 2, Elayi RCP 63), *ṣ(y)dn* in Punica xiv 2, xv 1 = abbrev. of *'š ṣdn* (for *'š ṣdn* however, v. supra, *ṣ(y)dn* as abbrev. of *'š ṣdn* improb.; the meaning 'copper' for *ṣdn* highly uncert.); Lidzbarski Handb 134 n. 4., CIS i sub 2998: *'š ṣdn* = *'š*$_4$ (= *š*$_{10}$) + n.l. = the one from Sidon (improb. interpret.; this interpret. of *ṣdn* imposs. in Punica xiv 2, xv 1) :: v.d.Branden BiOr xxxvi 158ff.: *ṣdn* = guard or guardian, *'š ṣdn* = Sing. cstr. of *'š*$_1$ + *ṣdn* = guard, i.e. one of the guard, or *'š* = Sing. abs. of *'š*$_1$ + *ṣdn* = guardian, i.e. one who is guardian, *hṣdn* = the guardian (cf. also id. ibid.: *ṣdnym* in KAI 60[1,7] = guardians, cf. however e.g. Cooke NSI p. 94, Röllig KAI a.l., Gibson SSI iii p. 149: = Plur. abs. of *ṣdny* (= Sidonian); id. ibid.: *'m ṣdn* in KAI 60[1] = the group of the *ṣdn*-association, cf. however e.g. Cook NSI p. 94f., Gibson SSI iii p. 149: = the community/people of Sidon (cf. also Röllig KAI a.l.))) - in *b'n ṣdn* (CIS i 5522[4]) *ṣdn* prob. = subst. Sing. abs., poss. meaning 'payment', 'money' (used in connection with manumission), cf. Février Sem iv 15: *b'n* = *b*$_2$ + *'n*$_2$ (= *'yn*$_1$) = without (:: v.d.Branden BiOr xxiii 142ff., xxxix 202: *b'n ṣdn* = *b*$_2$ + *'n* (= n.l.) + *ṣdn* (= n.l.) = in On of Sidon :: Segal sub ATNS 4[5]: in *b'nṣdn*, *nṣdn* = NIPH Inf. of *ṣdn* (= to be freed)) - in all instances *ṣdn* prob. derivatives of same root, *'š ṣdn*, *'š* poss. = *'š*$_4$ (v. supra) + (passive) verbal form of *ṣdn* (Pf. 3 p.s.m./f.?) = to emancipate, to manumit (?); *hṣ(y)dn* poss. = *h*$_1$ + nominal derivative of this root - the *ṣdn* in Herr SANSS-Amm 36 (= Jackson ALIA 77 n. 49), prob. = n.l. (cf. Avigad IEJ xvi 248, Garbini AION xxvii 483, Bordreuil & Lemaire Sem xxix 81, Jackson ALIA 77, 86, Aufrecht sub CAI 56).
v. *ḥsn*$_1$.

ṣdq$_1$ **OffAr** QAL Impf. 3 p.s.m. *yṣdq* Krael 10[15]; 1 p.s. *'ṣdq* Cowl 8[22], Aḥiq 139; 3 p.pl.m. *yṣdqwn* Cowl 10[19]; PA 'EL (:: Leand 31j: = QAL) Pf. 3 p.s.m. + suff. 1 p.s. *ṣdqny* Aḥiq 140 (cf. however Kottsieper SAS 149: l. *[y]ṣdqny* = PA 'EL Impf. 3 p.s.m. + suff. 1 p.s.) - ¶ verb QAL - **1)**

to be (considered as) just; *[mny] npqt lḥyty w'm mn 'ṣdq* Aḥiq 139: my misfortune has proceeded from myself (v. *lḥy*$_2$) and with whom shall I be justified? (cf. also Lindenberger APA 137, 260 n. 427; :: Grelot RB lxviii 188, DAE p. 442: with whom to obtain justice?) - **2)** to win one's case; *w'hk bdyn wl' 'ṣdq* Cowl 8[22]: (if) I start a lawsuit, I shall not win my case (cf. Muffs 6, cf. however Yaron RB lxxvii 415), cf. Cowl 10[19], Krael 10[15] - PA'EL to justify, to consider just, innocent; *[h]wh ly šhd ḥms wmn 'pw ṣdqny* Aḥiq 140: (if) there was a false witness against me, who then has justified me? (v. also supra).

ṣdq₂ **Ph** Sing. abs. *ṣdq* KAI 16, 43[11] (for both instances, v. infra); + suff. 1 p.s. *ṣdqy* KAI 26A i 12 - **Samal** Sing. + suff. 3 p.s.m. *ṣdqh* KAI 215[11]; + suff. 1 p.s. *ṣdqy* KAI 215[19] - **OldAr** Sing. cstr. *ṣdq* KAI 216[4], 219[4]; + suff. 1 p.s. *ṣdqy* KAI 216[4f.] - ¶ subst. - **1)** correct, justifiable conduct; *bṣdq 'by wbṣdqy hwšbny ... 'l krs' 'by* KAI 216[4ff.]: because of the righteousness of my father and my own righteousness .. he seated me on the throne of my father (cf. KAI 215[19], 219[4]); *['[by lw b'l ksp h' wlw b'l zhb bḥkmth wbṣdqh* KAI 215[10f.]: my father was a possessor of silver as well as a possessor of gold (v. *lw*) because of his wisdom and his righteousness (cf. KAI 26A i 12f.; on this use of *ṣdq*$_2$, cf. also Donner MiOr iii 96f.) - **2)** legitimacy; *ṣmḥ ṣdq* KAI 43[11]: the legitimate offspring/scion (indication of the legitimate heir of the throne), for this interpret. and translation, cf. e.g. Cooke NSI p. 86, Harr 140, Honeyman JEA xxvi 58, 63, v.d.Branden OA iii 248, 257f., Swetnam Bibl xlvi 29ff., 36f., Röllig KAI sub 16, Cazelles JANES v 67, Gibson SSI iii p. 137, 140; *bn ṣdq* KAI 16: the legitimate son (indication of the legitimate heir of the throne), for this interpret., cf. already Clermont-Ganneau RAO vi 346ff., Lidzbarski Eph ii 153ff., Elayi RCP 22, SCA 107f., and the literature just quoted supra (on the context, cf. also Gubel Syr lxvii 500ff., Bordreuil Trans iii 93f.); the *ṣdq* in *ṣmḥ ṣdq* and *bn ṣdq* might also be m. Sing. abs. of *ṣdq*$_3$ (cf. Harr 140) :: Loewenstamm CSBA 212f. n. 3: the *ṣdq* in these instances = indication of worthiness :: v.d.Branden PO ii 168ff.: the *ṣmḥ ṣdq* = someone belonging to the royal family who, although not being the legitimate heir, is designated to be the successor to the throne, the *bn ṣdq* = someone not belonging to the royal family, thus designated - a nom. derivative of the same root poss. in BASOR cxciii 8[4], cf. Sasson PEQ '79, 118, 122: l. *ṣdq* = Sing. abs. of *ṣdq*$_2$ (cf. Puech & Rofé RB lxxx 538), cf. also Shea PEQ '81, 105, 107: l. *ṣdq* (= Sing. abs. of *ṣdq*$_2$ (= justice, victory)) used adverbially, victoriously (less prob. interpret.); Fulco BASOR ccxxx 41, Jackson ALIA 10, 19, 25, Aufrecht sub CAI 59: l. *ṣdq[m]* (= m. Plur. abs. of *ṣdq*$_3$) (cf. also Smelik HDAI 84); cf. Puech & Rofé RB lxxx 532, 534, 538: l. poss. *ṣdq[* (= m. Sing. abs. of *ṣdq*$_3$) or *ṣdq[m]*; cf. however Horn BASOR cxciii 8, 11, Cross BASOR cxciii 18f.: readings *ṣdq* and *ṣdh* both poss. (cf.

Albright BASOR cxcviii 38: l. *ṣdh* (= Sing. + suff. 3 p.s.m. of *ṣd*$_2$);cf. also v.Selms BiOr xxxii 5ff., Shea PEQ '79, 19, 22) :: Horn BASOR cxciii 8, 11: or l. *ṣdh* (= QAL Part. pass. of *ṣdy*(= destroyed)) :: Shea PEQ '79, 17ff., 22: l. prob. *ṣdh* (= Sing. abs. of *ṣdh*$_3$(= ambush)) :: Dion RB lxxxii 32 (n. 55): l. *ṣrh[w]* (= Plur. + suff. 3 p.s.m. of *ṣr*$_2$ (against this reading, cf. also Garr DGSP 108)).
v. *ṣdq*$_3$.

ṣdq₃ **Ph** m. Sing. abs. *ṣdq* KAI 4[6] (:: Gray SVT xv 175: = Sing. abs. of *ṣdq*$_2$), 10[9] - **Pun** f. Sing. abs. *ṣdyq*ʿ(cf. FR 213, 229) KAI 154[3] - **Hebr** m. Plur. abs. *ṣdyqym* IEJ vii 244[3] - **OffAr** m. Sing. abs. *ṣdq* KAI 217[5], *ṣdyq*Cowl 44[6], ATNS 8[8] (for this reading, cf. Naveh IEJ xxxv 211, Shaked Or lvi 409, Porten & Yardeni sub TADAE B 5.6 :: Segal ATNS a.l.: l. *ṣbyt* = QAL Pf. 1 p.s. of *ṣby*$_1$),Aḥiq 126, 128, 167 (or = cstr.?, cf. Cowl p. 225, 245), 173 - **Palm** f. Sing. emph. *zdqt[ʾ]* CIS ii 3947[1] - **JAr** m. Plur. emph. *ṣdyqyh* MPAT-A 16[4] (= SM 17 :: Frey sub 981: l. *ṣdyqym*= m. Plur. abs., Hebrew form in Ar. context), 34[6] (= SM 69) - ¶ adj. - **1)** correct, justifiable in conduct; *pwlyʿ hṣdyqʿ* KAI 154[2f.]: P. the just woman (cf. also CIS ii 3947[1], v. *nhr*$_4$); *wṣdq ʾnh ʿm[* KAI 217[5]: I have been loyal towards ... (cf. Aḥiq 173) - **2)** legitimate; *mlk ṣdq wmlk yšr lpn ʾl gbl* KAI 4[6f]: the legitimate and rightful king in the sight of the gods of G. (for this interpret., cf. e.g. Herrmann MiOr vi 22f., Gibson SSI iii p. 18f., Butterweck TUAT ii 584 (cf. already Albright JAOS lxvii 157 (n. 36)), cf. however e.g. Dunand FB 30, Loewenstamm CSBA 212 n. 3, Elayi RCP 36: a just and right king (cf. also Röllig KAI a.l.: the king in question an usurper?); on this subject, cf. also *ṣdq*$_2$(cf. also Gray SVT xv 175f., Cazelles JANES v 62ff.)); cf. also KAI 10[9] - **3)** used in legal sense, being entitled to, having the right; *ṣdyq ʾ[nh lh]ḥsnwth* Cowl 44[6f.]: I have the right to transfer it (v. *ḥsn*$_1$ :: Cowl a.l.: *ṣdyq* = legally; for the restoration of the context, cf. e.g. Grelot DAE p. 95 (n. f), Porten & Greenfield JEAS p. 122, Porten & Yardeni sub TADAE B 7.3); *ʾnh ṣdyq bhm* ATNS 8[8] (v. supra): I am entitled to them (dam. context) - **4)** substantivated adj. - a) the just/righteous one: Aḥiq 126, 167; *ṣdyq mnk* Aḥiq 128: one who is more righteous than you are (v. *mn*$_5$) - b) the pious one (used especially as indication of the pious dead); *yhy lh ḥwlq ʿm ṣdyqyh* MPAT-A 16[3f.]: may his lot be with the pious ones (cf. MPAT-A 34[5f.]); *zkr ṣdyqym lbrkh* IEJ vii 244[2f.]: the memory of the pious ones may be blessed - the *zdq/zrq* in Hatra 333, 334[1] prob. = n.p. (cf. Degen NESE iii 109: l. in both instances *snṭrwq wzd/rq* :: As-Salihi Sumer xxxi 186f.: l. *snṭrwq wzdq* = Sanatruq the pious one :: Aggoula Sem xxvii 134: l. in Hatra 333 *snṭrwqw zdq* (= S. the pious one) and in Hatra 334: *snṭrwq zdq* (= S. the pious one; cf. also Vattioni IH sub 334, Tubach ISS 247 (n. 50)).

v. *ḥdy*$_5$, *ṣdq*$_2$.

ṣdqh **OffAr** Sing. abs. *ṣdqh* Cowl 30[27], 71[5]; emph. *ṣdqtʾ* Cowl 71[28], KAI 228A 15; + suff. 1 p.s. *ṣdqty* KAI 226[2]; cf. Frah i 14 (?, cf. Nyberg FP 61 :: Ebeling Frah a.l.: l. *ṣdh* = Sing. emph. of *ṣd*$_3$(= fortune) related to Akkad. *ṣaddu*) - **Nab** Sing. cstr. *ṣdqt* CIS ii 224[8] (= J 34) - ¶ subst. - **1)** righteousness, merit; *wṣdqh yhwh lk qdm YHW ʾlh šmyʾ mn gbr zy yqrb lh* ... Cowl 30[27f]: you will have a merit before YHW the god of the heavens more than a person who offers him ... (i.e. you will be favoured more than ... :: Aggoula Syr lxii 64: *ṣdqh* in this text = share, portion); *bṣdqty qdmwh šmny šm ṭb* KAI 226[2f.]: because of my righteousness before him (i.e. the god) he afforded me a good name (for this translation, cf. Vincent Rel 179, Rosenthal HUCA xxiii/1 426f. (also for litt. on this subject)) - **2)** grant: CIS ii 224[8] (= J 34; a grant of a tomb of a father to his daughter and her heirs), KAI 228A 15 (grant of annual revenue for a god and his temple bestowed upon him by other local gods), cf. also Rosenthal HUCA xxiii/1 425f., Aggoula Syr lxii 64 - **3)** justice: Cowl 71[28] (heavily dam. context) - **4)** the meaning in Cowl 71[5] highly uncert. (heavily dam. context).

ṣdt$_1$ v. *ḥdš*$_3$.

ṣdt$_2$ v. *ʾt*$_6$.

ṣhw$_1$ **Nab** Sing. cstr. *ṣhwt* CIS ii 354[2]; Plur. (?) emph. *ṣhwtʾ* CIS ii 350[2] - ¶ subst. exact meaning unknown; prob. indicating small building, or part of building (sanctuary, cella), for diff. interpret. proposals, cf. CIS ii sub 350, 354, Cantineau Nab ii 139, Milik RB lxvi 559f., Levinson NAI 208.

ṣhw$_2$ v. *ṣhwh*.

ṣhwh **OffAr** Sing. abs. *ṣhwh* Aḥiq 188 (cf. e.g. Kottsieper SAS 47, 228; Lindenberger APA 186: or = Sing. of *ṣhw*$_2$(= thirst), less prob. interpret.) - ¶ subst. thirst: Aḥiq 188 (prob. interpret., heavily dam. context, cf. Cowl a.l., Grelot DAE p. 446, cf. also Leand 43k', Kottsieper SAS 34).

ṣhr$_1$ **OldCan** Sing. abs. *ṣú-ú-ru-ma* EA 232[11] (cf. Rainey EA p. 91, cf. however CAD s.v. *ṣuʾru*, Sivan GAG 131, 270: l. *ṣú-uḫ-ru-ma*; on this word, cf. also Böhl 6d, 37l, Kossmann JEOL xxx 56) - ¶ subst. back.

ṣhr$_2$ **Mo** Sing./Dual + adv. ending (?, cf. e.g. Cooke NSI p. 12, Segert ArchOr xxix 222, v.Zijl p. 191 n. 3, Röllig KAI a.l., Gibson SSI i p. 80, Blau Maarav ii 143f. :: e.g. Silverman JAOS xciv 269, Jackson & Dearman SMIM 115) *ṣhrm* KAI 181[15] - ¶ subst. (after)noon; *ʿd hṣhrm* KAI 181[15]: until the (after)noon.

ṣwʾyt **Pun** word of unknown meaning in Punica iv A 8[4], cf. also Février CB viii 29, Schedl VT xii 344 (: root *ṣyy* = to erect (a tombstone/memorial)).

ṣwb v. *ḥwb*$_2$.

ṣwd v. *ṣrr*$_1$.
ṣwh v. *ṣwt*.
ṣwḥ **JAr** Naveh & Shaked AMB a.l.: l. poss. *ṣwḥ[t]* (= QAL Pf. 3 p.s.f. of *ṣwḥ* (= to shout)) in AMB 15[11] (uncert. reading).
ṣwy$_1$ **Hebr** PI'EL Pf. 3 p.s.m. + suff. 2 p.s.m. *ṣwk* TA-H 3[3]; 2 p.s.m. + suff. 1 p.s. *ṣwtny* TA-H 18[7f.] - ¶ verb PI'EL to command - **1)** + obj., to give someone an order: TA-H 18[7f.] - **2)** + obj. + *ʿl*$_7$, *ṣwk ḥnnyhw ʿl bʾr šbʿ ʿm mšʾ ṣmd ḥmrm* TA-H 3[3ff.]: Ch. has ordered you to go to B.-Sh. with the load of a pair of donkeys (for *ʿl*, v. however *ʿl*$_7$; for the context, v. also *mšʾ*; cf. Levine Shn iii 289).
ṣwy$_2$ v. *ṣwʿ*.
ṣwlh v. *mṣlh*.
ṣwm **OffAr** QAL Part. act. pl.m. abs. *ṣymyn* Cowl 30[15,20] - ¶ verb QAL to fast - a prob. form of this root *tṣm* (= QAL Impf. 2 p.s.m.) in DA xiic 2, cf. e.g. McCarter BASOR ccxxxix 51, 53, Levine JAOS ci 196, Hackett BTDA 38, 97, Puech FS Grelot 20, 27.
ṣwʿ **Ph** a subst. (Sing. abs.) *ṣwʿ* poss. in Mus li 286[1], reading of ʿ however uncertain., meaning uncertain. Prob. = indication of function, the sacrificer of the *ṣwʿt*-offering??, cf. also Honeyman Mus li 289, cf. however Sznycer RDAC '88 ii 59ff.: l. *ṣwy* poss. = Sing. abs. of *ṣwy*$_2$(= commander); cf. *ṣwʿh*.
ṣwʿh **Pun** Sing. abs. *ṣwʿt* KAI 69[3,4,5] (*[ṣw]ʿt*)[,6,7,9,13], 74[4,5], CIS i 3915[2] (*ṣw[ʿt]*) - ¶ subst. prob. meaning 'communal offering', cf. Dussaud Orig 142ff. (cf. e.g. also de Vaux SAT 44, Capuzzi StudMagr ii 64ff., 68ff., Amadasi ICO p. 175f.) :: Rosenthal ANET 656f.: = substitute offering? :: Ginsberg AJSL xlvii 52f.: = expiation offering (cf. also Röllig KAI a.l.) :: Cooke NSI p. 113, 117: = prayer-offering? (cf. also Lidzbarski KI p. 48); cf. Janowski UF xii 255f. for litt.; cf. *ṣwʿ* - for this offering, cf. also Urie PEQ '49, 70f., Amadasi Guzzo SSMA 111ff.
ṣwr$_1$ **Palm** QAL Pf. 3 p.pl.m. *ṣrw* Inv D 25[7]; Part. pass. pl.m. abs. *ṣyryn* Inv D 25[2] (reading however uncertain, cf. also Cantineau Syr xix 164) - ¶ verb QAL to paint; *ṣrw ṣwrtʾ hd[ʾ]* Inv D 25[7]: they have painted this painting; *ʾnšyʾ dṣyryn tnn* Inv D 25[2f.]: the men who have been painted here; on this root, cf. also Kaufman AIA 109f. - Vattioni Aug xvi 546: the *]sor* in IRT 886e 15 poss. = form of the root *ṣwr*$_1$ (highly uncert. interpret.) - Garbini PP xxxiii 425f.: l. *ṣr* (= QAL Pf. 3 p.s.m. of *ṣwr*$_1$ (= to incise, to cut)) in AMSMG xv-xvii 60 (highly uncert. reading and interpret., cf. also Amadasi Guzzo VO ii 4ff.: l. poss. *dr* (= Sing. cstr. of *dr*$_5$ (= pearl, mother-of-pearl, precious stone) ?)).
v. *mṣr*$_3$, *ṣwrh*.
ṣwr$_2$ cf. Frah x 29 (*ṣwlh*; cf. Benveniste Titres 62): neck.
ṣwrh **Palm** Sing. (or Plur.) emph. *ṣwrtʾ* Inv D 25[7] - ¶ subst. f. painting

(on the root of this word, cf. *ṣwr*$_1$).

ṣwt (cf. Leand 43j', or = *ṣwh*?) - **OffAr** Sing. cstr. *ṣwt* Cowl 37[14] - ¶ subst. order; *bṣwt mlk*ʾ Cowl 37[14]: by order of the king (cf. also Dion RB lxxxix 556).

ṣḥ v. *yrḥ*$_2$.

ṣḥb **Pun** Février sub IAM 4: l. prob. *yṣḥb* (= QAL/PIʿEL/YIPH Impf. 3 p.s.m. of *šḥb* (= to remove) in BAr '55/56, 32[4]; diff. reading, cf. Février BAr '55/56 a.l.: l. *ysḥb* = QAL Impf. 3 p.s.m. of *sḥb*$_1$.

ṣḥwh **OffAr** Sing. abs. *ṣḥwh* Aḥiq 188 (heavily dam. context) - ¶ subst. thirst.

ṣḥy **JAr** QAL Part. act. s.f. abs. *ṣḥyh* AMB 7[18,20]; s.f. emph. *ṣḥyth* AMB 7[20] - ¶ verb QAL to be thirsty.

ṣḥt v.Soden FS Christian 104: = desire (< root *ṣḥy*) > Akkad. *siḫittu* (imposs. interpret., cf. v.Soden Or xxxvii 267).

ṣṭwr **OffAr** Sing. emph. *ṣṭwr*ʾ BSOAS xxvii 272 iii 1 - ¶ word of unknown meaning (subst. or adj.) used as epithet after n.p.; poss. indication of title or function (cf. Sznycer JA ccliii 6) or = adj. < Iran. (= strong)??, cf. Bivar & Shaked BSOAS xxvii 276 n. 31 (for this interpret., cf. however Altheim & Stiehl AAW iii 70).

ṣy v. *ṣd*$_1$.

ṣyb cf. Frah iv 16 (*ṣyb*ʾ, *ṣyp*ʾ): fire-wood.

ṣybywn **JAr** Sing. + suff. 1 p.s. *ṣybywny* AMB 10[8] - ¶ subst. desire.

ṣyd$_1$ **OffAr** Sing. emph. *ṣyd*ʾ KAI 261[5] - ¶ subst. hunt; *kzy ṣyd*ʾ *ʿbd* ʾ*nh* KAI 261[5]: whenever I am hunting ...
v. *zʿr*$_2$, *ḥdš*$_3$,cf. *ṣd*$_1$.

ṣyd$_2$ **Hebr** Lemaire IH i 212: l. *ṣyd* in TA-H 52 (= Sing. abs. of *ṣyd*$_2$ (= hunter, fisherman) or = element *ṣd* known from Ph./Pun. onomastics). Prob. reading (cf. also Rainey with Aharoni TA a.l.), both interpretations improbable, cf. Rainey ibid.: *ṣyd* = n.p. :: Aharoni TA a.l.: l. *pšyd* = n.p. (cf. also Heltzer Shn ii 58) - Yadin & Naveh Mas a.l.: the *ṣyd*ʾ in Mas 440 = Sing. emph. of *ṣyd*$_2$ used as a nickname.

ṣydn v. *ṣdn*.

ṣyh **OldAr** Lipiński Stud 42: l. *ṣyh* (Sing. abs. = drought) in KAI 222B 37 (poss. reading; interpret. of context diff.).

ṣywʿn **Pun** Sing. abs. *ṣywʿn* NP 130[2] (for the reading, cf. Dérenbourg CRAI 1875, 260, 262, O.Blau ZDMG xxix 738f., Euting ZDMG xxx 284f., and with reserve Lidzbarski Handb 358, 438, Cooke NSI p. 147 :: Février RHR cxli 20: l. *sywʿt*(= Sing. abs. of *sywʿt*)) - ¶ subst. (funerary) stele.

ṣyy v. *ṣw*ʾ*yt*.

ṣyʿ **Nab** Sing. emph. *ṣyʿ*ʾ CIS ii 372[2], 375 (?), J 58, 119 - ¶ subst. m. goldsmith (for this interpret., cf. Jaussen & Savignac J i p. 216).

ṣyp v. *ṣyb*.

ṣypwn₁ v. *ṣpn₂*.
ṣypwn₂ v. *ṣpn₂*.
ṣypr v. *ṣpr₁*.
ṣyr **OffAr** Plur. + suff. 3 p.pl.m. *ṣyryhm* Cowl 30[10] - ¶ subst. hinge; *wṣyryhm dy dššy' 'lk nḥš* Cowl 30[10f.]: the hinges of those doors were bronze - on this word, cf. Kaufman AIA 96 :: Zimmern Fremdw 30: < Akkad.
ṣl₁ **OffAr** Sing. abs. *ṣl* Cowl 37[10], Krael 7[20] - ¶ subst. leather; *mšky ṣl* Cowl 37[10]: tanned skins (cf. Grelot DAE p. 389, Porten & Greenfield JEAS p. 80, Porten & Yardeni sub TADAE A 4.2 :: Grelot Sem xiv 67: rather = (small) bags of leather); *šnn zy ṣl prsyn* Krael 7[20]: a pair of Persian (sandals) of leather (cf. Grelot RB lxxviii 534, DAE p. 235 (n. y), Porten & Greenfield JEAS p. 55, Porten & Yardeni sub TADAE B 3.8) - > Akkad. *ṣallu* = tanned hide, cf. e.g. Salonen Wasserfahrzeuge 145, Fussbekleidung 77f., CAD s.v., v.Soden Or xxxvii 267, xlvi 194, AHW s.v. *ṣallu* II.
ṣl₂ **Hebr** Sing. cstr. *ṣl* AMB 4[19] - ¶ subst. shadow; *ṣl ḥmh* AMB 4[19f.]: the shadow of the sun (cf. also Naveh & Shaked AMB a.l.).
v. *š₁₀*.
ṣlb **Pun** word of unknown meaning inscribed on a hatchet (RES 125), poss. = QAL (or PI'EL?) Pf. 3 p.s.m. of root *ṣlb*; on this text and the hatchet on which it is written, cf. Chabot RES a.l.; Harr 141: cf. root *ṣlb* (Hebr. and J.Ar.) = to impale? (highly uncert. interpret.).
ṣlḥ₁ **OffAr** PA'EL Part. act. s.m. abs. *mṣlḥ* Aḥiq 125 (:: Sach p. 168: = APH Part. of *ṣlḥ₂* (= to make thrive)) - ¶ verb PA'EL to cut, to chop (cf. Perles OLZ '11, 502, Epstein ZAW xxxii 136, Nöldeke AGWG xiv/4, 15, Cowl a.l., Grelot RB lxviii 186, Ginsberg ANET 429, Lindenberger APA 114, 251 n. 338 (cf. ibid. 251 n. 339 for the context), Kottsieper SAS 22, 228 :: Grelot DAE p. 440 (n. l), Puech Sem xxi 12ff.: = to set on fire); *'yš mṣlḥ 'qn* Aḥiq 125: someone chopping wood :: Grimme OLZ '11, 535f.: someone penetrating a wood.
ṣlḥ₂ v. *ṣlḥ₁*.
ṣly **OffAr** PA'EL Impf. 1 p.pl. *nṣlh* Cowl 30[26]; Part. act. pl.m. abs. *mṣlyn* Cowl 30[15] - ¶ verb PA'EL to pray - **1)** + *l₅*, *wmṣlyn lYHW ... zy hḥwyn bwydrng* Cowl 30[15f.]: and we prayed to YHW ... that He may revenge us on W. (v. *ḥwy₁*) - **2)** + *'l₇*, *nṣlh 'lyk* Cowl 30[26]: we will pray for you - Degen NESE iii 16, 20ff.: l. *yṣly* in Cowl 49[2] (poss. reading (cf. however Porten & Yardeni sub TADAE B 4.1: l. prob. *ytly* (*ytly 'ly ksp* = I have (a claim) on you (for) silver?), on the uncert. interpret. of *ytly*, cf. Porten BASOR cclviii 50) :: Cowl a.l.: l. *'t* (= *'t₃*)+ *ly* (= *l₅* + suff. 1 p.s.)) = QAL Impf. 3 p.s.m. (+ *'l₇*; = to impose on (someone)), uncert. interpret., diff. context (cf. also Ullendorff JSS xxv 246).

ṣll **Pun** Solá-Solé Sef xx 277, 279: l. *mwṣl* (= Hoph Part. s.m. abs. of *ṣll* in Sef xx 277 (= ICO-Spa n.p. 3), reading uncert.) = purified (highly uncert. interpret. (cf. Amadasi sub ICO-Spa Np 3: = part of n.p.?)); for the problems involved, cf. also Fuentes Estañol sub CIFE 07.02.

ṣlm$_1$ **Ph** m. Sing. abs. *ṣlm* CIS i 34 (thus Hall Hebraica ii 242; ??, heavily dam. context, uncert. interpret.) - **OldAr** Sing. cstr. *ṣlm* Tell F 12 (Akkad. par. *ṣalam*); + suff. 3 p.s.m. *ṣlmh* Tell F 16 (Akkad. par. *ṣalam-šú*) - **OffAr** m. Sing. emph. *ṣlm›* KAI 225^{6,12}, RA lxxvii 78^1, AM-NS ii 169, 173 i (*ṣlm[›]*), ii 1, 174^1; + suff. 3 p.s.m. *ṣlmh* KAI 225^3, 226^2, SSI ii 37^1 (cf. Dupont-Sommer CRAI '66, 52f., Delcor Mus lxxx 305, Altheim & Stiehl AAW v/1, 73, Gibson SSI ii a.l. (for Sing. interpret., cf. also Degen Or xliv 124) :: Lipiński Stud 151 (cf. idem VT xxiii 368f.): = Plur. emph. :: Cross BASOR clxxxiv 8 (n. 16): = Plur. + suff. 3 p.s.m. (for Plur. interpret., cf. also Teixidor Syr li 329, cf. already Dupont- Sommer CRAI '66, 53)); Plur. emph. *ṣlmy›* BSOAS xxvii 272 iv 1 - **Nab** m. Sing. abs. *ṣlm* IEJ xxxvi 56^3; cstr. *ṣlm* RES 2117^5, *ṣnm* J 159^1 (for the reading, cf. also RES sub 1128A); emph. *ṣlm›* CIS ii 164^1, 349^1 (*[ṣ]lm›*), 354^1, RES 837C, RB lxxviii 237^1; f. Sing. emph. *ṣlmt›* RES 1092^1 - **Palm** m. Sing. abs. *ṣlm* CIS ii 3913 ii 129, Syr xvii 280^7 (= SBS 48^6, v. infra)^{,9} (= SBS 48^8), RIP 161^4 (v. infra), Inv xi 95, 98a, AAS xxxvi/xxxvii 165 no. 3^1; cstr. *ṣlm* CIS ii 3915^1, 3926^1, 3932^1, 3935^1, 3945^1, etc., etc., *ḥlm* (lapsus) CIS ii 4404^1; emph. *ṣlm›* CIS ii 3916^1, 3917^{1,6}, 3919^1, 3920^{1,2}, 3921^1, etc. etc.; Plur. abs. *ṣlmyn* CIS ii 3913 ii 130, Inscr P 36^1, DFD 13^{10} (*ṣ[l]myn*; dam. context); cstr. *ṣlmy* CIS ii 3913 ii 128; emph. *ṣlmy›* CIS ii 3914^1, 3930^3, 3931^1, 4125, 4129B 1, 4130^2 (*ṣlm[y›]*; Greek par. ἀνδρ[ιάντες]), etc. etc.; f. Sing. cstr. *ṣlmt* CIS ii 3947^1, 4179^1, 4244^1, 4301^1, 4343^1, etc., etc.; emph. *ṣlmt›* CIS ii 3954^1, 3969^1 (= Inv xi 84), 4409^1, 4527^1, Inv viii 92, DFD 163^5, Syr lxii 276 ii 1 (*ṣlmt* = printing error), AAS xxxvi/xxxvii 168 no. 9^1 (*ṣlmt* prob. = printing error) - **Hatra** m. Sing. cstr. *ṣlm*, cf. Assur 1^2 (*[ṣ]lm*), 5^2 (heavily dam. context); emph. *ṣlm›* 20^1, 21^1, 39, 56^1, 80^{1,6} (dam. context), 345^1, Mašr xv 512^1, etc., etc., cf. also Assur 15b 1, d 1, 16^1, etc.; + suff. 1 p.s. *ṣlmy* 288c 3 (cf. Degen NESE iii 83); f. Sing. emph. *ṣlmt›* 5^1, 30^1, 34^2, 35^1, 36^2, 37^1, 228^1 - ¶ subst. m. and f. statue: Tell F 12, CIS ii 164^1, 349^1, 3914^1, 3915^1, 3916^1, Hatra 20^1, 21^1, Assur 16^1, etc.; with the meaning 'image in bas-relief': KAI 225^{3,6,12}, 226^2, CIS ii 4125, 4129^1, 4130^3, 4135^1, 4136^1, Hatra 56^1 (?), etc., etc.; with meaning image painted on a wall: Assur 15b 1, c 1, d 1; the subst. in m.-form indicates an image in general or (specialized) an image of a god or a man (thus prob. also in Hatra 142^1, cf. Caquot Syr xli 259, Abbadi PIH 4 :: Vattioni IH a.l.: pro *›ltwm* (= n.p. m.) l. *›lt ws[my›]*); the subst. in f.-form indicates an image of a female deity

or a woman; for the m. subst. indicating images of females, cf. CIS ii 4444[1] (for the reading, cf. Chabot CRAI '40, 346: l. *ṣlm hgr b[t] zbyd*ʾ), Syr xxvi 44[2], Assur 15b 1 (v. also sub *mlk*$_3$); for the f. subst. + dem. pron. m. cf. CIS ii 3954 [1] (cf. Cantineau Gramm 145, Rosenthal Sprache 50); cf. *ʿbd lmlkw ... bʿlh ṣlm bt bʿl[š]mn* RIP 161[3f.]: he has made a statue for his lord M. in the temple of B.Sh. (cf. also *ṣlm mrkb swsy ṣlm bt bl[* SBS 48[6]: an equestrian statue, a statue in the temple of B. (:: Cantineau Syr xvii 280f.: poss. = ... a statue of the temple of B.)); *ṣlm*ʾ *znh prʿbdy* RA lxxvii 78: this image represents P.; *dnh ṣlm*ʾ *ḥrtt* RB lxxiii 237[1]: this is the statue of Ch. (on this diff. construction (lapsus?), cf. Starcky & Strugnell RB lxxiii 240f.; cf. also Hatra 144[1f.] (*ṣlm*ʾ *wrwd*), 36[2] (*ṣlmt*ʾ *dwšpry* = the statue of D. (on the name, cf. Aggoula Ber xviii 93, Abbadi PIH 14, 98)) :: Caquot Syr xxxii 241f.: l. *dy špry* = n.p. (cf. also Donner sub KAI 250) :: Safar Sumer viii 192f. (n. 37): l. *d wšpry* (= n.p.)); cf. also the comb. *lmlkw ḥyrn lṣlm* Inv xi 95: for M. Ch., for the statue (cf. Inv xi 98a, Inscr P 36[1]; *lṣlm rpbwl* Inv xi 98b 1: for the statue of R. (cf. Inv xi 92[1]; :: Silverman JAOS lxxxix 633f.: pro *lṣlm* l. *[lš]lm* = *l*$_5$ + Sing. cstr. of *šlm*$_2$)) - the σαλμα in Inv D 51[1] poss. = m. Sing. emph. (cf. Levi Della Vida FDE '22-23, 367f., du Mesnil du Buisson Inv D a.l.); cf. however Milik Syr xliv 290, 292ff.: part of n.p. - Aggoula Syr lxii 62f.: the *ṣlm* in KAI 228A 10 (*[ṣ]lm*), 12 = Sing. cstr. of *ṣlm*$_1$ (= lord), the *ṣlm* in KAI 228A 16 = Sing. abs. of *ṣlm*$_1$ (= lord), less prob. interpret., cf. e.g. Cooke NSI p. 196f., Donner KAI a.l., Gibson SSI ii p. 150: = n.d. (prob. interpret.) - Aggoula Syr lxii 66f.: the *ṣlm* in Atlal vii 109[4] = Sing. abs. of *ṣlm*$_1$ (= lord), less prob. interpret., cf. Livingstone Atlal vii a.l., Beyer & Livingstone ZDMG cxxxvii 286f.: = n.d. - on this word, cf. also Clines JNSL iii 19ff., Israel SAB i 79ff. -
v. *slm*$_2$, *šlm*$_2$.

ṣlm$_2$ **Pun** the diff. *ṣlm* in CIS i 6068[4] (= KAI 89) poss. = Sing. abs. (darkness), cf. Février sub CIS i 6068 (cf. already Lidzbarski Eph i 33, sub KI 85) :: e.g. Cooke NSI p. 135: l. *šlm* (= in full); cf. also Clermont-Ganneau RAO iii 315f., iv 95, Levi Della Vida RSO xiv 313 :: Ferron ZDMG cxvii 220ff.: l. *[ʿ]lm* (= Sing. abs. of *ʿlm*$_4$).

ṣlmh v. *ṣlm*$_1$.

ṣlmnyt **Nab** Plur. emph. *ṣlmnyt*ʾ IEJ xxix 112[7] - ¶ subst. small female idol, female statuette (cf. Naveh IEJ xxix 113, 119; very diff. context).

ṣlṣl **OffAr** Sing. cstr. *ṣl[ṣ]l* AJSL lviii 303B 6 (?; dam. context); emph. *ṣlṣl*ʾ AJSL lviii 304C 5 - ¶ subst. of uncert. meaning; Aimé-Giron AG p. 27: prob. meaning boat, cf. also R.A.Bowman AJSL lviii 309.

ṣlq$_1$ v. *ṣlqh*.

ṣlq$_2$ v. *ṣlqh*.

ṣlq$_3$ v. *ṣlqh*.

ṣlq$_4$ v. *ṣlqh*.

ṣlqh **Pun** Février Sem vi 23: the *ṣlq'tm* in KAI 145[9] = Dual or Plur. + suff. 3 p.s. of *ṣlqh* = column; for this highly uncert. interpret. and word division, cf. also RES sub 2221, context obscure :: v.d.Branden RSF i 166, 170 (div. otherwise): l. *'ṣlq* (= YIPH Impf. 1 p.s. of *ṣlq$_1$*(= to occupy oneself (with)) + *'tm* = *'t$_5$* (= *'yt$_3$*) + suff. 3 p.pl.m. :: Berger MAIBL xxxvi/2, 144, 161: l. *ṣlq* (= QAL Pf. 3 p.s.m. of *ṣlq$_4$*(= to cut)) + *'tm* = *'t$_5$* (= *'yt$_3$*) + suff. 3 p.pl.m. :: Krahmalkov RSF iii 188f., 195, 203 (div. otherwise): l. *ṣlq* (= QAL Part. act. s.m. abs. of *ṣlq$_2$*(= to cry aloud in pain)) + *'tm* (= *'t$_6$*+ suff. 3 p.s.m.) :: Halévy RS ix 281, 285 (div. otherwise): l. *ṣlq'* (= QAL/PI'EL Pf. 3 p.pl. of *ṣlq$_3$*(= to let sparkle, to decorate)) + *tm* (= QAL Pf. 3 p.s.m. of *tmm$_1$*)).

ṣmd$_1$ **Hebr** Sing. cstr. *ṣmd* TA-H 3[4f.] - ¶ subst. pair; Sing. *ṣmd ḥmrm* TA-H 3[4f.]: a pair of donkeys (for the context, v. also *mš'$_1$*) - Starcky MUSJ xlv 262, 272: prob. l. *ṣmd* in MUSJ xlv 262[7] (= Sing. abs./cstr. of *ṣmd$_1$*), cf. however Röllig NESE ii 2, 12: l. *ṣmd* (= the same word as *ṣmd$_2$*) in *b'l ṣmd* (KAI 24[15]; poss. = the lord of the club; for this interpret., cf. also Gordon Or xxi 123), or = *ṣmd$_1$*, or l. *ṣmr* = wool (cf. *'mr$_7$*;on the possibility of this reading, cf. already Starcky MUSJ xlv 272).

ṣmd$_2$ v. *ṣmd$_1$*.

ṣmdh v. *smr$_1$*.

ṣmw' **Hatra** Sing. emph. (?) *ṣmw''* 188[3] - ¶ word of unknown meaning, prob. indicating title or function (or surname; cf. Caquot Syr xli 267), diff. context.

ṣmḥ **Ph** Sing. cstr. (or abs.?) *ṣmḥ* KAI 43[11] - **Pun** Sing. abs./cstr. *ṣmḥ* KAI 162[2], 163[3] (for the reading in both texts, cf. Février AIPHOS xiii 162f., 166f., 170, cf. also Röllig KAI a.l.; uncert. interpret., obscure context; on both texts, cf. also Cross with Hackett BTDA 80, Hackett FS Cross 126, v.d.Branden BO xiv 195ff.); cstr. *ṣmḥ* Trip 41[2] - ¶ subst. offspring, scion; for the context of KAI 43[11], v. *ṣdq$_2$*; *ḥmlkt dryds ṣmḥ ḥn'* Trip 41[2]: Ch. D. the scion of Ch. (heavily dam. and diff. context; for this interpret., cf. Levi Della Vida RCL '63, 467 (n.10)).

ṣmr v. *ṣmd$_1$*.

ṣmq$_1$ **DA** QAL Impf. 3 p.s.f. *tṣmqn* xd 2 (for this form, cf. Hoftijzer DA p. 297; for the reading problems, cf. v.d.Kooij DA p. 161 :: Hackett BTDA 69 n. 73: poss. = QAL Impf. 2 p.pl.m. :: Garbini Hen i 171, 180 (div. otherwise): l. *tṣmq* = QAL Impf. 3 p.s.f. :: Garr DGSP 128: = QAL Impf. 3 p.pl.f.) - ¶ verb QAL to be dry, to wither; *ydh tṣmqn* DA xd 2: his hand will wither (cf. Hoftijzer DA a.l.).

ṣmq$_2$ **Pun** Sing. abs. *ṣmq* Trip 51[2] - ¶ subst. poss. meaning 'dried fruit' or special type of dried fruit (raisin?), cf. Levi Della Vida Or xxxiii 8f., 13f., Amadasi IPT 133.

ṣn v. *ṣ'n*.

ṣnl **OffAr** Shunnar CRM ii 283f., 287: l. *ṣnl'* = Sing. m. emph. of *ṣnl* (= delivered) in NESE i 11[6], improb. interpret. (cf. also Shunnar GMA 114f., Degen NESE i 11 (div. otherwise): l. *l'* (= *l'*$_1$)).

ṣnm v. *ṣlm* .

ṣn‛ (< Arab., cf. Cantineau Nab. ii 172, Altheim & Stiehl AAW i 191, Diem ZDMG cxxiii 228 n. 11, Or l. 354, O'Connor JNES xlv 218) - Nab. QAL Pf. 3 p.s.m. + suff. 3 p.s.m. *ṣn‛h* J 17[1] (on the form, cf. also O'Connor JNES xlv 223) - ¶ verb QAL to make + obj. (tomb) + *l*$_5$: J 17[1f.].

ṣnpr v. *ṣpr*$_1$.

ṣ‛ **OffAr** Plur. abs. *ṣ‛yn* Cowl 81[47,48] (for the context, cf. also Harmatta ActAntHung vii 361f.) - ¶ subst. plate, dish.

ṣ‛dw v. *t‛dwz*.

ṣ‛y **OffAr** QAL Impf. 3 p.pl.m. *yṣ‛wn* Aḥiq 168 (cf. Epstein ZAW xxxiii 232, Nöldeke AGWG xiv/4, 18, Leand 40f., Grelot RB lxviii 191f. (cf. also Lindenberger APA 172, 270f. n. 529, Kottsieper SAS 17, 228) :: Cowl p. 246: = PA‛EL Impf. 3 p.pl.m. of *yṣ‛*(= to spread > to fall ?)) - ¶ verb QAL to fall.

ṣ‛q **OffAr** QAL Impf. 3 p.pl.m. *yṣ‛qw* Cowl 52[6] (dam. context) - ¶ verb QAL to cry: Cowl 52[6] - Joüon MUSJ xviii 15, Silverman JAOS lxxxix 701 n. 63: Hebrew root in Aramaic context (cf. also *ṣ‛qh*).

ṣ‛qh **OldAr** this subst. = cry (Sing. abs.) poss. to be restored in KAI 222A 29f. (*[ṣ‛]qh*), cf. Brekelmans VT xiii 225ff. (cf. also Fitzmyer AIS 14f., 48, Degen AAG p. 11 n. 52, Lipiński Stud 29, Lemaire & Durand IAS 114, 133, Fitzmyer CBQ xxxix 263, Avishur SSWP 469 (n. 1)); restoration *[z‛]qh*(Sing. abs. with same meaning) also poss., cf. Brekelmans VT xiii 225ff. (cf. also Gibson SSI ii p. 30f., 40) :: Rosenthal ANET 660 (n. 5): l. *[n]qḥ* (= Sing. abs. of *nqḥ*(= mournful sounds)) :: Dupont-Sommer Sf p. 18, 20, 46, AH i/1, 4, i/2, 4: l. *[l]qḥ* (= QAL Part. act. s.m. abs. of *lqḥ*(= conqueror); cf. also Donner KAI a.l.); for KAI 222A 29f., v. also *hn*$_3$ - Dupont-Sommer Sf p. 99f., 102f.: this subst. prob. to be restored in KAI 223A 8f. (Sing. abs. *ṣ‛[qh]* (cf. also Fitzmyer AIS 80, 86, Lipiński Stud 53, Lemaire & Durand IAS 117); context however heavily dam. and highly uncert. interpret., cf. Degen AAG p. 17 n. 71) - cf. however also Silverman JAOS xciv 270: *ṣ‛qh* less prob. in Aramaic (cf. also *ṣ‛q*).

ṣ‛r$_1$ v.Soden Or xlvi 194: *ṣ‛r* (= grief, sorrow) > Akkad. *ṣar* = vehemently (cf. also idem AHW s.v.; improb. interpret.).

ṣ‛r$_2$ **Ph** f. Plur. abs. *ṣ‛rt* EI xviii 117[7] (= IEJ xxxv 83), cf. Diosc ii 114: ζεγαρ in (αμου)ζεγαρ(αφ) = small curled dock (*rumex crispus*), cf. Löw AP 402f. (poss. interpret.) - **Pun** m. Sing. + suff. 3 p.pl.m. *ṣ‛rnm* KAI 65[2f.] (*ṣ‛rn[m]*), 81[5] (for both texts :: Schiffmann RSF iv 51f.: =

Plur. abs. of *ṣʿrn* (= small one); for KAI 81[5] :: v.d.Branden PO i 204, 210: = m. Plur. + suff. 3 p.pl.m.) - ¶ adj. small; said of an object: EI xviii 117[7]; *ʾdrnm wʿd ṣʿrnm* KAI 81[5] (cf. KAI 65[2]): (from) their large one to their small one (i.e. (in) their totality).

ṣʿrn v. *ṣʿr*$_2$.

ṣp$_1$ v. *ṣpl*.

ṣp$_2$ > Akkad. *ṣuppu* (= strip of carded wool), cf. CAD s.v. *ṣuppu* C, v.Soden Or xxxvii 267 (cf. also idem AHW s.v. *ṣuppatu*, Or xlvi 195).

ṣpʾ v. *ṣpy*.

ṣph **Pun** Sing. (or Plur.?) abs. *ṣpʾt* KAI 126[9] - ¶ subst. prob. meaning: broad purple stripe or tunic with the same; *lʿbd bṣpʾt* KAI 126[9]: to use (a tunic) with broad purple stripe (cf. Lat. par. *lato clavo ... uti*); tunic with broad purple stripe was used by senators (in KAI 126[9] sign of special honour).

ṣpw v. *ṣbw*.

ṣpwn v. *ṣpn*$_2$.

ṣpḫ$_1$ v.Soden AHW s.v. *ṣappuḫu*, Or xlvi 194: Akkad. *ṣappuḫu* (= to press out (sc. water); cf. however Wiseman Irâq xx 80: = to scatter) < Ar. *ṣpḥ* (= to fall; highly uncert. interpret.).

ṣpḥ$_2$ **OffAr** Sing. emph. *ṣpḥʾ* RES 1300[8] (or = Sing. abs.f., cf. Leand 43 n'') - ¶ subst. f. recipient, jar.

ṣpy **JAr** Paʿel Impf. 1 p.s. *ʾṣpʾ* DBKP 20[42] - ¶ verb Paʿel to clear the title to a property (cf. Lewis DBKP p. 16, Yadin & Greenfield ibid. p. 145) - prob. < Arab., cf. Yadin & Greenfield ibid.

ṣpyt v.Soden Or xlvi 194: > *ṣāpītu/ṣābītu* = watchtower (cf. idem AHW s.v.).

ṣpl **Ph** Sing./Plur. + suff. 3 p.s.f. *ṣply* KAI 19[1f.] (v. infra) - ¶ subst. of unknown meaning (cf. Rosenthal JAOS lxxii 172: *ṣpl* indicating something belonging to or into the portico (cf. also Gibson SSI iii p. 119: = Plur. + suff. 3 p.s.f. of *ṣpl*) :: Lidzbarski sub KI 16: *ṣpl* = variant of *ṣpn* (= either *ṣpn*$_2$ (cf. also Lidzbarski Handb 359) or *ṣpn*$_3$ (= what is hidden, ἄδυτον)), cf. FR 56b (cf. also Cooke NSI p. 49, Chabot sub RES 1205, Levi Della Vida RSO xxxix 302, Milik DFD 424f., v.d. Branden GP p. 8, BO vii 70f.: *ṣpl* is variant of *ṣpn*$_2$) :: Dunand & Duru sub DD 4 (div. otherwise): l. *ṣp* (= Sing. abs. of *ṣp*$_1$(= doorstep)) + *ly* (= *l*$_5$ + suff. 3 p.s.f.) :: Halévy REJ xii 109f.: = Plur. (= annexes), improb. etymology; cf. also Röllig KAI a.l.).

ṣpn$_1$ **OffAr** Haph 1 p.s. + suff. 2 p.s.m. *hṣpntk* Aḥiq 49; Impf. 2 p.s.m. *thṣpn* Beh 57 (Akkad. par. *ta-pi-is-si-nu*), 58 (for this prob. reading, cf. Greenfield & Porten BIDG p. 50) - ¶ verb Haph to hide, to conceal; + obj. + *mn*$_5$ (from): Aḥiq 49 - Silverman Or xxxix 482: hebraism (uncert. interpret.).

ṣpn$_2$ **Hebr** Sing. abs. *ṣpwn* SM 49[7], DJD ii 22,1-9[3,12], 30[4,17] - **JAr**

Sing. abs. *ṣpn* MPAT 51[4] (:: Birnbaum PEQ '57, 130: l. *ṣpwn*);emph. *ṣpnh* MPAT 51[9], *ṣpwnʾ* MPAT 52[5] - ¶ subst. north, north side - **1)** prec. by *l*$_5$, *lṣpnh* MPAT 51[9] (for the diff. reading, cf. Milik Bibl xxxviii 264, Fitzmyer & Harrington MPAT a.l. (cf. also Milik RB lxi 183 (div. otherwise): l. *ʿl ṣpnh*); Abramson & Ginsberg BASOR cxxxvi 17 (div. otherwise): l. ...*ʾ ṣpnh*; or l. rather with Birnbaum PEQ '57, 130, Beyer ATTM 320: *wṣpnh*): to the north, at the north side - **2)** prec. by *mn*$_5$, *mn hṣpwn* SM 49[7]: from the north - used adverbially *ṣpn* MPAT 51[4], *ṣpwn* DJD ii 22,1-9[3,12], 30[4,17], *ṣpwnʾ* MPAT 52[5]: to the north, at the north side - Lemaire Syr lxi 341: l. *ṣpwn* (= Sing. abs.) in ATNS 52a 9 (uncert. interpret., cf. also Segal ATNS a.l.) - Naveh Mas a.l.: the *ṣypwn* in MAS 436 poss. = form of *ṣpn*$_2$ used as n.p., cf. however Yadin Mas a.l.: = form of *ṣypwn*$_2$(= soap, detergent), used as nickname - on *ṣpn*$_2$, cf. also Grave UF xii 221ff.
v. *mšpn*, *ṣpl*.

ṣpn$_3$ v. *ṣbw*, *ṣpl*.

ṣpr$_1$ **Pun** Sing. abs. *ṣpr* KAI 69[12] (:: Février JA ccxliii 51f.: = *ṣpr*$_2$, a certain type of perfume (cf. also Delcor Sem xxxiii 34ff.) :: v.d.Branden RSO xl 122f.: = *ṣpr*$_5$ (= very fine flour)),[15]; cstr. *ṣpr* KAI 69[11] (*[ṣ]pr*), CIS i 3915[5]; Plur. abs. *ṣyprm* Trip 51[7] (dam. context; cf. FR 107,1, cf. also Amadasi 135) - **DA** Sing. abs. (?) *ṣpr* i 11 (*ṣpr[*) - **OffAr** Sing. abs. *ṣnpr* Aḥiq 98; Plur. emph. *ṣnpryʾ* Aḥiq 199 (heavily dam. context); on the form *ṣnpr*,cf. Kottsieper SAS 54ff. - ¶ subst. - **1)** bird: KAI 69[12,15]; for *ṣpr ʾgnn*, v. *ʾgnn*, for the context, v. also *ṣṣ*$_1$ - **2)** special bird, sparrow: DA i 11 (cf. e.g. Hoftijzer DA a.l., H. & M.Weipert ZDPV xcviii 96, 103 :: Sasson UF xvii 288: coll. birds) - on Aḥiq 98, cf. e.g. Lindenberger APA 75.

ṣpr$_2$ v. *ṣpr*$_1$.

ṣpr$_3$ CAD s.v. *ṣippiri*: > Akkad. (< West-Semitic) = type of field (uncert. interpret.).

ṣpr$_4$ **JAr** Sing. abs. *ṣpr* IEJ xl 135[8]; emph. *ṣprʾ* IEJ xl 135[2] (on the reading problems, cf. Yardeni IEJ xl 138),[3], 140[2] (diff. reading) - ¶ subst. morning; *ṣpr wrmš* IEJ xl 135[8]: morning and evening.

ṣpr$_5$ v. *ṣpr*$_1$.

ṣprh$_1$ v.Soden Or xxxvii 267, xlvi 195: > Akkad. *ṣipparātu* = morning (cf. idem AHW s.v. *ṣippa(r)rātu* I; cf. also CAD s.v. *ṣipparātu* A: = West-Semitic loanword). Poss. interpret.

ṣprh$_2$ v.Soden Or xlvi 195: > Akkad. *ṣipirtu* = a special type of sash (cf. idem AHW s.v. *ṣipirtu* III). Uncert. interpret. (cf. CAD s.v. *ṣipirtu* A, cf. also CAD s.v. *ṣepēru* (concluding remarks)).

ṣṣ$_1$ **Pun** Sing. abs. *ṣṣ* KAI 69[11], 74[7], CIS i 3915[5] - ¶ subst. of uncert. meaning; CIS i sub 165, Harr 139: = wing > bird of wing = wild bird (highly uncert. interpret., cf. Lagrange ERS 474; cf. also Dussaud Orig

141: rather = hen, chicken (cf. also Delcor Sem xxxviii 90f.)) :: Röllig KAI a.l., Capuzzi StudMagr ii 59f.: *ṣpr ʾgnn ʾm ṣṣ* in KAI 69[11]: = pro *ṣpr ʾgnn* (v. *ʾgnn*) + *ṣpr ṣṣ* (= bird of wing = wild bird), cf. also Cooke NSI p. 120 :: v.d.Branden RSO xl 121: *ṣpr ʾgnn ʾm ṣṣ* pro *ṣpr ʾgnn* + *ṣpr ṣṣ* (= bird of nature); on this word, cf. also Ben-Chayyim LOT ii 607.

ṣṣ_2 cf. Frah xviii 2: bird of prey.

ṣṣ_3 Inscription *ṣṣ* on tags, meaning unknown, cf. Yadin IEJ xv 112, Yadin & Naveh Mas 13.

ṣṣn (*ṣṣnh*, cf. Leand 43s''') - **OffAr** subst. (Plur. abs. *ṣṣnn*) of unknown meaning in Cowl 55[12] (??; reading highly uncert., cf. Cowl p:161, Porten & Yardeni sub TADAE A 3.2 recto 7: or l. *ṣʾnn* ? (without interpret.)); Sach p. 135: = basket??; cf. also Ungnad ArPap 57: < Egypt.??

ṣql **OffAr** Harmatta ActAntHung vii 370: l. poss. *ṣqln* in Cowl 81[109] (= Plur. abs. of *ṣql* (= cloak, garment)). Cowl a.l.: l. *yql[* (without interpret.).

ṣr$_1$ **Hebr** Sing. abs. *ṣr* KAI 189[3], IEJ v 165 (dam. context, cf. e.g. Avigad IEJ v a.l., Puech RB lxxxi 202 (n. 28) :: Ussishkin BASOR cxcvi 19ff.: l. *ṣryḥ* = Sing. abs. of *ṣryḥ*$_1$ (cf. also Smelik HDAI 70)) - **OffAr** Sing. emph. *ṭwrʾ* ASAE xxxix 353[5] (uncert. reading, diff. context), 357[3] (uncert. reading); Plur. emph. *ṭwryʾ* Aḥiq 62; cf. GIPP 65 - **JAr** Plur. emph. *ṭwryh* AMB 9[8] - ¶ subst. - **1)** rock: KAI 189[3] (cf. e.g. Cooke NSI p. 14, Gibson SSI i p. 22f.: *bṣr* = in the rock, cf. also Michaud VT viii 299f.: inside the rock (cf. idem PA 68), cf. however H.P.Müller UF ii 234: *bṣr* = inside the mountain), IEJ v 165 (*ḥdr bktp hṣr* = chamber in the side of the rock/mountain, v. also supra) - **2)** mountain: AMB 9[8]; *ytqtl by[n] ṭwryʾ ... tryn* Aḥiq 62: he must be killed between two ... mountains (cf. e.g. Cowl a.l., Ginsberg ANET 428, Grelot DAE p. 450; or rather = between two rock formations?, crags?).

v. *swr*$_3$, *šr*$_2$.

ṣr$_2$ **Samal** Plur. abs. (casus obliquus; or rather + suff. 1 p.s.?, cf. Friedr 30*, Donner KAI a.l., Gibson SSI ii p. 76; for the *ṣ*, cf. e.g. Dion p. 97, 228, Gibson SSI ii p. 76, Garr DGSP 24, cf. however Degen ZDMG cxxi 132f.: *ṣr* in KAI 214[30] not = *ṣr*$_2$) *ṣry* KAI 214[30] - **DA** Plur. abs. *qrn* i 14 (cf. Hoftijzer DA a.l., H.P.Müller ZDPV xciv 62 (n. 39), ZAW xciv 218, 229 (cf. also Sasson UF xvii 288, 303 (n. 44)) :: Rofé SB 67: = Sing. of *qrn* (= skin); :: Garbini Hen i 180f., 185 = Sing. abs. of *qrn* (= bugle; cf. also Puech BAT 359, 362, FS Grelot 24, 28, Lemaire CRAI '85, 281: = horn) :: McCarter BASOR ccxxxix 51, 56: = Plur. abs. of *qr*$_5$ (= thread; cf. also Hackett BTDA 29, 52f., 132); on the subject, cf. also Levine JAOS ci 199; diff. context) - ¶ subst. enemy - Rocco StudMagr vii a.l.: l. *ṣrkm* (= Sing. + suff. 2 p.pl.m.) in StudMagr vii 12[1] (uncert. reading and interpret.).

v. *ʾrr*$_1$, *sd*$_2$, *sr*$_4$, *ṣdq*$_2$.

ṣrb$_1$ **Pun** Sing. cstr. *ṣrb* KAI 69[9], 74[5] - ¶ subst. of unknown meaning, only in the comb. *ṣrb ʾyl* (for *ʾyl*, v. *ʾyl*$_2$); CIS i sub 165: = the young of the *ʾyl* (cf. also e.g. Halévy JA vi/xv 492, Clermont-Ganneau JA vii/xi 480 n. 1, Lagrange ERS 474, Cooke NSI p. 120: = the young of a deer); Nöldeke ZDMG xl 737: *ṣrb* = sheep (cf. also Lidzbarski Handb 359), *ṣrb ʾyl* = ram; Capuzzi StudMagr ii 51: *ṣrb ʾyl* = African goat; Dussaud Orig 140f.: = animal belonging to the type of the *cerridae* (*ʾyl* indicating the male) :: v.d.Branden RSO xl 120: *ṣrb* = Sing. cstr. of *ṣrb*$_2$ (= milk), *ṣrb ʾyl* = sucking lamb.

ṣrb$_2$ v. *ṣrb*$_1$.

ṣrbwṣ v. *lbš*$_2$.

ṣrh$_1$ **Ph** Plur. + suff. 3 p.s.f. *ṣrty* KAI 27[17] (cf. e.g. Gaster Or xi 63, Gibson SSI iii p. 83, 87 :: Albright BASOR lxxvi 9, Cross & Saley BASOR cxcvii 45 (n. 20), Röllig KAI a.l., NESE ii 19, Lipiński RTAT 265, Garbini OA xx 284ff.: = Plur. + suff. 3 p.s.m.; cf. however also Caquot FS Gaster 49: = Plur. + suff. 1 p.s. :: Teixidor AO i 106: l. *ʾrty* (without interpret.)) - ¶ subst. f. co-wife.

ṣrh$_2$ **DA** Sing. abs. *ṣrh* i 10 (cf. Hoftijzer DA a.l., TUAT ii 142, Garbini Hen i 178, 185, Kaufman BASOR ccxxxix 73, Levine JAOS ci 197, 199, H.P.Müller ZAW xciv 218, 226, H. & M.Weippert ZDMG xcviii 95, 103, Smelik HDAI 79 :: Caquot & Lemaire Syr liv 198, Ringgren Mem Seeligmann 94, Lemaire BAT 317f., GLECS xxiv-xxviii 328, CRAI '85, 280, Puech BAT 359, 361, FS Grelot 17, 22, 28, Sasson UF xvii 288, 291, 299: l. *ṣdh* = Sing. abs. of *ṣdh*$_1$ :: McCarter BASOR ccxxxix 51, 55: l. *ṣrh* = QAL Pf. 3 p.s.m. of *ṣry*$_1$ (= to rip up; cf. Hackett BTDA 48, 98, 133) or PAʿEL Pf. 3 p.s.m. of *ṣry*$_1$ (= to lacerate)) - ¶ subst. distress.

ṣrwr **Hebr** Sing. cstr. *ṣrwr* Frey 661[5] - ¶ subst. bundle; *npšh bṣrwr hḥyym* Frey 661[5]: may her soul be in the bundle of the living (or: life).

ṣry$_1$ v. *ṣrh*$_2$.

ṣry$_2$ **OldCan** Sing. abs. *ṣú-ur-wa* EA 48[8] (for the reading, cf. Rainey EA p. 92: or l. *zu-ur-wa*?) - ¶ subst. balm, balsam - on this word, cf. Nielsen SVT xxxviii 61f., Knauf IUGP 16, Vitestam OrSu xxxvi-xxxvii 29ff.

ṣry$_3$ split > Akkad. *ṣurrû* (cf. v.Soden Or xxxvii 267, xlvi 195, AHW s.v.; cf. also CAD s.v.).

ṣryḥ$_1$ **Nab** Sing. emph. *ṣryḥʾ* CIS ii 213[3,4], 350[1], RES 1432[2]; Plur. emph. *ṣryḥyʾ* RES 1432[1] - ¶ subst. m. room, chamber (cf. Milik RB lxvi 556f., cf. also Jaroš AUSS xvi 57f.: = enclosed space) or rather = vault? (cf. Rösel ZDPV xcii 29 (n. 107)); for religious use: RES 1432[2]; as part of a tomb construction: CIS ii 213[3,4], 350[1] - < Arab.? (thus e.g. Cantineau Nab ii 172, Diem Or xlix 83, O'Connor JNES xlv 218f.).

v. *ṣr*$_1$.

ṣryḥ$_2$ **Palm** Plur. abs. *ṣryḥyn* (or rather *ṣdyḥyn*?)Inv x 44[4] - ¶ subst. (?) of unknown meaning; Starcky sub Inv x 44: = help??

ṣryk **Hebr** m. Sing. abs. *ṣryk* DJD ii 46[2,6,8] (uncert. reading) - ¶ adj. needing; *ʾyny ṣryk lʿmrk* DJD ii 46[2]: I do not need to insist upon you (v. however *ʿmr*$_3$).

v. *ṣrk*.

ṣrk **JAr** QAL Part. pass. pl.m. abs. *ṣrykyn* MPAT 58[3] - ¶ verb QAL to need; *ʾnḥnh ṣrykyn lh* MPAT 58[2f.]: we are in need of him.

v. *ṣryk*.

ṣrp$_1$ **Mo** QAL Part. act. s.m. abs. *ṣrp* Dir sig. 102 (= Vatt. sig. eb. 102 = CAI 27) - **OffAr** QAL Part. pass. s.m. abs. *ṣryp* Cowl 5[7], 28[11], Krael 5[15], 9[20], 11[6], *ṣrp* Krael 10[11], 12[20], ATNS 39[5] - ¶ verb QAL to purify; Part. act. goldsmith: Dir sig. 102; Part. pass. purified: *ksp kršn 5 bʾbny mlkʾ ksp ṣryp* Cowl 5[7]: silver, five *k.* according to the official weight, pure silver (cf. Krael 5[15], 9[20], 11[6], cf. also ATNS 39[5]); *ʾbygrnʾ ksp ṣryp kršn ʿšrh* Cowl 28[10f.]: a fine of 10 *k.* pure silver - on this root, cf. also Collini SEL iv 9f.

ṣrp$_2$ **OffAr** Sing. abs. *ṣrp* Cowl 38[3] - ¶ diff. word (subst.) in comb. *ʾbn ṣrp*, which prob. indicates some kind of precious stone, cf. Cowl p. 136, Grelot DAE p. 392, cf. also Porten & Yardeni sub TADAE A 4.3: dyer's stone; for the interpret. of *ʾbn ṣrp* as 'coloured/dyed stone', cf. Driver JRAS '32, 81, Grelot DAE p. 392 n. c, Porten & Greenfield JEAS p. 83, diff. interpret.: *ʾbn* = f. (against this interpret., cf. also Greenfield JCS xxi 91); Greenfield JCS xxi 91f.: poss. = stone/bead which has undergone a firing process and which greatly resembles a semi-precious stone :: Driver JRAS '32, 81: or *ʾbn ṣrp* = alum (cf. also Ug. *ʾabn ṣrp* on which, cf. e.g. Aistl 2360, Gordon Gloss 1652a, Liverani UF ii 100 (n. 24), Cutler & Macdonald UF ix 22) - cf. also Thompson Chemistry xlivf.

ṣrr$_1$ **Hebr** QAL Pf. 2 p.s.m. *ṣrrt* TA-H 3[5] (cf. Scagliarini Hen xii 137) - **OffAr** QAL Inf. *mṣr* IPAA 11[4], CRAI '70, 163[2bis] (for this reading, cf. Humbach IPAA 12 :: Dupont-Sommer CRAI '70, 163, 165: l. *mṣd* = HOPH Part. s.m. cstr. of *ṣwd*(= to hunt, to fish)) - ¶ verb QAL - **1)** to bind, to wrap up; *wṣrrt ʾtm bṣq* TA-H 3[5f.]: and you must wrap up the dough with them (sc. with the donkeys; for the context, v. *ʾt*$_6$ :: Hospers SV 103f.: and really prompt them (sc. the donkeys)) - **2)** to press, to oppress; *mṣr kwry* IPAA 11[4]: the torment of fish - cf. *qrr*$_1$.

ṣrr$_2$ > Akkad. *ṣurāru* = purse, cf. v.Soden Or xxxvii 267, xlvi 195, AHW s.v. *ṣurāru* III.

ṣrr$_3$ v. *sr*$_4$.

ṣṭ$_1$ v. *ṣd*$_2$.

ṣṭ$_2$ v. *ʾt*$_6$.

ṣtt **Pun** Sing. abs. *ṣtt* BAr-NS i/ii 228[2] (v. infra; :: Février BAr-NS i/ii 229: = HIPH Pf. 1 p.s. of *yṣt* (= to kindle, sc. the fire of the sacrifice)) - ¶ subst. of unknown meaning, prob. indicating some kind of votive offering :: Garbini AION xxv 260f.: *ṣtt* = variant of *štt* (< root *šyt*; = stele).

Q

q_1 v. *qb_1*.

q_2 v. *qrbn*.

q_3 **OffAr** abbrev. of unknown meaning in BSh 46[1] (cf. Naveh TeAv vi 191).

q'$_1$ v. *ql_1*.

q'$_2$ inscription *q'* on tags, meaning unknown, cf. Yadin IEJ xv 75, 112, Yadin & Naveh Mas p. 13.

q'l_1 **OffAr** the ideograms *q'ylt* (Nisa-b 70[2], 269[3], 447[2,4], 526[5], 556[2,4], 661[4], 676[4], Nisa-c 164[10] (diff. reading), 394[2]) and *q'ylw* (Nisa-b 73b 6) prob. derivatives of Semitic root *q'l* - Diakonov & Livshitz Nisa-b p. 49 and ibid. a.l.: poss. meaning of root = to measure (related to root *kwl_1/kyl_1/k'l*?) or related to root *qhl* (= to intend to, to be about)?? (cf. also GIPP 62).

q'l_2 v. *ql_1*.

q'm v. *qmḥ*.

qb_1 (< Egypt.?, cf. Ellenbogen 147) - **OffAr** Sing. abs. *qb* Cowl 45[8], ATNS 51[10], RES 1296[2], PSBA xxxvii 222[7] (:: RES sub 1793[2]: pro *qb* *1* l. *qwz* word of unknown meaning, prob. indicating some part of the process of making bread); emph. *qb'* ASAE xxvi 29[2]; Plur. abs. *qbn* ASAE xlviii 112A 2; cf. Frah xix 2 (*kb'*, *kp'*), xxx 1 (*kp'*) - **JAr** Plur. abs. *qbyn* MPAT 52[2] - cf. Greek κάβος in LXX - ¶ subst. m. measure of capacity, 1/6 of a *seah*, used for grain: Cowl 45[8], RES 1296[1f.], used for salt: ASAE xlviii 112A 2; in ASAE xxvi 29[2] *qb' rb'* (= the greater *qab*; context however dam.); for abbrev. *q*, cf. **OffAr** NESE iii 39[4,6,8,9], TA-Ar 1[2], 6[2], 8[3], 12[4], 16[3], 22[2], 30[1], BSh 27[2], 28[2], **JAr** MPAT 38[1,3], IEJ xl 142[2], 144[10,11] - for this measure, cf. e.g. Barrois ii 248ff., Trinquet SDB v 1224, 1229ff., EM iv 853ff., for the *qb* in Elephantine, cf. Porten Arch 72.

v. *qnyn*.

qb_2 **Palm** Plur. emph. *qby'* Syr lxii 279[6] (Lat. par. *gub*) - ¶ subst. indicating certain object; Al-As'ad & Teixidor Syr lxii a.l.: = crater, bowl (related to *gb_5*), uncert. interpret.

qbb **Ph** QAL Pf. 3 p.s.m. *qb* EpAn ix 5[5] - **Pun** QAL Pf. 3 p.s.f. *qbt* CIS i 4945[5] (cf. CIS i a.l. × Greenfield Sem xxxviii 157f., Krahmalkov

RSO lxi 75 n. 15: = QAL Pf. 3 p.s.f. + suff. 3 p.s.m. :: FR 164: = QAL Part. act. s.f. abs. :: Dahood Bibl xlix 364 n. 2, lx 433f.: = pass. Pf. 2 p.s.m.) - **DA** QAL Inf. abs. *qb* ix a 3; the foll. *nqb* ibid. = QAL Impf. 1 p.pl. or NIPH Impf. 1 p.pl. or Pf. 3 p.s.m. (uncert. interpretations, for the context, cf. Hoftijzer DA a.l., cf. also H.P.Müller ZDPV xciv 57 :: Dijkstra GTT xc 165 (n. 29): *nqb* = form of root *nqb*$_1$ (= to pierce)) - ¶ verb QAL to curse; *wqb ... qbt ʾdrt* EpAn ix 5[5]: and he cursed a mighty curse; *wʾš yrgz t mtnt z wqbt* (reading of *w* uncert.) *tnt* CIS i 4945[4ff.]: and whoever will disturb this gift, may T. curse (him) - Rocco AION xxiv 475ff.: l. *qbb* (= PI ʿEL/POL Imper. s.m.) in ll. 2, 3, 5, 6, 7 of GR ii 36 no. 20 and *qbbm* (= Pilel/POL Imper. s.m. + suff. 3 p.pl.m.) ibid. ll. 1, 4 (highly uncert. reading and interpret., cf. Polselli GR ii p. 36ff.: text is indecipherable) - Hoftijzer DA a.l.: the *qbt* in DA x a 3 prob. = form of this root (cf. also H.P.Müller ZDPV xciv 57) - Hoftijzer DA a.l.: l. poss. in DA ii 17 *qb* (= QAL Inf. cstr. (cf. also Levine JAOS ci 201f.)); uncert. reading, cf. v.d.Kooij DA p. 136: instead of *b* l. rather *h* (cf. also H.P.Müller ZAW xciv 238 (n. 63)) :: Caquot & Lemaire Syr liv 207f. (div. otherwise): l. *nlqy* = PA ʿEL Impf. 1 p.pl. of *lqy* (PA ʿEL = to beat; cf. also McCarter with Hackett BTDA 74: = to punish) :: Garbini Hen i 184f., 186, Lemaire CRAI '85, 277: l. *mlqy* = Sing. abs. of *mlqy*$_1$ (= punishment) :: Hackett BTDA 26, 30, 73, 94, 131: l. prob. *mlqh* = Sing. abs. of *mlqh* (= punishment).

qbh$_1$ **Ph** Sing. abs. *qbt* EpAn ix 5[5] (or = Plur. abs.?) - ¶ subst. curse; *qbt ʾdrt* EpAn ix 5[5]: a mighty curse (v. supra).

qbh$_2$ **Palm** Sing. emph. *qbtʾ* Ber iii 84[3], PNO 43[1] - ¶ subst. f. (cf. Cantineau Gramm 145, Rosenthal Sprache 50 for the comb. with m. dem. pronoun in PNO 43) vaulted room (cf. Milik DFD 178, 271: = building rather than tent (for this interpret., cf. Ingholt Ber iii 84ff.), cf. also Starcky sub PNO 43) :: Al-Asʿad & Teixidor Syr lxii 280: or = vessel, bowl? - Milik DFD 271: l. prob. *qbt[ʾ]* (= Sing. emph.) in DFD 271[6].

v. *qwq*$_2$.

qbwr **Palm** Sing. emph. *qbwrʾ* CIS ii 4160[1], 4163[2], 4165[1], 4166[2] (= Inv xii 16), Inv viii 62[1], 73[1], Syr xix 153[2] (*qbwr[ʾ]*), 160[2], RB xxxix 538[1], 539[1], RIP 166[2]; + suff. 3 p.s.m. *qbwrh* RB xxxix 539[1] - **JAr** Sing. abs. *qbwr* MPAT 89[1] (cf. Avigad IEJ xvii 105 :: Fitzmyer & Harrington MPAT a.l.: = Sing. cstr. (cf. also Puech RB xc 486f., 489 : or = Sing. cstr.?)) - ¶ subst. burial (place), tomb - **1)** tomb: MPAT 89[1] - **2)** in the comb. *bt qbwrʾ* in the Palm. texts (cf. Inv viii 73[1]: (*[bt] qbwrʾ*; RIP 166[2]: *[b]t qbwrʾ*; RB xxxix 539[1]: *bt qbwrh*): tomb (cf. the Greek parallels τὸν ταφεῶνα for CIS ii 4160[1], σπήλαιον ταφεῶνος for CIS ii 4163[2], Syr xix 160[1f.]), cf. also Gawlikowski Ber xxi 12f.

qbwrh v. *qbrh*.

qbylh v. *qblh*.

qbl_1 **Hebr** PI ‘EL Part. s.m. abs. *mqbl* EI xx 256[7] (?; on the problems, cf. Broshi & Qimron EI xx 258) - **OldAr** QAL Part. s.m. + suff. 3 p.s.m. *qblh* Tell F 12 (Akkad. par. *bēl di-ni-šú*) - **OffAr** QAL Pf. 3 p.s.m. *qbl* Cowl 37[3] (for both instances, cf. Driver JRAS '32, 80, Porten Arch 54 (n. 100), Porten & Greenfield JEAS p. 81, Grelot DAE p. 388 (n. d), Porten & Yardeni sub TADAE A 4.2 :: Cowl a.l.: = PA ‘EL Pf. 3 p.s.m., v. also *ptprs*), ATNS 10a ii 5 (context however heavily dam.), Driv F vii 1[1] (for the context, cf. Porten & Yardeni sub TADAE A 6.3); 2 p.s.m. *qblt* Krael 1[4,5] (:: Ginsberg JAOS lxxiv 156: in ll. 4, 5 *qblt* = QAL Pf. 1 p.s., ‘*ly* = lapsus for ‘*lyk*)·[6] (the following ‘*lyk* prob. lapsus for ‘*ly*, cf. Krael p. 136, cf. also Grelot DAE p. 212 :: Ginsberg JAOS lxxiv 156: *qblt* = QAL Pf. 1 p.s., ‘*lyk* correct, cf. also Porten & Greenfield JEAS p. 37 :: J.J.Rabinowitz Law 96 n. 14: *qblt* = PA ‘EL Pf. 1 p.s. (PA ‘EL = to agree), ‘*lyk* correct); 1 p.s. *qblt* Cowl 6[5], 7[4] (*qb[lt]*, for this reading, cf. Porten Arch 315, Porten & Greenfield JEAS p. 124, Grelot DAE p. 93 (n. b), Porten & Yardeni sub TADAE B 7.2 :: Cowl a.l.: l. *qryt* = QAL Pf. 2 p.s.m. of *qr’*$_1$, cf. also J.J.Rabinowitz Bibl xxxix 80); 1 p.pl. *qbln* SSI ii 28 obv. 4; Impf. 3 p.s.m. *yqbl* Krael 9[19,20], 10[12], 12[28]; 1 p.s. ’*qbl* Cowl 10[12], 47[7], Herm 2[10]; 3 p.pl.m. *yqblwn* Cowl 6[16], 10[18]; PA ‘EL Part. s.m. abs. *mqbl* Samar 1[8] (= EI xviii 8*), 2[7], 3[8]; cf. Frah xxi 12 (*mkblwn*), Paik 628, 629 (*mkbl*), GIPP 28 - **Nab** PA ‘EL Pf. 2 p.s.m. *qblt* MPAT 64 i 12 - **Palm** QAL Impf. 1 p.s. ’*qbl* Syr xvii 271[5] (heavily dam. context; cf. Cantineau Syr xvii 273, Lipiński BiOr xxxiii 234 :: Milik DFD 297: = PA ‘EL Impf. 1 p.s. :: Gawlikowski Syr li 98, 100: = APH Pf. 3 p.s.m. (= he has decreed)); Part. pass. s.m. abs. *qbyl* CIS ii 4050[8,10]; PA ‘EL Part. act. s.f. abs. *mqbl*’ RB xxxix 548[3]; APH Part. s.m. abs. *mqbl* CIS ii 4199[9]; s.m. emph. *mqbl*’ CIS ii 4171[2], 4195[6], 4199[8], Ber ii 78[2], 82[1], 86[5], 112[6], v 109 ii 7, RB xxxix 541[2], FS Miles 38[2], Syr lxii 277 i 5 (?, dam. context); s.f. abs. *mqbl*’ CIS ii 4199[5]; s.f. emph. *mqblt*’ CIS ii 4175[6f.], 4194[7], Ber ii 107[3], v 95[8]; m. pl. abs. *mqblyn* Ber v 125[8]; ITP Part. s.m. abs. *mtqbl* CIS ii 3913 ii 136 - **JAr** PA ‘EL Pf. 3 p.s.m. *qbl* MPAT 48[3]; 2 p.s.m. *qblt* RES 555 (?, dam. context); 1 p.s. *qblt* DBKP 17[40]; Part. act. s.m. abs. *mqbl* MPAT 50e 2, 52[8], IEJ xxxvi 206[5]; ITP Pf. 1 p.s. ’*tqblyh* MPAT 62[11] (lapsus for ’*tqbl(y)t*; Greek par. ἀπέσχον, cf. EI viii 50; cf. also Yadin & Greenfield sub DBKP 27) - ¶ verb QAL - **1)** to complain, to lodge a complaint - a) + obj., *hw qbl ptyprsn* Cowl 37[3]: he complained to the investigators (v. supra) - b) + l_5 (with) + ‘l_7 (concerning; followed by indication of object, not of person): SSI ii 28 obv. 4 - c) + l_5 (with) + ‘l_7 (concerning/against; followed by indication of person), ’*nh qblt l’ršm* ‘*l* ’*ḥtbsty* Dirv. 11[1]: I have complained to A. concerning A. - d) + ‘l_7 (against), *w’qbl* ‘*lyhn* Herm 2[10]: I will lodge a complaint against them (cf. Krael 9[20], cf. poss.

also Syr xvii 271[5]?, v. supra), RES 555? - e) + *ʿl$_7$* (against) + obj. (?), *wyqbl ʿlyky sgn wdyn* Cowl 8[13]: he will complain against you with prefect or judge (:: Joüon MUSJ xviii 38: *sgn* lapsus for *qdm sgn*) - f) + *ʿl$_7$* (against) + obj. (?) + *bšm* (because of), *qblt ʿlyk dyn wmrʾ bšm hyrʾ [znh]* Krael 1[5f.]: I have lodged a complaint against you with judge or lord because of this *hyr* (v. *hyr*) - g) + *ʿl$_7$* (against) + *bgw* (in this matter): Krael 1[4,5,6f.] (for Krael 1[4] :: J.J.Rabinowitz Law 95f.: *qbl* = PA ʿEL (= to agree) + *ʿl$_7$* (upon), for Krael 1[6], v. supra) - h) + *ʿl$_7$* (against) + *l$_5$* (with): Krael 9[19], 10[12f.] (for the *scriptio anterior wlbnyky* replaced by *wʿl bnyky*, cf. Porten & Szubin JAOS cvii 231) - i) + *ʿl$_7$* (against) + *l$_5$* (with) + *bšm* (because of): Krael 12[28] - j) + *ʿl$_7$* (against) + *ʿl dbr* (concerning): Cowl 6[16] - k) + *ʿl$_7$* (against) + *ʿl dbr* (concerning) + *qdm$_3$* (with): Cowl 6[5] - l) + *ʿl$_7$* (against) + *qdm$_3$* (with): Cowl 10[12f.,18], 47[7] - on this verb in this meaning, cf. also Joüon MUSJ xviii 37f., Kutscher JAOS lxxiv 238, J.J.Rabinowitz VT xi 65ff. - **2)** to be adversary of; *hdd lhwy qblh* Tell F 12: H. may be his adversary - **3)** to accept; Part. pass. accepted: CIS ii 4050[10]; *r[ʿ]ʾ wqbl l[rḥ]mnʾ* CIS ii 4050[8]: agreeable to and accepted by (i.e. the beloved one of?) the merciful one (in both instances dam. context; for the *r[ʿ]ʾ* in l. 8 and the *rʿʾ* in l. 10, cf. Milik DFD 48f.: = QAL Part. pass. s.m. abs. of *rʿy$_2$*, uncert. reading and interpret.) - PA ʿEL to accept, to receive - a) + obj.: MPAT 48[3f.] (a certain sum), Samar 3[8] (price) - b) + obj. + obj., *kspʾ ʾnh mqbl dmyn lʿlm* MPAT 52[8f.]: I receive the silver (as its) price forever (cf. IEJ xxxvi 206[5]) - c) + obj. + *mn$_5$* (from): Samar 2[7], cf. EI xx 256[7f.] (+ obj. + *hm$_2$* (= *mn$_5$*)) - d) + *mn$_5$*: Samar 1[8] (dam. context; for the context, cf. Porten BASOR cclxxi 86) - e) + *mn$_5$* + obj.: RB xxxix 548[3], DBKP 17[40f.] - APH Part. facing; *ʾksdrʾ mqblʾ* CIS ii 4195[6]: the exedra facing (sc. the entrance), cf. CIS ii 4194[7], 4199[5ff.], Ber ii 78[2], v 109 ii 7, cf. FS Miles 38[2]; *ʾksdrʾ mqblʾ mʿlyk* Ber ii 82[1]: the exedra facing (you) when you enter, cf. Ber ii 112[5f.]; *ʾksdrʾ mqbltʾ mʿrbytʾ* CIS ii 4175[6f.]: the exedra facing (the entrance), i.e. the western one, cf. Ber ii 107[2f]; *šṭrʾ klh mqblʾ tymnyʾ dydh dy ʾkšdrʾ* CIS ii 4171[2]: the complete wall facing the entrance, i.e. the southern one of the exedra (:: CIS ii a.l.: *mqblʾ tymnyʾ* ... = facing the south side), Ber ii 86[5f.]; *kptʾ mqbltʾ dy ʾksdrʾ mʿrbyʾ* Ber v 95[8]: the vaulted room facing (the entrance) of the western exedra (:: Ingholt Ber v 95: the vaulted space facing the western chamber); *ʾksdrʾ dnh mqblʾ dy mʿrtʾ dy mqbl bbʾ* CIS ii 4199[8f.]: this exedra facing (the entrance) which belongs to the hypogee, (and) which faces the gate (:: CIS ii a.l.: this exedra facing the hypogee (and) which is situated near the gate); *mqblyn gwmḥyn tltʾ* Ber v 125[8]: those which are situated facing (the entrance), i.e. the three niches (on these Palm. instances, cf. O'Connor FUCUS 364f.) - ITP - **1)** (active) to receive; *ʾtqblyh* (v. supra) *mn šmʿwn* ... *lkswt* ... *[ks]p*

d[y]nryn šṭyh MPAT 62[1f.] (= DBKP 27): I have received from Sh. for clothing the sum of six d. - **2)** (passive) to be received; *mks› [m]lḥ› ... yhw› mtqbl* CIS ii 3913 ii 134ff.: the salt tax will be received (:: Teixidor AO i 246: ... will be determined) - Gawlikowski TP 80: l. *] q[ ]l* in Inv xii 19[2] (= Inv iii 2), cf. also Milik DFD 240f.: l. *[m]q[b]l[›]* = APH Part. s.m. emph. (highly uncert. restoration, heavily dam. context) - PA‹EL > Akkad. *qubbulu* (= to accept), cf. v.Soden Or xxxvii 264, xlvi 193, AHW s.v. *qubbal*, cf. also CAD s.v. *qubbulu* A.
v. *qblh*.

qbl₂ Palm Plur. abs. *qblyn* SBS 48[5] - ¶ subst. m. meaning unknown; Cantineau Syr xvii 281: = mission, report (cf. also Milik DFD 310, 312, Dunant SBS a.l.); Gawlikowksi TP 27: *qblyn ›rb‹›* = four times over.

qbl₃ OffAr Cowl 15[36] (*scriptio anterior*; for the reading of the context, cf. Porten & Yardeni sub TADAE B 2.6), 26[7,23], 27[10], 30[25], 31[24], 32[10], 38[9], 43[4], 82[7], Aḥiq 52, 68, Krael 9[17], 10[7] (for the reading, cf. Milik RB lxi 251, Yaron JSS xiii 210, Porten & Greenfield JEAS p. 62, Porten & Szubin JAOS cvii 231, Porten & Yardeni sub TADAE B 3.11), Driv 6[4,5], 8[6], 9[2], F iv 7, MAI xiv/2, 66[5], KAI 260[5], 263, Samar 1[11] (= EI xviii 8*), 2[10], 3[9]; + suff. 3 p.s.m. *qblh* Cowl 8[27]; + suff. 2 p.s.m. *qblk* MAI xiv/2, 66[9] (for the reading, cf. Dupont-Sommer MAI xiv/2, 78, Porten & Yardeni sub TADAE B 1.1 :: Bauer & Meissner SbPAW '36, 415, 420, Koopmans 97: l. *qbl[h]* = + suff. 3 p.s.m.); + suff. 3 p.pl.m. *qblhm* Cowl 38[6]; cf. GIPP 56 - **Nab** CIS ii 164[3], IEJ xxxvi 56[3] (dam. context) - **Palm** CIS ii 3913 i 10; emph. *qbl›* Ber v 104[2]; + suff. 3 p.s.m. *qblh* Syr xix 156[2] - **JAr** + suff. 2 p.s.m. *qwblyk* MPAT 39[8] - ¶ (subst. front >) prep. - **1)** with local meaning, before; *›ntm qmw qblhm* Cowl 38[6]: you stand before them (i.e. be at their disposal) - **2)** > opposite; *wtplg ‹my bšnn 8 ḥmr qbl ḥmr* MAI xiv/2, 66[4f.]: and you will share with me in the eighth year *ḥomer* for *ḥomer* (i.e. each will have fifty procent of the yield) - **3)** with normative meaning, according to: Cowl 15[36] (for the context, cf. Porten & Yardeni sub TADAE B 2.6) - **4)** *qbl zy* with causal meaning, since; *›nh ... yhbth lk ... qbl zy* (v. supra) *l› ktb ‹l spr ›nttky* Krael 10[7]: as far as I am concerned ... I have given it to you since it is not written on your marriage document - **5)** preceded by prep. *l₅* - a) with local meaning, before, facing; *ḥl› zy lqbl byrt›* Cowl 26[7]: the river-bank (v. *ḥl₂*) facing the fortress; *‹d nyq› dy qym› lqblh* Syr xix 156[2]: to the *Nikè* that is situated before it; *bgll› dy lqbl hykl›* CIS ii 3913 i 10: on the stele which is in front of the temple (cf. Greek par. στήλη λιθίνη τῇ οὔσῃ ἀντικρὺς [ἱ]ερ[οῦ]); *drḥt› lqbl zy prbr lm‹rt›* KAI 260[5]: the tree (v. *drḥt*) in front of the precinct (v. *prbr*) belonging to the tomb (for this interpret. of *lqbl zy*, cf. Littmann Sardis 29, Cowley CRAI '21, 13, Cook JHS xxxvii 85, Torrey AJSL xxxiv 195,

Silverman JAOS xciv 271, Lipiński Stud 155 :: Kahle & Sommer KlF i 60: *lqbl zy prbr lmʿrtʾ* = as far as the precinct of this tomb extends, *lqbl zy* = according to, as, cf. also Donner KAI a.l. :: Lidzbarski ZA xxxi 125: *lqbl zy* = conjunction); *lqwblyk* MPAT 39^{8}: before you (i.e. at your disposal, cf. MPAT 51^{13} (v. infra)) - b) with normative meaning, according to, as; *ʾnt ʿbd lqbl znh zy hmrkryʾ ʾmrn* Cowl $26^{22f.}$: you are to act in accordance with this, which the accountants say; *lqbl zy ydkm mhškḥh hbw* Cowl 38^{9} (for the reading, cf. Porten & Yardeni sub TADAE A 4.3; v. also *škḥ*): give him as much as you can; *lmbnyh byb byrtʾ lqbl zy bnh hwh qdmyn* Cowl 30^{25}: to rebuild in the fortress Yeb as it was built formerly (cf. Cowl $32^{10f.}$); *ʿbd lqbl zy ʾnt ʿšt[* Aḥiq 68: do as you think best; *ʾnt lqbl zy ʾnh ʿbdt lk kn ... ʿbd ly* Aḥiq 51f.: as far as you are concerned, as I did to you, do thus to me; *hn ʾzd ytʿbd ... yty[dʿ] lmrʾn lqbl znh zy ʾnḥnh ʾmrn* Cowl $27^{8ff.}$: if an inquiry (v. *ʾzd*) is made ... let it be made known to our lord in accordance with this which we say; *šʾyl ptḥnwpy lqbl mly mnky* ATNS 4^{2}: P. was interrogated in accordance with the words of M.; *wyʿbd ptkr swsh ... lqbl zy qdmn ʿbd qdmy* Driv 9^{2}: and he will make a sculpture (v. *ptkr*) of a horse ... as he made for me before; *whlkʾ lqbl zy qdmn pmwn ʾbwhy hwh ḥšl yḥšl* Driv $8^{5f.}$: and he will pay (v. $ḥšl_1$) the tax just as his father P. paid before; *lqbl znh ʾsrʾ* Samar 1^{11} (= EI xviii 8*): according to this covenant (cf. Samar 2^{10}, 3^{9}); for KAI 263, v. *ʾsprn*; cf. also *sprʾ zk hnpqy wlqblh dyn ʿrry* (v. $ʿrr_1$) Cowl 8^{27}: produce this deed and in accordance with it start a process with him; *hbw [lh ...] ... ʿmyr lqbl rkšh* Driv $6^{2,4}$: give him fodder according to his horses (i.e. as much as his horses need); *ptpʾ znh hbw lhm mn pqyd ʿl pqyd lqbl ʾdwnʾ mn mdynh ʿd mdynh* Driv 6^{5}: give them this ration, each officer of you in turn, in accordance with the stages of his journey from province to province - c) with the meaning 'in return for', 'as compensation'; *ʾnh mptḥyh yhbt lky ... lqbl sbwl [zy yhbty ly]* Cowl 43^{3}: I M. have given (it) to you ... in return for the support you gave me - d) *lqbl zy* 'in return for that which' > because of; *yhbth lyhwyšmʿ lqbl zy sbltny* Krael $9^{16f.}$: I have given it to Y. because she has supported me; *dnh ṣlmʾ dy ʾqymw ʾl ʿbyšt lmlykt ... lqbl zy hw bnh byrtʾ* CIS ii $164^{1f.}$: this is the statue that the tribe of O. erected for M. ... because he built the temple - e) in a diff. expression *wʾḥryʾ lqbl ḥlqn 3* Cowl 82^{7}: and others according to 3 parts (i.e. and others divided into 3 parts (cf. Cowl a.l.; ?? dam. context)) - this word poss. also in MPAT 51^{13} (prec. by l_5, and + suff. 2 p.s.m.): *lwqblk* (??, reading and context uncert., cf. Milik RB lxi 183, cf. also Birnbaum PEQ '57, 116, v. also qny_2 :: Milik Bibl xxxviii 265: pro *lwqblk* l. *lqwblk*, cf. also Fitzmyer & Harrington MPAT a.l.).

qblh OffAr Sing. abs. *qbylh* Driv $12^{5,11}$, *qblt* Driv 4^{3} (for this form, cf. Wesselius AION xxx 267 :: Driv p. 50 : = Sing. abs. of *qblt*) - **Nab**

Sing. cstr. *qblt* MPAT 64 ii 8 (:: Fitzmyer & Harrington MPAT a.l.: = QAL Pf. 1 p.s. of *qbl*$_1$ :: Starcky RB lxi 166, 177: = PA ʿEL Pf. 1 p.s. of *qbl*$_1$) - ¶ subst. complaint; *qblt mlk wdyn* MPAT 64 ii 8: a complaint before king and judge; *qbylh šlḥ ʿlyk* Driv 12^5: he has sent a complaint about you (cf. Driv 12^{11}); *hn psmš[k] ʾḥr qblt mnk yšlḥ ʿly ḥsn tštʾl* Driv 4^3: if hereafter P. sends me a complaint about you, you will be strictly called to account.

qbln **Hebr** Sing. abs. *qbln* DJD ii 22^4, 30^{5,22} - ¶ subst. receiver; in DJD ii 22 and 30 indicating the one who has received a payment.

qbʿ$_1$ **JAr** ITP Pf. 3 p.s.m. *ʾtqbʿ* MPAT-A 11^1 - ¶ verb ITP to be composed (said of a mosaic).

qbʿ$_2$ **DA** QAL Part. act. pl.m. abs. *qbʿn* i 12 (cf. Hoftijzer DA a.l., H.P.Müller ZDPV xciv 61f. (nn. 35, 39), ZAW xciv 227f. :: e.g. Caquot & Lemaire Syr liv 200, Garbini Hen i 180, 185, Delcor SVT xxxii 58, McCarter BASOR ccxxxix 51, 56, Levine JAOS ci 197, Hackett BTDA 29, 50f., 133, Sasson UF xvii 288, 301 (n. 39), Knauf ZAH iii 16: = Plur. abs. of abs. *qbʿ*$_3$ (= hyena; cf. also Puech FS Grelot 28) :: H. & M. Weippert ZDPV xcviii 97f. (n. 108), 103: = Plur. abs. of *qbʿ*$_4$ used adverbially 'by cup' :: Rofé SB 67 n. 32: = Plur. abs. of *qbʿt* (= goblet > contents of goblet); for the interpret. with 'cup', cf. also Weinfeld Shn v/vi 146) - ¶ verb QAL to aggrieve: DA i 12 (cf. Hoftijzer DA a.l. :: H.P. Müll ZDPV xciv 61f. n. 39, ZAW xciv 218, 228 n. 84: = to rob).

qbʿ$_3$ v. *qbʿ*$_2$.

qbʿ$_4$ **Ph** Plur. abs. *qbʿn* Mus li 286^4, IEJ xxxii 120; cstr. *qbʿ* Mus li 286^7, IEJ xxxii 120 - **OffAr** Sing. emph. *qbʿʾ* Syr lxi 110 (on the reading problems, cf. Sznycer Syr lxi 115) - ¶ subst. m. cup, goblet; *qbʿ ksp* Mus li 286^7: silver cup (cf. Mus li 286^4: *qbʿm šl ksp*); in Syr lxi 110 indication of a small jar; for this word, cf. also Brown VT xxi 6 (: > Greek κύμβη, κύμβος, κύββα (highly uncert. interpret.), Cathcart RSO xlvii 57, Masson RPAE 75, Avigad & Greenfield IEJ xxxii 121ff., Amadasi Guzzo Sem xxxviii 20f.

v. *qbʿ*$_2$, *qs*.

qbʿt v. *qbʿ*$_2$.

qbr$_1$ **Ph** NIPH Impf. 3 p.pl. *yqbr* KAI 14^8 (cf. e.g. Röllig KAI a.l., Gibson SSI iii p.111 :: FR 141 n.: or = QAL Impf. 3 p.pl. :: Harr 142: = NIPH Impf. 3 p.s.m.) - **Pun** QAL Inf. cstr. *qbr* KAI 277^8 (v. infra); Part. pass. s.m. abs. *qybr* KAI 152^2 (for the reading, cf. Chabot sub Punica iv A 9; for the interpret., cf. Röllig BiOr xxvii 379; for the QAL, cf. also Röllig KAI iii p. 21; uncert. interpret. :: FR 143: = PI ʿEL/PU ʿAL Pf. 3 p.s.m. :: Friedr 145, v.d.Branden GP p. 79: = PU ʿAL Pf. 3 p.s.m. :: Février CB viii 28: = variant of *qbr*$_3$); s.f. abs. *qbrt* Handb 436C 8^4, Punica iv A 7^5 (cf. Hoftijzer VT xi 346 :: Harr 142: = PU ʿAL Pf. 2 p.s. :: Février CB viii 29: = Sing. abs. of *qbrh*; cf.

also Röllig KAI ii p. 136) - **Hebr** QAL Part. act. s.m. abs. *qwbr* DJD ii 46[5] - **Nab** QAL Impf. 3 p.s.m. *yqbr* CIS ii 197[3,7], 198[6], 199[4], 207[5], J 5[7]; 3 p.pl.m. *yqbrwn* CIS ii 212[6]; Inf. *mqbr* CIS ii 209[7], 210[5], 350[5]; QAL pass. Pf. 3 p.s.m. *qbyr* ADAJ x 44 ii 4 (= RB lxxii 95); ITP Impf. 3 p.s.m. *ytqbr* CIS ii 207[5], 208[3], 215[4], 217[3], 219[4], 222[4], 224[3], 350[3], J 5[3,4], 38[4] (*ytq[br]*); 3 p.s.f. *ttqbr* CIS ii 215[4]; 3 p.pl.m. *ytqbrwn* CIS ii 205[4], 209[3], 212[2], 219[3], 221[2], J 22[2] - **Palm** QAL pass. Pf. 3 p.s.m. *qbyr* Ber i 38[9] (cf. Cantineau Gramm 81, 84, Starcky ADAJ x 45 × Ingholt Ber i 40: = QAL Part. pass. s.m. abs.); 3 p.s.f. *qbyrt* Inv xii 17[5] (= RIP 105); Part. pass. pl.m. abs. *qbyryn* RIP 21[3]; s.f. abs. *qbyr›* RB xxxix 539[3] - **JAr** QAL Pf. 3 p.s.m. *qbr* MPAT 145C 2 (= Frey 1373; cf. e.g. Fitzmyer & Harrington MPAT a.l. :: Milik with Zayadine Syr xlvii 131, Beyer ATTM 342: = QAL pass. Pf. 3 p.s.m. :: Frey sub 1373: = Sing. cstr. of *qbr$_3$*); 1 p.s. + suff. 3 p.s.m. *qbrth* MPAT 68[6]; Part. pass. s.m. abs. *qbyr* MPAT-A 46[1]; ITP Impf. 3 p.s.m. *ytqbr* EI xx 161* - ¶ verb to bury, passim - **1)** + obj.: J 5[7] - **2)** + obj. + *b$_2$* (loci): CIS ii 212[6] - **3)** + obj. + *b$_2$* (instrum.), *yqbr mn dy yṣb› btqp› dy bydh* CIS ii 207[5f.]: he will bury whom he pleases in virtue of the warrant which is in his hand - **4)** + *b$_2$* (loci): KAI 14[8], CIS ii 197[3], Inv xii 17[5f.], RB xxxix 539[2]; cf. also *qwbr bmytyn* DJD ii 46[5]: burying (them) among the dead - **5)** + *b$_2$* (loci) + obj., *yqbr bh ›nwš* CIS ii 197[7]: he will bury someone therein, cf. CIS ii 198[6], 199[4f], 210[5] - **6)** + *tḥt*, *t‹t hbnt st qbrt* Punica iv A 7[4f.]: buried under this stone, cf. Handb 436C 8[4], cf. poss. also KAI 152[2] (v. supra) - **7)** in the comb. *ktb lmqbr* CIS ii 209[7]: a deed of burial; *tn› mqbr* CIS ii 350[5]: permission to bury - **8)** in the comb. *bym qbr ›lm* KAI 277[8f.]: on the day of the burial of the deity (cf. e.g. Dupont-Sommer JA cclii 292, 296f., Garbini ArchClass xvi 72f., OA iv 47, AION xviii 234, 246 (n. 37), RSF xvii 183ff., Levi Della Vida with Garbini OA iv 47, 51, Ferron OA iv 191ff., OA v 204, 206, Mus lxxxi 532ff., Février JA ccliii 11, Fitzmyer JAOS lxxxvi 286, 293f., Pfiffig OA v 218, v.d.Branden Meltô iv 101f., Vattioni AION xv 295f., Heurgon BAr-NS iv 247, 249f., Röllig KAI a.l., Soggin RSO xlv 245ff., Lipiński RTAT 261, Gibson SSI iii p. 154, 158, Avigad & Greenfield IEJ xxxii 127 :: Février OA iv 175: or = Sing. cstr. of *qbr$_3$*? :: Levi Della Vida with Vattioni AION xv 295: = Sing. cstr. of *qbr$_2$* (= someone who buries, inters) :: Milik (with Vattioni) AION xv 295f.: *qbr* = Sing. m. abs. of *qbr$_4$* (variant of *kbr$_3$* = mighty)) - QAL pass. to be buried; *qbyr* ... *‹l ymyn npš› dh* Ber i 38[9ff.]: he has been buried ... to the right of this portrait of the deceased (v. *npš*); for Part. pass. buried, v. supra - ITP to be buried: passim - **1)** + *b$_2$* (loci): CIS ii 207[5], 208[3], 209[3], 212[2], 215[4], 217[3], etc. - **2)** + *‹m$_4$* + *b$_2$*: EI xx 161*.

v. *ymn$_2$*, *‹yr$_1$*, *qbr$_3$*.

qbr$_2$ v. *qbr$_1$*.

qbr_3 **Ph** Sing. abs. *qbr* KAI 14[3,8], 30[2], Eph iii 54C 3; + suff. 1 p.s. *qbry* NESE i 3[1] (cf. Röllig NESE i a.l. :: Ullendorff JSS xviii 267 (div. otherwise): l. *qbr* (= Sing. abs.) + z_1 (used as relative pronoun)) - **Pun** Sing. abs. *qbr* CIS i 124[1] (context however dam.), 5945[2] (= TPC 7), RIL 803[1] (for the reading of the context, cf. Marcillet-Jaubert RevArch '59, 67), KAI 142[4,7] (??, dam. and diff. context; or rather (div. otherwise): l. *qbr* = QAL Part. pass. s.m. abs. of qbr_1), *qbʿr* KAI 128[2] (cf. FR 96c); cstr. *qbr* CIS i 137[1], 156[1], RES 6[1] (= CIS i 5943 = TPC 5), 7[1] (= CIS i 5942 = TPC 4), 14[1] (= CIS i 5944 = TPC 6), 239 (= CIS i 5954 = TPC 16), 249[1] (= CIS i 5955 = TPC 17), 501[1] (= CIS i 5961 = TPC 23), KAI 67[1], 70[1], 90[1] (= TPC 15), Mozia ix 163[1], CT xx (no. 79-80) 9[1], etc., etc., *qbʿr* KAI 93[1] (= TPC 12; cf. FR 96c), TPC 67[1] - **Hebr** Sing. abs. *qbr* Frey 661[2], 900[2], 994[1], 1394[1], RB lxxviii 248 i 1 (*qb[r]*); cstr. *qbr* Frey 620[1]; + suff. 3 p.s.m. *qbrw* Frey 668[1], 669[1] - **Samal** Sing. cstr. *qbr* KAI 215[21] - **OldAr** Sing. + suff. 3 p.s.m. *qb[rh]* KAI 223A 4f. (cf. Dupont-Sommer Sf p. 99, 101, 149, Fitzmyer AIS 80, 85f., Donner KAI a.l.; poss. restoration, cf. also Degen AAG p. 17 no. 71) - **OffAr** Sing. + suff. 3 p.s.m. *qbrh* Cowl 71[31] (for the reading of the *r*, cf. Cowl p. 182) - **Nab** Sing. abs. + Arab. ending *qbrw* J 17[1] (on this text, cf. also Diem Or l. 354 n. 51, O'Connor JNES xlv 223f.)[,7]; cstr. *qbr* RES 2043[1], 2044, 2045, ARNA-Nab 126; cstr. + Arab. ending *qbrw* J 18[2] (cf. also Diem Or l 354f.); emph. *qbrʾ* CIS ii 197[1], 206[1,2,4,5,6], 207[1,5], 212[2], 215[1], 350[1,5], RES 2035[1], ARNA-Nab 16[1] - **Palm** Sing. emph. *qbrʾ* CIS ii 4109A 1, B 1, 4112[2], 4113[2], 4114[2], 4116[1], 4121, 4122[1] (Greek par. τὸ μνημῖον), 4123bis 2, 4192 (Greek par. τάφος), 4202[1] (Greek par. μνημῖον), Inv vii 5[1] (Greek par. μνημεῖον), etc., etc. - ¶ subst. m. tomb, grave, passim (v. also pth_1; for the context of KAI 30[2], v. $šm_1$); cf. the foll. comb. - **1)** *qbrʾ dnh bt ʿlmʾ* CIS ii 4116[1]: this tomb, house of eternity (cf. CIS ii 4168[3], 4201[1], 4216, RB xxxix 523[1], Inscr P 12[1]), cf. also *yqr bt ʿlmʾ qbrʾ dnh* CIS ii 4192: a magnificent house of eternity, this tomb - **2)** *qbrʾ dnh wmʿrtʾ* CIS ii 4122[1]: this tomb and hypogee; *qbrʾ wmʿrtʾ* CIS ii 4206[2]: tomb and hypogee - **3)** cf. also *dnh qbrw ṣnʿh kʿbw* J 17[1]: this is the tomb which K. made (cf. Cantineau Nab i 112 :: Diem ZDMG cxxiii 228 n. 11: = .. a tomb ...) - this subst. (Sing. abs. *qbr*, preceded by article *ʾ*) prob. also in KAI 161[3] in comb. *ʾḥdr dl ʾqbr ʾyʿzm...*, the (funerary) chamber with the tomb, Y. (= n.p.) ... :: Février RA xlv 142f.: pro *ʾqbr ʾyʿzn* l. *ʾqbrʾ* (= article + Sing. abs. of *qbrh* (= funerary urn)) + *yʿzn* (= n.p.) :: Roschinski Num 112, 114: l. ... *ʾqbrʾ* (= Sing. + suff. 3 p.s.m. preceded by *ʾ* (either = $ʾ_8$ or = prosth. *ʾ*, cf. Röllig KAI a.l.: or *ʾqbrʾ* = form of qbr_3 + suff. 3 p.s.m.; cf. also Cooke NSI p. 149)) :: v.d.Branden RSF ii 143f.: pro *ʾqbrʾ* l. *ʾqrbʾ* = form of qrb_4 + suff. 3 p.s.m. (= entrance) - for qbr_3, cf. Gawlikowski Ber xxi 5 ff., Bénichou-Safar TPC p. 195ff., cf. also Negev IEJ xxi 52.

v. *b'r*, *byt_2*, *mṣbh*, *qbr_1*.

qbr_4 v. *qbr_1*.

qbrh **Hebr** Sing. cstr. *qbrt* Mosc var. B 2 (for the reading of the context, v. Ussishkin BiAr xxxiii 44) - **Nab** Sing. cstr. *qbrt* CIS ii 224^5; emph. *qbrt'* BAGN ii 87^1 - **JAr** Sing. emph. *qbwrt'* Frey 892^1, *qbwrth* MPAT-A 45^2, ZDPV xcvi 59^2, Frey 894^5 (for this prob. reading, cf. Kaplan EI xix 285, cf. also Klein MGWJ lxxv 374; or = Sing. + suff. 3 p.s.m./f.?, heavily dam. context; :: Pedersen Inscr Sem 7: l. poss. *qbwrt'* (= Sing. emph.) :: Frey a.l., Chabot sub RES 420: l. *qbwrtw* = Sing. + suff. 3 p.s.m.) - ¶ subst. f. tomb, grave: passim.
v. *$qbr_{1,3}$*.

qbš v. *dqr_1*.

qdd_1 v. *qr'_1*, *$šḥq_2$*.

qdd_2 v. *kdd_2*.

qdd_3 v. *kdd_3*.

qdh v. *kdh*. *qdwm* v. *qdm_3*.

qdwš v. *$qdš_3$*.

qdwšh **Hebr** Sing. cstr. *qdwšt* SM 75 - ¶ subst. holiness; introducing indication of person, *qdwšt mry rby 'ysy hkhn* SM $75^{1f.}$: his holiness my lord rabbi I. the priest (cf. e.g. Gutman, Yeivin & Netzer Qadm v 51, Naveh SM a.l.).

$qdḥ_1$ **Pun** PI'EL (?, or YIPH?) Part. s.m. abs. *mqdḥ* CIS i 352^3 - **OffAr**, cf. Frah app. 12 (*yḥk[d]ḥwn*; cf. Nyberg FP 99: = HAPH of *$qdḥ_1$* :: Ebeling Frah a.l. (sub app. 23): l. *yhq(w)'wn* = form of *kwy/qwy* (= to burn)) - ¶ verb PI'EL/YIPH (v. supra) Part. indication of function; CIS i sub 352: one who lights (sc. the lamps in the temple), cf. however Slouschz TPI p. 296: one who drills (in wood or metal); uncert. interpretations - HAPH to cause to burn: Frah app. 12 - a form of this root poss. in DJD ii 47^3, cf. Milik DJD ii a.l.

$qdḥ_2$ cf. Frah xviii 16 (*kdḥwn*, cf. Nyberg FP 49, 89 :: Ebeling Frah a.l.: l. *kšwn* = form of *kšy* (= to grow)).

qdy v. *mhdmr*.

qdym v. *qdm_3*.

qdyš v. *$qdš_3$*.

qdym v. *qdm_3*.

qdl **OffAr** Sing. + suff. 3 p.s.m. *qdlh* Aḥiq 134 (for this interpret., cf. also Grelot RB lxviii 188 :: Cowl p. 242: or (div. otherwise): l. *qdl* (= Sing. abs.) + *hk_2* (= variant of *hyk*)) - ¶ subst. m. neck; *mkdb gzyr qdlh* Aḥiq 134: a liar whose throat is cut (for the context, v. *gzr_1*).

qdm_1 **OffAr** QAL Part. act. s.m. abs. *qdm'* Sach 76 i A 4 (cf. Greenfield Or xxix 100 :: e.g. Sach p. 234, Lidzbarski Eph iii 256, Leand 47c, 61j: = Sing. emph. of *qdm_2* used adverbially); ITP Impf. 3 p.s.m. *ytqdm* Cowl 82^6; cf. Frah xx 2 (*kdmwn*; cf. Nyberg FP 50, 92 (cf. also Toll

ZDMG-Suppl viii 38) :: Ebeling Frah a.l.: l. *qymwn* = form of *qwm*$_1$) - **Nab** QAL Part. act. m. pl. cstr. *qdmy* BIA x 55[4] - ¶ verb QAL to precede; *ʿmrʾ zy lh qdmʾ mtmrṭ bkbʾ* Sach 76 i A 4f.: whose wool was previously pulled out by thorns (v. supra); Part. act. subst. chief; *qdmy šrkth* BIA x 55[4]: the chiefs of its corporation (v. *šrkh*), cf. Shahîd RoAr 140f. - PAʿEL to rise (early), to stand up: Frah xx 2 - ITP to present oneself, to be brought; *ytqdm byh* Cowl 82[6] (diff. and dam. context), Cowl p. 201: = let him come before him (cf. Driver JRAS '32, 86: let him be confronted by Yah, or: present himself before Yah), both interpretations of *byh* (= *b*$_2$ + suff. 3 p.s.m./*b*$_2$ + n.d.) highly uncert. - a form of this root (PAʿEL Pf. 3 p.s.m. *qdm*) in AJSL lviii 303A 10?? (dam. context), for the interpret., cf. AG p. 23, Bowman AJSL lviii 307 - Segal ATNS a.l.: a form of this root (*qdmt* = QAL Pf. 3 p.s.f.?) poss. in ATNS 66b 2?, or = Sing. abs. of *qdmh*$_1$ used adverbially (= previously??), heavily dam. context, highly uncert. reading.
v. *qdm*$_{2,3}$.

qdm$_2$ **Ph** Sing. abs. *qdm* KAI 43[12] (v. infra) - **OffAr** Plur. abs. *qdmn* Cowl 32[5,8], 33[9] (*qdm[n]*; for this prob. reading, cf. Porten & Yardeni sub TADAE A 4.10), 37[8], Aḥiq 46, 133 (*[q]dmn*), Driv 5[9], 7[1,5], 8[6], 9[2], ATNS 12[3], Sem xxxiii 94[3] (for the reading, cf. Porten Sem xxxiii 94, 97, Porten & Yardeni sub TADAE A 5.1 :: Sznycer HDS 168ff.: l. *qrbn* (= Sing. abs. of *qrbn*)), Beh 59 (cf. Greenfield & Porten BIDG p. 50f. :: Cowl a.l., Lindenberger APA 267 n. 498: l. *qmn* = QAL Part. act. pl.m. abs. of *qwm*$_1$ :: Cowl a.l.: or l. *qymn* = QAL Part. act. pl.m. abs. of *qwm*$_1$ :: Sach p. 196f., Ungnad ArPap p. 90: l. *qrwn*), *qdmyn* Cowl 30[25], 32[10]; cf. Nisa-b 447[1] (*qdm[n]*), 483[1], 526[1], 661[3], 676[1] (*qdmn*), GIPP 56 - **Palm** Plur. abs. *qdmyn* Syr xii 139[3] - **JAr** Plur. abs. *qdmyn* AMB 1[23] - ¶ subst. the time before; *yrḥ md yrḥ ʿd ʿlm kqdm* KAI 43[12]: month by month, for ever as aforetime (cf. e.g. Cooke NSI p. 83, 86, FR 251 II, Röllig KAI a.l., Gibson SSI iii p. 137 :: Clermont-Ganneau Et ii 176: *kqdm* = *k*$_3$ (= *ky*) + *qdm* (= PIʿEL Pf. 3 p.s.m. of *qdm*$_1$?) to be combined with the following words: *kqdm km hdlt hnḥšt* = for thus the bronze plaquette presents (i.e. according to the tenor of the bronze plaquette)) - Plur. - **1)** used adverbially, formerly, previously; *lmbnyh ... lqbl zy bnh hwh qdmyn* Cowl 30[25]: to rebuild it ... as it was built formerly; *qdmn šzbk* Aḥiq 46: he once saved you; *qdmn kzy mṣryʾ mrdw ʾdyn smšk* Driv 7[1]: previously when the Egyptians revolted, then P. ... (*smšk* = variant of *psmšk*, cf. Kutscher Kedem ii 70f., cf. however Driv p. 63: = lapsus for *psmšk* (cf. also ibid. p. 19 n. 3)); *ʿbydtʾ zyly yʿbdw kzy qdmn* Driv 5[9]: let them perform my service as before; *hn lw glyn ʾnpyn ʿl ʾršm qdmn lkn* Cowl 37[8]: if we had revealed our face before A. previously (v. *kn*$_4$; for the translation of the context, v. however *gly*); *kzy qdmn ʾmrt* ATNS 12[3]: as I said previously; cf. Driv 7[5], 8[6], 9[2], Beh

59 (v. supra) - **2)** preceded by prep. *l_5*, previously, formerly; *lmbnyh ... kzy hwh lqdmn* Cowl 32[8]: to rebuild it as it was before (cf. Cowl 32[10], cf. Nisa-b 447[1], 526[1], 556[1], 661[3]; cf. poss. also Syr xii 139[3]??, dam. context) - **3)** preceded by prep. *mn_5*, previously, formerly; *zy ... bnh hwh mn qdmn* Cowl 32[4f.]: which was built formerly; cf. Sem xxxiii 94[3] (v. supra) - **4)** prec. by prep. *l_5* and *mn_5*, *lmn qdmyn* AMB 1[23]: from the beginning (dam. context) - Rocco AION xix 551: l. *qdm* (= Sing. abs.) in ibid. l. 1, used adverbially (= forward), highly uncert. reading and interpret., cf. Amadasi GR i p. 45f.: text undecipherable.
v. *qdm_1*.

qdm_3 **Samal** KAI 215[21,23] - **OldAr** KAI 202B 13, 217[8] (*qd[m]*),[9] (dam. context), 222A 8, 9, 9f. (*[q]dm*), 10, 11, 12, Tell F 1, 15 (Akkad. par. *ina pani*) - **OffAr** Cowl 2[12,14], 6[5], 8[24], Aḥiq 10, 13, Krael 8[2] (the repetition of the phrase containing *qdm* in l. 3 lapsus, cf. Grelot DAE p. 240 n. b), ATNS 35[1], 43a 4, KAI 278[6], Pers 5[3], 13[4], 39[5], 40[4], Samar 7[17], etc., etc., cf. Warka 11, 14, 36, 39: *qu-da-am*, *qm* Del 105[1] (lapsus?); + suff. 3 p.s.m. *qdmwhy* Aḥiq 50, 107, Driv 3[6], Samar 3[4], *qdmwh* KAI 226[2], RES 1785F 5; + suff. 2 p.s.m. *qdmyk* Aḥiq 203 (*[q]dmyk*), Driv 1[1], 3[7], 5[2] (*qdm[y]k*); + suff. 2 p.s.f. *qdmyky* Krael 10[3]; + suff. 1 p.s. *qdmy* Driv 5[1], 9[2], KAI 233[9] (cf. e.g. Lidzbarski AUA p. 8, 11, R.A.Bowman UMS xx 277, 280, Dupont-Sommer Syr xxiv 31, 40, Donner KAI a.l., Gibson SSI ii p. 104, 107 :: Lidzbarski ZA xxxi 195, 199, Baneth OLZ '19, 56: l. *qdmh* = + suff. 3 p.s.m.), Samar 2[8], 6[9] (*[q]dmy*); + suff. 3 p.pl.m. *qdmyhm* ATNS 77a 4, Aḥiq 141; + suff. 1 p.pl. *qdmyn* Samar 9[11] (heavily dam. context), *qmyn›* Cowl 82[13] (??, heavily dam. context; highly uncert. interpret.); cf. Frah xxv 1 (*mdm*, lapsus for *qdm*, cf. Nyberg FP 101 :: Ebeling Frah a.l.: this interpret. less prob.), Paik 898 (*qdm*), Nisa-c 210[5], 287[3,4], (*qdmyk*), 287[3] (*qdmy*), Syn 300[1], 301[1], 302[2], 305[1], 310[1], DEP 153[3],, GIPP 33, 62, SaSt 19 - **Nab** CIS ii 320 F, 338[2], 393bis 3 (for the reading, cf. Chabot sub RES 1453), 401[2], 443[3], etc., *qm* RB xlii 415[5] (lapsus?); + suff. 3 p.s.f. *qdmyh* BSOAS xvi 227,81[5] (= RHR lxxx 4[5]; cf. Clermont-Ganneau RAO viii 242, Strugnell BASOR clvi 31 :: Littmann BSOAS xvi 229: + suff. 3 p.s.m.; on the problem, cf. also Starcky Syr xxxii 155); + suff. 3 p.pl.m. *qdmyhm* CIS ii 350[2] - **Palm** CIS ii 3951[5] (*qd[m]*; :: Gawlikowski Ber xix 74f.: l. *qr[b]* = PA‹EL Pf. 3 p.s.m. of *qrb_1*), 3973[8], 3998[1], PNO 2ter 5, Inv D 49, Inv xi 28[1], xii 31[1], RIP 127[3] (*qd[m]*), Ber iii 84[1], v 133[6] (:: Ingholt Ber v 133f.: = PA‹EL Pf. 3 p.s.m. of *qdm_1* (= to provide against)), etc.; + suff. 3 p.s.m. *qdmwhy* CIS ii 4168[3], Inv xii 2[4], 48[2], *qdymwhy* Inv xii 49[5], *qdmwh* PNO 52[3] (dam. context) - **Hatra** 2[2], 13[2], 16[1,2], 17, 23[1], 24[1], etc., etc., (cf. also Assur 6b 3, 12[3], 18[3], 23c 3, etc.), *qdwm*, cf. Assur 24, *qdw/ym*, cf. Assur 27i 3, *qmd* (lapsus), cf. Assur 17i 4; + suff. 3 p.s.m. *qmwhy* 23[3] (for the reading, cf. e.g. Caquot Syr xxix 102,

Milik RN vi/iv 54), *qmwh* 74^{1} (uncert. reading; cf. Milik DFD 401f., Vattioni IH a.l., cf. also Aggoula Ber xviii 96: l. *qm* ... (cf. Tubach ISS 264f. (n. 56)) :: Ingholt AH i/1, 44: l. *q<d>m* :: Safar Sumer xi 13, Caquot Syr xxxii 270: l. *qdm* (cf. also Donner sub KAI 256); or l. *qmd* = lapsus for *qdm*??); + suff. 2 p.s.m. *qdmyk* 147, 150, 230^{1}; + suff. 2 p.pl.m. *qdmykwn* 235^{2}; cf. also Jensen MDOG lx 17 n. 4: *qmd* (lapsus, idem ibid. 18 n. 6: *qdq* (lapsus)) - **JAr** Frey 845^{3} (= SM 104), 979^{2} (= MPAT-A 48), MPAT 37 ii 3, 40^{5}, 44 xxiii 2, 52^{12}, 56^{5}, AMB 7^{5}, etc., *qwdm* MPAT 41^{13}; + suff. 3 p.s.m. *q[d]mwy* AMB 9^{8}; + suff. 2 p.s.f. *qd[myk]* MPAT 42^{14} (heavily dam. context); + suff. 1 p.s. *qmy* MPAT 61^{24} (for this interpret., cf. Greenfield sub DBKP 17 :: e.g. Fitzmyer & Harrington sub MPAT 61 (div. otherwise): l. *qmyh* (= + suff. 3 p.s.f.)); + suff. 2 p.pl.m. *qdm[kn]* MPAT 52^{12} - ¶ (subst. used as) prep. - **1)** with local meaning, before; *šmt qdm [ʾlwr] nṣbʾ znh* KAI 202B 13f.: I have set up this stele before I. (cf. Tell F 1, 15); *ptkr znh hqm nnšt qdm ʾdrswn* KAI 258$^{1f.}$: this bas-relief N. has erected before A. (v. *ʾdrswn*); *wsgd[t] ... qdm ʾsrḥ[ʾdn]* Aḥiq 13: and I bowed down before A.; *qrbth qdm ʾsrḥʾdn* Aḥiq 10: I brought him before A.; *ʿbdy ʾḥḥpy zy psmšk yhqrb qdmyk* Driv 3^{7}: the slaves of A., that P. brought before you; *ʾksdrʾ wtmlʾ dqdmwhy* Inv xii 2$^{3f.}$: the exedra and the platform which is before it; *qbrʾ dnh bt ʿlmʾ wʾsṭwʾ dy qdmwhy* CIS ii 4168^{3}: this tomb, house of eternity and the portico which is before it (cf. also Inv xii 48$^{1f.}$, 49$^{4f.}$, RIP 127$^{3f.}$); *dqymy[n] qdm krsyh* AMB 7$^{4f.}$: who are standing in front of His throne (cf. KAI 215^{21}, RES 1785A 1f.); cf. *[ʾ]nh qdm mrʾy šlḥt* Cowl 16^{8}: I have sent (sc. a message) before (i.e. to) my lord; *bznh qdmy šlm ʾp tmh qdm[y]k šlm yhwy* Driv 5$^{1f.}$: there is peace here with me and there may be peace with you too (i.e. it is fine with me, hopefully it is fine with you too; cf. Driv 1^{1}; cf. also Driv p. 38, Whitehead JNES xxxvii 134 (n. 102)); *šlm qdmyk* Nisa-c 210^{5}, 287^{3,4}: may well-being be before you (i.e. may it be well with you); *lnqyh qdm ʾptw ʾlhʾ rbʾ* Cowl 72^{15}: as a libation for the great god A. (v. *nqyh*$_1$), cf. Cowl 72^{6,16,19}, CIS ii 3951^{5}, etc. - cf. also - a) before, in the presence of (sc. an authority); *qblt ʿlyk qdm dmydt wknwth dynyʾ* Cowl 6$^{5f.}$: I lodged a complaint against you before D. and his colleagues the judges; *ʾmr ydnyh ... qdm wydrng rb ḥylʾ* Cowl 25^{2}: Y. has declared in the presence of W. the commander of the garrison (cf. ATNS 35^{1}); *ršynkm qdm rmndyn prtrk* Cowl 20^{4}: we have sued you before R. the governor (for the reading *rmndyn*, v. *dn*$_1$; for the context, v. also *prtrk*); *mn hw zy yqwm qdmwhy* Aḥiq 107: who will maintain himself in his presence?; *ʾth ... lʾbwd ... qdm ʾwsy[ry]* Syr xli 285$^{3f.}$: he has come to Abydos before Osiris; *hḥsn qdmwhy* Samar 3^{4}: he took possession (sc. of a slave) in his presence (dam. context); *ʾ[t]ʾgr qdm mryns hygmwnʾ* CIS ii 3913 ii 65: it (sc. a contract) was (or: they were) laid down before

M. the prefect (cf. prob. also Sem xxiii 95 recto 2f.); *wʿdyʾ ʾln zy gzr brgʾ[yh ...] ... qdm mrdk wzrpnt* KAI 222A 7f.: the treaty which B. has concluded in the presence of M. and Z. (cf. prob. also KAI 278[5f.], for the problems of the context, v. *ḥgy*) - for *br(y)k qdm*, v. *brk$_1$* sub QAL (etc.) 6b - for *dk(y)r qdm* (and related formulae), v. *zkr$_1$* sub QAL A 2g, o, p, r, s, B a, b 3-6, C a 7-9, b 5, 9, 10, c 4, v. also *zkrn* sub A 1a, 2 - cf. also *qdm dšrʾ wʾ[lw]...* CIS ii 912: may W. be in the presence of D. ...; *šlm wʾlw ... qdm ʾlbʿly* CIS ii 1479: may the well-being of W. be before E. (cf. also Hatra 235[2]) - b) before, in the opinion of; *whʿdyt ḥṭʾyk qdmwhy* Aḥiq 50: I exculpated you before him; *ʾl yql šmk qdmyhm* Aḥiq 141: may your name not be lightly esteemed before them; *wlrḥmn yšymnk qdm drywhwš* Cowl 30[2]: and may he give you favour before D.; *ṣdqh yhwh lk qdm YHW* ... Cowl 30[27]: you will have a merit before YHW ... (cf. KAI 226[2f.]); *a-na-ʾ za-qi-it ú-ma-ʾ a-na-ʾ za-ka-a-a ma-a-a-[tu] qu-da-am ra-ab-ra-bi-e* Warka 10f.: I am pure, yes I am pure in the opinion of the great ones (cf. Warka 14, 16, 39); Milik DFD 401ff.: combine *mdʿn dbš qmwh* in Hatra 74 ll. 8 + 1 (for the reading, v. *mndʿm* and v. supra) = something evil before him (highly uncert. comb. and interpret.; Hatra 74[1,2] = rest of other inscription??) - c) in the comb. with *ʿrb$_5$*, *ʿrbʾ zy qdm kyšwš* CIS ii 65[1f.]: pledge which is before K. (i.e. given to K. as a security for rent which still has to be paid); *ʿrbʾ dy qdm mʿrtʾ* Ber v 133[4ff.]: the pledge before the tomb (i.e. poss. a pledge which serves as a security for the preservation of the tomb; v. supra); cf. also *dy ʾyty ly wdy ʾqnh ʾḥrʾyn w[ʿrbyn] lmrqʾ wlqymʾ zbnh dk qdm[kn] wqdm yrtkn* MPAT 52[11f.]: everything which belongs to me and which I shall acquire is a guarantee and security to clear and confirm that purchase for you and your heir (v. *mrq$_1$*, *qwm$_1$*) - d) before, incumbent upon; *šʿrn krn 45 qdm škḥ* Del 104[1f.]: 45 *kr* wheat to be repaid (with interest) by Sh. (cf. Del 79bis (= AM 66)) - e) before, sc. someone who has given an order; *lqbl zy qdmn ʿbd qdmy* Driv 9[2]: corresponding to that which he previously executed for me (cf. e.g. Pers 31[3], etc.) - f) Fales sub AECT 28: l. *z[y q]dm byt [ksp]ʾ* in CIS ii 20 (= Del 7); = household administrator (cf. the Akkad. *ša muḫḫi bīti*), the silver; uncert. interpret. :: Johns ADD iii 63: l. *zy qdm byt hyklʾ*: who is before the palace, cf. also Del a.l. :: Kaufman JAOS cix 99: *qdm* poss. = Sing. cstr. of *qdm$_4$* (= first fruit?) :: Stevenson ABC p. 127f.: l. *zy yqdm* (= PAʿEL Impf. 3 p.s.m. of *qdm$_1$*) *byt kspʾ* (= Sing. emph. of *ksp$_2$*, v. also *byt$_2$*, *ksp$_2$*) - **2)** with temp. meaning, before; *qdm knbwzy* Cowl 32[5]: before (the time of) C. (sc. before C. conquered Egypt); *tšlḥwn ly yt ʾlʿzr ... qdm šbh* MPAT 56[4ff.]: you must send me E. ... before the Sabbath; *qdm dnh* BASOR cclxiii 78[2]: before this (cf. however Jones BASOR cclxxv 43: *qdm* has local meaning) - **3)** prec. by prep. *b$_2$*, *bqmy* MPAT 61[24]: in my presence (v. supra), cf. *bmqm* in

MPAT 61[25] (v. *mqm$_1$*) - **4)** prec. by prep. *l$_5$*, before (loc.): FuF xxxv 173[6,9,11] (for this interpret., cf. Altheim & Stiehl FuF xxxv 173, ASA 245, 275), DM ii 38 iii 4 (+ n.d. in the introduction of a dedication) - **5)** prec. by prep. *mn$_5$* - a) from, before; *lhʿdyh bytʾ znh mn qdmyky* Krael 10[13]: to take away this house from you; *mn qdm ʾwsry myn qḥy* KAI 269[3]: from O. receive water; *lmhk* (v. *hlk$_1$*) *mn qdm rb ḥylʾ* Cowl 54[14]: to go from the presence of the commander of the army (heavily dam. context); cf. also *ʾsywth mn qdm mry šmyh* AMB 1[18]: his (?; v. *ʾsyw*) cure from the side of/on behalf of the Lord of Heavens - b) with the same meaning as *qdm*, *dkyr ʿbdt ... mn qdm dwšrʾ* CIS ii 393bis (for the reading, cf. RES 1453): may O. be remembered before D. (for comparable formulae, cf. *zkr$_1$* sub 2 A o 1, 2, q, u, B a 2, cf. also *zkrn* sub A 1); *šlm ḥyw mn qdm dwšrʾ* J 52: the well-being of Ch. be from D. (cf. J 169, 201, etc.; cf. Ribera AO i 114f.; cf. poss. also AMB 9[7f.] (v. however *tmh$_1$*)) - c) with temp. meaning, before; *hwyt ʾnty mn qdm dh* MPAT 40[5]: you have been my wife before now (i.e. up to this moment) - d) in diff. context: Hatra 23[3] - **5)** prec. by prep. *mn$_5$* and prep. *l$_5$*, *byt dh dʾwrḥwtyh* (v. *ʾrḥ$_2$*) *dmn* (v. *dmk*) *qdm ltrʿʾ* MPAT-A 48[2]: this hostel of his which is situated before the gate - Milik DFD 301: l. *q[dm]why* (= *qdm$_3$* + suff. 3 p.s.m.) in Syr xvii 353[10] (cf. also Gawlikowski TP 57) :: Cantineau Syr xvii 353f.: l. poss. *q[p]lwhy* (= Plur. + suff. 3 p.s.m. of *qpl$_2$* (= granary)) - Degen JEOL xxiii 419: l. *qdm* in Hatra 276 (improb. interpret., cf. Safar Sumer xxiv 28, Aggoula MUSJ xlvii 26, Abbadi PIH 194: l. *qym* = (part of) n.p.).
v. *yhb*, *mdm$_2$*, *mrzḥ*, *qrq$_1$*.

qdm$_4$ v. *qdm$_3$*.

qdmh$_1$ **Samal** Sing. + suff. 3 p.s.m. *qdmth* KAI 215[9] - **OffAr** Sing. abs. *qdmt* Cowl 38[10] (cf. Cowl a.l. :: Porten & Greenfield JEAS p. 82, Dion RB lxxxix 568: l. *qdmt[y]* (= Sing. + suff. 1 p.s., for this reading, cf. also Porten & Yardeni sub TADAE A 4.3)), ATNS 102a 2 (heavily dam. context); cstr. *qdmt* Cowl 30[17], Aḥiq 2; + suff. 3 p.s.m. *qdmth* Herm 2[15]; + suff. 2 p.s.m. *qdmtk* Aḥiq 101, SSI ii 28 rev. 4, Beh 54; + suff. 3 p.pl.m. *qdmthm* Cowl 71[3]; + suff. 3 p.pl.f. *qdmthn* Herm 1[9]; cf. Paik 899 (*qdmth*), MP 5, GIPP 62 - **JAr** Sing. cstr. *qdmt* MPAT 40[17], 52[4] - ¶ subst. - **1)** former state; *whyṭbh mn qdmth* KAI 215[9]: and he made it better than it was before (cf. e.g. Cooke NSI p. 174, 177, Donner KAI a.l. :: Rosenthal Forschung 78 n. 2: *qdmt-* functions as prep. 'before', *qdmth* = before him (i.e. before his time)) - a) used adverbially (*qdmt*): first; *šlḥ ʾgrt qdmt* Cowl 38[10]: send a letter first (dam. context, cf. also Leand 61i; v. supra :: Grelot VT xi 33: = immediately); cf. also ATNS 102a 2 (heavily dam. context) - **2)** used as preposition - a) with temp. meaning, before; *qdmt znh ... ʾgrt šlḥn* Cowl 30[17]: before that time we have sent a letter; *qdmt ml[w]hy [rb]h*

ʾḥyqr Aḥiq 2: before his words (i.e. before he spoke these words) A. was mighty (restoration of *rbh* uncert., cf. e.g. Baneth OLZ '14, 249 for the problems involved :: Montgomery OLZ '12, 535: *qdmt* used here as subst.: the beginning of ...); cf. poss. also Cowl 71^3 (dam. context), SSI ii 28 rev. 4 (dam. context) - b) with local meaning, before; *ʾl tqmy qdmth* Herm 2^{15}: do not stand before him, i.e. do not stand in his way (cf. e.g. Bresciani & Kamil Herm a.l., Milik Bibl xlviii 582, Grelot DAE p. 155, Porten & Greenfield JEAS p. 154, Gibson SSI ii p. 133, 135, Porten & Yardeni sub TADAE A 2.2 :: Kutscher IOS i 119: do not stand before him, i.e. do not serve upon him); for Herm 1^9, v. *lqḥ*; for Aḥiq 101, v. *qšh* - c) prec. by prep. *mn₅*, before (with temporal meaning); *mn qdmt dnh* MPAT 40^{17}: before this time (i.e. until this moment); *mn qdmt dnh* MPAT 52^4: formerly - *qdmtk* in Beh 54 of diff. interpret. (heavily dam. context; on this text, cf. also Greenfield & Porten BIDG p. 49) - in Nisa-b 1318^6 prob. l. *lqdmt* (= *l₅* + *qdmt*) = earlier (??, uncert. context).
v. *qdm₁*.

qdmh₂ **Pun** Plur. abs. *qdmt* KAI 69^{12}, 76A 3, 7 (in both instances in KAI 76 heavily dam. context) - ¶ subst. first-fruit.

qdmy **OffAr** Sing. m. emph. *qdmyʾ* Driv 7^1; Sing./Plur. m. emph. *qdmyʾ* AG 72 (uncert. reading, heavily dam. context); Plur. m. emph. *[qd]myʾ* Driv 7^8 - **Nab** Sing. f. emph. *qdmytʾ* CIS ii 158^5 (:: Cooke NSI p. 256f.: = Plur. f. emph.) - **Palm** Sing. m. abs. *qdmy* Ber ii 86^8; emph. *qdmyʾ* CIS ii 3913 i 9, Ber ii 84^1, 104^4; Plur. m. abs. *qdmyn* CIS ii 4171^2; emph. *qdmyʾ* CIS ii 3913 i 4; Sing. f. emph. *qdmtʾ* Syr xiv 177^5 (for the form, cf. Odeberg 230f., Dalman Grammatik 39,2), *qmytʾ* FS Miles $38^{1,2}$ - **JAr** Sing. f. emph. *qdmyth* MPAT-A 50^5 - ¶ adj. - **1)** with temp. meaning, preceding, first, earlier; *bzbnyʾ qdmyʾ* CIS ii 3913 i 4: in former times (cf. Greek par. ἐ[ν τ]οῖς πάλαι χρόνοις); *bgrmṭyʾ qdmtʾ* Syr xiv 177^5: during the first secretariat; *nmwsʾ qdmyʾ* CIS ii 3913 i 9: the former law (cf. Greek par. τοῦ πρώτου νόμου); *mḥrmtʾ qdmytʾ* CIS ii 158^5: the former sanctuary; *pqydʾ qdmyʾ* Driv 7^1: the former officer (cf. Driv $7^{7f.}$); *šth qdmyth* MPAT-A $50^{4f.}$: the first year - **2)** with local meaning, first; *qrqsʾ qdmyʾ* Ber ii 84^1: the first *qerqis*; *gwmḥʾ qdmyʾ* Ber ii $104^{3f.}$: the first niche (cf. CIS ii 4171^2, cf. also FS Miles $38^{1,1f.}$) - **3)** used adverbially, in the first place: Ber ii 86^8 - the same word (Sing./Plur. m. emph. *qdmyʾ*) poss. also in Hatra 238^1 (cf. Aggoula MUSJ xlvii 13, Degen JEOL xxiii 408, cf. however Vattioni IH a.l.: or = n.p.?).

qdns (< Greek κίνδυνος) - **Palm** Sing. abs. *qnds* SBS 45^9 - ¶ subst. danger; *mn qdns rb* SBS 45^9: out of great danger (cf. Greek par. ἐκ τοῦ ... μεγάλου κινδύνου).

qdr₁ **JAr** Sing. emph. *qdrh* MPAT 86 (or = Sing. m. emph. of *qdr₃* (=

dark, black?), cf. Fitzmyer & Harrington MPAT a.l.) - ¶ subst. potter or pot-seller (cf. Naveh IEJ xx 35, Beyer ATTM 345, 680, v. however supra :: Yadin with Naveh IEJ xx 35 n. 15: or = *qdr*$_2$ (= pot) used as a nickname).

qdr$_2$ **OffAr** Sing. abs. *qdr* Atlal vii 108 ii (diff. and heavily dam. context, cf. also Beyer & Livingstone ZDMG cxxxvii 292) - ¶ subst. pot (v. however supra).
v. *qdr*$_1$.

qdr$_3$ v.Soden Or xlvi 192, AHW s.v.: = darkened > Akkad. *qadduru* (highly uncert. interpret., cf. CAD s.v.: *qa-dur* prob. lapsus for *qa-lu*).
v. *qdr*$_1$.

qdš$_1$ **Ph** YIPH Pf. 3 p.s.m. *yqdš* KAI 42^4; 1 p.s. *yqdšt* KAI 43^{9,14} - **Pun** YIPH Pf. 3 p.s.m. *ʾyqdš* KAI 118^6 (uncert. reading), 121^2, 129^2, 138^6; HITP Pf. 3 p.s.m. *htqdš* KAI 138^1 - **Palm** PAʿEL Pf. 3 p.s.m. *qdš* Inv x 24^2, xii 23^3 (dam. context); Part. pass. s.m. abs. *mqdš* FS Miles 38^2; pl.m. abs. *mqdšyn* Ber v 124^3; APH Pf. 3 p.s.m. *ʾqdš* CIS ii 4162; 1 p.s. *ʾqdšt* Inv vii 2 (= CIS ii 4214; Greek par. ἀφιέρωσα) - **JAr** PAʿEL Part. pass. s.m. emph. *mqdšh* AMB 7^{11,16} - ¶ verb. PAʿEL to consecrate - a) + obj. (?) + *l*$_5$, *qdš mgdʾ lmdyth* Inv xii 23^3: he has consecrated a large gift (or: as a large gift) for his town; *bdyl dy qdš lh ḥdwdyn brh mn kysh l[...* Inv x 24$^{2f.}$: because he (sc. the uncle) has consecrated for him (sc. the father) his son Ch. to (god ...) at his own expense (cf. Greek par. ἱεράσαντα βήλῳ θεῷ ἐξ ἰδίων Αδδουδανην [υἱὸν αὐτοῦ]; for the interpret. of the text, cf. Seyrig Syr xxii 268) - b) Part. pass. - **1)** sacred; *bšmk ʾlh mqdšh* AMB 7^{11}: in Your name, sacred God (cf. AMB 7$^{15f.}$) - **2)** sanctified, sacred (said of a funerary niche in which a corpse has already been buried): Ber v 124^3, FS Miles 38^2 - YIPH/APH to consecrate; *bʾnʾ wʾyqdš* KAI 118^1: he has built and consecrated; *ḥydš wʾyqdš* KAI 138^6: he has renewed and consecrated; *btm pʿl wʾyqdš* KAI 121^2: at his own expense he made and consecrated (it; cf. Lat. par. *d(e) s(ua) p(ecunia) fac(iendum) coer(avit) idemq(ue) dedicavit*) - **1)** + obj., *lʾdn ... bnʾ wʾyqdš t ʿksndrʿ ...* KAI 129^2: he has built and consecrated the exedra to the lord ...; cf. *[qbr]ʾ dnh bnʾ wʾqdš ʾby[n]* CIS ii 4162: O. has built and consecrated this tomb (Greek par. Ὀβαιαν[ός ...] ... τὸ μνημεῖον ἔ[κτι]σεν καὶ ἀφιέρωσεν) - **2)** + obj. + *l*$_5$, *ytt wyqdšt ḥyt ... lʾdn ʾš ly lmlqrt* KAI 43^9: I have given and consecrated animals for my lord M.; cf. *[q]brʾ dnh dnbt wʾqdšt lbnyn wlbny bnyn* CIS ii 4214: I have completed (?, v. *dnb*) and consecrated this tomb for my children and grandchildren - **3)** + *l*$_5$, *wyqdšt lʾdn [ʾš ly]* KAI 43$^{14f.}$: I have consecrated to my lord - **4)** + *l*$_5$ + obj., *lʿnt ... bʿlšlm ... yqdš [ʾ]t m[z]bḥ* KAI 42$^{1,3f.}$: B. has consecrated the altar to A. (cf. Greek par. Ἀθηνᾷ ... Πραξίδημος ... τὸν βω[μὸ]ν ἀνέθ[ηκ]εν - HITP to be consecrated; *lbʿl ʾdr htqdš* KAI 138^1: consecrated to B. A. (cf.

e.g. Dussaud BAr '17, 165ff., Février Sem ii 26, Levi Della Vida RSO xxxix 309, Sznycer Sem xxx 37f., 41 :: Lidzbarski Eph iii 290, Röllig KAI a.l. (comb. with foll. n.p. *bʿlšylk*): B. has consecrated himself to B.A.).
v. *grš*$_1$.

qdš$_2$ **Ph** Sing. abs. *qdš* KAI 15, 16 (cf. e.g. Lipiński RSF ii 58, Gibson SSI iii p. 112f. :: Torrey JAOS xxiii 166, Röllig KAI a.l.: = Sing. m. abs. of *qdš*$_3$ :: e.g. Cooke NSI p. 401, 403: = n.l.), 17^1 (cf. e.g. Clermont-Ganneau CRAI '07, 606, Chabot sub RES 800, Röllig KAI a.l., Delcor CISFP i 780ff. :: e.g. Milik RB xlviii 572f., Gibson SSI iii p. 117, Teixidor Syr liii 315: = Sing. m. abs. of *qdš*$_3$); cstr. *qdš* KAI 14^{17} (cf. e.g. Lipiński RSF ii 58, Gibson SSI iii p. 109, 112f. :: e.g. Lagrange ERS 484, Röllig KAI a.l.: = Sing. m. abs. of *qdš*$_3$, cf. also Garbini AION xxvii 408, Elayi SCA 82 :: e.g. Cooke NSI p. 403 : = n.l.) - **Pun** Sing. abs. *qdš* CIS i 3779^6, KAI 277^1 (or in both instances = Sing. m. abs. of *qdš*$_3$?), BAr-NS vii 262f. l. 5; Plur. abs. *qdšm* KAI 145^2, CIS i 6000bis 4, 5 (= TPC 84; in both instances diff. and dam. context) - **Hebr** Sing. abs. *qdš* TA-H 104 (dam. context), BSh i p. 73 sub 4b, Hazor pl. ccclviiif 4, 5, IEJ xl 123 (in these prec. instances *qdš* = pottery mark, cf. also Barkay IEJ xl 126ff.; or = Sing. m. abs. of *qdš*$_3$?), Mas 449^3 (*qd[š]*), 451^3 (*qd[š]*), 452^4, 457; cstr. *qdš* RB lxxxviii 236 - **Palm** Plur. + suff. 3 p.s.m. *qdšwhy* Inv ix 1^5 (= Syr xiv 171) - **JAr** Sing. emph. *qwdšʾ* Mas 458, 460 (*[qw]dšʾ*) - ¶ subst. - **1)** sanctuary: CIS i 3779^6, KAI 277^1 (for both instances, v. however supra); *ʿštrt ʾš bgw hqdš* KAI 17^1: A. who is inside the sanctuary; *bšʿr hqdš* BAr-NS vii 262f. l. 4f.: in the gate of the sanctuary; *šr qdš ʿn ydll* KAI 14^{17}: the prince of the sanctuary of the *ydll*-spring (epithet of Eshmun, v. supra; v. also *šr*$_2$), cf. also *šr qdš* as epithet of Eshmun in KAI 15, 16 - **2)** sacred object; *qdš khnm* RB lxxxviii 236: sacred object belonging to the priests (cf. Lemaire RB lxxxviii 238f., BAR x 24ff., Avigad BiAr liii 160ff.); *ḥnk hyklʾ dy bl wyrḥbwl wʿglbwl ʾlhyʾ bqdšwhy* Inv ix 1$^{4f.}$: he dedicated the temple of B., Y. and A., the gods, with its sacred objects (cf. S. in RB xlv 312 :: Cantineau Syr xiv 172, sub Inv ix 1: *bqdšwhy* = with its shrines :: Dussaud with Cantineau Syr xiv 172: *bqdšwhy* = by his holy offerings (cf. Milik DFD 192, 199: by the holy meals offered by him) :: Drijvers SV 404: with its ceremonies (i.e. the ceremonies of the sanctuary in question) :: Gawlikowski TP 68: during their feast) - **3)** what is holy, hallowed; *lqwdšʾ* Mas 458 (inscription on jar): for hallowed things (cf. Yadin IEJ xv 84, 111, Yadin & Naveh Mas a.l.: *l* and *ʾ* in cursive script, rest in formal script; cf. Mas 460); *ṭhwr lqdš* Mas 456 (inscription on jar): clean for hallowed things (cf. Mas 457); *lṭhrt hqdš* Mas 452^4: for the purity of hallowed things; cf. also Mas 449$^{2f.}$ - the meaning of *qdšm* in KAI 145^2 uncert. diff. context, poss. = sacred

objects, cf. e.g. Cooke NSI p. 152f. (cf. also Février Sem vi 17, 20, Röllig KAI a.l., Sznycer Sem xxii 40) :: v.d.Branden RSF i 166f., Krahmalkov RSF iii 188, 190, 203: = shrines, sanctuaries (for the context, v. also *pḥnt*) - CIS i sub 3778: the *kd/rš* in KAI 78[5] poss. = *kdš*, variant of *qdš$_2$* (Sing. cstr.) = sanctuary, cf. also Harr 143, FR 39, Röllig KAI a.l., v.d.Branden GP p. 7 (uncert. interpret.) - du Mesnil du Buisson Syr xl 309f.: l. *ʾrwn* (= Sing. cstr. of *ʾrn$_1$*) *hqdš* (= *h$_1$* + Sing. abs. of *qdš$_2$*) in Syn 269 no. 2[2] (= SM 90), Hebrew in J.Ar. context (highly uncert. reading).
v. *qdš$_3$*, *qrbn*, *qrš$_2$*.

qdš$_3$ **Ph** Sing. m. abs. *qdš* KAI 27[18] (for the reading, cf. Cross & Saley BASOR cxcvii 45 (n. 14), Röllig NESE ii 19, 24, cf. also Caquot FS Gaster 48f., Gibson SSI iii p. 82, 87: l. *q[d]š*, for the reading of *d*, cf. already Torczyner JNES vi 24f., 29: l. *qdšy* (= Sing. + suff. 1 p.s. of *qdš$_2$* (improb. reading and interpret.)); for the interpret., cf. Caquot FS Gaster 48f., Röllig NESE ii 19, 24, cf. also Lipiński RTAT 265 × Cross & Saley BASOR cxcvii 45 (n. 14): = Sing. abs. of *qdš$_2$* (cf. however id. ibid. n. 21), cf. Zevit IEJ xxvii 112, 116, cf. also Gibson SSI iii p. 82f., 87: *q[d]š* = Sing. m. abs. of *qdš$_2$* or Sing. abs. of *qdš$_3$* :: v.d.Branden BO iii 43, 46: = Sing. cstr. of *qdš$_2$* :: du Mesnil du Buisson FS Dussaud 422, 424, 430, Dupont-Sommer RHR cxx 134f.: 143, 155f.: l.*qš* = n.d. (on the problem, cf. also Albright BASOR lxxvi 9 n. 29, Avishur PIB 254)); Plur. m. abs. *qdšm* KAI 4[5,7],14[9,22], *qdšn* KAI 27[12] (cf. Dupont-Sommer RHR cxx 134f., 140 (n. 3), Cross & Saley BASOR cxcvii 44f. (n. 10), Caquot FS Gaster 48, Röllig NESE ii 18, 22f., Garbini OA xx 283f., Gibson SSI iii p. 82f., 85, Segert GPP p. 111, cf. also Zevit IEJ xxvii 111f., Healy CISFP i 665 :: du Mesnil du Buisson FS Dussaud 422, 424, 427: *qdšn* = Sing. abs. of *qdšn* (holiness) :: Torczyner JNES vi 22, 28, Sperling HUCA liii 3, 7: *qdšn* = Plur. m. + suff. 1 p.pl. :: v.d.Branden BO iii 43, 45: = Plur. abs. of *qdš$_2$* :: Gaster Or xi 44, 59f.: poss. l. *qdšm* (= Plur. m. abs.), cf. also Avishur PIB 248, 252f. :: Albright BASOR lxxvi 8 n. 20: poss. l. *qdšt* (= Plur. f. abs.), cf. also Röllig KAI a.l.: l. *qdšm* or *qdšt*); Sing. f. abs. *qdšt* KAI 37A 7, Hill lxix 97 - **Pun** Sing. m. abs. *qdš* KAI 76B 2, 3 (cf. e.g. Cooke NSI p. 125f.; heavily dam. context in both instances), 104[1] (cf. e.g. Röllig KAI a.l. :: Cooke NSI p. 154: = Sing. abs. of *qdš$_2$*), 114[3], CIS i 172 (??, heavily dam. context), 4841[8] (cf. CIS i a.l. × Zevit IEJ xxvii 116 (n. 40): = Sing. abs. of *qdš$_2$*; v. also infra), Hofra 64[1], Punica xviii/ii 37 1 (for the reading, cf. Bertrandy & Sznycer sub SPC 104), xviii/iii 1[1f.] (cf. e.g. Chabot Punica a.l. :: Lidzbarski Handb 361: = Sing. abs. of *qdš$_2$*?), etc., *qydš* KAI 145[4] (on this form, cf. e.g. Krahmalkov RSF iii 191: */i/* in first syllable through vowel assimilation :: v.d.Branden RSF i 168: *-y-* = */u/* :: Berger MAIBL xxxvi/2: poss. = Sing. abs. of *qdš*2), Punica xii 10[1] (?, v. infra); Plur. m. abs. *qdšm* KAI 81[3] (:: v.d. Branden PO i 208: = Plur. abs. of *qdš*2); Sing. f. abs. *qdšt* KAI 76B 4 (or = Plur.?, dam. context), 161[3] (:: v. Selms FS v.d.Ploeg 264: = Plur. abs.), 162[3] (diff. context, cf. also Gruber UF xviii 147f.); Plur. f. abs. *qdšt* KAI 69[12], 74[9] - **Hebr** Sing. m. abs. *qdwš* Mas 672; Plur. m. abs. *qdwšym* IEJ vii 241[3]; Sing. f. abs. *qdšh* on coins of the first revolt, cf. Meshorer JC no. 148, id. Mas coin 1310, *qdwšh* ibid., cf. Meshorer JC no. 151, id. Mas coin 1320 - **OffAr** Plur. m. abs. *qdšn* Aḥiq 95 (cf. e.g. Baneth OLZ '14, 298, Ginsberg ANET 428 :: e.g. Cowl p. 223, Leand 43t': = Plur. abs. of *qdš*2 :: Grelot RB lxviii 182, DAE p. 436: l. *qdš*› = Sing. emph. of *qdš*2; on the subject, cf. Lindenberger APA 70, 233f. nn. 137-142, UF xiv 114ff.) - **Palm** Sing. m. emph. *qdyš*› JSS xxxiii 171 (*[q]dyš*›; dam. context); Plur. m. emph. *qdš*› CIS ii 4002[2], *qdyš*› CIS ii 4001[3] - **Waw** Sing. m. cstr. *qdyš* AMB 6[2] - **JAr** Sing. m. abs. *qdyš* AMB 3[23]; emph. *qdyš*› AMB 4[2], *qdyšh* MPAT-A 3[2] (*[qdy]šh*; = SM 60), 5[4] (*[q]dyšh*; = SM 64),[7], 13[3] (*[qdy]šh*; = SM 46), 30[2] (= SM 26), 34[2] (*qd[y]šh*; = SM 69), 35 (= SM 16), SM 84; Plur. m. emph. *qdyšy*› AMB 4[2], *qdyšyh* AMB 5[4], *qdšyh* AMB 7[4] (cf. Naveh & Shaked AMB a.l. :: Dupont-Sommer JKF i 203 (div. otherwise): l. *qdš* (= Sing. abs. of *qdš*2)); Sing. f. emph. *qdyšth* MPAT-A 13[1] (= SM 46) - ¶ adj. holy, passim - **1)** said of a deity - a) *h›lnm hqdšm* KAI 14[9,22]: the holy gods; *›l gbl qdšm* KAI 4[4f.,7]: the holy gods of Byblos; *l›dn l›ln ›qdš b‹lḥmn* KAI 104[1]: to the lord, to the holy god B.H. (for the reading *›qdš*, cf. e.g. Bertrandy & Sznycer sub SPC 29 :: Chabot sub Punica xviii/ii 31: l. *hqdš*); *bt skn b‹l ›qdš* CIS i 4841[6ff.]: the temple of S. the holy lord (v. however supra :: Milik Bibl xlviii 573 n. 4: = the Master of the Holy Ones): *l›lm hqydš* KAI 145[4]: to the holy god; *[l›]dn lb‹l hqdš* Hofra 64[1]: to the lord, to B. the holy one (cf. Punica xviii/iii 1[1f.]; cf. also KAI 27[18] (v. however supra)); *b‹l mn hqdš* Hofra 20[2f.]: B.H. the holy one (cf. prob. also *l›dn lb‹l ‹mn n›qydš* Punica xii 10[1]: to the lord, to B.H. the holy one; repetition of *n* prob. due to dittography, cf. Chabot Punica a.l.); cf. also the indication of the two anonymous gods in Palmyre, *trn ›[ḥy]› qdyš›* CIS ii 4001[3], *[trn ›ḥ]y› qdš›* CIS ii 4002[2]: the two holy brothers (cf. Cantineau Syr xii 135f., JA ccxxii 232f.; cf. the epithet of Ashtarte *mlkt qdšt* KAI 37A 7: the holy queen (cf. *mlk*3)) - b) substantivated adj., the holy one = god; *dr kl qdšn* KAI 27[12]: the community of all the gods (v. also supra), par. with *kl bn ›lm* = all the gods; *b‹l qdšn* Aḥiq 95: the lord of the gods (v. supra); cf. also *qdyš ›yl›* AMB 6[2]: the holy one of God (epithet of divine being); *ml›kyh qdšyh* AMB 5[4]: the holy angels - **2)** indicating human beings; *rby ›ny›nh w ... hqdwšym bnyw š[...* IEJ vii 241[2f.]: rabbi A. and ... the holy ones, the sons of ... (cf. Avigad IEJ vii a.l.), cf. also AMB 4[2], 6[2] - **3)** indicating cultic objects; *qdmt qdšt* KAI 69[12]: the holy first-fruits (cf. prob. KAI

74[9]) - **4)** indicating a place (and the people gathering there); *ʾtrh qdyšh* MPAT-A 5[7]: the holy place (i.e. the synagogue, cf. MPAT-A 3[2], 5[3f.], 13[2f.], 30[2], 35[1]); *qhlh qd[y]šh* MPAT-A 34[2]: the holy assembly (cf. SM 84[1]); *ḥbwrth qdyšth* MPAT-A 13[1]: the holy community - **5)** indicating a town; *lgbl qdšt* Hill lxix, 97: (coin) of holy Byblos; *yršlm qdšh* JC no. 148: holy Jerusalem (cf. JC no. 151); cf. also Sarfatti IEJ xxvii 204f. - **6)** said of an order given by God: AMB 3[23] - Milik DFD 195: l. *qdyš[ʾ]* (= Plur. m. emph.) in Syr xiv 279[2] (heavily dam. context, cf. Seyrig Syr xiv a.l.: l. *ydwš* without interpret.) - this word (Sing. m. abs. *qdš*) poss. also in AMB 3[13] (cf. however Naveh & Shaked AMB a.l.: = Sing. abs. of $qdš_2$ (= sanctity)).
v. $qdš_2$, $qrš_{1,2}$.

qdšn v. $qdš_3$.

qhy **Pun** Vattioni Aug xvi 551: a form of this root poss. in IRT 892[2]: *cavheni* (without further interpret.).

qhl₁ v. $qʾl_1$.

qhl₂ **JAr** Sing. emph. *qhlh* MPAT-A 34[2] (= SM 69), 40[1] (= SM 57) - ¶ subst. m. community: MPAT-A 40[1]; *kl qhlh qd[y]šh* MPAT-A 34[1f.]: the whole holy community (cf. poss. SM 84: *[qh]lh qdyšh*).
v. $ʾl_6$.

qwbh v. qwq_2.

qwbl v. qbl_3.

qwdm v. qdm_3.

qwdš v. $qdš_2$.

qwz v. qb_1.

qwy v. $qdḥ_1$.

qwl v. ql_1.

qwlwn (< Greek κόλων < Lat. *colonus*) - **Palm** Sing. abs. *qwlwn* CIS ii 4401[2] (cf. Greek par. κόλων) - ¶ subst. m. colonist, inhabitant of colonial town.

qwm₁ **Ph** Yiph Part. s.m. cstr. *mqm* KAI 44[2], Mus li 286[1] (v. infra) - **Pun** Qal Part. act. s.m. abs. *qʾm* Trip 51[3] (for this interpret., cf. Levi Della Vida Or xxxiii 10, 13 (cf. also Amadasi IPT 133): or = Qal Pf. 3 p.s.m.; diff. context, highly uncert. interpret.); Yiph Part. s.m. abs. *mqm* Trip 1 (v. infra); abs./cstr. *mqm* CIS i 227[4], 260[3], 261[4], 262[2], 377[4,5], 3351[5], 3352[6], 3788[4], 4863[5], 4864[5], 4865[6], 4866[3], 4867[5], 4868[4,5], 4869[6], 4870[5], 4871[3], 4872[4], 5979[1,2] (= TPC 41), 5980[1] (= TPC 42), 6000bis 2 (= TPC 84), KAI 70[3], 90[3] (= TPC 15), 93[4] (= TPC 12), *myqm* KAI 161[4] (for *mqm*, v. infra) - **Hebr** Qal Imper. s.m. *qm* KAI 198[1] (cf. e.g. Torczyner Lach i 159f., Hempel ZAW lvi 138, Michaud PA 90, Röllig KAI a.l., Lemaire IH i 130, cf. also Birnbaum PEQ '39, 107 (highly uncert. reading and interpret., cf. also Albright BASOR lxx 16: l. *ʾbw* = Qal Pf. 3 p.pl. of *ʾby* (= to want; cf. Kahle ZDMG xcii 274);

on the problem, cf. also Elliger ZDPV lxii 84f.) :: Gibson SSI i p. 48: l. *[h]qm* = HIPH Pf. 3 p.s.m.); HITP Impf. 3 p.s.m. *ytqym* EI xx 256^{10} - **DA** QAL Impf. 3 p.s.m. *yqm* i 5 - **Samal** QAL Pf. 3 p.s.m. *qm* KAI 214^{3,30} (:: Gibson SSI ii p. 76: = QAL Part. pass. :: Cook Maarav v/vi 65: = QAL Pf. 3 p. dual), 215^{2,6,8} (*[q]m*); 3 p.pl.m. *qmw* KAI 214^{2}; HAPH Pf. 3 p.s.m. *hqm* KAI 215^{18}; 1 p.s. *hqmt* KAI 214^{1,14} (*[h]qmt*); Impf. 3 p.s.m. *yqm* KAI 214^{28} - **OldAr** QAL Pf. 3 p.s.m. *qm* KAI 202A 3 - **OffAr** QAL Pf. 3 p.s.m. *qm* Cowl 22^{120}; 1 p.s. *qmt* MAI xiv/2, 66^{10}; 1 p.pl. *qmn* Krael 5^{13}; Impf. 3 p.s.m. *yqwm* Cowl 15^{26,29}, 42^{6} (*yqw[m]*), 46^{8}, Aḥiq 107, Krael 2^{7}, 5^{7}, 6^{16}, 7^{21,30} (*[y]qwm*), 8^{7}; 3 p.s.f. *tqwm* Cowl 15^{22}, *tqm* Krael 2^{9}; 2 p.s.m. *tqwm* Cowl 42^{7,13}, Aḥiq 101; 2 p.s.f. *tqmy* Herm 2^{15}; 1 p.s. *ʾqm* MAI xiv/2, 66^{10}; 3 p.pl.m. *yqmw* Cowl 50^{6}, *yqm[wn]* Cowl 61^{15} (?); Imper. s.m. *qwm* RES 1792A 6 (?, dam. context; for a poss. restoration of the context, cf. Grelot DAE p. 375 n. h), cf. Warka 18, 43: *qu-um*; s.f. *qwmy* JRAS '29, 108^{5}; pl.m. *qmw* Cowl 38^{6}; pl.f., cf. Warka 17, 42: *qu-ú-mi-ni*; Part. act. s.m. abs. *qym* ATNS 19^{2}, 20^{1}, 25^{3} (?, dam. and diff. contexts; Segal ATNS a.l.: = Sing. m. abs. of *qym$_2$*), NESE i 11^{7}, MAI xiv/2, 66^{13} (:: Grelot DAE p. 409 n. l: = QAL Part. pass. :: Bauer & Meissner SbPAW '36, 421: = Sing. abs. of *qym$_1$* (= pact)), RES 1785A 1; pl.m. abs. *qymn* RES 1785B 2, F 1 (or in both instances = pl.f. abs.?, dam. context), Cowl 30^{10} (for the reading, cf. e.g. Grelot DAE p. 409 n. l, Porten & Greenfield JEAS p. 90, Delsman TUAT i 255, Porten & Yardeni sub TADAE A 4.7 :: Nöldeke ZA xxi 199, Cowl a.l., Leand 39f, Lindenberger APA 267 n. 498: l. *qymw* = PA ʿEL Pf. 3 p.pl.m., cf. also Joüon MUSJ xviii 75ff. :: Sach p. 14: l. *qymw* = lapsus for *qysn* (= Plur. abs. of *qys* (= wood)), cf. also Barth ZA xxi 192: l. prob. *qysyn* = Plur. abs. of *qys* (= wood)); pl.f. abs. *qymn* Krael 3^{4}; PA ʿEL Pf. 3 p.s.f. *qymt* KAI 233^{9} (v. infra); HAPH/APH Pf. 3 p.s.m. *hqym* Aḥiq 12, *hqm* KAI 258^{1}; + suff. 1 p.s. *hqymny* Aḥiq 173 (cf. e.g. Cowl a.l. × e.g. Grelot RB lxviii 192, DAE p. 446, Lindenberger APA 176: = HAPH Imper. s.m. + suff. 1 p.s.; cf. also Kottsieper SAS 18, 156 (n. 195), 229); 2 p.s.m. *hqymt* Aḥiq 44, Cowl 64 xix 1 (cf. Greenfield & Porten BIDG 55); 1 p.s. *hqymt* Aḥiq 23; 3 p.pl.m. *hqymw* Samar 1^{5,11} (= EI xviii 8*), 3^{9}, 8^{5} (*hqym[w]*, heavily dam. context), 9^{6}; Impf. 1 p.s. + suff. 2 p.s.m. *ʾqmnk* RES 1792A 6; cf. Frah xx 3 (*ykʿymwn*), app. 19 (*qymwn*), Paik 411 (*hqʾym*, *hqʾymw*), 412 (*ykwymwn*), 900 (*qwmth*), 901 (*qym*), Nisa-b 587^{5} (*hqʾymt*), 884^{1} (*qʾymw*), cf. Lemosín AO ii 111, 267, Toll ZDMG-Suppl viii 28, 33, 36f., 39, GIPP 37, 52, 54, 62, SaSt 25 - **Nab** QAL Pf. 3 p.s.m. *qm* CIS ii 212^{5}; HAPH/APH Pf. 3 p.s.m. *hqym* CIS ii 161^{1}, 349^{2}, Atlal vii 109^{2,5} (in both instances *[h]qym*), *ʾqym* RB lxxiii 237^{3}; 3 p.pl.m. *hqymw* IEJ xxi 50^{2}, *ʾqymw* CIS ii 164^{1} - **Palm** QAL Pf. 3 p.s.m. *qm* CIS ii 3915^{2}, 3966^{5} (= RIP 156^{14}; reading *qwm* in Gawlikowski TP 91 prob. misprint), Syr xvii 353[4] (dam. context; *qm[*; cf. also Gawlikowski TP 57f., cf. however Milik DFD 301, 303: l. *qmḥ* (= Sing. abs. of *qmḥ*)), xix 75 i 4; 3 p.s.f. *qmt* Ber ii 107[9] (diff. context, v. infra); Part. act. s.m. abs. *qym* Inv ix 28[7,8] (= InscrP 31); s.f. abs. *qym*ʾ Syr xix 156[2], MUSJ xxxviii 106[6]; HAPH/APH Pf. 3 p.s.m. ʾ*qm* CIS ii 3927[3] (cf. Chabot sub CIS ii a.l. :: Milik DFD 3, Gawlikowski TP 51: l. ʾ*m[r]* = QAL Pf. 3 p.s.m. of ʾ*mr*$_1$ (= to permit, to grant)), ʾ*qym* CIS ii 3925[3], 3939[2], 3940[2], 3943[3], 3944[3], 3945[3], 3954[2], 3969[3] (or = Plur.?, dam. context), Ber xix 66[8] (Greek par. ἀνήγειρεν), etc.; 3 p.s.f. ʾ*qymt* CIS ii 3914[1], 3936[3], 3952[2], Inv x 90[2], 119[4], Inscr P 6[4], Syr xix 75 i 2, AAS xxxvi/xxxvii 165 no. 3[3]; 1 p.s. ʾ*qymt* CIS ii 3913 ii 76 (*[*ʾ*]qy[m]t*), 109 (cf. Greek par. εἵστημι); 3 p.pl.m. *hqymw* Syr xvii 351[12], ʾ*qymw* CIS ii 3924[3] (ʾ*qym[w]*), 3928[2], 3929[3], 3950[2], 3951[2], 3960[3], 3966[4] (= RIP 156[13]), Inv xi 100[2] (ʾ*qym[w]*), etc., ʾ*qym* CIS ii 3916[2], 3922[2], 3932[8], 3933[3], 3938[3], 3946[4], 3947[4], 3949[1], SBS 51[3], Inv xi 84[3]; Inf. abs. *mqmw* CIS ii 3956[4] (= Inv v 7) - **Hatra** QAL Impf. 3 p.s.f. *tqwm* 272[3] (cf. e.g. Safar Sumer xxiv 26 (n. 55) :: Degen JEOL xxiii 422: or = QAL Impf. 2 p.s.m.?; v. infra); APH Pf. 3 p.s.m. ʾ*qym* 20[2] (cf. e.g. Safar Sumer vii 180, Degen Or xxxvi 77 n. 1, ZDMG cxxi 125, Vattioni IH a.l. :: Donner sub KAI 242 (div. otherwise): l. *qym* = PAʿEL Pf. 3 p.s.m. (cf. also Altheim & Stiehl AAW ii 198)), 30[2], 65[3], 83[2], 112[4], 139[2], 140[4], 214[1] (cf. Degen WO v 223, cf. also Safar Sumer xxi 33; or = Plur.?), etc., etc., ʾ*yqym* (for this form type, cf. Altheim & Stiehl AAW ii 193f. :: Caquot Syr xxix 93: = lapsus for ʾ*qym*, cf. however idem GLECS ix 88, Syr xl 3), 5[2], 80[6], 229a 3 (Vattioni IH a.l.: ʾ*qym* (prob. misprint)); 3 p.s.f. ʾ*qy[mt]* 38[2] (cf. Milik DFD 337, Vattioni IH a.l. :: Safar Sumer viii 193f., Caquot Syr xxx 243: l. ʾ*qym[* = QAL Pf. 3 p.s.m.), ʾ*yqymt* 35[5]; 1 p.s. ʾ*qmt* 288a 7, ʾ*qymyt* 288c 2; 3 p.pl.m. ʾ*yqmw* 79[3] (:: Degen WO v 232: l. ʾ*yqymw* (prob. misprint)) - **JAr** QAL Pf. 3 p.s.f. *qmt* AMB 15[3] (dam. context); 3 p.pl.m. *qmw* Syn D A 5 (= SM 88), C$_2$ 4 (= SM 89b; for the reading, cf. Torrey Syn 268); Part. act. s.m. abs. *q*ʾ*m* MPAT 49 i 8, *qym* MPAT 40[9], 41[6] (cf. however Birnbaum JAOS lxxviii 16: = Sing. m. abs. of *qym*$_2$ (cf. also Milik DJD ii p. 112) or = QAL Part. pass. s.m. abs.), 45[2] (heavily dam. context), 47 recto 10, AMB 15[24]; s.m. emph. *qymh* AMB 9[5]; pl.m. abs. *qymy[n]* AMB 7[4] (for the reading, cf. Naveh & Shaked AMB p. 68, 74, Beyer ATTM 372 :: Dupont-Sommer JKF i 203: l. *qymy* = pl.m. cstr.); PAʿEL Inf. *qym*ʾ MPAT 45[4], 52[12], *mqymh* IEJ xxxvi 206[6] (for the form, cf. also Broshi & Qimron IEJ xxxvi 213); APH Pf. 3 p.s.m. ʾ*qym* AMB 9[6] - **Waw** QAL Part. act. pl.m. abs. *qymyn* AMB 6[3]; APH Imper. s.m. ʾ*qym* AMB 6[8,12f.] (cf. Dupont-Sommer Waw p. 20, highly uncert. interpret., cf. Gordon Or xviii 340f.: = APH Impf. 1 p.s. as part of n.d., Naveh & Shaked AMB a.l.: prob. = form of APH used as part of n.d. or = ʾ$_{12}$ (var. of h_5 = hʾ$_2$) + *qym* = QAL Part. act.

s.m. abs., used as part of n.d.) - ¶ verb QAL - **1)** to rise, to stand up: Warka 17, 18, 42, 43; *wyqm bl‘m mn mḥr* DA i 5: and B. stood up the next morning (cf. also Weinfeld Shn v/vi 141f.) - a) used to introduce a certain action - α) action described by *w* + finite verbal form, *wq[m] ’by whrpy nšy* KAI 215^{8}: and my father arose and released the women ...; *nqwm wnpṣl wnntn* Krael 3^{20}: we will stand up, clear the claim (v. *pṣl*) and give ...; *bdyl dy qm w‘drnn bkl ṣbw* Syr xix 75 i 4: because he arose and helped them in everything; *wtqm tmt wt’mr* Krael 2^{9}: T. will stand up and say (cf. Krael 2^{7}, MAI xiv/2, 86$^{10f.}$, CIS ii 3966^{5} (= RIP 156^{14})); for CIS ii 3924^{5} (= Inv ix 6a), cf. Gawlikowski Syr lx 63 n. 57; for Inv x 96, Syr xix 75 i 4, cf. Gawlikowski Syr lx 65 n. 71 - β) action represented by l_5 + Inf., *zy yqwm ltrk[wth]* Cowl 46^{8}: whoever shall arise to drive her away (cf. Krael 7^{30}; for the context, cf. Yaron JSS v 67f., Law 73f.) - b) + *‘l_7*, *zy yqwm ‘lyky ... yntn lk* Krael 5$^{7f.}$: whoever shall arise against you ... will have to give to you ... - c) + *‘l_7* + l_5 + Inf., *yqwm ‘l mptḥyh ltrkwth* Cowl 15$^{29f.}$: he will arise against M. to drive her away (for the context, cf. Yaron JSS v 66ff., Law 73f., Fitzmyer FS Albright ii 164f., Porten & Yardeni sub TADAE B 2.6; cf. Krael 6^{16}, 8^{7}) - d) + *qdmt*, *’l tqmy qdmth* Herm 2^{15}: do not stand up before him (i.e. do not stand in his way :: Kutscher IOS i 119: don't you (yourself) wait upon him) - **2)** to be standing, to be fixed; *’grwh qymn* Krael 3^{4}: his walls are standing (i.e. are in good repair, cf. Milik RB lxi 249; cf. also Hatra 272^{3}, v. supra, on this text, cf. also Degen JEOL xxiii 417, Aggoula MUSJ xlvii 23f., Safar Sumer xxix 89*); *wqm ‘yny* KAI 214^{30}: my eyes are fixed (cf. Dion p. 276f.); *yhy qym wmšlm* MPAT 40$^{9f.}$: let it be determined and paid (cf. MPAT 41^{6}, 47 recto 10 (dam. context)); cf. *qmt šnt 590* (for this reading, cf. Cantineau with Ingholt Ber iii 127) *byrḥ sywn* Ber ii 107$^{9ff.}$ (remark concluding text about the conveyance of part of tomb): it is agreed in the year 590 in the month S. (cf. Ingholt Ber ii 108 :: Milik DFD 301f.: pro *qmt* l. *q[y]mt* = PU‘AL Pf. 3 p.s.f. (= to be made valid)) - **3)** to stay; Aḥiq 101 (for the context, cf. Grelot RB lxviii 183, DAE p. 437, cf. however Lindenberger APA 81f.) - a) preceded by *’l_3* = to delay; *zy ’grt’ z’ [t]mṭ’ ‘lyk ’l tqwm ḥt mnpy l‘bq* Cowl 42$^{6f.}$: when this letter reaches you, do not delay, come down to M. at once (cf. Cowl 42^{13}; cf. also Dion RB lxxxix 562f.) - b) + *b_2* - α) with loc. meaning, *yqmw b’wṣr’* Cowl 50^{6}: they are in the Treasury (heavily dam. context); *hlyn tlt’ qymyn bm‘brt’* AMB 6$^{3f.}$: these three are standing in the ford (for this reading, cf. Naveh & Shaked AMB p. 62f., 66; for the context, v. *znh*, *m‘brh*); cf. also *qm bršhwn* CIS ii 3915$^{2f.}$: he was leading them - β) indicating equivalence, *wqm prs bšql* KAI 215^{6}: half a mina (v. *prs$_2$*) stood at a shekel - c) + *byd*, *ksp’ zy qm ywm’ hw byd ydnyh* Cowl 22$^{120f.}$: the silver which on that day was in the hand (i.e. in the possession) of Y. (cf. e.g Naveh & Shaked JAOS xci 381, Degen NESE i 19, Porten & Greenfield JEAS p. 147 :: Macuch JAOS xciii 60: the money which was collected that day is in the hand of Y.); the same comb. poss. in NESE i 11[7], v. however *yd* - d) + *btr*, *qym› btr gwmḥyn tlt› dy* ... MUSJ xxxviii 106[6f.]: standing beyond the three niches of ... - e) + *lqbl*, *nyq› dy qym› lqblh* Syr xix 156[2]: the *Nikè* which is situated before it - f) + *ʿl*$_7$, *wqm ʿl w›lt wbnyh dy* ... CIS ii 212[5]: it is incumbent upon W. and her sons, that ...; *dhw› qym ʿl ṭly›* Inscr. P 31[7f.] (= Inv ix 28): who is set over the servants (v. *ṭly*$_1$; cf. Inscr. P 31[8f.]); *dqmw ʿl ʿybyth* Syn D A 5f. (= SM 88): who are set over the work (cf. Syn D C$_2$ 4 (= SM 89b); for the reading of the context, cf. *ʿybydh*); *whbh lh bksp› zy yqw[m] ʿlwhy* Cowl 42[6]: give it to him for the silver which stands upon it (i.e. the price at which it is valued) - g) + *ʿm*$_4$ (cf. Tawil Or xliii 43ff.), *qmw ʿmy ›lhw* KAI 214[2]: the gods stood with me (cf. KAI 202A 3 (cf. Ross HThR lxiii 9f. (n. 32), Greenfield Proc v CJS i 176f., 183, FS Fitzmyer 50), 214[3], JRAS '29, 108[5f.]) - h) + *qbl*$_3$, *›ntm qmw qblhm* Cowl 38[6]: you, stand before them (i.e. be at their disposal) - i) + *qdm*$_3$ - α) used to indicate subservience, *ḥkym› qym qdm byl w›lhyn* RES 1785A 1f.: the wise one stands before B. and the gods (i.e. acts according to their will); *ml›kyh qdšyh dqymy[n] qdm krsyh d›lh rbh* AMB 7[4f.]: the holy angels who stand before the throne of the great God (for the reading, v. supra) - β) to stand firm in the presence of ...; *mn hw zy yqwm qdmwhy lhn zy ›l ʿmh* Aḥiq 107: who is he that can stand before him (sc. the king), except the one with whom God is (v. *›l*$_1$; cf. also Greenficld FS Fitzmyer 51) - j) Part. act. - α) existing, real; *ḥyh wqymh* AMB 9[5]: the One who lives and exists (i.e. God); *›l* (prob. reading) *qym* AMB 15[24]: the "existing" God - β) standing, i.e. in good order; *tql ›bd wt[q]l qym* MAI xiv/2, 66[13]: a worn shekel and a shekel in good state (cf. Dupont-Sommer MAI xiv/2, 81ff., Grelot DAE p. 74 (n. n) :: Couroyer RB lxxx 467: an invalid shekel and a current one :: Porten & Yardeni sub TADAE B 1.1: a lost (= forfeit) shekel and a lasting (= returnable) shekel; :: Teixidor JAOS cv 734: the *qym* in ATNS 19[2] poss. same meaning: in good condition, valid) - PAʿEL to confirm - **1)** + obj. + *qdm*$_3$, *lmrq› wlqym› zbnh dk qdm[kn]* MPAT 52[12]: to clear and to confirm this purchase for you (cf. MPAT 45[4]; cf. also IEJ xxxvi 206[6]; on the expression, cf. also Milik Bibl xxxviii 263, Yaron BASOR cl 27, J.J.Rabinowitz Bibl xxxix 487) - **2)** + *qdm*$_3$, *ydyhm ktbt wqymt qdmy* KAI 233[9]: their hands have written it and confirmed it in my presence (uncert. interpret., v. *ktb*$_1$; cf. Lidzbarski AUA p. 11, R.A.Bowman UMS xx 277, 280, Dupont-Sommer Syr xxiv 33, 40, Donner KAI a.l., Gibson SSI ii p. 105) - HAPH/APH (for YIPH in Ph./Pun., v. infra) - **1)** to place, to erect; *[dnh m]sgd› dy hqym [h]n›w* CIS ii 161[1f.]: this is the stele (v. *msgd*) that H. erected; *ṣlm›* *dnh dy nsʾ .. dy ʾqym lh bny šyrtʾ* CIS ii 3916[1f.]: this statue is that of N. ... which the members of the caravan erected for him - a) + obj. (inanimate), *[h]qmt nṣb hdd* KAI 214[14]: I have erected the statue of Hadad (v. *nṣb*$_3$; cf. CIS ii 3914[4], Hatra 80[6], 288c 2f.); *ʾqym ʿltʾ* FS Dussaud 885[4]: he has erected the altar; *ʾqym ʾrʿh* AMB 9[6]: He has set up the earth - b) + obj. + *b*$_2$ - α) *b*$_2$ with local meaning, *wyqm wth bmʾh* ... KAI 214[28]: and let him place him with hundred ... (?, diff. context, v. *mʾh*$_2$, *mt*$_6$) - β) *b*$_2$ with circumstantial meaning, *hqymny ʾl bṣdyq* ... Aḥiq 173: set me up, o God, as a righteous man ... (v. supra, v. also *ʾl*$_1$) - c) + obj. + *byn*$_2$, *ʾsrʾ hqymw bynyhm* Samar 1[11]: they established a covenant between them (cf. also Samar 1[5] (dam. context), 3[3] (dam. context)) - d) + obj. + *l*$_5$: Syr xvii 268[1ff.], SOLDV ii 514[2f.], DFD 163[5], Hatra 20[1f.] (statues), CIS ii 3927[4] (dedicated objects, v. *mḥrmh*); *ʾqmt prkʾ lgdʾ* Hatra 288a 7f.: I have erected the altar for Fortuna - e) + obj. + *ʿm*$_4$, *ʾqymnk ʿm[*... RES 1792A 6: I will place you with ... (?, dam. context, cf. also Grelot DAE p. 375) - f) + obj. + *qdm*$_3$: KAI 258[1f.] (statue), Atlal vii 109[5] (throne) - g) + *b*$_2$, *whqymt bbb hyklʾ* Aḥiq 23: I set (sc. him) in the gate of the palace (i.e. I gave him an official function; cf. Aḥiq 44) - h) + *byny* (between): Syr xvii 351[12] (dam. context) - i) + *l*$_5$ - α) *l*$_5$ used as *l*-comm.: RB lxxiii 237[3f.], CIS ii 164[1], 349[2], 3916[2], 3922[2f.], 3925[3], SBS 51[3], Hatra 5[2], 35[5], 193[3], 223[3] (statues), IEJ xxi 50[2] (tomb), Hatra 63[3,5] (standard), etc., etc.; cf. also *ṣlmʾ ... dʾqym lh dkrnh rpšʾ* Hatra 83[1ff.]: the statue ... which R. has erected for him as his memorial - β) *l*$_5$ used to indicate result of action, *hqym lbrh* Aḥiq 12: he set up as his son (i. e. he adopted him, cf. Cowl a.l., cf. however Grelot DAE p. 433: he brought his son ...) - j) + *l*$_5$ + obj.: Syr xiv 175[3], Inscr P 6[4f.] (statue) - k) + *l*$_5$ + obj. + *b*$_2$, *whqm lh mšky bʾrḥ* KAI 215[18]: he erected for him a decorated stone (v. *mšky*) by the way - l) + *ʿl*$_7$ (on) + obj.: CIS ii 3956[4f.] (statue) - **2)** to decide; *ʾqymt dy yhwʾ mtg[b]ʾ dnr* CIS ii 3913 ii 109f.: I have ordained that a *denarius* shall be levied (cf. Greek par. δην[άριον] εἴστημι πράσσεσθαι) - YIPH to erect; Part. one who raises, only in the comb. *mqm ʾlm/myqm ʾlm* (the one who raises the god), indicating religious function/title, cf. Harr 142, Sznycer Sem xxix 49f. and litt. mentioned below :: Chabot sub RES 13: *mqm* (= YOPH Part. s.m. cstr.) *ʾlm* = the one who is in charge of the sacred objects? :: Février JA ccxxx 296f.: *mqm* (= YOPH Part. s.m. cstr.) *ʾlm* = the one in charge of the god :: Heltzer AION xxv 293ff.: *mqm ʾlm* = imposed by the gods (improb. interpret., cf. Garbini AION xxvi 223f.) :: Mayer-Lambert JA ix/x 488: *mqm ʾlm* = the one who raises the gods, i.e. manufacturer of idols :: Honeyman Mus li 288, RHR cxxi 6f.: *mqm ʾlm* = establisher of gods, i.e. ordainer of things religious (cf. also Röllig FS Friedrich 412f. n. 7, sub KAI 44) :: Slouschz TPI p. 150: = whose place is with the gods (indication of a priest) :: (Rössler with) Roschinski Num 112, 114: the one who is placed with the gods, honorary title, *mqm/myqm* = YIPH Part. pass.; :: Berger RHR lxv 12: *mqm* ʾ*lm* poss. = *antistes*, title used in Mithras cult; poss. meaning: 'the one who revives the god', cf. e.g. Clermont-Ganneau RAO viii 164 (: the sacred reviver), de Vaux BMB v 17ff., Février JA ccliii 12, cclvi 5, Ferron StudMagr i 70, 78, Lipiński RAI xvii 32ff., Gibson SSI iii p. 145f. (for the problems, cf. also Amadasi ICO p. 183f.); cf. also the combinations - α) *mqm* ʾ*lm mlt* CIS i 5980 (= TPC 42), poss. = the one who raises the god Melqart, cf. Clermont-Ganneau RAO viii 164, Uffenheimer Lesh xxx 169, Lipiński RAI xvii 32 (n. 6), Ferron CT xix/3-4, 225f., Delcor RSF ii 65f., cf. however Berger RHR lxv 13, Lidzbarski Eph iii 286, Ferron Mus li 530: *mlt* = name of female deity (cf. also Février sub CIS i 5980: *mlt* = name of god or goddess) - β) *mqm* ʾ*lm mtrḥ* ʿ*štrny*, v. *mtrḥ* - γ) *mqm* ʾ*lm bš*ʾ*rm*, v. *bšr*$_2$; on the title *mqm* ʾ*lm*, cf. also Seyrig Syr xl 23 (n. 28), Teixidor Syr xlvi 320, lii 269 - the diff. *hmqm* ʿ*lm* in Trip 1 poss. = variant of the title *mqm* ʾ*lm*, cf. Berger RA ii 41f., Levi Della Vida Lib iii/ii 2f., Lipiński RAI xvii 37, 57, cf. however Levi Della Vida AttiTor '67, 395f.: *mqm* = Sing. abs. of *mqm*$_1$ (= (holy) place) + ʿ*l*$_7$ + *m*...; cf. Vattioni RB lxxviii 243: *hmqm* ʿ*lm* = place of eternity (indication of tomb; cf. also H.P.Müller WO ix 88 n. 48), on this text, cf. also Hoftijzer DA p. 224 n. 113: *mqm* prob. = *mqm*$_1$ - HITP the meaning of the HITP form in EI xx 256[10] highly uncert. (cf. Broshi & Qimron EI xx 259) - Lipiński Stud 43: l. a form of this root in KAI 222B 39 (*yqm* = QAL Impf. 3 p.s.m.), cf. however Lemaire & Durand IAS 115, 125, 139f.: l. *tqm* (= QAL Impf. 2 p.s.m.), uncert. reading - Segal ATNS a.l.: l. *qmn* in ATNS 28b 5 (= QAL Pf. 1 p.pl.), improb. reading, cf. Porten & Yardeni sub TADAE B 8.4: l. *d/rmn*, without interpret. - Segal ATNS a.l.: l. *qm* in ATNS 23b 2 (= QAL Pf. 3 p.s.m.) = to be standing or to be valid (context dam. and uncert.) - a form of this root poss. in ATNS 65b 6 (*qymn* = QAL Part. act. m. pl. abs., but reading uncert.; Segal ATNS a.l.: = Plur. m. abs. of *qym*$_2$) - a form of this root (*qym[*) in ATNS 75b 2, Segal ATNS a.l.: = form of *qym*$_2$ - Milik DFD 13f.: l. ʾ*qmw* = APH Inf. in DFD 13[17] (uncert. reading, heavily dam. context) - Milik DFD 75: l. *[*ʾ*]qym* (= APH Pf. 3 p.s.m./pl.m.) in Inv xi 85[1] :: Teixidor Inv xi a.l.: l. *[mt]qrh* (= ITP Part. s.m. abs. of *qr*ʾ$_1$) - a form of this root also in RIP 47[2]: *]*ʾ*qm[*?? - the *qymh* in Syn D B 7 (= SM 88[22]; for the reading, cf. already Torrey Syn p. 266 :: Obermann Ber vii 115: l. *qwl[h]* = Sing. emph. of *ql*$_1$) poss. = QAL Part. act. s.m. emph./s.f. abs. (cf. also Naveh SM a.l.).

v. ʾ*lp*$_3$, ʾ*mr*$_1$, *hwy*$_1$, *ywm*, *sm*ʾ, *qdm*$_{1,2}$, *qym*$_2$, *qr*ʾ$_1$, *tqm*$_{1,2}$.

qwm$_2$ **Nab** word of uncert. meaning in BSOAS xv 11,21b; n.p.?? Littmann BSOAS xv a.l.: = subst. < Arab. (Sing. abs.) = subsistance (highly uncert. interpret.).

qwmh **OffAr** Sing. emph. *qwmt*ʾ Cowl 26[11] - ¶ subst. of uncert. meaning, prob. indicating part of a boat: mast? (cf. Cowl a.l., Grelot DAE p. 290 (n. b), cf. however Holma Öfversigt af Finska Vetenskaps-Societetens Förhandlingar '15, B no. 5, 10f.), cf. however Porten & Yardeni sub TADAE A 6.2: or l. *qdmt*ʾ??

qwms (< Lat. *comes*) - **JAr** Sing. abs. *qwms* MPAT-A 26[4] (= SM 32) - subst. *comes*, count.

qws v. *qs*.

qwʿṭrbr (< Lat. *quattuorvir*, cf. Février RevEtAnc lv 359, Friedrich Or xxiv 157f.) - **Pun** Sing. abs. *qwʿṭrbr* KAI 125 - ¶ subst. *quattuorvir*: KAI 125 (Lat. par. *iiii-v[ir]*).

qwp$_1$ **OffAr** Sing. abs. *qwp* Krael 7[17] (:: Reider JQR xliv 340: = Sing. abs. of *qwp*$_2$ (= circle, sc. of ivory chips, worn as an ornament); v. *ḥṣ*$_4$; cf. however Porten & Yardeni sub TADAE B 3.8: l. *qpp* = Sing. abs. of *qpp* (= chest?)); cf. Frah-S$_1$ 8 (*kwp*ʾ) - ¶ subst. chest, large basket (cf. Krael a.l., Grelot RB lxxviii 526, DAE p. 235 (n. r)); *qwp 1 zy ḥwṣn tḥt lbšyh* Krael 7[17]: a chest of Palm. leaves under (i.e. in the context: for) her cloths; derivation from Akkad. *quppu* (cf. Zimmern Fremdw 34; on this word, cf. also Salonen Hausgeräte i 203f.) less prob., cf. Grelot RB lxxviii 526, Kaufman AIA 86f. (n. 283).
v. *tb*.

qwp$_2$ v. *qwp*$_1$.

qwph v. *qwpwt*.

qwpwt **JAr** the *qwpwt* in AMB 7[9] = part of magical name, cf. Scholem JGM 86, Naveh & Shaked AMB a.l. :: Dupont-Sommer JKF i 207: = Plur. abs. of *qwph* (= Hebr. word in Aramaic context) of unknown meaning.

qwpy v. *qp*$_2$.

qwq$_1$ v. *qqbtn*.

qwq$_2$ **JAr** Sing. emph. *qwq*ʾ MPAT 141[1] (Palm. script; for the reading, cf. Abel RB xxii 271, Fitzmyer & Harrington MPAT a.l. :: Frey sub 1222: l. *qyq*ʾ :: Milik DFD 271: l. *qwbt[*ʾ*]* = Sing. emph. of *qwbh* (= *qbh*$_2$)) - ¶ subst. ossuary (cf. RES sub 1779).

qwqm **OffAr**, cf. Frah xvi 11 (*kwkm*ʾ) = cauldron, cf. Nyberg FP 48, 87 :: Ebeling Frah a.l.: l. *qnqm*ʾ = form of *qnqm* (= cauldron (cf. Ar. *qmqm*)); cf. Cohen FS Bakoš 80.

qwrh **JAr** Sing. abs. *qwrh* IEJ xxxvi 206[2] - ¶ subst. of uncert. meaning in the comb. *byt qwrh* (reading *qyrh* also poss.); = beam?, Broshi & Qimron IEJ xxxvi 208: = oil-press beam?, *byt qwrh* = beam-house??

qwrys v. *qyrys*.

qḥk **DA** Qal Impf. 3 p.s.m. *yqḥk* i 13 (cf. Hoftijzer DA a.l., Caquot & Lemaire Syr liv 200, McCarter BASOR ccxxxix 51, 56, Levine JAOS ci 197, 199, H. & M.Weippert ZDPV xcviii 98, 103, Hackett BTDA 29, 51, 91, 133, Sasson UF xvii 288, 302 (n. 41) :: Rofé SB 67: l. *yqḥn* = NIPH Impf. 3 p.pl.m. of *lqḥ* :: Naveh IEJ xxxix 135: or *yqḥk* = QAL Impf. 3 p.s./pl.m. + suff. 2 p.s.m. of *lqḥ*, cf. also Puech FS Grelot 23f. (n. 48), 28, Weinfeld Shn v/vi 146; for a derivation from root *lqḥ*, cf. also Greenfield JSS xxv 250 :: Lemaire CRAI '85, 280: l. poss. *rqḥn* = QAL Part. act. pl.m. abs. of *rqḥ*$_1$) - ¶ verb QAL to laugh, + *l*$_5$ (at); for this root, cf. Greenfield JAOS lxxxii 290ff.

qḥm v. *qmḥ*.

qḥqḥ **OldAr** Dupont-Sommer Sf p. 62, 86, 149: l. *yqḥqḥ* in KAI 222B 45: = PALPEL Impf. 3 p.s.m. of *qḥqḥ* (= to laugh); uncert. reading × Fitzmyer AIS 18, 73 (div. otherwise): l. *yqrq* = QAL Impf. 3 p.s.m. of *qrq*$_1$ (cf. Lipiński Stud 52); on the reading problems, cf. also Degen AAG p. 16 (n. 68), GGA '79, 32.

qṭ **OffAr** Sing. abs. *qṭ* Sem ii 31 conc. 6; Plur. abs. *qṭyn* KAI 270B 6 (cf. Levine JAOS lxxxiv 19f., cf. also Porten Arch 275, Silverman JAOS xciv 272 :: e.g. CIS ii sub 137, Cooke NSI p. 203, Donner KAI a.l., Grelot DAE p. 138 (n. i): *qṭyn* = Sing. abs. of *qṭyn*$_2$ (= small, little), cf. Gibson SSI ii p. 124f. :: Dupont-Sommer ASAE xlviii 120, 127f.: = Plur. abs. of *qṭy*$_2$ (= cucumber)) - ¶ subst. of uncert. meaning; poss. = coin, cf. Levine JAOS lxxxiv 20 (cf. also Rosenthal AH i/2, 14, Grelot DAE p. 370 (n. j)); Grelot DAE ibid.: to be connected to the name of Egyptian coin *qd/t* :: Dupont-Sommer Sem ii 32, 36f.: = fine thread? :: Sanmartín UF xi 727 (n. 54): = linen?; *ḥt hmw bqṭ* Sem ii 31 conc. 6: pay them in coin (i.e. cash); *lʾ šʾr qṭyn* KAI 270B 4ff.: there are no coins left - the same word (Sing. emph.) in Cowl 42^{9}?? (*qṭʾ*) - on this word, cf. also Teixidor Syr xliv 178.
v.*ktb*$_1$.

qṭʾ v. *qṭ*.

qṭṭ v. *kdd*$_2$.

qṭy$_1$ > Akkad. *qaṭû* = to approach, cf. v.Soden Or xlvi 192 (cf. also CAD s.v. *qaṭû* v.).

qṭy$_2$ **OffAr** Plur. abs. *qṭyn* RES 493^{2} (for the reading, cf. RES 1801, Cowley PSBA xxxvii 221, Dupont-Sommer ASAE xlviii 128 :: Segal sub ATNS 19: poss. *qṭyn* = variant form of *ktn*$_1$ (= flax)) - ¶ subst. cucumber.
v. *qṭ*.

qṭyn$_1$ v. *qṭy*$_2$.

qṭyn$_2$ v. *qṭ*.

qṭyr$_1$ **Hatra** Sing. emph. *qṭyrʾ* 79^{13} (cf. e.g. Caquot Syr xl 5f., GLECS ix 88, Teixidor Syr xli 280, Altheim & Stiehl AAW iv 243, 248f., Vattioni IH a.l., cf. already Safar Sumer xvii 15 n. 28 :: Safar Sumer xvii 17 n. 39: *qṭyrʾ* = Sing. emph. of *qṭyr*$_2$ (= agreement)) - ¶ subst. oppression, violence; *l› ldbrhn ... bqṭyr›* Hatra 79[12f.]: may he not bring them under oppression.

qṭyr₂ v. *qṭyr₁*.

qṭl₁ (on the root (orig. *qtl*), cf. Moscati CGSL p. 56, Garr DGSP 72 n. 168 :: Segert AAG p. 108: orig. *qṭl*; for the different representations, cf. - a) for *qtl*, e.g. Friedr 10*b, Segert ArchOr xxxii 120, Dion p. 111ff. - b) for *kṭl*, e.g. Garb 271, Claassen AION xxi 296f., Kutscher IOS i 108 (n. 25), Kaufman AIA p. 121f.; cf. however also Greenfield Lesh xxxii 362 n. 20) - **Samal** QAL Part. pass. pl.f. abs. *qtylt* KAI 215[8] (dam. context) - **OldAr** QAL Impf. 3 p.s.m. *yqtl* KAI 223B 8f. (*[y]qtl*), 9, 224[18]; + suff. 3 p.s.m. *yqtlnh* KAI 222B 27; 3 p.pl.m. *yqtln* KAI 224[11]; Imper. s.m. *qtl* KAI 224[18]; pl.m. *qtlw* KAI 224[21] - **OffAr** QAL Pf. 3 p.s.m. *qṭl* TADAE A 5.5[3] (= RES 248B; dam. context), Beh 9 (Akkad. par. *id-du-ku*), Sem xiv 72 conv. 2 (?; *]qṭl*; to be divided otherwise?); 2 p.s.m. *[q]ṭlt* Cowl 71[13]; + suff. 3 p.s.m. *qṭl[thy]* Cowl 71[20]; 1 p.s. *[q]ṭlt* Beh 13 (Akkad. par. *[ni]-du-uk*); + suff. 3 p.s.m. *qṭlth* Aḥiq 49; + suff. 2 p.s.m. *qṭltk* Aḥiq 51; 3 p.pl.m. *qṭlw* Beh 3 (Akkad. par. *id-du-ku*), 5 (*[q]ṭlw*; Akkad. par. *id-du-ku*), 29 (*[q]ṭlw*; Akkad. par. *id-du-ku*), 33, 44, 48; Impf. 3 p.s.m. *yqṭl* Cowl 71[6]; 2 p.s.m. + suff. 1 p.s. *tqṭlny* Aḥiq 52; 3 p.pl.m. + suff. 2 p.s.m. *ykṭlwk* KAI 225[11]; Imper. s.m. *[q]ṭl* Beh 18 (Akkad. par. *du-[ú-]ku*); pl.m. *qṭlw* Beh 40 (Akkad. par. *du-ka-›*); Inf. *mqṭl* TADAE A 5.5[3] (= RES 248A; dam. context); Part. act. pl.m. abs. *qṭln* KAI 279[4] (cf. Dupont-Sommer JA ccxlvi 26, Garbini Kand 10 × Altheim & Stiehl EW ix 194: = QAL Pf. 3 p.pl.m.; cf. also Altheim & Stiehl GH i 401, ASA 275, Donner KAI a.l., Kutscher, Naveh & Shaked Lesh xxxiv 133, Coxon JNES xxxvi 297; :: Rosenthal EI xiv 97*f.: = QAL Inf. + Iran. inf. ending *-n*); QAL pass. Pf. 3 p.s.m. *qṭyl* Aḥiq 71; 3 p.pl.m. *qṭylw* Cowl 30[17], 31[16]; Part. pass. pl.m. emph. *qṭyly›* Beh 35; ITP Impf. 3 p.s.m. *ytqṭl* Aḥiq 62; cf. Frah xxii 4 (*yktlwn*; cf. Toll ZDMG-Suppl viii 28, 32 34), cf. also GIPP 62 - **Hatra** QAL Pf. 3 p.s.m. + suff. 3 p.s.f. *qṭlh* 30[8]; QAL Pass Impf. 3 p.s.m. *lqṭyl* 343[7] - **JAr** QAL Pf. 3 p.s.m. *qṭl* AMB 15[11]; Inf. *mqṭwl* AMB 15[17] - ¶ verb QAL to kill, passim - **1)** + obj.: KAI 222B 27, 223B 9, 224[11,18,21], Aḥiq 49, 51, 52, 61, Hatra 30[8]; *wmwt lḥh ykṭlwk* KAI 225[10f.]: and an evil death may they make you die - **2)** + b_2 (among): Beh 33 - **3)** + b_2 + obj., *qṭlw bhm 504[6]* Beh 3: they killed 5046 of them, cf. Beh 9, 29, 44 - **4)** + b_2 (with) + obj., *bṭ[l]h zy ›hwrmzd ḥyl› ... [q]ṭlt* Beh 13: with the protection of A. ... I killed the army - 5) + l_5 (introducing the object): Beh 3, 5, AMB 15[11,17] - **6)** + l_5?: Sem xiv 72 conv. 2 (diff. context, v. also supra) - QAL pass. to be killed: Cowl 30[17], 31[16], Hatra 343[7]; Part. pass., killed one: Beh 35; f. a killed woman: KAI 215[8] - ITP to be killed; *ytqṭl by[n] ṭwry› [›l]h tryn ḥlp ›ḥyqr znh* Aḥiq 62: let him be killed between these two mountains instead of this A.

qṭl₂ **OffAr** Sing. cstr. *qṭl* Aḥiq 46 (v. infra) - ¶ subst. killing, murder; *šzbk mn qṭl zky* Aḥiq 46: he has saved you from an undeserved death (litt. from the death of an innocent one, cf. Joüon MUSJ xviii 84 × Cowl p. 231: *qṭl* (= Sing. abs.) *zky* = an innocent death, cf. also Levine FS Morton Smith 43f. n. 30).

qṭn **Hebr** Sing. m. abs. *qṭn* Frey 1039[6], IEJ v 222 - ¶ adj. small; as nickname *hqṭn* Frey 1039[6], IEJ v 222: the small one, cf. also Lifshitz ZDPV lxxviii 68f. - cf. poss. also γάδον (= γὰρ παρ'αὐτοῖς τὸ ἐκ μικρῶν ᾠκοδομημένον) Etymologicum Magnum ..., ed. Th. Gaisford, Oxonii, 1848, s.v. - the same word used as name also in Punica xviii/ii 38[3]? (*ʾqṭn* = article + Sing. abs.?, highly uncert. interpret.).
v. *qṭ*.

qṭʿ₁ > Akkad. *qāṭû* = woodcutter (cf. v.Soden Or xxxvii 264, xlvi 192, AHW s.v., cf. also CAD s.v. *qāṭû* s.).

qṭʿ₂ > Akkad. *qettāʾu* = cane cutter (cf. v.Soden Or xxxvii 264, 269, xlvi 192, AHW s.v., cf. also CAD s.v.).

qṭr₁ **Ph** Puech Sem xxix 20f., 23: in KAI 30[5] l. *yqṭr* (= HIPH/PIʿEL Impf. 3 p.s.m./pl. of *qṭr₁* (= to make smoke/to send up in smoke)), heavily dam. text, uncert. reading and interpret.

qṭr₂ **OffAr** Sing. abs., cf. Warka 1, 27: *ki-ṭa-ri* (for this orthography, cf. Dupont-Sommer RA xxxix 41) - ¶ subst. knot (for the context, cf. Landsberger AfO xii 250f., Dupont-Sommer RA xxxix 55, Delsman TUAT ii 433).

qṭr₃ **OffAr** Sing. abs. *qṭr* WO vi 44A 8, REA-NS viii 170A 2, B 2 (:: Périkhanian REA-NS viii 170f. (div. otherwise): l. *qṭrbr* < Iran. = bearer of a crown, crowned one) - ¶ subst. crowner (cf. Périkhanian REA-NS iii 18, 22 (: = participle form)).

qṭrbr v. *qṭr₃*.

qṭrh v. *qṭrt*.

qṭryʾ (< Lat. *centuria*) - **Palm** Sing. cstr. *qṭryʾ* CIS ii 3908[4] - ¶ subst. division of troups, century; *qṭryʾ mksmws* CIS ii 3908[4]: *centuria Maximi* (cf. Lat. par.).

qṭrywn v. *qnṭryn*.

qṭryn v. *qnṭryn*.

qṭrt **Pun** Sing. abs. *qṭrt* CIS i 334[3f.]; abs./cstr. *qṭrt* KAI 76B 6 (v. infra), cf. *qṭ[rt]* in KAI 76B 3 (heavily dam. context) - ¶ subst. perfume: CIS i 334[3f.]; *qṭrt lbnt* KAI 76 B 6: perfume, frankincense (or: perfume, that is frankincense (interpreted as a construct state comb.)) - on this word, cf. Nielsen SVT xxxviii 52ff.
v. *ktrt*.

qydh v. *kdd₃*.

qydš v. *qdš₃*.

qywm **Palm** Sing. + suff. 3 p.s.m. *qywmh* CIS ii 3940[5], 3943[5] (*qyw[mh]*)

- ¶ subst. m. patron, protector (in both instances Greek par. προστάτην).

qyṭ v. *qṣ*$_1$.

qym$_1$ **OffAr** Sing. + suff. 3 p.s.f. *qymh* ATNS 8^{10} (cf. Porten & Yardeni sub TADAE B 5.6 :: Segal ATNS a.l.: = Sing. f. of *qym*$_2$); Plur. + suff. 3 p.pl.m. *qymyhm* ATNS 27^3 - ¶ subst. covenant (v. supra); *spr' zy qymyhn* ATNS 27^3: the document containing their covenants.
v. *qwm*$_1$.

qym$_2$ **Hebr** Sing. m. abs. *qym* DJD ii 24C 18, E 14 (*[q]ym*), EI xx 256^{11} - **Nab** Sing. m. abs. *qym* CIS ii 197^3, 198^{10}, 205^5, 206^6, 210^8 (= J 3; reading uncert.), 212^5 (:: Cantineau Nab ii 141: = Qal pass. Pf. 3 p.s.m. or Part. pass. s.m. abs. of *qwm*$_1$) - ¶ adj. - **1)** valid, legitimate; *wkl 'nwš dy ynpq bydh ktb mn khln pqym hw kdy bh* CIS ii 206$^{5f.}$: and everyone who will bring forward with his own hand a document from K., it shall be valid in accordance with what is in it; *pqym ktb' hw* CIS ii 198^{10}: that document shall be valid; *ktb qym lh* CIS ii 197^3: a document .. it shall be valid for him; *wmn [dy] y'bd k'yr dnh pl' 'yty lh qym* CIS ii 210$^{6ff.}$: and whoever will act contrary to this, there will not be anything legitimate for him (i.e. he will not be able to justify himself) - **2)** firm, enduring; *dy yhw' kpr' hw lw'lt ... qym l'lm* CIS ii 212$^{4f.}$: that this tomb will be an everlasting possession of W. - **3)** imposed, ordained; *pqym 'l wš[w]ḥ wbnth dy l' yzbnwn* CIS ii 205$^{5ff.}$ (= J 12): it is imposed upon W. and her daughters that they shall not sell; *qym 'ly l'mt kkh* DJD ii 24C 18f.: I am obliged to act according to its terms (sc. of the document); *wqym 'ly kwl š'š 'l hšṭr hz'* EI xx 256$^{11f.}$: and I am obliged to act according to what is (written) in this document - this word (Sing. f. abs.) prob. in PEQ '38, 238^1 (καιαμα), cf. Peters OLZ '40, 219 :: Beyer ATTM 353: = lapsus for καιαμαν = Plur. f. abs.; on the text, cf. also Milik LA x 154f.; or καιαμα = Qal Part. s.f. abs. of *qwm*$_1$?
v. *qwm*$_1$, *qym*$_1$.

qyn$_1$ v. *qny*$_1$. *qyn*$_2$ **JAr** Sing. emph. *qyn'* MPAT 89^{1,3,4} (:: Puech RB xc 484f., 486, 489: *qyn'* = Sing. emph. of *qyn*$_3$ (= *qn*$_2$ (= nest > cavity, chamber, dwelling, abode)) :: Beyer ATTM 329, 684: in all instances l. *qwn'* = Qal Part. pass. s.m. abs. of *qny*$_1$ (= something bought, acquired, property); for reading and interpret., cf. also Bennett Maarav iv 352) - ¶ subst. m. lament; *qyn' 'lm'* MPAT 89^{1,3}: a powerful lament (v. *'lm*$_2$); for the context of MPAT 89^4, v. *hykylyn*.

qyn$_3$ v. *qyn*$_2$.

qynh **Hatra** Sing. emph. *qynt'* 43^3 (*qynt[']*; for the reading, cf. Caquot Syr xxxii 50f. :: Safar Sumer ix 242 n. 7: l. *qyns[* = n.d.?), 202^2 (:: Teixidor Sumer xxi 88*: = Plur. emph., cf. also Aggoula MUSJ xlvii 41) - ¶ subst. singing, song; *rb qynt'* Hatra 202^2 (cf. 43^3): the master of the singing, choirmaster (cf. Caquot Syr xxxii 50f., xli 271, Safar Sumer

xviii 62 n. 73 :: Milik DFD 161: *qynt*ʾ = Sing. emph. of *qynw*/*qynt* (= forge), *rb qynt*ʾ = master of the smiths (cf. Vattioni IH a.l., cf. also Caquot Syr xli 271)).
v. *qn*ʾ*m*.

qynw v. *qynh*.

$qyny_1$ **Palm** Plur. emph. *qyny*ʾ CIS ii 3945[3] - **Hatra** Sing. emph. *qyny*ʾ 77[1] (cf. e.g. Safar Sumer xi 14 n. 49, Vattioni IH a.l. :: Caquot Syr xxxii 271: or = Sing. emph. of $qyny_2$ (= musician)), 190 - ¶ subst. smith; *qyny*ʾ ʿ*bd*ʾ *dhb*ʾ *wksp*ʾ CIS ii 3945[3f.]: gold smiths and silver smiths.

$qyny_2$ v. $qyny_1$.

qynt v. *qynh*.

qys v. qwm_1, *qysm*.

qysh v. $nṣb_5$.

qysm cf. Frah iv 7 = olive (??); Ebeling Frah a.l.: poss. = abbrev. of *qys* (= Sing. cstr. of *qys* (= tree)) *mšḥ*ʾ (= Sing. emph. of $mšḥ_3$), highly uncert. interpret.; cf. also Schaeder with Ebeling Frah a.l.: l. *kšmy* = sesame sprout, cf. however Nyberg FP 65: l. *kšm* = abbrev. of *k-šmn*ʾ (= Sing. emph. of $šmn_2$).

qysr v. *qsr*.

qyp **OffAr** diff. word *qy/sp* in heavily dam. context in OIC xxii p. 152, Kaufman a.l.: cf. perhaps Akkad. *qīpu* = agent.

qyṣ v. $qṣ_1$.

qyq v. qwq_2.

qyrʾ v. $qyrh_1$.

$qyrh_1$ (< Greek κύρα) - **JAr** Sing. abs. *qyrh* MPAT-A 26[2] (= SM 32), 28[1] (= SM 34), *qyr*ʾ Frey 661[3] - ¶ subst. lady, used as title; *qyrh qlnyq* MPAT-A 28: lady Kalonike (cf. MPAT-A 26[2], Frey 661[3]), cf. *qyrys*.

$qyrh_2$ **Samal** Plur. abs. *qyrt* KAI 215[4,15] (cf. e.g. Dion p. 140, Contini EVO ii 204 :: Garb 261, Segert AAG p. 194: = Plur. cstr. :: Sader EAS 163: = Sing. abs.) - ¶ subst. f. town.
v. $nṣb_5$.

$qyrh_3$ v. *qwrh*.

qyrys (< Greek κύριος) - **JAr** Sing. abs. *qyrys* MPAT-A 26[5] (= SM 32), 28[1] (= SM 34), *qyrs* MPAT-A 26[2,3,5] (= SM 32), *qwrys* MPAT-A 12[2] (= SM 71; for this interpret., cf. Frey sub 1195, Naveh SM a.l., Beyer ATTM 363, 683 :: Fitzmyer & Harrington MPAT a.l.: = n.p. :: Barag IEJ xxii 148: l. prob. *qwrws* = n.p.) - ¶ subst. lord, used as title; *qyrs slwsṭys* MPAT-A 26[3]: lord Sallustius (cf. MPAT-A 26[2,5,5f.], 28[1]), cf. $qyrh_1$.

qyrs v. *qyrys*.

qyšwʾ **Hebr** Plur. abs. *qyšw*ʾ*yn* SM 49[1] - ¶ subst. cucumber, marrow.

qyšt v. $qšt_2$.

qytdrh (< Greek καθέδρα) - **JAr** Sing. abs. *qytdrh* SM 107^{7} - ¶ subst. seat; in SM 107 uncert. and difficult context, cf. Naveh a.l.

ql$_1$ **Ph** Sing. abs. *ql* KAI 10^{3,8} (cf. Hoftijzer Mus lxxvi 197 n. 11 × FR 234, Röllig KAI a.l., Lane BASOR cxciv 41, Gibson SSI iii p. 96, Garr DGSP 99: = Sing. + suff. 1 p.s.), 33^{3} (for the reading, cf. Amadasi sub Kition A 1), 38^{2} (cf. however Gibson SSI iii p. 132f.: = Sing. + suff. 3 p.s.m.), 39^{3}, 41^{6}, CIS i 96^{3} (dam. context), RES 1213^{6} (cf. Hoftijzer Mus lxxvi 197 n. 11 :: Cross & Freedman JNES x 228: = Sing. + suff. 3 p.s.m.), DD 13^{3} (cf. however Gibson SSI iii p. 122: = Sing. + suff. 3 p.s.m.; for the context, v. *brk$_1$*), 14^{3}, 15^{3} (or = Sing. cstr.?, for the context, v. *brk$_1$*), Kition A 30^{3}; + suff. 3 p.s.m. *qly* DD 7^{4} (*ql[y]*, prob. restoration, cf. Chabot sub RES 504A), 8^{4} (= RES 504B); + suff. 3 p.pl.m. *qlm* CIS i 38 (dam. context; = Kition A 24), 88^{7}, Ber xii 45^{2} (dam. context) - **Pun** Sing. abs. *ql* CIS i 197^{6}, 638^{4}, 726^{3}, 890^{4}, 974^{4}, KAI 78^{1}, 98^{4} (or (div. otherwise) l. *qly* = Sing. + suff. 3 p.s.m.?), etc., etc., *qʾl* Punica xviii/ii 83^{4} (or = lapsus for *qlʾ* (= Sing. + suff. 3 p.s.m.)?); cstr. *ql* CIS i 3784^{7}, KAI 61A 6, MontSir ii 80^{3}, SMI 2^{2}, Moz vi 104^{3} (= SMI 23), 105^{4} (= SMI 24), ICO-Malta-pu 31^{4}, ICO-Spa 16^{5}; + suff. 3 p.s.m. *qlʾ* CIS i 180^{5}, 181^{5}, KAI 63^{3}, 68^{5}, 84, 88^{5}, Sem xxxvi 26^{4}, Punica xviii/ii 26^{4} (for the reading, cf. Bertrandy & Sznycer sub SPC 127 :: Chabot Punica a.l.: l. *lqʾ* (lapsus for *qlʾ*)), etc., etc., *qlʿ* Hofra 4^{4}, 104^{2}, 136^{3}, 151^{3}, 251^{3}, *qlm* CIS i 3604^{6}, KAI 77$^{3f.}$, Hofra 103^{4}, 142^{4}, 160^{4}, 221^{4}, *qly* CIS i 4464^{5}, KAI 167^{4}, Hofra 200^{2}, Antas 14 (or = Sing. + suff. 3 p.s.f.?, dam. context), *qlh* RES 340^{3}, *qlʾʿ* CIS i 3390^{3}, *qlʿʾ* CIS i 3709$^{6f.}$, *qwlʾ* Punica xi 19^{4}, 20^{3}, 25^{3}, 26^{4}, 28^{3}, xii 10^{4}, BAr '50, 144 ii 2, *qʾl[ʾ]* Punica xi 18^{4} (cf. Chabot a.l.), *qlš* (lapsus for *qlʾ*) Hofra 32^{3}, *mlʾ* (lapsus for *qlʾ*) Punica xii 6^{3}, cf. KAI 175^{4}: κουλω (cf. FR 79b, 234); + suff. 3 p.s.f. *qlʾ* CIS i 371^{6}, 395^{5}, 580^{3}, 600^{5}, 675^{4}, etc., etc., *qlʿ* CIS i 2005^{5}, *qlʿʾ* CIS i 3599$^{4f.}$, *qlm* KAI 164^{3} (for the reading, cf. Hofra sub 24 :: Röllig KAI a.l.: l. *qlʾ*; or = + suff. 3 p.s.m./pl.?); + suff. 1 p.pl. *qln* CIS i 418^{7} (reading of *n* uncert., reading *qly* (= Sing. + suff. 1 p.s.) poss.?); + suff. 3 p.pl.m. *qlm* CIS i 122A 3, KAI 47^{4} (= CIS i 122B), 146^{6}, 159^{7}, Punica xviii/iii 9^{4}, Eph i 44 iii 4 (for the reading, cf. Sznycer Sem xxxii 65 :: v.d.Branden RSF ix 11f., 16: l. *šlm* (= Pɪʿᴇʟ Pf. 3 p.s.m. of *šlm$_1$*)) - **Hebr** Sing. cstr. *ql* KAI 189^{2} (on the orthography, cf. Zevit MLAHE 20) - **DA** Sing. cstr. *ql* i 10 (diff. reading, cf. v.d.Kooij DA p. 107, Hoftijzer DA p. 202 :: Garbini Hen i 177f., 185: l. *q[n]* = Sing. cstr. of *qn$_2$* (= nest of birds, young birds), cf. also Delcor SVT xxxii 56f., H. & M.Weippert ZDPV xcviii 83, 94 (n. 85), 103, Puech BAT 359, 361, FS Grelot 22, 28 :: Lemaire BAT 318, CRAI '85, 280: l. poss. *q[ʾ]* = Sing. abs. of *qʾ* (= pelican)) - **OldAr** Sing. cstr. *ql* KAI 222A 29; + suff. 3 p.s.m. *qlh* KAI 201$^{4f.}$ (for the reading, cf. e.g. Cross BASOR ccv 38f., Gibson SSI ii p.

3, Shea Maarav i 166) - **OffAr** Sing. + suff. 3 p.s.m. *qlh* Aḥiq 107 (:: Kottsieper SAS 20, 229: = Sing. + suff. 3 p.s.m. of *ql*$_2$ (= messenger)); cf. Frah x 24 (*kʾlʾ*), GIPP 25 - **Palm** Sing. + suff. 3 p.s.f. *qlh* CIS ii 4080[5] - ¶ subst. m. - **1)** voice: passim; *k šmʿ qlm* KAI 47[3]: for he listened to their voice - **2)** sound: passim; *k šmʿ ql dbry* KAI 61A 5f.: because he listened to the sound of his words (v. *dbr*$_3$); *ql rḥmn* (v. also *rḥm*$_7$) DA i 10: the sound of the vultures; *ql knr* KAI 222A 29: the sound of the lyre.
v. *ʿrbh*, *qwm*$_1$, *qlbh*.

ql$_2$ v. *ql*$_1$.

qlbh **OldAr** Sing. cstr. *qlbt* KAI 222B 44 (for this reading, without interpret., cf. also Dupont-Sommer Sf p. 62, Fitzmyer AIS 18, Degen AAG p. 16, v. also infra) - ¶ subst. of unknown meaning and uncert. reading; Lipiński Stud 52: = scale-armour (cf. however Lemaire IAS 115, 140: l. *ql* (= Sing. cstr. of *ql*$_1$) *br* (= Sing. cstr. of *br*$_1$)).

qlby **OffAr** Sing. abs. *qlby* Cowl 72[2,3,8,10,13,15,16,17,19]; Plur. abs. *qlbyn* Cowl 72[3,4,5,14] - ¶ subst. of unknown meaning and etymology, prob. indicating liquid measure (cf. also Grelot Sem xxiii 103ff.: < Demotic < Greek κάλπαι (Plur. of κάλπη = pitcher, highly uncert. interpret.)), cf. *qlwl*.

qlh **Pun** Février AIPHOS xiii 164, 166, 170: the *qlt* in KAI 162[5], 163[3] = Sing. abs. of *qlh* (= curse), cf. also Röllig KAI (a.l.), v.d.Branden BO xiv 196, 200; highly uncert. interpret., diff. context.

qlwl (< Egypt., cf. Grelot DAE p. 99 n. b; cf. also CIS ii sub 146) - **OffAr** Sing. abs. *qlwl* Cowl 72[3,4,6,7,9,11,12] (*[q]lwl*),[13]; Plur. abs. *qlwln* Cowl 72[5,18] - ¶ subst. indicating liquid measure (greater than *qlby*).

qlyh cf. Frah-S$_2$ 112 (*klytʾ*) = cell, subterranean room.

qlyl **OffAr** Sing. m. abs. *qlyl* Aḥiq 38 (*qly[l]*), 112, KAI 276[2]; cf. GIPP 62 - ¶ adj. - **1)** light (> despised); *nšʾyt tbn wnsbt prn wlʾ wlʾ ʾyty zy qlyl mn twtb* Aḥiq 112: I have lifted straw and I have taken up bran, but there is absolutely nothing which is lighter (i.e. less respected) than a sojourner - **2)** light (> fast); *b[s]wsh ḥd qly[l]* Aḥiq 38: on a swift horse - **3)** small, used as a nickname; *zywḥ qlyl btḥš* KAI 276[2]: Z. the younger, the πιτιάξης (v. *btḥš*; cf. e.g. Metzger JNES xv 22, 23f., Donner KAI a.l., Kutscher, Naveh & Shaked Lesh xxxiv 310f., cf. also Tod JRS xxxiii 84 for the Greek par. Ζηουάχου τοῦ νεωτέρου πιτιάξου :: Nyberg Eranos xliv 235, 237: = Z. the small *bitaxš*) - v.Soden Or xxxvii 263, xlvi 192: > Akkad. *qallilu* = small, unimportant (cf. idem AHW s.v. *qallissu*), poss. interpret., cf. also CAD s.v. *qallilu*.

qll$_1$ **OldCan** Hiph Impf. 3 p.s.m. + suff. 1 p.s. *ya-qi-íl-li-ni* EA 245[38] (for this form, cf. Böhl 32a, n, Sivan GAG 176, 262) - **OffAr** Qal Impf. 3 p.s.m. *yql* Aḥiq 141; cf. Frah app. 9 (*qllwn*, prob. Paʿel form) - ¶ verb Qal (to be light >) to be less respected, despicable; *ʾl yql šmk* *qdmyhm* Aḥiq 141: let not your name be lightly esteemed before them (i.e. according to their opinion) - PA ‘EL to disturb, to confuse: Frah app. 9 - HIPH to despise, to disdain: EA 245[38] - Rocco AION xxiv 475f.: l. *qll* (= PI ‘EL/POL Imper. s.m.) in GR ii 36 no. 20[1] (highly uncert. reading and interpret., cf. Polselli GR ii a.l.).

qll$_2$ **Ph** Plur. abs. *qllm* KAI 51 verso 3 (heavily dam. context) - ¶ subst. jar (poss. interpret.).

qlm **Hebr** word of uncert. reading (*qlm/qln*) and interpret. on storage jar: TeAv ii 87[2].

qln v. *qlm*.

qlny ((< Greek κολωνεία) < Lat. *colonia*) - **Palm** Sing. emph. *qlny*› CIS ii 3932[2], 3939[4], Inv x 115[2] - ¶ subst. colony, used as indication of Palmyra; *›sṭr<ṭ> g› dy qlny›* CIS ii 3939[4]: the commander of the colony (cf. Greek par. στρατηγὸς τῆς λαμπροτάτης κολωνείας; cf. also in the Greek par. of CIS ii 3942 τῆς ... μητροκολωνείας as indication of Palmyra).

qlsṭr (< Greek, v. infra) - **Palm** Sing. emph. (or Plur.??) emph. *qlsṭr[›]* CIS ii 3951[5] - ¶ subst. of uncert. meaning, indicating an object; Milik DFD 115: = fence, rail (< Lat. *claustrum*, cf. also Gawlikowski TP 90; cf. however Greek κλεῖστρον with same meaning), prob. interpret. (cf. already Chabot sub CIS ii 3951: < Greek κλεῖστρον = bar, bolt) :: Mouterde with Cantineau sub Inv v 2: cf. Hebr. *qlsṭr* = basket :: Gawlikowski Ber xix 76 n. 38: < Greek κυλίστρα = place for horses to roll in, indicating in the context an area ending a colonnade (cf. also idem TP 90).

ql‘ **Ph** Sing. abs. *ql‘* RES 1214[2] - ¶ subst. (or QAL Part. act.) slinger or manufacturer of slings??

ql‘s **OffAr** Sing. abs. *ql‘s* Cowl 26[11] - ¶ subst. of unknown meaning, prob. indicating part of a ship used in connection with the mast (v. *qwmh*), maststep? (cf. Grelot DAE p. 290 n. b), cf. however also Cowl a.l.: sail?

ql‘rnt v. *‘rbh$_2$*.

qlqlh **OldAr** Plur. emph. *qlqlt›* Tell F 22 (Akkad. par. *tup-qí-na-te*) - ¶ subst. dung-hill, cesspit (cf. also Abou-Assaf, Bordreuil & Millard Tell F p. 21, 36, Kaufman Maarav iii 173, Greenfield & Shaffer AnSt xxxiii 123ff., RB xcii 56f., Shn v/vi 127) :: Andersen & Freedman FS Fensham 39: = basket - on this word, cf. also Millard JSS xxxi 1.

qm$_1$ **OffAr** *qm* in PF 2059[3], word of unknown meaning (or = abbrev.), prob. indicating dry measure.

qm$_2$ v. *qdm$_3$*.

qm$_3$ v. *qmḥ*.

qmz **Palm** du Mesnil du Buisson sub Inv D 52: the *qmzyn* ibid. = QAL Part. act. pl.m. abs. of *qmz* (= to be immersed, to be diminished (highly uncert. reading, interpret. and context)).

qmḥ **Hebr** Sing. abs. *qmḥ* TA-H $1^{5,7}$, $5^{3,5f.}$ (*qm[ḥ]*), 12^2, *qm* TA-H 8^2 (lapsus, cf. Aharoni TA a.l., Pardee UF x 306f., HAHL 41f.) - **OffAr** Sing. abs. *qmḥ* Driv $6^{3,4,5}$, ATNS 23a 2, $41^{1,8}$, 43b 5 (*[q]mḥ*), 89^1, TA-Ar 28^1 (*qm[ḥ]*), 29^1, 30^1, $36^{1f.}$ (cf. Naveh TA a.l.), Sach 76 i B 7 (for the context, cf. Porten Arch 132, 277), PF 704, 2059^3, JRAS '29, 108^{13}, cf. Frah iv 9 (*kḥm*ʾ :: Ebeling Frah a.l.: l. *qʾmʾ*) - **JAr** Sing. emph. *qmḥh* Syr xlv 101^{21} - ¶ subst. m. flour: passim; *qmḥ ḥwry* Driv 6^3: white flour; *hqmḥ hrʾšn* TA-H $1^{5f.}$: the first flour (cf. Pardee UF x 295: the flour of the first (i.e. earlier) grinding (cf. also id. HAHL 31, Hospers SV 103f.), cf. however Aharoni TA-H a.l., Gibson SSI i p. 52: flour from the earliest harvest, or flour of top quality (cf. Heltzer RDAC '88 i 169 n. 30; cf. also Lemaire IH i p. 157f.) :: Albright ANET 569 (n. 29): *qmḥ* = wheat, *qmḥ rʾšn* = old wheat); *qmḥ rmy* Driv 6^3: flour of inferior quality (?, v. *rmy*$_3$) - *qm* in TA-H $112^{1,2}$ poss. = abbrev. of *qmḥ* (cf. Rainey a.l.).
v. *qwm*$_1$.

qmy$_1$ v. *qdmy*.

qmy$_2$ v. *qdm*$_3$.

qmynʾ v. *qdm*$_3$.

qmyʿ **JAr** Sing. abs. *qmyʿ* AMB 1^{20}, $2^{1,11}$, 4^1, 13^2; emph. *qmyʿh* AMB 3^{14} - ¶ subst. m. amulet.

qml **OldAr** Sing. abs. *qml* KAI 222A 31 - ¶ subst. louse.

qmpwn (< Greek κάμπος) - **Hebr** Sing. abs. *qmpwn* SM 49^6 - ¶ subst. plain for exercise and amusement, *campus*.

qmṣ$_1$ **OffAr**, cf. Frah viii 8 (*kmṣʾ*): grasshopper.

qmṣ$_2$ v.Soden Or xlvi 193: > Akkad. *qenṣu* = handful (cf. also id. AHW s.v.), uncert. interpret. (cf. also CAD s.v.).

qmqm v. *qwqm*.

qmr$_1$ v. *ʿmr*$_7$.

qmr$_2$ Ebeling Frah a.l.: l. *qmryʾ* in Frah i 12 (= Semitic word *qmr* (= moon)); less prob. interpret., cf. Nyberg FP 61: Iran. word.

qmt$_1$ **Ph** Sing. (or Plur.) cstr. *qmt* KAI 43^{10} (v. infra) - ¶ subst. of unknown meaning, cf. Clermont-Ganneau Et ii 164 (cf. also Cooke NSI p. 83, 85); for this reading, cf. also Gibson SSI iii p. 136, 139f.: *qmt ʿm* (= Sing. abs. of *ʿm*$_1$) = some sort of sacred building (or place) of the people :: Honeyman JEA xxvi 63 (div. otherwise): l. *tqmt* (= Sing. cstr. of *tqmh*) *ʿm* = the establishment of the people (cf. also Lipiński RTAT 251 (n. 30): = the place of refuge of the people) :: v.d.Branden OA iii 248, 257: l. *qrt* (= Sing. cstr. of *qrh*$_1$ (= basin)) *ʿn* (= Sing. abs. of *ʿyn*$_2$) = the basin of the well.

qmt$_2$ **Pun** Sing. abs. *qmt* KAI 165^4 - ¶ subst. of unknown meaning (cf. Chabot sub Punica xvi 1, Röllig KAI a.l.); Levi Della Vida OA iv 65ff.:

= elevation, used figuratively > pre-eminence; Février BAr '51/52, 42: = elevation > burial mound (improb. interpret.); v.d.Branden RSF ii 146f.: = elevation > upper part of funerary monument (improb. interpret.).

qn$_1$ v. *kr$_2$*, *ṣ'n*, *qrb$_7$*.

qn$_2$ v. *qyn$_2$*, *ql$_1$*.

qn'$_1$ **Pun** Rocco AION xxiv 476, 478: l. *qn'n* (= PI'EL Imper. s.m. + suff. 1 p.pl. of *qn'$_1$* (= to be zealous for) in GR ii 36 no. 20[4] (highly uncert. reading and interpret., cf. Polselli GR ii a.l.)).

qn'$_2$ v.Soden Or xlvi 193: > Akkad. *qin'u* / *qi'u* = envy (highly uncert. interpret., cf. also CAD s.v. *qi'u* = envious, jealous person).

qn'$_3$ v. *qnh$_1$*, *qny$_1$*.

qn'm **Pun** Sing. abs. *qn'm* KAI 161[1], Trip 2[2] - ¶ subst. person (cf. Levi Della Vida Lib iii/2, 3f., Février RA xlvi 223, Röllig sub KAI 161, Roschinski Num 113f., Amadasi ITP 35 (n. 4) :: Berger RA ii 37f.: *qn'm* in KAI 161[1] = n.d. (cf. also Cooke NSI p. 148, Lidzbarski Handb 363) :: Février RA xlv 140f.: *qn'm* in KAI 161[1] = Plur. abs. of *qnh$_2$* (= variant of *qynh* (= funeral lamentation)), *myqdš qn'm* = funeral sanctuary); *p'l m'qr ... lqn'm* Trip 2[1f.]: M. made it for himself; *myqdš qn'm ... mkwsn* KAI 161[1]: sanctuary of the (divine) ... person of Micipsa - cf. *qnmy*.

qnh$_1$ **Pun** Sing. abs. *qn'* CIS i 3889[3], *qnh* CIS i 5967[2] (= TPC 29 :: Clermont-Ganneau sub RES 1229: l. prob. *'ph* = n.l.) - **OffAr**, cf. Frah iv 15 (*kny'*) - ¶ subst. f. reed; *sḥr qnh* CIS i 5967[2]: merchant of reed; *qn' zk'* CIS i 3889[3]: pure reed, prob. = aromatic reed, cf. Löw i 692ff., AP 341f., cf. also Nielsen SVT xxxviii 62f. :: Vattioni StudMagr x 24f. *qnh* = coll. animals - Février RA xlv 145f.: l. *q[n]m* (= Plur. abs. of *qnh$_1$*) in KAI 161[8]? (cf. also Röllig KAI a.l.; uncert. reading and interpret.) - this subst. (Sing. abs. *qnh*) also in Sach 78 i B 3 indicating linear measure? - > Greek κάννα, κάννη, Lat. *canna*, cf. e.g. Hehn KH 306f., Zimmern Fremdw 56, Masson RPAE 47f. - cf. also the *qnh* in FuB xiv 22[3] in heavily dam. context??

v. *'qn'*.

qnh$_2$ v. *qn'm*.

qnḥnty (< Egypt., *qnḥ* = chapel + *nty* = god, cf. Couroyer RB lxi 558f., lxviii 532ff., BiOr xxvii 252 (n. 26), Porten Arch 284) - **OffAr** *qnḥnty* Krael 9[9], 10[5] - ¶ compound subst. chapel of the god; *byt qnḥnty* Krael 9[9], 10[5]: the area of the chapel of the god (the god prob. being Chnum; on this chapel, cf. e.g. Porten Arch 284ff., 309) :: (Albright and Ranke with) Krael p. 241: = n.p. < Egypt.

qnṭnry (< Lat. *centenarium*) - **Pun** Sing. abs., cf. IRT 877[1]: *centenari* (for the reading, cf. Levi Della Vida OA ii 87 n. 48), KAI 179[2] (= IRT 889): *centeinari* - ¶ subst. *limes*-fortress.

qnṭryn ((< Greek κεντορίων, κεντυρίων) < Lat. *centurio*) - **Nab** Sing. emph. *qnṭryn*ʾ CIS ii 2171[1] - **Palm** Sing. emph. *qṭryn*ʾ Inv x 81[2], *qṭrywn*ʾ CIS ii 3962[1] (= Inv x 17), Inv xii 33[1] - ¶ subst. centurion, commander of a century (for the Nab. text, cf. Negev RB lxxxiii 225).

qny_1 **Ph** QAL Part. act. s.m. abs. *qn* KAI 26A iii 18 - **Pun** QAL Pf. 1 p.s., cf. Poen 932: *caneth* (cf. Sznycer PPP 63f., Garr DGSP 134), ibid. 942: *canthe* (cf. Sznycer PPP 123ff.; var. *canthi*; cf. however Schroeder 308 (div. otherwise): *canth* = QAL Inf. cstr. :: L.H.Gray AJSL xxxix 78: *canth* = QAL Inf. cstr. + suff. 1 p.s.; for Poen 932, 942, cf. also Vattioni StudMagr x 25); Part. act. s.m. abs. *qn* KAI 129[1]; YIPH Part. s.m. cstr. *mqny* CIS i 5522[2] (cf. v.d.Branden BiOr xxiii 143, GP p. 33, 107 :: Février Sem iv 15: = Sing. cstr. of *mqny* (= (possession >) slave; cf. also Swiggers BiOr xxxvii 340: perhaps = possession)) or = m_{12} (= mn_5) + QAL Part. pass. pl.m. cstr. of *qny* (= slaves); for the context, v. $trš_2$) - **Hebr** QAL Pf. 3 p.pl. *qnw* SM 49[12,26]; Impf. 1 p.s. ʾ*qnh* DJD ii 30[23]; Part. act. s.m. abs./cstr. *qn* IEJ xxii 195[3] (= BASOR ccxxxix 43) - **Samal** QAL Pf. 3 p.s.m. *qn* KAI 25[1] - **OffAr** QAL Pf. 3 p.s.m. *qnh* Cowl 30[16], Aḥiq 84 (cf. Leand 40f.; or = QAL Part. act. s.m. abs.?, cf. Lindenberger APA 55, Kottsieper SAS 229); 1 p.s. *qnyt* ATNS 50[1]; Impf. 3 p.s.m. *yqnh* Aḥiq 218 (reading highly uncert., cf. also Lindenberger APA 217: l. *hwh* = QAL Pf. 3 p.s.m. of hwy_1); 1 p.s. ʾ*qnh* ATNS 50[1]; Inf. *mqnh* ATNS 8[12] (cf. Porten & Yardeni sub TADAE B 5.6 :: Segal ATNS a.l.: l. *mšnh* (= PA‘EL Part. s.m. abs. of $šny_1$ (= to depart))); ITP Impf. 3 p.s.m. *y[t]qnh* Aḥiq 196; Part. s.m. abs. *mtqnh* Aḥiq 219 - **Palm** QAL Part. act. s.m. abs./cstr. *qn* RTP 220-223, *qwn* Syr xix 78[5] (this form poss. influenced by Can., cf. however Silverman Or xxxix 478 n. 1) - **Hatra** QAL Part. act. s.m. abs. *qnh* 23[3] - **JAr** QAL Impf. 1 p.s. ʾ*qnh* MPAT 39[8], 52[11], IEJ xxxvi 206[6,7], *[*ʾ*]qn*ʾ MPAT 41[12]; 1 p.pl. *nqnh* MPAT 51[13] (:: Milik RB lxi 188: = APH Impf. 1 p.pl.); Inf. *mqnh* MPAT 43[7], 50a 3 (*mqn[h]*; dam. context), 52[9] - ¶ verb QAL - **1)** to acquire: passim; *wkl dy* ʾ*yty ly wdy* ʾ*qnh* MPAT 52[11]: everything which belongs to me and which I shall acquire (cf. IEJ xxxvi 206[6], cf. also ATNS 50[1], IEJ xxxvi 206[7]; for MPAT 39[8] & 51[13], v. qbl_3); *wkl nksyn zy qnh* Cowl 30[16]: and all possessions which he gained (sc. illegally) - a) + obj.: Aḥiq 84 (slave), 218 (woman, dam. context, v. supra), SM 49[26] (place) - b) + mn_5: ATNS 8[12] (v. supra) - **2)** to possess: MPAT 52[9] - **3)** to make, to create - a) ʾ*l qn* ʾ*rṣ* KAI 26A iii 18, 129[1]: El creator of the earth (or poss. in some or all of these instances: El possessor of the earth (i.e. the lord of the earth, cf. Montgomery JAOS liii 116, Levi Della Vida JBL lxiii 1 n. 1, RSO xxxix 302, cf. also Humbert FS Bertholet 259ff., Katz JSS v 126ff.)); cf. also ʾ*lqnr*‘ in RTP 220-223, ʾ*lqwnr*‘ Syr xix 78[5] (for this reading, cf. Levi Della Vida with Littmann Or xi 293,

JBL lxiii 8 :: Cantineau Syr xix 78f.: l. *ʾlqwndʿ* = n.d.; cf. Greek par. Ποσειδῶνι; cf. also du Mesnil du Buisson TP 247ff.) and *bʿšmyn qnh dy rʿh/ʾ* Hatra 23[3] (cf. Caquot Syr xxix 102, xl 15); :: Honeyman PEQ '49, 36 n. 2: l. *ʾl qn ʾrṣ wšmm* pro *ʾl qn ʾrṣ wšmš* in KAI 26A iii 18f.; for the god 'Creator/Possessor of the earth', cf. also e.g. Pope SVT ii 49ff., UF xix 227, Levi Della Vida FS Friedrich 302ff., Otten MiOr i 135ff., Cross HThR lv 243f., Lipiński Royauté 418f., RTAT 260 (n. 75), Brown JSS x 207f., Weippert ZDMG-Suppl i 203f., Stolz BZAW cxviii 130ff., Habel JBL xci 321ff., Rey-Coquais Syr lv 361ff., Oppenheimer Shn ii 20ff., Hvidberg-Hansen TNT ii 79 n. 51, 84 n. 58, Mullen DCC 12ff., Mazar EI xvi 132ff., Fantar DM 97ff., Teixidor PP 25ff. - for the Hebr. *]qn ʾrṣ*, cf. also Miller BASOR cccxxxix 43ff.; cf. also de Moor FS Gordon ii 185f. - for the *el-ku-ni-ir-ša* in Hittite, cf. litt. mentioned above, especially Otten MiOr i 135ff. - b) prob. meaning 'to make' in KAI 25[1f.]; *smr z qn klmw*, sceptre (?, v. smr_2) which (v. *zy*) K. made (for this translat. of *qn*, cf. Landsberger Samʾal 42 n. 102, Galling BASOR cxix 16f., Röllig KAI a.l., Rosenthal ANET 655 (cf. also FR 63b, 176b; cf. also Gibson SSI iii p. 40f., Swiggers Or li 251, Sader EAS 160) :: Lipiński BiOr xxxiii 231: = to acquire (cf. also Gibson SSI iii p. 41) :: Galling BASOR cxix 17: or *qn* = QAL Pf. 3 p.s.m. of qyn_1 (= to forge; cf. also Dupont-Sommer RHR cxxxiii 21, 24ff.: qyn_1 = to ornate? (cf. Dion p. 26, 218)); cf. also Koopmans 16f., Segert AAG p. 298, 327, 405) - ITP to be bought: Aḥiq 196, 219 (in both instances dam. context) - Février RHR cxli 21f.: the *qnʾ* in NP 130[5] = QAL Part. act. s.m. abs. (the creator) preceded by *ʾtmy* (= YIPH Inf. of tmy_1 (= to invoke)), improb. interpret., diff. context, cf. also Lidzbarski Handb 438 n. 3 (div. otherwise): l. *myqnʾ* poss. = *mqnʾ* :: Dérenbourg CRAI 1875, 260, 265f. (div. otherwise): l. *my* (= Plur. cstr. of *mym*) *qnʾ* (= n.l. or Sing. abs. of $qnʾ_3$ (= reed)); cf. also Euting ZDMG xxx 286: unexplained - a form of this root also in CIS i 5510[7]?, cf. Chabot BAr '41/42, 391: *qnʾ* = QAL Inf. cstr. + suff. 3 p.s.m./f. (improb. interpret.); Février BAr '46/49, 172: = QAL Inf. cstr. + suff. 3 p.s.m./f. of wqy_1 (= to protect; improb. interpret.); Février sub CIS i 5510: = QAL Part. act. s.m. abs. (= the creator; improb. interpret.) - a form of this root in Krael 13[6] (*]qnh*??; for the reading, cf. Krael a.l. :: Porten & Yardeni sub TADAE A 3.9: l. *tnh* (= here)) - v.d.Branden BO xiv 196, 200: the *qnʾt* in KAI 162[5] = QAL Part. s.f. cstr.

v. *ʾqnʾ*, qyn_2, *šnym*.

qny_2 **Hebr** (?) Sing. abs. *qny* Mas 474 - ¶ word of uncert. meaning; Yadin & Naveh Mas a.l.: = either zealous (one), Zealot, or: silversmith.

$qnyh_1$ **Palm** Sing. cstr. *qnyt* RTP 306, 309; emph. *qnytʾ* RTP 307-308 - ¶ subst. of uncert. meaning; Cantineau Inscr p. 45: association (cf.

also RTP p. 148), less prob. interpret. :: Ingholt PBP 133 (n. 170): = worker in stucco :: Milik DFD 159ff.: = player on the lyre (cf. also Gawlikowski Ber xxii 146; cf. however also idem TP 36: or rather = metal-worker?); poss. to be connected with τῶν Κονέτων in SBS 52^3, for this connection, cf. Milik DFD 160, Gawlikowski TP 36 - on this word, cf. also Teixidor PP 107f.

qnyh$_2$ **Hatra** Sing. emph. *qnyt›* 342^5 - ¶ subst. poss. meaning female slave, in Hatra 342 // with *zmrh*; cf. however As-Salihi Sumer xxxiv 143f.: = Plur. emph. (= wailing-woman).

qnyn **OffAr** Sing. abs. *qnyn* Cowl 14^4; cstr. *q[n]yn* Aeg xxxix 4 recto 3 (for this uncert. reading, cf. Hoftijzer VT xii 342, Swiggers Aeg lx 93f. (for the reading problems, cf. also Porten & Yardeni sub TADAE A 3.11) :: Bresciani Aeg xxxix 6: l. prob. *qbyn* = Plur. abs. of *qb*$_1$); + suff. 3 p.s.m. *qnynh* Cowl 15^{19,30}, Krael 7^{30}, KAI 260^8; + suff. 3 p.s.f. *qnynh* Cowl 15^{22}, 46^1 (cf. Porten & Yardeni sub TADAE B 6.3 :: Cowl a.l.: = Sing. + suff. 3 p.s.m.), Krael 7^{27} (for this reading, cf. Porten & Yardeni sub TADAE B 3.8)^{,35}; + suff. 1 p.s. *qnyny* Cowl 15^{35} - ¶ subst. possessions, goods; for the context of = KAI 260^8 v. *ṭyn*.
v. *nks*$_3$.

qnyt v.Soden Or xxxvii 264, xlvi 193, AHW s.v. *qunātā*: > Akkad. *qunātā* = artichoke?? (uncert. interpret.; cf. CAD s.v. *qunātu*: poss. < Ar. root *qn‹* = woad (highly uncert. interpret.)).

qnm v. *qnmy*.

qnmy **Ph** KAI 14^{4,20} - ¶ indef. pronoun, whoever; *qnmy ›t* KAI 14^{4,20}: whoever you are; prob. < *qnm* (= person, cf. *qn›m* + *my*$_1$), cf. e.g. Lidzbarski Eph ii 164, Harr 144, FR 124b, v.d.Branden GP p. 62, Segert GPP p. 172, 181, Healey CISFP i 666, Amadasi Guzzo VO iv/2, 6, Gibson SSI iii p. 48; for other less prob. interpret. (among others *qnmy ›t* = Sing. + suff. 1 p.s. of *qnm* (= curse) + *›t*$_6$), cf. Munk JA v/vii 296, Stade FS Fleischer 223, Clermont-Ganneau Et ii 197 n. 2, RAO vi 203ff., 375f., Cooke NSI p. 33f., Prätorius ZDMG lviii 198, lx 167f., D(ussaud) Syr viii 365f., Torrey ZA xxvi 83f., Hirschfeld PEQ '27, 103f., Poeb 19 n. 3, Silverman JAOS xciv 268, Greenfield JNES xxxv 60, Avishur PIB 191f., Dahood Bibl lx 434.

qns$_1$ **OffAr** a form of this root (*›qns*) in MAI xiv/2, 66^{10}; Bauer & Meissner SbPAW '36, 420: = Qal (?) Impf. 1 p.s. of *qns*$_2$ related to Arab. *qnṣ*, and Ethiopic *qnṣ* (= to chase, to hunt, to jump > to act quickly (improb. interpret.)); Dupont-Sommer MAI xiv/2, 79: = Qal pass. Impf. 1 p.s. of *qns*$_1$ (= denominative of *qns*$_4$) = to be inflicted by a penalty; Yaron BiOr xv 19: = Aph Impf. 1 p.s. of *qns*$_3$ (related to *qss* = to cut) = to put an end to (less prob. interpret.; cf. also Porten & Yardeni sub TADAE B 1.1: = to block?); Grelot DAE p. 73 n. i: = subst. Sing. abs. (= penalty) < root *qns*$_1$ or < Egypt. (for this transl.,

cf. already Dupont-Sommer MAI xiv/2, 79) functioning as object of prec. *y[m]ḥnk* in l. 9 (v. *mḥ*ʾ).
qns$_2$ v. *qns$_1$*.
qns$_3$ v. *qns$_1$*.
qns$_4$ (< Greek κῆνσος < Lat. *census*, cf. Krauss GLL s.v.) - **Nab** Sing. abs. *qns* CIS ii 198[8], 209[8] - ¶ subst. fine; on this word, cf. Greenfield Mem Yalon 75ff.
v. *qns$_1$*, *šhd$_1$*.
qnʿ v. *qnyt*.
qnqm v. *qwqm*.
qs **Ph** l. *q[s]m* (= Plur. abs. of *qs* (= cup)) in CIS i 45?? (dam. context; uncert. reading, cf. Renan sub CIS i 45), cf. Greek par. ἀνὴρ [ἐ]κπωματοπ[οι]ός (= the man, the cupmaker) for *pʿl q[s]m* = manufacturer of cups (:: Slouschz TPI p. 87: or = Sing. abs. of *qsm*), cf. however Amadasi sub Kition B 36: poss. l. *qšm* = Plur. abs. of *qš$_1$* (= cup), Avigad & Greenfield IEJ xxxii 122: l. *q[bʿ]m* = Plur. abs. of *qbʿ$_4$* - Porten Bibl lvii a.l.: l. this noun (Sing. abs. *qws*) poss. in Bibl lvii 16[2] (reading of *w* however highly uncert., cf. Porten ibid.: or l. *qps* (< Egypt.) = basket?? or = certain kind of measure??).
qsṭ v. *qšṭ$_2$*.
qsṭwn (< Greek, v. infra) - **Palm** Sing. abs. *qsṭwn* CIS ii 3913 ii 69 - ¶ subst. f. (cf. Rosenthal Sprache 91 n. 3) of uncert. interpret.; Chabot CIS ii a.l.: < Greek ξεστῶν = gen. Plur. of ξέστης? (cf. Schiffmann PPT 173f.) = < Lat. *sextarius*, a measure, cf. however Cantineau Gramm 156: < Greek ξεστίον = ξέστης :: e.g. Cooke NSI p. 338: < Greek κόστος = a root used as spice (variant κόστον); *lmdyʾ dy qsṭwn ʿšr w[š]t* CIS ii 3913 ii 69f.: for the *modius*, which is 16 *sextarii* (?).
qsym **OffAr** word (?) of unknown meaning and interpret. in PF 695.
qsm$_1$ **Palm** Sing. emph. *qsmʾ* Syr vii 129[4], xvii 349[3] (*qsm[ʾ]*, v. infra) - ¶ subst. divination (cf. Ingholt Syr vii a.l., Cantineau Syr xvii a.l.); *bt qsm[ʾ]* Syr xvii 349[3]: the house of divination (part of the sanctuary of Bel?, cf. Cantineau Syr xvii a.l.; context heavily dam.); *ytb ʿl qsmʾ štʾ klh* Syr vii 129[3f.]: he presided over the divination the whole year; cf. however Milik DFD 153, 279ff.: *qsmʾ* = distributions (= Sing./Plur.? of *qsm$_2$*) - the same word poss. also in RIP 222[2]: *qsmʾ* (Sing./Plur. emph.), heavily dam. context (Gawlikowski RIP a.l.: = Sing. emph. of *qsm$_1$* or of *qsm$_3$* (= diviner)).
qsm$_2$ v. *qsm$_1$*.
qsm$_3$ v. *qsm$_1$*.
qsr ((< Greek καῖσαρ) < Lat. *caesar*) - **Nab** Sing. abs. *qysr* CIS ii 170[2], RES 2053[2]; Plur. abs. *qysryn* CIS ii 963[2] - **Palm** Sing. abs. *qsr* Syr xlviii 413[3], Inv ix 26 (*qs[r]*) - **JAr** Sing. abs. *qsr* MPAT 39[1], SM 88[4] (= Syn D A; dam. context), 89[3] (= Syn D C$_1$; *q[sr]*) - ¶ subst.

emperor.

qst v. *gšwt*.

qstr **OffAr** word of unknown meaning in Cowl 69[11].

q'dryg' (< Lat. *quadriga*, cf. FR 107.3, 208a) - **Pun** Sing. abs. *q'dryg'* KAI 122[2] - ¶ subst. chariot drawn by four horses.

q'n v. qrb_7.

q'r v. *znh*.

qp_1 **OffAr** Sing. emph. *qp'* Aḥiq 117 (v. however infra; on the reading, cf. Lindenberger APA 248 n. 303) - ¶ subst. of uncert. meaning; Epstein ZAW xxxii 135f.: = flood (Sing. abs. *qp'* < root *qp'*), cf. also Ginsberg ANET 429; Grelot DAE p. 439 (n. e): = mass of waters (< root *qpp*; cf. Kottsieper SAS 229); Montgomery OLZ '12, 536: *qp* = basket > boat; Lindenberger APA 105f.: = sea-snake? (cf. Akkad. *kuppû*??, cf. however id. ibid. 248 n. 307); on the word, cf. also Lindenberger APA 248 nn. 305, 306; for the context, v. *lb'*.

qp_2 **Palm** Plur. emph. *qpy'* Ber v 95[7] (for the reading, cf. Milik DFD 179 :: Ingholt Ber v 95, 97: l. *qwpy'* = Sing. emph. of *qwpy* (= posterior part)) - ¶ subst. exact meaning unknown; Milik DFD 179: = arch, *qpy' dy kpt'* Ber v 97[5f.]: the two halves of the arch on their pilasters (uncert. interpret.).

qp_3 v. *qb*.

qp_4 **OffAr** Sing. abs. *qp* Krael 7[19] (for this poss. reading, cf. Porten & Yardeni sub TADAE B 3.8) - ¶ subst. indicating some kind of object; Porten & Yardeni sub TADAE B 3.8: = chest?

qp'_1 **Ph** Sing. abs. *qp'* KAI 37A 3, 5 (for this prob. reading, cf. Amadasi sub Kition C 1 :: e.g. Peckham Or xxxvii 305, 309: l. *qr* (= Sing. abs. of qr_2)), 8, 12, 13, 15 (*q[p']*), B 3, 7, 11 - ¶ subst. indicating some type of coin, exact meaning unknown; Lidzbarski Handb 364: p'_1 and qp'_1 identical (improb. interpret.); Manfredi RSO lxi 83, 85f.: = tetrobol? v. qr_2.

qp'_2 v. qp_1.

qph **OffAr** Sing. emph. *qpt'* ASAE xlviii 112A 4 - ¶ subst. basket, cf. Dupont-Sommer ASAE xlviii 113; *qpt' 'lwhy* ASAE xlviii 112A 4: the basket is (meant) for it (sc. the salt; for this uncert. interpret., cf. Dupont-Sommer a.l.) - Yardeni IEJ xl 134: this subst. (Sing. abs., *qph*) poss. in IEJ xl 132[10] (*qph*),[11] (*qp'*), diff. context (= large vessel).

qpy > Akkad. *qapû* = to rise (cf. v.Soden Or xxxvii 263, xlvi 192, AHW s.v., cf. also CAD s.v.).

qpyd v. qpr_1.

qpyz v. qpr_1.

qpyls (< Greek κάπηλος, v. however infra) - **OffAr** Sing. abs. *qpyls* BASOR ccxx 55[2] (for the reading, cf. Geraty BASOR ccxx a.l., AUSS xix 138ff. (cf. also Skaist IEJ xxviii 107; Greek par. καπήλου; cf. however Naveh with Skaist IEJ xxviii 107 n. 7: l. *hnsq*? (= HAPH Pf. 3 p.s.m. of *slq*$_1$)) - ¶ subst. retail-dealer (cf. Skaist IEJ xxviii 107, cf. also Geraty AUSS xix 139f., FS Freedman 547 :: Geraty BASOR ccxx 55: = moneylender), v. also supra.

qpyr$_1$ v. *qpr*$_1$.

qpyr$_2$ v.Soden Or xlvi 192: > Akkad. *qapīru* = a certain measure of capacity (cf. idem AHW s.v.; uncert. interpret., cf. also CAD s.v.: *qapīru* = container).
v. *qpr*$_1$.

qpl$_1$ cf. Frah app. 5 (*kplwn*) = to shave, to erase (cf. Nyberg FP 98 (cf. also Toll ZDMG-Suppl viii 38) :: Ebeling Frah a.l.: l. *kprwn* = form of *kpr*$_2$ (= to sin)).

qpl$_2$ v. *qdm*$_3$.

qplwṭ (< Greek κεφάλωτον) - **Hebr** Plur. abs. *qplwṭwt* SM 49[3] - ¶ subst. leek with a head, porret.

qplrgyʾ (< Greek κεφαλαργία, cf. Naveh & Shaked AMB p. 92) - **JAr** Sing. abs. *qplrgyʾ* AMB 11[5] - ¶ subst. headache (cf. Segal JSS xxxi 97).

qps v. *qs*.

qpsws **JAr** Hachlili BASOR ccxxxv 56: the *qpswsʾ* in BASOR ccxxxv 24 no. 13a prob. = Sing. emph. of *qpsws* (= ossuary); highly uncert. interpret.; highly uncert. reading, cf. Hachlili a.l.: or l. *qnmwmʾ* = n.p.?

qpp v. *qwp*$_1$.

qpr$_1$ **OffAr** Sing. abs. *qpyr* Sach 80 vi A 4 (context however highly uncert.); emph. *qprʾ* RES 492A 5 (:: Halévy RS xii 60, 64: l. *sprʾ* = Sing. emph. of *spr*$_6$ (= sapphire)), *qpyrʾ* RES 492A 4, 6, 7 (for this reading in RES 492, cf. e.g. Lidzbarski Eph ii 238, Grelot DAE p. 139 n. h :: Halévy RS xii 59, 65: l. *spyrʾ* = Sing. emph. of *spr*$_6$ (= sapphire)), ASAE xxvi 29[3] (:: Lacau with Aimé-Giron ASAE xxvi 30 n. 1: l. poss. *qpydʾ* = Sing. emph. of *qpyd* (var. of *qpyz* < Iran. = a certain measure of capacity)) - ¶ subst. m. of unknown meaning, prob. indicating an object; Grelot DAE p. 139f. (n. h): net?; Aimé-Giron ASAE xxvi 30: or = basket? (the same word as *qpyr*$_2$) :: SC p. 50 = papyrus??

qpr$_2$ **Hebr** Sing. abs. *qpr* SM 6[3] - ¶ subst. used in the comb. *ʾlyʿzr hqpr* SM 6[2f.]: E. the *qpr* (on the meaning of this surname, cf. e.g. Urman IEJ xxii 22).

qṣ$_1$ **Hebr** Sing. abs. *qṣ* KAI 182[7] (cf. e.g. Cassuto SMSR xii 112, Albright BASOR xcii 23 (n. 38), Talmon Lesh xxv 199f., JAOS lxxxiii 183f., Röllig KAI a.l., Gibson SSI i p. 2, 4 (:: Dir p. 9 (n. 1): to be pronounced *qayiṣ*) :: Rathjen JBL lxxxiii 416f.: = Sing. abs. of *qṣ*$_1$ and of *qṣ*$_2$ (= end; play on words) :: Segal JSS vii 219f.: = QAL Imper. s.m. of (*qṣṣ* = to cut) or of *qyṣ* (= to gather summer fruits)) - **OldAr** Sing. emph. *kyṣʾ* KAI 216[19] (cf. e.g. Garbini 273, Degen AAG p. 42, Kutscher IOS i 108 n. 25, Claassen AION xxi 296, Kaufman AIA 121,

Segert AAG p. 108) - **JAr** Sing. emph. *qyṭ[ʾ]* Syr xlv 101[14] - ¶ subst. m. - **1)** summer; *byt kyṣʾ* KAI 216[19]: summer palace; *zrʿh [d]qyṭ[ʾ]* Syr xlv 101[14]: summer seed (heavily dam. context) - **2)** summer fruit; *yrḥ qṣ* KAI 182[7]: the month of the summer-fruit (cf. Dir p. 9, Mosc p. 18, and litt. quoted supra, cf. also Borowski AIAI 38) - Segal ATNS a.l.: l. poss. *kṣʾ* (= Sing. emph. of *kṣ* (= variant of *qṣ*$_1$)) in ATNS 69b 5 (uncert. reading and interpret.).

qṣ$_2$ v. *qṣ*$_1$, *qṣh*.

qṣ$_3$ **OffAr** Sing. f. emph., cf. Warka 17: *ka-ṣa-ta-ʾ*, 42: *ka-ṣa-ta-a* (for both instances :: Driver AfO iii 52: = Sing. emph. of *qṣt*$_2$ (= end)) - ¶ adj. prob. meaning: deficient, imperfect (cf. Gordon AfO xii 108, 117, cf. also Dupont-Sommer RA xxxix 48: broken) - poss. < root *qṣʾ*, cf. Gordon AfO xii 117, Dupont-Sommer RA xxxix 48; for *k* pro *q*, cf. Gordon AfO xii 112, Dupont-Sommer RA xxxix 48.

qṣb$_1$ **Pun** a form of this verb (= to cut) in KAI 145[9] (QAL Part. pass. s.m. abs.?); Février Sem vi 25: *qṣb* = Sing. abs. of *qṣb*$_3$ (= dressed stone, statue (cf. also v.d.Branden RSF i 166, 170: = emblem, sign)); cf. also Krahmalkov RSF iii 188f., 196, 204: *qṣb* = QAL Pf. 3 p.s.m.; highly uncert. context.

qṣb$_2$ **Palm** Plur. emph. *qṣbʾ* CIS ii 3913 ii 102 (cf. e.g. CIS ii a.l., Milik DFD 152, Schiffmann PPT 185, 320, cf. however Cooke NSI p. 329: = slaughtered animals (Plur. emph. of *qṣb*$_4$??), cf. however idem ibid. p. 339; Greek par. τοῦ σφάκτρου = tax paid for victims) - **JAr** Sing. emph. *qṣbʾ* Mas 512 - ¶ subst. butcher (for CIS ii 3913 ii 102, v. supra).

qṣb$_3$ v. *qṣb*$_1$.

qṣb$_4$ v. *qṣb*$_2$.

qṣh **Ph** Sing. cstr. *qṣt* KAI 26A i 21; Plur. abs. *qṣyt* KAI 26A i 14 (on this form, cf. Bron RIPK 64) - **Pun** Sing. abs. *qṣʾh* KAI 173[3] (?, cf. Levi Della Vida Atti Tor lxx 193, Röllig KAI a.l., Bron RIPK 64) - **Palm** Sing. emph. *qṣtʾ* Syr xl 34[4] (cf. Teixidor Sumer xviii 64, Syr xl 35), 47[4] (cf. however Starcky Syr xl 50f.: = Sing. emph. of *qṣt*$_2$, poss. interpret. for both Palm. instances :: Ingholt PBP 137 (nn. 144, 145): in both instances = Plur. emph. of *qṣt*$_3$ (= archer) related to *qšt*$_2$) - ¶ subst. end, border; *bqṣt gbly* KAI 26A i 21: at the edge of my territory (:: v.d.Branden Meltô i 44, 46, 80: in a district of ...); *hqṣʾh šhbhrm* KAI 173[3]: the edge of the wells (uncert. context, v. supra, v. *bʾr*); *dy hww ... bqṣtʾ tnn* Syr xl 33[2f.]: who were here at the border (for Syr xl 47[3f.], v. *rʾš*$_1$) - this word (Sing. abs. *qṣh*) poss. also in DA ii 15, uncert. interpret., cf. Hoftijzer DA a.l.; or = Sing. + suff. 3 p.s.m. of *qṣ*$_2$ (= end)?, cf. Hackett BTDA 30, 72, 94, 133.

v. *qṣy*.

qṣw **Ph** Teixidor Sem xxix 10f.: l. this subst. (Plur. cstr. *qṣwy*; = border) in RES 1204[1] (uncert. reading, highly uncert. interpret.).

qṣy **Ph** PI‘EL (cf. e.g. Röllig KAI a.l., FR 187 :: Gibson SSI iii p. 107ff.: = QAL (= to perish), cf. Ginsberg FS Gaster 143 n. 54 :: Levi Della Vida RSO xxxix 301: poss. = Sing. + suff. 3 p.pl.m. of *qṣh*) Impf. 3 p.pl. *yqṣn* KAI 14[22]; Inf. + suff. 3 p.s.m. *qṣtnm* KAI 14[9f.] - **Pun** PI‘EL Impf. 3 p.s.m. + suff. 3 p.s.m. *yqṣy’* CIS i 3784[3] - ¶ verb PI‘EL to cut > to extirpate; *wyqṣn hmmlkt h’ ... l‘lm* KAI 14[22]: and they (i.e. the gods) will extirpate that king forever; *b‘l ḥmn yqṣy’* CIS i 3784[2f.]: B.H. will cut him off, cf. KAI 14[9f.].

qṣ‘ **Hebr** Sing. abs. *qṣ‘* SM 49[3] - ¶ subst. cassia; cf. also Löw ii 113f.

qṣp **OldCan** NIPH Pf. 3 p.s.m. *na-aq-ṣa-pu* EA 82[51]; 1 p.s. *[na-]aq-ṣa-ap-ti* EA 93[5] (on these forms, cf. Sivan GAG 173, 262) - ¶ verb NIPH to be furious; cf. *kṣp*.

qṣṣ v. *qṣ$_1$*.

qṣr$_1$ **Hebr** QAL Impf. 3 p.s.m. *yqṣr* KAI 200[4]; Part. act. s.m. abs. *qṣr* KAI 200[3]; pl.m. abs. *qṣrm* KAI 200[10] - **OffAr** QAL Pf. 2 p.s.f. *qṣrty* Cowl 66 ix 2 (highly uncert. reading, dam. context) - ¶ verb QAL to harvest: KAI 200[4]; Part. act. harvester: KAI 200[10]; *‘bdk qṣr hyh ‘bdk* KAI 200[2f.]: as to your servant, your servant was harvesting (for this interpret., cf. e.g. Naveh IEJ x 131f., 134, Albright ANET 568, Gibson SSI i p. 28, Clifford CBQ xl 409, Hoftijzer FS Lebram 1ff., cf. also Garr DGSP 187 :: e.g. Vinnikov ArchOr xxxiii 547, Lemaire Sem xxi 61, 63, IH i 260, 262, Briend TPOA 134, Pardee Maarav i 36, 40f., HAHL 20f., Suzuki AJBI viii 5ff., Conrad TUAT i 250, Smelik HDAI 90, Weippert FS Rendtorff 460 (n. 26): your servant is a harvester, your servant was ...) - for KAI 200, cf. also Lemaire Sem xxi 77ff. (= IH i 266ff.) - on this root, cf. also Collini SEL iv 30f. n. 62 - and cf. Borowski AIAI 59. v. *gzr$_1$*, *kṣr$_1$*, *qṣr$_3$*.

qṣr$_2$ v. *mqṣr*.

qṣr$_3$ **Ph** Sing. abs. *qṣr* KAI 26A iii 2, C iv 5 - **Hebr** Sing. abs. *qṣr* KAI 182[5] (cf. e.g. Röllig KAI a.l., Gibson SSI i p. 2f. :: Segal JSS vii 219: = QAL Imper. s.m. of *qṣr$_1$* :: Driver PEQ ’45, 6 (n. 2; div. otherwise): l. *qṣrw* = QAL Pf. 3 p.pl. of *qṣr$_1$*); + suff. 3 p.s.m. *qṣr* KAI 200[6] (cf. Pardee Maarav i 35f., 46, HAHL 21f., 237 (cf. also Naveh Lesh xxx 70, Gibson SSI i p. 28f., Bruton JNES xlii 165) :: e.g. Delekat Bibl li 466, Garbini AION xxii 102, Lemaire Sem xxi 61, 71, IH i 261: = Sing. abs. (cf. also Rainey JBL cii 632) :: Cross BASOR clxv 43 n. 31, Amusin & Heltzer IEJ xiv 149f., 152 n. 10, Weippert FS Rendtorff 461 (n. 30): = lapsus for *qṣrh* (= Sing. + suff. 3 p.s.m.) :: Naveh IEJ x 131, 133, Yeivin BiOr xix 5, Suzuki AJBI viii 5, 11 (div. otherwise): l. *qṣrw* = Sing. + suff. 3 p.s.m. (cf. also Zevit MLAHE 21f., Garr DGSP 103) :: Albright with Cross BASOR clxv 45 n. 46, ANET 568 (n. 2; div. otherwise): l. *qṣrw* = QAL Part. act. pl.m. + suff. 3 p.s.m. of *qṣr$_1$*); + suff. 1 p.s. *qṣry* KAI 200[9] - ¶ subst. - **1)** harvest; *yrḥ qṣr š‘rm* KAI 182[4]: the month

of the barley harvest; *yrḥ qṣr wkl* KAI 182^5: the month of the wheat harvest and the measuring (?, v. *kl*$_2$; on this text, cf. e.g. Dir p. 8, Mosc p. 15f., Février Sem i 35f.) - **2)** what is harvested: KAI 200^{6,9} (cf. e.g. Weippert FS Rendtorff 461 n. 30); for KAI 200, cf. Lemaire Sem xxi 77 (= IH i 266f.), cf. also Cross BASOR clxv 46, Mettinger SSO 97 - on this word, cf. also Borowski AIAI 57ff.
v. *qšr*$_2$, *šmš*$_2$.

qṣr$_4$ (Cantineau Nab i 172: < Arab., less prob. interpret., cf. O'Connor JNES xlv 218) - **Nab** Sing. emph. *qṣrʾ* CIS ii 336^1 (reading of *ṣ* uncert. :: Nebe with Beyer & Livingstone ZDMG cxxxvii 292: l. *ḥgrʾ* = Sing. emph. of *ḥgr*$_4$ (= what is consecrated)) - ¶ subst. small room, cella; Catastini RSF xiii 6: this word also in RES 1204^1 (uncert. interpret.).
v. *qr*$_2$.

qṣr$_5$ v. *qr*$_2$.

qṣr$_6$ **OffAr**, cf. Frah-S$_2$ 115 (*kslʾ*) - **Nab** Plur. emph. *[q]ṣryʾ* HDS 151^1 (v. infra) - ¶ subst. poss. meaning camp (< Lat. *castra*), cf. Starcky HDS 154f., cf. however idem ibid.: or l. *[ḥ]ṣryʾ* = Plur. emph. of *ḥṣr*$_4$?, or l. *[ʾ]tryʾ* = Plur. emph. of *ʾtr*$_2$ (= *ʾšr*$_4$)?

qṣr$_7$ v. *kṣr*$_7$.

qṣrh **Pun** Sing. (or Plur.) abs. *qṣrt* KAI 69^{4,6,10,13}, 74^8 - ¶ subst. of unknown meaning indicating part of victim; Dussaud Orig 149: = chest (cf. also v.d.Branden RSO xl 117); cf. however Capuzzi StudMagr ii 65: = intestines; Rosenthal ANET 656f.: = neck; Levi Della Vida RSO xxxix 303f.: = short ribs; CIS i sub 165, Cooke NSI p. 118: = cuttings, *prosecta* (cf. also Lagrange ERS 470, 473); Prätorius ZDMG lx 175 (cf. also Röllig KAI a.l., Amadasi ICO p. 176f.): = knuckle - on this word, cf. also Amadasi Guzzo SSMA 116.

qṣt$_1$ (cf. BL 63h) - **Hebr** Sing. cstr. *qṣt* DJD ii 24B 7, C 7 - **OffAr** Sing. abs. *qṣt* Cowl 27^4, Krael 9^3; cstr. *qṣt* Cowl 29^3, 35^4; + suff. 3 p.s.f. *qṣth* Herm 2^7 (:: Porten & Yardeni sub TADAE A 2.2: = + suff. 3 p.s.m.) - **JAr** Sing. cstr. *qṣt* MPAT 48^5 (cf. Milik sub DJD ii 30; or = abs.??, heavily dam. context), 49 i 11 (*[q]ṣt* :: Beyer ATTM 318: l. *št* (= *št*$_5$ = *šš*$_3$)) - ¶ subst. part, share; *qṣt mn byty* Krael 9^3: a part of my house (cf. Cowl 27$^{4f.}$); *ksp š 2 ... mn qṣt kspʾ wnksyʾ zy ʿl spr ʾntwtky* Cowl 35$^{3ff.}$: (prob. transl.) silver, two *sh.* ... being part of the silver and the goods described in your marriage contract (cf. also Cowl 29^3; *mn* explained as *mn*$_5$ of identity), cf. Cowl a.l., Grelot DAE p. 86, 87, Porten & Yardeni sub TADAE B 4.5, cf. however id. ibid. B 4.6 (= Cowl 35): = from part of the silver (or perhaps = silver two *sh.* ... from the total (*qṣt* being Sing. cstr. of *qṣt*$_2$ = total) of the silver ... (*mn* explained as partitive *mn*$_5$); for this interpret., cf. Sach p. 62, Ungnad ArPap 24); *qṣt lḥm* MPAT 49 i 11: a little bread - the *nṣt* in MPAT 64 iii 4 poss. to be read *qṣt* (assuming that part of the *q* is obliterated, cf. Starcky RB lxi 178)

- *mn qṣt* in DJD ii 24B 7, C 7 (*[m]n*) of diff. interpret.: = part of? :: Milik DJD ii p. 127: *mnqṣt* = dissimilation < *mqṣt* = part.
v. *kṣt*.

qṣt$_2$ v. *kṣt*, *qṣ$_3$*, *qṣh*, *qṣt$_1$* (prob. the same word as *qṣt$_1$*).

qṣt$_3$ v. *qṣh*.

qq$_1$ **DA** Plur. abs. *qqn* i 16 (or = Plur. abs. of *qqh*?, cf. Hoftijzer DA a.l. :: McCarter BASOR ccxxxix 52, 56: = QAL Part. act. pl.m. abs. of *qqy* (= to decree) :: H.P.Müller ZAW xciv 218, 229ff. (n. 101): = Sing. cstr. of *qqn$_1$* (= certain type of plant); v. also infra) - ¶ subst. trouble, oppression (for the Plur., cf. Hoftijzer DA a.l.; cf. also Levine JAOS ci 197, 199: = acts of constraint (cf. also Hackett BTDA 29, 54f., 94, 133); on the problems, cf. also H. & M.Weippert ZDPV xcviii 100 (n. 123): or *qqn* = Sing. cstr. of *qqn$_2$* (= oppression)?, cf. also Weinfeld Shn v/vi 142, 146, Garr DGSP 95); *kl ḥzw qqn* DA i 16: all suffered oppression (cf. also Sasson UF xvii 288, 304 :: Caquot & Lemaire Syr liv 201: all saw restricted ones (in the context: saw the restriction of (the abundance of cattle)), cf. also Lemaire BAT 320, Puech FS Grelot 25, 28) - cf. *ʿq$_2$*.

qq$_2$ v. *qqbtn*.

qq$_3$ v. *qqbtn*.

qqb$_1$ v. *qqbtn*.

qqb$_2$ **DA** word of unknown meaning in DA iv g 1 (heavily dam. context), poss. = some kind of tree or green herbs (cf. Hoftijzer DA a.l.).
v. *qqbtn*.

qqbtn **OldAr** word(s) of unknown meaning in KAI 222A 32; Cantineau RA xxviii 172f.: = *qq* (Sing. abs. of *qq$_2$* (= pelican); cf. also Dupont-Sommer Sf p. 47) + *btn* (= Plur. abs. of *byt$_2$*); Hoftijzer DA p. 256: = *qqb* (= Sing. abs. of *qqb$_2$* (= tree)) + *tn* (= Sing. abs. of *tn$_2$* (= jackal)); Lipiński Stud 30, 50: = *qq* (= QAL Part. act. s.m. abs. of *qwq*/ *qqq* (= to demolish)) + *btn* (= Plur. abs. of *byt$_2$*), less prob. interpret.; Fitzmyer AIS 49 (cf. also Sader EAS 129): = *qq* (= Sing. cstr. of *qq$_3$* (= throat, neck)) + *btn* (= Sing. abs. of *btn$_2$* (= serpent), cf. also Halpern FS Lambdin 122); Dupont-Sommer Sf p. 47, 149: *qqbtn* (= Sing. abs.) = partridge? (cf. idem AH i/2, 6 (cf. also Koopmans 52: *qqbtn* indicating some kind of harmful animal)), less prob. interpret.; Lemaire & Durand IAS 134: poss. l. (div. otherwise) *lhqqbtn* = *l$_5$* + *hqqbtn* (= HAPH Inf. + suff. of *qqb$_1$* (= to make shear)) or l. <*y*>*qqb* (= QAL Impf. 3 p.s.m. of *qqb$_1$* (= to shear)) + *tn* (= Sing. abs. of *tn$_2$* (= jackal)), less prob. interpret.; Gibson SSI ii p. 31, 42: *qqbtn* = adj. (Sing. m. abs.), cut off, lopped off (improb. interpret., cf. also Garbini OA xv 352); Thomas JSS v 283: *qqbtn* (< root *qbb*) = withering, drought (improb. interpret.).

qqh v. *qq$_1$*.

qqy v. *qq$_1$*.

qqn$_1$ v. *qq*$_1$.
qqn$_2$ v. *qq*$_1$.
qqq v. *qqbtn*.
qr$_1$ **Mo** Sing. abs. *qr* KAI 181[11,12,24]; Plur. abs. *qrn* KAI 181[29] - ¶ subst. town; cf. *qryh* - the same word (= wall; Sing. abs.) prob. also in KAI 43[13] (*qr*), cf. e.g. Clermont-Ganneau Et ii 175, Chabot sub RES 1211, Honeyman JEA xxvi 58, 64, Röllig KAI a.l., Gibson SSI iii p. 137 :: e.g. Cooke NSI p. 83, 87 (div. otherwise): l. *bqr* (= Sing. abs. of *bqr*$_2$), cf. also Lidzbarski Handb 242, sub KI 36, Harr 91; for the context, v. *smr*$_1$ - on this word, cf. also Zimmerman SFAV 582ff., Dreyer FS v.Selms 17ff.
v. *nṣb*$_5$.
qr$_2$ **Ph** Sing. abs. *qr* KAI 37A 9, 11 (for the reading, cf. e.g. Peckham Or xxxvii 305, 315, Amadasi sub Kition C$_1$ :: e.g. CIS i sub 86, Röllig KAI a.l.: l. *qp*ʾ (= Sing. abs. of *qp*ʾ$_1$)), 15, 16, B 8, 10 - ¶ subst. indicating some kind of coin, exact meaning unknown (cf. also Manfredi RSO lxi 83: = the silver stater) - this word (Sing. abs. *qr*) poss. also in KAI 37A 6, cf. e.g. Cooke NSI p. 65, 67, Röllig KAI a.l., Puech Sem xxix 31 :: Amadasi Kition C$_1$ a.l.: l. poss. *qṣr* (= Sing. abs. of *qṣr*$_5$ (= small coin)) :: Masson & Sznycer RPC 26f., 40f., Delcor UF xi 153, Gibson SSI iii p. 125, 127f.: l. *qṣr* (= Sing. abs. of *qṣr*$_4$) :: Peckham Or xxxvii 305f., 310: l. *rṣd* (= Sing. abs. of *rṣd* (= watch, stand, guard)).
v. *qp*ʾ$_1$.
qr$_3$ **OffAr** Sing. abs. *qr* TC xiii 208 (for the reading, cf. Vattioni Or xlviii 145) - ¶ subst. indicating prob. a certain type of dry measure; Vattioni Or xlviii 145: = *kr*$_1$; Vattioni ibid.: l. *qr* (= Sing. abs.) in TC xii 58 (highly uncert. reading).
qr$_4$ v. *ṣr*$_2$.
qr$_5$ v. *ṣr*$_2$.
qrʾ$_1$ **Ph** QAL Pf. 3 p.s.m. *qr*ʾ KAI 10[2] (cf. FR 174, 276b also for litt. (cf. also Chiera Hen x 134); interpret. as Inf. (abs.; cf. also Amadasi Guzzo VO iii 89f., Gai Or li 254ff.) less prob.); 1 p.s. *qr*ʾ*t* KAI 10[7] - **Pun** QAL Pf. 1 p.s., cf. Poen 930, 940: *corathi* (var. in 940: *(suc)curati* pro *si corathi* :: Krahmalkov Or lvii 57, 60f.: *(suc)curati(m)* lapsus for *succart* (= *š*$_{10}$ + Sing. abs. of *qrt*$_1$) *caruti* = QAL Pf. 1 p.s. of *qr*ʾ$_1$ :: FR 80b, Friedrich OLZ '69, 47: *corathi* = lapsus for *carothi*, cf. also Sznycer PPP 52f.); 1 p.s. + suff. 3 p.pl.m., cf. Poen 1023: *coratim* (var. *corahim*, *coraphim*; cf. Sznycer PPP 144, J.J.Glück & Maurach Semitics ii 123, cf. however Schroed 297, 318, L.H.Gray AJSL xxxix 82: = QAL Pf. 1 p.s. + suff. 3 p.pl.m. of *qr*ʾ$_2$ (= *qry*$_1$)); Imper. s.m. *qr*ʾ KAI 145[14], 165[1] (cf. Février BAr '51/52, 41, 43, Levi Della Vida OA iv 67, Röllig KAI a.l., v.d.Branden RSF ii 146); Part. act. s.m. abs. *qr*ʾ CIS i 4883[4], 5510[6] (cf. Février CIS i a.l., cf. also id. BAr '46/49,

171, cf. already Chabot BAr '41/42, 390, 393) - **Hebr** QAL Pf. 1 p.s. *qr'ty* KAI 193[12]; Imper. s.m. *qr'* KAI 196[5]; Inf. cstr. *qr'* KAI 193[9] (cf. e.g. Cassuto RSO xvi 173, Torczyner Lach i p. 51, 55, Gibson SSI i p. 39, Lemaire IH i 101f. :: Sachs with Albright BASOR lxi 12f., Albright BASOR lxxiii 18, ANET 322, Röllig KAI a.l., Galling TGI 76: = QAL Imper. s.m. (cf. also Cross FS Iwry 43, 45) :: Dussaud Syr xix 264: = QAL Pf. 3 p.s.m.),[10], 196[13] (cf. e.g. de Vaux RB xlviii 197, 199, Albright BASOR lxxxii 23, Gibson SSI i p. 45 :: Albright BASOR lxx 15f. (div. otherwise, v. also *'z₂*): l. *yqr'* = QAL Impf. 3 p.s.m. (cf. also Elliger ZDPV lxii 79) :: e.g. Torczyner Lach i p. 202, Hempel ZAW lvi 135: *qr'* = QAL Pf. 3 p.s.m.; v. also *'z₂*); Part. act. s.m. abs. *qr'* KAI 189[2f.], *qwr'* Frey 896[1] (reading *qyr'* mistaken) - **Samal** QAL Pf. 3 p.s.m. + suff. 1 p.s. *qrny* KAI 214[13] (cf. e.g. Cooke NSI p. 162, 167, Lagrange ERS 492f., Friedrich ZS i 8, Friedr 28*a, Donner KAI a.l., Lipiński OLP viii 103 × Halévy RS i 151, Dion p. 381f.: = Sing. + suff. 1 p.s. of *qrn* (> power; cf. also Poeb 48 n. 4) :: Gibson SSI ii p. 66, 72 (div. otherwise): l. *yqrny* = QAL Impf. 3 p.s.m. + suff. 1 p.s. (poss. reading, improb. interpret.)) - **OffAr** QAL Pf. 1 p.s. *qryt* Cowl 7[10]; 1 p.pl. *qr'n* ATNS 94[2] (?, heavily dam. context); Impf. 3 p.s.m. *yqr'* ASAE xxxix 357[7] (uncert. reading, diff. and dam. context); 1 p.s. *'qr'* Cowl 7[7], Sach 78 i B 4; 3 p.pl.m. *yqr'wn* Aḥiq 117; Imper. s.m. *qr'* KAI 233[12] (:: R.A.Bowman UMS xx 277: = QAL Pf. 3 p.s.m.); Part. act. m. pl. abs. *qryn* AG 38[2] (heavily dam. context); cf. Frah xxiii 5 (*klytwn*), xxviii 31 (*klytwn*), app. 4 (*yklwn*, cf. Nyberg FP 98 :: Schaeder with Ebeling Frah a.l.: < root *gly* :: Ebeling Frah a.l.: < root *nkl₁*), Paik 543 (*klytn*), Nisa 132[3], 135[2], 137[3], 144[2], 145[2], 147[3], 148[2], 149[2], 150[2], etc. (*qry*). GIPP 25, 26, 62, SaSt 19 - **Nab** QAL Pf. 3 p.s.m. *qr'* RES 528 (?, uncert. interpret.); 2 p.s.m. *qr't* RES 1479[3] (context however dam.); Impf. 3 p.s.m. *yqr'* J 200; Imper. s.m. *qry* CIS ii 170[4] (context however diff., cf. Cantineau Nab i 78, 83 :: Levinson NAI 213: = QAL Part. pass. s.m. abs.); Part. act. s.m. abs. *qr'* IEJ xxxvi 56[1]; s.m. emph. *qr''* CIS ii 416, RES 1401[4]; ITP Impf. 3 p.s.m. *ytqr'* CIS ii 488B 1; Part. s.m. abs. *mtqr'* CIS ii 158[2], 486[1], 2615[1] (*[mt]qr'*), RES 529[3] (dam. and uncert. context), Syr xxxv 244[2], ADAJ xxi 145 n. 5 i 1 (uncert. reading; = RB xliv 269 no. 5); Ipt (< Arab., cf. Cantineau Nab i 73, 80, Garbini HDS 36, Diem Or xlviii 212) *mqtry* CIS ii 499[2], 1124[2] (*[m]qtry*), 1147[1], 1254[3], 1296[2], 1429[2], 1577[1] (*[m]qtr[y]*) - **Palm** QAL Pf. 3 p.s.m. *qr'* RIP 121[3], Inv xi 35[2], *qr* CIS ii 4034[5], 4038[4], 4046[7], 4047[3] (cf. CIS ii a.l. :: e.g. Cooke NSI p. 300: l. *q[ym]hy* = PA'EL Pf. 3 p.s.m. + suff. 3 p.s.m. of *qwm₁*, cf. also Díez Merino LA xxi 95), 4051[5], 4084[6], 4092[3], 4099[2], RIP 114[5], Inv xi 16[4], 19[5], 26[2], 37[4]; + suff. 3 p.s.m. *qryh* CIS ii 4011[5], RIP 120[4], *qrh* CIS ii 4047[5] (cf. Cantineau Gramm 74, Rosenthal Sprache 72; or rather = QAL Pf. 3 p.s.m.?); 3 p.s.f. *qr* (lapsus) CIS ii 4083[3];

+ suff. 3 p.s.m. *qrth* Ber iii 99^3; 3 p.pl.m. *qrw* CIS ii 4053^6, 4085^5, 4100^3, RIP 119^7, 124^5, Inv xi 1^5, 17^6; 1 p.pl. + suff. 3 p.s.m. *qryny* CIS ii 4048^6; ITP Part. s.m. abs. *mtqr'* CIS ii 3934^2, 3978^5, 4159^{3,5}, 4203^2 (Greek par. τοῦ ἐπικαλουμένου), 4288^6, RIP 96^3, Syr xii 120^3, 122^2, Ber ii 99 ii 1, xix 69^2, MUSJ xxxviii 106^2, *mtqrh* CIS ii 3923^2, 3966^2 (= RIP 156^{11}), 4114^3, Inv viii 9^4, xii 17^3 (= RIP 105), Syr lxii 273^2 (Greek par. ἐπικαλουμένου), etc., etc., *mqr'* CIS ii 3991^4, Syr lxii 257, AAS xxxvi/xxxvii 169 no. 10^4 (lapsus?, cf. Cantineau Gramm 86, Rosenthal Sprache 69 n. 5 (less prob. interpret.), cf. J.Ar. ITP forms with assimilated *t*, cf. Dalman Gramm p. 233, Odeberg 34), *mqrh* Ber ii 98^1 (lapsus?, v. however supra); s.f. abs. *mtqry'* CIS ii 4582^4; pl.m. abs. *mtqrn* Inv iv 3^2 (= CIS ii 4124; reading highly uncert.; Greek par. ἐπικαλουμένου) - **Hatra** QAL Impf. 3 p.s.m. + suff. 3 p.s.m. *lqryhy* 23^4 (for the reading, cf. Milik RN vi/iv 55, Caquot Syr xl 15f., Degen ZDMG cxxi 125, NESE ii 100, Vattioni IH a.l. :: Caquot Syr xxix 102f. (div. otherwise): l. *lqrwh* = QAL Impf. 3 p.pl.m. + suff. 3 p.s.m. (for the reading, cf. also Donner sub KAI 244)), 53^2, *lqrhy* 101^2 (for this reading, cf. Caquot Syr xl 11, Degen NESE ii 101, Vattioni IH a.l. :: Safar Sumer xvii 33f. (n. 81): l. *lqd(?)hy* = QAL Impf. of *qdd*$_1$ (= to cut off > to mutilate, to deface (sc. an inscription)), reading *lqrhy* however poss.) - **JAr** ITP Part. s.f. abs. *mtqryy'* AMB 11^5 (dam. context), *mtqryh* AMB 9^1 - ¶ verb QAL - **1)** to call - a) + obj., *qr' hmw* KAI 233^{12}: call them - b) + '*l*$_6$, *ql 'š qr' 'l r'w* KAI 189^2: a man's voice calling to his colleague - **2)** to call upon; + obj. + *l*$_5$ + Inf., *qrny lbn'* KAI 214^{13}: he (sc. the god Hadad) called upon me to build (v. however supra) - **3)** to invoke; *yth alonim walonuth si corathi* Poen 930: the gods and goddesses whom I invoke (cf. Poen 940) - a) + obj., *qr't 't* (v. '*yt*$_3$) *rbty b'lt gbl* KAI 10$^{7f.}$: I invoked my lady the mistress of Byblos (cf. KAI 10$^{2f.}$, CIS ii 4048^6, RIP 120^4); *qryh bkwl 'tr* CIS ii 4011^5: he has invoked him everywhere; *qrth bḥšwk'* (v. *ḥšk*$_2$) Ber iii 99^3: she has invoked him in darkness (i.e. in a difficult situation) - b) + *l*$_5$, *qr lh* CIS ii 4034^5: he has invoked him (cf. CIS i 5510^6, ii 4038^4, 4046^7, 4051^5, 4053^6, Inv xi 1^5, 17^6, etc., etc.); *qr lh bym' wbybš'* CIS ii 4047$^{3f.}$: he has invoked him at sea and on land; *qrw lh b'q'* RIP 119: they invoked him in distress - **4)** to call (i.e. to name); + *l*$_5$ + obj., *'l kn yqr'wn lqp' lb'* Aḥiq 117: therefore they call the flood (?, v. *qp*$_1$) *lb'* (v. *lb'*) - **5)** to read: KAI 196^5, J 200, RES 1479^3; *qr' lmm'l' mt'* KAI 145^{14}: read (it) from above to below (v. also *m'l*$_2$) - a) + obj.: KAI 193^{12}; *l' yd'th qr' spr* KAI 193$^{8f.}$: you cannot read a letter (v. also *yd'*$_1$), cf. KAI 196$^{13f.}$ - b) + obj. + *l*$_5$, *mn dy lqrhy l'dyn ktb'* Hatra 101^2: whoever will read this text (cf. Hatra 53$^{1f.}$) - c) + *l*$_5$ + obj., *'m nsh 'yš lqr' ly spr* KAI 193$^{9f.}$: no one has ever dared to read me a letter - d) Part. act., reader: RES 1401^4, CIS ii 416, Frey

896^1 (dam. context), cf. poss. also IEJ xxxvi 56^1 (cf. Negev IEJ xxxvi 58); in CIS i 4883^4 indication of function (herald?) - **6)** to declare - a) + l_5, *qryt lk* Cowl 7^{10}: I have (solemnly) declared in the presence of you (i.e. the opposing party) - b) + l_5 + *ʿl_7*, *ʾqrʾ lk ʿl ḥrmbytʾl* Cowl 7^7: I will make in your presence a (solemn) declaration by Ch. (for the meaning of *qrʾ* in Cowl 7 :: Milik RB xlviii 566: *qrʾ l ʿl* = to adjure someone to take an oath by (sc. the god) :: Porten Arch 316: = to call for/against someone to (sc. the god), cf. also Porten & Greenfield JEAS p. 124, Porten & Yardeni sub TADAE B 7.2 :: Cowl a.l.: = to challenge someone by (sc. the god) :: Joüon MUSJ xviii 62: *qrʾ* in Cowl 7 = to summon) - ITP to be given a nickname: passim; cf. also *ʿtʿqb br ʿgylw ... dmqrʾ qrʾ* AAS xxxvi/xxxvii 169 no. $10^{3f.}$: A. son of O. who is also called Q. (with Greek par. Ἴουλιος Ἀυρήλιος Αθηάκα[βος Ὀ]γήλου ..... [...] τοῦ καὶ Κω[ρρα]) - the form of this root in Sumer xx 19* ii 3 poss. to be read *mtqrʾ* (= ITP Part. s.m. abs.) :: Safar Sumer xx a.l.: l. *mhqrʾ* = HAPH Part. s.m. abs. (= the reciter) - a QAL Impf. 3 p.s.m. + suff. 3 p.s.m. poss. in Hatra 24^3: *lqryhy* (cf. Degen ZDMG cxxi 125 (: l. *lqry[hy]*), Vattioni IH a.l.) :: Milik RN vi/iv 55: l. *lqrwn* = QAL Impf. 3 p.pl.m. :: Pennachietti FO xvi 58ff.: l. *lqd[* = QAL Impf. of qdd_1 (= to tear; for the reading *lqd*, cf. also Safar Sumer vii 183, Caquot Syr xxix 103, Donner sub KAI 245) - a form of this root *[ʾt]qry* (ITP Pf. 3 p.s.m.; to be read) prob. in MPAT 64 i 11 (cf. Fitzmyer & Harrington MPAT a.l.).

v. *ʾmr_1*, *zkr_1*, *yqb*, *mhdmr*, *ntn*, *qbl_1*, *qwm_1*, *qry_1*.

qrʾ₂ Milik ADAJ xxi 150 n. 15: l. *yqrʾ* = QAL Impf. 3 p.s.m. of *qrʾ₂* (= *qry_1*) in ADAJ x 44 ii 2 (highly uncert. interpret., on the problems involved, cf. also Degen ZDPV lxxxii 297 (n. 140b)) :: Starcky ADAJ x 44f., RB lxxii 95, Levinson NAI 168 (div. otherwise) l. *yqr* = PUʿAL Pf. 3 p.s.m. of *yqr_1* (= to be honoured) or OPH Impf. 3 p.s.m. (of *yqr_1*) with same meaning.

v. *qrʾ₁*, *qry_1*.

qrb₁ **Hebr** QAL Part. act. pl.m. abs. *qrbym* DJD ii 42^5 (cf. Yeivin At i 99, Milik DJD ii a.l. :: Ginsberg BASOR cxxxi 26 n. 4: rather = m. pl. abs. of *qrb_9*) - **OffAr** QAL Pf. 3 p.s.m. *qrb* Aḥiq 110, Imper. s.m. *qrb* Aḥiq 194 (dam. context); PAʿEL Pf. 3 p.s.m. *qrb* KAI $229^{1f.}$ (*qr[b]*), JNES xv 2B, C (= SSI ii 25), xviii 154, ZDMG cxl 2^1; 1 p.s. + suff. 3 p.s.m. *qrbth* Aḥiq 10; 1 p.s. + suff. 2 p.s.m. *qrbtk* Aḥiq 50; Impf. 3 p.s.m. *yqrb* Cowl 30^{28}, 31^{27}; 3 p.pl.m. *yqrbwn* Cowl 30^{25} (under *q* an erased *h*, cf. e.g. Cowl a.l., Porten & Yardeni sub TADAE A 4.7), 32^9; 1 p.pl. *nqrb* Cowl 31^{25} (the interpret. of the Impf. forms as APH poss., but less prob.); HAPH Pf. 3 p.s.m. *hqrb* CIS ii 75 (v. infra), NESE ii 50 ii; Impf. 3 p.s.m. *yhqrb* Driv 3^7; 1 p.s. *ʾhqrb* Driv 3^6 - **Nab** PAʿEL Pf. 3 p.s.m. *qrb* CIS ii 174^1, 336^1, RES 83^2, 676^1, 2052^1, 2115, Syr xxxv

238[1], IEJ xi 128[1], 133[2], Atlal vii 105[1], MPAT 64 i 5 (*[q]rb*; :: Starcky RB lxi 165: = QAL Pf. 3 p.s.m.; cf. also Fitzmyer & Harrington MPAT a.l.); 3 p.pl.m. *qrbw* CIS ii 157[2]; Impf. 1 p.s. *ʾqrb* MPAT 64 i 10 - **Palm** PAʿEL Pf. 3 p.s.m. *qrb* CIS ii 3903[2], 3912[1], 3923[4] (*[q]rb*), 3966[5] (= RIP 156[14]), 3975[1], 3983[1] (= SBS 13), 3984[1], PNO 14[1], 16[2], RIP 126[1] (Greek par. ἀνέθηκεν), FS Collart 198[1] (dam. context), etc., etc.; 3 p.s.f. *qrbt* SBS 11[2]; 3 p.pl.m. *qrbw* CIS ii 3904, 3978[3], Inv xii 39, 48[2], SBS 10[2] (v. infra), 16[1], 25[1] (Greek par. ἀνέθηκαν), etc.; 3 p.pl.m. (or 3 p.s.m.?) *qrb* InscrP 35[1], Inv xi 99[1], Syr xvii 268[4] - **Hatra** PAʿEL Pf. 3 p.s.m. *qrb* 22, 222 (*[q]rb*, for this reading, cf. Aggoula MUSJ xlvii 43, Vattioni IH a.l., cf. however Safar Sumer xxi 38 n. 17, Degen WO v 227f.: l. *rb* = Sing. m. abs. of *rb*$_2$), app. 10[3], *qryb* 292[4], app. 3[2] (Greek par. ἔδωκεν) - ¶ verb QAL to be near, to approach - **1)** + *ʾl*$_6$, *hgyym* (v. *gy*) *qrbym ʾlnw* DJD ii 42[5]: the heathens are near to us (or: are approaching us; v. also supra) - **2)** + *l*$_5$ + Inf., *ʾryʾ ʾzl qrb lš[lmh lḥmrʾ]* Aḥiq 110: the lion came near to greet the ass - **3)** + *ʿl*$_7$, *qrb ʿly* Aḥiq 194: come near to me (dam. context) - PAʿEL to present: passim; *qrb ʿbdgdy [b]r lšglʾ* Hatra 22: A. the son of L. has offered (it; cf. Safar Sumer vii 181, Vattioni IH a.l., cf. also Abbadi PIH 25, 119f. :: Caquot Sem iv 55: l. *qrb ʿbdgdy lšglʾ*, A. has offered to Sh. (cf. also id. Syr xxix 101)) - **1)** + obj., *wʾqrb mh dy lk ʿmy* MPAT 64 i 10: I will give what I owe you; *qrb ʿmwdyʾ ʾln tryhwn wšrythwn wtṭlylh[n] mlkʾ* CIS ii 3984[1f.]: M. has offered these two columns, their architrave and the roof belonging to it (cf. also with other parts of (temple) buildings: SBS 2A 1f., B 1f., C 1f., D 1f., 17[1,3], 18[1], Inv xii 48[2]); *dkrn ṭb lmrʾ ʿlmʾ qrb bwly* RIP 126[1]: B. has offered a good memorial for the lord of the universe (sc. that he may remember); etc. - **2)** + obj. + *l*$_5$, *ʿltʾ dh lmlkbl wlʾlhy tdmr qrb ṭbrys ... wtdmryʾ lʾlhyhn* CIS ii 3903: T. has offered this altar to M. and the gods of Tadmor ... and the Tadmoreans (have offered it) to their gods (cf. CIS ii 3975[1,3], Inv xi 46[1], SBS 24[1ff.], MUSJ xlii 177[7ff.], PNO 16[1ff.]; with other objects, cf. RIP 143[1], Inv xii 22[2,4], 39, CIS ii 3983[1] (= SBS 13), SBS 1A 1, B 1 (= InscrP 30), 10[2ff.], etc.) - **3)** + obj. + *ʿl*$_7$, *wmḥtʾ wlbwntʾ wʿlwtʾ yqrbwn ʿl mdbḥʾ ... bšmk* Cowl 30[25f.]: they will offer the meal-offering and the incense-offering and the burnt-offering on the altar ... on your behalf (cf. Cowl 31[25], 32[9f.]) - 4) + obj. + *qdm*$_3$, *qrbth qdm ʾsrḥʾdn mlk ʾtwr* Aḥiq 10: I presented him before E. the king of A. (cf. Aḥiq 50) - **5)** + *l*$_5$ (introducing object), *lṣlmyn ... qrbw mqymw ... wyrḥbwlʾ* InscrP 6: M. and Y. have offered statues - **6)** + *l*$_5$ (used as so-called *l*-comm.), *qrb tbrʾ ... wmqym ... lbl ...* Inv xi 99: T. and M. have offered ... to Bel; *[ʾl]h try gmlyʾ dy qrbw zydw wʿbdʾlgʾ ... ldwšrʾ* CIS ii 157[1ff.]: these are the two camels which Z. and A. offered ... to D.; cf. also JNES xv 2B, C, xviii 154, ZDMG cxl 2[1f.], CIS ii 174[1f.], 336, 3978[3f.], Syr xxxv 238, Atlal vii 105[1f.] (for the reading, cf. Beyer

& Livingstone ZDMG cxxxvii 291), Inv xi 11[4f.], SBS 3, RES 2052[2ff.], PNO 20, etc. - **7)** + l_5 + obj., *gbr zy yqrb lh ʿlwh wdbḥn* Cowl 30[28], 31[27]: a man who offers to him burnt-offering and sacrifices; *lbʿlšmn qrb kptʾ wʿršʾ ʾgtgls* CIS ii 3912: A. has offered to B. the vaulted room and the couch (cf. Greek par. Διὶ μεγίστῳ Ἀγαθάνγελος ... τὴν καμάραν ᾠκοδόμησεν καὶ τὴν κλίνη[ν] ... ἀνέθηκεν) - **8)** + mn_5, *qrb mn kysh* Inv xii 19[1] (= Inv iii 2 = InscrP 47): he has offered it on his expense - **9)** + mn_5 + l_5 + obj., *qryb mn ʿbdʾ hdyn lšmš ʾlhʾ dnrʾ 100* Hatra app. 3[2ff.]: he offered from this construction (i.e. as a part of the expenses needed for this construction) to the god Sh. 100 *denarii* - 10) cf. also the foll. comb. - a) *bnʾ wqrb* CIS ii 3966[5] (= RIP 156[14]): he built and offered - b) for *ʿbd wqrb*, v. $ʿbd_1$ - HAPH to present, to offer: NESE ii 50 ii - **1)** + l_5, *lʾkdbn ... srsʾ zy hqrb lhdd* CIS ii 75: (seal belonging) to A. ... the eunuch, who made offering to H. (cf. e.g. CIS ii a.l., Naveh AION xvi 21, xviii 450 :: Gall 151: who worships H., cf. Lipiński RSF ii 55; or *hqrb* = HOPH Pf. 3 p.s.m.?, who was offered/consecrated to H.?; cf. also Vattioni Aug ix 369) - **2)** + qdm_3, *ʿbdy ʿḥḥpy zy psmšk yhqrb qdmyk* Driv 3[7]: the slaves of A. whom P. will present before you (cf. Driv 3[6]) - a form of this root in KAI 219[2]: *qrbn* = Sing. abs. of *qrbn* of = PA ʿEL Pf. 1 p.pl. of qrb_1 (cf. e.g. Lidzbarski Handb 364, Donner KAI a.l.; for interpret. as form of *qrbn*, cf. also Sznycer HDS 171) or = QAL Part. pl.m. of qrb_1 or Plur. abs. of qrb_9 - a form of this root in ATNS 67a 1 (*qrbw* = QAL/PA ʿEL Pf. 3 p.pl.m. or Imper. pl.m.) + l_5 (dam. context).

v. br_1, hwy_1, ndr_1 qdm_3, qrb_2, *qrbh*.

qrb_2 **Mo** Sing. cstr. *qrb* KAI 181[23] (*qr[b]*),[24] - **Hebr** Plur. abs. *qrbyn* AMB 4[18] - ¶ subst. midst; *bqrb* = inside; *br ʾn bqrb hqr* KAI 181[24]: there was no cistern inside the town (cf. KAI 181[23]) - Kaufman JAOS cix 100: l. *mn qrb* in TH rs 1 = mn_5 + Sing. cstr. of qrb_2 :: Lipiński Stud 118, 121: *qrb* = Sing. cstr. of qrb_5 (= amount) :: Fales sub AECT 53: *mn* = mn_4, *qrb* = QAL Part. act. s.m. abs. of qrb_1 or < Akkad. :: Jensen in Tell Halaf p. 361 (div. otherwise): l. *qrbn* = n.p. :: Friedrich TH p. 71ff. (div. otherwise): l. *qrbnn*? (= n.p.), cf. also Degen NESE i 51f. - Plur. intestines: AMB 4[18] (uncert. and diff. context).

qrb_3 **OffAr** Sing. abs. *qrb* Beh 2 (Akkad. par. *ta-ḫa-za*), 3 (Akkad. par. *ṣa-al-tu₄*), 4 (Akkad. par. *ṣa-al-tu₄*), 10 (Akkad. par. *taḫaza*), 19 (for the reading, cf. Greenfield & Porten BIDG p. 34f. :: Cowl a.l.: l. *[qr]bʾ* (Sing. emph.; Akkad. par. *ṣal-tu₄*), 20 (Akkad. par. *ṣa-al-tu₄*), 43 (Akkad. par. *ṣa-al-tu₄*); emph. *qrbʾ* 2 (Akkad. par. *ṣal-tu₄*), 10 (Akkad. par. *ṣa-al-tu₄*), 29 (Akkad. par. *ṣa-al-tu₄*), 33 (Akkad. par. *ṣa-al-tu₄*) - ¶ subst. battle; for the context, v. $ʿbd_1$; > Akkad. *qarābu*, cf. v.Soden Or xxxvii 264, xlvi 192, AHW s.v., cf. CAD s.v., cf. also Kaufman AIA 30 :: Zimmern Fremdw 13: qrb_3 poss. < Akkad.

qrb$_4$ v. *qbr$_3$*.
qrb$_5$ v. *qrb$_2$*.
qrb$_6$ v. *qrb$_1$*, *qrbn*.
qrb$_7$ cf. Frah vii 9 (*krb*ʾ): sheep, cf. Nyberg FP 43, 70 :: Ebeling Frah a.l.: l. *q*ʿ*n*ʾ (= form of *qn$_1$* (= cattle)).
v. *kr$_2$*, *ṣ*ʾ*n*.
qrb$_8$ **OffAr** Giron AE a.l.: l. *qrb*ʾ (= Sing. emph. of *qrb$_8$* (= sacrifice)) in AE '23, 42 no. 11[1] (uncert. interpret., dam. context).
qrb$_9$ **OffAr** Sing. m. abs. *qrb* Cowl 1[5], 13[10], Krael 1[9], CRAI '47, 181 conv. 2 (= OA iii 56, heavily dam. and uncert. context), *qryb* Cowl 5[9], 6[13], 20[10], 43[5], Krael 5[5]; Plur. m./f. abs. *qrybn* RES 1785F 1, 3 - **Palm** Sing. m. + suff. 3 p.s.m. *qrybh* Ber ii 76[1]; Plur. + suff. 3 p.s.m. *qrybwhy* Ber ii 77[2] - ¶ adj. - **1)** near; + *lwt*, *qrybn lwt byl* RES 1785F 1f.: near to Bel (i.e. prob. the planet Jupiter), cf. RES 1785F 3 - **2)** substantivated adj., relative; ʾ*ḥ w*ʾ*ḥh qrb wrḥy[q b*ʿ*]l dgl wb*ʿ*l qryh* Cowl 13[10]: a brother or sister, a relative or someone not related, soldier or civilian (cf. Cowl 1[5], 5[8f.], 6[12f.], 43[5f.], Krael 1[8f.], 5[5], cf. also Cowl 20[10]), for this interpret. of *qrb wrḥyq*, cf. Cowl p. 3, cf. however Yaron Bibl xli 265f.: *qrb wrḥyq* = someone near and someone far away (in local sense; cf. also Porten & Szubin Maarav iv 49f., Porten & Yardeni sub TADAE B 2.1 and elsewhere) :: Peiser OLZ '08, 24, Krael p. 136, Grelot DAE p. 77 (a.e.): *qrb wrḥyq* = a close or distant relative; the *qryb* in Palm. (Ber ii 76[1], 77[2]): = relative rather than cousin (thus Milik DFD 113) - a form of this word poss. in ATNS 12[2] (*qrb[*; reading uncert.).
v. *qrb$_1$*, *qrbh*.
qrbh (or *qrbw*?) - **OffAr** Sing. cstr. *qrbt* KAI 268[1] (:: Lipiński OLP viii 111: = QAL Part. act. s.f. abs. of *qrb$_1$* (= being nearby > the departed one)); emph. *qrbt*ʾ KAI 267[1] (:: Lipiński OLP viii 109f.: = QAL Part. act. s.f. emph. of *qrb$_1$*; v. supra) - ¶ subst. approach; *lqrbt bnt l*ʾ*wsry* KAI 268[1f.]: for approach of B. to Osiris (i.e. the appearance of B. before Osiris after death, cf. e.g. Cooke NSI p. 201, Donner KAI a.l., REHR 39f., Gibson SSI ii p. 120); cf. also KAI 267[1f.] - this word, *qrbt*ʾ (= Sing. emph.; or = s.f. emph. of *qrb$_9$*? :: Baneth OLZ '14, 252: or = f. form with accusative ending), poss. used adverbially (= immediately after, then) in Aḥiq 45 (*[qr]bt*ʾ), 56, 59 (cf. Baneth OLZ '14, 252, Cowl p. 232, Leand 61 l, Grelot DAE p. 449f.) - the *qrbt*ʾ in Cowl 75[2] poss. = the same word.
qrbw v. *qrbh*.
qrbwn v. *qrbn*.
qrbn **Hebr** Sing. abs. *qrbn* BiAr xxxiii 55 (or = J.Ar.?) - **Nab** Sing. abs. *qrbwn* BASOR cclxiii 77[1] (:: Hammond, Johnson & Jones ibid. 78: = abstract Plur. of *qrb$_6$* (= gifts)) - **JAr** Sing. abs. *qrbn* MPAT 107[1] (= Frey 1407), cstr. *qrbn* MPAT 69[2] - ¶ subst. offering: passim; *qrbn*

ʾlh mn dbgwh MPAT 69[2]: an offering to God from the one within it (sc. in the ossuary; cf. e.g. Testa SGC 449ff., Fitzmyer JBL lxxviii 62ff. (= ESBNT 96ff.), Falk HThR lix 311f., Fitzmyer & Harrington MPAT a.l., cf. also Baumgarten JANES xvi/xvii 7, cf. however Milik RB lxv 409: = malediction (cf. also Greenfield JNES xxxv 60)); for *qrbn* in BiAr xxxiii 55, cf. also Zeitlin JQR lix 135, Baumgarten JANES xvi/xvii 7 - the exact meaning of *qrbwn* in BASOR cclxiii 77[1] (dam. context) uncert. (cf. also Jones BASOR cclxxv 42) - Aharoni sub TA-H 103: l. *q* + sign in TA-H 102, 103, *q* prob. = abbrev. of *qrbn* (or, less prob., of $qdš_2$; cf. however Cross BASOR ccxxxv 75ff.: l. *qš* = abbrev. of $qdš_2$, Ph. script, and cf. Herzog, M. Aharoni, Rainey & Moshkovitz BASOR ccliv 12, 15, 32: l. *qk* = *q* (= abbrev. for *qdš* (= Sing. cstr. of $qdš_2$)) + *k* (= abbrev. for *khnm* (= Plur. abs. of khn_1)) = set aside for the priests (less prob. reading)) - Yadin & Naveh Mas a.l.: the *q* in Mas 459 = abbrev. for *qrbn* or $qdš_2$?
v. qdm_2, qrb_1.

qrdm Ph Kornfeld sub Abydos 15: l. *qrdm* (= Sing. m. abs. (= strong)) in RES 1349[1] (highly uncert. reading and interpret.; RES a.l. (dividing otherwise): l. *bn* (= Sing. cstr. of bn_1) *grmlqrt* (= n.p.)).

qrh_1 v. qmt_1.

qrh_2 v. $sḥr_2$. $qrḫ_1$ v.Soden Or xxxvii 264, xlvi 192, AHW s.v.: > Akkad. *qarāḫu* = to freeze, to become frosted (poss. interpret.; cf. however CAD s.v.).

$qrḥ_2$ v.Soden Or xxxvii 264, xlvi 192, AHW s.v.: > Akkad. *qarḫu* = ice (poss. interpret.; cf. however CAD s.v.).

$qrḥ_3$ v.Soden Or xxxvii 270f., xlvi 192, AHW s.v. *qarruḫu*: = bald > Akkad. *qarūḫu* = old (less prob. interpret.; cf. CAD s.v. *qarāḫu*: *qaruḫu* poss. = sherbet; cf. also Fales OA xvi 68).

qrḥh Mo Mazar EM iv 923: the *qrḥh* in KAI 181[3,21,24,25] (= Sing. abs.; < Akkad. *qirḫu*) = acropolis, citadel (less. prob. interpret.; *qrḥh* prob. = n.l., cf. e.g. also v.Zijl 78ff., Lipiński Or xl 338) - on this word, cf. also Ahlström RANR 16.

qrṭys OffAr Segal ATNS a.l.: the *qrṭys* in ATNS 125[3] = subst. Sing. abs. (= document) < Greek χάρτης (cf. also Teixidor JAOS cv 733: l. *krtys* < Greek χάρτης; less prob. reading), heavily dam. context, uncert. interpret.

qrṭsṭws v. *qrṭsṭs*.

qrṭsṭs (< Greek κράτιστος, cf. Cantineau Gramm 156, Rosenthal Sprache 92) - **Palm** Sing. abs. *qrṭsṭs* CIS ii 3939[1] (reading *qrṭysṭs* mistaken), 3942[1], *qrṭsṭws* CIS ii 3940[1], 3941[1] (*q[rṭs]ṭws*), 3943[1]; Plur. emph. *qrṭsṭʾ* CIS ii 3946[1], *qrṭsṭwʾ* CIS ii 3947[3] (cf. Rosenthal Sprache 23, Joüon Syria xix 188f.) - ¶ adj. mightiest, most excellent; used as epithet, *spṭmys wrwd qrṭsṭs* CIS ii 3939[1]: S. W. the most excellent man (cf. Greek par.

Σεπτί[μιον Οὐορρώδην τὸ]ν κράτιστον), cf. CIS ii 3940[1], 3941[1], 3942 and the Greek par. to these texts; *spṭmyw' zbd'* ... *wzby* ... *qrṭsṭw'* CIS ii 3947[2f.]: the Septimii Zabdâ and Zebbai ... most excellent men (cf. Greek par. Σεπτίμιοι Ζάβδας ... καὶ ... Ζαββαῖος ... οἱ κράτιστοι).

qrṭr Pun Rocco SicArch xiii 27: l. *qrṭr* (= Sing. abs.) < Greek κρατήρ = crater, in Pun. inscription; highly uncert. reading (for other reading proposals, cf. SicArch xiii a.l.).

qry_1 Hebr QAL Impf. 3 p.s.m. *yqrh* TA-H 24[16]; Inf. cstr. *qrt* KAI 189[4] (on this form, cf. also Scagliarini Hen xii 140; :: Shea FUCUS 431, 435f.: or = QAL Inf. cstr. of qr'_1) - **OffAr** QAL Pf. 3 p.s.m. *qrh[* Cowl 71[18] (?, heavily dam. context) - ¶ verb to meet; + obj., *pn yqrh 't h'yr dbr* TA-H 24[16f.]: lest anything should happen to the city - Inf. cstr. preceded by l_5: towards, opposite to: KAI 189[4] - L.H.Gray AJSL xxxix 79: the *ucommucro* in Poen 945 poss. = equivalent to *wkmqr'* (= *w* + k_1 + HOPH Part. s.m. abs. of qry_1) = and as that which is made to happen; Schroed 312: l. *ucommutro* = equivalent *wkmṭr'* = *w* + k_1 + *mṭr'/h* (= Sing. abs. of *mṭr'/h* (= duty)); highly uncert. interpretations, cf. also the varr. *umcomuoro*, *umcomuero*; prob. to be related to *chon chem* in Poen 935 (for this text, v. kwn_1, kn_4) - Milik ADAJ xxi 150 n. 15: l. *yqr'* (= QAL Impf. 3 p.s.m. of qry_1 (= to happen)) in ADAJ x 44 ii 2 (= RB lxxii 95[2]), highly uncert. interpret.; derivation from the root yqr_1 (cf. Starcky RB lxxii 95, ADAJ x 44f.) also less prob.; on the problems, cf. also Weippert ZDPV lxxxii 297 (n. 140 b).

v. *kbh*, nqr_1, $qr'_{1,2}$.

qry_2 OffAr Plur. abs. *qry* WO vi 44C 5 (for the reading and interpret., cf. Naveh WO vi 44f. :: Tiratsian VDI lxvii 89: l. $qrṣ_2$ (= Sing. abs.) = part); emph. *qry[']* WO vi 42D 2 (for the interpret., cf. Naveh WO vi 45 :: Périkhanian REA-NS iii 43: l. *qry[']* (= Sing. emph. of qry_2) or l. *qry[t']* (= Sing. of *qryh*)?), REA-NS viii 170A 5, B 5 - ¶ subst. village; *ḥlq 'rq byn qry* WO vi 44C 3ff.: he divided the land between the villages (cf. also WO vi 44B 3ff., REA-NS viii 170 A 5, B 5).

v. *qryh*.

qry_3 v. qrt_1.

qryb v. qrb_9.

qryh OldAr Sing. abs. *qryh* KAI 224[12]; cstr. *qryt* KAI 222B 36 (cf. e.g. Dupont-Sommer Sf p. 62, 64, 83, Donner KAI a.l., Fitzmyer AIS 19 × Lipiński Stud 41, Lemaire IAS 115, 124, 139 (div. otherwise): l. *qryt'* (= Sing. emph., v. infra)) - **OffAr** Sing. abs. *qryh* Cowl 5[9], 13[10], 20[11], 46[6], MAI xiv/2, 66[3] (cf. Dupont-Sommer MAI xiv/2, 71f. :: Torrey AJSL lviii 396f.: = Sing. emph. of qry_2; for the reading of the context, cf. Porten & Yardeni sub TADAE B 1.1)[,18]; emph. *qryt'* KAI 278[2] (or = Plur.?, cf. also Dupont-Sommer DHC 11f., Garbini RSO xl 136,

Naveh AION xvi 33, Donner KAI a.l., Gibson SSI ii p. 156), HDS 9^6, ATNS 22^1, $57^{2,3,4}$, 68^7 (dam. context), 100^3 (heavily dam. context); + suff. 3 p.s.m. *qryth* HDS 9^3 (for the reading, cf. Fales AION xxviii 278ff. :: Caquot HDS 9, 13, Lipiński Stud 79f., WGAV 375f.: l. *ʿrsth* = Sing. + suff. 3 p.s.m. of *ʿrsh* (= tenancy) < Akkad. (cf. however Kaufman AIA 49)); Plur. emph. *qrytʾ* ATNS 1^9 (reading however highly uncert., cf. Porten & Yardeni sub TADAE B 8.8); cf. Nisa 96^5, 242^5, 504^5, 542^4, 594^3, 647^8, 650^6, etc. (*qrytʾ*; cf. also in Nisa 200^5, 601^1, 754^6), GIPP 62 - **Palm** Sing. abs. *qryʾ* RTP 6 (cf. Caquot RTP p. 148: or = Sing. emph. of *qry*$_2$?; or = Plur. emph.? :: Chabot sub RES 1686: l. *mry* (without interpret.)); emph. *qrytʾ* PNO 39, 42^4, 51, 78^2, Sem xxii 59^5, *qrtʾ* MUSJ xxxviii 133^6 (for the reading, cf. Starcky MUSJ xxxviii 134); Plur. emph. *qryʾ* CIS ii 3913 ii 112 (:: Teixidor GHPO 42: or < Greek χώρα, cf. however Graf GHPO 173) - ¶ subst. town, village (for diff. shades of meaning, cf. Caquot RTP p. 148); *bqryt ʾymʾm* KAI 222B 36 (v. however supra and v. *mlk*$_1$): in the town E.; *bqryh krb* MAI xiv/2, 66^{18}: in the town K.; *kršy qrytʾ* KAI 278^2: the town K. (v. however supra), cf. ATNS 57^2; *bʿl qryh* Cowl 13^{10}, $20^{10f.}$, 46^6: citizen; *bʿl dgl wqryh* Cowl 5^9: soldier or civilian; *ḥzn qrytʾ* HDS 9^6: the mayor of the city; *bny qrytʾ* PNO $78^{1f.}$: the people of the village; *dyrʾ dy qrytʾ* Sem xxii $59^{4f.}$: the community of the village (v. also *dyr*); *gdh dy qrytʾ* PNO $42^{3f.}$: the "Fortune" of the village, cf. PNO 51, MUSJ xxxviii 133^6; *gnyʾ dy qrytʾ* PNO 39^1: the *genii* of the village; *qryʾ* RTP 6: the town (?, poss. = Palmyre, cf. however *qryʾ* in CIS ii 3913 ii 112 = the villages, indicating townships around Palmyre (cf. Greek par. τῶν [χω]ρίων)) - on this word, cf. also Dreyer FS v.Selms 18f.
v. *qr*$_1$, *qry*$_2$, *qrt*$_1$.

qryq **OffAr** Segal ATNS a.l.: l. this noun (Sing. abs. *qr[y]q* = fugitive) in ATNS 47 i 5 (context however heavily dam.).

qryqr **OffAr** Plur. abs. *qryqrn* ATNS 33^1 - ¶ subst. fugitive.

qrn **Pun** Dual + suff. 3 p.s.m. *qrny* KAI 69^5 - **Palm** Sing. emph. *qrnʾ* Syr xvii 271^1, Ber ii 78^2 - ¶ subst. f. - **1)** horn: KAI 69^5 - **2)** corner: Syr xvii 271^1 (cf. also Milik DFD 289, Gawlikowski Syr li 97, 100), Ber ii 78^2 - v.d.Branden Meltô i 69f., 76: l. this word (Sing. cstr. *krn*), as part of divine epithet in KAI 26A ii 19, iii 2, 4, improb. interpret., cf. e.g. Röllig KAI a.l., Gibson SSI iii p. 60: prob. = part of n.l.
v. *ṣr*$_2$.

qrnyt **Hebr** (?) the *qrnyt* in IEJ xii 10^2 diff. word of unknown meaning; Avigad IEJ xii a.l.: = name of plant (prob. thyme) used as nickname or = word related to n.l. Cyrene :: Milik DF 81 (n. 11): l. poss. *qrnyh* (or lapsus for *qrnyh*?) = Sing. m. emph. of *qrny* (= the one from Cyrene).

qrs$_1$ ((< Greek κάρρος) < Lat. *carrus*) - **Palm** Sing. abs. *qrs* CIS ii 3913 i 13 - ¶ subst. cart, waggon; *ṭʿwn qrs* CIS ii 3913 i 13: a waggon-load (Greek par. γόμος καρρικὸς), cf. also Teixidor Sem xxxiv 69f.

qrs$_2$ v.Soden Or xlvi 192, AHW s.v. *qarsu*: > Akkad. *qarsu* = dry, hard? (highly uncert. interpret., cf. also CAD s.v. *qarrišu*).

qrplgs Edom (?) Sing. abs. *qrplgs* BASOR lxxx 8[1] - ¶ subst. (?) word of unknown meaning, prob. indication of some kind of liquid (mentioned in the same context as wine); Glueck BASOR lxxx 9: the interpret. as rendering of Greek καρπολόγος (= tax gatherer (cf. Albright with Glueck BASOR lxxx 9 n. 12)) less prob.

qrṣ$_1$ v. *krṣ*.

qrṣ$_2$ v. *qry$_1$*.

qrq$_1$ **DA** HAPH Pf. 3 p.s.f. *hqrqt* i 17 (prob. interpret., cf. e.g. Hoftijzer DA p. 219, 274, Hackett BTDA 29, 55, 91, 133, Or liii 63 (n. 28) :: Caquot & Lemaire Syr liv 202, Delcor SVT xxxii 59: *nmr* = subj.; on the problems, cf. also Garbini Hen i 181f., H. & M.Weippert ZDPV xcviii 102 (n. 137f.), Garr DGSP 24) - **OldAr** QAL Impf. 3 p.s.m. *yqrq* KAI 224[4,19]; Part. act. s.m. abs. *qrq* KAI 224[4] (cf. e.g. Fitzmyer AIS 108, Donner KAI a.l., Degen AAG p. 69, Gibson SSI ii p. 52 :: Dupont-Sommer BMB xiii 32: or rather = QAL Inf. abs.?); s.m. + suff. 1 p.s. *qrqy* KAI 224[19]; + suff. 3 p.pl.m. *qrqhm* KAI 224[19f.] - **OffAr** QAL Pf. 3 p.s.m. *qrq* Beh 30 (*qr[q]*; cf. Greenfield & Porten BIDG p. 38f. :: Cowl a.l.: l. *qd[m]* = *qdm$_3$*; Akkad. par. *iḫ-liq-ma*; cf. also Greenfield FS Rundgren 52), 46 (*[q]rq*, cf. Greenfield & Porten BIDG p. 44f., cf. also Greenfield FS Rundgren 52 :: Ungnad ArPap 89: l. *[ʿ]rq* = QAL Pf. 3 p.s.m. of *ʿrq$_3$* (= to flee) :: Cowl a.l.: l. *[ʿ]rq* = Sing. cstr. of *ʿrq$_4$*; Akkad. par. *iḫ-liq*); 3 p.pl.m. *qrqw* KAI 233[9,13], Driv 3[5], ATNS 86a 6 (dam. context); Impf. 3 p.pl.m. *yqrqn* KAI 233[16]; Inf. *mqrq* ATNS 26[6]; Part. act. pl.m. cstr. *qrqy* KAI 233[18]; pl.m. + suff. 1 p.s. *qrqy* KAI 233[17] (Dupont-Sommer Syr xxiv 40f.: the forms of *qrq* in KAI 233 < root *qrq$_2$* = to tear, to slander (cf. however idem BMB xiii 32; cf. also Lidzbarski AUA p. 11f.)); cf. Frah xx 12 (*ʿlykwn*), var. in FP p. 54 sub 2: *ʿlyk*; cf. also Toll ZDMG-Suppl viii 35 - **JAr** QAL Pf. 3 p.s.m. *ʿrq* AMB 15[14] (reading of *q* uncert.); 3 p.s.f. *ʿrqt* AMB 15[2]; Impf. 3 p.pl.m. *yʿrqwn* AMB 11[8] - ¶ verb QAL to flee, to fly, passim - **1)** + *ʾl$_6$* (= towards): KAI 224[19] - **2)** + *l$_5$*, *lmqrq lṣd pnh* ATNS 26[6]: to flee in the direction of P. (v. also *pnh$_1$*) - **3)** + *mn$_5$*, *yqrq mny* KAI 224[4]: he will flee from me (cf. Driv 3[5], AMB 11[8], 15[2,14] (v. however supra)); Part. act. fugitive; *qrqy* KAI 224[9]: a fugitive of mine (i.e. someone fleeing from me), cf. KAI 224[19f.], 233[17,18] - HAPH to make flee DA i 17 (uncert. context) - on the root of this verb, cf. e.g. Baneth OLZ '19, 55, Driv p. 46f., Greenfield JAOS lxxxii 291 n. 9, Fitzmyer AIS 108, Degen AAG p. 37 n. 25, Blau PC 47 n. 8, 132, Hoftijzer DA p. 219 n. 99, Gibson SSI ii p. 52 - Gibson SSI ii p. 104f., 107: l. *qrq* (= QAL Inf.

abs.) in KAI 233[9] (uncert. reading).
v. *qḥqḥ*.

qrq₂ v. *qrq₁*.

qrqyn **Pun** Garbini AION xxv 437ff.: the *qrqyn* in RSF iii 51B 3 = subst. (Sing. abs. ; < Greek κηρυκεῖον, cf. also idem FSR 181) = herald's staff (*bt qrqyn* = indication of religious function); improb. interpret., cf. Fantar RSF iii a.l.: *qrqyn* = n.p. (prob. interpret.).

qrqs (< Greek κερκίς?, cf. Hiortsoe with Ingholt Ber ii 83) - **Palm** Sing. emph. *qrqs᾿* Ber ii 82[1], 84[1], 85[10]; Plur. emph. *qrqsy᾿* Ber ii 97[1], 98[1], 100 i 2 - ¶ subst. m. of uncert. meaning poss. indicating arch; *qrqs᾿ qdmy᾿* Ber ii 84[1]: the first arch (poss. = the arch at the entrance of the central exedra); *lgw mn qrqs᾿* Ber ii 85[9f.]: further inside than the arch (i.e. beyond the arch); *šṭr᾿ ymny᾿ dy bt᾿* (v. *bt᾿*) *qrqsy᾿* Ber ii 97[1]: the right wall between the arches (poss. = the right of the first part of the central exedra); *btr ᾿ksdr᾿ bt᾿ trn qrqsy᾿* Ber ii 98[1] (for the reading, cf. Cantineau with Ingholt Ber iii 127): beyond the exedra between the two arches (poss. = the internal part of the central exedra), cf. also Ber ii 100 i 2.

qrq῾ **JAr** Sing. emph. *qrq῾᾿* MPAT 51[8] - ¶ subst. ground, terrain; *bnyh wqrq῾᾿* MPAT 51[8]: what is built upon and the vacant site (v. also *bny₁*) - the same word poss. also in Cowl 75[1]? (*qrq[῾ ...*), diff. reading, dam. context.

qrr₁ **DA** a form of this root (= to be cold) poss. in DA ii 29 (heavily dam. context); cf. Hoftijzer DA a.l.: or = form of root *qrr₂* (= to be inimical (v. *ṣrr₁*)).
v. *yqr₂*, *mqrh*.

qrr₂ v. *qrr₁*.

qrš₁ **Ph** diff. word in Syr xlviii 396[6], uncert. interpret.; Lipiński RSF ii 51f.: = QAL Pf. 3 p.s.m. of *qrš* (= to clot, used to indicate the desiccation of the field (cf. also id. RTAT 267)); v.d.Branden BiOr xxxiii 13: = QAL Pf. 3 p.s.m. of *qrš* (= variant of *krš* (= to be in the midst of)); Gaster BASOR ccix 18f., 23: *qrš* = QAL Imper. s.m. of *qrš* (= to freeze, to be(come) a solid mass); Liverani RSF ii 36f.: *qrš* = QAL Imper. s.m. of *qrš* (= variant of *qrs* (= to bow down > to succumb)); Caquot Syr xlviii 403: *qrš* = QAL Part. act. s.m. abs. (or *nomen agentis*) of *qrš* (= to cut off, to crunch), indicating ogre; Röllig NESE ii 29, 31f., de Moor JEOL xxvii 111 (n. 21): *qrš* = Sing. abs. of *qrš* (= dwelling-place, residence, abode); Garbini OA xx 289f., 292: *qrš* = QAL Pf. 3 p.s.m. of *qrš* (= to be solid > to resist) :: Teixidor AO i 108 (div. otherwise): l. *qršk* (without interpret.) :: Cross CBQ xxxvi 486ff. n. 23, Avishur PIB 267, 270, UF x 35, Gibson SSI iii p. 89, 91: l. *qdš* = Sing. m. abs. of *qdš₃*.

qrš₂ **Palm** Caquot RTP p. 148f.: the *qrš* in RTP 694, 695, 697-699,

700 (*q[r]š*), 701 (*[q]rš*) poss. = adj. Sing. m. abs. (= heavy, thick, said of wine); highly uncert. interpret., cf. du Mesnil du Buisson TMP 485: l. *qdš* = Sing. m. abs. of *qdš*$_3$ (= consecrated; cf. also Díez Merino LA xxi 94 n. 46, Lipiński EI xx 131*f.); cf. also Milik DFD 191ff.: l. *qdš* = Sing. abs. of *qdš*$_2$ (= sacredness), used as indication of sacred banquet; cf. also Dunant sub SBS-Tess 12.

qrt$_1$ **Ph** Sing. abs. *qrt* KAI 26A ii 9, 17, iii 5, 7, 15, C iv 6, 17, EpAn ix 5[4] (or = n.l.?, cf. Mosca & Russell EpAn ix 13) - **Pun** Sing. abs. *qrt* KAI 92 (= CIS i 5948 = TPC 10), RCL '66, 201[5] - **OffAr** Sing. emph. *qrt*ʾ ATNS 52b ii 9 (:: Segal ATNS a.l.: = Sing. emph. of *qryh*)] - **JAr** Sing. emph. *qrth* MPAT-A 22[4] (= SM 70[11]; :: Dothan Lesh xxxv 212f.: l. *qryyh* = Sing. emph. of *qry*$_3$ (= Scriptures or reading (sc. of them); against Dothan, cf. Barag Tarbiz xli 453f.; v. also infra), 32[1] (for the reading, cf. Naveh sub SM 39, Beyer ATTM 386 :: Hüttenmeister ASI 183f.: l. *[ʾ]tth* = f. Sing. + suff. 3 p.s.m. of *ʾš*$_1$ :: Frey sub 885 (with reserve), Fitzmyer & Harrington MPAT a.l.: l. *wrth* (without interpret.)), SM 83 - ¶ subst. f. town, cf. however Margalit ZAW xcix 398: in KAI 26A ii 9 etc.: = the fortified acropolis within and above the town; in RCL '66, 201[5] prob. indicating Carthage; in KAI 92 poss. indication of Carthage, cf. e.g. Lidzbarski Eph ii 174f., Février sub CIS i 5948, cf. however Clermont-Ganneau RAO v 317f.: rather = n.l., *Cirta*?; for the context of KAI 92, v. *sḥr*$_2$; for the context of RCL '66, 201[5], v. *ʿmq*$_2$ - *bny qrth* SM 83: the inhabitants of the town; *rzh dqrth* MPAT-A 22[4]: the secret of the town (:: Dothan Lesh xxxv 211 ff: l. *rzh dqryyh* = the secret of (the reading of the Tora in Hebrew)) - on this word, cf. also Bordreuil Maarav v/vi 18ff.

v. *qrʾ*$_1$.

qrt$_2$ v. *yqr*$_2$.

qrtgr v. *yqr*$_2$.

qš$_1$ v. *qs*.

qš$_2$ v. *qšb*$_1$.

qš$_3$ v. *š*$_{10}$.

qš$_4$ v. *qrbn*.

qšb$_1$ **Hebr** a form of this root prob. in KAI 188[2]; Albright PEQ '36, 212f.: l. *hqšb* (= Hiph Imper. s.m. of *qšb*$_1$ (= to pay attention; cf. also Mosc p. 37f., Röllig KAI a.l.)) or (dividing otherwise): l. *hqšbw* (= Hiph Imper. pl.m. of *qšb*$_1$; cf. also Michaud PA 62 n. 5, Milik DJD ii p. 97 n. 2, Gibson SSI i p. 14, Teixidor Syr l. 418) :: Lipiński OLP viii 86: l. *hqšbw* = Hiph Pf. 3 p.pl. :: Birnbaum Sam p. 12: l. poss. *hqš* (= *h*$_1$ + Sing. abs. of *qš*$_2$ (= straw)) + *bw* (= *b*$_2$ + suff. 3 p.s.m.), cf. also Galling ZDPV lxxvii 180ff. :: Lemaire RB lxxix 567, 569, IH i 247 (dividing otherwise): l. *wšbw* (= *w* + Qal Pf. 3 p.pl. of *šwb*; against this reading, cf. Lipiński BiOr xxxv 287).

v. *ʿšr$_4$*.

qšb$_2$ > Akkad. *qašbu* (= dried dates), cf. v.Soden Or xlvi 192, AHW s.v. (cf. also CAD s.v.).

qšh **OffAr** Sing. m. abs. *qšh* Aḥiq 101; Plur. m. emph. *qšyʾ* Cowl 6^{11}, 8^{8} - ¶ adj. hard, difficult; *mndʿm qšh* Aḥiq 101: something difficult (cf. Lindenberger APA 81); *myʾ qšyʾ* Cowl 6^{11}, 8^{8}: the difficult/rough waters (i.e. the cataract, sc. in the Nile near Assuan).

qšḥt **Pun** *qšḥt* in CIS i 6058 prob. = n.p., cf. Lidzbarski Eph i 297, Harr 145, Benz p. 407 :: Clermont-Ganneau sub CIS i 6058: abbrev. of *qdš ḥmlkt*; on this word, cf. also Février CIS i a.l.

qšṭ$_1$ **OffAr** HAPH Pf. 3 p.s.m. *hqšṭ* Cowl 4^{3} (diff. and dam. context); Part. s.m. abs. *mhqšṭ* KAI 279^{1} - **Palm** PA ʿEL (?) Impf. 3 p.s.m. *yqšṭ* CIS ii 4218^{5} - ¶ verb PA ʿEL (?) to be justifiable; *wlʾ yqšṭ lmn dy ypthyhy ʿd ʿlmʾ* CIS ii $4218^{5f.}$: and it is unjustifiable for the one who opens it forever (i.e. the one who opens it, cannot vindicate himself forever) - HAPH to make right, to act correctly; *qšyṭʾ mhqšṭ* KAI 279^{1}: he has realized what is right/the truth (i.e. he has embraced Buddhism, *dharma*; cf. Greek par. εὐσέβεια[ν] ἔδειξεν τοῖς ἀνθρώποις; for the interpret., cf. also Dupont-Sommer JA ccxlvi 23f., Altheim & Stiehl GH i 398, 407, EW ix 192, x 244, Kutscher, Naveh & Shaked Lesh xxxiv 132, Donner KAI a.l.) :: Garbini Kand 7f., Rosenthal EI xiv 97*: the one who promotes truth/the right-doer (cf. also Altheim GH v 397) :: Levine JAOS lxxxvii 186: the truthful one, doer of truth.

qšṭ$_2$ **Palm** Sing. emph. *qšṭ[ʾ]* CIS ii 3913 ii 131; + suff. 3 p.s.f. (?) *qš[ṭ]h* CIS ii 4209 (or l. rather *qš[ṭy]h*? = Plur. + suff. 3 p.s.f.; Greek par. δικαίοις); Plur. + suff. 3 p.s.m. *qšṭwh* Syr xix 156^{3}; + suff. 3 p.pl.m. *qšṭyhwn* Ber ii 102 ii 5, 110^{1} (Greek par. δικαίοις), 112^{7}, *qsṭyhwn* Ber ii 104^{5} - ¶ subst. - **1)** what is legally right; *qšṭ[ʾ ʾ]tḥzy ly dy ...* CIS ii 3913 ii 131: I think it is legally right that ... - **2)** legal right; *gwmḥyʾ ʾln trn ... wqsṭyhwn rḥqt ʾmw* Ber ii $104^{1, 5f.}$: A. has transferred these two niches and their rights (i.e. the legal rights pertaining to the possession of these niches), cf. CIS ii 4209 (v. supra), Syr xix 156^{3} (:: Cantineau Syr xix 156: *qšṭ* = *qšṭ$_4$* (= variant of *qšṭ$_1$*)), Ber ii 102 ii 5, 110^{1}, 112^{7}.

qšṭ$_3$ v. *qšṭ$_2$*.

qšṭ$_4$ v. *qšṭ$_2$*.

qšṭ$_5$ v. *qšṭ$_2$*.

qšy **OffAr** APH (cf. Seidel ZAW xxxii 296; cf. however Kottsieper SAS 230: = PA ʿEL; or = QAL?) Impf. 1 p.s. *ʾqšh* Aḥiq 140 - ¶ verb APH (?, v. supra) to strive (cf. e.g. Grelot RB lxviii 189, cf. already Seidel ZAW xxxii 296; cf. also Lindenberger APA 138f.) + *ʿm$_4$* (with).

qšyṭ **OffAr** Sing. m. emph. *qšyṭʾ* KAI 279^{1} - ¶ substantivated adj., what is right, truthful (indication of Buddhist belief, *dharma*) :: Levine JAOS lxxxvii 186: = adj. modifying the prec. noun, the truthful one.

For the context, v. *qšṭ₁*.

qšyš **Palm** m. Sing. emph. *qšyš*ʾ CIS ii 4501[2] - **Hatra** Sing. abs. *qšš* 344[2]; emph. *qšyš*ʾ 202[18] (cf. Aggoula Ber xviii 93, Vattioni IH a.l. (reading *qšyš* prob. printing error) × Milik DFD 368: = Plur. emph., cf. however Teixidor Sumer xxi 87*: = n.p.), 290[3], 342[4], Ibr 9[1], *qšš*ʾ 232B 4 (or = n.l.??; v. also *ḥpyw*), *qšys*ʾ 338[3] (this reading cannot be checked); Plur. emph. *qšyšy*ʾ, cf. Assur 11[2,4] (uncert. combination, cf. also Aggoula Assur a.l.), *qšyš*ʾ 336[4] (cf. Safar Sumer xxxiv 70, 74 n. 11 :: Vattioni IH a.l.: = Sing. emph.), 343[3] - ¶ subst. (or substantivated adj.) old one, elder; *wḥtry*ʾ *qšyš*ʾ *wdrdq*ʾ Hatra 336[3f.], 343[3]: and the Hatreans, the old and the young ones (:: Safar Sumer xxxiv 70: l. *bḥtry*ʾ :: Vattioni IH a.l.: l. (*rbyt*ʾ) *bḥtry*ʾ *qšyš*ʾ *wdrdq*ʾ = the majordomus among the Hatreans, the old one and the young one ...); *qšyš*ʾ *dy dyr*ʾ CIS ii 4501[3]: elder of the community (prob. religious function, cf. Aggoula Ber xviii 93, Syr lx 102, Milik DFD 367f., Gawlikowski TP 79, Starcky Sem xxii 60 (n. 4), 64, 65 (n. 1), cf. also Segal Irâq xxix 9f.) :: Clermont-Ganneau RAO iii 108: indication of senator of Palmyre (cf. also Lidzbarski Eph i 87, Chabot sub CIS ii 4501, v. also *dyr*); in Hatra 290[3], 338[3] epithet: elder (perhaps indication of function, cf. e.g. Safar Sumer xxiv 12, Aggoula Ber xviii 93, 100, Degen NESE iii 86 (for Hatra 290[3]): = religious function, priest, cf. however Safar Sumer xxxiv 72, 74 n. 20 (for Hatra 338[3]): = cheikh); Degen JEOL xxiii 404, Aggoula MUSJ xlvii 8: the *qšš*ʾ in Hatra 232B 4 = indication of religious function, priest, cf. also Safar Sumer xxiv 9: = the abstenious one, ascetic (v. however also supra); Milik DFD 368: the *qšyš*ʾ in Hatra 202[18] = the elders, presbyters (v. however supra) - Segal ATNS a.l.: the *]kšyš* in ATNS 22[1] = variant form of this noun (Sing. cstr.), heavily dam. context, uncert. interpret.
v. *gšyš*.

qšyšw **JAr** Sing. + suff. 3 p.s.m. (or Sing. emph.?) *qšyšwth* Syn D A 4 (= SM 88), C_1 4 (for the reading, cf. Torrey Syn 267; = SM 89a), C_2 3 (= SM 89b) - ¶ subst. eldership; *bqšyšwth dšmwʾl khnh* Syn D A 4f.: during the eldership of the priest Sh. (cf. also Syn D C_1 4f., C_2 3f.).

qšr₁ **OffAr** Yaron JSS ii 47: the *qšr* in MAI xiv/2, 66[17] = QAL Pf. 3 p.s.m. of *qšr₁* (= to bind; uncert. interpret., cf. Dupont-Sommer MAI xiv/2, 67, 87: = n.p.) - a form of this root poss. also in CIS ii 42b: *mqšrn* = PAʿEL Part. pass.m. pl. abs.??, *šʿry*ʾ *mqšrn* = gathered barley?? (or cf. Fales sub AECT 15: l. *mqšrn šʿry*ʾ = attached (?): the barley ...), reading of *m* highly uncert. (cf. Fales sub AECT 15: or l. *30 qšrn* (= QAL Part. pass. pl.m. abs.) *šʿry*ʾ = 30 (*emārus*), attached, the barley ...), cf. also CIS ii a.l.; Stevenson Contracts p. 120: l. *qšrn* (= Sing. cstr. of *qšrn*) *šʿry*ʾ (= Plur. emph. of *šʿr₅* (= interest)) = the bond of interest, improb. interpret.; cf. however Kaufman JAOS cix 98: l. poss.

30 ḥmrn (= Plur. abs. of *ḥmr$_6$* (= *emāru*)); on this text, cf. also Del p. 44, Contini SEL iv 30f. n. 62.
v. *ʿšr$_4$*.

qšr$_2$ **Hebr** Michaud Syr xxxiv 47f.: l. *hqšr* = *h$_1$* + Sing. abs. of *qšr$_2$* (= conspiracy), in KAI 195[8] (cf. also Gibson SSI i p. 43f.; highly uncert. reading, cf. also Lemaire IH i 117f.: l. *hqṣr* = *h$_1$* + Sing. abs. of *qṣr$_3$* (cf. also Conrad TUAT i 623; highly uncert. reading)).
v. *bqš*.

qšrh v. *gšwt*.

qšrn v. *qšr$_1$*.

qšš v. *qšyš*.

qšt$_1$ **Pun** Sing. abs. *qšt* Hofra 100[3] (context however dam.) - **Samal** Sing. + suff. 3 p.s.m. *qšth* KAI 214[26,32] (on both instances, cf. Garr DGSP 45) - **OldAr** Sing. cstr. *qšt* KAI 222A 39; emph. *qštʾ* KAI 222A 38 - **OffAr** Sing. + suff. 3 p.s.m. *qšth* Aḥiq 191; + suff. 2 p.s.m. *qštk* Aḥiq 126 (*[q]štk*), 128; Plur. abs. *qštn* CRAI '70, 163[2] (v. infra), IPAA 11[5]; cf. Frah xiv 3 (*qšwtʾ*) - ¶ subst. arch, bow; *pʿl qšt* Hofra 100[3] (context however dam.): manufacturer of arches/bows; interpret. of *qštn* in CRAI '70, 163[2], IPAA 11[5] diff., Dupont-Sommer CRAI '70, 166: = f. Plur. abs. of *qšt$_1$* or = Plur. abs. of *qšt$_2$* (= measure of distance, linear measure (so far as an archer may travel on horseback; improb. interpret., cf. de Menasce IOS ii 291, Humbach IPAA 13)), cf. Humbach Indologen-Tagung '71, 167: = hunting-weapon, Humbach IPAA 13: = indication of locality or building.
v. *qšṭ$_2$*.

qšt$_2$ **Hebr** Sing. abs. *qšt* Frey 1162[9] (= SM 45), *qyšt* SM 70[4] - **Palm** Sing. abs. *qšt* Inv viii 121[4] (:: Rosenthal with Cantineau Syr xix 166: = n.p.); emph. *qšṭʾ* CIS ii 3908[3], RTP 60 (cf. du Mesnil du Buisson TMP 459f.), 94 (cf. du Mesnil du Buisson ibid.); Plur. cstr. *qštʾ* Syr xxxvi 106[14]; emph. *qšṭʾ* Inv D 19[2], 33[4], RTP 78, 91, 142, *qštʾ* RTP 942 (dam. context; for the RTP texts, cf. Mesnil du Buisson TMP 459f. a.e., Milik Syr xxxvii 95 :: Caquot RTP p. 157: rather = n.p. :: Gawlikowski TP 103: *qšṭʾ* in RTP 142 = Sing. m. emph. of *qšṭ$_4$* (= just)?; for the interchange of *t* and *ṭ*, cf. Cantineau Gramm 39) - ¶ subst. m. archer; in Frey 1162[9] (= SM 45), SM 70[4] indication of sign of the zodiac - Puech RB xc 504: l. poss. *qšt* (= Sing. abs. of *qšt$_2$*) in Frey 1288[2] (uncert. reading and interpret., Frey a.l.: l. *bn* (= Sing. cstr. of *bn$_1$*) *št* (= n.p.)).
v. *qṣh*, *qšt$_1$*.

qt v. *qtn*.

qtyt **OffAr**, cf. GIPP 55 (*ktyt*): solidly (< root *qtt* = to be fixed).

qtl v. *qṭl$_1$*.

qtn **OffAr** word of unknown meaning in ATNS 19[8], 52a 3, 81[4] (poss. = Sing. abs. of *qtn* or Plur. abs. of *qt* (= noun)). Segal sub ATNS 19:

= variant form of *ktn*$_1$ (= flax; uncert. interpret.).
qtr v. *mqtb.*
qtrwd v. *smypr.*

R

r$_1$ **Pun** in the expression *ʿt r* (KAI 62^4, 69^1 (*ʿt [r]*), CIS i 170^1 (*ʿt.r*), 3919^4, Punica ivA 1^3, 5^2, Karth xii 48^3, RCL '66, 201^2) - ¶ abbrev. Février & Fantar Karth xii 48: = abbrev. of abstract noun derived from root *rbb*$_1$, indicating public office (prob. interpret.; cf. Jongeling VO vi 250, cf. also Mahjoubi & Fantar RCL '66, 204, Dupont-Sommer CRAI '68, 123) :: e.g. CIS i sub 132, 3919, Lidzbarski Handb 366, sub KI 56, Cooke NSI p. 106, Slouschz TPI p. 128f., Röllig sub KAI 62, Ferron Mus xcviii 50f.: = abbrev. of form of *rb*$_1$ or of *rbn.*
v. *nʿtr.*
r$_2$ v. *rbʿ*$_3$.
r$_3$ **Palm** abbrev. *r* in MO xv 178^3, *ḥbyby r* = Ch. the great? (*r* abbrev. of *rb*ʾ = Sing. m. emph. of *rb*$_2$?, uncert. interpret.).
r$_4$ v. *rb*$_2$.
rʾy **Pun** Schroed 19 n. 1: the *iar* in Augustine Enarr in Ps 123^5 (on Ps 124^5) = QAL Impf. 3 p.s.m. (highly uncert. interpret.; cf. also Penna CISFP i 893ff.) - **Mo** QAL Impf. 1 p.s. *ʾrʾ* KAI 181^7; HIPH Pf. 3 p.s.m. + suff. 1 p.s. *hrʾny* KAI 181^4 - **Hebr** QAL Pf. 2 p.s.m. *rʾt* DJD ii 17A 3 (cf. Scagliarini Hen xii 137); Impf. 1 p.pl. *nrʾh* KAI 194^{12} (cf. e.g. Torczyner Lach i p. 84, Albright BASOR lxxxii 21, ANET 322, Cassuto RSO xvi 176, Röllig KAI a.l., Gibson SSI i p. 42, Lemaire IH i p. 110 × Gordon BASOR lxvii 32, Ginsberg BASOR lxxx 11: = NIPH Part. s.f. abs.); HIPH Impf. 3 p.s.m. *yrʾ* KAI 196^1; + suff. 2 p.s.m. *yrʾk* KAI 195^7 (for this reading, cf. Albright BASOR lxx 15, cf. also e.g. de Vaux RB xlviii 196, Röllig KAI a.l., Gibson SSI i p. 43f. :: Torczyner Lach i p. 95, 97: l. *ydʿ[n]k* = HIPH Impf. 3 p.s.m. + suff. 3 p.s.m. of *ydʿ*$_1$) - **DA** QAL Imper. pl.m. *rʾw* i 7 - ¶ verb QAL to see - **1)** + obj., *lʾ nrʾh ʾt ʿzqh* KAI 194$^{12f.}$: we do not see A. (v. however supra); *wlkw rʾw pʿlt ʾlhn* DA i 7: come, see the works of the gods (cf. Hoftijzer DA a.l.) - **2)** + *b*$_2$, *wʾrʾ bh wbbth* KAI 181^7: I saw (my desire) upon him and his house (i.e. I was revenged upon him) - HIPH to show - **1)** + obj. + obj., *yrʾ YHWH ʾt ʾdny ʾt hʿt hzh šlm* KAI 196$^{1f.}$: the Lord give my lord to see the present moment in good health (cf. e.g. Bergman with Albright BASOR lxii 32, Albright BASOR lxx 15, Röllig KAI a.l., Gibson SSI i p. 45, Lemaire IH i p. 120 (on the formula, cf. also Dion RB lxxxix 542 n. 98) :: de Vaux RB xlviii 197: may the Lord give my lord to see this happy moment :: Gordon BASOR lxx 17: may the Lord make

my lord see this present signal! Peace! (v. *'t$_6$*) :: Torczyner Lach i p. 117 (div. otherwise): l. ... *'th 'th zh šlm* = (while) thou (art) even now in peace; for the interpret. of *šlm* in this text, v. *šlm$_2$*); on this text, cf. also Pardee HAHL 100; cf. prob. also KAI 195[7] (for the context, v. also *qšr$_2$*, v. also supra) - **2)** + obj. + *b$_2$*, *wky hr'ny bkl šn'y* KAI 181[4]: because he let me see (my desire) upon all my adversaries (i.e. he revenged me upon them).

v. *h'$_1$*, *ḥr'$_1$*, *ntn*, *ryt*.

r'yšy v. *ršy$_4$*.

r'm$_1$ **OffAr** word of unknown meaning (Plur. abs. *r'mn*) in Cowl 81[110] (cf. also Grelot DAE p. 116 n. r); Driver JRAS '32, 86: = wild ox, *br'mn 2 ptḥn* = carved with two wild oxen (v. also *ptḥ$_2$*).

r'm$_2$ v. *šty$_3$*.

r'rb Ebeling Frah a.l.: l. *r'rb* in Frah viii 6, poss. = contamination of derivative *'rb* = *'rb$_9$* (= raven) with *rrb* (= variant of *ǵrb* (= raven)), or = onomatopaic word of unknown origin?; less prob. interpret., cf. Nyberg FP 44, 73: l. here Iranian word.

r'š$_1$ **OldCan** Sing. + suff. 1 p.pl. *ru-šu-nu* EA 264[18] (cf. Sivan GAG 30, 128, 265) - **Ph** Sing. abs./cstr. *r'š* Syr xlviii 403[3] (for interpret. as abs., cf. Caquot Syr xlviii 406, Gaster BASOR ccix 19, 25, Cross CBQ xxxvi 488f., Röllig NESE ii 29, 32f., Garbini OA xx 290, 292; for interpret. as cstr., cf. Lipiński RSF ii 52f., v.d.Branden BiOr xxxiii 13, Avishur PIB 267, 270f., UF x 32, 35, Gibson SSI iii p. 90f., de Moor JEOL xxvii 111; for the context, v. *mgmr$_1$* :: Teixidor AO i 108: l. *d'š* (without interpret.)), Syr xlviii 403[4] (for interpret. as abs., cf. Gaster BASOR ccix 19, 25, Röllig NESE ii 29, 32f., for interpret. as cstr., cf. Caquot Syr xlviii 404f., 406, Lipiński RSF ii 52f., v.d.Branden BiOr xxxiii 13, Avishur PIB 267, 270f., Gibson SSI iii p. 90f., de Moor JEOL xxvii 111; cf. however Garbini OA xx 290ff. (dividing otherwise): l. *dbr* (= Sing. abs. of *dbr$_3$*) *'š* (= *š$_{10}$*); for the context, v. also *ḥlm$_3$*); + suff. 3 p.s.m. *r'š* KAI 24[15,16] (cf. e.g. FR 112,1 sub 3 I, 234a :: Torrey JAOS xxxv 369: = Sing. abs. used adverbially (= completely)) - **Pun** Sing. cstr. *r'[š]* CIS i 6000bis 6 (= TPC 84); Plur. cstr. *r'š'* KAI 145[9] (cf. Février Sem vi 20, 23, 26, cf. however Cooke NSI p. 155, Lidzbarski Eph i 50: = Sing. + suff. 3 p.s.m./f.?, cf. also Berger MAIBL xxxvi/2, 144, 161: l. *r'š'* = Sing. + suff. 3 p.s.m. :: v.d.Branden RSF i 166, 170 (div. otherwise): l. *r'š* (= Sing. abs.) :: Krahmalkov RSF iii 189, 194, 203: l. *r'š'* = variant of *rš'* (= Sing. m. abs. of *rš'* (= the guilty one))), *rš'* KAI 172[2] (for the context, v. *myṭb*) - **Mo** Sing. + suff. 3 p.s.m./f. *ršh* KAI 181[20] (v. infra) - **Hebr** Sing. abs. *rwš* RB lxv 409[15]; cstr. *r'š* KAI 189[6], on Hasm. coins, cf. Meshorer JC no. 22, 23, 24 (*[r]'š*), 25 (id.), *rwš* DJD ii 42[2] (for this reading, cf. e.g. de Vaux RB lx 270, Birnbaum PEQ '55, 22, Milik DJD ii a.l. :: Lehmann

& Stern VT iii 391f.: l. *ryš* (= Sing. cstr. of *ryš* (= variant of *r'š$_1$*)) :: Yeivin At i 96 (div. otherwise): l. *ryšh* = Sing. emph. of *ryš*) - **DA** Sing. + suff. 2 p.s.m. *r'šk* ii 11; cf. also the *r'š[* in viii b 1 - **OldAr** Sing. + suff. 1 p.s. *r'šy* KAI 224[11] - **OffAr** Sing. abs. *r'š* Cowl 11[5]; cstr. *r'š* Cowl 6[1], Samar 1[1] (= EI xviii 8*), *ryš* FX 136[15] (cf. however Dupont-Sommer FX 149: l. rather *r'š*); emph. *rš'* Cowl 10[6]; + suff. 3 p.s.m. *r'šh* Krael 2[8], 7[22]; + suff. 3 p.s.f. *r'šh* Cowl 15[23], Krael 2[9], 7[25]; + suff. 3 p.pl.m. *r'šhw[m]* Beh 38 (Akkad. par. *qaqqadi-šú-nu*); Plur. cstr. *r'šy* Cowl 82[5]; cf. Paik 926 (*ryšh*), 927 (*l'yšh*), Frah x 7 (*l'yšh*), GIPP 26, 63 SaSt 21, cf. Toll ZDMG-Suppl viii 29 - **Nab** Sing. abs. *r'š* MPAT 64 iii 2; cstr. *r'š* RB xlvi 405[2] (v. infra), *ryš* BAGN 88[2] (*ry[š]*),[5] - **Palm** Sing. cstr. *rš* CIS ii 3944[2], Inv x 29[4], Syr xl 47[3]; emph. *rš'* CIS ii 3913 ii 42, Syr lxii 257, AAS xxxvi/xxxvii 169 no. 10[2] (*rš[']*); + suff. 3 p.pl.m. *ršhwn* CIS ii 3915[3], 3916[4]; Plur. emph. *rš'* RTP 39 (cf. Starcky RTP a.l., cf. however Gawlikowski Sem xxiii 119 (n. 2): or = Sing. emph. :: Milik DFD 284f.: l. *dš'* = fresh herbs > spring) - **JAr** Sing. cstr. *rš* MPAT-A 53, *ryš* MPAT-A 50[3]; emph. *rš'* Frey 1144, 1145 (or in both instances = n.p.?); + suff. 3 p.s.m. *ryšh* AMB 5[5]; + suff. 3 p.s.f. *ryšh* AMB 11[4,10]; + suff. 1 p.s. *r'šy* AMB 14[8] - ¶ subst. m. head, passim - **1)** head, part of the body: EA 264[18], KAI 24[15,16], 224[11] (v. *b'y$_1$*), AMB 5[8], 11[4,10], 14[8]; *wm[']t 'mh hyh gbh hṣr 'l r'š hḥṣb[m]* KAI 189[5f.]: a hundred cubits was the height of the rock above the head of the masons - figurative use related to this meaning > person, *ksp šn'h br'šh* Cowl 15[23]: the divorce-money is on her head (i.e she will have to pay ... :: Driver AnOr xii 55: = the money for divorce in its full amount), cf. Krael 2[8,9], 7[22,25]; *'mry' ... lrš' ḥd 'sr' ḥd* CIS ii 3913 ii 42: lambs ... one *assuarius* per head (i.e. for every animal) - **2)** head, first rank; *qm bršhwn* CIS ii 3916[4]: he stood at their head (cf. Beh 38, CIS ii 3915[2f.]) - **3)** head, chief, leader; *[r]'š ḥbr yhwdym* Hasm. coins (cf. Meshorer JC no. 25; cf. also ibid. no. 22-24): the head of the community of the Jews; *r'šy 'd[t']* Cowl 82[5]: the heads of the congregation (v. *'dh$_1$*); *rš šyr'* Inv x 29[4]: the leader of the caravan; *rš tdmwr* CIS ii 3944[2f.]: the chief of Tadmor (cf. Greek par. ἔξα[ρχον Παλμυ]ρηνῶν; cf. also Altheim & Stiehl AAW ii 252, Milik DFD 317 :: Ingholt PBP 123: = a supreme officer of the Palmyrene militia? (cf. also id. ibid. 127f., 130ff.)), cf. BAGN 88[2f.,5] (cf. Altheim & Stiehl AAW v/1, 307f.), cf. AAS xxxvi/xxxvii 169 no. 10[2], Syr lxii 257; *rš' hslky* KAI 172[2]: the heads (i.e. senators) of Sulcis (for the context, v. *myṭb*); *nṭyr'l br zyd'l r'š 'yn l'bn* RB xlvi 405[1f.]: N. the son of Z., the chief of the source L. (for this word division and interpret., cf. Starcky RB lxvi 215ff., Glueck DD 138, 615 n. 1011 :: Savignac RB xlvi a.l.: l. *nṭyr'l br zyd' lr'š'yn l'bn* = N. the son of Z. for *r'š'yn* (= n.d.) of L. (cf. also Broome RB lxii 246ff.: *r'š* = mountain, *'yn* = source, *l'bn* =

n.d., *r'š 'yn l'bn* = indication of deity); for *'yn l'bn* = n.l., cf. Albright with Glueck BASOR lxvii 14); *rwš hmḥnyh* DJD ii 42[2]: the head of the camp (v. *mḥnh*), a civil function (cf. Starcky RB lxiv 203, Sonne PAAJR xxiii 87f.); or a strictly military function?, cf. Milik DJD ii a.l. (cf. also de Vaux RB lx 273: military governor of a district); cf. also RTP 39, v. supra; *rš mrym* MPAT-A 53: the chief of the citizens (v. *mr'*); this meaning prob. also in KAI 30[1] - **4)** elite, elite troops; *[w]'qḥ mm'b m'tn 'š kl ršh* KAI 181[19f.]: and I took two hundred men from Moab, all its elite troops (cf. also Albright ANET 320, Briend TPOA 91, de Moor UF xx 154) :: Demsky Shn vii/viii 256f.: *r'š* here = sum, amount :: v.Zijl p. 191, Gibson SSI i p. 76, 81: *rš* = division (cf. also Segert ArchOr xxix 215 n. 81, 219, 223, 230, 233, 244, 267, Röllig KAI a.l., cf. also Jackson & Dearman SMIM 98, 117: its entire unit) :: e.g. Cooke NSI p. 13, Segert Arch xxix 215 n. 81, 219, 223, 230, 233, 244, 267, Röllig KAI a.l., Andersen Or xxxv 91, 93, Liver PEQ '67, 25f., Miller PEQ '74, 17: *ršh* = Plur. + suff. 3 p.s.m./f. = its chiefs (cf. also Reviv CSI p. 26, de Geus SV 26, Garr DGSP 108, H.P.Müller TUAT i 649) :: Praetorius ZDMG lix 34: *ršh* = Plur. + suff. 3 p.s.m./f. of *rš$_2$* (= poor (one)) cf. also Lidzbarski Eph ii 152 :: Nöldeke Inschrift 14: *kl ršh* = every chief of it (i.e. the chiefs of the people) - **5)** beginning; *šnt 21 r'š mlkwt' kzy 'rtḥššš mlk' ytb bkrs'h* Cowl 6[1f.]: in the 21st year, at the beginning of the kingship (i.e. in the period after the death of the old king and before the formal coronation of the new one, cf. Muffs 192 n. 7) when king A. sat on his throne (cf. Samar 1[1]); *lryš* (v. supra) *yrḥ'* FX 136[15]: at the beginning of the month (cf. Greek par. κατ' ἑκάστην νουμηνίαν), cf. MPAT-A 50[3f.] - **6)** top; *br'[š ']ṭr* CIS i 6000bis 6: at the top of the gable (v. *'ṭr$_2$*) - **7)** extremity; *dy 't' brš qṣt'* Syr xl 47[3f.]: who has come to the extremity of the border (for this uncert. interpret., cf. Starcky Syr xl 50f.; *brš* rather = as the earliest?; v. also *qṣh*) - **8)** principal (capital as distinguished from the interest): Cowl 10[6], 11[5] (cf. e.g. Kutscher JAOS lxxiv 243, Muffs 5f.); *[sl]'yn 'rb' m'h kps r'š rbyn* MPAT 64 iii 2: four hundred *s.* bearing interest as part of the principal (v. *ps$_1$*) - v.Soden Or xlvi 193: > Akkad. *ra'su* (/*re'su*, *rāšu*; = chief), cf. also idem AHW s.v. *ra'su* (uncert. interpret.) - Fitzmyer & Harrington MPAT a.l.: l. *r'š* (= Sing. cstr.) in MPAT-A 1[1] (cf. also Klein BJPES ii 47ff.), less prob. reading, cf. already Ginsberg BJPES ii 47f.: l. *brwk* (= n.p.; cf. also Naveh sub SM 21, Beyer ATTM 371).
v. *'š$_1$*, *byt$_2$*, *mšn$_2$*, *r'š'*, *rš't*.

r'š$_2$ v. *'š$_1$*.

r'šn **Hebr** Sing. m. abs. *r'šn* TA-H 1[5f.] - ¶ adj. first; for the context of TA-H 1[5f.], v. *qmḥ*.

r'št **Ph** Sing. cstr. *r'št* KAI 31[1] - **Pun** Sing. abs. *ršt* KAI 120[2] - ¶ subst. - **1)** the choicest; *r'št nḥšt* KAI 31[1]: the choicest bronze (cf.

e.g. Cooke NSI p. 52, 54, cf. also Röllig KAI a.l., Dahood Bibl lx 434f., cf. however Ginsberg JANES v 145 n. 60, Gibson SSI iii p. 68: the first yield of copper, i.e. the first yield of a new mine or a certain year) - **2)** first fruit; for KAI 120, v. *šlm*$_3$ - for the inscription *br*ʾ*šyt* on jar, cf. Naveh with Lipiński BiOr xxxv 287.

rb$_1$ **Ph** Sing. cstr. *rb* KAI 26A iii 5, 27[12] (cf. Dupont-Sommer RHR cxx 140, v.d.Branden BO iii 45, Röllig NESE ii 18, 22, Avishur PIB 248, Garbini OA xx 283f., Gibson SSI iii p. 83, 85 :: du Mesnil du Buisson FS Dussaud 424, Albright BASOR lxxvi 8, Gaster Or xi 60f., Röllig KAI a.l.: = Sing. m. cstr. of *rb*$_2$ (cf. also Gibson SSI iii p. 85) :: Cross & Saley BASOR cxcvii 45 (n. 19), Mullen DCC 274 = Plur. m. cstr. of *rb*$_2$ :: Torczyner JNES vi 22, 28, Sperling HUCA liii 3, 7 = Sing. m. abs. of *rb*$_2$) - **Hebr** Sing. cstr. *rwb* MPAT-A 13[4] (= SM 46) - ¶ subst. multitude; ʾ*rk ymm wrb šnt* KAI 26A iii 5f.: length of days and multitude of years; *rb dr kl qdšn* (v. *qdš*$_3$) KAI 27[12]: the numerous assembly of the holy ones; *rwb šlwm* MPAT-A 13[4]: much peace.
v. *ṣbyt*. *r*$_1$, *rb*$_2$.

rb$_2$ **Ph** Sing. m. abs./cstr. *rb* CIS i 64[3] (= Kition B 9); abs. *rb* RES 930[2]; cstr. *rb* KAI 34[1,2,3,4] (= Kition B 45), 37A 15 (= Kition C 1A 14), 43[2,6], 51 rs. 2, 59[2], DD 16[1,2], Kition A 30[2], Syr xlviii 396[2], RDAC '84, 103; + suff. 1 p.pl. *rbn* DD 12[1]; Sing. f. abs. *rbt* KAI 10[2,15]; + suff. 3 p.s.m. *rbty* CIS i 13[3] (= Kition A 27), RES 535[4f.]; + suff. 3 p.s.f. *rbty* KAI 33[3] (= Kition A 1); + suff. 1 p.s. *rbty* KAI 10[3,7], 17[1], 48[2] (or = Plur.?), Mus li 286[6,7]; + suff. 1 p.pl. *rbtn* KAI 14[15], ATNS ix 1 (heavily dam. context); Plur. m. abs. *rbm* KAI 9A 4, 26A iii 9, 10, C iv 10, 11 (*r[b]m*) - **Pun** Sing. m. abs. *rb* KAI 78[8], 81[6,8], 95[1], 118[2], CIS i 229[5,6], 230[5], 231[3], 232[5], etc., *rr* (lapsus) RES 910[2] (= CIS i 6012 = TPC 86; cf. possibly also *rp* Punica xviii/iii 5[3] (or l. *rb*?, cf. Chabot Punica a.l., for this reading, cf. also Bertrandy & Sznycer sub SPC 99; or *rp* = QAL Part. act. s.m. abs. of *rp*ʾ$_1$?, cf. Chabot ibid.)); cstr. *rb* KAI 65[10], 81[8,9], 93[3] (= TPC 12), 95[1] (= TPC 50), 96[8] (= CIS i 5523), 101[3], 118[2], 120[1], 145[16], RES 249[2] (= CIS i 5955), 538[1] (= CIS i 5946 = TPC 8), Hofra 74[2], 75[3], etc.; Sing. f. abs. *rbt* KAI 78[2], 79[1], 83, 85[1], etc., etc., *rb*ʾ*t* KAI 164[1], *rt* (lapsus) CIS i 408[1], 960[1], 984[1], 1303[1], 3046[1], 3138[1], 3160[1], 3767[1], *rb* (lapsus) CIS i 475[1], 489[1], 1590[1], 2390[1], 3522[1], 4471[1], 4546[1], *r*ʾ*t* (lapsus) CIS i 3129[1] (cf. *lrbtnt* representing *lrbt tnt*, cf. CIS i 642[1], 910[1], 2615[1], 3175[1], 5073[1]; cf. also *lhrbt* KAI 172[3] = *l*$_5$ + *h*$_1$ + *rbt* (cf. e.g. FR 118a) :: Röllig FS Friedrich 416, KAI a.l.: or *h* is representation of *shewa*; and cf. *l*ʾ*rbt* KAI 94[1], CIS i 4680[1], Hofra 132[1ff.] (= *l*$_5$ + ʾ$_9$ (= *h*$_1$) + *rbt*), cf. CIS i sub 2992, Berthier & Charlier Hofra a.l., FR 118a, 119 :: Röllig KAI a.l.: ʾ = representation of *shewa*, cf. also CIS i sub 4680: = lapsus); + suff. 3 p.s.m. (or f.) *rby* (lapsus for *rbty*) CIS i 419; + suff. 1 p.pl. *rbtn* CIS i 1116[1], 2848[1], 3696[1], RES 7 (= CIS i

5942 = TPC 4), Hofra 16[1], etc., *rb'tn* Hofra 4[1f.], 85[1f.] (*[r]b'tn*), 153[2], 167[1f.] (*rb'[tn]*), KAI 72B 3 (for this reading, cf. Amadasi sub ICO-Spa 10 :: e.g. Solá-Solé Sef xv 50 (cf. also idem Sem iv 30), Röllig KAI a.l., Delcor Sem xxviii 44f., FR 97b: l. *rbbtn* = lapsus for or variant of *rbtn*), *rbnn* (lapsus for *rbtn*) CIS i 747[1], cf. KAI 175[2]: ρυβαοων (lapsus for ρυβαθων :: Röllig KAI a.l.: = lapsus for ρυβαθουν (cf. also Levi Della Vida RSO xxxix 311, Degen ZDMG cxxi 129), cf. *l'r[bt]n tnt* in CIS i 5599[1f.], for the reading , v. *'dn₁*); Plur. m. abs. *rbm* CIS i 5510[9]; Plur. f. abs. *rbt* KAI 81[1] (cf. e.g. Lidzbarski sub KI 69, Röllig KAI a.l., FR 230a; or = Sing.?, cf. also Cooke NSI p. 127), 161[2] (cf. e.g. Cooke NSI p. 149 × or = Plur. cstr. (v. infra) :: Février RA xlv 142: = Sing. f. cstr., used to indicate a male person, cf. also Röllig KAI a.l., Roschinski Num 112); cstr. *rbt* KAI 101[2] (cf. Röllig KAI a.l. (cf. also Février RA xlv 142) :: Lidzbarski SbPAW '13, 301 (div. otherwise): l. *rb tm.t*), 119[1] - **Mo** Plur. m. abs. *rbn* KAI 181[5] - **Amm** Plur. m. abs. *rbm* Ber xxii 120[7] - **Hebr** Sing. m. abs. *rb* Frey 900[2] (cf. Greek par. Ραβ), 1218; + suff. 1 p.s. *rby* Frey 994B 2, 1055, SM 6[3], 75[1,5], IEJ v 221[1] (Greek par. ραββι), cf. Frey 1052: ριββι; Plur. f. abs. *rbwtynw* SM 49[26] - **OldAr** Sing. m. abs. *rb* KAI 222B 7, Tell F 6 (Akkad. par. *rabî*): Plur. m. + suff. 3 p.s.m. *rbwh* KAI 222A 39, 40, 223B 3, C 15f. (:: Kaufman BiOr xxxiv 94: = Plur. + suff. 3 p.s.m. of *rby₂* (= noble)) - **OffAr** Sing. m. abs. *rb* Aḥiq 60, ATNS 42b 5 (diff. context), Beh 45 (Akkad. par. *ra-bu-ú*), Cowl p. 269 i 3 (for the context, cf. Greenfield & Porten BIDG 22; Akkad. par. *rabû*), CIS ii 38[6] (= Del 21 = AECT 3), Pers 7[4], 10[4], 14[2], 16[3], 18[2], 39[4], 64[4], 88[3], FuF xxxv 173[1,2]; cstr. *rb* Cowl 1[3], 16[7], 20[5], 25[2,4], 30[7], 38[3], 54[14], 69[8] (for the reading, cf. Porten & Yardeni sub TADAE B 8.5), RES 438[2], 966[1] (dam. context), Krael 8[2,3], AG 2[2] (cf. Segal Maarav iv 70 :: Aimé-Giron AG a.l. (div. otherwise): l. *rbk* = Sing. cstr. of *rbk₂* (= mixture?)), KAI 276[4,6], PTT 4-8 (?, on seal, cf. Cameron PTT p. 89, cf. also Greenfield JAOS lxxxii 298 n. 89); emph. *rb'* Cowl 30[18], 42[6] (*[r]b'*), 63[13], 72[15], 81[32,33], ATNS 103[2], RES 492A 7, 956[4], 1785G, ASAE xxvi 29[2], xxxix 355[3], BSOAS xxvii 272 v 2, Syr xli 285[5]; Sing. f. abs. *rbh* Or lvii 34[6], 35[3,6,8]; emph. *rbt'* Krael 4[3,6], 9[4,11], 10[6], 12[13,21], Sach 76 i 3, Sem xxi 85 conc. 3; Plur. m. cstr. *rby* Cowl 80[3] (for the reading, cf. Porten & Yardeni sub TADAE A 5.5), Aḥiq 33 (:: Kaufman BiOr xxxiv 94: = Plur. cstr. of *rby₂* (= noble)), Samar 7[7] (dam. and diff. context); emph., cf. Warka 36: *ra-ab-bi-e*; cf. Frah xii 6 (*lb'*), Paik 916 (*rb'*), 917 (*rb'*, *lb'*), Sogd ii 231, B 269, Bb 141, Ka 15, 18, 22, ML 595, Ta 483, 486, Syn 315 ii, Syr xxxv 317[41], 319[48], BSOAS xxxiii 152[14] (*lb'*), GIPP 26, 62, SaSt 21f. - **Nab** Sing. m. cstr. *rb* CIS ii 196[4], 442[2] (dam. context), RB lxiv 215[1], ADAJ xxi 139[1] (= CIS ii 476), *rbw* RES 1097[2] (= CIS ii 192; for the ending -*w*, cf. e.g. Diem ZDMG cxxiii 227ff.: < Arab., also for literature); emph. *rb'* CIS ii 349[3],

350[1]; Sing. f. emph. *rbt*ʾ RB xliii 574[1] (for the reading, cf. Milik ADAJ xxi 144 n. 3), xliv 266[1,2,3] - **Palm** Sing. m. abs. *rb* RTP 196, SBS 45[9] (Greek par. μεγάλου), 61a; cstr. *rb* CIS ii 3913 i 10 (Greek par. Ραβ; v. ʾ*sr*$_1$), 3932[5], 3936[2], 3946[3], 3947[2,3], 3948[2], RTP 27, 30-33, 35, RIP 126[2], 127[8]; emph. *rb*ʾ CIS ii 3911[8], 3913 ii 44, 3946[3], etc., etc.; Sing. f. abs. *rb*ʾ CIS ii 3915[4]; emph. *rbt*ʾ CIS ii 3914[4], AAS xxxvi/xxxvii 167 no 7[4] (Greek par. μεγ[άλην]) - **Hatra** Sing. m. cstr. *rb* 43[2], 56[2], 140[5], 202[3]; emph. *rb*ʾ 25[1] (for the reading, cf. e.g. Altheim & Stiehl AAW ii 201, Ingholt AH i/1, 45, Degen ZDMG cxxi 125, Vattioni IH a.l. :: Milik RN vi/iv 55f.: l. *rw*ʾ (var. form of *rb*ʾ) :: Safar Sumer vii 183, Caquot Syr xxix 104: l. *drb*ʾ = *d*$_3$ + *rb*ʾ (cf. also Donner sub KAI 246)), 67[3], 107[4,6], 110, 202[5], 218[2], 231 (?, heavily dam. context), 288a 7, *rwb*ʾ 24[1] (for this reading, cf. e.g. Milik RN vi/iv 55 (n. 2), Aggoula Ber xviii 90, Pennacchietti FO xvi 59, Vattioni IH a.l. (cf. also Safar Sumer vii 182: l. *r.b*ʾ) :: Caquot Syr xxix 103, Degen WO v 236, ZDMG cxxi 125, Donner sub KAI 245: l. *rb*ʾ = Sing. m. emph.; or = Plur.?); Sing. f. cstr. *rbt* Hatra 31[3] (for this reading and poss. interpret., v. ʾ*mr*$_2$); Plur. m. emph. *rb[*ʾ*]* 173 (for this reading, cf. Milik DFD 105, Vattioni IH a.l. :: Caquot Syr xli 265: l. *dy*?; cf. however Safar Sumer xviii 50: no text to be read), *rwb*ʾ 15[2] (for this reading and interpret., cf. e.g. Aggoula Ber xviii 91 (cf. also Vattioni IH a.l.: or = Sing. emph.) :: Safar Sumer vii 183, Caquot Syr xxix 104, Altheim & Stiehl AAW ii 201: l. *rb*ʾ = Sing. m. emph. (for this reading, cf. also Ingholt AH i/1, 45) :: Milik RN vi/iv 55f.: l. *rw*ʾ (= variant of *rb*ʾ = Sing. m. emph.)), 26[3] (cf. e.g. Aggoula Ber xviii 91, Vattioni IH a.l. (cf. also Safar Sumer vii 184: l. *r.b*ʾ) :: Milik RN vi/iv 56, DFD 105: l. *rwb*ʾ = Sing. m. emph. :: Caquot Syr xxix 104: l. *rb*ʾ = Sing. m. emph. :: Altheim & Stiehl AAW ii 202: l. *drb*ʾ = *d*$_3$ + *rb*ʾ (= Sing. m. emph.)) - **Waw** Sing. m. emph. *rb*ʾ AMB 6[1]; Sing. f. emph. *rbt*ʾ AMB 6[4] - **JAr** Sing. abs. *rb* MPAT-A 27[1] (= SM 33 = Frey 857; cf. however Naveh sub SM 33: poss. = lapsus for *rby* (= Sing. m. + suff. 1 p.s.)), EI xii 146a 3 (or = Hebr.?); emph. *rb*ʾ MPAT 44,15[1] (heavily dam. context), 68[2], MPAT-A 17[1] (= SM 7), AMB 1[8], 7[5,15], Mas 461, etc.; + suff. 1 p.s. *rby* MPAT-A 3[1] (= SM 60 = Frey 1199), 22[9] (= SM 70[17]), 41[2] (for the reading, cf. Naveh SM 29), 48[1] (= SM 15 = Frey 979), Frey 892[2], AMB 3[5]; + suff. 1 p.pl. *rbnw* MPAT 58[3]; Sing. f. abs. *rbh* AMB 7[4] (diff. context, v. *srrw*); Plur. m. emph. *rbyh* MPAT-A 34[2] (= SM 69) - ¶ **A)** adj. - **1)** numerous; *ymn rbn* KAI 181[5]: numerous (many) days (i.e. during a long period); *ywmt rbm* Ber xxii 107: numerous (many) days (cf. Dion RB lxxxii 26 n. 8); ʾ*rṣt rbt* KAI 161[2]: numerous lands (or wide lands? × Plur. *rbt* used to indicate male person (div. otherwise): l. *rbt mmlk*ʾ*t* KAI 161[2]: the overlord of kings (v. also supra)) - **2)** big, large, vast, wide; *t*ʾ*t*ʾ *zylk rbt*ʾ Sach 76 i 3: your large ewe (cf. Greenfield

Or xxix 99); *byt› [r]b›* Cowl 42[6]: a large house (cf. IEJ xxxvi 206[2]); *hwn rb znh* Pers 14[2]: this large mortar; *ṣryḥ› rb›* CIS ii 350[1]: the large room (v. *ṣryḥ*$_1$); *bslq› rbt›* CIS ii 3914[4]: the great portico (cf. AAS xxxvi/xxxvii 167 no. 7[4]); *bb› rb›* Syr xvii 274[3] (cf. SBS 24[3f.]): the great gate; *ḥyl› rb›* CIS ii 3946[2], 3947[2f.]: the great army (mentioned in the same context as *ḥyl› dy tdmwr* CIS ii 3946[3f.], 3947[3]: the garrison of T., cf. Greek par. of CIS ii 3947 mentioning ὁ μέγας στρατηλάτης and ὁ ἐνθάδε στρατηλάτης); *qdns rb* SBS 45[9]: a great danger; *hykl› rb›* Hatra 107[6]: the great temple; *mkn› rb›* Hatra 202[5]: the great altar; *m‹brt› rbt› d›wqynws* AMB 6[3ff]: the great ford of the Ocean; cf. *rbt› ... z‹yrt›* Sem xxi 85 conc. 3: great ... small - **3)** important, great; *mlk rb* KAI 222B 7: the great king (cf. Noth ZDPV lxxvii 146, cf. also Fitzmyer AIS 61; cf. also FuF xxxv 173[1] (inscription from Georgia)); *mr› rb* Tell F 6: the great lord (epithet of Hadad); *›ptw ›lh› rb›* Cowl 72[15]: A. the great god; *šmš ›lh› rb›* ASAE xxxix 355[2f.]: Sh. the great god; *›lht› rbt›* RB xliv 266[1,2,3]: the great goddess; *b‹lšmyn rb›* RES 956[3f.]: the great B. (cf. Hatra 24[1], v. however supra; interpret. *mrn wb‹šmn rwb›* = our lord and B., the great ones, preferable?); *mrn wmrtn wbrmryn wb‹šmyn ›lh› rwb›* Hatra 25[2]: our lord, our lady, and the son of our lords and B., the great gods (cf. Hatra 26[2f.]); *b‹lšmn rb› wrḥmn›* CIS ii 3988[1]: the great and the merciful B.; *byl rb› mlk›* RES 1785G: the great B., the king; *bl ›lh› rb›* Syr xiv 177[4]: B. the great god (cf. Syr xli 285[5], Hatra 107[4], 272[2]); l. poss. also ... *›lh]› rb› d‹rb* Hatra 231[1]: ...] the great god(s) of Arabia (cf. Aggoula MUSJ xlvii 5f. :: Safar Sumer xxiv 7 (n. 4): *rb› d‹rb*: cheikh of the Arabs (reading *rb›* pro *rb› d‹rb* in IH a.l. erroneous)); *yšm‹›l rb› gybr› wdḥyl›* AMB 1[8]: I. (an angel), the great, mighty and terrifying one; *br t›wn rb›* AMB 7[1]: the great B.; *rb ›rsw* RTP 196: A. is great (cf. RTP 190); *bkl [ṣ]bw klh rb› wz‹r›* CIS ii 3915[4]: in every matter be it great or small (etc.); *khn› rb›* Cowl 30[18]: the high-priest (v. also Mas 461); *›pkl› rb›* Hatra 67: the high-priest; *kmr› rb›* Hatra 25[1]: the high-priest (v. also *kmr*$_2$ and v. supra); *msyq› rb›* Hatra 218[2]: the chief tax-collector (v. *msyq*) - **B)** substantivated adj. - **1)** important man; *kl qhlh q[dy]šh rbyh wz‹yryh* MPAT-A 34[1f.]: the complete holy community, the important people and the unimportant ones (cf. prob. also Warka 36) - a) indication of high court official; *znh [›ḥy]qr rb* Aḥiq 60: this Aḥiqar was a high court official; cf. KAI 222A 39, 40, 223B 3, 224[15f.], Aḥiq 33 - b) used as title preceding names of male persons: *rb ywdn* Frey 900[2f.]: *rab* Y. (cf. Frey 1218, MPAT-A 27[1], EI xii 146a 3); *rby yṣḥq* Frey 994B 2: *rabbi* Y. (cf. Frey 892[2], MPAT-A 48[1], SM 6, etc.); *rbnw bṭnyh br mysh* MPAT 58[3]: our lord B. the son of M.; cf. also *rbwtynw* SM 49[26]: our rabbis; Fitzmyer & Harrington MPAT a.l.: l. *r* (= abbrev. of *rby*) in MPAT-A 43[1] (cf. already Klein ZDPV li 137; cf. however Goldhar with Klein ibid.: l. *d* (= d_3), cf. also Naveh sub SM 5) - c) used as title for a deity; *lrbn* DD 12[1]: for our lord (without specification); *lhrbt l›lt* KAI 172[3]: for the lady A.; *lrbt l›m› wlrbt lb‹lt* ... KAI 83: for the lady Amma and the lady Ba‹alot; *hrbt b‹lt gbl* KAI 10[2,15]: the Lady, the mistress of G. (cf. *rbty b‹lt gbl* KAI 10[3,3f., 7,7f.]); *lrbt l‹štrt* CIS i 135[1]: to the lady Ashtarte (cf. *lrbty l‹štrt* RES 535[4ff.], KAI 17[1], Mus li 86[6,7]); *rbty ‹štrt* KAI 33[3]; *lrbt l‹štrt wltnt* KAI 81[1]: to the ladies Ashtarte and Tinnit (v. however supra); *lrbty l›m h›zrt* CIS i 13[3]: to his lady the ... mother (v. *›zr*$_4$); *rbt ḥwt ›lt mlkt* ... KAI 89[1] (= CIS i 6068): the lady Ch., the goddess, the queen (v. *mlk*$_3$); *lrbt ltnt pn b‹l* CIS i 181[1], 182[1], etc., etc.: to the lady T., face of Ba‹al (v. *pnh*$_1$; cf. *lrbt pn b‹l* CIS i 4449[1f.], *l›m lrbt pn b‹l* CIS i 380[4f.]; *rbtn tnt p‹n b‹l* KAI 102[1f.]: our lady T., face of Ba‹al, *lrbtn ltnt* CIS i 1116[1]: to our lady T.; *lrby* (v. supra) *lt[nt p]n b‹l* CIS i 419: to his lady T., face of Ba‹al (cf. *l›dn lrbt tnt* CIS i 2685[1], *l›dn ltnt* CIS i 3048[1], 3913[1f.], 4328[1], Hofra 120, *l›dn lrbt ltnt* CIS 4796[1f], 4994[1], *lrbt lb‹l* CIS i 4130[1])); *lrbty l›lm ›drt ›s ›lm ‹štrt* KAI 48[2]: to my lady (/ladies, v. supra) the mighty goddess Isis (and) the goddess Ashtarte; cf. also without name of Tinnit following, *lrbt* CIS i 580[1], 2983[1], RES 789[1], *rbtn* RES 7 (= our lady) - d) used as epithet following n.p.; *›bh br khnh ›l‹z* (on the spelling of this name, cf. E.S.Rosenthal IEJ xxiii 74 n. 10, Teixidor Syr li 327) *br ›hrn rbh* MPAT 68[1f.]: A. the son of E., the priest, the son of A., the elder (cf. also Dion Bibl lvi 418f.; :: E.S. Rosenthal IEJ xxiii 74: = the high-priest); the epithet *rb›* in BSOAS xxvii 272 v 2, SBS 60[10], 61e 3, CIS ii 4562[2], RIP 79A 3, 143[3], Ber ii 91[1], 93[1], RTP 233 (for this text, cf. Ingholt FS Michałowski 471, cf. however Caquot RTP p. 165: prob. = n.p.), Hatra 110, 288a 7, FuF xxxv 173[2] poss. = the important one, the elder, or = indication of function?, for the interpret. as elder in Palm. texts, cf. Ingholt FS Michałowski 471ff. (cf. also Teixidor Syr xlv 379f.); the same word without emph. ending, *rb*, poss. also as epithet in SBS 61a (diff. reading); cf. also the epithet *›bwn rb›* in SBS 60[11], 61e 4: our great father - e) used as epithet following n.d., v. supra; cf. also *mlk‹štrt rbt ›lpqy* KAI 119[1]: M. the lady of Lepcis (cf. RES 2052[5f.]), cf. however di Vita Or xxxvii 201ff., Pardee Mem Craigie 61f.: *rbt* (f. form) referring to two male gods *šdrp›* and *mlk ‹štrt* (cf. already Solá-Solé Sef xxi 255f.) - **2)** as indication of tutor: RES 1097[2] (cf. Greek par. τροφεὺς) - **3)** head, chief, commander; *rb ›rṣ* KAI 43[2,6]: chief of the land (exact meaning unknown, indication of high government official, cf. e.g. Honeyman JEA xxvi 59, Röllig KAI a.l., Gibson SSI iii p. 138, Elayi RCP 11); *rb dgl›* Cowl 69[8] (v. supra): commander of a detachment; for *rb dḥšyhy*, v. *dḥš*; for *rb ḥz‹nm*, v. *ḥzy*$_1$; *rb ḥyl› zy swn* RES 438[3]: commander of the garrison of Syene (cf. Cowl 16[7], 25[2,4], 30[7], Krael 8[2,3]); *rb ḥyl›* Cowl 1[3], 20[5], 38[3], 54[14]: the commander of the garrison (cf. e.g. Verger RCL '64, 82ff., RGP 179ff., Frye BAG 90, Lipiński Stud 179, 184); *rb ḥylʾ rbʾ ... rb ḥylʾ dy tdmwr* CIS ii 3946[3f.], 3947[2f.]: the commander of the great army ... the commander of the garrison of T.; *rb ḥn ʾnm* Hofra 82[3]: prob. indication of chief of a certain clan (v. *nʾn*); for *rb ḥrm*, v. *ḥrm*$_4$; for *rb ḥrš*, v. *ḥrš*$_4$; for *rb khnm/rb hkhnm* and related functional indications, v. *khn*$_1$; for *rb kṣrʾ*, v. *kṣr*$_3$; *rb mʾt* KAI 101[3], RES 1502: commander of a century (cf. however Elayi RCP 51; cf. Cowl 80[3]; cf. Plur. KAI 101[2] (for Lib. par., cf. Chaker AION lvi 544f.)); *rb mzrḥ* KAI 145[16]: the head of a *mzrḥ* (v. *mzrḥ*$_1$); *rb mḥnt* KAI 120[1]: the commander of an army (i.e. *consul*), used as title of roman emperor, cf. also *rb tʾḥt rb mḥnt* KAI 118[2]: *proconsul* (for these two titles, cf. e.g. Clermont-Ganneau RAO vii 100ff., Lidzbarski Eph iii 60, Levi Della Vida AfrIt vi 8, PBR xix 67, Angeli Bertinelli CISFP i 255f. and the Greek translations of *consul* and *proconsul*: στρατηγός ὕπατος and στρατηγός ἀνθύπατος); for *rb mrzḥʾ*, v. *mrzḥ*; for *rb (h)mšṭrt*, v. *mšṭrh*; *rb mšrytʾ* CIS ii 196[4], RB lxiv 215[1f.]: the commander of the camp, indication of a military function (cf. Savignac & Starcky RB lxiv 200ff.); for *rb mtrm*, v. *mtr*$_1$; for *rb smyʾ*, v. *smʾ*; for *rb (h)sprm*, v. *spr*$_2$; for *rb srs*, v. *srs*; for *rb srsrm*, v. *srsr*$_2$; *rb ʿyn* RIP 127[8]: caretaker of the source; *rb ʿyn ʿl ʾpqʾ* RIP 126[2f.]: caretaker of the source at E. (cf. Greek par. ἐπιμελητὴς ... Ἔφκας πηγῆς; cf. Starcky RB lxiv 216f.); for *rb pršyʾ*, v. *prš*$_2$; for *rb qyntʾ*, v. *qynh*; *rb šwq* CIS ii 3932[5]: market-superintendant (cf. Greek par. ἀγορανομήσαντα); *rb šyrtʾ* CIS ii 3936[2], 3948[2]: the leader of a caravan (cf. Greek par. resp. [ἀ]ρχέμπορον and σ[υν]οδιάρχῃ); *rb šʿrm* DD 16[1,2]: the chief of the door-keepers; for *rb hšpṭm* Karth xii 46[2]: the chief of the suffetes; for *rb trbṣ*, v. *trbṣ* - cf. also *rb* as indication of function or title in Punic texts (cf. KAI 81[5], CIS i 229[5,6], 230[5], 231[3], 232[5], 5510[6,7,9f.,10], etc., etc.; cf. *wylk rbm ʾdnbʿl ... hrb wḥmlkt ... hrb* CIS i 5510[9f.]: and the *rab* s will come (?, v. *hlk*$_1$), A. ... the *rab* and Ch. ... the *rab*; cf. also Krahmalkov RSF iv 155f., Huss 465); cf. also the foll. titles *rb šny* RES 930[2]: second *rab*, *rr* (lapsus, v. supra) *šlšʾ* RES 910[2]: third *rab* (exact meaning of these titles unknown, cf. also Lidzbarski Eph i 147; Slouschz TPI p. 43: *šny* indication of the place of the *rab* in question in the hierarchy (cf. also Cooke NSI p. 42); Teixidor Sem xxix 15: = the *duumvir*, one of the two magistrates of the town (cf. also idem Syr lvi 382); for *rb šlšʾ*, v. also *šlšy*) - **4)** the *rb ʿn* In Syr xlviii 396[2] prob. = the great eyed one (prob. indicating a demon), cf. e.g. (Dupont-Sommer with) Caquot Syr xlviii 399f., 403, Gaster BASOR ccix 19, Röllig NESE ii 29f., Liverani RSF ii 37, Avishur PIB 267f., UF x 30, 33, Gibson SSI iii p. 89f., de Moor JEOL xxvii 111 :: v.d.Branden BiOr xxxviii 13: = the lord of the rain :: Lipiński RSF ii 51: = abundant source - **C)** in the expression *brbm* KAI 9A 4 (dam. context), 26A iii 9, 10 = extremely, largely (cf. e.g. Dupont-Sommer

RA xlii 174 (cf. also H.P.Müller TUAT i 644) :: Röllig KAI a.l.: in KAI 9A 4 = among the great ones (cf. also Février Sem ii 23, Cross IEJ xxix 44), in KAI 26A = among many :: Gibson SSI iii p. 62: in KAI 26A = consisting of many, as many (against Gibson's interpret., cf. Pardee JNES xlvi 138 (n. 15)) :: v.d.Branden Meltô i 56f., 80 = during a long time (poss. abbrev. for *bymm rbm*) :: Obermann Conn xxxviii 32f.: = *b*$_2$ + *rb* (= Inf.) + suff. 3 p.pl.m. (in their affluence); *wbrbm yld* KAI 26A iii 9: may it (i.e. the people) bear (v. *yld*$_1$) abundantly; *wbrbm y'dr wbrbm y'bd l'ztwd* KAI 26A iii 10f.: and may it (i.e. the people) grow extremely mighty and may it serve A. extremely well (for KAI 26A, cf. also Amadasi-Guzzo VO iii 100f.) - **D)** f. used as title for male person; *rbt m't* KAI 101[2]: commanders of a century - l. prob. *rbm* (= Plur. m. abs.) in MUSJ xlv 262[3] (cf. Röllig NESE ii 2, 8, Cross IEJ xxix 41, 44 :: Schiffmann RSF iv 172: = Sing. + suff. 3 p.pl.m. of *rb*$_1$) - Milik DFD 49: l. Sing. m. emph. *rb[']* in RTP 197 (uncert. reading) - Aggoula Syr lxii 66f., 74f.: the *rb* in Atlal vii 109[6] = Sing. m. abs. of *rb*$_2$ (= fortress, temple; in the context indicating a temple in Têma), less prob. interpret., cf. also Beyer & Livingstone ZDMG cxxxvii 286f.: l. *db* or *rb* = n. l. - Roschinski Num 112, 115: the *rb'* in KAI 161[9] = Sing. m. + suff. 3 p.s.m. (uncert. interpret., diff. context) - Albright FS Horn 508: l. *rb* (Sing. m. cstr.) in Or xxi 184[2] (diff. context, uncert. interpret.) - R.A.Bowman Pers a.l.: l. *rb* (= Sing. m. abs.) in Pers 43[4] (improb. reading, cf. Naveh & Shaked Or xlii 455: no visible traces) - Segal ATNS a.l.: l. *rb'* (= Sing. m. emph.) in ATNS 103[2] (improb. interpret., cf. Zauzich Ench xiii 117f.: = part of n.l.) - Teixidor Sumer xx 78*, Syr xliv 189: l. *rb* (= Sing. m. abs.) in Hatra 209[2] (improb. reading, cf. Aggoula Ber xviii 99: pro *rb br'šy* (= n.p.) l. *d brr'šy* (= n.p.; reading of first *r* uncert.) :: Milik DFD 391, Vattioni IH a.l.: l. <*d*>*zbyd* (= n.p.) *'šy* (= n.p.)) - for the diff. *rb 'br lspt*, v. *'br*$_1$.

v. *'lh*$_1$, *byrby*, *brk*$_1$, *d't*, *db*, *dnb*, *yhb*, *ytn*$_1$, *kb*, *kpwtk*, *mr'*, *npš*, *sbb*$_2$, *prb*, *qrb*$_1$, *r*$_3$, *rb*$_1$, *rbh*, *rby*$_{1,3}$, *rbyt*, *rbmg*, *rbtkh*, *rd*$_2$, *rḥ*$_1$, *r'y*$_1$, *šṭrb*, *šr*$_2$.

rb$_3$ v. *brk*$_1$.

rb'$_1$ v. *rby*$_1$.

rb'$_2$ v. *rp'*$_1$.

rb'$_3$ **OffAr** Sing. abs. *rb'* Cowl 42[5] - ¶ subst. interest (for the restoration of the dam. context, cf. Porten & Yardeni sub TADAE A 3.8).

rb'n v. *rbn*.

rbb$_1$ **DA** a form of this root (*hrbt(y)*) in x b 1, poss. = Haph Pf. 3 p.s.f. or 2 p.s.f. of *rbb*$_1$ (= to make great), highly diff. and heavily dam. context, for other poss. solutions, cf. Hoftijzer DA a.l.

v. *dnb*.

rbb$_2$ **Nab** Sing. + suff. 3 p.s.m. *rbbh* ADAJ x 44 ii 5 (for the reading, cf. Milik ADAJ xxi 151 n. 16 :: Starcky RB lxxii 95, ADAJ a.l.: l. *rbnh*

= Sing. + suff. 3 p.s.m. of *rbn* :: Milik ADAJ xxi a.l.: *rbbh* = lapsus for *rbnh*) - ¶ subst. foster-father (< Arab.?).

rbd **Pun** QAL (/PI<EL) Pf. 3 p.s.m. *rbd* KAI 124^2 - ¶ verb QAL (/PI<EL) to pave; *wt hmḥz rbd* KAI 124^2: he has paved the *forum* (cf. Lat. par. *forum ...d(edit) f(aciendum) c(uravit)*); etymology proposed by v.d.Branden PO i 436 less. prob.; cf. also Amadasi IPT 64.

rbh **OffAr** Sing. abs. *rbh* RES 1367^1, 1372B 1 (v. infra) - ¶ subst. poss. meaning master, sir; *rbh trkmnh* RES 1367^{1f}, 1372B 1: master T. (for this interpret., cf. also Grelot DAE p. 339 n. d; cf. however Lidzbarski Eph iii 104: *rbh* = Sing. m. emph. of *rb*$_2$).
v. *rby*$_2$.

rbw$_1$ **Waw** Sing. abs. *rbw* AMB 6^8 (for the reading and interpret., cf. Naveh & Shaked AMB a.l. :: Gordon Or xviii 339f.: l. *rbw* = orthogr. variant of (or lapsus for) *rbwn* (= master, lord) :: Dupont-Sommer Waw p. 19: l. *dkw* = Sing. abs. of *dkw* (= purity), cf. also id. AIPHOS xi 121f.) - ¶ subst. greatness, magnificence; for the context of AMB 6^8, cf. Naveh & Shaked AMB a.l., Segal JSS xxxi 97.
v. *rbyt*.

rbw$_2$ v. *rb*$_2$.

rbw$_3$ **OffAr** cf. Sogd 232, B 270, Ka 19, Ve 119, ML 595 - **Palm** CIS ii 3934^5 - ¶ cardinal number, ten thousand.

rbw>n v. *rby*$_3$.

rbwn v. *rbw*$_1$, *rbn*.

rbw<$_1$ v. *rb<*$_3$.

rbw<$_2$ **JAr** Sing. emph. *rbw<[h]* SM 110 - ¶ subst. m. square (cf. however Meitlis Tarbiz liii 465f. = eating and drinking place for the Beth Midrash (cf. also Naveh EI xx 305)).

rbw<h **Palm** Sing. emph. *rbw<t>* MUSJ xxxviii 106^{6,9} - ¶ subst. exact meaning unknown, indicating part of tomb construction, rectangular room (cf. Ingholt MUSJ xxxviii 112 :: Gawlikowski MFP 209: = quarter?) - the same word as *rb<h*$_2$?

rby$_1$ **Hebr** PI<EL Part. s.m. abs. *mrb[h]* DJD ii 30^{19}; HIPH Inf. abs. *hrbrh* AMB 1^1 (v. infra) - **OldAr** PA<EL Impf. 1 p.s. *>rb>n* KAI 222B 30 (for this reading and interpret., cf. Greenfield JSS xi 103f., Lemaire & Durand IAS 115, 138, cf. also Fitzmyer AIS 68, Sader EAS 131 (on the problems involved, cf. Degen AAG p. 14f. n. 64) :: Lipiński Stud 37f.: = QAL Impf. 1 p.s. of *rb>*$_1$ (= to esteem highly, to extol) :: e.g. Dupont-Sommer Sf p. 62: l. *>rb>m* without interpret. :: Weinfeld DDS 125 n. 4 (div. otherwise): l. *>rb>* (= PA<EL Impf. 1 p.s.) - **OffAr** QAL Pf. 3 p.s.m. *rb>* Aḥiq 18 (cf. Baneth OLZ '14, 250f., Cowl p. 228, Leand 40d, f (cf. also Grelot DAE p. 448, Kottsieper SAS 50) :: e.g. Sach p. 151, Driver JRAS '32, 87: = Sing. m. emph. of *rb*$_2$ :: Lipiński Stud 38: = QAL pass. of *rb>*$_1$ (= to esteem highly)); Impf. 3 p.s.m. *yrbh* Cowl

10^{4,6}, 11^{2,5,9}, ATNS 35^2, LidzbAss 6^3 (= AECT 51), *yrby* LidzbAss 5^4 (= AECT 50; cf. however Kaufman JAOS cix 100: l. *yrbh* (= QAL Impf. 3 p.s.m.)?); Part. act. s.m. abs. *rbh* Cowl 11^9; PA ʿEL Pf. 3 p.s.m. *rbh* Cowl 81^{47} (cf. Cowl a.l., Leand 40v :: Grelot DAE p. 111: = QAL Part. act. s.m. abs.); 1 p.s. *rbyt* Aḥiq 25; Impf. 3 p.s.m. *yrbh* Aḥiq 114 (cf. Cowl a.l., Grelot DAE p. 439, cf. also Lindenberger APA 101, cf. however e.g. Ginsberg ANET 429, Grelot RB lxviii 185, Kottsieper SAS 21, 230: = QAL); 1 p.pl. *nrby* Cowl 81^{70} (v. however infra) - **Nab** QAL Part. act. m. pl. abs. *rbyn* MPAT 64 iii 2 - **Palm** PA ʿEL Pf. 3 p.s.m. *rby* Ber v 131 - ¶ verb QAL to be great, to become great - **1)** to come of age; *bry rb*ʾ Aḥiq 18: my son is an adult now - **2)** to grow, to increase, said of money which bears interest (cf. Muffs 185; cf. also Kaufman AIA 90); cf. MPAT 64 iii 2; *mrbyt* (v. *mrby*) *yhwh r*ʾ*š wyrbh* Cowl 11^5: interest, it will become (part of) the capital and it will bear interest; *kn mṭt mrbyt*ʾ *lrš*ʾ *yrbh mrbyt*ʾ *krš*ʾ Cowl 10^6: if the interest is added to the capital, it shall bear interest like the capital - a) + *b*$_2$, *brb*ʿ*h yrby* LidzbAss 5$^{3f.}$ (= AECT 50): and it will bear interest equivalent to a quarter of it (i.e. it will bear 25% interest (cf. also Lipiński Stud 103f.); cf. LidzbAss 6$^{3f.}$ (= AECT 51); cf. also ATNS 35^2 (for the reading, cf. Porten & Yardeni sub TADAE B 4.7) - b) + *b*$_2$ + ʿ*l*$_7$, *bmrbyth yrbh* ʿ*ly ksp ḥlrn 2 ltql 1 lyrḥ 1* Cowl 10$^{4f.}$: it shall increase at my expense with its interest namely a sum of two *ḥallur* silver per *shekel* per month (i.e. it shall bear a monthly interest of 5%, v. *ḥlr*; for the division of clauses, cf. Grelot DAE p. 82 :: Cowl a.l., Porten & Greenfield JEAS p. 111, Porten & Yardeni sub TADAE B 3.1: *bmrbyth* part of prec. clause), cf. Cowl 11$^{2f.}$ - c) + ʿ*l*$_7$, *wyhwh rbh* ʿ*ly* Cowl 11^9: it will increase at my expense (i.e. I will have to pay interest) - PA ʿEL - **1)** to make numerous; ʾ*yš z*ʿ*yr wyrbh mlwhy* Aḥiq 114: if an unimportant man becomes loquacious ... (or: if an unimportant man becomes great, his words ...; v. supra); *hmrb[h] hrby[h]* DJD ii 30^{19}: (said of trees) which increase (their) yield; *wpgr*ʾ ʾ*rb*ʾ*n* ʿ*l pgr* KAI 222B 30: I will multiply (i.e. pile) corpse upon corpse - **2)** to bring up; *[br* ʾ*ḥ]ty zy* ʾ*nh rbyt* Aḥiq 25: my sister's son whom I brought up (cf. Ber v 131) - **3)** to make to increase; *nrby lg 1 bm 1 p* Cowl 81^{70}: we will lend 1 *log* at an interest of 1 obol (v. *m*ʿ*h*) and a half (for this interpret., cf. Cowl a.l., cf. also Harmatta ActAntHung vii 365, 367, cf. however Grelot DAE p. 113 (n. f): pro *nrby* l. *ndby* (= n.p.)) - HIPH Inf. abs. (*hrbh*) used adverbially, *[m]ymynk hrbh m*ʾ*d* AMB 1^1: on your right there are very many - Lipiński Stud 118, 121: l. *[y]rb[wn]* = QAL Impf. 3 p.pl.m. of *rby*$_1$ in TH 1 vs. 6f. (cf. Fales sub AECT 53; uncert. reading, cf. also Friedrich TH a.l.: l. *db[* in l. 7 (cf. also Degen NESE i 50: l. *]b[* in l. 7)) - Friedrich TH a.l.: l. twice *yrbn* in TH 4 recto 3 (= AECT 56), one instance = QAL Impf. 3 p.pl.m. of *rby*$_1$, cf. however Lipiński Stud 135,

138: the second word in this line = *yrbn* = n.p. (cf. also Degen NESE i 55f.), Lipiński ibid.: the first word of this line = *ʾdrn* (= n.p.) - Porten & Yardeni sub TADAE A 4.5: l. poss. *rbyn* (= QAL Pf. 1 p.pl. (= to grow, to increase)) in Cowl 27[1] (highly uncert. reading and interpret., cf. also Grelot DAE p. 401f. (n. c): l. *zrbyn* = Plur. abs. of *zrb*$_2$ (= anguish, distress)).
v. *zky*$_2$.

rby$_2$ (or *rbh*?, cf. Leand 43g^{0}) - **OffAr** Sing. emph. *rbyʾ* Aḥiq 38, 41, 54, 56, 58, 59 (*[r]byʾ*) - ¶ subst. great one, officer: Aḥiq 38, 41, 54, 56, 58, 59 - Kaufman AIA 87: < Akkad. (?).
v. *rb*$_2$, *rbyt*.

rby$_3$ **OffAr** Sing. + suff. 3 p.s.m. *rbyh* KAI 236A vs. 5 (= AECT 49), TH 4 vs. 3 (= AECT 56; for the reading, cf. Lipiński Stud 135 :: Garr DGSP 107: = Plur. m. + suff. 3 p.s.m. of *rb*$_2$; dam. context; cf. also Degen NESE i 55) - ¶ subst. interest: KAI 236A vs. 5, TH 4 vs. 3; this word (Sing. emph. *rbyʾ*) poss. also in ATNS 36[1] (diff. and dam. context) - *rbwʾn* in Sem xxxvi 89[2,4] prob. meaning interest, poss. = Plur. f. abs. belonging to this noun (cf. also Gawlikowski Sem xxxvi 92).

rby$_4$ cf. Frah xi 19 (*lpydʾ*, *lpyʾ*) = boy, adolescent; Frah xi 20 (*lpytʾ*) f. = girl; cf. Frah xiii 8 (*lp(m)h* = lapsus for *rbh* (= boy), cf. Nyberg FP 82 (:: Ebeling Frah a.l.: l. *rpyh*)).

rbyh **Hebr** Sing. abs. *rbyh* DJD ii 30[19] - ¶ subst. produce, yield.

rbyʿ **OffAr** word of uncert. meaning in ATNS 186[1]; poss. = subst. (s.m. abs.) fourth (part), square (diff. and dam. context).
v. *rbʿ*$_3$.

rbyʿy v. *rbʿy*.

rbyt **Hatra** Sing. cstr. *rbyt* 384; emph. *rbytʾ* 16[1] (for this reading, cf. Milik RN vi/iv 53, Teixidor Sumer xxi 88*, Degen WO v 235, Vattioni IH a.l. :: Safar Sumer vii 179 (n. 29): l. *rbwtʾ* = Sing. emph. of *rbw*$_1$ (= magnificence), used as indication of rank or occupation (cf. also Caquot Syr xxix 98, Altheim & Stiehl AAW ii 196, Donner sub KAI 241)), 60[2] (*[r]bytʾ*, for this reading, cf. Aggoula Ber xviii 95, MUSJ xlvii 60f. (n. 3), Vattioni IH A.l. :: Safar Sumer xi 5, Caquot Syr xxxii 263, Donner sub KAI 252: l. *bytʾ* = Sing. emph. of *byt*$_2$), 94, 109, 116[2], 144[2,4], 195[2], 218[1], 221[1], 223[2,4,5], 224[3,5], 251, 278[2,3], 336[3], 345[7], 362[1,4], 364[2,4] (cf. also Assur 15a 4; cf. also Assur 15a 3: *rbtʾ*), *rbyʾ* 224[2] (lapsus, cf. Safar Sumer xxi 39, Degen WO v 229; rather than Sing. emph. of *rby*$_2$) - ¶ subst. (< *rb*$_2$ + *byt*$_2$) majordomus, passim; *rbytʾ dy brmryn* Hatra 109: the majordomus of Barmarayn (cf. Hatra 223[4], 224[5]); *rbytʾ dmrʾn* Hatra 195[2]: the majordomus of our lord (cf. also Hatra 345[7], 362[4]); *rbytʾ dmrtn* Hatra 364[4]: the majordomus of our lady; *rbyt ʾlt* Hatra 384: the majordomus of AlLat.; *rbytʾ dy ʿrb* Hatra

223^2: the majordomus of Arabia (or: of the Arabs; for the meaning of *ʿrb*, v. *mlkʾ d(y) ʿrb* sub *mlk*$_3$; cf. also Hatra 364^2); *rbytʾ bḥṭryʾ* Hatra 336^3: the majordomus among the Hatreans (or: in Hatrean territory?) - Vattioni IH a.l.: l. *rbyt* in Hatra 41^1 (cf. Milik DFD 372: l. *rbyt[ʾ]*; heavily dam. context), cf. however Safar Sumer viii 195, Caquot Syr xxx 244: l. *dbyt* = *d*$_3$ + form of *byt*$_2$ - Milik DFD 387: l. perhaps *rbytʾ* in Hatra 202$^{21:1}$ (improb. reading, cf. Teixidor Sumer xxi 88*: l. *rb.* (= part of n.p.; for this reading, cf. also Vattioni IH a.l.: = form of *rb*$_2$)).

rbk$_1$ v. *rkb*$_1$.

rbk$_2$ v. *rb*$_2$.

rbmg (< Akkad., cf. Zimmern Fremdw 6; cf. also Lipiński ZAH i 72) - **OffAr** Sing. emph. *rbmgʾ* KAI 265 (for the poss. reading, cf. (Gregoire with) Benveniste REJ lxxxii 57 × Lidzbarski Eph iii 67: l. *rb* (= Sing. cstr. of *rb*$_2$) *ḥ[ylʾ]* (= Sing. emph. of *ḥyl*$_2$), cf. also Donner KAI a.l., Lipiński Stud 174ff. :: Gregoire CRAI '08, 439, 443, 444 (n. 1): l. *rb* (= Sing. cstr. of *rb*$_2$) *ḥgʾ* (= Sing. emph. of *ḥg* (= master of a guild/company)) - ¶ subst. high (military) official (cf. Greek par. στρατηγ[ὸ]ς).

rbn **OffAr** Sing. + suff. 1 p.s. *rbʾny* AM-NS ii 171 i 1, ii 1 (for this interpret., cf. Altheim & Stiehl Suppl 91f., ASA 54, 276, Shaked BSOAS xxvii 287 n. 75); Plur. cstr. *rbny* Cowl 3^{11} - **Palm** Plur. cstr. *rbny* RTP 37, 38 - **Waw** Sing. abs. *rbwn* AMB 6^{12} - ¶ subst. - **1)** master, chief - a) indicating deity: AMB 6^{12} - b) indicating the chief of a group of people; *rbny ʿwntʾ dy bl* RTP 37: the chief of the *ʿwnh* (v. s.v.) of Bel (cf. RTP 38) - **2)** officer, authority: Cowl 3^{11} - > Akkad. *rab-bānē*, cf. Zadok RA lxxvii 189f.

v. *dkw*, *r*$_1$, *rbb*$_2$, *rbnšqw*.

rbnw **Palm** Sing. cstr. *rbnwt* CIS ii 3919^4, 3928^4, 3970, InscrP 31^1, Inv xii 44^1, RIP 127^1, Syr vii 129^2, DFD 271^1 (= Syr xlviii 413); + suff. 3 p.s.m. *rbnwth* AAS xxxvi/xxxvii 169 no. 10^5, Syr lxii 257 - ¶ subst. presidency, curatorship, leadership; *brbnwt mrzḥwth* CIS ii 3919^4: during his presidency of the confraternity (cf. CIS ii 3970, InscrP 31^1, DFD 271^1, Syr vii 129^2); *brbnwt šyrt[ʾ] dy [zbdʿ]tw* CIS ii 3928$^{4f.}$: during Z.'s leadership of the caravan; *brbnwt ʿynʾ* Inv xii 44^1: during the curatorship of the source (cf. RIP 127^1).

rbnšqw (prob. < combination of *rbn* + *šq*$_1$ + ending *-ū(t)*) - **Palm** Sing. + suff. 3 p.s.m. *rbnšqwth* Inv x 115^2 - ¶ subst. office of a market-overseer.

rbʿ$_1$ **Palm** the diff. *mrbʿʾ* in Syr xiv 188^3 prob. = PAʿEL (/APH) Inf. of *rbʿ*$_1$ (meaning uncert.); Milik DFD 33: = to clear (goods) by paying a 25% tax.

rbʿ$_2$ v. *rbʿ*$_3$.

rbʿ$_3$ **Ph** Sing. abs. *rbʿ* Mus li 286^4 - **Pun** Sing. abs. *rbʿ* KAI 69^{9,11}

- **Hebr** Sing. abs. *rbyʿ* on coins of the first revolt, cf. Meshorer JC no. 162; cstr. *rbʿ* Dir pes. 10a, b, on coins of the first revolt, cf. Meshorer JC no. 150, 160 - **OldAr** Plur. cstr. *rbʿy* KAI 216^4, 217^2 - **OffAr** Sing. abs. *rbʿ* RES 1794^{12,13}; cstr. *rbʿ* CIS ii 11; + suff. 3 p.s.m. *rbʿh* LidzbAss 5^3 (= AECT 50), 6^3 (= AECT 51); Plur. abs. *rbʿn* RES 1794^{3,14} - **Nab** Sing. abs. *rbʿ*, *rbwʿ* on coins, cf. Meshorer NC no. 81, 82 - **Palm** Sing. abs. *rbʿ* RTP 194, 570, 571 (*[r]bʿ*); emph. *rbʿʾ* Inv x 29^2, 113^2; Dual abs. *rbʿyn* RTP 709 (uncert. interpret., cf. (Caquot with) du Mesnil du Buisson TMP 484f. n. 2, 492 :: du Mesnil du Buisson TMP 485: or = QAL Part. act. pl.m. abs. of *rbʿ*$_2$ (= to lie down) :: Milik DFD 190: l. *dbʿyn* = d_3 + QAL Part. act. pl.m. abs. of *bʿy*$_1$ :: Starcky & Caquot RTP a.l. and p. 149: l. *rbʿy[ʾ]* = Plur. emph. of *rbʿ*$_3$) - ¶ subst. m. - **1)** quarter: Mus li 286^4, LidzbAss 5^3 (= AECT 50), 6^3 (= AECT 51), RTP 194, 570, 571, 709 (v. supra; v. also infra); *rbʿ nṣp* Dir pes. 10a: a quarter of a *nṣp* (v. s.v.); *rbʿ hšql* on coins of the first revolt: a quarter of a *shekel* (cf. Meshorer JC no. 150, 160); for *rbʿ šl* Dir pes. 10b, v. *šql*$_3$; *rbyʿ* on coin of the first revolt, a quarter (of a *shekel*; cf. Meshorer JC no. 81, 82); *š 2 m 1 rbʿ 1* RES 1794^{12}: two *shekel* and 1 1/4 *m.* (v. *mʿh*$_1$), cf. RES 1794^{3,14,23}; *rbʿ* on Nab. coins: a quarter of a *shekel* (for the coins with Hebr. and Nab. inscription, cf. Meshorer Proc v CJS i 82f. (Hebr.)); *ksp rbʿ šlšt* KAI 69^{9,11}: three quarters of (a *shekel*) silver; cf. also - a) *rbʿy ʾrqʾ* KAI 216^4: the four quarters of the earth (cf. KAI 217^2) - b) *rbʿ ʾrq[ʾ]* CIS ii 11: a quarter of *mina* of the land (i.e. the official *mina*, cf. Akkad. par.: ... *ša šarri*) - c) *dy rbʿʾ* Inv x 29^2, 113^2: the one of the quarter, i.e. the tax-farmer collecting the 25% tax (cf. Seyrig Syr xxii 264ff. and Greek par.: τεταρτώνην and τεταρτώνῃ) - **2)** abbrev. *r* - a) in Elephantine texts - α) *šʾ 1 r 2* Cowl 24^7: barley, 1 ardab and 2 quarters (cf. Cowl 24^{16,28}, 81^{36}) - β) *ḥntn s 1 r 1* Cowl 81^2: wheat, 1 *seah* (v. *sʾh*$_1$) and 1 quarter (cf. Cowl 81$^{136f.}$) - γ) *ʾmn 4 r 2* Krael 7^7: four cubits and two quarters (cf. e.g. Grelot DAE p. 233, Porten Arch 305ff., Porten & Greenfield JEAS p. 53; cf. also Krael 7^9 × Krael p. 210, 317: *r* in ll. 7, 9 poss. = abbrev. for *rgl*$_2$ (= foot, i.e. 1/3 of a cubit)) - δ) *ksp šql 1 r 2* Cowl 15^{12}: silver 1 *shekel* and a quarter (cf. Cowl 15^{24}, Krael 7^{26}, cf. also *š 1 r 2* Cowl 81^{61}: 1 *shekel* and 2 quarters (cf. Cowl 81^{64,85}; cf. also Sem xxxvii 51$^{5,7\text{-}10,13\text{-}19}$ (text of unknown provenance)); cf. also *r 2* in Sem xxxvii 51^{21} (cf. ibid. l. 22)) - ε) *ksp r 2* Cowl 15^{13}: silver 2 quarters (of a *shekel*), cf. Cowl 81^{62,63,65,67}, etc., etc. - ζ) *ksp kršn ʿšrh b[ʾbn]y mlkʾ ksp r 2 lkrš 1* Cowl 20^{15}: 10 *karš* silver according to the official weight, silver of a purity of two quarter to one *karš*, sc. of a purity of 95% (cf. Cowl 25^{16}, 43^3, Krael 4$^{15,21f.}$; cf. also *ksp kršn 20 hw ʿšrn bʾbny mlkʾ ksp r 2 lʿšrtʾ* Cowl 6$^{14f.}$ (cf. Cowl 8^{14,21}, 9^{15}), *krš šqln 2 bʾbny mlkʾ ksp r 2 l 10* Cowl 15$^{6f.}$ (cf. Cowl 15^{14}, Krael 7^{32})), for this interpret., cf. Cowl p. xxxi and

the following formulae, ***ksp kršn 5 b'bny mlk' ksp ṣryp*** Cowl 5[7]: 5 ***karš*** silver according to the official weight, pure silver (cf. Cowl 28[10f.], Krael 5[15], etc.), ***ksp [šqln 3 +] 1 [b']bny ptḥ ksp š 1 l 10*** Cowl 11[2]: silver 4 ***shekel*** according to the weight of Ptah, silver of a purity of 1 ***shekel*** to 10 ***shekels***, i.e. of a purity of 90% (cf. also Yaron Lesh xxxi 287f., JSS xiii 202f., Grelot RB lxxxii 290 :: Lidzbarski Eph iii 76ff.: these texts refer to an agio of 5 (or 10) %, cf. also Porten Arch 66f., 305ff., Couroyer BiOr xxvii 250, RB lxxvii 465 n. 2, Fitzmyer FS Albright ii 153, WA 256 :: Wag 221ff.: referring to a type of tax (of 5 or 10%) on conveyance of money) - b) in other Off.Ar. texts from Egypt - α) BIFAO xxxviii 58[1,4,7,9] (prob. indication of *rb'*, perhaps a quarter of *m* (v. *m'h*$_1$) is meant :: Segal Maarav iv 72: in l. 4 pro *r 1* l. *kn* (= *kn*$_4$), in l. 7 pro *r* l. *k* = abbrev. of *krš*$_1$, id. ibid. 73: in l. 9 no sign *r*), cf. also the diff. *m 3 r 2 m* in BIFAO xxxviii 58[9] (v. *m'h*$_1$) - β) NESE iii 43[8]: *r 2 r 1* (Degen NESE iii 44, 47: = 3 quarters; uncert. interpret.) - c) in a text from Tell Arad: TA-Ar 41 obv. 8, 9 (cf. Aharoni TA a.l.: *r* indicating *rb'*$_3$, or some measurement of length) - d) in Palm. texts: RTP 506: *r 2* (poss. = two quarters, cf. Starcky RTP a.l. :: Milik DFD 186: *r* = symbol indicating *denarius*), RTP 758: *r m* (or *r 2*, v. *mkl*$_1$; Starcky RTP a.l.: = a quarter of a *m*, or two quarters, or l. *d m* or *d 2* = resp. honey, a measure, or: two (measures of honey) :: Milik DFD 186: l. *r* = symbol for roman *denarius*, cf. also id. ibid. 186f.: the *rb'* in RTP 570, 571 also indication of roman *denarius*) - e) in texts from Palestine - α) BSh 37[2] (*mr* = 1/4 *m'h*?, v. also *m'h*$_1$) - β) Syr iv 245[1,9], 246[2,5] (for the reading, cf. Milik DJD ii p. 90, Naveh TeAv vi 188 :: Dussaud Syr iv a.l.: = symbol for number 10) - γ) DJD ii 9[1-5], 10[1-4,6] (in DJD ii poss. submultiple of *k* = *krš*?, v. also *krš*$_1$; in both texts *m* occurring as submultiple of *r*, v. also *m'h*$_1$); or in these texts *r* = abbrev. of *rb't* (v. *rb'y*) - δ) Mas 597-602, *r* prob. indicating *denarius* - ε) IEJ xxxviii 164A 9, 10, B i 1, 4-6, ii 1-4 - *r* as abbrev. of *rb'*$_3$ prob. also in ATNS 106[4] - the same word (Sing. cstr. with prosth. *alef*) prob. also in Sem xxxvi 89[1] (*'rbw'*; cf. also Gawlikowski Sem xxxvi 92 :: idem Sem xxxvi 89, 92: = f. abs. of *'rb'*).
v. *zz*, *rb'*$_5$, *rb'h*$_1$.

rb'$_4$ **OffAr** Sing. abs. *rb'* KAI 226[5] - ¶ subst. (member of) fourth generation; *bny rb'* KAI 226[5]: members of the fourth generation (cf. e.g. Röllig ZA lvi 240 n. 58, Greenfield ZAW lxxvii 91 n. 11, FS Fitzmyer 49, Tawil Or xliii 63ff.)

rb'$_5$ **JAr** Plur. abs. *rb'yn* MPAT 40[10,23] (v. however infra) - ¶ subst. Plur. fourfold; *mšlm lrb'yn* MPAT 40[10]: paid fourfold (cf. MPAT 40[23]), cf. however Koffmahn DWJ 153f.: *rb'yn* = Plur. abs. of *rb'*$_3$, *mšlm lrb'yn* = paid in four instalments and Beyer ATTM 308, 588: pro *rb'yn* l. *ṭb'yn* = Plur. abs. of *ṭb'*$_2$ (= coin).

rb῾$_6$ v. *rb῾y*.

rb῾h$_1$ **Samal** Plur. cstr. *rb῾t* KAI 215[14] (cf. e.g. Dion p. 132, cf. however Donner KAI a.l.: = Plur. cstr. of *rb῾*$_3$) - ¶ subst. quarter; *rb῾t ᾽rq* KAI 215[14]: the four quarters of the earth.
v. *rb῾y*.

rb῾h$_2$ **Nab** Sing. emph. *rb῾t᾽* CIS ii 160[1], RES 482[1], 2092[1] (*[r]b῾t᾽*), ClRh ix 142[3], BASOR cclxix 48[1] - ¶ subst. f. prob. meaning: cella, rectangular sanctuary, cf. also Jones, Hammond, Johnson & Fiema BASOR cclxix 49: poss. = (quadrangular) shrine :: Levinson NAI 215: = slab on which corpse is placed :: Levi Della Vida ClRh ix 144: = rectangular object > inscribed tablet - cf. *᾽rb῾n* - the same word as *rbw῾h*? - for this word, cf. also Meitlis Tarbiz liii 465f., Urman Tarbiz liii 531ff.

rb῾w **Palm** Sing. cstr. *rb῾wt* CIS ii 4206[4] - ¶ subst. prob. meaning quarter (diff. context).

rb῾y **Hebr** Sing. m. abs. *rby῾y* SM 106[1]; f. abs. *rb῾t* TeAv v 85 (= Lach xxix 1), Mosc pes. 1 (v. however infra; Delavault & Lemaire RSF vii 32f., Bron & Lemaire CISFP i 767f.: = Ph.); cstr. *rb῾t* Dir pes. 23 - ¶ ordinal number, fourth; *mšmr hrby῾y* SM 106[1]: the fourth division of duty (v. *mšmr*); *brb῾t* TeAv v 85 (= Lach xxix 1): in the fourth (sc. regnal year, cf. Ussishkin TeAv a.l., cf. also Lemaire Or lii 445) - f. substantivated: quarter; *šql plg rb῾t* Mosc pes. 1: a *shekel*, the half of a quarter (cf. e.g. Dir a.l.; or rather read *plg rb῾t šql*??; cf. however Scott BASOR clxxiii 55: l. *plg rb῾* (= Sing. m. abs. of *rb῾y*) = a fourth part or l. *plg* (= Sing. abs. of *plgh*$_2$) *rb῾t* = a fourth part?; cf. also Delavault & Lemaire RSF vii 32f.); *hn wḥṣy hlg wrb῾t hlg* Dir pes. 23: a *hin* and three quarters of a *log* (Garbini Ant xxxii 428, JSS xii 112: *rb῾t* in Mosc pes. 1, Dir pes. 23 = Sing. cstr. of *rb῾h*$_1$) - a form of this word (*rb῾y*) poss. also in BiAr xlii 170[3] (diff. and dam. context).
v. *᾽rb῾y*, *rb῾*$_3$.

rbnšqw (prob. < combination of *rbn* + *šq*$_1$ + ending -*ū(t)*) - **Palm** Sing. + suff. 3 p.s.m. *rbnšqwth* Inv x 115[2] - ¶ subst. office of a market-overseer.

rbṣ **OffAr** QAL Part. act. s.m. abs. *rbṣ* FX 136[16] (reading uncert., cf. Dupont-Sommer FX 150) - ¶ verb QAL to sprinkle; meaning in the context of FX 136[16] uncert., Dupont-Sommer FX 137, 150: > to sacrifice? (for the context, cf. also Garbini SMEA xviii 271f., Contini OA xx 232).

rbrb **OldAr** Plur. m. abs. *rbrbn* KAI 216[10,13f.]; m. cstr. *rbrby* KAI 223A 7 (context however heavily dam.) - **OffAr** Plur. m. abs. *rbrbn* Cowl 31[9]; m. emph., cf. Warka 11: *ra-ab-ra-bi-e*; cf. Syn 315 ii - **Palm** Plur. f. abs. *rbrbn* Inv x 44[6], DFD 13[4] - **JAr** Plur. abs. *rbrn* (lapsus for *rbrbn*) AMB 4[2] (for this uncert. reading and interpret., cf. Naveh

& Shaked AMB a.l.); emph. *rbrby[h]* MPAT-A 32[1] (for the reading, cf. Naveh sub SM 39, Beyer ATTM 386 :: e.g. Frey sub 885, Fitzmyer & Harrington MPAT a.l.: l. *dbrby* = d_3 + Sing. abs. of *brby* (= variant of *byrby*), cf. also Hüttenmeister ASI 183f.) - ¶ adj. - **1)** big, large; *tr‘n rbrbn 5* Cowl 31[9]: five great gates; *npqn rbrbn* Inv x 44[6]: great costs - **2)** great, important, mighty; *mlkn rbrbn* KAI 216[10]: mighty kings (cf. KAI 216[13f.]) - **3)** substantivated adj., the great one, adult; *qu-da-am ra-ab-ra-bi-e u-ma-ʾ [k]i-da-di-e* (v. *kdd$_2$*) Warka 11: before the adults and the children.

rbšqh (< Akkad., cf. e.g. Kaufman AIA 140 n. 11, Fales AECT p. 56) - **OffAr** Plur. abs. *rbšqn* Del 30[2] (for the reading, cf. Fales sub AECT 16, on the form, cf. also Fales ibid. p. 67f. :: Del a.l.: l. *bbšqn* = n.p.) - ¶ subst. chief-cupbearer; *mt rbšqn* Del 30[2]: the province of the chief-cupbearers (cf. also Fales AECT p. 174f.).

rbt$_1$ v. *rbyt*.

rbt$_2$ v. *sbb$_2$*.

rbtn **JAr** Beyer ATTM 372: l. *rbtnn* (= Plur. f. abs. of *rbtn* (= mighty)) in AMB 7[8] (uncert. reading, highly uncert. interpret., diff. context).

rbtkh **OffAr** word of unknown meaning in Cowl 75[1,7]; CIS i 150: = Sing. f. + suff. 2 p.s.m. of *rb$_2$*, your lady (improb. interpret.).

rgg **OffAr** PA‘EL Impf. 2 p.s.m. *trgg* Aḥiq 136 - ¶ verb PA‘EL to desire, to covet; *wʾl trgg lkbyr zy ymn‘ mnk* Aḥiq 136: do not covet a great thing which is withheld from you - Otzen ZAW c Suppl 241ff.: the *rgm* in graffiti from Hama = *rg* + *m* (= abbrev.?), *rg* = QAL Part. pass. s.m. abs. of *rgg*? (= acceptable?, accepted?); highly uncert. interpret.
v. *hrg$_1$*.

rgz$_1$ **Ph** QAL Inf. abs. *rgz* KAI 13[7]; cstr. *rgz* KAI 9A 5, MUSJ xlv 262[2]; YIPH Impf. 2 p.s.m. + suff. 1 p.s. *trgzn* KAI 13[4,6,7] - **Pun** YIPH Impf. 3 p.s.m. *yrgz* CIS i 4945[4f.] - **OffAr** QAL Part. act. s.m. abs., cf. Warka 19, 23: *ra-gi-zu*; ITP Part. s.m. abs., cf. Warka 19, 23: *mi-it-ra-ag-ga-zu* - ¶ verb QAL - **1)** to be troubled; *lrgz ‘ṣmy* KAI 9A 5: in order that my bones are troubled (cf. MUSJ xlv 262[2]) - **2)** to be furious: Warka 19, 23 - YIPH to trouble, to disturb, to remove; *wrgz trgzn* KAI 13[7]: and you will in fact disturb me (i.e. my mortal remains), cf. KAI 13[4,6]; *wʾš yrgz hmtnt z* CIS i 4945[4f.]: and who will remove this gift - ITP to become furious: Warka 19, 23.
v. *rgz$_2$*.

rgz$_2$ **Samal** Sing. abs. *rgz* KAI 214[23] (cf. however Dion p. 273, 488 n. 7 = QAL Inf. cstr. of *rgz$_1$*),[26] (for this interpret., cf. e.g. also Dion p. 131) - **OffAr** Plur. emph., cf. Warka 20: *ru-ga-zi[-e]*, 24: *ru-ga-zi-e*; + suff. 3 p.s.m., cf. Warka 30: *ru-ga-za-a-ʾi[-i]* - **Palm** Sing. emph. *rgzʾ* RIP 142[2] - ¶ subst. Sing./Plur. anger; *š‘tʾ drgzʾ* RIP 142[2]: the hour (i.e. the time) of the anger (i.e. of the punishment), cf. Gawlikowski

RIP a.l., TP 95, Aggoula Syr liv 284 :: Michałowski FP v p. 114, Milik DFD 294: = the hour of the earthquake.

rgl$_1$ **Pun** PI‹EL (?) Part. s.m. abs. *mrgl* CIS i 5933[4f.] (or l. *mdgl*?) - ¶ verb PI‹EL (?) Part. meaning unknown, indicating dependent function, Février CIS i a.l.: = servant at the feet of ... (improb. interpret.).

rgl$_2$ **Hebr** Sing. + suff. 2 p.pl.m. *rglkm* DJD ii 43[6] - **Samal** Dual cstr. *lgry* KAI 215[16] (on this form, cf. e.g. Cooke NSI p. 179, Friedr 42*, Koskinen ZDMG cxiv 56, Dion p. 117, Segert AAG p. 109, Garbini AION xxvi 127, Swiggers Or li 253 (n. 42)) - **OffAr** Sing. abs. *rgl* ATNS 28b 4; + suff. 2 p.s.m. *rglk* Aḥiq 123; + suff. 1 p.s. *rgly* Aḥiq 206 (or = Dual + suff. 1 p.s.?); + suff. 3 p.pl.m. *rglhm* Aḥiq 122 (:: Nöldeke AGWG xiv/4, 15: or = Dual + suff. 3 p.pl.m.); Dual + suff. 3 p.s.m. *rglwhy* Cowl 30[16], 31[15], Aḥiq 80 (*rglw[hy]*); Plur. abs. *rgln* ATNS 28b 4; emph. *rgly›* Beh 1 (Akkad. par. *girri*; :: Ungnad ArPap p. 84, Lemaire Or lv 349: l. *dgly›* = Plur. emph. of *dgl*); cf. Frah x 41 (*lglh*), Paik 663 (*ngryn*), 664 (*lglh*), MP 5 (*ngryn*), GIPP 27, 59, SaSt 22, cf. Toll ZDMG-Suppl viii 29, 32 - **Palm** Sing. + suff. 3 p.s.f. *rglh* CIS ii 4058[6] (dam. context) - ¶ subst. f. - **1)** foot: Aḥiq 80, 122, 123, 206, Cowl 30[16], 31[15], CIS ii 4058[6]; *kp rgl* ATNS 28b 4: the sole of the foot; cf. *š›ny ntn t kblym brglkm* DJD ii 43[5f.]: that I will put fetters on your foot (i.e. on your feet?) - l. poss. *rglyk* (= Dual + suff. 2 p.s.m.) in RES 1790[5], reading of *r* uncert., cf. also in the ll. 3 and 4 *[r]glyk* - **2)** leg: ATNS 28b 4 (cf. Segal ATNS a.l.; uncert. interpret.; or = time?) - **3)** time; *btrty rgly›* Beh 1: a second time (poss. interpret., cf. Cowl a.l., Greenfield & Porten BIDG p. 29, cf. also Lidzbarski Eph iii 258, Leand 60d).
v. *dgl*, *kp$_1$*, *rb‹$_3$*.

rgly **Palm** Sing. abs. *rgly* CIS ii 3913 ii 3 (*rgl[y]*), 6 (Greek par. σώμα[τος]), 81; Plur. abs. *rglyn* CIS ii 3913 ii 80 - ¶ subst. man, person; *whn zbwn› ypq ‹ly[m]yn ytn lkl rgly [d] 12* CIS ii 3913 ii 6: and if the buyer exports slaves he has to pay 12 *d.* for everyone (of them), cf. CIS ii 3913 ii 2f., 81; *wdy m‹l rglyn ltdmr* CIS ii 3913 ii 80: and who imports people (i.e. slaves) into Tadmor.

rgm **Hatra** the diff. *mrgym* in 281[12] prob. = Part. pass. s.m. abs. of this root (cf. Safar Sumer xxvii 5, Aggoula Syr lii 183 :: Degen AION xxvii 489, NESE iii 72: = APH Inf. abs.). Prob. meaning: accursed (cf. Safar Sumer xxvii 5 :: Aggoula Syr lii 182f., Sem xxvii 143, Degen AION xxvii 489, NESE iii 68, 72: meaning of the root *rgm* = to stone (cf. also Tubach ISS 274, 275 n. 114: = APH Part. s.m. abs. (= to stone))); cf. also *lrgym* (= QAL pass. Impf. 3 p.s.m.) in Hatra 343[9], cf. Aggoula Syr lxiv 92: = to be stoned, uncert. interpret. (v. also supra).
v. *›rgmyt*.

rg‹ **Hebr** Sing. abs. *rg‹* AMB 1[4] - ¶ subst. of uncert. interpret.; Naveh

& Shaked AMB a.l.: poss. = sudden calamity.

rgš **OffAr** QAL Impf. 3 p.s.m. *yrgš* Aḥiq 29 - ¶ verb QAL to be excited, to be furious (:: Cowl p. 221. Gressmann ATAT 454: = to be troubled).

rd_1 v. *bdd_1*.

rd_2 **Ph** the poss. *rd* inn RES 250[3] (for the reading, cf. Dunand & Duru sub DD 5 (cf. also Lidzbarski Eph i 281f.): = QAL Part. act. s.m. abs. of *rdy* (= to press), *rd* indicating poss. cellarer, cf. however Catastini RSF xiii 10: < root *rdy* = governor) word of unknown meaning (prob. indication of title or function; cf. also Chabot sub RES 250: l. *r[b]* = Sing. m. abs. of *rb_2*).

rd_3 **Ph** the diff. *rd* in KAI 27[27] poss. = QAL Inf. cstr. of *rdd* (= to trample down; cf. Röllig NESE ii 19, 26) :: de Moor JEOL xxvii 108 (n. 12): = Inf. cstr. of *yrd* :: Cross & Saley BASOR cxcvii 47 nn. 35, 39: l. *dr* = Sing. abs. of *dr_1* (= household, home circle, *ldr* = home; cf. Caquot FS Gaster 51, Lipiński RTAT 266, Garbini OA xx 286, Gibson SSI iii p. 83, 88: *ldr* = forever, cf. also Avishur PIB 248, 255f.: *ldr* = from my house) :: Baldacci BiOr xl 129: l. *ldr* poss. = *l_2* (= *l'_1*) + QAL Inf. abs. of *dwr_1* (= to dwell) :: du Mesnil du Buisson FS Dussaud 424f., 433, Albright BASOR lxxvi 10 (n. 38), Gaster Or xi 44, Röllig KAI a.l., v.d.Branden BiOr xxxiii 13 (div. otherwise): l. *ld* = QAL Imper. s.f. of *yld_1* :: Torczyner JNES vi 27, 29: pro *wlrd* l. *ḥld* = Sing. abs. of *$ḥld_2$* (= morning); on this problem, cf. also Garr DGSP 181.

rd' **OffAr** QAL Pf. 1 p.s. *rdyt* Cowl 16[4] - ¶ verb QAL to plough (dam. context).

rdd v. *rd_3*.

rdh_1 v. *mwddw*.

rdh_2 v. *mwddw*.

rdwt'lh' **Nab** unexplained combination of words in CIS ii 456, this reading proposed by Euting with Brünnow ProvAr i 210 uncert.; poss. = *rdwt* + *'lh'* (= Sing. emph. of *$'lh_1$*).

rdḥh v. *drḥt*.

rdy **OffAr** Segal ATNS a.l.: l. a derivative of this root, *rdn* (= Plur. abs. (= ploughman)) in ATNS 52b i 13 (heavily dam. context).
v. *yrd*, *mddh*, *rd_2*, *rd'*.

rds v. *r's*.

rdp **JAr** PA'EL Pf. 3 p.pl.m. *rdpw* AMB 15[15]; Part. pass. s.m. emph. *mrdph* MPAT 68[3f.] - ¶ verb PA'EL to pursue, persecute; *rdpw btrh* AMB 15[15]: they chased him; Part. pass. the persecuted one (cf. also Beyer ATTM 347, 692: the expelled one) - > Akkad. *radāpu*, cf. v.Soden Or xxxvii 265, xlvi 193, AHW s.v., cf. also v. Soden Or ibid., AHW s.v. *radpi(u)*, *ridpu* (= resp. quickly, persecution), both words < Ar.

rhṭ **OffAr** QAL Imper. s.f., cf. Warka 16: *ri-ḫu-ṭi-'*, 41: *ri-ḫu-ṭi-i* (for the forms in Warka, cf. Gordon AfO xii 111, cf. also Kaufman JAOS

civ 89); cf. Frah xx 5 (*lḥṭwn*) - ¶ verb QAL to hasten oneself, to run; *ḫa-gi-ir-ta-ʾ ri-ḫu-ti-i* Warka 41: you, limping one, run, cf. Warka 16.
v. *rhyṭ*.

rhyṭ **JAr** Plur. cstr. (?) *rhyṭy* Syn D A 10 (= SM 88; for this reading, cf. Obermann Ber vii 108, Naveh SM a.l.; × Obermann Ber vii 108: *rhyṭy* = Plur. abs. :: Obermann ibid.: or = Plur. emph. :: Torrey Syn 263, 265: l. *rhṭw* = QAL Pf. 3 p.pl.m. of *rhṭ*) - ¶ subst. beam, rafter? (cf. Obermann Ber vii a.l., Naveh sub SM 88 :: Obermann ibid.: or = column).

rhn **OffAr** QAL (?) Pf. 3 p.pl.m. *rhnw* CIS ii 43^2 (= Del 26 = AECT 13) - **Nab** QAL (?) Impf. 3 p.s.m. *yrhn* CIS ii 197^6, 198^5, 214^5, 217^6; ITP Impf. 3 p.s.m. *ytrhn* CIS ii 208^4 - ¶ verb QAL (?) to give as a pledge, to mortgage: CIS ii 197^6, 198^5, 214^5 - **1)** + obj.: CIS ii 217^6 - **2)** + l_5 + l_5 + b_2, *rhnw lʾsrḥm lšndlh bksp* ... CIS ii 43$^{2f.}$: they gave A. to S. as pledge for silver ... (for this interpret., cf. Del p. 45f.) - ITP to be given as a pledge: CIS ii 208^4 - for this root, cf. also Lipiński ActAntHung xxii 382f., WGAV 382f., Greenfield Mem Yalon 76ff. - Cantineau Nab ii 172, O'Connor JNES xlv 216f., 219: < Arab. (uncert. interpret., cf. also Levinson NAI 78).
v. *dhm*.

rw v. *rb*$_2$.

rwb$_1$ v. *rb*$_1$.

rwb$_2$ v. *rb*$_2$.

rwbh **OffAr** word of unknown meaning in Sach 76 i B 7, cf. also Koopmans 150.

rwz v. *rz*.

rwḥ$_1$ **Pun** YIPH Inf. cstr. + suff. 3 p.s.m. *yrḥy* CIS i 5510^6 (cf. Février BAr '46/49, 171, CIS i a.l., FR 187, cf. however Chabot BAr '41/42, 390, 393: = Plur. + suff. 3 p.s.m. of *yrḥ*$_2$) - **Palm** APH Impf. 3 p.s.m. *yrḥ* MUSJ xxxviii 106^{11}; Inf. *mrḥ* MUSJ xxxviii 106^9 - ¶ verb YIPH/APH - **1)** to widen, to enlarge: MUSJ xxxviii 106^{9,11} - **2)** to set at large, to relieve; + obj.: CIS i 5510^6 (v. however supra).

rwḥ$_2$ v. *rḥ*$_1$.

rwḥ$_3$ **OffAr** Sing. abs. *rwḥ* Aḥiq 168 (cf. Grelot RB lxviii 191, DAE p. 445 × e.g. Cowl a.l., Ginsberg ANET 430, Lindenberger APA 171, Kottsieper SAS 17, 231 = Sing. abs. of *rwḥ*$_4$ (= *rḥ*$_1$), cf. also Gressmann ATAT 461) - **Palm** Sing. emph. *rwḥʾ* CIS ii 4058^5 (cf. Milik DFD 181f. :: e.g. CIS ii a.l.: = Plur. emph. of *rwḥ*$_4$ (= *rḥ*$_1$)), 4100^5, RIP 119^8, MUSJ xxxviii 106^8 - ¶ subst. - **1)** tranquility, respite; *ywm rwḥ* Aḥiq 168: a calm day (v. however supra); *dy qrw lh bʿqʾ wʿnn brwḥʾ ln* RIP 119$^{7f.}$: because they invoked him in distress and he answered us by giving us respite - **2)** room, space: MUSJ xxxviii 106^8.
v. *rḥ*$_1$.

rwḥ$_4$ v. *rwḥ*$_3$, *rḥ*$_1$.
rwḥ$_5$ v. *rḥ*$_1$.
rwy$_1$ **DA** QAL Part. act. pl.m. cstr. *rwy* ii 4 (cf. Hoftijzer DA a.l. × Caquot & Lemaire Syr liv 202: = QAL Imper. s.f. (cf. also Rofé SB 68, BAT 366, Levine JAOS ci 201, Ringgren Mem Seeligmann 94, McCarter with Hackett BTDA 79) or = PA ʿEL Imper. s.f. :: Levine JAOS ci 201: or = QAL Pf. 3 p.s.m. :: Hackett BTDA 29, 56, 94, 134: = Sing. m. abs. of *rwy*$_3$ (= full)); PA ʿEL Impf. 3 p.s.m. *yrwy* ii 6 (cf. Hoftijzer DA a.l. :: e.g. Caquot & Lemaire Syr liv 203, Hackett BTDA 29, 58f., 98, McCarter with Hackett BTDA 79: = QAL Impf. 3 p.s.m. (cf. also Rofé SB 68, H.P. Müll ZAW xciv 219, 232 (n. 119), Levine JAOS ci 201) :: Garbini Hen i 182, 185: = QAL Pf. 3 p.s.m. or Part. act. s.m. abs.) - **OldAr** QAL Impf. 3 p.s.m. *yrwh* Tell F 20 (or l. *yrwy*?, cf. Wesselius BiOr xl 181, Kaufman JAOS civ 572, Gropp & Lewis BASOR cclix 53), *yrwy* Tell F 21 (in both instances Akkad. par. *u-šá-ba-a*) - **OffAr** ITP Impf. 3 p.s.f. *ttrwh* Aḥiq 189 (dam. context) - **JAr** APH Imper. s.m. *ʾrwy* Syr xlv 101^{8,14} (in both instances heavily dam. context) - ¶ verb QAL to saturate oneself: Tell F 20, 21; *rwy ddn* DA ii 4: those who saturate themselves with love (v. however supra) - PA ʿEL to saturate: DA ii 6 (dam. context) - APH to irrigate: Syr xlv 101^{8,14} - ITP to be saturated: Aḥiq 189 (dam. context), or: to get drunk?
v. *ryt*.
rwy$_2$ cf. Sogd B 270: to speak, to answer (= *rʿy*$_2$?), cf. Benveniste Sogd B p. 214, cf. *rny*.
rwy$_3$ v. *rwy*$_1$.
rwm$_1$ **Edom** HIPH Pf. 3 p.s.m. *hrm* TeAv xii 97^5 (dam. and diff. context, cf. also Israel RivBib xxxv 341) - **OldAr** APH Pf. 3 p.pl.m. *hrmw* KAI 202A 10; Impf. 2 p.s.m. *thrm* KAI 224^5 (cf. e.g. Dupont-Sommer BMB xiii 26, Donner KAI a.l., Fitzmyer AIS 97, 109, Degen AAG p. 20, 76, Gibson SSI ii p. 46, 53, Lemaire & Durand IAS 118, 144 :: Puech RB lxxxix 584: l. *thhm* (= lapsus))^{,6} - **OffAr** ITP Impf. 3 p.s.m. *ytrwm* Aḥiq 138 (for the reading, cf. Lindenberger APA 259 n. 421; for the form, cf. Leand 39a, h, Lindenberger APA 135, 259f. n. 422, Kottsieper SAS 152ff. :: Beyer ATTM 488: = lapsus for *ytrwmm*); cf. Nisa-b 587^4 (*hrymt*), GIPP 54 - **JAr** PA ʿEL Part. pass. s.m. emph. *mrwmh* AMB 7^{16} (cf. Naveh & Shaked AMB p. 71, 75, 277 :: Beyer ATTM 372f.: = lapsus for *mrwmmh* = POL Part. s.m. emph. :: Dupont-Sommer JKF i 204, 208f. (div. otherwise): l. *rwmh* = Sing. emph. of *rwm*$_2$ (= heighth; cf. however Dupont-Sommer JKF i 216 n. 21: or l. *mrwmh* = Sing. emph. of *mrwm* (= heighth) used as epithet of God); cf. also Scholem JGM 86) - ¶ verb HAPH - **1)** to elevate, to put up; *whrmw šr mn šr ḥzrk* KAI 202A 10: they put up a wall higher than

the wall of Ch. (cf. Greenfield Proc v CJS i 177f. (n. 15)) - **2)** used figuratively; *wlthrm nbšhm mny* KAI 224[5f.]: you may not make their souls higher than mine (for the exact meaning of this expression, cf. e.g. Gibson SSI ii p. 47, 53: you shall not alienate ..., Fitzmyer AIS 97, 109: you must not incite them ... (cf. also Donner KAI a.l., Sader EAS 134), Rosenthal BASOR clviii 29: you must not cause them to be disdainful of me, Rössler TUAT i 187: you must not take sides against me, Dupont-Sommer Sf p. 129, 149: you must not subtract them from me (cf. also Ben-Chayyim Lesh xxxv 247, Lemaire & Durand IAS 129, 144) :: Lipiński Stud 55: you must not give more weight to their throat than to me) - ITP to take pride in; *[zy] l› ytrwm bšm ›bwhy* Aḥiq 108: whoever takes no pride in his father's name - Garbini AION xxxv 263f.: the *›tr‹m‹›* in Karth x 132[2]: = ITP Pf. 3 p.pl. of *rwm$_1$* (= to be changed into higher beings; highly uncert. interpret.) :: Février Karth a.l.: l. *›p* (= *›p$_2$*) + *r‹m‹›* (= Sing. f. abs. of *rm$_2$*) - a form of this root (*mtrym* = ITP Part. s.m. abs.?) prob. in FuF xxxv 173[3] (diff. and uncert. context; cf. Altheim & Stiehl FuF xxxv 175, ASA 250, 276).
v. *mwddw*, *rmh$_1$*, *šty$_3$*.

rwm$_2$ v. *rwm$_1$*.

rwmn v. *rmn$_1$*.

rwndkn (< Iran., cf. Naveh WO vi 45 n. 21) - **OffAr** Sing. abs. *rwndkn* WO vi 44A 4, C 3, D 4 (*rwnd[kn]*; or (div. otherwise): l. *›rwnd[kn]*, v. *mlk$_3$* :: Dupont-Sommer Syr xxv 56 (dividing otherwise): l. in text A *nwn›* (= Sing. emph. of *nwn*) + *kn* (= *kn$_5$*)), REA-NS viii 170A 1, B 1 - ¶ adj. the one belonging to *rwnd*.

rwṣ **OldAr** QAL Pf. 1 p.s. *rṣt* KAI 216[8] - ¶ verb QAL to run; *wrṣt bglgl mr›y mlk ›šwr* KAI 216[8f.]: and I have run at the wheel of my lord the king of Assur (prob. said of the vassal-king riding a horse or a chariot alongside the chariot of his lord, cf. Landsberger Sam›al 68 n. 174).

rwq **OffAr** QAL Impf. 3 p.pl.m. *yrwqn* Aḥiq 133 (on the reading, cf. Lindenberger APA 256 n. 393 :: Cowl p. 242: = QAL Impf. 3 p.pl.m. of *rqq$_2$* or = lapsus for *yrqwn* (= idem of *rqq$_2$*), cf. Leand 39c: cf. also Lindenberger APA 129, 256 n. 392, 279, Kottsieper SAS 82) - ¶ verb QAL to spit; *wyrwqn b›npwhy* Aḥiq 133: they will spit him in the face.

rwš v. *r›š$_1$*.

rwšh **JAr** the diff. *mrwšt* in MPAT-A 2[3] poss. = *m$_{12}$* (= *mn$_5$*) + *rwšt*; Naveh sub SM 58: *rwšt* poss. = lapsus for *rwšth* = Sing. + suff. 3 p.s.m. of *rwšh* (= possessions; uncert. interpret.) :: Fitzmyer & Harrington MPAT a.l.: *mrwšt* = Sing. abs. of *mrwšt* (= basin?; cf. also Lietzmann ZNW xx 253) :: Avi-Yonah QDAP ii 155: l. *mryšt* = Sing. abs./cstr. = roof (cf. also Vincent & Carrière RB xxx 582ff., Hüttenmeister ASI 324) :: Klein SeYi 109: l. *mrwšh* = Sing. abs. (= basin) :: Frey sub 1197: l. *mryšt* (= Sing. abs.) = basin (cf. also Sukenik ASPG 75: l. *mry/wšt[h]*, poss. = Sing. emph. of *mryšh* (= basin)) :: Beyer ATTM 392, 689: l. *mryšt<h>* = Plur. emph. of *mryš/mr'š* (= beam) :: Krauss REJ lxxxix 398f. (div. otherwise): l. *nbršt* = Sing. abs. (= lamp, indication of *menorah*).

rwšm OffAr Sing. abs. *rwšm* Samar 2[2] - ¶ subst. (slave) mark.

rwt v. *ytr*$_1$.

rz (< Iran., cf. e.g. Telegdi JA ccxxvi 254f., Hinz AISN 203) - **JAr** Sing. abs. *rwz* AMB 3[3] (or = Hebr.?); emph. *rzh* MPAT-A 22[4] (= SM 70[12]) - ¶ subst. m. secret, mystery; for the context of MPAT 22[4], v. *qrt*$_1$; cf. *'rz*$_3$.

v. *nwr*$_3$.

rz' Palm Plur. abs. *rz'yn* CIS ii 3932[5] - ¶ subst. prob. meaning: expense; *wḥsk rz'yn šgy'n* CIS ii 3932[5]: he spent money in a most generous way (v. *ḥsk*), cf. Hoffmann with Lidzbarski Handb 368, Lidzbarski Eph i 239, Cooke NSI p. 280, Cantineau sub Inv iii 31.

rzḥ v. *mrzḥ*.

rzm$_1$ **Waw** APH Impf. 1 p.s. *'rzm* AMB 6[12] (for this interpret., cf. Gordon Or xviii 339, 341, Naveh & Shaked AMB p. 63, 68, 277 :: Dupont-Sommer Waw a.l. (div. otherwise): l. *'r* (= Sing. cstr. of *'r*$_1$) *mwbk* (= Sing. + suff. 2 p.s.m. of *mb'*)) - ¶ verb APH to swear, to invoke; *'rzm bk* AMB 6[12]: I invoke you.

rzm$_2$ v. *'zn*$_2$.

rzn Ph Sing. abs. *rzn* KAI 26A iii 12, C iv 13; Plur. abs. KAI 26A iii 12, C iv 13 - **Pun** Sing. cstr. *rzn* KAI 145[5] (:: Krahmalkov RSF iii 192: = Sing. abs.) - ¶ subst. m. prince; *mlk bmlkm wrzn brznm* KAI 26A iii 12: a king among kings and a prince among princes (on this type of formula, cf. Demsky EI xiv 8ff., cf. also R.Kutscher & Wilcke ZA lxviii 125f.; cf. also Pardee JNES xlvi 141f.); used as epithet for a deity in *rzn ymm* KAI 145[5]: the prince of the seas (cf. Berger MAI xxxvi/2, 157, 175, Cooke NSI p. 152, 154, Röllig KAI a.l.: or = prince of the days (for this interpret., cf. Février Sem vi 18, v.d.Branden RSF i 166, 168) :: Krahmalkov RSF iii 192, 201 (v. also supra): *rzn ymm* = ruler since ancient times; cf. also Fantar DM 101f.) - Jongeling SEL vi 127ff.: l. *rzn* in KAI 162[1] (uncert. interpret. :: v.d.Branden BO xiv 196f.: l. *bht* (= Sing. abs. of *byt*$_2$)).

rḥ$_1$ **Pun** Sing. abs. *rḥ* CIS i 6000bis 4 (v. infra); cstr. *rḥ* KAI 79[11], CIS i 4937[5]; Plur. cstr. *rḥt* CIS i 5510[2], KAI 89[4] (= CIS i 6068; cf. Février CIS i a.l. (poss. interpret.; cf. already Lidzbarski Eph i 33f., KI sub 85) :: Levi Della Vida RSO xiv 313, FR 146, Röllig KAI a.l., NESE ii 32 (div. otherwise): l. *'brḥt* = YIPH Pf. 1 p.s. of *brḥ*$_1$ (= to loose; cf. also Clermont-Ganneau RAO iv 95, Cooke NSI p. 136: = to pay) :: Zurro Bibl lxii 546f.: = YIPH Pf. 1 p.s. of *brḥ*$_2$ (= to sustain a loss (economically)) :: Ferron ZDMG cxvii 222 (div. otherwise): l. *'brḥt* =

flight) - **Hebr** Sing. abs. *rwḥ* AMB 4^{15}; Plur. abs. *rwḥwt* AMB 15^{25} - **OldAr** Sing. abs. *rwḥ* KAI 224^2 (cf. e.g. Dupont- Sommer BMB xiii 30f., Fitzmyer AIS 104, Or xxxviii 583, Donner KAI a.l., Grelot RB lxxv 284, Gibson SSI ii p. 52, Puech RB lxxxii 615 :: Degen AAG p. 27f.: poss. = Sing. cstr. of *rwḥ₃* (= relief; cf. already Nober VD xxxvii 173f.); cf. however also Garbini AION xix 13: or = Sing. abs. of *rwḥ₅* (with consonantal *w* (= variant of *rḥ*)) - **Nab** Sing. emph. *rwḥʾ* IEJ xxix 112^1 - **JAr** Sing. abs. *rwḥ* AMB 3^4 (or = Hebr.?), $12^{1,12}$ (dam. and diff. context),^{32} (heavily dam. context), $13^{7,11}$ (dam. context), 14^3 (uncert. reading); cstr. *rwḥ* AMB $1^{20,21}$; emph. *rwḥʾ* AMB 12^9 (dam. context), *rwḥh* AMB 7^6, 9^1, *rwḥ* AMB 7^{12} (prob. lapsus for *rwḥh,* cf. Naveh & Shaked AMB p. 70, cf. already Dupont-Sommer JKF i 208, 210, cf. also Beyer ATTM 372); + suff. 3 p.s.m. *rwḥyh* Frey 668^2; Plur. emph. *rwḥth* AMB 2^9 - ¶ subst. f. - **1)** wind, breath: KAI 224^2 (v. *bʿy₁*) - **2)** spirit (prob. > soul :: e.g. CIS i sub 3785, Krahmalkov RSF iv 154 (n. 4): > intent (cf. also Février sub CIS i 5510: = *consilium*); *wkl ʾš lsr t ʾbn z ... wšpṭ tnt pn bʿl brḥ ʾdm hʾ* KAI $79^{6ff.,10f.}$: everyone who removes this stone ... T. will judge the soul of this man (cf. CIS i $4937^{1ff.}$; cf. also *[br]ḥt hʾdmm hmt wbrḥt ʾzrtnm* CIS i 5510^2: the souls of these men and the souls of their *familia* (v. *ʾzrh₁*; dam. context)); the same poss. also in CIS i 6000bis 4?, *rḥ dl qdšm* CIS i 6000bis 4: a spirit concerned with holy things (??, cf. Ferron StudMagr i 73f., 78 :: Février BAr '51/52, 75: *rḥ* = Qal Pf. 3 p.s.m. of *rwḥ₂* (= to take delight)?, *dl* to be translated 'in' (cf. also idem CIS i a.l.); for the interpret. of *rḥ*, cf. already Lidzbarski Eph i 166f., Chabot sub RES 13); *tšry rwḥyh* Frey 668^2: may his soul rest - **3)** spirit, demon: IEJ xxix 112^1, AMB 2^9, 12^1, 13^7, etc.; *rwḥh byšth* AMB 7^6: the evil spirit (cf. AMB 3^4, 7^{12}; *rwḥ zkr wnqbh* AMB 4^{15}: the male and female spirit; *rwḥh dmtqrʾ ʾšth* ... AMB 9^1: the spirit which is called fever: *rwḥ grmyh* AMB $1^{20,21}$: the spirit of the bones, i.e. the spirit that causes sickness of the bones > the actual sickness (cf. Naveh & Shaked AMB a.l.); this meaning poss. also in *brḥt ṣlm* CIS i 6068 = by the demons of darkness (??, cf. already Lidzbarski sub KI 85 (cf. also idem Eph i 33), v. also *ṣlm₂*) - Ferron StudMagr i 74, 77f.: l. *rḥ[y]* in CIS i 6000bis 4 (= Sing. + suff. 3 p.s.m.), highly uncert. reading, cf. Février BAr '51/52, 75: l. *r[bm* (= Plur. m. abs. of *rb₂*) + *w]?*, cf. also Février CIS i a.l.: l. *r[...)* - Ferron StudMagr i 76ff.: l. *brḥ* (= *b₂* + Sing. abs. of *rḥ₁*) in CIS i 6000bis 8 (poss. reading, uncert. interpret.) :: Février BAr '51/52, 79, CIS i a.l.: l. *yrḥ* = n.p. (for the reading problems, cf. Lidzbarski Eph i 169).
v. *mdnḥ, mtrḥ, rwḥ₃*.

rḥ₂ v. *lqḥ*.

rḥb **Ph** Yiph Pf. 3 p.s.m. *yrḥb* KAI 26A i 4 (for this form, cf. FR 267b, also for litt.; interpret. as Inf. (abs.) less prob.) - ¶ verb Yiph to enlarge, to extend; *yrḥb ʾnk ʾrṣ ʿmq ʾdn lmmṣʾ šmš wʿd mbʾy* KAI 26A i 4f.: I extended the land of the plain of A. from the rising of the sun to its setting.

rḥbh **OldAr** Sing. abs. *rḥbh* KAI 222A 10 (v. infra) - ¶ subst. open land (cf. e.g. Donner KAI a.l., Gibson SSI ii p. 29, 36f. (cf. also Degen AAG p. 48, Lemaire & Durand IAS 120), cf. however Dupont-Sommer Sf p. 33, Fitzmyer AIS 36 (cf. also Rosenthal ANET 659, Zadok AION xliv 530f., Sader EAS 128 (n. 43): = n.g.))

rḥh v. *dḥy*.

rḥy **OffAr** cf. Frah ii 18 (*lḥyʾ*): mill - Dual abs. (*rḥyn*) in text in unknown West-Semitic dialect: Sem xxxviii 52[1] (or = fraud?, cf. however Bordreuil & Pardee Sem xxxviii 65ff.).

rḥym **OffAr** Sing. m. cstr. *rḥym* Aḥiq 115 (for the reading, cf. Lindenberger APA 247 n. 292); f. abs. *rḥymh* Aḥiq 92 (cf. however Lindenberger APA 102, Kottsieper SAS 231: = Qal Part. pass.f. s. abs. of *rḥm*$_1$; against this interpret., cf. Muraoka JSS xxxii 187) - **Palm** Sing. m. *rḥm* Syr xvii 280[4] (for this poss. interpret., cf. Milik DFD 310, 312 (cf. however Dunant sub SBS 48: = subst. or adj. or verbal form of root *rḥm*$_1$); heavily dam. context; cf. however also Gawlikowski Ber xxii 146 (div. otherwise): pro *rḥm md/r[* l. *wkmrʾ* (= *w* + Plur. emph./cstr. of *kmr*$_2$)), *rḥym* CIS ii 3932[7], InscrP 6[2], 32[2], Inv x 62[2], 102[4], Syr xiv 175[2]; Plur. m. cstr. *rḥymy* CIS ii 3930[3], 3931[3], *rḥymʾ* CIS ii 3914[3] - **Hatra** Sing. m. abs. *rḥym* 20[4], 25[3], 34[8], 35[8], 52[5], 80[5] (*rḥy[m]*), 107[8], 116[3], 272[2], 286[6] (*rḥy[m]*, for this reading, cf. Degen NESE iii 77, Vattioni IH a.l.), 311[3], 337[4], Mašr xv 513 ii 5 (diff. and dam. context; :: Aggoula Sem xxvii 128f.: = Qal Part. act. s.m. abs. of *rḥm*$_1$; v. infra), 408[5]; cstr. *rḥym* Hatra 362[3] - ¶ adj. (or = Qal Part. pass. of *rḥm*$_1$?, cf. e.g. Altheim & Stiehl AAW ii 202) - **A)** - **1)** with active meaning, loving, attached to; *rḥymʾ mdythwn* CIS ii 3914[3]: patriotic (v. *mdnh*; cf. CIS ii 3930[3], 3931[3], 3932[7], InscrP 32[2], Inv x 62[2], 102[4], Syr xiv 175[2f.], cf. poss. Syr xvii 280[4], cf. Milik DFD 310, 312, Lindenberger APA 247 n. 293); *rḥym mḥwzh* Inscr P 6[2]: patriotic; for the obscure, poss. comparable *rḥymʾ ʾdyʾ* Inv viii 180[2], v. *ʾdy*$_2$ - **2)** in the expression *rḥym lh* (and comparable ones) with active meaning (cf. e.g. Degen JEOL xxiii 418, cf. also e.g. Safar Sumer vii 183, xviii 34 (for Hatra 116), Krückmann AfO xvi 148 (for Hatra 25), As-Salihi Sumer xxxiv 71 (for Hatra 337), Milik DFD 353 (for Hatra 35)) or passive meaning (cf. e.g. Safar Sumer xxiv 27 (for Hatra 272), Vattioni IH a.l.); *mn drḥym lh* Hatra 52[5]: whoever loves him/whoever is beloved by him (cf. Hatra 20[4] (for the context, v. *kl*$_1$), 25[3], 34[8], 35[8], 80[5], 107[8], 116[3], 272[2], 337[4], 408[5]); cf. also *mn dy rḥym lmn dy lmrn* Hatra 311[3f.] (diff. context): poss. = whoever is beloved by the one belonging to our lord (cf. however Degen NESE iii 102: prob. loss of text between *rḥym* and *lmn*) - **B)** substantivated adj. - **1)** beloved one; *rḥym ʾlhn* Aḥiq 115: a favorite of the gods (cf. e.g. Lindenberger APA 247 n. 293 :: Lidzbarski Eph iii 255 (n. 2): loving the gods); *rḥym ʾlhʾ wʾnšʾ* Hatra 362^3: beloved by gods and men - **2)** something cherished; *tltʾ rḥymh lšmš* Aḥiq 92: three things are cherished by Shamash (for the context, cf. Lindenberger UF xiv 113) - Caquot Syr xl 13: l. poss. *r[ḥym]* (= Sing. abs.) in Hatra app. 4^{10}, less prob. interpret. (cf. Safar Sumer xvii 39 n. 101: no room for reading *r[ḥym lh]*), cf. also Milik DFD 395: l. poss. *ddh* (= d_3 (= *zy*) + d_3 + suff. 3 p.s.m.; poss. interpret.) :: Aggoula Sem xxvii 138, 143: pro *dd/r[* ... l. *ddkrh* (= d_3 + QAL Pf. 3 p.s.m. + suff. 3 p.s.m. or Part. act. s.m. + suff. 3 p.s.m. of *dkr*₁ (= *zkr*₁)) :: Starcky with Teixidor Syr xli 275 n. 2: l. d_3 + form of *verbum dicendi* - v.Soden Or xxxvii 265, xlvi 193, AHW s.v. *reʾmu*: > Akkad. *reʾmu* (highly uncert. interpret.).

rḥyq v. *rḥq*₃.

rḥl₁ v. *zḥl*.

rḥl₂ **DA** Plur. abs. *rḥln* i 11 - ¶ subst. ewe.

rḥm₁ **Pun** YIPH Pf./Impf. 3 p.s.m. + suff. 3 p.s.m. *yrḥmh* Punica xviii/iii 4^7 (for this interpret., cf. Février JA cclv 63; or l. rather (div. otherwise) *yrḥm* (= YIPH Pf./Impf. 3 p.s.m.) followed by article) - **OffAr** QAL Pf. 3 p.s.m. + suff. 3 p.s.m. *rḥmh* Aḥiq 11; + suff. 1 p.s. *rḥmy* Aḥiq 51; 2 p.s.m. *rḥmt* Krael 12^{23}; 2 p.s.f. *rḥmty* Cowl $8^{10,19}$, Krael 9^{21}; 2 p.pl.m. *rḥmtn* Cowl 25^9; Impf. 3 p.s.m. *yrḥm* Aḥiq 153; 2 p.s.m. + suff. 3 p.s.f. *trḥmnh* Sach 76 i A 7 (cf. Sach p. 234, Perles OLZ '11, 503, Leand 33a, Greenfield Or xxix 100, Grelot DAE p. 377 :: Lidzbarski Eph iii 256: l. *trḥʿnh* = QAL Impf. 2 p.s.m. + suff. 3 p.s.f. of *rḥʿ* (= *rḥṣ*₁)); Part. act. s.m. abs. *rḥm* AE '23, 40 no. $2^{3,8}$; cf. SbPAW '33, 135 - **Nab** QAL Part. act. s.m. abs. (or cstr.?) *rḥm* CIS ii 196^7, 197^5, 198^3, 199^9, etc., etc. - **Hatra** QAL Pf. 3 p.s.m. (or Part. act. s.m. abs.) *rḥm* 389^2, 405^6 - **JAr** QAL (or PAʿEL?) Impf. 2 p.pl.m. *trḥmwn* Mas 554^1; Imper. pl.m. *[r]ḥmw* Mas 554^4 - ¶ verb QAL - **1)** to love, to care for; + obj., *mn dy rḥm lh klh* Hatra $405^{6f.}$: everyone who loves him (cf. Hatra 389^2), cf. also Aggoula Syr lxii 284; cf. also the foll. expressions - a) *rḥm ʿmh* CIS ii 196^7 and on coins (cf. Meshorer NC no. 48, 49, 49a, 51-53, 65, 83, etc.): the one who loves his people (epithet of king Haretat iv of the Nabateans; in this combination the notion of protection is included) - b) *ʾp šgyʾ snḥʾryb mlkʾ rḥmny ʿl zy* ... Aḥiq 51: king S. was well pleased with me that ... - c) *ʾḥr rḥmh ʾsrḥʾdn* Aḥiq 11: then A. got a liking for him - **2)** to have compassion; *trḥmwn ʿly* Mas 554^1: have pity on me (v. however supra) - **3)** to like, to want; *lmn zy rḥmty tntnn* Cowl $8^{9f.}$: to whomsoever you like you may give it (cf. Cowl 8^{19}, 25^9, Krael 9^{21}, 12^{23}; for this and parallel expressions, Szubin & Porten BASOR cclii 36ff.; cf. also J.J.Rabinowitz Bibl xxxvi 76f., Law 19f., Yaron Bibl xli 386f., Muffs 24, 41 (n. 2), 133

n., Hurvitz VT xxxii 260f.); *bywm trḥmnh* Sach 76 i A 6f.: on the day that you want it - YIPH to bestow as a favour; + obj., *yrḥm hnm* Punica xviii/iii 4[7]: he may bestow kindness (upon him), cf. Février JA cclv 63 (v. also supra) - a form of this root prob. in KAI 222B 42, cf. Lemaire & Durand IAS 115, 140: l. *trḥm* (= PA ʿEL Impf. 2 p.s.m., to pity; cf. also Lipiński Stud 44f.), for the reading, cf. also Degen AAG p. 15 and with different division of words, Dupont-Sommer Sf p. 85: l. poss. *ntrḥm*, which eventually might be explained as ITP Impf. 1 p.pl. (= to pity; for this reading and word division, cf. also Fitzmyer AIS 18, Donner KAI a.l.) :: Silverman JAOS xciv 270: l. *ntrḥm* = form of root *nḥm*₁ - Segal ATNS a.l.: l. poss. a form of this root (*ʾrḥm*) in ATNS 33a 2 (context however heavily dam. and reading uncert.) - for this root, cf. also Schmuttermayr Bibl li 499ff., Sperling JANES xix 149ff.
v. *rḥym*, *rḥm*₄.

rḥm₂ v. *rḥmh*₂.

rḥm₃ **OffAr** Plur. abs. *rḥmn* Cowl 18², 25¹¹,¹⁴, 30², 31², 38², 43³ (cf. Ungnad sub ArPap 35, Porten JNES xlviii 176, Porten & Yardeni sub TADAE B 5.5 :: Cowl p. 146: l. rather *rḥmt* (= Sing. abs. of *rḥmt* (= gift)), cf. also Muffs 133 (nn. 3, 5), 202), Krael 4⁴,¹², 7⁴, 9⁵,¹²,¹⁷, 10⁹ - **Palm** Plur. emph. *rḥmʾ* CIS ii 3935⁴ (cf. Rosenthal Sprache 76 :: Cantineau Gramm 96: = Sing. emph. :: Lidzbarski Handb 368: = Sing. abs. of *rḥmh*₁ :: Dérenbourg JA vi/xiii 366, Nöldeke ZDMG xxiv 106: = Sing. emph. of *rḥm*₆ (= marble)) - **JAr** Plur. abs. *rḥmyn* AMB 7a 1, 7b 1 - ¶ subst. Plur. affection, love, mercy: AMB 7a 1, 7b 1; *nksyʾ* ... *brḥmn yhbt lkm* Cowl 18²: I have given you possessions in affection (cf. Cowl 25¹¹,¹⁴, 43³, Krael 4⁴,¹², 7⁴¹, 9⁵,¹²,¹⁶ᶠ·, 10⁹; here also the notion is included of giving without payment, unconditionally, cf. Krael p. 172, Yaron Bibl xli 255 n. 3; on this and parallel formulae, cf. Szubin & Porten BASOR cclii 35ff., cf. also Muffs 25f., 40ff., 128, 132 n. 2, 133 n., n. 5, 135, 185, Yaron RB lxxvii 410, Levine FS Morton Smith 42); *wlrḥmn yšymnk qdm drywhwš mlkʾ* Cowl 30²: and may he give you favour before king Darius (cf. Cowl 31², 38²ᶠ·; cf. Dion RB lxxxix 531f.); *ṣlm ṣ[lwqws] ʿqʾ* ... *dy ʾqym [lh b]wlʾ wdmws lyqrh mn rḥmʾ* CIS ii 3935¹,³ᶠ·: statue of S. O. ... which the Senate and the People have erected for him in his honour in appreciation - this word (Plur. abs.) prob. to be restored in KAI 200¹³ᶠ· (or l. 13), cf. e.g. Cross BASOR clxv 44 (n. 39), Amusin & Heltzer IEJ xiv 150, 154 n. 23, Naveh IEJ xiv 159, Röllig KAI a.l., Lemaire Sem xxi 75, Gibson SSI i p. 28, Pardee Maarav i 35, Suzuki AJBI viii 5, 20f. :: Yeivin BiOr xix 5f.: l. *bḥ[m]* (= *b*₂ + Sing. abs./cstr. of *ḥm*₂).
v. *rḥm*₄, *rḥmn*.

rḥm₄ **OldAr** Sing. abs. *rḥm* KAI 224⁸ (cf. e.g. Fitzmyer AIS 96, 111, Donner KAI a.l., Degen AAG p. 20, 69 n. 56, Gibson SSI ii p. 46,

Lemaire & Durand IAS 119, 129 :: e.g. Dupont-Sommer BMB xiii 32, Sf p. 128, 130, AH i/1, 5 (dividing otherwise): l. *rḥmh* = Sing. + suff. 3 p.s.m. of *rḥm₃* :: Garbini RSO xxxiv 46, Segert ArchOr xxxii 126 n. 11: l. *rḥmh* = Plur. + suff. 3 p.s.m. of *rḥm₃*) - **OffAr** Plur. + suff. 2 p.s.m. *rḥmyk* Cowl 30[24], 31[23] (cf. e.g. Cowl a.l., Grelot DAE 411 (n. b), Porten & Greenfield JEAS p. 92, 96 :: Wag 21, Joüon MUSJ xviii 77, Galling TGI 87: = Plur. + suff. 2 p.s.m. of *rḥm₃*), Aḥiq 176 (:: Kottsieper SAS 18, 231: or = Plur. + suff. 2 p.s.m. of *rḥm₃* - **Nab** Plur. cstr. *rḥmy* RES 53[1] - **Palm** Sing. + suff. 3 p.s.m. *rḥmh* CIS ii 3939[4], 3940[5], 3941[5] (*rḥm[h]*), 3943[5], 3973[8], AAS xxxvi/xxxvii 169 no. 10[5], etc.; Plur. + suff. 3 p.s.m. *rḥmwhy* CIS ii 3960[6], *rḥmwh* CIS ii 4061[7]; + suff. 3 p.pl.m. *rḥmyhn* PNO 87[3] - **Hatra** Sing. + suff. 3 p.s.m. *rḥmh* 13[3] (cf. e.g. Krückmann AfO xvi 146 n. 37, Milik Syr xliv 298, Aggoula Ber xviiii 88 (cf. also Donner sub KAI 240) :: Safar Sumer vii 178, Caquot Syr xxix 96: = QAL Part. pass. s.m. emph. of *rḥm₁*; the reading *rḥm*ʾ with Vattioni IH a.l. mistake), 381[2]; + suff. 3 p.s.f. *rḥmh* 36[6] (cf. Milik DFD 371f., Safar Sumer xxix 95*, Vattioni IH a.l. :: Safar Sumer viii 192, Caquot Syr xxx 241f., Maricq Syr xxxii 273, Donner sub KAI 250: = QAL Imper. s.m. + suff. 3 p.s.m. (Donner ibid.: + suff. 3 p.s.m./f.)) - **JAr** Plur. emph. *rḥmy*ʾ MPAT 89[3] - ¶ subst. (or = QAL Part. act. of *rḥm₁*?) friend, colleague: Cowl 30[24], 31[23] (for the context of Cowl 30, 31, v. *ṭbḥ₁*), Aḥiq 176, CIS ii 3939[4], 3941[5], 3960[6], 4061[7], Hatra 13[3], 36[6], 381[2]; cf. *rḥmh* CIS ii 3939[4]: his friend (Greek par. [τ]ὸν ἑαυτοῦ φίλον; cf. AAS xxxvi/xxxvii 169 no. 10[5] (Greek par. τὸν φίλον)); cf. the foll. combinations - **1)** *gyrh wrḥmh* CIS ii 3973[8]: his *cliens* and friend - **2)** *rḥmh wqywmh* CIS ii 3940[5]: his friend and protector (cf. Greek par. τὸν φίλον καὶ προστάτην, cf. also CIS ii 3943[5]); cf. also *bny qryt*ʾ *wrḥmyhn* PNO 78[1ff.]: the people of the village and their friends; *rḥmy gd*ʾ RES 53[1]: those who feel attached to the Gad.
v. *rḥmn*.

rḥm₅ **DA** Sing. abs. *rḥm* ii 13 - ¶ subst. womb (for the context of DA ii 13, v. *ʿl₅*).
v. *ptḥ₁*, *rḥmh₁*.

rḥm₆ v. *rḥm₃*.

rḥm₇ **DA** Plur. abs. *rḥmn* i 10 (for the reading problems, cf. v.d.Kooij DA p. 107f. :: Garbini Hen i 171, 177f., 185: l. *rḥ[p]n* = QAL Part. act. pl.m. abs. of *rḥp* (= to brood), cf. also Delcor SVT xxxii 56f.) - ¶ subst. vulture.

rḥm₈ v. *rḥym*.

rḥmh₁ **OffAr** Sing. abs. *rḥmh* Krael 6[14] (cf. Kutscher JAOS lxxiv 236 :: Krael p. 196: = Sing. emph. of *rḥm₅* (= womb > love)), *rḥmt* Cowl 9[7], Krael 12[26,31] (cf. Wesselius AION xl 267: = accusative form :: Leand 61i: = Sing. cstr. (cf. also Grelot VT xi 33: = Sing. cstr.

used adverbially)); + suff. 3 p.s.f. *[r]ḥmth* Aḥiq 91 - ¶ subst. love, affection; *[mn r]ḥmth* Aḥiq 91: out of love for her (for the context, v. *rkn*); *yhbt lk bty› ›lh brḥmh* Krael 6[14]: I have given you these houses in affection (here the notion is included of giving without payment, unconditionally, cf. e.g. Krael a.l., Porten Arch 226, Muffs 43f., 132 n. 2) - used adverbially, *l› šlyṭ ›nt lzbnh wlmntn rḥmt l›ḥrnn* Cowl 9[6f.]: you do not have the power to sell it or to give it unconditionally/as a present to others (cf. Krael 12[26,31]).
v. *rḥm*₃.

rḥmh₂ **Mo** Plur. abs. *rḥmt* KAI 181[17] - ¶ subst. female slave (cf. however Lemaire Syr lxiv 208: poss. = QAL Part. act. pl.f. abs. of *rḥm*₂ (= to be pregnant) = pregnant woman).

rḥmh₃ **Pun** Plur. (?) abs. *rḥmt* CIS i 340 - ¶ subst. marble, marble slab; *p‹l hrḥmt* CIS i 340: mason making marble slabs (poss. interpret., cf. CIS i a.l., Slouschz TPI p. 298).

rḥmwt v. *lqḥ*.

rḥmn **OldAr** Sing. m. abs. *rḥmn* Tell F 5 (Akkad. par. *rēmēnû*) - **OffAr** Sing. m. abs. *rḥmn* Aḥiq 53, 107 (v. infra; :: Kottsieper SAS 12, 231: = lapsus for *rḥmn›* (= Sing. emph.)), 223 (dam. context; cf. however Lindenberger APA 219, Kottsieper SAS 14, 231: l. prob. *rḥmy* = Plur. + suff. 1 p.s. of *rḥm*₄) - **Palm** Sing. m. emph. *rḥmn›* CIS ii 3974[3], 3988[1], 3989[1], 4001[2], 4002[1], 4007[2], RIP 119[2] (for this reading, cf. Gawlikowski RIP a.l. :: Al-Hassani & Starcky AAS iii 160 ii (div. otherwise): l. *›rḥmn›*), etc., etc., *rḥm›* (lapsus) CIS 3981[3], 4027[2] - **JAr** Sing. emph. *rḥmnh* MPAT-A 22[10] (= SM 70[18]), 39[3] (= SM 42[4]; for the interpret., cf. Ben-Dov Qadm vi 61, Naveh SM a.l., Beyer ATTM 389, 694 (cf. Fitzmyer & Harrington MPAT p. 353) :: Fitzmyer & Harrington MPAT a.l.: = Sing./Plur. + suff. 1 p.pl. of *rḥm*₃ (= generosity; cf. also Hüttenmeister ASI 274)), SM 107[4] (:: Hüttenmeister ASI 97: l. *rḥmym* (= Plur. abs. of *rḥm*₃)) - ¶ adj. merciful; *›srḥ›dn mlk› rḥmn hw kmnd‹* Aḥiq 53: king A. is merciful, as is known (v. *mnd‹*₁); cf. *mlk krḥmn* Aḥiq 107: a king is merciful (for this poss. interpret., cf. Seidel ZAW xxxii 292; *k* = *kaph veritatis*, v. *k*₁) :: Grelot RB lxviii 184, DAE p. 438: as merciful as a king is, (so ...) :: Grimme OLZ '11, 532, Ginsberg ANET 429: a king is like the Merciful One, cf. also Lindenberger APA 93, 244 n. 261, UF xiv 110, Watson OA ii 255f. :: Sach p. 165, Gressmann ATAT 459: the king is like a merciful one? - used as epithet of gods (cf. also Kaufman AIA 106, Maarav iii 165); *›lh rḥmn* Tell F 5: the merciful god (epithet of Hadad); *rḥmn›* DM ii 37 ii 2: the merciful one (prob. indication of the anonymous god); cf. also - 1) *lb‹lšmn rb› wrḥmn›* CIS ii 3988[1] (= RIP 128): to B. the great and merciful one - **2)** *mr› ‹lm› ṭb› wrḥmn›* CIS ii 3989[1] (= RIP 131): the lord of the universe, the good and merciful one (prob. = Ba‹alshemayn) - **3)** *‹zyzw ›lh› ṭb›*

wrḥmn› CIS ii 3974$^{2f.}$: A. the good and merciful god - **4)** *lbryk šmh l‹lm› ṭb› wrḥmn›* CIS ii 3996$^{1f.}$: to the one whose name is blessed in eternity, the good and merciful one (cf. CIS ii 4001$^{1f.}$, 4002^{1}, 4007$^{1f.}$, 4014$^{1f.}$, 4016$^{1f.}$, DM ii 37 i 1f., 39 ii 1f., etc.), cf. *bryk šmh l‹lm› ṭb› wlrḥmn›* CIS ii 4034$^{1f.}$, *lbrk šmh l‹lm› ṭb› wrḥmn› wtyr›* CIS ii 4046$^{1ff.}$ (cf. also CIS ii 4075$^{1ff.}$), *lbry[k] šm[h] rḥmn›* CIS ii 4088$^{1f.}$ (cf. also RIP 107^{1f}, 114$^{2ff.}$), *lbryk šmh l‹lm› wrḥmn›* RIP 137^{1}, *lbryk šmh rḥmn› ṭb›* CIS ii 4033$^{1ff.}$ (cf. CIS ii 4022$^{1f.}$ (= PNO 73), cf. also CIS ii 4009$^{1ff.}$, 4018$^{1f.}$, 4077$^{1f.}$, Inv xi 31$^{1ff.}$, xii 45$^{2f.}$, DM ii 38 ii 5f., 40 i 2), *bryk šmh l‹lm› rḥmn ṭb› wtyr›* CIS ii 4038$^{1f.}$ (cf. CIS ii 4028$^{1ff.}$, 4041$^{1f.}$, 4042$^{1f.}$, RIP 121$^{1f.}$, 122^{1f}, Syr xvii 348$^{1f.}$, Inv xi 13$^{1ff.}$, 20$^{1f.}$, 29$^{1ff.}$ (= CIS ii 4075)), *lbryk šmh l‹lm› rḥmn› wḥnn› wtyr›* CIS ii 4084$^{1ff.}$, *lbryk šmh l‹l[m]› rḥmn› wtyr›* RIP 119$^{1f.}$, *lbryk šmh l‹lm› ›lh› d/rṭy wrḥmn›* PNO 72$^{3f.}$ (v. *rṭy*), *[b]ryk šmh l‹lm› ṭb› wrḥmn› wskr›* Inv xi 38$^{1ff.}$; cf. also *lrḥmn›* (without preceding n.d.; indication of the anonymous god) CIS ii 4025^{3} (cf. CIS ii 4091^{2}, Inv xi 1^{6}, 37^{2}, xii 45^{9}), cf. also *lrḥmn› ṭb›* PNO 42$^{2f.}$, RIP 120^{2}, 121^{3}, CIS ii 4092^{1}, 4093^{1}, 4099$^{1f.}$, Inv xi 26$^{1f.}$, *rḥmn› ṭb› wtyr›* CIS ii 4051$^{4f.}$ (cf. CIS ii 3981$^{3f.}$) - **5)** used to indicate God: the Merciful One; *lšmh drḥmnh* MPAT-A 22^{10}: in the name of the Merciful One; *mn drḥmnh wmn d‹mlh* MPAT-A 39$^{2f.}$: out of what belongs to the Merciful One and out of his own effort (for the reading, v. *‹ml*$_2$).
v. *‹lm*$_4$.

rḥmnyt **Palm** Sing. emph. *rḥmnyt›* Sem xxvii 117^{5} - ¶ subst. mercifulness, mercy; in Sem xxvii 117^{5} deified (cf. Aggoula Sem xxvii 119; poss. interpret.).

rḥmt v. *rḥm*$_3$.

rḥ‹ v. *rḥm*$_1$, *rḥṣ*$_1$.

rḥp v. *rḥm*$_7$.

rḥpn v. *ḥsn*$_3$.

rḥṣ$_1$ **OffAr** Qal Impf. 1 p.s. + suff. 3 p.s.f. *›rḥ‹h* Sach 76 i B 3 - ¶ verb Qal to wash; + obj.: Sach 76 i B 3.
v. *pḥṣ*, *rḥm*$_1$, *rḥṣ*$_2$.

rḥṣ$_2$ **Hebr** Sing. abs. *rḥṣ* KAI 186^{3}, 187$^{2f.}$, Dir ostr 16^{3}, etc., etc. (cf. e.g. Dir p. 37f., Röllig KAI a.l., Israel RSO xlix 17ff., Lipiński OLP viii 85f., BiOr xxxv 285 × e.g. Noth ZDPV l 220, Savignac RB xliv 292f., Mosc p. 27, Sasson JSS xxvi 1ff., Stager JSS xxviii 241ff., Lemaire IH i 31, 47: = Qal Part. pass. s.m. abs. of *rḥṣ*$_1$ (= washed > pure), *šmn rḥṣ* = refined oil) - ¶ subst. washing; *šmn rḥṣ* KAI 186^{3}: oil for washing (= cosmetic oil? (cf. Knauf ZAH iii 15: prob. = personal hygiene), cf. however Sasson JSS xxvi 1ff., Stager JSS xxviii 244 n. 9 (v. supra)).

rḥq$_1$ Qal Pf. 1 p.s. *rḥqt* Cowl 13^{7,16}, 14^{6}, 25^{4}, 67 v 2, Krael 1^{7}; 1 p.pl. *rḥqn* Krael 3^{11,13}; Impf. 3 p.s.m. *yrḥq* NESE i 11^{8}; Imper. s.m. *r[ḥ]q*

Aḥiq 194 (dam. context; for this reading, cf. Lindenberger APA 192, Kottsieper SAS 13, 231 :: Cowl a.l.: l. *r[ḥy]q* = PA‘EL Imper. s.m) - **Palm** QAL (:: Cantineau Gramm 85f. : = PA‘EL) Pf. 3 p.s.m. *rḥq* CIS ii 4173[1], 4174[1], Ber ii 85[4], 102 i 2, 112[2], v 110[3]; 3 p.s.f. *rḥqt* CIS ii 4175[3], RIP 163b 2; 1 p.s. *rḥqt* CIS ii 4206[1]; 3 p.pl.m. *rḥq* CIS ii 4171[1], 4172[1], RB xxxix 526B 2, FS Miles 50 ii 4 (subj.: two women); PA‘EL (:: Rosenthal Sprache 61: = QAL; cf. also Nöldeke ZA xx 145 n. 2) Pf. 3 p.s.m. *rḥq* Ber ii 78[1], 82[1], 84[1], 86[3,9,13], 101[3], 103[6], 110[1] (Greek par. ἐξεχώρησεν), v 104[1], Syr lxii 277 ii 2 (context however dam.); 3 p.s.f. *rḥqt* CIS ii 4199[12], Ber ii 93[1], 104[5], 107[4], Syr xiv 185[2]; 1 p.s. *rḥqt* Ber ii 96[2]; 3 p.pl.m. *rḥq* CIS ii 4173[3] (or = 3 p.s.m.?), 4204[2] (or = 3 p.s.m.?), Ber ii 97[1], 98[1], 99 ii 1, v 124[3] (:: Ingholt Ber v 125f.: = 3 p.s.m.), Syr xix 156[3] (or = 3 p.s.m.?); APH Pf. 3 p.s.m. *ʾrḥq* RB xxxix 542 i 2 (dam. context), Ber ii 88[3]; 3 p.pl.m. *ʾrḥq* Ber v 95[6] - ¶ verb QAL to withdraw oneself, to go away, to leave; + *mn*$_5$: NESE i 11[8] (cf. also Porten Or lvii 80), Aḥiq 194 (v. supra); cf. the foll. legal uses: - 1) to renounce a right on property - a) + *mn*$_5$, *rḥqt mnh* Cowl 13[7]: I have withdrawn myself from it (i.e. I have renounced the right I had on it), cf. Cowl 13[16], Krael 3[11,13]; cf. also *rḥqt mnkm mn byt yznyh* Cowl 25[4]: I ceded all my rights on the house of Y. to you (for this text, cf. Porten & Szubin JAOS cii 654) - b) + *l*$_5$ + *mn*$_5$ (or + *mn*$_5$ + *l*$_5$), *zbdbwl ... rḥq lnqrys mn sṭrʾ mdnḥyʾ dy ʾksdrʾ* CIS ii 4173[1]: Z. has ceded to N. the eastern wall of the exedra (cf. CIS ii 4171[1], 4172[1], 4174[1ff.], 4175[2ff.], 4206[1f.], Ber ii 85 ii 2ff., 102 i 2f., 112[2ff.], v 110[3f.], RB xxxix 526B 2ff., RIP 163b 2f.) - **2)** to renounce a legal claim; + *mn*$_5$, *rḥqt mnky* Cowl 14[6]: I renounce any claim on you (cf. Cowl 67 v 2 (dam. context), Krael 1[7]); for the use of *rḥq* in Off.Ar., cf. Rundgren ZAW lxx 210ff., Kutscher JAOS lxxiv 238, Yaron Bibl xli 383ff., Law 81f., 103, RB lxxvii 411, Muffs 25ff., 48ff., 118ff., 154 n. 1, 178 (cf. also Malul ZA lxxv 72) - PA‘EL to part with, to renounce legal rights on - **1)** + obj. + *l*$_5$ (or + *l*$_5$ + obj.), *sṭrʾ dnh m‘rbyʾ ... rḥq ... bny yrḥy ... lywlys ʾwrlys* CIS ii 4204[1ff.]: the sons of Y. have ceded to Y.A. this western wall (cf. Ber ii 78[1f.], 82[1f.], 84[1f.], 86[3ff.,9,12ff.], 96[2f.], 102 ii 1ff., 104[1ff.], 107[1ff.], 110[1f.], v 104[1f.], 124[1ff.], Syr xiv 184[1ff.], xix 156[1ff.], FS Miles 50 ii 4ff.) - **2)** + *l*$_5$: CIS ii 4173[3], 4199[12] - **3)** + *l*$_5$ + *b*$_2$, *nwrbl wʾqʾt ... šwtpt wrḥqt lb‘ly ... bʾksdrʾ tymnʾ* Ber ii 93[1ff.]: N. and A. have associated themselves with and transferred to B. the southern exedra (i.e. prob. a share in the southern exedra; the transl. ... transferred the southern exedra (cf. Ingholt Ber ii 94) less prob.) - **4)** + *l*$_5$ + *mn*$_5$ + obj. (or + *mn*$_5$ + obj. + *l*$_5$, or + *mn*$_5$ + *l*$_5$ + obj.), *ywlys ʾwrlys ‘gʾ ... rḥq lywlys ʾwrlys lmlkʾ ... mn ṭksys dy gwmḥyn trn* Ber ii 100 ii 2ff.: Y.A.O. has ceded to Y.A.L. from the row of niches two (niches); *rḥq lbsʾ wlrsyqʾ ... mn šṭrʾ ymnyʾ ... qwmḥyn štʾ* Ber ii 97[1f.]: they have ceded to B. and R.

six niches of the right wall (cf. Ber ii 98[1f.], 99 ii 1f.) - APH to part with, to renounce; *ʾwrlys ḥyrn ... ʾrḥq lʾwrlyʾ ṣmy ... mn gwmḥyn trn* Ber ii 88[2f.]: A.Ch. has ceded to A.S. from the niches two (niches); *mqymw ... wʾqmt ... ʾḥbr lšlmn ... wltymw wʾrḥq lhwn mn pnyn trtn* Ber v 95[2ff.]: M. ... and A. ... have ceded to S. and T. and have transferred to them from the stretches two (stretches; v. *pnyh*) - a derivative of this root prob. also in DA ii 16 (cf. Hoftijzer DA a.l., Hackett BTDA 73; for the context, v. also *pḥz₂*).
v. *šbq₁*.

rḥq₂ **DA** Sing. abs. *rḥq* i 15 (for the reading problems, cf. Hoftijzer DA a.l.) - ¶ subst. distance; *wšmʿw ḥršn mn rḥq* DA i 15: and the deaf heard from afar.

rḥq₃ **Amm** Plur. f. abs. *rḥqt* Ber xxii 120[8] - **OffAr** Sing. m. abs. *rḥyq* Cowl 1[6], 5[9], 6[13,15], 13[10] (*rḥy[q]*), 14[11], 20[15], 41[7], 43[5], Krael 5[5], *rq* (lapsus) Krael 1[9]; Plur. m. abs. *rḥyqn* Cowl 20[9], 28[11]; cf. Frah xxv 21 (*lḥyk*), GIPP 27, SaSt 22 - **Nab** Sing. m. abs. *rḥq* J 3[6] (= CIS ii 210) - Sing. m. abs. (*rḥq*) in an unknown West-Semitic dialect: Sem xxxviii 52[2] (or fraud?, cf. however Bordreuil & Pardee Sem xxxviii 57) - ¶ adj. far, far-away - **1)** temporal, *bywmt rbm wbšnt rḥqt* Ber xxii 120[7f.]: for many days and far-away years (cf. also Dion RB lxxxii 25) - **2)** used in a legal sense, followed by *mn₅*, *wʾnh rḥyq mn kl dyn* Cowl 14[11]: I am far from every process (i.e. I renounce all suit); *whw ... rḥyq mn ʾlh nksyʾ* Cowl 20[15]: and he ... is far from these goods (i.e. he has no claim on these goods); *ʾnh mnḥm wʿnnyh rḥyqn ʾnḥnh mnk* Cowl 20[9]: I M. and A., we are far from you (i.e. we renounce all claim on you; cf. Cowl 28[11], Sem xxxviii 52[2]); *wʾnt rḥyq mn kl dyn zy yqblwn ʿlyk* Cowl 6[15f.]: and you are far from every process (you are quit of all claim) that they may bring against you, cf. also the *rḥyq* + *mn₅* in Cowl 41[7], context however dam. - **3)** far, i.e. not related (contrasting with *qrb₉*), *ʾnwš rḥq* J 3[5f.]: someone outside the family - **4)** substantivated, someone who is not a relative: Cowl 1[6], 5[9], 6[13], 13[10], 43[5], Krael 1[9], 5[5] (for this interpret., v. *qrb₉*) - Röllig NESE ii 2, 7f.: l. prob. *rḥqm* (= Plur. m. abs.) in MUSJ xlv 262[3] (cf. also Schiffmann RSF iv 176), prob. reading :: Cross IEJ xxix 41, 44: l. *wdrkm* = *w₂* + Plur. abs. of *drk₃* (excised word).

rṭb₁ v. *rṭb₂*.

rṭb₂ **DA** Sing. m. abs. *rṭb* ii 5 - ¶ adj. moistened (cf. however Hackett BTDA 29, 58, 134: or = Sing. abs. of *rṭb₁* (= moist > foliage)?).

rṭy **Palm** word of unknown meaning (*rṭy/dṭy*) in PNO 72[5]. Ingholt & Starcky PNO a.l.: epithet to the preceding *ʾlhʾ*.

ry v. *prr₁*.

ryb **OldAr** QAL Impf. 3 p.s.m. *yrb* KAI 224[17,26] - ¶ verb QAL to be in conflict with, to strive with; *whn yrb br[y] zy yšb ʿl khsʾy* (v. *krsʾ*)

ḥd ʾḥwh KAI 224[17]: and if my son, who will sit on my throne, will strive with one of his brothers (cf. e.g. Fitzmyer AIS 99, Limburg JBL lxxxviii 299f., Gibson SSI ii p. 49, 55 :: Lipiński Stud 47f.: and if one of his brothers contests the right of my son who sat upon my throne :: Hartman CBQ xxx 259: a *ʿm$_4$* forgotten by lapsus after *yrb*? :: Dupont-Sommer BMB xiii 29: *ryb* used absolutely without object; cf. Koopmans 66f.); cf. also KAI 224[26] (heavily dam. context).

rys **JAr** Plur. emph. *[r]ysyʾ* AMB 5[6] - ¶ subst. Plur. eye-lids.

ryq$_1$ v. *trq*.

ryq$_2$ **OffAr** Sing. m. abs. *ryq* CRAI '70, 163[2], IPAA 11[5] - **JAr** Sing. m. abs. *ryq* MPAT 44 i 7 - ¶ adj. void, invalid: MPAT 44 i 7; substantivated: nonsense; *mh ʿbd ryq* IPAA 11[5]: what is the doing of what is vain, senseless (v. *ʿbd$_3$*; for the context of CRAI '70, 163[2], cf. also Humbach IPAA p. 12 (n. 11)), cf. *rq$_2$*.

ryš v. *rʾš$_1$*.

ryt **Mo** Sing. abs. *ryt* KAI 181[12] - ¶ subst. poss. meaning spectacle (cf. e.g. Lidzbarski Handb 366, Cooke NSI p. 11, Bernhardt ZDPV lxxvi 145 (n. 31), Gibson SSI i p. 76, 79 (< *rʾy*; cf. also Nöldeke Inschrift 12: 'Augenweide') :: Ryckmans JEOL xiv 81: a sacrifice to fulfill an obligation (cf. also Röllig KAI a.l., Liver PEQ '67, 24f. (n. 33); < *rwy$_1$*) :: Albright BASOR lxxxix 16 n. 55, ANET 320, Briend TPOA 91, Jackson & Dearman SMIM 98, 111f.: = satiation (< *rwy$_1$*; cf. Michaud PA 38, Andersen Or xxxv 96, 104), cf. also de Moor UF xx 153 (a treat) :: Beeston JRAS '85, 143f., 147: = technical term for annexation :: Halévy RS viii 289: = contraction of *rʿyt* (= satisfaction) :: Lemaire Syr lxiv 206f.: l. poss. *hyt* = QAL Pf. 3 p.s.f. of *hyy*; on this subject, cf. also Segert ArchOr xxix 215, 219, 243, 247, 258, 266, Reviv CSI p. 21, Garr DGSP 50, Mattingly SMIM 235f.).

rkb$_1$ **Hebr** HIPH Impf. 2 p.s.m. *trkb* TA-H 1[6f.] (cf. Otzen VT xx 289ff., Aharoni TA a.l., Lemaire IH i 155, 158, Pardee UF x 295f., HAHL 31f., 237 :: Freedman IEJ xix 55f.: = PI ʿEL/HIPH Impf. 2 p.s.m. of *rkb$_2$* (= to grind; cf. Albright ANET 569 (n. 30)) :: Brock VT xviii 396f.: = HIPH 2 p.s.m. of *rkb$_4$* (= to scrape together) :: (Ben-Chayyim with) Aharoni IEJ xvi 3 (n. 6): poss. = lapsus for *trbk* (= pass. Impf. 3 p.s.f. of *rbk$_1$* (= to be prepared, mixed)); cf. also Cathcart VT xix 121ff.: = passive Impf. 3 p.s.f. of *rkb$_2$*, Sasson VT xxx 44ff.: = active Impf. 2 p.s.m. of *rkb$_2$*) - **OffAr** QAL Part. act. s.m. abs. *rkb* Aḥiq 38; + suff. 3 p.s.m. *rkbh* Driv 9[2]; pl.m. abs. *rkbyn* ATNS 62[2] (:: Segal ATNS a.l.: = Plur. abs. of *rkby* (= charioteer)); cstr. *rkby* Beh 30 (or in Driv 9[2], Beh 30 = *rkb$_5$*? (= rider, horseman)); HAPH Pf. 3 p.s.m. *hrkb* Aḥiq 191; 2 p.s.m. *hrkbt* Aḥiq 128; Impf. 2 p.s.m. *thrkb* Aḥiq 126 (for the reading, cf. also Lindenberger APA 117f.) - **Palm** PA ʿEL Part. act. s.m. abs./cstr. *mrkb* SBS 48[6] - ¶ verb QAL to ride, to mount (sc. a

horse); *swsh ʿm rkbh* Driv 9[2]: a horse with its rider (v. however supra); *rkb b[s]wsh ḥd qly[l]* Aḥiq 38: riding on a swift horse; *ḥylʾ zʿy[rʾ] rkby swsyn* Beh 30: a small troop mounted on horses (Akkad. par. *ú-qu i-ṣi e-li ṣeri ša sisē*; v. however supra); *rkbyn swsyn* ATNS 62[2]: mounting horses - PAʿEL to ride, to mount (sc. a horse); *ṣlm mrkb swsy* SBS 48[6]: an equestrian statue (cf. Greek par.: ἔφιππον ἀν[δριά]ντα) - HIPH/HAPH - **1)** to load; + obj.: TA-H 1[6] (sc. upon a donkey, cf. Aharoni sub TA-H 1, Lemaire IH i 155, 158, Pardee UF x 295f., Heltzer RDAC '88 i 169 n. 31 (cf. also Conrad TUAT i 250) :: Otzen VT xx 289ff.: to load upon a wagon; on the text, cf. also Barrick JBL ci 501f.) - **2)** to shoot (with arrow as object) - a) + obj.: Aḥiq 191 (?, dam. context; cf. also Barrick VT xxxv 356) - b) + obj. + *l*$_5$, *ʾl thrkb ḥṭk lṣdyq* Aḥiq 126: do not shoot your arrow at a righteous man (cf. Aḥiq 128).
v. *rkn*.

rkb$_2$ v. *rkb*$_1$.

rkb$_3$ v. *rqy*$_1$.

rkb$_4$ v. *rkb*$_1$.

rkb$_5$ v. *rkb*$_{1,6,7}$.

rkb$_6$ **Samal** Sing. abs. *rkb* KAI 215[3] (dam. context),[10] (v. infra) - **OldAr** Sing. abs. *rkb* KAI 202B 2 (cf. e.g. Black DOTT 247, Donner KAI a.l., Degen AAG p. 47 × e.g. Lipiński Stud 23, Gibson SSI ii p. 11, 16, de Moor UF xx 162: = Sing. abs. of *rkb*$_5$ (= rider)) - ¶ subst. chariot (v. however supra): KAI 202B 2; *bʿly rkb* KAI 215[10]: commanders of chariots (cf. e.g. Dion p. 39, Dahood Or xlv 382) :: Gibson SSI p. ii 79, 82: commanders of cavalry (*rkb* = *rkb*$_5$ with collective meaning) :: e.g. Cooke NSI p. 174, 177, Degen ZDMG cxxi 133: = charioteers :: Landsberger Samʾal 50 (n. 127): = indication of certain type of gods :: e.g. Donner KAI a.l., Sader EAS 167f. (n. 44): = owners of chariots.

rkb$_7$ **OffAr** Plur. + suff. 2 p.s.m. *rkbyk* Aḥiq 205 (or = Plur. + suff. 2 p.s.m. of *rkb*$_5$?, cf. Sach p. 178 :: Baneth OLZ '14, 353: = Plur. + suff. 2 p.s.m. of *rkb*$_8$ (= saddle)) - ¶ subst. the act of riding, ride; *wʾnh rkbyk lʾ ʾḥzh* Aḥiq 205: I will not see your acts of riding (sc. on me; i.e. I will not be ridden by you; v. however supra).

rkb$_8$ v. *rkb*$_7$.

rkby v. *rkb*$_1$.

rkybh v. *rkysh*.

rkyk **OffAr** Sing. m. abs. *rkyk* Aḥiq 100, 105 - ¶ adj. soft; *rkyk mmll mlk* Aḥiq 100: soft is the speech of a king (cf. Aḥiq 105; for the last-mentioned text, cf. Lindenberger APA 91).

rkysh (prob. < Akkad.) - **OffAr** Sing. abs. *rkysh* Cowl 81[29] - ¶ subst. harness, saddlery (cf. Grelot DAE p. 109 n. v) :: Harmatta ActAntHung vii 351: l. *rkybh* (= saddle) :: Driver JRAS '32, 83: l. *rkysh* = string.

rkl **OffAr** Plur. emph. *rklyʾ* Cowl 38[4]; + suff. 2 p.s.m. *rklyk* Beh 55 (for the reading, cf. also Greenfield and Porten BIDG p. 48) - ¶ subst. merchant: Cowl 38[4]; context of Beh 55 obscure.

rklh v. *nklh*.

rkn **OffAr** Qal Pf. 3 p.s.m. *rk[n]* Aḥiq 91 (for this reading, cf. e.g. Epstein ZAW xxxiii 134, Cowl a.l., Grelot DAE p. 436, Kottsieper SAS 11, 144, cf. however Sach 162, Lindenberger APA 64, 231 n. 110: l. *rk[b]* = Qal Pf. 3 p.s.m. of *rkb*$_1$ (= to mount)); cf. Frah app. 6 (*yḥrkn[w]n*, cf. Nyberg FP 54, 99: = Haph form :: Ebeling Frah a.l.: l. *yhwqwn* = poss. form of *yqy* (= to hear)) - ¶ verb Qal to bend, to bow; + *l*$_5$ (for): Aḥiq 91, v. however supra - Haph to lean (sc. one's ear): Frah app. 6.

rkrk v. *rqrq*.

rkš **OffAr** Sing. abs. *rkš* TA-Ar 6[1]; emph. *rkš*› Aeg xxxix 4 recto 2, verso 1; + suff. 3 p.s.m. *rkšh* Driv 6[4] - ¶ subst. coll. horses: Aeg xxxix 4 recto 2, verso 1, Driv 6[4]; *bny rkš* TA-Ar 6[1]: colts (cf. Naveh TA a.l.; or = horses??) - Albright FS Ubach 135 (n. 25), FS Horn 508: l. *rkšn* (= Plur. abs.) in IEJ i 220[2] (highly uncert. reading), cf. Zayadine Syr li 134 (div. otherwise): l. *br šnb* (= n.p.); cf. also Lemaire Syr lxi 251, 254; cf. Puech with Lemaire Syr lxi 254: l. *br šnp* (= n.p.).

rm$_1$ **Hebr** Sing. abs. *rm* DJD ii 24F 11 (heavily dam. context) - ¶ subst. height.

rm$_2$ **Ph** Plur. m. abs. *rmm* KAI 15 - **OffAr** Sing. m. abs. *rm* Aḥiq 142, 150 (?, dam. context) - ¶ adj. high, elevated: KAI 15 (for the context, v. *šmym*); ‹*m zy rm mnk* Aḥiq 142: with someone higher than you (for the context, cf. Lindenberger APA 142, 262 n. 444; cf. Aḥiq 150 (v. supra)) - *mlkrm* in Dir ostr 64 = n.p. (cf. e.g. Jirku OLZ '25, 281, Noth IP 118 n. 2 :: Dir a.l.: *rm* = Sing. m. abs. of *rm*$_2$).

v. *mym*, *rwm*$_1$.

rm› v. *ḥrm*$_1$, *rmy*$_1$.

rmbk (< Iran., cf. Périkhanian REA-NS viii 10) - **OffAr** Sing. abs. *rmbk* REA-NS viii 9 - ¶ subst. m. plate, dish.

rmh$_1$ **DA** Sing. abs. *rmh* ii 8 (cf. e.g. Hoftijzer DA a.l., Levine JAOS ci 200f., Hackett BTDA 30, 62, 134 :: e.g. Caquot & Lemaire Syr liv 204: = Qal Part. act. s.f. abs. of *rwm*$_1$) - ¶ subst. vermin.

rmh$_2$ **OffAr**, cf. Frah ix 7 (*rmt*›): mountain.

rmy$_1$ **OffAr** Qal Pf. 3 p.s.m. *rm*› FX 136[17] (for this uncert. interpret., cf. Teixidor Syr lii 289 :: Dupont-Sommer CRAI '74, 137, 149, FX 150f., Mayrhofer FX 184, Teixidor JNES xxxvii 184 (n. 17): l. *dm*› = Sing. emph. of *dm*$_2$ (< Iran.; = domain, fief), cf. also Contini OA xx 232f.); cf. Frah xx 16 (*lmytwn*), Paik 929 (*rmy*), 930 (*[r›]my*; ?), 931, 932 (*lmytn*), GIPP 27, 63, SaSt 22 - **Palm** Qal Pf. 3 p.s.m. *rm*› Syr xiv 184[2] (or l. *dm*› = Qal Pf. 3 p.s.m. of *dm*› (= to estimate); cf. Cantineau Syr xiv a.l., Gawlikowski TP 44) - ¶ verb Qal - **1)** to throw, cf. Frah

xx 16, Paik 929-932 - **2)** to decide: FX 136[17], Syr xiv 184[2] (for both instances, v. however supra).
v. *dmn$_1$*, *ḥrm$_1$*.

rmy$_2$ v. *dmn$_1$*.

rmy$_3$ **OffAr** Sing. m. abs. *rmy* Driv 6[3] - ¶ adj. of inferior quality (?); *qmḥ rmy* Driv 6[3]: = flour of inferior quality? (cf. Driv p. 60), cf. however Hinz NWAP 40, AISN 198: < Iran. = fine, excellent, *qmḥ rmy* = flour of high quality; cf. also Whitehead JNES xxxvii 133 n. 90: = type of wheat.

rmk cf. Frah vii 4 (*lmk’*): mare.

rmn$_1$ **OffAr** Sing. emph. *rmn’* Aḥiq 165; cf. Frah iv 21 (*lwmn’*, *lwlmn’*, *lmwn’*) - ¶ subst. pomegranate; for this word, cf. Borowski AIAI 116f.

rmn$_2$ (< Egypt., cf. Grelot RB lxxviii 529f., DAE p. 235 (n. v)) - **OffAr** Sing. abs. *rmn* Krael 7[18] (for the reading, cf. also Porten & Greenfield JEAS p. 54 :: Krael a.l.: l. *dmn* (= *dmn$_1$*)) - ¶ subst. basket (cf. Grelot RB lxxviii 529f.).

rms **OffAr** Porten Or lvii 18: the *rms* in Or lvii 16[3] = form of root *rms* (= to tread)?? (heavily dam. context; reading *dms* also poss.).

rmṣ (< Arab., cf. Milik BIA x 57, O'Connor JNES xlv 228f.) - **Nab** PA‘EL Pf. 3 p.s.m. + suff. 3 p.pl.m. *rmṣhm* BIA x 55[5] - ¶ verb PA‘EL to pacify; + obj. BIA x 55[5] (cf. also O'Connor JANES xviii 73).

rmš **JAr** Sing. abs. *rmš* IEJ xl 135[8]; emph. *rmš’* IEJ xl 132[8], 135[4,5,7], 140[3] (on the reading, cf. Yardeni IEJ xl 142) - ¶ subst. evening; *lrmš’* IEJ xl 132[8], 135[4,5,7]: in the evening; *ṣpr wrmš* IEJ xl 135[8]: morning and evening.

rnbt v. *dnb*.

rnh v. *‘rbh$_2$*.

rny **OffAr**, cf. Sogd B 270: to speak, to answer (= *r‘y$_2$*??), cf. Schaed 235f. -
v. *rwy$_2$*.

rnn **Palm** du Mesnil du Buisson Inv D p. 23f.: l. QAL Part. act. pl.m. emph. (*rnny’*) of *rnn* (= to announce, to sing) in Inv D 40[3] (uncert. interpret.).

rsy (< Egypt., cf. Couroyer RB lxi 252f., Kutscher JAOS lxxiv 237) - **OffAr** Sing. f. abs. *rsy* Krael 10[3] (:: Krael a.l.: l. *dsy* (= Plur. cstr. of *ds* (= flight (of stairs))??) - ¶ adj. southern.

rsp Ebeling sub Frah xxvii 12: l. *rspyn’* (= autumn), incorrect Plur. of *rsp* (= glow), highly uncert. interpret., cf. also Nyberg FP 56, 107: l. *lsp’n’* = either form of *rspn* (< Akkad. *rasāpu/rasābu* = to strike) or form of root *rsb* (= to trample), both interpret. highly uncert.

rspyn v. *rsp*.

rspn v. *rsp*.

r‘$_1$ **Hebr** Sing. + suff. 3 p.s.m. *r‘w* KAI 189[2,3,4] (on the form, cf. CF

50, Pardee CBQ xliv 504, Rainey JBL cii 632) - **OffAr** Sing. + suff. 3 p.s.m. *rʿh* Aḥiq 222 (Kottsieper SAS 232: or = Sing. + suff. 3 p.s.m. of *rʿh*$_3$ (= friend) or = Sing. abs. of *rʿh*$_4$ (= herdsman, shepherd); for the reading problems, cf. Lindenberger APA 219); Plur. abs. *rʿyn* Aḥiq 113 (the *y* prob. = *mater lectionis* :: Driver JRAS '32, 88: the *y* is root consonant, = noun < root *rʿy*$_3$ (= friend) :: Nöldeke AGWG xiv/4, 14: *rʿyn* = QAL Part. act. pl.m. abs. of *rʿy*$_1$ (= shepherd) :: Cowl p. 239, Leand 43u: = Plur. abs. of *rʿ*$_2$, cf. also Ginsberg ANET 429 :: Kottsieper SAS 21, 232: = Plur. abs. of *rʿy*$_5$; on this form, cf. also Lindenberger APA 100) - ¶ subst. m. friend, colleague, neighbour; *nšm]ʿ* (or *[wyšm]ʿ*) *ql ʾš qrʾ ʾl rʿw* KAI 189[2f.]: a man's voice was heard calling to his colleague (cf. KAI 189[2,4]); *byt rʿh* Aḥiq 222: the house of his neighbour; *byn rʿyn ṭbn* Aḥiq 113: between good friends (cf. Ungnad ArPap sub 57, Driver JRAS '32, 882, v. also supra) - Leand 43f[00]: in Aḥiq 113, 222 prob. loan from Hebr. (??).

v. *ʾšr*$_4$, *rʿy*$_1$.

rʿ$_2$ **Ph** Sing. m. abs. *rʿ* KAI 26A i 9, iii 17; Plur. m. abs. *rʿm* KAI 26A i 15 - **JAr** Sing. f. abs. *rʿh* AMB 13[10] - ¶ adj. bad, wicked; *ʾšm rʿm* KAI 26A i 15: wicked men; *ʿyn rʿh* AMB 13[10]: an evil eye - substantivated adj. - **1)** evil; *kl hrʿ ʾš kn bʾrṣ* KAI 26A i 9: all evil that was in the country (:: Gibson SSI iii p. 47: every evildoer) - **2)** malice: KAI 26A iii 17.

v. *rʿ*$_1$.

rʿʾ v. *rʿy*$_1$.

rʿh$_1$ **Hebr** Sing. abs. *rʿh* TA-H 40[15] - ¶ subst. evil.

v. *rʿy*$_1$.

rʿh$_2$ **Ph** Sing. abs. *rʿt* KAI 60[4] (v. infra; :: Milik Bibl xlviii 573 n. 1: l. *dʿt* = QAL Inf. cstr. of *ydʿ*$_1$) - ¶ subst. decision (prob. < root *rʿy*, cf. Gibson SSI iii p. 150f. (cf. also Lidzbarski Handb 369, Cooke NSI p. 97f.) :: e.g. Chabot sub RES 1215, Harr 147, FR 207, Röllig KAI a.l.: < Ar. *rʿy* = Can. *rṣy*); *ʾyt rʿt z lktb ... ʿlt mṣbt ...* KAI 60[4f.]: to write down this decision ... on a stele of ....

rʿh$_3$ v. *rʿ*$_1$.

rʿh$_4$ v. *rʿ*$_1$.

rʿh$_5$ v. *rʿy*$_6$.

rʿw **JAr** Sing. + suff. 1 p.s. *rʿwty* MPAT 50f., 51[3], *rʿty* MPAT 40[2, 13]; + suff. 2 p.pl.m. *rʿwtkwn* SM 102[1] (= Frey 826b) - ¶ subst. free will; *mn rʿwty* MPAT 51[3]: out of my own free will (cf. MPAT 40[2], 50f.; cf. also Koffmahn DWJ 66f.); the context of SM 102[1] diff., poss. *mn rʿwtkwn* = because of your wish (cf. Naveh SM a.l.: i.e. because of your decision, cf. however Albright with du Mesnil du Buisson RB xlv 76 n. 1: with your permission, by your leave (cf. also Torrey Syn p. 275), Vincent with du Mesnil du Buisson RB xlv 76 n. 1: out of your

kindness, du Mesnil du Buisson RB xlv 76: out of your generosity).
v. *lhbh*.

r'y$_1$ **Ph** QAL Part. act. pl.m. abs. *r'm* KAI 37B 8 (:: e.g. CIS i sub 86, Cooke NSI p. 69, Harr 147, v.d.Branden BO viii 261: poss. = Plur. abs. of *r'$_1$*) - **OffAr** QAL Pf. 3 p.s.m. *r'>* Sumer xx 13[4]; 3 p.pl.m. *r'w* Sumer xx 15[5]; Part. act. s.m. emph. *r'y>* JRAS '29, 108[3] - **Palm** QAL Pf. 3 p.s.m. *r'>* RTP 190 (cf. du Mesnil du Buisson TMP 237 (n. 7), diff. reading :: Starcky RTP a.l.: l. *rb>* = Sing. m. emph. of *rb$_2$*) - ¶ verb QAL to feed, to graze; *dy r'w tnn* Sumer xx 15[5]: who pastured (sc. their animals) here (cf. Sumer xx 13[4]); Part. act. shepherd; *npn> r'y> qn zy sḥmry* JRAS '29, 108[3]: N. the shepherd of the cattle of S. (cf. also KAI 37B 8) - Milik DJD a.l.: the *r't* in DJD ii 17A 4 (heavily dam. context) poss. = QAL Pf. 2 p.s.m./1 p.s. of *r'y$_1$* (highly uncert. interpret.; or preferably = Sing. cstr. (?) of *r'h$_1$*) - Porten & Yardeni sub TADAE A 2.2: the *r'yh* in Herm 2[16] poss. = QAL Part. act. s.m. emph. of *r'y$_1$* (less prob. interpret., cf. e.g. Grelot DAE p. 489, Gibson SSI ii p. 133, 135: = n.p.).
v. *yd'$_1$*, *r'$_1$*.

r'y$_2$ v. *qbl$_1$*, *rwy$_2$*, *rny*.

r'y$_3$ v. *r'$_1$*, *r'y$_6$*, *rṣy*.

r'y$_4$ **OffAr** Sing. abs. *r'y* Cowl 73[6,13,15,17] - ¶ subst. of unknown meaning; prob. countable object.

r'y$_5$ **OldAr** Sing. abs. *r'y* Tell F 2 (Akkad. par. *ri-i-ti*) - ¶ subst. pasture (on this word, cf. also Abou-Assaf, Bordreuil & Millard Tell F p. 28, Kaufman Maarav iii 164, Gropp & Lewis BASOR cclix 47); cf. however Andersen & Freedman FS Fensham 16f.: = food, provender.
v. *r'$_1$*.

r'y$_6$ **Palm** Caquot RTP p. 182: the *r'y>* in RTP 175 and the *r'yy>* in RTP 176 poss. = Sing. emph. of *r'y$_6$* (= shepherd, herdsman), cf. also Drijvers FS Widengren 369 n. 1, CBE 168 (n. 105), cf. however Caquot RTP p. 182f.: or = QAL Part. act. s.m. emph. of *r'y$_3$* (= to be favourable), cf. *rqy$_1$* (cf. Milik DFD 48) :: du Mesnil du Buisson TMP 237: *r'y>* = Plur. emph. of *r'h$_5$* (= meadow, pasture), *r'yy>* = Sing. m. emph. of *r'yy* (= pastoral); in both instances uncert. interpret.

r'yt v. *ryt*.

r'yn v. *z'r$_2$*, *lqwt*.

r'yy v. *r'y$_6$*.

r's **Pun** Sing. abs. *r's* Trip 2[1] (for the reading, cf. Levi Della Vida Lib iii/ii 3f., cf. however Amadasi IPT 35: or l. *rds* (without interpret.)) - ¶ subst. of unknown meaning; prob. indication of function or title (:: e.g. Lidzbarski Handb 369: l. *r'ṣ* = sculptor?).

r'' v. *>rṣ$_1$*, *zr'$_2$*, *mrq$_3$*, *rqy$_2$*.

r'ṣ v. *r's*.

r‘q **Pun** Plur. abs. *r‘qym* Karth xii 50[2] - ¶ word (subst.?) of unknown meaning, Février & Fantar Karth xii 50, 57: = Plur. abs. of *rqy‘* (= foundation), v.d.Branden RSF v 57, 59: = Plur. abs. of rq_1 (= ruins) :: Krahmalkov RSF iii 178ff.: = Plur. m. abs. of rq_2 (= worthless), *r‘qym* = worthless people.

r‘š v. $r’š_1$.

r‘š‘ **Pun** Sing. abs. *r‘š‘* KAI 136[5] - ¶ subst. of unknown meaning, prob. indication of function; *wkn‘ š‘nt ‘sr wšmn r‘š‘* KAI 136[4f.]: she was *r‘š‘* during 18 years :: Février Sem v 64 (div. otherwise): l. *r‘š* (= Sing. cstr. of $r’š_1$; cf. also v.d.Branden BiOr xxxvi 157), for the context, v. also *mš‘rt* and cf. also Garbini FSR 182.

rp’₁ **Ph** PI‘EL Part. s.m. abs. *mrp’* CIS i 41[3] (= Kition A 26; for this interpret., cf. e.g. CIS i a.l. × Vattioni Bibl xl 1012: = Sing. abs. of *mrp’* (= healing), cf. also Loewenstamm CSBA 320 n. 1a, Dahood CISFP i 595) - **Pun** QAL (cf. FR 187) Pf. 3 p.s.m. + suff. 3 p.s.m. (or = PI‘EL?) *rpy’* KAI 66[2]; Part. act. s.m. abs. *rp’* CIS i 321[3], 322[3f.], 323[5], 3513[3] (dam. context), 4884[6], 4885[5], Hofra 92[2], RES 79[7], 1546[3], *rb’* Trip 4 (Greek par. ἰατροῦ, Lat. par. *medici*), 5 (Greek par. ἰατρός, Lat. par. *medicus*), cf. Poen 1006: *rufe* (cf. Sznycer APCI 211) - **Hebr** QAL Part. act. s.m. abs. *rp’* IEJ xxxvi 29 no. 4 (= EI xviii 80 no. 4), *rwp’* AMB 3[19]; PI‘EL Part. s.m. abs. *mrp’* AMB 1[20] - **OffAr** QAL Impf. 3 p.pl.m. *yrpwn* Aḥiq 154 (cf. however Halévy RS xx 68: = PA‘EL of rpy_1 (= to relax, to slacken), cf. Kottsieper SAS 46 (n. 122): = QAL or PI‘EL of root rpy_1 (cf. ibid. 232: = QAL); cf. also Lindenberger APA 154) - ¶ verb QAL (?, v. supra) to heal, to cure, passim; + obj.: KAI 66[2], Aḥiq 154 (dam. context); cf. *hrwp’ kl h’rṣ* AMB 3[19]: the One who heals the whole earth (epithet of God); substantivated Part., physician: CIS i 321[3], 322[3f.], 323[5], Trip 4, 5, IEJ xxxvi 29 no. 4, etc. - PI‘EL to cure, *hmkh whmrp’ lrwḥ grmyh* AMB 1[20]: He who afflicts and cures the spirit of the bones (i.e. the actual illness); *mrp’* poss. epithet of a deity in *b‘l mrp’* = B. the healer (CIS i 41[3]), v. however supra - Levi Della Vida LibSamal. iii/ii 107: l. *r‘b’* (= QAL Part. act. s.m. abs.) in KAI 131, cf. however Levi Della Vida with Amadasi IPT 47 (n. 3): l. *hr/t/n.d.b’* (without interpret.).

v. *bwp*, rb_2.

rp’₂ **Ph** Plur. abs. *rp’m* KAI 13[8], 14[8] - **Pun** Plur. abs. *r’p’m* KAI 117[1] - ¶ subst. m. Plur. *manes*, shades; cf. *l‘l[nm] ’r’p’m* KAI 117[1]: to the divine shades (cf. Lat. par. *D(is) M(anibus) Sac(rum)*); cf. also Karge Rephaim 609ff., Gray PEQ ’49, 127ff., Ferron MC 70ff., Duprez JDG 60ff., de Moor ZAW lxxxviii 330f., Caquot SDB vi 344ff., L’Heureux RACG 111ff., 201ff., 215ff., 227ff., HThR lxvii 265ff., Healy UF x 89ff., Xella CISFP i 405f., Horwitz JNSL vii 37ff., Levine & de Tarragon JAOS civ 654ff., Spronk BAAI 161ff., 210f., 227ff., Smith & Bloch-

Smith JAOS cviii 280ff.

rp'h **OffAr** Sing. abs. *rp'h* Aḥiq 100 (:: Kottsieper SAS 12, 20, 197: l. *dp'h* = Sing. f. abs. of *dp'* (= hot, warm)) - ¶ subst. healing, cure (on this word, cf. Lindenberger APA 79).

rpwy **Hebr** Sing. abs. AMB 3^{19} - ¶ subst. healing.

rpy_1 **Hebr** PI'EL Inf. cstr. *rpt* KAI 196^6 - **Samal** HAPH Pf. 3 p.s.m. *hrpy* KAI 215^8 - ¶ verb PI'EL to loosen; + obj. (hands) = to discourage (someone): KAI 196^6 (for the context, cf. Ginsberg BASOR lxxi 27, Pardee HAHL 101) - HAPH to release; + obj. (prisoners): KAI 215^8.
v. rp'_1.

rpy_2 v. rby_4.

rpyh v. rby_4.

rpq v.Soden Or xlvi 193: > late Babylonian *ripqu* = hoeing (less prob. interpret.).

rṣd v. qr_2.

rṣwn **Hebr** Sing. + suff. 1 p.s. *rṣwny* DJD ii 24B 6 (*rṣwn[y]*), C 6, E 5 - ¶ subst. will; *'n[y m]rṣwny ḥkrt* DJD ii 24C 5f.: I have rented out of my own free will (cf. DJD ii 24B 6f., E 5).

rṣy **Hebr** QAL Pf. 3 p.s.m. *[r]ṣh* TA-H 40^7 (heavily dam. context, uncert. restoration) - **OffAr** QAL Pf. 3 p.pl.m. *r'yw* Samar 2^4, 3^4 (dam. context) - ¶ verb QAL - **1)** to want: TA-H 40^7 - **2)** to be satisfied; *r'yw ḥd mn ḥd 'sr'* Samar 2^4: they were mutually satisfied with the bond (diff. context) - cf. rqy_1.
v. $'rṣ_1$, $ḥrš_2$.

rṣp **Palm** QAL Part. pass. s.m. abs. *rṣyp* CIS ii 3913 ii 101 - ¶ verb QAL to fix, to prescribe; Part. pass. in CIS ii 3913 ii 101 poss. meaning: fixed, established (cf. CIS ii a.l. for reading and interpret.) - Lipiński RAI xvii 41 n. 2, RSF ii 54f.: the *rṣp* in SG-phoen 18 = QAL Part. pass. s.m. abs. (= attached (to)), *'š lmlqrt rṣp* = who is attached to M. (less prob. interpret.; part of n.d.?? :: e.g. Dussaud Syr xxv 229, Conrad ZAW lxxxiii 181 n. 192: *rṣp* = Reshef).

$rṣṣ_1$ v. rqy_2.

$rṣṣ_2$ = chicken > Akkad. *raṣṣīṣu* (cf. v. Soden Or xxxvii 265, xlvi 193, AHW s.v.).

rq_1 v. zrq_1, *r'q*.

rq_2 v. *r'q*, cf. also ryq_2.

rq' v. $rqḥ_1$.

rqb **OldAr** Lipiński Stud 42: l. a form of this root (HAPH Pf. 3 p.s.m. *[h]rqb*) = to eat through in KAI 222B 37 (highly uncert. reading).

rqh = swamp > Akkad. *raqqatu* (cf. Kaufman AIA 88, v.Soden Or xlvi 193; uncert. interpret., cf. also Perles OLZ '18, 70: *rqh* < Akkad.).

rqw v. $'rṣ_1$.

rqwn v. *nklh*.

rqḥ$_1$ **Ph** QAL Part. act. s.m. abs. *rqḥ* RES 1316 - **Pun** QAL Part. act. s.m. abs. *rqḥ* CIS i 3056[2] (for the context, v. *ldp*), 3784[6], 4886[4], 4887[5], *rqh* CIS i 3628[3], *rq*ʾ (?, same word?) CIS i 315[5f.] (cf. also Slouschz TPI p. 244 :: CIS i a.l.: = < *rq*ʿ$_1$, *obtusor*, the one who flattens), 358[4]; PIʿEL Part. s.m. abs. *mrqḥ* Hofra 263[2] (or = subst.? :: Berthier & Charlier Hofra a.l.: = n.p.?) - **DA** QAL Part. act. s.f. cstr. *rqḥt* i 13 (cf. Hoftijzer DA a.l., Levine JAOS ci 197, 199, H.P. Müll ZAW xciv 218, 228 (n. 88), Puech FS Grelot 28 × e.g. Caquot & Lemaire Syr liv 200, Garbini Hen i 180, 185, McCarter BASOR ccxxxix 51, 56: = QAL Pf. 3 p.s.f.; cf. also H. & M.Weippert ZDPV xcviii 98, Hackett BTDA 51) - ¶ verb QAL to pound spices, to prepare perfumes; *rqḥt mr* DA i 13: one who prepares myrrh (or: perfume with myrrh; according to Weinfeld Shn v/vi 145: one who prepares myrrh-unguent for burial; v. however supra); Part. act. perfumer: CIS i 3056[2], etc. - PIʿEL Part. perfumer: Hofra 263[2].
v. *qḥk*.

rqḥ$_2$ **OffAr** Sing. emph. *rqḥ*ʾ ATNS 45b 5 - ¶ subst. perfume; *rqḥ zy mšḥ* ATNS 45b 5: perfume of oil.

rqy$_1$ **Samal** QAL Impf. 3 p.s.m. *yrqy* KAI 214[18] (*[y]rqy*),[22] - **OldAr** QAL Inf. abs. *rqh* KAI 224[18] (cf. e.g. Fitzmyer AIS 189, Degen AAG p. 77, Beyer ZDMG cxx 201); PAʿEL (:: Dupont-Sommer BMB xiii 34, Garbini RSO xxxiv 51: = QAL) Impf. 2 p.s.m. *trqh* KAI 224[18,19] - **OffAr**, cf. Frah app. 17 (*lkḥwn*) for this poss. interpret., cf. Nyberg FP 100 :: Ebeling Frah a.l.: l. *rkybwn* = form of *rkb*$_3$ (= to consider) - ¶ verb QAL to take pleasure in, to look favourably upon; *w*ʾ*l yrqy bh* KAI 214[22]: and may he not look favourably upon it (sc. upon the sacrifice), cf. KAI 214[18]; in Frah app. 17: = to think, to ponder (v. however supra) - PAʿEL (v. supra), to make peace; *rqh trqh bnyhm* KAI 224[18]: you will truly make peace between them (cf. e.g. Rosenthal BASOR clviii 29 n. 5, Donner KAI a.l., Lipiński Stud 56f., Gibson SSI ii p. 49, cf. also Fitzmyer CBQ xx 451: you *prevail* between them), cf. KAI 224[19] - cf. *rṣy*.
v. ʾ*rṣ*$_1$, *r*ʿ*y*$_6$, *rqy*$_2$.

rqy$_2$ **OldAr** QAL (?) Impf. 2 p.s.m. + suff. 3 p.pl.m. *trqhm* KAI 224[6]; 1 p.s. + suff. 3 p.pl.m. ʾ*rqhm* KAI 224[6]; Imper. pl.m. *rqw* KAI 224[6] (cf. e.g. Hoftijzer DA p. 196 n. 28 (cf. also Lemaire & Durand IAS 145, Garr DGSP 140) :: Gibson SSI ii p. 53: poss. = lapsus for *rqy* (= QAL Imper. s.m.) :: (Spitaler with) Degen AAG p. 20 n. 83, 78: *rqw šm* = lapsus for *rqwhm* (= Imper. pl.m. + suff. 3 p.pl.m.) :: Rosenthal BASOR clviii 29 n. 6: *rqw* = QAL Inf.); Inf. abs. *rqh* KAI 224[6] - ¶ verb QAL (?) of uncertain meaning; in the context poss. = to capture, cf. also Garbini RSO xxxiv 50f., l. here root *rqy*$_2$ = *rqq*$_1$ = *r*ʿʿ = *rṣṣ* (Can.; cf. also Ben-Chayyim Lesh xxxv 248, Sader EAS 134 (n. 58), v. also infra) :: Fitzmyer AIS 97, 110: = PA῾EL form of *rqy*$_1$ (= to placate; v. infra), cf. also Rosenthal BASOR clviii 29 n. 5, 6 (v. infra), Degen AAG p. 77f., Gibson SSI ii p. 47, 53, Lipiński Stud 55, Lemaire & Durand IAS 129, 144 :: Dupont-Sommer BMB xiii 32: = forms of the root *rqq*$_1$ = *r῾῾* (= to constrain, to capture; cf. also id. AH i/2, 6) - for *rqw*, cf. also Fitzmyer CBQ xx 450: = detain :: Ben-Chayyim Lesh xxxv 248 (v. also supra) :: Rosenthal BASOR clviii 29 n. 6 = QAL Inf. of *rqy*$_1$ - for the problems of KAI 224^6, cf. Degen AAG p. 20 n. 82, Gibson SSI ii p. 47, 53.

rqyn v. *lqwt*.

rqy῾ **JAr** Sing. abs. *rqy῾* AMB 1^{14}, 7^{14} - ¶ subst. heaven: AMB 1^{14}; *lrqy῾h mlyh slqh* AMB 7^{14}: may the words rise up to heaven (for the context, v. also *mlh*) - cf. *rq῾*$_2$ (sub *bny*$_1$).

v. *r῾q*.

rqm$_1$ **Pun** QAL Part. act. s.m. abs. *rqm* CIS i 4912^3 - ¶ verb QAL to embroider; Part. substantivated: embroiderer (on this root, cf. Vattioni SEL vii 129ff.).

rqm$_2$ **OffAr** Sing. emph. *rqm᾽* TA-Ar 41 obv. 9 - ¶ subst. embroidery (?, uncert. context).

rq῾$_1$ **OffAr** Segal ATNS a.l.: l. *rq῾* in ATNS 46^5 = PA῾EL Imper. s.m. of *rq῾*$_1$ (= to spread), diff. and dam. context, uncert. reading.

v. *rqḥ*$_1$.

rq῾$_2$ cf. *rqy῾* - v. *bny*$_1$.

rq῾h **OffAr** Plur. abs. *rq῾n* Cowl 26^{14}; emph. *rq῾t᾽* Cowl 26^{20} (:: Cowl p. 91: = Sing. emph.) - ¶ subst. of uncert. meaning, to be connected with the rigging of a ship: = ship's shroud?? (cf. Grelot DAE p. 291 n. k (cf. also Cowl a.l., Segal sub ATNS 46: = awning), cf. however Holma Öfversigt af Finska Vetenskaps-Societetens Förhandlingar '15, B no. 5, 15f.: = tissue, type of sail?? and cf. Porten & Yardeni sub TADAE A 6.2: = plating??

rqp v. *šrgb*.

rqq$_1$ v. *rqy*$_2$.

rqq$_2$ v. *rwq*.

rqrq Ebeling Frah a.l.: indication of *rqrq* (= certain kind of bird) in Frah viii 3, 4 (*rk/qrq, k/qr/lk/q*; less prob. reading, cf. Nyberg FP 44, 72: l. here Iran. words).

rrb v. *r᾽rb*.

rš$_1$ v. *mšn*$_2$, *r᾽š*, *rš᾽t*.

rš$_2$ v. *r᾽š*.

rš$_3$ **DA** Garbini Hen i 181, 185: the *rš[* in xd 4 = Sing. abs. of *rš*$_3$ (= poverty), highly uncert. interpret., heavily dam. context.

rš᾽ v. *rš᾽t*, *ršy*$_1$.

rš᾽t **Ph** Sing. abs. *rš᾽t* KAI 26A iii 6, C iii 20 - ¶ subst. f. old age (cf. Bron AION xxxv 545f., RIPK 105f., Gibson SSI iii p. 51, 53, 62, Goldenberg with Tur-Sinai HalSe iii 410f., Swiggers BiOr xxxvii 340, Barré JANES xiii 1ff., Maarav iii 189ff., Lipiński SV 49 :: Honeyman Mus lxi 54, Vaccari with O'Callaghan Or xviii 187, Gordon JNES viii 115, Obermann JAOS Suppl ix 31 n. 83, Röllig KAI a.l, Greenfield ActOr xxix 11 n. 33, IEJ xxxii 180, Gevirtz JNES xxx 90, VT xxxvii 159f., Dahood FS Ziegler ii 40 n. 2, Or li 283f., Kaufman AIA 89 n. 296, Lipiński RTAT 260, Puech RB lxxxviii 98, Pardee JNES xlii 66 (cf. however id. JNES xlvi 138), Healy CISFP i 665: *rš›t* = authority (< root *rš›*, cf. also Alt WO i 283, v.d.Branden Meltô i 52, 54, 81, Del Olmo Lete AO i 289) :: Davies & Hawkins Heth viii 272ff.: = abundance, prosperity :: Lipiński OLZ '82, 458: or = Sing. cstr. (= enjoyment, pleasure) :: H.P.Müller TUAT i 644: = property (< root *rš›/y* (= to acquire)) :: Dupont-Sommer RA xlii 174: pro *rš›t n‹mt* l. *rš* (= Sing. cstr. of *r›š*$_1$ (= high degree)) + *›tn‹mt* (= Sing. abs. of subst. *tn‹mh* prec. by *aleph prosth.*; = delight) :: Friedrich FuF xxiv 79: l. *dš›t* (= Plur.? abs. of *dš›h* (= young verdure), cf. also Levi Della Vida RCL '49, 277, 286: > prosperity?); *rš›t n‹mt* KAI 26A iii 6: good old age (cf. Barré Maarav iii 191ff.).

ršd **OffAr** a form of this root (QAL/PA‹EL Impf. 1 p.s.) *›ršd* (reading of *d* uncert.) in Sach 78 i A 3, meaning unknown.

ršh$_1$ **JAr** Sing. abs. *ršh* MPAT 51^{5,9} - ¶ subst. authority; *wršh l› ›yty lk ‹my bgw drth dyly* MPAT 51$^{9f.}$: you have no authority with me inside my courtyard (i.e. over my courtyard), cf. MPAT 51^{5}.

ršh$_2$ v. *wršh*.

ršw$_1$ **OffAr** Sing. cstr. *ršwt* Cowl 26^{17} - ¶ subst. Grelot DAE p. 292 (n. o): prob. = debt (cf. Akkad. *rāšūtu*); *ršwt mṣn* Cowl 26^{17}: (according to Grelot ibid.) amount of the bill (meaning of *mṣn* derived from context), cf. however Porten & Yardeni sub TADAE A 6.2: *d/ršwt* not to be combined with *mṣn* :: Cowl a.l.: *ršwt* = government of, *mṣn* = lapsus for *mṣrn* (= Egypt) :: Holma Öfversigt af Finska Vetenskaps-Societetens Förhandligar, '15 B no. 5, 16f.: *ršwt* = adj. strong (said of wood), *mṣn* = Plur. abs. of *mṣ* (= indication of certain kind of wood? (cf. also Whitehead JNES xxxvii 133 n. 90, Segal sub ATNS 40 (also *mṣn* indication of kind of wood))).

v. *ršwt*.

ršwt **Hebr** Sing. abs. *ršwt* DJD ii 22,1-9^{5}, *ršt* DJD ii 22,1-9^{6}; + suff. 3 p.s.m. *ršwtw* DJD ii 30^{28} - **JAr** Sing. abs. *rš[w]t* MPAT 48^{5} - ¶ subst. - **1)** authority; *ršwt šl‹lm* DJD ii 22,1-9^{5}: everlasting ownership (cf. also DJD ii 22,1-9^{6}, MPAT 48^{5}) - **2)** private property, territory, terrain; *ršwtw wbytw* DJD ii 30^{28}: his terrain and his house - the same word (Sing. emph. *ršwt›*) poss. in ATNS 40^{3} (cf. Teixidor JAOS cv 733: = *ršw*$_1$ (cf. also Grelot RB xcii 450f.); Segal ATNS a.l.: = Sing. emph. of

ršw2 (= a kind of wood); cf. also Williamson JEA lxxiii 268).
v. *rštwʾ*.

ršy1 **Samal** QAL Impf. 3 p.s.m. *yršy* KAI 214[27,28] (cf. however e.g. Dion p. 219, Gibson SSI iii p. 74f.: = APH (cf. also Stefanovic COAI 176)) - **OldAr** QAL Impf. 2 p.s.m. *tršh* KAI 224[9] - **OffAr** QAL Pf. 3 p.s.m. *ršh* Cowl 8[24], ATNS 4[6] (cf. Porten & Yardeni sub TADAE B 8.7 :: Segal ATNS a.l.: = QAL Part. act. s.m. abs.); suff. 2 p.pl.m. *rškm* Cowl 25[12]; 1 p.s. + suff. 2 p.pl.m. *ršytkm* Cowl 25[12]; 1 p.pl. *ršyn* Cowl 20[16]; + suff. 2 p.s.m. *ršynk* Cowl 28[9]; + suff. 2 p.pl.m. *ršynkm* Cowl 20[4,7]; Impf. 3 p.s.m. *yršh* Cowl 8[26], Krael 9[19], 12[27]; + suff. 2 p.s.m. *yršnk* Krael 12[27]; + suff. 2 p.s.f. *yršnky* Cowl 8[12], 13[9], 43[10], Krael 9[18,19], 10[12] (for a haplography in this text, cf. Porten & Szubin JAOS cvii 231); + suff. 2 p.pl.m. *yrškm* Cowl 25[15]; 1 p.s. + suff. 2 p.s.m. *ʾršnk* Cowl 9[13]; + suff. 2 p.s.f. *ʾršnky* Cowl 8[20], 43[4] (*ʾršnk[y]*), Krael 4[13]; 3 p.pl.m. *yršwn* Cowl 20[11,13,14], 25[14]; + suff. 2 p.pl.m. *yršwnkm* Cowl 20[11] (*yršw[nk]m*; for the reading problems, cf. also Porten & Yardeni sub TADAE B 2.9)[,13]; 1 p.pl. *nršh* Cowl 25[10], 28[9], Krael 12[26]; + suff. 2 p.s.m. *nršnk* Krael 12[25]; Inf. *mršh* Cowl 28[8]; Part. act. s.m. abs. *ršh* Cowl 44[5] - **Nab** QAL Part. act. (or = adj. *ršy3*?) s.m. abs. *ršy* CIS ii 209[4], 210[3], 214[5], 217[4], 219[3], 223[2], 224[9]; pl.m. abs. *ršyn* CIS ii 212[3] - **JAr** QAL Part. act. (or = adj. *ršy3*?) s.m. abs. *ršy* MPAT 51[6]; s.f. abs. *ršyʾ* MPAT 40[6,17]; pl.m. abs. *ršyn* MPAT 45[8] (cf. however Beyer ATTM 314: l. *[r]šʾyn*), *ršʾyn* MPAT 52[9] - ¶ verb QAL - **1)** to have authority, to have a right to (cf. also Zimmern Fremdw 17 n. 4: < Akkad.?, cf. however Kaufman AIA 89) - a) + *b2*, *ršy ʾlʿzr bzbn bth dk* MPAT 51[6]: E. has authority by the purchase of that house - b) + *b2* + *l5* + Inf., *ʾt ršyʾ bnpšky lmhk* MPAT 40[5f.]: you are free on your part to go (cf. MPAT 40[17f.]); *ršʾyn zbnyʾ ... bʾtrʾ dk ... lmqnh ...* MPAT 52[9]: the buyers have the right ... over this site ... to acquire (it) ... (cf. also Geller BSOAS 51, 316) - c) + *zy*-phrase, *wlʾ ršy ʾnwš ... dy yzbn kprʾ dnh* CIS ii 209[4f.]: no one has the right ... to sell this tomb (cf. CIS ii 212[3], 214[5], 219[3f.], 223[2], 224[9]; cf. Greenfield Mem Yalon 67f.) - d) + *l5* + Inf., *wlʾ ršy ʾnwš lmktb bkprʾ dnh* CIS ii 210[3f.]: no one has the right to make an inscription on this tomb - e) + *l5* + *ʿl7*, *wltršh ly ʿly[h]* KAI 224[9]: you shall not assert your authority over me therein (for this interpret., cf. e.g. Fitzmyer AIS 112, Gibson SSI ii p. 49, 54, Lipiński Stud 56, cf. also Greenfield SVT xxxii 111 (or l. *ʿlʾ* (= in this matter) pro *ʿly[h]*?), cf. Lemaire & Durand IAS 119, 129, 145) :: e.g. Dupont-Sommer BMB xiii 32, AH i/2, 6: you must not contest it with me (cf. Donner KAI a.l., Rosenthal ANET 660; cf. also Sperling JANES i/1, 39) - **2)** to suit, to start a process (for this meaning, cf. Joüon MUSJ xvii 36ff., Porten Arch 192 n. 15, Kaufman AIA 89, Muffs 31 n. 2, 197) - a) + obj.: Cowl 20[7,11,13], 25[12] - b) + obj. + obj., *ʾršnky dyn wdbb* Cowl 8[20]: I will institute against you suit or process (cf. Cowl 8^{12}, 9^{13}, 25^{15}, Krael 9$^{18,19f.}$, 10^{12}, 12^{27}) - c) + obj. + obj. + *bšm*, *yršnky dyn wdbb bšm byt› zk* Cowl 13^{9}: he will institute against you suit or process in the matter of this house (cf. Cowl 43^{4}) - d) + obj. + obj. + *‹l›* (about it): Cowl 28^{9} - e) + obj. + *bšm*: Cowl 43^{10} - f) + obj. + *‹l dbr* + obj., *›ršnky ‹l dbrh dyn* Krael 4^{13}: I will institute suit against you concerning it - g) + obj. + *‹l›* (about it): Cowl 20^{14} - h) + obj. + *b$_2$* + *qdm$_3$*, *ršynkm bdyn ... qdm rmndyn* Cowl 20^{4}: we have instituted a process ... against you before R. (the magistrate) - i) + *l$_5$*, *yršwn lbnykm* Cowl 20^{11}: they will start a suit against your sons (cf. Cowl 20^{13}, 25^{10,14}, Krael 9^{19}, 12$^{26,27f.}$) - j) + *l$_5$* + *‹l$_7$* (concerning): Cowl 44$^{5f.}$ (?, dam. context) - k) + *l$_5$* + *‹l dbr*, *nršh lbr ... lk ... ‹l dbr pṭwsyry ‹bd› zk* Cowl 28$^{9f.}$: we will start a suit against a son of yours ... in the matter of P. this slave - l) + *‹l$_7$* (concerning): Cowl 8$^{26f.}$, 20^{16} - m) + *‹l$_7$* (against) + *‹l dbr*, *lmršh ‹lyk ... ‹l dbr pṭwsyry* Cowl 28^{8}: to bring suit against you ... in the matter of P. - n) + *‹l$_7$* (concerning) + *qdm$_3$* (before): Cowl 8^{24} - **3)** for the meaning in KAI 214^{27,28}, v. *šḥt$_1$* - the *ršh* in NESE ii 87 ii 2 a form of this root?, cf. Altheim & Stiehl AAW v/1, 75, cf. also Degen NESE ii 88: *ršh* = form of *ršy$_1$* or = n.l. or l. *mšh* = form of *mšy* or = n.l. :: Altheim & Stiehl AAW v/1, 75: or l. *ršm* (= Qal Pf. 3 p.s.m. of *ršm*)?? (on this text, cf. also Teixidor Syr xlvii 373) - on this root, cf. also Greenfield Mem Yalon 79ff.

v. *yrš*, *nks$_3$*, *nš$_1$*, *rš›t*, *škḥ*.

ršy$_2$ v. *ndš*.

ršy$_3$ v. *ršy$_1$*.

ršy$_4$ **Palm** Sing. m. emph. *ršy›* Syr xii 139^{6}, *r›yš[y›]* Syr xvii 351^{8} (or = Plur.?, dam. context); Plur. (or = Sing.?) m. emph. *r›yšy›* Syr xvii 353^{6} (dam. context) - ¶ adj. principal, supreme; *[ml]k› ršy›* Syr xii 139^{6}: supreme king; in Syr xvii 353^{6} prob. substantivated, cf. also Milik DFD 303.

ršy‹ **OffAr** Sing. m. emph. *ršy‹›* Aḥiq 171; Plur. m. abs. *ršy‹n* Aḥiq 168 - ¶ adj. wicked, substantivated adj., wicked person: Aḥiq 168, 171 (on this text, cf. Greenfield FS Moran 196ff.).

ršm v. *byk*, *ršy$_1$*, *šym$_1$*.

rš‹ v. *r›š$_1$*.

ršp **Ph** Plur. abs. *ršpm* KAI 15, RES 766A 3, B 2, etc. - ¶ subst. in all instances in the comb. *›rṣ ršpm* (for which, v. *›rṣ*), exact meaning of *ršp* unknown, cf. for the diff. interpret.: Meyer ZAW xlix 13ff.: *ršpm* = flames, the gods of flames/of the fire (cf. also v.d.Branden BO xxiii 43f., GP p. 33), Albright FS Haupt 147ff.: *ršpm* = *manes*, shades (cf. also Röllig KAI a.l.), Lewy HUCA xviii 472: *ršpm* = Plur. *magnitudinis* of n.d. *ršp*, Vattioni AION xv 53, 61: *ršpm* = Plur. of *ršp* indicating either gods in general or gate-keeper gods.

ršt$_1$ v. *ršwt*.
ršt$_2$ v. *r'št*.
rštw v. *rštw'*.
rštw' **OffAr** diff. word in MAI xiv/2, 66^7 (or l. *dštw'*?, cf. also Porten & Yardeni sub TADAE B 1.1); Dupont-Sommer MAI xiv/2, 75: poss. = lapsus for *ršwt'* (= Sing. emph. of *ršwt* (= authority)), *phy ly rštw' mn npšk* MAI xiv/2, 66$^{6f.}$: and further this I demand from you (for a comparable transl., cf. also Grelot DAE p. 72); Bauer & Meissner SbPAW '36, 419: *rštw'* (= Sing. emph. of *rštw* (= first)) = in the first place (cf. also Koopmans 97).
rt v. *bn$_1$*.
rt'$_1$ v. *rty*.
rt'$_2$ v. *rty*.
rtb$_1$ v. *ktb$_1$*.
rtb$_2$ **Nab** Savignac RB xliii a.l.: l. *rtb'* (= Sing. m. emph. of *rtb$_2$* (= strong, solid)) in RB xliii 575 no. 17 (cf. however for the correct reading and interpret. Strugnell BASOR clvi 29f.: l. *ktb'* prec. by Arab. article *'l* = n.d. (cf. also Albright BASOR clvi 37f., Milik & Teixidor BASOR clxiii 22ff., Hoftijzer RelAr 21 (n. 35)) :: Milik & Starcky Syr xxxv 247 (n. 3): l. *nṣb'* = Sing. emph. of *nṣb$_3$*).
rty **OffAr** Pa'el Imper. s.m. *rt'* Aḥiq 177 - ¶ verb Pa'el to pity; + obj. (for this interpret., cf. Cowl p. 246, Grelot DAE p. 446, Silverman JAOS lxxxix 696 (n. 32), Lindenberger APA 181), cf. also Epstein ZAW xxxiii 232, Baneth OLZ '14, 352, Cowl p. 246: or = to admonish?; cf. Leand 40d, o; cf. however Kottsieper SAS 47f., 233: = Sing. abs. of *rt'$_2$* (= blockhead, nitwit).
rtm$_1$ **Ph** Qal Pf. 3 p.s.m. *rtm* KAI 27^{16} (for this reading and interpret., cf. Caquot FS Gaster 48f., Avishur PIB 248, 253, Garbini OA xx 284, 286 (cf. also Lipiński RTAT 265, Zevit IEJ xxvii 111 (n. 12), Gibson SSI iii p. 82f., 86) :: Dupont-Sommer RHR cxx 134f., 141f.: *rtm* = Sing. cstr. of *rtm$_2$* (= fodder, pasture) :: du Mesnil du Buisson FS Dussaud 422, 424: l. *dtm* = *d$_3$* + *tm* (= Sing. m. abs. of *tm$_3$*) :: v.d.Branden BO iii 46: l. *dtm* = *d$_3$* + Qal Pf. 3 p.s.m. of *tmm$_1$* :: Albright BASOR lxxvi 9, Gaster Or xi 42 n. 5, 62, Röllig KAI a.l., NESE ii 18, 23f., Cross & Saley BASOR cxcvii 44f. (n. 13), Xella AION xxii 276, Dahood Bibl xlviii 543, l. 353, RPIM 129, Sperling HUCA liii 4, 9, de Moor JEOL xxvii 108: l. *tm* = Sing. m. abs. of *tm$_3$* :: Torczyner JNES vi 24f., 29: l. *[b]tk* = *b$_2$* + Sing. cstr. of *twk* (= centre)) - ¶ verb Qal to bind; *'š rtm py* KAI 27^{16}: whose mouth one has bound (for par., cf. also Tawil Or xliii 61ff.).
rtm$_2$ v. *rtm$_1$*.
rtq$_1$ v. *trq*.
rtq$_2$ **JAr** Aph Pf. 3 p.pl.m. *'rtqw* AMB 15^8 - ¶ verb Aph to knock;

ʾrtqw ʿl [... AMB 15[8]: they knocked on ... (cf. also Naveh & Shaked AMB a.l.).
rtt$_1$ v. *ytr*$_1$.
rtt$_2$ **JAr** PAʿEL Part. s.f. abs. *mrttʾ* AMB 14[3] - ¶ verb PAʿEL to shake, to make tremble; *rwḥ* (uncert. reading) *mrttʾ* AMB 14[3]: a spirit that shakes (sc. someone).

Š

š$_1$ **Ph** Sing. abs. *š* KAI 24[8] (cf. e.g. Röllig KAI a.l., Gibson SSI iii p. 35 :: Sperling UF xx 333: = Sing. abs. of *š*$_2$ (= barley, related to *šʾh*$_1$)),[11], 26A iii 2, C iv 6 - ¶ subst. sheep.
v. *ʾhb*, *mlk*$_5$, *mlš*$_1$, *mt*$_6$.
š$_2$ v. *š*$_1$.
š$_3$ v. *šṭr*$_2$.
š$_4$ v. *šlm*$_2$.
š$_5$ v. *šnh*$_2$.
š$_6$ v. *šʿrh*.
š$_7$ v. *šṭ*$_1$, *šql*$_3$.
š$_8$ v. *šmn*$_2$.
š$_9$ v. *špṭ*$_2$.
š$_{10}$ **Ph** *š* CIS i 112b 2, *ʾš* KAI 10[2], 13[3], 14[4], 18[1], 24[1,4,6,7] (for l. 6 and 7, cf. FR 124c, 258a, 325, cf. already e.g. Lidzbarski Eph iii 228f., 237, Torrey JAOS xxxv 366, Landsberger Samʾal 51 × e.g. Bauer ZDMG lxvii 686, Poeb 35, Dupont-Sommer Syr xxiv 46, Collins WO vi 185, Avishur PIB 208, 211, Gibson SSI iii p. 34, 36f.: = Sing. abs. of *ʾš*$_2$ (cf. also de Moor UF xx 167, Sperling UF xx 329ff.) :: Fales WO x 12: in l. 6 = *ʾš*$_6$ (= *yš*), in l. 7 = *ʾš*$_2$ :: Schuster FS Landsberger 443: = Sing. abs. of *ʾš*$_1$), 26A i 2, 27[16] (cf. e.g. Albright BASOR lxxvi 9 n. 23, Cross & Saley BASOR cxcvii 45, Röllig KAI a.l., Gibson SSI iii p. 83 :: du Mesnil du Buisson FS Dussaud i 422, 424, 430: l. *qš* = n.d. (cf. also Dupont-Sommer RHR cxx 134f., 141) or n.l. or m. Sing. abs. of *qš*$_3$ (= old) :: v.d.Branden BO iii 46: *qš* = Sing. abs. of *qš*$_2$ = stubble), 30[1] (for the context, v. *ʾš*$_1$; cf. e.g. H.P.Müller ZA lxv 108f., Masson & Sznycer RPC 15, 17 :: v.d.Branden Meltô i 33 n. 40: l. *ʾš* = Sing. cstr. of *ʾš*$_1$ :: Dupont-Sommer RA xli 202f.: l. *ʾš[mn]* = n.d. being part of n.g.), 34[1], 43[4], CIS i 8[2] (= DD 2), DD 13[1], 14[1], Syr xlviii 396[4] (cf. Caquot Syr xlviii 403, Gaster BASOR ccix 19, Cross CBQ xxxvi 488 (n.22), Röllig NESE ii 29, Garbini OA xx 288f., 292, de Moor JEOL xxvii 111 :: Gibson SSI iii p. 89f.: = Sing. abs. of *ʾš*$_2$ or Sing. + suff. 3 p.s.m. of *ʾš*$_2$ (*ʾš*$_2$ = fire > lightning; cf. already Lipiński RSF ii 51f., RTAT 267, v.d.Branden BiOr xxxiii 13, Avishur PIB 267, 269, UF x 31, 34) ::

Liverani RSF ii 37: = Sing. abs. of *ʾš*$_1$ (= everyone; cf. also Baldacci BiOr xl 129), Hill 52 no. 5 (for this reading, cf. e.g. Clermont-Ganneau RAO ii 80f., Cooke NSI p. 46 n. 3, 349f., Dussaud THSA 59) × e.g. Babelon p. cix and 86, Lewy HUCA xviii 439 (n. 68): l. *ʾm* (= Sing. abs. of *ʾm*$_1$), cf. also Hill a.l., for the reading *ʾm*, cf. also Bordreuil & Tabet Syr lxii 180, Bordreuil GHPO 304), etc., etc., *ʾm* KAI 14^{15} (lapsus :: Swiggers BiOr xxxvii 341: = Sing. + suff. 1 p.s. of *ʾm*$_1$) - **Pun** *š* KAI 118^{1}, 173^{3}, CIS i 315^{5}, 317^{4}, 2096^{3}, 5947, Punica xi 1^{1}, Karth x 131^{1}, 132^{2} (for the reading of the context, cf. Fantar Sem xxv 72f.), CT xx (79/80), 9^{1} (or pro *prkʾ š* preferably l. (div. otherwise) *prk* (= n.p.) *ʾš*), etc., etc., *ʾš* KAI $69^{5,13}$, 72^{2}, 73^{5}, 74^{1}, 112^{1}, 113^{2}, 116^{2}, 156, 159^{1}, 173^{1}, CIS i 180^{2}, 181^{2}, 3975^{3}, 4956 (in both last-mentioned instances *šʾ* prob. misprint), Antas 61^{1}, 65^{1}, Moz iv 97^{2} (= SMI 11), vi 98^{2} (= SMI 18), 99^{2} (= SMI 19), MontSir ii 80^{1}, Karth xii 53^{2} (:: Krahmalkov RSF iii 179, 184: = variant of *z*$_1$), etc., etc., *ʿš* CIS i 387^{2}, 770^{2}, 1328^{1}, 2535^{3}, 3771^{3}, 4335^{2}, 4698^{2}, 4961^{1}, 5000^{3}, RES 329^{2}, CB vi 22 (?, v. infra), *šʾ* Hofra $11^{2f.}$ (:: Berthier & Charlier Hofra a.l.: *šʾ* = variant of *z*$_1$), Punica xviii/ii 127^{2}, *šʿ* CIS i 654^{4}, *ʾ* (lapsus) CIS i 668^{4}, 866^{2} (or l. *ʾ[š]?*), 2683^{3}, 2984^{2}, 3577^{3}, 4447^{4}, 5145^{2}, *ʾd* (lapsus) RES 362^{2}, CIS i 1828^{2}, *ʾm* (lapsus) CIS i 475^{3}, *ʾn* (lapsus) CIS i 5289^{3}, *ʾšʾ* (lapsus for *ʾš ndrʾ*??) CIS i 4755^{3}, *šʾš* (lapsus?, cf. also Février JA cclv 61, or = *š*$_{11}$ (= variant of *z*$_1$) + *ʾš*?, cf. Chabot Punica a.l.) Punica ix 9^{1}, *ʾt* (lapsus) CIS i 3677^{2}, cf. KAI 178^{1}, Poen 930: *sy*, cf. Poen 933: *sy* (in *syllohom*; cf. Schroed 310, FR 33 n. 1, 121, 239, 282.3c, Sznycer PPP 73 :: L.H.Gray AJSL xxxix 77f.: *syllohom* = Sing. + suff. 3 p.pl.m. of *ṣl*$_2$ (= shadow > protection)), cf. Poen 1023: *sy* (variants *si*, *su*), cf. IRT 886e (= Aug xvi 547): *sy* in *sylo* (cf. Levi Della Vida OA ii 82, Vattioni Aug xvi 546f.), cf. IRT 879^{1}: *sy* (second *sy*, cf. Vattioni AION xvi 41, Aug xvi 544, cf. also Levi Della Vida OA ii 85, 91 (div. otherwise): l. *sysy* poss. = lapsus for *sy* (= *š*$_{10}$) :: Krahmalkov RSF iii 184 (div. otherwise): l. *ysy* = *ʾz*$_1$ (= *z*$_1$)), cf. IRT 906^{2}: *[s]y* (poss. reading, cf. Levi Della Vida OA ii 73, cf. however Vattioni AION xvi 50ff.: l. *y* = *w* (cf. also idem Aug xvi 550)), cf. IRT 906^{3}: *ꝭy* (in *ꝭyly*, cf. Levi Della Vida OA ii 73 :: Vattioni AION xvi 50ff., Aug xvi 550 (div. otherwise): l. *ꝭ* (= abbrev. of *sestertii*) + *y* (= *w*)), cf. Poen 930, 935: *si*, cf. Poen 940: *si* (in *sicorathi* variant *succorati*), cf. Poen 949: *si* (cf. Schroed 292, Sznycer PPP 129 :: L.H.Gray AJSL xxxix 78, 80: = *zh* = *z*$_1$ (= here)), cf. Poen 943: *si* (in *silli*, cf. Schroed 291f.; uncert. interpret., cf. Sznycer PPP 126, cf. also L.H.Gray AJSL xxxix 77f.), cf. Poen 1141: *si* (in *silli*), cf. Poen 944: *se* (cf. Sznycer PPP 126f.; v. however *ʾš*$_1$), cf. Apul 47: *se* (or div. otherwise: *esse*?), cf. KAI 179^{3}: *su* (= IRT 889; or l. *sy*?, cf. e.g. Vattioni AION xvi 45, Aug xvi 551), cf. Poen 935: *ys* (cf. Sznycer PPP 84), cf. Poen 936: *ys* (cf. Sznycer PPP

87, cf. however Schroed 290, 312, L.H.Gray AJSL xxxix 77f., J.J.Glück & Maurach Semitics ii 110: = *yš*), cf. Poen 940: *is* (poss. interpret., cf. Sznycer PPP 117f., Krahmalkov Or lvii 57, 61 :: L.H.Gray AJSL xxxix 77ff.: l. *istymihy* (pro *isthymhimihy*) = HITP Impf. 3 p.pl.m. of *šmḥ* (= to rejoice) :: J.J.Glück & Maurach Semitics ii 103 (div. otherwise): l. *isthym* (= Sing./Plur. + suff. 3 p.pl.m. of *ʾšh*$_3$ (= sacrifice)), cf. Poen 948: *us* (cf. Sznycer PPP 128 :: Schroed 292, L.H.Gray AJSL xxxix 78 : = *yš*), cf. Poen 946: *s* (cf. Sznycer PPP 127 :: Schroed 291f., 312, L.H.Gray AJSL xxxix 77f.: *s* = *yš*), cf. Poen 947: *s* (in *sitte*, v. *ʾt*$_6$), cf. KAI 175[3]: υς, Diosc iii 96: ες - **Amm** (cf. Sivan UF xiv 229, Jackson ALIA 60, 79f., Lipiński BiOr xliii 449) *š* SANSS-Amm 36 (= CSOI-Amm 80 = Jackson ALIA 77 no. 49 = CAI 56), *ʾš* AUSS xiii 2[6] - **Hebr** *š* DJD ii 22,1-9[5,6], 24B 4, 11, 12, C 7, SM 49[6,7,8,10,12,13], 75[2,4], 76[2,3,5], etc., *šh* SM 6[3] (in comb. *šhlrby*), EI xx 256[8], (combined with *yš*) *šʾyš* DJD ii 24C 7 - ¶ particle introducing phrase/subordinate clause (v. also infra) - A) with relative function - **1)** introducing subordinate clause - a) introducing verbal clause - α) with antecedent, *my bbny ʾš yšb tḥtn* KAI 24[13f.]: any of my sons who shall sit in my place; *ḥwrn ʾš rtm py* KAI 27[16]: H whose mouth is bound (v. *rtm*$_1$); *ʾrṣt ʿzt ... ʾš bl ʿn kl hmlkm* KAI 26A i 18f.: strong lands ... which none of the kings have been able to subdue; *ʾnk yḥwmlk ... ʾš pʿltn hrbt bʿlt gbl [m]mlkt ʿl gbl* KAI 10[1f.]: I am Y. ... whom the lady the mistress of G. has made king over G.; *ʿṣmt ʾš pʿlt* KAI 14[19]: the mighty deeds which I performed; *wkl ʾdm ʾš ysp lpʿl* KAI 10[11]: and every man who will do further work; *k[p]rt ḥrṣ ... ʾš ytn ʿbdk* DD 13[1]: the chiselled sphinx (v. *ḥrṣ*$_5$, *kprt*) ... which your servant gave; *kl ʾš ytn l mtš* EpAn ix 5[6f.]: all that M. has given him; *ʿbn ʾš ṭʿnʾ lmʿryšʿt* Punica ix 1[1]: the stone which is erected for M.; *mtnt ʾš ytn lbʿl ḥmn ytnbʿl ...* Moz ix 156[1f.] (= SMI 37): gift which Y. has given to B.H.; *mqdšm šnm ʾš pʿl bʿl tnsmt* KAI 137[1]: the two sanctuaries which the citizens of T. have made; *qmdʾ ʾš ʿlʾ bbn mʾt mʿqr* KAI 124[3]: C. who became the adoptive son of M.; *kl šthpṣ* DJD ii 30[23]: everything you want; *my š ytn lk thṭyn* DJD ii 44[8f.]: whoever will bring you the grain; *hkhn ... šʿšh hpsypws* SM 75[2f.]: the priest ... who made the mosaic; cf. also the foll. constructions, *bmqmm bʾš kn ʾšm rʿm* KAI 26A i 14f.: in the places where there were wicked men; cf. also *kl šyš ly wšʾqnh* DJD ii 30[23]: everything I have and which I will acquire; for *mʾš* v. *mh*$_2$ - β) without so-called antecedent, *ʾš ndr ʿbdʾlm* KAI 18[1]: what A. has voted; *ʾš ytnʾt ʾnk* KAI 54[2]: what I have erected; *ʾš pʿl ʾšmnḥlṣ* RES 1214[1f.]: what E. has made; *sml ʾz ʾš ytn mlk mlkytn* CIS i 91[1]: this statue is the one which king M. gave; *mzbḥ z ʾš ynḥ bnḥdš* KAI 58: this altar is the one which B. has erected; *wʾnḥn ʾš bnn btm lʾln ṣdnm* KAI 14[17f.]: we were it who built temples for the gods of the Sidonians; *ʾš ndr ḥmlkt ...* Moz vi 98[2f.]: which Ch.

has voted; *š ndr bdmlqrt* CIS i 761[2]: that which B. has voted; etc., etc. - b) introducing nominal clause - α) with antecedent, *wp‘l ’yt kl ’š ‘lty mšrt* KAI 60[3f.]: and he did all that was required by him by way of service; *bšnt 31 l’dn mlkm ptlmys ... ’š h’ št 57 l’š kty* KAI 40[1f.]: in the 31st year of the lord of kings P. ... that is the 57th year of the men of K.; etc.; *kl ’š lsr t ’bn z* KAI 79[6ff.]: everyone who wants to remove this stone (cf. CIS i 3784[1f.]; cf. also FR 268.2); *qṣt ‘pr š’yš b‘yr* DJD ii 24C 7: part of (v. *qṣt*$_{1}$; ?) the terrain which is in I.; *kl šyš ly* DJD ii 30[23]: everything which is mine; *mn hywm ‘d swp ‘rb hšmṭh šhm šnym šlmwt* DJD ii 24E 8ff.: from this day until the end of the Eve of the Release that is (a number of) complete years; *h‘pr šhw’ šly* DJD ii 24E 6: the plot which is mine; cf. also *nsy’ [yš]r’l bmḥnh šywšb bhrwdys* DJD ii 24E 2: the prince of Israel in the encampment (i.e. in the field) who resides in H. - **2)** introducing a phrase - a) prepositional phrase - α) with antecedent, *wbyrḥ mp‘ ’š bšnt 4 l’dn mlkm ptlmyš ...* KAI 43[6]: in the month M. in the 4th year of the lord of kings P.; *’rṣt dgn h’drt ’š bšd šrn* KAI 14[19]: the splendid corn-lands (v. *’rṣ*$_{1}$) in the plain of Sh. (cf. also EpAn ix 5[2f.,4f.] (cf. Mosca & Russell EpAn ix 14)); *l’šmn ’š b‘n ydl* MUSJ xlix 493[2]: to E. who is at the source Y.; *wl’dmm ’š ‘l dl* KAI 37A 6: and for the men who were at the door; *hmzbḥ nḥšt zn ’š bḥṣr z* KAI 10[4]: this altar of bronze which is in this court; *mlkt hbn’ ’š bmqdšm ’l* KAI 137[2]: the building activities in these sanctuaries; *hqdš ’š ly* KAI 17: her sanctuary (× Gibson SSI iii p. 117: *’š* starting new clause (cf. also Teixidor Syr liii 315) :: e.g. Röllig KAI a.l., Coxon PEQ ’83, 76: my sanctuary; v. also *qdš*$_{2}$); *’š ’lm ’š lmlqrt* Lévy SG-Ph 18: the prophet (v. *’š*$_{1}$) of M. (cf. Lévy SG a.l., Lipiński RSF ii 54f., cf. also Cooke NSI p. 361, Miller UF ii 182 (n. 27) :: Herr SANSS-Ph 5 (div. otherwise): l. *’š’l* (= n.p.) *m’š ...*); *l’dn ’š ly* KAI 43[9]: to my lord; *qb‘m šl ksp* Mus li 286[4]: goblets of silver; *whdlht ’šl* KAI 18[3f.]: its doors; *h’š šl’* NP 130[3]: her husband; *NP] ’š b‘m hkrl’* Antas 61[1]: NP who belongs to the assembly of K. (cf. Antas 51[1f.]; for par., v. *‘m*$_{1}$); *NP ’š ‘l knṣwl‘t* Karth xii 50[1]: NP who was charged with the consulship (v. *knṣwl‘t*); *hmḥšbm ’š ln* RCL ’66, 201[7]: their accountants (v. *ḥšb*$_{1}$; for this interpret., cf. Mahjoubi & Fantar RCL ’66, 209 × Dupont-Sommer CRAI ’68, 117, 131: = our accountants); *hmks’m ’š b‘mq qrt* RCL ’66, 201[5]: the *mks’m* who are in the lower town (v. *‘mq*$_{2}$); *bymarob syllohom* Poen 933: under their protection; *bani silli* Poen 1141: my son of mine (variant *bene siilli*); *hprnsyn šl byt mškw* DJD ii 42[1]: the administrators of B.M.; *kl šbw w‘lyw mkrty* DJD ii 30[4]: everything which is in or on it I have sold; *’štw šl dwsts* DJD ii 30[25f.]: the wife of D.; *hgll’ym šhṣlkm* DJD ii 43[4]: the Galileans who are with you; *ršwt šl‘lm* DJD ii 22,1-9[5]: an everlasting ownership; *mškbh šl prṭywsh* Frey 570[1f.]: The tomb of P. - β) without so-called antecedent, *šhy šlw* DJD ii 42[4]: that she is his - b) non-prepositional phrase - α1) with antecedent and with possessive meaning, *hkhnt šrbtn* RES 7[1f.] (= CIS ii 5942 = TPC 4): the priestess of our lady; *[m‹š]n ‹ṣmm šytnmlk* RES 951: urn for the bones of Y.; *mnṣbt š btb‹l* Punica xx 1[1]: the stele of B.; *›rš bn š mgnm* CIS i 315[4f.]: A. son of M.; *‹mt ›š ‹štrt* CIS i 263[3]: the female servants of A. (:: v.d.Branden BiOr xxxvi 158: *›š* = Plur. cstr. of *›š*$_1$; v. *›mh*$_2$); *‹bd›šmn š›zrt ‹bd›šmn bn bd‹štrt* CIS i 3712[3ff.]: A. belonging to the *familia* of A. the son of B.; *›štm š zw›sn* Punica xi 1[2f.]: the wife of Z.; *alonim ualonuth ... sy macom syth* Poen 930: the gods and goddesses of this place; *m‹šn š‹ṣmm* RES 950D 1: the urn for the bones ...; *wks›t šhnskt l›lm ›wgsṭs* KAI 122[1]: the throne for the statue of the divine August (v. *nskh*); *hbnm š›bnm* KAI 100[2]: the builders of stones (i.e. the stone masons); *hḥršm šyr* KAI 100[6]: the wood-craftsmen; *felioth iadem si rogate* KAI 178[1f.]: the handiwork of R. (v. *yd*); *›š b‹mt ›š ‹štrt* CIS i 263[3f.]: who belongs to the slavegirls of Ashtarte (v. *›mh*$_2$; :: CIS i sub 263, Slouschz TPI p. 235, Harr 79: = Sing./Plur. cstr. of *›š*$_1$ (cf. also FR 240.7: = Plur. cstr. of *›š*$_1$); cf. also CIS i 3776[4]); *ḥtm š ṣry* JKF i 44: seal of S.; etc., etc.; cf. *brkmlqrt [›]š ‹[z]rb‹l bn grskn bn mgn bn ḥmlkt bn knt* ... KAI 77[1f.]: B. (property) of (i.e. servant of/client of?) A. the son of G. the son of M. the son of Ch. the son of K.; cf. KAI 64[2], CIS i 317[4], 2705[4], 2791[4f.], etc.; cf. also *mgn bn bd› šḥpṣb‹l* KAI 49[36]: M. son of B. servant of Ch. (cf. e.g. Röllig KAI a.l., cf. also Benz 125, 316 :: Zevit JANES vii 107: *ḥpṣb‹l* = Qal Pf. 3 p.s.m. of *ḥpṣ*$_2$ + n.d.) - α2) with antecedent and without possessive meaning, *h‹pr šhzh* DJD ii 24C 9: this plot (cf. Milik DJD ii p. 127f.) - β) without so-called antecedent, *š ›m‹štrt* RES 509: (tomb) of A.; *š b‹štrt* Hofra 110: (vow) of B.; *š b‹lšlk ... mtnt ›š ṭn› lb‹l* Hofra 250[1ff.]: (vow) of B. ... the gift he erected for B.; *š ‹m mḥnt* Müll ii 75: (coin) of the people of the camp (v. also *‹m*$_1$; cf. coins with inscription *‹m mḥnt*) - B) subordinate clause with non-relative function - a) introducing verbal clause, *‹l kkh š l› thy ›mwr* ... DJD ii 42[6]: for that reason that you will not say ...; *pqdty ... š lh ›ḥr hšbt yṭlwn* DJD ii 44[8ff.]: I order ... that they must not (?) bring it after the Sabbat (diff. context); *tsl‹ hzw› ›n mqbl hmk š›prk* EI xx 256[1f.]: I am accepting this *sela‹* from you with the understanding that I will repay you; with principal clause deleted (at the beginning of a letter after introductory formula; cf. Pardee JBL xcvii 339), *šyd‹ yhy lk š ...* DJD ii 42[2f.]: let it be known to you, that ...; *štšlḥ ... ḥmšt kwryn ḥ[ṭy]n* DJD ii 44[2f.]: you must send 5 *kor* grain - b) introducing nominal clause, *yd‹ yhy lk šhprh ... šhy šlw* DJD ii 42[2ff.]: let it be known to you that the cow ... that she is his - C) preceded by prep., *›ḥr ›š p‹l ṣyw‹n* NP 130[2]: after he made a funerary monument; *km ›š qr›t* ... KAI 10[7]: when I called (v. also *km*$_2$); *kmh š ‹št[y] lbn ‹plwl* DJD ii 43[6f.]: as I have done to B.A. (v. also *km*$_2$);

for other instances of $\check{s}_{10}$ preceded by prep., cf. poss. DJD ii 22,1-9[6], 24B 11, 30[26], 46[7] - for *ʾlly š*, v. *ʾlly* - e.g. Lidzbarski Handb 322, 371, 445, Eph i 318f., Clermont-Ganneau RAO iii 106f., Cooke NSI p. 186f., Loewenstamm Lesh xxiii 82, Donner KAI a.l., Stiehl with Altheim & Stiehl AAW i 232, Kaddari PICS 105 n. 13, Segert AAG p. 327: l. *š* (= $\check{s}_{10}$) at the beginning of KAI 225[1] (*š* + *šnzrbn*; cf. also Delsman TUAT ii 573), incorrect reading and interpret.: l. *šnzrbn* = n.p. (cf. Kokovtsov with Lidzbarski Eph i 318f., Kaufman JAOS xc 270f., cf. also Degen ZDMG cxxi 134f., GGA '79, 25, Teixidor Syr xlviii 461, Gibson SSI ii p. 95f., Stefanovic COAI 288 (n. 1) (for the reading, cf. already Clermont-Ganneau Et ii 193f.: l. *š* (= $\check{s}_{10}$) + *nzrbn* = n.p., cf. also Halévy RS iv 281, 369f., Hoffmann ZA xi 208ff.)) - e.g. Lidzbarski Handb 371, 445, Eph i 318f., Clermont-Ganneau Et ii 193f., 201, Cooke NSI p. 190, Loewenstamm Lesh xxiii 82, Donner KAI a.l., Stiehl with Altheim & Stiehl AAW i 232, Kaddari PICS 105 n. 13, Segert AAG p. 327 (cf. also Delsman TUAT ii 574): the *šʾgbr* in KAI 226[1] = $\check{s}_{10}$ + *ʾgbr* (= n.p.), incorrect interpret., *šʾgbr* = n.p. (cf. Kokovtsov with Lidzbarski Eph i 318f., Kaufman JAOS xc 270f. (cf. also Degen ZDMG cxxi 134f., GGA '79, 25, Teixidor Syr xlviii 461, Gibson SSI ii p. 97f.)) - Fales sub AECT 30 (= Del 4): l. $\check{s}_{10}$ in AECT 30 (improb. reading and interpret., cf. Kaufman JAOS cix 99) - Dupont-Sommer JKF i 203f.: l. *l šlw zh* in AMB 7[2] (= l_5 + ($\check{s}_{10}$ + l_5 + suff. 3 p.s.m.) + z_1; cf. *mn šlw zh* in l. 7), improb. interpret., cf. Naveh & Shaked AMB p. 68, 72: l. *lšlwnh* resp. *mn šlwnh* = prep. (l_5 resp. mn_5) + n.p. - for the etymology of *š*, *ʾš*, etc., cf. e.g. Harr 55, Gevirtz JNES xvi 124ff., Hoftijzer VT viii 289 n. 1, Garbini ISNO 105f., FR 95a, 121, 122b, v.d.Branden GP p. 15, 60, Segert GPP p. 75, 108 - for the syntactic use in Ph. and Pun., cf. FR 291, 310.2-3, Schuster FS Landsberger 431ff., Segert GPP p. 171f., 219, 260f., cf. also Levine EI xviii 147ff. -
v. *ʾš*$_{1,2}$, *byt*$_2$, z_1, *ḥrš*$_7$, *yš*, *mʾš*$_1$, *mlk*$_5$, *mṣbh*, *nš*$_1$, *nšʾ*$_1$, *sʿd*, *ʿrkh*$_1$, *ʿšy*, *pʿr*$_2$, *šʾl*$_1$, *šḥṭ*$_3$.

š$_{11}$ v. z_1.

šʾ$_1$ v. z_1.

šʾ$_2$ v. $\check{s}_{10}$.

šʾ$_3$ v. *mlš*$_1$.

šʾh$_1$ v. *š*$_1$, *šʾh*$_2$.

šʾh$_2$ **Samal** Sing. abs. *šʾh* KAI 215[6,9] (cf. Landsberger Samʾal 63 n. 164, Dupont-Sommer Sf p. 37, Pleiade 635, Greenfield Or xxix 99, Lesh xxxii 363 (n. 21), Albright HTS xxii 44, Dion p. 37, 39, 94, 415, Younger JANES xviii 97, Sader EAS 167 :: Halévy RS ii 167f., Cooke NSI p. 173f., 176, Donner KAI a.l., JSS xii 279, Gibson SSI ii p. 79, 83: = *šʾh*$_1$ (= corn (cf. also Delsman TUAT i 629)); on this subject, cf. also Avishur SSWP 463 n. 1) - **OldAr** Sing. abs. *šʾt* KAI 222A 21 (for the form, cf. Wesselius AION xxx 265f. :: Degen AAG p. 54 n. 24: = segolate form or archaic form); Plur. abs. *š'n* KAI 222A 23, *s'wn* Tell F 20 (Akkad. par. *lahrātu*; for the form, cf. Abou-Assaf, Bordreuil & Millard Tell F p. 41, Zadok TeAv ix 122, Kaufman Maarav iii 149, 169, Wesselius BiOr xl 182, Pardee JNES xliii 256, Israel ASGM xxiv 79f., Greenfield & Shaffer RB xcii 50f., Gropp & Lewis BASOR cclix 53, Huehnergard BASOR cclxi 93, Andersen & Freedman FS Fensham 36, Garr DGSP 96 :: Vattioni AION xlvi 364: or = representing *s'hwn*? = their cattle?; cf. also Huehnergard ZDMG cxxxvii 276 n. 36) - **OffAr** Sing. emph. *t't'* Sach 76 i A 2 - ¶ subst. sheep, ewe; *wkbrt ḥṭh wš'rh wš'h wšwrh* KAI 215[9]: and wheat and barley and sheep and cows were plentiful (v. *šwrh*); *wšb' š'n yhynqn 'mr* KAI 222A 23: seven sheep shall suckle a lamb (cf. Tell F 20) - for the etymology, cf. Albright BASOR cx 16 n. 48, Greenfield Or xxix 99, ActOr xxix 12 n. 38, Degen WO iv 57 (n. 46), ZDMG cxix 175 n. 23 (cf. also Baneth OLZ '32, 451 n. 1, Driver JSS xiii 38, Pardee JNES xxxvii 196, xliii 256, Younger JANES xviii 97); for less prob. interpret., cf. Dupont-Sommer Sf p. 37f., Fitzmyer AIS 41 and further Perles OLZ '11, 503, Lidzbarski Eph iii 256, Joüon MUSJ xviii 18f.

š'h$_3$ v. *šn'h*.

š'h$_4$ v. *s'h$_1$*.

š'wl **OffAr** Sing. abs. *š'wl* Cowl 71[15]; cf. Frah ii 20 (*šwlh*; cf. Nyberg FP 64, cf. also Ebeling Frah a.l.) - ¶ subst. *sheol*, netherworld (= n.g.).

š'wr v. *š'r$_2$*.

š'y$_1$ v. *nš'$_1$*, *šhynn*.

š'y$_2$ cf. Paik 941: *š'ywt*; prob. verbal form of this root; meaning unknown.

š'ylh v. *š'l$_1$*.

š'ys v. *šš$_1$*.

š'k **Pun** Plur. abs. *š'km* Trip 18[2] (poss. interpret., cf. Levi Della Vida Lib iii/ii 20; or = Sing. abs. of *škm$_2$*??, cf. also Levi Della Vida Lib iii/ii 20 n. 4, Février JA ccxxxvii 89) - ¶ subst. of uncert. meaning; poss. = container.

š'l$_1$ **Pun** QAL Impf. 1 p.s. + suff. 3 p.pl.m., cf. Poen 939 *yslym* (cf. Sznycer PPP 107, J.J.Glück & Maurach Semitics ii 114 :: Schroed 290f., 314 (div. otherwise): l. *ysl* (= QAL Impf. 1 p.s.) *ymmon* (= *hmwn$_2$*) :: Zevit JANES vii 107 (div. otherwise): l. *ys* (= *š$_{10}$*) *lymmon* (= *l$_5$* + *mn$_5$*) = from), cf. Poen 949: *ussilim* (cf. Sznycer PPP 129: *ussilimlim* dittography for *ussilim*, cf. also L.H.Gray AJSL xxxix 77 :: Schroed 291f., 315: *ussilimlimmim* dittography for *ussilimmim* = lapsus for *ussilimmun* (= QAL Impf. 1 p.s. + *hmwn$_2$*) :: Zevit JANES vii 107 (div. otherwise): l. (as reconstructed text) *iusim* (= QAL Part. act. m. pl. abs. of *yṣ'*) + *limin* (= *l$_5$* + *mn$_5$*) = from); HITP Impf.

1 p.s. + suff. 3 p.pl.m., cf. Poen 931: *ysthyalm* (variants: *isthyalm*, *istialm*; cf. L.H.Gray xxxix 76ff.), cf. Schroed 290, 306, Sznycer PPP 58 :: J.J.Glück & Maurach Semitics ii 104 (div. otherwise): l. *mysthyalm* (= HITP Part. m. pl. abs.) - **Hebr** QAL Impf. 3 p.s.m. *yš'l* TA-H 18[2f.] - **Samal** QAL Impf. 3 p.s.m. *yš'l* KAI 214[23]; 1 p.s. *'š'l* KAI 214[4] (*'š'[l]*),[12] - **OffAr** QAL Pf. 3 p.s.m. *š'l* Aḥiq 77 (heavily dam. context), Driv 12[3] (cf. Porten & Yardeni sub TADAE A 6.15 :: Driv p. 82: rather = lapsus for *š'lt* (= QAL Pf. 1 p.s.), cf. also Grelot DAE p. 325), ATNS 51[3] (heavily dam. context); + suff. 3 p.s.m. *š'lh* Aḥiq 11; + suff. 3 p.s.f. *š'lhy* JRAS '29, 108[14] (dam. context); 2 p.s.m. (or 1 p.s.) *š'lt* Cowl 47[5] (reading uncert., heavily dam. context); 1 p.s. *š'lt* Krael 7[3], 14[2] (*š'[l]t*, for the reading, cf. Porten & Yardeni sub TADAE B 6.1, Porten AN xxvii 85); 1 p.pl. *š'ln* ATNS 1[7]; Pf. pass. 3 p.s.m. *š'yl* ATNS 1[5], 4[2,9], 90[1] (heavily dam. context), 134[2] (heavily dam. context); 3 p.s.f.*š'ylt* ATNS 3[6], 12[1] (heavily dam. context); 1 p.s. *š'ylt* Cowl 7[6] (*š'yl[t]*; for this reconstruction, cf. Epstein ZAW xxxii 143 n. 4, Porten & Greenfield JEAS p. 124, Porten Or lvi 92, Porten & Yardeni sub TADAE B 7.2 :: Leand 43h'', Joüon MUSJ xviii 61: l. *š'yl[h]* :: Cowl p. 20f.: l. *š'yl[']*; v. infra), 16[3] (dam. context); 3 p.pl.m. *š'ylw* ATNS 13[1]; 2 p.pl.m. *š'yltm* Cowl 20[8]; Impf. 3 p.s.m. *yš'l* KAI 233[12] (*[yš]'l*), Cowl 30[2], 31[2] (*[y]š'l*), 40[1] (*[y]š'l*); + suff. 3 p.s.m. *yš'lh* ASAE xxxix 357[4] (uncert. reading and interpret., cf. also Aimé-Giron ASAE xxxix 359f.); 3 p.pl.m. *yš'lw* Cowl 37[2], 39[1], 41[1] (*yš'[lw]*), 56[1], AG 52[4] (dam. context), NESE i 11[1]; + suff. 1 p.s. *yš'lwnny* Cowl 65 viii 1; Imper. s.m. *š'l* KAI 233[12] (:: Bowman UMB xx 277 : = QAL Pf. 3 p.s.m.), Cowl 16[9] (or preferably l. *[y]š'l*? = QAL Impf. 3 p.s.m., cf. Porten & Yardeni sub TADAE A 5.2), Sem xiv 72 conv. 4 (dam. context); Part. act. m. s. abs. *š'l* Krael 16E 3, Herm 1[3,6], 6[2] (dam. context), 8[7] (*[š]'l*; heavily dam. context), RES 495B 4, 6 (= CIS ii 138; cf. however e.g. Degen NESE i 33f.: = QAL Pf. 3 p.s.m.); pl.m. abs. *š'ln* Herm 6[7]; ITP Impf. 2 p.s.m. *tšt'l* Driv 4[3], 12[8], F ii A 25[1] (dam. context); 3 p.pl.m. *yšt'lw* Cowl 76[4] (for this reading, cf. Porten & Yardeni sub TADAE A 5.4; dam. context); 2 p.pl.m. *tšt'lwn* Driv 7[9]; cf. Nisa-c 362[1] (*š'ylw* = QAL Pf. 3 p.pl.m.), cf. also GIPP 64 - **Nab** APH Impf. 3 p.s.m. *yš'l* CIS ii 206[4] - **Palm** APH Pf. 1 p.s. *'š'lt* MUSJ xxxviii 106[3] - ¶ verb QAL to ask, passim - **1)** to ask for information, to interrogate - a) + obj. (indicating the one to whom the question is directed): Poen 939, 949, Aḥiq 11, ATNS 1[7] - b) + obj. (indicating the one to whom the question is directed) + direct discourse, *š'lhy lm mh tb'y* JRAS '29, 108[14]: he asked her: what do you want?; *š'l hmw hṣd[']* ... KAI 233[12]: ask them: is it true ...? - c) + l_5 (indicating the one to whom the question is directed), *mlk' š'l lgbry'* Aḥiq 77: the king interrogated the men (dam. context) - d) + l_5 + $'l_7$, *š'l* (v. however supra) *ltrwḥ wdyn' '[l] dnh* Cowl 16[9]:

ask T. and the judge about this - e) + *'l_7* (concerning) + n.p.: RES 495B 4, 6 (dam. context), Herm 1[6] - **2)** to ask for something - a) + obj. + *mn_5* (from), *wmh 'š'l mn 'lhy* KAI 214[12]: and what I asked from the gods; *ḥlky' gbrn 5 š'l* (v. supra) *mn [nḥ]tḥwr* Driv 12[3]: he has asked N. for the Cilicians, 5 men - b) + *mn_5* + *l_5* (object) + *l'ntw*, *wš'lt mnk lnšn yhwyšm' šmh 'ḥtk l'ntw* Krael 7[3]: and I asked from you the woman named Y. your sister as a wife - **3)** with object *šlm* - a) with divine being as subject (cf. Fales JAOS cvii 457f.), *šlm mr'n 'lh šmy' yš'l šgy' bkl 'dn* Cowl 30[1f.]: may the God of Heavens favour our lord exceedingly at all times (cf. Cowl 31[2], 37[1f.], 39[1], 40[1], 56[1], NESE i 11[1]; cf. Birkeland ActOr xii 81ff., cf. also Cowl p. 53f., Krael p. 286f., Leand 33a, Porten & Greenfield ZAW lxxx 227, Fitzmyer JBL xciii 214f., Dion RB lxxxix 531 (n. 26), 534ff., Loewenstamm CSBA 437f. :: Brockelmann GVG i 526, Joüon MUSJ xviii 6, 55: l. in these texts instead of QAL: HAPH (= to grant) + obj. *šlm* (= well-being), cf. also Grelot VT iv 354 n. 1) - b) with human being as subject (cf. Fales JAOS cvii 458), *ḥrwṣ š'l šlmhn* Herm 1[3]: Ch. asks after their welfare (cf. Herm 6[2,7]) - cf. also *YHWH yš'l lšlmk* TA-H 18[2f.]: may the Lord favour your well-being (cf. also Pardee JBL xcvii 338, Dion RB lxxxix 541ff., Sarfatti Maarav iii 79f.) - QAL passive, to be interrogated, to be examined: Cowl 16[3], 20[8], ATNS 1[5], 3[6], 4[9] (dam. context), 13[1]; cf. also *wlqḥt lnpš[k] 'bdt š'yl[t]* (v. also supra) Cowl 7[6]: "you took it (and) made it your own". I was interrogated (for this interpret., v. also *'bd_1*, cf. e.g. Porten Arch 316, Grelot DAE p. 93, Porten & Greenfield JEAS p. 124, Porten & Yardeni sub TADAE B 7.2 :: e.g. Cowl p. 20f., J.J.Rabinowitz Bibl xxxix 80 (combining *'bdt* with the foll. *š'yl[]*), cf. also Joüon MUSJ xviii 61); *š'yl ... lqbl mly mnky* ATNS 4[2]: he was interrogated with regard to what M. had said - APH to lend: CIS ii 206[4]; + obj.: MUSJ xxxviii 106[3] - ITP - 1) to ask: Poen 931 - **2)** to be called to account: Driv 4[3], 7[9], 12[8] (cf. Driv p. 50, cf. also Grelot DAE p. 305 (n. c), Whitehead JNES xxxvii 134 :: Benveniste JA ccxlii 304f.: = to punish (cf. also Rundgren ZAW lxx 214f.) :: J.J.Rabinowitz Bibl xli 73f.: = to be accused) - Solá-Solé RSO xli 98, 102f.: l. *š'l* in ICO-Spa 16[3] (= QAL Part. s. m. abs. (= oracle priest, cf. also Delcor FS Ziegler i 32, Ross HThR lxiii 13 n. 38), improb. interpret. (cf. also Heltzer OA vi 266, 268: *š'l* in combination *bny š'l* = borrowed sons > sons devoted to the deity; v.d.Branden RSO xliv 104, 106: *š'l* = something consecrated (sc. to a deity); Krahmalkov OA xi 210ff.: *š'l* = Sing. abs. of *š'l_2* (= request)), preferably l. (div. otherwise) *bn* (v. *bn_1*) *yš'l* (= n.p.), cf. Puech RSF v 85f., 88, Gibson SSI iii p. 65f., Fuentes Estañol sub CIFE 14.01; on this text, cf. also Amadasi sub ICO-Spa 16 - Krahmalkov OA xi 212: l. in KAI 48[2f.] *'š'l* (= QAL Impf. 1 p.s.; uncert. interpret.; cf. also Lidzbarski Eph i 155, 158, Röllig KAI a.l.

(div. otherwise): l. *'š* (= *š*$_{10}$) + *'l[* - a form of this root (*šy'l[*) in ATNS 7[5], Segal ATNS a.l.: restore *š'yl[t]* (= QAL pass. Pf. 3 p.s.f. or *š'yl[w]* (= QAL pass. Pf. 3 p.pl.m.), for the last-mentioned restoration, cf. also Lemaire Syr lxi 341 - a form of this root in Or lvii 16[4] (*š'l*).
v. *'lym*, *'lm*$_1$, *šwy*$_1$.

š'l$_2$ v. *š'l*$_1$.

š'lh **DA** Sing. cstr. *š'lt* ii 15; + suff. 2 p.s.m. *š'ltk* ii 16 - ¶ subst. what one asks for; *š'lt mlk* DA ii 15: what a king asks for (cf. Hoftijzer DA a.l., Garbini Hen i 186; interpret. as "consultation of an oracle", cf. Caquot & Lemaire Syr liv 207, less prob.; on the problems cf. also Amadasi BTDA 72).

š'lwm v. *šlm*$_2$.

š'lm v. *šlm*$_2$.

š'n$_1$ **OffAr** Sing. (or Dual?) + suff. 1 p.s. *š'ny* Aḥiq 206 - ¶ subst. shoe, sandal - Blau PC 116 (n. 9): < Akkad. (cf. also e.g. Zimmern Fremdw 38, Vollmer ZAW lxxx 345f., poss. interpret.) :: Kaufman AIA 30 n. 1: derivation from Akkad. excluded; on this word, cf. also Perles OLZ '11, 503 - the same word (Sing./Dual + suff. 1 p.s. *š'ny*) poss. also in Aḥiq 210 (diff. reading, dam. context).

š'n$_2$ v. *šn'*$_1$.

š'plt **OffAr** Segal ATNS a.l.: l. this word of unknown meaning in ATNS 52b ii 3, poss. to be related to *'pl*$_1$? (reading however uncert.).
v. *mšplt*.

š'r$_1$ **OffAr** QAL Pf. 3 p.s.m. (× Part. act. s.m. abs.) *š'r* Sach 76 i B 7 (cf. Porten Arch 132, 277); ITP Pf. 3 p.s.m. *'št'r* Krael 12[6]; Impf. 3 p.s.m. *yšt'r* Cowl 11[9] - ¶ verb QAL to remain, to rest; *' qmḥ š'r tnh* Sach 76 i B 7: an *ardab* of flour remains here - ITP to remain; *mrbyth zy yšt'r 'ly* Cowl 11[9]: the interest on it which is outstanding against me; *l' 'št'r ln 'lyk mn dmy'* Krael 12[6]: none of the price was outstanding to us from you (on these formulae, cf. Muffs 76f., 173 n. 4, 181f., Yaron RB lxxvii 413f., cf. also Levine FS Morton Smith 46f.).
v. *psšrt*, *š'r*$_2$.

š'r$_2$ **Hebr** Sing. cstr. *š'r* SM 49[1,19,21,24] - **OffAr** Sing. abs. *š'r* ATNS 48[3], Cowl 81[61,62,63,77,106,118] (for the dam. context, cf. Harmatta Act-AntHung vii 373),[131] (*[š]'r*),[132]; cstr. *š'r* ATNS 38[20] (or abs.?, dam. context), KAI 270B 5 (cf. e.g. Porten Arch 275, Levine JAOS lxxxiv 20 (cf. also Dupont-Sommer ASAE xlviii 128f.) :: e.g. Röllig KAI a.l., Gibson SSI ii p. 124f.: = Sing. abs. :: CIS ii sub 137: or = QAL Part. act. s.m. abs. of *š'r*$_1$; for the context, v. *qṭ*) - **Palm** Sing. cstr. *š'r* Ber ii 96[2], *š'wr* DFD 37[4] - **JAr** Sing. cstr. *š[']wr* Syr xlv 101[15]; emph. *š'r'* MPAT 48[4] - ¶ subst. rest; *š'r 'ksdr'* Ber ii 96[2f.]: the rest of the exedra; *š'wr pḥz'* DFD 37[4f.]: the rest of the tribes; *nkys lqn 6 br 3 š'r 1* Cowl 81[63]: Nikias, 6 *log* at 3 quarters, remainder 1 (i.e. prob. 3 quarters of which N. has still one to pay, cf. also Grelot DAE p. 112 n. b); *bš'r šny šbw'* SM 49[21]: in the rest of the years of the seven year period (cf. SM 49[1]; cf. also *byš'r šny šbw'* SM 49[19,24]); etc. - Segal Irâq xxxi 174: the *šr* ibid. l. 4 poss. = Sing. cstr. of *š'r*$_2$ (highly uncert. interpret.) - cf. also the comb. *'d š'r* in ATNS 38[20], 48[3] (up to the remainder ...), exact meaning however uncert., in both instances heavily dam. context - a form of this word poss. in ATNS 24[6] (*š'r[)*, context however heavily dam.

v. *'r'l*, *š'r*$_3$, *š'ry*.

š'r$_3$ Pun Sing. abs. *š'r* KAI 69[4,6,8,10], CIS i 170[2] (*[š]'r*) - ¶ subst. meat, flesh - this word Sing. + suff. 3 p.s.m./f. (*š'rm*) poss. also in KAI 163[3] (cf. Février AIPHOS xiii 167, Röllig KAI a.l.; uncert. context, diff. interpret.) - this word poss. also in KAI 162[2] (Sing. + suff. 3 p.s.f. *š'rm* (cf. Février AIPHOS xiii 165, Röllig KAI a.l.; uncert. context, diff. interpret.)) - Sznycer GLECS x 102: the *sar* in OA ii 83[3] poss. = Sing. abs. of *š'r*$_3$ (= child; uncert. interpret.; cf. also Polselli StudMagr xi 40f. (div. otherwise): l. *ysar* (= n.p.)) :: Levi Della Vida OA ii 84: poss. = Sing. cstr. of *š'r*$_2$ used to indicate the rest (sc. of the family) :: Vattioni AION xvi 40f. (div. otherwise): l. *ysary* (= Sing. abs. or Sing. + suff. 3 p.s.m. of *'šr*$_4$), cf. also Vattioni Aug xvi 539.

v. *bšr*$_2$.

š'r' Nab word of unknown meaning in CIS ii 493[3]; n.p. or indication of function?

š'rh v. *š'ry*.

š'ry OffAr Sing. cstr. *š'rt* Krael 7[23] (*š[']rt*)[,26,27] (or = Sing. cstr. of *š'rh*?), *š'ryt* ATNS 29 ii 2 (dam. context), *šyryt* Cowl 30[11] (cf. e.g. Cowl a.l., Grelot DAE p. 409, Porten & Greenfield JEAS p. 90, Porten & Yardeni sub TADAE A 4.7 :: Galling OLZ '37, 474ff.: l. *šydyt* = Sing. cstr. of *šydy* (= box)); cf. Nisa-b 211[3], 798[5] (*š'ry*, for the form, cf. Altheim & Stiehl AAW ii 217, GMA 476f. :: Diakonov & Livshitz Nisa-b p. 40f.: = Plur. cstr. of *š'r*$_2$), cf. also GIPP 64 - **Nab** Sing. cstr. *š'ryt* CIS ii 350[3], J 57[1] (= CIS ii 235), *šryt* RES 2025[3] (or = n.d.?) - ¶ subst. rest, remainder.

šb OffAr Sing. m. abs. *šb* Aḥiq 6, 17, *sb* (= *sb*$_2$, variant of *šb*; cf. e.g. Coxon ZDMG cxxix 20) Krael 9[17]; m. emph. *šb'* Aḥiq 35 - **JAr** Sing. m. emph. *sb'* MPAT 89[1] (cf. however Beyer ATTM 329, 589: l. *ṭb'* = Sing. m. emph. of *ṭb*$_2$; on reading and interpret., cf. also Bennett Maarav iv 253), 110[2] (cf. Frey sub 1299 :: Fitzmyer & Harrington MPAT a.l.: or = n.p.) - ¶ adj. old; *šb 'nh* Aḥiq 17: I am old (cf. Aḥiq 6); *'nh ymyn sb* Krael 9[17]: I am old of days; *['ḥ]yq[r] zk šb'* Aḥiq 35: the mentioned A. the old man - substantivated adj., elder: MPAT 89[1]; *šm'wn sb'* MPAT 110[2]: S. the elder - Segal ATNS a.l.: l. *sby* (= Sing. + suff. 1 p.s.) = grandfather in ATNS 44 i 2 (less prob. interpret., prob. = part of n.p.,

cf. also Porten & Yardeni sub TADAE B 8.2).
v. *šmym.*

šb'$_1$ **OffAr** word of unknown meaning in Del 44 (poss. = n.p.) - v. *yšbr.*

šb'$_2$ v. *šb'$_6$*.

šbb$_1$ (< Akkad., cf. Kaufman AIA 101; cf. however Yeivin Lesh xxxviii 151f.) - **Palm** Plur. + suff. 3 p.pl.m. *šbbyhwn* SBS 25[3] - ¶ subst. neighbour - the same word (*šbb[*) poss. also in Inv xii 41[1] (cf. also Aggoula Sem xxix 115: l. *šbb[y]* = Sing. + suff. 1 p.s.).

šbb$_2$ = spark, v.Soden Or xlvi 195: > Akkad. *šibūbu* (cf. also idem AHW s.v.; uncert. interpret.).

šbh$_1$ v. *šbṭ$_2$*.

šbh$_2$ v. *yšb$_1$*.

šbwḥh v. *šbṭ$_2$*.

šbw' **Hebr** Sing. abs. *šbw'* SM 49[1,5,19,21,24], 76[3] (dam. context) - ¶ subst. septennate, seven years period.

šbw'h **JAr** Sing. abs. *šbw'h* MPAT-A 46[3] - ¶ subst. oath; *wbšbw'h dkl dypth ... yhy m'yt ...* MPAT-A 46[3ff.]: with an oath that anyone who will open ... may die ...

šbzbn **OffAr** word of unknown meaning in ATNS 43 i 2 (the *ḥzr šbzbn* in ATNS 43 i 2 to be related to the *ḥzr zbn* in ATNS 43 ii 2?? (diff. and dam. context, uncert. reading)).

šbḥ$_1$ **Hatra** PA'EL Part. Sing. m. emph. *mš[b]ḥ'* 404[1] (v. infra) - **Palm** PA'EL Pf. 3 p.s.m. + suff. 3 p.s.m. *šbḥh* SBS 45[8] - ¶ verb PA'EL to praise + obj.: SBS 45[8]; *mrt mš[b]ḥ'* Hatra 404[1] Mrt the glorious (cf. Aggoula Syr lxvii 402f.:: Abdallah Sumer xliii 116 n. 31: *mrt* = f. Sing. abs. of *mr$_4$*) - > Akkad. *šubbuḫu*, cf. v.Soden Or xlvi 195 - a derivative of this root poss. in IEJ xxxvii 27 no. 4[3] (= QAL Part. pass. s.m. abs.?), *yn 'z šbḥ* improved wine from Gaza? (v. also *yyn*), cf. Naveh IEJ xxxvii 30.

šbḥ$_2$ v. *zbḥ$_1$*.

šbṭ$_1$ **JAr** Dupont-Sommer JKF i 203, 207: l. in AMB 7a 10 *šbṭ* (= QAL Imper. s.m. of *šbṭ$_1$* (= to hit)), reading however highly uncert., cf. Naveh & Shaked AMB a.l.: l. *šb?*, Scholem JGM 86: l. *yšb[t]* = magical name.

šbṭ$_2$ **OldAr** Sing. abs. *šbṭ* Tell F 23 (Akkad. par. *šib-ṭu*) - ¶ subst. affliction; *mwtn šbṭ zy nyrgl* Tell F 23: the pest, the affliction of Nergal (cf. also Kaufman Maarav iii 148 (n. 27), Greenfield & Shaffer Irâq xlv 116, Shn v/vi 128, RB xcii 58, Dion FS Delcor 146f., Greenfield FS Rundgren 150).

šby$_1$ **OffAr** Pf. 3 p.s.m. *šbh* KAI 233[15]; 2 p.s.m. *šbyt* Cowl 71[14]; 3 p.pl.m. *šbw* FS Driver 54 conv. 1 - ¶ verb QAL to capture, to make captive; *wšby' zy šbyt bz' šnt'* Cowl 71[14]: the prisoners you have cap-

tured this year; *wšby šbh šrkn mn drsn* KAI 233[15]: Sargon deported prisoners from D.; *l› šbw lntn tmh* FS Driver 54 conv. 1: they have not deported N. there.
v. *šbt$_2$*, *šwb*.

šby$_2$ **Samal** Sing. cstr. *šby* KAI 215[8] - **OffAr** Sing. abs. *šby* KAI 233[15,16] (*šb[y]*); emph. *šby›* Cowl 71[14] - ¶ subst. (with collective meaning) captives, prisoners; *whrpy šby y›dy* KAI 215[8]: he released the captives of Y.; for KAI 233[15], Cowl 71[14], v. *šby$_1$*.

šbyḥyt **Palm** Inv x 44[7] - ¶ adv. laudably, commendably.

šbyṭ **OffAr** Sing. abs. *šbyṭ* Cowl 15[9], 36[2] (cf. Porten & Greenfield JEAS p. 118, Porten & Yardeni sub TADAE B 6.2, Porten GCAV 258, AN xxvii 90; cf. however Cowl a.l.: reading *šbyṭ* imposs.), Krael 7[9] (dam. context) - ¶ subst. m. indicating some article of dress; Cowl p. 48: poss. = closely-woven stuff > shawl (cf. e.g. Porten & Greenfield JEAS p. 20, 52, cf. also Grelot DAE p. 193 (n. h), Porten & Yardeni sub TADAE B 2.6); Kutscher JAOS lxxiv 236: = smooth garment.

šbyl **Hebr** *šbyl* DJD ii 47[4] - ¶ subst. in comb. *bšbyl* DJD ii 47[4]: because of (context however dam.).

šby‘y **Hebr** Sing. m. abs. *šby‘y* SM 106[4]; Sing. f. abs. *šby‘yt* SM 49[1,19,21,23]; cstr. *šby‘yt* SM 49[5] - ¶ ordinal number, seventh; *šby‘yt šny šbw‘* SM 49[5]: the seventh year of the seven years period.

šbyt v. *ḥšb$_1$*.

šbl **Ph** word of unknown meaning in KAI 1[2], poss. subst. (Sing. abs.) indicating some kind of erasing instrument (cf. e.g. Donner WZKMU '53/54, 157 n. 16, Röllig KAI a.l., Galling TGI 49 (n. 4), Gibson SSI iii p. 16) × Teixidor Syr lxiv 139f.: l. *gbl* (= n.l.) :: Albright JAOS lxvii 156 n. 27: l. *šbl* = road, way (for other interpretations, cf. Torrey JAOS xlv 274, Levi Della Vida RSO xxxix 301); for the reading, cf. Ronzevalle MUSJ xii 22 :: Dussaud Syr v 141: l. *šrl* = n.l. (Hades) :: Dussaud Syr vi 107: l. *šrl* = Sing. abs. of *šrl* (= sword) :: Vincent RB xxxiv 189: l. *šrl* = *šr<š>* (= Sing. abs. of *šrš$_2$*) *l<h>* (= *l$_5$* + suff. 3 p.s.m.) :: v.d.Branden BO xxiii 46, Mašr liv 732f., 735: l. *šrl* (= Sing. abs. of *šr$_7$*) + *l<h>* (=*l$_5$* + suff. 3 p.s.m.) :: Aimé-Giron ASAE xlii 317f.: l. *šrl* = *šr›l* (= n.d.) :: Vinnikov VDI xlii 146: l. *tbl* (?) (= Sing. abs. of *tbl$_2$*) = n.l., (inhabited) world (cf. also Gaster Irâq vi 140 n. 222) :: Albright JPOS vi 77, JPOS vii 122ff.: l. *mtbl* (= *mn$_5$* + *tbl*).

šb‘$_1$ **Ph** (**Hebr**?) Impf. 3 p.pl.m. *yšb‘w* KA 11[2] - **OldAr** Impf. 3 p.s.m. *yšb‘* KAI 222A 22, 23, 23f. (*[yš]b‘*), 223A 1 - **OffAr** Qal Impf. 2 p.s.m. *tšb‘* Aḥiq 127, 129 - Itp Impf. 3 p.s.m. *yštb‘* Aḥiq 189 - **Palm** Qal Impf. 3 p.s.m. *yšb‘* CIS ii 4218[7] - ¶ verb Qal to be sated: passim; for KAI 222A 22-24, cf. Hillers 22, 61f.; for KA 11[1], cf. e.g. Scagliarini RSO lxiii 211 (with literature); *wlḥm wmn lm› yšb‘* CIS ii 4218[7]: that he will not be sated with bread and water - Itp to be sated; *yštb‘ k‘s* *mn lḥm* Aḥiq 189: let him that is vexed be satisfied with bread (or preferably: let he gorge himself?, cf. Grelot RB lxviii 193, DAE p. 446, Lindenberger APA 187).

šbʿ$_2$ **Hebr** HIPH Part. s.m. abs. *mšbyʿ* AMB $4^{28,31}$ (*mšby[ʿ]*) - **JAr** APH Pf. 1 p.s. *[ʾš]bʿt* AMB 12^{9}; Part. s.m. abs. *mšbʿ* AMB 8^{3}, 9^{4}, + pers. pron. 1 p.s. affixed *mšbʿnh* AMB 1^{21} - ITP Part. s.m. abs. *[m]štbʿ* AMB 15^{18} - ¶ verb HIPH/APH to adjure + *ʿl$_7$*, *mšbyʿ ʾny ʿlykm* AMB 4^{28}: I adjure you (cf. AMB 1^{21}, $8^{3f.}$, 9^{4}, 12^{9}); *mšby[ʿ] ʾny ʿlykm bšm ymynw* AMB $4^{31f.}$: I adjure you by His right hand; cf. the expression *ʿlyk bḥy* AMB 1^{23}: (I adjure you) by the Living One, and *ʿlyk rwḥh d ...* AMB 9^{1}: (I adjure) you, oh spirit, which ... (for the reading cf. Naveh & Shaked AMB a.l. :: Greenfield Mem Kutscher xxxviii: pro *ʿlyk* l. *lyk*) - ITP to swear, *[ʾnh m]štbʿ lkwn bmn d ..* AMB $15^{17f.}$: I swear to you in (the name of) the One who ...
v. *šbt$_1$*.

šbʿ$_3$ **Ph** Sing. abs. *šbʿ* KAI 26A i 6, ii 7, 13, 16, iii 7, 9, C iv 7, 9 - ¶ subst. plenty, abundance (v. also *trš$_1$*).
v. *šbʿ$_6$*.

šbʿ$_4$ v. *špḥ$_1$*.

šbʿ$_5$ **Pun** v.d.Branden RSF ix 11f., 15: l. *šbʿ* (= Sing. cstr. of *šbʿ$_5$* (= oath)) in Eph i 42 iii 3; improb. reading, cf. Sznycer Sem xxxii 60, 64f.: l. *ʿbd* = part of n.p.

šbʿ$_6$ **Ph** m. cstr. *šbʿ* KAI 27^{17} - **Pun** m. abs. *šbʿ* KAI 76B 6 (dam. context); cstr. *šbʿ* 136^{3}, 137^{5}, 148^{3}, Punica v 4^{6}, vi 2^{4}, xii 29^{3}, BAr '55/56, 32^{4} (= IAM 4); f. abs. *šbʿt* Hofra 59^{4}, 60^{4}, 61^{3} - **Mo** f. cstr. *šbʿt* KAI 181^{16} - **Hebr** m. *šbʿ* Frey 624^{2} (dam. context) - **OldAr** m. cstr. *šbʿ* KAI 222A 21, 22, 23, 24, 27, 223A 1, 5 (*[š]bʿ*), 6 (*[š]bʿ*); f. *šbʿ[t]* KAI 202A 8 - **OffAr** m. abs. *šbʿ* Krael 6^{4}, RES 438^{4}, TH 2 vs. 4; f. abs. *šbʿh* Krael 7^{23}; cf. Frah xxix 7 (*šbʾ*) - **Nab** m. abs. *šbʿ* CIS ii 170^{1}, 182^{3}, 201^{4}, RES 2053^{2}, BASOR cclxiii 78^{4}, on coins, cf. Meshorer NC no. 25, 26; f. *šbʿh* CIS ii 333^{5}, J 22^{4} - **Palm** m. abs. (or cstr.?) *šbʿ* Sem xxxvi 89^{6}; m. emph./f. abs. *šbʿʾ* RTP 758 (cf. Milik DFD 185 :: Caquot RTP p. 165: = n.p.); f. abs. *šbʿʾ* CIS ii 3952^{3}; f. emph. *šbʿtʾ* CIS ii 3987^{3}, Inv xi 70^{4}, xii $45^{6f.}$ (?, v. infra), 47^{1} (dam. context), RTP 292 (cf. du Mesnil du Buisson BiOr xvii 237, Milik DFD 164 :: Caquot RTP p. 159: = n.p.), Syr xxxvi 104 no. 5 (cf. du Mesnil du Buisson BiOr xvii 237, Milik DFD 164 :: Dunant Syr a.l.: = n.p.) - **JAr** m. abs. *šbʿ* MPAT 62^{13} (= DBKP 27), IEJ xl 144^{10} (dam. context); f. abs. *šbʿh* MPAT $41^{1,15}$, IEJ xl 135^{3}, 144^{7} (*šbʿ[h]*; dam. context) - ¶ cardinal number, seven: passim; used in dating, *bʿsr wšbʿ lyrḥ mpʿ* KAI 137^{5}: on the 17th day of the month M.; *bšbʿt ʾrbʿm št lmlkm* Hofra $59^{4f.}$: in the 47th year of his reign (instance with no discongruence of gender); *šnt šbʿ ʾrtḥššš mlkʾ* RES 438^{4}: in the 7th year of king A.; *šnt šbʿ lqldys*

qysr CIS ii 170[1f.]: in the 7th year of the emperor Claudius (cf. CIS ii 182[3], 201[4], RES 2053[2]); *bywm 'sr wšb'h bsywn* J 22[3f.]: on the 17th day of Siwan; *[by]rḥ šbṭ šnt 443 ywm šb't'* CIS ii 3987[3]: in the month Shebat of the 443 on the 7th day; *šb'h bh* IEJ xl 135[3]: the seven(th day) in her (i.e. the week); etc. - Lipiński Stud 108, 110; the *šb'* in Lidzb Ass vi 4 = representation of Akkad. *seba* (= seven, used as name of month (cf. also Fales sub AECT 51)), less prob. interpret., cf. also Lidzbarski Lidzb Ass a.l. - this word poss. also in BiAr xlii 170[2] (*šb'*) or = Sing. abs. of *šb'$_3$* (less prob. interpret.) - the meaning of the diff. *šb't'* in Inv xii 45[6f.] poss. = the seventh generation? :: Naveh JAOS cii 184: = the seven ones :: Aggoula Sem xxix 116: = Sing. emph. of *šb'h$_1$* (= satiety) :: Teixidor Sem xxx 61f.: = Sing. emph. of *šb'h$_1$* (= flourishing) - Aggoula Assur a.l.: l. *šb''* (= f. abs.?) in Assur 27e 2 (uncert. interpret., diff. context).
v. *p'l$_2$*.

šb'h$_1$ **Pun** Sing. abs. *šb't* NP 130[1] (cf. Février RHR cxli 20, Sem vi 19f. :: e.g. Cooke NSI p. 147 (div. otherwise): l. *rš* (= n.p.) *b't* (= Sing. cstr. of *bt$_2$* (= f. of *bn$_1$*)), KAI 145[6] (cf. Février RHR cxli 20, Sem vi 19f., Röllig KAI a.l., v. d Branden RSF i 166, 169, 171 :: Krahmalkov RSF iii 189: = Sing. abs. of *šb'h$_2$* (= eulogy) :: Berger MAIBL xxxvi/2, 158f.: = Sing. abs. of *šbt$_3$* (= rest)),[11] (cf. Février RHR cxli 20, Sem vi 19f., Röllig KAI a.l., v.d.Branden RSF i 166, 171 :: Krahmalkov RSF iii 188, 197: = Plur. abs. of *šb'h$_2$* (= laudation)), Karth xii 50[2] (cf. Février & Fantar Karth xii a.l., v.d.Branden RSF v 57, 59f. :: Krahmalkov RSF iii 181, 204: = QAL Pf. 3 p.s.m. of *šbt$_1$* (= to come to an end)), Karth xii 51[1] (cf. Février & Fantar Karth xii a.l., v.d.Branden RSF v 57, 60 :: Krahmalkov RSF iii 178, 181, 204: = QAL Pf. 3 p.s.m. of *šbt$_1$* (= to come to an end)), Karth xii 53[2] (cf. Février & Fantar Karth xii a.l., v.d.Branden RSF v 57, 60 :: Krahmalkov RSF iii 173 (n. 12), 178, 186, 204: = Sing. abs. of *šb'h$_2$* (= eulogy)), Karth xii 54[2] (cf. Février & Fantar Karth xii a.l., v.d.Branden RSF v 57, 60) - ¶ subst. poss. meaning abundance, passim (cf. Février RHR cxli 20, Sem vi 19f., Röllig sub KAI 145, v.d.Branden RSF v 59f.; cf. however Février & Fantar Karth xii 50f.: = contribution (cf. also Bron RIPK 44)); *ytn šb't* KAI 145[11]: a sumptuous gift (?, v. also *ytn$_2$*); *y'tn' t 'šb't* Karth xii 53[2]: they have given abundantly.
v. *šb'$_6$*, *špḥ$_1$*.

šb'h$_2$ v. *šb'h$_1$*.

šb'h$_3$ **JAr** Beyer ATTM 372: l. *šb'th* (= Sing. emph. of *šb'h$_3$* (= oath)) in AMB 7[10f.], less prob. reading and interpret., cf. Naveh & Shaked AMB a.l. (div. otherwise): l. *šb[..] tḥt* (v. s.v.).

šb'yn v. *šb'm*.

šb'm **Pun** *šb'm* KAI 133[3], 136[3], 171[4], Punica x 2[4], xi 1[4] (cf. e.g.

Lidzbarski Handb 437, reading *sbʿm* (cf. Chabot Punica a.l.) less prob.), xii 27[3] - **Samal** *šbʿy* (casus obliquus) KAI 215[3] - **OffAr** *šbʿn* Cowl 26[11,15] - **Palm** *šbʿyn* CIS ii 4053[5] - **JAr** *šbʿyn* MPAT 52[7], Mas 578[2] (*[š]bʿyn*), *šybʿyn* Mas 566[3] - ¶ cardinal number, seventy: passim; used in dating, *šnt ḥmš mʾh wšbʿyn wtšʿ* CIS ii 4053[4f.]: the year 579; on the context of KAI 215[3], cf. Fensham PEQ '77, 114f.

šbʿn v. *šbʿm*.

šbṣ v. *šʿbṣ*.

šbq₁ **OffAr** QAL Pf. 3 p.s.m. *šbq* Aḥiq 90 (cf. however Kottsieper SAS 233: = QAL Part. act. s.m. abs.); 2 p.s.m. *šbqt* Aḥiq 176 (:: Kottsieper SAS 18, 233: or = Pf. 1 p.s.?); 1 p.s. *šbqt* Krael 5[4], ASAE xxvi 27[2]; + suff. 2 p.s.m. *šbqtk* Aḥiq 175; + suff. 2 p.s.f. *šbqtky* Krael 5[4]; 3 p.pl.m. *šbqw* Aḥiq 162; + suff. 3 p.s.m. *šbqwhy* Cowl 69[5]; 1 p.pl. *šbqn* Cowl 27[1]; Impf. 3 p.s.m. *yšbq* Cowl 54[15], ATNS 35[5]; + suff. 1 p.s. *yšbqn[y]* KAI 266[7] (cf. e.g. Ginsberg BASOR cxi 25, Fitzmyer Bibl xlvi 52, WA 239, Gibson SSI ii p. 113, Porten BiAr xliv 36, Porten & Yardeni sub TADAE A 1.1 :: Dupont-Sommer with Ginsberg BASOR cxi 25 n. 4b: l. *tšbqn[y]* = Impf. 2 p.s.m. + suff. 1 p.s. (cf. Degen ZDMG cxxi 125, 136f.) :: Dupont-Sommer Sem i 51, Donner KAI a.l.: l. *šbqn[y]* = Imper. s.m. + suff. 1 p.s.); 2 p.s.m. *tšbq* Cowl 42[11], ATNS 26[3,5,9]; 1 p.s. *ʾšbqn* Aḥiq 82 (on this form, cf. Lindenberger APA 226 n. 51, Kottsieper SAS 136); + suff. 3 p.s.m. *ʾšbqnh* AE '23, 40 no. 2[8] (diff. context); 3 p.pl.m. *yšbqwn* Cowl 54[6], ATNS 26[8]; Imper. s.m. *šbq* Aḥiq 171; Inf. *mšbq* Aḥiq 193; Part. act. s.m. abs. *šbq* Herm 2[15], 3[4,10] (or = Imper. s.m.?, cf. Greenfield IEJ xix 200 (n. 10), cf. also Bresciani & Kamil Herm p. 427: = Imper. s.m.); pl. abs. *šbqn* Cowl 30[23], 31[23]; pass. s.m. abs. *šbyq* FX 136[18]; s.f. abs. *šbyqh* Krael 5[9,10]; ITP Pf. 3 p.s.m. *ʾštbq* Driv 8[2,4]; Impf. 3 p.pl.m. *yštbqw* Driv 5[9] (forms of this root also in Cowl 69 xiii (*]šbq[*), Sach 79 i 3 (*šbq*)); cf. Frah xxi 6 (*šbkwn*), Paik 945 (*šbqw*), 946 (*šbkw*), GIPP 34, 64, SaSt 23 - **Nab** QAL Pf. 3 p.s.m. *šbq* MPAT 64 i 7; 2 p.s.m. *šbqt* MPAT 64 i 13 - **Hatra** QAL Impf. 3 p.s.f. *tšbw[q]* 342[6] - **JAr** QAL Part. act. s.m. abs. *šbq* MPAT 40[2,13] - ¶ verb QAL to leave, to leave alone, to leave behind, to abandon, to set free, to allow, to permit, etc.: passim - a) + obj., *ʾl yšbqn[y]* KAI 266[7]: let not him abandon me; *mnṭrtn lʾ šbqn* Cowl 27[1]: we did not leave our posts; *dy tšbw[q] m[q]mh* Hatra 342[6]: who leaves her place; *lʾ šbqwhy* Cowl 69[5]: they did not let him go (prob. out of prison); *ʾzt šbqtky bmwty* Krael 5[4]: I set you free at my death (cf. Benveniste JA ccxlii 298f. < Iran., cf. however Greenfield AAASH xxv 113); *wḥwby yšbq* ATNS 35[5]: he will remit my debt; cf. Cowl 54[6] (cf. also Porten & Yardeni sub TADAE A 3.1), Aḥiq 162 - b) + obj. + b_2, *šbqtk bstr ʾrzʾ* Aḥiq 175: I left you behind in the secret hiding-place; *lmšbq zhb bydk* Aḥiq 193: to leave gold in your hand - c) + obj. + l_5, *wšbq kl gšr zy tškḥ lmmh* Herm

3[10]: leave every beam you can find with M. (cf. Porten & Greenfield ZAW lxxx 225, JEAS p. 156, Porten Arch 101, Hayes & Hoftijzer VT xx 103, Hoftijzer SV 113f., Grelot DAE p. 158, Swiggers AION xlii 137, Porten & Yardeni sub TADAE A 2.4 × Bresciani & Kamil Herm a.l., Milik Bibl xlviii 583, Gibson SSI ii p. 136: combine *lmmh* with next clause) - d) + *ʾl*$_6$: ATNS 26[9] (context however dam.) - e) + *b*$_2$, *šbq bydh* Aḥiq 171: leave it to him; *wyhwy ... šbq bbth* Herm 2[15]: and let he leave (them) in his house (v. however supra) - f) + *l*$_5$ (obj.), *šbqt lrḥmyk* Aḥiq 176: you have abandoned your friends; *wšbqt lyhyšmʿ* Krael 5[4]: I set free Y.; *lh šbq ʾnh lh* Herm 3[4]: I will not leave him alone - g) + *l*$_5$ (for, to): ATNS 26[8] (to allow; dam. context), MPAT 64 i 13 (to remit; dam. context); cf. prob. also Cowl 42[11] (cf. however Grelot DAE p. 131: + *l* obj.) - h) + *l*$_5$ + Inf., *lʾ tšbq lmnpq* ... ATNS 26[3]: you will not allow to go forth - i) + *l*$_5$ + *l*$_5$ + Inf., *lʾ šbqn ln lmbnyh* Cowl 30[23]: they do not allow us to build it (cf. Cowl 31[23]) - j) + *ʿl*$_7$, *ʾšbqn ʿl lbbk* Aḥiq 82: I leave (sc. you) to your own heart (i.e. I leave you to yourself) - cf. also *ktwny zy šbqt byt byt YHH* ASAE xxvi 27[1f.]: my tunic which I left in the temple of YHH (cf. Aimé-Giron ASAE xxvi 28: *byt byt* prob. = dittography :: Dupont-Sommer JA ccxxxv 80f., 86f., Grelot DAE p. 368f.: *byt byt YHH* = in the house of the House of YHH (i.e. in an outbuilding dependent of the Temple of YHH)); *wlʾ šbq bny ddy wlʾ ʾyty lh yld* MPAT 64 i 7f.: and my uncle B. did not leave and has no offspring (i.e. prob. he died intestate and without offspring, cf. Starcky RB lxi 165, 172 :: J.J.Rabinowitz BASOR cxxxix 13: i.e. he did not have children nor was a child born to him posthumously) - Part. pass. freed, set free: Krael 5[9,10] (for the context, v. *ṭl*$_2$, *šmš*$_2$); *wrmʾ znh šbyq zy lh* FX 136[17f.]: this is decided, what is his is exempt (cf. Teixidor Syr lii 288; cf. Greek par. καὶ ἔδοσαν αὐτῷ ἀτέλειαν τῶν ὄντων; v. also *rmy*$_1$) - ITP to be left; *bgh ... ʾštbq* Driv 8[2]: his fief ... was abandoned (sc. during the disturbances), cf. Driv 8[4]; *yštbqw* Driv 5[9]: let them be released (sc. from prison) - Teixidor Syr xliv 185: l. *šbq* (= QAL Pf. 3 p.s.m.) in IrAnt iv 122[1] (prob. reading, cf. also Dupont-Sommer IrAnt iv 123 :: Dupont-Sommer IrAnt iv a.l.: l. *šbwr* (= n.p.); for the reading, cf. also Naveh AION xvi 34) - a form of this root (*šbq*) in Cowl 69[13] (dam. context) - Porten & Yardeni sub TADAE A 3.8: l. *[š]byqt* (= QAL Pf. pass. 3 p.s.f.) in Cowl 42[12] (heavily dam. context; poss. reading; Cowl a.l.: l. *[rḥ]qt* = QAL Pf. 1 p.s. of *rḥq*$_1$) - a form of this root prob. also in ATNS 55[2] (*šbq[*) - the form *tšbqn* in Samar 2[8] (dam. context) poss. lapsus for *tštbqn* (= ITP Impf. 2 p.s.f.).

šbq$_2$ **JAr** Plur. abs. *šbq[yn]* MPAT 40[21] - ¶ subst. Plur. divorce; *gṭ šbq[yn]* MPAT 40[21]: writ of divorce.

šbr$_1$ **Ph** QAL Pf. 1 p.s. *šbrt* KAI 26A i 8 (cf. e.g. Röllig KAI a.l., FR 131, Bron RIPK 51, Gibson SSI iii p. 47, 57, Puech RB xcii 292

:: O'Callaghan Or xviii 185: = Sing. cstr. of *šbrh*$_1$ (= totality, group), cf. Gevirtz Maarav v/vi 145ff., 153ff.: = Sing. cstr. of *šbrh*$_1$ (= band, assembly), cf. also Fuentes Estañol VF s.v. *šbrt* :: Gordon JNES viii 109, 113: = Sing. cstr. of *šbrh*$_1$ (= council) :: v.d.Branden Meltô i 36, 38, 81: = Plur. cstr. of *šbrh*$_2$ (= statue); cf. also Alt WO i 280) - **OldAr** QAL Impf. 3 p.s.m. *yšbr* KAI 222A 38; QAL pass. Impf. 3 p.s.f. *tšbr* KAI 222A 38 - **OffAr** QAL Pf. 3 p.pl.m. *tbrw* Cowl 30[9]; Impf. 3 p.s.m. *ytbr* Aḥiq 106; Part. pass. s.m. abs. *tbyr* Aḥiq 190; pl.m. abs. *tbyrn* Cowl 26[13]; cf. Frah xxi 5 (*tblwn*), cf. Toll ZDMG-Suppl viii 33f. - ¶ verb to break; + obj., *kn yšbr ʾnrt* (cf. Greenfield JSS xi 100ff.) *whdd [qšt mtʿʾl] wqšt rbwh* KAI 222A 38f.: so shall I. and H. break the bow of M. and the bow of his nobles (cf. Hillers TC 60); *wʿlʿy tnyn ytbr* Aḥiq 106: and it breaks the ribs of a dragon; *wʿmwdyʾ zy ʾbnʾ ... tbrw hmw* Cowl 30[9]: the pillars of stone ... they broke them; *šbrt mlṣm* KAI 26A i 8: I broke the wicked ones (v. *lyṣ*) - Part. pass. broken; *mʾn ṭb ks[h] mlh blbbh w ... tbyr hnpqh brʾ* Aḥiq 109: a good vessel hides a thing within itself but ... a broken one let it go forth; cf. Cowl 26[13]: broken (said of beams; cf. Grelot DAE p. 291 n. j) - Caquot & Lemaire Syr liv 204: l. *yšbr* (= QAL Impf. 3 p.s.m.) in DA ii 9 (cf. also Garbini Hen i 172, 186; poss. reading; reading *yšbq* also poss., cf. v.d.Kooij DA p. 123: *q* more prob. than *r* :: Hackett BTDA 26, 30, 65, 84, 96, 130 (div. otherwise): l. poss. *yšb* = QAL Part. act. s.m. abs. of *yšb*$_1$).
v. *bwʾ*, *tnrw*.

šbr$_2$ **JAr** QAL/PAʿEL Pf. 3 p.s.f. *šbrt* MPAT 88[2] - ¶ verb QAL/PAʿEL of unknown meaning; Naveh IEJ xx 37: to fail to give birth (highly uncert. interpret.); cf. also Tzaferis Proc v CJS i 3 (Hebr.), Beyer ATTM 345, 702: = to have a difficult delivery (cf. also Hestrin IR p. 258); Fitzmyer & Harrington MPAT p. 228f.: = *šbr*$_3$ (variant of *sbr*$_1$ (= to hope for)), improb. interpret. :: Yeivin in Prolegomenon to G.A.Smith Jerusalem[2], New York 1972, p. lxxviii (div. otherwise): pro *dy šbrt* l. *ryš* or *dyš brt* ... = R. or D. daughter of ...

šbr$_3$ v. *šbr*$_2$.

šbrh$_1$ v. *šbr*$_1$.

šbrh$_2$ v. *šbr*$_1$.

šbšqltʾ **Ph** word (?) of unknown meaning and uncert. reading in RES 1918 (on a bronze object representing the head of a horse or a dog; cf. also Lidzbarski Eph i 272f.).

šbt$_1$ **Pun** YIPH Inf. cstr. (prec. by *l*$_5$) *lšbt* CIS i 5510[3] - **Hebr** QAL Inf. cstr. *šbt* KAI 200[5f.] (cf. Delekat Bibl li 463, Gibson SSI i p. 29 (or = Pf. 1 p.s. of *šwb* or Sing. abs. of *šbt*$_2$, cf. also Gibson JSS xxiv 114), Pardee Maarav i 44, Booij BiOr xliii 644 (cf. also Garbini AION xxii 99: *šbt* = derivative of root *šbt*$_1$ (= end of forced labour/corvee); Talmon BASOR clxxvi 32: = derivative of root *šbt*$_1$ (= time off, dismissal);

cf. also Röllig KAI a.l.) :: Veenhof Phoenix xi 248: = QAL Inf. cstr. of *yšb*$_1$ (or: = Sing. abs. of *šbt*$_2$) :: Amusin & Heltzer IEJ xiv 150, 152, Vinnikov ArchOr xxxiii 547, Albright ANET 568, Suzuki AJBI viii 5, 11ff., Weippert FS Rendtorff 461 n. 29: = Sing. abs. of *šbt*$_2$ (= Sabbat; cf. Lemaire Sem xxi 70, IH i 263f.: = public holiday; cf. also Briend TPOA 135, Lemaire FS Cazelles 277 (n. 2)) :: Naveh IEJ x 133f., Yeivin BiOr xix 5f.: = QAL Inf. cstr. of *yšb*$_1$ + suff. 1 p.s. :: Naveh Lesh xxx 70: poss. = QAL Inf. cstr. of *yšb*$_1$ + suff. 3 p.s.m.; cf. also Cross BASOR clxv 45 (n. 45), Pardee HAHL 20, 22, 237) - ¶ verb QAL to finish working, to stop: KAI 200$^{5f.}$ (cf. Gibson SSI i p. 29, Pardee Maarav i 44 :: Delekat Bibl li 463: = to observe the Sabbath) - YIPH to destroy: CIS i 5510^3 - the diff. *nšbt* in KAI 3^3 poss. = YIPH Impf. 1 p.pl. of *šbt*$_1$ (with meaning: to bring to an end, to settle), cf. Albright BASOR xc 36 (n. 8), JAOS lxvii 159 (n. 50), Iwri JAOS lxxxi 33, Gibson SSI iii p. 11 (cf. also Albright BASOR lxxiii 12 (n. 14): = to make an end) :: Dunand BMB ii 103, 105: = to abandon (sc. an amount of silver) :: Dupont-Sommer ArchOr xvii^1, 161ff.: *nšbt* = QAL Pf. 1 p.s. of *nšb*$_1$ (// *nsb*; = to receive; cf. also Healy CISFP i 664f.) :: Torczyner Lesh xiv 161, 165: = QAL Pf. 2 p.s.m. of *nšb*$_1$ (// *nsb*) :: Obermann JBL lviii 234f., 242: *nšbt* = QAL Pf. 2 p.s.m. of *nšb*$_2$//*nšp* (= to desire) :: v.d.Branden RSF ii 139: = NIPH Pf. 3 p.s.m. of *šbt*$_1$ (= to come to an end, to cease, said of destruction) :: McCarter & Coote BASOR ccxii 19f.: l. *nšbʿt* = NIPH Pf. 1 p.s. of *šbʿ*$_2$ (= to swear) :: Segal sub ATNS 38: poss. to be related to diff. *nšb[*, *nšbʾ* in respectively ATNS 38^{2,5} (v. *nšb*$_3$).
v. *ḥšb*$_1$, *yšb*$_1$, *šbʿh*$_1$.

šbt$_2$ **Hebr** Sing. abs. *šbt* DJD ii 44^{6,10}, AMB 4^{30} - **OffAr** Sing. abs. *šbh* Sem ii 31 conc. 2, RSO xxxii 404^1, FS Driver 54 conc. 5 (:: Naveh AION xvi 25: or = QAL Pf. 3 p.s.m. of *šby*$_1$ (= to capture)?); *šbh* poss. = hypercorrect form of the abs. besides the emph. *šbtʾ* :: Grelot DAE p. 370 n. e: late Aramaic form :: Dupont-Sommer Sem ii 33, RSO xxxii 407, MAI xv/1, 75f.: *šbh* = f. form < root *šb*, *šbt* also < root *šb* (cf. however Pelletier VT xxii 441); Reider JQR xliv 339: *šbh* = not Sabbat, cf. also Segal PEQ '74, 163) - **JAr** Sing. abs. *šbt* Syn D B 8 (= SM 88^{23}; for this reading, cf. Torrey Syn D p. 266, cf. however Naveh SM a.l.: l. *šbh* :: Obermann Ber vii 115f.: l. *šbwḥ[h]*? = praise, or *šbwḥ[ʾtʾ]*), *šbh* MPAT 56^6, IEJ xl 132^7, 140^4, 144^7 (diff. reading)^{,13,14}; emph. *šbtʾ* IEJ xl 132^3, 135^{1,3,6,8}, 140^{1,2} - ¶ subst. - **1)** week; *mšbt lšbt* AMB 4^{30}: from week to week; *ywm ḥd bšbh* IEJ xl 132^7: the first day of the week - **2)** Sabbath; *yhw bw ʾṣlk t šbt* DJD ii 44$^{5f.}$: let them be there with you during the Sabbath; *mḥr bšbh* Sem ii 31 conc. 2: tomorrow at the Sabbath; *ʿd ywm šbh* RSO xxxii 404^1: until the Sabbath day (cf. IEJ xl 132^3, 135^{3,8}, 140^2); for *ʿrwbt šbtʾ* IEJ xl 135^{1,6}, 140^1 v. *ʿrwbh* -

for the Sabbath in Elephantine, cf. Dupont-Sommer MAI xv/1, 81ff., Porten Arch 122ff., JNES xxviii 116ff. - for Greek representations, cf. Pelletier CRAI '71, 71ff., VT xxii 436ff. - the words *šbt'* (ATNS 72a 1) and *šbt[* (ATNS 72b 1; diff. reading, cf. also Garbini RSO lxi 212) prob. no forms of $šbt_2$ (cf. also Segal ATNS a.l.: preferably = n.p.) :: Garbini RSO lxi 212: in ATNS 72a 1: reading *šbt'* mistaken, pro *t* l. *r*.
v. $šbt_1$.

šbt₃ v. $ḥšb_1$, $yšb_1$, $šb'h_1$.

šbt₄ v. *tb'h*.

šbt₅ = dill > Akkad. *šibittu* (cf. v.Soden AHW s.v., Or xlvi 195).

šg'₁ **OffAr** Haph Impf. 2 p.s.m. *thšg'* Aḥiq 137 (cf. Cowl p. 224, 242, Grelot RB lxviii 188, DAE p. 442, Kottsieper SAS 16, 234 :: Ginsberg ANET 429: = Haph Impf. 2 p.s.m. of $šg'_2$ (= to make great); for this form, cf. also Lindenberger APA 134) - ¶ verb Haph to lead astray; *'l thšg' lbb'* Aḥiq 137: lead not your heart astray (for the context, cf. Lindenberger APA 134, 259 nn. 418, 419) - Milik Bibl xlviii 555: the *yšg'* in RES 1795A 2 = Qal Impf. 3 p.s.m. of $šg'_1$ (= to lose one's way, to go astray (uncert. interpret.; for the context, v. *ntn*)); cf. $šgy_1$ - > Akkad. *šagû*, cf. v.Soden AHW s.v. *šagû* II, Or xlvi 195.
v. $šg'_3$.

šg'₂ v. *sgyl*, $šg'_1$.

šg'₃ **OffAr** Sing. m. abs. *šg'* Cowl 54[8], KAI 270A 4 (cf. e.g. Euting Epigraphische Miscellen ii 1 no. 99, Dupont-Sommer ASAE xlviii 123, Donner KAI a.l., Gibson SSI ii p. 124 :: CIS ii sub 137: = Qal Part. act. s.m. abs. of $šg'_1$), Sem xxi 85 conc. 5, *šgy'* Cowl 27[19], 30[2], 41[2], Aḥiq 29, 51, 74, Beh 60, Krael 13[1], Driv 2[1] (*šg[y]'*, for the reading, cf. Yardeni with Porten & Szubin JNES xlvi 39ff.), 3[1], 5[1], 11[5] (for the reading, cf. Porten & Yardeni sub TADAE A 6.14; diff. context), 13[1], RES 1785E 5 (= KAI 264), F 3, 4, AE '23, 40 no. 2[3,8] (diff. context), *šgy* Cowl 41[1]; m. cstr. *šgy'* Aḥiq 106 (:: Lindenberger APA 92, 243f. n. 259: or = $šgy'_1$, subst. to be distinguished from $šgy'_2/šg'_3$ (= multitude)), 165 (*šg[y']*; for the restoration, cf. Lindenberger APA 269 n. 512); Plur. m. abs. *šgy'n* Aḥiq 50, 116, Beh 51 (Akkad. par. *ma-a-du*); f. cstr. (or Sing. f. cstr.) *šgy't* Aḥiq 87 (dam. and diff. context); cf. DEP 153[1], Nisa-c 210[4], 287[2] (*šgy'*), GIPP 64 - **Nab** form *šgy'[* in MPAT 64 ii 2 (heavily dam. context) - **Palm** Plur. m. abs. *šgy'yn* CIS ii 3914[3] (*šgy'[yn]*), 3932[5], SBS 45[6]; f. abs. *šgy'n* CIS ii 3949[3], Inv x 44[4], DFD 13[4], *šgyn* CIS ii 3913 i 4 (Greek par. πλεῖστα), 6, *šgy'n* CIS ii 3932[5] - **JAr** Sing. m. abs. *sgy* MPAT 89[4] (?, heavily dam. context :: Beyer ATTM 329, 644: l. poss. *s[y]gy* = Plur. cstr. of *syg* (= fence, enclosure) :: Puech RB xc 488f.: l. poss. *mḥyy* = Pa'el Part. s.m. abs. of *ḥyy* (= to restore)), MPAT-A 22[10] (v. infra); Plur. m. abs. *sgyn* SM 25[2] (dam. context) - ¶ adj. - **1)** numerous, abundant; *sbl šgy'* Aḥiq 74: abundant sustenance;

wlywmn ʾḥrnn šgyʾn Aḥiq 49f.: and many days after; *zbnyn šgyn* CIS ii 3913 i 6: many times (Greek par. πλειστάκις); *wḥsk rzʾyn šgyʾn* CIS ii 3932[5]: he spent money in a most generous way (v. *ḥsk*); cf. Aḥiq 116, Beh 51, CIS ii 3913 i 4, 3914[3], 3932[5], 3949[3], Inv x 44[4], SBS 45[6] - **2)** substantivated adj., multitude; *bšgyʾ bnn lbbk ʾl yḥdh* Aḥiq 106: let not your heart rejoice in a multitude of children; *mh ṭb šg[yʾ] kby[k]* Aḥiq 165: what is the good of your many thorns - **3)** used adverbially, abundantly, very; *ʾnt ʾḥty šgyʾ ḥkym[* RES 1785E 5 (= KAI 264): you my sister are very wise; *šgyʾ yrgš* Aḥiq 29: he will be most furious; *šlm mrʾn ʾlh šmyʾ yšʾl šgyʾ* Cowl 30[1f.]: may the God of Heavens favour our lord exceedingly; *šlm wšrrt šgyʾ hwšrt lk* Driv 3[1]: I send you much greetings of peace and prosperity (i.e. I send you my very best wishes); cf. Cowl 41[1,2], Krael 13[1], Driv 5[1], 13[1], KAI 270A 4 (v. supra), Aḥiq 51, Beh 60 (cf. also Cowl 27[19] (dam. context), 54[8] (dam. context)); *NP NP ... dsgy sgy hnwn ʿbdw l ...* MPAT-A 22[10]: NP, NP ... who have exerted themselves exceedingly for ... (for the reading *dsgy sgy* (and interpret.), cf. Naveh sub SM 70, Beyer ATTM 364 :: e.g. Fitzmyer & Harrington MPAT a.l., Hüttenmeister ASI 113: pro *dsgy sgy* l. *drgy* (= Plur. abs. of *drg*$_2$) *sgy* (= Plur. m. abs.)) - Caquot & Lemaire Syr liv 196: l. *šg[yn]* (= Plur. m. abs.) or *šg[yt]* (= Plur. f. abs.) in DA i 7, cf. also Garbini Hen i 175: l. *šg[yʾ]* = Sing. m. abs., cf. also Delcor SVT xxxii 54, Lemaire BAT 318 (less prob. reading and interpret., cf. Hoftijzer DA p. 274: l. poss. *šg[r]* = n.d. (cf. also Rofé SB 65f., H. & M. Weippert ZDPV xcviii 87 (n. 39); cf. also e.g. McCarter BASOR ccxxxix 51, 53, Levine JAOS ci 196, 198, Hackett BTDA 25, 29, 38f., Puech BAT 356, 361, Sasson UF xvii 287, 294 n. 21, Wesselius BiOr xliv 594, 596: l. *šd[yn]* = Plur. abs. of *šdy*$_2$ (for the reading problems, cf. v.d.Kooij DA p. 106)).
v. *ksp*$_2$, *sgd*$_1$, *sgyl*, *šgy*$_1$, *šym*$_2$.

šgb$_1$ **OldAr** QAL (cf. e.g. Fitzmyer AIS 69, Degen AAG p. 69 (n. 55) :: Dupont-Sommer Sf p. 150, Donner KAI a.l.: = PA ʿEL; cf. also Ben-Chayyim Lesh xxxv 250) Inf. *šgb* KAI 222B 32 - ¶ verb QAL to protect, to save + obj.

šgb$_2$ v. *šrb*$_2$.

šgd v. *sgd*$_3$.

šgy$_1$ **Ph** QAL Part. act. pl.f. abs. *šgyt* KAI 43[9] (cf. Clermont-Ganneau Et ii 163, Honeyman JEA xxvi 62f., Gibson SSI iii p. 137, 139 :: e.g. Lidzbarski sub KI 36, Röllig KAI a.l., v.d.Branden OA iii 248, 256, FR 14, Silverman JAOS xciv 268, Lipiński RTAT 251: = Plur. f. abs. of *šgʾ*$_3$ (= numerous)) - ¶ verb QAL to roam, to stray; *ḥyt šgyt bgbl šd nrnk* KAI 43[9]: roaming beasts in the territory of the plain of N. - cf. *šgʾ*$_1$.

šgy$_2$ v. *šgʾ*$_3$.

šgy$_3$ cf. Frah xiii 14 (*šgy*ʾ < root *šg*ʾ$_1$ (= to err)) = criminal, sinner :: Ebeling Frah a.l.: l. *šzg*ʾ (from *šzg* = sinner), cf. Akkad. *šaqṣu*.

šgyʾ$_1$ v. *šg*ʾ$_3$.

šgyʾ$_2$ v. *šg*ʾ$_3$.

šgr **DA** cf. e.g. Caquot & Lemaire Syr liv 201, McCarter BASOR ccxxxix 52, 56, Hackett BTDA 41, 94, 134: the *šgr* in DA i 16 = Sing. abs. of *šgr* (= litter of cattle), improb. interpret., cf. Hoftijzer DA p. 273f., TUAT ii 144f., Rofé SB 65f., H.P.Müller ZDPV xciv 64f. (nn. 48, 49, 50, 52), ZAW xciv 229f., Garbini Hen i 181, 185, Hvidberg-Hansen TNT ii 153 n. 73, Delcor SVT xxxii 59, H. & M. Weippert ZDPV xcviii 100f., Puech FS Grelot 21, Smelik HDAI 82: = n.d. (cf. also Ringgren Mem Seeligmann 96) :: Levine JAOS ci 198f., 203f.: *šgr wʿštr* name of one goddess (cf. also Sasson UF xvii 285, 295f., AUSS xxiv 148); on *šgr* in DA, cf. also Winter FG 491f.

šd$_1$ **OldCan** Sing. abs. *ša-te-e* EA 287^{56} - **Ph** Sing. abs. EpAn ix 5^{6}; cstr. *šd* KAI 14^{19}, 43^{9}, Mus li 286^{1} (dam. and diff. context), EpAn ix 5^{2,4}; Plur. abs. *šdyt* EpAn ix 5^{8} - **Pun** Sing. abs. *šd* Trip 51^{3} (diff. context); cstr. *šd* KAI 118^{2}, 153^{4} (or in both instances = Plur.??); cf. Diosc iv 175: (θορφαθ) σαδοι (cf. Löw AP 407), iii 96 (σισσιμανες) σαδε (cf. Löw AP 409), i 97: (βιλλε) σαδε (cf. Löw AP 410), Apul 47: *sade*) - ¶ subst. field, plain; *šd* ʾ*m krm* EpAn ix 5^{6}: field or vineyard; *bšd šrn* KAI 14^{19}: in the plain of Sh.: *bgbl šd nrnk* KAI 43^{9}: in the territory of the field of N.; *bšd lwbym* KAI 118^{2}: in the plain of the Libyans (cf. KAI 153^{4}, cf. Clermont-Ganneau with Chabot sub Punica xxv 3 (p. 226 n. 3 = JA xi/xi 285 n. 3), Février JA ccxxxix 87; cf. also Levi Della Vida PBR xix 68: *šd lwbym* prob. = *Provincia Africa* (cf. also idem RSO xxxix 306, Angeli Bertinelli CISFP i 256, Nomenclatura 44, 133f., Amadasi IPT 111) :: Delgado ILC 237 (div. otherwise): l. *lbymy* = *l*$_5$ + *b*$_2$ + Plur. + suff. 1 p.s. of *ym*$_2$ (= *ywm*) - Levi Della Vida Or xxxiii 11, 13: the *šd* in Trip 51^{3} = farm, landed property (uncert. interpret., diff. context) - this word (Sing. cstr.) poss. in RES 1512^{1} (Ph. text from Egypt): *šd* ʾ*lnm* = field of the gods (= necropolis??), cf. Lidzbarski Eph iii 126 (highly uncert. interpret.; cf. the combinations *šdqr/dy* and *šdbnhʿm* in resp. RES 1510B, 1511 (fragments of comparable origin)) - Slouschz TPI p. 62ff.: l. *šd* (= Sing. cstr.) in *šdkš* in CIS i 112b 1, 2, c 1 = the plain (> territory) of Kush (poss. interpret.; cf. also Lidzbarski sub KI 43: *šd* = plain) - Milik Bibl lxvi 550f.: l. *šd* (= Sing. cstr.) in KAI 190^{1} (cf. also Lemaire IH i 239f., Smelik HDAI 72) :: e.g. Mosc p. 46 (div. otherwise): l. *šrš* (= n.p.; cf. also Gibson SSI p. 25f.); on the reading and interpret. of this text, cf. also Dir p. 74ff., Mosc p. 44ff.

v. *šdh*$_1$, *šr*$_2$.

šd$_2$ v. *mšr*$_2$.

šd$_3$ v. *šdy*$_2$.

šd$_4$ v. *šdy$_2$*.
šd$_5$ v. *šrgb*.
šdd OldAr Lipiński Stud 46f.: l. *[y]šdnk* in KAI 223B 10 (= QAL Impf. 3 p.pl.m. + suff. 2 p.s.m. of *šdd* (= to throw down); highly uncert. reading); cf. Dupont-Sommer Sf p. 105, Donner KAI a.l., Fitzmyer AIS 82, Degen AAG p. 18: l. *]nk* (both signs uncert.).
v. *mšr$_2$*.
šdh$_1$ Ph Caquot Syr xlviii 400, 403: the *šdh* in Syr xlviii 396^{4,5} = variant form of *šd$_1$* (cf. also Gaster BASOR ccix 19f., Lipiński RSF ii 51f., v.d.Branden BiOr xxxiii 13, Avishur PIB 267, 270, UF x 31, 34f., de Moor JEOL xxvii 111, Cross CBQ xxxvi 488f., Garbini Sem xxxviii 134f.), uncert. interpret., cf. also Röllig NESE ii 29, 31: poss. = Sing. abs. of *šdh* (= *šd$_1$*), interpret. as Sing. + suff. 3 p.s.m. of *šd$_1$* less prob.
šdh$_2$ Nab word of obscure meaning in CIS ii 2642^3 (or l. *šrh*?; = n.p.?).
šdḥ Ph/Hebr (?) the *šdḥ* in Lev iii 92 prob. = n.p. (cf. Stager BASOR cxciv 48 (n. 12)) :: Landgraf Lev iii 92f.: or = Sing. abs. of *šdḥ* (= sweet, intoxicating wine (< Egypt.)).
šdy$_1$ OffAr, cf. Frah xiv 4 (*šdyt(w)n*), Paik 947 (*šdy*), 948 (*šdyw*), 949 (*šdytn*), GIPP 34, 64, SaSt 23 - **Palm** ITP Part. pl.m. abs. *mštdn* CIS ii 3913 ii 108 (Greek par. <ρειπτουμένων>) - ¶ verb QAL to shoot: Frah xiv 4, Paik 947-949 - ITP to be thrown away; *pgryn dy mštdn* CIS ii 3913 ii 108: dead bodies which are thrown away (sc. outside the town) - v.Soden Or xxxvii 267, xlvi 195: > Akkad. *šadû* (N), cf. also idem AHW s.v. *šadû* IV.
v. *ʾšd*.
šdy$_2$ DA Plur. abs. *šdyn* i 8 (cf. Hoftijzer DA p. 275f., Caquot & Lemaire Syr liv 196; cf. also Puech FS Grelot 17, 21, 27: l. *šdyn* = Plur. abs. in i 7) - **OffAr**, cf. GIPP 34, 35, SaSt 23 - **Palm** Plur. emph. *šdyʾ* Syr xii 130^9 (reading of *y* uncert.; (Littmann with) Cantineau Syr xiv 194: = Plur. emph. of *šd$_3$* (= *šyd$_1$*; < Akkad., cf. Zimmern Fremdw 69, Kaufman AIA 101) = demon (cf. also Gawlikowski TP 64f.) :: Cantineau Syr xii a.l.: = n.d. :: Milik DFD 48: = Plur. emph. of *šd$_4$* (= certain type of construction)) - ¶ subst. indicating certain type of god (for DA, cf. Hoftijzer DA p. 275f., Rofé SB 65 (n. 26), H.P.Müller ZDMG xciv 65ff., ZAW xciv 223, H. & M. Weippert ZDPV xcviii 88 (n. 42), Hackett BTDA 85ff., BiAr xlix 218ff., Fulco CBQ xlviii 110 (cf. also Sasson UF xvii 306f., AUSS xxiv 148ff.)).
v. *šgʾ$_3$*.
šdk OffAr HAPH Part. s.m. abs. *mhšdk* Cowl 37^9 - ¶ verb HAPH to appease; + obj., *mhšdk ʾnpyn* Cowl 37^9: appeasing our anger.
šdn Hatra Milik DFD 338: l. *šdnʾ* (= Sing. emph. of *šdn* (= overseer)) in Assur 33f. 2 (cf. already Jensen MDOG lx 19 n. 2; uncert. interpret.; cf. also O'Connor JANES xviii 72, DRBE 608, 612); cf. however Ag-

goula Assur a.l.: *šdn* = fool.
v. *šr$_2$*.

šdq$_1$ **OffAr** QAL Part. pass. s.m. abs. *šdyq* Cowl 40[3] (for the reading, cf. Porten & Yardeni sub TADAE A 3.6 :: Driver JRAS '32, 82: l. *šryq* (= QAL Part. pass. s.m. abs. of *šrq$_1$* (= torn), cf. already Baneth OLZ '14, 298) :: Cowl a.l.: l. *śryq* (= adj., Sing. m. abs. < root *ś/srq* (= to be empty) = distressed, cf. also Grelot DAE p. 129 (n. a) :: Epstein ZAW xxxiii 144: = QAL Part. act. of *šrq$_2$* (= to steal)) - ¶ verb QAL to tear apart; *ʿlyk lbby šdyq* Cowl 40[3]: my heart is torn for you.
v. *šrq$_5$*

šdq$_2$ **Mo** word of unknown meaning in KAI 181[34] (heavily dam. context); Michaud PA 42 n. 5: = QAL Pf. 3 p.s.m. of *šdq* (= to fall abundantly (said of rain)), poss. interpret., cf. also Baumgartner BiOr xviii 89.

šdr$_1$ **OffAr** PAʿEL Pf. 3 p.s.m. *šdr* Aḥiq 165; 1 p.s. *šdrt* ATNS 69a (dam. context, or = 2 p.s.m. or 3 p.s.f.?); cf. Frah xxiii 3 (*šdrwn*, cf. also *špr$_2$*), Paik 950 (*šdrwn*), DEP 154 recto 1, verso 2, GIPP 34 (cf. Toll ZDMG-Suppl viii 38f.) - **Palm** PAʿEL Pf. 3 p.s.m. + suff. 3 p.s.m. *šdrh* Syr xii 139[3] - **JAr** PAʿEL Impf. 2 p.pl.m. *tšdrwn* MPAT 59[2]; HITP Imper. s.m. *htšdr* MPAT 55[3] - ¶ verb PAʿEL to send - **1)** + obj.: Syr xii 139[3], MPAT 59[2] - **2)** + obj. + *l$_5$* (to): ATNS 69a - **3)** + *l$_5$*, to send a message to: Aḥiq 165 - HITP to make an effort + *ʿm$_4$*: MPAT 55[3f.] (dam. context) - a form of this root (ITP Impf. 3 p.s.m. *yštd[r]*) poss. to be restored in ATNS 46[1] (= to be sent) - Segal Maarav iv 71 : l. *šdr* (= PAʿEL Pf. 3 p.s.m. or Imper. s.m. in AG 4 bis 2 (highly uncert. reading).
v. *ysd$_1$*, *šrkh*.

šdr$_2$ **OffAr** ITP Pf. 3 p.pl.m. *ʾštdrw* Cowl 38[4] - ¶ verb ITP to intercede + *ʿm$_4$* (with): Cowl 38[4].

šdr$_3$ **OffAr** Torrey JAOS liv 32: the *šdr* in JAOS liv 31[3] = PAʿEL (?) Pf. 3 p.s.m. of *šdr$_3$* (= to make rows), highly uncert. interpret., diff. context.

šdr$_4$ v. *sdr*.

šdt v. *šrr$_1$*.

šh$_1$ v. *mt$_6$*.

šh$_2$ v. *š$_{10}$*.

šhd$_1$ **OffAr** QAL Pf. 3 p.pl.m. *šhdw* Cowl 82[6] - **Palm** QAL Pf. 3 p.s.m. *šhd* SBS 45[7], *shd* CIS ii 3919[3], 3932[6], Inv x 85, 115[2] (Greek par. μεμαρτυρῆσθαι); 3 p.s.f. *šhdt* SBS 48[4] (Greek par. ἐ[μαρ]τύρησαν) - ¶ verb QAL to give testimony - **1)** + *l$_5$*, *wshd lh yrḥbwl ʾlhʾ ... dy ... rḥym mdyth* CIS ii 3932[6f.]: the god Y. has testified concerning him that he is patriotic (cf. Inv x 85, SBS 45[7]) - **2)** + *l$_5$* + *b$_2$*, *šhdt lh bdgm bwlʾ wdms* SBS 48[4]: the Senate and the People have testified concerning him by

decree - **3)** + *ʿl*$_7$ (concerning): Cowl 82[6] - **4)** + *ʿl*$_7$ + *l*$_5$, *wʿl hnn shd lh ʾlhʾ* Inv x 115[2]: and therefore the god has testified concerning him - the *šhd* in J 11[8] (= CIS ii 211) prob. = QAL Pf. 3 p.s.m. (or Part. act. s.m. abs.), *wšhd bdnh lʿnt dwšrʾ* J 11[8]: and may the curse uttered by D. be a witness against this (cf. Guidi RB xix 421ff., cf. also J a.l., Cantineau Nab ii 149) :: J a.l.: l. *šhr* = QAL Pf. 3 p.s.m. of *šhr*$_1$ (= to watch; cf. also Cantineau Nab ii 149) :: CIS ii sub 211: l. *qns* = Sing. abs. of *qns*$_4$ (= to justify, to declare).
v. *šhd*$_2$, *šḥq*$_2$.

šhd$_2$ **OldAr** Plur. abs. *šhdn* KAI 222A 12 - **OffAr** Sing. abs. *šhd* Cowl 5[16-19], 6[17-21], Krael 2[15], 3[23b,24], CIS ii 35[3] (= Del 31; for the reading, cf. Fales AECT 11), Syr xxxvii 100A 1, TH 2 recto 1, 2 (= AECT 54), LidzbAss 4[12] (= KAI 236 = AECT 49), etc., etc.; cstr. *šhd* Aḥiq 140; Plur. abs. *šhdn* TH 2 recto 3 (= AECT 54), 4 recto 1 (= AECT 56; for the poss. reading, cf. Degen NESE i 55f., Lipiński Stud 134f., Kaufman JAOS cix 100; cf. however Friedrich TH 4 a.l.: reading *šhd/šhdn* imposs.), LidzbAss 1[5] (= AECT 46), 2[6] (= KAI 234 = AECT 47), 3[6] (= KAI 235 = AECT 48), 5[5] (= AECT 50), 6[5] (= AECT 52; *scriptio anterior*, cf. Lidzbarski a.l., Lipiński Stud 110), Sem xxiii 95 verso 6 (= AECT 58); emph. *šhdyʾ* Cowl 1[8], 2[19], 3[22], Krael 2[14], 4[23], MAI xiv/2, 66[15], TH 1 recto 3 (*šhdy[ʾ]*; = AECT 53), etc., etc., *šhdy* (lapsus) Krael 3[22b]; cf. Paik 952 (*šhdyn*), GIPP 64 - **Palm** Sing. abs. *šhd* MUSJ xxxviii 106[13,14] - **JAr** Sing. abs. *šhd* MPAT 39[10] (cf. however Beyer ATTM 307: l. *mʾmrh* = Sing. + suff. 3 p.s.m. of *mʾmr*, cf. also Bennett, Maarav iv 256, cf. already Yadin IEJ xii 254 n. 47, Koffmahn DWJ 88),[11], 40[27-29], 42[27], 51[19,20], 52[17] (*[š]hd*),[20], FS Loewenstamm ii 305 ii 2, DJD ii 40[2], EI xx 256[16] (Ar. in Hebr. context); emph. *šhdh* MPAT-A 55 (= SM 77) - ¶ subst. (prob. orig. QAL Part. act. of *šhd*$_1$) - **1)** witness; *šhd ḥms* Aḥiq 140: a false witness; *[NP] šhd mn ḥbrn* MPAT 52[20]: NP a witness from Hebron - **2)** function indication (notary?): MPAT-A 55, FS Loewenstamm ii 305 ii 2 (cf. Naveh sub SM 77, FS Loewenstamm ii 303ff.) - Degen NESE iii 16, 26: pro *šhdyʾ* (= Plur. emph.) in Cowl 49[5] l. *šhd* (= Sing. abs.), prob. reading (cf. also Porten & Yardeni sub TADAE B 4.1) - Krael a.l., Grelot DAE p. 241: l. *šhd* (= Sing. abs.) in Krael 8[10] (improb. reading, cf. Porten & Greenfield JEAS p. 120, Porten & Yardeni sub TADAE B 3.9 (div. otherwise): l. *šhrʿqb* (= n.p.)).

šhdw **Nab** Sing. emph. *šhdtʾ* MPAT 61[25] (= DBKP 15) - ¶ subst. testimony.
v. *šrr*$_1$.

šhy$_1$ **DA** QAL Part. act. s.m. abs. *šhh* ii 14 (× Hackett BTDA 30, 71, 98: = QAL Pf. 3 p.s.m., cf. also Garr DGSP 53) - ¶ verb QAL to be in a bad state, to be desolate (for the context, v. *nqr*$_1$); for this interpret., cf. also Levine JAOS ci 200, 202, H.P.Müller ZAW xciv 219, 236f.

šhy$_2$ v. *šhynn*.

šhyn v. *šhynn*.

šhynn **OffAr** word of uncert. meaning in Aḥiq 168; derivative of root *šhy*? (= rest, tranquillity), cf. Sach p. 175, Cowl a.l., Grelot RB lxviii 191, DAE 445; cf. however Lindenberger APA 171f.: = ruin, vacancy; Gressmann ATAT 461 (n. b): = desolate region; Kottsieper SAS 34ff., 234: to be related to root *š*ʾ*y$_1$* (= to rage), *šhynn* (= Plur. abs. of *šhyn*) = gale, tempest; for other interpret., cf. also Epstein ZAW xxxiii 232: = Plur. abs. of *šhyn* (= cold; cf. however Nöldeke with Epstein ZAW xxxiii 312); Stummer OLZ '14, 254: *šhynn* = lapsus for *šhyn* (= Plur. abs. of *šhy$_2$* (= desolation)).

šhm v. *šmm$_3$*.

šhr$_1$ v. *šhd$_1$*.

šhr$_2$ **OffAr** the diff. *šhr* in Sem xxiii 95 verso 5 prob. = n.d. (cf. Fales AION xxvi 546f., Lipiński ActAntHung xxii 377, 379, Kaufman Conn xix 120, 123).

šwʾ v. *šwy$_1$*.

šwb **Mo** Hiph Impf. 3 p.s.m. + suff. 3 p.s.f. *yšbh* KAI 181$^{8f.}$ (cf. e.g. Cooke NSI p. 2, 9, CF 39, Vriezen & Hospers PI 19, Michaud PA 37 (n. 2), Fitzmyer AIS 120, Miller Or xxxviii 461ff., de Moor UF xx 151 (n. 14), Smelik HDAI 35, Jackson & Dearman SMIM 97 (n. 7), 110 × Gressmann ATAT 441: *yšbh* = haplography for *yšb* (= Qal Impf. 3 p.s.m. of *yšb$_1$*) *bh* (= *b$_2$* + suff. 3 p.s.f.), cf. e.g. v.Zijl 190, Röllig KAI a.l., Andersen Or xxxv 99, Liver PEQ '67, 15, Galling TGI 52, Albright ANET 320, FR p. 39 n. 2, Lipiński Or xl 340 n. 67, Dahood Or xli 318 (on this problem, cf. also Ullendorff DOTT 198, Segert ArchOr xxix 210 (n. 64), 226, 265, Gibson SSI i p. 79)); 1 p.s. ʾ*šb* KAI 181^{12} (× e.g. Cooke NSI p. 11, Beeston JRAS '85, 144f.: or = Qal Impf. 1 p.s. of *šby$_1$*) - **Hebr** Hiph Pf. 3 p.s.m. *hšb* KAI 195^{6}; Impf. 1 p.pl. *nšb* TA-H 111^{4}; Imper. s.m. *hšb* KAI 197$^{4f.}$ (poss. reading, cf. Gibson SSI i p. 47, Lemaire IH i p. 127, Pardee HAHL 107); Inf. cstr. *hš[b]* KAI 200$^{12f.}$ (cf. e.g. Röllig KAI a.l., Gibson SSI i p. 28f., Lipiński BiOr xxxv 287 :: Delekat Bibl li 470: l. *hš[*ʿ*t]* = Hiph Inf. cstr. of *š*ʿ*y$_1$* (= to look)) - **OldAr** Qal Pf. 3 p.s.f. *šbt* KAI 224^{25}; Haph Pf. 3 p.s.m. *hšb* KAI 224^{20} (cf. e.g. Donner KAI a.l., Fitzmyer AIS 117, Degen AAG p. 76, Gibson SSI ii p. 49, 55 × Garbini RSO xxxiv 48: = Hoph); 3 p.pl.m. *hšbw* KAI 224^{24}; Impf. 2 p.s.m. + suff. 3 p.pl.m. *thšbhm* KAI 224^{6}; 1 p.s. ʾ*hšb* KAI 224^{20} - **OffAr** Qal Impf. 3 p.s.m. *yšb* Sem xxiii 95 verso 4 (cf. Fales AION xxvi 545ff., idem sub AECT 58 and AECT p. 85, Lipiński ActAntHung xxii 377, Kaufman Conn xix 124f.), *ytb* ATNS 21^{2} (diff. and dam. context; or = Aph Impf. 3 p.s.m.? :: Segal ATNS a.l.: = Qal Impf. 3 p.s.m. of *ytb$_2$* (= to give, to pay)); 1 p.s. ʾ*twb* Cowl 45^{5} (cf.

Cowl a.l., Porten RB xc 566f., Porten & Yardeni sub TADAE B 7.1 :: Grelot DAE p. 97 (n. g): = APH Impf. 1 p.s.); HAPH/APH Pf. 3 p.s.m. *htyb* Cowl 20^{7}, ATNS 59^{4}; 3 p.pl.m. *ʾtbw* Cowl 34^{6}; Impf. 3 p.s.m. *yhtb* KAI 233^{11}; + suff. 3 p.s.m. *yhtybnhy* Aḥiq 126 (:: Lindenberger APA 118, 280: poss. = lapsus for *yhtybwnh* (= HAPH Impf. 3 p.pl.m. + suff. 3 p.s.m.)); 1 p.pl. *nhtyb* Samar 4^{10}, 7^{13} (*[n]htyb*); Imper. s.m. *htb* Driv $12^{7,10}$; Part. s.m. abs. *mhtyb* AG 34^{2} - **Nab** QAL Impf. 3 p.s.m. *ytwb* CIS ii 223^{4} - **JAr** APH Impf. 1 p.s. *ʾtyb* DBKP 17^{41}; + suff. 2 p.s.f. *ʾtbn[k]* MPAT 42^{10} (dam. context (cf. also Beyer ATTM 310: l. *ʾtb* = APH Impf. 1 p.s.)) - ¶ verb QAL - **1)** to return, to come back: Cowl 45^{5} (dam. context); *ytwb ḥlqh lʾṣdqh* CIS ii 223^{4}: his portion will return to his legitimate heir; cf. KAI 224^{25} - **2)** + *ʿl_7*, *mn ʿl mn yšb* Sem xxiii 95 verso 4 (= AECT 58): whoever returns (in suit) against the other - HIPH/HAPH/APH to return, to hand back - **1)** + obj., *wyšbh kmš* KAI $181^{8f.}$: K. restored it (v. however supra); *hn hšb zy ly ʾhšb [zy lhm]* KAI 224^{20}: if he returns (v. however supra) mine, I will return theirs; *mndʿm ʾḥrn zy lqḥt klʾ htb hb lmspt* Driv $12^{6f.}$: restore anything else that you have taken, all of it, to M. (cf. Driv $12^{9f.}$, TA-H 111^{4}); for KAI 224^{24}, v. *šybh* - **2)** + obj. + *ʾl_6*, *hšb ʿbdk hsprm ʾl ʾdny* KAI 195^{6}: your servant has returned the letters to my lord - **3)** + obj. + *l_5*, *yhtb hmw lʾpq[nrbyl]* KAI 233^{11}: he will give them back to A. (cf. KAI 224^{6}, DBKP 17^{41}) - **4)** + obj. + *ʿl_7*, *wyhtybnhy ʿlyk* Aḥiq 126: he (i.e. the god) will return it (i.e. the arrow) to you; *wnksyʾ zy lqḥw ʾtbw ʿl mryhm* Cowl 34^{6}: the goods they have taken, they returned to the owners of it - **5)** + *l_5*, *lʾ htyb lh* Cowl 20^{7}: he did not return it to him (cf. AG 34^{7} (dam. context), ATNS 59^{4} (dam. context; Segal ATNS a.l.: = to reply to)) - **6)** + *mn_5* + obj., *wʾšb mšm ʾt ʾrʾl* KAI 181^{12}: I brought back from there the A. (v. however supra; v. *ʾrʾl*) - the *ʾttb* in KAI 259^{2} prob. = haplography for *ʾt_4* (v. *ʾnth_2*) *ttb* (= APH Impf. 2 p.s.m.), cf. Hanson BASOR cxcii 11, Teixidor Syr xlvii 374, Gibson SSI ii p. 154f. (v. *bʿy_1*) - Lipiński Stud 144f.: l. *y[h]šb* in NESE i $48^{1f.}$ (= HAPH Impf. 3 p.s.m.), improb. interpret. (cf. Degen NESE i 40ff. (div. otherwise): l. *ʾyš* = n.p.; for other solutions also involving personal names, cf. Degen NESE i a.l.) - a form of the HAPH prob. in ATNS 35^{3}? (Segal ATNS a.l.: restore *[yh]tyb* = HAPH Impf. 3 p.s.m. (uncert. interpret., cf. Porten & Yardeni sub TADAE B 4.7: l. *[k]tyb* (= QAL Part. pass. s.m. abs. of *ktb_1*)) - Segal ATNS a.l.: l. poss. *tb* (= QAL Pf. 3 p.s.m.) in ATNS 61a 4 (improb. reading, cf. Porten & Yardeni sub TADAE B 8.4: l. *mn* = *mn_5*) - Beyer ATTM 316: l. *ʾtybt* (= APH Pf. 1 p.s.) in MPAT 50e 3 (diff. and uncert. reading).

v. *bn_1*, *bny_1*, *$yšb_1$*, *$lyš_1$*, *$qšb_1$*, *$šbt_1$*, *tbʾh*, *twb_5*.

šwbk cf. Frah xv 11: head-band, hair-net (*šwbkʾ*, *šwpkʾ*); for this interpret., cf. Ebeling Frah a.l., Nyberg FP 85.

šwh **JAr** *šwh* MPAT 56[5] - ¶ adv. immediately (cf. Margain Sem xxix 122; on this word, cf. also Naveh & Shaked AMB p. 72).
šwzb v. *šzb*.
šwzy **OffAr** Sing./Plur. emph. *šwzyʾ* Driv 7[4] - ¶ subst. of uncert. meaning, poss. = disturbance, trouble (cf. Driv p. 64f.), cf. also Grelot DAE p. 314 n. h :: Kutscher Kedem ii 73: *šwzyʾ* = n.l.
šwzp v. *šzb*.
$šwṭ_1$ **JAr** Pol Part. pl.f. abs. *mšwṭṭn* MPAT-A 22[5] (= SM 70[13]; cf. Naveh SM p. 151 :: Fitzmyer & Harrington MPAT p. 353: = < root *$šṭṭ_1$* (= to roam)) - ¶ verb Pol to roam; *dyn dʿynwh mšwṭṭn bkl ʾrʿh* MPAT-A 22[5]: the Judge whose eyes range over all the earth - the *šṭ* in KAI 222A 24 in the comb. *yhkn bšṭ* of diff. interpret.; cf. Dupont-Sommer Sf p. 40f.: *šṭ* = Qal Inf. cstr. of *$šwṭ_1$* (= to roam, to rove about), combined with following *lḥm* = in search for food (cf. e.g. also Donner KAI a.l., Hillers TC 72f., (Kutscher with) Greenfield ActOr xxix 13f. n. 39, Fitzmyer AIS 44, Garbini AION xvii 91f., Degen AAG p. 75, Rosenthal ANET 659, Dahood Bibl liv 353f.); Gibson SSI ii p. 31, 38: *šṭ* = Qal Inf. of *$šwṭ_2$* (= to be consumed, to burn), *bšṭ lḥm* = while the bread gets burnt (cf. also Puech RB lxxxix 576ff., 581f.; cf. however Garbini OA xv 353); Lipiński Stud 28 (n. 1): *šṭ* = Qal Inf. of *$šwṭ_3$* (= to be lacking), *bšṭ lḥm* = during a food shortage (cf. already Hoftijzer DISO s.v. *$šwṭ_1$*); Lemaire Henoch iii 161ff., Syr lxii 33, 35: *šṭ* = Sing. cstr. of *$šṭ_1$* (= piece), *bšṭ lḥm* = for a piece of bread (cf. also Lemaire & Durand IAS 121); Swiggers HTSO 320f.: *št* = Qal Inf. of *yšṭ* (= to throw oneself towards, to rush to); Epstein Kedem i 39: *bšṭ* = Qal Inf. of *pšṭ* (= to stretch, to straighten), *bšṭ lḥm* = to stretch the thread; all these interpret. less prob., resp. improb.; correct interpret. of context depends on interpret. of *bnth* (v. *br_1*), *lḥm* (v. *$lḥm_4$*), *yhrgn* (v. *hrg_1*); on this text cf. also Kaufman Maarav iii 172.
v. *šyṭ*.
$šwṭ_2$ v. *$šwṭ_1$*.
$šwṭ_3$ v. *$šwṭ_1$*.
$šwṭ_4$ v. *šyṭ*.
$šwy_1$ **OffAr** Qal Part. act. s.m. abs. *šwh* Cowl 15[8] (*[š]wh*)[,9,11,13], Krael 2[4], 7[7,8,10,11,12], 14a, *šʾh* Krael 7[9] (for the reading, cf. Porten & Yardeni sub TADAE B 3.3; for the reading problems, cf. Krael a.l.); s.f. abs. *šwyh* Cowl 15[12], Krael 2[5]; pl.f. abs. *šwyn* Cowl 15[13]; Paʿel Pf. 1 p.s. *šwyt* KAI 264[7] (v. infra); Itp Pf. 1 p.pl. *ʾštwyn* Cowl 28[2] (cf. Joüon MUSJ xviii 18, 75, cf. however Margain Sem xxix 120 (n. 2)) - **Palm** Qal Pf. 3 p.s.m. *šwʾ* Sem xxvii 117[7] - **JAr** Qal Pf. 3 p.pl.m. *šww* MPAT 62[13] (for the diff. reading, cf. Greenfield DBKP 27 a.l.; Yadin EI viii 50, Fitzmyer & Harrington MPAT a.l.: l. *šw[y]n* = Qal Part. act. pl.m. abs.; cf. Greek par. εἶσιν); Part. act. s.m. abs. *šwʾ*

MPAT 89^3; PA ʿEL Imper. pl.m. *šwyw* AMB 7^1 (cf. Naveh & Shaked AMB a.l. :: Beyer ATTM 372: l. *šwy* (= PA ʿEL Imper. s.m.) + *l*$_5$ :: Dupont-Sommer JKF i 204 (div. otherwise): l. *šwy* = Sing. abs. of *šwy*$_4$ (= price (cf. also Levine with Neusner HJB v 360: = accord)) :: Scholem JGM 86f. (div. otherwise): l. *šyyl* = QAL Part. act. s.m. abs. of *šʾl*$_1$); HAPH Imper. s.m. + suff. 3 p.s.m. *hšwhy* MPAT 49 i 11 (dam. context; cf. however Beyer ATTM 318: l. *hškḥ* = HAPH Pf. 3 p.s.m. of *škḥ*; uncert. reading) - ¶ verb QAL to equal, to be equal, to be of the same value; *lbš 1 zy ʿmr šwh ksp šqln 7* Krael 2$^{4f.}$: 1 woollen garment worth in silver 7 shekels (cf. Cowl 15$^{7f.,9f.,11}$, etc., etc.); *[y]rḥyn tltʾ šw[y]n* MPAT 62^{13}: three equal months (cf. Greek par. EI viii 50^{10}: μηνῶν τελίων τρῖς); *qynʾ ʿlmʾ ... zy hwyt šwʾ* MPAT 89^3: an everlasting lament of which you are worthy (cf. Fitzmyer & Harrington MPAT a.l.; highly uncert. interpret., cf. Avigad IEJ xvii 105: without interpret.); *šwʾ mn tnn lšlmyt* Sem xxvii 117$^{7f.}$: he accepts (agrees to) here the agreement of (v. *šlmy*; cf. Aggoula Sem xxvii 119, Teixidor Syr lvi 399 (highly uncert. interpret.)) - PA ʿEL to make, to appoint, to put; *ʿl zk šwyt lk ʾntt by* (v. *lb*) KAI 264$^{7ff.}$: therefore I have made you the lady of the house (for this interpret. of *šwyt*, cf. Chabot sub RES 1785E, Donner KAI a.l., Margain Sem xxix 121 :: Lidzbarski Eph i 69: *šwyt lk* barbarism for *šwytk* :: Clermont-Ganneau RAO iii 65 n. 5: *šwyt* = QAL Pf. 1 p.s. of *šwy*$_2$ variant of *swy* (= to desire) :: Lipiński Stud 180f.: *šwyt* = QAL Pf. pass. 1 p.s., I have been adjoined (cf. however Degen WO ix 171)); *šwyw rḥmyn mn šmyh* AMB 7^1: put mercy from heaven - HAPH to divide + obj.: MPAT 49 i 11 (v. however supra) - ITP to agree; *ʾnḥnh ʾštwyn kḥdh* Cowl 28$^{2f.}$: we have agreed together (cf. however Porten & Yardeni sub TADAE B 2.11: = we were equal as one (= we owned jointly)) - a form of this root prob. also in Syr xlv 101^9 (*šwʾ[*), uncert. reading, dam. context - the diff. *šwy* in IEJ iv 98^2 (twice) poss. = QAL Part. pass. s.m. abs. (Ar. form in Hebr. context??) = placed, made??, cf. also Avigad IEJ iv a.l.

v. *šyy*, *šnʾh*.

šwy$_2$ v. *šwy*$_1$.

šwy$_3$ **Nab** QAL Part. pass. s.m. abs. *[š]wh* BIA x 55^4 (uncert. restoration) - ¶ verb to place, to establish; Part. pass. established; *lmhwʾ [š]wh mn ydhm* BIA x 55^4: that it may be established by their hands (said of temple; cf. also O'Connor DRBE 619 n. 19), v. however supra.

šwy$_4$ v. *šwy*$_1$.

šwy$_5$ **OffAr** Sing. abs. *šwy* Cowl 15^{15} - ¶ subst. indicating certain object made of reed; Grelot RB lxxviii 517ff.: poss. = small box, casket (cf. also idem DAE p. 194 n. k) :: Staerk JAP p. 29 n. α, Peiser OLZ '07, 626, Epstein JJLG vi 366 n. 2, Cowl a.l., Porten & Greenfield JEAS p. 20, Fitzmyer FS Albright ii 156, WA 259, Delsman TUAT i

261, Porten & Yardeni sub TADAE B 2.6: poss. = couch, bed. v. *tb*.

šwywy v. *š'rh*.

šwyr v. *š'rh*.

šwm$_1$ **Hebr** Sing. cstr. *šwm* DJD ii 22,1-9^{2} - ¶ subst. estimate, valuation: DJD ii 22,1-9^{2} (dam. context).

šwm$_2$ v. *šm$_2$*.

šwm'r cf. Frah ix 2: cat (*šwm'lh*); Ebeling Frah a.l., Nyberg FP 73: cf. J.Ar. *šwnr-*, cf. also Syriac/J.Ar. *šwrn-*, cf. also *šrn*.

šwmyn v. *šmym*

šwn v. *mṣ'$_1$*.

šw'$_1$ v. *šy'$_1$*.

šw'$_2$ v. *šy'$_1$*.

šwpk v. *šwbk*.

šwq v. *šq$_1$*.

šwr$_1$ v. *šr$_6$*.

šwr$_2$ **OldCan** QAL Pf. 1 p.s. *širti* EA 252^{14} (cf. Rainey EA p. 93, Halpern & Huehnergard Or li 229) - ¶ verb QAL to be maligned.

šwr$_3$ v. *šr$_2$*, *šrt$_1$*.

šwr$_4$ **Hebr** m. Sing. abs. *šwr* Frey 855^{2} (= SM 27), 1162^{2} (= SM 45), 1206^{2} (= SM 67), SM 70^{3} - **Samal** f. Sing. abs. *šwrh* KAI 215^{6,9} (for both instances, cf. Landsberger Sam'al 63 n. 164, Dupont-Sommer Sf p. 40, Pleiade 635, Greenfield Or xxix 99, Lesh xxxii 363 n. 21, Dion p. 37, 39, 74, 94, 401, Younger JANES xviii 97, Sader EAS 167 :: Sachau AS i 72, Halévy RS i 225f., 240f., Cooke NSI p. 173f., 176, Donner KAI a.l., Gibson SSI ii p. 79, 83, Delsman TUAT i 629: = Sing. abs. of *šwrh$_1$* (= millet); on the subject, cf. also Avishur SSWP 463 n. 1) - **OldAr** m. Sing. abs. *swr* Tell F 20 (Akkad. par. *lâtu*); f. Sing. abs. *šwrh* KAI 222A 23 - **OffAr** Sing. abs. *twr* Cowl 33^{10}, FX 136^{17} (cf. Greek par. βοῦν); emph. *twr'* IPAA 11^{6}, CRAI '70, 163^{3} (for the reading, cf. Humbach IPAA p. 13 :: Dupont-Sommer CRAI '70, 163, 166: l. *tmh$_3$*); Plur. abs. *twrn* PF 693; cf. Frah vii 2 (*twr'*, *twl'*), cf. Lemosín AO ii 266 - **Palm** m. Sing. emph. *twr'* RTP 59, 159, 252 (*t[w]r'*), 325, 585 - ¶ subst. m. ox, bull, f. cow; in Frey 855^{2} (= SM 27), 1162^{2} (= SM 45), 1206^{2} (= SM 67), SM 70^{3} indicating sign of the Zodiac; as sacrificial animal, cf. Cowl 30^{10}, FX 136^{17}; used to indicate meat in sacrificial meals: RTP 59, 159, 252, 325, 585 (cf. Milik DFD 190 :: du Mesnil du Buisson TMP 400ff.: *twr'* in these instances = divine epithet) - used collectively, *[wšb'] šwrh yhynqn 'gl* KAI 222A 23: and seven cows shall suckle a calf (cf. however Blau IOS ii 57f.: *šwrh* is non-collective noun, for this problem, cf. also *ssh*; cf. KAI 215^{6,9}; cf. also m. form *swr* with collective meaning in Tell F 20, cf. also Sasson ZAW xcvii 101 :: Greenfield & Shaffer Irâq xlv 111, 115: or = lapsus pro *swrn* (=

Plur. abs.; cf. also idem RB xcii 55) :: Gropp & Lewis BASOR cclix 53: = lapsus for *šwrh* (= f. Sing. abs.)) - on this word, cf. also Péter VT xxv 486ff. - Dupont-Sommer CRAI '70, 169: the diff. *trt*ʾ in CRAI '70, 163[3bis] poss. = f. Sing. emph. of *šwr$_4$* used as n.l. (Humbach IPAA 15: or l. *trṣ*ʾ (without interpret.)) - Plut Sulla 17,8: θωρ οἱ φοίνικες τὸν βοῦν καλοῦσιν (Altheim & Stiehl ASA 228: θωρ Aramaic rather than Phoenician).
v. *tnb*, *twrh*.

šwr$_5$ v. *šr$_1$*.

šwrh$_1$ v. *šwr$_4$*.

šwrh$_2$ v. *šwr$_4$*.

šwrh$_3$ **Hebr** Sing. abs. *šwrh* Mas 449[1], 450[1] (*šwr[h]*), 452[1] - ¶ subst. f. row.

šwšn v. *ššn$_1$*.

šwšp **Nab** Sing. emph. *šwšp*ʾ ADAJ xx 129[3] - ¶ subst. of uncert. meaning, prob. indicating function; Milik & Starcky ADAJ xx a.l.: = paranymph? (uncert. interpret.).

šwtp (denominative verb, v. *šwtpw*) - **Palm** QAL Pf. 3 p.s.m. *štp* FS Collart 161[9]; 3 p.s.f. *šwtpt* Ber ii 93[1]; 3 p.pl.m. *šwtpw* RIP 24[4]; ITP Part. s.m. abs. *mšttp* CIS ii 3913 ii 79 - ¶ verb QAL to associate oneself with; *šwtpw ḥnbl ... wprštn*ʾ *... lzbd*ʿ*th* RIP 24[4f.]: Ch. and P. ... associated themselves with Z. (i.e. they sold a part of the tomb belonging to them to him); cf. Ber ii 93[1]; *štp tym*ʾ *... bmnth šm*ʿ*wn* FS Collart 161[9]: T. asssociated himself with Sh. for his share (i.e. he ceded a part of his portion to Sh., cf. also Dunant FS Collart 162ff.) - ITP to become associated to: CIS ii 3913 ii 79 (dam. context; cf. Cantineau Gramm 93).

šwtpw (< Akkad., cf. Zimmern Fremdw 46, Littmann Syr xix 171, Rosenthal Sprache 90, Kaufman AIA 105 (cf. however idem ibid. 57 n. 124, 150f.; cf. also v.Soden JSS xxii 83) - **Palm** Sing. cstr. *šwtpwt* RB xxxix 548[6,7] - ¶ subst. association; *yhbt lh wb*ʿ*dt p[l]gwt mnt[*ʾ*]* ʾ*ḥd*ʾ *... bšwtpwt mlkw ... wšwtpwt* ʿ*gylw ...* RB xxxix 548[4ff.]: she has sold and ceded (v. *b*ʿ*d$_1$*) half of one share ... in association of M. and of O. (i.e. so that M. and O. are now each proprietor of a part of this share).
v. *šwtp*.

šzb (< Akkad., cf. Zimmern Fremdw 69, Kaufman AIA 105 (n. 373), 123 n. 36) - **OffAr** Pf. 3 p.s.m. + suff. 2 p.s.m. *šzbk* Aḥiq 46; + suff. 1 p.pl. *šzbn* Or lvii 16[5] (heavily dam. context); 3 p.pl.m. + suff. 1 p.s. *šzbwny* Cowl 38[5]; Impf. 3 p.s.m. *yšzb* AG 32[1] (?, dam. context; or = part of n.p.?); 1 p.pl. + suff. 2 p.s.m. *nšbzbnk* Cowl 54[9] (dam. context; for this reading, cf. Porten & Yardeni sub TADAE A 3.1 recto 8 :: Cowl a.l.: l. prob. *nšzbn[hy]* = Impf. 1 p.pl. + suff. 3 p.s.m.) - **Nab** Pf. 3 p.s.m. *šyzb* RES 83[12f.], 468[5], 1434[6] (*š[y]zb*),[12], 2058, RB xlii 408[2,5],

IEJ xi 135[4], xiii 113[4], *šzb* RES 471[4] - **Palm** Pf. 3 p.s.m. + suff. 3 p.s.f. *šwzbh* SBS 45[9] (cf. Greek par. διασώσαντα) - ¶ verb to save, to deliver - **1)** + obj., *ʾštdrw ʿm wydrng wḥrnwpy ... ʿd šzbwny* Cowl 38[5]: they interceded with W. and Ch. ... until they got me free (:: Wag 29: until they freed me); for *š(y)zb* in Nab. texts in epithets of king Rabel II, v. *ḥwy$_2$*); cf. Or lvii 16[5] - **2)** + obj. + *mn$_5$*, *šwzbh mn qdns rb* SBS 45[9]: he saved it (sc. the caravan) from great danger; *šzbk mn qṭl zky* Aḥiq 46: he saved you from being killed innocently (v. *qṭl$_2$*) - Milik DFD 294: l. *[š]wzpnwn* (= Pf. 3 p.s.m. + suff. 3 p.pl.m.) in RIP 142[2] (cf. also Aggoula Syr liv 284; highly uncert. interpret., Gawlikowski sub RIP 142, TP 95 (div. otherwise): l. *pnwn* = PAʿEL Pf. 3 p.pl.m. of *pny* (= to save; uncert. interpret.)) - Milik DFD 294: l. *šwzph* = Pf. 3 p.s.m. + suff. 3 p.s.m. in Inv xi 35[4] (uncert. reading, cf. Teixidor a.l.: l. *šlwm* = n.p. (uncert. reading)).

šzg v. *šgy$_3$*.

šḥ$_1$ **Pun** Sing./Plur. cstr. *šḥ* KAI 76B 2 - ¶ subst. shrub: KAI 76B 2 (dam. context; CIS i sub 166: = branch, Levi Della Vida AfrIt vi 11f.: = a bundle of mixed herbs or shrubs).
v. *šḥ$_2$*.

šḥ$_2$ **Pun** Plur. abs. *šḥm* KAI 120[2] (v. infra) - ¶ subst. indicating wooden tool or recipient (cf. Sznycer Sem xii 46ff., Garbini AION xv 338; derivation from Akkad. (Sznycer) less prob. (Garbini) :: Levi Della Vida AfrIt vi 11f.: = form of *šḥ$_1$*).

šḥ$_3$ v. *šḥsgm*.

šḥd$_1$ **OldAr** QAL Impf. 3 p.pl.m. *yšḥdn* KAI 224[28] - ¶ verb QAL to bribe + obj. : KAI 224[28] (dam. context; cf. Greenfield ActOr xxix 10, Lemaire & Durand IAS 147, cf. also Tadmor & Cogan Bibl lx 499ff.) - a derivative of this root also in AG 87a 19 (*šḥdnʾ*)?? (dam. context, diff. reading).

šḥd$_2$ **OffAr** Sing. abs. *šḥd* Cowl 37[4] - ¶ subst. bribe, gift: Cowl 37[4]; this word also in Sach 77 iii 2, 4 (Sing. emph. *šḥdʾ*)? (dam. context, diff. reading) - the same word (*šḥd* = Sing. abs.) prob. also in ATNS 42b 5, 43b ii 3 (context however dam.; Segal ATNS a.l.: = Sing. abs. of *šḥr$_1$* (= indication of herb; less prob. interpret.)).

šḥṭ$_1$ **OffAr** a form of this root (*nšḥṭ*) in Cowl 15[10]; poss. = NIPH Part. s.m. abs. (cf. Lidzbarski Eph iii 80: = loan from the language of Phoenician merchants (cf. also Cowl a.l., Grelot DAE p. 193 n. i), cf. also Leand 21b), meaning uncert. SC p. 44: poss. = drawn out > fine-spun (cf. Cowl a.l., Porten & Greenfield JEAS p. 20, Porten & Yardeni sub TADAE B 2.6); Grelot DAE p. 193: = with fringes; Wag 61 n. 1: = carded (on *nšḥṭ*, cf. also Perles OLZ '08, 28, Porten Arch 88 n. 133).

šḥṭ$_2$ v. *ḥṭṭ$_1$*.

šḥṭ$_3$ **Pun** Solá-Solé Sef xx 278f.: the *šḥṭ* in ICO-Spa-NPu 3 = Sing.

abs. of *šḥṭ₃* (= knife), improb. interpret., cf. Amadasi ICO a.l.: poss. = *š₁₀* + (part of) n.p. (for the problems, cf. also Fuentes Estañol sub CIFE 07.02).

šḥym v. *šḥm*.

šḥl v.Soden Or xxxvii 267, xlvi 195: *šḥl* = bucket > Akkad. *šaḫi(l)lu* (cf. also idem AHW s.v.).

šḥly **OldAr** Plur. abs. *šḥlyn* KAI 222A 36 - ¶ subst. Plur. poss. indicating some type of cress (cf. Dupont-Sommer Sf p. 52f., Donner KAI a.l.; cf. also Fitzmyer JAOS lxxxi 199f., AIS 53, Gibson SSI ii p. 42: = weeds). For the context of KAI 222A 36, cf. Hillers TC 23.

šḥlyn v. *šlḥ₁*.

šḥm **Palm** Sing. m. emph. *šḥm*ʾ Ber v 110[5], *šḥym*ʾ RIP 163[2], Ber ii 96[3]; f. emph. *šḥymt*ʾ Syr xiv 185[1]; Plur. emph. *šḥymy*ʾ Ber v 95[7] - ¶ adj. common, profane, said of burial niches (etc.): not used before (cf. Cantineau Syr xiv 186, Ingholt MUSJ xlvi 178, Aggoula MUSJ xlix 488 :: Aggoula MUSJ xlvii 70: = empty).

šḥsgm **Pun** word (?) of unknown meaning in KAI 66[1]; v.d.Branden BMB xiii 94: = *šḥ* (= Sing. cstr. of *šḥ₃* (= comptroller, overseer) + *sgm* (= Plur. abs. of *sg₁* (= basket)), highly uncert. interpret.; cf. also Cooke NSI p. 109 (div. otherwise): = *š₁₀* + *ḥsgm* (= indigenous n.p., or functional indication or title) = son/servant of Ch., cf. also Harr 93: *ḥsgm* = n.p.?; Amadasi sub ICO-Spa 9: *ḥsgm* prob. = Plur. abs. par. with Lat. par. *soc(iorum)*; cf. also CIS i sub 143, Röllig KAI a.l.; *šḥsgm* par. with *soc(iorum) s(ervus)* in Lat. par. and with κατὰ πρόσταγμα in Greek par.

šḥpn **Ph** the *šḥpn* in KAI 49[19] poss. = *š₁₀* + *ḥpn* (= n.p.; = servant of Ch.), cf. Lidzbarski Eph iii 101, Chabot RES sub 1313, Röllig KAI a.l. :: Silverman JAOS xciv 269: l. *šṭpn*.

šḥq₁ **OffAr** Qal Part. pass. s.m. abs. *[š]ḥyq* Cowl 42[10] - ¶ verb Qal to rub; Part. pass. rubbed, worn out (said of a garment); or l. *[s]ḥyq*?, cf. Ungnad ArPap sub 17 (without interpret.), Porten & Yardeni sub TADAE A 3.8: = worn.

v. *šḥq₂*.

šḥq₂ **Hatra** Qal Pf. 2 p.s.m. + suff. 3 p.s.m. *šḥqth* 232e 2 (cf. Degen JEOL xxiii 405 (cf. also Tubach ISS 269 (n. 86)) :: Aggoula MUSJ xlvii 10: = Qal Pf. 2 p.s.m. + suff. 3 p.s.m. of *šḥq₁* (= to crush, to force back); for the reading, cf. also Safar Sumer xxiv 10); Impf. 3 p.s.m. *lšḥq* 24[3] (for the poss. reading, cf. Degen ZDMG cxxi 125 :: Safar Sumer ix 14*: l. *šhrw* (= n.d.) :: Vattioni IH a.l.: l. *lšhd* = Qal Impf. 3 p.s.m. of *šhd₁* (cf. also Milik RN vi/iv 55: l. *šh-*) :: Pennacchietti FO xvi 62 n. 4: l. *lqd* = Qal Impf. 3 p.s.m. of *qdd₁* (= to damage)? :: Safar Sumer vii 183: l. poss. *šnpyr* (= Sing. m. abs. of *špr₄*; cf. also Caquot Syr xxix 103, Donner sub KAI 245)); + suff. 3 p.s.m. *lšḥqh* 23[3] (cf.

Ingholt AH i/1, 45, i/2, 50, Degen ZDMG cxxi 125, JEOL xxiii 405 :: Caquot GLECS ix 88, Syr xl 15: = QAL Impf. 3 p.s.m. + suff. 3 p.s.m. of *šḥq*$_1$ (= to damage) :: Caquot Syr xxix 102 (div. otherwise): l. *lšḥqb* (without interpret.; cf. also Donner sub KAI 244) :: Milik RN vi/iv 54: l. *lšhdh* = QAL Impf. 3 p.s.m. + suff. 3 p.s.m. of *šhd*$_1$ (= to give testimony about; cf. also Vattioni IH a.l.), 125^3 (cf. Degen JEOL xxiii 405 :: Caquot Syr xli 256: = QAL Impf. 3 p.s.m. + suff. 3 p.s.m. of *šḥq*$_1$ (= to damage; cf. Safar Sumer xviii 37 (div. otherwise): l. *šḥqh*) :: Vattioni IH a.l.: l. *lšhdh* = QAL Impf. 3 p.s.m. + suff. 3 p.s.m. of *šhd*$_1$) - ¶ verb QAL to laugh, to smile kindly upon: Hatra 24^3 - **1)** + obj.: Hatra 23^3, 125^3 - **2)** + obj. + *mn*$_5$, *šḥqth mn bytk lmn dlṭrh* Hatra 232e 2ff.: may you smile kindly from your temple upon him (sc.) the one who will guard it (for this interpret., cf. Degen JEOL xxiii 405) - Rocco StudMagr vii a.l.: l. *šḥq* = QAL Imper. pl.m. in StudMagr vii 12^1, uncert. reading and interpret.

šḥr$_1$ v. *šḥd*$_2$.

šḥr$_2$ **OffAr** Sing. emph. *šḥrʾ* FuF xxxv 173^5 - ¶ subst. of uncert. meaning; Altheim & Stiehl FuF xxxv 176, ASA 253, 276: < Iran. = town (highly uncert. interpret.).

šḥrṣ (< Akkad., cf. Cross EI xviii 11*f.) - **OffAr** Sing. abs. *šḥrṣ* Samar 1^3 (= EI xviii 8*), 3^2, 4^3 (*šḥ[rṣ]*), 6^3, 9^4 - ¶ subst. exact, fixed price (cf. also Freedman & Andersen FS Fitzmyer 19).

šḥrt **Mo** Sing. abs. *šḥrt* KAI 181^{15} - ¶ subst. dawn.

šḥt$_1$ **Ph** PIʿEL/YIPH (cf. Gibson SSI iii p. 39; cf. FR 18.2, 146: = YIPH) Impf. 3 p.s.m. *yšḥt* KAI 24$^{15(bis)}$ (:: Baldacci BiOr xl 126f.: in the first instance *yšḥt* = QAL, in the second one HIPH (sic)),^{16} (or = 3 p.pl.??) - **Samal** PAʿEL Inf. *šḥt* KAI 214^{27,28} (cf. e.g. Cooke NSI p. 170: = Inf. cstr. :: Gibson SSI ii p. 75, iii 39: = QAL Inf. (cf. also Donner KAI a.l.: = PAʿEL Inf. or Sing. abs. of *šḥt*$_2$) :: Dion p. 128, 383 n. 17: = QAL Part. act. s.m. abs.); Pf. 2 p.s.m. *šḥt* KAI 214^{31} (cf. Gibson SSI ii p. 76 :: idem ibid.: or = QAL Pf. 2 p.s.m. :: Donner KAI a.l.: = PAʿEL Pf. 3 p.s.m. :: Dion p. 35, 128: = QAL Part. act. s.m. abs.); HAPH Pf. 3 p.s.m. *hšḥt* KAI 214^{29} - **OffAr** HAPH Impf. 3 p.pl.m. *yhšḥtwn* Aḥiq 19, 155 (on the dam. context cf. also Kottsieper SAS 138) - ¶ verb PIʿEL/PAʿEL/YIPH/HAPH to destroy - **1)** + obj., *wmy yšḥt hspr z yšḥt rʾš bʿl ṣmd* KAI 24^{15}: and whoever will destroy this inscription may B.S. smash his head (cf. KAI 24^{16}); *yršy šḥt bʾšr ḥd ʾḥyh* ... KAI 214^{27}: he will plot to make destruction in the region (??, v. *ʾšr*$_4$) of one of his brothers (cf. KAI 214^{31}; poss. interpret., diff. context); *yršy šḥt* KAI 214^{28}: he will plot to make destruction (poss. interpret., diff. context) - a form of this root in KAI 215^2: *šḥt* (heavily dam. context).

v. *ʾšḥh*, *ḥtt*$_1$, *tḥt*.

šḥt$_2$ **Samal** Sing. abs. *šḥt* KAI 215[7]; + suff. 3 p.s.m. *šḥth* KAI 215[2] (cf. e.g. Dion p. 152, Gibson SSI ii p. 82 :: Garb 261, Schuster FS Landsberger 441: = Sing. abs. of *šḥth*) - ¶ subst. destruction: KAI 215[2] (for this text, cf. also Tawil Or xliii 54 n. 9); *ʾbn šḥt* KAI 215[7]: (litt.) the stone of destruction (combination of diff. interpret.; D.H.Müller WZKM vii 38, 45f., 127, 138, Gibson SSI ii p. 79, 88, Donner KAI a.l., Delsman TUAT i 629: poss. = indication of leader of rebellion :: Sader EAS p. 167 (n. 42): = the fathers of destruction (relating *ʾbn* to *ʾb*$_1$, cf. already Landsberger Samʾal 63); v. also *ʾbn*$_2$).
v. *šḥt*$_1$.

šḥt$_3$ **OffAr** word of unknown meaning and uncert. reading in CIS ii 26 (= Del 103).

šḥt$_4$ v. *ʾšḥh*.

šḥth v. *šḥt*$_2$.

šṭ$_1$ **Ph** Sing. cstr. *šṭ* CISFP i 765, 766 (= RES 1504) - **OldAr** Sing. cstr. *šṭ* CISFP i 763 - ¶ subst. of uncertain meaning, Bron & Lemaire CISFP i 764: = indication of a certain measure, used in inscriptions on weights, *šṭ šql ḥmt* CISFP i 763: "fraction" of a shekel of H. (cf. CISFP i 765, 766), cf. also Lemaire Hen iii 166 :: Bordreuil Syr lxvii 489: *šṭ* = *š* (= abbrev. of *šql*$_3$) + *ṭ* (= abbrev. of *ṭbʿ* = Qal Part. pass. s.m. abs. of *ṭbʿ*$_1$ (= to standardize)).
v. *šwṭ*$_1$, *šṭrb*.

šṭ$_2$ v. *šṭṭ*$_2$.

šṭṭ$_1$ v. *šwṭ*$_1$.

šṭṭ$_2$ **OffAr** Plur. abs. *šṭṭn* Cowl 42[8] - ¶ subst. of uncert. meaning; Grelot DAE p. 131 (n. c): poss. < Egypt., = hem, fringe? :: Cowl a.l.: = Plur. abs. of *šṭ*$_2$ (= line; cf. also Leand 52b).

šṭy **OffAr** Qal Part. act. s.m. abs., cf. Warka 18, 43: *ša-ṭi-e* - ¶ verb Qal to be stupid; Part. act.: stupid - Porten Or lvii 18: the *šṭy* in Or lvii 16[3] poss. = Qal Part. act. s.m. abs. or < Egypt.?

šṭyn cf. Frah x 15 (*šṭynʾ*): silly, cf. Nyberg FP 45, 75 :: Ebeling Frah a.l.: l. *dḥkynʾ* = form of *dḥk* (= laughter).

šṭp v. *šsp*$_2$.

šṭr$_1$ **Pun** Qal Part. act. s.m. abs. *šʿṭr* BAr '55/56, 32[1] (dam. context) - **JAr** Qal Part. act. m. s. emph. *šṭrʾ* MPAT 51[2] (for the reading, cf. Milik Bibl xxxviii 266, Fitzmyer & Harrington MPAT a.l. :: Birnbaum PEQ '57, 110, 122: l. *šṭyʾ* :: Abramson & Ginsberg BASOR cxxxvi 17ff.: l. *šyʿʾ* = Sing. of *šyʿ*$_2$ (= plasterer) :: Milik RB lxi 183, 185: l. *šryʾ* = Qal Part. act. s.m. emph. of *šry*$_1$) - ¶ verb Qal to inscribe, to write; Part. act. substantivated, scribe: BAr '55/56, 32[1] (cf. also Heltzer AO ii 229), MPAT 51[2]; :: Zimmern Fremdw 29: < Akkad. (cf. Kaufman AIA 101 n. 352) - Aggoula Sem xxvii 117ff.: l. *mšṭ[rtʾ]* = Aph/Paʿel Part. pass. s.f. emph. in Sem xxvii 117[8] (= written);

uncert. interpret., diff. context :: Starcky with Teixidor Syr lvi 399: = Part. pass. (= proscribed).
v. *sṭr*$_1$, *ʿṭr*$_2$, *tʾrh*.

šṭr$_2$ (< Akkad., cf. Zimmern Fremdw 19, 29, Harmatta ActAntHung vii 345, Kaufman AIA 101, cf. O'Connor JNES xlv 219) - **Hebr** Sing. abs. *šṭr* EI xx 256^{9,12} - **OffAr** Sing. abs. *šṭr* Cowl 81^{5,16,17,19,20} (*[š]ṭr*)$^{,22\text{-}25,26}$ (*šṭ[r]*), Del 81[1] (*š[ṭ]r*), 82[1]; cstr. *šṭr* CIS ii 67, Del 48, 49, 51, 53 (= AM 67), FuB xiv 13[1], 18[1], etc., etc.; emph. *šṭrʾ* Samar 6[6] (*šṭ[rʾ]*), 7[14], 8[12], 9[16] (*šṭ[rʾ]*, heavily dam. context) - **Nab** Sing. abs. *šṭr* CIS ii 221[5]; cstr. *šṭr* CIS ii 204[3], MPAT 64 i 2, 3, 9, 10, 11, iii 4, 6; emph. *šṭrʾ* MPAT 64 i 8, iii 3 (*š[ṭ]rʾ*); Plur. abs. *šṭryn* MPAT 64 ii 4; cstr. *šṭry* CIS ii 350^{4,5} - **Palm** Sing. cstr. *šṭr* CIS ii 3913 i 8 - **JAr** Sing. emph. *šṭrʾ* MPAT 41[14], 47 i recto 10, *šṭrh* MPAT 40^{11,24}, IEJ xxxvi 206[7] - ¶ subst. m. document, passim; *šṭr šytʾ* Del 58: document of S. (i.e. document concerning a debt of S.), cf. Del 64[1], FuB xiv 18[1]; *šṭr rḥymʾl zy tmrn krn [40]* Del 72: document of R. concerning 40 *k*. of dates (i.e. concerning a debt of R.); *šṭr zbdnnʾ zy qnʾ* Del 71: document of Z. concerning small cattle (i.e. concerning a debt of Z.); *šṭr ʾrqt ngryʾ zy yhb hydwry ... lrybt* Del 77[1]: document concerning the fields of the carpenters, which H. has given (on loan) to R.; *šṭr bnḥ zy ksp hlkʾ zy pryʿ* Del 79$^{1f.}$ (= AM 110): document concerning the "gift" (v. *bnḥ*) of the silver of the tax, which is paid (cf. Del 78); *šṭr ḥnṭn* (v. *ḥṭh*) *kr 1* Del 79bis (= AM 66): document concerning 1 kor barley; *šṭr btʾ* Del 93: document concerning the house (prob. = receipt for paid rent); *šṭr bḥmrn 40* Cowl 81[16]: document on 40 she-asses (i.e. bond for 40 she-asses :: Grelot DAE p. 108: = invoice for 40 she-asses), cf. Cowl 81 passim; *šṭr ksp ... qdm blʾṭr* FuB xiv 13f.: document concerning silver ... (which is) incumbent upon B.; *šṭr ʾgwrn* FuB xiv 24[1]: document concerning bricks; *šṭr mwhbtʾ* CIS ii 204$^{3f.}$: document/deed of gift; *šṭr ʾgryʾ* CIS ii 3913 i 8: document concerning the lease (cf. Greek par. τῇ ... μισθώσει); for *šṭr ʿdwʾ*, v. *ʿdw*; for *šṭry ḥrmyn*, v. *ḥrm*$_3$ - the diff. *š* in the beginning of Cowl 24$^{2\text{-}18}$ poss. = abbrev. of *šṭr*$_2$?? (cf. Grelot DAE p. 271 n. a :: Cowl p. 81: = abbrev. of a word meaning "portion", "ration"? (*šyʿwr?*) :: Sach p. 87: = abbrev. of *šql*$_3$ :: Grelot DAE p. 271ff.: or = abbrev. of *šʿrn* (= Plur. abs. of *šʿrh*)).

šṭr$_3$ **OffAr** Sing. abs. *šṭr* Cowl 25^{13,16}, Driv 12[5]; cstr. *šṭr* Cowl 5[5]; cf. Frah ii 11, 14, Paik 767 (*šṭrʾ*), 958 (*šṭrʾ*, *štrʾ*), GIPP 34, 65, SaSt 23 - **Palm** Sing. abs. *šṭr* RB xxxix 539[2], *sṭr* Ber ii 86[11], v 124[2]; cstr. *sṭ[r]* Syr xii 139[5] (dam. context); emph. *šṭrʾ* CIS ii 4171[2], Ber ii 98[1], 99 ii 1, *sṭrʾ* CIS ii 4173[1], 4174[3], 4175[5], 4204[1], Ber ii 78^{1,2}, 86^{5,9}, 97[1] (for the reading, cf. Cantineau with Ingholt Ber iii 126 :: Ingholt Ber ii a.l. : l. *šṭrʾ*), 104[1], v 106[3], Syr xix 156[1] (Greek par. πλευρὸν), RB xxxix 532[2], MUSJ xxxviii 106^{10,12}; Plur. emph. *šṭrʾ* Ber v 95[6], *sṭryʾ* FS Miles 38[2] -

JAr Sing. cstr. *sṭr* AMB 7^{15} - ¶ subst. m. - **1)** side: Cowl 5^{5}; *slqh bsṭr krsyh d'lh rbh* AMB 7^{14f}: may they rise up at the side of the throne of the great God (cf. however Naveh & Shaked a.l.: or = variant of *bstr* (= behind) < Iran.) - **2)** wall: CIS ii 4171^{2}, 4173^{1}, 4174^{3}, 4175^{5}, Ber ii 98^{1}, 99 ii 1, MUSJ xxxviii 106^{10,12}, FS Miles 38^{2}, etc. - **3)** in the comb. *š/sṭr mn* - a) with the exception of, excluding; *dy mn dy yṣb' yḥpr lh mn lgw šṭr mn 'ksdr' gwy'* RB xxxix 539^{2}: that whoever wants will dig at the interior excluding the interior exedra; *rḥq lh sṭr' mdnḥy' ... sṭr mn gwmḥ' ḥd bry'* Ber ii 86$^{9ff.}$: he transferred to him the eastern wall ... with exception of the one niche the outer; cf. Cowl 25^{13,16}, Ber v 124^{2} - b) apart from; *hb lmspt ḥlky' 'lk 5 šṭr mn zy yhbw bbb'l gbrn 5* Driv 12$^{4f.}$: give these 5 Cilicians to M. apart from those who have been given at B., 5 men.

šṭrb **Samal** the diff. *šṭrb[* in KAI 215^{6} (or l. *šṭrbt*?, cf. Gibson SSI ii p. 78, cf. already e.g. Cooke NSI p. 176, cf. however Lipiński OLP viii 102) poss. indication of a measure?, exact meaning unknown; cf. also Bron & Lemaire CISFP i 764: poss. = *šṭ* (= Sing. abs. of *šṭ*$_1$) + *rb* (= Sing. m. abs. of *rb*$_2$).

šy$_1$ **Hebr** Sing. abs. *šy* IEJ xii 30^{2} - **Samal** Sing. abs. *šy* KAI 214^{18} (cf. Lagrange ERS 494, Montgomery JAOS liv 422, Greenfield RB lxxx 50ff., Gibson SSI ii p. 67, 73, cf. also Donner KAI a.l., Greenfield FS Cross 70 :: Poeb 47 n. 1, Dion p. 104, 422: = Sing. abs. of *šy*$_2$ (= conformity), *šy l* = like; context however diff.) - ¶ subst. gift, donation: IEJ xii 30^{2}; v. also supra - the *šy* on seal of unknown provenance in SANSS-Hebr 163 prob. = *šy*$_1$, cf. Avigad IEJ xvi 245, Herr SANSS a.l. (seal however most prob. forgery) - Puech Sem xxix 22: l. this subst. (Sing. abs. *]šy*) in KAI 30^{3} (uncert. interpret., heavily dam. context), cf. however Dupont-Sommer RA xli 202, 204: l. *[lb]šy* (= Sing. + suff. 3 p.s.m. of *lbš*$_2$ (cf. also Masson & Sznycer RPC 17, H.P.Müller ZA xlv 110, 113) :: Honeyman Irâq vi 107: l. *[y]nšy* = passive Impf. 3 p.s.m. of *nšy*$_1$ (= to be forgotten).

šy$_2$ v. *šy*$_1$.

šyb **OffAr** Kottsieper SAS 14, 23, 234: l. poss. *yš[y]b* (= Qal Impf. 3 p.s.m. of *šyb* (= to become grey, old)) in Aḥiq 212 (uncert. reading, heavily dam. context).

šybh **OldAr** Sing. cstr. *šybt* KAI 224^{24} - ¶ subst. restoration; *hšbw 'lhn šybt by[t 'by]* KAI 224^{24}: the gods have restored the fortunes of my father's house (cf. e.g. Vogt Bibl xxxix 274, Noth ZDPV lxxvii 149 (n. 85), Donner KAI a.l., Greenfield ActOr xxix 4, Gibson SSI ii p. 51, 56).

šyb'yn v. *šb'm*.

šyd$_1$ (< Akkad., cf. Zimmern Fremdw 69, Kaufman AIA 101) - **OffAr**, cf. Frah S$_2$ 154, 155 (*šyd'*), Paik 960 (*šyd'*) - **JAr** Sing. abs. *šyd* AMB

13^7; emph. *šydh* AMB 7a 6, 12b 3 - ¶ subst. demon (cf. *šydh*). v. *šdy₂*.

šyd₂ **Nab** Sing. emph. *šyd*ʾ RES 1088^2 (for this reading, cf. Nöldeke ZA xxiii 184 n. 1 :: Torrey JAOS xxviii 350: l. *šyr*ʾ = Sing. emph. of *šyr₃* (= leader of caravan)), RB xlii 415^5, ***syd***ʾ BSOAS xvi 224,75^2 (cf. Littmann BSOAS a.l., cf. also Cantineau Nab i 43) - ¶ subst. m. plasterer (cf. also Joüon MUSJ xviii 92 n. 6).

šydh **JAr** Plur. emph. *šydth* AMB 2^8 - ¶ subst. female demon (cf. *šyd₁*).

šydy v. *š*ʾ*ry*.

šyzb v. *šzb*.

šyzbw v. *mqlw*.

šyḥh **JAr** Sing. abs. *šyḥh* AMB 1^{17} - ¶ subst. talk, whisper: AMB 1^{17} (diff. context).

šyṭ **OffAr** Sing. emph. *šyṭ*ʾ RCL '62, $259^{2,3,4}$; Plur. emph. *šyṭy*ʾ RCL '62, 259 iii 3, 5 (for the reading *šyṭ*, cf. Naveh AION xvi 35f. :: Bresciani RCL '62, p. 259 (n. 3), 262: or l. *šwṭ*ʾ/*šwṭy*ʾ, same forms of *šwṭ₄* (= oarsman)) - ¶ subst. (or QAL Part. act. of *šwṭ₁*) sailor.

šyy **Ph** Liverani RSF ii 36ff.: the *šyy* in Syr xlviii $396^{3,6}$ = QAL Pf. 3 p.s.m. of *šyy* (= to be equal), variant of *šwy₁*, less prob. interpret., cf. Gibson SSI iii p. 91; Cross CBQ xxxvi 488 (n. 20): = Sing. abs. of *šyy* (= spoiler), less prob. interpret.; de Moor JEOL xxvii 111 (n. 19): *šyy* (= adj. Sing. m. abs. < root *šyy/š*ʾ*y*) = murderous, ʾ*l šyy* = the murderous god, less prob. interpret.; v. also ʾ*l₃*.

šym₁ **Ph** QAL Pf. 3 p.pl. *šm* KAI 14^5 (:: Dahood Ps i 310, Rosenthal ANET 662: = passive form) - **Pun** QAL Pf. 3 p.s.m. *šm* KAI 61A 2f., B 2f. (*š[m]*) - **Samal** QAL Pf. 3 p.s.m. *šm* KAI $215^{1,10}$; 1 p.s. *šmt* KAI 214^{29}, 215^{20}; Impf. 2 p.pl.m. *tšm[w]* KAI 215^4 (cf. e.g. Donner KAI a.l., Gibson SSI ii p. 78f., 82f. :: Landsberger Samʾal 62f. n. 160: l. *tšmṭ* = QAL Impf. 3 p.s.f. of *šmṭ* (= to be drawn, said of a sword) :: Koopmans 72: l. *tšm[ṭw]* = QAL Impf. 2 p.pl.m. of *šmṭ*) :: Halévy RS i 224, 240: l. *tšm[d]* = HAPH Impf. 3 p.s.f. of *šmd₁* (= to exterminate) - **OldAr** QAL Pf. 3 p.s.m. *šm* KAI 201^1, 202A 1, Tell F 1, 16 (Akkad. par. *iz-qu-up*); 1 p.s. *šmt* KAI 202B 13; + suff. 3 p.s.f. *šmth* KAI 202B 6; 3 p.pl.m. *šmw* KAI 202A 7 (cf. Montgomery JAOS liv 424, Greenfield ActOr xxix 9, 16, Degen AAG p. 9 (cf. also Rössler TUAT i 179) :: e.g. Dupont-Sommer Sf p. 17, 19, Fitzmyer AIS 12f., Gibson SSI ii p. 28f. (div. otherwise): l. *šm* = QAL Pf. 3 p.s.m.), 9, 222B 6; Impf. 3 p.s.m. *yšym* Tell F 12 (Akkad. par. *i-šak-ka-nu*), *lšm* Tell F 11 (Akkad. par. *liš-kun*; :: Andersen & Freedman FS Fensham 25: prob. = *l₁* + QAL Pf. 3 p.s.m. :: Vattioni AION xlvi 361: = *l₅* + Sing. abs. of *šm₁*); 1 p.s. ʾ*šm* KAI 222C 19 (cf. e.g. Dupont-Sommer Sf p. 88, 91, Donner KAI a.l., Fitzmyer AIS 20, 76, Gibson SSI ii p. 34, 43 :: Lemaire &

Durand IAS 116, 126, 141: l. *›šn[h]* = PA‹EL Impf. 1 p.s. of *šny*₁); 3 p.pl.m. *yšmw* KAI 222C 23 (cf. e.g. Dupont-Sommer Sf p. 87, Donner KAI a.l., Fitzmyer AIS 20, Gibson SSI ii p. 34 :: Lemaire & Durand IAS 116, 126, 141: l. *yšnw* = PA‹EL Impf. 3 p.pl.m. of *šny*₁); ITP Impf. 3 p.pl.m. *y[t]šmn* KAI 223C 3 (cf. Gibson SSI ii p. 45, Lemaire & Durand IAS 128, 142f., cf. also Rosenthal ANET 660; poss. interpret., cf. also Lemaire & Durand IAS 143: or l. *yšmn* = QAL Impf. 3 p.pl.m. (cf. already Milik Bibl xlviii 570 n. 3) :: e.g. Dupont-Sommer Sf p. 117, 120, Donner KAI a.l., BiOr xxvii 248, Fitzmyer AIS 82f., 90, Degen AAG p. 19, 69, 112 (n. 20): l. *y[r]šmn* = QAL pass. Impf. 3 p.pl.m. of *ršm* (= to be engraved)) - **OffAr** QAL Pf. 3 p.s.m. + suff. 1 p.s. *šmny* KAI 226[3]; 2 p.s.m. *šmt* ATNS 50[4] (dam. context; or = 3 p.s.f. or 1 p.s.?); 1 p.s. *šmt* Beh 35 (Akkad. par. *áš-ku-un*); 3 p.pl.m. *šmw* ATNS 14[5], KAI 226[6], Sem xxiii 95 recto 2, verso 3 (= AECT 58); + suff. 3 p.s.m. *šmh* KAI 228A 4 (cf. e.g. Gibson SSI ii p. 150f. × e.g. CIS ii sub 113, Lidzbarski Handb 374, Cooke NSI p. 196f., Koopmans 146, Donner KAI a.l.: = Pf. 3 p.s.m. + suff. 3 p.s.m.); + suff. 1 p.s. *šmwny* KAI 226[7]; Pf. pass. 3 p.s.m. *šym* Cowl 26[22,23,25], Driv 10[5]; 1 p.s. *šymt* FS Driver 54 conc. 2; 3 p.pl. *šymw* BSOAS xiii 82[7] (or = QAL Imper. pl.m., cf. Shaked JRAS '69, 122, cf. also Kutscher, Naveh & Shaked Lesh xxxiv 128); Impf. 3 p.s.m. + suff. 2 p.s.m. *yšymnk* Cowl 30[2]; 2 p.s.m. *tšym* Aḥiq 130; 1 p.s. *›šym* Driv 3[6]; 3 p.pl.m. *yšmw* Driv 13[5], F v 1[1], *yšymwn* Aḥiq 115; Imper. s.m. *šm* Driv 1[3], 3[7], ATNS 26[15]; Part. pass. s.m. abs. *šym* Cowl 17[2] (*š[y]m*; for this poss. reading, cf. (Segal with) Porten RB xc 410, Porten & Yardeni sub TADAE A 6.1, Lipiński Or lvii 435 :: Avigad with Porten Arch 52 n. 90: l. *šlm* (= PA‹EL Imper. s.m. of *šlm*₁) :: Cowl a.l.: l. *šlmt* = PA‹EL Pf. 2 p.s.m. (cf. Sach p. 35, Grelot DAE p. 281) :: Torrey with Sprengling AJT xxiv 418 n. 1: l. *šlḥt* = QAL/PA‹EL Pf. 2 p.s.m. of *šlḥ*₁), 38[10]; s.f. abs. *šymh* Aḥiq 95; pl.m. abs. *šmn* KAI 233[7] (cf. e.g. Lidzbarski AUA 11, Donner KAI a.l., Gibson SSI ii p. 103, 107, cf. also Dupont-Sommer Syr xxiv 38 :: Dupont-Sommer Syr xxiv 38: or = QAL Pf. 1 p.pl. :: Bowman UMS xx 277: = QAL pass. Pf. 1 p.pl. :: Lidzbarski ZA xxxi 198: = Sing. abs. of *šmn*₂), *šymn* Cowl 69B 2 (for the reading, cf. Porten & Yardeni sub TADAE B 8.5 :: Cowl a.l.: l. *šymw*); ITP Impf. 3 p.s.m. *ytšm* Driv 5[8], *ytšym* Cowl 27[21], ATNS 15[3], Aḥiq 80; cf. Frah app. 10 (*symwn*), cf. Toll ZDMG-Suppl viii 36; a form of this root (*šym*) in Driv F xi 16 (heavily dam. context) - ¶ verb QAL to place, to put, to set up, passim; cf. also *‹dy ›lhn hm zy šmw ›lhn* KAI 222B 6: this is the treaty of the gods which the gods have set up (i.e. concluded) - **1)** + obj.: KAI 202B 6 (dam. context), Tell F 12, ATNS 50[4] (dam. context) - **2)** + obj. + *b*₂, *yšymwn ṭb bḥnkh lm›mr* Aḥiq 115: they will put something good in his palate (i.e. his mouth) to speak; cf. KAI 214[29]; *tšm[w] ḥrb* *bbyty* KAI 215$^{4f.}$: you will set the sword against my house (v. supra; v. also *ḥrb*$_2$); *šmym lšm bh* Tell F 11: and may he put my name on it - **3)** + obj. + *l*$_5$, *nṣb zn šm brrkb l'bh* KAI 215^1: B. has set up this statue for his father (cf. KAI 215^{20}), cf. also Dion FS Delcor 142; *wyšmw tḥtyh [l‘]lyth* KAI 222C 23f.: may they (sc. the gods) make his lower part his upper part (i.e. may the gods overturn him) - **4)** + obj. + *‘l*$_7$, *wšmw kl mlky' 'l mṣr ‘l ḥzrk* KAI 202A 9: all these kings laid siege to Ch. (cf. also Greenfield Proc v CJS i 177) - **5)** + obj. + *qdm*$_3$, v. *'m*$_2$ - **6)** + *b*$_2$ + obj., *'y šm bn mnm* KAI 14^5: they have not laid anything in it (cf. e.g. Röllig KAI a.l., Dahood PNSP 53, Gibson SSI iii p. 107, cf. also FR 254 :: e.g. Cooke NSI p. 31, 34: with me) - **7)** + *l*$_5$, *nṣb ... 'š šm nḥm lb‘l ḥmn* KAI 61A 1ff.: the stele which N. has set up for B.Ch. (cf. KAI 201$^{1f.}$, 202A 1, cf. also ATNS 26^{15} (context however dam.)); *'hpk ṭbt' w'šm [l]lḥyt* KAI 222C 19f.: I shall change the good and turn it into evil - **8)** + *l*$_5$ + obj. + *qdm*$_3$, *wlrḥmn yšymnk qdm drywhwš mlk'* Cowl 30^2: and may he give you favour before king D. (cf. Dion RB lxxxix 531f.) - **9)** + *‘m*$_4$ + obj., *wlšmw ‘my m'n ksp wnḥš ‘m lbšy šmwny* KAI 226$^{6f.}$: they did not put with me any vessel of silver or bronze, with my garments they laid me (sc. in my grave) - **10)** + *qdm*$_3$, *dmwt' zy hdys‘y zy šm qdm hdd* Tell F 1: statue of H. which he put before H. (cf. Dion FS Delcor 142) - **11)** + *qdm*$_3$ + obj., *šmt qdm ['lwr] nṣb' znh* KAI 202B 13f.: I have set up this stele before I.; cf. Tell F 16 - **12)** cf. the following combinations of *šym* with object - a) + *ṭ‘m*$_2$, *'nt šm ṭ[‘]m* Driv 1^3: you, give an order (cf. Driv 3^7, ATNS 14^5); cf. also *'nh 'šym lhm ṭ‘m* Driv 3^6: I will give an order concerning them (on this combination, cf. Greenfield Trans iii 90f.) - b) + *šlm*$_2$, *[kzy] 'lhy' šlm yšmw lk* Driv 13^5: that the gods may grant you peace (cf. also Driv F v 1^1); cf. also *wšmw šlm bynyhm* Sem xxiii 95 verso 3 (= AECT 58): and they made peace between them - c) + *šm ṭb*, *šmny šm ṭb* KAI 226^3: he afforded me a good name (cf. Tawil Or xliii 58ff.) - for the context of KAI 215^{10}, v. *kpyr*, *mt*$_5$; context of Beh 35 dam.; with meaning to establish, to determine in Frah app. 10 - Qal pass. to be placed, to be put; *[bm]sgr' symt* FS Driv 54 conc. 2: I was put in prison; + *l*$_5$ in Cowl 69B 2 (dam. context; v. supra); with subj. *ṭ‘m*$_2$, *kzy šym ṭ‘m* Cowl 26^{22}: according to the order issued (cf. Cowl 26^{23,25}); cf. also *mny šym lhytyh bb'l* Driv 10^5: I have given an order to bring (it) to B. (for the construction, cf. Driv p. 77, Kutscher PICS 149ff.); Part. pass.: established, *bš[my]n šymh hy* Aḥiq 95: she is established in heaven :: Lindenberger APA 68ff.: or = she has been established by Šamayn); *‘m klby' šmn* KAI 233^7: put with the dogs (dam. context; v. supra; cf. Donner KAI a.l., Gibson SSI ii p. 107) - Itp - **1)** to be put; *wytšym 'rḥ' brglw[hy]* Aḥiq 80: and a fetter (?, v. *'rḥ*$_5$) is put on his feet - **2)** with subject *ṭ‘m*$_2$, *mnk ytšm ṭ‘m ...* Driv

5[8]: let an order be issued by you (cf. Cowl 27[21], ATNS 15[3]) - Ingholt PNO p. 176: the *smt* in PNO 6d prob. = Qal Pf. 3 p.s.f. of *sym* (= *šym*$_1$), highly uncert. interpret., cf. also Milik DFD 343: prob. = n.p. - Roschinski Num 112, 115: l. *sm*ʾ in KAI 161[9] = Qal Pf. 3 p.s.m. + suff. 3 p.s.m. of *šym*$_1$ (highly uncert. interpret., diff. and dam. context).
v. *ʾš*$_1$, *ʾšm*$_4$, *dmk*, *ʿṣb*, *šm*$_{1,4}$, *šmʾl*, *šmym*.

šym$_2$ **OffAr** Sing. emph. *šymʾ* Cowl 38[10] - ¶ subst. m. of uncert. meaning; poss. = account, amount; *šymʾ šym ʾḥrwhy bbyt ʿnny* Cowl 38[10]: the amount is fixed with respect to (i.e. for) it in the house of A. (cf. Cowl a.l., Porten & Greenfield JEAS p. 82; cf. however also Grelot DAE p. 393 (n. m): the amount has been fixed after him (i.e. according to his indications) at (the expense of) the house of A., and cf. Porten & Yardeni sub TADAE A 4.3: l. *šgyʾ* (= Sing. m. abs. of *šgʾ*$_3$) *šym ʾḥrwhy* = (a) great (loss), there is backing; very diff. context).
v. *šm*$_1$.

šym$_3$ **OffAr** Sing. abs. *šym* Cowl 26[10,19] - ¶ subst. of unknown meaning, cf. Holma Öfversigt af Finska Vetenskaps-Societetens Förhandlingar '15, B 5, 6f., Cowl a.l., Grelot DAE p. 289; cf. also Whitehead JNES xxxvii 133 n. 90: part of boat (without further explanation).

šym$_4$ v. *ʾš*$_1$.

šymh **OffAr** Sing. emph. *šymtʾ* KAI 228A 18 - ¶ subst. of unknown meaning; cf. Gibson SSI ii p. 150f.: < Akkad. = property (cf. also Winckler AltorForsch i 184: = crown property < Akkad., less prob. etymology); the interpret. as "treasury" (cf. e.g. CIS ii sub 113, Lidzbarski Handb 375, Cooke NSI p. 198, Donner KAI a.l., Aggoula Syr lxii 62) less prob.; cf. also Lagrange ERS 503: = property (not < Akkad.).

šyn **OffAr** Sing. abs. *šyn* FuF xxxv 173[12] - ¶ subst. of uncert. meaning; Altheim & Stiehl FuF xxxv 173, ASA 276: = peace.

šys v. *šš*$_1$.

šyʿ$_1$ **Palm** for the diff. word (?) *ʾšyʿ* in Syr xvii 271[9], cf. Gawlikowski Syr li 99: < root *šyʿ* (= to help); cf. also Milik DFD 298f.: poss. < root *yšʿ*$_1$/*šwʿ*$_1$ (= to save) :: Cantineau Syr xvii 274: < root *šwʿ*$_2$ (= to smooth, to efface) :: Gawlikowski Syr li 99: or = < root *šʿʾ* (= to polish, to cover) :: Milik DFD 299: or = < root *nsʿ* (= to tear out, to pull out).

šyʿ$_2$ v. *šṭr*$_1$.

šyʿh$_1$ **Palm** Plur. cstr. *šyʿt* RTP 285 - ¶ subst. poss. meaning "protectress", "female auxiliary" (cf. Syriac/Palm. root *syʿ* = Arab. *šyʿ*, cf. Caquot RTP p. 149 :: Caquot ibid.: or = Sing. cstr. of *šyʿh*$_2$ (= troop; cf. also du Mesnil du Buisson TMP 445).

šyʿh$_2$ v. *šyʿh*$_1$.

šyʿwr v. *šṭr*$_2$.

šyph **Hebr** Sing. abs. *šyph* SM 49[3] - ¶ subst. bark (for the context of

SM 49[3], v. *ʾgd$_1$*).

šyr$_1$ **Ph** QAL Part. act. pl.m. abs. *šrm* KAI 37A 7 (for the reading, cf. (Cross with) Peckham Or xxxvii 305, 311 (n. 1), cf. also Amadasi sub Kition C 1, Gibson SSI iii p. 124, 128, Masson & Sznycer RPC 26, 41f. :: e.g. CIS i sub 86, Cooke NSI p. 65, 67, Röllig KAI a.l.: l. *ʾdm* = Plur. cstr. of *ʾdm$_1$* :: v. d Branden BO viii 252 (div. otherwise): l. *ʾdmm* = Plur. abs. of *ʾdm$_1$*) - ¶ verb QAL to sing; Part. act.: singer. v. *mšʿrt*, *ʿšr$_4$*.

šyr$_2$ **Hebr** Sing. cstr. *šyr* AMB 3[1] - ¶ subst. song; *šyr tšbḥwt* AMB 3[1]: a song of praise.

šyr$_3$ v. *šyd$_2$*.

šyrh **Palm** Sing. abs. *šyrʾ* Inv x 29[4]; cstr. *šyrt* Inv x 90[3] (v. infra); emph. *šyrtʾ* CIS ii 3916[2], 3928[2,4] (*šyrt[ʾ]*), 3933[3], 3936[2,4], 3948[2], 3963[2], Inv x 81[4], 90[2], 124[2], SBS 45[8] (*šyr[tʾ]*; Greek par. [συν]οδίαν)[,10] (Greek par. συνοδία)[,13], Syr xix 74[2], 75 i 3; Plur. abs. *šyryn* DFD 13[11] (dam. context; Greek par. συνοδιῶν), *šyrn* Inv x 44[5] (:: Inv x a.l.: l. *šyryn*) - ¶ subst. caravan; for comb. with *šyrh*, v. *br$_1$*, *rʾš$_1$*, *rb$_1$*, *rbnw*; cf. also *[brb]nwt šyrtʾ* SBS 45[13]: during (his) leadership of the caravan (cf. Greek par. συνοδιάρχων).

šyry v. *šʾry*.

šyš$_1$ v. *šš$_1$*.

šyš$_2$ v. *dhmpṭypṭyš*.

šyšm v. *ššm*.

šyt$_1$ **Ph** QAL Pf. 3 p.s.m. *št* KAI 26A i 11, ii 9, 17 (for these instances, cf. FR 267b, also for litt.; interpret. as Inf. (abs.), cf. also Gai Or li 254ff., less prob.), iii 14, 16 (in both instances :: FR 166: = QAL Part. act. s.m. abs., cf. also Röllig CISFP i 382), EpAn ix 5C 3; 1 p.s. *št* KAI 26C iv 16, 18; + suff. 3 p.s.m. *šty* KAI 24[11]; + suff. 3 p.pl.m. *štnm* KAI 26A i 16; 3 p.pl. *št* KAI 24[13] (cf. e.g. Röllig KAI a.l., Gibson SSI iii p. 35, 38 :: Torrey JAOS xxxv 365, Sperling UF xx 335f.: = QAL Pf. 1 p.s.); Impf. 2 p.s.m. *tšt* KAI 10[13]; YIPH Pf. 1 p.s. *yšt* KAI 43[7] - **Pun** QAL Pf. 3 p.pl. *št* KAI 69[17,18,20], 74[11] (or = QAL Part. pass. s.m. abs.?, cf. also Lidzbarski Handb 375, Cooke NSI p. 122, Schuster FS Landsberger 436 n. 25; cf. however CIS i sub 165[18]; :: Harr 148: in KAI 69[17,18] *št* = QAL pass. Pf. 3 p.s.f.); Inf. cstr. *št* KAI 76B 8 - **Hebr** QAL Impf. 2 p.s.m. *tšyt* AMB 4[18] - ¶ verb QAL to place, to put, to establish, passim - **1)** + obj., *whspr z št phlʾš hspr* EpAn ix 5C 3: and this inscription P. the scribe has set down (cf. Mosca & Russell EpAn ix 24); *wšt šm* KAI 26A iii 14: and he will put up his (own) name (sc. on the gate); cf. KAI 26C iv 16; for *št nbš* KAI 24[13], v. *npš* - **2)** + obj. + *ʾt$_6$*, *wʾm ʾbl tšt šm ʾtk* KAI 10[13]: and if you do not put my name beside your own; *wšt ʾnk šlm ʾt kl mlk* KAI 26A i 11f.: and I made peace with every king - **3)** + obj. + *ʿl$_7$*, *wšt šm ʿly* KAI 26A iii 16: he will put his

name thereon; cf. KAI 26C iv 18; cf. also *bl tšyt lb nkl ʿlyh* AMB 4[18f.]: do not place an evil heart (or an evil man's heart) on her - **4)** + obj. + *tḥt*, *wʾnk ʾztwd štnm tḥt pʿmy* KAI 26A i 16f.: and I A. placed them under my feet (on the context, cf. Greenfield EI xiv 74) - **5)** + double object, *šty bʿl ʿdr* KAI 24[11]: I made him owner of a flock; *wšt ʾnk šm ʾztwdy* KAI 26A ii 9f.: I called its name A. (cf. KAI 26A ii 17f.; v. *šm$_1$*) - **6)** + *b$_2$*, *[k]l mšʾt ʾš ʾybl št bps z* KAI 69[18]: every payment which is not put (i.e. written down) on this tablet (cf. KAI 69[17,20], 74[11]) - **7)** + *ʿlt*, *lšt ʿlt hḥdrt* KAI 76B 8: to place (it) near the chamber (v. *ḥdrh*, *ʿlt*) - YIPH to place, to erect; *yšt bmqdš mlqrt ʾyt mš pn ʾby* KAI 43[7]: I placed a statue representing my father in the sanctuary of M. (for the context, v. *pnh$_1$*) - a form of the same root prob. in KAI 1[1]: *kšth bʿlm*, cf. e.g. Tawil JANES iii 33ff., Lesh xxxvii 99ff.: = *k$_3$* (= *ky*) + *šth* (= QAL Pf. 3 p.s.m. + suff. 3 p.s.m. of *šyt$_1$*) *bʿlm* (= Sing. cstr. of *byt$_2$* + Sing. abs. of *ʿlm$_4$*; cf. already Jenni ZAW lxiv 208, cf. also Garr DGSP 182) = when he put him in his grave (cf. also Penar NSPBS 49, Avishur PIB 159f., Gibson SSI iii p. 14f., Garr DGSP 110; poss. interpret.; cf. already Torrey JAOS xlv 272: *bʿlm* lapsus for *bt ʿlm*?? (less prob. interpret.)); for the same interpret. of *kšth*, cf. Torrey JAOS xlv 270, 272, Friedrich FS Dussaud 43, v.d.Branden Mašr liv 732f., FR 20, 166; for the same interpret. of *šth*, cf. Lidzbarski NGWG '24, 46f., Vinnikov VDI xlii 142, Galling TGI 49 :: Lidzbarski NGWG '24, 46f., Galling TGI 49: *k* = *kʾ$_2$* :: Friedrich FS Dussaud 43, Röllig KAI a.l., Galling TGI 49: *bʿlm* = *b$_2$* + Sing. abs. of *ʿlm$_4$* (= in eternity), cf. Lidzbarski NGWG '24, 45f.: = for eternity (cf. also v.d.Branden Mašr liv 732f.) :: Vinnikov VDI xlii 142: *ʿlm* = world :: Dussaud Syr v 136, 139: *kšth* = *k$_1$* + Sing. + suff. 3 p.s.m. of *št$_1$* (= dwelling place), cf. also Bauer OLZ '25, 131 :: Vincent RB xxxiv 185: *kšth* = *k$_1$* + QAL Part. pass. s.m. + suff. 3 p.s.m. of *šyt$_1$* (= as his dwelling) :: Albright JAOS lxvii 155 n. 19: *kšth* = lapsus for *kšbth* (= *k$_1$* + QAL Inf. cstr. + suff. 3 p.s.m. of *yšb$_1$*; cf. also Galling WO i 422) :: Slouschz TPI p. 2f.: l. *kštr bʿlm* = *k$_3$* (= *ky*) + QAL Pf. 3 p.s.m. of *štr$_2$* (= to go) + *b$_2$* + Sing. abs. of *ʿlm$_4$* (when he went to his eternal world) or l. *kšth bʿlm* = *k$_3$* (= *ky*) + QAL Pf. 3 p.pl. + suff. 3 p.s.m. of *šyt$_1$* + Plur. abs. of of *bʿl$_2$* - the diff. *šʾt* in KAI 145[4] of uncert. interpret., Clermont-Ganneau RAO iii 336f., Février Sem vi 18, Röllig KAI a.l., FR 166: = QAL Part. act. s.m. abs. of *šyt$_1$*, cf. however v.d.Branden RSF i 166, 168, Krahmalkov RSF iii 188, 191, 202: = QAL Inf. cstr. of *nšʾ$_1$*, cf. also the discussion with Berger MAIBL xxxvi/2, 157 - the *št* in CIS i 5510[10] poss. = QAL Pf. 3 p.pl. (cf. Krahmalkov RSF ii 173).
v. *ʾš$_1$*.

šyt$_2$ **OldAr** Sing. abs. *šyt* KAI 223A 5 - ¶ subst. thorns (heavily dam. context).

šyt$_3$ v. *ʾḥd$_4$*.

škb Ph QAL Part. act. s.m. abs. *škb* KAI 9A 3, 13[2,5], 14[3], MUSJ xlv 262[1]; s.f. abs. *škbt* KAI 11 (cf. e.g. Gibson iii p. 100 :: Baldacci BiOr xl 130: = QAL Pf. 1 p.s.) - **Pun** NIPH Part. s.f. abs. *nškbt* NP 130[6] - **Hebr** QAL Part. act. s.f. abs. *šwkbt* Frey 634[1] - **DA** QAL Impf. 2 p.s.m. *tškb* ii 11 (:: Garbini Hen i 186 : = APH Impf. 2 p.s.m. (= to put)) - **OffAr** QAL Impf. 1 p.s. *ʾškb* AE '23, 40 no. 2[3,8]; cf. Frah xix 18 (*škb-ḥ-un*), cf. Toll ZDMG-Suppl viii 38 - ¶ verb QAL, to repose, to lie down; *tškb mškby ʿlmyk* DA ii 11: you will sleep the sleep of death (cf. Hoftijzer DA a.l.; for the text, v. also *ʿlm$_4$*); *bmškb zn ʾš ʾnk škb* KAI 9A 3: in this tomb where I repose; + *b$_2$*, *ʾnk škb bʾrn zn* MUSJ xlv 262[1]: I repose in this sarcophagus (cf. KAI 11, 13[2,5], 14[3]); + *ʿm$_4$*: AE '23, 40 no. 2[3,8] (diff. and dam. context) - NIPH (to lie down >) to die, to be laid to rest: NP 130[6].
v. *mškb$_2$*.

škh v. *šky$_1$*.

škḥ OffAr HAPH/APH Pf. 3 p.s.m. *hškḥ* Cowl 30[14] (cf. however Porten & Greenfield JEAS p. 90, Porten & Yardeni sub TADAE A 4.7: l. *hškḥh* = HAPH Pf. 3 p.s.m. + suff. 3 p.s.m.), 31[13]; 2 p.s.m. *hškḥt* Cowl 42[7,8]; 1 p.s. *hškḥt* Cowl 13[5], Aḥiq 76, Driv F 1a 2 (dam. context), Aeg xxxix 4 recto 2 (diff. context), *ʾškḥt* Herm 3[11], 4[9]; + suff. 3 p.s.f. *ʾškḥth* Herm 4[4]; 3 p.pl.m. *hškḥw* Cowl 38[4], AG 88[7] (:: Aimé-Giron AG a.l.: l. *hšdḥw*); 1 p.pl. *[h]škḥn* Cowl 4[5]; Impf. 3 p.s.m. *yškḥ* Herm 2[15]; 2 p.s.m. *thškḥ* Aḥiq 34, Krael 11[11], *tškḥ* Cowl 10[9,10,17], Herm 3[10]; 1 p.s. *ʾškḥ* Herm 2[12]; 3 p.pl.m. *yhškḥwn* Cowl 38[7], ATNS 26[14]; 3 p.pl.f. *yškḥn* RES 492B 6 (cf. Ben-Chayyim EI i 139; diff. context, cf. also RES 1800, cf. however Grelot DAE p. 141 n. r: = APH Impf. 3 p.s.m. + energic ending); 2 p.pl.m. *tškḥwn* Cowl 37[10]; Imper. s.f., cf. Warka 16, 41: *aš-ka-ḫi-i*; Part. s.f. abs. *mhškḥh* Cowl 38[9] (for this prob. reading, cf. Porten & Yardeni sub TADAE A 4.3 :: e.g. Cowl a.l.: l. *mh* (= *mh$_2$*) + *ymnh* (= PAʿEL Impf. 3 p.s.m. of *mny*)); ITP Pf. 3 p.s.m. *ʾštkḥ* Cowl 27[2,13]; 3 p.pl.m. *ʾštkḥwn* Cowl 34[4]; Impf. 3 p.s.m. *yštkḥ* Cowl 35[11] (*[y]štk[ḥ]*; for this prob. reading cf. Porten JNES xlviii 166, Porten & Yardeni sub TADAE B 4.6 :: Cowley a.l.: l. *[r]štk[y]* = QAL Pf. 1 p.s. + suff. 2 p.s.f. of *ršy$_1$*), 44 (*scriptio anterior* l. 2; for the reading, cf. Porten & Yardeni sub TADAE B 7.3); cf. Frah xx 13 (*ḥškḥwn*), cf. also Toll ZDMG-Suppl viii 39, Nisa 194[4], 644[6], etc. (*hškḥw*), GIPP 54 - **Nab** ITP Impf. 3 p.s.m. *yštkḥ* BASOR cclxiii 78[3] - **Palm** ITP Pf. 3 p.s.m. *ʾštkḥ* Syr xvii 280[4] (for the reading, cf. Milik DFD 310 :: Dunant sub SBS 48 (div. otherwise): l. *štt* = f. cstr. of *šš$_3$*) - ¶ verb HAPH/APH to find, passim; *lqbl zy ydkm mhškḥh* Cowl 38[9]: as much as you can (v. also supra) - **1)** + obj., *hn hškḥt ksp [ḥ]t lʿbq* Cowl 42[7]: if you found the silver, come down immediately (cf. Cowl 4[5], 37[10] (?), Herm 2[15], 3[10]);

aš-ka-ḫi-i ḫa-ba-ra-an Warka 16: find the others (cf. Warka 41, Herm 4^9) - **2)** + obj. + describing element, *kzy knbwzy ʿl lmṣryn ʾgwrʾ zk bnh hškḥ* (v. however supra) Cowl $30^{13f.}$: when C. came to E. he found this temple (already) built (cf. Cowl 31^{13}, $38^{3f.}$, Herm 4^4) - **3)** + obj. + l_5, *kzy mlh bʾyšh lʾ yhškḥwn lkm* Cowl $38^{6f.}$: that they will not find fault with you - **4)** + obj. + l_5 + Inf., *wlʾ hškḥt ksp ... lšlmh lky* Cowl 13^5: I have not found silver to pay you (cf. Herm 2^{12}, 3^{11}) - **5)** + l_5 (obj.), *hškḥt lʾḥyq[r]* Aḥiq 76: I have found A. - **6)** + l_5 (with), *kl ʿrbn zy tškḥ ly* Cowl 10^9: any security that you will find with me ... (cf. Cowl $10^{10,17}$) - **7)** + l_5 + b_2, *zy thškḥ ly byb wbswn ...* Krael 11^{11}: which you will find with me in Y. and S. - **8)** + mn_5 + obj., *yhškḥwn mn tmh gbrn kšyrn* ATNS 26^{14}: let them find from there capable men - ITP to be found; *ʾštkḥ rḥm md[ynth]* Syr xvii 280^4: he was found patriotic (for the reading and interpret., cf. Milik DFD 310ff.) - **1)** + b_2, *gbryʾ zy ʾštkḥw bbbʾ* Cowl 34^4: the men who were found at the gate - **2)** + l_5, *wmndʿm mḥbl [lʾ] ʾštkḥ ln* Cowl 27^2: nothing bad was found with us (v. *ḥbl*$_1$), cf. Cowl 27^{13} - **3)** + $ʿl_7$, *pyprʿ mh dy yštkḥ ʿl[why]* BASOR cclxiii 78^3 (for this prob. context reading, cf. Jones BASOR cclxxv 43): and he shall pay, which is found against him - the diff. *ʾštḥ* in Inv x 127^3 poss. = lapsus for *ʾštkḥ* (= ITP Pf. 3 p.s.m.), cf. Greek par. ἐνδέδειχται (cf. also Milik DFD 311) - a form of this root prob. in Cowl 42^3 (*h[š]kḥt* = HAPH Pf. 2 p.s.m./1 p.s.), for the reading cf. Porten & Yardeni sub TADAE A 3.8 :: e.g. Cowley a.l.: l. poss. *yntn* = QAL Impf. 3 p.s.m. of *ntn*.

v. *šwy*$_1$.

šky$_1$ **Pun** Rocco AION xix 552f.: l. *šktk* in GR i 61 no. 31 B1 (= GR ii 88 no. 70) = QAL Pf. 1 p.s. + suff. 2 p.s.f. of *šky*$_1$ (= to implore) or Sing. + suff. 2 p.s.f. of *škh* (= ship), reading and interpret. highly uncertain, cf. Guzzo Amadasi GR a.l.

šky$_2$ v. *šry*$_1$.

škynh **Hebr** Sing. cstr. *škynt* AMB 1^3 - ¶ subst. divine presence.

škytyt **Palm** CIS ii 3932^6 - ¶ adv. honourably (cf. Greek par. καλῶς).

škl **OldAr** Lipiński Stud 34f.: l. *hšklh* (= HAPH Pf. 3 p.s.m. + suff. 3 p.s.m. of *škl* (= to leave childless) in KAI 222B 12 (very diff. and dam. context; uncert. interpret.; reading however poss.).

škll **JAr** Pf. 3 p.s.m. *škll* EI xx 305 iii 4 (heavily dam. context) - ¶ verb, to finish, to decorate.

škm$_1$ **DA** Hoftijzer DA a.l.: l. *škmtʾ* in i 3f. = Plur. emph. (= mountainous regions?); less prob. combination and interpret. (cf. also Greenfield JSS xxv 251), diff. and dam. context; cf. e.g. Caquot & Lemaire Syr liv 194f., McCarter BASOR ccxxxix 51f., Ringgren Mem Seeligmann 93, Lemaire BAT 318, GLECS xxiv-xxviii 333f. (combining fragments otherwise): l. resp. *bkh* (v. *bky*$_1$) and *kml[y]ʾ* (= k_1 + Plur. emph. of *mlh*; on this reading and interpret., cf. also Koenig Sem xxxiii 77ff.; less prob. reading); cf. e.g. Rofé SB 61, Levine JAOS ci 196, 198, BAT 329, 333, H. & M. Weippert ZDPV xcviii 83f., 86, Hackett BTDA 25, 33, 37, Or liii 59 n. 15, Puech BAT 360, FS Grelot 17f., Wesselius BiOr xliv 593f.: l. *bkh* and *kmš›* (= k_1 + Sing. cstr. of *mš›*$_1$; less prob. reading); Garbini Hen i 171, 173, 175: l. *bkh* and *kml›* (*ml›* = subst. or Inf. < root *ml›*$_1$ indicating 'wrath' or 'being in wrath' (improb. interpret.); cf. also H. & M. Weippert ZDPV xcviii 84 (n. 28)).

škm$_2$ **Pun** the *škm* in KAI 153^5 poss. = Sing. abs. of *škm*$_2$ (= subst. of unknown meaning); Février JA ccxxxvii 89: = hypogee (highly uncert. interpret. and word division). Or div. otherwise l. *t›škmst* = n.l.??
v. *š›k*, *twm*$_1$.

škn$_1$ **Ph** QAL Part. act. pl.m. abs. *šknm* KAI 37A 7 (for the reading, cf. CIS i sub 86, Cooke NSI p. 65, 67, Slouschz TPI p. 77f., Röllig KAI a.l., Masson & Sznycer RPC 26, 43ff., Healy BASOR ccxvi 53, 55, Amadasi sub Kition C 1 :: Gibson SSI ii p. 124, 128: l. *šknm* = Plur. abs. of *škn*$_3$ (= variant of *skn*$_2$), cf. also e.g. Harr 149, Röllig KAI a.l. :: Peckham Or xxxvii 305, 311f. (nn. 3, 1; cf. also idem JNES xxxv 286): l. *škny* = Sing. + suff. 3 p.s.f. of *škn*$_2$ (= habitation, dwelling-place)) - **OffAr** QAL Part. act. s.m. abs. *škn* IPAA 12^{10} (diff. context), abs./cstr. *škn* Krael 12^2 - **JAr** PA‹EL Pf. 3 p.s.m. *škn* MPAT-A 39^1 (for the reading, cf. Naveh sub SM 42, Beyer ATTM 389 :: Ben-Dov Qadm vi 61: l. *šrn* = PA‹EL Pf. 3 p.pl.m. of *šry*$_1$ (= to establish) :: Fitzmyer & Harrington MPAT a.l.: l. *šrn* = PA‹EL Pf. 1 p.pl. of *šry*$_1$) - ¶ verb QAL to dwell, to reside; *YHW ›lh› škn yb* Krael 12^2: YHW the God dwelling in Yeb (cf. Yaron JSS iv 309, Segert ArchOr xxiv 403, Porten Arch 107ff.); *›š šknm* KAI 37A 7: who reside (cf. CIS i sub 86, Cooke NSI p. 66, 67, Masson & Sznycer RPC 43f. (uncert. interpret.; cf. e.g. Healy BASOR ccxvi 53: = who perform)) - PA‹EL to establish, to present; *dškn hdh skwpth* MPAT-A 39$^{1f.}$: who established this lintel ... - a form of this root also in CIS i 135^{2,3}: *škn*?? - poss. also a form of this root (QAL Part. act. s.m. abs./cstr.) in Frey 900^4: *škn lwd* = inhabitant of Lydda (for this reading, cf. Clermont-Ganneau RAO iv 142f., Lidzbarski Eph iii 190, Pedersen InscrSem sub 2) - Ferron StudMagr i 77: l. *sk[n]* in CIS i 6000bis 7 = QAL Part. act. s.m. abs. of *skn*$_1$ (= variant of *škn*$_1$), improb. interpret. (cf. Février CIS i a.l.: l. *sk[* = part of n.p. and Lidzbarski Eph i 168f.: l. *sk[r* = form of *skr*$_4$ (= *zkr*$_2$), cf. also Chabot sub RES 236).

škn$_2$ **OffAr** Segal ATNS a.l.: l. *škn* (= Sing. abs. of *škn*$_2$ (= dwelling)) in ATNS 44 ii 2, *byt škn* = dwelling-place (less prob. interpret., prob. *bytškn* = n.p., cf. also Porten & Yardeni sub TADAE B 8.2).
v. *mškn*$_3$, *škn*$_1$.

škn$_3$ v. *škn*$_1$.

škr$_1$ **Ph** QAL Pf. 3 p.s.m. *škr* KAI 24[7] (cf. Gibson SSI iii p. 37 (cf. also Teixidor JBL ciii 454), cf. FR 267b also for litt. (cf. also Chiera Hen x 134); interpret. as Inf. (abs.), cf. also Amadasi Guzzo VO iii 89f., less prob. (:: Garbini FSR 104ff.: < root *škr$_2$* = to be abundant, to be opulent?)) - **Palm** QAL Pf. 3 p.s.f. *skrt* Inv x 115[2] - ¶ verb QAL - **1)** to hire; *wškr ʾnk ʿly mlk ʾšr* KAI 24[7f.]: I hired against him the king of A. (cf. Smend with Lidzbarski Eph iii 230, Halévy RS xx 28, Bauer ZDMG lxvii 686, lxviii 228, Torrey JAOS xxxv 365, 367 (interpret. *škr* as QAL Part. act. s.m. abs.), Röllig KAI a.l., Swiggers RSO xlv 2f., Gibson SSI iii p. 35, 37, Sperling UF xx 332 (nn. 86, 88) :: Landsberger Samʾal 51f.: *škr* = QAL Part. pass. s.m. abs. or subst. (Sing. abs.) or QAL Part. pass. s.m. (or subst. Sing.) + suff. 3 p.s.m. (I was a (or his) mercenary against the king of Assur) :: Lidzbarski Eph iii 229f.: or = he hired against me the king of Assur, or: the king of Assur hired him against me (cf. also Poeb 35) :: Dahood CBQ xxii 405: = QAL Part. act. s.m. abs. of *škr$_3$* (= to be drunk > to be helpless, cf. also idem CBQ xxx 519, Ps iii 88) - **2)** to reward: Inv x 115[2] (+ *l$_5$* obj.).
v. *mkr$_2$*.

škr$_2$ v. *škr$_1$*.

škr$_3$ v. *škr$_1$*.

škr$_4$ **OffAr** Sing. emph. *škrʾ* RES 492B 3 (= RES 1800) - ¶ subst. prob. meaning salary, reward (interpret. of context however diff., cf. also Grelot DAE p. 140 n. o) - this subst. Sing. emph. (*skrʾ*) also in Inv D 15[4]? (diff. context, cf. also Dussaud Syr vi 203) - on this word, cf. Chiera RSO lvii 46f.
v. *škr$_6$*.

škr$_5$ (< Arab.?, cf. Cantineau Gramm 42, 150; cf. also Diem Or xlix 76) - **Palm** Sing. m. abs. *škr* MUSJ xlii 177[10] (v. however infra); emph. *škrʾ* CIS ii 3973[4], 3983[2] (= SBS 13), Inscr P 30[2] (= SBS 1b), PNO 5, etc., *skrʾ* CIS ii 4013[2], PNO 4, 13[3f.], 37[5], Rob 373[3], Inv xi 11[6] (*sk[rʾ]*; or rather = Plur. emph.?, cf. Aggoula Sem xxix 110), 38[3]; Plur. emph. *škryʾ* PNO 7a, 48[4], SBS 7[2], 14[2], Syr xii 135[2], Sem iii 47[8], *skryʾ* CIS ii 3974[1], PNO 39, Inv xii 32[3], *škrʾ* FS Collart 327[5] - ¶ adj. rewarding; used as divine epithet; *ʾlhʾ škr[ʾ]* (or preferably *škr*??, cf. also MUSJ xlii 177[9f.] *ʾlhʾ ṭb wškr*) MUSJ xxxviii 133[7]: the rewarding god; in other instances combined with *ṭb$_2$*, cf. e.g. *ʾlhʾ ṭbʾ wškrʾ* SBS 3[2]: the good and rewarding god (cf. CIS ii 4013[2]); *qnyʾ ṭbʾ wškrʾ* FS Collart 327[4f.]: the good and rewarding *genii* (for the formula *ṭbʾ wškrʾ*, cf. also Drijvers FS Widengren 365f.); cf. also *ṭbʾ wrḥmnʾ wskrʾ* Inv xi 38[2f.]: the good, merciful and rewarding one; used for diff. deities.

škr$_6$ **OffAr** Sing. abs. *škr* Driv 6[3], ATNS 20[2] (or = Sing. abs. of *škr$_4$*?), 42[3,4], 81[6] (or = Sing. abs. of *škr$_4$*?, dam. context); cf. Frah v 9 (*škl*, *šklʾ*) - ¶ subst. ale, mead (cf. Driv p. 60); in Frah v 9 some kind of intoxicating drink.

škt **Pun** Rocco AION xix 552: l. *šktk* (= Sing. + suff. 2 p.s.f. of *škt* (= ship)) in GR i no. xxxi b 1 (= GR ii no. 70), highly uncert. reading and interpret. (cf. also Amadasi Guzzo sub GR i no. xxxi and Polselli sub GR ii no. 70).

šl v. *šql*$_3$.

šl᾽ v. *gll*.

šlb$_1$ cf. Frah-S$_2$ 162 (*šlb᾽*) = spout of a vessel.

šlb$_2$ **Pun** Plur. abs. *šlbm* KAI 69[4,6,8,10], *᾽šlbm* CIS i 170[2], KAI 74[4] (*᾽šl[bm]*; cf. FR 95a :: Capuzzi StudMagr ii 66 n. 106: ᾽ poss. = article) - ¶ subst. indicating some part of the sacrificial animal, exact meaning unknown: fat, entrails or ribs (cf. CIS i sub 165, Cooke NSI p. 119, Röllig KAI a.l., Capuzzi Stud Magr ii 66; Lagrange ERS 473: = leg, thigh :: v.d.Branden RSO xl 125: = Dual abs. (= kidneys)) - on this word, cf. also Cathcart AO v 11ff.

šlh$_1$ **OldAr** Sing. abs. *šlh* Tell F 3 - ¶ subst. rest (for the context and Akkad. par., v. *᾽dqwr*).

šlh$_2$ v. *᾽dqwr*.

šlh$_3$ v. *᾽dqwr*.

šlw (< Arab., cf. Cooke NSI p. 223, Cantineau Nab. ii 172, O'Connor JNES xlv 218f.) - **Nab** Sing. abs. *šlw* CIS ii 198[6] - ¶ subst. the body after its decaying.

šlwm v. *šlm*$_2$.

šlwš v. *šlš*$_1$.

šlwt = negligence > Akkad. *šilûtu/šilētu*, cf. v.Soden Or xxxvii 268, xlvi 195, AHW s.v. *silûtu* II.

šlḥ$_1$ **Ph** QAL (or PI῾EL?) Pf. 3 p.s.m. *šlḥ* KAI 24[6]; 2 p.s.f. *šlḥt* KAI 50[3,5f.]; 3 p.pl. + suff. 1 p.s. *šlḥn* KAI 26A ii 11; for KAI 37A 15, 17, v. *šlḥ*$_3$ - **Pun** QAL (or PI῾EL?) Imper. s.m. *šlḥ* Trip 51[7] (?, reading *š* uncert., diff. and dam. context; cf. also Amadasi IPT 131, 135: reading of *ḥ* uncert., poss. = QAL Pf. 3 p.s.m.) - **Hebr** QAL (or PI῾EL?, except in KAI 194[8], TA-H 16[1], 21[1]) Pf. 3 p.s.m. *šlḥ* KAI 193[1,18], 194[2,4], 196[3], Lach xviii 2; + suff. 3 p.s.m. *šlḥh* KAI 193[21]; 2 p.s.m. *šlḥth* KAI 193[6] (or = 2 p.s.m. + suff. 3 p.s.m.?; for the reading *šlḥth ᾽l ῾bdk*, cf. Ginsberg BASOR lxxi 26, Albright BASOR lxxiii 18 (cf. also Lemaire IH i p. 100), cf. however e.g. Torczyner Lach i p. 51: l. *šlḥ* (= QAL Pf. 3 p.s.m.) *᾽dny l῾bdk* (cf. also Diringer Lach iii 332, Röllig KAI a.l.) :: Gibson SSI i p. 38: l. *šlḥ ᾽d[ny ᾽]l ῾[b]dk*), 194[4] (for this poss. reading, cf. de Vaux RB xlviii 195 (cf. also Lemaire IH i p. 110) :: e.g. Torczyner Lach i p. 79: l. *šlḥ ᾽dny* (cf. also e.g. Röllig KAI a.l., Gibson SSI i p. 41)); 1 p.s. *šlḥty* TA-H 16[4], 24[8], *šlḥt* DJD ii 17A 1 (diff. and uncert. reading; cf. also Aharoni BASOR cxcvii 30 n. 44, Scagliarini Hen xii 137, Pardee HAHL 122; for the context, cf. Dion RB lxxxvi 554f.); 3 p.pl. *šlḥw* TA-

H 61[1] (or = Imper. pl.m.??); 2 p.pl.m. *šlḥtm* TA-H 24[13]; Impf. 2 p.s.m. *tšlḥ* TA-H 16[10], DJD ii 44[2]; Imper. s.m. *šlḥ* TA-H 5[2], 6[2], 13[4] (cf. Pardee UF x 309f. (uncert. interpret., cf. v.Dyke Parunak BASOR cxxx 27f. (div. otherwise): l. *nšlḥw* = Niph Pf. 3 p.pl.) :: Aharoni TA-H a.l. (div. otherwise): l. *šlḥw* (= Qal Imper. s.m. + suff. 3 p.s.m.)), 14[3], 17[5], AMB 3[19]; + suff. 3 p.s.m. *šlḥnw* TA-H 4[2] (cf. e.g. Aharoni TA a.l., Lemaire IH i p. 166, Pardee UF x 302, HAHL 36f. :: Israel OA xvii 241: = Imper. s.m. + suff. 1 p.pl.); Inf. abs. *šlḥ* DJD ii 17A 1 (uncert. reading); Inf. cstr. *šlḥ* TA-H 40[14]; + suff. 2 p.s.m. *šlḥk* KAI 193[7]; Part. act. s.m. abs. *šlḥ* KAI 194[8] (cf. e.g. Albright BASOR xcvii 26, cxliv 26, Cross BASOR cxliv 24, Röllig KAI a.l., Gibson SSI i p. 41, Pardee HAHL 92 (cf. also Lemaire IH i p. 110) :: e.g. Torczyner Lach i p. 79, 82: l. *yšlḥ* = Qal Impf. 3 p.s.m.), TA-H 16[1], 21[1]; pl.m. abs. *šlḥ[m]* TA-H 40[2] (or rather l. *šlḥ[w]*? (= Qal Pf. 3 p.pl.), cf. Pardee UF x 324, HAHL 64); a form of this root prob. in KAI 197[3], cf. e.g. Torczyner Lach i p. 135: l. *šlḥ[t]* = Qal Pf. 2 p.s.m. (less prob. interpret.), cf. also Gibson SSI i p. 47: l. *nšlḥ* (= Niph Pf. 3 p.s.m., less prob. interpret.), Röllig KAI a.l.: l. *yšlḥ* (= Qal Impf. 3 p.s.m.) or l. (div. otherwise) *lḥm* (= Sing. abs. of *lḥm*4; for this interpret., cf. also Michaud Syr xxxiv 52, 54, PA 88, Lemaire IH i 127); forms of this root also in TA-H 16[9], 62[1]: *]šlḥ[-* **OldAr** Qal (or Pa ʿel?, except KAI 222B 34) Impf. 3 p.s.m. *yšlḥ* KAI 202B 21, 222B 25, 34 (for this reading, cf. Ronzevalle MUSJ xv 260 facsimile no. 4 l. 15, Degen AAG p. 15, 68, GGA '79, 33, Kaufman BiOr xxxiv 95, Lemaire & Durand IAS 115, 124, 139, Kottsieper SAS 138 :: e.g. Dupont-Sommer Sf p. 62, 150, Fitzmyer AIS 18, 70, Lipiński Stud 39, Segert AAG p. 260, Hopkins BSOAS xl 142: l. *mšlḥ* = Qal Inf.), 224[8]; 2 p.s.m. *tšlḥ* KAI 222B 37 (dam. context), 224[17,21]; 1 p.s. *ʾšlḥ* KAI 223B 6, 224[8]; 3 p.pl.m. *yšlḥn* KAI 222A 30 - **OffAr** Qal (or Pa ʿel?, except Part. forms) Pf. 3 p.s.m. *šlḥ* Cowl 30[7], 31[6], 40[3], 64 xx 2 (dam. context), Beh 38 (Akkad. par. *iš-pur-ma*), Driv 4[1], 8[1,2], 12[1,5,8], F v 1[2] (dam. context), ATNS 27[5] (?, dam. context), 77b 3, 102a 2 (?, *šlḥ[)*, RES 492B5, 1792B 5, 6, Sem xxxiii 94[2] (for this prob. interpret., cf. Porten Sem xxxiii 96, Porten & Yardeni sub TADAE A 5.1 :: Sznycer HDS 168f.: = Imper. s.m.), AE '23, 42 no. 9[4] (dam. context); 2 p.s.m. *šlḥt* Cowl 41[5], ATNS 33a 1 (dam. context, or = 3 p.s.f. or 1 p.s.?); 2 p.s.f. *šlḥty* Herm 1[5]; 1 p.s. *šlḥt* Cowl 16[8], 54[2], Beh 25 (Akkad. par. *al-ta-par*), 26* (cf. Greenfield & Porten BIDG 38; Akkad. par. *aš-pur*), Driv 7[5], F vii 7 (or = 3 p.s.f., 2 p.s.m.?, dam. context), RES 1300[4], 1792A 1, B 7, 8, KAI 233[13] (or = 2 p.s.m.?), JRAS '29, 108[2], RHR cxxx 20 conc. 2, conv. 2, RSO xxxv 22[5], Herm 2[17], 3[5,13], 4[12], 5[9], 7[1,4]; 3 p.pl.m. *šlḥw* Cowl 26[6], 30[19]; 2 p.pl.f. *šlḥtn* Herm 5[8]; 1 p.pl. *šlḥn* Cowl 30[18,29], 31[17,28]; Impf. 3 p.s.m. *yšlḥ* Aḥiq 62 (*[yš]lḥ*), Driv 4[3], 12[11], NESE iii 48[10]; + suff. 2 p.s.m.? *[y]šlḥn[k]* Aḥiq

201 (for the reading, cf. Lindenberger APA 200); 2 p.s.m. *tšlḥ* Driv F vi 10^{2} (dam. context); 1 p.s. *ˀšlḥ* Cowl 41^{3}, KAI 233^{19}; 3 p.pl.m. *yšlḥwn* NESE iii 48^{8}; Imper. s.m. *šlḥ* Cowl 38^{10}, 40^{4} (dam. context; for this prob. reading, cf. Porten & Yardeni sub TADAE A 3.6 :: e.g. Cowl a.l. (div. otherwise): poss. l. *thšlḥ* (= HAPH Impf. 2 p.s.m.)), 42^{10}, Sach 76 i B 2, 80 i 3 (dam. context), iii B 2 (dam. context), RES 1298B 1, 3 (or = Pf. 3 p.s.m.?; dam. context), PSBA '15, 222^{8} (= RES 1793), RES 1810^{1} (for the reading, cf. Sznycer HDS 169; or = QAL Pf. 3 p.s.m.?), RHR cxxx 20 conc. 4, ASAE xxvi 24 A 2 (or = Pf. 3 p.s.m.?, cf. Segal Maarav iv 70; dam. context), Sem xiv 72 conv. 5 (dam. context), Herm $3^{6,7}$, *šḥ* RES 1296^{2} (lapsus, cf. e.g. Grelot DAE p. 137 :: Lidzbarski Eph iii 122 (div. otherwise): l. *šḥly* = lapsus for *šlḥy* (= QAL Imper. s.f.) :: Aimé-Giron sub AG 3a (div. otherwise): l. *šḥlyn* = indication of a certain substance); + suff. 3 p.s.m. *šlḥhy* RES 1795B 2 (context however dam.); s.f. *šlḥy* Herm 1^{12}, $2^{6,8,9,10,16}$; pl.m. *šlḥw* Cowl 54^{15} (?, dam. context); Inf. *mšlḥ* KAI 266^{7}; Part. act. s.m. abs. *šlḥ* Cowl 38^{9}, PSBA '15, 222^{10} (= RES 1793^{5}); s.f. abs. *šlḥt* Herm 1^{11} (for this form, cf. Wesselius AION xxx 266); pl.m. abs. *šlḥn* Cowl 17^{3}; QAL pass. Pf. 3 p.s.m. *šlyḥ* ATNS 26^{12}, 29^{7} (dam. context); Part. pass. s.m. abs. (or rather = QAL pass. Pf. 3 p.s.m.?) *šlyḥ* Cowl 21^{3}, 26^{6}; PAʿEL Part. act. s.m. + suff. 3 p.s.f. *mšlḥh* Aḥiq 98 (cf. e.g. Grelot DAE p. 437, Lindenberger APA 76 (idem ibid. 236 n. 168: or + suff. 3 p.s.m.?), Muraoka JSS xxxii 188 :: Grimme OLZ '11, 531, Ginsberg ANET 428, Bibl lvi 256: = Part. pass. s.f. abs., cf. also Nöldeke AGWG xiv/4, 12 :: Leand 31b: = Part. pass. + suff. 3 p.s.f. (cf. also Cowl a.l., Grelot RB lxviii 183) :: Kottsieper SAS 235: = PAʿEL Part. + suff. 3 p.s.m.) - HAPH/APH Pf. 1 p.s. (or 3 p.s.f. or 2 p.s.m.) *hšlḥt* Cowl 67 ii 2 (dam. context); + suff. 3 p.s.m., cf. Warka 30: *áš-làøh-te-e*; ITP Impf. 3 p.s.m. *yštlḥ* Cowl $26^{4,21}$, 30^{24}, Driv 3^{5}; 3 p.s.f. *tštlḥ* Driv 10^{2}; cf. Paik 964-965 (*šlḥw*), GIPP 64 - **JAr** QAL (or PAʿEL?) Pf. 1 p.s. *šlḥt* MPAT 54^{1}, 60^{1}; Impf. 3 p.s.m. *yšlḥ* AMB 3^{15}; 2 p.s.m. *tšlḥ* MPAT 60^{1}; 2 p.pl.m. *tšlḥn* MPAT 57^{2}, *tšlḥwn* MPAT 56^{4}; 3 p.pl.m. *yšlḥn* MPAT 60^{3}; Imper. s.m. *šlḥ* MPAT $60^{3,4}$ - ¶ verb QAL (or PIʿEL/PAʿEL?) to send; cf. *kkl ˀšr šlḥ ˀdny kn ʿšh ʿbdk* KAI $194^{2f.}$: in accordance with all (the instructions) my lord has sent, so your servant has acted - **1)** + obj., *šlḥ ˀdny ˀ[t sp]r hmlk* KAI $196^{3f.}$: my lord has sent the letter of the king; *šlḥt ˀrtwrzy šmh* Beh 25: I sent someone named A. (cf. Cowl 38^{10}, ATNS 33a 5, RES $1296^{2f.}$, RHR cxxx 20 conv. 2, RSO xxxv 22^{5}, TA-H 4^{2}, 14^{3}, $16^{9f.}$, 40^{14}); *[ms]pt qbylh ... lˀ yšlḥ* Driv 12^{11}: M. will not send a complaint; *wšlḥy kl ṭʿm zy hwh bbyty* Herm 1^{12}: send (a report/letter about) every matter that has happened in my house; *hwyt ˀšlḥ šlmk* Cowl 41^{3}: I used to send you a greeting (cf. RES $1793^{5f.}$; cf. Dion RB lxxxix 557f.); *šlḥ rpwy* AMB 3^{19}: send healing; cf. also *mspt šlḥ grdˀ ...*

zy mr᾽ty ktš Driv $12^{8f.}$: M. has sent (a message): he has beaten up the domestic staff of my lady; *wlh šlḥtn hn ḥy ᾽nh whn mt ᾽nh* Herm $5^{8f.}$: and you did not write (to ask) whether I was alive or dead; cf. also *šlḥ l᾽mr zy l᾽ yškḥn* RES 492B 5f.: he has sent me the message that they will not find ... (v. *škḥ*) - **2)** + obj. + indication of place, *wšlḥtm ᾽tm rmt ...* TA-H 24^{13}: and you shall send them to R. ... - **3)** + obj. + *᾽l*$_6$, *šlḥh ‹bk ᾽l ᾽dny* KAI 193^{21}: your servant has sent it (sc. the letter) to my lord (cf. KAI 224^{8}, for the context, v. *šlm*$_1$) - **4)** + obj. + *b*$_2$, *wyšlḥn ᾽lhn mn klmh ᾽kl b᾽rpd* KAI 222A 30: and the gods will send caterpillars, lice (and) devourers over A. (v. *klmh*$_1$, *mn*$_2$); *ltšlḥ lšn bbyty wbny bny* KAI 224^{21}: you shall not let loose your tongue in my house nor among my sons (cf. also Fitzmyer AIS 116, Sperling JANES ii 104, Tawil CBQ xlii 32ff., Lemaire & Durand IAS 146 :: Rosenthal BASOR clviii 30 n. 10: or = < *šlḥ*$_2$ (= to strip/to bare the tongue); *wlykhl bry [l]yšlḥ yd bbr[k]* KAI 222B 25: my son will not be able to stretch out (his) hand against your son (cf. KAI 222B 34; cf. Greenfield FS Fitzmyer 49) - **5)** + obj. + *bšm*: Herm $1^{5f.}$ (v. *šm*$_1$); for + obj. + *bšm* + *‹l*$_7$: Cowl 30^{29}, 31^{28}, v. also *šm*$_1$ - **6)** + obj. + *bny*, *ltšlḥ lšnk bnyhm* KAI $224^{17f.}$: you shall not loose your tongue among them (cf. also Fitzmyer AIS 116, Sperling JANES ii 104, Sader EAS 135) :: Rosenthal BASOR clviii 30 n. 10: or = < *šlḥ*$_2$ (= to strip/to bare the tongue; cf. also Greenfield ActOr xxix 6) - **7)** + obj. + *l*$_5$, *ml᾽kty ᾽šlḥ lk* KAI 233^{19}: I shall send my report to you (v. *ml᾽kh*$_2$), cf. TA-H $16^{4f.}$; *šlm wḥyn šlḥt lk* RHR cxxx 20 conc. 2f.: welfare and life I sent to you (cf. Herm 3^{5}, 7^{1}; cf. Fitzmyer JBL xciii 215, Fales JAOS cxvii 458f.); *šlm yqyh hwy šlḥt lh* Herm 1^{11}: send greetings for Y. to him (cf. e.g. Hoftijzer SV 109 × e.g. Porten & Greenfield ZAW lxxx 226, 228, Milik Bibl xlviii 550, 581, Gibson SSI ii p. 130, Swiggers AION xli 146: send greetings from Y. to him (or her?)); *brk[h] šlḥt lky* JRAS '29, $108^{1f.}$: a blessing I send you; *kl zy tṣbh šlḥ ly* Herm 3^{7}: write me everything you want; *wšlḥ ythn lmḥnyh* MPAT 60^{4}: send them to the camp - **8)** + obj. + *l*$_5$ + Inf., *w᾽nšw šlḥ lqḥt ...* KAI $193^{17f.}$: he sent his men to take ... (:: Smelik HDAI 113: as to his men, he has sent (a message) to take (them)); *šlḥn lbnt* KAI 26A ii 11: they sent me (i.e. they ordered me) to build; *lmšlḥ ḥyl lhṣltn[y]* KAI 266^{7}: to send an army to save me (v. *ḥṣl*$_1$); *mlk᾽ [yš]lḥ [᾽]ḥryn pgrh zy ᾽ḥyqr ... lmḥzh* Aḥiq 62f.: the king will send others to see the body of A. ...; *kl šlḥ yd llḥm* KAI 24^{6}: and each stretched out his hand to eat (v. *lḥm*$_2$; :: Tawil CBQ xlii 35ff.: *šlḥ yd* here = to plot (against this interpret., cf. Sperling UF xx 328f. (n. 53)) - **9)** + obj. + *mlwt*, *šlḥ ᾽ḥryn mlwtk* MPAT 60^{3}: send others from you - **10)** + obj. + *‹l*$_7$, *᾽grh ḥdh l᾽ šlḥw ‹lyn* Cowl 30^{19}: they did not send us any letter (cf. Cowl $31^{6,17}$, 41^{5}, NESE iii $48^{8f.}$); *zn zn hww šlḥn ‹ly* Cowl 17^{3}: every type do send to me (v. also *hwy*$_1$); *᾽grh* *šlḥn mr>n w<l YHWH nn* Cowl 30[18]: we have sent a letter to our lord and to Y. (before *mr>n* a *<l* prob. left out by mistake, cf. Cowl a.l., or perhaps *mr>n* = acc. dir.??); *qblt mnk yšlḥ <ly* Driv 14[3]: he will send me a complaint about you; *>p qbylh šlḥ <lyk* Driv 12[5]: he has also sent a complaint about you; cf. also Cowl 40[4], v. supra - **11)** + obj. + *<l$_7$* + *l>mr*, *>grt šlḥ <l ... brh l>mr ...* Cowl 30[7f.]: he has sent a letter to ... his son of the following content ... - **12)** + obj. + *<l dbr* + *l$_5$*, *wšlḥ >grh <l dbr kn lṣ>[* Cowl 40[3]: and send a letter about this to S. - **13)** + obj. + *qdm$_3$*: KAI 233[13] (dam. context) - **14)** + *>l$_6$*, *spr >šr šlḥth >l <bdk* KAI 193[5f.]: the letter you sent to your servant (for the reading of the text, cf. also Cross FS Iwry 45); *m>z šlḥk >l <bdk* KAI 193[7f.]: since you have written to your servant - **15)** + *b$_2$*, *yšlḥ b>sywth* AMB 1[15]: he will send forth his healing - **16)** + *l$_5$*, *šlḥy ly* Herm 2[8]: write to me (cf. Herm 2[9,10,16], MPAT 54[1] (dam. context), Cowl 54[15], RES 1792A 1f. (for the context, cf. Grelot DAE p. 374 (n. c)), cf. also RES 1792B 5, 6 (for the context, v. *spr$_3$*), 1795B 2 (dam. context); *hksp >š šlḥt ly* KAI 50[3]: the silver you have sent me; *šlḥ ly* Sach 76 i B 2f.: write to me (i.e. inform me; cf. also Sem xxxiii 94[2] (v. supra)); *šlḥ lzp* TA-H 17[5]: send it to Ziph (for the uncert. reading *zp*, cf. Aharoni TA a.l., cf. however idem BASOR clxxxiv 14: pro *lzp* l. *ly* (cf. also Lipiński OLP viii 92 (poss. reading); on the problems, cf. also Pardee UF x 314f., Lemaire Or lii 446)); cf. also *šlḥ lšlm >lyšb* TA-H 16[1f.]: he sends greetings to E. (cf. TA-H 21[1f.]; on this formula cf. Pardee JBL xcvii 334); cf. RES 1298 B 5 (dam. context) - **17)** + *l$_5$* + Inf., *hnh šlḥty lh<yd bkm* TA-H 24[18f.]: see, I have sent a message to warn you; *<bdk hwš<yhw šlḥ lhg[d]* KAI 193[1f.]: your servant H. has written to inform ... - **18)** + *l$_5$* + obj., *šlḥ ly lbš>* RHR cxxx 20 conc. 4: send me the garment; cf. also *lšlmkn šlḥt sprh znh* Herm 2[17]: to greet you I have sent this letter (cf. Herm 4[12f.], 5[9], 7[4]), cf. also Fitzmyer JBL xciii 217, WA 194, Sarfatti Maarav iii 80; cf. *šlḥ ly >mt t<bdn psḥ>* RES 1793[4f.]: write me: when will you celebrate the Passover? (cf. Cowl 54[2ff.]); cf. prob. also ASAE xxvi 24[2] (l. rather *ly* instead of *<ly*, cf. Aimé-Giron ASAE a.l., hardly room to restore *<*) - **19)** + *l$_5$* + nota obj. *yt*, *tšlḥwn ly yt >l<zr* MPAT 56[4]: you are to send me E. (cf. MPAT 60[1]) - **20)** + *l$_5$* + *byd*, *šlḥ ly byd <qbh* Herm 3[6]: send me (a message/it) through A. - **21)** + *l$_5$* + *byd* + obj., *šlḥt lk byd >ḥwh> ... <nz ḥd* RES 1300[4f.]: I send you through her brother ... one goat - **22)** + *l$_5$* + *l$_5$* + Inf., *wšlḥt lh lmḥwh* RES 1792B 7: I have sent a message to him to notify (v. *ḥwy$_1$*; cf. RES 1792B 6) - **23)** + *l$_5$* + *l$_5$* + obj., *lšlmkn šlḥt l[kn] sprh znh* Herm 3[13]: to greet you I send you this letter (cf. however Porten & Greenfield JEAS p. 156, Porten & Yardeni sub TADAE A 2.4: *l]* = erasure) - **24)** + *l$_5$* + *lwt* + obj., *wyšlḥn lmḥnyh lwtk llbyn* MPAT 60[3]: and let they send to the camp, to you, *lulabs* - **25)** + *m>t* + *>l$_6$* + obj.: TA-H 6[2f.] (dam.

context) - **26)** + *m*ʾ*t* + *mn*$_5$, *šlḥ m*ʾ*tk m*ʿ*wd hqmḥ* TA-H 5[2f.]: send from you from the surplus of the flour (cf. also Levine Shn iii 292) - **27)** + ʿ*l*$_7$, *šlḥ* ʾ*nh* ʿ*lykm* Cowl 38[9]: I inform you; *wkzy yntn hmw lk šlḥ* ʿ*ly* Cowl 42[10]: and when he will give them to you, inform me; *šlḥy* ʿ*l tby wtwšr* Herm 2[6f.]: write to T. to send ...; cf. Driv 4[1], 8[1], 12[1], NESE iii 48[10], cf. also in dam. context Driv F v 1[2], Cowl 64 xx 2, ATNS 27[5], AE '23, 42 no. 9[4]; cf. also ʿ*l znh šlḥn hwd*ʿ*n* Cowl 30[28f.]: about this we have sent (and) given instructions (on the formula, cf. also Dion RB lxxxix 552f.) - **28)** + ʿ*l dbr*, *šlḥ* ʾ*dny* ʿ*l dbr byt* ... KAI 194[4f.]: my lord has written about B. - **29)** + ʿ*l*$_7$ + ʿ*l*$_7$, *šlḥt* ʿ*lykm* ʿ*l znh* Driv 7[5]: I have written you about it - **30)** + ʿ*m*$_4$ + obj. + *lwt*, *tšlḥ* ʿ*mhn ... gbryn lwt yhwntn* MPAT 60[1f.]: you are to send with them (sc. the asses) ... men to Y. - **31)** + *qdm*$_3$ + *l*ʾ*mr*, *[*ʾ*]nh qdm mr*ʾ*y šlḥt l*ʾ*mr k*ʿ*šq* ʿ*byd ly* Cowl 16[8]: I have sent to (?) my lord (a message) with the following contents: a wrong was done to me (context however dam.; or rather translate: ... before my lord. I have sent ...?) - **32)** QAL pass. to be sent; *mn mlk*ʾ *šlyḥ* ʿ*l* ʾ*rš[m]* Cowl 21[3]: word was sent from the king to A. (cf. Cowl 26[6], ATNS 26[12], 29[7]) - PAʿEL (v. supra); *ṣnpr hy mlh wmšlḥh gbr l*ʾ *l[qḥ]* Aḥiq 98: a word is like a bird, when a man sends it forth, he cannot recapture it - HAPH - **1)** to send; + *l*$_5$: Cowl 67 ii 2 (?, dam. context) - **2)** to undress, *áš-làḫ-te-e šá-am-Lat. ru-ga-za-a-*ʾ*i[-i]* Warka 30: I strip him of his mantle of anger - ITP - **1)** to be sent; cf. *yštlḥ lm ... ytyhb ...* Cowl 26[21]: let it be reported that it will be delivered - a) + *mn*$_5$ + ʿ*l*$_7$, ʾ*grt mn mr*ʾ*y tštlḥ* ʿ*l nḥtḥwr* Driv 10[2]: a letter will be sent from my lord to N. (cf. Cowl 30[24]; f. subject with m. verbal form, cf. Driver FS Cohen 234; cf. also Kutscher PICS 150f.) - b) + ʿ*l*$_7$: Cowl 26[4] (context however dam.); *yštlḥ* ʿ*l* ʾ*rtwn[t]* Driv 3[5]: let A. be informed - a form of this root (*šlḥ*) in HDS 168[2] (dam. context) - Segal ATNS a.l.: l. *[š]lḥh* in ATNS 35[4] (= QAL Pf. 3 p.s.m. + suff. 3 p.s.m./f.; uncert. reading and interpret., cf. Porten & Yardeni sub TADAE B 4.7: l. poss. *[*ʾ*]ḥh* = f. Sing. abs. of ʾ*ḥ*$_1$) - a form of this root prob. in RES 492A 4 (= RES 1800), cf. Lidzbarski Eph ii 237f., 401, Grelot DAE p. 139 - for the use of *šlḥ* in resp. QAL/PIʿEL, cf. also Rubinstein Lesh xxxviii 11ff.

v. ʾ*mr*$_1$, *šym*$_1$, *šlḥ*$_3$, *šlm*$_2$, *tnh*.

šlḥ$_2$ v. *šlḥ*$_1$.

šlḥ$_3$ **Ph** Sing. abs. *šlḥ* KAI 37A 15, 17 (for this reading and interpret. of both instances, cf. (Cross with) Healy BASOR ccxvi 53, 56 × e.g. Gibson SSI iii p. 124, 129f.: = QAL Part. pass. of *šlḥ*$_1$ (= deputed, commissioned, on duty :: Amadasi Kition C 1 a.l.: = PUʿAL Pf. 3 p.s./pl.m. of *šlḥ*$_1$?? :: Peckham Or xxxvii 305f., 316f.: = passive conjugation Pf. 3 p.pl. (cf. also Masson & Sznycer RPC 26f., 54, Delcor UF xi 160f.) :: CIS i sub 86 (div. otherwise): l. prob. *lḥ* = *l*$_5$ + *ḥ* (poss. = abbrev. of *ḥbrm* (= Plur. abs. of *ḥbr₂*; cf. also Cooke NSI p. 67, v.d.Branden BO viii 257); cf. also Röllig KAI a.l.: *ḥ* poss. = abbrev. of *ḥbry* (= Plur. + suff. 3 p.s.m. of *ḥbr₂*) :: v.d.Branden BO viii 257: or l. *lḥ* = QAL Part. s.m. abs. of *lwḥ* (= one who bakes the tablets)) - ¶ subst. deputy (v. supra).

šlḥ₄ **Palm** Sing. emph. *šlḥ›* CIS ii 3913 ii 142 - ¶ subst. skin (cf. Cooke NSI p. 331, 340, CIS ii a.l., Schiffmann PPT 124, 322; or = *šlḥ₅* (= weapon)?, cf. Cooke NSI p. 340, Schiffmann PPT 195, cf. also Reckendorff ZDMG xlii 415).

šlḥ₅ v. *šlḥ₄*.

šlṭ₁ **OffAr** QAL (or PA‹EL?) Impf. 3 p.s.m. *yšlṭ* Krael 4[20] - **Nab** QAL (or PA‹EL?) Pf. 3 p.pl.m. *šlṭw* CIS ii 196[5] (= RES 674) - **Palm** QAL Part. pass. s.m. abs. *šlyṭ* MUSJ xxxviii 106[9] (*šlyṭh* misprint for *šlyṭ lh*); APH Pf. 1 p.s. + suff. 3 p.s.m. *›šlṭh* CIS ii 3956[3] (for this reading, cf. Cantineau sub Inv v 7, cf. also Milik DFD 116, Gawlikowski TP 89) - ¶ verb QAL (or PA‹EL?) to exercise power over - a) *›yš ›ḥrn l› yšlṭ bbyth* Krael 4[20]: no one else will have power over the house; cf. also *l› yh› šlyṭ lh lmrḥ* MUSJ xxxviii 106[8f.]: he will not be allowed to enlarge ... - b) to be in command; *bbyt šlṭwnhm dy šlṭw ... šnyn tltyn wšt* CIS ii 196[5f.]: in their governmental office during their office during a period of 36 years - APH to give power + obj.: CIS ii 3956[3] (diff. context; for litt., v. supra) - Kaufman AIA 98f.: > Akkad. *šalāṭu*? :: Magnanini AION xviii 378f., Muffs 153 n. 4, 177f.: legal use < Akkad.
v. *šlyṭ*.

šlṭ₂ = sheath, quiver (cf. Borger VT xxii 385ff.; cf. also Hinz NWAP 58f.) > Akkad. *šalṭu*, cf. v.Soden Or xxxvii 267, xlvi 195, AHW s.v.

šlṭ₃ v. *šlyṭ*.

šlṭwn v. *šlṭn*.

šlṭn **OffAr** Sing. emph. *šlṭn›* NESE iii 48[12] - **Nab** Sing. + suff. 3 p.pl.m. *šlṭwnhm* CIS ii 196[5] (= RES 674) - **Palm** Sing. emph. *šlṭn›* PNO 2ter 7 - ¶ subst. - **1)** power, control; *yhb l›bgl šlṭn› b›tr› klh* PNO 2ter 6f.: he gave A. control over the whole region; *šlṭn› ... lzbnwth* NESE iii 48[12f.]: authority ... to sell it - **2)** government; *bbyt šlṭwnhm* CIS ii 196[5]: in their governmental office.

šly **OldAr** QAL Imper. pl.m. *šlw* KAI 224[5] - ¶ verb QAL to stay quietly, to be at rest; *šlw ‹l ›šrkm* KAI 224[5]: stay quietly where you are (for the context, cf. Greenfield ActOr xxix 4) - > Akkad. *šulû* (to be negligent, to neglect), cf. v.Soden Or xxxvii 268, xlvi 195, AHW s.v. *šelû* IV.

šlyh **OffAr** Plur. abs. *šlyn* Aḥiq 130 (cf. Cowl a.l., Leand 43m'; or = Sing. abs. of *šlyn*?? (cf. Kottsieper SAS 235), cf. also Ungnad ArPap sub 58, Lindenberger APA 124) - ¶ subst. rest, tranquillity - Puech & Rofé RB lxxx 532: l. *šlyh* (= Sing. abs.) in BASOR cxciii 8[7] (highly uncert. reading, cf. Puech ibid. 546: l. rather *šth* or *šsh*; cf. also Fulco

BASOR ccxxx 42).

šlyṭ OffAr Sing. m. abs. *šlyṭ* Cowl $5^{11,14}$, 8^{11}, $9^{6,11}$, 10^{16}, 28^{6}, Krael 2^{11} (*scriptio anterior*, cf. Hoftijzer & Pestman BiOr xix 216, Yaron JSS xiii 205f., cf. also Porten & Yardeni sub TADAE B 3.3)^{,12} (on the reading of the context, cf. Yaron JNES xx 130, JSS xiii 205), 3^{11}, $5^{6,9}$, 6^{9}, 8^{9}, 11^{10}, 12^{33}, Driv 2^{4}, Samar 1^{4} (= EI xviii 8*; on the dam. context, cf. also Porten BASOR cclxxi 86), 4^{5}, *šlṭ* (or = QAL Part. act. s.m. abs. of *šlṭ*$_1$?), Cowl $2^{16,17}$, 3^{19} (*[š]lṭ*, for the reading, cf. Porten & Yardeni sub TADAE B 4.3); f. abs. *šlyṭh* Cowl 8^{9}, 9^{9}, 15^{10}, 46^{7} (*šlyṭ[h]*, cf. Porten & Yardeni sub TADAE B 6.3 :: Cowl a.l.: l. *šlyṭ* = Sing. m. abs.), Krael 2^{11}, 6^{10} (*š[l]yṭh*), 7^{33}, $9^{11,21}$, *šlyṭ*ʾ Krael $9^{13,15}$; Plur. m. abs. *šlyṭn* Cowl $9^{7,10,13}$, 10^{8}, Krael $4^{17,19}$, 8^{5}, 9^{21}, 10^{9}, 12^{33}, Samar 7^{16}; cf. Frah xii 1 (*šlytʾ*) - ¶ adj. having authority, having power (cf. e.g. also Yaron Law 72f., J.J.Rabinowitz JJP xiii 150ff., Hoftijzer BiOr xxi 222, Muffs 39 n. 3, 41 n. 2, Fitzmyer FS Albright ii 160, WA 262, Gottlieb JSS xxvi 196f., Greenfield EI xvi 56f.): passim; *wʾnty yhwyšmʿ ... šlyṭh* Krael $9^{20f.}$: and you Y. will have authority (i.e. as a proprietor); cf. also Frah xii 1: = ruler (substantivated adj.) - **1)** + b_2, having authority over, being proprietor of, being entitled to; *wʾnt šlṭ bprsn* Cowl 2^{16}: you have a right to our salary; *lʾ ʾyty ly br wbrh ʾḥrnn ... šlyṭ bʾrqʾ zk lhn ʾnty wbnyky* Cowl $8^{10f.}$: I have no other son or daughter ... who has right to that plot, except you and your children; *ʾnty šlyṭh bh* Cowl 8^{9}: you have authority over it; *ʾnt ydnyh šlyṭ bpṭwsyry ʿbdʾ zk* Cowl 28^{6}: you Y. have authority over P., this slave; *mḥr ʾw ywm ʾḥrn ymwt ʿnnyh tmt hy šlyṭh bkl nksn zy yhwwn byn ʿnny wtmt* Krael $2^{10f.}$: (when) some day or other A. will die, T. will have rights to all the goods that are joint possessions of A. and T. (v. *byn*$_2$; cf. also Greenfield SVT xxxii 125f.; on these lines cf. also Gottlieb JSS xxvi 194ff.); *br ly wbrh ... lʾ šlyṭ bky wbyhyšmʿ brtky* Krael $5^{5f.}$: a son of mine or a daughter (of mine) ... will have no authority over you or over your daughter Y. (cf. Cowl 8^{11}, $9^{7,10,11,13}$, etc.) - **2)** + b_2 + l_5 + Inf., *ʾp šlyṭʾ ʾnty bplg drgʾ lmslq wmnḥt* Krael 9^{15}: further you will have a right to half the stairs to go up and to descend; *ʾnt ... šlyṭ bʿrbny lmḥd* Krael 11^{10} (for the reading, v. *ʾḥz*, *ʿrbn*): you have the right to seize my attachable property (sc. as a pledge) - **3)** + l_5, *šlyṭ yhwnwr lnḥ[myh]* Samar 4^{5}: Y. has authority over N. (the authority of a master over his slave), cf. Samar 1^{4} - **4)** + l_5 + Inf., *wʾnt šlyṭ lmbnh* Cowl 5^{11}: you have the right to build; *wʾnt šlyṭ lmptḥ trʿʾ zk* Cowl 5^{14}: you have the right to open this gate; *ʾnh wbr wbrh ly ... lʾ šlyṭn lmšnth* Krael $8^{5f.}$: nor I or a son or a daughter of mine will have the right to mark him; *psmšk brh šlyṭ YHWH lmnšʾ dšnʾ zky* Driv 2^{4}: his son P. shall have the right to accept that donation (cf. Cowl $9^{6,9}$, $10^{8f.,16f.}$, Krael 8^{9}) - **5)** + ʿl_7,*wgbr ʾḥrn lʾ šlyṭ ʿlyky wʿl yhyšmʿ brtky* Krael $5^{9f.}$: and no one else will have authority over you or over your daughter Y.

šlyn v. *šlyh*.

šlk$_1$ Pu PI‘EL Part. s.m. cstr. *mšlk* KAI 126[6] - ¶ verb PI‘EL to save, *mšlk bn› ‘m* KAI 126[6]: saviour of the sons of the people (cf. Levi Della Vida RCL ’49 406, Röllig KAI a.l., Amadasi IPT 68).

šlk$_2$ **Mo** Plur. abs. *šlkn* KAI 181[4] (for the reading, cf. e.g. Nöldeke Inschrift 9, LC ’87, 60, Clermont-Ganneau JA viii/ix 89, Lidzbarski Eph i 4f., KI sub 1, Cooke NSI p. 8, Segert Arch Or xxix 236, 244, Röllig KAI a.l., Gibson SSI i 74, 78 (cf. also Briend TPOA 90, H.P.Müller TUAT i 647) :: e.g. Smend & Socin IKM 12f., 17f., Lidzbarski Handb 310, 415, Michaud PA 36 n. 3, v.Zijl 189 (n. 7), Reviv CSI p. 15, Auffret UF xi 110f. (n. 7), de Moor UF xx 152, Jackson & Dearman SMIM 94, 97 (n. 6), 105f. (n. 52): l. *mlkn* = m. Plur. abs. of *mlk$_3$*) - ¶ subst. assailant (or = Plur. abs. of *šlk$_3$* (= assault?)); for litt. v. supra :: Dahood FS Horn 430f.: = Plur. abs. of *šlk$_4$* (= cormorant > greedy, rapacious person)).

šlk$_3$ v. *šlk$_2$*.

šlk$_4$ v. *šlk$_2$*.

šll$_1$ v. *šlm$_1$*.

šll$_2$ v. *gll*.

šlm$_1$ **Ph** PI‘EL Inf. cstr. *šlm* KAI 60[7] - **Pun** PI‘EL Pf. 3 p.s.m. *šlm* KAI 115[1], Hofra 11[3] (cf. Février Hofra a.l.; improb. interpret., rather = n.p., cf. Jongeling NINPI 207, cf. already Berthier & Charlier Hofra a.l.), 118[1], 121[3], 221[4] (diff. reading, dam. context), 235[2]; 1 p.s. *šlmty* Punica xviii/i 31[3] (on this form, cf. Sznycer APCI 218); Inf. cstr. *šlm* CIS i 5510[6] - **Hebr** PI‘EL Impf. 3 p.s.m. *yšlm* TA-H 21[4] - **OldAr** PA‘EL Impf. 2 p.pl.m. *[tš]lmn* KAI 222B 24 (cf. e.g. Dupont-Sommer Sf p. 61, 77, 150, Degen AAG p. 14 n. 61 :: Fitzmyer AIS 66, 157: = APH; cf. also Donner KAI a.l.: = PA‘EL or APH) - **OffAr** QAL Impf. 2 p.s.m. *tšlm* Krael 11[11] (?, cf. Kutscher JAOS lxxiv 237; Kutscher ibid.: or = lapsus for *tštlm* (= ITP Impf. 2 p.s.m.)? :: Krael p. 264, 318: = PA‘EL); PA‘EL Pf. 1 p.s. *šlmt* Cowl 11[7], 29[6] (*[š]lmt*), 82[5] (?, dam. context), Krael 11[5,8]; + suff. 2 p.s.m. *šlmtk* Cowl 10[7,11,14]; 3 p.pl.m. *šlmw* Cowl 10[16], Krael 11[9]; 1 p.pl. *šlmn* Cowl 42[2] (for the restoration of the context, cf. Porten & Yardeni sub TADAE A 3.8); Impf. 3 p.s.m. *yšlm* ATNS 177[1] (*yšlm[*; ?, dam. context); 2 p.s.m. *tšlm* Driv 12[8]; 1 p.s. *›šlm* Krael 11[4,7], Samar 1[9] (= EI xviii 8*), *›šlmn* Cowl 35[5] (:: Kaufman BiOr xxxiv 95: = lapsus for *›šlmnhy*); + suff. 3 p.s.m. *›šlmnhy* Cowl 11[3,5] (for the reading cf. Porten BASOR cclviii 43, cf. also Porten & Yardeni sub TADAE B 4.2),[10]; + suff. 2 p.s.m. *[›š]lmnk* Cowl 64 xxvii 2 (dam. context); 3 p.pl.m. *yšlmwn* Cowl 10[15], Krael 11[9]; 1 p.pl. Samar 8[10] (*nšl[m]*); Inf. *šlmh* Cowl 13[5]; Part. act. s.m. abs. *mšlm* Cowl 11[7] - **Palm** PA‘EL Part. act. s.m. abs. *mšlm* Ber ii 93[2]; APH pass. Pf.

3 p.s.m. *ʾšlm* Syr xiv 179[2] (?, cf. Rosenthal Sprache 62 n. 1, Milik Syr xliv 295 n. 1; or = APH?); 3 p.s.f. *ʾšlmt* CIS ii 3976[4] (cf. Cantineau Gramm 90) - **JAr** PA ʿEL Impf. 2 p.s.m. *[t]šlmn* MPAT 36[2]; Imper. pl.m. *šlmw* Mas 554[2] (?; *]šlmw* :: Yadin IEJ xv 111, Beyer ATTM 349: l. *[t]šlmn* = PA ʿEL Impf. 3 p.pl.m.); Part. pass. *mšlm* MPAT 40[10] (cf. however Beyer ATTM 308, 711 (dividing otherwise): l. *mšlmnh* = PA ʿEL Part. + encl. of 1 p.s.),[23] (*[mš]lm*; cf. however Beyer ATTM 308: l. *[mš]lmn[h]*) - ¶ verb QAL (v. supra) to be (re)paid; + b_2, *wtlqḥ lk ... ʿd tšlm bkspk* Krael 11[10f.]: you may take for yourself ... until you have been repaid your money - PI ʿEL/PA ʿEL - **1)** to (re)pay - a) + obj., *šlmn ksp kršn 10* Cowl 42[2]: we have paid 10 *k.* silver - b) + obj. + b_2, *lʾ šlmtk bkspk* Cowl 10[7]: I have not repaid you your money (cf. Cowl 10[11f.,14]) - c) + obj. + l_5, *ʾšlmnhy l[k]* Cowl 11[3]: I will repay it to you (cf. Cowl 11[5,10]) - d) + l_5 (obj.), *[t]šlmn lkspʾ ...* MPAT 36[2]: you are to pay the silver ...; cf. Mas 554[2] - e) + l_5 (to), *ksp ... zy ʾhwh mšlm lk* Cowl 11[7]: the silver which I pay you (cf. Cowl 13[5], 35[5]) - f) + l_5 + obj., *hmw yšlmwn lk kspʾ znh* Cowl 10[15]: they will pay you that silver (cf. Cowl 10[16], 11[7f.], Krael 11[9,9f.]) - g) + l_5 + $ʿl_7$, *ln šlm ʿl kl mntʾ ... zy yhbnh* Cowl 17[2]: pay (v. supra) us (for) the whole *mntʾ* (v. *mnh*$_1$) ... which we have given - h) + $ʿl_7$, *]šlmt ʿl rʾšy ʿd[tʾ]* Cowl 82[5]: I paid to the heads of the congregation (dam. context) - i) cf. also combinations with - α) *yhb*, *kspʾ znh [lʾ š]lmt yhbt lk* Cowl 29[6]: this silver which I have not paid you (cf. Krael 11[5,8]) - β) *ntn*, *ʾšlm wʾntn lk kntnyʾ ʾlk* Krael 11[4]: I will repay to you this emmer (v. *knt*$_2$); *ʾšlm [ʾ]ntn lk* Samar 1[9] (= EI xviii 8*) = I shall pay you; cf. Krael 11[7], Cowl 35[5] - j) + *ḥlpt* + obj., *ydʿ hgw lšlm ḥlpt ʾyt ʾdmm ʾš pʿl* KAI 60[7]: the community knows how to requite the men who have done ... - **2)** to give restitution for; *mh zy lqḥt zyny tšlm* Driv 12[8]: for what you have taken you will give restitution as for something being lost (uncert. interpret.) - **3)** to give (someone) his due; *yšlm YHWH lʾdn[y]* TA-H 21[4]: may the Lord give my master his due (cf. also Pardee HAHL 58) - **4)** to accomplish + obj., *šlmty ʾt ndry* Punica xviii/i 31[3f.]: I have accomplished my vow (cf. Hofra 27[1f.] (= KAI 115), 43[4f.], 118[1], 121[3], 235[2f.]; *[tš]lmn ʿdyʾ ʾln* KAI 222B 24: you will have to accomplish these treaty-stipulations - **5)** Part. pass. paid; *yhy qym wmšlm* MPAT 40[9f.]: let it be determined and paid (cf. MPAT 40[23], dam. context) - APH pass. to be entrusted + *ʿl ydwh* (to him): CIS ii 3976[4] (said of source); for Syr xiv 179[2], v. supra (uncert. context) - Milik RN vi/iv 56 n. 2, Syr xliv 297, Vattioni IH a.l.: l. *šlm* in Hatra 49[4] (= PA ʿEL Pf. 3 p.s.m.; uncert. reading) - a form of this root (*htšlm* = HITP Pf. 3 p.s.m.) poss. in EI xx 256[10] (reading however uncert.; cf. also Broshi & Qimron EI xx 259) - Lemaire RB lxxix 569, IH i 246, Lipiński OLP viii 86, BiOr xxxv 287: the *šlm* in KAI 188[1] = PI ʿEL Pf. 3 p.s.m. (cf.

already Michaud PA 62 n. 2; uncert. interpret.), cf. however Birnbaum Sam p. 12f., Albright ANET 321, Gibson SSI i p. 15: = n.p. :: Albright PEQ '36, 12, Mosc p. 38, Milik DJD ii p. 97 n. 2 (cf. also Michaud PA 62 (n. 2)): = Sing. abs. of *šlm$_2$* :: Röllig KAI a.l.: or = Pi ‘el Imper. s.m. of *šlm$_1$* :: Sukenik PEQ '33, 153, Dir p. 71f.: or = Sing. m. abs. of *šlm$_4$* :: Galling ZDPV lxxvii 175ff. (div. otherwise): l. *šl* (= Qal Pf. 3 p.s.m. of *šll$_1$* (= to rob)), for discussion of other possibilities, cf. also Sukenik PEQ '33, 153, Dir p. 71f., Röllig KAI a.l. - Beyer ATTM 362, 711: l. *[y]štlm[wn]* in SM 53[4] = Itp Impf. 3 p.pl.m. (heavily dam. context) - a form of this root (*šlmm*?) in KAI 51 verso 5 (heavily dam. context), Aimé-Giron BIFAO xxxviii 3, 6, Röllig KAI a.l.: = Plur. abs. of *šlm$_3$* - a form of this root in ATNS 46[3] (Segal ATNS a.l., Shaked Or lvi 410: = Sing. abs. of *šlm$_6$* (= full)) - Delavault & Lemaire RSF vii 10 sub no. 14: l. *šl[m]* (= Pi ‘el Pf. 3 p.s.m.??) on Ph. fragment, cf. however Naveh HThR lxi 70 - Lemaire IH i 121: the *šlm* in KAI 196[10] = Pi ‘el Pf. 3 p.s.m. of *šlm$_1$*, cf. however e.g. Röllig KAI a.l., Gibson SSI i p. 45f. (div. otherwise): l. *[yr]šlm* = n.l. - a form of this root also in SM 49[19] (Aph/Pa ‘el Part. pass. s.m. abs.?) *mšlm*, for the diff. interpret. of the context, cf. Sussman Tarbiz xliii 129f., Hüttenmeister ASI 374f., L.I.Levine ASR 153).
v. *mlk$_5$*, *mšlm*, *mšlmw*, *ṣb’$_3$*, *ql$_1$*, *šym$_1$*, *šlm$_2$*, *šlmy*.

šlm$_2$ **Ph** Sing. abs. *šlm* KAI 26A i 11, iii 3, C iii 18, 50[2,3] - **Pun** Sing. abs. *šlm* CIS i 5510[6] (cf. Chabot BAr '41/42, 393 :: Février BAr '46/49, 171)[,7] (cf. Février BAr '46/49, 172, sub CIS i 5510 :: Chabot BAr '41/42, 391, 394: = Pi ‘el Pf. 3 p.pl. of *šlm$_1$*)[,11] (poss. interpret., cf. Krahmalkov RSF ii 173f. :: Chabot BAr '41/42, 392, 394, Février BAr '46/49, 172f., sub CIS i 5510: = Pi ‘el Pf. 3 p.pl. of *šlm$_1$*), KAI 142[7] - **Amm** Sing. abs. *šlm* BASOR cclxiv 47[2] (= CAI 144) - **Edom** Sing. abs. *šlm* TeAv xii 97[2] - **Hebr** Sing. abs. *šlm* KAI 192[2f.], 193[3], 195[2] (uncert. reading), 196[2] (v. infra), *šlwm* IEJ vii 243[3], Frey 293, 499, 558, 593[4], 596[6] (for the reading *šlwm* pro *š’lm*, cf. Lifshitz Prol Frey p. 45), 974 (= SM 1), etc., etc., *š’lwm* Frey 397, 579, *šwlm* IEJ iv 98[1,2], *šl’š* Frey 574[1] (lapsus for *š’lm*?), cf. Frey 1034: σαλομ (cf. also Frey 1037, 1038 (σαλο[μ])), Frey 1113: σαλλομ; cstr. *šlm* TA-H 16[1f.,2], 21[1,2], DJD ii 17A 1; + suff. 2 p.s.m. *šlmk* TA-H 18[3] - **OldAr** Sing. abs. *šlm* KAI 224[8] (cf. e.g. (Milik with) Fitzmyer AIS 96, 111f., Rosenthal ANET 660, Grelot RB lxxv 284, Gibson SSI ii p. 46, 53, Lipiński Stud 55, Lemaire & Durand IAS 119, 145 :: Fitzmyer CBQ xx 458f.: l. *šlm* = Pa ‘el Inf. of *šlm$_1$* (= to greet) :: Dupont-Sommer BMB xiii 32, Degen AAG p. 20, 69, Puech RB lxxxix 583: l. *šlḥ* (= Qal Inf. of *šlḥ$_1$*) :: Dupont-Sommer Sf p. 150: l. *šlḥ* (= Pa ‘el Inf. of *šlḥ$_1$*); cstr. *šlm* Tell F 8 (Akkad. par. *šulum*; :: Kaufman Maarav iii 165f., Andersen & Freedman FS Fensham 21: or = Pa ‘el Inf. of *šlm$_1$*?, cf. also Muraoka

AN xxii 99f.) - **OffAr** Sing. abs. Cowl 37², Aḥiq 110, Krael 13⁴, Driv 1¹, 2¹ (for the reading, cf. Yardeni with Szubin & Porten JNES xlvi 39ff.), 3¹, 5¹,², Herm 1², 2², 3², SSI ii 28 obv. 3, RHR cxxx 20 conc. 2, Sem xxiii 95 verso 3 (= AECT 58), KAI 270A 7 (cf. e.g. Cooke NSI p. 203, Donner KAI a.l., Levine JAOS lxxxiv 19, 21f., Porten Arch 275, Gibson SSI ii p. 124 :: Dupont-Sommer ASAE xlviii 125 (div. otherwise): l. *šlmy* = Pa ʿel Imper. s.f. of *šlm₁*), etc.; cstr. *šlm* Cowl 17¹, 21², 30¹, Aḥiq 120, Krael 13¹, Herm 1¹,²,¹¹, NESE i 11¹, Sem xiv 72 conc. 1, etc., etc.; + suff. 2 p.s.m. *šlmk* Cowl 41²,³,⁵,⁷, 56¹, RES 1793⁸ (= PSBA xxxvii 222²), RSO xxxii 403¹, RHR cxxx 20 conv. 2; + suff. 2 p.s.f. *šlmky* Cowl 39¹, Herm 1¹², 6²,⁷, 7⁴, Sem xxi 85 conc. 2; + suff. 3 p.pl.m. *šlmhn* Herm 1³ (:: Degen GGA '79, 26: + suff. 3 p.pl.f.); + suff. 2 p.pl.m. *šlmkm* Cowl 37⁴ (dam. context), *šlmkn* Herm 2¹⁷, 3¹³, 4¹²; + suff. 2 p.pl.f. *šlmkn* Herm 5⁹; cf. Frah xxvi 5 (*šrmʾ*), DEP 153², Nisa-b 31a 1, 902 rev. 1, 2, 3, 5, Nisa-c 210²,³,⁵,⁶,⁸, etc., cf. also GIPP 34, 64 - **Nab** Sing. abs. *šlm* CIS ii 355, 357, 362, 367, 368, etc., etc., *links* *ššlm* (lapsus) CIS ii 370bis, *šl* (lapsus) CIS ii 2108¹, 2432¹, 2433¹, *šml* CIS ii 1906 (lapsus), *šm* (lapsus) CIS ii 3193; cstr. *šlm* RES 676⁴; emph. *šlmʾ* BIA x 55⁴ (for this reading, cf. also Teixidor Syr xlvii 378 :: Altheim & Stiehl AAW v/2, 24f.: l. *ṣlmʾ* (m. Sing. emph. of *ṣlm₁*)); + suff. 3 p.s.m. *šlmh* RES 676³ - **Palm** Sing. abs. *šlm* CIS ii 3903³, 4124³ (for the reading, cf. Cantineau Inv iv 3), RB xxxix 546⁵ (*[š]lm*), PNO 67, RTP 252, 993, Inv xi 85², 88², SBS 60¹¹, 61e 4, RIP 166⁶, Syr xl 34⁴, MUSJ xlii 177²; emph. *šlmʾ* CIS ii 3915³, DFD 37³ - **JAr** Sing. abs. *šlm* MPAT 36¹, 55¹,⁵, 57², 58³, 60⁵, 89¹,³,⁴, MPAT-A 50⁸, Syr xlv 101²² (dam. and diff. context), Mas 554¹, *slm* MPAT 53¹, *šlwm* (Hebr. in Ar. context) MPAT-A 1⁵, 12⁷, 22¹⁰, 27³, 28²,⁴, 29⁵, 33¹ (Ar. context?), 35, 51⁹, 52⁸,⁹; emph. *šlmh* MPAT-A 30¹ (cf. Naveh sub SM 26, Dothan HT 53 :: Fitzmyer & Harrington MPAT p. 353: or = Sing. + suff. 3 p.s.m.?), Syn D A 14 (= SM 88); + suff. 3 p.s.m. *šlmh* SM 46³ (= MPAT-A 13 :: Bahat Qadm v 57, ASR 85: = Sing. emph.) - ¶ subst. - **1)** welfare, well-being, health; *wbrk bʿl ... ʾyt ʾztwd ḥym wšlm wʿz ʾdr* KAI 26A iii 2f.: and may Baʿal ... bless A. with life, health and powerful strength (cf. *wbrk bʿl ... ʾyt ʾztwd bḥym wbšlm wbʿz ʾdr* KAI 26C iii 16ff.); *lšlm byth wlšlm zrʿh wlšlm ʾnšwh* Tell F 8f.: for the well-being of his house, of his descendants and his people (Akkad. par. *šulum biti-šú zere-šú u niše-šú*); *šlmk šmʿt* Cowl 41²: I have heard that it is well with you; *ʾgrt ḥdh bšlmk lʾ šlḥt ʿly* Cowl 41⁵: you did not send one letter to me about your welfare (cf. Dion RB lxxxix 558); *šlm nbwšh tnh* Herm 2²ᶠ·: it is well with N. here (cf. Herm 6⁸ᶠ·); *šlm yhwy lk* Aḥiq 110: I wish you well (the lion greeting the ass; cf. Herm 1³ᶠ·); *šlm ly tnʾ* Cowl 57¹: it is well with me here (for this interpret., cf. Porten & Greenfield IOS iv 23, ZAW lxxx 227, cf. also Porten IrJu 16*, Dion

RB lxxxix 555); *šlm ʾmk wynqyʾ klʾ* SSI ii 28 rev. 5: it is well with your mother and all the children (cf. e.g. Gibson SSI ii a.l. :: Naveh AION xvi 27: greeting to your mother ...; cf. also Alexander JSS xxiii 165: greetings from your mother ...); *ʾlhyʾ šlm yšmw lk* Driv 13[5]: may the gods grant you well-being; *msgdʾ dy qrb ... [y]mlk ʿl šlmh* RES 676[1ff.]: stele which Y. offered for his welfare; *mtḥzqyn btqwnh dʾtrh [qdy]šh wbšlmh* SM 46[2f.]: contributing to the repair of the synagogue and its welfare (:: Fitzmyer & Harrington sub MPAT-A 13: ... and its completion); *yhy šlmh ʿl kl mn d ...* MPAT-A 30[1]: may there be well-being for everyone who ...; *qbr bšlm* KAI 142[7]: buried in peace (?, v. *qbr*$_3$); *wʾšlḥ mlʾky ʾ[l]wh lšlm ʾw lkl ḥpṣy* KAI 224[8]: I send my messenger to him (to ask) after his welfare or on any matter of business that I have; *ʿl šlmʾ dy ...* BIA x 55[4]: for the well-being of ... (beginning of an inscription, Greek par. ὑπὲρ αἰωνίου διαμονῆς κρατήσεως τῶν ... and ἐπι νείκῃ καὶ αἰωνίῳ διαμονῇ ...); *rwb šlwm* MPAT-A 13[4] (= SM 46): much well-being - a) in greeting formulae introducing a letter (cf. Fitzmyer JBL xciii 214, Dion RB lxxxix 536); *[mnḥ]m br mʿzy šlm* MPAT 36[1]: M. the son of M. greetings; *[šmʿ]wn lyntn ... [š]lm* MPAT 57[1f.]: Sh to Y. ... greetings (cf. MPAT 53[1], DJD ii 42[2], 43[3], Mas 554[1] (dam. context), etc.); *ʾgrt šmʿwn ... šlm lyhwntn ...* MPAT 55[1f.]: letter of Sh. ... greetings! to Y. ...; *mn mykyh ʿl ʾ[ḥwṭb] šlmky* Sem xxi 85 conc. 1f.: from M. to A. greetings to you; *mšmʿwn ... lyšʿ ... šlwm* DJD ii 43[1ff.]: from Sh. to Y. greetings (cf. DJD ii 42[2], 44[1f.], 46[2]); *[ʾl ʾ]ḥy prwr ʾḥwk bltr šlm l ...* KAI 233[1]: to my brother P. your brother B., greetings to ... (cf. Dion RB lxxxvi 555ff.); *šlm ydnyh* Sem xiv 72 conc. 1: greetings to Y. (cf. FS Driver 54 conc. 1; for this type of formula, cf. Dion RB lxxxix 554); *šlm ʾḥwṭb ʾl yšgʾ* RES 1795A 1f.: greetings of A. to Y.; *šlm byt nbw* Herm 1[1]: greetings/blessings to the temple of N. (cf. Herm 2[1], 3[1], 4[1]; cf. Fitzmyer JBL xciii 212, Dion RB lxxxvi 561ff., Fales JAOS cvii 455f.); *brk ʾnt [l ... zy yḥ]wny ʾnpyk bšlm* SSI ii 28 obv. 3: may you be blessed by ... so that he may may show me your face in health (i.e. may he (sc. the god) let me see you again in good health; cf. Dion RB lxxxix 555); *brktky lptḥ zy yḥzny ʾpyk bšlm* Herm 1[2]: I bless you by Ptah that he may let me see you again in good health (cf. Herm 2[2], 3[2], 4[2], 5[2]); *yšmʿ YHWH ʾt ʾdny šmʿt šlm* KAI 191[1ff.]: may the Lord let my lord hear tidings of welfare (cf. KAI 193[2f.]); *yrʾ YHWH ʾt ʾdny ʾt hʿt hzh šlm* KAI 196[1f.]: the Lord may give my lord to see the present moment in good health (for this interpret. of *šlm* as *šlm*$_2$, cf. Torczyner Lach i p. 203, cf. also e.g. Bergman with Albright BASOR lxxii 32, Gordon BASOR lxx 17 (other interpret. of context), Gibson SSI i p. 46, Pardee HAHL 243 :: e.g. Albright BASOR lxiii 37: *šlm* = Sing. m. abs. of *šlm*$_6$; for the context, v. *rʾy*); *ʾlhyʾ kl yšʾlw šlmky bkl ʿdn* Cowl 39[1]: may all the gods seek your welfare (i.e. favour you) at all times (cf. Cowl 17[1], 21[2], 30[1f.], 38[2], 56[1], Krael 13[1], NESE i 11[1]; v. *š'l*$_1$); *YHWH yš'l lšlmk* TA-H 18[2f.]: may the Lord seek your welfare (v. *š'l*$_1$); *šlm wḥyn šlḥt lk* RHR cxxx 20 conc. 2f.: I send you welfare and life (cf. Herm 3[5]; cf. poss. also DJD ii 17A 1 (v. *šlḥ*$_1$); cf. Dion RB lxxxvi 554f., 562ff.); *'ḥk ḥnnyhw šlḥ lšlm 'lyšb* TA-H 16[1f.]: your brother Ch. sends for the welfare of E. (cf. TA-H 21[1f.]; cf. Dion RB lxxxvi 558ff.); *šlm wšrrt šgy' hwšrt lk* Driv 3[1]: I send you much welfare and prosperity (cf. Driv 5[1], 13[1], Cowl 42[1], v. *šrrt*; cf. also SSI ii 28 obv. 1; cf. Dion RB lxxxvi 565f.; cf. also Nisa-c 210[3], 287[1]); *brktk lb'l ṣpn wlkl 'l tḥpnḥs yp'lk šlm* KAI 50[2f.]: I bless you by B.S. and all the gods of T., may they procure you well-being (cf. Dion RB lxxxvi 575f.); *šlm 'ḥy bkl 'dn* RES 1300[3] (abbreviated salutation) the well-being of my brother at all times (cf. NESE iii 48[3f.]; :: Joüon MUSJ xviii 56: Greetings, my brother, at all times); *šlm 't* BASOR cclxiv 47[2]: are you well? (cf. TeAv xii 97[2]); *šlm 't 'p 'nk šlm* KAI 50[2]: are you well? I am well too (cf. Dion RB lxxxvi 575f.); *wk't bznh qdmy šlm 'p tmh qdm[y]k šlm yhwy* Driv 5[1f.]: and now, it is well with me here, may it be well also with you over there (cf. also Driv 1[1], Cowl 37[2]) - b) in greeting formulae in letters; *šlm NP* Herm 1[2]: greetings to NP (cf. Herm 2[3f.,4,16f.], Cowl 39[1f.], 40[1], Krael 13[6], RSO xxxv 22[2,5], etc.; cf. Fitzmyer JBL xciii 216f., WA 193f., Fales JAOS cvii 456); *šlm bytk wbnyk* Cowl 34[7]: the greeting to/best wishes for your house and your children (cf. Herm 4[12]); *šlm yqyh hwy šlḥt lh* Herm 1[11]: be so good to send the greetings/best wishes for Y. to him; *ḥrwṣ š'l šlmhn* Herm 1[3]: Ch. sends them his best wishes (cf. e.g. Hoftijzer SV 108 :: Gibson SSI ii p. 130: Ch. asks after their welfare; cf. Herm 6[2,7]); *hwyt 'šlḥ šlmk* Cowl 41[3]: I used to ask for your welfare; *hw' šlwm* DJD ii 44[8]: the best wishes - c) in formulae at the end of a letter; *lšlmkn šlḥt sprh znh* Herm 4[12f.]: I have written this letter for your welfare (i.e. to send you my best wishes; cf. Herm 1[12f.], 2[17], 3[13], 5[9], 7[4]; cf. also RHR cxxx 20 conv. 2 :: Dupont-Sommer RHR a.l.: to satisfy you; cf. Dion RB lxxxvi 563ff.); *hwy šlḥ šlm ynq'* PSBA xxxvii 222[10f.] (= RES 1793[5f.]): send greetings to the child(/children??, v. *ynq*$_2$; :: Grelot DAE p. 376 (n. g): send tidings of the baby :: Dupont-Sommer REJ '46/47, 49f. (n. 37): send Sh. the child); *hw' šlm* MPAT 55[5]: the best wishes (cf. MPAT 58[3], 60[5], DJD ii 42[7], 44[8], 46[12], 48[6]); *'hwh šlwm wkl byt yšr'l* DJD ii 42[7]: the best wishes for you and all Israel - *šlm 'ḥy bl wnbw šmš wnrgl* RHR cxxviii 30[2f.]: (may) B., N., Sh. and N. (favour) the well-being of my brother (?, or: greetings to my brother. B., N., Sh. and N. ..., end of text on reverse being lost); for greeting formulae, cf. also Galling ZDPV lxxvii 177, Fitzmyer JNES xxi 21, Porten EI x 180ff. - for combination of *šlm* with *'l*$_7$, cf. Nisa-b 902 rev. and for combination of *šlm* with *qdm*$_3$, cf. Nisa-c 210[5] - d) in tomb inscriptions - α) *šl(w)m* on its own: CIS ii 4124^3 (v. supra), SBS 60^{11}, RIP 166^6, Frey 552, 579^4, 596^6, MPAT-A 50^8 (= Frey 1208), etc. (cf. also MPAT 89^{3,4}) - β) *šlwm lywdn* Frey 1087 (cf. Frey 607) - γ) *yhy šlwm ‘l mnwḥtw* Frey 622^4: peace be on his resting-place (cf. Frey 558, 630b 4f.) - δ) *šlwm ‘l mškbh* Frey 1536^2: peace be over his tomb (cf. Frey 593^4, 595$^{1f.}$) - ε) *šlwm ‘l NP* Frey 609 (cf. also *šlwm šlwm ‘lh* (v. *‘l$_7$*) MPAT-A 51$^{9f.}$) - ζ) *šlwm ‘l yšr’l* Frey 599^4 (cf. Frey 293, 397, etc.); cf. also *šlwm ‘l yšrwn l‘wlm* Frey 1175^1; cf. also *šlwm ‘l yšr’l ’mn ’mn šlwm šmw’l* Frey 650^1 and *šlwm ‘l yšr’l šlwm* MPAT-A 52$^{8f.}$ - η) *bšlwm* Frey 499, cf. prob. also Frey 1437: l. *bšlwm* pro *lšlwm*? - e) in dedicatory and comparable inscriptions - α) *šlm* on its own: CIS ii 3903^3, cf. Inv xi 85^2, 88^2, DFD 23^3, IEJ xiii 118, MPAT-A 1^5, 12^7 (= Frey 1195), 22^{10}, SM 70^{18} - β) *šlwm ‘l yšr’l* SM 68 (cf. SM 38, 70^8, Frey 884) - γ) *šlwm ‘l yšr’l ’mn* SM 75^6 - δ) *šlwm ‘l kl yšr’l ’mn ’mn slh* MPAT-A 33$^{1ff.}$ (= SM 50 = Frey 866); cf. also the *šlm šlm ’m[n]* (diff. reading) as graffito near pentagram: RB xcii 273 - ε) *’mn ’mn slh šlwm* MPAT-A 27^3, 28^{2,4} - ζ) *šlwm ‘l yšr’l w‘lynw w‘l bnynw ’mn* SM 111 - η) *yhy šlwm bmqwm hzh wbkl mqwmwt yšr’l* SM 1; cf. *yhy šlwm ‘l hmqwm hzh w‘l kl mqwmwt ‘mw yšr’l [’]mn slh* SM 3 - θ) *’mn [...] slh šlwm* MPAT-A 35; v. also *’mn$_5$* - f) at the end of an amulet: AMB 8^{12} - g) in commemorative inscriptions and graffiti (cf. Sumer xx 18* ii 1, 19*^{5}, 20* i 8; for the graffiti, cf. Ahlström FS Widengren 324ff.) - cf. the following combinations - α) *NP šlm* CIS ii 355, 357, 362, 367, 368, 370, J 78 (for the reading, cf. Milik sub ARNA-Nab 112), etc., etc. - β) *šlm NP* CIS ii 370bis, 371, 372, 373, 374, IEJ xxxi 66 ii, etc. (the *šlm NP* in J 71 (= RES 1113) incorrect reading for *NP*, cf. Milik sub ARNA-Nab 104); this combination also in BSOAS xv 10 no. 19^2 :: Littmann a.l.: = PA‘EL Pf. 3 p.s.m. of *šlm$_1$* (= to greet; cf. also the text *šlm NP* on two Nab. lamps, cf. Savignac with G. & A. Horsfield QDAP ix 195 no. 413-414, cf. also Hammond BASOR cxlvi 12, Khairy PEQ ’84, 118) - γ) *šlm NP bṭb* CIS ii 228, 496, 497, 498, 501, Qedem vi 14 no. 17, Sumer xx 13*^{5}, IEJ xxxi 69 no. 9, etc. - δ) *šlm NP bṭb l‘lm* ADAJ xxvi 203 - ε) *šlm NP bḥyr* CIS ii 1499 - ζ) *šlm NP ḥyr bṭb* CIS ii 1631 - η) *šlm NP bṭb wšlm* CIS ii 561, 629, 691, 738, 1305, Qedem vi 61 no. 237, etc. (cf. also *šlm NP wNP bṭb wšlm bl’* CIS ii 757, *šlm NP wNP wNP wNP wNP bṭb wšlm mn qdm[* CIS ii 3048) - θ) *šlm NP bṭb šlm* CIS ii 811 - ι) *šlm NP bkl ṭb* CIS ii 767, 2273, 2296, 2356, 2444, 3029, EI x 183 no. 29, etc. - κ) *šlm NP šlm bṭb* IEJ xxvii 228 no. 27 - λ) *šlm NP wdkyr* CIS ii 2717 - μ) *šlm NP bryk l‘lm* CIS ii 491 - ν) *šlm šlm NP* CIS ii 1436, 1516 - ξ) *šlm šlm šlm NP* CIS ii 536$^{1ff.}$, 2108, 2433 - ο) *šlm šlm NP bṭb* CIS ii 1948 - π) *šlm NP šlm* CIS ii 1505, 1633, 1702, EI x 184 no. 31, etc. - ρ) *šlm šlm NP šlm* CIS ii 2387 - σ) *šlm NP ‘d ‘lm* CIS ii 2680 - τ) *šlm NP mn qdm dwšr’* ARNA-Nab 54 (= J 52), RES 1401$^{1f.}$ - υ) *šlm lNP*

J 71 - φ) *lNP šlm* J 45 - χ) *šlm NP wdkyr bṭb* CIS ii 3010 - ψ) *NP [b]ṭb wšlm* CIS ii 2783 - ω) *šlm wdkyr NP bṭb lʿlm* ARNA-Nab 67 - αα) *NP šlm bryk* RES 1414, 1419 - ββ) *ʿbdw šlm br ḥwrw br tlmw* CIS ii 426C (for the reading, cf. RES 1443) - γγ) *bryk NP šlm* CIS ii 418bis - δδ) *bryk NP bṭb wšlm* CIS ii 1150 - εε) *dkyr NP šlm* CIS ii 376, 409, PNO 67; cf. also *dkyr NP qdm bl wʾrṣw šlm bṭb* MUSJ xlii 177[1f.] - ζζ) *dkyr NP bšlm* CIS ii 750 - ηη) *dkyr NP bṭb wšlm* CIS ii 401, 509, 2501 - θθ) *wdkyryn NP NP bṭb wbšlm* ARNA-Nab 73, 90 (= J 18) - ιι) *dk[y]r NP bṭb šlm* CIS ii 2098 - κκ) *dkyr bṭb wšlm NP bṭb*: CIS ii 619 - λλ) *dkyr NP bkl ṭb wšlm* CIS ii 1257 - μμ) *dkyr ṭb lʿlm ʿlmn NP bṭb wšlm* CIS ii 1841 - νν) *NP dkyr bṭb wšlm lʿlm mn qdm dwšrʾ wmntw* J 184 (the second part prob. = CIS ii 320F) - ξξ) *dkyr bṭb wšlm NP ʿd ʿlm* CIS ii 2072 - οο) *dkyr wbryk NP šlm* CIS ii 3186 - ππ) *dkyr bṭb NP wšlm* EI x 184 no. 31b - ρρ) *dkyr bṭb wšlm NP bṭb* CIS ii 613, 619 - σσ) *NP šlm wdkyr bṭb lʿlm* BSOAS xvi 226, 78 - ττ) *dkrwn ṭb wšlm lNP* CIS ii 407, 459, 3072, J 180[1f.] (= CIS ii 316) - υυ) *dkrwn ṭb lNP šlm* CIS ii 426E (for the reading, cf. RES 1445) - φφ) *dkrwn ṭb wšlm lNP šlm* IEJ xi 130 no. 5 - χχ) *bly šlm NP* ARNA-Nab 75 (v. *blʾ*$_3$; v. also *bly*$_3$), cf. also CIS ii 266, 285 - ψψ) *šlm NP bṭb wšlm blʾ* CIS ii 757 (v. however *blʾ*$_2$) - ωω) *lʾ šlm[* ARNA-Nab 16[3] (:: Joüon MUSJ xviii 96f.: *šlm* in several of these formulae = QAL Pf. 3 p.s.m. of *šlm*$_1$: *salvus sit*) - **2)** peace, good relations; *wʿbd šlmʾ bynyhm* CIS ii 3915[3]: he made peace between them (he reconciliated them), cf. Sem xxiii 95 verso 3 (= AECT 58); *ʿbd šlmʾ bthwmy mdytʾ* DFD 37[3]: he established peace in the region of the town; *wšt ʾnk šlm ʾt kl mlk* KAI 26A i 11f.: I made peace with every king - **3)** cf. the foll. diff. texts - a) the *šlm* in KAI 3[2] of uncert. interpret., cf. - α) Albright BASOR xc 36 n. 6: = Sing. abs. of *šlm*$_2$ (= reconciliation; cf. Obermann JBL lviii 234, 242, Iwry JAOS lxxxi 33, v.d.Branden RSF ii 138f.: = peace) - β) Dupont-Sommer ArchOr xvii/1, 162: = *šlm*$_4$ (= payment; cf. Röllig KAI a.l., McCarter & Coote BASOR ccxii 18f.) - γ) Gibson SSI iii p. 11: or = PIʿEL Imper. s.m. of *šlm*$_1$ (= to pay, to make restitution) :: δ) Dunand BMB ii 102: = lapsus for *šqlm* (= Plur. abs. of *šql*$_3$) - b) the *šlm* supposed in KAI 46[3f.] poss. = Sing. abs. of *šlm*$_2$ (cf. e.g. Dupont-Sommer CRAI '48, 15f., JA cclii 300, Röllig KAI a.l.), or = Sing. m. abs. of *šlm*$_6$ (= being at peace, intact), cf. Ferron RSO xli 285f., 288, Cross BASOR ccviii 15f.), or = PIʿEL Pf. 3 p.s.m. of *šlm*$_1$ (cf. Février RA xliv 124, Cross CMHE 220 no. 5), or = QAL Pf. 3 p.s.m. of *šlm*$_1$ (cf. v.d.Branden Mašr lvi 286, 289, Delcor Syr xlv 331, 345, 351, Bunnens EPM 34f., 37f.) :: Peckham Or xli 459, 463: = QAL Inf. abs. of *šlm*$_1$ :: e.g. CIS i sub 144, Cooke NSI p. 110f., Slouschz TPI p. 136f. (div. otherwise): l. *šlmh* = PIʿEL Pf. 3 p.s.m. + suff. 3 p.s.f. of *šlm*$_1$ (= to complete, cf. also Lidzbarski Handb 376), cf. however Albright BASOR lxxxiii 19: l. *š[... hʾ]dm* (for the text, cf. also Gibson SSI iii p. 27) - c) for the *šlm* supposed in KAI 46[4f.], v. *ṣbʾ*$_3$ - d) the *šlmh* in CIS ii 53[1] poss. = Sing. emph., context however diff., cf. also CIS ii a.l. - e) the *šlm* in TA-H 18[8] = Sing. abs. of *šlm*$_2$ (cf. Aharoni TA-H a.l., Gibson SSI i p. 53, Lipiński OLP viii 92, Pardee UF x 315, 317f., HAHL 55, 241, Levine Shn iii 289, Hospers SV 104, Smelik HDAI 105) × Albright ANET 569 (n. 22), Weinberg ZAW lxxxvii 364f.: = n.p. :: Freedman IEJ xix 56 (cf. also Conrad TUAT i 252), Lemaire IH i 180ff.: = PUʿAL Pf. 3 p.s.m. of *šlm*$_1$ :: Fritz WO vii 138f.: = PIʿEL Pf. 3 p.s.m. of *šlm*$_1$ (= to acquit a vow) :: Levine IEJ xix 49f.: = Sing. abs. of *šlm*$_3$ - f) this word (Sing. abs. *šlm*) poss. in BASOR cxciii 8[8], cf. Puech & Rofé RB lxxx 532, 534, 542, cf. also Dion RB lxxxii 32f. (*[š]lm*), Fulco BASOR ccxxx 41 (*šlm*), Sasson PEQ '79, 118, 124 (*[š]lm*), Shea PEQ '81, 105, 108 (*[š]lm*), cf. already Horn BASOR cxciii 13, cf. however Horn BASOR cxciii 13: l. *[ʾ]lm* (= Sing. abs. of *ʾlm*$_2$), cf. also Cross BASOR cxciii 17 (*ʾlm*), v.Selms BiOr xxxii 7f. (*[ʾ]lm*), cf. however also Albright BASOR cxcviii 38: l. *[ʾ]lm* = Plur. abs. of *ʾl*$_1$ - g) Krahmalkov RSF iii 178f., 186, 204: the *šlm* in Karth xii 54[1] = Sing. abs. (cf. v.d.Branden RSF v 57, 62, BiOr xxxvi 202) :: Février & Fantar Karth xii 54: = *š*$_{10}$ + *l*$_5$ + suff. 3 p.pl.m. - h) Naveh IEJ xx 37, Tsaferis Proc v CJS i 3 (Hebr.): the *šlwm* in MPAT 88[2] poss. = Sing. abs. of *šlm*$_2$?, cf. however also Fitzmyer & Harrington MPAT a.l., Beyer ATTM 345, 740: = n.p. - i) Teixidor Syr xlviii 481: l. prob. *šlm* (= Sing. abs.) in AAW v/1, 85[1] :: Altheim & Stiehl AAW a.l.: l. *ṣlm* = Sing. cstr. of *ṣlm*$_1$ - **4)** the σαλάμ in AnthGraeca vii 419, 7 (the way the Syrian is greeted) prob. = Aramaic - **5)** the *š* in RES 904 (uncert. reading) = abbrev. of *šlm*$_2$??

v. *ʿlm*$_4$, *ṣlm*$_1$, *šʾl*$_1$, *šym*$_1$, *šlm*$_1$.

šlm$_3$ **Pun** Sing. cstr. *šlm* KAI 69[3,5,7,9,11], KAI 120[2] - ¶ subst. indicating certain type of sacrifice/offering; for *šlm kll*, v. *kll*$_2$; *šlm hršt* KAI 120[2]: poss. = offering of first fruit (cf. also Sznycer Sem xii 45f. :: Février with Sznycer Sem xii 46 n. 2 (div. otherwise): l. *bʿlšlm* = n.p. (supposing that a preceding *bn* has been left out by mistake)) - Puech Sem xxix 20f., 24f.: l. *šlmm* (= Plur. abs.) in KAI 30[3] (*š[l]mm*) and 30[7] (in both instances heavily dam. and uncert. text).

v. *ʾl*$_1$, *šlm*$_{1,2}$, *territory*.

šlm$_4$ **OffAr** Sing. abs. *šlm* Irâq xxxiv 136 (= AECT 60) - ¶ subst. settlement, payment; *spr šlm zy ḥzʾl* Irâq xxxiv 136: document concerning the settlement with Ch. (i.e. repayment of silver to him; cf. also the *šulmu* in Akkad. main text (cf. also Hawkins with Millard Irâq xxxiv 137, Kaufman JAOS cix 100); *zy ḥzʾl* to be combined with *spr (šlm)*?, cf. Fales sub AECT 60).

v. *šlm*$_{1,2}$.

šlm$_5$ v.Soden Or xlvi 195, AHW a.l.: = completion > Akkad. *šullāmu*, used to describe certain type of horse (highly uncert. interpret.).

šlm$_6$ **Hebr** Plur. f. abs. *šlmwt* DJD ii 24E 10 - ¶ adj. complete; *šnym šlmwt* DJD ii 24E 9f.: complete years - this word (Sing. m. emph. *šlm*ʾ) poss. also in RES 1785F 4 - poss. also on Nab. coins (Sing. m. abs.), cf. Meshorer NC no. 112, 113 (cf. also idem ibid. p. 58f.).
v. *slm$_2$*, *šlm$_{1,2}$*.

šlm$_7$ **Pun** Sing. m. abs. *šlm* Trip 51[1,6,8] (:: Levi Della Vida Or xxxiii 7, 14, Amadasi IPT 132: = verbal noun of root *šlm* related to PIʿEL) - ¶ adj. settled, paid (in the combination *lkn šlm* Trip 51[1]: to be settled (cf. Trip 51[6,8])).
v. *ṣbʾ$_3$*.

šlmy **Palm** Sing. cstr. *šlmyt* Sem xxvii 117[8] - ¶ subst. agreement (cf. Aggoula Sem xxvii 119; diff. context, cf. also Teixidor Syr lvi 399 (cf. also Starcky with Teixidor ibid.: *šlmyt* = PAʿEL Inf. of *šlm$_1$* (improb. interpret.) = payment)).

šlʿ v. *gll*.

šlp$_1$ cf. Frah app. 15: = to draw.

šlp$_2$ = blade of a knife > Akkad., cf. v.Soden Or xlvi 195, AHW s.v. *šulāpu*.

šlš$_1$ **Ph** m. *šlš* KAI 19[8], 51 verso 2 (dam. context), RES 453; f. *šlšt* KAI 40[4], Mus li 286[2,7] - **Pun** m. *šlš* KAI 62[1], 127[4] (for the reading, cf. Levi Della Vida FS Friedrich 309 n. 15), 130[2], 134[2], 152[3], 277[7], RES 173[2], 1543[5], BAr-NS i-ii 224[4], *šʿlš* KAI 144[3], cf. August Ep ad Rom 13: *salus* (cf. FR 45, 76a, 79b, 197a, 242, Penna CISFP i 891); f. *šlšt* KAI 69[9,11] - **Hebr** m. *šlš* KAI 189[2], on coins of the first revolt, cf. Meshorer JC no. 156: *šlwš* (cf. Meshorer Mas Coin 3000); f. *šlšh* TA-H 8[2f.], SM 106[11], *šlwšt* IEJ vii 245, DJD ii 24E 12 (*šlw[št]*) - **DA** f. *šlšh* ii 34 (heavily dam. context) - **OffAr** m. abs. *tlt* Driv 6[3], IEJ xxv 118[2] (for script and language, cf. Naveh ibid. 120ff.); emph. *tlt*ʾ Aḥiq 92 (:: Kottsieper SAS 19, 104, 238: used instead of ordinal number); f. abs. *tlth* Cowl 26[10,11,15,18,19,20], Aḥiq 39, Krael 12[5], Driv 6[4]; cstr. *šlšt* CIS ii 3b (for the reading, cf. Degen NESE iii 11ff., GGA '79, 27 n. 54, 30 :: CIS ii a.l. and litt. quoted with Degen NESE iii 11f.: l. *šlš*ʾ = f. abs.); cf. Frah xxix 3 (*tlt*ʾ) - **Nab** m. abs. *tlt* CIS ii 199[9], 219[7], Syr xxxv 244[5], on coins, cf. Meshorer NC 11, 11a, 21, 52; f. abs. *tlth* CIS ii 206[7] (:: CIS ii a.l.: l. *tlt*), 963[2] - **Palm** m. abs. *tlt* CIS ii 3984[4], Inv x 54[7], RB xxxix 548[5,7]; f. abs. *tlt*ʾ CIS ii 4173[2], Inv x 115[1], Ber ii 82[1], 84[1], 85[8], 95, 99 i 2, 100 i 2, 112[4], v 125[8], SBS 15[1] (*t[l]t*ʾ), 16[1], 17[1], MUSJ xxxviii 106[7,8], Sem xxxvi 89[6], *tl*ʾ DM ii 43 ii 2 (for the reading, cf. Al-Asʿad & Teixidor DM a.l.), *tlth* RIP 199[13] - **Hatra** f. cstr. *tltt* 72 - **JAr** m. abs. *tlt* MPAT 44 i 1, 51[1], 52[2], MPAT-A 27[3] (= SM 33), 50[6], 51[6], DJD ii 66 (?, heavily dam. context), IEJ xxxvi 206[1], DBKP 17[41]; cstr. *tlt* MPAT-A 27[2] (= SM 33); + suff. 3 p.pl.m. *tltyhwn* MPAT-A

27^2 (= SM 33), *tltyhn* AMB 7a 22 (× Naveh & Shaked AMB p. 76: = lapsus for *tlthyn*), *tlthyn* AMB 7a 17; f. abs. *tlth* MPAT 52^2, 62^{13}, Syr xlv 101^{15}, MPAT-A 40^4 (for the reading, cf. Naveh Lesh xxxviii 298f., SM sub 57, Hüttenmeister ASI 304f. :: Fitzmyer & Harrington MPAT a.l.: l. *tg* (= Sing. cstr. of *tg*$_2$ (= sum) < Greek ταγή) + *try* = cstr. of *tryn*), 52^3 (for the correct reading, cf. Sukenik Kedem ii 87), EI xx 307 vii 2 (heavily dam. context), *tltl* MPAT 62^{13} (diff. reading, cf. Greenfield sub DBKP 27; lapsus?; cf. Yadin EI viii 50, Fitzmyer & Harrington MPAT a.l.: l. *tlt›*) - **Waw** f. abs. *tlt›* AMB 6^3 - ¶ cardinal number, three: passim; *‹mwdy› ›ln tlt›* SBS 16^1: these three columns; *gwmḥyn tlt›* MUSJ xxxviii 106^7: three niches; *tltt klbn* Hatra 72: three dogs (v. also *klb*$_1$); *ḥnṭyn s›yn tlt wqbyn tlth* MPAT 52^2: wheat, three *seah* and three *qab*; *tlth ywmyn* Syr xlv 101^{15}: three days; *rb‹ šlšt* KAI 69^{9,11}: 3/4 shekel; *mšmr šlšh [‹š]r* SM 106$^{11f.}$: the thirteenth division (v. *mšmr*); *tltyhwn* MPAT-A 27^2: the three of them; *hmwn tlthyn* AMB 7a$^{16f.}$: those three; *hlyn tlt›* AMB 6^3: these three; used in chronology, *lmlky šnt šlš 3 byrḥ krr* KAI 277$^{7f.}$: of my reign, the third year in the month K. (cf. RES 453); *šlš ḥmšm št l‹m ...* KAI 19^8: the 53rd year of the people of ...; *bym ‹šrt wšlšt lyrḥ* Mus li 286^2: on the thirteenth day of the month; *mn hšlšh ‹šr lḥdš* TA-H 8$^{2f.}$: from the thirteenth day of the month; *šnt ‹šr wtlt lḥrtt* CIS ii 199^9: the thirteenth year of Ch. (cf. CIS ii 219^7, Syr xxxv 244^5); *šnt tlt lḥrt yšr›l* MPAT 51^1: the third year of the liberation of Israel; *bywm tlth bhd‹šr ywmyn byrḥ ›lwl* MPAT-A 52$^{3f.}$: on the third day (of the week; i.e. on Tuesday), the eleventh day of the month E. - Savignac with G. & A. Horsfield QDAP ix 195 no. 415-418: l. *tlt* on Nab. lamps = *tlt*$_1$ or *tlt*$_2$ (= *šlš*$_1$); cf. also Albright with Hammond BASOR cxlvi 12 n. 9: poss. = something like "thrice", cf. however Negev NPW 29: l. *›lt* (= n.d.) and Khairy PEQ '84, 117f.: l. *r›yt* = Arab. I have seen.
v. *šlšy*.

šlš$_2$ In unknown West-Semitic dialect, Sing. abs. (*šlš*), Sem xxxviii 52^2, Bordreuil & Pardee Sem xxxviii 58: = guarantee (uncert. interpret.; text fraud?, cf. however Bordreuil & Pardee Sem xxxviii 65ff.).

šlš$_3$ v. *šlšy*.

šlš› v. *šlšy*.

šlšy **Ph** Sing. m. abs. *šlš›* CIS i 6012^2 (= TPC 86) - **Hebr** Sing. f. abs. *šlšt* TA-H 20^1 (v. infra) - **JAr** Sing. f. emph. *tlytyt›* IEJ xl 132^1 (on the context, cf. Yardeni IEJ xl 133) - ¶ ordinal number, third; in *rr šlš›* CIS i 6012^2: third *rab* (v. *rb*$_2$; exact meaning of title unknown (cf. also Slouschz TPI p. 207: or = Sing. + suff. 3 p.s.m. of *šlš*$_3$ (= captain); less prob. interpret.)) - *bšlšt* TA-H 20^1 prob. = in the third (year), cf. Aharoni TA a.l., cf. also Weippert ZDPV lxxx 183, Gibson SSI i p. 51, Lemaire IH i p. 184, Herzog, M.Aharoni, Rainey & Moskovitz BASOR

ccliv 27, 29 :: Lipiński OLP viii 91: *šlšt* = a third part (of a *bat*; cf. also idem BiOr xxxv 287) - the *šlšt* in Dir pes. 20 = Sing. f. abs. of *šlšy* or f. abs. of *šlš*$_1$ (cf. e.g. Clermont-Ganneau RAO iv 196, Dir p. 281, Bron & Lemaire CISFP i 767; on this weight cf. also Scott BASOR clxxiii 54 n. 1).
v. *zz*.

šlšlt **JAr** Plur. abs. *šlšln* AMB 9[6], *šwšln* AMB 11[6] - ¶ subst. chain.

šlšm **Ph** *šlšm* KAI 41[5] - **Pun** *šlšm* CIS i 3917[1], KAI 130[2], Punica ivA 8[3f.], xi 6[5], 16[3], Trip 51[5] - **Mo** *šlšn* KAI 181[2] - **OldAr** *šlšn* KAI 219[3] - **OffAr** *tltyn* Krael 8[8] - **Nab** *tltyn* CIS ii 196[6], 206[9], 207[7], ARNA-Nab 16[2], BAGN 88[7], BASOR cclxiii 78[4] - **Palm** *tltyn* Sem xxxvi 89[2] - **JAr** *tltyn* MPAT-A 52[6], *tltlyn* MPAT 62[13] (lapsus; cf. also Yadin & Greenfield sub DBKP 27) - ¶ cardinal number, thirty: passim; *šlšm h›š* CIS i 3917[1]: the thirty men; *ḥw‹ š‹nt šlšm* Punica ivA 8[3f.]: she lived thirty years (cf. Punica xi 16[2f.]); *šlšn št* KAI 181[2]: thirty years; *šnyn tltyn wšt* CIS ii 196[6]: 36 years (cf. BAGN 88[7f.]); *kršn tltyn* Krael 8[8]: 30 *karsh*; used in chronology, *bšnt šlšm 30 lmlk mlkytn* KAI 41[4f.]: the thirtieth year of king M.; *tltlyn* (v. supra) *b›lwl›* MPAT 62[13]: in the thirtieth of (the month) Elul; *bhšlšm lyrḥ* Trip 51[5]: on the thirtieth of the month; *šnt tltyn wḥmš lḥrtt* CIS ii 206[9]: the 35th year of king Ch. (cf. CIS ii 207[7], ARNA-Nab 16[2], BASOR cclxiii 78[4]); *šnt ›rb‹ m›h wtltyn wḥmš šnyn lḥrbn byt mqdšh* MPAT 52[5ff.]: the year 435 of the destruction of the Temple.

šlšn$_1$ v. *šlšm*.

šlšn$_2$ **Ph** Sing. abs. *šlšn* Hill cxxvii - ¶ subst. prob. meaning a thirtieth (sc. of a *mine*), cf. also Harr p. 151, Betlyon CMP 40ff., 64 n. 19, Puech RB xcii 287.

šm$_1$ **Ph** Sing. abs. *šm* KAI 18[6], 26A iii 13, iv 1 (for iii 13, iv 1 :: Ginsberg FS Gaster 140 n. 39: = Sing. + suff. 3 p.s.m.); cstr. *šm* KAI 14[18] (v. infra), 26A iii 13, iv 2; + suff. 3 p.s.m. (acc.) *šm* KAI 26A iii 14, 16, C iv 16 (cf. e.g. Bron RIPK 115, Gibson SSI iii p. 62 :: Röllig KAI a.l.: = Sing. abs. :: Dupont-Sommer Sem iii 38 n. 2, Hoftijzer Mus lxxvi 196 n. 9: = + suff. 1 p.s.); + suff. 3 p.s.f. (acc.) *šm* KAI 26A ii 10, 18 (cf. Cross & Freedman JNES x 230, Gibson SSI iii p. 60 (cf. also Bron RIPK 87, 131) :: Dupont-Sommer RA xlii 166: = Sing. cstr.); + suff. 1 p.s. *šm* (acc.) KAI 10[12] (cf. Dupont-Sommer Sem iii 41, Hoftijzer Mus lxxvi 197, Röllig KAI a.l., Gibson SSI iii p. 95, 99 :: e.g. CIS i sub 3, Cooke NSI p. 24, Baldacci BiOr xl 130: = form of *šym*$_1$ (cf. also Dahood UHP 11: or = QAL Inf. abs. of *šym*$_1$)),[13] (cf. Dupont-Sommer Sem iii 42, Hoftijzer Mus lxxvi 197, Gibson SSI iii p. 95 :: Röllig KAI a.l.: = Sing. abs. :: Cooke NSI p. 19: = *šm*$_4$??), *šmy* (acc.) KAI 26A iv 18 (cf. Dupont-Sommer Sem iii 38 n. 2), *šmy* KAI 43[3] - **Pun** Sing. abs. *šm* Punica xii 29[3]; cstr. *šm* KAI 124[1], 165[6], CIS i 6000bis 6 (= TPC 84;

cf. Février BAr '51/52, 77, CIS i a.l. (cf. also Ferron StudMagr i 75f., 78: the *mšm* in CIS i 6000bis 6 = mn_5 + Sing. cstr. of $šm_1$ or = Part. of root *šm/šmy* (= according to)) :: Lidzbarski Eph i 167, 169 (div. otherwise): l. *šmm* = Sing. + suff. 3 p.pl.m.); + suff. 3 p.s.m. *šmy* CIS i 6000bis 6 (= TPC 84; cf. Février BAr '51/52, 77, CIS i a.l., Ferron StudMagr i 78 :: Lidzbarski Eph i 166f., 169: = + suff. 1 p.s.), *š‘m’* Trip 40^4 (diff. and dam. context); + suff. 1 p.s. *šmy* KAI $79^{9f.}$; Plur. cstr. *šm’t* KAI 145^{12}; + suff. 3 p.pl.m. *šm’tm* Karth xii 54^2 - **Hebr** Sing. abs. *šm* AMB 4^{12}; cstr. *šm* TA-H 1^4, AMB 1^{13}; + suff. 3 p.s.m. *šmw* AMB 4^2 - **Samal** Sing. cstr. *’šm* KAI $214^{16,21}$ - **OldAr** Sing. abs. *’šm* KAI 222C 25; cstr. *šm* KAI 202C 2; + suff. 1 p.s. *šmy* Tell F 11, 16; + suff. 1 p.s. + *-m*, *šmym* Tell F 11 (:: Vattioni AION xlvi 361: = QAL Part. pass. of $šmm_1$ (= to be hostile to, to damage)); + suff. 3 p.s.m. *šmh* Tell F 12; + suff. 3 p.pl.m. *’šmhm* KAI 223B 7 - **OffAr** Sing. abs. *šm* KAI 226^3; cstr. *šm* Cowl 8^{12}, 13^9, 14^8, Aḥiq 85, Krael $1^{5,6,9}$, ATNS 51^{11}, etc., etc.; + suff. 3 p.s.m. *šmh* Cowl $28^{4,5,9}$, Aḥiq 1, Krael 8^3, Driv 3^1, Herm 1^6, ATNS 5^1, 9^3, 17^1, Beh 7 (*[š]mh*; Akkad. par. *šu-um-šú*), Pers 36^1, Samar 1^2 (= EI xviii 8*), etc., etc.; + suff. 3 p.s.f. *šmh* Cowl 28^{13}, Krael 2^3, $5^{2,4}$, 6^3, 7^3, ATNS 55a ii 4, Beh 2, 12 (Akkad. par. *šu-um-šú*), 17 (Akkad. par. *šu-um-šú*), 18 (*šm[h]*, for the reading, cf. Greenfield & Porten BIDG 34), 27* (for the reading, cf. also Greenfield & Porten BIDG 38; Akkad. par. *šu-um-šú*); + suff. 2 p.s.m. *šmk* KAI 225^{10}, Cowl 30^{26}, 31^{25}, Aḥiq 141; + suff. 1 p.s. *šmy* KAI 233^{12}, Cowl 6^{14} (for the *scriptio anterior šm* (= Sing. cstr.), cf. Porten & Szubin Maarav iv 50), 8^{16}, $25^{12,13}$, Aḥiq 170, RES 1298B 4; + suff. 3 p.pl.m. *šmhm* ATNS $8^{9,12}$, 10a 6; + suff. 1 p.pl. *šmn* Cowl 30^{29}, 31^{28}; Plur. cstr. *šmht* Cowl 22^1, $34^{2,4}$, 66 i 1 (*[š]mht*); + suff. 3 p.pl.m. *šmhthm* ATNS 19^8, TADAE A 4.6^{15} (*š[m]hthm*), Aḥiq 116; cf. Frah xxx 41 (*šm*), Paik 966 (*šmh*), 967 (*šm*), SbPAW '33, 149, Nisa-b 458^2 (*šmh*), BSOAS xxxiii 152^6, GIPP 64, SaSt 23 - **Nab** Sing. cstr. *šm* MPAT 64 i 4; + suff. 1 p.s. *šmy* MPAT 64 ii 2; + suff. 3 p.pl.m. *šmhn* MPAT 64 iii 6 (or preferably = Plur. abs.?, cf. also J.J.Rabinowitz BASOR cxxxix 14) - **Palm** Sing. cstr. *šm* SBS 45^5 (Milik DFD 310f.: l. also Sing. cstr. *šm* in SBS 48^6; uncert. and diff. reading, cf. Cantineau Syr xvii 280, Dunant SBS a.l.); + suff. 3 p.s.m. *šmh* CIS ii 3992^1, 3993^1, 3994^2, etc., etc. - **Hatra** Sing. + suff. 3 p.s.m. *šmh* 335^3 (heavily dam. context; cf. Degen NESE iii 110) - **JAr** Sing. cstr. *šm* AMB $2^{10,13,15}$, $7^{2,8,13}$ (cf. Dupont-Sommer JKF i 203f., Scholem JGM 85f. :: Naveh & Shaked AMB a.l.: l. *šm[k]* = Sing. + suff. 2 p.s.m.), etc.; emph. *šm’* AMB 12^{15}; + suff. 3 p.s.m. *šmh* MPAT-A 22^{10} (= SM 70^{18}), SM $88^{21,22}$ (for the reading, cf. Naveh SM a.l.; heavily dam. context, cf. also Torrey sub Syn D B 6,7), AMB 9^4, 11^7, *links šmh* (lapsus) AMB 15^{20} (or = Sing. emph.?); + suff. 2 p.s.m. *šmk* AMB 7^{11} (cf. Naveh & Shaked AMB a.l., cf. however Dupont-Sommer JKF i 203, Scholem JGM 85f.: l. *šm* (= Sing. abs.) + *d* (= d_3 (= *zy*)), cf. also Beyer ATTM 372: l. *šmd* = Sing. abs. of *š*md_2 or = lapsus for *šmh* (= Sing. + suff. 3 p.s.m. of *š*m_1) + *d* (= d_3) ?); + suff. 3 p.pl.m. *šmhtwn* MPAT-A 34[4] (= SM 69) - ¶ subst. m. - **1)** name: passim; cf. *pṭwsyry šmh* Cowl 28[4]: one named P. (cf. Cowl 33[1], Aḥiq 1, 5, Beh 7, Krael 2[3], 5[2], Driv 3[1,3], Pers 36[1], ATNS 17[1], IPAA 11[9], Samar 1[2] (= EI xviii 8*), etc., etc.); *bkndr šmh* Beh 12: in a place named K. (cf. Beh 27, etc.); *tgr šmh brtʾ* Beh 2: a fortress named T. (for this use of *šm*, cf. Kutscher JAOS lxxiv 241, Lindenberger APA 31 n. 24, Lipiński LDA 104); cf. *ktb šm hym* TA-H 1[4]: write down the date (cf. Pardee UF x 294, HAHL 31) - **2)** *šm* indicating both the name and the one bearing the name; *šmʾt hmzrḥ* KAI 145[12]: the names of those belonging to the community (v. *mzrḥ*); *bryk šmh* indication of Palm. deity: the one whose name is blessed (cf. CIS ii 3932[1], 3993[1], 3994[1f.], etc., etc.); *z mṣbt skr šm ʿbdʿ[...* DD 10[1f.]: this is the memorial stele for the name of A. (cf. also KAI 43[3]); cf. also *šm* in AMB 4[12] prob. indicating the Name of God - 3) name, reputation (cf. also Tawil Or xliii 58ff.); *šmny šm ṭb* KAI 226[3]: he afforded me a good name; *lkny ly lskr wšm nʿm tḥt pʿm ʾdny* KAI 18[6f.]: that it may be for me a memorial and a good name beneath the feet of my lord (:: Dahood Bibl liii 396: *šm* here = monument; cf. Punica xii 29[3]); *[w]ʾl ygl šmk qdmyhm* Aḥiq 141: that your name may not be lightly esteemed before them; *wʾl yrt šr[š]h ʾšm* KAI 222C 24f.: may his posterity inherit no name; *šm ʾztwd ykn lʿlm km šm šmš wyrḥ* KAI 26A iv 2f.: may the name of A. last forever like the name of the sun and the moon (on the context, cf. Greenfield FS Albright ii 266ff., Amadasi Guzzo VO iii 93f.; cf. KAI 26C v 5ff.); *[zy] lʾ ytrwm bšm ʾbwhy* Aḥiq 138: whoever takes no pride in his father's name; *ʾdm šm* KAI 26A iii 13, iv 1: a man of renown (cf. e.g. Bron RIPK 112f., cf. also Pardee JNES xlvi 141f. :: Rosenthal ANET 654 (n. 6): = a man who is (just) called a man (i.e. an ordinary human being without title of any sort), cf. also Ginsberg FS Gaster 140 (n. 39), Tawil Or xliii 58f. n. 57f., Ceresko JLNS 57, Swiggers BiOr xxxvii 340, Kutler JANES xiv 74f.; on this expression, cf. also Demsky EI xiv 8ff. and R.Kutscher & Wilcke ZA lxviii 125f.) - **4)** *šm* indicating the name of someone living on in his posterity; *ysḥw šmk ... mn ḥyn ... wyhʾbdw zrʿk* KAI 225[9f.]: may they pluck out your name ... from among the living and may they cause your seed to perish (v. *ḥ*y_2); *ynsḥwhy wzrʿh wšmh mn ʾnpy tymʾ* KAI 228A 14f.: may they remove him and his seed and his name from T. (cf. KAI 223B 7); *lʾ yhn[pq] ṣlmšzb ... mn bytʾ znh wl[zr]ʿh wšmh km[ryʾ bb]ytʾ znh [lʿlmʾ]* KAI 228A 21f.: they shall not remove Ṣ. ... from this temple nor his seed nor his name (from being) priests in this temple forever - **5)** *šm* indicating the name of someone living on by the preservation of that name; *ʾm ... ymḥ šm ʾztwd bšʿr z ... wmḥ bʿlšmm ... ʾyt mmlkt hʾ* ... KAI 26A iii 12ff., 18f.: if someone effaces the name of A. from this gate, may B.Sh. efface that king; *wmn ... ybl ... wšmym lšm bh wzy yld šmy mnh wyšym šmh* ... Tell F 10ff.: and whoever ... takes (it) ... may he put my name on it, and who effaces my name from it and places his own name... (Akkad. par.: ... *šumī-ma ... šumē ... šum-šú*) - **6)** *šm* in a divine epithet, indicating the manifestation of a deity; *ʿštrt šm bʿl* KAI 14^{18}: A. the name of B. (cf. e.g. CIS i sub 3, Cooke NSI p. 37f., Gibson SSI iii p. 113 :: Dillmann Monatsber. d. Ber Akad. 1881, 606ff.: *šm* = Dual cstr. of *šmym* (cf. also e.g. du Mesnil du Buisson BiOr xviii 110, Röllig KAI a.l.)) - **7)** *šm* (stat. cstr.) preceded by prep. - a) prec. by *b*$_2$ - α) in the matter of, on account of, because of (cf. Ginsberg JAOS lxxiv 156, Kutscher JAOS lxxiv 242, Muffs 31 n. 2, Kaufman AIA 39); *ʾgrnky dyn wdbb ... bšm nksyʾ ʾlky* Cowl 14$^{7f.}$: I will institute suit or process against you ... in the matter of those goods (cf. Cowl 8$^{12f.}$, 13^{9}, Krael 1$^{5f.}$, 10$^{15f.}$, 12^{25,29}); *grytky dyn wdbb ... bšm mwmʾh dky* Cowl 14$^{8f.}$: I institute suit or process against you on account of this oath; this meaning prob. also in Aḥiq 85 (v. *šrḥw*); cf. also *yhb ... ksp r 3 bšm ksp mlḥʾ* OLZ '27, 1043$^{1ff.}$: he has paid 3 *r.* silver in the matter of (i.e. as) salt-tax (?, v. *ksp*$_2$) - β) in the name of; *ygrnk bšmy* Cowl 6^{14}: he will sue you in my name (cf. Cowl 25$^{10ff.,12f.}$); *yhnpqwn ʿlyky spr ḥdt wʿtyq bšmy* Cowl 8$^{15f.}$: they will produce a deed against you, new or old, in my name (cf. also RES 1298B 3f.?); cf. also *ʾp klʾ mlyʾ bʾgrh ḥdh šlḥn bšmn* Cowl 30^{29}: also the whole matter we have sent in a letter in our name; *wkl ʾš lsr tʾbn z by py ʾnk wby py ʾdm bšmy* KAI 79$^{6ff.}$: and whoever will remove this stone ... without my personal order or the order of anyone (acting) in my name (cf. MPAT 64B 2, cf. poss. also MPAT 64A 3f.); *bšm bwlʾ [wdm]s* SBS 45^{5}: in the name of the Council and the People (cf. Greek par. δημοσίοις); *bšmk ʾlh mqdšʾ* ... AMB 7^{11}: in your name, o sacred God, may ... (cf. AMB 7$^{2,8,13f.}$); *wʿlwtʾ yqrbwn ... bšmk* Cowl 30$^{25f.}$: they will offer burnt-offerings ... in your name (i.e. on your behalf), cf. Cowl 31^{25}; *spr lh šlḥty bšmh* Herm 1$^{5f.}$: you have not sent him a letter in his name (i.e. addressed to him, cf. e.g. Bresciani & Kamil Herm a.l., Porten & Greenfield ZAW lxxx 226, Gibson SSI ii p. 130f., Hoftijzer SV 108, 110 n. p, Porten & Yardeni sub TADAE A 2.3 (uncert. interpret.), or rather = concerning him? :: Kutscher IOS i 110, 112: you have sent a letter to him in his name (i.e. directly)); *gʿwrw ʾšth wʿryth ... bšm ...* AMB 2^{8,10}: drive out fever and shiver ... in the name of ... (cf. AMB 2$^{11ff.}$, 9^{4}), cf. also AMB 4^{24}, 11^{7}; *mšby[ʿ] ʾny ʿlykm bšm ymynw* AMB 4$^{31f.}$: I adjure you by His right hand - b) prec. by prep. *l*$_5$, for the sake of; *dsgy* (v. *šgʾ*$_3$) *sgy ʾnwn ʿbdw lšmh drḥmnh* MPAT-A 22^{10}: who have exerted themselves exceedingly for the sake of (i.e. for) the Merciful One (or rather: for the Name of the Merciful One? :: Fitzmyer & Harrington MPAT a.l.: in the name of) - c) prec. by prep. *l$_5$* + *mn$_5$* + *b$_2$*, *lmbšm g'y* KAI 124: in the name of G. (cf. Lat. par. *nomine [C]*; :: v.d.Branden PO i 434f.: in honour of G.) - d) prec. by prep. *'l$_7$*, *'mt' zyly zy sṭyrh 'l šmy* ATNS 8[3]: my slave girl who is marked with my name (for the reading of the context, cf. Shaked Or lvi 409); *'l šm* RES 492B 7f. of uncert. interpret., cf. Halévy RS xii 64, 66: = addressed to him; Lidzbarski Eph ii 240f.: on his name?; Grelot DAE 141: (marked) by his name (for the context, v. *ktb$_1$*, *'lym*) - v.d.Branden OA iii 252, Meltô i 33 n. 40: l. in KAI 30[1f.] *'š šm* = a man of renown (imposs. interpret.: l. *'š [...]//[...]m*, cf. e.g. Masson & Sznycer RPC 15, Gibson SSI iii p. 29 - Levi Della Vida Or xxxiii 7f.: a form of this word in Trip 51[1] (*š'm'*), cf. however Amadasi IPT 132: = Pl cstr. of *šym$_2$* (= place of deposit), uncert. interpret., diff. context.

v. *'š$_1$*, *bšm$_1$*, *šym$_1$*, *šmh*, *šmym*, *šmš$_{1,2}$*, *tm$_3$*.

šm$_2$ **Hebr** Sing. abs. *šwm* SM 49[4] - **Samal** Plur. abs. (casus obl.) *šmy* KAI 214[6] (:: Segert AAG p. 209: = Plur./Dual abs. (casus obl.) of *šmym*) - **OffAr**, cf. Frah vi 3 (*twm'*) - ¶ subst. garlic.

šm$_3$ v. *hš*.

šm$_4$ **Ph** *šm* KAI 14[16,17] (for both instances, v. *'dr$_1$*), 26A ii 1 - **Pun** *š'm* Trip 51[2] (diff. context, cf. Levi Della Vida Or xxxiii 9) - **Mo** *šm* KAI 181[12,17,30,33] - **Hebr** *šm* KAI 194[5], TA-H 17[4]; (+ loc. ending -*h*) *šmh* KAI 194[8], TA-H 24[20] - **DA** *šm* i 8 (dam. context; :: Hackett BTDA 43f., 98, 134: = Qal Inf. abs. of *šym$_1$* (cf. also Garr DGSP 181) :: Rofé SB 66: = pass. form of *šym$_1$*), ii 7 - **Samal** *šm* KAI 214[8] (dam. context) - **OldAr** *šm* KAI 224[6] (v. *rqy$_2$*) - ¶ adverb there: passim (:: H.P.Müller ZAW xciv 219, 233: in DA ii 7 with temporal meaning "then"); *wdnnym yšbt šm* KAI 26A i 21f.: and I settled the D. there; *wyšbny šm m'drm* KAI 14[17]: and we established him (i.e. the god) there glorifying (him), cf. KAI 14[16]; *'yn šm 'dm* KAI 194[5]: there is no one there - **1)** prec. by prep. *mn$_5$*, from there; *wlqḥt mšm 1 šmn* TA-H 17[3f.]: and you must take from there 1 (measure of) oil (or l. with Lipiński OLP viii 92: *wlqḥ gm šm 1 šmn*?; cf. KAI 181[12,17,30,33]) - **2)** followed by local ending -*h*, there; *pn tb' 'dm šmh* TA-H 24[20]: lest Edom should come there (cf. KAI 194[8]) - cf. the etymologically related *tmh*, *tmn*.

v. *šmh*, *tm$_3$*.

šm$_5$ v. *šmšm*.

šm'wl v. *šm'l*.

šm'l **Hebr** Sing. abs. *šm'wl* AMB 4[13]; + suff. 2 p.s.m. *šm'wlk* AMB 1[1] - ¶ subst. the left side; *mšm'wlk* AMB 1[1]: on your left; *šm'wl* AMB 4[13]: the left, i.e. the North - Sing. cstr. *šm'l* (= the left) poss. to be read in the Ph. text RES 1204[1] (cf. Clermont-Ganneau Et i 89, cf. also

Catastini RSF xiii 6; reading however uncert., cf. Cooke NSI p. 43 :: Teixidor Sem xxix 10 (div. otherwise): l. *šm* (= QAL Part. pass. s.f. abs. of *šym*$_1$) + *ʾl*$_6$ - cf. *šml*$_1$.

šmd$_1$ v. *šym*$_1$, *šmr*$_1$.

šmd$_2$ **Nab** Plur. abs. *šmdyn* (or l. *šmryn*?) CIS ii 198[3] - ¶ subst. of unknown meaning; CIS ii sub 198, Cooke NSI p. 223: = curse (poss. interpret.); J sub 16 (cf. also Roschinski BJ clxxx 159): indication of fixed sum to be paid as a fine (less prob. interpret.); cf. also Levinson NAI 219.

v. *šm*$_1$.

šmh **DA** Hoftijzer DA a.l.: the diff. *šmh* in DA ii 13, 14 poss. = subst. Sing. abs. (= (place of) horror; cf. also Puech RB lxxxv 116, Garbini Hen i 186), cf. however Caquot & Lemaire Syr liv 206: = Sing. + suff. 3 p.s.m. of *šm*$_1$ (diff. and dam. context) :: McCarter BASOR ccxxxix 59 n. 4: = *šm*$_4$ + adv. ending *-h* (cf. also Levine JAOS ci 200, Garr DGSP 117); on the problem, cf. also Hackett BTDA 69.

šmwnh v. *šmn*$_4$.

šmḥ **Amm** QAL Impf. 3 p.s.m. *yšmḥ* Ber xxii 120[6] (:: Shea PEQ '78, 110f., Coote BASOR ccxl 93, Aufrecht sub CAI 78: = PIʿEL Impf. 3 p.s.m. (cf. also Becking BiOr xxxviii 275 (n. 21)) :: Baldacci VT xxxi 367: = HOPH Impf. 3 p.s.m. (= to be congratulated) - ¶ verb QAL to be glad, to rejoice (cf. e.g. Zayadine & Thompson Ber xxii 138ff., Cross BASOR ccxii 12f., Loretz UF ix 171 :: Krahmalkov BASOR ccxxiii 56 (n. 6): to be connected with following *b*$_2$, to rejoice because of).

v. *š*$_{10}$, *tmk*.

šmṭ **OffAr**, cf. Frah xviii 13 (*šmyṭwn*): to detach, to extricate; cf. Toll ZDMG-Suppl viii 35.

v. *šym*$_1$.

šmṭh **Hebr** Sing. abs. *šmṭh* DJD ii 24B 14, C 12, E 9 - **JAr** Sing. abs. *šmṭh* MPAT 39[7] (:: Beyer ATTM 307: l. *šmṭth* = Sing. emph.; on the reading problems, cf. also Bennett Maarav iv 256); emph. *šmṭth* MPAT-A 50[5], 51[5] (*šmṭt[h]* :: Beyer ATTM 369: l. *šmṭ[h]* = lapsus for *šmṭth*), 52[5] - ¶ subst. release; *šnt šmṭh* MPAT 39[7]: the year of the Release (for the context, cf. Koffmahn DJW 86f.); *mšth qdmyth dšmṭth* MPAT-A 50[4]: in the first year of the Release (cf. MPAT-A 51[5], 52[4f.]); *mn hywm ʿd swp ʿrb hšmṭh* DJD ii 24E 8f.: from this day until the Eve of the Release (cf. DJD ii 24B 14, C 12).

šmy v. *šm*$_1$.

šmym **OldCan** Plur./Dual abs. *ša-mu-ma* EA 211[17], *ša-me-ma* EA 264[16] (or l. *ša-mì-ma* ?) - **Ph** Plur./Dual abs. *šmm* KAI 15, 27[13] - **Pun** Plur./Dual. *šmm* KAI 145[4] (cf. e.g. Février Sem vi 20, Röllig KAI a.l., v.d.Branden RSF i 166, 168 :: Krahmalkov RSF iii 188, 191f., 204: = Sing. + suff. 3 p.s.m. of *šm*$_1$); cf. Sanch 34c: σαμημ (in Σαμημρουμος;

cf. also FR 76a, 78d, 86a, 226a), Augustinus Quaest in Hept vii 16: *samen* - **Hebr** Plur./Dual abs. *šmym* DJD ii 43[3] - **DA** Plur./Dual. *šmyn* i 8 - **OldAr** Plur./Dual abs. *šmyn* KAI 202B 25 (*šmy[n]*), 222A 11 (*šmy[n]*), 26, B 7, Tell F 2 - **OffAr** Plur./Dual abs. *šmyn* KAI 266[3], Herm 4[1], Aḥiq 94 (for this reading, cf. e.g. Baneth OLZ '14, 297, Grelot DAE p. 436, Lindenberger APA 68, 233 n. 130, Kottsieper SAS 12, 235 :: e.g. Cowl a.l.: l. *šmt* = Qal Pf. 2 p.s.m. of $šym_1$); emph. *šmy›* KAI 266[2], Cowl 30[2,15,28], 31[27], 32[4], 38[3,5], 40[1], RES 1785B 3; cf. Frah i 9 (*šmy›*) - **Nab** Plur./Dual. *šmy›* CIS ii 236[2] (prob. interpret., cf. Milik DFD 410) - **Palm** Plur./Dual emph. *šm[y]›* Ber iii 99[1] (for this reading, cf. Milik DFD 182 :: Ingholt Ber iii 99ff. (div. otherwise): l. *nšmt›* (= Plur. emph. of *nšmh* (= soul); for the reading, cf. Al-Hassani & Starcky AAS iii 149 n. 1) - **JAr** Plur./Dual emph. *šmy›* Frey 845 (*[š]my›*; = SM 104), *šmyh* SM 53[3], Syn D A 12 (for the reading, cf. e.g. Naveh sub SM 88[12] :: Torrey Syn p. 263, 265: l. *šby›* = Plur. emph. of *šb* (cf. also Ellis & Ingholt Syn 463) :: Obermann Ber vii 110: l. *šmyy* = orthogr. variant of *šmy›*), AMB 1[18], 7[1], *šwmy›* MPAT-A 42[5] (= SM 20), *šwmyh* MPAT-A 22[7] (= SM 70[15]), AMB 3[6], 9[5] - ¶ subst. m. Plur./Dual heaven(s): passim; for the context of DA i 8, v. skr_6; for the context of KAI 266[3], v. rm_2; *wy‹qwr ytyh mn tḥwt šwmyh* MPAT-A 22[7]: and may He uproot him from beneath the heavens; heaven and earth combined in *klmh lḥyh b›rq wbšmyn* KAI 222A 26: all manner of evil in earth and heaven; *b›lt šmm w›rṣ* KAI 27[13]: by an oath of heaven and earth (i.e. an oath under invocation of heaven and earth), cf. KAI 266[2]; for the context of Tell F 2, v. *gwgl* - in the title *›lḥ šmy›* Cowl 30[2,28], 32[3f.], 38[3,5]: the God of Heavens (epithet of YHW; cf. Vincent Rel 100ff.; cf. also AMB 3[6]), cf. also *mr› šmy›* Cowl 13[15]: the Lord of Heavens (epithet of YHW; cf. MPAT-A 42[4f.] (= SM 20), AMB 1[18]); *›lhy šmy[n]* KAI 202B 25: the gods of heaven (dam. context); *mlkt šmyn* Herm 4[1]: the queen of heavens (prob. = Ashtarte, cf. Bresciani & Kamil Herm a.l., Milik Bibl xlviii 561, Gibson SSI ii p. 138, Olyan UF xix 161ff.; on this goddess, cf. also Winter FG 502ff., Koch UF xx 97ff.) - heaven as indication of God's abode; *brkth mn šmyh* Syn D A 12 (= SM 88): the blessing from Heaven; *rḥmyn mn šmyh* AMB 7[1]: mercy from Heaven; cf. also *m‹yd ›ny ‹ly t šmym* DJD ii 43[3]: I take the Heavens as witness against myself - *šmm rmm* KAI 15 ("the high heavens") indication of one of the wards of Sidon, cf. e.g. Cooke NSI p. 402, Torrey JAOS xxiii 162ff., Eissfeldt Ras Schamra 62ff., 109f., Milik Bibl xlviii 575 n. 6, Teixidor Syr xlvi 332, Olyan UF xix 167f. :: e.g. Lidzbarski Eph ii 53, Houtman VT xxvii 346, Gibson SSI iii p. 112: = name of a shrine or sacred precinct (cf. also Mullen DCC 170, Mettinger SPDS 121; v. also $›rṣ_1$) - l. poss. *šmyn* (Plur./Dual abs.) in KAI 222B 23 (uncert. and diff. reading) - the diff. *lmrtšmn* on ring (RB

lxvii 249) poss. = l_5 + f. Sing. cstr. of *mr›* + Plur./Dual abs. of *šmyn* (for the lady of the heavens).
v. *›dr*$_1$, *šm*$_{1,2}$.

šmyn v. *šmym*.

šmyny Hebr m. Sing. abs. *šmyny* SM 106[6] - ¶ ordinal number, eighth.

šmkh v.Soden Or xlvi 195 (cf. also idem AHW s.v. *šamakātā*): > Akkad. (= onion); uncert. interpret.

šml$_1$ **Palm** Sing. emph. *šml›* CIS ii 4173[2], 4199[7], RB xxxix 538[1], FS Collart 161[4], *sml›* RB xxxix 532[2], Ber ii 85[10], 93[2], 102 ii 3, 5, 104[3,5], v 125[8], FS Miles 38[1,2], 50 ii 7, 8; + suff. 2 p.s.m. *šmlk* RB xxxix 548[6], *smlk* CIS ii 4174[5], 4195[8], 4204[1], Ber ii 77[1], 82[1], 84[1], 88[7], 110[1] (Greek par. ἐωνίμοις), v 109 ii 10, RIP 163b 3; + suff. 1 p.pl. *smln* Ber ii 86[8,10] - ¶ subst. - **1)** left: passim; *›ksdryn trn ... m‹lyk bb› dy ymynk wdy smlk* Ber ii 110[1]: two exedras ... when you enter the doorway on your right and on your left; *b›ksdr› sml›* FS Miles 50 ii 7f.: in the exedra to the left - a) preceded by *mn*$_5$, to the left of; *›ḥbrth gwmḥyn tmny› mn ymynk ›rb‹› wmn smlk ›rb‹›* Ber v 109[6,8ff.]: I have made him a partner (in) eight niches, four on your right and four on your left (cf. CIS ii 4195[6ff.]) - b) prec. by *‹l*$_7$ - α) *‹l š/sml›*, at the left side; *gwmḥyn ... št› m‹lyk ›ksdr› ‹l sml›* Ber v 124[7f.]: six niches ... at the left side, when you enter the exedra (cf. CIS ii 4173[2], 4199[7], Ber ii 85[10], 93[2], 102 ii 3, 5, 104[3], RB xxxix 538[1], FS Miles 38[1,2], 50 ii 7, FS Collart 161[4]) - β) *‹l š/sml*, at the left side of; *sṭr› dnh ... m‹lyk bb› ‹l smlk* CIS ii 4204[1]: this wall ... when you enter the doorway on your left (cf. CIS ii 4174[5], RB xxxix 548[6], Ber ii 77[1], 82[1], 84[1], 86[8,10], 88[7], RIP 163b 3) - **2)** with special meaning, north; *gb› dy sml› dy ›ksdr›* RB xxxix 532[2]: the north side of the exedra (v. also *gb*$_1$); *pnn lsml›* Ber ii 104[5]: empty at the north side - this word (Sing. abs. *šml*) also on IfN 314? (cf. G.Herrmann ibid. p. 45) - cf. *šm›l*.

šml$_2$ v. *šlm*$_2$.

šml› OffAr (orig. SHAPH of *ml›*$_1$) Impf. 2 p.s.m. (or 3 p.s.f.?) *tšml›* ATNS 52b 8 (v. infra) - ¶ verb (orig. SHAPH) to complete; *tšml› mly[* ATNS 52b 8: you(?) shall complete the affairs of ... (reading however uncert.).

šmlh OffAr Sing. cstr., cf. Warka 20, 24, 30, 31: *šá-am-lat* - ¶ subst. mantle; *šá-am-Lat. ru-ga-zi-e* Warka 24: the mantle of wrath (cf. Warka 20, 30); *šá-am-Lat. di-ma-a-a-›[i-i]* Warka 31: his mantle of calmness (?, v. *dmy*$_2$) - Michaud Syr xxxiv 47f., PA 86: l. in KAI 195[5] *šm[l]h* (Sing. abs.)? (improb. reading and interpret., cf. e.g. Röllig KAI a.l., Gibson SSI i p. 44).

šmly Palm Sing. m. abs. *smly* Ber ii 112[5]; emph. *šmly›* CIS ii 4175[6], *smly›* CIS ii 4172[1], Ber v 124[1]; Plur. m. abs. *smlyn* Ber ii 112[4] - ¶ adj. northern, north: passim; *m‹rby wsmly* Ber ii 112[5]: at the north-western side (v. *m'rby*).

šmm$_1$ **Pun** Schroed 321, L.H.Gray AJSL xxxix 83: a form of this root *estimim* (HITP Impf. 1 p.s.) with the meaning "to be upset, to be perturbed" poss. in Poen 1142 (uncert. interpret. :: J.J.Glück & Maurach Semitics ii 125: *estimim* = Sing. abs. of *'š$_1$* + Sing. m. abs. of *tmym*).
v. *šm$_1$*.

šmm$_2$ v. *šmym*.

šmm$_3$ **Nab** word of uncert. meaning in J 2^3 (for the reading, cf. Lidzbarski Eph iii 268 :: Jaussen & Savignac sub J 2: l. *šhm* = n.p.); for poss. interpretations, cf. Cantineau Nab ii 151; prob. = n.p. or tribal name.

šmn$_1$ v. *yšmn*.

šmn$_2$ **Pun** Sing. abs. *šmn* KAI 69^{12} (:: Lagrange ERS 471, 475: = Sing. abs. of *šmn$_3$* (= fatted animal); v. also *zbḥ$_2$*), 74^9 - **Edom** Sing. cstr. (?) *šmn* RB lxxiii 399^1 - **Hebr** Sing. abs. *šmn* Mosc var. 10, TA-H 4$^{1f.}$, 6^5 (dam. context), 7^8 (dam. context), 10^3, 12^1, 13^2 (*[š]mn*), 14^3 (dam. context), 17$^{4,8f.}$, SM 49^{5,23}; cstr. *šmn* KAI 186^3, 187^2, Dir ostr 16^3, 17$^{2f.}$, 18^2, 20^2 (*[š]mn*), 21$^{2f.}$, 53^2, 55^3, 59^1 - **OffAr** Sing. abs. *šmn* ATNS 69a - **Palm** Sing. abs. *šmn* RTP 707, 708 - ¶ subst. oil; in the TA-H texts 4$^{1f.}$, 7^8, 10^3, 12^1, 13^2, 14^3, 17$^{4,8f.}$ prob. indication of a jar of oil; for RTP 707, 708, cf. Milik DFD 190: = oil or animal fat?; for *šmn rḥṣ*, v. *rḥṣ$_2$* - abbrev. *š* prob. in IEJ xv 141 (cf. Dothan IEJ a.l., Weippert ZDPV lxxx 191f., Puech TK 302, 308 n. 16) - Puech FS Grelot 24: l. *šmn* (= Sing. abs.) in DA x d 1 - Lipiński RTAT 251 n. 30: l. *[š]mn* in KAI 43^{10} (poss. reading, uncert. interpret., cf. also Gibson SSI iii p. 139) - Lemaire Sem xxxv 14: l. this word poss. on sherd (Sing. abs./cstr. *šmn*; reading however highly uncertain) - on this word, cf. Borowski AIAI 119ff.
v. *bzz$_1$*, *mny*, *qysm*, *šmn$_2$*.

šmn$_3$ v. *šmn$_2$*.

šmn$_4$ **Ph** m. *šmn* CIS i 92^2, *šmnh* KAI 27$^{17f.}$ (for the form, cf. e.g. FR 102 Anm., Röllig KAI a.l. :: Dahood UF i 18, Bibl lii 396 n. 2 (div. otherwise): l. poss. *šmn* + *h* (= article)) - **Pun** m. *šmn* KAI 111^3, 136^5, RES 168^3, *šmn'* Punica x 1^5 - **Hebr** m. *šmnh* DJD ii 24B 17; f. *šmnh* TA-H 8^4, *šmwnh* DJD ii 30^{21}, AMB 4^{17} - **OffAr** f. *tmnyh* Krael 7^{16}; cf. Frah xxix 8 (*twmny'*) - **Nab** m. *tmwn'* CIS ii 214^4, 215^5 (cf. Cantineau Nab i 48) - **Palm** f. *tmny'* CIS ii 3913 ii 49, 50, 4173^2, 4195^7, Ber v 124^6 - **JAr** f. *tmnyh* MPAT 52^7, AMB 9^3, *tmn[y]'* MPAT 51^6 (for this reading, cf. Milik RB lxii 253, Fitzmyer & Harrington MPAT a.l., Puech RQ ix 214, 217 :: Milik RB lxi 183, 186: l. *tmn[y] my'* = eight hundred :: Birnbaum PEQ '57, 130: pro *tmny' w* l. *tmnyh* (cf. also Abramson & Ginsberg BASOR cxxxvi 17f.: l. *tm[n]yh*; diff. reading,

diff. context) - ¶ cardinal number, eight; used in chronology, *bšnt šmn 8 lmlky* CIS i 92[2]: in the eighth year of his reign; *b‘sr wšmn lyrḥ* KAI 111[2f.]: on the eighteenth of the month; *‘d hšmnh ‘šr lḥdš* TA-H 8[3f.]: until the eighteenth of the month; *šnt ’rb‘yn wtmwn’ lḥrtt* CIS ii 214[3f.]: the 48th year of Ch. (cf. CIS ii 215[6]).
v. *smnh*.

šmnh v. *šmn*$_4$.

šmnm Pun *šmnm* Punica ix 6[2] (*[šm]nm*), xiv 3[3], KAI 130[2], RES 172[2], NP 130[6], *šmn* KAI 128[3] (in the comb. *šmnšš*, cf. FR 99c: < *šmnm šš* :: Levi Della Vida RCL ’49, 410: sixty eight would have been *šmnm wšš* (*w* left out by mistake?)) - **Hebr** *š[mw]nym* DJD ii 30[21] - **OffAr** *tmnyn* Cowl 26[10,14] (for the form, cf. Degen GGA ’79, 30) - ¶ cardinal number, eighty.

šms v. *šmš*$_2$.

šm‘$_1$ **Ph** QAL Pf. 3 p.s.m. *šm‘* KAI 38[2], 39[3], 41[6], CIS i 88[7] (= Kition F 1), RES 504A 4 (= DD 7), 504B 5 (= DD 8), 1213[5], DD 13[3], Kition A 30[3]; 3 p.s.f. *šm‘* KAI 10[8]; Impf. 3 p.s.f. *tšm‘* KAI 33[3] (= Kition A 1); 2 p.s.m. *tšm‘* KAI 14[6] - **Pun** QAL Pf. 3 p.s.m. *šm‘* KAI 47[3], 61A 5, 63[3], 104[3], 110[4], 113A 3, 129[4], Punica xviii/ii 29[3f.] (for the reading, cf. Bertrandy & Sznycer SPC sub 19 :: Chabot Punica a.l. l.: *m‘* (lapsus for *šm‘*)); etc., etc., *šm’* KAI 98[4], 106[3], 111[5], 112[3], Hofra 30[3f.], 33[3], 34[4f.], 216[3] (v. *l*$_1$), NP 76[3] (for the context reading, cf. Amadasi Guzzo VO vi 185f.), 78[2] (:: Schroed 265 (div. otherwise): l. *šm’’*), Sem xxxvi 30[4], etc., etc., *š‘m’* CIS i 3244[3], RES 303[2], Hofra 69[3], 153[3], Punica xi 18[3f.] (*š‘m[’]*; v. *l*$_1$), 25[3], etc., *šmḥ* RES 340[5], 1536[2], Hofra 141[3], 156[3], Punica xviii/ii 22[3f.], 26[4], *šmw* Punica xi 31[3], *šmn* (lapsus) CIS i 5268[2] (dam. context), *šm* KAI 114[3], Hofra 121[3], *šb‘* RES 1554[3], Punica xviii/ii 40[2], 3 p.s.f. *šm‘* CIS i 327[5], 418[6f.], 497[4], 508[4], 926[6], 3777[2], etc., *šm’* CIS i 180[4], 1577[3], 4571[9], 4717[4]; 2 p.s.m. *šm’t* Hofra 181[3f.] (dam. context); 3 p.pl.m. (or = 3 p.s.m.?) *šm‘* CIS i 181[4f.], 182[3], 185[5], 192[4], 197[5], etc., etc., *šm’* CIS i 213[5], 258[5], 319[1f.], 329[3], 363[4], etc., etc., *šm‘’* CIS i 953[4], KAI 119[8], *šm* CIS i 973[5], 1330[3], 2672[5], 3390[3], 3399[4], RES 336[5], etc., *š‘m’* CIS i 5718[8], *š‘m* CIS i 4831[5], *šb‘* CIS i 3599[4], *š‘* (lapsus) CIS i 2005[5], 2214[4], *š’* (lapsus) Hofra 135[3], *šmd* (lapsus) CIS i 2867[3], *šk’* (lapsus) CIS i 2443[4], cf. KAI 175[4]: σαμω (cf. v.d.Branden BiOr xxiii 145, FR 131, Röllig KAI a.l.: = 3 p.s.m. :: FR 132b Anm.: = pausal form); Impf. 3 p.s.m. *yšm‘* Antas p. 61[2] (dam. context), Hofra 32[3] (× Février with Berthier & Charlier Hofra p. 34 (div. otherwise): l. *šm‘* = QAL Pf. 3 p.s.m., v. *l*$_1$; on this form, cf. also Sznycer APCI 213 (n. 12)); 2 p.s.m. *tšm‘* KAI 77[3], RES 1535[2], Hofra 3[2], 4[4], 5[2], 10[3], etc., *tšm’* KAI 108[4], Hofra 2[3], 46[2f.], 67[4], 80[3], *tšmḥ* RES 337[2], *tš‘m’* Hofra 70[3], 161[3] (:: Garbini AION-SL iv 92f.: = *iqattal*-form?), *tšm* CIS i 4938[4]; 3 p.s.f. *tšm‘* CIS i 252[5], 506[3], 1109[4], 1180[4], 2775[2], etc., *tšm’*

CIS i 411^{5}, 2075^{4}, 2944^{6}, 4003$^{4f.}$, 4320^{4}, etc., *tšmʿʾ* CIS i 3604^{5} (cf. however FR 133: = 2 p.pl.m.), *tšm* CIS i 1144, 4475^{5}, 4664^{4}; 3 p.pl. *yšmʿ* CIS i 380^{5}, 391^{4}, 2723^{4}, 3638^{5}, 3822^{5}, KAI 78^{1}, etc., *yšmʾ* CIS i 5690^{6}, *ymʿ* Hofra 60^{5} (lapsus), *yšmʿʾ* CIS i 3709^{6}, 4358^{7}; Alt ZAW lx 156ff.: Impf. forms beginning with *t-* forms of resp. 3 p.s.m. and 3 p.pl.m., cf. also FR 129 Anm. (less prob. interpret.)) - **Hebr** Qal Impf. 3 p.s.m. *yšmʿ* KAI 200^{1} (cf. e.g. Naveh IEJ x 131, 134, Yeivin BiOr xix 5, Lemaire Sem xxi 62, Pardee Maarav i 36f. :: Gibson SSI i p. 29: = Hiph); 2 p.s.m. *tšmʿ* DJD ii 17A 2; Inf. cstr. *šmʿ* TA-H 111^{7}; Hiph Impf. 3 p.s.m. *yšmʿ* KAI 192^{1}, 193^{2}, 194^{1}, 195^{1} - **DA** Qal Pf. 3 p.pl.m. *šmʿw* i 15 (:: Levine JAOS ci 197: = Qal Imper. pl.m.); Imper. pl.m. *šmʿw* i 12 (cf. Hoftijzer DA a.l., H.P.Müller ZDPV xciv 61f. n. 35 (cf. also Rofé SB 67, Levine JAOS ci 197, H. & M. Weippert ZDPV xcviii 98, Puech FS Grelot 28) :: Caquot & Lemaire Syr liv 200: = Qal Pf. 3 p.pl.m. (cf. also e.g. Garbini Hen i 185, Delcor SVT xxxii 58, McCarter BASOR ccxxxix 51, Hackett BTDA 29, 98)) - **OldAr** Qal Pf. 3 p.s.m. *šmʿ* KAI 201^{4}; Impf. 3 p.s.m. *yšmʿ* KAI 222B 21, 223B 3; 2 p.s.m. *tšmʿ* KAI 223B 4; 3 p.pl.m. *yšmʿn* KAI 223B 2 (bis), 3; Inf. *mšmʿ* Tell F 9 (Akkad. par. *še-me-e*; :: Vattioni AION xlvi 360: or = subst. *mšmʿ* (Sing. cstr. = answer, sc. to prayer)); Itp Impf. 3 p.s.m. *ytšmʿ* KAI 222A 29 - **OffAr** Qal Pf. 3 p.s.m. *šm[ʿ]* Cowl 71^{10} (dam. context); 1 p.s. *šmʿt* Cowl 40^{2}, 41^{2}; 3 p.pl.m. *šmʿw* ATNS 102a 4 (heavily dam. context; or = Imper. pl.m.?); Impf. 3 p.s.m. *yšmʿ* Aḥiq 93; 2 p.pl.m. *tšmʿwn* RES 492A 3; Imper. s.m. *šmʿ* Beh 53; pl.m. *šmʿw* Aḥiq 59; Part. act. s.m. abs. *šmʿ* Aḥiq 29; pl.m. abs. *šmʿn* Cowl p. 269 i 2 (for the reading and the context, cf. Greenfield & Porten BIDG 22; Akkad. par. of *šmʿn ly*: *i-šem-mu-ʾ-in-ni*); Part. pass. s.m. abs. *šmyʿ* Driv 7^{3}, SSI ii 28 rev. 6; Itp Pf. 3 p.s.m. *ʾštmyʿ* Aḥiq 70 (for this form, cf. Cowl p. 233, Leand 34e, Lindenberger APA 297 n. 1); Impf. 3 p.s.m. *yštmʿ* Cowl 18^{3}, Krael 7^{42}; Imper. pl.m. *ʾštmʿw* Driv 4^{3}; Part. pl.m. abs. *mštmʿn* Driv 4^{1,3*} (*mštm[ʿ]n*); cf. Frah xxiii 7 (*ʿšmhn*), Paik 156, 158, 159 (*ʾšmʿyw*; for the prosthetic vowel in this ideogram, cf. Coxon ZAW lxxxix 275f.), GIPP 19, 47, cf. Toll ZDMG-Suppl viii 37f., 40 - **Palm** Qal Pf. 3 p.s.m. *šmʿ* CIS ii 4080^{5}; Part. pass. s.m. emph. *šmyʿʾ* CIS ii 4100^{1} - **Hatra** Qal Part. pass. s.m. emph. *šmyʿʾ* 404^{1} - **JAr** Part. act. s.m. abs. *šmʿ* MPAT 49 i 5 - ¶ verb Qal - **1)** to hear, to become acquainted with; *šlmk šmʿt* Cowl 41^{2}: I heard about your welfare (cf. Aḥiq 93); *šmʿt kʿmlʾ zy ʿmlt* Cowl 40^{2}: I have heard of the trouble that you took; *šmʿ hwyt zy ʾmr* MPAT 49 i 5: I have heard that he said ... (cf. Beh 53); cf. also Part. pass. + *l*$_5$, *šmyʿ ly kzy pqydyʾ* ... Dri 7^{3}: I hear that the officers ... (cf. Friedrich AfO xviii 125, Kutscher Kedem ii 73, PICS 134ff.), cf. SSI ii 28 rev. 6 (*šmyʿ ln lʾmr*) - **2)** to hear (implying the reaction upon what is heard); meaning "to obey" in KAI 222B 21, 223B 2 (bis), 3, 4 - a) + obj., *šmʿ mlqrt qlm* CIS i 88[7]: M. has heard their voice (i.e. he has given ear to them), cf. KAI 10[8] (cf. also Greenfield Proc v CJS i 180ff.), 38[2], 41[6], 61[5], CIS i 180[4f.], DD 7[4], 8[5], 13[3], etc., etc.; *yšmʿ ʾdny hšr ʾt dbr ʿbdh* KAI 200[1f.]: may my lord the commander hear the word of his servant (i.e. give ear to what his servant says; cf. Dion RB lxxxvi 576f.); cf. also Tell F 9 - b) + *b$_2$*, *šmʿ bqlh* CIS ii 4080[5]: he has listened to her voice - c) + *l$_5$*, *wšmʿ lqlh* KAI 201[4f.]: he has listened to his voice (cf. Aḥiq 59) - **3)** Part. pass. renowned, famous: CIS ii 4100[1]; *šmyʿʾ dy nbw ʾlhʾ* Hatra 404[1f.]: messenger of the god N. (uncert. interpret.) - HIPH to let (someone) hear + double object, *yšmʿ YHWH ʾt ʾdny šmʿt šlm* KAI 192[1f.]: may the Lord give my lord to hear favourable tidings (cf. KAI 193[2f.], 194[1f.], 195[1f.]; on this formula, cf. Pardee JBL xcvii 335, Dion RB lxxxix 542 n. 98) - ITP - **1)** to be heard; *wʾl ytšmʿ ql knr bʾrpd* KAI 222A 29: and let the sound of the lyre not be heard in A. (cf. Hillers TC 57, Greenfield ActOr xxix 15, McCarthy CBQ xxxv 183); *ʾštmyʿ bm[dynt ʾtwr]* Aḥiq 70: it was heard in the city of A. (i.e. the rumour went in the city of A.) - **2)** to pay attention to (implying the reaction upon what is to be heard); *lʾ yštmʿ lh* Krael 7[42]: one will not pay attention to him (cf. Yaron Bibl xli 391); *ʾrmpy ʿm ḥylʾ ... lʾ mštmʿn ly* Driv 4[1]: A. with the army ... do not obey me (cf. Driv 4[3,3*f.]) - Cantineau sub Inscr P 31: the diff. *šmʿ* in Inscr P 31[9] = QAL Pf. 3 p.s.m.? (highly uncert. interpret.), cf. Aggoula Sem xxxii 111, 116: = QAL Pf. 3 p.pl.m. or Imper. pl.m., cf. also Gawlikowski Syr xlviii 415, TP 76, Milik DFD 277: = Sing. abs. of *šmʿ$_2$* (= reputation, renown; in the combination *šmʿ ṭbyt* (= good reputation); highly uncert. interpret., v. also *ṭbyt*) - a form of this root in ATNS 144[1] (*]šmʿ*).

v. *ypʿ$_1$*, *mšmʿh*, *sml$_1$*.

šmʿ$_2$ v. *šmʿ$_1$*.

šmʿh **Hebr** Plur. (cf. e.g. Röllig sub KAI 192; or = Sing.?, cf. e.g. Gibson SSI i p. 37) cstr. *šmʿt* KAI 192[2], 193[3,4] (?), 194[2], 195[2] - ¶ subst. tidings; *šmʿt ṭb* KAI 194[2]: good tidings (for a possible reading of *šmʿt ṭb* (or eventually *šmʿt ṭbt*), cf. Cross FS Iwry 43, 45); *šmʿt šlm* KAI 192[2f.], 193[3]: favourable tidings; *šmʿt šlm wṭb* KAI 195[2]: favourable and good tidings (reading however uncert.).

šmr$_1$ **Pun** QAL Part. act. s.m. cstr. *šmr* KAI 62[7]; Part. pass. s.m. abs. *šmr* CIS i 6067a 1, b 1 (for this interpret., cf. Lidzbarski Eph i 172f., FR 139 × RES sub 19, 20, Février sub CIS i 6067: = QAL Imper. s.m.); NIPH Pf. 3 p.s.f. *nšmrʾ* NP 130[5] (cf. Cooke NSI p. 147f., Février RHR cxli 21; diff. context) - **Hebr** QAL Part. act. s. + suff. 1 p.pl. *šmrn* KA 7[2]; pl.m. abs. *šmrm* KAI 194[11]; NIPH Imper. s.m. *hšmr* KAI 193[21] - **OffAr** (:: Joüon MUSJ xviii 15: *šmr$_1$* in Aramaic = Hebraism) ITP Impf. 3 p.s.m. *[y]štmr* Aḥiq 160 (for this reading, cf. Ungnad ArPap p.

77, Grelot RB lxviii 190, Puech Sem xxi 14 n. 2, Lindenberger APA 161, 266 nn. 488, 489 :: Kottsieper SAS 10, 17, 235: l. *[mš]tmd* = ITP Part. s.m. abs. of *šmd*$_1$ (= to curse) :: Cowl a.l.: l. *[y]ʿmd* (= QAL Impf. 3 p.s.m. of *ʿmd*$_1$ (= to stand)), cf. also Gressmann ATAT 461); Imper. s.m. *ʾštmr* Aḥiq 97, 101 (on the ITP instances of *šmr*$_1$, cf. Lindenberger APA 74, 235 n. 155) - ¶ verb QAL - **1)** to guard; *nṣr wšmr* CIS i 6067a 1: protected and guarded (v. however supra; cf. CIS i 6067b 1; on CIS i 6067 a, b, cf. Greenfield Sem xxxviii 156); Part. act. guardian, inspector; *šmr mḥṣb* KAI 62[7]: the inspector of the quarry; said of God: *šmrn* KA 7[2]: our Guardian (for this interpret., cf. e.g. Naveh BASOR ccxxxv 28, 29 n. 7 :: e.g. Gilula Shn iii 129ff., Tigay NOG 26: = Samaria (cf. also Emerton ZAW xciv 2ff., Scagliarini RSO lxiii 207 (with literature)) - 2) to observe, to watch; + *ʾl*$_6$, *ʾl mšʾt lkš nḥnw šmrm* KAI 194[10f.]: we are watching for the beacons of L. - NIPH to be on your guard: KAI 193[21] - ITP to be on your guard - **1)** + *l*$_5$, *ʾštmr lk* Aḥiq 97: watch on your behalf (i.e. beware; for the prec. *pmk* prob. being last word of the prec. clause, cf. Ungnad ArPap p. 71, Baneth OLZ '14, 298, Ginsberg ANET 428, Grelot RB lxviii 182, DAE 437 (n. b) :: Cowl a.l., Gressmann ATAT 458, Lindenberger APA 73f.: *pmk* = object of *ʾštmr*), cf. Aḥiq 101 - **2)** + *ʿm*$_4$, *[y]štmr ʾyš ʿm ʾlhn* Aḥiq 160: a man will abide by the gods (cf. Lindenberger APA 161: ... is in the care of the gods × Fitzmyer CBQ xlvi 317: = ... does beware of th gods (?)) - a form of this root prob. also in BAr '55/56, 31 ii 2 (reading uncert.), Février sub IAM 3: l. *tšʿmrnʾ* (= PI ʿEL Impf. 2 p.s.m. + energic ending) :: Février BAr '55/56 a.l. (div. otherwise): l. *tšmrn* = QAL Impf. 2 p.s.m. + energic ending :: Garbini AION-SL iv 92f.: l. *tšʿmrn* = QAL Impf. (*iqattal*-form?) 2 p.s.m. + suff. 3p.s.m. v. *mrnr*.

šmr₂ Ph Sing. cstr. *šmr* KAI 48[2] - ¶ subst. exact meaning unknown: guard?, or preservation? (for the context, v. *nʾlk*).

šmrg Samal word of unknown meaning in KAI 215[16]. Halévy RS vii 344, 354, Zimmern ZDMG lviii 950, Montgomery JAOS liv 424, Dion 203ff.: = SHAPH Pf. 3 p.s.m. of *mrg* (= *mrṣ*$_2$/*mrq*$_2$/*mrʿ*$_1$ (= to be sick; cf. also Delsman TUAT i 630)), cf. also Rabin EI ix 150: or = SHAPH of *mrg* (= to spoil), Halévy RS i 235, 241: = SHAPH of *mrg* (= *mrq*$_2$) = to pine away, to collapse; highly uncert. interpret., cf. also Cooke NSI p. 179: prob. = n.p., Donner KAI a.l.: = n.p. or n.l., Gibson SSI ii p. 85: perhaps = n.l. - on this word, cf. also Garr DGSP 24, Stefanovic COAI 176.

šmrh Pun Sing. abs. *šmrt* KAI 81[4] (:: Clermont-Ganneau RAO iii 12: or = Plur. abs.?, cf. also CIS i sub 3914) - ¶ subst. poss. meaning protection; *ḥgr hšmrt* KAI 81[4]: poss. = protecting wall (cf. e.g. CIS i sub 3914, Röllig KAI a.l., v.d.Branden PO i 204, 209), cf. however

Cooke NSI p. 129: *šmrt* poss. = watchtower (cf. also Halévy RS ix 81f., Lidzbarski sub KI 69); Lidzbarski Eph i 23, sub KI 69: or *šmrt* = thorns, *ḥgr hšmrt* = thorn fence; Milik Bibl xlviii 564: *ḥgr hšmrt* = the court of the guard (v. also *ḥgr*$_2$).

šmš$_1$ **Pun** PI ʿEL Pf. 3 p.s.m. *šmš* CIS i 6000bis 5 (= TPC 84 :: Lidzbarski Eph i 166f., 169: l. prob. *šmy* (= Sing. + suff. 1 p.s. of *šm*$_1$)) - **Palm** PA ʿEL Pf. 3 p.s.m. *šmš* CIS ii 3924^5, 3932^3, 3934^3, Syr vii 129^3; Part. pl.m. cstr. *mšmšy* RTP 304 - **Hatra** ITP Part. pl.m. abs. *mštmšyn* Hatra 408^7 - ¶ verb PA ʿEL - **1)** to serve + obj., *ʾlnm šmš* CIS i 6000bis 5: he served the gods; *dy šmš ʾlhyʾ* Syr vii $129^{3f.}$: who served the gods - **2)** to occupy a certain function; *wšmš kdy hwʾ tnn q[r]spynws hygmwnʾ* CIS ii 3932^3: he was in function (said of a *strategos*) when C. was prefect there; *dy šmš wšpr lhwn bʾsṭrṭgwth* CIS ii $3934^{3f.}$: he was in function and they were pleased by him during his office as *strategos*; *wšmš bmgdʾ r[bʾ]* CIS ii 3924^5: he exercised his function by (giving) large gifts (dam. context); Part., *mšmšy pḥdyʾ* RTP 304: the officials of the tribes (indicating a religious function, cf. Caquot RTP p. 150, Milik DFD 158) - ITP to be served: Hatra 408^7 - a form of this root (*mšmšh[m]*) in BIA x 55^4, poss. = PA ʿEL Part. pass. + suff. 3 p.pl.m. substantivated: their venerated object/place (said of a temple) :: Milik BIA 56: = PA ʿEL Inf. + suff. 3 p.pl.m. of *šmš*$_1$ (same interpretation but with diff. translation with O'Connor DRBE 606).

šmš$_2$ **Ph** Sing. abs. *šmš* KAI $13^{7f.}$, 14^{12}, 19^1, 26A i 4f., 19, 21, ii 2, iv 3, C v 7, 27^{26} (:: v.d.Branden BO iii 47: l. *šrš* = Sing. abs. of *šrš*$_2$) - **Pun** Sing. abs. *šmš* KAI 78^6, CIS i 5510^5 - **Samal** Sing. abs. *šmš* KAI $215^{13,14}$ - **OldAr** Sing. emph. *šmšʾ* KAI 222C 5 - **OffAr** Sing. abs. *šmš* Cowl $6^{8,9}$, 8^6, 13^{15}, $25^{6,7}$, 67 xiii 2 (dam. context; or part of n.p.?), Krael 3^9, $4^{10,11}$, 6^7, $9^{3,8,11}$, $10^{3,4}$, $12^{7,9,15,17,18}$, Aḥiq 138 (*šm[š]*, cf. e.g. Cowl p. 224 (cf. however p. 243), Gressmann ATAT 460, Ginsberg ANET 429 × Grelot DAE p. 442 (n. l), Lindenberger APA 135, 260 n. 424, UF xiv 112f.: = n.d. (cf. also Kottsieper SAS 16, 236) :: Ungnad ArPap p. 75: l. *šm[šʾ]* = Sing. emph. :: Nöldeke AGWG xiv/4, 16: l. *šm[šh]* = Sing. + suff. 3 p.s.m. (cf. also Epstein ZAW xxxii 137) :: Torczyner OLZ '12, 402: l. *šmh* (= Sing. + suff. 3 p.s.m. of *šm*$_1$)); emph. *šmšʾ* Cowl 21^8; cf. Frah i 11 (*šmsyʾ*) - ¶ subst. m. (cf. Aḥiq 138) sun: KAI 27^{26}, Aḥiq 138; *ʾl ykn lm šrš ... bḥym tḥt šmš* KAI $14^{11f.}$: may they have no root ... among the living under the sun (cf. also Elayi SCA 238); *zrʿ bḥym tḥt šmš wmškb ʾt rpʾm* KAI $13^{7f.}$: posterity among the living under the sun and a resting-place with the shades; *bḥym ʿl pn šmš* CIS i 5510^5: during (their) life (or: among the living?) in the face of the sun (i.e. publicly); *šm ʾztwd ykn lʿlm km šmš wyrḥ* KAI 26A iv 2f.: may the name of A. last forever like the name of the sun and the moon (cf. KAI 26C v 6f.); v. *mbʾ*, *mdnḥ*, *mwṣʾ*, *mʿrb* - for *šmšʾ*

in Krael 5[9] (on the form, cf. Krael p. 185, Segert AAG p 109) in the combination *mn ṭl' lsmš'* (from the shadow to the sun), v. *ṭl₂* :: Krael a.l., Volterra RSO xxxii 692: *smš'* = n.d. (Shamash) - l. poss. *šmš* (= Sing. abs.) in KAI 200[11] (for this reading, cf. e.g. Naveh IEJ x 133, Cross BASOR clxv 43 (n. 35) :: Yeivin BiOr xix 4: l. *[ywm]* = Sing. abs. of *ywm*; cf. also Röllig KAI a.l.), cf. however Lemaire Sem xxi 73, IH i 15: l. *[qṣr]* (= Sing. abs. of *qṣr₃*), on the problem, cf. also Pardee Maarav i 49ff.

šmšgl cf. Frah vi 2: onion (for this reading cf. Ebeling Frah a.l., cf. however Nyberg FP 69: l. *šamšer* (Iran. word).

šmšm Hebr Plur. abs. *šmšmyn* SM 49[3,20] - **OffAr** Sing. abs. *šmšm* ATNS 42b 1; Plur. abs. *šmšmn* ATNS 43b 3; cf. Frah iv 8 (*šm*, abbrev.), Nisa-c 52[2] (*šmšmn*), GIPP 64 - ¶ subst. sesame - for this word, cf. Borowski AIAI 99 - cf. *ššmn*.

šn₁ v. *znh*, *ngdwt'*, *npš*.

šn₂ v. *šnn*.

šn'₁ Mo QAL Part. act. pl.m. + suff. 1 p.s. *šn'y* KAI 181[4] - **DA** QAL Impf. 2 p.s.m. *tšn'n* ii 10 (or = pass. Impf.?, cf. Hoftijzer DA p. 292 (cf. also p. 297, cf. also Puech RB lxxxv 116), cf. also Lemaire CRAI '85, 277 × Knauf ZDPV ci 190: = QAL Impf. 2 p.pl.m. :: Rofé SB 68: = QAL Impf. 2 p.s.m. + suff. 3 p.s.f. :: Levine JAOS ci 200, Hackett BTDA 30, 65f., 94, 98: = QAL Impf. 2 p.s.m. + suff. 3 p.s.m. (cf. also Garr DGSP 111, 169) :: Garbini Hen i 183, 186: = QAL Impf. 2 p.s.m. + energic ending of *šn'₂* (= *šny₁*; cf. H.P. Müll ZAW xciv 234) :: Caquot & Lemaire Syr liv 204f.: = QAL Impf. 2 p.s.m. + suff. 1 p.s./1 p.pl.) - **OldAr** QAL Part. act. pl.m. + suff. 3 p.s.m. *šn'wh* KAI 224[12]; + suff. 1 p.s. *šn'y* KAI 222B 26, 223B 14 (diff. reading), 224[10,11] - **OffAr** QAL Pf. 3 p.s.m. *šn'* RES 1789 (??, dam. context); 1 p.s. *šn't* Cowl 15[23,27], Krael 2[7,9], *šnyt* Krael 7[21]; + suff. 2 p.s.m. *šny[t]k* Krael 7[25]; Impf. 3 p.s.f. *tšn'* Krael 7[24]; + suff. 2 p.s.m. *tšn'nk* Cowl 9[8]; Part. act. pl.m. + suff. 1 p.s. *š'ny* Aḥiq 174 (prob. lapsus for *šn'y*, cf. e.g. Sach p. 176, Cowl p. 246, Segert AAG p. 341, Lindenberger APA 178, 279 (cf. also Kottsieper SAS 236); cf. however Puech RB xcv 591: l. poss. *bḥny* (= QAL Part. pass. + suff. 1 p.s. of *bḥn* (= my chosen one), highly uncert. interpret.)); cf. SbPAW '33, 148 - **Palm** QAL Part. pass. pl.f. abs. (or = adj.?) *šnyn* CIS ii 4058[5] - ¶ verb QAL to hate; substantivated Part. act., enemy, adversary: KAI 181[4], 222B 26, 223B 14, 224[10,11,12]; cf. also the following formulae used in cases of divorce - **1)** + obj. (pron. suff.), *whn yh[wy]š[m'] tšn' lb'lh ... wt'mr lh šny[t]k* Krael 7[24f.]: and if Y. hates her husband and says to him: I hate you (cf. Cowl 9[8]) - **2)** + *l₅*, *wy'mr šn't ltmt 'ntty* Krael 2[7]: and he says: I hate my wife T. (cf. Krael 7[21]); *šn't lb'ly 'nny* Krael 2[9]: I hate my husband A. (cf. Cowl 15[23], Krael 7[24f.]); cf. Cowl p. 28, Krael p. 148,

J.J.Rabinowitz Law 40, Kutscher JAOS lxxiv 238, Yaron JSS iii 32ff., Verger RGP 118ff. - Part. pass. (v. however supra): hated; *rwḥ' šnyn* CIS ii 4058[5]: evil spirits (dam. context).
v. *b'y*$_1$, *šn'h*, *šnh*$_2$.

šn'$_2$ v. *šn'*$_1$.

šn'$_3$ v. *šnh*$_5$.

šn'$_4$ v. *šny*$_1$.

šn'h **Ph** Sing. abs. *šn't* KAI 26A iii 17 - **OffAr** Sing. abs. *šn'h* Cowl 15[23], 18[1], Krael 7[22] (for the reading *šn['']h*, cf. Porten & Yardeni sub TADAE B 3.8),[25,34] (cf. Ginsberg JAOS lxxiv 159 :: Krael a.l., Segert AAG p. 385: = QAL Part. pass. s.f. abs. of *šn'*$_1$),[37] (*[š]n'h*; for the reading, cf. Yaron JSS iii 24 n. 2, Porten & Greenfield JEAS p. 56, Porten & Yardeni sub TADAE B 3.8 :: Krael a.l.: l. *[š]n'hy* = QAL Pf. 3 p.s.m. + suff. 3 p.s.f. of *šn'*$_1$?),[39] (cf. Ginsberg JAOS lxxiv 159 :: Krael p. 318: = QAL Part. pass. s.f. abs. of *šn'*$_1$), *šn'* Krael 2[8] (:: Krael p. 148: = lapsus for *šn'h* or = QAL Part. pass. s.m. abs. of *šn'*$_1$),[40] (:: Ginsberg JAOS lxxiv 159: *šn'hy* = phonetic orthography for *šn'h hy* :: Krael p. 220: *šn'hy* = QAL Part. act. s.m. + suff. 3 p.s.f. of *šn'*$_1$), *š'h* Krael 2[9] (lapsus; for the reading, cf. Yaron JSS xiii 207 n. 1, cf. also e.g. Porten & Greenfield JEAS p. 38, Porten & Yardeni sub TADAE B 3.3 :: Krael a.l., Grelot DAE p. 214: l. *šwh* = QAL Part. act. s.m. abs. of *šwy*$_1$); + suff. 3 p.s.m. *šn'th* Aḥiq 132 - ¶ subst. - **1)** hate: KAI 26A iii 17 - **2)** hatefulness; *šn'th kdbt špwth* Aḥiq 132: his hatefulness is the untruthfulness of his lips - **3)** divorce; *wy'bd lh dyn šn'h* Krael 7[39]: he shall apply to her the provisions of divorce (cf. Cowl 18[1] (dam. context); cf. Porten GCAV 256); *ksp šn'h* Cowl 15[23], Krael 7[25]: the divorce money (i.e. the amount of silver to be paid by the partner divorcing), cf. Krael 2[8] (*ksp šn'*), 2[9] (*ksp š'h*, v. supra); *šn'h hy* Krael 7[34,39] (*šn'h [hy]*), *šn' hy* Krael 7[40] (v. supra; cf. also Krael 7[37]): this means divorce (i.e. an action mentioned before is equated to the pronouncement of the divorce formula), cf. Yaron JSS iii 23f., v 69f. :: J.J.Rabinowitz Law 55, Grelot RB lxxxii 290: it is (ground for) divorce.

šnby (< Akkad., cf. Bauer & Meissner SbPAW '36, 419, Dupont-Sommer MAI xiv/2, 75f., Kaufman AIA 103 :: Grelot DAE p. 73 (n. f; div. otherwise): l. poss. *[pw]šnby* < Egypt. = amount of tax still due) - **OffAr** Sing. abs. *šnby* MAI xiv/2, 66[7] (dam. context) - ¶ subst. two-thirds; cf. *snb*.

šnh$_1$ v. *šny*$_1$.

šnh$_2$ **OldCan** Sing. abs. *ša-ni-ta* EA 362[66] - **Ph** Sing. abs. *št* KAI 18[5], 19[8], Mus li 286[5]; abs./cstr. *št* KAI 18[4], 19[5], 40[2], 52[4] (dam. context), 60[1], CIS i 94[2]; cstr. *št* CIS i 4[1]; Plur. abs. *šnt* KAI 26A iii 6, C iii 20; abs./cstr. *šnt* KAI 14[1] (cf. e.g. Gibson SSI iii p. 108 :: Swiggers BiOr xxxvii 338: = Sing.), 32[1] (= Kition A 2), 33[1] (= Kition A 1), 38[2], 39[1], 40[1], 41[4], 43[4,5,6,8], CIS i 13[1] (= Kition A 27), 88[1,6] (= Kition F 1), Kition A 29[1], 30[1]; + suff. 3 p.s.m. *šntw* KAI 4[5], 6[3], 7[5], 10[9] - **Pun** Sing. abs. *št* KAI 110[4], 111[4], 112[5], 130[3], 137[5], 152[3], RES 336[5], Hofra 57[4], 59[4], 61[4], *š‘t* Punica xv 2[4], cf. IRT 894[7]: *sath* (?, diff. context; cf. Levi Della Vida OA ii 86 n. 44, cf. however Vattioni Aug xvi 552: without interpret.); abs./cstr. *št* KAI 101[1], 141[3]; cstr. *št* KAI 66[2], 77[3], 80[1], 101[2], 118[2], 130[1], 137[1], 159[5], 163[4] (diff. and dam. context), 173[3], CIS i 124[3], 179[6], 3920[3], 5510[8], Antas p. 65[4] (dam. context), Hofra 21[2], 90[2], RES 79[2], *[š]‘t* Punica ix 9[2], RSF xvii 244[1]; Plur. abs. *šnt* KAI 277[9,10] (cf. e.g. Dupont-Sommer JA cclii 292, 296f., Röllig KAI a.l., Gibson SSI iii p. 154 :: Lipiński RSF ii 61, RTAT 261 n. 79: = QAL Part. act. pl.f. abs. of *šny*$_3$ (= to shine)), cf. PBSR xxii 115f[2,4]: *sanu* (for this form, cf. FR 231); abs./cstr. *šnt* KAI 134[2], 151[3], 171[3], 277[7], Punica ivA 7[3], D 4[2], E 15[3], vi 1[3], ix 1[3], xii 28[3], RSF i 130[1], etc., etc., *š‘nt* KAI 133[3], 135[3], 136[2f.,4], 140[7], 142[3], 143[4], 144[2], 148[2], 149[4], 158[2], 169[3], Punica ivA 8[3], v 3[2], vi 2[3f.], ix 2[4], xv 2[4], Sem xxxvi 33[2], etc., etc., *š‘n’t* KAI 142[2] (*š‘n’[t]*), Punica ix 3[3], xiv 8[2], Trip 40[4] (diff. and dam. context), *šnwt* Punica xiv 4[3], *š‘nwt* Punica xiv 3[3], Karth x 133[3,4] (reading *šnwt* misprint; cf. Fantar Sem xxv 72 :: Garbini AION xxv 262, 264: l. *‘nwk* = QAL Inf. cstr. of *ḥnk*$_1$ :: Février Karth a.l.: l. *‘nwk* = *’nk*), cf. *sanu* OA ii 83[4], KAI 180a, d (*sanu[]*), IRT 879[3] (cf. e.g. Levi Della Vida OA ii 85, 92, Vattioni AION xvi 41, Aug xvi 554, Krahmalkov RSF iii 184f. :: Krahmalkov RSF vi 28ff.: *sanu* has double meaning, a) years, b) QAL Part. pass. s.m. abs. of *šn’*$_1$), 894[5] (for this form, cf. FR 231), *sanuth* KAI 180c, e (cf. e.g. Röllig KAI a.l. :: Vattioni AION xvi 53, Aug xvi 540: pro *sanuth* l. *sanu cii*) - **Mo** Sing. abs. *št* KAI 181[2,8] (the same word also in KAI 181[34]?? (dam. context)) - **Amm** Plur. abs. *šnt* Ber xxii 120[7] - **Hebr** Sing. abs. *šnh* SM 13, IEJ vii 239[4], DJD ii 22,1-9[9], 24B 16, C 14, 18, 30[27], AMB 4[30,31], *št* KAI 183[1], 184[1], 185[1], 186[1], 187[1], etc., etc.; cstr. *šnt* Sam 16[2] (uncert. reading), on coins of the first revolt, cf. Meshorer JC no. 153, 156, 161, 162, 163 (cf. also Meshorer Mas coin 1358, 3000, 3492, 3493), on coins of the second revolt, cf. Meshorer JC no. 165, 166, 168, 170, 171, 172, 173, 176, DJD ii 22, 1-9[1], 24B 1 (*š[n]t*), C 1 (*[š]nt*), D 1, E 1, 29[1,9],30[8], *št* Dir ostr 22[1], 23[1], 27[1], 28[1], etc., etc.; Plur. *šnym* IEJ vii 239[7], DJD ii 24C 12 (*šn[ym]*), E 9; cstr. *šny* SM 49[5,19,21,24], DJD ii 24A 12 (heavily dam. context), E 10 - **Samal** Sing. cstr. *šnt* KAI 215[1] (dam. context) - **OldAr** Sing. cstr. *šnt* KAI 232, MDAIA ciii 62 (for the reading, cf. Bron & Lemaire RA lxxxiii 37f., Eph‘al & Naveh IEJ xxxix 193, 196 :: Kyrieleis & Röllig MDAIA ciii 65 (div. otherwise): l. *bšn* (= n.g.)); Plur. abs. *šnn* KAI 222A 27, 223A 5, 6; + suff. 3 p.s.m. *šnwh* Tell F 8 (Akkad. par. *šanāti-šú*) - **OffAr** Sing. abs. *šnh* Cowl 10[7], ATNS 25[1] (heavily dam.

context)^{,3}, 52a 3, 8, KAI 228A 20, FX 136$^{12,12f.,17}$; cstr. *šnt* Cowl 1^{1}, 2^{1}, 5^{1}, Krael 1^{1}, 2^{1}, ATNS 10a i 7, 19^{2,5,6}, Pers 2^{5}, 3^{5}, FuB xiv 18^{3}, BSh 1^{1}, 2^{1}, 27^{1}, Samar 1^{1} (= EI xviii 8*), etc., etc., *št* KAI 228A 1; emph. *šnt›* Cowl 21^{3}, 71^{14}, 81^{39,112}, ATNS 2^{4}, 3^{3}, 36^{2}, 108^{2}, FuB xiv 15^{4}, 20^{3}; Plur. abs. *šnn* Cowl 45^{8}, 71^{9}, Krael 4^{17,18}, Driv 11^{4} (for the reading, cf. Porten & Yardeni sub TADAE A 6.14), MAI xiv/2, 66^{1,4,5}, KAI 279^{1}; cf. Frah xxvii 1 (*šnt*), xxviii 31 (*šnt*), Paik 971 (*šnt*), Syn 300^{2}, 301^{1}, 302 ii 2, 305^{1}, 310^{1}, ZDMG xcii 441A 1, 2, 3, 442B 1, 2, 3, Nisa 2^{1}, 3^{1}, 4^{1}, 5^{1}, 6^{1}, 7^{1}, 8^{1}, 9^{1}, etc. (*šnt*), Nisa 156^{4} (*št*, prob. lapsus), Nisa 17^{2} (*š*, abbrev.), BSOAS xxxiii 147^{1}, 152^{8}, GIPP 34, 64, SaSt 23 etc. - **Nab** Sing. cstr. *šnt* CIS ii 158^{4}, 195^{5}, 196^{8}, 197^{4}, etc., etc. *št* J 285 (diff. context), IEJ xvii 250^{3}, 252^{3}; Plur. abs. *šnyn* CIS ii 196^{6}, 333^{7} (dam. context), BAGN 88^{7}; cstr. *šny* CIS ii 196^{6} - **Palm** Sing. abs. *šn›* Syr xvii 274^{4}; cstr. *šnt* CIS ii 3902^{2}, 3909^{4}, 3913 i 1, Syr lxii 257 (Greek par. ἔτους), etc., etc.; emph. *št›* Syr vii 129^{4}, SBS 34^{2}; Plur. abs. *šnyn* CIS ii 4358^{6}, 4359^{6}, 4562^{2}, 4616^{7}, Inv viii 168^{4}, RIP 25^{10}, 39A 4, 103c 5, AAS iii 24 i 6, ii 6; cstr. *šnt* CIS ii 3908^{5} (:: Rosenthal Sprache 78 n. 2: = lapsus) - **Hatra** Sing. cstr. *šnt* 34^{1}, 35^{1}, 36^{1}, 62^{1}, 65^{1}, 80^{9}, 82^{1}, 131 (incomplete?), 214^{1}, 272^{1}, 288a 1, b 5, 290^{1} (*[š]nt*), 293^{1}, 294^{1}, 338^{1}, app. 5^{1}, 6^{1}, 10^{1}, (cf. Assur 1^{1}, 4^{1}, 17 i 1, etc.); Plur. abs. *šnyn* 30^{5} (for this reading, cf. Aggoula MUSJ xlvii 29 (:: idem ibid.: or l. *šnwn*), cf. however Safar Sumer viii 186, ix 16*, Caquot Syr xxx 236, Donner sub KAI 248, Ingholt AH i/1, 45: l. *šnt*) - **JAr** Sing. cstr. *šnt* MPAT 39^{7}, 40^{1,12}, 41^{1}, 43 i 3, 51^{1}, 62^{13} (= DBKP 27), 149^{2}, SM 88^{2} (:: Torrey Syn D p. 263: l. *šnh* = Sing. abs.)^{,3} (= Syn D A), 89^{1,3} (= Syn D B), MPAT-A 50^{6}, 51^{5,6}, 52^{4} (:: Beyer ATTM 370: l. *št* = lapsus for *šth* = Sing. emph.)^{,5}, IEJ xl 132^{1}, 135^{1}, *št* SM 88^{9} (= Syn D A; :: Torrey Syn D p. 263: pro *bšt ḥdh* l *bšnt šyt* :: Obermann Ber vii 97: l. *bšth[*; cf. also Naveh EI xx 308); emph. *šth* MPAT-A 11^{1} (= SM 43), 50^{4}; Plur. abs. *šnyn* MPAT-A 50^{7}, 51^{7}, 52^{7} - ¶ subst. f. year (in Cowl 10^{7} *šnh* apposition to *tnyn*?), passim; *kl yrḥn wšnn* Cowl 45^{8}: during all the months and years (cf. Yaron JNES xx 128f.); *šnh wšnh* DJD ii 24B 16: every year (cf. DJD ii 24C 14, 18, D 15, 30^{27}); *šnh bšnh* KAI 228A 20: year after year (= every year; cf. FX 136$^{12f.}$ (Greek par. κατ' ἕκαστον ἐνιαυτὸν), 137^{17} (Greek par. κατ' ἐνιαυτὸν)), cf. poss. also ATNS 25^{2} (*šnh [b]šnh*); *mšnh lšnh* AMB 4$^{30f.}$: from year to year; *lšnt›* FuB xiv 20^{3}: yearly; *bšt› dh* SBS 34^{2}: in this year; *šnym šlmwt šny [m]ksh* DJD ii 24E 9f.: complete years, fiscal years - **1)** in constructions indicating someone's age - a) Plur. abs. + cardinal number, *šnt šnm* Punica ivE 15^{3} (cf. e.g. Punica ix 2 ii 2, 6 ii 3, x 1^{5}, RES 168^{3}); *š‹n›t ‹sr wḥmš* Punica ix 3^{3} (cf. e.g. Punica ix 4$^{2f.}$, KAI 105); *š‹nt šlšm* Punica ivA 8$^{3f.}$ (cf. e.g. KAI 149^{4}, Punica ivD 4$^{2f.}$, vi 1$^{3f.}$); *šnt ›rb‹m w›ḥd* Punica ix 1$^{3f.}$ (cf. e.g. KAI 148$^{2f.}$, 169$^{3f.}$, RES 172, Punica xii 23$^{2f.}$,

28^{3}, CIS ii 3908^{5}, cf. *sanu lxxiii* OA ii 83^{4} (cf. KAI 180a), cf. also *avo sanuth xxv* KAI 180c beside *sanu av lxvi* PBSR xxii 115f^{2} (cf. ibid. l. 4f.), cf. also *šanu N lxxx* IRT 894$^{5f.}$ (cf. also the mistake *š‘nt mspr š‘t* Punica xv 2^{4}: litt. years, the number of the years, and *š‘nt* without indication of number KAI 142^{3}, and *šnwt w›ḥd* Punica xiv 4^{3} (the tens left out)); *šnyn 9* Inv viii 168^{4} (cf. Cowl 71^{9} (dam. context), Krael 4^{17,18}, CIS ii 4358B 6f., 4359$^{6f.}$, 4562$^{6f.}$, 4616$^{7f.}$, RIP 25$^{9f.}$ (*[br] šnyn 33*, Greek par. ἔτη λγ'), 39$^{4f.}$, etc.), *šnyn 18* Hatra 30$^{4f.}$ (v. supra) - b) cardinal number + Plur. abs., *tš‘ šnym* IEJ vii 239$^{6f.}$: nine years - c) cardinal number + Sing. abs., *šmnm št* NP 130^{6} (cf. *ššm št wšlš* KAI 152^{3}); *‘šrym wštym šnh* IEJ vii 239$^{3f.}$; cf. also indicating the length of a period *šlšn št* KAI 181^{2} (cf. KAI 181^{8}) - **2)** constructions used in chronology - a) in combinations with numerals and/or dates, events; *bšnt ›sr w›rb‘ 14 lmlky* KAI 14^{1}: in the fourteenth year of his reign (cf. KAI 32^{1}, 33^{1}, CIS i 13^{1}, etc.); *bšnt 11 l›dn mlkm ... ›š hmt l‘m lpṭ šnt 33* KAI 43$^{4f.}$: in the eleventh year of the lord of kings ... that is the 33rd year of the people of L.; *bšnt 31 l›dn mlkm ... ›š h› št 57 l›š kty* KAI 40$^{1f.}$: in the 31st year of the lord of kings ... that is the 57th year of the people of K.; *bšt 14 l‘m ṣdn* KAI 60^{1}: in the fourteenth year of the people of S. (cf. KAI 18$^{4f.}$); *bšt m[lk]y mlk bd‘štrt* CIS i 4$^{1f.}$: in the year that king B. mounted the throne; *šlš ḥmšm št l‘m [ṣr]* KAI 19: the fifty-third year of the people of Tyre (cf. KAI 18$^{5f.}$); *bššt ›rb‘m št lmlky* KAI 111$^{3f.}$: in the 46th year of his reign (cf. KAI 110$^{3f.}$, Hofra 57$^{3ff.}$, RES 336^{5}, 1539$^{3f.}$, etc.); *bšt ‘srm w›ḥt lmlkm* KAI 141$^{3f.}$: in the twenty-first year of his reign; *bšt h‘šrt* KAI 183^{1}: in the tenth year (cf. KAI 184$^{1f.}$, 185^{1}, 186^{1}, 187^{1}, etc.); *bšt 15* Dir ostr 22^{1}: in the fifteenth year (cf. Dir ostr 23^{1}, 27^{1}, 28^{1}, etc.); *bšt h15* Dir ostr 24^{1}: in the fifteenth year (cf. Dir ostr 31^{1}, 45^{1}); *mlk› ›lksndrws šnt k[* on Hasmonean coins, cf. Naveh IEJ xviii 21f.: king Alexander the twenty-(...) year (cf. also Kindler ibid. 188f.); *šnt ›ḥt lg›lt yšr›l* on coins of the second revolt, cf. JC no. 165: the first year of the liberation of Israel (cf. JC no. 166, 168, 170, 171, etc.; cf. also MPAT 43 i 3, 51^{1}, DJD ii 22,1-9^{1}, 24B 1f., C 1f. (dam. context), D 1f., E 1f., 29 i 1, 30^{8}); *šnt 27 ldrywš mlk›* Cowl 1^{1}: the 27th year of king D.; *šnt 15 ḥšy›rš mlk›* Cowl 5^{1}: the 15th year of king Xerxes (etc., etc.); *›škr šnt 3* Pers 24^{6}: the tax of the third year; *bšt 22* KAI 228^{1}: in the twenty-second year; *bšnt 3* Pers 57^{4}: in the third year (for the reading, cf. Degen BiOr xxxi 125 n. 6, cf. Pers 65^{5}); *bšnn 7 lm[l]k› drwš* MAI xiv/2, 66^{1}: in the seventh year of king D. (cf. MAI xiv/2, 66^{4,5}); *šnt ḥd ›rtḥššš mlk›* FX 136$^{1f.}$: the first year of king A. (cf. Syr xli 285$^{1f.}$, on this text, cf. also Teixidor Syr xli 287 n. 3); *šnt 14* FuB xiv 18^{3}: the fourteenth year (sc. of Artaxerxes I, cf. Akkad. par.); *šnt tḥrb ḥr* JAOS liv 31^{2}: the year that Ch. was devastated (for this diff. text, v. also *ḥrb*$_1$); *bšnt ›rb‘yn* *wšt lh* CIS ii 196[8]: in his 46th year; *šnt tšʿ lḥrtt* CIS ii 197[4]: the 9th year of Ch.; *bšnt ḥmš lʿbdt* ADAJ xx 121[2ff.]: in the fifth year of O. (cf. BASOR cclxiii 78[4], cclxix 48[4f.]); *šnt 2 lʾṭlh* BASOR cclxix 48[7]: the second year of A. (cf. Jones, Hamm, Johnson & Fiema ibid. 52, 55: date of the term of office of a local priest (cf. also BSOAS xvi 227, no. 81[7f.], for the reading of this text, cf. Strugnell BASOR clvi 32)); *šnt mʾtyn wḥmšyn wʾḥd* BAGN 88[6f.]: the year 251 (etc., etc.); *28 šnt* IEJ xi 137[3]: the 28th year (cf. also *468 šnt* CIS ii 4046[9f.]); *šnt trtyn lhprkyʾ* IEJ xiii 118: the second year of the eparchy (cf. also IEJ xiii 119[4]); *šnt 461* CIS ii 3909[4]: the year 461 (of the seleucid era; cf. also Hatra 31[1], Assur 21 ii 1, etc.); *b[š]nt 457* CIS ii 3911[1]: in the year 457 (of the seleucid era; etc.); *šnt št* MPAT 40[1]: the sixth year (sc. of the eparchy, cf. Milik DJD ii p. 106; cf. MPAT 41[1], cf. Milik DJD ii p. 111); *šnt tlt mʾ wštyn wrbʿ šnyn lḥrbn byt mqdšh* MPAT-A 50[6ff.]: the 364th year after the destruction of the Temple (cf. MPAT-A 52[7]); *šnt tlt mʾ [wtlt] mn šnyn lḥrbn byt mqdšh* MPAT-A 51[6ff.]: the 303rd year after the destruction of the Temple (cf. also *lmspr ʾrbʿ mʾwt wtyšʿym wʾrbʿ šnh lḥrbn hbyt* SM 13: in the year 494 of the destruction of the Temple); *šnt šmṭh dh* MPAT 39[7]: this the year of the Release; *šth qdmyth dšmṭth* MPAT-A 50[4f.]: the first year of the Release; cf. possibly also *mn št 6 lšntʾ 10* FuB xiv 15[4]: from the sixth to the tenth year (sc. of Darius II, cf. Akkad. par.; for the diff. reading and interpret., cf. Jakob-Rost & Freydank FuB xiv a.l.); cf. the ideogrammatic *hnʿlt ʿl šnt* 176 Nisa-c 280bis 3: he brought (it) for the year 176 (cf. Nisa-c 164[10f.], 179[5], 218[4], 223[9f.], 240[5], 394[8f.]; cf. also *ʿl š* in Nisa-b 740[6]); cf. also *šnh 6* ATNS 52a 8: the sixth year (cf. ATNS 52a 2) - b) in combination with the names of eponyms; *bšt ḥ[nb]ʿl* CIS i 124[3f.]: in the year of Hannibal (cf. CIS i 179[6f.]); *št ʾšmnʿs.m. ... hrb wḥnʾ hrb* CIS i 5510[8f.]: the year that E. and Ch. were *rb*; *bšt špṭm ḥmlkt wʿbdʾšmn* KAI 66[2]: in the year that Ch. and A. were suffetes (cf. CIS i 3920[3], RES 79[7], KAI 130[1], 173[3f.]); *bšt rb tʾḥt rb mḥnt ... lwqy ʿyly lʿmyʿ* KAI 118[2]: in the year that Lucius Aelius Lamia was proconsul (cf. also Hofra 21[1], 90[2f.]; cf. also Sumer xx 15[6] (*šnt zbydʾ ḥwml*; cf. Safaitic par. *šnt bn ḥwml*)? - Plur. indicating a period; *ymt yḥmlk wšntw ʿl gbl* KAI 4[5f.]: the days of Y. and his years over G. (i.e. his reign (or: his life and his reign ...?); cf. KAI 6[3], 7[5], 10[9]); *šny ḥrtt mlk nbṭw* CIS ii 196[6f.]: the reign of Ch. king of N.; *wyšmḥ bywmt rbm wšnt rḥqt* Ber xxii 120[6ff.]: and may he be glad for many days and far-away years; *wšnt lmʾš ʾlm šnt km hkkbm ʾl* KAI 277[9ff.]: and may the years of the divine statue be years like (the years of) these stars (v. *kkb*) - abbrev. *š* on coins of the first and second revolt, cf. Meshorer JC no. 151, 152, 154, 155, 157 (?), 158, 159, 176, 177, 178, 179, etc. etc. (cf. also Meshorer Mas coin 1343, 2989, 3490, 3595) and on Nab. coins, cf. Meshorer NC no. 15-17a; cf. also abbrev.

s in texts in transcription: Aug xvi 541 no. 17[2], 541 no. 21[3] - cf. poss. *šnt dy hww bny ḥgy* Syr xlvii 413[4f.]: the year that the B.Ch. were ... (reading of *šnt* however uncert., cf. Teixidor Syr xlix 443) - the *šnh* in KAI 233[16,20] = Sing. abs.? (cf. Dupont-Sommer Syr xxiv 45, 48, Donner KAI a.l.; cf. however Baneth OLZ '19, 57f., Gibson SSI ii p. 105, 109: = *šnh*$_6$ (= variant of *tnh*) - for Cowl 10[7], v. *tnyn*$_2$.
v. *kšt*, *šnm*$_1$, *št*$_6$.

šnh$_3$ **Samal** Sing. abs. *šnh* KAI 214[24] - ¶ subst. sleep.

šnh$_4$ **OffAr** Sing. emph. *šnt᾿* RES 1300[6] - ¶ subst. of uncert. meaning; poss. = the neck of a recipient for liquids, cf. Grelot DAE p. 143 n. c :: Lidzbarski Eph iii 24: = point ('Spitzen', 'Zacken').

šnh$_5$ **Pun** Sing. abs. *šnh* CIS i 4859[4], *šn᾿* CIS i 359[5], 5955[1,2] - ¶ subst. of uncert. meaning, indication of function (prob. religious function; cf. CIS i 5955 *ḥmlkt khn bʿl šmm bn ʿzrbʿl hšn᾿ bn ᾿šmnʿs.m. hšn᾿ bn mhrbʿl rb hkhnm*), related to the root *šny*$_1$? (or = Qal Part. act. of *šny*$_1$?); Lidzbarski Eph i 248 n. 1: = the one who changes clothes (cultic function) × Slouschz TPI p. 191: *šn᾿/h* = second priest (i.e. the priest just below the high-priest in the hierarchy, cf. Huss 543f. n. 338: priest second class), cf. also Clermont-Ganneau RAO v 69: *šn᾿* = variant of *šny*$_5$ (doubtful interpret.; cf. also CIS i sub 4859).

šnh$_6$ v. *šnh*$_2$.

šnhbw v. *ngdwt᾿*.

šnz = to swerve, to deflect > Akkad., cf. v.Soden Or xlvi 195, cf. idem AHW s.v. *šanāzu*.

šnṭ$_1$ v. *šnṭ᾿*.

šnṭ$_2$ **OffAr** Sing. f. abs. *šnṭt* Herm 4[4] (for the ending, cf. Wesselius AION xl 266; v. infra) - ¶ adj. (?) of uncert. meaning; Bresciani & Kamil Herm a.l., Porten & Greenfield ZAW lxxx 221: = striped?, Grelot RB lxxiv 435: poss. = ridiculous (cf. also idem DAE p. 160 n. a) :: Porten Arch 267: = torn? (cf. Grelot RB lxxiv 435: = poss. interpret.; Porten & Greenfield JEAS p. 59, Porten & Yardeni sub TADAE A 2.1: = frayed?; cf. however Hayes & Hoftijzer VT xx 105 n. 1); or *šnṭt* = variant of *šnṭ᾿* (= sheet of linen)?, cf. Milik Bibl xlviii 552f., 583 (cf. also Greenfield Lesh xxxii 367 n. 46) - on *šnṭ*$_2$, cf. also Gibson SSI ii p. 138.

šnṭ᾿ (< Egypt., Kutscher JAOS lxxiv 236, Couroyer RB lxi 559, Milik Bibl xlviii 552f., Porten Arch 89, Grelot DAE p. 234 n. 1 :: Kraeł 211: < Akkad.) - **OffAr** Sing. abs. *šnṭ᾿* Krael 7[11] (cf. Kutscher JAOS lxxiv 236, Couroyer RB lxi 559, Milik Bibl xlviii 553 :: Krael p. 211: = Sing. emph. of *šnṭ*$_1$ (= dress)) - ¶ subst. m. some type of garment/dress.
v. *šnṭ*$_2$.

šny$_1$ **OffAr** Paʿel Impf. 3 p.s.m. *yšnh* Samar 2[6]; 1 p.pl. *nšnh* Samar 7[11]; Itp Impf. 2 p.s.m. *tštnh* Aḥiq 201 (diff. and dam. context, cf. also

Lindenberger APA 200) - **Nab** PA‘EL Impf. 3 p.s.m. *yšn’* J 12[8] (= CIS ii 205), 17[7]; ITP Impf. 3 p.s.m. *ytšn’* CIS ii 350[4] - **JAr** HAPH Inf. *hšnyh* EI xx 161* - ¶ verb PA‘EL to change - **1)** + obj., *mn yšn’ ’l qbrw d’* J 17[7]: the one who will change this tomb - 2) + *b$_2$*, *hw yšnh b’sr’ znh* Samar 2[6]: he will renege on this bond, cf. Samar 7[11] - **3)** + *mn$_5$*: J 12[5] (reading of context uncert.) - HAPH to change: EI xx 161* - ITP to be changed; *wl’ ytšn’* CIS ii 350[4]: and that it will not be changed; exact meaning in Aḥiq 201 uncert. (to be changed?, cf. Cowl p. 226, Gressmann ATAT 462, cf. also Lindenberger APA 200, or to change oneself?), dam. context - Dupont-Sommer Sem i 53: l. *šnywy* in KAI 266[9] = PA‘EL Pf. 3 p.pl.m. + suff. 3 p.s.m. of *šny$_1$* (cf. also e.g. Meyer FS Zucker 256, Donner KAI a.l., cf. also Galling TGI 72) :: Fitzmyer Bibl xlvi 55, WA 241: = Plur. + suff. 3 p.s.m. of *šny$_4$* (= change, alteration?) :: Gibson SSI ii p. 113, 116: l. *šnywh* = PA‘EL Pf. 3 p.pl.m. + suff. 3 p.s., improb. readings, cf. Porten BiAr xliv 36, Porten & Yardeni sub TADAE A 1.1, Delsman TUAT i 634: l. *šndwr* = n.p. (prob. reading and interpret.) - on the Nab. material cf. also Greenfield Mem Yalon 82f. - Milik sub DJD ii 72, Fitzmyer & Harrington MPAT a.l.: l. *mtn’* (= PA‘EL Part. s.m. abs.) in MPAT 49 i 3 (less prob. reading, cf. also Beyer ATTM 318, 640: l. *mtnṣḥ* = ITP Part. s.m. abs. of *nṣḥ$_1$* (= to prevail)).

v. *mṣ’$_1$*, *mšnh*, *qny$_1$*, *šym$_1$*, *šn’$_1$*, *šnh$_5$*.

šny$_2$ v. *šn’$_1$*.

šny$_3$ v. *šnh$_2$*.

šny$_4$ v. *šny$_1$*.

šny$_5$ **Ph** Sing. m. abs. *šny* KAI 14[6], RES 930[2] - **Hebr** Sing. f. abs. *š[ny]h* SM 76[3] (dam. context) - ¶ ordinal number, second, other; *w’l y‘msn bmškb z ‘lt mškb šny* KAI 14[5f.]: and let nobody carry me away from this resting-place to another resting-place; *rb šny* RES 930[2]: second *rab* (v. *rb$_2$*) - cf. *tnyn$_2$*.

v. *šnh$_5$*, *twb$_5$*, *tny$_3$*.

šnym **Ph** m. abs. *šnm* RES 827, *’šnm* KAI 32[3] (= Kition A 2); cstr. *’šn* CIS i 88[6] (= Kition F 1) - **Pun** m. abs. *šnm* KAI 64[1], 127[3] (for the reading of this line, cf. Levi Della Vida FS Friedrich 309), 130[3], 137[1,6], 151[3], Punica ivE 15[3], Eph i 42 iii 3 (= Sem xxxii 60 :: v.d.Branden RSF ix 11f., 15f. (div. otherwise): l. *qn* (= QAL Pf. 3 p.s.m. of *qny$_1$*) *nn* (= Sing. abs. of *nn* (= posterity)), cf. OA ii 83[2]: *lisnim* (= *l$_5$* + *šnym*; cf. Levi Della Vida OA ii a.l., Sznycer GLECS x 102 :: Vattioni AION xvi 40: *isnim* = Sing. + suff. 3 p.s.m. of *’š$_1$* (cf. however idem Aug xvi 539)); for the form, cf. FR 242, 243, Segert GPP 63.2, cf. however Brugnatelli QMS 27 (n. 64)); cstr. *šn* CIS i 122[2], KAI 47[3], Mozia vi 102[2] (= SMI 22), *’šn* CIS i 4596[5] - **Hebr** m. abs. *šnym* TA-H 7[7], SM 106[10], AMB 1[19], Mas 587 (heavily dam. context); f. abs. *štym* on coins

of the first revolt, cf. Meshorer JC no. 153 (cf. also Meshorer Mas coin 1358), IEJ vii 239[3], EI xx 256[1], Frey 630b 4, DJD ii 24B 1 (*šty[m]*), C 1, D 1 (*št[ym]*), E 1 (*št[ym]*), I 1, 29 i 1, 9, 30[21]; f. cstr. *šty* Mas 585[3] - ¶ cardinal number, two: passim; *mqdšm šnm* KAI 137[1]: two sanctuaries; *dnʿryʾ ḥmšm wšnm* KAI 130[3]: 52 *denarii*; *bn šnt šnm* Punica ivE 15[3]: a boy of two years; *bt ʿšrym wštym šnh* IEJ vii 239[3]: a woman of the age of 22 years; *ʾšn bn [ʾd]nšmš* CIS i 88[6]: the two sons of A. (cf. FR 313; cf. also Mozia vi 102[2] (= SMI 22)); *šty ʾmwt* Mas 585[3]: two cubits - used in chronology, *bšnm lyrḥ* Eph i 42 iii 3 (v. supra): on the second day of the month (cf. TA-H 7[6f.]); *šnt štym* on coins of the first revolt, cf. Meshorer JC no. 153: the second year; *šnt štym lgʾlt yšrʾl* DJD ii 29 i 1: the second year of the liberation of Israel (cf. DJD ii 24B 1f., C 1f., D 1f., E 1f., I 1f., 29 i 9, EI xx 256[1]) - Levi Della Vida OA ii 86: l. this number (m. abs. *çnim*) poss. in the text PBR xxviii 54.7[4] (context however dam. and diff.; cf. for other reading Vattioni Aug xvi 553 sub no. 65) - cf. *tryn*.
v. *ʾš$_1$*.

šnyt$_1$ v. *šnt$_2$*.

šnyt$_2$ **Pun** Sing. cstr. CIS i 6011B 3 (= TPC 85) - ¶ subst. of uncert. meaning, poss. = second wife (cf. Février sub CIS i 6011).

šnyth **OffAr** Sing. abs. *šnyth* Krael 5[3] (v. infra); cstr. *šnytt* Cowl 28[4,6] - ¶ subst. mark; *šnytt mqrʾ ʾrmyt* Cowl 28[4]: a mark (with) legend in Aramaic (cf. Cowl 28[6]); *ʾmth zy šnyth ʿl ydh* Krael 5[3]: his slave-girl, on whose hand is a mark (cf. however Krael a.l., Milik RB lxi 249: ... who is marked on her hand, *šnyth* = Qal Part. pass. s.f. abs. of *šnt$_1$*) - for this word, cf. Kaufman AIA 102f.

šnm$_1$ **Samal** word of unknown meaning in KAI 214[4] :: Tawil Or xliii 48ff.: = Plur. abs. of *šnh$_2$* (imposs. interpret.).

šnm$_2$ v. *šnym*.

šnn **OffAr** Sing. abs. *šnn* Krael 7[20] (v. however infra); cstr. *šnn* Cowl 15[16], Krael 2[5] - ¶ subst. pair (for this interpret., cf. Grelot RB lxxviii 534f., DAE p. 195 n. q, Porten & Greenfield JEAS p. 20, 39, Porten & Yardeni sub TADAE B 2.6/3.3 :: Cowl p. 49: = knife?? :: Kutscher JAOS lxxiv 234 n. 6: cf. Assyrian *šēnān* = two shoes (cf. Epstein ZAW xxxiii 225) :: Nöldeke ZA xx 147: = kind of measure (Sing. abs.)); *šnn mšʾn 1* Cowl 15[16], Krael 2[5]: a pair of mules (v. *mšʾn*); in Krael 7[20] prob. the same word (for interpret., v. supra :: Reider JQR xliv 339: *šnn* = bag; or *šnn* in this text = Plur. abs. of *šn$_2$* (= sandal?)); cf. also Porten Arch 91.

šnpyr v. *špr$_4$*.

šnṣy (< Akkad., cf. Driv p. 54: derivative of root *mṣy* (prob. interpret.) :: Kaufman AIA 104: prob. = reflection of babylonianized pronunciation of native Ar. form *šmṣy* (= Shaph of root *mṣy*) :: Pavlovsky

Bibl xxxvi 546: = derivative of Akkad. *ušēṣi* (root *yṣ’*)) - **OffAr** Pf. 3 p.pl.m. *šnṣyw* Driv 5[4*] (heavily dam. context, cf. Porten & Yardeni sub TADAE A 6.7)’[7] - ¶ verb to succeed; *l’ šnṣyw lmn‘l bbyrt’* Driv 5[7]: they did not succeed in entering the fortress.

šnt$_1$ **OffAr** Qal Inf. + suff. 3 p.s.m. *mšnth* Krael 8[6,7,9]; + suff. 2 p.s.f. *mšntky* Krael 5[7]; Part. pass. s.m. abs. *šnyt* Cowl 28[4,6] - ¶ verb Qal to mark; + obj., *w’nš l’ šlyṭ lmšnth* Krael 8[8f.]: no one shall have power to mark him (i.e. with a mark indicating slave-status), cf. Krael 5[6f.], 8[5f.,6f.]; Part. pass. marked; *ywd šnyt ‘l ydh* Cowl 28[4]: a mark has been made on his hand (cf. Cowl 28[5f.]; for the context, v. however *ywd$_1$*). v. *šnyth*.

šnt$_2$ **OffAr** Sing. emph. *šnt’* Driv 7[7], *šnyt’* ATNS 2[1] (for this prob. reading, cf. Porten & Yardeni sub TADAE B 8.9 :: Segal ATNS a.l. (div. otherwise): l. *nš’t’* = Sing. emph. of *nš’h* (= load)), 5[8], 9[2], 10a i 5, 164a 1 - ¶ subst. mark: Driv 7[7] (for the context, v. *sṭr$_1$*), ATNS 2[1], 5[8], 9[2], 10a i 5, 164a 1 (in all instances prob. slave marks); on this word, cf. also Kaufman AIA 102f. - the same word prob. also in ATNS 97a 1 (*šnyt[]*).

šsḥmr **OffAr** Goetze Ber viii 99: l. poss. Sing. abs. *šsḥm[r]* in RES 245 (< Iran.) = imperial chamber of accounts? (cf. also Hinz NWAP 42, AISN 134).

š‘$_1$ **Pun** word of unknown meaning in KAI 161[8] (context obscure, word division uncert.); Février RA xlv 146: = Sing. abs. of *š‘$_1$* (= offering (of perfume)), highly uncert. interpret., cf. also Roschinski Num 112, 115: combine *š‘wtm* (without interpret.), to be combined with *š‘t*??

š‘$_2$ **OffAr** word of unknown meaning in RES 1300[6] (diff. context); Lidzbarski Eph iii 24: = adj. Sing. m. abs. (= smooth, polished); Grelot DAE p. 143 n. c: = subst. Sing. abs. (= plaster).

š‘$_3$ v. *tš‘$_1$*.

š‘$_4$ v. *š$_{10}$*.

š‘’ v. *šy‘$_1$*.

š‘bṣ **Pun** word of unknown meaning and diff. reading in Karth xii 51[3], cf. Février & Fantar Karth xii a.l. (or: l. *š‘rṣ*?); Krahmalkov RSF iii 177f., 182, 204: poss. = Qal Pf. 3 p.s.m. of *šbṣ* verb denoting act or aspect of speaking; v.d.Branden RSF v 56, 60: l. *š‘rṣ* = *š$_{10}$* + Sing. abs. of *‘rṣ* (= orthographical variant of *’rṣ$_1$*).

š‘d **OffAr** word of uncert. meaning in Sumer xx 13[4]; Milik DFD 258: = Sing. abs. of *š‘d* (= happiness), less prob. interpret., cf. Safar Sumer xx a.l.: l. *š‘d[y]* = nl.

š‘h **Palm** Sing. emph. *š‘t’* RIP 142[2] - ¶ subst. hour, time; for the context of RIP 142[2], v. *rgz$_2$*.

š‘w$_1$ v. *š‘wh*.

š‘w$_2$ **Palm** du Mesnil du Buisson TMP 604f.: l. *š‘wt* (= Sing. cstr. of *š‘w$_2$* (= play)) in RTP 184 (less prob. reading, cf. RTP a.l., Milik DFD 118: l. *t[b]‘wt* or *s‘wt*).

š‘wh OldAr Sing. emph. *š‘wt’* KAI 222A 35, 37, 39 (for this form, cf. Fitzmyer AIS 52, cf. also Degen AAG p. 48 :: Segert ArchOr xxxii 125: = Sing. emph. of *š‘w$_1$* (= wax)) - ¶ subst. f. wax; for parallels of the context, cf. Fitzmyer AIS 52f., Hillers TC 19ff. (with notes), Weinfeld Shn i 73.

š‘y$_1$ v. *šwb*, *št‘$_1$*, *tš‘m*.

š‘y$_2$ v. *št‘$_1$*.

š‘y$_3$ v. *tš‘$_1$*.

š‘yd Palm Plur. m. emph. *š‘yd’* PNO 14[4] (:: Milik DFD 343: Sing. m. emph.; cf. also Ingholt & Starcky PNO a.l.) - ¶ adj. helpful (or: lucky?); for a discussion of both root and meaning, cf. PNO a.l., Cantineau Gramm 43 (cf. also Stark PNPI 115).

š‘yrh v. *š‘rh*.

š‘l$_1$ OldAr Sing. abs. *š‘l* KAI 222A 33 - **OffAr**, cf. Frah ix 6 (*t’lh*), 8 (*t’rh*, for the reading, cf. Nyberg FP 44, 74 :: Ebeling Frah a.l.: l. poss. *mtmh* < Akkad. = jackal) - ¶ subst. fox, jackal (for par. of KAI 222A 33, cf. Hillers TC 44); *t’rh kzb’* Frah ix 8: false fox = jackal - Puech FS Grelot 17, 23, 28: l. poss. *š‘l[n]* (= Plur. abs.) in DA i 12 + vii a (uncert. interpret.; cf. also Lemaire CRAI ’85, 280: l. *š‘l* (= Sing. abs.)).

š‘l$_2$ OffAr word of uncert. meaning in ATNS 43b i 2, 3, poss. = subst. Sing. abs.; Segal ATNS a.l.: = handful.

š‘l$_3$ v. *yš‘$_1$*.

š‘m v. *tš‘m*.

š‘‘$_1$ v. *tš‘m*.

š‘‘$_2$ OffAr Segal ATNS a.l.: a derivative of this root in ATNS 43b 1 2 (*]mš‘’*), prob. = subst. (*mš‘*) Sing. emph. (= trowel; heavily dam. context, uncert. interpret.).

š‘r$_1$ OldCan Sing. abs. *ša-aḫ-ri* EA 244[16] - **Ph** Sing. abs. *š‘r* KAI 18[3], 26A iii 14, 15, 16, 18 - **Pun** Sing. abs. *š‘r* RCL ’66, 201[1]; cstr. *š‘r* PEQ ’61, 151 (= ICO-Malta 8), BAr-NS vii 262[4] (prob. interpret., cf. Fantar ibid. 263f.) - **Mo** Plur. + suff. 3 p.s.f. *š‘ryh* KAI 181[22] - **Hebr** Sing. abs. *š‘r* SM 49[9] - ¶ subst. m. gate (in most instances indicating the town gate: EA 244[16], KAI 26A iii 14, 15, 16, 18, 181[22], RCL ’66, 201[1], SM 49[9]; indicating temple gate in KAI 18[3]) - Teixidor Syr lvi 384f.: l. poss. *]š‘r* (= Sing. abs./cstr.) in KAI 33[3] (= Kition A 1), uncert. reading - cf. *šr‘$_1$*, *tr‘$_1$*.

v. *ktr$_1$*, *š‘r$_2$*.

š‘r$_2$ Ph Plur. abs. *š‘rm* DD 16[1,2] (cf. Dunand & Duru DD a.l. :: Chéhab BMB xiii 52: = Plur. abs. of *š‘r$_1$* :: Milik DFD 60f.: = Plur. abs. of *š‘r$_3$*) - **Hebr** Sing. cstr. *š‘r* SVT xl 10 - ¶ subst. porter, doorkeeper; *rb š‘rm* DD 16[1,2]: the chief of the door-keepers; *š‘r hmsgr* SVT xl 10: the porter of the prison.

š‘r₃ **Palm** Milik DFD 60: l. *š‘r’* in SBS 25[3] = Plur. emph. of *š‘r₃* (= manager of the practical side of religious feasts); improb. interpret., cf. Cantineau Syr xvii 347, Dunant sub SBS 25, Gawlikowski Ber xxii 144: l. *š‘d’* = n.p.
v. *š‘r₂*.

š‘r₄ cf. Frah x 9 (*š’lh*), 20 (*š’lh*).
v. *mlš₁*.

š‘r₅ v. *qšr₁*.

š‘r₆ **OldAr** Plur. abs. *š‘ryn* Tell F 19 (cf. Zadok TeAv ix 119, Greenfield & Shaffer Irâq xlv 113, 115, RB xcii 53, Puech RB xc 596 (cf. also idem Shn v/vi 124), Muraoka AN xxii 111 n. 25, Greenfield FS Rundgren 150, Stefanovic COAI 235 (n. 4), Gropp & Lewis BASOR cclix 46, Huehnergard BASOR cclxi 93, Vattioni AION xlvi 363 :: Abou-Assaf, Bordreuil & Millard Tell F p. 25, Wesselius SV 56, Kaufman Maarav iii 163: = Plur. abs. of *š‘rh* (on the subject, cf. also Sasson ZAW xcvii 100 n. 13)) - ¶ subst. measure: Tell F 19 (for the context, cf. Greenfield & Shaffer RB xcii 54).

š‘rṣ v. *š‘bṣ*.

š‘rh **Hebr** Plur. abs. *š‘rm* KAI 182[4], 188[3] - **Samal** Sing. abs. *š‘rh* KAI 215[6,9]; Plur. abs. (casus obl.) *š‘ry* KAI 214[5] - **OldAr** Plur. abs. *š‘rn* Tell F 22 - **OffAr** Plur. abs. *š‘rn* Cowl 2[5,7,8], 3[4], 4[5], 10[10], Herm 3[9], ATNS 85[2], CIS ii 38[1] (= Del 21 = AECT 3), 39[1] (= Del 23 = AECT 9), 40[1] (= Del 22 = AECT 6), TH 1 vs. 1 (= AECT 53), 2 vs. 1 (= AECT 54), LidzbAss 1[1] (= AECT 46), Sem ii 31 conc. 5, etc., etc.; Plur. cstr. *[š‘]ry* MAI xiv/2, 66[13] (cf. Dupont-Sommer MAI xiv/2, a.l. :: Grelot DAE p. 74: = Plur. + suff. 1 p.s.); emph. *š‘ry’* CIS ii 42[1], TH 1 vs. 4, 6 (*š‘r[y’]*; heavily dam. context; = AECT 53), rect. 2 (= AECT 53), LidzbAss 4[15] (= KAI 236 = AECT 49), ASAE xxvi 25B 2 - **JAr** Plur. abs. *s‘ryn* MPAT 38[1], *s‘ry* Syr xlv 101[15] (*s‘r[y]*),[16] - ¶ subst. Sing./Plur. barley - for the diff. text CIS ii 42, v. *qšr₁* - Dupont-Sommer MAI xiv/2, 66, 74: l. poss. *š‘yry* = Plur. + suff. 1 p.s. in MAI xiv/2, 66[6] (cf. also Grelot DAE p. 72 (cf. however Porten & Yardeni sub TADAE B 1.1: l. *šwywy* = equally?) :: Bauer & Meissner SbPAW '36, 415, 418: l. *šwyry* = Plur. cstr. of *šwyr* (= corn)) - abbrev. *š* in Cowl 24[1,2,3,6,7], BSh 1[2], 2[2], 4[2], 27[2], 28[2], TA-Ar 1[2], 2[1], IEJ xl 142[2], etc., etc. (cf. also Frah iv 2) - Israel BiOr xxxvii 6: l. Sing. cstr. (*s‘rt*) in NESE ii 66, poss. reading, less prob. interpret., cf. also Degen NESE ii a.l.: l. *s‘dt* = n.p. - for this word, cf. also Borowski AIAI 91f.
v. *prs₂*, *šṭr₂*, *š‘r₆*, *š‘rt*.

š‘rrt v. *š‘rt*.

š‘rt **Amm** word of unknown meaning (Sing./Plur. abs.) in BASOR cclxiv 47[3]; Yassine & Teixidor BASOR cclxiv a.l.: prob. not identical with *š‘rh*, but = she-goat or poss. = Se‘irite woman - the diff. *š‘rrt* in BASOR cclxiv 47[2] lapsus for *š‘rt*??; cf. also Aufrecht sub CAI 144: *š‘rt* = form of *š‘rh* (= barley) and *š‘rrt* = lapsus for *š‘rt*.

š‘t Pun word of unknown meaning in KAI 160[2,3,5], cf. Röllig KAI a.l.; Février Sem iv 21: poss. = spices (uncert. interpret.).
v. *š‘*$_1$.

šp$_1$ OffAr Sing. abs. *šp* Cowl 26[11,19] - ¶ subst. of unknown meaning indicating part of a ship; Grelot DAE p. 289 n. w: prob. = beam (without etymology, but prob. < Egypt.) :: Holma Öfversigt af Finska Vetenskaps-Societetens Förhandlingar '15, B no. 5, 8: yard of a ship :: Krael p. 304: = measure of length - Porten & Yardeni sub TADAE A 4.2: l. prob. *špn* in Cowl 37[10] (= Plur. abs. of *šp*$_1$ (= boards; prob. reading)).
v. *prs*$_2$.

šp$_2$ v. *'bšp*.

šp$_3$ Ph Sing. abs. *šp* Syr liii 328 no. 138 (for the reading, cf. also Lipiński OLP xiv 144) - ¶ subst. of uncert. meaning; Lipiński OLP xiv 145f.: = cup > oil-lamp, uncert. interpret. (cf. Amadasi Guzzo Sem xxxviii 25).

šph OldAr Dual + suff. 2 p.s.m. *šptyk* KAI 224[14f.]; + suff. 3 p.s.m. *šptwh* KAI 224[15,16] - **OffAr** Plur. + suff. 3 p.s.m. *špwth* Aḥiq 132 (cf. Leand 43d); cf. Frah x 19 (*šptyn*), cf. Toll ZDMG-Suppl viii 32 - ¶ subst. lip; for the context of KAI 224[14ff.], v. *nš'*$_1$.

špḥ$_1$ Ph Sing. cstr. *špḥ* EpAn ix 5[6] - **Pun** Sing. abs. *špḥ* KAI 69[16], CIS i 6000bis 7 (= TPC 84) - ¶ subst. clan, family (cf. Clermont-Ganneau RAO iii 27f., Cooke NSI p. 121, Röllig KAI sub 69, Février sub CIS i 6000bis; for older interpret., cf. CIS i sub 165; :: Lidzbarski Handb 381: = servant (cf. however idem Eph i 47f.) :: v.d.Branden BMB xiii 94: = slave who sprinkles water over the hands of his master (< root *špḥ* = to sprinkle water)); *'dr špḥ* CIS i 6000bis 7: the head of the clan (on this title, cf. also Huss 503); *špḥ klš* EpAn ix 5[6]: the family of K. - the *[š]pḥ* in KAI 125 poss. = the same word (cf. also Levi Della Vida RevEtAnc lv 359; reading and interpret. however uncert.; cf. Février & Fantar Karth xii 51: l. *[š]bḥ* = Sing. abs. of *šb‘*$_4$ (related to *šb‘h*$_1$; = expenses), cf. also Levi Della Vida RevEtAnc lv 360: l. poss. *[z]bḥ* (= Sing. abs. of *zbḥ*$_2$) :: Février RevEtAnc lv 358f.: l. *[š]pḥ* = Sing. abs. of *špḥ*$_2$ (= generosity)).

špḥ$_2$ v. *špḥ*$_1$.

špḥh v. *šp‘t*.

špṭ$_1$ Pun QAL Pf. 3 p.s.f. *špṭ* KAI 79[10], 4937[4] - **DA** NIPH (cf. Hoftijzer DA a.l. × Caquot & Lemaire Syr liv 207, H.P. Müll ZAW xciv 219, 237: = QAL (cf. also Niehr HR 60f.)) Impf. 1 p.pl. *nšpṭ* (cf. also McCarter

with Hackett BTDA 74) ii 17 (:: Puech RB lxxxv 116, Garbini Hen i 184, 186, Hackett BTDA 26, 30, 73, 94, 131: l. poss. *mšpṭ*, cf. also Lemaire CRAI '85 277: = Sing. abs. of *mšpṭ*) - **OffAr** QAL Impf. 3 p.pl.m. *yšpṭwn* Aḥiq 104 (cf. Leand 23d, Niehr HR 62 :: Joüon MUSJ xviii 15: = NIPH Impf. 3 p.pl.m.; on this instance, cf. also Lindenberger APA 87f., 242 nn. 244, 246); 1 p.pl. *nšpṭ* Cowl 52^5 (dam. context :: Joüon MUSJ xviii 15: = NIPH Impf. 1 p.pl., cf. also Silverman JAOS lxxxix 701 n. 63) - ¶ verb QAL - **1)** to begin a process, to litigate; + *ʿm_5*, *[lm]h yšpṭwn ʿqn ʿm ʾšh* Aḥiq 104: why should wood strive with fire? - **2)** to judge; + *b_2*, *wšpṭ tnt pn bʿl brḥ ʾdm hʾ* KAI $79^{10f.}$: T. the face of Baʿal will judge the soul of this man (cf. CIS i $4937^{4ff.}$; cf. also CIS i $5632^{6f.}$) - **3)** + *ʿl_7* prob. in Cowl 52^7 (*[š]pṭ*), heavily dam. context - NIPH to litigate; + *l_5*, *lk nšpṭ* DA ii 17: we will litigate with you (cf. Hoftijzer DA a.l., v. however supra; for the context, v. *lšn*) - Slouschz TPI p. 327: the diff. *špṭ* in CIS i 226^3 = QAL Pf. 3 p.s.m., cf. however CIS i sub 226: = Sing. cstr. (?) of *šp$ṭ_2$* (both interpretations less prob.; *psnʿm š špṭ* CIS i $226^{2f.}$: prob. = P. belonging to (i.e. client of) S.) - on the root, cf. also Stol BiOr xxix 276f.
v. *šp$ṭ_2$*.

šp$ṭ_2$ **Ph** Sing. abs. *špṭ* KAI 36^2 (= Kition B 31), 58, RES $1204^{3,4,7}$ - **Pun** Sing. abs. *špṭ* KAI 65^5, $69^{1,2}$, 78^8, 82, $87^{5,6}$, etc., etc.; Plur. abs. *špṭm* KAI 66^2, 77^3, $81^{5,6}$, 96^3 (= CIS i 5523), etc.; > Lat. *sufes* - ¶ subst. m. (= QAL Part. act. of *šp$ṭ_1$*) magistrate - 1) in KAI 36^2, 58, RES $1204^{3,4,7}$ (respectively from Cyprus, Piraeus and Tyre) indication of a function, the exact substance of which is unknown (on RES 1204, cf. also Teixidor Sem xxix 12ff.) - **2)** in North-Africa (Carthage and towns influenced by it) indication of the highest functionaries (cf. Ehrenberg PW ii/7, 643-651, Gsell HAAN ii 193ff., v 129ff., Huss 458ff., cf. also Yaron FS Daube 352f.) - a) for Carthage, cf. e.g. KAI 78^8, 82, $87^{5,6}$, $93^{2,3}$ (= TPC 12), etc.; *ʿsrm št l[...] špṭm bqrtḥdš[t]* CIS i $5632^{2f.}$: the twentieth year of [...] the suffetes in Carthage (diff. and dam. context); the suffetes in function during one year are used as eponyms of that year, cf. *bšt špṭm ʾdnbʿl wʾdnbʿl bn bdmlqrt* KAI 77^3: in the year of the suffetes A. and A. the son of B. (cf. KAI 96^3, CIS i 3920^3); *lmbyrḥ ḥyr špṭm ʿbdmlqrt w[...] ... špṭm špṭ wḥnʾ ... wrb ʿbdmlqrt ...* KAI $81^{5f.}$: from the month Ch. of the suffetes A. and ... [until] ... of the suffetes Sh. and Ch. and the *rab* A.; *[bšt] špṭm špṭ wʾdnbʿl ʿt r ʾdnbʿl bn ʾšmnḥlṣ bn b[... ... ml]qrt bn ḥnʾ wḥbrnm* RCL '66, $201^{2f.}$: [in the year of] the suffetes Sh. and A. in the time of the magistracy of A. the son of E., the son of B. [... (and) ...]... son of Ch. and their colleagues; cf. also *št šʿbdʾšmn wḥnʾ* CIS i $4824^{5f.}$: the year of A. and Ch. (or: *š* = abbrev. of *špṭm*?) - b) outside Carthage, *bšt špṭm ḥmlk wḥmlk bn ʾnkn* KAI $137^{1f.}$: in the year of the suffetes Ch. and Ch. the son of A. (cf. RES

79[1]); more than two suffetes seem to be indicated in KAI 159[6]; cf. also *ʿt r ʿyknʾ bn ʾdrbʿl wbrk bn sʿldyʾ rb ʾyknʾ* ... Karth xii 48[3f.]: at the time of the magistracy (v. *r*₁) of A. the son of A. and B. the son of S., A. being *rab* (the two first mentioned magistrates poss. being suffetes, cf. Février & Fantar Karth xii 46ff., Niehr HR 68 (n. 245); cf. also the *rb hšpṭm* in Karth xii 46[2]) - α) cf. also the instances from Tripolitania, *byrḥ ḥyr špṭm bʾlpqy ʾrš wbdmlq[rt]* KAI 119[3]: in the month Ch. being suffetes in Lepcis A. and B.; *ʾdnbʿl bn ... wʿbdmlqrt bn ... špṭm* KAI 120[2]: A. and A. being suffetes (cf. Lat. par. ... *[su]fetib(us)*), cf. KAI 122[2]; *bšt hšpṭm ʿbdmlqrt ... wʾrš* KAI 130[1]: in the year of the suffetes A. and A. - β) cf. also the instances from Sardinia: Antas p. 61[2], 65[2,3], 83[2]; cf. *bšt špṭm ḥmlkt wʿbdʾšmn* KAI 66[2]: in the year of the suffetes Ch. and A.; *bšt špṭm bbʿl hrʾmy ... wmʿrqh* ... KAI 173[3f.]: in the year of the suffetes B. the Roman and M. - **3)** combination of *špṭ* with other functions in the same person - a) *špṭ zbḥ* (comb. only in Tripolitania), cf. *špṭ zbḥ ʾdr ʿzrm* KAI 120[3] (cf. Lat. par. *sufes flamen praefectus sacrorum*), cf. also KAI 121[1f.] (*zbḥ špṭ ʾdr ʿzrm*; Lat. par. *flamen sufes praef(ectus) sacr(orum)*); *ʾdr ʿzrm z[bḥ lʾlm] wʾspʿsyʿnʾ šp[ṭ] zbḥ lk[l hʿ]t* KAI 126[1f.] (Lat. par. *praefectus sacrorum flamen divi Vespasiani sufes flamen perpetuus*) - b) *hšpṭ hšʿṭr* BAr '55/56, 32: the suffete (and) scribe - c) *hšpṭ mqm ʾlm* ... CIS i 3351[5f.]: the suffete, raiser of the god ... (v. *qwm*₁), cf. also CIS i 3352[6ff.], 4867[5ff.], 4868[3f.], RES 1566[5f.]; *hšpṭ rb hkhnm mqm ʾlm* RES 553[3f.]: the suffete, the high priest, the raiser of the god - for this word, cf. also Richter ZAW lxxvii 68ff., Niehr HR 65ff., Bunnens EPM 287f., 392, Krahmalkov BASOR ccxlix 93f.
v. *špṭ*₁.

špy₁ **OffAr** QAL Part. pass.m. pl. abs. *špyn* Aḥiq 113 - ¶ verb QAL to smooth; Part. pass. (or adj.?, cf. Kottsieper SAS 236) smooth, calm (said of water).

špy₂ v. *ʾbšp*.

špyq **OffAr** *špyq* Driv 7[3,7] - ¶ adv. (prob. Sing. m. abs. of adj. (= QAL Part. pass. of *špq*₁?)) sufficiently; *grd ʾmnm wspzn špyq bʿw* Driv 7[6f.]: acquire a staff of craftsmen of various types in a sufficient way (i.e. a sufficient staff ...) - on this root, cf. also Blau PC 121, 133.

špyr v. *špr*₄.

špl **OffAr** HAPH Impf. 3 p.s.m. *yhšpl* Aḥiq 150 (:: Kottsieper SAS 16, 236); cf. Frah app. 7 (*yšplwn*, cf. Nyberg FP 54, 99: = PAʿEL form of *špl*??, cf. however Ebeling Frah a.l.: l. *yhnṣlwn* < root *nṣl*) - ¶ verb HAPH + *l*₅, to humiliate (dam. context).

špn₁ = to make smooth, v.Soden Or xlvi 195 (cf. also idem AHW s.v. *šapānu*) > Akkad.; uncert. interpret.

špn₂ v. *mšpn*.

špʿh v. *špʿt*.

šp‘r v. *p‘r₂*.
šp‘t **Pun** diff. word in Karth xii 54[1]; Krahmalkov RSF iii 178, 186, 204: = Sing. abs. of *šp‘h* (= abundance, wealth), cf. also v.d.Branden RSF v 57, 62 :: Février & Fantar Karth xii a.l.: = variant of *špḥt* = Sing. abs. of *špḥh* (= clan).
špq₁ v. *špyq*.
špq₂ **OffAr** Sing. emph. *špq'* JKF i 46[2] - ¶ subst. richness, abundance (word division and interpret. of context highly uncert., v. also *‘md₂*).
špr₁ **Palm** QAL Pf. 3 p.s.m. *špr* CIS ii 3916[3], 3917[5], 3923[3], 3929[4], Inv x 39[3] (= Inscr P 6), 115[2,3], 131[3], SBS 38[5], 39[5], etc., etc.; 3 p.pl.m. *šprw* CIS ii 3930[4] - ¶ verb QAL to please, to act pleasantly, to do good; + *l₅*, *bdyl dy špr lhwn* Inv x 131[3f.]: because he has pleased them (sc. by his acts); *mn dy špr lhn wl'lhyhwn* CIS ii 3929[4f.]: because he pleased them and their gods; *bdyl dy ‘bd lhn bb' w... wšpr lhwn bkl ṣbw* CIS ii 3917[2ff.]: because he made for them the gate and ... and pleased them in every thing; *mn dy špr lhwn bkl gns klh w‘dr bn[yn] dy bl wyhb mn kysh* Syr xii 122[4f.]: because he pleased them in every way, namely he helped the fabric (?) of Bel (v. *bnyn*) and gave from his own purse; *wšpr lhwn b'sṭrṭgwth wmgd lbwl' zwzyn rbw* CIS ii 3934[3ff.]: he acted pleasantly towards them (i.e. Senate and People) during his office as *strategos* and gave generously to the Senate (a gift of) 10.000 *zuzin* - v. Weiher STU ii 120: Aramaic form of root *špr₁* is base of Akkad. formation *na-aš-pa-ru-ú* (prob. interpret.) - a form of this root in ATNS 7[1] (*]špr*), Segal ATNS a.l.: restore *[y]špr* (= QAL Impf. 3 p.s.m.).
v. *špr₄*.
špr₂ Ebeling Frah a.l.: in Frah xxiii 3 l. *šprwn* (= form of *špr₂* (= to send)); improb. reading, cf. Nyberg FP p. 93, 97: l. *šdrwn* (v. *šdr₁*).
špr₃ v. *špr₂*.
špr₄ **OldAr** Sing. m. abs. *špr* KAI 224[29] (context however heavily dam.) - **OffAr** Sing. m. abs. *špyr* Aḥiq 108, 159 (poss. reading, cf. Puech RB xcv 591), KAI 276[9] (for the context, v. *hwy₁*, *prnwš*; :: Grelot Sem viii 13: = orthogr. variant of Sing. f. abs. *špyrh*); emph. *špyr'* KAI 264[6] (for the context, v. *ḥkm₂*); Sing. f. abs. *špyrh* Cowl 81[33] (*špyr[h]*, dam. context), Aḥiq 92 (:: Lindenberger APA 66: = QAL Part. pass. s.f. abs. of *špr₁*; against this interpret., cf. Muraoka JSS xxxii 187), *šprt* Herm 2[12] (for the form, cf. Wesselius AION xxx 266); cf. Frah xxvi 2 (*špyl*), Paik 972 (*špyl*), BSOAS xxxiii 152[19], GIPP 34, 64, SaSt 23 - **Palm** m. Sing. abs. *špyr* Inv x 53[4], Syr xiv 191[3] - **Hatra** Sing. m. abs. *špr* 309, cf. also Assur 27d 3, *špyr* 50[2], *šnpyr* 23[2,5], 25[2,3], 26[3], 52[3], 53[4,6], 58[3] (*šnp[yr]*), 74[3], 77[2], 81[2], 90, 118, 182, etc. (cf. also Assur 17 i 5, 25g 5, 28a 4, etc.), *šnpr* 178[2], cf. also Assur 32h 3 (*š[n]pr*) (cf. Vattioni IH a.l., cf. however Safar Sumer xviii 51, Caquot Syr xli 265: l. *šnpyr*) - ¶ adj. beautiful, magnificent; said of an

object: Herm 2[12]; *špyr mlk lmḥzh kšmš* Aḥiq 108: magnificent is a king to look at, as Shamash; *špyr› ›nt mn ›lhn* KAI 264[6]: you are more beautiful than the goddesses; *hkyn ṭb wšpyr YHWH hyk zy br ›ynš l› dm‹ YHWH mn ṭbwt* KAI 276[9ff.]: she was so nice and pleasant that no one was her equal in beauty (v. also *ṭbwt*) - adj. f. substantivated, something pleasant, pleasure; *trtyn mln špyrh ... lšmš* Aḥiq 92: two things are a pleasure to Sh. - used adverbially, *bdyl dy hlk ‹mh špyr* Inv x 53[4]: because he behaved himself well towards him - for the use of the combination *ltb wlš(n)p(y)r* in Hatra, v. *zkr*$_1$.
v. *dkyw*, *p‹r*$_2$, *šḥq*$_2$.

špry› **Pun** Gandolphe Sem xxxviii 128ff.: the diff. *špry›* in CIS 4106[5f.] poss. = *š*$_{10}$ + *pry›* (= n.l.).

šṣp$_1$ **Pun** v.d.Branden BiOr xxxvi 158: the *šṣpm* in CIS i 274[3] = QAL Part. act. pl.m. abs. of *šṣp*$_1$ (Part. = oracle priest casting lots), less prob. interpret., cf. CIS i a.l., Benz 185: = n.p.

šṣp$_2$ **Pun** Sing. abs. *šṣp* KAI 69[11] - ¶ subst. of unknown meaning, indication of certain type of sacrifice; Lagrange ERS 474: = sacrifice of expiation, cf. also Urie PEQ '49, 70f. (< root *šṭ/ṣp*; ?), Capuzzi StudMagr ii 73f. :: v.d.Branden RSO xl 120f.: sacrifice connected with divination/auspices, cf. already CIS i sub 165 (cf. also v.d.Branden BiOr xxxvi 158) :: Dussaud Orig 321: sacrifice connected with exorcism (on this sacrifice, cf. also Amadasi Guzzo SSMA 113).

šq$_1$ (< Akkad., cf. Zimmern Fremdw 43, Kaufman AIA 93f., 141) - **DA** Plur. cstr. *šqy* ii 8 (dam. context, *šqy[*, cf. Hoftijzer DA a.l. (cf. also idem TUAT ii 146) :: Levine JAOS ci 200f.: l. *šqy* = Plur. cstr. of *šq*$_5$ (= desire; cf. Weinfeld Shn v/vi 146) :: Hackett BTDA 30, 63, 95, 135: poss. = Plur. cstr. of *šq*$_6$ (= sepulchre) :: Greenfield JSS xxv 252, Rofé BAT 366: = Plur. cstr. of *šq*$_3$ (cf. also Lemaire CRAI '85, 276)) - **OffAr** Sing. cstr. *šwq* Krael 3[8,10], 4[10,11], 10[4], 12[19,21]; emph. *šq›* Cowl 13[14], *šwq›* Cowl 5[12,14]; cf. Frah ii 12 (*šwk›*) - **Nab** Sing. cstr. *šwq* MPAT 64 iii 5; Plur. emph. *šqy›* MPAT 64 i 2 - **Palm** Sing. abs. *šwq* CIS ii 3932[5] - ¶ subst. - **1)** street: Cowl 5[12,14], 13[14]; *šwq mlk›* Krael 3[8]: the king's street (a street in Elephantine; cf. Krael p. 77, Porten Arch 95), cf. Krael 3[10], 4[10,11], 10[4f.], 12[19,21] - **2)** market: CIS ii 3932[5] - **3)** exact meaning in MPAT 64 i 2, iii 5 uncert.; Starcky RB lxi 167: poss. = souk; Fitzmyer & Harrington MPAT a.l.: = market; cf. also J.J.Rabinowitz BASOR cxxxix 13: *‹l šqy›* in MPAT 64 i 2: = on the markets, technical phrase meaning "publicly" (compare ἐν ἀγυιᾷ in Egyptian papyri) - the same word prob. also in Cowl 82[4] (*šwq*), Sing. cstr. (?, dam. context) - Lipiński Stud 54: the *šq* in KAI 223B 15 = status pronominalis of *šq* (= [your] street), cf. Lemaire & Durand IAS 117, 127: l. *šq[km]* = your streets - v.Soden Or xlvi 196: *šq*$_1$ (< Akkad. *sūqu*) > Akkad. *šūqu*; less prob. interpret.

v. *rbnšqw*.

šq$_2$ **OffAr** Sing. abs. *šq* Aḥiq 103 (v. *hwn$_1$*); Plur. abs. *šqn* EI xv 67^{*2} (diff. context), *šqqn* Cowl $30^{15,20}$, $31^{14,19}$ (*šqq[n]*; for this form, cf. Leand 52b) - ¶ subst. - **1)** sack: EI xv 67^{*2} (v. however supra) - **2)** sackcloth: Cowl $30^{15,20}$,$31^{14,19}$, Aḥiq 103; > Greek σάκ(κ)ος, cf. Masson RPAE 24f.

šq$_3$ **OffAr** Driv AnOr xii 58: the *šq›* in RES 496^1 = Sing. emph. of *šq$_3$* (= thigh), heavily dam., highly uncert. context, v. also *ntn*; cf. Frah x 38 (*škh*) = leg :: cf. Ebeling Frah a.l.: = posterior (= *šq$_4$*) :: Schaeder with Ebeling Frah a.l.: l. *šqh* = lapsus for *šth* (v. *št$_2$*).

v. *šq$_1$*.

šq$_4$ v. *šq$_3$*.

šq$_5$ v. *šq$_1$*.

šq$_6$ v. *šq$_1$*.

šqd$_1$ **Pun** Qal Impf. 2 p.s.m. *tšqd* KAI 76B 5 - ¶ verb Qal to pay attention to; *wtyn ... lqḥt tšqd* KAI 76B 5: and take care to use figs (context however dam.).

šqd$_2$ **Ph** Aimé-Giron BIFAO xxxviii 6f.: l. poss. *šqdm* (= Plur. abs. of *šqd$_2$* (= almond)) in BIFAO xxxviii 3^6 (reading however rather *šqrm*, cf. Aimé-Giron BIFAO a.l.) - on this word, cf. Borowski AIAI 131f.

šqdh v. *šqrh*.

šqh v. *›dqwr*.

šqwp **Hebr** Sing. abs. *šqwp* SM 1 (= Frey 974) - **JAr** Sing. emph. *šqwph* MPAT-A 10^2 (= SM 4) - ¶ subst. m. lintel - for this word and its relation to *›yskwph*, cf. Kaufman AIA 37 (n. 33).

šqṭ **Hebr** Pi‹el Inf. cstr. *[š]qṭ* KAI $196^{6f.}$ (for this restoration and interpret., cf. Gibson SSI i p. 46, cf. however Torczyner Lach i p. 113f., Röllig KAI a.l.: l. *[hš]qṭ* = Hiph Inf. cstr.) - ¶ verb Pi‹el (v. supra) to make limp + obj. (hands): KAI $196^{6f.}$.

šqy$_1$ **OffAr** Haph Inf. *hšqy›* Cowl 27^7 - **JAr** Aph Imper. s.m. + suff. 3 p.s.m. *›šqynh* Syr xlv 101^{16} (dam. context) - ¶ verb Haph/Aph - **1)** to give to drink (with animate object); *wmyn l› ḥsrh lhšqy› ḥyl›* Cowl 27^7: it (sc. the well) did not lack water to give the garrison to drink - **2)** to irrigate (with inanimate object: a field): Syr xlv 101^{16}.

v. *šqy$_2$*.

šqy$_2$ **OldCan** f. Sing. abs. *ša-qī-tu$_4$* EA 369^8 (or rather = syllabic representation of the preceding sumerogram?) - **OffAr** m. Plur. emph. *šqy›* IEJ xiv 27 (cf. Avigad PEQ '68, 43f., Milik DFD 152, Gibson SSI ii p. 5f., cf. however Mazar a.o. IEJ xiv 27f., Naveh AION xvi 19: = m. Sing. emph. :: Teixidor Syr xliv 179: *lšqy›* = *l$_5$* + Haph Inf. of *šqy$_1$*) - **Palm** m. Sing. abs. *šq›* MUSJ xxxviii 133^5 - ¶ subst. (poss. < Qal Part. act. of *šqy$_1$*) - **1)** cup-bearer, butler: m. IEJ xiv 27, f. EA 369^8 (v. however supra) - **2)** irrigator; *lyrḥbwl lšq› l›rq* MUSJ xxxviii $133^{4f.}$:

to Y. the one who gives water to A.

šqy$_3$ v. *byt$_2$*.

šql$_1$ **Pun** QAL Pf. 3 p.pl. *šql* RCL '66, 201[5] (for this interpret., cf. Garbini RSO xliii 13 × Mahjoubi & Fantar RCL '66, 208f., Dupont-Sommer CRAI '68, 117, 128: = QAL Part. act. pl.m. cstr.); Impf. 3 p.pl.m. *yšql[›]* Trip 51[1]; Part. act. s.m. abs. *šql* CIS i 6003 (for this interpret., cf. Lidzbarski Eph i 295 × Slouschz TPI p. 203: or = *šql$_4$* (subst.) ?); YIPH Part. s.m. abs./cstr. *myšql* KAI 121[1], 126[5] (on this form, cf. FR 147b (uncert. interpret.)) - **Hebr** QAL Part. act. m. s. abs. *šwql* DJD ii 24B 15, C 13, D 15, F 14 - **OffAr** QAL Pf. *šqlw* Sem xxiii 95 recto 6 (= AECT 58); Impf. 3 p.s.m. + suff. 3 p.s.m. *ytqlnhy* Cowl 71[6]; 3 p.s.f. *ttql* Cowl 15[24]; cf. Frah xix 3 (*tklwn*), BSOAS xxiv 355?? (*tglwn*), for the ideogram *tgdwn* poss. = *tglwn*, cf. Gignoux FS Nyberg 271f. - ¶ verb QAL - **1)** to weigh out; *wttql l[›s]ḥwr ksp šqln 7 r 2* Cowl 15[24]: she shall weigh out to A. silver 7½ shekel (cf. Trip 51[1f.], Sem xxiii 95 recto 6ff. (= AECT 58)); *›h› šwql lk ... ḥnṭyn* DJD ii 24B 15f.: I will pay you ... (in) barley ... (cf. DJD ii 24C 13ff., D 15); the *šql mḥtt* in RCL '66, 201[5] of uncert. interpret., v. supra (v. also *mḥth*; cf. Dupont-Sommer CRAI '68, 117,128: = to weigh (cf. also Ferron Mus xcviii 59), Garbini RSO xliii 13: to stabilize :: Mahjoubi & Fantar RCL '66, 208f.: = to polish, to decorate) - Part. act., poss. indication of function: CIS i 6003 (cf. e.g. Lidzbarski Eph i 295: tax-collector, Slouschz TPI p. 203: function connected with weighing (cf. also Heltzer UF xix 435; on this text, cf. also RES 15) - **2)** used figuratively, *wytqlnhy blbh* Cowl 71[6]: he considered it in his heart (uncert. interpret., diff. reading of *lbh*, v. *lb*; or: = and he will pay it ...?) - YIPH to ornate, to decorate; *myšql ›rṣ* KAI 121[1], 126[5]: who adorns his country (cf. Lat. par. *ornator patriae* in both instances) - on this word, cf. Kaufman AIA 100.
v. *šqlh*.

šql$_2$ **Palm** Part. act. s.f. abs. *šql›* CIS ii 3913 ii 48, 49, 51 (*šql[›]*), 127, 128; pl.f. abs. *šqln* CIS ii 3913 ii 126 - ¶ verb QAL to take; *mn dy šql› dynr [›w] ytyr* CIS ii 3913 ii 48: one (sc. a prostitute) who takes a *denarius* or more (Greek par. ... λαμβά]νουσιν ...[..., cf. also CIS ii 3913 ii 49, 51, 126, 127, 128 - on this word, cf. Kaufman AIA 100 - on the root, cf. also Greenfield UF xi 325ff.

šql$_3$ **Pun** Sing. abs. *šql* KAI 69[7]; cstr. *šql* CISFP i 765 - **Hebr** Sing. abs. *šql* IEJ xii 30[2], Mosc pes. 1 (cf. however Delavault & Lemaire RSF vii 32, Bron & Lemaire CISFP i 768: = Ph.), on coins of the first revolt, cf. Meshorer JC no. 149, 150, 152, 155, 159, 160 (cf. also Meshorer Mas coin 1313, 1343, 2989, 3490, 3595), *šl* Dir pes. 10 (prob. lapsus, cf. Delavault & Lemaire RSF vii 31, Bron & Lemaire CISFP i 769; interpret. of *šl* as abbrev. less prob., for a discussion of older litt., cf. Dir p. 269ff.; cf. also Delavault & Lemaire RSF vii 31, Bron &

Lemaire CISFP i 769f.: = Ph.); cstr. *šql* on coins of the first revolt, cf. Meshorer JC no. 148, 151, 154, 158, 164 (cf. also Meshorer Mas coin 1310, 1320, 2985) - **Samal** Sing. abs. *šql* KAI 215^{6} (for the context, v. *qwm_1*) - **OldAr** Sing. cstr. *šql* CISFP i 763; Dual cstr. *šqly* Syr lx 341 - **OffAr** Sing. abs. *šql* Cowl $15^{12,14}$ (v. infra), Krael $7^{12,14}$, $12^{6,14}$, AOF ii $133^{2,3,4,7}$ (= AECT 52), *tql* Cowl 10^{5}, MAI xiv/2, 66^{13} (for the context, v. *qwm_1*); Plur. abs. *šqln* Cowl 10^{3}, $15^{5,6,8,10,11}$, Krael $1^{3,7}$, $2^{5,6,10,16}$, ATNS 20^{2}, CIS ii 13a, 14, 43^{4} (= Del 26 = AECT 13), Sem xxiii 95 verso 1 (= AECT 58), LidzbAss 5^{1} (= AECT 50; *šql[n]*; cf. also Lipiński Stud 104 :: Lidzbarski sub LidzbAss 5: l. *šql* = Sing. abs.), etc., etc., *tqln* Krael 2^{8}, IEJ xiv 186^{1} (*tq[ln]*) - **JAr** Sing. abs. *tql* MPAT 52^{8}; emph. *tql*ʾ Mas 554^{3}; Plur. cstr. *tqly* IEJ xxxvi 206^{5} - ¶ subst. m. shekel (weight, coin); *tqly ksph* IEJ xxxvi 206^{5}: silver shekels (cf. also Broshi & Qimron IEJ xxxvi 210f.); *mḥzy 1 zy nḥš šwh šql 1 r 2* Cowl $15^{11f.}$: a mirror of bronze worth in silver one shekel and a half; *šqly ḥmt* Syr lx 341: two shekels of Hamat (cf. CISFP i 763, 765); *šql yšrʾl* on coins of the first revolt: shekel of Israel; *šql 5* Cowl 15^{14} prob. lapsus for *šqln 5* (cf. Cowl p. 48); the shekel in Israel. prob. around 11.4 gr. (for exception of 13.43 gr., cf. Lemaire Sem xxvi 33f., but cf. the coins of the first revolt, cf. Sperber PEQ '67, pp 108f. no. 19-21), for a discussion, cf. Barrois ii 252ff., Wambacq VD xxix 341f., Liver HThR lvi 182 n. 18, Trinquet SDB v 1240ff., EM iv 862ff., Scott BiAr xxii 32ff., BASOR clxxiii 55ff., cc 62ff., PEQ '65, 128ff., de Vaux IAT i 310ff., Aharoni BASOR clxxxiv 16ff., cci 35, Kerkhof BASOR clxxxiv 20f., Yeivin Lesh xxxi 249, Ben-David PEQ '68, 145ff., '70, 105f., Meshorer Proc v CJS i 81ff., Dever HUCA xl/xli 176ff., Lemaire Sem xxvi 40ff., Lemaire & Vernus Sem xxviii 56 - for the shekel in the Elephantine texts, cf. e.g. Revillout RevEgypt. xiii 158ff., Porten Arch 62ff. - for the abbrev. *š*, cf. Mosc var. 11^{2} (= SSI i p. 17B), TA-H 16^{5}, $65^{1,2}$ (dam. context), 81^{1} (dam. context), IEJ xii 29 no. 4, Del 70^{2}, 80^{2}, 81^{1}, 91^{2} (= CIS ii 64), MAI xiv/2, 66^{12}, Cowl 11^{2} (for the context, v. *$rbʿ_3$*)$,^{3}$, $22^{2,3,4}$, 35^{3}, 50^{9}, $61^{13,15}$, 63^{2}, 78^{3}, $81^{18,31}$, ATNS 51^{3}, 52a 6 (?), 66a 9 (?), 72b 3, 81^{2} (?), 147^{4} (?), Herm $2^{6,7}$, 6^{4}, RES 1784, $1794^{3,7,11,12}$, NESE i $11^{4,5}$, iii 43^{7}, Samar 1^{8} (= EI xviii 8*), 2^{3}, 4^{3}, 7^{11}, Mas 424^{2}, 426^{1}, BSh $16^{2,3}$ (uncert. interpret., heavily dam. context), IEJ xxxviii 164A 1-8, 11, 13, B i 2, 3, ii 7, Sem xxxvii $51^{6,7,8}$, etc. - Israel BiOr xxxvii 6: l. abbrev. *š* in NESE ii 6 $^{1-5}$ (prob. reading and interpret. :: Degen NESE ii a.l.: the *š* in ll. 2, 4 = part of n.p., in l. 3 l. ʿ = part of n.p., in l. 5 l. prob. *d* = part of n.p.) - Segal ATNS a.l.: l. *š* (= abbrev.) in ATNS 9^{5} (highly uncert. reading, cf. Porten & Yardeni sub TADAE B 8.6: l. numbers) - for this word, cf. also Kaufman AIA 29 - > Greek σίγλος, σίκλος, cf. Masson RPAE 34 ff.

v. *prs_2*, *$šṭ_1$*, *$šṭr_2$*, *$šlm_2$*.

šql$_4$ v. *šql$_1$*.
šqlh **Pun** the *š'qlt* in Karth xii 53[3] word of diff. interpret.; v.d.Branden RSF v 61: = Sing. abs. of *šqlh* (= money), cf. however Février & Fantar Karth xii 53: div. *š'ql* (= QAL Pf. 3 p.s.m. of *šql$_1$*) + *t* (= *t$_1$* = *'yt$_3$*), he decorated ... :: Krahmalkov RSF iii 178, 185, 204: = QAL Part. pass. s.f. abs., weighed out (said of a certain capital).
šqmh v. *šqqh*.
šqp **OffAr** QAL/PA'EL Pf. 3 p.pl.m. + suff. 1 p.s. *šqpwny* ATNS 28b 4 - ¶ verb QAL/PA'EL to strike; *šqpwny rgln 2* ATNS 28b 4: they struck me on (my) legs two times.
šqq (< Akkad., cf. Zimmern Fremdw 43, Kaufman AIA 93f., 141 - v.Soden Or xlvi 196: *šqq* (< Akkad. *sūqāqu*) > Akkad. *šūqāqu*, less prob. interpret.) - **OffAr** Sing. abs. *šqq* IPAA 11[3] (reading of first *q* uncert., v. also infra) - **Palm** Sing. emph. *šqq'* CIS ii 4199[7]; Plur. abs. *šqqn* CIS ii 4199[3] - ¶ subst. orig. meaning street, place; in CIS ii 4199 indication of part of tomb construction (// with *plṭy* in Ber ii 84[1], 85[7], cf. Ingholt Ber ii 84, FS Miles 48 (n. 59)), prob. identical with *exedra*; in IPAA 11[3] in the comb. *mn šryryn šqq*, Humbach IPAA 11f.: prob. = from the street/way of the loyal ones (if interpret. correct, non-Aramaic word order), or *šqq* = used figuratively, way of life?
šqqh **Palm** Sing. emph. *šqqt'* FS Miles 38[1,2] - ¶ subst. street - in FS Miles 38[1,2] indication of part of tomb construction (cf. also Ingholt FS Miles 48: almost synonymous with exedra) - the same word poss. also in Inv D 20[2]: *šqqt'* (= Sing. emph.), for this reading, cf. Cantineau Syr xix 164, Gawlikowski TP 32f., *bny šqqt'* poss. = market vendors (:: Cantineau Syr xix 164: = inhabitants of the street; cf. also Gawlikowski TP 32f.) :: Milik DFD 342: l. *šqmt'* (for this reading, cf. also Ingholt Ber v 98 n. 7) = Plur. emph. of *šqmh* (= manufacturer of wine-skins) :: du Mesnil du Buisson Inv D a.l.: pro *bny šqqt'* l. *bnyšm* (= n.p.) *mt'* (= n.p.).
šqr **OldAr** QAL/PA'EL (on this problem, cf. e.g. Fitzmyer AIS 107, Donner KAI a.l., Degen AAG p. 70, Gibson SSI ii p. 38) Pf. 2 p.s.m. *šqrt* KAI 222B 38, 224[9] (*š[q]rt*)[,14,19,20,27]; 2 p.pl.m. *šqrtm* KAI 222B 23, 223B 9, 14 (cf. Dupont-Sommer Sf p. 105, 113, Donner KAI a.l., Fitzmyer AIS 82, Degen AAG p. 18, 70 × Lemaire & Durand IAS 117 (div. otherwise): l. *šqrt* (= QAL/PA'EL Pf. 2 p.s.m.)), 224[4,7,16,23] (*[š]qrtm*) (cf. Dupont-Sommer Sf p. 76, 151, Donner sub KAI 222B 13, Hillers TC 32f., Degen AAG p. 70, Silverman JAOS xciv 270f. :: Fitzmyer CBQ xx 456: = 2 p.s.m. + mimation, cf. also Fitzmyer AIS 107, Donner KAI sub 224[4]); Impf. 3 p.s.m. *yšqr* KAI 222A 14, 15, 24 - ¶ verb QAL/PA'EL (v. supra) to be false (to), to betray - 1) + *b$_2$*, *šqrt b'dy' 'ln* KAI 222B 38: you have violated these treaty-stipulations (cf. KAI 224[7,9,19,20,27]) - **2)** + *l$_5$*, *šqrtm lkl 'lhy 'dy'* KAI

222B 23: you have betrayed all the gods of the treaty (cf. KAI 223B 9, 14, 224[4,14,16f.,23]) - on *šqr* + b_2 or + l_5 in OldAr., cf. Greenfield FS Fitzmyer 51 - a derivative of this root in DA x c 1.

šqrh OffAr the *šqrtʾ/šqdtʾ* in IrAnt iv 122[1] = Sing. emph. of *šqrh/šqdh*, word of unknown meaning (cf. Naveh AION xvi 34); Dupont-Sommer IrAnt a.l.: l. *šqrh* = pyre (cf. also Teixidor Syr xliv 185).

šr$_1$ OldAr Sing. abs. *šr* KAI 202A 10; emph. *šwrʾ* KAI 202A 17 - **OffAr** Sing. abs. *šwr* Cowl 27[5]; emph. *šwrʾ* Cowl 27[6]; Plur. abs. *šwrn* ATNS 100[1] (uncert. interpret., heavily dam. context) - **Hatra** Sing. emph. *šwrʾ* 272[1], 290[4] (*šw[rʾ]*), 336[10], 343[6], Ibr 9[2] - ¶ subst. m. wall; *šwrʾ wʾbwlʾ dy bnʾ byt ʾlhʾ nṣr[w]* Hatra 272[1]: the wall and the gateway which he built in the house of the god N. (cf. also Hatra 290[4]); *šwrʾ zk bnh bmnṣyʿt byrtʾ* Cowl 27[6]: this wall was built in the midst of the fortress (cf. Cowl 27[5], cf. also on this wall Porten Arch 284, Grelot DAE p. 402f. n. h); *whrmw šr mn šr ḥzrk* KAI 202A 10: they put up a rampart higher than the wall of Ch.; *šwrʾ dy kpʾ* Hatra Ibr 9[2]: a wall of stone.

v. *šrgb*.

šr$_2$ Ph Sing. abs. *šr* KAI 15, 16; cstr. *šr* KAI 15 (:: Milik Bibl xlviii 575f. n. 6: l. *šd* (= Sing. abs. of *šd$_1$*) :: Teixidor JBL ciii 455: l. *šd* (= Sing. cstr. of *šd$_1$*); for the reading *šr*, cf. André & Bordreuil Syr lxvii 499f.) - **Hebr** Sing. abs. *šr* KAI 200[1,12], Vatt sig. eb. 99 (= SANSS 68; poss. interpret., cf. also Amusin & Heltzer IEJ xiv 150; interpret. as n.p. (cf. Dir sub sig. 99) less prob.); cstr. *šr* KAI 193[14], Vatt sig. eb. 394 (= HBTJ 10), 402, TA-H 26[2] (??, *šr[*; dam. context, cf. also Aharoni TA-H a.l., Pardee UF x 323, HAHL 62); Plur. abs. *šr[m]* KAI 196[4] - **OffAr** Sing. cstr. *šr* RES 245 (reading however uncertain) - **Palm** Sing. + suff. 1 p.pl. *šrn* RTP 333 (cf. Caquot RTP p. 150, cf. also Gawlikowski TP 103, cf. however Milik DFD 339: l. *šdn[ʾ]* = Sing. emph. of *šdn*); cf. also du Mesnil du Buisson TMP 412) - ¶ subst. m. prince, high functionary; *[sp]r hmlk w ... spry hšr[m]* KAI 196[3f.]: the letter of the king and ... the letters of the high functionaries; *šr mlk* RES 245: officer of the king (v. however supra); *šr hṣbʾ* KAI 193[14]: the commander of the army; *šr hʿr* Vatt sig. eb. 394 (= HBTJ 10; cf. also Conrad TUAT ii 569), 402: the governor of the city (cf. Avigad FS Cross 204f.); for the *šr* in KAI 200, cf. Yeivin BiOr xix 3, Amusin & Heltzer IEJ xiv 150f., Delekat Bibl li 458f., Lemaire Sem xxi 62, 77, IH i 261f., 266, Pardee Maarav i 38ff., Suzuki AJBI viii 34ff., 47 n. 98; *šr qdš* KAI 15, 16: prince of the sanctuary (v. *qdš$_2$*), title of the god Eshmun (cf. also Meyer ZAW xlix 13 (n. 3) :: Hoffmann ThLZ xxvii 633: *šr* = QAL Part. act. s.m. abs. of *šwr$_3$* (= to guard) *qdš* (= sanctuary or = n.l.?)), cf. also *ʾšmn [š]r qdš ʿn ydll* KAI 14[17]: Eshmun the prince of the sanctuary of the Y. spring (for the reading *[š]r* instead

of *šd* in this instance, cf. also Xella CISFP i 404f. :: Caquot ACF '78, 575); *šmš šrn rb*ʾ RTP 333: Shamash our great prince (uncert. reading, v. supra) - *ṣdn šr* KAI 15: Sidon the Prince (prob. name of a ward of Sidon (cf. also *ʾrṣ$_1$*, *mšl$_1$*), cf. Lidzbarski Eph ii 52, sub KI 8 :: Cooke NSI p. 401ff., Clermont-Ganneau RAO v 225, 228f.: l. *ṣdn šd* (= Sing. abs. of *šd$_1$*): = Sidon of the plain (cf. e.g. Milik Bibl xlviii 575f. n. 6, Gibson SSI iii p. 113, Elayi RCP 14, SCA 83f.) :: Torrey JAOS xxiii 165: l. *ṣr* (= Sing. cstr. of *ṣr$_1$*) *nšr* (= Sing. abs. of *nšr$_2$*) :: Hoffmann ThLZ xxvii 633: l. *šr* = QAL Imper. pl.m. of *šwr$_3$* (= to guard); cf. also Röllig KAI a.l.) - Lipiński Stud 140f.: l. *šr* (= Sing. abs.) in TH 5 obv. 6 (= AECT 57) = indication of Assyrian king (highly uncert. reading and interpret.; for the reading, cf. also Degen NESE i 56).
v. *dl$_1$*, *sd$_2$*, *srn*, *srsr$_2$*, *ʿšr$_4$*.

šr$_3$ **DA** Sing. abs. *šr* ii 35 - ¶ subst. heavy rain (cf. Hoftijzer **DA** a.l., cf. also Rofé SB 68) :: Dijkstra GTT xc 165 (n. 30): = acid?

šr$_4$ v. *šyr$_1$*.

šr$_5$ v. *šʾr$_2$*.

šr$_6$ **Palm** O'Connor FUCUS 363f.: the diff. *šrk* in Ber ii 102 ii 5: = *šr* + suff. 2 p.s.m. (prob. interpret.); O'Connor ibid.: *šr* prob. = derivative of *šwr$_1$* (= to pass.) or of cognate of *swr$_1$* (= to turn away) :: Ingholt Ber ii 103: or = Sing. abs. of *šrk* (= remaining part, rest).

šr$_7$ v. *šbl*.

šrʾ$_1$ v. *šry$_1$*.

šrʾ$_2$ v. *šry$_1$*.

šrʾ$_3$ v. *šry$_1$*.

šrb$_1$ **Palm** Sing. emph. *šrbʾ* Syr lxii 57^5 - ¶ subst. of uncert. meaning, indicating an object; Caquot Syr lxii 59: = burner??

šrb$_2$ **OldAr** Plur. + suff. 3 p.s.m. *šrbwh* KAI 224$^{13f.}$ (for this reading, cf. Fitzmyer AIS 114, Gibson SSI ii p. 48, 54, Lemaire & Durand IAS 119, 145 (: or l. *šgbwh*?, cf. also Puech RB lxxxix 584, 587), cf. however Dupont-Sommer BMB xiii 33, Sf p. 128, 150: l. *šgbwh* = Plur. + suff. 3 p.s.m. of *šgb* (= great, mighty; cf. e.g. Segert ArchOr xxxii 120, Donner KAI a.l.), cf. also Degen AAG p. 21, 52: = Plur. of *šgb* (= troops) and Noth ZDPV lxxvii 150 (n. 89): *šgb* = watchman, watchpost) - ¶ subst. of uncert. meaning; Fitzmyer AIS 114: = noble, Rosenthal BASOR clviii 29 n. 8, Gibson SSI ii p. 54: = member of a clan (cf. also Kaufman AIA 154).

šrbh v. *šrkh*.

šrgb **Palm** Sing. emph. *šrgbʾ* Inv xii 48^2, 49^6 (cf. Gawlikowski TP 84, Bounni & Teixidor Inv xii a.l. :: Dupont-Sommer CRAI '66, 188f. (div. otherwise): = *šr* (= Sing. cstr. of *šr$_1$*) + *gbʾ* (= Sing. emph. of *gb$_2$*) :: Teixidor Syr xlv 380f. (div. otherwise): = *šr* (= Sing. cstr. of *šr$_1$*) + *gbʾ* (= Sing. emph. of *gb$_1$*) :: Aggoula Sem xxix 117 (div. otherwise): l.

šd (= Sing. cstr. of *šd*$_5$ (= base, support)) + *gb*ʾ (= Sing. emph. of *gb*$_2$ (= pitcher, basin))) - ¶ subst. of unknown meaning, cf. Gawlikowski TP 84 (:: Gawlikowski Syr xlviii 410 n. 3 = one word consisting of two elements < Akkad., *šr* (= circle), *gb* (= basin) = circular crater :: Starcky CRAI '66, 174: = derivative of root *rqp* with *š*- prefix).

šrdl$_1$ v. *dl*$_1$.

šrh v. *šdh*$_2$.

šrw **OffAr** Sing. emph. *šrt*ʾ Cowl 72^{2,3,10,17,18,24} - ¶ subst. dinner, banquet (cf. also CIS ii sub 146, Grelot Sem xxiii 103).

šrḥ **Palm** Sing. emph. *šrḥ*ʾ RIP 142^3 (cf. however Milik DFD 294 (div. otherwise): l. *ʿšrt*ʾ = f. emph. of *ʿšr*$_3$; v. also *ywm*) - ¶ subst. of unknown meaning.

šrḥw **OffAr** Sing. emph. *šrḥw[t*ʾ*]* Aḥiq 170 (cf. however Kottsieper SAS 10, 237: l. *šrḥw[ty]* = Sing. + suff. 1 p.s.); + suff. 3 p.s.m. *šrḥwth* Aḥiq 85 (cf. also Kottsieper SAS 47) - ¶ subst. prob. meaning (bad smell >) bad name, bad reputation, cf. e.g. Baneth OLZ '14, 296, Nöldeke AGWG xiv/4, 11, Joüon MUSJ xviii 84f., Grelot DAE p. 445 (n. h; for Aḥiq 170), cf. however Sach p. 161, Cowl p. 222, Ginsberg ANET 428, Grelot DAE p. 435 (for Aḥiq 85), Kottsieper SAS 17, 19, 237: = wantonness (on this word, cf. also Lindenberger APA 55f. (cf. also ibid. 173)); *bšm šrḥwth* Aḥiq 85: because of his bad reputation.

šry$_1$ **OldAr** QAL Impf. 2 p.s.m. + suff. 3 p.s.m. *tšryh* KAI 224^{18} - **OffAr** QAL Impf. *yšrh* Cowl 71^7 (reading of *r* uncert.); ITP Part. s.m. abs. *mšrth* KAI 261^6; cf. Frah xxi 7 (*šlytwn*) - **Nab** QAL Imper. s.m. *šr*ʾ IEJ xxix 112^8 (twice; reading of first *šr*ʾ uncert.; cf. Naveh IEJ xxix 113, 119; diff. context) - **Palm** PAʿEL Pf. 3 p.s.m. *šry* Syr xiv 188^3 (cf. however Milik DFD 33: l. *šky*? = Sing. abs. of *šky*$_2$ (= expectation)) - **Hatra** QAL Part. act. s.m. abs. *šr*ʾ app. 4^{4,8} (:: Tubach ISS 400 (n. 694), 402: < root *šr*ʾ$_2$ = to make fluid, to procure water :: Altheim & Stiehl AAW v/1, 83f.: = QAL Pf. 3 p.s.m. of *šr*ʾ$_3$ (= to exorcize)) - **JAr** QAL Impf. 3 p.s.f. *tšry* Frey 668^2 - ¶ verb QAL - **1)** to release; + obj., ʾ*srh w[*ʾ*l] tšryh* KAI 224^{18}: imprison him and do not let him go free (cf. also Cowl 71^7 (dam. context; v. supra)); cf. IEJ xxix 112^8 (v. supra) - **2)** to reside; *šr*ʾ *bḥṭṭ* Hatra app. 4^4: who resides in Ch. (v. *ḥṭṭ*$_2$), cf. Hatra app. 4^8 (for the context, v. *mlḥ*$_5$); cf. also *tšry rwḥyh* Frey 668^2: may his soul rest - PAʿEL to begin; + *l*$_5$ + Inf.: Syr xiv 188^3 (v. however supra) - ITP to encamp: KAI 261^6 (:: e.g. Nöldeke ZA vii 351, 353, Cooke NSI p. 194, Donner KAI a.l., Gibson SSI ii p. 155: = to take a meal) - v.Soden Or xlvi 195, AHW s.v. *šerû* III: > Akkad. *šerû* (poss. interpret., cf. also CAD s.v. *šerû* C).

v. *zry*$_1$, *ntyn*, *šṭr*$_1$, *škn*$_1$, *šrt*$_1$.

šry$_2$ v. *srṭ*.

šry$_3$ v. *š*ʾ*ry*.

šry$_4$ v. *ntyn*.
šryq v. *šdq$_1$*.
šryr **OffAr** Sing. m. abs. *šryr* Cowl 30^3, 31^3; emph. *šryr›* Cowl 70^2; Plur. m. abs. *šryryn* CRAI '70, 163^2, IPAA 11^3; cf. Frah xiii 10 (*šll›*) - ¶ adj. firm, strong; *ḥdh wšryr hwy bkl ‘dn* Cowl 30^3: may you be happy and strong at all times (cf. Cowl 31^3; cf. also Porten EI xiv 167, Dion RB lxxxix 532); *ḥy› ḥdh wšryr› mr›y yhwy* Cowl 70^2: that my lord be alive, happy and strong; cf. also *šryryn šqq* IPAA 11^3: street/way of the loyal ones (v. *šqq*), for this meaning, cf. also CRAI '70, 163^2 (:: Dupont-Sommer CRAI '70, 164: *šryryn* = the prosperous ones); cf. also Frah xiii 10: = firm, true.
šryt **Palm** Sing. emph. *šryt›* SBS 19^2, 20^4; + suff. 3 p.s.f. *šryth* SBS 1a 1, 1b 1 (= Inscr P 30), 3^1, 7^1, 8^1, Syr xvii 274^1; + suff. 3 p.pl.m. *šrythwn* SBS 13^1 (= CIS ii 3983), 14^1, 17^2, 19^2, CIS ii 3955^5, 3984^2 - **JAr** Plur. emph. *šryt[›]* MPAT 51^7 - ¶ subst. beam: MPAT 51^7; in Palm. texts indication of architrave, entablature - > Akkad. *šārītu* (cf. v.Soden Or xlvi 195, AHW s.v., cf. also CAD s.v.).
šrk v. *šr$_6$*.
šrkh (< Arab., cf. Milik BIA x 57, O'Connor JNES xlv 228f.) - **Nab** Sing. cstr. *šrkt* BIA x 55^4 (Greek par. ἔθνος); + suff. 3 p.s.f. *šrkth* BIA x 55^4 - ¶ subst. federation, confederation; *šrkt tmwdw* BIA x 55^4: the confederation of T. (prob. of the Thamudian clans), on the subject, cf. Milik BIA x 57, Graf & O'Connor BySt iv 56, 65f., Shahîd RoAr 138ff., 141 n. 13, O'Connor JANES xviii 73, 80, DRBE 603, 607, 612; cf. however Shahîd RoAr 141 n. 13: or l. *šrbt* (= Sing. cstr. of *šrbh* (= tribe, people))?, for this reading, cf. also O'Connor DRBE 608, 612 :: Teixidor Syr xlvii 378: l. *drbt* = those belonging to the Robat tribe - Milik DFD 338f.: l. *šr[k]t* (= Sing. cstr. of *šrkh* (= thiasos)) in Assur 33f. 2 (cf. also O'Connor JANES xviii 72, 80, DRBE 608, 612), uncert. reading and interpret. (cf. also Aggoula Assur a.l. (div. otherwise): l. *šdr* = PA‘EL Pf. 3 p.s.m. of *šdr$_1$*? (uncert. reading and interpret.)).
šrl v. *šbl*.
šrm v. *šrn*.
šrn **OldAr** Sing. abs. *šrn* KAI 222A 33 (cf. e.g. Dupont-Sommer Sf p. 48, Greenfield JSS xi 98ff., Fitzmyer AIS 50 :: Fensham JNES xxii 185f.: l. *šrm* = Sing. abs. of *šrm* (= wild-ass)) - ¶ subst. wild cat; on the word, cf. also Kaufman AIA 154 - cf. *šwm›r*.
šr‘$_1$ **DA** Naveh IEJ xxix 136: the *šr‘›* in DA 267 no. 1, 2 = Sing. emph. of *šr‘$_1$* = gate, cf. also Knauf ZDPV ci 189 (cf. also Lemaire GLECS xxiv-xxviii 322: poss. = Sing. emph. of *šr‘$_2$* (= gatekeeper)?, cf. also idem CRAI '85, 273f. (n. 27)); less prob. interpret., cf. Hoftijzer DA a.l.: = n.d. or n.g. -cf. also *š‘r$_1$*, *tr‘$_1$*.
šr‘$_2$ v. *šr‘$_1$*.

šrp$_1$ **OffAr** QAL Pf. 3 p.pl.m. *šrpw* Cowl 30[12], 31[11] - **Hatra** QAL Impf. 3 p.s.m. *lšrp* 293[3] (cf. Degen NESE iii 92ff. :: Teixidor Syr lii 291, Vattioni IH a.l.: l. *yšrp* = QAL Impf. 3 p.s.m. :: As-Salihi Sumer xxviii 27, 20*: l. *bšrp*, cf. also Aggoula MUSJ xlix 471f.: l. *bšrp* = *b*$_2$ + Sing. abs. of *šrp*$_2$ (= dung of cow)) - ¶ verb QAL to burn; + obj.: Hatra 293[3f.] (bones); + obj. + *b*$_2$, *wmṭll ʾgwrʾ zk bʾštʾ šrpw* Cowl 31[10f.]: and the roof of this temple they have burnt by fire (cf. Cowl 30[11]).

šrp$_2$ v. *šrp*$_1$

šrṣh Nab Naveh IEJ xxix 113, 117: l. *šrṣt* = Sing. cstr. of *šrṣh* (= profusion) in IEJ xxix 112[4] (highly uncert. context).

šrq$_1$ **Hebr** Sing. abs. *šrq* KAI 190[2] (v. infra) - ¶ verb QAL to card.; Part. act. carder: KAI 190[2] (cf. Milik RB lxvi 551, Smelik HDAI 72 :: Milik HDS 84: *hšrq* > n.p. (cf. also Lemaire IH i 240)) - Milik RB lxvi 550f.: l. *šrqm* (= QAL Part. act. pl.m. abs.) in KAI 190[1] = carders (cf. also Lemaire IH i 239, 241, Smelik HDAI 72) :: Mosc p. 46 (div. otherwise): l. *bqyhw* (= n.p.), cf. also e.g. Röllig KAI a.l., Gibson SSI i p. 25f.; on the reading and interpret. of the text, cf. Dir p. 74ff., Mosc p. 44f.

v. *šdq*$_1$, *šrq*$_5$.

šrq$_2$ v. *šdq*$_1$.

šrq$_3$ v. *šrq*$_5$.

šrq$_4$ cf. Frah app. 1 (*šlkwn*) = to paint (cf. also Frah S$_1$ 6).

šrq$_5$ **OffAr** Sing. m. abs. *šrq* Aḥiq 100 - ¶ adj. sharp: Aḥiq 100 (cf. e.g. Cowl p. 223, Grelot DAE p. 437; cf. also Sach p. 164, Baneth OLZ '14, 298: = QAL Part. act. of *šrq*$_1$ (= tearing, cutting, cf. also Halévy RS xx 52) :: Epstein ZAW xxxii 134f., Nöldeke AGWG xiv/4, 12: = QAL Part. act. of *šrq*$_3$ (= to glide), smooth :: Koopmans 142f.: or = *šrq*$_6$ (= bloody) :: Kottsieper SAS 12, 20, 234: l. *šdq* = QAL Part. act. s.m. abs. of *šdq*$_1$ (= to cut), for this reading and interpret., cf. also Sach p. 164); on this word, cf. also Lindenberger APA 80, 238 nn. 196, 197.

šrq$_6$ v. *šrq*$_5$.

šrr$_1$ **Palm** APH Pf. 3 p.s.m. *ʾšr* CIS ii 3913 ii 120 (Greek par. ἐσημιώσατο); 3 p.s.f. *ʾšrt* CIS ii 3913 i 3 (Greek par. ἐψηφίσθη); APH pass. Pf. 3 p.s.m. *ʾšr* CIS ii 3913 i 9 (cf. CIS ii sub 3913, Cantineau Gramm 90, Rosenthal Sprache 56 :: e.g. Reckendorff ZDMG xlii 385, 399, Cooke NSI p. 334: = APH), Syr xiv 179[2] (cf. Rosenthal Sprache 62 n. 1, Milik Syr xliv 295 n. 1, DFD 343) - **JAr** HAPH Pf. 3 p.s.f. *hšrt* MPAT 61[24] (Greek par. ἐμαρτυροποιησάμη; for the reading, cf. Greenfield sub DBKP 15 :: e.g. Fitzmyer & Harrington MPAT a.l. (div. otherwise): l. *šdt* (= lapsus for *šhdt* = Sing. cstr. of *šhdw*)) - ¶ verb HAPH/APH to decide, to establish, to declare - 1) + obj., *ʾšrt mdy ktyb mn lṭht* CIS ii 3913 i 3f.: it established what is written below - **2)** + *b*$_2$, *whyk dy ʾšr qrblwn ... bʾgrtʾ* CIS ii 3913 ii 120f.: and as C. ... established in the letter - **3)**

+ *bqmy* + *k*$_1$, *bqmy hšrt bbth kkl dy* ... MPAT 61^{24}: B. has declared in my presence in accordance with everything that ... (i.e. has confirmed everything that) - APH pass. to be approved, to be decided; *ˀšr lˀgwrˀ* CIS ii 3913 i 9: it was approved by the tax farmer (cf. CIS ii sub 3913, Rosenthal Sprache 56, cf. also Nöldeke Gramm 247; Greek par. κυρωθῇ τῷ μισθουμένῳ); *ˀšr wˀšlm* Syr xiv 179^2: it is decided and executed.

šrr$_2$ v. *srr*$_1$.

šrr$_3$ **Nab** Naveh IEJ xxix 112f., 116: the *šrrnˀ* in IEJ xxix 112^2 = Sing. + suff. 1 p.pl. of *šrr*$_3$ (= steadfastness, faithfulness), interpret. of context highly uncert.

šrrt **OffAr** Sing. abs. *šrrt* Cowl 42^1 (for this reading, cf. Driv p. 44 n. 1, Bresciani RSO xxxv 20, Grelot DAE p. 130 n. b, Porten & Yardeni sub TADAE A 3.8), Driv 2^1 (for the reading, cf. Yardeni with Szubin & Porten JNES xlvi 39ff., cf. also Porten & Yardeni sub TADAE A 6.4), 3^1, 5^1, 13^1, SSI ii 28 obv. 1; cf. DEP 153^2, GIPP 64, v. also infra - ¶ subst. firmness, strength (cf. Porten EI xiv 168, cf. also Fales JAOS cvii 459); *šlm wšrrt šgyˀ hwšrt lk* Driv 3^1: I send you many greetings and strength (cf. Fitzmyer JBL xciii 215, Dion RB lxxxix 537; cf. Cowl 42^1, Driv 2^1, 5^1, 13^1, SSI ii 28 obv. 1; cf. also the combination of *šlm* and *šrrt* in Nisa-c 136, 210^{2,4,6,8}, 287^1, 398, etc.).

šrš$_1$ **Pun** Vattioni Aug xvi 547: the *sarasthi* in IRT 886f 5f. = Pf. form of *šrš*$_1$ (= to root, to deroot; improb. interpret.).

šrš$_2$ **Ph** Sing. abs. *šrš* KAI 14^{11}, 43^{16} (dam. context, for which, cf. Honeyman JEA xxvi 58, Lipiński RTAT 251 (n. 37), Gibson SSI iii p. 137, 141), Mus li 286^3 (× Lane BASOR cxciv 44: = Sing. + suff. 1 p.s.); cstr. *šrš* KAI 26A i 10; cf. Diosc ii 163: σοιρις (cp συρις quoted from Diosc ii 193 in FR 96c, 194b) - **OldAr** Sing. + suff. 3 p.s.m. *šršh* KAI 202B 28 (*š[r]šh*, dam. context), KAI 222C 24f. (*š[rš]h*) - ¶ subst. root; used figuratively, *ˀl ykn lm šrš lmṭ wpr lmˁl* KAI 14$^{11f.}$: may they have no root below nor branches/fruit (v. *pry*$_2$) above (:: Ginsberg FS Driver 74f.: *šrš* = root plus the trunk of the tree), on the expression, cf. Watson UF viii 374, Avishur PIB 77f.; > offspring: KAI 26A i 10, 222C 24f., Mus li 286^3, the same meaning prob. also in KAI 43^{16} (dam. context).

v. *šbl*, *šmš*$_2$.

šrt$_1$ **Pun** PIˁEL Pf. 3 p.s.m. *šrt* CIS i 5510^7 (diff. context; cf. Février BAr '46/49, 171, CIS i a.l. :: Chabot BAr '41/42, 390, 393 (div. otherwise): l. *[m]šrt* = Sing. abs. of *mšrt*$_3$ (= raising, preservation < root *šwr*$_3$, *šry*$_1$); for the context, v. *qny*); Part. s.m. abs. *mšrt* CIS i 5510^4 (cf. Février BAr '46/49, 170f., CIS i a.l. :: Chabot BAr '41/42, 390, 393: = Sing. abs. of *mšrt*$_3$); Inf. cstr. *šrt* NP 130^4 (diff. context, uncert. interpret.; cf. e.g. Cooke NSI p. 147) - ¶ verb PIˁEL to serve; v.d.Branden BiOr xxxvi 159 n. 36: in CIS i 5510 in the sense of military service;

v. supra - Dupont-Sommer RDAC '84 a.l.: the *šrt›* in RDAC '84, 198 no. 5b2 = derivative of this root (= the officiant, the officiating priest), less prob. interpret., cf. also Puech Sem xxxix 104f.: = n.p.
v. *›šr₇*.

šrt₂ v. *›šr₇*, *psšrt*.

šrt₃ v. *›šr₇*, *mš‹rt*.

šš₁ **OffAr** Sing. abs. *šš* Krael 7[18] (cf. e.g. Ginsberg JAOS lxxiv 159, Kutscher JAOS lxxiv 236 :: Krael a.l.: = *šš₃*); emph. *šys›* (emended by superscription to *š›ys›*) AM ii 174[4] (v. infra) - **Palm** Sing. emph. *šyš›* Inv xii 48[2] - ¶ subst. alabaster, marble; *›bn šš* Krael 7[18]: alabaster stone (for this interpret., cf. e.g. Ginsberg JAOS lxxiv 159, Kutscher JAOS lxxiv 236, Segert ArchOr xxiv 392, Couroyer RB lxxviii 520f., Grelot DAE p. 235; v. supra); *kwrsy› š›yš›* (v. supra) AM ii 174[4]: prob. = a marble stool (for this interpret., cf. Henning AM a.l., Bivar & Shaked BSOAS xxvii 288f., cf. however ibid. 290 (n. 92), where other interpret. of context is proposed :: Altheim & Stiehl Suppl 94f.: l. *kwrsy› bš›ys›*); *›stw› dy šyš›* Inv xii 48[1f.]: a marble portico - Segal ATNS a.l.: l. prob. *šš* (Sing. cstr.) *swn* in ATNS 24[7] (= alabaster of Sewan), highly uncert. reading and interpret.

šš₂ **Samal** Dupont-Sommer JKF i 207: the *šš* in AMB 7a 9 either = *šš₂* (= linen) or = *šš₃* (improb. interpret., cf. Scholem JGM 86, Naveh & Shaked AMB p. 74: = part of name).
v. *ššn₁*.

šš₃ **Pun** m. *šš* KAI 128[3], 130[1], Punica ix 6b 3, xii 32[4], RES 172[2], *š›š* KAI 142[2]; f. *ššt* KAI 111[3], 112[4] - **Hebr** m. *šš* Frey 622[2], SM 51[2]; f. *ššh* TA-H 7[4], IEJ vii 239[8]; cstr. *ššt* DJD ii 24D 16 - **OffAr** m. *št* ATNS 26[6], 64b 9 (dam. context); f. *šth* Cowl 43[3], ATNS 77a 2, 136[1] (dam. context); cf. Frah xxix 6 (*št›*) - **Nab** m. *št* CIS ii 196[6,8], 200[10], 207[7], RES 471[3], IEJ xxi 50[5], on coins, cf. Meshorer NC no. 23, 24 - **Palm** m. *št* CIS ii 4175[8], Sem xxxvi 89[2,3]; f. *šth* Sem xxxvi 89[7], *št›* CIS ii 3913 ii 51 (*[š]t›*), 3955[5], 3970[1], 4194[6], RIP 155 (dam. context), Ber ii 97[2], v 125[8]; cstr. *štt* Ber v 106[4]; emph. *štt›* Syr xiv 171[6]; + suff. 3 p.pl.m. *šttyhwn* CIS ii 3914[4] - **Hatra** f. emph. *štt›* 49[3] - **JAr** m. *št* MPAT 40 i 12, EI xx 305 iii 1 (heavily dam. context), Mas 561[2], 575[3,4], 583[3], *šyt* SM 88[3], 89[2]; f. abs. (?) *štt* Frey 1098[4]; f. abs. *šth* IEJ xxxvi 206[5] (dam. context), xl 135[1]; abs. (?) *štyh* MPAT 62[12] (= DBKP 27; Greek par. ἕξ) - ¶ cardinal number, six: passim; *d[y]nryn štyh* MPAT 62[12]: six *denarii*; *štt gwmḥwhy* Ber v 106[4]: his six niches; *tr‹y› ›ln šttyhwn* CIS ii 3914[4]: these six gates; *št m›h* Sem xxxvi 89[3]: six hundred; used in chronology, *bššt ›rb‹m št lmlky* KAI 111[3f.]: in the 46th year of his reign (cf. KAI 112[4f.]); *bšnt ‹šryn wšt lrb›l* RES 471[3]: in the 26th year of R. (cf. CIS ii 196[8], 207[7]); *ywm štt›* Syr xiv 171[6]: on the sixth day; *hššh lḥdš* TA-H 7[4f.]: the sixth day of the month (cf. IEJ xl 135[1]); *‹l*

štt' bṭbt Hatra 49[3]: on the sixth day of Tebet (cf. Milik RN vi/iv 56 n. 2, Syr xliv 297, Vattioni IH a.l. :: Caquot Syr xxxii 54: l. *lṭbt*); *bšnt ḥmš m'h ḥmšyn wšyt* SM 88[2f.]: in the 556th year.
v. *'ḥd*$_4$, *qṣt*$_1$, *škḥ*, *šš*$_{1,2}$.

ššbyn (< Akkad., cf. Zimmern Fremdw 46, Kaufman AIA 94, 138 n. 3) - **Palm** Sing. + suff. 3 p.s.m. *ššbynh* Inv viii 137[7] - ¶ subst. m. best man.

ššy$_1$ > Akkad. *šāšītu* (= part of/accessory for a lantern), cf. v.Soden Or xxxvii 267, xlvi 195, AHW s.v. (cf. also CAD s.v.).

ššy$_2$ **Hebr** Sing. m. abs. *ššy* SM 106[3] - ¶ ordinal number, sixth.

ššm **Pun** *ššm* KAI 149[4], 152[3], Punica ivA 6[3], xi 4[4], xvi 2[2], BASOR lxxxvii 31[3] (= KAI 127 = IRT 294; for this reading, cf. Levi Della Vida FS Friedrich 309), Karth x 133[4] (for the reading, cf. Fantar Sem xxv 72 :: Février Karth x a.l.: l. *šlm* = n.p. :: Garbini AION xxv 264: l. *šlm* (= Sing. abs. of *šlm*$_3$), cf. also Jongeling NINPI 207), *šyšm* KAI 157[3], *š['š]m* KAI 142[2] (cf. also FR 109; highly uncert. restoration) - **OffAr** *štn* Cowl 26[12] - **Nab** *štyn* J 17[5] - **Palm** *štyn* RIP 103c 5 - **JAr** *štyn* MPAT-A 50[6] - ¶ cardinal number, sixty; cf. e.g. *bn ššm št wšlš* KAI 152[3]: at the age of 63 years; *'w' [š']nt šyšm w'mš* KAI 157[2f.]: he lived sixty-five years; used in chronology, *bšnt m'h wštyn wtryn* J 17[5f.]: in the 162nd year; *šnt tlt m' wštyn wrb' šnyn lḥrbn byt mqdšh* MPAT 50[6f.]: in the 364th year after the destruction of the Temple.

ššmn **Ph** Sing. abs. *ššmn* BIFAO xxxviii 3[7] (:: Segal sub ATNS 42: = Plur.) - ¶ subst. sesame; for the interpret. of BIFAO xxxviii 3[7], cf. also Aimé-Giron ibid. p. 7; on this word, cf. also Masson RPAE 57f. - cf. *šmšm*.

ššn$_1$ **OffAr** Bresciani Aeg xxxix 5: l. *šwšnn* in Aeg xxxix 4 recto 3 = Plur. abs. of *ššn*$_1$ (= lily), *šwšny'* ibid. recto 4 = Plur. emph. of *ššn*$_1$ (cf. Porten FS Bresciani 439f., cf. also Porten & Yardeni sub TADAE A 3.11); improb. interpret., in Aeg xxxix 4 recto 3 pro *šwšnn šš* (= Sing. abs. of *šš*$_2$; thus Bresciani Aeg a.l.), or pro *šwšnn* + numerical signs (thus Porten FS Bresciani 439f., Porten & Yardeni TADAE a.l.), l. (div. otherwise) *šwšnnš* (= n.p.) *zy*, cf. Hoftijzer VT xii 342 (cf. also Swiggers Aeg lx 93f.); pro *šwšny'* in Aeg xxxix 4 recto 4 l. *šwšnnš* (= n.p.), cf. Hoftijzer VT xii 342 (cf. also Swiggers Aeg lx 93f.) :: Milik Aeg xl 80: l. *šwšnn* in Aeg xxxix 4 recto 3 = Plur. abs. of *šwšny* (= nisbe adj. from *šwšn*) and l. *šwšny'* in Aeg xxxix 4 recto 4 = Plur. emph. of *šwšny* (cf. Porten FS Bresciani 439, cf. also Porten & Yardeni sub TADAE A 3.11) - for *ššn* (= lily), cf. also Greek σοῦσον (adj. σούσινος, cf. also Lat. *susinus*), cf. also Masson RPAE 58f.

ššn$_2$ v.Soden Or xlvi 196: = animal, servant > Akkad. *šušānu*, *šušannu* (cf. also v.Soden AHW s.v. *šušānu*); improb. interpret.

št$_1$ v. *šyt*$_1$.

št$_2$ **OffAr** Sing. + suff. 3 p.s.m., cf. Warka 35: *šá-te-e*; cf. Frah x 39 (*šth*) - ¶ subst. buttocks, anus: Frah x 39; this meaning prob. in Warka 35 (cf. Gordon AfO xii 117, Landsberger ibid. 254 n. 27).
v. *šq*$_3$.
št$_3$ v. *šnh*$_2$, *št*$_6$.
št$_4$ v. *mlk*$_5$.
št$_5$ v. *qṣt*$_1$, *šš*$_3$.
št$_6$ **Pun** Garbini AION xxv 259ff.: the *št* in BAr-NS i/ii 228^2 = pron. des.m. f. (poss. interpret.) :: Février BAr a.l.: = Sing. cstr. of *šnh*$_1$.
štʾ v. *šty*$_1$.
šth v. *tḥt*.
štw **OldAr** Sing. emph. *štwʾ* KAI 216^{18} - ¶ subst. winter.
šty$_1$ **DA** Qal Imper. pl.m. *štyw* i 12 (cf. Hoftijzer DA a.l., Levine JAOS ci 197, H.P.Müller ZAW xciv 218, 226f., Garr DGSP 136f., Puech FS Grelot 23, 28 :: Caquot & Lemaire Syr liv 200: = Qal Pf. 3 p.pl.m. (cf. also e.g. Garbini Hen i 185, McCarter BASOR ccxxxix 51, 55f., H. & M. Weippert ZDPV xcviii 97, 103, Hackett BTDA 29, 50, 98)) - **Samal** Qal Pf. 3 p.s.m. *štʾ* KAI 214^9 (on this form, cf. also Garr DGSP 135); Impf. 3 p.s.f. *tšty* KAI 214^{22} - **OffAr** Qal Impf. 3 p.s.m. *yšth* Aḥiq 99; 2 p.s.m. *tšth* Cowl 71^{22} (dam. context); 2 p.pl.m. *tštw* Cowl 21^7; Part. act. pl.m. abs. *štyn* Cowl 27^8, 30^{21} (cf. e.g. Degen GGA '79, 38 :: Leand 40f.: = Pf. 1 p.pl.), 31^{20} (:: Leand ibid.: idem); cf. Frah xix 15 (*ʿšthn*), Paik 12, 22, 162 (*ʾštywn*), 163 (*ʿšth*), 164 (*[ʿ]šth*), GIPP 19f., 47, for the prosthetic vowel in the ideograms, cf. Altheim GH iv 92f., Coxon ZAW lxxxix 275f., Toll ZDMG-Suppl viii 37 - **Palm** Qal Part. act. s.m. abs. *štʾ* CIS ii 3973^5 - **JAr** Qal Part. act. s.f. abs. *štyh* AMB 7^{18,21} - ¶ verb Qal to drink, passim; *ḥdh ṣḥyh wlʾ štyh* AMB 7$^{17f.}$: one who is thirsty but does not drink (cf. AMB 7$^{20f.}$) - **1)** + obj.: Cowl 30^{21}, 31^{20}, Aḥiq 93; *ʾlhʾ ṭbʾ wškrʾ dy lʾ štʾ ḥmr* CIS ii 3973$^{4f.}$: the good and rewarding god who does not drink wine (cf. Hoftijzer RelAr 41, Milik DFD 211f.); *štyw ḥmr* DA i 12: drink wrath (for this interpret., cf. Hoftijzer DA p. 207ff., v. however *ḥmr*$_3$) - **2)** + *b*$_2$ + obj., *bb[rʾ z]k myʾ štyn* Cowl 27^8: they drank water in that well - **3)** + *ʿm*$_4$, *wtšty nbš pnmw ʿm h[dd]* KAI 214^{22}: and may the soul of P. drink with Hadad (v. also *npš*).
v. *mglb*, *šty*$_2$.
šty$_2$ **DA** the *šty* in ii 18 poss. = nom. derivative (Sing. abs.) of root *šty*$_1$ (= to drink), cf. Hoftijzer DA a.l. (heavily dam. and diff. text): drink, beverage, drinking bout??, cf. also H.P. Müll ZAW xciv 219, 238, cf. however Puech RB lxxxv 116 (div. otherwise): l. poss. *mšty* (= Sing. abs. of *mšty* (= drink, drinking)) and cf. Hackett BTDA 26, 30, 74, 98, 135: l. poss. *nšty* (= Qal Impf. 1 p.pl. of *šty*$_1$) :: McCarter with Hackett BTDA 74 (div. otherwise): l. *ʿnšty* (= Qal Pf. 1 p.s. of *ʿnš*$_1$).
šty$_3$ **OffAr** diff. word in KAI 279^3 in the comb. *wbkl ʾrqʾ rʾm šty*; cf.

Benveniste JA ccxlvi 39: poss. *r'm* (< Iran.) = peace, happines and *šty* (< Iran.) = establishment (on the whole earth there was peaceful abode; cf. also Hinz AISN 198), cf. also Silverman JAOS xciv 272: *šty* (< Iran.) = happiness, *r'm šty* = joy and peace (for this interpret., cf. already Benveniste JA ccxlvi 39, Kutscher, Naveh & Shaked Lesh xxxiv 130, 132f., Rosenthal EI xiv 97*: used as hendiadys); Altheim GH ii 171, Altheim & Stiehl EW x 244, ASA 276, GMA 348: *r'm* = QAL Part. act. s.m. abs. of *rwm*$_1$ and *šty* (< Iran.) = joy, on the whole earth joy arose (cf. Garbini Kand 10, 18, Donner KAI a.l. :: Altheim & Stiehl GH i 398, 400, 407, EW ix 192, 193: pro *r'm šty* l. *w'p šty* = *w* + *'p*$_2$ + *šty* (< Iran.) = rejoicing, there was rejoicing :: Levi Della Vida Editto 20, 22, 34: l. *w'p šty* (*šty* = everywhere ??) (cf. also Nober VD xxxvii 372); cf. also Greek par. καὶ πάντα εὐθηνεῖ κατὰ πᾶσαν γῆν).

štym v. *šnym*.

štyn v. *ššm*.

štmh diff. word in Frah iii 4, according to the context indicating something connected with water (sea, canal), Junker with Ebeling Frah a.l.: = canal, aqueduct, cf. also Nyberg *štmt'* poss. = lapsus for *štqt'* poss. = a canal which is navigable; interpret. however uncert. :: Ebeling Frah a.l.: = director, leader (for this word, cf. Kaufman AIA 101, 142, 147f. n. 39, Widengren HDS 226ff.: < Akkad. < Sum.).

štn v. *ššm*.

št'$_1$ **Ph** QAL Impf. 3 p.s.m. *yšt'* KAI 26A ii 4 (cf. e.g. Röllig KAI a.l., FR 133, 263.3, Gibson SSI iii p. 49, 59 :: Lipiński OLZ '82, 459: or = YIPH Pf. 3 p.pl., cf. also v.d.Branden Meltô i 82); NIPH Part. pl.m. abs. *nšt'm* KAI 26A ii 4 - ¶ verb QAL to fear, to dread: KAI 26A ii 4 - NIPH to be feared, to be dreaded; *bmqmm 'š kn lpnm nšt'm 'š yšt' 'dm llkt drk* KAI 26A ii 3ff.: in places which were formerly dreaded, where a man was afraid to walk on a road - the *tšt'* in BASOR cxciii 8^6 prob. form of this root, Cross AUSS xiii 12 n. 34, Shea PEQ '79, 18, 20: = pass. conjugation Impf. 2 p.s.m. (+ *b*$_2$ = to be feared among; cf. also Garr DGSP 119, 121: poss. = NIPH), cf. however Dion RB lxxxii 30ff.: = QAL Impf. 2 p.s.m. (cf. also R.Kutscher Qadm v 28, Jackson ALIA 10, 22f., 26, Smelik HDAI 84) :: Puech & Rofé RB lxxx 534, 541, Sasson PEQ '79, 118, 123: = QAL Impf. 2 p.s.m. + *b*$_2$ (= to stand in awe of) :: Sivan UF xiv 230: = QAL Impf. 3 p.s.m. :: Shea PEQ '81, 105, 108: l. *htšt'* = HITP Pf. 3 p.s.m. of *št'*$_2$ (= to be looked upon, to be favoured) :: Cross BASOR cxciii 19 (n. 16): = Gt Impf. 3 p.s.f. of *š'y*$_2$ (= to be offered; cf. also Fulco BASOR ccxxx 41f.) :: Albright BASOR cxcviii 38, 40: = Gt Impf. 2 p.s.m. of *š'y*$_1$ (= to trust) :: Aufrecht sub CAI 59: = causative stem of *š'y*$_1$ (= to gaze in awe) :: v.Selms BiOr xxxii 6, 8 (div. otherwise): = *t*$_1$ (= *'yt*$_3$) + Sing. abs. of *št'*$_3$ (= plaque); on the problem, cf. also Garbini AION xxx 254f.

v. *tḥt.*

št'$_2$ v. *št'$_1$*.

št'$_3$ v. *št'$_1$*.

št't v. *tḥt.*

štp v. *šwtp.*

štpn v. *šḥpn.*

štq **OldAr** PA'EL Impf. 2 p.s.m. *tštq* KAI 222B 8 (cf. also Greenfield Lesh xxxii 364, Bibl l 100f. :: e.g. Dupont-Sommer Sf p. 71, 151, Fitzmyer AIS 17, 61, Donner KAI a.l., Degen AAG p. 68: = QAL Impf. 3 p.s.f.) - **OffAr** QAL Pf. 3 p.s.m., cf. Warka 7: *šá-ti-iq*; Impf. 1 p.s. *'štq* Aḥiq 121 (dam. context; for this context, cf. Lindenberger APA 110f., 250 n. 324); Part. act. s.m. abs., cf. Warka 2: *šá-ti-iq* (v. infra) - ¶ verb QAL to be silent; *ba-a-a ma-li-e mi-il-in-ni šá-ti-iq* Warka 7: the house full of words became silent; *šá-ti-iq mi-in si-ip-pa-a di-a-ba-ba-'* Warka 2, sentence of diff. interpret., *šá-ti-iq* used adverbially (silently), cf. Gordon AfO xii 108, 117 (: silently from the threshold which is at the gate) :: Dupont-Sommer RA xxxix 42: *šá-ti-iq* = the silent one > instrument which silences :: Driver AfO iii 49: *šá-ti-iq* = QAL Pf. 3 p.s.m. (there is silence from the threshold to the door) :: Landsberger AfO xii 251f. (div. otherwise): pro word divider + *šá-ti-iq* l. *mi-šá-ti-iq* (= PA'EL Part. s.m. abs.) = that which silences - PA'EL to make silent, to neglect; *w'l tštq ḥdh mly spr' zn[h]* KAI 222B 8: and do not neglect one of the words of this text - v.Soden Or xxxvii 267, xlvi 195, AHW s.v. *šatāqu* II: > Akkad. *šatāqu* = to be silent (less prob. interpret., cf. CAD s.v. *etēqu* A sub 4g).

štqh v. *štmh.*

štr$_1$ **OffAr** QAL Pf. 3 p.s.m. *štr* Aḥiq 125 (:: Puech Sem xxi 14 n. 3, Lindenberger APA 114, Kottsieper SAS 237: = QAL Part. act. s.m. abs. :: Sach p. 168: = Sing. cstr. of *štr$_3$* (= *str$_2$*); v. also infra) - ¶ verb QAL to destroy (cf. Nöldeke LZ '11, 1506, Perles OLZ '11, 502, Epstein ZAW xxxii 136, Ginsberg ANET 429, Grelot RB lxviii 186, DAE p. 440, Kottsieper SAS 237); *'yš gnb zy štr by* Aḥiq 125: a thief (or: a man who is stealing) who has broken into a house (cf. also Cowl p. 224, 240, Lindenberger APA 114f.).

štr$_2$ v. *šyt$_1$*.

štr$_3$ v. *štr$_1$*.

štt **OffAr** Segal ATNS a.l.: the *yšttw* in ATNS 52b ii 10 prob. = PA'EL Impf. 3 p.pl.m. of *štt* (= to flow); uncert. interpret., diff. and dam. context.

T

t_1 v. *'yt_3*, *šqlh*, *št'$_1$*.
t_2 v. *mwt_1*.
t_3 v. *tmr_2*.
t_4 as abbrev. of *tr(w)mh* (= heave-offering, contribution for the sanctuary) on wine and oil amphoras from Masada, cf. Yadin IEJ xv 111f.
t'h v. *š'h_2*.
t'wh v. *'wy_2*.
t'wm **Hebr** Plur. abs. *t'wmym* SM 45^3 (= Frey 1162), 70^3 - ¶ subst. Plur. twins; indicating sign of the Zodiac *Gemini*: SM 45^3, 70^3.
v. *twm_1*.
t'wn **JAr** Dupont-Sommer Waw p. 12: the *t'wn* in AMB $6^{1,11}$ < Greek θεόν (cf. also Gordon Or xxii 416), *br t'wn* AMB $6^{1,11}$: = son of God (cf. however Naveh & Shaked AMB a.l., Puech RB xcv 586: = name of divine being).
t'kl cf. Frah xix 11 (*t'ykl'*), cf. Nyberg FP 50, 91 (cf. also Nyberg with Ebeling Frah a.l.) :: Ebeling Frah a.l.: l. *t'gwl'*, to be related to Akkad. *takultu*.
t'n **Amm** Sing. abs. *t'n* AUSS xiv $145^{1,2}$ - ¶ subst. coll. meaning, figs: AUSS xiv $145^{1,2}$.
t'nh **Hebr** Plur. abs. *t'nym* DJD ii 30^{18} - **OffAr** Plur. abs. *t'nn* PF 2024^2 - **JAr** Plur. emph. *t'ny'* MPAT 52^6 - ¶ subst. - **1)** fig: PF 2024^2 - **2)** fig-tree: MPAT 52^6; *ht'nym hzytym h'ṣ ...* DJD ii 30^{18}: the fig-trees, the olive-trees, the trees which ...; for this word, cf. Borowski AIAI 114ff.
t'r **Ph** Sing. abs. *t'r* KAI 14^{12} - **Pun** Sing. + suff. 3 p.pl.m. *t'rm* KAI 120^3, 121^2 (for the reading in both instances, cf. Février BAr '51/52, 77 :: Levi Della Vida AfrIt vi 104, 108f., Röllig KAI a.l.: pro *bt'rm* l. *bn* (= Sing. cstr. of *bn_1*) *'rm* (= n.p.)), 138^5 - ¶ subst. - **1)** in the expression *bt'rm btm* KAI 121^2, 138^5, *bt'rm* prob. = according to their plan, for *btm*, v. *tm_1* (for this interpret., cf. Février BAr '51/52, 77, Sem ii 26, RA l 188, cf. also Levi Della Vida AttiTor lxx 191 n. 2; cf. KAI 120^3 (*bt'rm*[) - **2)** in KAI $14^{11f.}$, *'l ykn lm šrš lmṭ wpr lm'l wt'r bḥym tḥt šmš*, that they have not roots below nor branches above, nor a *t'r* among the living under the sun; Février RA l. 188, Avishur PIB 195: *t'r* = renown, imposing presence (cf. also Röllig KAI a.l., Gibson SSI iii p. 111 :: CIS i sub 3, Cooke NSI p. 36, Harr 154: *t'r* = form, comeliness (cf. also Greenfield FS Albright ii 265) - the *t'rm* in KAI 119^7 poss. = the same word Sing. + suff. 3 p.pl.m., *w't 'btm w't t'rm* KAI 119^7: of diff. interpret., poss. = their fathers and their dignity (cf. Février RA l 188f.; cf. also Röllig KAI a.l.) × Levi Della Vida RCL '55, 560f.: = the houses and their outline; cf. also Amadasi IPT 81f. - cf.

t᾽rh.

t᾽rh **Pun** Sing. abs. *t᾽rt* CIS i 6000bis 6 (= TPC 84; or cstr.?, v. infra) - ¶ subst. plan, design: CIS i 6000bis 6 (diff. and dam. context, cf. also Bonnet SEL vii 113; the word following *wt᾽rt* prob. to be read *wt᾽rt* (dittography erased by stone mason) :: Lidzbarski Eph i 166, 169: l. poss. *[tp᾽r]t* (= Sing. abs. of *tp᾽rh* (= glory, splendour)) :: Ferron StudMagr i 75, 77: l. *k[t]bt* = QAL Pf. 1 p.s. of *ktb_1* :: Février sub CIS i 6000bis: l. *w[š]ṭrt* = QAL Pf. 1 p.s. of *$šṭr_1$* (cf. also Bonnet SEL vii 114)) - cf. *t᾽r*.

tb (< Egypt., cf. Grelot RB lxxviii 519, DAE p. 235 n. t) - **OffAr** Sing. abs. *t[b]* Krael 7[17] (for this restoration, cf. Grelot RB lxxviii 519, Porten & Greenfield JEAS p. 54 (uncert. interpret., cf. also Grelot RB lxxviii 519f.: or l. *tm* < Egypt. = Sing. abs. of *tm_2* (= mat. of rush or straw) or l. *tn* < Egypt. = Sing. abs. of *tn_1* (= basket)) :: Krael a.l.: l. *t[wy]* (= variant of *$šwy_5$*) or *t[b᾽]* (= variant of *tbh* (= box)), cf. also Porten Arch 94 n. 165: l. *t[wy]* - ¶ subst. m. basket; Grelot DAE p. 235 n. x: l. poss. also *tb* (Sing. abs.) in Krael 7[19] (for the reading of *t*, cf. Krael p. 206, 214, cf. also Porten Arch 94: l. *t[wy]* = Sing. abs. of *twy*, cf. however Porten & Greenfield JEAS p. 54: l. *q[wp]* = Sing. abs. of *qwp_1*, and cf. Porten & Yardeni sub TADAE B 3.8: l. *qp* (= chest?).

tb᾽ v. *tb*.

tb᾽h **Ph** Honeyman JEA xxvi 57, 63: l. *tb᾽t* in KAI 43[10] (= Sing. cstr. of *tb᾽h* (= coming)), uncert. interpret., cf. Gibson SSI iii p. 139, cf. however Lipiński RTAT 251 n. 30 (div. otherwise): l. *šbt* (= QAL Pf. 1 p.s. of *šwb*) *b᾽t* (= QAL Pf. 1 p.s. of *bw᾽*) :: Clermont-Ganneau Et ii 164, Chabot sub RES 1211 (div. otherwise): *b᾽t* = Sing. cstr. of *b᾽h* (= produce) :: v.d.Branden OA iii 248, 256f.: pro *šbt b᾽t* l. *zbḥt* (= QAL Pf. 1 p.s. of *$zbḥ_1$*) + *hḥy[t]* (= *h_1* + Sing. abs. of *$ḥyh_2$*).

tbb v. *$bʿy_1$*.

tbh v. *tb*.

tby v. *byk*.

tbk Ebeling Frah a.l.: l. *tb/twb* (pro *tp*; = letter) + Iran. phonetic complement *-k* in Frah xv 3 (less prob. interpret., cf. Nyberg FP 47, 85: l. Iran. word).

tbl_1 **Pun** Levi Della Vida OA ii 88, 92: pro *mbula* in PBSR xxviii 53 text 5[10f.] (= Vattioni Aug xvi 550) l. *tabula* (< Lat.) = tablet; *ys felu tabula* = who made the tablet (// *hanct[ ]ulam instituerunt* ibid. l. 6f.); poss. interpret.

tbl_2 **OffAr** Sing. emph. *tbl᾽* Cowl 26[4] (*[t]bl᾽*)[,8], AJSL lviii 303B 5 (= AG 15) - ¶ subst. prob. = dry riverbank (cf. Grelot Sem xx 26, DAE p. 286 (n. f; cf. also Porten & Yardeni sub TADAE A 6.2), cf. already Aimé-Giron AG p. 33, R.A.Bowman AJSL lviii 308 :: Cowl a.l.: = *tbl_3* (= rope, measuring line), *ʿl tbl᾽* = according to measure,

accurately (cf. already Perles OLZ '11, 498; cf. also Epstein ZAW xxxiii 141, Sprengling AJT xxi 428: *‹l tbl›* = by a rope).
v. *šbl*.
tbl$_3$ v. *tbl$_2$*.
tbn$_1$ **OffAr** Sing. abs. *tbn* ATNS 23b 1 (:: Segal ATNS a.l.: perhaps = Sing. abs. of *tbn$_2$* (= certain weight); < Egypt., Aḥiq 112, Lesh xxxvii 270[1]; cf. Frah iv 6 - **Palm** Sing. emph. *tbn›* CIS ii 3913 ii 59 (Greek par. ἀχύρων) - ¶ subst. straw.
v. *lbnh$_1$*, *tbnh$_2$*, *tnb*.
tbn$_2$ v. *tbn$_1$*.
tbnh$_1$ v. *tnb*.
tbnh$_2$ **Pun** Roschinski Num 112, 115: l. *tbnm* (= Plur. abs. of *tbnh$_2$* (= building) in KAI 161[5] (prob. interpret.)) :: Février RA xlv 144: l. *trnm* = Plur. abs. of *trn$_1$* (= mast), cf. Röllig KAI a.l., cf. also v.d.Branden RSF ii 144f., 147: *trn* = wooden peristyle - Roschinski Num 112, 115: l. *tbnm* (= Plur. abs. of *tbnh$_2$*) in KAI 161[7], poss. reading, diff. context :: Röllig KAI a.l. (div. otherwise): l. *znm* = Plur. abs. of *zn$_1$* :: Février RA xlv 145: *znm* = Plur. abs. of *zn$_2$* (= perfume), cf. also Watson Bibl liii 194 :: v.d.Branden RSF ii 144f., 146: l. *znm* = Plur. abs. of *zn$_3$* (= decoration) - Roschinski Num 112: the *tbnm* in KAI 161[10] = Plur. abs. of *tbnh$_2$* (poss. interpret., diff. and dam. context) :: Février RA xlv 147: = Plur. abs. of *tbn$_1$*.
tb‹ cf. Paik 982: to ask.
tbr v. *šbr$_1$*, *tnrw*.
tbrh$_1$ **Pun** Sing. (or Plur.) abs. *tbrt* KAI 74[2,3] - ¶ subst. exact meaning unknown, indicating part of victim; Cooke NSI p. 124: = cuttings?; Février CB viii 42: = edible parts (sc. of the victim), cf. CIS i sub 167: the part of the victim which is not put on the altar :: Dussaud Orig 150f.: = horns (for discussion of the problem, cf. Capuzzi StudMagr ii 65f.).
v. *t‹br*.
tbrh$_2$ **Nab** unexplained word in RES 1449[2]; family name??
tbrḥ v. *brḥ$_1$*.
tbrk v. *brk$_1$*.
tg$_1$ (< Iran., cf. Caquot RTP p. 150) - **Palm** Sing. emph. *tg›* RTP 111, 112, Syr xxxvi 104 no. 2 - ¶ subst. crown; *tg› dy bl* RTP 111, 112, Syr xxxvi 104 no. 2: crown of Bel (on this comb., cf. du Mesnil du Buisson TMP 65, Milik DFD 150).
tg$_2$ v. *šlš$_1$*.
tgm (< Greek τάγμα) - **Palm** Sing. emph. *tgm›* CIS ii 3945[3] (cf. Greek par. συντέ[λεια]) - ¶ subst. m. corporation; *tgm› dy qyny› ‹bd› dhb› wksp›* CIS ii 3945[3f]: the corporation of the gold- and silversmiths.
tgr$_1$ (< Akkad., cf. Zimmern Fremdw 16, Kaufman AIA 107, Widen-

gren HDS 225f.) - **OffAr** Sing. abs. *tgr* BSh 47[1], 48[2] - **Palm** Plur. emph. *tgry*ʾ CIS ii 3960[6], Inv x 29[3], 44[6], 114[3], 127[3], Inscr P 7[3] (*tgry[*ʾ*]*), 9[6], 34[5], Syr xii 122[2] (*t[g]ry*ʾ), DFD 13[5] (diff. reading), *tgr*ʾ CIS ii 3913 i 7 (Greek par. ἐμπόρων), ii 115 (or = Sing.?), 3933[3] - **Hatra** Plur. emph. *tgry*ʾ 65[5] (for this interpret., cf. Aggoula MUSJ xlvii 29f., Vattioni IH a.l. :: Safar Sumer xi 8f. (div. otherwise): l. *gdy*ʾ (= Sing. emph. of *gdy*$_3$), v. also *yqr*$_2$) - ¶ subst. m. merchant; for CIS ii 3913 ii 115, v. *ḥšbn*$_1$; the same word (Sing. emph. *tgr*ʾ) also in CIS ii 2084[3] (**Nab**.)?, cf. Nöldeke with Euting Sin Inschrift sub 208 (cf. however CIS ii a.l.: l. *tḥ*ʾ = indication of function??)- cf. *tgrw*.

tgr$_2$ **Hebr** Sing. abs. *tgr* DJD ii 30[25] - **JAr** Sing. abs. *tgr* MPAT 45[5], 46[3] (*[t]gr*), IEJ xxxvi 206[7] (*tg[r]*) - ¶ subst. claim.

tgrw **Palm** Sing. emph. *tgrt*ʾ CIS ii 3913 ii 124 - ¶ subst. trade, business; *bdyldy* ʾ*yt bhwn tgrt*ʾ CIS ii 3913 ii 124: because there is trade through them (i.e. they are an article of merchandise); cf. *tgr*$_1$.

tdḥ v. *trḥ*$_2$.

tdyr **JAr** Plur. f. abs. *tdyrn* MPAT-A 26[7] (= SM 32) - ¶ adj. regular, constant; *myṣwtwn tdyrn bkl* ʾ*tr* MPAT-A 26[7]: their acts of charity are constant everywhere.

tdmr **Nab** word of highly uncert. reading and unknown meaning in RES 1421; = family name?

tdq v. *trq*.

th (< Arab.) - **Nab** Cantineau Nab i 60: l. *th* pro *dnh* in J 17[1]?? (= demonstrative pronoun; for this poss. reading, cf. also Jaussen & Savignac J a.l.), cf. also Diem Or l. 354 n. 50, O'Connor JNES xlv 222f.

thgy v. *hgy*$_1$.

thl v. *hll*.

thlk v. *hlk*$_2$.

thm **OffAr** subst. (?) s.m. abs. (*thm*), word of diff. reading and uncert. meaning in RES 1300[6]; prob. indicating an object; Grelot DAE p. 143 n. c: = amphora (< Egypt. *thm* = recipient for liquids), poss. interpret.

tw$_1$ **Pun** Sing. abs. *tw* KAI 277[6] (v. infra) - ¶ subst. cella, shrine; *wbn tw* KAI 277[5f.]: and he has built (= Qal Pf. 3 p.s.m. of *bny*$_1$) the shrine (cf. Friedrich FS Altheim i 207f., Röllig WO v 109f., 114, KAI a.l., Lipiński RencAss xvii 35 n. 2, RTAT 261, Garbini AION xxiii 275, FSR 213f., RSF xvii 182, 187, Delcor RSF ii 64 (for this division of words, cf. Altheim & Stiehl AAW iv 225f., Anatolica i 88f. :: idem ibid. *tw* = Piʿel Pf. 3 p.s.m. of *twy*$_1$ (= to give a sign, to determine) :: Roschinski TUAT ii 604: *tw* = Sing. abs. of *tw*$_2$ (= sign, in the context indicating the sanctuary)) × Garbini OA iv 41, AION xviii 243, 246 (div. otherwise): l. *bntw* = Qal Pf. 1 p.s. of *bny*$_1$ + suff. 3 p.s.m. (cf. Nober VD xliii 204, Fitzmyer JAOS lxxxvi 287, 292, Février JA cclvi 4f., 7); for both interpret., cf. Gibson SSI iii p. 154, 156f. :: Ferron Mus lxxxi 524, 528, 534: *bntw* = prep. *bnt* + suff. 3 p.s.m. :: Fischer & Rix GGA '68 68f.: = *b$_2$* + *ntw* (without interpret.) :: Garbini ArchClass xvi 70f., 74, Dupont-Sommer JA cclii 291ff., CRAI '65, 15: l. *bmtw* = Sing. + suff. 3 p.s.m. of *bmh* (cf. Moscati RSO xxxix 260, Février CRAI '65, 10f., OA iv 176, Ferron OA iv 182, 184, 186ff., 193, Delcor Mus lxxxi 242, 246); on the problem, cf. also Pfiffig OA v 207ff., Silverman JAOS xciv 272, Amadasi ICO p. 165).

tw$_2$ v. *tw$_1$*.

twb$_1$ v. *yšb$_1$*, *šwb*.

twb$_2$ v. *twb$_5$*.

twb$_3$ v. *twp*.

twb$_4$ v. *twb$_5$*.

twb$_5$ **OffAr** *twb* Cowl 1[7], 9[12], FuF xxxv 173[10] (diff. context; cf. also Altheim & Stiehl ASA 277), *twb*ʾ Driv 12[11] (on this form, cf. Driv p. 84), Aḥiq 44 (?, dam. context, cf. already Baneth OLZ '14, 252 :: Cowl p. 231: = Sing. emph. of *twb$_2$* (= recompense, cf. also Grelot DAE p. 449) :: Epstein ZAW xxxii 133: = Sing. emph. of *twb$_4$* (= saliva); cf. also Leand 43p; cf. Frah xxix 2 (cf. Nyberg FP 57, 108), xxx 29 (cf. Nyberg FP 58, 110) :: Ebeling Frah a.l.: l. in both instances *tny* (= *tny$_4$* = *šny$_5$*), xxx 42:2, GIPP 35, 65, SaSt 24, cf. also Nisa-b 1693[4]?? (*tw/yb*), cf. Diakonov & Livshitz PaSb ii 136 n. 4 - **Palm** *twb* Ber ii 86[8], iii 99[4] (dam. context) - **Hatra** *twb* app. 4[7] (cf. e.g. Caquot Syr xl 13, Vattioni IH a.l. :: Safar Sumer xvii 39f. (n. 96): = part of n.p.) - ¶ adv. (Leand 61i, Driv p. 84: orig. = Qal Imper. of *twb$_1$* (uncert. interpret.)) - **1)** again; *kn kzy [ms]pt qbylh twb*ʾ *l*ʾ *yšlḥ* Driv 12[11]: so that M. will not again send a complaint - **2)** moreover, also, *wtwb plg*ʾ *hw bnyk mn mbtḥyh hmw šlyṭn bh* ʾ*ḥryk* Cowl 9[2f.]: and also as to that part, your children by M. have power over it after you; *ywlys* ʾ*wrlys ... rḥq lywlys* ʾ*wrlys ... sṭr*ʾ *mqbl*ʾ *dy* ʾ*ksdr*ʾ *... ymny*ʾ *... qdmy wtwb rḥq lh sṭr*ʾ *mdnḥy*ʾ Ber ii 86[1ff.]: J.A. has ceded to J.A. the wall facing (the entrance) of the exedra at the right side in the first place and moreover he has ceded to him the eastern wall; cf. Hatra app. 4[7] - **3)** still, *wmnt*ʾ *zylky twb* Cowl 1[7]: and the share will still be yours (cf. Joüon MUSJ xviii 29, Skaist AAALT 31ff. :: Yaron Bibl xli 270f., Law 88: *twb* = again (cf. also Grelot DAE p. 77, Porten & Greenfield JEAS p. 106) :: Cowl a.l.: connect *twb* with the foll. *šhdy*ʾ = and the witnesses are ... - the same word also in RES 528[1], 529[1]?? (dam. context, diff. interpret.).

twb$_6$ v. *tbk*.

twbʾ v. *twb$_5$*.

twd v. *yrd*.

twhy **JAr** Beyer ATTM 372: l. *twhyh* (Sing. f. abs. of *twhy* (= terrible)) in AMB 7[11] (improb. reading and interpret., cf. Naveh & Shaked AMB a.l. (div. otherwise): l. *YHWH* (= n.d.)).

twḥyt **Palm** Sing. cstr. *twḥyt* Inv i 2^1 (for this reading, cf. Cantineau Inv i a.l., Dunant sub SBS 44B, Milik DFD 11 :: Chabot sub CIS ii 3959: l. *ywṣyt* = (edict) ?), Inv x 44^1, DFD 37^1 - ¶ subst. decision; *btwḥyt bwlʾ wdms* Inv x 44^1: by decision of the Senate and the People (cf. Greek par. προστάγματι ...); cf. *mn twḥyt bwlʾ wdmws* Inv i 2^1: by decision of the Senate and the People (cf. DFD 37^1); for the etymology of this word, cf. Cantineau Gramm 112, 151, 161: < root *wḥy* (cf. Arab.) semantically comparable to root *ḥwy*$_1$ in Aramaic (cf. also Rosenthal Sprache 65 n. 4) :: Joüon Or ii 118: semantic comparability of both roots mistaken; cf. also *yḥʾ*.

twy$_1$ v. *tw*$_1$.

twy$_2$ **OldAr** Sing. abs. *twy* KAI 222A 28 - ¶ subst. indicating crop-consuming insect (prob. winged), for this interpret., cf. Tawil BASOR ccxxv 59f., cf. already Weinfeld Bibl xlvi 424 n. 2, DDS 124 n. 2, cf. also Lemaire & Durand IAS 133 :: Fitzmyer AIS 46: = some sort of blight (cf. also Rosenthal ANET 660, Gibson SSI ii p. 31, 39) :: Ben-Chayyim Lesh xxxv 245f.: = desert, wilderness :: Lipiński Stud 28f.: = complaint :: Koopmans BiOr xvii 52: = wild sheep/ox :: Greenfield ActOr xxix 13 n. 40, Lesh xxxii 363 n. 25, JBL lxxxvii 241: = lapsus for *thwy* (= QAL Impf. 3 p.s.f. of *hwy*$_1$); for the problems involved, cf. also Dupont-Sommer Sf p. 44, Donner KAI a.l.

twy$_3$ v. *tb*.

twyn v. *mnrtwyn*.

twk v. *rtm*$_1$.

twlʿ **OffAr** Sing. abs. *twlʿ* Driv 13^3 - ¶ subst. red/purple colour; *gldy twlʿ 2* Driv 13^3: two red/purple-coloured skins; on the word, cf. Driv p. 86 - cf. *tlʿ*.

twlʿh **OldAr** Sing. abs. *twlʿh* KAI 222A 27 - ¶ subst. f. worm (devouring the vegetation); *wšbʿ šnn tʾkl twlʿh* KAI 222A 27: and seven years the worm (coll.) will devour; for this word, cf. Borowski AIAI 156.

twlt v. *tlt*$_1$.

twm$_1$ **Pun** Garbini AION xxv 262ff.: l. *štwmm* in Karth x 133^2 (= *š*$_{10}$+ Sing. + suff. 3 p.s.m. of *twm*$_1$ (= twin), cf. *tʾwm* (highly uncert. interpret.) :: Février Karth x a.l.: l. *škʾm* = Sing. abs. of *škm*$_2$ (= burial vault); cf. Fantar Sem xxv 71ff. (div. otherwise): l. *nymmʾ* = n.p.

twm$_2$ v. *šm*$_2$.

twmnyʾ v. *šmn*$_4$.

twn **OffAr** Sing. emph. (or + suff. 3 p.s.m.?) *twnh* Krael $4^{3,6}$; Plur. + suff. 2 p.pl.m. *twnykm* Cowl 21^9 - **Nab** Plur. emph. *twnyʾ* MPAT 64 iii 5 - **Palm** Sing. emph. *twnʾ* Inscr P 31^6 (or = Plur. emph.??; v. infra), Syr xlviii 413^9 (heavily dam. context; or = Plur. emph.??, v. infra) -

JAr Sing. emph. *twnh* IEJ xxxvi 206[2] (dam. context, diff. reading) - ¶ subst. room, chamber; in Inscr P 31[6], Syr xlviii 413[9] poss. = the inner room, cella (cf. Cantineau Inscr P a.l., Ingholt Ber iii 90, du Mesnil du Buisson RES '41/45, 79f., Gawlikowski Syr xlviii 419, TP 79 (cf. Aggoula Sem xxxii 14, cf. also Milik DFD 272ff.: = Plur. emph. (= *naoi*)), cf. however Février Rel 170: = Plur. emph., the rooms) - the same word (Sing./Plur. emph. *twn'*) prob. also in Ber iii 88[3] (for the interpret. as Sing., cf. Ingholt Ber iii a.l., Gawlikowski TP 79; for the interpret. as Plur., cf. Milik DFD 274; for the context, v. also dkh_1) - Starcky RB lxi 179: the *tny* in MPAT 64 iv 1 = Plur. cstr., cf. also Fitzmyer & Harrington MPAT a.l. (less prob. interpret., heavily dam. context).

twp Ebeling Frah a.l.: l. *twp'* in Frah xv 12: = garment (*p* pro *b*, cf. Ar. *tōtāḇā*, Arab. *ṯawb* (highly uncert. interpret., cf. Nyberg FP 48, 85: l. Iran. word)).

twpḥ cf. Frah iv 19: = apple; Ebeling Frah a.l.: influenced by Arab. (less prob. interpret.).

twpr **Palm** Sing. emph. *twpr'* CIS ii 4172[2], 4173[2], 4174[6], RB xxxix 526B 3 - ¶ subst. of unknown meaning, prob. indicating part of tomb construction (for a discussion, cf. Chabot sub CIS ii 4172).

twqp **Hebr** Sing. + suff. 3 p.s.m. *twqpw* AMB 4[33] - ¶ subst. vigour, strength.

$\mathbf{twr_1}$ v. ytr_1.

$\mathbf{twr_2}$ v. $šwr_4$, *twrh*, *tnb*.

$\mathbf{twr_3}$ v. *yrd*.

twrh **OffAr** the *twrh* in Cowl 82[10] word of diff. interpret. Cowl a.l.: poss. = Sing. + suff. 3 p.s.f. of twr_2 (= $šwr_4$ (= ox)), less prob. interpret. :: Cowl a.l.: or = *Torah*.

twrms (< Greek θέρμος, cf. Löw AP 394f.) - **Hebr** Plur. abs. *twrmsyn* SM 49[3] - ¶ subst. m. lupine; *htwrmsyn hybyšyn* SM 49[3f.]: the dried lupines.

twt **OffAr** Sing. abs. *twt* PF 215 - ¶ subst. mulberry (on the etymology of this word, cf. Hinz NWAP 84, AISN 238f.).

twtb **OffAr** Sing. abs. *twtb* Aḥiq 112 - ¶ subst. sojourner (cf. Lindenberger APA 99, 246 n. 280).

tzgbs **OffAr** Word of uncert. reading and interpret. in Pers 1[3] (cf. R.A.Bowman Pers p. 68, 73).

tḥ' v. tgr_1.

tḥwm v. *tḥm*.

tḥwt v. *tḥyt*, *tḥt*.

tḥyt (< Egypt., cf. Couroyer RB lxi 252, Kutscher JAOS lxxiv 237, Grelot DAE p. 231 n. p) - **OffAr** Sing. abs. *tḥyt* Krael 6[10] (for this reading, cf. Milik RB lxi 250, Grelot DAE p. 231 (n. p), Porten &

Greenfield JEAS p. 50, Szubin & Porten BASOR cclxix 39, Porten & Yardeni sub TADAE B 3.7 :: Krael a.l.: l. *tḥwt* (= variant of *tḥt*), 6[13], 9[4,13,15] - ¶ subst. porch; *plg trbṣ› hw plg tḥyt mṣryt* Krael 9[4]: half of the court, that is half of the *tḥyt* in Egyptian (v. also *mṣryt*); cf. also Porten Arch 95 n. 173, 98 n. 185 (explication of *tḥyt* as "court" less prob., cf. Erichsen Demotisches Glossar p. 377 s.v. *ḫyt*).

tḥm **Hebr** Sing. cstr. *tḥm* Frey 1183 (cf. RES 386), *tḥwm* SM 49[9,10,11,27]; Plur. abs. *tḥwmym* DJD ii 30[3]; cstr. *tḥwmy* SM 49[13], DJD ii 30[16]; + suff. 3 p.s.m. *tḥwmw* DJD ii 22[12], 30[18] - **OffAr** Sing. abs. *tḥm* Sem xxiii 95 recto 5 (cf. Bordreuil Sem xxiii 100, 102, Fales AION xxvi 542, 545, 547, idem sub AECT 58, Lipiński ActAntHung xxii 377, WGAV 377, Kaufman JAOS cix 100 :: Kaufman Conn xix 120, 122: l. *lḥm* = Sing. abs. of *lḥm*$_4$; for this reading cf. also Teixidor Syr lvi 391: or = Sing. abs. of *lḥm*$_5$ (= threat??)); cstr. *tḥwm* KAI 259[1], 278[1]; emph. *tḥwm›* KAI 278[6]; Plur. cstr. *tḥmy* Krael 3[7], *tḥwmy* Cowl 6[7], 13[13], Krael 4[8], 9[8], 12[9]; + suff. 3 p.s.m. *tḥmwhy* Krael 3[17], *tḥwmwhy* Cowl 8[5], 25[4,8], 66 xiii (*tḥwmwh[y]*; dam. context), Krael 4[12], 9[12], 10[3,7,11,14,16] (for *scriptio anterior* cf. Porten & Szubin JAOS cvii 231), 12[17,22], ATNS 49[3], *tḥ[w]m[w]h* Krael 6[9] (dam. context) - **Nab** Plur. abs. *tḥwmyn* MPAT 64 iii 6; + suff. 3 p.s.f. *tḥwmyh* MPAT 64 i 2 - **Palm** Plur. cstr. *tḥwmy* DFD 37[3]; emph. *tḥwm›* CIS ii 3913 ii 111 (Greek par. των ὅρων), 119, 145; + suff. 3 p.s.f. *tḥwmyh* CIS ii 3913 ii 3, 64, 81 (*tḥ[wm]yh*) - **JAr** Sing. + suff. 3 p.s.m. *tḥwmh* MPAT 52[5]; Plur. cstr. *tḥmy* IEJ xxxvi 206[4], *tḥwmy* MPAT 52[3], *tḥwm›* MPAT 51[8] (:: Fitzmyer & Harrington MPAT a.l.: = Sing. emph.) - ¶ subst. border, boundary, territory within boundary (often difficult to distinguish); *h› tḥwmy ›rq› zk ... byty lmw‹ šmš mnh wbyt qwnyh ... lm‹rb šmš lh* Cowl 6[7ff.]: these are the limits of this terrain ... my house is to the east of it and the house of Q. ... to the west of it (cf. Cowl 13[13ff.], Krael 4[8ff.], MPAT 51[8f.], 52[3f.], IEJ xxxvi 206[4]); *znh tḥwm krbyl wkršy qryt›* KAI 278[1f.]: this is the territory of K. and K. the cities ... (cf. Garbini RSO xl 137), the translation "this is the boundary of ..." less correct (for this transl., cf. e.g. Dupont-Sommer CRAI '61, 19, DHC 11f., Gibson SSI ii p. 156); for the context of *tḥwm›* in KAI 278[6], v. *ḥgy*; *‹d tnh tḥwm* ... KAI 259[1]: to here (extends) the territory of ... (cf. e.g. Donner KAI a.l.; the translation "the boundary of ..." less correct (for this transl., cf. e.g. Torrey ZA xxvi 91, Driver AnOr xii 50, Hanson BASOR cxcii 11, Gibson SSI ii p. 154)); *yhw› mt[›‹]l br mn tḥwm› ›w m›pq* CIS ii 3913 ii 111: it shall be imported from without the borders or exported (cf. CIS ii 3913 ii 119, 145); *‹lymy› dy mt›‹lyn ltdmr ›w ltḥwmyh* CIS ii 3913 ii 2f.: the slaves who are imported into Tadmor or its borders (i.e. its territory; cf. CIS ii 3913 ii 64, 80f.); *‹bd šlm› btḥwmy mdyt›* DFD 37[3]: he established peace within the boundaries (i.e. in the territory) of the town; *tḥm gzr* Frey 1183: the boundary of G./the territory of G. (on this inscription, cf. Reich EI xviii 167ff., IEJ xl 44ff., Rosenfeld IEJ xxxviii 235ff., Schwartz IEJ xl 47ff.; cf. SM 49[9,10,11,27]; cf. also *tḥwmy ʾrṣ yšrʾl* SM 49[13]); *ʾtrʾ dk btḥwmh wbmṣrh* MPAT 52[5f.]: this place within its boundary and its border - Zimmern Fremdw 9: < Akkad. (improb. interpret., cf. Kaufman AIA 105f. (cf. also Koopmans 160); v.Soden JSS xxii 83: < Iran.?).

tḥn v. *ḥnn₁*.

tḥnh v. *ḥnh₁*.

tḥnyt v. *nwḥ₁*.

tḥt **Ph** Sing. cstr. *tḥt* KAI 2[3] (cf. e.g. Dussaud Syr v 143, Röllig KAI a.l., Gibson SSI iii p. 17 :: Dahood UHP 40: = QAL Impf. 2 p.s.m. of *ḥtt₁* = to smash, cf. Dahood Bibl xlv 410), 13[7], 14[12], 18[7], 26A i 16, EpAn ix 5[4,5]; + suff. 1 p.s. *tḥtn* KAI 24[14]; + suff. 3 p.pl. *tḥtnm* KAI 14[9] - **Pun** Sing. cstr. *tḥt* KAI 152[2], NP 66[4] (= Punica iv A 6), Punica iv A 8[4], *tʾḥt* KAI 118[2], *tʿt* Punica iv A 7[4], KAI 145[8] (cf. e.g. Février Sem vi 20, 26, Röllig KAI a.l.; context however diff., cf. also Cooke NSI p. 155 (div. otherwise): l. *štʿt* = Plur. abs. of *šth* (= pillar) :: v.d.Branden RSF i 166, 169f. (div. otherwise): l. *[ʾ]štʿt* = Plur. cstr. of *ʾšt₁* (= incense-burner in pillar form) :: Krahmalkov RSF iii 187, 189, 194, 204 (div. otherwise): l. *[n]štʿt* = NIPH Part. s.f. abs. of *štʿ₁* :: Berger MAIBL xxxvi/2, 161: = n.d. (cf. also Halévy RS ix 280, 285)), 145[2] (for this interpret., cf. e.g. Röllig KAI a.l. (cf. also Sznycer Sem xxii 41), cf. however e.g. Cooke NSI p. 153 (div. otherwise): l. *štʿt* = Plur. abs. of *šth* (= pillar), v d Branden RSF i 166f. (div. otherwise): l. *štʿt* = Plur. cstr. of *šth* (= pillar; cf. also Sznycer Sem xxii 41) :: Krahmalkov RSF ii 187 (div. otherwise): l. *štʿtʾ* = Plur. + suff. 3 p.s.m. of *šth* (= pillar; cf. also Clermont-Ganneau RAO iii 327 (:: id. ibid. *štʿt* = representation of Greek στοά)) :: Lidzbarski Eph i 48: *tʿt* = n.d. different from Egypt. god Thot (cf. also Halévy RS ix 270f.) :: Berger MAIBL xxxvi/2, 150ff.: *tʿt* = n.d. (Thot)) - **Hebr** Sing. abs. *tḥt* IEJ xxxii 195[1] (heavily dam. context) - **DA** Sing. cstr. *tḥt* ii 11 (cf. e.g. Hoftijzer DA a.l., Rofé SB 68, Garbini Hen i 186, Levine JAOS ci 200, 202, H.P.Müller ZAW xciv 219, 234, cf. however Hoftijzer DA a.l.: or = HAPH/APH Impf. 3 p.s.f. of *ḥtt₁*? :: Puech RB lxxxv 116 (div. otherwise): l. poss. *[y]štḥt* = ITP Impf. 3 p.s.m. of *šḥt₁*; diff. and dam. context) - **OldAr** Sing. + suff. 3 p.s.m. *tḥth* KAI 222A 6 (cf. e.g. Dupont-Sommer Sf p. 151, Donner KAI a.l., Gibson SSI ii p. 35 :: Degen AAG p. 56: + suff. 3 p.s.f. :: Fitzmyer AIS 190: = Sing. m. + suff. 3 p.s.m. of *tḥty* (cf. also the remarks of Hartman CBQ xxx 258)); + suff. 2 p.pl.m. *tḥtk[m]* KAI 224[7] - **OffAr** Sing. abs. *tḥt* Krael 6[9], 9[4]; cstr. *tḥt* Cowl 26[12], Krael 2[13], 7[17,19], Sem ii 31 conv. 2, xiv 71 i 3, Or lvii 35[4,5], 39 ii 1 (*[t]ḥt*), FS Volterra vi 530 A 3, cf. Warka 3, 25, 33: *ti-ḫu-ú-tú* (cf. Garbini HDS

33f.) - **Nab** Sing. + suff. 3 p.s.m./f. *tḥth* ADAJ xxvi 366[3] (heavily dam. context) - **Palm** Sing. abs. *tḥt* CIS ii 3913 i 4; cstr. *tḥwt* Ber i 38[13], RB xxxix 526B 3, 548[4] - **JAr** Sing. cstr. *tḥt* AMB 7[11] (dam. context; v. *šbʿh*$_3$), *tḥwt* MPAT-A 22[7] (= SM 70[15]) - ¶ **1)** subst. what is lower, what is below; *šbw ltḥtk[m]* KAI 224[7]: stay where you are; *kl ʿly ʾrm wtḥth* KAI 222A 6: all of upper and lower Ar. (for the construction, cf. Degen AAG p. 88; v. also *ʿly*$_2$); cf. also the following expressions - a) *mn ltḥt, mdy ktyb mn ltḥt* CIS ii 3913 i 4: what is written below (Greek par. τὰ ὑποτεταγμένα) - b) *tḥt mn, wtḥt mnh byt prsʾ hw* Krael 9[4]: and beneath it (i.e. the staircase) is the *byt prsʾ* (v. *prs*$_3$; *wtḥt* later added above the line) - c) *mn tḥt* in dam. context in Krael 6[9]: *ktybn bsprʾ mn tḥt wm[nʿ]l* (or *m[nʿ]l[ʾ]?*, cf. Grelot DAE p. 230 n. n; :: Porten & Greenfield JEAS p. 48: pro *sprʾ* l. *sprʾ [znh]* (cf. also Szubin & Porten BASOR cclxix 30, 36, Porten & Yardeni sub TADAE B 3.7)): written in the document, (both) what is below and what is above (possibly referring to ground-floor and the upper storey of the house ceded (for this poss. interpret., cf. Grelot DAE p. 230 n. n), cf. also Szubin & Porten BASOR cclxix 36f., 41) :: Grelot DAE p. 230 n. n: habitual formula in the redaction of a contract, what is written here below and here above :: Grelot DAE p. 230 n. n: possibly = geographical indication - **2)** used as prep. - a) with local meaning, under; *krmm bšd zbl tḥt qrt* EpAn ix 5[4]: vineyards in the field of the Prince below the city (or: below Q.?), cf. EpAn ix 5[4f.]; *tʿt hbnt st qbrt* Punica ivA 7[4f.]: buried below this stone (cf. KAI 152[2f.], NP 66[4] (= Punica ivA 6), Punica ivA 8[4f.]; *aḫ-ḫi-te-e ti-ḫu-ú-tú li-iš-šá-ni-ʾ* Warka 3: I put it under my tongue (cf. Warka 25); *qbyr ... tḥwt ʿlʾ brt yrḥy* Ber i 38[9,13ff.]: he was buried below A. the daughter of Y. (cf. Ingholt Ber iii 126); cf. KAI 2 (*tḥt zn* = under this, cf. e.g. Röllig KAI a.l., Gibson SSI iii p. 17 :: Cecchini UF xiii 28f.: = this subterranean room (indicating sarcophagus)), 145[2] (v. however supra), Cowl 26[12] (diff. context), RB xxxix 526B 3 (diff. context); for Krael 7[17], v. *qwp*$_1$ (cf. prob. Krael 7[19]); for KAI 13[7f.], 14[12], MPAT-A 22[7], v. *šmym, šmš*$_2$; for KAI 18[6f.], 26A i 16f., v. *pʿm*$_2$ - b) with meaning, in the place of, instead of, in exchange for; *wmy bbny ʾš yšb tḥtn* KAI 24[13f.]: any of my sons who shall sit in my place (i.e. who shall reign in my place); *wʾl ykn lm bn wzrʿ tḥtnm* KAI 14[8f.]: and may they have no son nor seed in their place (i.e. to succeed them); *mwdyʾ lmlkw ... dy mqblʾ mnh ksp dnryn mʾh wʿsryn wtḥwt hln yhbt lh ...* RB xxxix 548[3f.]: she acknowledges to M. ... that she has received from him silver, 120 *denarii*, and in exchange of which she has given him ...; *mh zy hwšrt tḥt ḥmr* (v. *ḥmr*$_5$) ... *hwšrth* Sem ii 31 conv. 1ff.: what I sent, it is in exchange for wine that I sent it (for this interpret., cf. e.g. Grelot DAE p. 370 n. m); *rb tʾḥt rb mḥnt* KAI 118[2]: *proconsul* (v. *rb*$_2$) - c) preceded by prep. *mn*$_5$, with local meaning, from below; *na-šá-a-a-tú*

... *ḫa-la-ṭi-i-ni mi-in ti-ḫu-ú-tú [liš-šá-ni-e]* Warka 32f.: I have taken the mixtures (v. *ḥlṭ*$_2$) from under his tongue - d) preceded by prep. *mn*$_5$, with figurative meaning; *l› ›kl ›nṣl lplṭy mn tḥt lbbk* Krael 2[13f.]: I will not be able to take away P. from under your heart (v. *lbb*$_2$; i.e. from under your authority) - e) preceded by prep. *mn*$_5$, followed by prep. *l*$_5$: IEJ xxxii 195[1] - a form *tḥt* poss. also in RB xxxix 526B 3, context however heavily dam. - Lemaire & Durand IAS 117, 126: poss. l. a form of this word *tḥtyhm* (= Plur. + suff. 3 p.pl.m.) in KAI 223A 10 (highly uncert. reading) - Altheim & Stiehl FuF xxxv 173, 176: l. *lytḥty* in FuF xxxv 173[8]: = *ly* (= *l*$_5$) + Plur. cstr. of *tḥt*.
v. *tḥyt, tt›*.

tḥty **OffAr** Sing. m. abs. *tḥty* Krael 4[8], 9[13], 10[2], 12[12,13] - ¶ adj. which is below, only in the combination *by tḥty*: lower house, indication of one-storey-house on the roof of which a lighter building was possible (cf. Couroyer RB lxi 556f., cf. also Kutscher JAOS lxxiv 236, Yaron JNES xx 129, Porten Arch 98 n. 183); *mbny by tḥty* Krael 9[12f.], 10[2], 12[13]: the construction of a one-storey-building; prob. more than one building of this type could be erected within a house enclosure).

tḥtyh **OldAr** Sing. + suff. 3 p.s.m. *tḥtyth* KAI 222C 23 - **OffAr** Sing. abs. *tḥtyh* Cowl 6[10], 8[4,6], 25[5,6], Krael 3[8], 4[6,9], ATNS 52a 9 (for the problems of the context, cf. also Lemaire Syr lxi 341), 87[2] (*tḥty[h]*), 113[3], *tḥty›* Cowl 13[13], Krael 9[6,10], 10[6], 12[8,16,20]; emph. *tḥtyt›* Krael 6[11] (heavily dam. context; for the reading and the *scriptio anterior*, cf. Szubin & Porten BASOR cclxix 33), Driv 5[6], 7[1*] - ¶ subst. - **1)** which is below; *wyšmw tḥtyh [l‹]lyth* KAI 222C 23f.: may they make its lower part its upper part (said of a house that is to be overturned; cf. also Levine FS Morton Smith 53 n. 58) - **2)** in Elephantine papyri "lower end" indicating the South (cf. Krael p. 79f.; for the discussion, v *‹lyh*); cf. the following combinations - a) *btḥtyh* Cowl 25[6]: at the lower end (cf. ATNS 52a 9 (cf. also Lemaire Syr lxi 341)) - b) *tḥty› lh* Cowl 13[13]: at the lower end of it (cf. Cowl 25[5], Krael 4[9], 10[6], 12[20]) - c) *tḥty› mnh* Krael 9[10]: at the lower end of it - d) *ltḥtyh lh* Cowl 6[10]: at the lower end of it (cf. Cowl 8[6], Krael 3[8]) - e) *mn tḥtyh l‹lyh* Cowl 8[4]: from the lower end to the upper end (cf. Krael 9[6], 12[8]) - f) *mn ‹lyh ltḥtyh* Krael 12[16]: from the upper end to the lower end - g) *mn ‹lyh ‹d tḥtyh* Krael 4[6]: from the upper end to lower end - **3)** Löwer Egypt: Driv 5[6], 7[1*] (cf. also Levine FS Morton Smith 52) - the same word (Sing. abs. *tḥty›*) also in AG 5[5]?? (heavily dam. context).
v. *w*$_2$.

tḥtn **Hebr** Plur. abs. *tḥtnm* TA-H 25[2] - **OldAr** Sing. abs. *tḥtn* NESE ii 40 i - ¶ adj. lower; *[m]‹nym tḥtnm ... m‹lynm* TA-H 25[2f.]: from lower Anim ... from upper (sc. Anim); in NESE ii 40 i written on an object, that probably has to be placed in a lower position (cf. also Lemaire

Sem xxvi 66).

tyl› **Pun** word (?) of unknown meaning in Karth xii 50[2]; Février & Fantar Karth xii a.l., v d Branden RSF v 57, 59: = Sing. + suff. 3 p.s.m. of *tl* (= ruin) :: Krahmalkov RSF iii 178, 180, 204: = PI‘EL Pf. 3 p.s.m. of tly_1 + obj. (= to hang someone).

ṭṭlyl **Palm** Sing. emph. *ṭṭlyl›* CIS ii 3911[3], Inv xii 48[2], SBS 20[4]; + suff. 3 p.s.f. *ṭṭlylh* SBS 1a 1, 1b 1, 3[1], 7[1], 9 (*ṭṭly[lh]*), 43[5], Syr xii 130[2], DFD 162[4]; + suff. 3 p.pl. *ṭṭlylhwn* CIS ii 3955[6], 3983[1] (= SBS 13), SBS 17[2] (*ṭṭlylhw[n]*), 19[3], *ṭṭlylh[n]* CIS ii 3984[2] - ¶ subst. roofing (cf. Garbini OA xiv 176).

tyṭr (< Greek θέατρον) - **Nab** Sing. emph. *tyṭr›* CIS ii 163[2] (for this text, cf. RES 803, 804, 2023) - ¶ subst. f. (?, cf. dem. pronoun *d›*, cf. however Cantineau Nab i 58) theatre, in CIS ii 163 part of temple construction, cf. Starcky & Strugnell RB lxiii 243 :: Littmann PAAES iv 89, Negev IEJ xi 128f., xv 192f.: = portico.

tym v. mwt_1.

tymn **Palm** Sing. m. emph. *tymn›* Ber ii 93[2]; Plur. m. emph. *tymn›* Ber ii 107[2] - ¶ adj. (cf. Ingholt Ber ii 94) southern; the same word (Sing. f. abs. *tymnh*) prob. also in Aḥiq 134, cf. e.g. Cowl p. 242, Grelot DAE p. 442 :: Lindenberger APA 130f.: < root $›mn_1$, indication of a female religious functionary of some sort (cf. also idem ibid. 257 n. 402) :: Kottsieper SAS 45f., 207: < root ymn_1 (= to stay on the right side), *btwlh tymnh* = a young woman who stays on the right side > a betrothed young woman? - cf. *tymny*.

tymny **Palm** Sing. m. emph. *tymny›* CIS ii 4171[2], 4204[1], Ber v 95[7]; f. emph. *tymnyt›* CIS ii 4173[2]; Plur. m. abs. *tymnyyn* CIS ii 4174[3] - ¶ adj. southern; cf. *tymn*.

tyn **Pun** Sing. abs. *tyn* KAI 76B 5 - **OffAr**, cf. Frah iv 25 - ¶ subst. m. fig; in KAI 76B 5 prob. used with collective meaning.

typt (< Iran., cf. Benveniste JA ccxxv 185f., cf. also Schaed 263 n. 1, Eilers Beamtennamen 126, Henning BZAW ciii 143 n. 36, v. also infra) - **OffAr** Plur. emph. *typty›* Cowl 27[9] - ¶ subst. indicating a function, prob. = police officer connected with the court, for a discussion with litt., cf. Porten Arch 50 (n. 83), Hinz AISN 236.

tyq v. *ṭyq*.

tyr (< Akkad., cf. Zimmern Fremdw, Cantineau Gramm 153, Rosenthal Sprache 89, Kaufman AIA 106, v.Soden JSS xxii 83) - **Palm** Sing. m. emph. *tyr›* CIS ii 3981[4], 4028[3], 4038[2], 4041[2], RIP 119[2], Inv xi 20[2], 29[3] (:: CIS ii 4075: l. *lyr›* = lapsus), etc. - ¶ adj. compassionate, in all instances used as epithet of a deity; v. also *rḥmn*.

tyš‘ym v. *tš‘m*.

tk_1 **Ph** verbal form of uncert. derivation and meaning in KAI 26A ii 5; cf. Ginsberg with Levi Della Vida RCL '49, 284: = QAL Impf.

3 p.s.f., cf. also Starcky MUSJ xlv 262f., Röllig NESE ii 3, Dahood Or xlvi 475, li 284, Bron RIPK p. 85, Gibson SSI iii p. 49, 59: < root hlk_1/hwk (= to go), cf. also Greenfield EI xiv 75ff., H.P.Müller TUAT i 642 :: Gordon JNES viii 114, Alt WO i 281, Röllig KAI a.l., Teixidor Syr xlix 430, Schiffmann RSF iv 172 (div. otherwise): l. *tkl* = QAL Impf. 3 p.s.f. of *ykl* (cf. also Rosenthal ANET 654, Garr DGSP 187f.) :: Schub Lesh xxxviii 148 n. 7: *tk* = QAL Impf. 3 p.s.f. of kwn_1 :: Lipiński OLZ '82, 458f., SV 48, 50 n. e: *tk* = QAL Impf. 3 p.s.f. of *tkk* (= to travel, to tread; cf. also Del Olmo Lete AO i 289: prob. < root *wky* or *nky*) :: Honeyman Mus lxi 52, PEQ '49, 32f.: *tk* = Sing. abs. of tk_2 (= severity, subjugation; cf. also Marcus & Gelb JNES viii 119, Obermann JAOS Suppl ix 25, Dunand BMB viii 27, v.d.Branden BMB xiii 92f.) :: Dupont-Sommer RA xlii 172, JKF i 302f.: *tk* = Sing. abs. of tk_3 (= center; cf. also Swiggers UF xii 440, BiOr xxxix 339) :: Friedrich FuF xxiv 78: *tk* = Sing. cstr. of tk_3 :: Zolli Sef x 169: *tk* = Sing. abs. of tk_4 (= passage) :: Pedersen ActOr xxi 52 (div. otherwise): l. *tkl* = Plur. cstr. of tkl_2 (= Sing. strength, Plur. troops); on tk_1, cf. also Weippert GGA '64, 192.

tk_2 v.Soden AHW s.v. *tukku* II > (?) Akkad. = (act of) oppression.
v. tk_1.

tk_3 v. rtm_1, tk_1.

tk_4 v. tk_1.

tk_5 **Nab** l. poss. *tkʾ* (= Sing. emph. of tk_5 (= throne)) in J 257?? (cf. J ii p. 200, reading and interpret. highly uncert.).

tk_6 v.Soden Or xlvi 196, AHW s.v. *takku* > Akkad. = tablet? (uncert. interpret.).

tk_7 **Pun** Garbini AION xxv 441f.: the τοιχοι in StudMagr vi 46[2] = Plur. cstr. of tk_7 (= gutter).

tkd **Pun** YIPH/YITP Pf. 3 p.pl. *ʾytkdʾ* KAI 119[4] (v. infra) - ¶ verb YIPH/YITP to decide (meaning derived from context), or = YITP Pf. 3 p.pl. of root $kdd_1/kdy/kwd/ykd/$*ʾkd*?, for a discussion, cf. also Levi Della Vida RCL '55, 557f., Or xxxiii 10f., RSO xxxix 307, Röllig KAI a.l., Sznycer APCI 217 (n. 36), Sem xxx 38, Amadasi IPT 77, 134 :: Février RA l 186: = YITP Pf. 3 p.pl. of root $ʾḥd_2$ - a form of the same derivation also in Trip 51[3]: *ʾtkd* (Pf. 3 p.s.m.), cf. Levi Della Vida Or xxxiii 10f., 14, Amadasi 134, Röllig BiOr xxvii 379, cf. however Vattioni AION xvi 38f. (div. otherwise): l. $ʾt_5$ + Sing. abs. of kd_1 (= amphora).

tkh_1 **Ph** Sing. cstr. *tkt* KAI 10[5] (or = Plur.?, cf. e.g. Gibson SSI iii p. 97; cf. also Röllig KAI a.l.) - ¶ subst. middle; *btkt ʾbn* KAI 10[5]: in the centre of the stone.
v. *mtkh*.

tkh_2 **Hatra** Sing. (or Plur.??) *tktʾ* 292[4] (v. however infra) - ¶ subst. girdle, belt (cf. Safar Sumer xxvii 13 n. 37; cf. also Degen NESE iii

89f.: = necklace, collar) :: Aggoula Syr lii 194: < Iran. = bed (cf. also Vattioni IH a.l.).

tkwnh **OffAr** Sing. abs. *tkwnh* Cowl 15^6, Krael 7^5; emph. *tk[w]nt'* Krael 7^{15}; + suff. 3 p.s.f. *tkwnth* Krael $7^{22,27}$ - ¶ subst. ready cash (cf. Krael p. 209, Greenberg with Muffs 51 n. 1, Greenfield FS Iwry 81ff. (cf. e.g. also Grelot DAE p. 193, Fitzmyer FS Albright ii 143, 152, WA 255, Porten & Greenfield JEAS p. 21, Porten & Yardeni sub TADAE B 2.6 and elsewhere) :: Cowl p. 46f.: = cost of furniture).

tky v. *tkk*.

tkyn v. kpy_1.

tkk **Pun** QAL Impf. 1 p.s. *'tk* CIS i 6068^2 (= KAI 89, cf. already Lidzbarski Eph i 31f., Clermont-Ganneau RAO iv 92 (n. 1); or < root *ntk* with same meaning as *tkk*, cf. FR 151, 164, 165 :: Clermont-Ganneau RAO iii 305, 308f.: = $'t_6$ + suff. 2 p.s.f.) - **Palm** QAL Pf. 3 p.s.m. + suff. 3 p.s.f. *tkh* SBS 45^{10} (cf. Degen WO viii 131; cf. Greek par. περιστάντος αὐ[τ]ήν; :: Dunant SBS a.l.: < root *tky* (= to menace)) - ¶ verb QAL + obj. - **1)** to bind, *'tk 'nky mṣlḥ 'yt 'm'[š]trt* ... KAI 89^2: I M. bind A. (sc. by magical means) :: Lipiński OLZ '82, 458 (n. 2): = to trample - **2)** to menace, *qdns rb d[y] hw tkh* SBS $45^{9f.}$: the great danger which threatened her (sc. the caravan).
v. tk_1.

tkl_1 **OffAr** ITP Impf. 2 p.s.f. *ttkly* Sem ii 31 conc. 4f. (cf. Greenfield IEJ xix 203 n. 24, Kutscher IOS i 119, Grelot DAE p. 370 n. f (cf. also Porten JNES xxviii 116) :: Dupont-Sommer Sem ii 35: = ITP Impf. 2 p.s.f. of kl'_1); Part. s.m. abs. *mtkl* Herm 7^2 (cf. Greenfield IEJ xix 203 n. 24, Kutscher IOS i 119, Gibson SSI ii p. 143 :: Bresciani & Kamil Herm p. 427, Coxon JAOS xcviii 418 (n. 12): = APH (or PA'EL) Part. s.m. abs.) - ¶ verb ITP to trust, to entrust, to rely; + $'l_7$, *'l ttkly 'l mšlmt* Sem ii 31 conc. 4f.: do not rely on M. (cf. Herm 7^2) - for this root, cf. also Kaufman AIA 106 (n. 377).

tkl_2 v. tk_1.

$tklh_1$ Sing. cstr. *tklt* KAI 37A 1 (for the reading, cf. Masson & Sznycer RPC 28); + suff. 1 p.s. *tklty* KAI 18^4 (v. infra) - **Pun** Sing. abs. *tkl't* KAI 173^1 (v. infra); cstr. *tklt* KAI 119^5, *tkl't* Trip 3^1 (cf. Sznycer Sem xii 48 n. 4, Elmayer LibStud xiii 50 (cf. however, for the problems of this reading Amadasi-Guzzo FS Delcor 5ff.)) - ¶ subst. expense (cf. Février JA ccxxxix 6ff., Masson & Sznycer RCP 27ff. (cf. also Delcor UF xi 148) :: Levi Della Vida OA iv 68ff.: = addition, complement; v. infra); *'yt hš'r z ... p'lt btklty* KAI $18^{3f.}$: this gate ... I made at my own expense (cf. also Lidzbarski sub KI 12, Röllig KAI a.l. :: Levi Della Vida OA ii 74: with its complement (+ suff. 3 p.s.m., cf. also idem RSO xxxix 302) :: Röllig KAI a.l.: or = in its totality?? (+ suff. 3 p.s.m.) :: Cooke NSI p. 45, 47: in fulfilment of it (+ suff. 3 p.s.m.) :: Prätorius

ZDMG lx 167: *tklty* = Sing. + suff. 1 p.s. of *tklh*$_2$ (= care < *ykl*); on this text, cf. also Prätorius ZDMG lxvii 131); *tklt yrḥ ʾtnm* KAI 37A 1: the expense of the month E. (cf. also e.g. Lidzbarski Handb 296, KI sub 29, Röllig KAI a.l., Gibson SSI iii p. 126 :: Cooke NSI p. 66, Amadasi sub Kition C$_1$: = sum, total (cf. Peckham Or xxxvii 307 (n. 1): = accounts, cf. also idem JNES xxxv 286) :: Levi Della Vida OA ii 74: = addition, complement); *btklt mqm* KAI 119^5: at the expense of the sanctuary (cf. also Février RA l 187, Röllig KAI a.l. :: Levi Della Vida RCL '55, 553, 559: *tklt* preferably = inside); *btṣʾt wtklʾt* KAI 173^1: at the outlay and expense ... (:: Röllig KAI a.l.: *tklʾt* = Plur. abs. (= the extremities) :: Levi Della Vida OA ii 74: *tklʾt* = addition, complement (cf. also idem OA iv 69: *tklʾt* poss. = Plur. abs., cf. also Amadasi sub ICO-Sard 8)) - the same word (Sing. abs. *thychleth*) prob. also in IRT 906^4, cf. Levi Della Vida OA ii 73f.: = addition, Vattioni AION xvi 52, Aug xvi 550: = completion, Masson & Sznycer RPC 30: = expenses (diff. context, uncert. interpret.) - on this word, cf. also Milano VO i 84, 89ff. - cf. also *tṣʾh*.

tklh$_2$ v. *tklh*$_1$.

tkryk Nyberg FP 48, 85: poss. l. this noun (= wrapping) in Frah xv 12 (uncert. reading and interpret.), cf. also Ebeling Frah a.l.: l. Iran. word.

tl **OldAr** Sing. abs. *tl* KAI 222A 32 - **OffAr** Plur. cstr. *tly* CIS ii 111^1; cf. Frah x 17 (*tlh*, cf. Nyberg FP 45, 76 :: Ebeling Frah a.l.: l. *mḥrh* = form of *mḥr*$_1$ (= nose) - ¶ subst. 1) *tell*, heap of ruins; *wthwy ʾrpd tl* KAI 222A 32: and may A. become a heap of ruins (for the context, cf. Hillers TC 44f., 53f.); in CIS ii 111^1 poss. meaning *tumulus* - **2)** nose: Frah x 17 - for this word, cf. Kaufman AIA 108.

v. *tylʾ*.

tlʾym **OldAr** Cazelles VT xviii 150 n. 3: the *tlʾym* in KAI 224^{25,26} = Sing. abs. of *tlʾym* (= people, populated region; highly improb. interpret., cf. Noth ZDPV lxxvii 155ff., cf. also Dupont-Sommer BMB xiii 30, 35, Fitzmyer AIS 192, Röllig KAI a.l., Gibson SSI ii p. 51: = n.g.).

tlgw v.Soden Or xlvi 196, AHW s.v. *tilgūtu*: > Akkad. *tilgūtu* = chilblain? (uncert. interpret.).

tlḥ **OffAr** Itp Part. pl.m. abs. *mtlḥy[n]* EI xv 67*^{1} (on the reading, cf. Cross EI xv a.l.) - ¶ verb Itp to break into pieces, to crumble: EI xv 67*^{1} (on the problems of the context, cf. Cross EI xv a.l.).

tlṭ v. *lwṭ*.

tly$_1$ **OffAr** Qal Impf. 2 p.s.m. + suff. 3 p.s.m. *[t]tlnhy* Cowl 71^{19}; Itp Impf. 3 p.s.m. *ytly* Cowl 81^{39} - **JAr** Qal Pf. 3 p.s.m. *tlh* AMB 9^5 - ¶ verb Qal to hang + obj.: AMB 9^5 (the Heavens; cf. Naveh & Shaked AMB a.l.), Cowl 71^{19} (person; ?, heavily dam. context) - Driver JRAS '32, 83: the *tlk* in Cowl 71^{33} prob. = Qal Pf. 3 p.s.m. + suff. 2 p.s.m.

(dam. context) - a derivative of this root poss. also in MPAT 64 ii 4 (context however diff. and dam.), cf. also Starcky RB lxi 176 - ITP Cowl 81[39], meaning uncert., Cowley a.l.: = to be held in suspense, to be held back (said of wine) or: not to be reckoned in the account (cf. however Harmatta ActAntHung vii 354f.: l. poss. *btny* = *b*$_2$ + Sing. abs. of *tny*$_2$ (= agreement); on this text, cf. also Grelot DAE p. 110 n. f) - Rocco StudMagr vii a.l.: l. *tl* (= QAL Imper. pl.m.) in StudMagr vii 12[5] (uncertain reading, highly uncert. interpret.).
v. *tyl*ʾ.

tly$_2$ **OffAr** Sing. abs. *tly* ASAE xlviii 112B 1; + suff. 3 p.pl.m. *tlyhm* Cowl 30[8] (or = Plur. + suff. 3 p.pl.m.?; cf. also Leand 53z) - ¶ subst. weapon (cf. e.g. Barth ZA xxi 191 :: Nöldeke ZA xxi 198: = something appending > followers, cf. also Wag 20 n. 1); in Cowl 30[8] par. with *znyhwm* in Cowl 31[8]; cf. Dupont-Sommer ASAE xlviii 114f.: = pick, pickaxe?, Puech CISFP i 566: = axe?

tlyt **OffAr** Plur. abs. *tlytn* ATNS 76[3] - ¶ subst. third, third in rank, captain: ATNS 76[3] (context however dam.).

tlyty **JAr** Milik Syr xlv 101: l. poss. Plur. abs. of *tlyty* (*tlytyn*) = third in l. 13 (diff. and dam. text).
v. *šlšy*.

tlmd **Pun** Vattioni Aug xvi 545f.: the *[th]lemis* in IRT 886b 8 poss. = *tlmd*, cf. the *[th]lemisa* in IRT 886e 11 (meaning: student??); highly uncert. interpret., diff. context.

tlʿ **OffAr** Harmatta ActAntHung vii 370: l. poss. *tlʿyn* (= Plur. abs. of *tlʿ* (poss. = purple texture)) in Cowl 81[110], uncert. reading, cf. Cowl a.l.: l. *mlʿtyn* - cf. also *twlʿ*.

tlpḥt **OffAr** Naveh IEJ xxxv 211: l. this word (Sing. abs.) = lentils poss. in ATNS iii :: Naveh ibid. (div. otherwise): *pḥt* = Sing. cstr. of *pḥh* :: Segal ATNS a.l.: l. *]ṭ l* (= *l*$_5$) *gḥt* (= n.p.).

tlš v. *lwš*.

tlt$_1$ **Nab** Sing. cstr. *tlt* CIS ii 213[3]; Plur. abs. *tltyn* CIS ii 213[4] - ¶ subst. third part; *tlt kpr*ʾ CIS ii 213[3]: a third part of the tomb; *tltyn tryn mn kpr*ʾ CIS ii 213[4]: two third of the tomb - Beyer ATTM 316: l. *twlt* (= Sing. cstr.) in MPAT 50 e 4 (diff. and uncert. reading).
v. *šlš*$_1$.

tlt$_2$ v. *šlš*$_1$.

tltw **JAr** Sing. abs. (?) *tltwt* DJD ii 25, 7-8[2] (for the heavily dam. context, cf. Beyer ATTM 312) - ¶ subst. third part (??, v. supra).

tltyn v. *šlšm*.

tm$_1$ **Ph** Sing. abs. *tm* Syr xlviii 403[5] (v. infra) - **Pun** Sing. abs. *tm* KAI 72B 4, 104[2f.], 105[3], 106[2], 108[4], 118[3], 121[2], 132[2], 138[4] (cf. e.g. Röllig KAI a.l., Sznycer Sem xxx 40f. :: Février Sem ii 25f. (div. otherwise): l. prob. *bnm* = derivative of *bny*$_1$),[5], Hofra 29[2], RES 333[2], Trip 51[6], BAr

'21 cclx (for this reading cf. Levi Della Vida LibAnt i 61 n. 6 :: Chabot BAr '32-'33, 448: l. *nm* (without interpret.) :: Dussaud BAr a.l.: l. *ṣqmbtm* = n.p.; on this text, cf. also Jongeling NINPI 10ff.), etc., etc., *tn* Hofra 37^3 (reading of *n* diff.), 44^4, 50^3 (for this form, cf. Hoftijzer VT viii 290 n. 4), cf. IRT 828^3: *them* (cf. Levi Della Vida OA ii 78, 92, Vattioni AION xvi 49, Aug xvi 538); + suff. 3 p.pl.m. *tmnm* KAI 130^{1,2,3} - ¶ subst. totality, completion, integrity - **1)** > sum, price, *tmnm dn‘ry› m›t šlšm wšlš btm* KAI 130$^{1f.}$: their price was in total 133 *denarii* (cf. KAI 130^{2,3}); *htm* in Trip 51^6 poss. = total sum (cf. also Levi Della Vida Or xxxiii 13f., Amadasi IPT 135; diff. context) - **2)** in the combination *btm* - a) in total, in all: KAI 130^2 (quoted supra) - b) totally, *p‘l› btm* KAI 132^2: he made it totally (i.e. completely at his own expense), cf. KAI 72B 4, Trip 73 - α) *btṣ›tm btm* KAI 118^3, 129^3, Trip 13^3, 52^2: completely at his own expense (v. *tṣ›h*) - β) *bt›rm btm p‘l* KAI 121^2: he made (them) completely according to their plan (v. *t›r*; cf. Lat. par. *d(e) s(ua) p(ecunia) fac(iendum) coer(avit)*), cf. KAI 138^5 - γ) *p‘l lmbmlktm btm* KAI 126^{11}: he made them according to the work necessary for them (v. *ml›kh$_1$*) completely at his own expense; cf. KAI 124^2, cf. Lat. par. *d(e) s(ua) p(ecunia) f(aciendum) c(uravit)* - δ) cf. also IRT 828^3: *fel baiaem bithem* (he made it during his life at his own expense) - ε) for *btm* in *lmb[š]pḥ btm*, v. *špḥ$_1$* - b) in perfect state (said of sacrifice), *mlk ›dm* (v. *mlk$_5$*) *bšrm* (v. *bšr$_2$*) *btm* KAI 106$^{1f.}$: a human sacrifice his offspring in perfect state (cf. Hoftijzer VT viii 291, Röllig KAI a.l. :: Roschinski TUAT ii 608: *btm* not referring to the sacrifice, but to the act of sacrificing :: Albright YGC 205 n. 79: *btm* = completely :: Février RHR cxliii 10, JA ccxlviii 186 n. 17: *btm* = at his own expense (cf. also Cazelles SDB v 1341) :: Garbini GLECS xi 144f.: *btm* = Sing. + suff. 3 p.s.m. of *bt$_2$* :: v.d.Branden BO xv 203f. RSF ix 14: *btm* = *bn tm* (= Sing. abs. of *bn$_1$* + Sing. m. abs. of *tm$_3$*) :: Charlier Karth iv 25ff., 45f.: = part of n.l.; for this expression, cf.also Berthier & Charlier sub Hofra 28), cf. KAI 104$^{2f.}$, 105^3, 108$^{3f.}$, RES 332^2, Hofra 30^2, 34^4, etc. - the *btm* in Syr xlviii 403^5 prob. = *b$_2$* + Sing. abs. of *tm$_1$* (= fully, completely; cf. Lipiński RSF ii 53f., Röllig NESE ii 29, 34f., v.d.Branden BiOr xxxiii 13, Gibson SSI iii p. 90, 92 (cf. also Cross CBQ xxxvi 488f.: perfectly)) :: Gaster BASOR ccix 19, 25f., de Moor JEOL xxvii 111 (n. 23): *tm* = Sing. cstr. of *tm$_1$* :: Caquot Syr xlviii 405f., Avishur PIB 267, 271, UF x 32, 36: *btm* = Sing. abs. of *btm* (= serpent) :: Garbini OA xx 291f.: l. *btn* = Sing. abs. of *btn$_2$* (= serpent). v. *›b$_1$*, *ytm*, *m‘zrh*, *mqm$_1$*, *mtm$_3$*, *tm$_3$*, *tmh$_2$*.

tm$_2$ v. *tb*.

tm$_3$ **Pun** Sing. m. abs. *tm* KAI 107^4, 134^3, 145^7, 152^3, CIS i 3746^7, 4929^3 (:: Benz p. 186, 429: = n.p.), 5740^4, 5741^8, Hofra 38^4, 45^3, cf. Poen 1006: *sam* (variant reading *tam*; cf. Schroed 295, 317, Sznycer

PPP 142, J.J.Glück & Maurach Semitics ii 120 (cf. however Sznycer PPP 142 n. 2: or *sam* = Sing. abs. of $šm_1$) :: L.H.Gray AJSL xxxix 81, 84: *sam* = $šm_4$); f. abs. *tm'* Punica xii 23[3] (cf. FR 213, 229), Trip 38[1] (:: Levi Della Vida LibAnt i 58, FR 95b (div. otherwise): l. *'tm'* (= form with prosth. *alef*)) - ¶ adj. - **1)** perfect, undamaged (said of sacrifice), *bšrm bn tm* CIS i 3746[6f.]: his offspring, an unblemished son (cf. however CIS i 5507[4], 5695[5]: *bn ty*, cf. also Roschinski TUAT ii 608: *bntm* and *bnty* = prep. bnt_1 (= *pnt*) + suff. 3 p.s.m.; less prob. interpret.), *bšrm bn' tm* KAI 107[4]: his offspring, his unblemished son (cf. CIS i 4929[3] (*bn tm*), 5740[4] (*bn tm*), 5741[8] (*bn tm*), Hofra 38[3f.] (*bn' tm*), 45[3f.] (*bn tm*)); for this interpret., cf. Hoftijzer VT viii 290f. (or preferably div. otherwise: l. *bn 'tm* = *bn* + $'_2$ (= article) + tm_3?, cf. also v.d.Branden RSF ix 14) :: Février JA ccxlviii 172 (div. otherwise): *bntm* = b_2 + *ntm* (= NIPH Inf. of tmm_1 or = verbal noun derived from this root), *bntm* = at (his) expense (cf. also Février sub CIS i 5740, 5741: *bn* (in *bntm*) = variant of b_2 + Sing. abs. of tm_1) :: Garbini GLECS xi 144f.: *bntm* = Plur. + suff. 3 p.s.m. of bt_2 :: Charlier Karth iv 25ff., 45f.: = part of n.l.) - **2)** perfect, honest (said of the way someone led his life): KAI 134[3], 152[3], Punica xii 23[3] (v. $ḥy_1$); this meaning prob. also in KAI 145[7]; the same word with same meaning poss. also in KAI 166[4]?? :: Février Sem xi 7: pro *tm* at the beginning of l. 4 l. *km* (= km_2); for the reading *tm*, cf. Chabot sub Punica xi 7 (the interpret. of *tm* as n.p. (cf. e.g. Lidzbarski Handb 386) less prob.) - the *thum* in Poen 945 form of this word?, cf. e.g. L.H.Gray AJSL xxxix 77, cf. however Sznycer PPP 127: no interpret. poss. - the τιμ in αμουτιμ (Diosc ii 114) = tm_3?, cf. the αμουζεγαραφ sub $ṣ'r_2$.
v. *ytm*, rtm_1, tm_1, $tmh_{2,3}$.

tm'₁ v. tm'_2.

tm'₂ **Ph** Sing. cstr. *tm'* KAI 1[2] - **Pun** Sing. abs. *tm'* CIS i 151[3] (cf. also Février JA ccxlvi 443f., Amadasi sub ICO-Sard-NPu 2, cf. also Pili BO xxii 216: = cstr.; for the context, v. also mqr'_2), Hofra 104[3] - ¶ subst. m. indication of function; prob. meaning (derived from context): chief, commander; *tm' mḥnt* KAI 1[2]: commander of an army (on the context, cf. Demsky EI xiv 8ff., cf. also R.Kutscher & Wilcke ZA lxviii 125f.); *htmy' 'š bgrgšn* (?) Hofra 104[2]: the commander in G. - Gevirtz JNES xxvi 15f.: the same word as Greek ταμίας = overseer, manager :: Torrey JAOS xlv 273: = nominal form < Akkad. *tamû* (= to speak) :: Albright JPOS vi 80: = QAL Part. act. s.m. cstr. (in KAI 1) of tm'_1 < Akkad. *tamû* (cf. Harr 155, Slouschz TPI p. 3; against both improb. interpret., cf. Brockelmann FS Eissfeldt 66, Gevirtz VT xi 146f. n. 8) :: Brockelmann FS Eissfeldt 66: = Part. of root *tm'* = variant form of root *tmk* :: Baldacci BiOr xl 124f.: = noun with preformative *t-* < $m'h_2$ (= century, company) = centurion :: Aimé-Giron ASAE xlii 315:

< root *'mm* (< Akkad. or < Arab.) :: Yeivin Lesh xxxvi 248f.: = QAL Pf. 3 p.s.m. of *tm'*$_1$ (= to command) - the same word also in RES 304[2] (Clermont-Ganneau RAO v 108: *tm'* = QAL Pf. 3 p.pl.m. of *tmm*$_1$ (= to complete; cf. also Chabot sub RES 306; improb. interpret.)) and in RES 906[2]??, in both instances diff. and dam. context.
v. *tš'*$_1$.

tm'$_3$ v. *tmw'nty*, *tmy*$_2$.

tm'm Ebeling Frah a.l.: l. in Frah xxx 31 *tm'm* = complete; cf. *tmym* (improb. reading, cf. Nyberg FP 58, 110: l. Iran. word).

tmh$_1$ **JAr** QAL Part. act. pl.m. abs. *tmhyn* AMB 9[7] (reading however highly uncert.) - ¶ verb to be astonished, to be terrified (v. however supra).

tmh$_2$ **Pun** Sing. abs. *tmt* KAI 121[1], 126[6] - ¶ subst. perfection; *mḥb d't htmt* KAI 121[1], 126[6]: who loves the perfect knowledge (cf. Lat. par. *amator concordiae*; v. also *yd'*$_1$) - the same subst. (Sing. abs. *tm'*) prob. also in KAI 161[5], *tm' 'dr'* = the splendid perfection, cf. Février RA xlv 143f., Röllig KAI al :: FR 42 n. 1, 213, 229: = Sing. f. abs. of *tm*$_3$ :: Roschinski Num 112: = Sing. + suff. 3 p.s.m. of *tm*$_1$ - Février AIPHOS xiii 170: the *t'mt* in KAI 162[6] poss. = Sing. abs. of *tmh*$_2$ (uncert. interpret., diff. context), cf. however v.d.Branden BO xiv 196, 200: l. *t'ṣmṭ* (= Sing. abs. of *t'ṣmh* (= happiness)) - Torrey JAOS xxxv 365f.: l. *tm[t]* (= Sing. abs.) in KAI 24[4] (uncert. interpret., cf. e.g. Gibson SSI iii p. 36: prob. = n.p. :: Collins WO vi 184f.: l. *tm* (= Sing. abs. of *tm*$_1$) :: Sperling UF xx 326f.: l. *tm[m]* = Sing. m. abs. of *tmm*$_2$ (= perfect)).

tmh$_3$ **OffAr** Cowl 5[4], 25[6], 27[15], 30[6,9,11], 31[6], 33[10], 38[5], Aḥiq 48, 72, Krael 12[22], Driv 1[1], 2[4], 5[2], 10[2], ATNS 14[2], 26[6,9,12,14], 61a 4, 107[2], 133[1], AG 8 recto 2 (uncert. reading), FS Driver 54 conv. 1, AE '23, 41 no. 3/4, 5[6], 8[6]; cf. Frah xxv 3, 45, Paik 1000, GIPP 35, 65, SaSt 22, 24 - **Nab** ADAJ x 44[4] (= RB lxxii 95) - ¶ adv. there: passim; *lmbnh 'gr 1 tmh* Cowl 5[3f.]: to build a wall there; *tmh hwyt msbl lk* Aḥiq 48: there (i.e. in my house) I provided for you; *l' šbw lntn tmh* FS Driver 54 conv. 1: they have not deported N. there; *'tyn tmh 'lykm* Cowl 38[5]: they are coming there to you; *qbyr tmh* ADAJ x 44[4]: buried there (sc. in the place where he died, namely Jorash; text found in Petra) - prec. by prep. - a) by *l*$_5$, *ltmh* Frah xxv 45: there - b) by *mn*$_5$, *mn tmh tnpq wtn'l byt' znh* Krael 12[22]: from there (sc. the gate) you may leave and enter this house (cf. e.g. Krael a.l., Grelot DAE p. 259 × Porten & Greenfield JEAS p. 71, Porten & Yardeni sub TADAE B 3.12: *byt' znh* beginning of new clause :: J.J.Rabinowitz Law 124ff.: *mn tmh* = from now henceforth (less prob. interpret., cf. Yaron RIDA v 207, cf. also Cowl 5[12,14]); *mnd'm mn tmh l' mhytyn 'ly* Driv 10[2]: they bring me nothing from there; *'gwr' zy YHW 'lh' zy byb byrt' yh'dw mn tmh*

Cowl 30^6: let them remove the temple of YHW the God from there (i.e. let them destroy it (cf. Cowl 31^6)); ***mn tmh ... mn mlk' šlyḥ*** ATNS 26^{12}: from there ... there was sent from the king; ***yhškḥwn mn tmh gbrn kšyrn*** ATNS 26^{14}: they will find from there suitable men - the same word most prob. also in KAI 269^2, *l' 'mrt tmh* KAI 269^2: she has not spoken there (sc. in the other world, cf. Lévy JA ccxi 297ff. :: Nöldeke with CIS ii 141, Lidzbarski Handb 386, Grelot Sem xvii 73, 75, DAE p. 342 (n. r): there (i.e. on earth) :: Donner KAI a.l.: = here (cf. also Degen ZDMG cxxi 137) :: Shea JAOS ci 216: to be combined with mn_5 in l. 3 as compound prep. :: Lipiński OLP viii 112, 115: prob. = Sing. f. abs. of tm_3 :: Torrey JAOS lviii 396: = Sing. f. abs. of tm_3 used adverbially, totally :: Cooke NSI p. 205f.: poss. = ever) - cf. $šm_4$, *tmn*.
v. $šwr_4$.

tmw'nty (< Egypt., v. infra) - **OffAr** *tmw'nty* Krael 9^9 - ¶ subst. < Egypt.: *tmw'* (= tm'_3 = tmy_2) + *nty*: = the road of the god, cf. Couroyer RB lxi 557f., lxviii 531f., 536, lxxv 80, 82, BiOr xxvii 251f., Porten Arch 285, 309, Grelot DAE p. 244 (nn. g, h), Porten & Greenfield JEAS p. 58, Porten & Yardeni sub TADAE B 3.10 :: Krael a.l.: *tmw'nty* < Egypt. = indication of some sort of building (cf. also Cazelles Syr xxxii 85: *tmw'nty* < Egypt. = tm'_3 (= tmy_2 (= ward)) + *nty* (= of the god)) - cf. tmy_2.

tmwn v. $šmn_4$.

tmḥy v. *tms*.

tmy$_1$ v. qny_1.

tmy$_2$ (< Egypt., v. infra) - **OffAr** Sing. abs. *tm'* Krael 4^{10}, *tmy* Krael 3^8 - ¶ subst. way (< Egypt., cf. Couroyer RB lxi 557f., lxviii 530ff., lxxvii 465, BiOr xxvii 251f., Grelot DAE p. 217 n. e :: Erichsen with Krael p. 160, Porten & Greenfield JEAS p. 40, 45: < Egypt. = town (cf. Krael p. 79f., Ginsberg JAOS lxxiv 154, Porten Arch 285 n. 16, 308f.: = ward (cf. also Cazelles Syr xxxii 85)) :: Albright with Krael p. 160f.: or = < Egypt., what belongs to :: Couroyer RB lxi 253: = part of temple) - cf. *tmw'nty*.

tmy' v. tm'_2.

tmydh **JAr** the diff. *tmydh* in AMB 1^{14} (reading of *t* uncert.) = wine ?? (cf. Naveh & Shaked AMB a.l.; highly uncert. interpret.).

tmyk v. $smyk_1$.

tmym **OffAr** Sing. m. abs. *tmym* Samar 1^2 (= EI xviii 8*), 2^2 (*tm[ym]h*); cf. Nisa-c 285^4 (*[t]mym*)?? (heavily dam. context) - ¶ adj. without blemish (said of a slave): Samar 1^2, 2^2 - > Akkad., cf. v.Soden Or xxxvii 268, xlvi 196, AHW s.v. *tamīmu*.
v. $šmm_1$.

tmys (< Egypt., cf. Glanville ZÄS lxviii 12f., Grelot DAE p. 291 n. h) **OffAr** Sing. abs. *tmys* Cowl $26^{13,20}$ - ¶ subst. of uncert. meaning, indicating part of a boat; cf. Glanville ZÄS lxviii 13: = decking, panelling (cf. also Grelot DAE p. 291 n. h, Porten & Yardeni sub TADAE A 6.2).

tmyr v. *tmr*$_2$.

tmk **Ph** QAL Pf. 1 p.s. *tmkt* KAI 24^{13} - **Pun** QAL Pf. 3 p.pl. *tmk* CIS i 5510^{10} (cf. Krahmalkov RSF ii 173f. × Février BAr '46/49, 172, sub CIS i 5510: = QAL Inf. abs. (v. also infra) :: Garbini RSO xlii 12, FSR 165 n. 13: = PI‘EL Pf. 3 p.pl. (= to hang)) - **Nab** PA‘EL Part. pl.m. abs. *mtm[ky]n* BIA x 55^{4} (for this prob. reading and interpret., cf. Milik BIA x 56) - ¶ verb QAL to take, to seize; for KAI 24^{13}, v. *yd*; context of CIS i 5510^{10} diff., Krahmalkov RSF ii 173ff.: *wtmk hmt ’yt ’grgnt* = they took Agrigentum, cf. also v.d.Branden RSF v 140, BiOr xxxvi 203, v however *gnh*$_1$ (interpret. of *wtmk* as *w*$_2$ + Inf. abs. used adverbially less prob., thus Février BAr '46/49, 172: steadily) - PA‘EL Part. ruler, *mtm[ky]n [l]k[l ‘]l[m’]* BIA x 55^{4}: the rulers of the whole world (said of two Roman emperors; cf. Greek par. τῶν θειοτάτων κοσμοκρατόρων and αὐτοκρατόρων) - Sznycer PPP 116ff.: pro *thymihy* in Poen 940 l. *thymchy* = QAL Part. act. pl.m. cstr. = protectors of ... (poss. interpret., cf. however Schroed 302f. (div. otherwise): emend *isthymhimihy* to *isthymmihy* (= HITP Impf. 3 p.pl.m. of *šmḥ* (= to rejoice over); cf. also L.H.Gray AJSL xxxix 79: emend to *isthymihy* :: Krahmalkov Or lvii 57, 61f.: emend to *timlacun*, *thymlachun* (= QAL Impf. 2plm of *mlk*$_1$) + *alt* (= *‘lt*)).
v. *tm’*$_2$.

tml$_1$ (< Greek θυμέλη) - **Palm** Sing. emph. *tml’* Inv xii 2^{3} - ¶ subst. platform: Inv xii 2^{3}.

tml$_2$ v. *ll*$_2$.

tmm$_1$ **Ph** QAL Pf. 3 p.s.m. *tm* KAI 60^{1} - **Pun** QAL Impf. 1 p.s., cf. Poen 931: *ythmum* (cf. Schroed 305, L.H.Gray AJSL xxxix 77f., FR 164, 165, Sznycer PPP 58 :: J.J.Glück & Maurach Semitics ii 103f. (div. otherwise): l. *ythm* = QAL Impf. 3 p.s.m.); cf. also the form *tumam* in Poen 941, Sznycer PPP 122: *tumam* = lapsus for *itumam* (haplography?; = PU‘AL Impf. 3 p.s.m.; cf. L.H.Gray AJSL xxxix 79: = POL Impf. 3 p.s.m., cf. Schroed 307f.: = *tmm*$_3$ (adv. = totally)) - ¶ verb QAL to be completed, to be decided, *tm bd ṣdnym ... l’ṭr* KAI 60^{1}: it was resolved by the Sidonians ... to crown (for a discussion of the context, cf. Krahmalkov RSO lxi 76ff.) - Février BAr-NS i-ii a.l.: the *’tm* in BAr-NS i-ii 229 = YIPH Pf. 3 p.s.m. of *tmm*$_1$ (uncert. interpret.) - Février AIPHOS xiii 166, 170: the *’tm* in KAI 163^{1} = YIPH Pf. 3 p.s.m. of *tmm*$_1$ (= to complete, to accomplish).
v. *ytm*, *mwt*$_1$, *mtm*$_3$, *ṣlqh*, *rtm*$_1$, *tm*$_3$, *tm’*$_2$.

tmm$_2$ v. *tmh*$_2$.

tmm$_3$ v. *tmm*$_1$.

tmn **JAr** *tmn* MPAT 49 i 10, 51[3] - ¶ adv. there; *slqt mn tmn lmṣd'* MPAT 49 i 10: I went up from there to M.; *šṭr' mn tmn* MPAT 51[2f.]: the scribe from there (sc. from the place just mentioned); cf. $šm_4$, tmh_3. v. mn_5.

tmnh v. $šmn_4$.

tmnḥh v. $mnḥh_3$.

tmny v. *tms*.

tmnyn v. *šmnm*.

tms **OffAr** Sing. emph. *tms'* Cowl 15[12] (*tm[s']*; for this reading, cf. Krael p. 212, Porten Arch p. 93, Fitzmyer FS Albright ii 155, WA 257f., Porten & Greenfield JEAS p. 20, Grelot DAE p. 194 n. j, Porten & Yardeni sub TADAE B 2.6/3.8 :: Cowl a.l.: l. *tm[ḥy]* = Sing. abs. of *tmḥy* (= tray) :: Lidzbarski Eph iii 131: l. *tmny* (without interpret.)), Krael 7[13] - ¶ subst. f. bowl, dish.

tmr_1 v. $'mr_1$.

tmr_2 **Pun** Sing. abs. *t'm'r* Trip 51[4] - **Hebr** Plur. abs. *tmryn* SM 49[5,23] - **OffAr** Plur. abs. *tmrn* Del 46[1], 72[2], 75[2], Irâq iv 18[2], FuB xiv 17[2], 18[2], 19[1], 20[3]; emph. *tmry'* Cowl 81[111] - **Nab** Plur. emph. *tmyry'* DBKP 22[31] (lapsus?) - **JAr** Sing. emph. *tmr'* Syr xlv 101[4] (heavily dam. context) - ¶ subst. - **1)** date-palm; *b'mqt šht'm'r* Trip 51[4]: in the valley of the palm-tree (cf. Levi Della Vida Or xxxiii 14, Amadasi IPT 134; cf. also FR 107.4); ... *zy yhbw 'l tmry zy pḥy* Cowl 81[111]: (objects, v. $nḥš_6$) which they put (or: were put) on the date-palms of P. (cf. however Harmatta ActAntHung vii 371: or *tmry'* = dates); *gny tmyry'* DBKP 22[31]: the palm orchards - **2)** date; (in Aramaic dockets): Del 46[1], 72[2], 75[2], Irâq iv 182[2], FuB 17[2], 18[2], 19[1], 20[3]; (in Hebr. text): SM 49[23], cf. also *tmryn 'psywt* SM 49[5]: dates from E. - abbrev. *t* in Frah v 3 - for this word, cf. Borowski AIAI 126ff.

tmr_3 **Ph** Sing. abs. *tmr* KAI 49[27] - ¶ subst. indication of occupation, prob. = seller of dates (cf. also Lidzbarski Eph iii 102).

tmr_4 v. nmr_2.

tn_1 v. *tb*.

tn_2 v. *qqbtn*.

tn' **OffAr** Sing. abs. *tn'* CIS ii 69 - **Nab** Sing. cstr. *tn'* CIS ii 350[5] - ¶ subst. - **1)** account; *tn' zy lbnn* CIS ii 69 (= Del 89): an account concerning bricks - **2)** permission; *tn' mqbr* CIS ii 350[5]: a permission to bury.

tnb **OffAr** Sing. + suff. 3 p.s.m. *tnbh* TA-Ar 38[3] (v. infra) - ¶ subst. of uncert. meaning; Naveh sub TA-Ar 38: = lapsus for *tbnh* (= Sing. + suff. 3 p.s.m. of tbn_1), cf. also Teixidor Syr xliv 179 :: Aharoni & AmIran. IEJ xiv 141f.: = Sing. abs. of *tnbh* (= fruit)? :: Naveh AION xvi 31f.: l. *twrh* = Sing. + suff. 3 p.s.m. of twr_2 (= $šwr_4$); Naveh sub TA-Ar 38: *byt tnbh* = his shed of straw (poss. interpret.; :: Naveh ibid.:

same meaning as *mtbnh* in l. 2).
tnbh v. *tnb*.
tnh **OffAr** Cowl 4[6] (dam. context), 27[4], 30[5,24,27], 31[5,23,26], 34[7], 40[4] (for this poss. reading, cf. Porten & Yardeni sub TADAE A 3.6 :: Cowl a.l. (div. otherwise): l. *thšlḥ* (= HAPH Impf. 2 p.s.m. of *šlḥ$_1$*)), Krael 13[7], Driv 7[3], 11[1], AG 61[2], Herm 1[4,9], 2[3,10], CRAI '70, 163[3bis] (diff. context), SSI ii 28 obv. 4, rev. 5, KAI 259[1], 261[5], ATNS 5[7] (*]tnh*; highly uncert. reading, cf. also Porten & Yardeni sub TADAE B 8.3), RSO xxxv 22[2] (for the reading, cf. Porten FS Bresciani 434, Porten & Yardeni sub TADAE A 3.4 :: Bresciani RSO xxxv 23: l. *tnm* = part of n.p.), etc., etc.; cf. GIPP 27, 35, 65, SaSt 22, 24 - ¶ adv. here; *wyhwdy› kl zy tnh* Cowl 30[26f.]: all the Judeans that are here; *šlm ln tnh* Cowl 37[2]: we are alright here (cf. Herm 1[3f.], 2[2f.], 6[8]); *tnh ... šmy‹ ly* Driv 7[3]: I have heard here; *tnh ›nh qblt l›ršm ‹l ›ḥtbšty* Driv 11[1]: I have complained here to A. concerning A. (cf. Herm 2[10]); *[m]ṭ›t spynt› tnh ‹lyn* Krael 13[7]: the ship has reached us here; etc. - **1)** prec. by prep. *‹d$_7$*, *‹d tnh tḥwm* ... KAI 259[1]: to this point (extends) the boundary of ...
v. *pnh$_1$*, *qny$_1$*, *šnh$_2$*.
tnw›r Ebeling Frah a.l.: the *tnw›r* in Frah x 37 = posterior (*tnw›r* = *tnwr*), improb. interpret., cf. also Nyberg FP 45, 78: l. Iran. word here.
tnwr$_1$ v. *tnr$_2$*.
tnwr$_2$ v. *tnw›r*.
tny$_1$ **JAr** PA‹EL Part. s.m. abs. *mtn›* MPAT 49 i 3 - ¶ verb PA‹EL to recount - Sznycer PPP 89ff.: the *tnu* in Poen 936 = QAL Pf. 3 p.pl. of *tny$_1$* (= to repeat, to tell), uncert. interpret., cf. also Schroed 290, 312, L.H.Gray AJSL xxxix 77, FR 93, 254: = *›t$_6$* + suff. 1 p.pl. (cf. also Friedrich OLZ '69, 47 n. 4).
tny$_2$ v. *tly$_1$*.
tny$_3$ **OffAr** word of unknown meaning in Cowl 75[6] (dam. context); Cowl a.l.: perhaps = *tny$_4$* (= *šny$_5$*; used adverbially, = again)??, cf. however CIS ii sub 150 = QAL Imper. s.f. of *ntn*.
tny$_4$ v. *twb$_5$*, *tny$_3$*.
tnyn$_1$ **OffAr** Sing. abs. *tnyn* Aḥiq 106 - ¶ subst. dragon.
tnyn$_2$ **OffAr** Sing. m. abs. *tnyn* Cowl 10[7] (v. infra), 63[13] (dam. context) - ¶ ordinal number, second; *mṭ› tnyn šnh* Cowl 10[7]: a second year has arrived (cf. Cowl a.l., Grelot DAE p. 82, Porten & Greenfield JEAS p. 111, Porten & Yardeni sub TADAE B 3.1; cf. however Sach p. 110, Ungnad ArPap 46f.: *tnyn* = Sing. cstr. of noun (= repetition), *mṭ› tnyn šnh* = (when) the same time next year arrives - this word (Plur. m./f. abs. *tnynn*) prob. also in ATNS 42b 5 (context however diff. and dam.; :: Segal ATNS a.l.: = of the second harvest or of second quality?), cf. also the *tnyn* (Sing. m. abs.) in ATNS 43b ii 3, 4, xxii 1, the *tnynn*

(Plur. m./f. abs.) in ATNS 86b 2, 3 (*tnyn[n]*) and the *tnynh* (Sing. f. abs.) in ATNS 43b ii 4 - cf. *šny*$_5$.

tnn **OffAr** Sumer xx 13^4, 15^5 - **Palm** CIS ii 3932^3, Inscr P 78^7, Syr xiv 184^2, xl 34^4, xlvii 113^4, Inv D 25^3, Sem xxvii 117^7, SBS 45^{11} - ¶ adv. here; *kdy hwʾ tnn q[r]spynws hygmwnʾ* CIS ii 3932$^{3f.}$: when C. was prefect here; *ʾnšyʾ dṣyry[n] tnn* Inv D 25$^{2f.}$: the men that have been painted here; *ʿlh brt ʾydʿn ... ʾmh wʾbwh tnn* Inscr P 78$^{1ff.}$: A. the daughter of I. ... her mother and her father are (buried) here; *rʿw tnn* Sumer xx 15^5: they pastured (sc. their animals) here (cf. Sumer xx 13^4) - **1)** preceded by prep. *l*$_5$, *mn dy yʿl ltnn swm nkry* Syr xiv 184^2: whoever will bring in here the corpse of a stranger - **2)** preceded by prep. *mn*$_5$, *mn tnn* Sem xxvii 117^7: here (??, diff. context).

tnʿmh v. *ršʾt*.

tnr$_1$ v. *tnrw*.

tnr$_2$ **Pun** Plur. abs. *tnrm* RCL '66, 201^6 - **OldAr** Sing. abs. *tnwr* Tell F 22 (cf. Akkad. par. *tinūru*) - ¶ subst. oven, stove; *lʾpn btnwr lḥm* Tell F 22: let them bake bread in the oven; on this word, cf. Kaufman AIA 108.

tnrw **OffAr** word of uncert. reading in FuF xxxv 173^{13} (cf. Altheim & Stiehl ibid. 177: or l. *tbrw* = QAL Pf. 3 p.pl.m. of *tbr* (= to overcome); uncert. interpret. :: Altheim & Stiehl ibid. 177: = PAʿEL Pf. 3 p.pl.m. of *tnr*$_1$ (= to heat, to excite, denominative of *tnr*$_2$); cf. idem ASA 276f.).

tsbh **Hebr** Sing. cstr. *tsbt* KAI 194^9 (v. infra) - ¶ subst. turning (interpret. of context diff.); *tsbt hbqr* KAI 194^9: the survey-tour of the morning (cf. Aharoni TA-H p. 16, Pardee HAHL 91, 93 (cf. also Levine Shn iii 288 and cf. Dahood Or xlvi 330: after the morning round), cf. already Torczyner Lach i p. 82 (div. otherwise): l. *tsbth* (= Sing. + suff. 3 p.s.m.) = his inspection-tour (less prob. word division; cf. also Talmon BASOR clxxvi 31, Yeivin BiOr xix 7 n. 52)) × *tsbt hbqr* = when morning comes (cf. Elliger PJB '38, 49, ZDPV lxii 71, Röllig KAI a.l., Galling TGI 77 (n. 5), Lemaire IH i 110, 112, Lipiński OLP viii 90 (cf. also Sasson ZAW xciv 106f.)) :: Albright BASOR xcvii 26, ANET 322, Cross BASOR cxliv 25: during the next morning (cf. also Gibson SSI i p. 42f., Briend TPOA 144, Smelik HDAI 116) :: Gordon BASOR lxvii 31, de Vaux RB xlviii 195, May BASOR xcvii 25 (div. otherwise): *tsbth* (= Sing. + suff. 3 p.s.f.) = its vicinity :: Cassuto RSO xvi 175f. (div. otherwise): *tsbth* (= Sing. + suff. 3 p.s.m.) = his return (cf. also Chapira RES '45, 123) :: Hempel ZAW lvi 133 (div. otherwise): *tsbth* (= Sing. + suff. 3 p.s.m.) = his following; on this word, cf. also Thomas JThSt x 10 - v. also *bqr*$_3$.

tshd **OffAr** Sing. emph. *tshdʾ* Cowl 71^{10} - ¶ subst. of uncert. reading and interpret. CIS ii sub 145: poss. = testimony (cf. however Cowl p. 181, Leand 2q).

t‘bh Ph Sing. cstr. *t‘bt* KAI 13[6] - ¶ subst. abomination; *k t‘bt ‘štrt hdbr h’* KAI 13[6]: for such an act is an abomination for A.
t‘br Pun Garbini AION xxv 264: l. *t‘br* (word of unknown meaning, to be connected to *tbrh*$_1$?) in Karth x 133[3] (reading poss., cf. however Février Karth x a.l., Fantar Sem xxv 72f.: l. *n‘b’* (= n.p.)).
t‘gwl v. *t’kl.*
t‘dwz Nab word of uncert. reading and unknown meaning in RES 836 (cf. Cantineau Nab ii 157); cf. also Lidzbarski Eph ii 263: l. *ṣ‘dw* or *m‘dw*?? (without interpret.).
t‘dyt OffAr Segal ATNS a.l.: l. poss. this subst. (Sing. emph. *t[‘]dyt’*) = passage in ATNS 26[5] (reading however highly uncert.).
t‘l v. *š‘l*$_1$.
t‘lbh Pun Plur. (?) abs. *t‘lbt* CIS i 5952[2] (= TPC 14; v. however infra) - ¶ subst. poss. indication of object: box?, pyxis? (for this interpret., cf. Clermont-Ganneau RAO v 50, Chabot sub RES 500, Février CIS i a.l. (for the reading, cf. also Delattre with Clermont-Ganneau RAO v 50, cf. however Chabot sub RES 240, Lidzbarski Eph i 299f.: l. *t‘lyt* (= Plur. (?) abs. of *t‘lyh*, prob. = aquaduct), cf. also Slouschz TPI p. 195: *t‘lyh* = gutter, Chabot sub RES 500: (*si vera lectio*) *t‘lyh* = pestle)) - Chabot Punica xi ad 14: the *t‘l[* in Punica xi 14[5] to be restored to *t‘l[yt]*, cf. however Février sub CIS i 5952: to be restored to *t‘l[bt].*
t‘lh Ph Sing. abs./cstr. *t‘lt* RES 1204[1] (for this interpret., cf. Teixidor Sem xxix 10 :: e.g. Cooke NSI p. 43, Chabot sub RES 1204 (div. otherwise): l. *‘lt* (= prep.)) - ¶ subst. canal: RES 1204[1] (v. supra, diff. context).
t‘lyh v. *t‘lbh.*
t‘n v. *‘yn*$_2$.
t‘ṣmh Pun Sing. abs. *t‘ṣmt* KAI 165[7] - ¶ subst. greatness; *dl šm t‘ṣmt* KAI 165[6f.]: possessor of a great name (cf. also Chabot sub Punica xvi 1, Levi Della Vida OA iv 68).
v. *kbdh, tmh*$_2$.
t‘qh v.Soden Or xxxvii 268, xlvi 196 (cf. also idem AHW s.v. *te’iqtu*): = injury, damage > Akkad. (uncert. interpret.).
t‘r v. *‘dy*$_1$.
tp v. *tbk.*
tp’rh v. *t’rh.*
tpd Pun word of unknown meaning and highly uncert. reading in Antas 18, cf. Garbini AION xix 328, cf. however Fantar Antas a.l. (div. otherwise): l. *’štp* = n.p.
tplh$_1$ **OffAr** Sing. abs. *tplh* Cowl 81[30] - ¶ subst. of unknown meaning, prob. indicating a certain countable object, according to the context made of silver; poss. < Egypt., cf. Grelot DAE p. 109 n. w; Harmatta ActAntHung vii 351: = small box; :: Cowl a.l.: = phylactery (= *tplh*$_2$)

??
tplh$_2$ **Pun** Sing. abs. *tplt* KAI 162[4] (diff. and uncert. context) - ¶ subst. prayer (v. however supra).
v. *tplh$_1$*
tpsh **OffAr** Sing. abs. *tpsh* Cowl 55[1] (heavily dam. context) - ¶ subst. (?) of unknown meaning, poss. indicating countable object.
tpp **Ph** Pol Part. s.m. abs. *mtpp* KAI 49[7] (for this reading, cf. Lidzbarski Eph iii 97) - **OldAr** Qal Imper. s.m. + suff. 3 p.s.m. *tph* KAI 224[13] (for this reading and interpret., cf. Dupont-Sommer BMB xiii 33, Degen AAG p. 21, 73 × Dupont-Sommer BMB xiii 33: or = Imper. pl.m. + suff. 3 p.s.m.? × Fitzmyer AIS 98, 114, Gibson SSI ii p. 54: l. *tkh* = Qal Impf. 2 p.s.m. of *nky$_1$* :: Puech RB lxxxix 585f., Lemaire & Durand IAS 145: l. *tph* = lapsus for *tkh*); pl.m. + suff. 3 p.s.f. *tpwh* KAI 224[13] (for this reading and interpret., cf. Dupont-Sommer BMB xiii 33, Degen AAG 21, 73 (n. 68) × Gibson SSI ii p. 54, Sader EAS 135 (n. 60): *tpwh* = lapsus for *tkwh* (= Qal Impf. 2 p.pl.m. + suff. 3 p.s.f. of *nky$_1$*) :: (Cross with) Fitzmyer AIS 98, 114: *tpwh* = lapsus for *tkwh* (= Paʿel Impf. 2 p.s.m. + suff. 3 p.s.f. of *nky$_1$*; cf. also Greenfield ActOr xxix 5 n. 11) :: Puech RB lxxxix 585f., Lemaire & Durand IAS 145: l. *tpnh* = lapsus for *tknh* (= Qal Impf. 2 p.s.m. + suff. 3 p.s.f. of *nky$_1$*)) - ¶ verb Qal to strike; *nkh tpwh bḥrb* KAI 224[12f.]: strike it with the sword (sc. the town; note the combination with Qal Inf. abs. of *nky$_1$*, v. however supra); cf. KAI 224[13f.] - Pol to drum, Part. drummer: KAI 49[7] (cf. FR 164) - on derivatives of this root, cf. also Masson RPAE 94f.
tpr v. *prr$_1$*.
tṣʾh **Pun** Sing. abs. *tṣʾt* KAI 173[1] (:: Röllig KAI a.l.; v. infra); cstr. *tṣʾt* KAI 122[2] (v. infra); + suff. 3 p.s.m. *tṣty* Trip 38[5], *tṣʾtm* KAI 118[3] (v. infra), 129[3] (v. infra), Trip 13[3], 52[2], BAr '21, cclx (for the reading, cf. Levi Della Vida LibAnt i 61 n. 6 :: Dussaud BAr a.l. (div. otherwise): l. *bn* (= Sing. cstr. of *bn$_1$*) *tšqmbtm* (= n.p.)); + suff. 3 p.pl.m. *tṣtnm* Punica xx 1[4] (:: Chabot Punica a.l.: l. *tstnm*; for the reading, cf. also Levi Della Vida LibAnt i 59 n. 2) - ¶ subst. expense (cf. Février JA ccxxxix 6ff., Levi Della Vida RSO xxxix 306, Masson & Sznycer RPC 30 :: Levi Della Vida AttiTor lxx 191, PBR xix 68: = extremity, outer part, cf. also Röllig sub KAI 118, 122, 129, 173; cf. also Clermont-Ganneau RAO vii 112f.); *bnʾ bʿnyʿ btṣtnm* Punica xx 1[4]: his sons have built it at their own expense; *nplʿ btṣty* Trip 38[5]: it (i.e. a tomb) was constructed at his own expense; *btṣʾtm btm* KAI 118[3]: completely at his own expense (cf. also Levi Della Vida RSO xxxix 306; cf. KAI 129[3], Trip 13[3], 52[2]); *btṣʾt wtklt* KAI 173[1]: at the outlay and expense of ... (v. *tklh$_1$*); *btṣʾt mqm* KAI 122[2]: at the expense of the sanctuary (context however diff., v. *mqm$_1$*, *nʿtr*; cf. also Amadasi IPT 57) - cf. also *tklh$_1$*.

tṣbwt **Palm** Sing. + suff. 3 p.s.m. *tṣbwth* CIS ii 4204^{2} - ¶ subst. decoration; cf. *tṣbyt.*

tṣbyt **Palm** Sing. emph. *tṣbyt᾿* Inv xii 23^{2}, CIS ii 4001^{12} (*tṣbyt[᾿]*) or l. *tṣbyt[h]* = + suff. 3 p.s.?); + suff. 3 p.s.m. *tṣbyth* CIS ii 3985^{2} (= RIP 152), 4201^{2}, PNO 7a, Inscr P 47^{1} (dam. context), Inv xii 19^{1} (dam. context), 48^{2}, 49^{7}, *tṣbth* Syr xix 156^{2}; + suff. 3 p.s.f. *tṣbyth* CIS ii 3902^{1} (?), 4209^{3} (Greek par. [κοσ]μῷ), Ber iii 84^{4}; + suff. 3 p.pl.m. *tṣbythwn* CIS ii 3952^{4} - ¶ subst. decoration (cf. *tṣbwt*) - Milik DFD 176: a form of this word also in Inv xi 78^{1} (highly uncert. reading, cf. also Gawlikowski TP 75).

tṣbt v. *tṣbyt.*

tṣlw **OldAr** Sing. + suff. 3 p.s.m. *tṣlwth* Tell F 5 (Akkad. par. *ṣi-pu-šú*), 9 (Akkad. par. *ik-ri-bi-a*) - ¶ subst. f. prayer; *lmšmʿ tṣlwth* Tell F 9: to hear his prayer; *zy tṣlwth ṭbh* Tell F 5: the prayer to whom is good (:: Wesselius SV 56: whose intercession is good), cf. also Stefanovic COAI 234 n. 2; cf. Dion FS Delcor 143: poss. < Akkad.? (for this uncertain interpret., cf. also Andersen & Freedman FS Fensham 19); on the form, cf. also Kaufman Maarav iii 165, Greenfield FS Rundgren 150.

tq᾿ **JAr** Naveh sub SM 20, EI xx 307: l. *tq᾿* (= Sing. emph.?, < Greek θήκη (= ark, chest)) in MPAT-A 42^{4} (prob. reading, diff. interpret. :: e.g. Fitzmyer & Harrington MPAT a.l., Hüttenmeister ASI 14: l. *tr᾿* (= Sing. emph. of *trʿ*$_{1}$) :: Beyer ATTM 399: l. *tr᾿* = lapsus for *᾿tr᾿* (= Sing. emph. of *᾿tr*$_{2}$ (= *᾿šr*$_{4}$)).

tqbh **OffAr** Sing. abs. *tqbh* Herm 4^{5} (= gen.), *tqbt* Herm 2^{11} (= acc.; for these forms, cf. Wesselius AION xxx 266) - ¶ subst. of unknown meaning, indicating a countable object; Bresciani & Kamil Herm p. 388: = garment? (cf. also Milik Bibl xlviii 553, 582: not < Egypt., indication of some sort of cloak, < root *qby/qbb*; cf. also Swiggers AION xlii 139) :: Porten & Greenfield ZAW lxxx 223 (n. 22), Porten Arch 267f. (n. 7), Grelot DAE p. 155 (n. e): < Egypt. = vessel, vase (cf. also Porten & Greenfield JEAS p. 154, 159, Porten & Yardeni sub TADAE A 2.1/2.

tqby v. *tqbr.*

tqbr **OffAr** Sing. abs. *tqbr* Sem ii 31 conv. 1 (v. infra) - ¶ subst. (?) of unknown meaning; Grelot DAE 370 n. l.: poss. < Egypt., cf. however Dupont-Sommer Sem ii 37f.: poss. < Iran., indication of Persian functionary?; cf. also Grelot DAE p. 370 n. l: or (div. otherwise) l. *tqbrmh* < Egypt. (meaning unknown) :: Grelot RB lxxiv 586: poss. l. *tqby* (< Egypt.).

tqbrmh v. *tqbr.*

tqwmh **Hebr** Sing. abs. *[t]qwmh* DJD ii 45^{4} - ¶ subst. existence; *᾿yn lhm [t]qwmh* DJD ii 45^{4}: they cannot survive.

tqwn **JAr** Sing. emph. *tqwnh* MPAT-A 13^{2} (= SM 46) - ¶ subst. repair;

tqwnh d›trh [qdy]šh MPAT-A 13[2f.]: the repair of the synagogue.

tqwph **Hebr** Sing. cstr. *tqwpt* SM 27[13-16], 45[13-16] (= Frey 1163), 67[15,16] (= Frey 1207) - ¶ subst. solstice, equinox; *tqwpt nysn*, *tqwpt tmwz*, *tqwpt tyšry*, *tqwpt ṭbt* SM 45[13f.]: spring equinox, summer solstice, autumnal equinox, winter solstice (occurring in a depiction of the Zodiac), cf. SM 27[13ff.], 67[15f.].

tql$_1$ v. *šql$_1$*.

tql$_2$ v. *šql$_3$*.

tqm$_1$ (< Egypt., cf. Grelot Sem xiv 68ff., RB lxxviii 533, DAE p. 335 n. a, Farzat Sem xvii 77ff., Bresciani & Kamil Herm p. 389, Porten Arch 92f. (nn. 159-161), Gibson SSI ii p. 143) - **OffAr** Sing. abs. *tqm* Cowl 15[16], 37[10], Krael 2[6], 7[20], Herm 2[13], 3[12], 4[7], 5[5], ATNS 92[1], Sem xiv 72 i conv. 1 - ¶ subst. castor oil (for this interpret., cf. Grelot Sem xiv 63ff., cf. also Porten & Greenfield ZAW lxxx 223 (n. 23), Fitzmyer FS Albright ii 157f., WA 260, v. also supra; cf. already Krael p. 214: or = oil or ointment and Milik RB lxi 249: type of parfum or a spice) :: Krael p. 147, 214: or = jar? (cf. also Reider JQR xliv 339) :: Joüon MUSJ xviii 58: a certain object, piece of furniture? :: Cowl p. 49, 134, Leand 39b: = Qal Impf. 3 p.s.f. of *qwm$_1$*; *dbš tqm* Cowl 37[10]: honey, castor oil (cf. Grelot Sem xiv 67 :: Milik RB lxi 249: = honey with seasoning :: Krael p. 147: = honey of the jar? (i.e. a jar of honey?)). v. *tqm$_2$*.

tqm$_2$ **OffAr** Sing. emph. *tqm›* AG 99[2] - ¶ subst. poss. meaning sanctuary (< root *qwm$_1$*, cf. also Joüon MUSJ xviii 57f. :: Joüon ibid.: = colony) :: Aimé-Giron AG a.l. p. 98 (cf. also idem BIFAO xxxviii 35f.): = subst. used adverbially, ordinarily (cf. also Verger RGP 43, Milik Bibl xlviii 557, Grelot Sem xiv 65) :: (Dupont-Sommer with) Bresciani & Kamil Herm p. 389: = castor grove (cf. *tqm$_1$*; cf. also Grelot DAE p. 335 n. a), cf. also Farzat Sem xvii 79f.: *tqm›* in AG 99[2] = castor grove, prob. = the same word as *tqm$_1$* :: Segal sub ATNS 21: = Sing. emph. of *tqm$_1$* (= castor oil)) - *lš›yl kmr› zy nbw ytb tqm› bswn* AG 99: of Sh. the priest of Nebo who dwells in the sanctuary in Sewan (epithet to be connected with Nebo) - the same word poss. also (Sing. emph. *tqm›*) in Sem xiv 72 ii 2 (heavily dam. context).

tqmh v. *qmt$_1$*.

tqn$_1$ **Hebr** Pi‹el Impf. 2 p.s.m. *ttqn* DJD ii 44[4]; Part. pl.m. abs. *mtqnyn* SM 49[24] - **Palm** Pa‹el Impf. 3 p.s.m. *ytqn* RB xxxix 539[4] - **JAr** Pa‹el Imper. s.m. *tqn* MPAT 60[4] - ¶ verb Pi‹el/Pa‹el to prepare: MPAT 60[4] (+ obj.), RB xxxix 539[4] (+ l_5 + obj.); *ttqn lhn mqwm* DJD ii 44[4f.]: prepare for them a place; in SM 49[24]: to set in order > to make things legally fit for use by giving the priestly dues (cf. Jastrow s.v. *tqn*, cf. also Yadin IEJ xi 48f., BK 129, Beyer ATTM 352, 726, v.Bekkum SV 123).

tqn₂ **OffAr** Sing. abs. *tqn* FuF xxxv 173^{10}; cstr. *tqn* FuF xxxv 173^{9} (v. infra) - ¶ subst. fortress: FuF xxxv $173^{9,10}$ (for this highly uncert. interpret., cf. Altheim & Stiehl FuF xxxv 173, 176, ASA 277).

tqp₁ **Nab** Sing. abs. *tqp* CIS ii 197^{3}, 207^{3}, 210^{4}, 215^{3}, 222^{4}, 224^{3}, J $5^{3,6}$; emph. *tqp›* CIS ii 207^{6} - ¶ subst. (v. however infra) valid document, title (on the meaning of this word, cf. Muffs 208, Kaufman AIA 46, Lipiński Stud 142 n. 4 (cf. also Loewenstamm HUCA xlii 119)); *tqp mn ›rws dnh* CIS ii 207^{3}: a valid document of the said A.; *dy ynpq bydh tqp mn yd hn›w dnh dy ytqbr* J $5^{2f.}$: who produces himself a valid document by the hand of the said H. that he may be buried; *dy ynpq bydh mn yd hynt d› ktb ›w tqp dy ...* CIS ii $224^{2f.}$: who produces by himself a writ or a valid document to ... from the hand of the said H.; *yqbr mn dy yṣb› btqp› dy bydh kdy bktb› hw* CIS ii $207^{5f.}$: he will bury whom he pleases in virtue of the valid document he owns, according to what is in that writ; cf. also *ktb tqp* CIS ii 197^{3}, 215^{3}, 222^{4}: a writ of (i.e. containing) a valid title (or in these instances *tqp* = Sing. m. abs. of *tqp₂* (= adj., valid)?), cf. also Greenfield Mem Yalon 73f.

tqp₂ v. *tqp₁*.

tr **Pun** Solá-Solé Sef xv 48: l. *trm* (= Plur. abs. of *tr* (= necklace)) in ICO-Spa 2; *kd trm ›drm* = a jar for splendid necklaces (highly uncert. reading and interpret., cf. Amadasi sub ICO-Spa 2, Sem xxxviii 18).

tr› v. *tq›*, *tr‹₁*.

tr›h **Pun** Sing. abs., cf. Poen 939: *thera* (for this interpret., cf. L.H.Gray AJSL xxxix 80, Sznycer PPP 106, FR 203, 284.1b n. :: e.g. Schroed 314, Glück & Maurach Semitics ii 113f.: = Sing. abs. of *tr‹₁*) - ¶ subst. observation; *bodi aly thera* Poen 939: while I am on the look-out.

trb cf. Frah vii 17 (*tlb›*): fat (subst.), cf. also Lemosín AO ii 267.

trbh **Pun** Sing. abs. *trbt* KAI 162^{4}, 163^{3} - ¶ subst. (?) of uncert. meaning; Février JA ccxliii 55, AIPHOS xiii 164, 170: = offspring (cf. also Röllig KAI a.l.).

trbṣ (< Akkad., cf. e.g. Zimmern Fremdw 42, Kaufman AIA 107, Whitehead JNES xxxvii 124 n. 27) - **OffAr** Sing. abs. *trbṣ* KAI $276^{5,6}$; emph. *trbṣ›* Krael $9^{4,7,14,15}$, Driv 7^{7}, *trbṣh* Krael 10^{3} (cf. Krael p. 249 × e.g. Grelot DAE p. 248, Porten & Greenfield JEAS p. 63, Porten & Szubin JAOS cvii 233, Porten & Yardeni sub TADAE B 3.11: = Sing. + suff. 3 p.s.m.); + suff. 3 p.s.m. *trbṣh* Krael 3^{4} (cf. Milik RB lxi 249, Porten & Greenfield JEAS p. 40 :: Driver PEQ '55, 92: = Sing. emph.), KAI 260^{7} - ¶ subst. m. - **1)** porch, gateway (cf. *plg trbṣ› hw plg tḥyt mṣryt* Krael 9^{4}: half of the *trbṣ* that is half of the *tḥyt* (v. s.v.) in Egyptian; *trbṣh hw bbh* (v. *bb₁*) Krael 10^{3}: its *trbṣ* that is its gateway), this meaning also in Krael $9^{7,14,15}$; *trbṣh ›r‹ wl› bnyh* Krael $3^{4f.}$: its *trbṣ* is vacant and not built upon (for an interpret. of *trbṣ* in this instance as "courtyard", cf. e.g. Krael a.l., Ginsberg JAOS lxxiv 157, Kutscher JAOS lxxiv 234f., Hoftijzer VT ix 312f., Grelot DAE p. 216, Porten & Greenfield JEAS p. 40, Porten & Yardeni sub TADAE B 3.4; an interpretation as "porch-building" is not to be excluded: the (place of) the porch-building is vacant ...) - **2)** used figuratively to indicate the room where the personnel/slaves of the household stay and prob. also to indicate the people staying there; *whnʿlw btrbṣʾ zyly wsṭrw bšntʾ zyly* Driv 7[7]: bring (them; i.e. slaves) in my *trbṣ* and mark (v. *sṭr*$_1$) them with my mark; *trbṣh byth qnynh ṭyn wmyn wmndʿmth* KAI 260[7f.]: his *trbṣ* (i.e. prob. all his personnel/slaves), his house (i.e. his family), his possessions, earth and water, everything that is his (:: Lipiński Stud 155: *trbṣh* = his garden) - this meaning prob. also in the title *rb trbṣ* KAI 276[4f., 6] indication of high functionary in Parthian administration (cf. Greek par. resp. πιτιάξου and ἐπιτρόπου βασιλέως), for this title and its relation to the function of a *bṭhš*/πιτίαξ, cf. e.g. Altheim LuG ii 41ff., Frye SOLDV i 316ff., Altheim & Stiehl Suppl 77ff., ASA 83ff., AAW i 254, GMA 284, GH i 249 (cf. also GMA 482).

trgwl cf. Frah viii 1 (*trgwlʾ*): cock < Akkad. (cf. Kaufman AIA 108), cf. *trnʾwl.*

trdm **OffAr** l. *trkmnh* in CIS ii 129B 1 (= n.p.; cf. also Lidzbarski Eph iii 103f., Chabot sub RES 1367) :: CIS ii a.l.: l. *trdmnʾ*: = Sing. + suff. 1 p.pl. of *trdm* (= sleep).

trḥ$_1$ v. *mtrḥ.*

trḥ$_2$ **OffAr** word of unknown meaning and uncert. reading (reading *tdḥ* also poss.) in IPAA 11[8] (cf. Humbach IPAA p. 15).

try$_1$ (< Egypt., cf. e.g. Couroyer RB lxi 252f., Kutscher JAOS lxxiv 235, cf. also Ginsberg JAOS lxxiv 158, Grelot DAE p. 221 n. a :: Krael p. 172, Segert AAG p. 343: = m. cstr. of *tryn*) - **OffAr** Sing. abs. *try* Krael 4[3,6], 9[4,11], 10[3,6], 12[13,21] - ¶ subst. f. room, house consisting of one room (for litt., v. supra, cf. also Kutscher PICS 142 :: Porten Arch 98, Porten & Greenfield JEAS p. 45, 58, 59, 63, 68, 73: = side (cf. however Porten & Yardeni sub TADAE B 3.5/10)); *mbny by tḥty hw try rbtʾ zyly* Krael 12[13]: the construction of a one-storey-building that is my great room (cf. also Krael 4[3,6], 9[4,11], 10[6], 12[13,21]); *try rsy* Krael 10[3]: the southern room; prob. more than one building of this type could be erected within a house enclosure; v. *tḥty.*

try$_2$ v. *try*$_3$.

try$_3$ **Hatra** the diff. *tryʾ* in Hatra app. 4[6a] prob. = m. emph. of *tryn*, cf. Milik DFD 395 (for the interpret. of this word as "two", cf. Segal Irâq xxix 9 n. 28) :: Safar Sumer xvii 38 (n. 94): = Sing. emph. of *try*$_2$ (= instructor (< Greek; cf. also Caquot Syr xl 12f.: related to Syriac *trʾʾ* = instructor, tutor; cf. also Teixidor Syr xli 273) :: Altheim & Stiehl AAW v/1, 82f., Tubach ISS 401 (n. 696): l. *trʿʾ* (= Sing. emph.

of *tr*ʿ$_2$) :: Aggoula Sem xxvii 138: l. *bny*ʾ (= QAL Part. act. m. s. emph. of *bny*$_1$), cf. also Vattioni IH a.l.

tryn **OffAr** m. abs. *tryn* Cowl 26^{8,11,12,14,18,19}, 82^{11}, Krael 7^{6,40} (*[t]ryn*), Driv 6^4, Aḥiq 56, 58, 62; + suff. 3 p.pl.m. *tryhw[m]* ATNS 5^6 (uncert. reading, cf. Porten & Yardeni sub TADAE B 8.3 (div. otherwise): l. *try* (= m. cstr.) *g*(x)); f. abs. *trtyn* Krael 7^{38}, Driv 6^3 (*trt[y]n*), Aḥiq 92; cstr. *trty* Beh 1 (v. *rgl*$_2$); cf. Frah xix 2 (*tryn*), GIPP 35, SaSt 24 - **Nab** m. abs. *tryn* CIS ii 196^2, 212^8, 213^4, J 176, DBKP 22^{33}; cstr. *try* CIS ii 157^1, J 2^1, RB lxxiii 244^1; f. abs. *trtyn* CIS ii 186^3 (diff. context), 224^{14}, RES 2036^2, IEJ xiii 118^2, DBKP 22^{33}, on coins, cf. Meshorer NC no. 20 (*trty[n]*), 50; cstr. *trty* CIS ii 196^1, MPAT 64 i 12, iii 5, iv 1 (dam. context) - **Palm** m. abs. *tryn* Sem xxxvi 89^{2,4,5}, *trn* CIS ii 3913 ii 130, 3956^5, 4001^3 (for the context, cf. Cantineau JA ccxxii 232f.), 4171^2, 4172^2, 4174^5, Inv xi 7^3 (= Inscr P 74), Ber ii 110^1 (Greek par. δυεῖν), FS Miles 38^2, etc., etc.; emph. *try*ʾ RTP 244 (cf. Caquot RTP p. 150, cf. also Gawlikowski TP 113 n. 20; identical text (*try[*ʾ*]*) in SBS-Tess 4), SBS 35^2 (context however dam., uncert. interpret.); + suff. 3 p.pl.m. *tryhwn* CIS ii 3984^1, SBS 10^4, *trwyhn* CIS ii 3931^2, 4129^1, *trwyhwn* CIS ii 3914^1, 3930^1, Inv x 119^1, xi 83^1 (on the form *trwy-*, cf. Cantineau Gramm 128 :: Rosenthal Sprache 41); f. abs. *trtyn* Sem xxxvi 89^5, *trtn* CIS ii 3913 ii 26, 31 (*trt[n]*), 58, 3973^1 (*[t]rtn*), 3976^2, 4173^1, 4174^8, 4199^4, Ber ii 104^4, v 95^6, Sem xxxvi 89^{3,7} (uncert. reading, cf. Gawlikowski Sem xxxvi 92), cf. Inv D 51^1: θαρθην; emph. *trty*ʾ CIS ii 3959^2 (= SBS 44); + suff. 3 p.pl.m. *trtyhn* Syr xix 78^4 - **Hatra** + suff. 3 p.pl.m. *tryhwn* 408^2 - **JAr** m. abs. *tryn* MPAT 48^4, EI xx 305 ii (*[t]ryn*; heavily dam. context), DBKP 21 back (?, highly uncert. reading, cf. Yadin & Greenfield DBKP a.l.; Greek par. δύω); cstr. *try* MPAT 60^1, *tr* MPAT 60^2 (lapsus); f. abs. *trtyn* MPAT 39^1, 67^3 (= Frey 1300), *trtn* MPAT 51^6, SM 88^3 (= Syn D A 3), 89^3 (for this reading, cf. Torrey sub Syn D C 1^3, cf. however Naveh sub SM 89: l. *trtyn* :: Obermann Ber vii 94: l. rather *trty* = f. abs.) - ¶ cardinal number, two: passim; cf. the foll. constructions - **1)** ʾ*mn tryn* Cowl 26^{12}: two cubits; *kršn tryn* Krael 7^6: two *karsh*; *gbrn ḥlkyn tryn* Driv 6^4: two Cilician men; *zmnyn tryn* CIS ii 196^6: two times; *tltyn tryn* CIS ii 213^4: two thirds; *ksp sl*ʿ*yn* ʾ*lpyn tryn* CIS ii 212^8: a sum of two thousand *s.*; ʾ*ksdryn trn* RB xxxix 541^3: two exedrae; *ṣlmyn trn* CIS ii 3913 ii 130: two statues; *gwmḥyn trn* CIS ii 4174^5: two niches; *gwmḥyn trn gwyyn* Ber ii 88^4: the two inmost niches; *sl*ʿ*yn trtn* MPAT 51^6: two *s.*; ʾ*myn trtyn* MPAT 67^3: two cubits; etc., etc. - **2)** *trtyn mln* Aḥiq 92: two things; *trtyn zbnyn* CIS ii 186$^{3f.}$: two times (diff. context); θαρθην γοβνιν Inv D 51^1: two cheeses (v. *gbn*$_2$) - **3)** *trn* ʾ*[ḥy]*ʾ *qdyš*ʾ CIS ii 4001^3: the two holy brothers; *trtn kpy*ʾ Ber ii 104^4: the two vaulted rooms; *trn ṣtry*ʾ FS Miles 38^2: the two walls - **4)** *try ḥmrn* MPAT 60^1:

two asses; *tr gbryn* MPAT 60[2]: two men (v. supra) - **5)** *try gmly›* CIS ii 157[1]: two camels; *try gwḥy›* J 2[1]: two niches; *trty npšt›* CIS ii 196[1]: the two stelae; *trty ḥnwt›* MPAT 64 i 12, iii 5: the two shops - **6)** *gwmḥy› trn qdmyn* CIS ii 3971[2]: the two foremost niches - **7)** *gbry› ›lk tryn* Aḥiq 56: these two men; *gwmḥy› ›ln trn* Ber ii 104[1]: these two niches - **8)** *[t]rtn ‹lwt› ›ln* CIS ii 3973[1]: these two altars - **9)** *ṣlmy› ›ln trwyhwn* CIS ii 3914[1]: these two statues; *‹mwdy› ›ln tryhwn* SBS 10[4]: these two columns; *prsd› tryhwn* Hatra 408[2]: the two columns; etc. - used in chronology, *šnt trtn* SM 88[3]: the second year (cf. IEJ xiii 118[1f.], SM 89[3]); *byrḥ ›yr šnt ḥmš m›h wtrtn* CIS ii 4173[1]: in the month I. in the 502nd year (cf. CIS ii 4174[7f.]); *šnt trtyn lrb›l* CIS ii 224[13f.]: the second year of R. (cf. RES 2036[1f.], J 17[5f.], Nab. coins (v. supra)) - for the context of Krael 7[38,40], v. *dyn*$_1$ - for the context of CIS ii 3959[2], v. *grmṭws* - a form of this word poss. also in ATNS 103 (*try[*; heavily dam. context) - Aggoula Syr lxiii 364: l. *[t]rynh* = Sing. + suff. 3 p.s.m. in Hatra 369 (= his lieutenant), uncert., reading and interpret., cf. also An-Nagafi Sumer ???: l. *]dynh* (without interpret.) - cf. *šnym*.
v. *šlš*$_1$, *try*$_{1,3}$.

tryṣyt **OffAr** Altheim & Stiehl FuF xxxv 173: l. *tryṣyt* in FuF xxxv 173[5] = adv., indeed (cf. also idem ASA 277; highly uncert. interpret.).

tryš v. *trš*$_2$.

trk$_1$ **OffAr** PA‛EL Impf. 2 p.s.m. *ttrk* Krael 2[14] (on the reading, cf. also Yaron JSS xiii 207 n. 1, Porten BiAr xlii 82); Inf. + suff. 3 p.s.f. *trkwth* Cowl 15[30], 46[8] (*trk[wth]*), Krael 7[30]; + suff. 2 p.s.f. *trktky* Krael 6[16] - **JAr** PA‛EL Part. s.m. abs. *mtrk* MPAT 40[2,13] - ¶ verb PA‛EL to chase - **1)** + obj. + *mn*$_5$, *ltrkwth mn byth zy ›ṣḥwr* Cowl 15[30]: to chase her from the house of A. (cf. Krael 6[16], 7[30]) - 2) + *l*$_5$, *ttrk l›mh tmt* Krael 2[14]: you will chase away his mother T.; *šbq wmtrk mn r‛ty ... ›nh ... lky* MPAT 40[2f.]: I divorce and repudiate you of my own free will ... (cf. MPAT 40[13f.]) - for the context of Cowl 15, Krael 7, cf. Yaron JSS v 66f., Law 55, Verger OA iii 53f., RGP 126ff.
v. *trq*.

trk$_2$ **JAr** Plur. abs. *trkyn* MPAT 40[7,20] - ¶ subst. Plur. repudiation; *spr trkyn wgṭ šbqyn* MPAT 40[7f.]: a document of repudiation and a writ of divorce (cf. MPAT 40[20f.]).

trn$_1$ v. *tbnh*$_2$.

trn$_2$ v. *tryn*.

trsyt **OffAr** Sing. + suff. 2 p.s.m. *trsytk* ATNS 25[2] - ¶ subst. provisions, sustenance.

trn›wl cf. Frah viii 3 (*tln›wl(y)›*): rooster - cf. *trgwl*.

tr‛$_1$ **OffAr** Sing. abs. *tr‛* Krael 9[15], FuF xxxv 173[8] (uncert. context), cf. Warka 13: *ta-ra-ḫa*, Warka 38: *ta-ra-ḫi* (for the forms in Warka, cf. Garbini HDS 32); cstr. *tr‛* Cowl 5[3], Aḥiq 44; emph. *tr‛›* Cowl 5[12,14],

Krael 12[21], Driv F iia 13[1], AM-NS ii 171 i 3 (:: Altheim & Stiehl Suppl 90, 92f. (div. otherwise): l. *bḥr'* (= n.p.)), *tr'* AM-NS ii 171 ii 3 (:: Altheim & Stiehl Suppl 93 (div. otherwise): l. *bḥr'* (= n.p.)); for these forms from AM-NS, cf. Shaked BSOAS xxvii 287 n 76; Plur. abs. *tr'n* Cowl 30[9], 31[9]; + suff. 3 p.s.f. *tr'yh* Aḥiq 168; cf. GIPP 65 - **Nab** Sing. emph. *tr''* CIS ii 170[3] - **Palm** Sing. emph. *t[r]''* RB xxxix 541[3]; Plur. emph. *tr'y'* CIS ii 3914[4]; + suff. 3 p.s.m. *tr'why* CIS ii 3917[3], 3958[4] (= SBS 49), Inv xii 48[2], JSS xxxiii 171[3], *tr'wh* PNO 7a, *tr'w* SBS 39[2] (dam. context) - **Hatra** Sing. emph. *tr''* 380 - **JAr** Sing. emph. *tr'h* MPAT-A 1[4] (= SM 21), 21 (= SM 11), 48[2] (= SM 15; :: e.g. Frey sub 979: l. *tr''* (= Sing. emph.)), IEJ xxxvi 206[3], AMB 15[7] (dam. context); Plur. abs. *tr'yn* AMB 15[5] - ¶ subst. m. - **1)** gate - a) of a town, cf. *ta-ra-ḫa ú-ma-' ia-a-ti-ib-a-a-'i-i* Warka 13: the gate and those who are sitting in it (cf. Warka 38) - b) of a palace; ... *zy hqymt btr' hykl'* Aḥiq 44: the one whom you have placed in the gate of the palace (i.e. whom you gave an (administrative) function at the court); cf. Aḥiq 23: *whqymt bbb hykl'* (cf. also Kaufman AIA 40f.) - c) of temple; *tr'n zy 'bn ... zy hww b'gwr' zk* Cowl 30[9f.]: the gateways of stone, which were in that temple (cf. Cowl 31[9]), CIS ii 3914[4] (cf. however Gawlikowski Ber xix 76 n. 37: in this text = doorleaf), PNO 7a, Inv xii 48[2] (v. *mlbn*); cf. prob. also SBS 39[2], dam. context - d) of a synagogue: MPAT-A 1[4], 21 (context however dam.) - e) of a tomb construction: RB xxxix 541[3] - f) of a house; *wyhbt ly tr' byt zylk lmbnh 'gr 1 tmh* Cowl 5[3f.]: you gave me the gateway of your house to build a wall there (exact meaning of the passage not clear), cf. Cowl 5[12,14], Krael 9[15], 12[21], Aḥiq 168; cf. also *[d]lt tr'h dbyth* IEJ xxxvi 206[3]: the door (?) of the gate of the house - **2)** door (of a gate), *bb' wtr'why* CIS ii 3917[3]: the gate and its doorleaves (or the porch-building and its doors) - > Akkad., cf. v.Soden Or xxxvii 268, xlvi 196, AHW s.v. *taraḫu* - cf. *š'r₁*, *šr'₁*.
v. *šr'*, *tq'*, *tr'h*, *tr'₂*.

tr'₂ **Hatra** Plur. emph. *tr''* 202[9,11] (cf. Milik DFD 386f., Vattioni IH a.l. :: Caquot Syr xli 271, Aggoula Ber xviii 101: = Sing. emph. :: Safar Sumer xviii 63, Teixidor Sumer xxi 87* no. 4: = Sing. emph. of *tr'₁*) - ¶ subst. gate-keeper, janitor.
v. *try₃*.

tr'₃ v. *trq*.

tr'h = breach, rift > Akkad., cf. v.Soden Or xxxvii 268, xlvi 196, AHW s.v. *terḫutu*.

trṣ **Palm** PA'EL Pf. 3 p.pl.m. *trṣw* Inv xii 49[8] - ¶ verb PA'EL to settle, to arrange (for the context, v. *ṣbw*).
v. *mwddw*.

trṣ' v. *šwr₄*.

trq **Ph** QAL (?, or PI'EL?) Pf. 3 p.s.m. *trq* KAI 26A I 9 (cf. FR

267b also for litt.; interpret. as Inf. abs. less prob.) - ¶ verb QAL (?, or PI‘EL?) meaning derived from context, to destroy or to drive out; uncert. etymology; Honeyman PEQ ’49, 52: *trq* = *ṭrq* (cf. Hebr., Ar., Arab.); = to strike (cf. H.P.Müller TUAT i 641: = to strike, to smash, cf. Akkad. *tarāku(m)*); Alt WO i 281: *trq* secondary formation < root *ryq*$_1$ (cf. Pedersen ActOr xxi 50, cf. also Zolli Sef x 167); Lipiński SV 48, 50 n. d: *trq* = to remove, to take away (cf. Akkad. *tarāqu*; highly uncert. etymology); Marcus & Gelb JNES viii 19: l. *tdq*, *tdq* = secondary formation < root *dqq* (:: Leveen & Moss JJS i 193: = lapsus for *ydq* (= YIPH form of root *dqq* = to crush)); Dupont-Sommer RA xlii 170: or *trq* = *trk*$_1$ (cf. J.Ar. and Akkad.; for this interpret., cf. also Dupont-Sommer Oriens ii 122, v.d. Branden Meltô i 40, 82, Bron RIPK 53f., Lipiński OLZ ’82, 458, Gibson SSI iii p. 57) :: Dupont-Sommer ibid.: or *trq* = *tr‘*$_3$ (cf. J.Ar. and Syriac; = to break, to shatter (cf. Healy CISFP i 665)) :: Levi Della Vida RCL ’49, 283: poss. *trq* = lapsus for *rtq*$_1$ (= to chain, to put in fetters), cf. also Del Olmo Lete AO i 288.

trš$_1$ **Ph** Sing. abs. *trš* KAI 26A iii 7, 9, C iv 7, 9 (*tr[š]*) - ¶ subst. must, new wine; *b‘l šb‘ wtrš* KAI 26A iii 9: owners of plenty (sc. of grain) and of new wine (cf. e.g. Obermann Conn xxxviii 32, Gordon JNES viii 115, Röllig KAI a.l., v.d.Branden Meltô i 56f., Dahood Bibl liii 397, Ps iii 348, Fensham VT xxii 298 (n. 4), Gibson SSI iii p. 51f., 57, Bron RIPK 107f. (cf. also Alt WO i 283, Dahood Bibl xlvii 278f., Ginsberg FS Gaster 138, Greenfield Sem xxxviii 155f., H.P.Müller TUAT i 644) :: Honeyman PEQ ’49, 53: *trš* = *trš*$_2$ (= heritage, possessions), cf. also Février Sem iv 15, RHR cxli 20: = *trš*$_2$ (= riches), Lipiński SV 48: = *trš*$_2$ (= well-being) in KAI 26A i 6) - on this word, cf. also Brown VT xix 168ff., Delcor APCI 228ff., Borowski AIAI 113.
v. *trš*$_2$.

trš$_2$ **Pun** Sing. abs. *trš* CIS i 5522[2] (v. infra) - ¶ subst. of uncert. interpret.; prob. = derivative of root *yrš*: heritage?; *mqny htrš mbmyp‘l ’dn* CIS i 5522[2]: the one who acquired the heritage because of an act of (his) master (:: v.d.Branden BiOr xxiii 143: *trš* = *trš*$_1$, *mqny htrš* = wine merchant) :: Février Sem iv 15, CIS i a.l. (div. otherwise): l. *mqny htršm bmyp‘l ’dn*, *tršm* = Plur. abs. of *trš*$_2$ (= hereditary possession), *mqny htršm* = hereditary slave; on the expression, cf. also Elayi RCP 62f. - v.d.Branden Meltô i 69f., 82: l. this word (Sing. abs. *tryš*) in KAI 26A ii 19, iii 2, 4 (= abundance) as part of divine epithet; improb. interpret., cf. e.g. Röllig KAI a.l., Gibson SSI iii p. 60: prob. = part of n.l.
v. *trš*$_1$.

trtyn v. *tryn*.

trtn$_1$ **OffAr** Bordreuil Syr lxv a.l.: the *trtn* on seal (Syr lxv 445) =

title (Sing. abs.) < Akkad. (= indication of high official), uncertain interpret. (on this word, cf. also Lipiński ZAH i 73).

trtn$_2$ v. *tryn*.

tš’$_1$ **Pun** Sing. abs. *tš’* Hofra 103^2 - ¶ subst. indication of function, prob. = lapsus for *tm’$_2$*, cf. Février with Berthier & Charlier Hofra p. 85, JA ccxlvi 444, Roschinski Num 109.

tš’$_2$ v. *tš‘$_2$*.

tšbḥwt **Hebr** Sing. abs. *tšbḥwt* AMB 3^1 - ¶ subst. praise; *šyr tšbḥwt* AMB 3^1: a song of praise.

tšy‘y v. *tš‘y*.

tškb **Palm** the reading *tškb[’]* in CIS ii 3972^3 (= Sing. emph. of *tškb* (= couch?)) less prob., l. rather *tšbb[’]* (= n.p.), cf. Ingholt PaS 19 n. 2, Rosenthal Sprache 67, 74 n. 2.

tšlwmh **JAr** Sing. emph. *tšlwmt’* MPAT 39^7 (*tšlwm[t’]*), 45^6, *tš[lm]th* MPAT 51^{13} - ¶ subst. indemnity.

tšlmh v. *tšlwmh*.

tšmyš **Palm** Sing. cstr. *[tš]myš* CIS ii 3913 ii 58 (Greek par. χρήσεως); emph. *tšmyš’* CIS ii 3913 ii 70 - ¶ subst. use (:: Teixidor AO i 245: = administration); *[ltš]myš ‘ynn trtn dy m[y] dy bmdyt’ d 800* CIS ii 3913 ii 58: for the use of two wells of water which are in the city, 800 *denarii*; *[w]m’ dy ytb‘’ ytn [lh]n ltšmyš’* CIS ii 3913 ii 70: what is required (sc. of the salt), he will give to them (sc. to the tax-collectors) for use.

tš‘$_1$ **Palm** CIS ii sub 4100: l. *[t]š‘’* in CIS ii 4100^1 = Sing. emph. of *tš‘$_1$* (= reputation, renown; cf. also Díez Merino LA xxi 137); highly uncert. interpret., cf. e.g. Aggoula Sem xxvii 118f.: l. *]š‘’* = Sing. emph. of *š‘$_3$* or *š‘y$_3$* (= reputation); cf. also Milik DFD 298f.: l. *[y]š‘’* = Sing. emph. of *yš‘$_3$* (= Saviour); cf. also Rosenthal Sprache 74 n. 2.

tš‘$_2$ **Pun** m. *tš‘* KAI 130^2, Hofra 61^3, Sem xxxvi 35^4 - **Hebr** m. *tš‘* IEJ vii 239^6 - **OffAr**, cf. Frah xxix 9: *tš’* - **Nab** m. *tš‘* CIS ii 197^4, 198^3, 220^3 - **Palm** m. *tš‘* CIS ii 4053^5, Sem xxxvi 89^4; f. *tš‘h* Sem xxxvi 89^3, *tš‘’* CIS ii 4229^2, Inv xi 23^7 (= CIS ii 4010) - **JAr** m. *tš‘* MPAT 52^8, IEJ xxxvi 206^5, Mas 564^4 (heavily dam. context) - ¶ cardinal number, nine; used in chronology, *ywm tš‘’ byrḥ ’b* Inv xi 23^7: on the ninth day in the month A.; *]tš‘ lyrḥ* Hofra 61^3: on the ... ninth day of the month; *šnt tš‘ lḥrtt* CIS ii 197^4: the ninth year of Ch. (cf. CIS ii 198$^{2f.}$, 220^3); *šnt ḥmš m’h wšb‘yn wtš‘* CIS ii 4053$^{4f.}$: the 579th year.

tš‘y **Hebr** m. abs. *tšy‘y* SM 106^7; f. abs. *tš‘t* KAI 185^1, Dir ostr 4^1, 8^1, 9^1, 10^1, 12^1, 14^1 (*tš[‘t]*), *tš‘yt* Lach xx 1 - ¶ ordinal number, ninth; *bšt htš‘t* KAI 185^1: in the ninth year (cf. Dir ostr 4^1, 9^1, 10^1, 12^1, 14^1); *btš‘yt* Lach xx 1: in the ninth (year), prob. interpret., dam. context (cf. Diringer Lach iii p. 339 n. 1, Lemaire IH i 134 :: Lipiński BiOr xxxv 287: *tš‘yt* poss. = indication of a ninth part of a *bat*); *[m]šmr htšy‘y* SM 106^7: the ninth division (v. *mšmr*).

tš‘yt **Palm** Sing. emph. *tš‘yt›* Sem xxvii 117^4 - ¶ subst. renown (cf. Aggoula Sem xxvii a.l.).

tš‘m **Ph** *tš‘m* KAI 3^2 (diff. and uncert. context; for this interpret., cf. Dunand BMB ii 102, Torczyner Lesh xiv 158 n. 1, 160f., Dupont-Sommer ArchOr xvii^1 162, Röllig KAI a.l., FR 242 :: v. d Branden RSF ii 139, BiOr xxxvi 203: = QAL Impf. 2 p.s.m. of *š‘m* (= to reconcile) :: Albright BASOR xc 36 n. 5: = QAL Impf. 2 p.s.m. of *š‘y*$_1$ + enclitic *mem* (= to see, to look for, to take an interest in, to care for) :: Obermann JBL lviii 233f., 242: = QAL Impf. 2 p.s.m. of *š‘‘*$_1$ (= to enjoy), cf. Iwry JAOS lxxxi 33, McCarter & Coote BASOR ccxii 18, cf. already Albright BASOR lxxiii 11f. for the interpret. of this word as Impf. 2 p.s.m.; cf. also Gibson SSI iii p. 11) - **Pun** *tšm* Punica xx 1^5, *ṭyšm* Punica v 4^2, xii 23^2 - **Hebr** *tyš‘ym* SM 13^1 - **JAr** *tš[‘]yn* MPAT 48^4 - ¶ cardinal number, ninety; used in chronology, *lmspr ›rb‘ m›wt wtyš‘ym w›rb‘ šnh lḥrbn hbyt* SM 13^1: in the year 494 of the destruction of the Temple.

tš‘yn v. *tš‘m*.

tt› **OffAr** word of unknown meaning in FuF xxxv 173^{11} (Altheim & Stiehl FuF xxxv 173, 177, ASA 277: = variant of *tḥt›* (= Sing. emph. of *tḥt*), highly uncert. interpret.).

ttr v. *‘wtr*.

B. Porten

Glossary of New Readings from TADAE C

C 3.7 is published here for the first time (the abbreviation C = Cowl).

ʾb₁ v. *ʾlh₁*.

ʾgr₂ Sing. + suff. 3 p.s.f. *bʾgrh* 3.28[89] (:: *s.grh* C 81[12]) - ¶ subst. wages.

ʾdyhbn Sing. (?) abs. (?) *ʾryhbn/ʾdyhbn* 3.7Ev1[15], 3.7Ev2[6]; v. *ʾryhbn* - ¶ subst. of unknown meaning.

ʾhb₁ v. *ʾwpsth*.

ʾwpsth Sing. abs. or + suff. 3 p.s.m. *ʾwpsth* 3.21[4] (:: *ʾhbth* C 75[3], cf. *ʾhb₁*), 3.21[9] (:: *ʾḥwth* C 75[8], cf. *ʾḥ₁*) - ¶ subst. land.

ʾzl v. *yd*.

ʾḥ₁ f. Sing. + suff. 3 p.s.m./1 p.s. *ʾḥt[h]/ʾḥt[y]* 1.1[6] (:: *ʾḥr[y]* Aḥiq 6); v. *ʾwpsth* - ¶ subst. f. sister.

ʾḥr₄ *[ʾ]ḥr* 1.1[13] (:: *[ʾt]wr* Aḥiq 13) - ¶ adv. then.

ʾḥr₅ *ʾḥry [ʾ]ḥry ʿwy[...]* 1.1[213] (:: nothing Aḥiq 214); + suff. 1 p.s. *ʾḥry* 2.1[77] (:: *ʾ .r.* BIDG) - ¶ prep. after.

ʾḥry Sing. m. abs. *ʾḥry* 3.27[29] (:: *ṣmy* C 83[28]) - ¶ adj. other.

ʾyty *ʾyty* 1.1[115] (:: *ʾtn[* Aḥiq 179) - ¶ subst. (pseudo verb) there is.

ʾkrpk/ʾkdpk Sing. abs. *ʾkrpk/ʾkdpk* 3.7Gr2[26], 3.7Gr3[5,13], etc., etc. - ¶ subst. a kind of wood.

ʾl₃ *ʾ[l]* 1.1[81] (:: *[zy]* Aḥiq 97),[146] (*wʾ[l]* :: *w[...* Aḥiq 146) - ¶ adv. not (prohibitive).

ʾlh₁ Plur. + suff. 3 p.pl.m. *ʾlhyhm* 1.2[19] (:: *ʾbhyhm* C 71[2], cf. *ʾb₁*) - ¶ subst. god.

ʾlk v. *zk₂*.

ʾlp₃ Plur. abs. *ʾlpn* 3.14[39] (:: *ʾlp* thousand C 24[40], cf. *ʾlp₅*) - ¶ subst. boat.

ʾlp₅ v. *ʾlp₃*.

ʾm₁ Sing. + suff. 3 p.s.m. *ʾmh* 4.9[1] (:: *plgh* C 74[1], cf. *plg₃*) - ¶ subst. mother.

ʾmh *ʾmh* 3.21[7] (:: *ʾmt* C 75[6]) - ¶ word of unknown meaning.

ʾmr₁ Qal Pf. 3 p.s.m. *]ʾmr[* 3.8II[10] (:: ... AG 16v[5]), *kn ʾmr* 3.8IIIB[30] (:: *..b* AG 15v[3]); Pf. 1 p.s. *w[ʾmrt]* 1.1[14] (:: nothing Aḥiq 14); inf. cstr.

lʾm[r] 3.13[56] (:: *l...* C 61.1[5]) - ¶ verb QAL to say.

ʾnb v. *ʿnb*.

ʾnzʿrrh Sing. emph. *ʾnzʿrrtʾ* 1.1[89] (:: *ʾp zʿrrtʾ* Aḥiq 105, cf. *zʿrrh*) - ¶ subst. medlar.

ʾnp$_2$ Dual + suff. 3 p.s.m. *ʾnpwhy* 1.1[115] (:: *why* Aḥiq 179) - ¶ subst. face.

ʾswt Sing. cstr. (?) *ʾswt* 3.7Dr1[7], 3.7Kr2[25], 3.7Kr4[2], etc., etc. - ¶ subst. meaning unknown.

ʾp$_2$ *[ʾ]p hw* 3.8IIIB[33] (:: *...b]gw* AG 13v[1]) - ¶ adv. moreover.

ʾṣyl v. *ḥṣyp*.

ʾrdb abbrev. *ʾ* 3.14[23] (:: ..... C 24[24]) - ¶ subst. ardab.

ʾrz$_2$ Sing. abs. *ʾrz* 3.7Gr3[24,25], 3.7Fr 2[25], etc., etc. - ¶ subst. cedar.

ʾrḥ$_2$ Sing. emph. *ʾrḥʾ* 1.1[122] (:: *ʾrḥh* Aḥiq 187, cf. *ʾrḥ$_2$*) - ¶ subst. way.

ʾryhbn Sing. abs. (?) *ʾdyhbn/ʾryhbn* 3.7Ev1[15], 3.7Ev2[6]; v. *ʾdyhbn* - ¶ subst. of unknown meaning.

ʾš$_1$ m. Sing. abs. *ʾy[š]* 1.2[21] (:: *ʾy[* C 71[28]); f. Sing. cstr. *ʾtt* 3.4[6] - ¶ subst. m. man, f. woman, wife.

ʾšh$_2$ Sing. emph. *ʾštʾ* 1.1[222] frag a[3] (:: ....ʾ Aḥiq 218 C) - ¶ subst. fire.

ʾšl$_1$ Plur. abs. *ʾšln* 3.23[1] (*[ʾ]šln* :: *]šln* ATNS 87[1]),[4] (*].tḥq ʾšln* :: *]ptḥqy .šln* ATNS 87[4]), 3.24[3] (:: *ʾšl.[* ATNS 106[3]),[4] (*kl [ʾ]šln* :: *].ln* ATNS 106[4]) - ¶ subst. aroura, surface measure.

ʾšr$_4$ Sing. + suff. 3 p.s.m.? *(ydʿ) ʾt[rh]* 1.1[190] (:: nothing Aḥiq 191) - ¶ subst. place.

ʾšrn Sing. emph. *[ʾ]šrnʾ* 3.8IIIB[32] (:: *...šrn.* AG 15v[5]) - ¶ subst. material.

bylwp v. *zlwḥ*, *tlpḥ*.

byt$_2$ Sing. cstr. *(b)byt* 1.1[121] (:: *.b.t* Aḥiq 186); + suff. 1 p.s. *[mn by]ty* 1.1[139] (:: *[mny]* Aḥiq 139); emph. *bytʾ* 3.27[30] (:: *myrytʾ* C 83[29], cf. *myryt*) - ¶ subst. house.

bmyt Sing./Plur. *bmyt[* 3.8IIIA frag.b[1] (:: ....*ṭ*.... AG 7[1]) ,[2] (:: *bmys* AG 7[2]) - ¶ subst. of unknown meaning.

bswlh Sing. abs. (?) *bswlh* 1.1[217] (:: *b[ʿ]wlh* Aḥiq 218) - ¶ subst. of unknown meaning.

bʿy$_1$ QAL Impf 3 p.s.m. + suff. 2 p.s.m. *ybʿk* 1.1[43] (:: *yrʿk* Aḥiq 43, cf. *yrʿ*) - ¶ verb QAL to seek.

bqr PAʿEL Pf. 3 p.pl.m. *bqrw* 3.7Ar2[19], 3.7Br1[15], 3.7Cr2[3], etc., etc. - ¶ verb PAʿEL to inspect, examine.

br$_1$ m. Sing. cstr. *br* 3.28[92] (:: *bb* C 81[16]), 3.8IIIA[6] (*[b]r* :: . AG 5[6]); Sing. emph. *w[brʾ]* 1.1[1] (:: *[...* Aḥiq 1); + suff. 1 p.s. *]bry[* 1.1[8] (:: *brh [* Aḥiq 8, cf. *br$_1$*); f. Sing. cstr. *brt* 3.15[14] (*[.... br]t* :: nothing C 22[14]),[17] (*b[rt]* :: *b[r]* C 22[17]),[97] (*[.]l[.. br]t* :: nothing C 22[94]), 3.18[4] (:: *byt* ATNS 45a[2]),[5] (:: *byt* ATNS 45a[3]),[6] (*b]rt* :: ... ATNS 45a[4]), 3.26[22] (*[b]rt[* :: ... AG 87b[4]) - ¶ subst. m. son, f. daughter.

br' mn *br' mn* 3.28[48] (:: *br'mn* C 81[110]) - ¶ words of unknown meaning.

btm'sr Sing. abs./cstr. (?) *btm'sr* 3.28[114] (:: *bṭm'sw* C 81[40]) - ¶ subst. of unknown meaning.

gby$_1$ QAL Part. pass. s.m. abs. *gby* 3.7Ar2[1], 3.7Br1[11,19], etc., etc. - ¶ verb QAL to collect.

gbr$_2$ Sing. abs. *gb[r]* 1.1[218] (:: *g[rh]* Aḥiq 219, cf. *grh*$_2$) - ¶ subst. man.

gdy$_2$ Sing. + suff. 2 p.s.f. *gdyky* 1.1[209] (:: *š'ny* Aḥiq 210, cf. *š'n*$_1$) - ¶ subst. kid.

gw *gw* 3.19[3] (:: *grwm* C 73[3]), 3.8IIIB[19sl] (*bgw* :: *yd* AG 11r[7]) - ¶ subst. inside; preceded by prep. *b*$_2$ in, inside.

gwy$_2$ Sing. m. emph. *gwy'* 3.19[1] (:: *gpy'* C 73[1], cf. *gp*$_1$), *mn gnz' g[wy']* 3.19[21] (:: *mpš* C 73[4] left) - ¶ adj. internal.

gn$_1$ v. *grb*$_1$.

gnz Sing. emph. *gnz'* 3.19[1] (:: *gp'* C 73[1], cf. *gp*$_1$),[21] (*mn gnz' g[wy']* :: *mpš* C 73[4] left), 3.19frag[2] (*gnz'[* :: *gpy'* C 73[8] left, cf. *gp*$_1$) - ¶ subst. treasury.

gp$_1$ v. *gwy*$_2$, *gnz*.

grb$_1$ Plur. abs. *gnbyn* 3.28[115] (:: *gn b 46* C 81[41], cf. *gn*$_1$) - ¶ subst. flagon.

grh$_2$ v. *gbr*$_2$.

db Sing. emph. *db'* 1.1[168] (:: *rb'* Aḥiq 120, cf. *db*) - ¶ subst. bear.

dgl$_1$ Sing. cstr. *(l)dgl* 3.19[4] (:: *ls..l* C 73[4]) - ¶ subst. detachment.

dwgy Sing. cstr. 3.7Gr1[12], 3.7Gr2[22], 3.7Gr3[16], etc., etc. - ¶ subst. sea-going vessel.

dwgyt Sing. abs. *dwgyt* 3.8I[10] (or cstr. (?), *[d]wgyt[* :: *.g.l.../...t..* AG 18r[3] + 12v[1]), 3.8IIIB[26] (*bgw dwgyt* :: *...kygzt .* AG 10rb[6]); Sing. cstr. *dwgyt* 3.8IIIB[19sl] (*dw[gy]t ḥnh.[* :: *by...t ḥzh* AG 15rb[6bis]); Sing. emph. *dwgyt'* 3.8II[7] (*[dwg]yt'* :: *.t'* AG 16v[2]), 3.8IIIA[3] (*[dw]gyt'* :: *..yt'* AG 5[3]), 3.8IIIB[24] (:: *p.yt'* AG 13r[6]), 3.8IV frag a[7] (*[dw]gyt'* :: ... *yt'* AG 39[3]); + suff. 3 p.s.m. *dwgyth* 3.8IV frag a[5] (:: ...... AG 18r[3] + 12v[1]); + suff. 1 p.s. *dwgyty* 3.8IV frag a[9] (:: *dwgyt'* AG 39[5]). ¶ subst. fishing boat.

dm$_1$ v. *nmr*$_2$.

dmn Plur. cstr. *dmy* 3.7Jv2[3], 3.7Kv2[4,6], etc., etc. - ¶ subst. Plur. price, value

dš Plur. cstr. *[d]ššy* 1.1[97] (:: *..š* Aḥiq 161) - ¶ subst. door

h'$_1$ m. Sing. *hw* 1.1[128] (:: *hd* Aḥiq 128, cf. *h'*$_1$), 3.8IIIB[33] (*[w']p hw* :: *...b]gw* AG 13v[1]) - ¶ pers. pron. he, it.

h'$_2$ *[kz]y/[h]'* 1.1[18] (:: *h'* Aḥiq 18, cf. *h'*$_2$) - ¶ interj. behold!

hw v. *h*ʾ$_1$.

hwy$_1$ QAL Pf. 3 p.s.m. *hwh* 1.1^{211} (:: *hy.* Aḥiq 212),^{217} (:: *yqnh* Aḥiq 218, cf. *qny$_1$*), 2.1^3 (*[hwh ʿlw]hy* :: *[brʾšhwm]* BIDG); 3 p.pl.m. *h[ww]* 1.1^{40} (:: *ḥ[zny]* Aḥiq 40); Inf. + suff. 3 p.pl.m. *mhwyhwn* 3.28^{118} (:: *mhny zwzn* C 81^{44}, cf. *mhny*, *zz*) - ¶ verb QAL to be.

hwn$_1$ v. *nšq$_1$*.

hlʿtyk *hlʿtyk* 3.28^{47} (:: *.lʿtyk* C 81^{109}),^{48} (:: *mlʿtyn* C 81^{110}, cf. *tlʿ*) - ¶ subst. of unknown meaning.

hn$_1$ v. *yyn*.

zbn$_1$ QAL Part. act. pl.m. abs. or Pf. 1 p.pl. *zbnn* 3.8IIIB^{32} (:: *z......* AG 15v^5) - ¶ verb QAL to buy.

zhb Sing. abs. *zhb* 3.7Jr2^{20} , 3.7Ar2^2, 3.7Ar3^{23}, etc., etc. - ¶ subst. gold.

zz v. *hwy$_1$*.

zy *zy* 1.1^{211} (:: nothing Aḥiq 212); in comb. *kzy [kz]y/[h]ʾ* 1.1^{18} (:: *hʾ* Aḥiq 18) - ¶ conj. who, which/of; in comb. *kzy* when.

zk$_2$ Plur. *ʾlk* 3.19 frag^3 (:: *wlk* C 73^9 left) - ¶ pron. Plur. those.

zkrn Sing. abs. *zkrn* 3.8IIIB^{28} (*zkrn]* :: ... AG 11v^2),^{34} (*z]krn* :: *...mn* AG 13v^2), 3.13^{24} (:: *1 l.* C 62,3^5),^{44} (:: *zkwr* C 63^8) - ¶ subst. memorandum.

zlwḥ Plur. abs. *zlwḥn* 3.13^7 (*zlwḥ[n]* :: *bylwp* C 61^7, cf. *bylwp*),^{17} (*zlw[ḥn]* :: *1 lp* C 61^{17}),^{21} (*zlwḥ[n]* :: *wl.* C 62,3^2),^{25} (*zl[wḥn]* :: *1 l* C 62,3^6) - ¶ subst. sprinkler (?).

znh *(b)znh* 3.28^{73} (:: *ḥnyh* C 81^{127}) - ¶ dem. pron. this.

zʿr$_2$ Sing. m. abs. *[zʿy]r* 1.1^{136} (:: nothing Aḥiq 136); *[zʿ]rh* 3.28^{122} (:: *rbh* C 81^{48}) - ¶ adj. little, small.

zʿrrh v. *ʾnzʿrrh*.

zph Sing. abs. *(b)zph* 3.28^{58} (:: *...ph* C 81^{121}) - ¶ subst. loan.

zrʿ$_2$ Sing. + suff. 3 p.pl.m. *zr[ʿhwm]* 2.1^{78} (:: *lzr[ʿ]* BIDG) - ¶ subst. seed.

ḥgb *ḥgb* 3.8IIIB^{25} (:: *ḥ..* AG 10rb^5) - ¶ word of unknown meaning.

ḥdš$_1$ Plur. m. abs. *ḥdtn* 3.7Fv2^{19}, 3.7Fv3^{15}, 3.7Gv3^2, etc., etc. - ¶ adj. new.

ḥdt$_1$ v. *ḥdš$_1$*.

ḥwy$_1$ v. *ḥzy$_1$*.

ḥzy$_1$ QAL Pf. 3 p.s.m. *ḥzh* 1.1^{220} (*]ḥzh k[.]h* :: ... *mh* Aḥiq 221),^{221} (:: *znh* Aḥiq 222); Impf. 3 p.s.m. + suff. 3 p.s.m. *yḥznhy* 1.1^{86} (:: *yḥ[wn]hy* Aḥiq 102); 2 p.s.m. *tḥzh* 1.1^{80} (:: *tḥwh* Aḥiq 96, cf. *ḥwy$_1$*) - ¶ verb QAL to see.

ḥyh$_1$ Sing. abs. *[w/k]lḥyh* 1.1^{181} (:: *[ʿd y]ḥyh* Aḥiq 86) - ¶ subst. animal.

ḥlp$_4$ *]ḥ[l]p* 3.8IV frag a^5 (:: ... AG 39^1) - ¶ prep. instead of.

ḥmh$_2$ Sing. + suff. 1 p.s. *ḥmty* 1.1^{140} (:: *ḥmt[ʾ]* Aḥiq 140, cf. *ḥmh$_2$*) - ¶ subst. wrath.

ḥmwš Sing. abs. *ḥmwš* 3.7Cr1[10], 3.7Cr2[11], 3.7Dr3[17], etc., etc., *kḥmwš* 3.7Dr1[7,13], 3.7Kr2[25], etc., etc. - ¶ subst. of unknown meaning.

ḥmd$_2$/r$_3$ Sing. cstr. *ḥmd/r* 1.1[88] (:: *ḥmr* Aḥiq 104, cf. *ḥmr$_3$*) - ¶ subst. delight/heat.

ḥmr$_3$ v. *ḥmd$_2$*.

ḥmr$_4$ v. *ḥmr$_5$*.

ḥmr$_5$ Sing. abs. *ḥmr* 3.7Ar2[7,15], 3.7Cr2[14], *ḥm* 3.28[92], 3.28[92] (*ḥm k›n* :: *ḥmr›n* C 81[16], cf. *ḥmr$_4$*), *mr* 3.19[33] - ¶ subst. wine.

ḥmš$_2$ v. *ḥmšy*.

ḥmšy Plur. f. emph. *ḥmšt[›]* 3.28[22] (:: *ḥmšt..* C 81[83], cf. *ḥmš$_2$*) - ¶ subst. fifth (?).

ḥṣyp Sing. m. abs. *ḥṣy[p]* 1.1[143] (:: *›ṣy[l]* Aḥiq 143, cf. *›ṣyl*) - ¶ adj. impudent.

ḥrš *[ḥr]š›* 3.28[110] (:: *...z›* C 81[34]) - ¶ word of unknown meaning.

ṭbḥ$_1$ Sing. emph. *ṭbt›* 3.8II[1] (*]mn ṭbt›* :: *... mn ṭbt .....* AG 16r[1]) - ¶ subst. goodness.

ṭyn Sing. cstr. *ṭyn* 3.7Gr2[25], 3.7Gr3[4,12], etc., etc. - ¶ subst. clay (?).

ṭlpt Sing. abs. *ṭlpt* 3.7Gv4[1] - ¶ subst. of unknown meaning.

ṭ‹m$_2$ Sing. abs. *ṭ‹m* 3.8IIIB[30] (:: *.... b....* AG 14v[3]),[34] (*[ṭ‹]m* :: *d....p....* AG 10v[1]) - ¶ subst. order.

ybl$_1$ HAPH Pf. 3 p.pl. *hyblw* 3.28[56] (:: *bzyly* C 81[119]) - ¶ verb HAPH to bring.

yd Sing. cstr. *(l)yd* 3.8IV frag a[8] (:: *..›zlyn* AG 39[4], cf. *›zl*); Plur. + 3 p.s.m. *[bydwh]y* 1.1[135] (:: nothing Aḥiq 135), *‹lyd* 3.8IIIB[35] (:: .... AG 10v[2]), 3.12[10,11,31] (:: *‹lyk* C 72[5,6,20]), *‹l y[d]* 3.1[4] (:: nothing RES 1791) - ¶ subst. hand; preceded by prep. *‹l$_7$* by the hand of.

yd‹$_1$ QAL Pf. 3 p.s.m. *yd‹ (›t[rh])* 1.1[190] (:: nothing Aḥiq 191) - ¶ verb QAL to know.

yhb QAL Pf. 1 p.s. *yhbt* 1.1[9] (*y[hb]t* :: *h[šgyt* Aḥiq 9), 3.13[10] (or 3 p.s.f. *]zy yhbt* :: absent C 61[10]) - ¶ verb QAL to give.

yw Sing. abs. *yw* 3.7Br1[3], 3.7Cr2[11], 3.7Er1[11?], etc. - ¶ subst. a liquid measure.

ywm Sing. emph. *ywm›* 1.1[80] (:: *ytr›* Aḥiq 96, cf. *ywm*), 3.19[2] (*[y]wm›* :: *[‹]lym›* C 73[2]),[20] (*ywm[›]* :: *r›* C 73[3] left); Plur. abs. *ywmn* 1.2[5] (*ywmn ḥm[šh]* :: *wmnḥ[m]* C 71[21]); + 2 p.s.m. *[y]wmyk* 1.1[202] (:: *[q]dmyk* Aḥiq 203, cf. *qdm$_3$*) - ¶ subst. day.

yḥṭ QAL Part. pass. abs. s.m. *yḥyṭ* 1.1[133] (:: *[..]yṭ* Aḥiq 133); Inf. cstr. *lmyḥṭ* 3.8IV 7 (:: *lmṣry›* AG 12v[3]) - ¶ verb QAL to set up.

yyn Sing. abs. *yn* 3.1[2] (:: *hn* RES 1791, cf. *hn$_1$*), 3.1[1] (*[y]n[..]n[* :: nothing RES 1791) - ¶ subst. wine.

yld$_1$ QAL Impf. 3 p.s.f. *wtld* 1.2[26] (:: *tlk* C 71[33]) - ¶ verb QAL to bear a child.

ym$_1$ Sing. emph. *ym›* 3.7Gv5[22], 3.7Kv2[1,3], etc., etc. - ¶ subst. sea.

yrḥ$_2$ Sing. cstr. *yrḥ* 3.13^{12} (:: *ywm* C 61^{12}), 3.26^{4} (*[byr]ḥ* :: .... AG 87a^{7}) - ¶ subst. month.
yrʻ v. *bʻy$_1$*.
yšr$_1$/pšr$_1$ HAPH Pf. 3 p.s.m. *hwšr/hpšr* 3.13^{50} (:: *hpšr* C 63^{14}, cf. *pšr$_1$*) - ¶ verb HAPH to dispatch.
ytr$_3$ Sing. m. abs. *ytyr* 3.7Dv2^{1} - ¶ substantivated adj. surplus.
kby v. *ksy$_1$*.
kd$_1$ Plur. abs. *kndn* 3.7Ar2^{7,15}, 3.7Cr1^{13}, etc., etc. - ¶ subst. jar.
kdb$_3$ Sing. m. abs. *k[d]yb* 2.1^{65} (:: *ʻ[....]* BIDG) - ¶ substantivated adj. liar.
kkr v. *sbr$_2$*.
knd v. *kd$_1$*.
knt Plur. abs. *kntn* 3.8IIIB^{25} (:: *k.tn* AG 10rb^{5}), 3.16^{6} (*[k]ntn* :: *tw p* Krael 17^{6}), 3.17b^{5} (:: *kwtnw* AG 77^{5}) - ¶ subst. emmer.
ksy$_1$ QAL Pf. 3 p.s.m. *ksh* 3.13^{34} (:: *ksp ..* C 63^{1}); Impf. 2 p.s.m. *tksh* 1.1^{84} (:: *tkbh* Aḥiq 100, cf. *kby*) - ¶ verb QAL to cover.
ksy$_2$ Sing. + suff. 2 p.s.m. *ksyky* 1.1^{167} (:: *nsyky* Aḥiq 119, cf. *nsyk*) - ¶ subst. covering.
ksp$_2$ Sing. abs. *ksp* 1.2^{22} (:: *]sw* C 71^{29}), 3.15^{20} (*[ksp]* :: nothing C 22^{20}) - ¶ subst. silver.
kp$_1$ Plur. abs. *kp[n]* 3.13^{26} (:: *bḥ.* C 62,3^{7}); *kʼ* 3.7Br1^{3}, 3.7Dr1^{1}, 3.7Dr2^{13}, etc., etc. - ¶ subst. hand = 1/3 of a cubit, 1/3 of a jar; ladle.
krš$_1$ Plur. abs. *kr[šn]* 3.28^{56} (:: .. C 81^{119}) - ¶ subst. measure of weight.
kt Sing. emph. *(mn) ktʼ* 3.28^{80} (:: *nṣbtʼ* C 81^{2}) - ¶ subst. aftergrowth.
lʼ$_1$ *lʼ* 1.1^{97} (:: *lh* Aḥiq 161)^{,211} (*w[l]ʼ* :: *z...* Aḥiq 212) - ¶ adv. not.
lbb$_2$ Sing. abs. *lb[b]* 1.1^{82} (:: *l[qḥ]* Aḥiq 98); + suff. 2 p.s.m. *[llb]bk* 1.1^{84} (:: *[lʼḥw]k* Aḥiq 100) - ¶ subst. heart.
lwṭ QAL Impf. 2 p.s.m. *tl[w]ṭ* 1.1^{80} (:: *t[b]ṭ* Aḥiq 96) - ¶ verb QAL to damn.
lyly Sing. abs. *[ly]lh* 1.1^{80} (:: *[kl m]lh* Aḥiq 96) - ¶ subst. night.
lq Sing. abs. *lq* 3.7Gr2^{2,12}, 3.7Gr4^{13}, etc., etc.; Plur. abs. *lqn* 3.7Gr3^{6,14}, 3.7Fr1^{21}, etc., etc. - ¶ subst. oar (?).
lqḥ QAL Pf. 3 p.s.m. *(w)lqḥ* 3.13^{50} (:: *wl ...[* C 63^{14}) - ¶ verb QAL to take.
ltqs[*ltqs[* 3.13^{18} (:: *2* C 61^{18}) - ¶ word of unknown meaning.
mʼh$_2$ Sing. cstr. *mʼt* 3.13^{54} (:: *myt* C 62,1^{3}, cf. *mwt$_1$*) - ¶ subst. century
mʼkl Sing. cstr. *[ky mk]l* 1.1^{131} (:: *[tšlm]* Aḥiq 131) - ¶ consumption, food.
mʼn Plur. cstr. *mʼny* 3.8II^{6} (*[mʼ]ny* :: .... AG 16v^{1}), 3.13^{10} (*[m]ʼny* :: *ʻny* C 61^{10}) - ¶ subst. vessel.
mwt$_1$ v. *mʼh$_2$*.
mym Plur. abs. *my[n]* 1.1^{95} (:: *mt[ngdh]* Aḥiq 159) - ¶ subst. water.

myn$_1$ v. *mym*.
myryt v. *byt$_2$*.
mlwt (< Coptic *mlot* [Zauzich]) Sing. abs. *mlwt* 3.7Gr3^{25}, 3.7Fr2^{26}, 3.7Gv2^{22}, etc., etc. - ¶ subst. board (?).
mn$_5$ *mn gnzʾ g[wyʾ]* 3.19^{21} (:: *mpš* C 73^{4} left) - ¶ prep. from.
mndh$_1$ Sing. emph. *mndtʾ* 3.7Ar2^{1}, 3.7Ar3^{19}, 3.7Br1^{11}, etc., etc. - ¶ subst. payment, duty.
mnh$_1$ Sing. cstr. *mnt* 3.7Ar2^{4}, 3.7Br1^{22}, 3.7Cr2^{10}, etc., etc. - ¶ subst. portion.
mnyn Sing. abs. *mnyn* 3.7Gr3^{23}, 3.7Fr1^{19}, 3.7Fr2^{24}, etc., etc. - ¶ subst. amount.
mnṣyʿh Sing. cstr. *mnṣ[yʿt]* 1.2^{7} (:: *mnṣ[ḥn]* C 71^{16}); Sing. emph. *mṣyʿtʾ* 3.28^{112} (:: *mṣy..ʾ* C 81^{38}) - ¶ subst. middle, midst.
mʿnh Sing. abs. *mʿnh* 1.1^{162} (:: *mʿ[l]h* Aḥiq 114, cf. *ʿly$_1$*) - ¶ subst. utterance, concern.
mʿšr Sing. abs. *mʿšr* 3.7Kr2^{19}; emph. *mʿšrʾ* 3.7Fr2^{12} (*wmʿšrʾ*), 3.7Gr3^{2,9}, etc., etc. - ¶ subst. tithe.
mrʾ Sing. + suff. 3 p.s.m. *(l)m[rʾ]h* 1.2^{23} (:: *(l)[ ]š* C 71^{6+30}); Plur. + suff. 3 p.pl.m. *mrʾyhm* 1.1^{73} (:: *mrʾy h[n]* Aḥiq 73), 1.2^{24} (:: *mrʾh[* C 71^{7}, cf. *mrʾ*) - ¶ subst. master.
mrby Sing. emph. *mrbytʾ* 3.81V frag a^{10} (:: *mb.tʾ* AG 39^{6}) - ¶ subst. interest, excess.
mšḥ$_3$ Sing. abs. *mšḥ* 3.7Ar2^{8}, 3.7Br1^{3}, 3.7Cr1^{10}, etc., etc., *mš* 3.29^{6}; Sing. emph. *mšḥʾ* 3.7Ar2^{4}, 3.7Br1^{18,22}, etc., etc. - ¶ subst. oil.
mšḥh v. *mšḥt*.
mšḥt Sing. + suff. 3 p.s.m./f. *mšḥth* 3.7Cr2^{5}, 3.7Er1^{16}, etc., etc. - ¶ subst. measurement.
ngd$_3$ Plur. + suff. 3 p.s.m. *ngdwhy* 1.1^{10} (:: *sgdwhy* Aḥiq 10, cf. *sgd$_2$*) - ¶ subst. chief.
ngʿ$_1$ v. *pgʿ$_1$*.
ngr$_2$ v. *sgd/r*.
nhr$_2$ Sing. emph. *nhrʾ* 3.13^{34} (:: *bʾ* C 63^{1}) - ¶ subst. river (?).
nḥš$_2$ Sing. abs. *(zy) nḥš* 3.13^{13} (:: .. *ksp (?) š* C 61^{13}), 3.7Kr4^{21}, 3.7Gr2^{10}, 3.7Gr3^{21}, etc., etc. - ¶ subst. bronze, copper.
nḥt$_1$ QAL Inf. cstr. *lmnḥt* 3.16^{1} (:: *mpḥt* Krael 17^{1}, cf. *nḥt$_3$*) - ¶ verb QAL to go down, bring down.
nḥt$_3$ v. *nḥt$_1$*.
nkry Sing. abs. *mn nk[ry]* 1.1^{159} (:: *[zptʾ ?]* Aḥiq 111) - ¶ subst. stranger.
nmr$_2$ Sing. abs. *nrm* 1.1^{210} (:: *wdm* Aḥiq 211, cf. *dm$_1$*) - ¶ subst. leopard.
nsyk v. *ksy$_2$*.
nsk QAL Inf. cstr. *lmnsk* 3.13^{7} (:: *lg* C 61^{7}) - ¶ verb QAL to pour.

npq$_1$ HAPH Pf. 3 p.pl. *hnpqw* 3.7Gv5[16], 3.7Kv2[1,4], etc., etc.; Impf. 3 p.s.m. *wyhnpq* 1.2[22] (:: *wʾtnpq* C 71[29], cf. *npq*$_1$) - ¶ verb HAPH to take out (= to ship).

npqh Sing. emph. *[n]pqtʾ* 3.17[b5] (:: *..qtʾ* AG 77[5]); Plur. abs. *npqn* 3.27[20] (:: *swqn* C 83[19]) - ¶ subst. outlay.

nrm v. *nmr*$_2$,

nšʾ$_1$ QAL Impf. 3 p.s.m. *ynšʾ* 1.1[193] (:: *ypšr* Aḥiq 194, cf. *pšr*$_1$) - ¶ verb QAL to carry.

nšq$_1$ HAPH Impf. 2 p.s.m. *thnšq* 1.1[87] (:: *thn šq* Aḥiq 103, cf. *hwn*$_1$) - ¶ verb HAPH to kindle.

ntn QAL Pf. 1 p.s.m. *[w]ntnt* 3.28[79] (:: .... C 81[1]); Impf. 3 p.pl.m. *zʾ yntnw* 3.8IV frag. a[7] (:: *zy* .... AG 39[3]); 2 p.pl.m. *wtntnw* 3.8IV frag. a[8] (:: *..p...* AG 39[4]); Inf. cstr. *lmntn* 3.8IIIA frag. b[3] (:: *ʾnt.* AG 7[3]) - ¶ verb QAL to give.

ntr$_5$ Sing. emph. *ntrʾ* 3.7Kv2[4,6,8], etc., etc. - ¶ subst. natron.

sbr$_2$ Sing. abs. *sbr* 3.27[31] (:: *kl* C 83[30]); Plur. abs. *sbrn* 3.27[30] (:: *kkrn* C 83[29], cf. *kkr*) - ¶ subst. m. porter.

sgd/r Sing. emph. *sgd/rʾ* 3.13[45] (:: *ngrʾ* C 63[9], cf. *ngr*$_2$) - ¶ subst. of unknown meaning.

sgd$_2$ v. *ngd*$_3$.

swyr Sing. emph. *swyrʾ* 1.1[183] (:: *swydʾ* Aḥiq 88, cf. *swyr*) - ¶ subst. hiding place (?).

sy (< Egypt. *sy*) Sing. abs. *sy* 3.7Gr3[24], 3.7Fr2[25], 3.7Gv2[21], etc., etc. - ¶ subst. beam (?).

smkt Sing. abs. *smkt* 3.7Ar2[9,17], 3.7Br1[4], etc., etc. - ¶ subst. support (?).

sny Sing. abs. *sny* 3.7Fv2[14], 3.7Fv3[10], 3.7Gv2[11], etc., etc. - ¶ subst. a kind of iron.

sp$_1$ Plur. abs. *spn* 3.7Ar2[8,16,18], etc., etc. - ¶ subst. jar (?).

spynh Sing. abs. *spynh* 3.7Ar2[20], 3.7Br1[8], 3.7Cr2[4], etc., etc.; cstr. *spynt* 3.7Fr1[6], 3.7Jv2[4,6], etc., etc.; emph. *spyntʾ* 3.7Dr1[11], 3.7Fv3[18], etc., etc., 3.12[23] (*[s]pyntʾ* :: *]pṣtʾ* C 72[23] right); Plur. abs. *b/wspynn* 1.2[8] (:: *ʾḥrnn* C 71[24]) - ¶ subst. ship, boat.

spl Sing. emph. *splʾ* 3.28[109] (:: *wzwlʾ* C 81[33]) - ¶ subst. bowl.

spr$_2$ Sing. emph. *sprʾ* 3.8IIIB[37] (:: ...ʾ AG 10v[4]) - ¶ subst. scribe.

spt QAL Part. pass. pl. m./f. abs. *spytn* 3.7Ar2[18], 3.7Cr1[16], 3.7Cr2[2], etc., etc. - ¶ verb QAL to coat with pitch (?).

ʿbd$_1$ QAL Pf. 1 p.s. *ʿbdt l[* 2.1[71] (:: .... BIDG); 3 p.pl.m. *ʿb[dw]* 3.8IIIB[24] (:: *ʿb[d]* AG 10rb[4]); Impf. 3 p.s.m. *yʿbd* 1.2[21] (:: nothing Aḥiq 71[28]); ITP Impf. 3 p.s.m. *ytʿbd* 3.8IV frag. a[3] (:: *yt....* AG 17[3]) - ¶ verb QAL to do, make - ITP to be done/made.

ʿbd$_2$ Sing. abs. *kʿ[bd]* 1.1[72] (:: *ʿ[ʾyš]* Aḥiq 72) - ¶ subst. servant.

ʿbr$_4$ Sing. emph. *ʿbwrʾ* 3.28[79] (:: *ʿnbyʾ* C 81[1], cf. *ʿnb*) - ¶ subst. grain.
ʿwyr/l Sing. m. abs. *[ʾ]ḥry ʿwy[l/r]* 1.1[213] (:: nothing Aḥiq 214) - ¶ substantivated adj. blind man/child.
ʿl$_7$ *ʿ[l]* 3.16[2] (:: nothing Krael 17[2]) - ¶ prep. on, to.
ʿlh$_6$ Sing. emph. or Sing. + suff. 3 p.s.m. *ʿlth* 3.25[16] (:: *ʿlnh* C 78[1], cf. *ʿln$_3$*) - ¶ subst. income.
ʿly$_1$ v. *mʿnh*.
ʿly$_2$ Sing. m. emph. *ʿlyʾ* 3.28[88] (:: *ʿl..* C 81[11]) - ¶ adj. superior.
ʿlym m. Plur. cstr. *ʿlymy* 3.27[30] (:: *ʿl* C 83[29]) - ¶ subst. lad.
ʿll$_1$ HAPH Pf. 3 p.pl.m. *[hnʿ]lw* 3.19[1] (:: *]ʿln* C 73[1], cf. *ʿln$_3$*) - ¶ verb HAPH to bring in.
ʿln$_3$ v. *ʿlh$_6$*, *ʿll$_1$*.
ʿmr$_7$ Sing. cstr. *qmr* 3.7Fv2[12], 3.7Fv3[8], 3.7Dv1[11], etc., etc. - ¶ subst. wool.
ʿnb Plur. + 2 p.s.m. *ʾnbyk/bʾbyk* 1.1[101] (:: *[bʾn]byk* Aḥiq 165); v. *ʿbr$_4$* - ¶ subst. fruit.
ʿnz Sing. emph. *ʿnzʾ* 1.1[209] (:: *w[lʾ]* Aḥiq 210), 1.1[209] (*[lʿnz]ʾ* :: *...k* Aḥiq 210) - ¶ subst. goat.
ʿṣ Sing. cstr. *ʿq* 3.7Ar2[17], 3.7Br1[4], 3.7Cr2[1], etc., etc.; Plur. abs. *ʿqn* 3.7Gr3[23], 3.7Gr4[6,20]; cstr. *ʿqy* 3.7Gr2[26], 3.7Gr3[5,13], etc., etc. - ¶ subst. wood.
ʿq$_1$ v. *ʿṣ*.
ʿrb$_7$ Sing. emph. *ʿrbʾ* 3.28[102] (:: *ʿ...* C 81[26]) - ¶ subst. guarantor.
ʿtq Sing. m. abs. *ʿtyq* 3.7Gr2[2,12], 3.7Fr2[2], etc., etc.; Plur. m./f. abs. *ʿtyqn* 3.7Fr1[21], 3.7Gv3[3] - ¶ adj. old.
pgʿ$_1$ QAL Impf. 3 p.s.m. + suff. 1 p.s. *ypgʿny* 1.1[212] (:: nothing Aḥiq 213); Part. act. s.m. abs./cstr. *pgʿ* 1.1[101] (:: *n]gʿ* Aḥiq 165, cf. *ngʿ$_1$*),[102] (:: *ngʿ* Aḥiq 166) - ¶ verb QAL to meet, to touch.
pḥn *pḥn* 3.28[49] (:: *pḥy* C 81[111]) - ¶ word of unknown meaning.
pkd/rn Sing. abs. *pkd/rn* 3.7Gr3[20], 3.7Fr1[14], 3.7Fr2[19], etc., etc. - ¶ subst. a kind of iron.
plg$_3$ Sing. abs. *plg* 3.7Br1[23], 3.7Ar2[7,15], 3.7Cr2[14], 3.28[25], etc., etc. - ¶ subst. half.
v. *ʾm$_1$*.
psld/ršy Sing. abs. *psld/ršy* 3.7Br1[9], 3.7Dr3[3,10], etc., etc. - ¶ subst. of unknown meaning.
pʿmy Sing. abs. *pʿmy* 3.7Jv1[25], 3.7Fv2[18], 3.7Fv3[14], etc., etc. - ¶ subst. a kind of wood.
pq (< Coptic *poge, poke* [Zauzich]) Sing. abs. *pq* 3.7Jv1[24], 3.7Fv2[17], 3.7Fv3[13], etc., etc. - ¶ subst. plank (?).

przl Sing. abs. *przl* 3.8II[6] (:: .... AG 16v[1]); Sing. cstr. *przl* 3.7Gr3[20], 3.7Fr2[19], 3.7Fr3[14], etc., etc. - ¶ subst. iron.
pryš Sing. *pryš.[.].* 1.1[207] (:: *pryšh* Aḥiq 208, cf. *prš$_1$*) - ¶ subst. separation or QAL Part. pass. of *prš$_1$*, separate.
prmnkr Plur. emph. *prm[nkry›]* 3.8IIIB[1] (:: *prm......* AG 14r[1]) - ¶ subst. foreman.
prs$_2$ abbrev. *p* 3.17[b4] (:: *špz* AG 77[4]); Sing. emph. *prs›* 3.26[4] (:: *pbs›* AG 87a[7]) - ¶ subst. allotment.
prš$_1$ v. *pryš.*
pšr$_1$ v. *yšr$_1$*, *nš›$_1$*.
ptḥ$_1$ or **ntḥ** QAL Part. pass. s.m. abs. *p/ntyḥ* 1.1[98] (:: *[ptyḥ]* Aḥiq 162) - ¶ verb to tear, to open.
pty$_3$ Sing. abs. *(b)p[ty]* 3.13[47] (:: *(b).[* C 63[11]) - ¶ subst. width.
ṣbyt Sing. cstr. *[ṣ]byt* 1.1[3] (:: *[ṣb]yt* Aḥiq 3, cf. *ṣbyt*) - ¶ subst. bearer of seal.
ṣlṣl Sing. emph. *ṣlṣl›* 3.8IIIB[24] (:: *›l.n›* AG 13r[6]) - ¶ subst. sailboat (?).
ṣpn$_1$ HAPH Impf. 2 p.s.m. + suff. 3 p.s.m. *thṣpnhy* 2.1[71] (:: *thṣpn* BIDG, cf. *ṣpn$_1$*) - ¶ verb HAPH to hide.
qbl$_3$ + suff. 3 p.s.m. *(l)qblh* 1.2[24] (:: *(l)qbrh* C 71[31], cf. *qbr$_3$*) - ¶ subst. preceded by prep. *l$_5$* opposite.
qbr$_3$ v. *qbl$_3$*.
qdm$_2$ Plur. abs. *(l)qdmn* C3.8II[7] (:: *(l)h bgw* AG 16v[2]); v. *ywm* - ¶ subst. the time before.
qdm$_3$ + suff. 3 p.pl.m. *qdmyhm* 1.2[20] (:: *qdmthm* C 71[3], cf. *qdmh$_1$*); ¶ (subst. used as) prep. before; preceded by prep. *l$_5$* formerly.
qdmh$_1$ v. *qdm$_3$*.
qmr$_1$ v. *‹mr$_7$*.
qndt‹› Sing. abs. *qnd/rt‹›* 3.7Gr1[12], 3.7Gr3[16], 3.7Ev1[16], etc., etc. - ¶ subst. a large sea-going vessel.
qndtšyry Sing. abs. *qnd/rtšyry* 3.7Gr2[22], 3.7Fr2[4], 3.7Jv2[7], etc. - ¶ subst. a small sea-going vessel.
qnh$_1$ Sing. abs. *]qnh[* 3.13[6] (:: .... C 61[6]); Plur. abs. *qnn* 3.13[6] (*[q]nn* :: .... C 61[6]),[15] (:: *yqm[wn]* C 61[15], cf. *qwm$_1$*),[20] (:: *q.* C 62,3[1]) - ¶ subst. rod.
qny$_1$ QAL Impf. 3 p.s.m. *l› [yqnh]* 1.1[195] (:: *l› y[t]qnh* Aḥiq 196, cf. *qny$_1$*); v. *hwy$_1$* - ¶ verb QAL to acquire.
qnrt‹› Sing. abs. *qnr/dt‹›* 3.7Gr1[12], 3.7Gr3[16], 3.7Ev1[16], 3.7Ev 2[19], etc., etc. - ¶ subst. a large sea-going vessel.
qnrtšyry Sing. abs. *qnr/dtšyry* 3.7Gr2[22], 3.7Fr2[4], 3.7Jv2[7], etc. - ¶ subst. a small sea-going vessel.
qrb$_1$ QAL Imp. 2 pl. m. *[q]rb[w]* 1.1[57] (:: *[hqšy]b[w]* Aḥiq 57) - ¶ verb QAL to approach.

qryh Sing. abs. *qr[y]h* 1.1^{95} (:: *q[št]h* Aḥiq 159); emph. *qryt›* 3.21^{2} (*qry[t›]* :: *qrq[‹]* C 75^{1})^{,3} (:: *qrbt›* C 75^{2}, cf. *qrbh*)^{,4} (*q[ryt›]* :: *q[rq‹]* C 75^{3})^{,5} (*qryt›* :: *qr[bt›* C 75^{4}), 3.24^{1} (*[qr]yt›* :: *]yt›* ATNS 106^{1})^{,2} (*[q]ryt›* :: *].yt›* ATNS 106^{2})^{,3} (*[qry]t›* :: *]t›* ATNS 106^{3}) - ¶ subst. town, city.

rb$_2$ Sing. m. + suff. 3 p.pl.m. *rbhm* 2.1^{4} (:: *rbhw[m]* BIDG) - ¶ substantivated adj. commander.

rb‹$_3$ Plur. abs. *rb‹n* 3.28^{29} (:: .... *br* C 81^{90})^{,30} (:: *b* C 81^{91})^{,53} (:: ... C 81^{115}) - ¶ subst. fourth.

rbtkh v. *rstkh*.

rḥm$_4$ m. Plur. cstr. (?) *rḥmy* 1.1^{222} (:: *rḥmn* Aḥiq 223) - ¶ subst. friend.

rḥq$_1$ QAL Imp. 2 p.s.m. *[rḥ]q* 2.1^{165} (:: *]q* BIDG) - ¶ verb QAL to withdraw.

ryqn Plur. m. abs. *ryqnn* 3.7Ar2^{18}, 3.7Br1^{5}, 3.7Cr2^{2}, etc., etc. - ¶ adj. empty.

rkb$_1$ QAL Pf. 3 p.s.m. *rkb* 1.1^{186} (:: *rk[n]* Aḥiq 91, cf. *rkn*) - ¶ verb QAL to mount.

rkn v. *rkb*$_1$.

rstkh Sing. abs. *rstkh* 3.21^{1,8} (:: *rbtkh* C 75^{1,7}, cf. *rbtkh*) - ¶ subst. market.

r‹y$_4$ Sing. abs. *r‹y* 3.19^{8} (:: *brt* C 73^{8})^{,18} (:: *pš[* C 73^{1} left)^{,19} (*r[‹y]* :: ... C 73^{2}) - ¶ subst. a measure or quantity (?).

š›n$_1$ v. *gdy*$_2$.

šg‹ QAL Impf. 3 p.s.m. *[y]šg‹* 2.1^{72} (:: *]šg‹* BIDG) - ¶ verb QAL to be abundant.

šdq Sing. m. abs. *šdq* 1.1^{84} (:: *šrq* Aḥiq 100, cf. *šrq*$_5$) - ¶ adj. sharp.

šwy$_3$ QAL Impf. 3 p.s.m. *wyšwh* 1.2^{24} (:: *wyšrh* C 71^{7}, cf. *šry*$_1$) - ¶ verb QAL to place.

šwšn Sing. emph. *šwšn›* 3.26^{15} (:: ..*šḥdn›* AG 87a^{19}) - ¶ subst. *shushan*-official.

šzb QAL Impf. 3 p.s.m. *yšzb* 1.1^{211} (:: nothing Aḥiq 212) - ¶ verb QAL to rescue.

šṭr$_2$ v. *š‹rh*.

šym$_1$ QAL Pf. 3 p.pl.m. *šmw* 3.8IIIB^{30} (:: ....*b*..... AG 14v^{3})^{,34} (*šm[w]* :: ...*š* AG 10v^{1}) - ¶ verb QAL to issue (an order).

škḥ ITP Pf. 3 p.s.m. *›štkḥ* 3.7Ar2^{4}, 3.7Br1^{18,22}, etc., etc.; 3 p.pl.m. *›štkḥw* 3.7Gr2^{23}; Impf. 3 p.s.m. *wyštk[ḥ]* 1.1^{173} (:: *yšt[mr ?]* Aḥiq 125) - ¶ verb ITP to find oneself, to be found.

šmwš Sing. abs. *šmwš* 3.7Gr2^{25}, 3.7Fr2^{23}, 3.7Gv2^{19}, 3.7Dv1^{15} - ¶ subst. of unknown meaning.

šmym Plur. abs. *šmyn [* 1.1^{189} (:: ..*šmt[* Aḥiq 94, cf. *šmym*) - ¶ subst. heaven.

šmyn v. *šmym*.

šmr$_1$ Itp Impf. 3 p.s.m. *[y]štmr* 1.1[96] (:: *[y]‘md* Aḥiq 160, cf. *šmr$_1$*) - ¶ verb Itp to guard oneself.

šnh$_2$ Sing. cstr. *[š]nt* 3.16[7] (:: *..t* Krael 17[7]) - ¶ subst. year.

š‘rh abbrev. *š* 3.14[23] (:: ..... C 24[24]), 3.17[b4] (:: *špz* AG 77[4]); Plur. abs. *š‘rn* 3.28[83] (:: *šṭr* C 81[5], cf. *šṭr$_2$*) - ¶ subst. Plur. barley.

š‘tsm Sing. abs. *š‘tsm* 1.2[5] (:: *]š‘trm* C 71[21]) - ¶ subst. of unknown meaning.

šrḥw Sing. emph. *šrḥw[.]’* 1.1[106] (:: *šrḥw[t’]* Aḥiq 170, cf. *šrḥw*) - ¶ subst. foulness (?).

šry$_1$ v. *šwy$_3$*.

šrq$_5$ v. *šdq*.

šty$_1$ Qal Impf. 2 p.s.m. *tšth* 1.1[191] (:: nothing Aḥiq 192) - ¶ verb Qal to drink.

tḥt *tḥt* 3.8IIIB[31] (:: ......*l th.n* AG 15v[4]) - ¶ prep. under.

tly$_1$ Qal Impf. 3 p.s.m./1 p.s. + suff. 3 p.s.m. *[y/’]tlnhy* 1.2[3] (:: *[t]tlnhy* C 71[19], cf. *tly$_1$*); Part. pass. s.m. abs. *tly* 3.28[113] (:: *ytly* C 81[39], cf. *tly$_1$*) - ¶ verb Qal to hang; substantivated Part. pass. stretched out (wine strainer).

tl‘ v. *hl‘tyk*.

tlpḥ *tlpḥn* 3.13[5] (*tlpḥ[n]* :: *bylwp* C 61[5]),[16] (:: *w* .... C 61[16]) - ¶ word of unknown meaning.

tmh$_3$ *]tmh* 2.1[4] (:: *[š]mh* BIDG) - ¶ prep. there.

tshd v. *tshr’*.

tshr’ (< Egypt. *t’ shr.t*) Sing. abs. *tshr’* 1.2[1] (:: *tshd’* C 71[10], cf. *tshd*) - ¶ subst. barque.

tqyn *tqyn’* 2.1[70] (:: *t...* BIDG) - ¶ word of unknown meaning.

A Selective Glossary of Northwest Semitic Texts in Egyptian Script

Richard C. Steiner and Adina Mosak Moshavi

Almost all of the material in this glossary is drawn from the Aramaic text in demotic script (papyrus Amherst 63 + papyrus Michigan-Amherst 43b), with only a sprinkling of entries from three New Kingdom documents in hieratic script: the London Medical Papyrus (British Museum 10059), papyrus Anastasi I (British Museum 10247), and ostracon Cairo 25759. Other Egyptian documents have been omitted altogether, either because the transliterated Northwest Semitic material which they contain consists solely of individual words or names rather than texts or because none of it meets the selection criterion set forth below.

Citation of Texts

For each form in the glossary a source is given. For the New Kingdom material, publications are cited; but for the Aramaic text in demotic script, only the column numbers (as they appear on the papyrus today; Vleeming & Wesselius renumber 4A as 4, 4B as 5, 5 as 6 ..., 22 as 23) and line numbers are given. The immediate source of all the material from that text is R.C. Steiner's forthcoming edition of the text, based on the Nachlass of C.F. Nims. That edition (and hence this glossary) incorporates many corrections of Vleeming and Wesselius to the articles of Nims and Steiner, which we gratefully acknowledge here.

Selection of Forms

Our goal has been to include only forms which can serve as a firm basis for conclusions about the history of Northwest Semitic, forms which are no less reliable than those found in more conventional texts. In almost all cases, we have adhered strictly to this goal, preferring to err on the side of caution. Thus, we have reluctantly omitted many hapaxes which contain too high a percentage of ambiguous consonants or which are embedded in a context which is not fully deciphered. Only in cases of unusual interest have we made an exception and included forms whose interpretation must be considered, for the time being, as less than probable: ***ʾmry špr*** "choice lambs", ***šršy*** "caning", ***rkb-škb*** "upper and lower millstones", ***ḥmt ... tnnn*** "venom. ... serpents".

Abbreviations

AH S.P. Vleeming and J.W. Wesselius, "An Aramaic Hymn from the Fourth Century B.C.", BiOr xxxix (1982), 501-509. (11/11-19)
APA I. Kottsieper, "Anmerkungen zu Pap. Amherst 63", ZAW c (1988), 217-244. (11/11-19)
ART R.A.Bowman, "An Aramaic Religious Text in Demotic Script", JNES iii (1944), 219-231. (7/3-6)
AS R.C. Steiner and C.F. Nims, "Ashurbanipal and Shamash-shum-ukin: A Tale of Two Brothers from the Aramaic Text in Demotic Script", RB xcii (1985), 60-81. (17/1-22/9)
AT R.C. Steiner, "The Aramaic Text in Demotic Script: The Liturgy of a New Year's Festival Imported from Bethel to Syene by Exiles from Rash", JAOS cxi (1991), 362-363. (3/6-11, 4A/9-13, 15/10-12, 16/1-19)
BS S.P. Vleeming and J.W. Wesselius, "Betel the Saviour", JEOL xxviii (1983-1984), 110-140. (6/1-18)
ENS A. Shisha-Halevy, "An Early North-West Semitic Text in the Egyptian Hieratic Script", Orientalia xlvii (1978), 145-162.
NSI R.C. Steiner, "Northwest Semitic Incantations in an Egyptian Medical Papyrus of the Fourteenth Century B.C.E.", JNES li (1992), 191-200.
PA R.C. Steiner, "Papyrus Amherst 63: A New Source for the Language, Literature, Religion, and History of the Arameans", to appear in the proceedings of "Aramaic and the Arameans: new sources and new approaches", held June 26-27, 1991 at the Institute of Jewish Studies (London), JSS monograph.
PV R.C. Steiner and C.F. Nims, "A Paganized Version of Ps 20:2-6 from the Aramaic Text in Demotic Script", JAOS ciii (1983), 261-274
PVP M. Weinfeld, "The Pagan Version of Psalm 20:2-6 – Vicissitudes of a Psalmodic Creation in Israel and its Neighbors", EI xviii (1985), 130-140 (11/11-19)
SGA E.Y. Kutscher, *Studies in Galilean Aramaic*, Ramat-Gan, 1976.
SPA S.P. Vleeming and J.W. Wesselius, *Studies in Papyrus Amherst 63*, vol. I, Amsterdam., 1985.
SPA II S.P. Vleeming and J.W. Wesselius, *Studies in Papyrus Amherst 63*, vol. II, Amsterdam., 1990 (9/9-10/16). Inasmuch as this appeared in 1991, after the DISO cut-off date, it was not used in preparing this glossary. Happily, there is almost complete agreement between the material selected for the glossary and SPA II, extending even to rare words and expressions like *šršy* and *ʿby ry*.
SS H.-W. Fischer-Elfert, *Die satirische Streitschrift des Papyrus Anastasi I*, Ägyptologische Abhandlungen, vol. xliv (Wiesbaden, 1986).
YCO R.C. Steiner and C.F. Nims, "You Can't Offer Your Sacrifice

and Eat it Too: A Polemical Poem from the Aramaic Text in Demotic Script", JNES xliii (1984), 89-114. (6/1-18)

Editorial Symbols

⌜ ⌝ enclose signs whose reading is less than certain because of the damaged condition of the papyrus of the ambiguity of the writing.
[ ] enclose signs restored by the editor in places where no traces remain.
< > enclose signs added by the editor.
{ } enclose signs deleted by the editor.
( ) enclose explanatory editorial additions which involve no emendation, e.g., word-final *matres lectionis*, quiescent *alephs* (except when their presence is signalled indirectly), one of two "shared" consonants, and totally assimilated consonants.
- connects words which, in contemporary Aramaic texts, are normally separated by a space but in the demotic text are treated as a single word. In other words, the hyphen marks the absence of an expected determinative. It should be noted, however, that the scribe does not normally add a determinative to words ending in a sign which contains its own internal determinative (e.g. $\overline{r}$, $\overline{rn}$, $\overline{Mn}$) or a sign which comes after the determinative in normal demotic writing (e.g. $\dot{w}$); nor does he add a second determinative to words which contain a non-final determinative (e.g. ʿ$r^{wl}y$).
| indicates the occurrence of a determinative in a position where a contemporary Aramaic scribe would not normally have left a space.
/ separates alternatives. (It is also used to separate line numbers from column numbers in citations from pAmherst 63.)

Acknowledgments

Major funding for work on the Aramaic text in demotic script was provided by the Texts Program of the National Endowment for the Humanities (an independent federal agency of the United States Government), the Littauer Foundation, and Yeshiva University. The Dutch Organization for Scientific Research defrayed the costs of R.C. Steiner's trip to Holland in 1990 to finalize the arrangements for this glossary. Inge Dupont and William Voelkle of the Pierpont Morgan Library, Ludwig Koenen and Karla M. Vandersypen of the University of Michigan, Janet H. Johnson and John A. Larson of the Oriental Institute, and Zvi Erenyi of the Gottesman Library at Yeshiva University have gone out of their way to make resource of their respective institutions available for this project. Michael Oppenheim, with great efficiency and dedication, created a program to assist in the generation of the glossary; Lenny Brandwein, with infinite patience and good humor, supervised the computerization of the project, helping us with hardware problems and innumerable other details; Stanley Ocken has been very helpful in this area, as well. The demotists of the Oriental Institute contributed a great deal to the decipherment of the non-alphabetic demotic signs. Robert Ritner put his superb paleographic skills at the disposal of C.F. Nims and R.C. Steiner for hours on end; George R. Hughes, Richard Jasnow, and Janet H. Johnson also served as demotic consultants. On the Semitic end, there have been many consultants, among them Robert D. Biggs, Joshua Blau, Daniel Boyarin, J.A. Brinkman, H.Z. Dimitrovsky, Barry Eichler, M. Elat, Moshe Greenberg, J.C. Greenfield, Victor Hurowitz, Peter Machinist, Alan R. Millard, S. Shaked, Matthew Stolper, and H. Tadmor. We wish to express our sincerest gratitude to all of the above and also to the editors of DISO for inviting us to contribute this appendix to their monumental work.

Glossary

ʾb Sing. abs. *ʾb* (:: SPA = l. *rb* mighty) 12/5; + suff. 1 s. *ʾby* 9/15, 10/6,15; + suff. 2 s.m. *ʾ{ʾ}bk* 18/8; + suff. 2 s.f. *ʾbky* 18/8; Plur. cstr. *(ʾ)bhy* 18/8 - ¶ subst. father.

ʾbs Qal Imper. s.m. *ʾbs* (*e.b.s*^{m}) 15/11 - ¶ verb Qal to stuff.

ʾgn Sing. + suff. 2 s.m. *ʾgnk* 8/6 - ¶ subst. krater.

ʾdm Sing. abs. *b(ʾ)dm* 12/11, *ʾdm* 16/4 - ¶ subst. man.

ʾdr Sing. m. abs. *ʾd|r* (:: SPA = *ʾt/d/ṯr* I took) 19/3; f. abs. *ʾdyr(h)* (:: SPA = *ʾt/d/ṯyr* I took) 19/5 - ¶ adj. mighty.

ʾḫ Sing. abs. *ʾḫ-* 20/4; Sing. + suff. 1 s. *ʾḫy* 11/6, *ʾḫ(y)* 17/7, *ʾḫ(y)-* 20/18, 22/9; + suff. 2 s.m. *ʾ⌜ḫ⌝k* 19/17, *ʾḫk* 20/5, 21/4; + suff. 3 s.m. *wʾḫ⌜h⌝* 20/4; + suff. 1 pl. *ʾḫn* 17/10; Plur. + suff. 1 s. *ʾḫy* (*eḫy*^{m}) 16/3 - ¶ subst. brother.

ʾḫh Sing. cstr. *ʾḫt* 19/12; Sing. + suff. 1 s. *ʾḫty* (*eḫty*^{m}) 16/4, *ʾḫt(y)* 18/16 - ¶ subst. sister.

ʾybl Sing. abs. *ʾy|bl* 5/7, *ʾybl* (:: BS = I was brought) 6/4 - ¶ subst. ram.

ʾymh Sing. abs. *ʾym(h)-* 5/1 - ¶ subst. terror.

ʾkl Qal Pf. 3 pl.m. *ʾklw* 17/17; Impf. 1 pl. *n(ʾ)kl* 6/6; Imper. pl.m. *⌜ʾ⌝klw* 17/15 - ¶ verb Qal to eat.

ʾl 6/12 - ¶ adv. not.

ʾl *ʾl-* 11/16 (*2) - ¶ dem. pronoun these.

ʾl *ʾl-* 18/14, 21/1; + suff. 1 s. *ʾly-* 16/9 - ¶ prep. to.

ʾlh Sing. cstr. *(ʾ)lh-* 9/21, *ʾlh-* 10/6,14; emph. *ʾlh(ʾ)* (:: BS = l. *ʾlhn* Sing. + suff. 1 pl.) 6/2; + suff. 1 s. *ʾlh(y)* (:: BS = l. *ʾlhn* Sing. + suff. 1 pl.) 6/2,3; + suff. 1 pl. *ʾlhn* 6/9; Plur. abs. *[ʾl]|⸢h⸣n* 4A/10, *ʾlhn* 4A/12, *bʾlhn* 12/2, *b(ʾ)lhn* 12/11(*2), 12/12 - ¶ subst. god.

ʾlh Sing. + suff. 1 s. *ʾlt(y)-* 13/17, *ʾl⸢t⸣(y)-* 14/3; + suff. 1 pl. *ʾl|tn* 14/1 - ¶ subst. goddess.

ʾlp Sing. emph. *ʾlp(ʾ)* 8/6 - ¶ subst. bull.

ʾlp Sing. cstr. *ʾlp-* 8/13 - ¶ subst. thousand.

ʾm Plur. + suff. 2 s.m. *w(ʾ)m|{m}htk* 5/4 - ¶ subst. mother.

ʾmr Sing. abs. *ʾmr* 6/4; Plur. cstr. *⸢ʾmr⸣y* 12/1 - ¶ subst. lamb.

ʾmr QAL Pf./Impf. 3 s.m. *w(ʾ)ymr/wy(ʾ)mr* 17/14, 20/1,15, 21/5, 22/7, *w(ʾ)y|mr/wy(ʾ)|mr* 18/12; Pf.3 s.m. *w(ʾ)ymr* 19/13, *ʾmr* 19/14, 20/2,6, *ʾymr* 20/13, *(ʾ)mr-* 20/13, *wʾymr* 20/17, 21/2; 3 pl.m. *ʾymrn* 19/10, *(ʾ)ymr(w)* 21/1; 1 pl. *ʾmrnu* NSI, p. 195; Impf. 1 s. *ʾmr* NSI, p. 195 - ¶ verb QAL to say.

ʾmrh Plur. + suff. 1 s. *⸢l⸣|ʾmr|ty* 19/16, *lʾmr|ty* 20/7; + suff. 2 s.m. *lʾmrtk (r..mrt.k*^{m}*)* 21/6; + suff. 3 s.f. *lʾmrt(h)* (:: SPA = *lʾmrt?* at speaking) 20/6 - ¶ subst. remark.

ʾn *(ʾ)⸢n⸣-* 16/3; *(ʾ)n* 16/3 - ¶ adverb where.

ʾnh *ʾn(h)-* 6/15, 14/5, 16/3, 19/12, *ʾn(h)* 10/8(*2), 18/3, *⸢d⸣[ʾ]n(h)* 20/14 - ¶ pers. pronoun I.

ʾnḥnh *w(ʾ)nḥn(h)* 4A/9, *ʾnḥn(h) (e.nḥ.n.*^{m}*)* 11/17 - ¶ pers. pronoun we.

ʾnp Du. + suff. 2 s.f. *⸢ʾn⸣pyk⸢y⸣* 22/8; + suff. 3 s.m. *ʾnpwh⸢y⸣* 20/19; + suff. 3 s.f. *ʾnpy|h* 8/15, *ʾnp⸢y⸣h* 19/9, *ʾnpyh (ṣīnṣpyh.*^{m}*)* 20/12 - ¶ subst. face.

ʾnth *(ʾ)t(h)-* 15/3, *ʾ⸢t⸣(h)-* 16/3, *(ʾ)nt(h)* 16/16, *⸢ʾ⸣nt(h)* (:: SPA = woman) 17/7, *w(ʾ)nt(h)* 18/4 - ¶ pers. pronoun s.m. you.

ʾnth Sing. + suff. 1 s. *ʾnt(y)/⸢y⸣* 16/7 - ¶ subst. wife.

ʾnty *ʾnty* 8/7, 13/2,3, *(ʾ)nty* 13/1,17, 15,3, 16/17, *(ʾ)nt(y)* 16/16, *ʾty* 13/17, 14/1,3(*2), *(ʾ)nty/(ʾ)ty* 14/1, *ʾ⸢t⸣y* 16/7 - ¶ pers. pronoun s.f. you.

ʾsw Sing. *ʾstm* NSI, p. 195 - ¶ subst. healing.

ʾsy QAL Part. act. s.m. *ʾsym* NSI, p. 195 - ¶ verb QAL to heal.

ʾrz Plur. abs. *ʾrzn* 17/2 - ¶ subst. cedar.

ʾrḫ Sing. abs. *ʾrḫ-* 16/16 - ¶ subst. cow.

ʾrk APH Impf.2 s.m. *t(ʾ)rk-* 8/9 - ¶ verb APH spread (only in comb. *ʾʾrk gp*).

ʾrk Sing. cstr. *b(ʾ)rk* 8/12 - ¶ subst. length.

ʾrġ see *ʾrq*.

ʾrq Sing. abs. *w(ʾ)rq* 22/7; emph. *ʾrq(ʾ)* (*.rqᵐ*) 17/6,11 - ¶ subst. land, earth.

ʾty QAL Pf. 3 s.m./Part. act. s.m. abs. *d(ʾ)t(h)* 19/10, *[d](ʾ)⌜t⌝(h)* 21/1; Imper. s.m. *ʾt(y)-* 19/17, 20/5, 21/4 - APH Imper. s.m. *ʾyty* (*ey̅t̅y̅*) 15/11 - ¶ verb QAL to come - APH to bring.

b prep. Spatial: in, among, into (+ subst.); *bkpy* 6/3,9; *bpym(y)* 6/3,9; *bġnhn* 6/4; *bḥ̣t{ʾ}r|thn* 6/4-5; *bpmhn* 6/7,11; *bpm{n}hn* 6/10; *bšmyn* 8/12; 11/12; 15/14; *bhyklyk* 8/13; *bhyklwhy* 8/17; *bhyklyk(y)* 9/6; *bgw* 9/23; 10/7,15; *kblbn* 11/14,15; *bʾlhn* 12/2; *b(ʾ)lhn* 12/11(*2),12; *b(ʾ)dm* 12/11; *bym(ʾ)* 13/9; *bḥšby(h)* 15/2; *bḫrṣ* 15/7; *bgnnky* 16/8; *bbytn* 16/12; *bšmwhy* 16/14; *bb[b]* 18/17 - Spatial: at, on, along (+ subst.); *bq/kr(h)* 8/7; *b(ʾ)rk* 8/12; *bʾqbhn* 14/5; *bk⌜t⌝pk* 16/5; *brš* 20/17 - Spatial: from (+ subst.); *bhyk⌜l⌝(ʾ)* 20/19 - Temporal: on, during (+ subst.); *brš<y>-* 4B/8; *byrḫ-* 15/2 - Circumstantial: in (+ subst.); *bšlm* 9/14; 10/13; 17/7; ⌜*bšlm*⌝ 9/20; *bš|rwšy* 10/11-12 - Instrumental: with (+ subst.); *bqšt* 11/16; *bḥnt* 11/16; *bḥmt(y)* 14/6; *btrwd* 15/11.

bb Sing. abs. *lb⌜b⌝* 3/7; cstr. *bb* 13/7, *bb[b]* 18/17 - ¶ subst. gate.

bṭ (cf. Syriac; <Iran.) Plur. emph. *bṭy(ʾ)* 15/11(*3) - ¶ subst. duck.

byn *byn* 4A/10,11, *by(n)* 15/6, *by|⌜n⌝-* 17/2 - ¶ prep. among.

byt Sing. cstr. *byt* 18/9,12,14, 20/7(*2), 8(*2), 21/7,8(*3), *l|byt* 18/10, *lbyt* 18/13, *lby[t]* 22/6; + suff. 2 s.m. *bytk* 8/9,12; + suff. 1 pl. *bbytn* 16/12 - ¶ subst. house.

bny QAL Impf. 1 s. *ʾbn(y)* 10/9; Impf. 3 s.m. *yb|ny* 13/4-5; Impf. 3 pl.m. *ybnw* (*y.b̅n̅w̅*) 8/12,13; Impf. pass. 3 s.m. *ybn(h)-* (:: SPA = Impf. 3 pl.m.) 20/8 - ¶ verb QAL to build.

bsm QAL Pf. 2 s.f. *bsmt* (*b.smtᵐ*) 18/11 - PA ʿEL Pf. 2 s.f./1 s. *bsmty* 17/2; Part. pass. s.m. emph. *m|bsm(ʾ)* 16/13 - ¶ verb QAL to be pleasing - PA ʿEL to perfume.

bsm Sing. abs. *bsm* (:: SPA = pleased) 17/3; Plur. cstr. *wb{s}my* 20/9, *[wb]smy* 21/9 - ¶ subst. perfume.

bsr Sing. + suff. 3 s.m. *bsr(h)* 6/6 - ¶ subst. flesh.

bṣ Sing. abs. *bṣ* 19/4 - ¶ subst. linen.

br Plur. + suff. 2 s.m. *bnyk* 5/4, 8/2, 20/9,10; Plur. cstr. *bny* 7/11,12; + suff. 3 s.m. ⌜*b*⌝*n(w)hy* 21/9, *bnwh[y]* 21/10 - ¶ subst. son (also in combs. *bny zmrn, bny lḫnn*).

brh Plur. + suff. 2 s.m. *bn|tk* 8/2, *wbntk* 20/9,11; + suff. 3 s.m. *wbnt⌜h⌝* 21/9 - ¶ subst. daughter.

brk QAL pass. Part. s.m. abs. ⌜*b*⌝*[r]yk-* 13/1, *bryk-* 15/3(*2), 16/16(*2), 17; pl.m. abs. *brykn* 13/1 - PA ʿEL Impf.3 s.m. *ybrk* 4A/17, 11/18, 12/16,

16/15; + suff. 2 s.m. *yb⌜rkk⌝* 7/2, *ybrkk* 7/3,4,5,6,9,11, 12/4; + suff. 2 s.f. *ybrkky* 4A/19; + suff. 2 s.m. *tbrkk* 7/2,4,5,6 - ¶ verb QAL pass. to be blessed - PA ʿEL bless.

brkh Plur. + suff. 2 s.m. *brktk* 11/19 - ¶ subst. blesSing.

bš Sing. abs. *lbš* 6/3,9 - ¶ subst.evil.

gw Sing. cstr. *bgw* 9/23; 10/7,15 - ¶ subst. midst.

gys Sing. abs. *g⌜ys⌝* 20/17 - ¶ subst. detachment.

gnh Sing. + suff. 1 s. *gnty* (:: SPA = *qnty*? you lament) 17/2 - ¶ subst. garden.

gnn Sing. + suff. 2 s.f. *bgnnky* (*bk.n.nky*^{m}) 16/8 - ¶ subst. bridal chamber.

gp Sing. abs. *gp* 8/9 - ¶ subst. wing.

gšr Plur. cstr. *gšwry-* (*kšw̱r̄y*) 8/9 - ¶ subst. beam.

d conj. that (+ 1st word of rel. clause): *dʿlyk* 9/18; *dcd* 15/2; *dyld* 17/5,10; *dl(ʾ)* (:: SPA = *dl-*) 17/9; *dlhwwn* 17/14; *dl[h]⌜w⌝wn* 18/1; *dh(w)* 19/2; *d(ʾ)t(h)* 19/10; *⌜d⌝[ʾ]n(h)* 20/14; *[d](ʾ)⌜t⌝(h)* 21/1 - prep. of + subst.: *dprzln* 17/11; *dmrn* 16/12; *dlḥm* (:: SPA = *drḥm*) 20/16.

dʾ *hd(ʾ)-* 8/15 - ¶ dem. pronoun this.

dhb Sing. abs. *dhb* 15/8; + suff. 1 pl. *wdhb|nn* 9/11 - ¶ subst. gold.

dwr QAL Part. act. s.m. cstr. *d(ʾ)r* 8/6, *d(ʾ)r* (:: SPA = *dr* the generation) 12/14(*2), *wd(ʾ)r* 8/10 - ¶ verb QAL reside.

dḥl QAL Impf. 2 s.m. *tdḥl* 6/12; 3 pl.m. *wy|{y}dḥlw* 4A/7 - ¶ verb QAL to fear.

dkr QAL Impf. 3 s.m. + suff. 2 s.m. *ydkrk* 15/2 - ¶ verb QAL to remember.

dm Sing. + suff. 3 s.m. *dm(h)* 6/6 - ¶ subst. blood.

dnḥ QAL Pf.3 s.m. *dnḥ* 18/6; Part. act. s.m. abs. *wdnḥ* (*w.t.n.ḥ.*^{m}) 8/11 - ¶ verb QAL to rise.

h (+ dem. pronoun) *hd(ʾ)-* 8/15 - ¶ presentative particle here.

hw *hw-* 9/13, *wh(w)* 10/13, *dh(w)* 19/2 - ¶ pers. pronoun he.

hwy QAL Pf.3 s.m. *hw(h)* 17/11; Pf.3 s.f. *hwt* (*h.ẇt*^{m}) 17/6; Pf. 3 pl.m. *dl(ʾ)hww* (:: SPA = *dlhww lamed*-imperfect) 17/9, *dlhwwn* (:: SPA = *lamed*-imperfect) 17/14, *dl[h]⌜w⌝wn* (:: SPA = *lamed*-imperfect) 18/1; Impf. 2 s.m. *thw(y)* 8/6; Impf.3 s.m. *yhw(y)* 4A/12, 8/4 - ¶ verb QAL to be.

hy *⌜h⌝(y)* 2/5, *h(y)* 9/18, *hy* 19/12 - ¶ pers. pronoun she.

hy *hwy* 13/1; 16/16 - ¶ vocative particle O.

hykl Sing. cstr. *[h]yk⌜l⌝* 18/17; emph. *mhykl(ʾ)* 19/8; Sing. emph. / + suff. 3 s.m. *mhykl(ʾ)/mhykl(h)* 18/7; Sing. emph. *bhyk⌜l⌝(ʾ)* 20/19; Plur. + suff. 2 s.m. *bhyklyk* 8/13; + suff. 2 s.f. *bhyklyk(y)* 9/6; + suff. 3 s.m. *bhyklwhy* (*b.hyk.rwhy*^{m}) 8/17 - ¶ subst. temple, palace.

h(l)k QAL Impf.1 s. *ʾhk{w}* (:: SPA = Imper.pl.m.) 18/13; 2 s.m. *thk* (*t̄hk.*^{m}) 20/17 - ¶ verb QAL to go, to walk.

hn *hn* 20/6 - ¶ conjunction if.

w + verb: *wšmʿny* 1/18, 3/4, 4A/4, *wyʿmd* 3/7, *wy|ydḥlw* 4A/7, *wyqwmw⌜n⌝* 4A/11, *wnšmn* 6/5,6, *wnks(y)* 6/6, *wnrw(y)* 6/7, *wd(ʾ)r* 8/10, *wdnḥ* 8/11, *w(ʾ)ymr/wy(ʾ)mr* 17/14, 20/1,15, 21/5, 22/7,*wymll* 17/14, 20/13, 21/2,*w(ʾ)y|mr/wy(ʾ)|mr* 18/12, *wymn[l]⌜l⌝* 19/1, *w(ʾ)ymr* 19/13, *wt|tb* 19/16, *wlt<b>* 20/6, *wym⌜n⌝ll* 20/15, *wmrq(w)* 20/16, *wʾymr* 20/17, 21/2, *wyml⌜l⌝* 20/18, *wtt<b>* 21/6, *wy⌜m⌝[ll]* 22/7 - + subst.: *wknr* 1/11, *w(ʾ)m|{m}htk* 5/4, *wdkh|nn* 9/11, *w(ʾ)dry* 10/6, *wsnm|pr* 11/9-10, *wnh⌜š⌝* 11/11, *wmyn* 18/6,9, *wʾḫ⌜h⌝* 20/4, *wqy|ṭrn* 20/8, *wbs{s}my* 20/9, *wbntk* 20/9,11, *wḥn⌜ty⌝k* 20/17, *wqyṭrn* 21/9, *wbnt ⌜h⌝* 21/9, *w(ʾ)rq* 22/7 - + pers. pronoun: *wh(w)* 10/13, *w(ʾ)nth* 18/4, *w(ʾ)nḥn(h)* 4A/9 - + prep.: *wʾ(l)-* 6/14, *wʾm-* 8/2 - ¶ conjunction.

zbḥ (< Hebr) - QAL Impf. 1 pl. *nzbḥ* (*n.s.b.ḥ*^{m}) 12/2 - ¶ verb QAL to sacrifice.

zwʾh Sing. emph. *zwʾt(ʾ)* 5/2 - ¶ subst. trembling.

zmr Plur. abs. *zmrn* (*s.m.r̄n̄*) 7/11; + suff. 2 s.m. *⌜z⌝[m]ry⌜k⌝* 5/10 - ¶ subst. musician, singer (also in comb. *bny zmrn*).

zġr Plur. m. abs. *zġyrn* (*s.hyr̄n̄*) 19/11; 21/2 - ¶ adj. small.

zph Sing. emph. *zpt(ʾ)* (:: SPA = *spd*? mourning) 20/8, 21/9 - ¶ subst. tar (in comb. *zptʾ wqṭrnʾ*; cf. Arab. *zift waqaṭrān*).

ḥzy QAL Pf.1 pl. *ḥzy⌜n⌝* 4A/9; 3 pl.m. + suff. 2 s.f. *ḥzwk[y]* 4A/6; Impf. 2 s.m. *(t)ḥz(y)* (:: SPA = *ḥzy*? is seen) 20/10; Imper. s.m. *ḥz(y)* 8/7; APH Impf. 3 s.m. + suff. 1 s. *ly⌜ḥz⌝[ny]* (:: SPA = *lyḥzw*? let them not see) 22/8 - ¶ verb QAL to see - APH to show, to let see.

ḥṭrh Plur. + suff. 3 pl.m. *bḥṭ{ʾ}r|thn* (:: SPA = under their sticks) 6/4-5 - ¶ subst. sheep-fold.

ḥyy PAʿEL Impf. 3 m.pl. *yḥyn/yḥy(w)-* 20/18, *yḥ⌜y⌝(w)* 22/9 - ¶ verb PAʿEL to keep alive.

ḥyn Plur. abs. *ḥyn* 17/7 - ¶ subst. Plur. life.

ḥys Sing. m. abs. *ḥ⌜y⌝s* (:: SPA = l. *ḥzz* n.g.) 10/17 - ¶ adj. forbearing.

ḥlw/mḥlw Plur. emph. *mn-ḥlwy(ʾ)/m{n}ḥlwy(ʾ)* (:: SPA = l. *mn ṭlwyʾ* of the young) 6/10 - ¶ subst. sweet.

ḥmh Sing. abs. *ḥ⌜m⌝(h)* 6/11; + suff. 1 s. *bḥmt(y)* 14/6; + suff. 2 s.m. *⌜ḥmt⌝|k-* 15/14 - ¶ subst. venom.

ḥnṭh Plur. abs. *⌜ḥ⌝mṭm* (= *ḥnṭn*) 16/3 - ¶ subst. wheat.

ḥnqh Sing./Plur. *ḥmqtu* NSl,pp. 193, 198 - ¶ subst. strangulation-demon.

ḥnt Sing. abs. *bḥnt* 11/16; Plur. + suff. 2 s.m. *wḥn⌜ty⌝k* 20/17 - ¶ subst. spear.

ḥsd Plur. m. + suff. 2 s.m. *lḥsyd|{d}yk* 11/18-19 - ¶ subst. pious one.

ḥrmh Sing. emph. *ḥrmt(ʾ)* 7/10 - ¶ subst. consecrated animal.

ḥšb Sing. + suff. 3 s.m. *bḥšby(h)* 15/2 - ¶ subst. mind.

ḫyl Sing. cstr. *ḫyl* 15/13,14, 21/2; emph. *ḫyl(ʾ)* 19/10, 21/1; + suff. 2 s.m. *ḫylk* 15/13,14 - ¶ subst. force, troop.

ḫmr Sing. abs. *ḫmr* 14/3; emph. *ḫmr(ʾ)* 15/12; + suff. 3 s.m. *ḫmr(h)* 17/16,18 - ¶ subst. wine.

ḫmr QAL Pf.3 s.m. *ḫmr* (*ḫ.mr̄*^{m}) 18/5 - ¶ verb QAL to become angry (cf. Aḥiqar 47).

ḫsr PA ʿEL Impf.3 s.m. *lyḫ|sr* 11/15-16 - ¶ verb PA ʿEL to leave unfulfilled.

ḫrṣ Sing. abs. *bḫrṣ* (*b.ḫrt.s.*^{m}) 15/7 - ¶ subst. gold.

ṭbḫ Sing. + suff. 2 s.m. ⌜*ṭ*⌝*bḫ{t}*<*k*> 5/7; Plur. abs. *ṭpḫn* 8/5 - ¶ subst. butcher.

ṭws QAL Impf.2 s.m. *tṭs* 8/9 - ¶ verb QAL to fly.

ṭmr QAL Part. pass. pl.m. abs. *ṭmrn* 9/10 - ¶ verb QAL to hide.

ṭnr Sing. abs. *ṭnr* 10/6 - ¶ subst. flint.

ṭʾn Sing. + suff. 2 s.m. *ṭʿ{ʾ}ynk* 2/5 - ¶ subst. burden.

ṭpsr Sing. abs. *ṭpsr* 20/16 (*2) - ¶ subst. scribe.

ṭrd QAL Impf. 1 s. *ʾṭr*⌜*d*⌝ 22/2 - ¶ verb QAL to banish.

ybl QAL Impf. pass. 3 pl.m. *yblw* (:: SPA = Pf. 3 pl.m.) 18/10; Imper. s.m. *bl* 20/5; Energic Imper. s.m. *bln* 19/17, 21/4 - ¶ verb QAL to bring, to lift.

yd Sing. + suff. 3 s.f. *ydy(h)* 13/5; + suff. 3 pl.m. *ydhn* 5/4, *ydh(n)* (:: SPA = *ydh*? Sing. + suff. 3 s.m.) 22/3; Du. + suff. 3 s.m. *ydwhy* (*y.t.why*^{m}) 3/11; + suff. 3 s.f. *ʾ*⌜*y*⌝*dyh* 9/18, *ʾydyh* 9/18; + suff. 1 pl. *ydyn* 8/5 - ¶ subst. hand; side (latter meaning only in comb. *ʿl yd*).

ydʿ Qal Part. act. s.m. *ydiʿ* NSI, p. 193, fn. 17 - ¶ verb QAL to know.

ywm Plur. abs. *ywmn* 17/9, 18/1, ⌜*y*⌝*mn* 17/13; cstr. *ymy-* 18/8, *ymy* 18/8 - ¶ subst. day.

yyn Sing. abs. *yyn* (*y.yn.*^{m}) 12/6, *kyyn* 17/16, *kyy*⌜*n*⌝ 17/18 - ¶ subst. wine (< Hebr).

yld QAL pass. Pf.3 s.m. *dyld* 17/5,10 - ¶ verb QAL pass. to be born.

yld Sing. abs. *yld* 16/5 - ¶ subst. boy.

ym Sing. emph. *ym(ʾ)* 9/9, *bym(ʾ)* 13/9 - ¶ subst. sea.

yʿṣh Plur. + suff. 1 pl. *yʿṣt*<*n*> (:: APA = *yʾṭ sd*<*n*> our heart's plan) 11/15 - ¶ subst. plan (< Hebr).

yṣʾ QAL Impf. 3 s.m./pl. *yṣ(ʾ)* NSI, pp. 198-199 - ¶ verb QAL to go out.

yqr Sing.m. abs. *yq*⌜*r*⌝ 4A/12, *yqr-* 18/4 - ¶ adj. glorious.

yrḫ Sing. cstr. *byrḫ-* 15/2 - ¶ subst. month.

ytb OPH Impf. 3 s.f. *twt[b]* 4A/11 - ¶ verb OPH to be seated.

k prep. Comparative: like, as - + subst.: *ktnn* 8/8, *knšr* 8/9, *ksn* 8/11,

ksn 8/12, *kpṣy-* 10/6, *ktnnn* 15/14, *kyyn* 17/16, *kyy⌜n⌝* 17/18 - + pers. pronoun: *kk* (:: SPA = n.g.) 10/17, 12/12 - + prep.: *kblbn* 11/14,15 - Temporal, at: *pkʿt* 16/4.
kbr Sing. f. emph. *kbrt(ʾ)* 14/1 - ¶ adj. mighty.
kbš Sing. cstr. *kbš-* 4A/13 - ¶ subst. stool (only in comb. *kbš lgr*).
kd *kd-* 20/10 - ¶ conjunction when.
kh *k(h)* 19/17, 20/5, *k(h)-* 21/4 - ¶ demonstrative adv. here.
khnh Sing. abs. *khn(h)* 8/13 - ¶ subst. priestess.
kwh Plur. + suff. 2 s.m. *kwyk* (*k.wyk.*^{m}) 13/7(*2); Plur. + suff. 3 s.f. *lkwyh* 11/10 - ¶ subst. window.
kwkb Plur. abs. *kwkbn* 8/12, 10/2, 15/6 - ¶ subst. star.
kl Sing. cstr. *kl* 5/3, 8/5, 9/9, 11/16, 13/1, *kl-* 8/11,15, 11/15; + suff. 3 pl.m. *klhn* 5/5 - ¶ subst. all, every.
kly PAʿEL Impf. 1 s. *ʾkl(y)* (:: BS = I shall detain) 6/15 - ¶ verb PAʿEL to cause to perish.
kmr Sing. abs. *kmr* 16/8; Plur. + suff. 2 s.m. *kmryk* 5/8 - ¶ subst. priest.
knr Sing. abs. *wknr* (*w̄k.n.r̄*) 1/11, *knr* 5/10, *k⌜n⌝r* 17/3; cstr. *knr* 12/9(*2); Plur. emph. *knry(ʾ)* 16/11 - ¶ subst. lyre.
ksy QAL Impf. 1 pl. *wnks(y)* (*w.n.q.s.*^{m}) 6/6 - ¶ verb QAL to become corpulent (cf. Deut 32:15; see YCO).
ksp Sing. emph. *ksp(ʾ)* 15/8; + suff. 1 pl. *kspn* 9/11 - ¶ subst. silver.
kp Sing. + suff. 1 s. *bkpy* 6/3,9 - ¶ subst. hand.
krh (or *qrh*) Sing. abs. *bkl/qr(h)* 8/7; + suff. 1 pl. *k/qrtn* (:: SPA = *qrʾtn*? our calling) 12/2 - ¶ subst. banquet.
krm Plur. emph. *k⌜r⌝my(ʾ)* 4B/8 - ¶ subst. vineyard.
krsy Sing. emph. *krsy(ʾ)* (*kr$\overline{sy}$*) 13/19, *kr|sy(ʾ)* 13/19; + suff. 3 pl.m. *kr⌜s⌝hn* 4A/11 - ¶ subst. throne.
ktp Sing. + suff. 2 s.m. *bk⌜t⌝pk* 16/5 - ¶ subst. shoulder.
l prep., Spatial, to, toward: + subst. *lb⌜b⌝* 3/7, *⌜l⌝mt* 17/17, *l|byt* 18/10, *lbyt* 18/13, *l|bbl* 19/9, *l|bbl* 20/17, *lby[t]* 22/6; + pers. pronoun *l(y)-* 9/3; Interpersonal to: *lmrty* 4B/3, *⌜l⌝sr|[m]gy* 17/14-15, *ls|rṭr(h)* 19/1, *lmly* 19/16, *⌜l⌝|ʾmr|ty* 19/16, *lʾmrt(h)* 20/6, *lmly* 20/7, *lʾmr|ty* 20/7, *ltwrtn(ʾ)* 20/15,18, *lsrmwgy* 21/2, *lmlyk* 21/6, *lʾmrtk* 21/6; + pers. pronoun *lk* 12/2, *(l)k* 18/4, *lh* 20/6, *(l)ky* 20/13 - Possessive, belonging to: + subst. *lkwyh* 11/10, *lḥsyd|{d}yk* 11/18-19; + pers. pronoun *lk-* 9/11, *lk* 9/11,12; Accusative: *lbbl* 20/18 - Ethical dative (+ pronoun): *lk* 16/4 - Pleonastic (+ prep.): *ltḥtyk* 12/13, *lthtyky* 12/14.
l + verb: *lyḫ|sr* 11/15-16, *dlhwwn* (:: SPA = *lamed*-imperfect) 17/14, *dl[h]⌜w⌝wn* (:: SPA = *lamed*-imperfect) 18/1, *l{h}šmʿ* 20/6, *wlt<b>* 20/6, *ltšmʿ* 20/6, *lttb* 20/7, *ly⌜ḥz⌝[ny]* 22/8; + subst. (adj. not?): *lbš* 6/3,9, *ltr|tyn* 6/3,9 - ¶ adv. not (see also *lʾ*).

l' *dl(')* (:: SPA = *dl-lamed*-imperfect) 17/9 - ¶ adv. not (see also *l*).
lb Sing. + suff. 1 pl. *kblbn* 11/14,15 - ¶ subst. heart.
lbš APH Pf.3 s.m. *'lbš* 5/4; Imper. s.m. + suff. 3 pl.m. *'l|bšwnn-* (:: SPA = Pf. 3 pl.m. + suff. 3 pl.m.) 18/10 - ¶ verb APH to clothe, to dress.
lgr Sing. + suff. 2 s.m. *lgrk* 6/15; + suff. 3 s.f. *lgr[h]* 4A/13; Du. + suff. 2 s.m. *lgr⌜yk⌝* 19/17, *lgryk (r.kr̄yk.^{m})* 21/4; + suff. 2 s.f. *lgryky* 20/5 - ¶ subst. foot.
lḥm Sing. abs. *lḥm (rḥm ^{br})* 18/6,9; + suff. 3 s.m. *lḥm⌜h⌝* 17/15, *lḥm(h)* 17/17 - ¶ subst. bread.
lḥm Sing. abs. *dlḥm* (:: SPA = *drḥm*? loves) 20/16 - ¶ subst. war.
lḫn Plur. abs. *l⌜ḫ⌝nn* 7/12 - ¶ subst. temple servitor (only in comb. *bny lḫnn*).
lmh *lm(h)-* 18/4 - ¶ interrogative pronoun why.
lqḥ QAL Impf. 1 pl. *nqḥ* (:: SPA = *ngḥ*? we shall fight) 21/7 - ¶ verb QAL to capture.
lšn Sing. + suff. 3 pl.m. *lšnhn* 6/8, *lšn|hn* 6/10,11-12 - ¶ subst. tongue.
mgdl Sing. abs. *mgdl(')* 13/5 - ¶ subst. tower.
mdbḥ Sing. abs. *mdbḥ* 8/13 - ¶ subst. altar.
mh *m(h)* 11/7, *m(h)-* 20/13 - ¶ interrogative pronoun what.
mzg Qal Pf. 3 pl.m. *mzgw* 12/6 - ¶ verb Qal to mix.
mḥlw see *ḥlw*.
mḫ' QAL Impf. 3 pl.m. *ym{⌜'⌝}ḫ<⌜'⌝>(w)* 20/18 - ¶ verb QAL to strike (see also *mḫy*).
mḫy QAL Impf. 3 s.m. *y⌜m⌝ḫ(y)* 5/7, *ymḫ(y)* (*y.mḫ.^{m}*) 5/7; Impf. 3 pl.m. *ymḫ(w)* 22/8 - QAL passive Impf. 3 s.m. *ymḫ(h)* 6/14 - ¶ verb QAL to strike (see also *mḫ'*).
mṭr APH. Imper. s.m. *'mṭr-* 9/10 - ¶ verb APH to cause to rain.
my *m(y)* 12/11(*2),12 - ¶ interrogative pronoun who (< Hebr).
myn Du. abs. *wmyn* 18/6,9; + suff. 3 s.m. *myh* 11/8 - ¶ subst. Du. water.
myp'h Plur. + suff. 2 s.m. *myp'|tk* 8/11,15-16 - ¶ subst. manifestation.
mlh Sing. cstr. *mlt* 18/7; Plur. + suff. 1 s. *lmly* 19/16; 20/7; + suff. 2 s.m. *lmlyk* 21/6 - ¶ subst. word.
mly QAL Part. act. s.f. abs. *mly(h)* 11/9 - HAPH Impf. 3 s.m. *yhmly* 11/15, *yhmly-* 11/15 - ¶ verb QAL to be full - HAPH to fulfill.
mlk Sing. abs. *mlk* 19/2; Sing. emph. *mlk(')* 3/9, 13/18, 17/5,14, 18/3,5,7,11,12,15,17, 19/17, 20/5,13,15, 21/2,4, 22/7, *⌜m⌝l⌜k⌝(')* 20/17; Plur. abs. *mlkn* 4A/6, 18/7, 20/3, 21/3 - ¶ subst. king.
mlkh Sing. cstr. *mlkt* 4A/9; Sing. + suff. 1 s. *mlkt(y)* 9/5, *mlkty* 13/2

- ¶ subst. queen.

mll PA ʿEL Impf. 3 s.m. *wymll* 17/14, 20/13, 21/2, *wymn|[l]⌜l⌝* 19/1, *wym⌜n⌝ll* 20/15, *wyml⌜l⌝* 20/18, *wy⌜m⌝[ll]* 22/7 - ¶ verb PA ʿEL to speak, to address.

mn prep. Spatial, from: *⌜m⌝n-* 4A/11, *mn-* 4B/8, 16/3(*4), 18/1,3,9, 12, 19/6,17, 20/5,7(*2),11,12, 21/4,7,8, *⌜mn⌝-* 16/11; + subst. *my ⌜{ʾ}r⌝wšlm* 16/4, *mhykl(ʾ)* 19/8 - Temporal, from, since: *mn-* 18/8(*2) - Partitive, some: *mn-* 6/10 - Comparative, more than, too ... for: *mn-* 13/1, 19/10,11, 21/1,2; + suff., *mnk* (:: SPA = *mn* + n.g) 10/17 - Causal, from, through: *mn-* 8/8(*2) - Pleonastic: *mn-* 6/8,10,11.

mn *mn-* (:: SPA = from) 10/17(*2), *mn* 13/4,17; 14/1,3 - ¶ interrogative pronoun who.

mndh Sing. emph. *mnd|t(ʾ)* (:: SPA = *mnt d-*? the share which is) 17/16, *mnd⌜t⌝(ʾ)* 17/18 - ¶ subst. tribute.

mnḫr Plur. emph. *mnḫr[y](ʾ)* 7/13 - ¶ subst. nostril.

msḥy Sing. emph. *m{n}sḥy|t(ʾ)* 18/10, *m{n}s⌜ḥ⌝yt(ʾ)* 18/13 - ¶ subst. bath (only in comb. *byt msḥy*; see also *mšḥy*).

mʿyn Du. + suff. 3 s.m. *myʿwhy* 5/11 - ¶ subst. Du. belly.

mr Sing. abs. *mr* 20/2, 21/2; cstr. *mr* 7/17, 18/7; Sing. + suff. 1 pl. *dmrn* 16/12, *mrn* 17/5,10, 18/7 - ¶ subst. lord.

mrh Sing. + suff. 1 s. *lmrty* 4B/3; + suff. 1 pl. *mrtn* 16/16 - ¶ subst. lady.

mrwy Sing. + suff. 3 s.m. *mrwhy* 14/3 - ¶ subst. intoxication.

mrkb Sing. cstr. *⌜m⌝rkb* 13/18 - ¶ subst. seat.

mrkbh Sing. emph. *mrkbt(ʾ)* 19/8, *mr[kb]t(ʾ)* 20/19, *mrkb[t](ʾ)* 21/12 - ¶ subst. chariot.

mrq QAL Imper. pl.m. *wmrq(w)* (:: SPA = *wmlkʾ*? and the king) 20/16 - ¶ verb QAL to polish (in comb. *mrq ḥnt*; cf. Jer 46:4).

mrr Plur. emph. *mnrr|y(ʾ)* 6/8 - ¶ subst. bitters.

mrrh Sing. emph. *mr<y>r{y}(h)* 6/11 - ¶ subst. venom.

mšʾl Sing. cstr. *mšʾl-* (:: SPA = *mšʾlh*; see PVP, p. 133; ApA) 11/16 - ¶ subst. request.

mšḥy Sing. emph. *⌜mš⌝ḥyt(ʾ)* 18/14 - ¶ subst. bath (only in comb. *byt mšḥy*; see also *msḥy*).

mšḥt Sing. + suff. 3 pl.m. *mšḥt(h)n* (:: SPA = *mšḥtn*? our measure) 18/11 - ¶ subst. sin (see also *sḥt*).

mt Sing. cstr. *mt* 17/15, *⌜l⌝mt* 17/17; emph. + suff. 1 s. *mt(ʾ)/mt(y)* 10/8 - ¶ subst. land.

nbl Sing. abs. *[n]bl* 1/11, *nbl* 5/10, 12/8, *nb<l>* (:: SPA = *l.-nk* for you) 12/9 - ¶ subst. harp.

nhr Sing. emph. *nhr(ʾ)* 9/2 - ¶ subst. river.

nḥš Sing. abs. *wnḥ⌜š⌝* 11/11; Plur. abs. *nḥšn* (*n.ḥ.š.n*^{m}) 17/11 - ¶ subst.

bronze.

nḥt OPH Impf. 3 pl.m. *yḥtw* 18/5 - ¶ verb OPH to be brought down.

nḫrh Plur. + suff. 2 s.m. *nḫrtk* 8/8 - ¶ subst. snort.

nḫtm Sing. + suff. 2 s.m. *nḫt|mk* 5/5 - ¶ subst. baker.

nṭr Sing. + suff. 2 s.f. *⌜n⌝ṭrky* 15/4 - ¶ subst. guard.

ny *ny* 9/3, 14/3, 20/2, 21/6, *n(y)* 9/10, 20/2,18, 21/2(*2), *(n)y-* 18/10 - ¶ precative particle.

nsy Plur. emph. *nsy(ʾ)* 5/5 - ¶ subst. chief.

nsy QAL Pf. 3 s.f. *nst* 9/18(*2); 3 pl.m. *nsw* 22/3; Impf. 3 s.m. *ynsy* 5/10(*2); 3 pl.m. *ynsw* (*yn$\overline{sw}$*) 7/11; Imper. s.m. *s(y)* 16/5 - ¶ verb QAL to carry, to lift, to pick up.

nsk Plur. + suff. 2 s.m. *nsy|kyk* 5/3 - ¶ subst. prince.

npq QAL Pf. 3 s.m. *npq-* 19/8, *npq* 20/11, *np⌜q⌝* 20/18; 3 pl.m. *npqw* (*np.kẇ*) 18/1; Imper. pl.m. *pqw* 18/14; Inf. cstr. + suff. 2 s.m. *mnpqk* 7/20; Inf. abs. *mnpq* 20/12 - APH Impf. 1 s. *ʾnpq{w}* (:: SPA = Imper. pl.m.) 18/12; Imper. pl.m. *ʾnpqw* (:: SPA = Pf. 3 pl.m.) 18/9 - ¶ verb QAL to go out - APH to take out.

nṣy QAL Part. act. pl.m. abs. *nṣyn* (*n.tsyn*^{m}) 20/4 - ¶ verb QAL to quarrel.

nšr Sing. abs. *knšr* 8/9 - ¶ subst. eagle.

sbl QAL Impf. 3 s.f. *tsbl-* 2/5; + suff. 2 s.m. *tsblk* 2/4 - ¶ verb QAL to carry.

sb‘ QAL Impf. 1 s. *p(ʾ)sb‘-* 13/8 - ¶ verb QAL to become satiated.

sgy Sing. m. abs. *sg(y)* 19/10 - ¶ adj. large (see also *šgy*).

swsy Sing. abs. *sws(y)* 19/3; Plur. abs. *swsyn* 14/4,5 - ¶ subst. horse.

swt Sing. abs. *swt* 7/8 - ¶ subst. holocaust aroma.

sym QAL Pf. 1 s. + suff. 3 s.m. *smthy* (:: SPA = Pf. 2 s.m. + suff. 3 s.m.) 19/2; 3 s.m. + suff. 1 s. *sm|tny* 6/4, *smtn(y)* 6/10; 3 s.f. *smt* 19/9, 20/12; Impf. 2 s.m. *tsm* 15/2; 3 s.m. + suff. 2 s.m. *ysmk* 15/3 - ¶ verb QAL to put, to set; to grant; to make.

sky QAL Part. act. pl.m. emph. *sky(ʾ)* 19/9,10, *s⌜kʾ⌝y(ʾ)* 21/1, *s[k]⌜y⌝(ʾ)* 21/1 - ¶ verb QAL to keep watch, to look out.

slq QAL Pf. 3 pl.m. *slqw* 19/9, *slq⌜w⌝/(w)* 21/1; Imper. s.m. *slq* 15/9 - APH Part.act. s.m. abs. *⌜m⌝sq* 16/4 - ¶ verb QAL to go up - APH to bring up.

smn Sing. *smun* NSI, p. 198 - ¶ subst. a type of disease.

sn Sing. abs. *ksn* 8/11,12 - ¶ subst. moon.

snwr Plur. emph. *snwry(ʾ)* ($\overline{snw}$*.ry.*^{m}) 13/6 - ¶ subst. blinding light (cf. Gen 19:11, etc.; see PA).

snpr Sing. abs. *wsnm|pr* 11/9-10 - ¶ subst. lapis lazuli.

s‘d QAL Impf. 3 s.m. + suff. 1 s. *[y]⌜s‘|dny⌝{-}* 9/20, *ys<‘>dny* 10/13, *ys‘dny* 10/14; + suff. 1 pl. *ys‘|dn* 9/13, *ys‘dn* 9/14, 11/14, *ys‘⌜d⌝n-*

9/21 - ¶ verb QAL to help.

sph Plur. + 2 s.f. *sp{ʾ}wtky* (*spewtky*^{m}) 16/9 - ¶ subst. lip.

spr Sing. *supr* NSI, p. 193, fn. 17 - ¶ subst. scribe.

srp see *šrp*.

str Sing. emph. *str(ʾ)* 16/13 - ¶ subst. hideaway.

ʿb Sing. + suff. 2 s.m. *ʿb|k* 9/3-4; Plur. cstr. *ʿ|by* (*ʿ.*^{m}*by*^{m}) 9/9 - ¶ subst. cloud.

ʿbd QAL Impf. 3 s.m. *p|yʿbd* 5/6, *yʿbd* 5/8; Part. act. pl.m. cstr. *ʿbdy* 19/11 - ¶ verb QAL to make (also in comb. *ʿbd qrb*).

ʿbd Sing. + suff. 1 s. ⌜ʿ⌝*bdy* 6/12 - ¶ subst. servant.

ʿd *ʿd* 8/1, 18/2, *dʿd* 15/2 - ¶ prep. until.

ʿdh Sing. cstr. *ʿdt* 5/3 - ¶ subst. assembly.

ʿdn PAʿEL Part. act. pl.m. abs. ⌜*m*⌝*ʿdnn* 4B/9 - ¶ verb PAʿEL to delight.

ʿṭh Sing. emph. *ʿṭt(ʾ)* (*ʿ.t.t*^{m}) 18/11 - ¶ subst. advice.

ʿyn Sing. abs. *ʿy(n)-* 8/7; Du. + 1 s. *ʿyny* 16/1 - ¶ subst. eye.

ʿkšb Sing. emph. *ʿksb(ʾ)-* (*ʿkš.b*) 14/5 - ¶ subst. viper (cf. Ps 140:4; see PA).

ʿl prep., Spatial, upon, on: *ʿl* 6/15, 12/8, 14/4, 16/6, 17/3, 19/8,9, 20/19, 21/12; *ʿl-* 16/14; + suff. 3 s.m. *ʿlwhy* 8/5,7 - Spatial, over: *ʿl* 13/7,18,19(*2) - Spatial, by: *ʿl* 13/5 - Spatial, to: *ʿl* 12/16, 15/11, 17/2, 18/3,7, 19/17, 20/5, 21/4; + suff. 1 s. *ʿly* 15/9, 15/10(*2); + suff. 2 s.m. *ʿlyk* 7/18; + suff. 3 s.m. *ʿlw*⌜*h*⌝*y* 20/14 - Temporal, during: *wʿ(l)-* 6/14; + suff. 3 s.m. *ʿl|{l}w*⌜*hy*⌝ 21/10 - Causal, on account of: *ʿl* 11/6 - Affective, against, to detriment of: *ʿl* 18/5; + suff. 1 s. *ʿly* 19/2, 22/3; + suff. 2 s.m. *ʿlyk* 20/10 - Affective, to: *ʿl* 18/11.

ʿlm Plur. abs. *ʿlmn* 8/1, 15/2 - ¶ subst. eternity.

ʿm *wʿm-* 8/2, *ʿm* 8/12, 20/10, *ʿm-* 21/10 - ¶ prep. with.

ʿmd QAL Impf. 3 s.m. *wyʿmd* 3/7 - ¶ verb QAL to stand still.

ʿny QAL Pf. 3 s.m. *ʿn(h)* 20/13, *ʿn(h)-* 17/14, 18/12, 19/13, 20/1,15,17, 21/1,2,5, ⌜ʿ⌝*[n](h)-* 22/7; 3 s.f. *ʿn*⌜*t*⌝ 19/14, *ʿnt* 20/2,6; Pf. 3 pl.m. *ʿnwn* (*ʿ.n.ẇ.n*^{m}) 19/10; Impf. 3 s.m. + suff. 1 pl. *yʿnn* 11/11,12,17; Part. act. s.m. abs. *ʿny* (:: BS = Part. pl.m. abs. with *n* deleted) 6/12 - ¶ verb QAL to speak up, to answer.

ʿnh Sing. abs. *pkʿt* 16/4 - ¶ subst. time (only in comb. *kʿt* now).

ʿpr Sing. cstr. *ʿpr* 17/11 - ¶ subst. soil.

ʿqb Sing. + suff. 3 pl.m. *bʿqbhn* (*b.ʿ.kbh.n*^{m}) 14/5 - ¶ subst. heel (in comb. *ʿkšb bʿqb* [*swsyn*]; cf. Gen. 49:17).

ʿrb Sing. m. abs. *ʿrb* 20/9, *ʿr*⌜*b*⌝ 21/9 - ¶ adj./subst. sweet smelling / Arabia (only in comb. *bsmy ʿrb*).

ʿrs Sing. + suff. 2 s.m. *ʿrsk* 8/13 - ¶ subst. bed.
ġll QAL Impf. 2 s.m. *tġl* (*t̄ḫ.rᵐ*) 3/9; Imper. s.m. *ġl-* (*ḫ.r*) 16/4; Inf. cstr. + suff. 2 s.m. *mnġlk* 7/20; Inf. abs. *mn⌜ġ⌝l* 3/9 - HAPH Pf. 3 s.m. *hn⌜ġ⌝l-* (:: SPA = Impf. 3 s.m.) 21/9; Imper. s.m. *hnġl* (*hnḫrᵐ*) 20/9 - (H)oph. Pf. 3 pl.m. *hnġlw* (*hnḫ.rẇ*) 18/2; Part. act. s.f. abs. *mnġl(h)* 4A/10 - ¶ verb QAL to enter - HAPH to bring in - (H)oph. to be brought in.
ġlm Sing. abs. *ġlm* (*ḫrm.ᵐ*) 16/4; emph. *ġlm(ʾ)* 16/3 - ¶ subst. lad.
ġn Sing. + suff. 3 pl.m. *bġnhn* (*b.ḫ.nh.n.ᵐ*) 6/4 - ¶ subst. coll. flocks.
p + verb: *p*|*yʿbd* 5/6, *p(ʾ)sbʿ-* 13/8; + adv. *pkʿt* 16/4 - ¶ conjunction.
pḥ/pḥh Sing. cstr./abs. *pḥ/pḥ(h)* 18/4; emph./abs. *pḥ(ʾ)/pḥ(h)* 19/2 - ¶ subst. governor.
plg QAL Impf. 1 s. *ʾplg* 18/4 - ¶ verb QAL to show (only in comb. *plg yqr*).
pm Sing. + suff. 1 s. *pym(y)* (*p̄yᵐ.*) 3/8, *bpym(y)* 6/3,9; + suff. 3 pl.m. *bpmhn* 6/7,11, *bpm{n}hn* 6/10 - ¶ subst. mouth.
pṣ Plur. cstr. *kpṣy-* (*k.ptsy*) 10/6 - ¶ subst. splinter (only in comb. *pṣy-ṭnr*).
przl Plur. abs. *pr*|*zln* 11/11, *dprzln* (*ṭprs.rnᵐ*) 17/11 - ¶ subst. iron.
ptr Sing. abs. *ptr(ʾ)* 15/11; + suff. 2 s.m. *ptwrk* 8/4; 16/6 - ¶ subst. table.
ṣdq Sing. m. emph. *ṣdq(ʾ)* (*t̄s.t.k.ᵐ*) 10/12 - ¶ subst. righteous one.
ṣwʾr Plur. + suff. 3 pl.m. *ṣwʾrthn* (*t̄sw̄ert.hnˢʷ*) 6/15 - ¶ subst. neck (with ʾ; see PA).
ṣwd QAL Pf. 3 s.m. *ṣd* 5/5 - ¶ verb QAL to hunt.
ṣwr see *ṣwʾr*
ṣlw Sing. + suff. 1 s. *ṣlt(y)* (:: SPA = *ṣltʾ* Sing. emph.) 12/16 - ¶ subst. prayer.
ṣr Plur. abs. *ṣrn* 18/8, *ṣyrn* 19/10, 21/1; emph. *ṣry(ʾ)* 18/1,9,12, *ṣyry(ʾ)* (*t̄syr̄y.ᵐ*) 18/5, *⌜ṣ⌝ry(ʾ)* 18/14 - ¶ subst. emissary.
qb Sing. cstr. *qb* 16/5 - ¶ subst. kab (a measure).
qbr Sing. emph. *qbr(ʾ)* 16/11 - ¶ subst. grave.
qdm *qwdm* 4A/8; + suff. 2 s.m. *qdmyk* 6/15 - ¶ prep. in front of.
qwm QAL Impf. 3 pl.m. *wyqwmw⌜n⌝* 4A/11, *yqwmn* 8/5, 12/8, *p*|*yqmn* 8/6; Imper. s.m. *qm* (:: SPA = Pf. 3 s.m.) 10/17, 12/16, *q⌜m⌝* (:: SPA = Pf. 3 s.m.) 12/17 - ¶ verb QAL to rise; to stand; to stand in attendance (only in comb. *qwm ʿl*).
qṭn QAL Impf. 3 pl.m. *yqṭnw* 10/5,6 - ¶ verb QAL to become thin.
qṭrn Sing. emph. *wqy*|*ṭrn(ʾ)* 20/8, *wqyṭrn(ʾ)* (*w̄kyt.r̄.nᵐ*) 21/9 - ¶ subst. pitch (cf. SGA, p. 33; see also *zph*).
ql Sing. cstr. *ql* 16/11; + suff. 3 pl.m. *qlhn* 7/11 - ¶ subst. voice, sound.

qrb Qal Part. act. s.f. abs. *qrb(h)* 7/18 - Pa ʿel Imper. s.m. *qrb* 15/9,10; 16/9 - ¶ verb Qal to come near - Pa ʿel to come near.
qrb Sing. abs. *qrb* 19/11 - ¶ subst. war.
qrh see *krh*.
qry Qal Impf. 3 pl.m. *yqrw* 18/15 - ¶ verb Qal to call.
qryh Sing. abs. *qry(h)* 10/9; 11/9 - ¶ subst. city.
qšt Sing. abs. *bqšt* 11/16, *qšt* 19/5, + suff. 2 s.m. *qštk* 15/14 - ¶ subst. bow.
rb Sing. + suff. 1 s. *rbiy* NSI, pp. 196-197; + suff. 1 pl. *rbun* NSI, p. 193; Plur. + suff. 3 pl.m. *rbyhn* 4A/8 - ¶ subst. official, lord.
rbd Sing. abs. *rbyd* 16/14 - ¶ subst. bedspread.
rbn Sing. abs. *rbwn* 8/8 - ¶ subst. lord.
rwy Qal Impf. 1 s. *ʾrw(y)* 13/8; 1 pl. *wnrw(y)* (*w.nr̄w.*^{m}) 6/7; Imper. s.m. *rwy* 12/8 - Aph Impf. 2 s.m. + suff. 1 s. *tr⌜w⌝n-* 14/3 - Itp Impf.3 pl.m. *yt⌜rw⌝w* 14/2 - ¶ verb Qal to become saturated, drunk - Aph to intoxicate - Itp to become drunk.
rḥ Plur. + suff. 2 s.m. *rwḥtk* 8/8 - ¶ subst. breath.
rḥ Sing. + suff. 1 s. *rḥy* 17/2 - ¶ subst. scent.
rḥm Qal pass. Part. s.f. abs. *rḥm(h)* 13/5; + suff. 1 s. *rḥmty* 16/12 - Pa ʿel Part. act. s.m. abs. *mrḥ⌜m⌝* 12/6 - ¶ verb Qal pass. to be beloved - Pa ʿel to be merciful.
rḥġ see *rḥq*.
rḥq Qal Pf. 3 s.m./Part. act. s.m. abs. *r|ḥq* (*r̄.*^{m}*ḥ.k*^{m}) 3/10-11 - ¶ verb Qal to wash.
ry Sing. abs. *ry* (*r̄y*^{m}) 9/10 - ¶ subst. moisture (in comb. *ʿby ry*; cf. Job 37:11).
rym Qal Impf. 1 s. *ʾrm* 9/21; 10/13; 1 pl. *nrm* 9/14 - Polel Impf. 3 s.m. + suff. 1 s. *yrmmn* 9/15; + suff. 1 pl. *yrmmn* 10/15; + suff. 1 s./pl. *yrmmn* 10/6 - Aph Imper. 2 s.m. *ʾrym-* 8/7; Part. act. s.m. abs. *mrym* 9/9 - ¶ verb Qal to be exalted, raised up - Polel to raise - Aph to lift (in comb. *ʾrym ʿyn*), to cause to rise.
rkb Aph Pf. 3 s.m. + suff. 3 s.m. *ʾrkb(h)* 20/19; 3 pl.m. + suff. 3 s.m. *ʾrkb|h* 21/12; + suff. 3 s.f. *ʾrkbh* 19/8 - ¶ verb Aph to seat (in vehicle).
rkb Sing. *rkbu* ENS, pp. 157-58 - ¶ subst. upper millstone (cf. Deut 24:6, etc.; see also *škb*).
rm Plur. m. abs. *rmn* (*r̄.M̄n̄*) 11/2 - ¶ adj. high, lofty.
rpʾ Qal Part. act. s.m. emph. *rp(ʾ)* 21/14; s.m. + suff. 1 s. *rpy* NSI, pp. 198-199; pl.m. + suff. 2 s.m. *wrpyk* 20/9,11; pl.m. + suff. 3 s.m. *wr[p]why* 21/11 - ¶ verb Qal to heal.
rprp Itp Impf. 3 pl.m. *ytrprpwn* (*y.t.r.pr.pẇn.*^{m}) 8/5 - ¶ verb Itp to slacken.
rqmh Sing. emph. *ryqmt(ʾ)* 18/10, *rq⌜m⌝t(ʾ)* 18/13, *rqmt(ʾ)* 18/15 - ¶ subst. embroidered garment.

rš Sing. cstr. *brš* 20/17; Plur. cstr. *brš<y>-* 4B/8 - ¶ subst. head.
šgy Sing. m. abs. *šg(y)* 21/1 - ¶ adj. large (see also *sgy*).
šgl Sing. cstr. *šgl* 16/12; emph. *šgl(ʾ)* 13/3 - ¶ subst. (queen) consort.
šwb QAL Impf. 3 s.m. *yšb* 12/16 - ¶ verb QAL to give heed (< Hebr, cf. Prov 1 :23; see also *twb*).
šḥt PA ʿEL Pf. 3 s.m. *šḥt* (*š.*$\overline{\text{ḥt}}$) 19/2 - ¶ verb PA ʿEL to sin against.
šyr QAL Part. act. s.m. abs. *šr-* (< Hebr; :: SPA = song) 12/8,9, *š(ʾ)r* 16/8 - POLEL Pf. 1 s./2 s.f. *šrrty* (*š.rrty*^{m}) 17/2 - ¶ verb QAL to sing, to play instrument - POLEL to play music.
škb Sing. *škbu-* ENS, pp. 157-158 - ¶ subst. upper millstone (in comb. *škb-rkb*; cf. m Baba Batra 2:1).
šlḥ QAL Pf. 1 s. + suff. 2 s.f. *šlḥtky* (*š.rḥt.ky*^{m}) 20/14; Imper. s.m. *šlḥ-* 9/3, *šlḥ* 11/13 - QAL pass. Impf. 3 s.m. *yšlḥ* 22/2 - ¶ verb QAL to send - QAL pass. to be sent.
šlm Sing. abs. *šl*⌜*m*⌝ 15/2, *bšlm* 9/14, 10/13, ⌜*bšlm*⌝ 9/20; cstr. *bšlm* 17/7 - ¶ subst. safety, peace (also in comb. *šlm ḥyn*).
šm Sing. + suff. 3 s.f. *šmh* 10/9 - ¶ subst. name.
šmyn Du. abs. *šmyn* 7/17; 12/14(*2), *bšmyn* 8/12, 11/12, 15/14, ⌜*š*⌝*[my]*⌜*n*⌝ 22/6; emph. *šmy(ʾ)* 10/2, 17/11,12; + suff. 3 s.m. *šmwhy* 8/12, *bšmwhy* (*b*$\overline{\text{šmw}}$*hy*^{m}) 16/14 - ¶ subst. Du. heavens.
šmn QAL Impf. 1 pl. *wnšmn* 6/5,6 - ¶ verb QAL to become fat.
šmʿ QAL Pf. 3 s.m. *l{h}šmʿ* (:: SPA = *lhšmʿ*? APH Pf. 3 s.m.) 20/6; Impf. 2 s.m. *ltšmʿ* 20/6; Imper. s.m. *šmʿ* 18/7, 19/16; Imper. s.m./Imper. s.m. + suff. 1 s. *šmʿ-ny/šmʿny* 20/2, *smʿ-n(y)/šmʿn(y)* 20/2, 21/2(*2), *wšmʿny* 3/4, 4A/4, ⌜*š*⌝*mʿny* 12/1 - ¶ verb QAL to hear.
šn Sing. abs. *šn* 11/9 - ¶ subst. ivory.
šnh Sing. emph. *šnt(ʾ)* 17/5,10; Plur. abs. *šnn* 4B/8, 17/10,14, 18/1; + suff. 2 s.m. *šn*⌜*t*⌝*k* 6/14 - ¶ subst. year.
špr Sing. f. abs. *špr(h)* 8/14, ⌜*šp*⌝*r(h)* 8/15 - ¶ adj. beautiful.
špr Sing. abs. *špr* 12/1 - ¶ subst. beauty (in comb. *ʾmry špr*; cf. Gen 49:21).
šqy Plur. abs. *šqyn* 8/7 - ¶ subst. butler.
šr Sing. cstr. *h(ʾ)-šr-nb<l>* (:: SPA = l. *nšyrnk*) 12/9, *šr-* 12/9 - ¶ subst. music.
šr Sing. abs. *šr* 5/4 - ¶ subst. shackle.
šr Sing. cstr. *šr* 19/9, *šr-* 21/1; Plur. + suff. 3 s.f. *šwryh* (*š.wr̄.yh.*^{m}) 11/10 - ¶ subst. wall.
šrp QAL Impf. 3 s.m. *yšrp-* 20/10 - ¶ verb QAL to burn.
šrr Sing. m. emph. *šrr(ʾ)* 13/17, *šr*⌜*r*⌝*(ʾ)* 14/3 - ¶ adj. powerful.
šršy Sing. abs. *bš|rwšy* (*b.š*^{m}*r̄ẇšy*^{m}) 10/11-12 - ¶ subst. caning (cf. Ezr 7:26).

šty QAL Pf. 3 s.m. *[ʾ]⌜š⌝t(h)* 17/17; Impf.1 pl. *nšty* 6/6; Imper. s.m. *šty* 12/7, *ʾš⌜t⌝(y)* 17/15; + suff. 3 s.m. *(ʾ)yšthy* 8/8 - ¶ verb QAL to drink.

štn *štn* 7/11, *št⌜m⌝* 7/12 - ¶ subst. sixty.

twb QAL Pf. 3 s.m. *wlt<b>* (:: SPA = *wlʾtʾ*? did not arrive) 20/6; Impf. 2 s.m. *wt|tb* 19/16, *lttb* 20/7, *wtt<b>* (:: SPA = *wtʾtʾ*? you came) 21/6 - ¶ verb QAL to give heed (litt., return; cf. Ug. *ṯb;* see also *šwb*).

twr Plur. + suff. 1 pl. *twryn* 9/12 - ¶ subst. bovine.

tḥt *tḥt* 6/8,10,11; 11/2; + suff. 2 s.m. *ltḥtyk* (*r.t.ḥtyk.*^{m}) 12/13; + suff. 2 s.f. *ltḥtyky* 12/14 - ¶ prep. under.

tkmh Sing. + suff. 1 s. *tkmty* (*t.qm.t̄ȳ*) 14/4 - ¶ subst. back.

tmk QAL Part. act. s.m. cstr. *tmk* (:: SPA = *dmkh*? who beats) 22/6 - ¶ verb QAL to hold.

tmnḥ Sing. emph. *tm|nḥ(ʾ)* 5/9 - ¶ subst. devotee/offering.

tmr Sing. abs. *tmr* 6/10 - ¶ subst. date.

tnn Sing. abs. *ktnn* 8/8 - ¶ subst. smoke.

tnn Plur. abs. *ktnnn* 15/14 - ¶ subst. serpent (in comb. *ḥmt...tnnn*; cf. Deut 32:33).

trwd Sing. abs. *btrwd* (*b.trw.t*^{m}) 15/11 - ¶ subst. spoon.

tryn *[b]tr⌜t⌝y* 16/1, *t{y}ryn* 20/3, *try(n)* 21/3 - ¶ subst. two.

trtyn Sing. abs. *ltr|tyn* 6/3,9 - ¶ subst. duplicity/slander.

trtn Sing. emph. *twrtn(ʾ)* 18/6, 20/17, 21/2, *ltwrtn(ʾ)* 20/15,18, *t⌜wr⌝[t]n(ʾ)* 21/10, *[l]twrt⌜n⌝(ʾ)* 22/7 - ¶ subst. general.

HANDBUCH DER ORIENTALISTIK

Abt. I: DER NAHE UND MITTLERE OSTEN

ISSN 0169-9423

Band 1. Ägyptologie

1. *Ägyptische Schrift und Sprache.* Mit Beiträgen von H. Brunner, H. Kees, S. Morenz, E. Otto, S. Schott. Mit Zusätzen von H. Brunner. Nachdruck der Erstausgabe (1959). 1973.
   ISBN 90 04 03777 2
2. *Literatur.* Mit Beiträgen von H. Altenmüller, H. Brunner, G. Fecht, H. Grapow, H. Kees, S. Morenz, E. Otto, S. Schott, J. Spiegel, W. Westendorf. 2. verbesserte und erweiterte Auflage. 1970. ISBN 90 04 00849 7
3. HELCK, W. *Geschichte des alten Ägypten.* Nachdruck mit Berichtigungen und Ergänzungen. 1981. ISBN 90 04 06497 4

Band 2. Keilschriftforschung und alte Geschichte Vorderasiens

1-2/2. *Altkleinasiatische Sprachen [und Elamitisch].* Mit Beiträgen von J. Friedrich, E. Reiner, A. Kammenhuber, G. Neumann, A. Heubeck. 1969. ISBN 90 04 00852 7

3. SCHMÖKEL, H. *Geschichte des alten Vorderasien.* Reprint. 1979. ISBN 90 04 00853 5

4/2. *Orientalische Geschichte von Kyros bis Mohammed.* Mit Beiträgen von A. Dietrich, G. Widengren, F. M. Heichelheim. 1966. ISBN 90 04 00854 3

Band 3. Semitistik

Semitistik. Mit Beiträgen von A. Baumstark, C. Brockelmann, E. L. Dietrich, J. Fück, M. Höfner, E. Littmann, A. Rücker, B. Spuler. Nachdruck der Erstausgabe (1953-1954). 1964. ISBN 90 04 00855 1

Band 4. Iranistik

1. *Linguistik.* Mit Beiträgen von K. Hoffmann, W. B. Henning, H. W. Bailey, G. Morgenstierne, W. Lentz. Nachdruck der Erstausgabe (1958). 1967. ISBN 90 04 03017 4

2/1. *Literatur.* Mit Beiträgen von I. Gershevitch, M. Boyce, O. Hansen, B. Spuler, M. J. Dresden. 1968. ISBN 90 04 00857 8

2/2. *History of Persian Literature from the Beginning of the Islamic Period to the Present Day.* With Contributions by G. Morrison, J. Baldick and Sh. Kadkanī. 1981. ISBN 90 04 06481 8

3. KRAUSE, W. *Tocharisch.* Nachdruck der Erstausgabe (1955) mit Zusätzen und Berichtigungen. 1971. ISBN 90 04 03194 4

Band 5. Altaistik

1. *Turkologie.* Mit Beiträgen von A. von Gabain, O. Pritsak, J. Benzing, K. H. Menges, A. Temir, Z. V. Togan, F. Taeschner, O. Spies, A. Caferoglu, A. Battal-Tamays. Reprint with additions of the 1st (1963) ed. 1982. ISBN 90 04 06555 5
2. *Mongolistik.* Mit Beiträgen von N. Poppe, U. Posch, G. Doerfer, P. Aalto, D. Schröder, O. Pritsak, W. Heissig. 1964. ISBN 90 04 00859 4
3. *Tungusologie.* Mit Beiträgen von W. Fuchs, I. A. Lopatin, K. H. Menges, D. Sinor. 1968. ISBN 90 04 00860 8

Band 6. Geschichte der islamischen Länder

5/1. *Regierung und Verwaltung des Vorderen Orients in islamischer Zeit.* Mit Beiträgen von H. R. Idris und K. Röhrborn. 1979. ISBN 90 04 05915 6

5/2. *Regierung und Verwaltung des Vorderen Orients in islamischer Zeit.* 2. Mit Beiträgen von D. Sourdel und J. Bosch Vilá. 1988. ISBN 90 04 08550 5

6/1. *Wirtschaftsgeschichte des Vorderen Orients in islamischer Zeit.* Mit Beiträgen von B. Lewis, M. Rodinson, G. Baer, H. Müller, A. S. Ehrenkreutz, E. Ashtor, B. Spuler, A. K. S. Lambton, R. C. Cooper, B. Rosenberger, R. Arié, L. Bolens, T. Fahd. 1977.
ISBN 90 04 04802 2

Band 7.
Armenisch und Kaukasische Sprachen. Mit Beiträgen von G. Deeters, G. R. Solta, V. Inglisian. 1963. ISBN 90 04 00862 4

Band 8. Religion
1/1. *Religionsgeschichte des alten Orients.* Mit Beiträgen von E. Otto, O. Eissfeldt, H. Otten, J. Hempel. 1964. ISBN 90 04 00863 2
1/2/2/1. BOYCE, M. *A History of Zoroastrianism. The Early Period.* Rev. ed. 1989. ISBN 90 04 08847 4
1/2/2/2. BOYCE, M. *A History of Zoroastrianism. Under the Achaemenians.* 1982. ISBN 90 04 06506 7
1/2/2/3. BOYCE, M. and GRENET, F. *A History of Zoroastrianism. Zoroastrianism under Macedonian and Roman Rule.* With F. Grenet. Contribution by R. Beck. 1991. ISBN 90 04 09271 4
2. *Religionsgeschichte des Orients in der Zeit der Weltreligionen.* Mit Beiträgen von A. Adam, A. J. Arberry, E. L. Dietrich, J. W. Fück, A. von Gabain, J. Leipoldt, B. Spuler, R. Strothman, G. Widengren. 1961. ISBN 90 04 00864 0

Ergänzungsband 1
1. HINZ, W. *Islamische Maße und Gewichte umgerechnet ins metrische System.* Nachdruck der Erstausgabe (1955) mit Zusätzen und Berichtigungen. 1970. ISBN 90 04 00865 9

Ergänzungsband 2
1. GROHMANN, A. *Arabische Chronologie und Arabische Papyruskunde.* Mit Beiträgen von J. Mayr und W. C. Til. 1966. ISBN 90 04 00866 7
2. KHOURY, R. G. *Chrestomathie de papyrologie arabe.* Documents relatifs à la vie priveé, sociale et administrative dans les premiers siècles islamiques. 1992. ISBN 90 04 09551 9

Ergänzungsband 3
Orientalisches Recht. Mit Beiträgen von E. Seidl, V. Korošc, E. Pritsch, O. Spies, E. Tyan, J. Baz, Ch. Chehata, Ch. Samaran, J. Roussier, J. Lapanne-Joinville, S. Ş. Ansay. 1964. ISBN 90 04 00867 5

Ergänzungsband 5
1/1. BORGER, R. *Das zweite Jahrtausend vor Chr.* Mit Verbesserungen und Zusätzen. Nachdruck der Erstausgabe (1961). 1964. ISBN 90 04 00869 1
1/2. SCHRAMM, W. *[Einleitung in die assyrischen Königsinschriften, 2:] 934-722 v. Chr.* 1973. ISBN 90 04 03783 7

Ergänzungsband 6
1. ULLMANN, M. *Die Medizin im Islam.* 1970. ISBN 90 04 00870 5
2. ULLMANN, M. *Die Natur- und Geheimwissenschaften im Islam.* 1972. ISBN 90 04 03423 4

Ergänzungsband 7
GOMAA, I. *A Historical Chart of the Muslim World.* 1972. ISBN 90 04 03333 5

Ergänzungsband 8
KORNRUMPF, H.-J. *Osmanische Bibliographie mit besonderer Berücksichtigung der Türkei in Europa.* Unter Mitarbeit von J. Kornrumpf. 1973. ISBN 90 04 03549 4

Ergänzungsband 9
FIRRO, K. M. *A History of the Druzes.* 1992. ISBN 90 04 09437 7

Band 10
STRIJP, R. *Cultural Anthropology of the Middle East. A Bibliography.* Vol. 1: 1965-1987. 1992. ISBN 90 04 09604 3

Band 11

ENDRESS, G. & GUTAS, D. (eds.). *A Greek and Arabic Lexicon.* (*GALex*) Materials for a Dictionary of the Mediæval Translations from Greek into Arabic.

Fascicle 1. Introduction—Sources—ʾ – ʾ-kh-r. Compiled by G. Endress & D. Gutas, with the assistance of K. Alshut, R. Arnzen, Chr. Hein, St. Pohl, M. Schmeink. 1992. ISBN 90 04 09494 6

Fascicle 2. ʾ-kh-r – ʾ-ṣ-l. Compiled by G. Endress & D. Gutas, with the assistance of K. Alshut, R. Arnzen, Chr. Hein, St. Pohl, M. Schmeink. 1993. ISBN 90 04 09893 3

Band 12

JAYYUSI, S. K. (ed.). *The Legacy of Muslim Spain.* Chief consultant to the editor, M. Marín. 2nd ed. 1994. ISBN 90 04 09599 3

Band 13

HUNWICK, J. O. and O'FAHEY, R. S. (eds.). *Arabic Literature of Africa.*

Volume I. *The Writings of Eastern Sudanic Africa to c. 1900.* Compiled by R. S. O'Fahey, with the assistance of M. I. Abu Salim, A. Hofheinz, Y. M. Ibrahim, B. Radtke and K. S. Vikør. 1994. ISBN 90 04 09450 4

Band 14

DECKER, W. und HERB, M. *Bildatlas zum Sport im alten Ägypten. Corpus der bildlichen Quellen zu Leibesübungen, Spiel, Jagd, Tanz und verwandten Themen.* Bd.1: Text. Bd. 2: Abbildungen. 1994. ISBN 90 04 09974 3 (Set)

Band 15

HAAS, V. *Geschichte der hethitischen Religion.* 1994. ISBN 90 04 09799 6

Band 16

NEUSNER, J. (ed.). *Judaism in Late Antiquity.* Part One: The Literary and Archaeological Sources. 1994. ISBN 90 04 10129 2

Band 17

NEUSNER, J. (ed.). *Judaism in Late Antiquity.* Part Two: Historical Syntheses. 1994. ISBN 90 04 09799 6

Band 18

OREL, V. E. and STOLBOVA, O. V. (eds.). *Hamito-Semitic Etymological Dictionary.* Materials for a Reconstruction. 1994. ISBN 90 04 10051 2

Band 19

AL-ZWAINI, L. and PETERS, R. *A Bibliography of Islamic Law, 1980-1993.* 1994. ISBN 90 04 10009 1

Band 20

KRINGS, V. (éd.). *La civilisation phénicienne et punique.* Manuel de recherche. 1995 ISBN 90 04 10068 7

Band 21

HOFTIJZER, J. and JONGELING. K. *Dictionary of the North-West Semitic Inscriptions.* With appendices by R.C. Steiner, A. Mosak Moshavi and B. Porten. Part One: ʾ - L.
Part Two: M - T. 1995
ISBN 90 04 09817 8 (*Vol. 1*)
ISBN 90 04 09820 8 (*Vol. 2*)
ISBN 90 04 09821 6 (*Set*)

